T0377399

GEOGRAPHERS OF THE
ANCIENT GREEK WORLD

VOLUME I

Ancient Greek geographical writing is represented not just by the surviving works of the well-known authors Strabo, Pausanias, and Ptolemy, but also by many other texts dating from the Archaic to the Late Antique period. Most of these texts are, however, hard for non-specialists to find, and many have never been translated into English. The present volumes, the work of an international team of experts, present the most important thirty-six texts in new, accurate translations. In addition, there are explanatory notes and authoritative introductions to each text, which offer a new understanding of the individual writings and demonstrate their importance: no longer marginal, but in the mainstream of Greek literature and science. The book includes twenty-eight newly drawn maps, images of the medieval manuscripts in which most of these works survive, and a full Introduction providing a comprehensive survey of the field of Greek and Roman geography.

GRAHAM SHIPLEY is Professor of Ancient History at the University of Leicester, and the author of many studies of Greek history that bring together written sources, archaeology, and landscape, such as *The Greek World after Alexander* (2000) and *The Early Hellenistic Peloponnese* (Cambridge, 2018). In 2019, he was elected a member of the international association GAHIA, 'Geography & Historiography in Antiquity'.

About the Author

D. Graham J. Shipley, a native of Northumberland and alumnus of the Royal Grammar School, Newcastle upon Tyne, is Professor of Ancient History and a Public Orator at the University of Leicester, where he was a founding member of the highly regarded School of Archaeology & Ancient History. He is the author of many studies of Greek history that bring together written sources, archaeology, and landscape.

A Literae Humaniores graduate of Wadham College, Oxford, he held research fellowships at Wadham and Balliol, and then at St Catharine's College, Cambridge, before his appointment at Leicester. He has been Visiting Fellow at the British School at Athens, and has held a British Academy–Leverhulme Senior Research Fellowship. He is a fellow of the Royal Astronomical Society, the Royal Geographical Society, the Royal Historical Society, and the Society of Antiquaries of London, as well as a Senior Fellow of the Higher Education Academy. He holds a D.Phil. from Oxford, and was awarded a D.Litt. by examination in 2020. His interest in local identities led him to inaugurate the successful campaign for a registered flag for the historic county of Leicestershire.

A former Chair of the Council of University Classical Departments and member of the UK Education Honours Committee, he currently serves on the Oxford Classical Texts Committee of Oxford University Press. In 2019 he was elected a member of GAHIA, the Asociación Internacional 'Geography & Historiography in Antiquity'.

Selected works by the same author

A History of Samos 800–188 BC
(Clarendon Press, 1987; revised Modern Greek edition, 2021)

(edited with J. W. Rich)
War and Society in the Greek World and *War and Society in the Roman World*
(Routledge, 1993)

(edited with J. B. Salmon)
Human Landscapes in Classical Antiquity: Environment and Culture
(Routledge, 1996)

(with W. G. Cavanagh, J. H. Crouwel, R. W. V. Catling)
Continuity and Change in a Greek Rural Landscape: The Laconia Survey
(British School at Athens, 1996–2002)

The Greek World after Alexander: 323–30 BC
(Routledge, 2000; Spanish translation, 2001; Modern Greek edition, 2012)

(edited with J. Vanderspoel, D. J. Mattingly, L. Foxhall)
The Cambridge Dictionary of Classical Civilization
(Cambridge University Press, 2006)

Pseudo-Skylax's Periplous: The Circumnavigation of the Inhabited World
(Exeter University Press, 2011; 2nd edition, Liverpool University Press, 2019)

The Early Hellenistic Peloponnese, 338–197 BC: Politics, Economies, and Networks
(Cambridge University Press, 2018)

GEOGRAPHERS
OF THE
ANCIENT GREEK
WORLD

Selected Texts in Translation
VOLUME I

BY

D. Graham J. Shipley

*Professor of Ancient History at the
University of Leicester*

with contributions by

Colin E. P. Adams	Daniela Dueck	Ralph Morley
David C. Braund	James W. Ermatinger	Oliver Nicholson
Stanley M. Burstein	Robert C. Helmer	Thomas Russell
J. Brian Campbell	Yumna Z. N. Khan	Richard J. A. Talbert
Katherine J. Clarke	Aidan Liddle	

Completed with the assistance of

Ancient World Mapping Center, University of North Carolina, Chapel Hill
Arts & Humanities Research Council
Loeb Classical Library Foundation

CAMBRIDGE
UNIVERSITY PRESS

Shaftesbury Road, Cambridge CB2 8EA, United Kingdom

One Liberty Plaza, 20th Floor, New York, NY 10006, USA

477 Williamstown Road, Port Melbourne, VIC 3207, Australia

314–321, 3rd Floor, Plot 3, Splendor Forum, Jasola District Centre, New Delhi – 110025, India

103 Penang Road, #05-06/07, Visioncrest Commercial, Singapore 238467

Cambridge University Press is part of Cambridge University Press & Assessment, a department of the University of Cambridge.

We share the University's mission to contribute to society through the pursuit of education, learning and research at the highest international levels of excellence.

www.cambridge.org
Information on this title: www.cambridge.org/9781009174893

DOI: 10.1017/9781009194211

First published 2024

Printed in the United Kingdom by CPI Group Ltd, Croydon CR0 4YY

A catalogue record for this publication is available from the British Library.

Library of Congress Cataloging-in-Publication Data
NAMES: Shipley, D. Graham J., editor.
TITLE: Geographers of the ancient Greek world : selected texts in translation / [compiled] by D. Graham J. Shipley.
DESCRIPTION: Cambridge, United Kingdom ; New York, NY : Cambridge University Press, 2024. | Includes bibliographical references and index.
IDENTIFIERS: LCCN 2023052633 | ISBN 9781009174893 (set ; hardback) | ISBN 9781009194204 (v. 1 ; hardback) | ISBN 9781009184229 (v. 2 ; hardback) | ISBN 9781009174930 (set ; ebook)
SUBJECTS: LCSH: Geography, Ancient – Sources.
CLASSIFICATION: LCC G87.A1 G28 2024 | DDC 910.92/238–dc23/eng/20231220
LC record available at https://lccn.loc.gov/2023052633

ISBN – 2 volume set 978-1-009-17489-3 Hardback
ISBN – Volume I 978-1-009-19420-4 Hardback
ISBN – Volume II 978-1-009-18422-9 Hardback

Κύπριδος οὗτος ὁ χῶρος, ἐπεὶ φίλον ἔπλετο τήνᾳ
    αἰὲν ἀπ' ἠπείρου λαμπρὸν ὁρῆν πέλαγος,
ὄφρα φίλον ναύτῃσι τελῇ πλόον· ἀμφὶ δὲ πόντος
    δειμαίνει λιπαρὸν δερκόμενος ξόανον.

Kypris' place is this, since it was her own joy ever
    to look from land at the shining open sea (*pelagos*)
and complete sailors' own journey for them. Around her
    the main (*pontos*) is fearful, beholding the bright carved statue.

Anyte of Tegea (C3e),
Anthologia Graeca 9. 144 (my translation)

Contents

VOLUME I

PART II: CLASSICAL PERIOD

PART III: HELLENISTIC PERIOD

VOLUME II

PART IV: ROMAN PERIOD

PART V: LATE ANTIQUE PERIOD

Figures

Maps

All drawn by the Ancient World Mapping Center, University of North Carolina, Chapel Hill.

SYMBOLS AND LEGEND

ASIA	largest region, continent, etc.
CRETE	larger region/people, large island, body of water, etc.
ARKADIA	smaller region/people, local body of water, etc.
Chobos	river, cape, mountain, smaller island
• **name**	larger settlement
• name	smaller settlement
+	sacred place, sanctuary
■	(in Arrian) military fort

▲ mountain

▼ (in *PME*) emporion nomimon

▽ (in *PME*) small *emporion*

Tables

Contributors

Colin E. P. Adams is Professor of Ancient History at the University of Liverpool and has held positions at the Universities of St Andrews and Leicester. He took his doctorate (on transport in Roman Egypt) at the University of Oxford. A specialist in the economic and social history of Roman Egypt, he has also published widely on ancient travel and geography, including *Travel and Geography in the Roman Empire* (edited with R. Laurence, 2001) and *Travel and Geography in Ancient Greece and the Near East* (edited with J. Roy, 2007). He was elected a Fellow of the Society of Antiquaries of London in 2015.

David C. Braund is Emeritus Professor of Black Sea and Mediterranean History at the University of Exeter. Greek geographers have featured in all his books and many of his various articles on antiquity, such as *Rome and the Friendly King: The Character of Client Kingship* (1984), *Scythians and Greeks* (edited, 2004), and *The Black Sea Region in the Context of the Roman Empire* (edited with A. Chaniotis and E. K. Petropoulos, 2022).

Stanley M. Burstein is Professor Emeritus of History at California State University, Los Angeles, where he taught from 1968 to 2004. He received his BA, MA, and Ph.D. degrees in Ancient History from the University of California at Los Angeles. He was president of the Association of Ancient Historians from 1990 to 1993. His research has placed particular emphasis on the encounter between Greeks and non-Greek peoples in the Black Sea basin and Ancient North-East Africa. He is the author of many publications, including *Outpost of Hellenism: The Emergence of Heraclea on the Black Sea* (1976), *Agatharchides of Cnidus, On the Erythraean Sea* (1989), *Graeco-Africana: Studies in the History of Greek Relations with Egypt and Nubia* (1995), *The Reign of Cleopatra* (2004), *Ancient African Civilizations* (edited; 2nd edition, 2009), and *The Essential Greek Historians* (edited, 2022).

J. Brian Campbell is Emeritus Professor of Roman History at the Queen's University of Belfast. He completed his D.Phil. at Worcester College, Oxford, and his published work includes studies of army and society, land survey, and rivers in the Roman world, among them *The Writings of the Roman Land Surveyors* (2000) and *Rivers and the Power of Ancient Rome* (2012). He has held a Leverhulme Senior Research Fellowship, was visiting scholar at Wolfson College, Oxford, and St John's College, Oxford, and in 2005 was Visiting Fellow at All Souls College, Oxford.

Katherine J. Clarke is Professor of Greek and Roman History at the University of Oxford, and a Fellow of St Hilda's College. She is particularly interested in the relationship between space and time in historical narratives, and in geographical traditions as reflective of changing geopolitical realities. She has published widely on ancient geography and history, including *Between Geography and History: Hellenistic Constructions of the Roman World* (1999), *Making Time for the Past: Local History and the Polis* (2008), and *Shaping the Geography of Empire: Man and Nature in Herodotus' Histories* (2018). She was elected a Fellow of the British Academy in 2023.

Daniela Dueck is Professor of Ancient History at Bar Ilan University. She has published studies of ancient geography including *Geography in Classical Antiquity* (2012), *The Routledge Companion to Strabo* (edited, 2017) and *Illiterate Geography in Classical Athens and Rome* (2021). Her research interests include the distribution of geographical knowledge in Classical antiquity through texts—whole or fragmentary—and beyond texts, orally or visually.

James W. Ermatinger is Professor of History and Interim Dean, Education & Human Services, at the University of Illinois Springfield, and previously Dean of the College of Liberal Arts & Sciences at the University of Illinois Springfield (2009–20). He has published extensively on Roman economic history, including *The Economic Reforms of Diocletian* (1996). He and Bob Helmer began working on the *Stadiasmos* at Lourdes University in 1998.

Robert C. Helmer is President of Baldwin Wallace University, Berea, Ohio, having previously served as President of Lourdes University for ten years. He completed his doctorate at Marquette University with a dissertation on the Ethiopic and Greek fragments of the *Apocalypse of Peter*, and has published on early Christian origins and apocalyptic literature. He and Jim Ermatinger began working on the *Stadiasmos* at Lourdes University in 1998.

Yumna Z. N. Khan is an independent scholar and speech/language pathologist. She has taught at Birkbeck College London and King's College London, as well as several universities in the Boston area, where she lives and works. She completed her doctorate on Dionysios Periegetes at the University of London, and has presented and published on the poetry of the *Periegesis*.

Aidan Liddle, a graduate of Hertford College, Oxford, is an independent scholar and British diplomat, currently serving as UK Ambassador and Permanent Representative to the Conference on Disarmament in Geneva. He has published *Arrian, Periplus Ponti Euxini* (2003).

Ralph Morley is an independent scholar and barrister. He studied Classics at Trinity College, Cambridge, where he was a Senior Scholar and a University Classical Scholar. He practises in admiralty, maritime, and commercial law at 7 King's Bench Walk, Temple, London. Ralph has also worked on Avienus for ToposText, a digital humanities platform mapping the ancient world by reference to primary sources.

Oliver Nicholson read Modern History at Trinity College, Oxford, where he went on to write a D.Phil. thesis on Lactantius, arguably the brains behind Constantine the Great. Seven years in six positions, two continents, three countries, four states, and the District of Columbia culminated in thirty years teaching Late Antiquity and Latin Patristics at the University of Minnesota. He has now retired to his native Devonshire, where he seeks solace in local history, pedestrian cynegetics, and (still) writing about Lactantius. He was the General Editor of the *Oxford Dictionary of Late Antiquity* (2018).

Thomas Russell earned his doctorate at St Hilda's College, Oxford, before taking up a position as Lecturer of Classics and Ancient History at Balliol College. He is now a teacher, and is Head of Classics and Latin at the Royal Grammar School, Worcester. He is the author of *Byzantium and the Bosporus: A Historical Study, from the Seventh Century BC until the Foundation of Constantinople* (2017).

D. Graham J. Shipley is Professor of Ancient History at the University of Leicester. He completed his D.Phil. at the University of Oxford, and was awarded a D.Litt. by examination in 2020. He is a fellow of learned societies including the Royal Geographical Society and the Society of Antiquaries of London, and in 2018 was elected to the Asociación Internacional 'Geography & Historiography in Antiquity'. He is the author of many studies of Greek history that bring together written sources, archaeological evidence, and landscape, including *A History of Samos* (1987), *The Laconia Survey* (co-author, 1996–2002), *The Greek World after Alexander* (2000), and *The Early Hellenistic Peloponnese* (2018). His previous work on geographical texts includes *Pseudo-Skylax's Periplous* (2nd edition 2019).

Richard J. A. Talbert is Research Professor of History at the University of North Carolina, Chapel Hill, USA. His publications include the *Barrington Atlas of the Greek and Roman World* (2000), *Rome's World: The Peutinger Map Reconsidered* (2010), *Roman Portable Sundials: The Empire in Your Hand* (2017), *Challenges of Mapping the Classical World* (2019), *World and Hour in Roman Minds: Exploratory Essays* (2023), and a translation (with Brian Turner) of *Pliny the Elder's World: Natural History, Books 2–6* (2022).

Preface

His duties required him, however, to lecture on a wide variety of subjects,
including physical geography, about which he became, perhaps because of
his reluctance to travel, an acknowledged authority.

Scruton, *Kant* (2001), 4

Ancient geography is a field of which one may truly say one only sees further by standing on the shoulders of giants. First among those are the ancient writers themselves,
particularly Menippos, Arrian, and Markianos, to whom we owe the preservation of
a dozen or more works. They continue with antiquarians and scholar-rulers of the
Byzantine world, such as the patriarch St Photios and the emperor Constantine VII
Porphyrogennetos; post-Renaissance copyists, collectors, and founders of European
libraries; the great editors and heads of early printing-houses who both preserved
and disseminated, for the most part calling a halt to the erosion of the textual legacy
of antiquity; then the scholars, initially writing in Latin and then in the vernacular,
from the Vos brothers to the likes of Gronov, Hudson, and Gail,[1] who assembled
compendious volumes of what they sometimes called the 'minor' geographers
('minor' variously connoting brevity, lack of literary pretensions, or fragmentary
preservation), building a firmer chronology and refining the texts. Finally came
the academics and independent scholars—almost innumerable now, in our world
of multiplying universities and increasingly rapid communication—whose insights
have clarified our understanding of the ancient writers' aims, the mutual interaction
between their texts, and ultimately the complex relationships between ancient texts
and the 'real' Graeco-Roman world of mountains and islands, cities and harbours,
travel and conquest, administration and exploration. To survey the gamut of ancient
geographical writing is to be awe-struck at the richness, familiarity, strangeness, and
ultimately sophistication of past societies and the universes of meaning that they
created and inhabited.

ACKNOWLEDGEMENTS

Completion of this work would have been impossible without substantial funding
for research leave granted by the Loeb Classical Library Foundation (for the spring
semester of 2020) and—at a crucial juncture during the Covid-19 pandemic—by the
Ancient World Mapping Center, University of North Carolina, Chapel Hill. In 2022,
the Center also prepared the maps from my specifications with their customary effi-
ciency, creativity, and meticulous attention to detail.

[1] e.g. G. I. Vossius 1624; I. Vossius 1639; Gronovius 1697; Hudson 1698–1712; Gail 1826–31.

The Loeb Classical Library Foundation and the Arts & Humanities Research Council generously funded earlier periods of leave during my work on Pseudo-Skylax ([1]Shipley 2011; [2]Shipley 2019), which has borne further fruit in Chapter 7.

I thank the College of Social Sciences, Arts, & Humanities, University of Leicester, for granting me research leave in 2017, 2020, and 2022, and colleagues in the School of Archaeology & Ancient History—a wonderfully supportive department—who shouldered additional duties as a result: especially, in 2020, Neil Christie, Naoíse Mac Sweeney, and Nikki Rollason.

Publication has been facilitated by Michael Sharp at Cambridge University Press, as well as his colleagues Katie Idle and Liz Davey; and by the anonymous readers who approved the initial proposal and those whose detailed comments vastly improved the draft text (where their suggestions, including additional references, have been adopted, it is done silently to avoid cluttering the notes, except in the case of the technical information on Mnaseas 14). I am grateful to Bethan Lee for her eagle-eyed copy-editing, Jonathan Bargus for the text design, and to Annette Copping and Jane Burkowski for their help at the proofs stage. At earlier stages, generous advice was received from Chuck Grench at University of North Carolina Press.

For generous assistance and frequent timely advice over many years, I am grateful above all to two leading experts, Kai Brodersen and Richard Talbert. They have guided me in matters of selection, structure, and approach, have been endlessly patient with innumerable enquiries, and at a more detailed level have often assisted by locating images of manuscripts and out-of-print works.

As regards the content of the volumes, it is my pleasant obligation to thank the fourteen contributors, who have been diligent and energetic by turns: Colin Adams, David Braund, Stanley Burstein, Brian Campbell, Katherine Clarke, Daniela Dueck, Jim Ermatinger, Robert Helmer, Yumna Khan, Aidan Liddle, Ralph Morley, Oliver Nicholson, Thom Russell, and Richard Talbert himself. They have shared ideas and knowledge far beyond the scope of their own chapters. I am particularly appreciative of the friendly collaboration I have enjoyed with Stanley Burstein and Richard Talbert over our joint chapters. (Contributors' own acknowledgements will be found in their respective chapter introductions.)

Four further scholars have made a marked difference to particular chapters. Egidia Occhipinti's meticulous critiques of my Agatharchides translation saved me from many errors and greatly improved the choice of words. I thank Silvia Panichi for extended discussions which have been of enormous benefit to the chapter on Artemidoros. Frances Pownall has generously shared her expertise with regard to Hekataios. It has been a privilege to be able to draw upon the expertise of Nigel Wilson with reference to Photios' summary of Agatharchides and the Munich 'fragment' of Artemidoros.

For comments on the Introduction and other chapters, I thank, as well as many of those above, Dominic Berry (Avienus), David Blackman (Timosthenes), George Boys-Stones (Ps.-Aristotle), Mark Humphries (Markianos), Lindsay Judson (Ps.-Aristotle),

Chiara Maria Mauro (Ps.-Skylax), Lucijana Šešelj (Ps.-Skylax), Paul Smee (Introduction), and on multiple chapters or the text as a whole Richard J. G. Evans, Myles Harman, Jan Haywood, Brady Kiesling, Robin Lane Fox, David Mattingly, Gillian Ramsey, and Charlotte Van Regenmortel. Naturally, any remaining errors in all my own chapters are my responsibility.

At various stages of development, I received support and helpful advice from †Lionel Casson; Hans-Joachim Gehrke and the other editors of 'Jacoby V', Veronica Bucciantini and Felix Maier; Grant Parker; Duane W. Roller; and James Romm.

Besides the above, those who have generously shared their expertise include Alexander Arenz (on Herakleides Kritikos), Mary Beagon (Pliny the Elder), Gordon R. Campbell, Richard Catling, Cynthia Damon (Eratosthenes), Anca Dan, Klaus Geus, Tom Harrison (*AWP*), Richard Janko, Anne Kolb (Artemidoros), Jeremy McInerney (Herakleides Kritikos), John Marincola, Céline Marquaille-Telliez, Andy Merrills, and Robert Parker (the epitaph in Dionysios of Byzantion). I thank John Waś for many years of profound wisdom about text formatting and copy-editing matters.

As on a previous occasion, I thank Christian Förstel, Bibliothèque Nationale de France, for assistance with study images of part of the manuscript of the *Nikomedean Periodos* ('Ps.-Skymnos'); and staff at the David Wilson Library, University of Leicester, especially the former subject librarian for Archaeology & Ancient History, Jackie Hanes, and her predecessor Evelyn Cornell; and those at the Institute of Classical Studies, especially Sue Willetts. In the years before online publication became ubiquitous, the staff of the former University of Leicester Bookshop, especially Mark Burrows and Yasmin Master, helped locate foreign publications.

For sustained interest and encouragement, I owe a debt of gratitude to numerous colleagues named above as well as (among others) Amy Arden, Carla Brain, Alastair Buchan, Anna-Sophie Bulder, Katie Carlill, Christy Constantakopoulou, Susan Deacy, Andrew Erskine, Florentia Fragkopoulou, Francisco José González Ponce, Colin Haselgrove, †Hermann Kienast, Katarína Kompauerová, Janie Masséglia, Tamar Miller, Astrid Möller, and Sarah Scott.

Besides many of the above, the following colleagues among others have been generous in sharing (or offering to share) their own or others' publications relevant to the project, or in facilitating access to publications: Hans Beck, Serena Bianchetti, Graeme Bourke, Efrosyni Boutsikas, Alan C. Bowen, Sergio Brillante, D. J. Butterfield, Giovanni Buzzi, Paul Christesen, Nino Crisà, Michael Curtis, Edwin de Vries, Philippe Della Casa, Nathan Dennis, †Jehan Desanges, Jane L. Draycott, Roberta Fabiani, Kilian Fleischer, Dina Frangié, John Franklin, Olivier Gengler, Klaus Geus, Eric Guiry, Sven Günther, Victor Gysembergh, Daniel Hanigan, Robert Hannah, Michael Hendry, Michael Hillgruber, Collin Hilton, Marko Jelusić, Molly Jones-Lewis, Paul Keyser, Hartmut Krech, Stefan Krmnicek, Jane Lightfoot, Nick Lowe, Francesco Lubian, Carlo Lucarini, Michael Lurie, Adalberto Magnava, Shushma Malik, Didier Marcotte, Toph Marshall, Ivan Matijašić, Ugo Carlo Luigi Mondini, Jason Morris, Massimo Nafissi, Jim O'Donnell, Marta Otlewska-Jung, Floris Overduin, Irene Pajón Leyra, Athina

Papachrysostomou, Georgios Papantoniou, Christopher Pelling, Philomen Probert, Enrico Prodi, Michael Rathmann, Andres Reyes, Marco Riccardo, Anna Santoni, David Seamon, Nicholas V. Sekunda, David Sider, Ian Storey, †Gocha Tsetskhladze, John Tully, Christopher Tuplin, Mattia Vitelli Casella, Javier Williams, Christina Williamson, and (over many years) Nicola Zwingmann. I apologize for any inadvertent omissions. Further acknowledgements in respect of my earlier work on Ps.-Skylax may be found in Shipley 2011, viii–ix (²Shipley 2019, x–xi).

The inspiration I have drawn from the novels of Anthony Powell, the joyous playing of Lisa Batiashvili, the Hot Club of Cowtown, Alison Krauss, and Andy Schumm and his bands, the determination of Leicester Tigers, the wisdom of J. R. R. Tolkien, and the dedication of the supporters of the 'A Flag for Leicestershire' campaign (2014–21) is gratefully acknowledged.

Almost last but far from least, I thank the late, great Yi-Fu Tuan for his interest in this project, and am saddened that he did not live to see it published.

My greatest debt, as always, is to Anne, Joseph, and Dorothea.

PERMISSIONS

Sources for images of manuscripts are credited in the List of Figures below.

Katherine Clarke and I are grateful to Professor Duane W. Roller and to Cambridge University Press for permission to quote from his translation of Strabo (Roller 2014) in Chapters 8, 12, and 18–19. The Press has also allowed us to quote a lengthy fragment of Poseidonios (Chapter 19 no. 46) in the translation by Kidd 1999.

Aidan Liddle and I thank Bloomsbury Publishing for permission to adapt his translation of Arrian's *Periplous* in Liddle 2003.

D.G.J.S.   *Leicestershire, 20 June 2022*

NOTE

The pace of publication on ancient geography is continually accelerating; and my research largely ended in 2020. Only partial account has been taken in Chapter 7 of Brillante 2020 (on Pseudo-Skylax); likewise, in Chapter 32, of Guillaumin and Bernard 2021 (on Avienus), which appeared in the last stages of preparing these volumes.

On the other hand, L. Scott 2021 (on Pytheas), and Roller 2022b (on Hanno, the *Nikomedean Periodos*, and Avienus), appeared too late to be taken into account, as did the volume edited by González Ponce and Chávez Reino 2021. A new translation of Pliny the Elder's geographical books (Turner and Talbert 2022), a commentary on those books (Roller 2022a), and the revised Loeb volume containing the Hippocratic *Airs, Waters, and Places* (Potter 2022) were due to appear as this work went to press. More recent still, Brodersen 2023a includes a new Greek text and German translation of both Arrian's *Periplous* and the late antique Pseudo-Arrianic *Euxine*, while Brodersen 2023b does the same for Theophrastos, *On Winds*, as well as Aristotle's *Meteorologika*, 2. 4–6.

Glossary

This includes technical terms in English and may also serve as a guide to how technical terms in Greek or Latin are normally translated (cf. Introduction, §IX. 2–3). Head-words in italics are transliterated from Greek unless otherwise stated. Key terms forming related clusters (i.a. for classes of writing, bodies of water, 'compass' directions, stopping-places for ships) are in **bold** type. These clusters, and others, are grouped at the end of the list.

Wind names are in lower case here, but are often capitalized as proper names in the main body of the book. For additional, local names for winds, see the introduction to Chapter 10.

For distances and dimensions, see the list of 'Units of measure' that follows.

Cross-references of the form §X, §III, etc. refer to sections of the Introduction.

aigialos: shore

Aithiopikos kolpos (Aithiopian gulf): the east-central Atlantic, the great bight off W Africa

akra: (feminine noun) cape

akron, pl. *akra*: (neuter noun) point (in the sense of cape), extremity

akrōtērion: promontory

aktē: headland

anabasis: voyage inland, moving away from the sea (lit. a 'going up')

anagraphē: record, register

anametrēsis: measurement (in the sense of a set of measurements of a region or the *oikoumenē*; cf. Eratosthenes 41 below, and appendix to Chapter 36)

anaplous: voyage upstream (lit. a 'sailing up'), as in the *Anaplous of the Bosporos* by Dionysios of Byzantion (Chapter 30)

anatolē, pl. *anatolai*: lit. 'rising(s)' of the sun, i.e. East (see §X. 3. b)

anemos: wind

aparktias: due north wind

apēliōtēs: due east wind (lit. 'from the sun')

Arabikos kolpos (Arabian gulf): the enclosed sea between Egypt and the Arabian peninsula; the modern *Red Sea* (*see also* Erythraian sea)

archaic (or Archaic): a period term based on the history of art, denoting the archaeological and artistic phase between the end of 'Geometric' art around 700 BC and the beginning of the Classical period. More helpfully, a general chronological label for the 7th and 6th centuries BC (700–500 BC).

argestēs: one of the north-westerly winds (see §X. 3. b)

arktos, pl. *arktoi*: lit. 'bear' and 'bears', i.e. the north (see §X. 3. b)

bēmatistēs, pl. *bēmatistai*: pacer, who measures long distances by counting his steps

bibliothēkē: library, especially as the title of a compendious work (e.g. by Diodoros or Photios)

boreas (or *borrhas*): north wind, the north (see §X. 3. b); sometimes a NNE wind

cadaster: a map of property boundaries, based on a land survey

chōra: land, territory

chōrion: settlement, locality

chōrographia: regional description (lit. 'land- or territory-writing') (see §III. 1. d)

classical: generally, the ancient periods from the earliest written sources in Greek (*c.*750–725 BC) to the beginning of Muslim conquests in the 7th c. AD. Written with a capital initial as 'Classical', the term refers more narrowly to the period of Greek history between the end of the Persian invasion of mainland Greece in 479 BC to the death of Alexander the Great in 323 (or his accession in 336, or sometimes the battle of Ipsos between his Successors in 301). In archaeological typology, it may begin in 480 with the destruction of the temples on the Athenian Acropolis, which provide a firm dating criterion for some artefacts. More generally, it is a shorthand to refer (without undue precision) to the 5th and 4th centuries (500–300).

codex, pl. codices: normally a manuscript book made up of rectangular leaves sewn together at the left

corpus: a collection (lit. 'body' in Latin) of texts, especially one arranged by an editor, ancient or modern

cubit: see *pēchys* under 'Units of measurement' below

diagnōsis: 'determination' (in the sense of a text enumerating geographical information, see §VIII. 2. a)

diaplous: sea crossing (lit. a 'sailing through'), by direct navigation rather than by following the coast. (Also, a manoeuvre in a sea battle, sailing through the enemy lines.)

dysis, pl. *dyseis*: setting(s) of the sun (lit. 'sinking(s)'), i.e. the west (see §X. 3. b)

dysmē, pl. *dysmai*: equivalent to *dysis*

ēiōn: shore, beach

ēōs: dawn, the east (see §X. 3. b)

ēpeiros: mainland, continent (also the region of Epeiros in NW Greece)

epitomē: summary, abridgement, précis

Erythraian sea (*Erythra thalassa*): the western Indian Ocean including the modern *Red Sea*; lit. either 'red sea' or 'sea of Erythras' (see §X. 2)

etēsiai: lit. 'annuals' (masculine noun), the prevailing NNW winds of the Aegean in summer; or other annual winds elsewhere

Ethiopian gulf: see *Aithiopikos kolpos*

ethnikon, pl. *ethnika*: the term for a communal name such as 'Athenian' or 'Hellenic' (lit. the 'national (name)'). From about the late Classical or early Hellenistic period, refers especially to the type of city surname appended (since earliest Greek history) to a free citizen's name, as in *Hekataios Milēsios*, 'Hekataios (citizen) of Miletos'. See also *ethnos*.

ethnos, pl. *ethnē*: nation(s); general term for a community at any scale (see §X. 3. c) *euronotos*: one of the south-easterly winds, between Euros and Notos (see §X. 3. b)

euros: one of the south-easterly winds (see §X. 3. b)

Euxine: English version of *euxeinos*, 'hospitable'; in Greek, usually combined with Pontos, 'the hospitable main', as a designation (possibly apotropaic) for the Black Sea

folio: strictly a 'leaf' of a manuscript or codex with bound pages, with two faces—the first or right-hand face being the 'recto' (often abbreviated 'r'), the reverse the 'verso' (v); more loosely, a page in the sense of one of the two sides of a leaf

fragment: see §VII. 3

gē: the Earth, or earth/land/ground in general (see *gēs periodos*)

genos, pl. *genē*: race (see §X. 3. c)

gens, pl. *gentes* (Latin): nation (the Latin writers often seem to use it to translate Greek *ethnos*), race, people

geōgraphia: lit. 'earth-writing' or 'earth-drawing'; see §II. 1; a geographical writing may be called *geōgraphika* (e.g. Strabo) or *geōgraphoumena* (e.g. Artemidoros) rather than a *geōgraphia*

gēs periodos: lit. 'way round the Earth', i.e. circuit of the Earth in narrative form (also *periodos gēs*)

Great Sea, *see megalē thalassa*

hellenistic (or Hellenistic): lit. 'Greekifying', a term coined in the 19th c. to refer to the period from Alexander the Great's conquest of the Persian empire to the beginning of the Christian era. Originally conceived as the period of fusion between Judaism and Hellenic religion, the term is nowadays used either to describe the overlaying of Hellenic culture and administration upon parts of the Near East, or as a simple chronological marker for the period beginning at Alexander's death in 323 BC (or sometimes his accession in 336, or the battle of Ipsos between his Successors in 301) and the Roman acquisition of Egypt in 30 BC. (Earlier scholarship may end the period with the Roman destruction of Corinth in 146.) More helpful, a general chronological marker for the last three centuries BC (300 to 1 BC).

hellēspontias: another name for *apēliōtēs* (see Chapter 10, introduction and appendix)

hespera: lit. 'evening'; the west (see §X. 3. b)

historia: lit. 'enquiry'; a narrative, historical account, history

hormos: anchorage

hyphormos: minor anchorage

hypotypōsis: outline (as a form of writing)

iapyx: one of the north-westerly winds (see §X. 3. b)

Imperial: as a period term, loosely denotes the first three centuries AD (approx. AD 1–300), following the foundation of the Principate by Augustus

isēmerinos: lit. 'equal in day', 'equidiurnal', i.e. equinoctial (which strictly means 'equal in night'); hence as a noun (understanding *kyklos*, 'circle'), an equinox, or the (terrestrial or celestial) Equator

kaikos: one of the north-easterly winds (see §X. 3. b)

keras or *kerōs*: lit. 'horn'; often an inlet or bay;[2] also a promontory;[3] or one limb of a bow[4]

kirkios: one of the north-westerly winds (see §X. 3. b)

klima, pl. *klimata*: lit. 'inclination', a zone of latitude (between two parallels of latitude); hence a climatic zone

kolpos: gulf or bay (occasionally capitalized when in roman type as part of a name, e.g. Mesanites Kolpos)

late antique, or late Roman: denotes approximately the 4th to 6th centuries AD (300–600); sometimes equates to 'early Byzantine' (i.e. from the division of the Roman empire under Diocletian and/or the refoundation of Byzantion as Constantinople in 324)

late Roman: *see* late antique

Libyē (*Libya* in Latin): Africa as a whole (the ancients were unaware of the extent of central and southern Africa)

limēn, pl. *limenes*: harbour (see §IX. 3)

lips: one of the south-westerly winds (see §X. 3. b)

megalē thalassa: 'Great Sea', usually the outer Ocean; in *Stad.*, the Mediterranean

mesēmbria (*mesēmbriē* in Ionic dialect): lit. 'midday', hence the south (see §X. 3. b)

mesēmbrinos (or *mesēmbrinos kyklos*): lit. 'midday circle', i.e. meridian, line of longitude

mesēs: a north-north-easterly wind (see Chapter 10, appendix)

mile: see 'Units of measure' below

milion (μίλιον), pl. *milia* (μίλια), 'mile': late antique Greek translation of Latin *mille passuum* (see 'mile, Roman' under 'Units of measure' below)

mundus (Latin): world, cosmos

notos: south wind, the south (see §X. 3. b)

oikoumenē: 'the inhabited', the feminine gender implying *gē*, 'Earth'; i.e. the band of the Earth's surface known to be inhabited (essentially Europe, Asia, and Africa other than parts deemed uninhabitable such as the far South and far North)

ōkeanos, Okeanos: the outer Ocean surrounding all the (then known) continents: Europe, Asia, and Libyē

olympias: one of the north-westerly winds (see §X. 3. b)

orbis (Latin): the world, as in *orbis terrae* (or *terrarum*), 'the circle of land(s)', conceived as a collection of inhabited lands

palimpsest: a manuscript that has been erased and reused once or more than once, the earlier text(s) remaining discoverable (e.g. in ultra-violet light)

paraplous, pl. *paraploi*: coastal sailing (lit. a 'sailing beside'), i.e. a voyage along a coast rather than across open sea or up a river

---

[2] e.g. the Horn of the West, a bay at Hanno §14; or the Keras of Byzantion (mod. *Golden Horn*), Dionysios of Byzantion §5 etc. Cf. Roller 2006, 38–41.

[3] e.g. Artemidoros 98 §14 = Strabo 16. 4. 14; Ps.-Aristotle 3. 5; *PME* §38.

[4] e.g. *Hypotyposis* §51.

pelagos: open sea (see §IX. 3) (capitalized when in roman type as part of a name, e.g. Barbarikon Pelagos; 'open sea' is hyphenated if another name precedes it, e.g. 'Cretan open-sea')

periēgēsis: tour, guided tour (lit. a 'leading round') of a particular region (large or small); occasionally *periēgētikon*

perimetros: circumference

periodos, pl. *periodoi*: circuit (lit. 'road round', 'way round'); see also *gēs periodos*

periplous, pl. *periploi*: circumnavigation (lit. a 'sailing round'), whether the record of an actual voyage or a literary narration (see §III. 1)

Persikos kolpos ('Persian gulf'): as in modern parlance, the enclosed sea between the Arabian peninsula and Iran

phoinix or *phoinikias*: one of the south-easterly winds (see §X. 3. b)

phylon, pl. *phyla*: tribe (see §X. 3. c)

pinax, pl. *pinakes* (*tabula(e)* in Latin): board or tablet (cf. *CGL*; in text, may refer to a list (such as a table of contents), or map, or other illustration (see Introduction, §V)

polis, pl. *poleis*: city, city-state

pontos: main, i.e. a particular sea (see §IX. 3). As a proper name in English, Pontos (*Pontus* in Latin) in roman type refers either to the Black Sea or to a region of N Asia Minor on its S shore

pyrgos, pl. *pyrgoi*: tower (see §III. 3. j)

quaternion: a sequence of 16 pages formed by sewing together four sheets, each folded double

recto: *see* folio

Red Sea: (*a*) same as Erythraian sea (see definition above); (*b*) in modern parlance, in a narrower sense, the enclosed sea between Egypt and the Arabian peninsula

Rubrum mare (Latin): lit. 'red sea', i.e. *Erythra thalassa* (see 'Erythraian sea' above)

salos: roadstead (lit. a 'swell'), a place to anchor in safe, open water (see §IX. 3)

skirōn: one of the north-westerly winds

stade (*stadion*): see 'Units of measure' below

stadiasmos: lit. 'stading', i.e. a stade table or list of places with distances between them in stades (as in the title of the work in Chapter 31)

tabula (Latin): see *pinax*

testimonium (pl. testimonia): see §VII. 3

thalassa (*thalatta* in Attic dialect): sea (see IX. 3) (occasionally capitalized when in roman type as part of a name, e.g. Sapra Thalatta)

thraskias: one of the north-westerly winds (see §X. 3. b)

tropē: lit. 'turning', 'turning-point', i.e. a solstice

tropikos (*kyklos*): lit. 'circle of turning', one of the two Tropics (of Cancer or Capricorn)

verso: *see* folio

zephyros: the west wind, hence the west (see §X. 3. b)

SELECTED CLUSTERS OF GREEK AND LATIN TERMS

coastal features: *akra, akron, akrōtērion, aktē, ēiōn, hormos, hyphormos, keras, kolpos, limēn, salos*

directions (*see also* winds): (north) *arktos, boreas*; (east) *anatolē, ēōs*; (south) *mesēmbria, notos*; (west) *dysis/dysmē, hespera, zephyros*

distance measures: *parasangēs, pēchys, plethron, schoinos, stadion*; Latin *mille passūs/mille passuum*

forms of graphic representation: *pinax*; Latin *tabula*

forms of text: *chōrographia, epitomē, geōgraphia* (and related terms), *gēs periodos* (or *periodos gēs*), *hypotypōsis, periēgēsis, periēgētikon, periplous*

geographical areas: *chōra, ēpeiros, gē, oikoumenē*; Latin *orbis, orbis terrarum*

sea areas: *keras, kolpos, pelagos, pontos, ōkeanos, thalassa*

sea journeys: *anaplous, diaplous, paraplous, periplous*

winds (*see also* directions): *aparktias, apēliōtēs, argestēs, boreas, etēsiai, euronotos, euros, hellēspontias, iapyx, kaikos, kirkios, lips, mesēs, notos, olympias, phoinix/phoinikias, skirōn, thraskias, zephyros*. For additional, local names see introduction to Chapter 10 (also Fig. 10.1).

UNITS OF MEASURE

For more detail, see Dilke 1987, 26–8. Headwords in roman type at the beginning of an entry are English. ᴸ marks Latin words.

Alphabetical list

cubit: see *pēchys*

fathom: either 6 feet (182.88 cm) or $^1/_{1000}$ nautical mile (1.852 m, *c*.6.076 feet); see *orguia*

foot: 12 inches = 30.48 cm

furlong = 220 yards = $^1/_8$ English/US mile = 201.168 m (sometimes used to translate *stadion*, though not in this work)

inch: 25.4 mm

mile (1), nautical = 1,000 fathoms = 1,852 m, corresponding to 1′ (1 minute) of arc of the Earth's surface

mile (2), English/US = 1,760 yards = 5,280 feet = 1,609.344 m

mile (3), Roman = ᴸ*mille passūs* or ᴸ*mille passuum* (pl. ᴸ*milia passuum*): Roman mile of *c*.1,478.5 m

nautical mile: *see* mile (nautical)

orguia, 'fathom' = $^1/_{100}$ stade

parasang (English word) = Greek *parasangēs* (Persian *farsang*): roughly an hour's march or *c*.3 miles (*c*.5 km)

ᴸ*passus* '(double) pace' = $^1/_{1000}$ Roman mile = *c*.1.48 m (*c*.4 feet 10 inches); but half a fathom at Poseidonios 17 *pēchys*, 'cubit' = *c*.18 inches (*c*.46 cm), usually measured from wrist to elbow[5]

plethron, pl. *plethra* = *c*.100 feet (*c*.30 m)

schoinos, pl. *schoinoi*: a variable measure of distance in Egypt; see 'Equivalances' below

stade (Greek *stadion*, pl. *stadia*), lit. 'running track'; variable but commonly thought to
average *c*.606 English/US feet (*c*.185 m).[6] (See, further, under 'Equivalences' below.)

yard: 3 feet = 91.44 cm

Equivalences (longest first)

schoinos = 30–120 stades = *c*.5.3–*c*.23.6 km (depending on value of *stadion*)

parasang = 30–60 stades = *c*.5.3–*c*.11.8 km (depending on value of *stadion*)

[L]*mille passūs* or [L]*mille passuum*, a Roman mile (*milion* in Greek) = 8⅓ or 8¼ or 8 (the
commonest value) or 7½ stades = 1,000 (double) paces

stadion ('stade') = 6 *plethra* = 600 Greek feet, variously calculated as (for example) *c*.177.7 m
(*c*.194 yds) or *c*.179.5 m (*c*.196 yds) or *c*.185.1 m (*c*.202 yds, the commonest value) or *c*.197.5
m (*c*.216 yds); sometimes (but not in this book) translated 'furlong' (i.e. 220 yds, *c*.201
m). The variation in the computed length of the *stadion* is not surprising if we consider
that the surviving race-courses at Delphi, Epidauros, Athens, and Olympia imply races
of 177.3 m (*c*.193.9 yds), 181.3 m (*c*.198.3 yds), 184.3 m (*c*.201.6 yds), and 192.3 m (*c*.210.3
yds) respectively, for a double run ('there and back again').[7]

plethron = 100 feet = *c*.30 m

orguia ('fathom') = 6 feet = *c*.1.8 m

pēchys (pl. *pēcheis*), 'cubit' = *c*.18 inches = *c*.46 cm (e.g. Eudoxos of Knidos 31)

[L]*pēs* (pl. *pedēs*), 'foot'; see *pous*

pous (plural *podes*), 'foot' = *c*.1 foot = *c*.30 cm (e.g. Arrian §2)

spithamē (pl. *spithamai*), 'handspan' (thumb to little finger) = *c*.8 inches = *c*.20 cm (see
Agatharchides 100a–b; Artemidoros 98 §19)

daktylos (pl. *daktyloi*), 'finger' (e.g. '4 fingers' = *c*.2.8 inches = *c*.7 cm, Poseidonios 51)

---

[5] Dilke 1987, 23.   [6] Russo 2013 argues for an older suggestion of *c*.157.5 m.
[7] Schulzski 2006.

Abbreviations

Abbreviations of the names of classical authors and their works, modern journals, corpora, etc., follow the conventions of the *Oxford Classical Dictionary* unless otherwise specified. (Abbreviations are avoided in the main text of a chapter introduction.) Some of these are nevertheless listed below for convenience. Papyri are cited in forms such as *P. Oxy.* 42. 3000.

Short forms (e.g. Ps.-Skyl., Artem.) are sometimes used in footnotes, especially after the first occurrence of a name within a chapter and especially when a chapter, line, or section number follows. An author's or text's initial(s) (e.g. H. for Hekataios, PS for Pseudo-Skylax) may be used within footnotes in the relevant chapter only. Special short forms (e.g. Hek for Hekataios, *Nik* for the *Nikomedean Periodos*) are used in the Index and listed at the top of that section. Other forms are used in the Concordance and listed there.

'Pliny' is always Pliny the Elder unless 'the Younger' is specified. I cite his *Natural History* in the style '2. cxii. 242', where 2 is the book, cxii the traditional chapter (derived from Pliny's tables of contents in book 1), and 242 the number in the modern series of shorter sections most often used today. The 'Plinian' numbers are roman to indicate that the modern sections are a continuous series within each book, not subdivisions of the Plinian. The series of chapter numbers found in Mayhoff's Teubner edition (Mayhoff 1875–97), where (for example) ch. cxii of book 2 is Mayhoff's 108, is not indicated, but readers should be aware that it is sometimes used, as in Dicks's edition of Hipparchos' geographical fragments (Dicks 1960).

A similar system is used for Diogenes Laërtios: thus 8. viii. 86–91 refers to the life of Eudoxos of Knidos, the eighth biography in book 8, comprising sections 86–91 of that book.

Likewise, sections of Agathemeros are cited in the form 'ii. 5', where ii is one of the five parts into which the work is traditionally divided and 5 the section number in the continuous series running through the whole work.

'Introduction' (capitalized) denotes the main Introduction to this book, 'introduction' normally the introduction to another specific chapter.

Otherwise, arabic numerals are used for chapters and sections within texts. The 'section' sign § is used for cross-references to sections of a continuous text (e.g. Ps.-Skylax) or of the Introduction, but not for fragments and testimonia.

An ellipsis of the form . . . within a quoted ancient text always indicates material omitted by the translator. In all other places, such as in quotations from modern authors, ellipses are of the form [. . .]. Ellipses are not used at the start or end of a quotation unless the sense is incomplete, though they may be used when a quotation begins with a chapter or section number but the quotation is not from the beginning of the passage.

An em rule (—) on its own is a normal dash, but [—] always indicates a gap or illegible passage in the original text, not an editorial deletion.

CENTURY DATES

In editorial text, whole centuries are contracted ('2nd century', not 'second century'). In footnotes, 'century' is shortened to 'c.'.

In footnotes, the Time-line, and occasionally elsewhere, dates BC follow the style of the Copenhagen Polis Centre. For example:

C8	8th century BC
C7f	first half of 7th century BC
C6s	second half of 6th century BC
C5e	early 5th century BC
C4m	mid-4th century BC
C3l	late 3rd century BC
C2a	first quarter of 2nd century BC
C1b	second quarter of 1st century BC
C1c AD	third quarter of 1st century AD
C2d AD	fourth quarter of 2nd century AD

Sometimes, to avoid ambiguity, 'BC' is appended. For centuries AD where the era is obvious, and from the 10th onwards except in the Time-line, 'AD' is omitted.

SPECIAL SIGNS AND ABBREVIATIONS

This list includes several which, while familiar to scholars, may be less so to the student or general reader (such as §, fl., sc.).

*	(in 'Selected Further Reading' lists) a 'critical edition', i.e. with at least a revised original text and usually an *apparatus criticus* or the equivalent
†	(in a translation) an obelus (dagger) after a word indicates that it is uncertain; a pair of obeli may also enclose a sequence of words
§	section
§§	sections
·	(in Chapters 8, 12, 18–19) raised point placed before and after passages of Strabo translated by Graham Shipley (to distinguish from passages quoted or adapted from Roller 2014)
⟨ ⟩	insertion by an editor
[abc]	(in translated papyri and inscriptions) letters missing in the original and added by an editor

[—]	(in translated manuscripts) illegible or missing text (length not indicated)
‹ ›	(in Chapter 31 only) insertion by Helm
« »	(in Chapter 31 only) insertion by Müller
~	(when comparing different ancient or modern texts) approximately the same as
≈	(in measurements) approximately equals
⌟	(in Agatharchides 98 and Artemidoros 4) end of a passage designated as a fragment in Burstein 1989, if it does not coincide with the beginning of another

ad loc.	*ad locum* (when citing a commentary on a text), 'on (this) place', i.e. 'referring to this passage'
Agatharch.	Agatharchides
Agathem.	Agathemeros
anc.	ancient
Anth. Gr.	*Anthologia Graeca*, ed. Beckby 1965
app.	appendix
Ar	archaic (period)
Arr.	Arrian
Artem.	Artemidoros
Avien.	Avienus
AWP	Hippocratic *Airs, Waters, and Places*
Barr.	R. J. A. Talbert (ed.), *Barrington Atlas of the Greek and Roman World* (Princeton, NJ, 2000)
BMCR	*Bryn Mawr Classical Review*
BNJ	*Brill's New Jacoby*, 1st edition, ed. I. Worthington (Leiden, 2007–)
BNJ²	*Brill's New Jacoby*, 2nd edition, ed. I. Worthington (Leiden, 2016–)
BNP	*Brill's New Pauly*, ed. H. Cancik *et al.* (Leiden, 2002–11)
C.	Cape
cf.	compare (Latin *confer*)
CGL	J. Diggle (ed.), *The Cambridge Greek Lexicon* (Cambridge, 2021)
Cl	Classical (usually in the sense of the narrow period, C5–C4 BC, rather than the whole of the 'classical' age)
cod.	codex
COD¹²	A. Stevenson and M. Waite, eds, *The Concise Oxford English Dictionary*. 12th edition (Oxford, 2011)
DB	Dionysios of Byzantion
Diagn.	*Diagnōsis en epitomēi tēs en tēi sphairai geōgraphias* [see Introduction, §VIII. 2. a]
Dik.	Dikaiarchos
Dion. Byz.	Dionysios of Byzantion

Dion. Kall.	Dionysios son of Kalliphon
Dion. Peri.	Dionysios Periegetes
DK	Dionysios son of Kalliphon
DP	Dionysios Periegetes
EANS	P. T. Keyser and G. L. Irby-Massie, *The Encyclopedia of Ancient Natural Scientists: The Greek Tradition and its Many Heirs* (London–New York, 2008)
ed. pr.	*editio prior*, the 'original publication' (in the era of printing) of an ancient text
edn	edition
Epit. Art.	Markianos' epitome of Artemidoros (lost)
Epit. Men.	Markianos' epitome of Menippos
Erat.	Eratosthenes
esp.	especially
Eud.	Eudoxos (of Knidos)
Eux.	Pseudo-Arrian, *Circumnavigation of the Euxine*
Exp.	*Expositio*
f.	formerly
FGrH i–iii	F. Jacoby *et al.*, *Fragmente der griechischen Historiker*, i *Genealogie und Mythographie*; ii *Zeitgeschichte*; iii *Horographie und Ethnographie* (Leiden, 1923–58) [see Introduction, §VII. 3]
FGrH iv	J. Bollansée *et al.* (eds), *Felix Jacoby, Die Fragmente der griechischen Historiker Continued*, iv: *Biography and Antiquarian Literature* (Leiden, 1998–)
FGrH v	H.-J. Gehrke and F. Meier (eds), *Die Fragmente der griechischen Historiker*, v: *Geographie* (Leiden, 2011–)
FHG	C. W. L. Müller, *Fragmenta historicorum Graecorum*, 5 vols (Paris, 1841–70)
fl.	*floruit*, 'flourished' (date when an author was alive)
fo.	folio (leaf of a bound manuscript capable of having writing on both sides)
GGM	C. W. L. Müller, *Geographi Graeci minores*, 3 vols (Paris, 1855–61)
H.	(in Agatharchides) section no. from Henry's Photios
Hekat.	Hekataios (of Miletos)
Hipparch.	Hipparchos
HK	Herakleides Kritikos
Hl	hellenistic (period)
Hyp.	*Hypotypōsis*
I.	Island
i.a.	*inter alia*, 'among other things'; or *inter alios*, 'among other people'
ibid.	*ibidem*, 'in the same place' (i.e. the same work)
id.	*idem*, 'the same author' (male)
iid.	*iidem*, 'the same authors' (male)

Is.	Islands
Isid.	Isidoros
Jacoby V	same as *FGrH* v (Leiden, 2011–)
l.	line (followed by number)
L.	Lake
lit.	literally
ll.	lines (followed by numbers)
Mark.	Markianos
mi	mile(s) (English/US, not Roman)
Mnas.	Mnaseas
mod.	modern
Nik.	the anonymous *Nikomedean Periodos*, misleadingly known today as 'Pseudo-Skymnos'
NP	*Der neue Pauly*
ODB	A. P. Kazhdan (ed.), *The Oxford Dictionary of Byzantium* (Oxford, 1991)
ODLA	O. P. Nicholson (ed.), *The Oxford Dictionary of Late Antiquity* (Oxford, 2018)
pl.	plural
PLRE	A. H. M. Jones *et al.* (eds), *The Prosopography of the Later Roman Empire* (Cambridge, 1971–92), 3 vols.
PME	*Periplus maris Erythraei* (*Circumnavigation of the Erythraian Sea*)
Pos.	Poseidonios
PS	Pseudo-Skylax
Ps.-Arist.	Pseudo-Aristotle, *On the Cosmos* (*De mundo*)
Ps.-Plut.	Pseudo-Plutarch
Ps.-Skyl.	Pseudo-Skylax
Pyth.	Pytheas
r	recto (right-hand page)
r.	(before a date) 'ruled', 'reigned'
R.	River
sc.	*scilicet* (Latin), equivalent to 'that is to say'
SK	Skylax of Karyanda
Skym.	Skymnos (of Chios)
Stad.	Pseudo-Hippolytos, *Stadiasmos*
s.v.	(before title of entry in dictionary or encyclopaedia) *sub voce* (Latin), 'under the word . . .'
TIB 12	A. Külzer, *Ostthrakien* (Tabula Imperii Byzantini, 12; Vienna, 2008)
Tim.	Timosthenes
trans.	translated by; translation
v	verso (left-hand page)
vel sim.	*vel similiter* (Latin), 'or similarly'

INTRODUCTION

GREEK GEOGRAPHY AND GEOGRAPHERS

D. Graham J. Shipley*

[I]t is never wrong to plug your own line; it is almost always wrong to write off others.

(Attributed to O. H. K. Spate, Tuan 1974b, iii)

I. AIMS

These volumes cover most of the short or fragmentary ancient Greek geographical writings (a few of them preserved only in Latin versions), from the archaic period (*c.*700–*c.*500 BC) to the late antique (*c.* AD 300–600). Some have not been Englished before now; most are found only in specialist publications, usually in other languages; and they have not previously been gathered together in a form accessible to contemporary readers.[1] Together they are often classed misleadingly as 'the minor Greek geographers'. The book aims to restore these hitherto largely recondite voices to their deserved, prominent position within the canon of Greek literature, as well as to render them better audible beyond an audience of specialists. Some, such as **1** Aristeas and **30** Dionysios of Byzantion, emerge into the limelight with the aid of new research presented in these volumes. The chapters on others, such as **7** Pseudo-Skylax, **9** Dikaiarchos, **18** Artemidoros, **34** Markianos, and **36** the Pseudo-Arrianic *Euxine*, respond to recent scholarship in order to communicate a new perspective and context.[2]

The juxtaposition of sources from across almost 1,300 years of Antiquity enriches the understanding of ancient Greek geographical thought that we gain from the few surviving 'major' works (for which see §VI. 1): in particular, by highlighting similarities, inter-relationships, and differences, and especially when we emphasize (as in this Introduction) the social and cultural contexts within which geographical investigation took place and within which geographical writings were composed (see further §III. 3).[3] The hope is that the result will be many times greater than the sum of its parts.

* I thank, among others, Oliver Nicholson, Paul Smee, and Charlotte Van Regenmortel, and especially the Press's anonymous readers, for invaluable comments on this Introduction.

[1] The original undertaking was partly inspired by Warmington 1934, whose selection of extracts, occupying 255 pages, includes many used in the present volumes, but is arranged thematically rather than by author.

[2] In this Introduction, bold numbers (as in '**1** Aristeas') are those of authors or texts in the present volumes.

[3] For a similar attempt to contextualize Greek 'science' in its social milieu, see Shipley 2000, ch. 9.

The contributors have aimed to provide readable translations while maintaining the highest standards of accuracy and, as far as practicable, consistency within and between chapters. Where sufficiently continuous text survives, they aspire to offer a version that is faithful but fluent; an aim that serves not only to engross the general reader but also to enable students, teachers, and researchers in Classics, Ancient History, and Geography to reflect upon the most up-to-date scholarly ideas. Chapter introductions, annotations, and 'selected further reading' lists are designed to make the texts accessible and encourage readers to take things to the next level in their exploration. Ultimately, the aim is to stimulate further research into the cultural context within which these works were written, as well as into ancient perceptions and representations of landscapes, seascapes, and the peoples inhabiting them.

II. WHAT IS, AND WAS, GEOGRAPHY?

II. 1. INVESTIGATING

Geography, at first sight, may seem a clearly defined concept: at its simplest, the study of the Earth.[4] The term *geōgraphia*, which etymologically means 'earth-writing' or 'earth-drawing', was perhaps invented by Eratosthenes.[5] As a modern profession, however, geography is internally disparate, even loose and disconnected, because of the breadth of the range of its aims.

Typically divided into physical geography and human geography (with further subdivisions), professional geography today draws upon other subjects such as geology, seismology, volcanology, climatology, economics, sociology, political science, media studies, development studies, and international relations. Among these, only the 'earth sciences' and physical geography can in some sense be called 'pure' sciences that do not necessarily take account of the human factor; though geologists can apply their expertise in the service of archaeology, for example through geomorphology (the study of changes in land-forms) and pedology (soil science). The social sciences, as applied in geography today, express the desire to expose and challenge human practice, ostensibly in order to ameliorate human society (relations with the animal kingdom are mostly left to other physical sciences and social sciences). It is not clear that any such aim activated ancient geographical writers, other than perhaps the advancement of trade.

Also on the human side, 'historical geography' (sometimes practised by academics in history departments rather than departments of geography) tends to reconstruct the past geography of a region, or the representation of geographical thought in past

---

[4] More fully in *COD*[12]: '1 the study of the physical features of the earth and of human activity as it relates to these. 2 the relative arrangement of places and physical features. 3 [. . .] a geographical area; a region'.

[5] e.g. Dan, Crom, *et al.* 2016, 576; Roller 2015, 122.

societies (for example in their literature), rather than focusing on 'the history of geography' as such; the last does not engage many geographers today. The present book stands close to both of these last two areas (both currently to some extent backwaters within academic geography), bringing together writers who had differing interests from one another or combined disparate aspects of geography in their writing.

More active areas in recent writing about the ancient Mediterranean have been eco-history and environmental history, especially under the influence of *Annales* history, a loose grouping rather than the 'school' it is often dubbed. Its pioneers such as Marc Bloch, Lucien Febvre, and (for the Mediterranean) Fernand Braudel broke with Francophone traditions of diplomatic and military history to create *histoire totale* ('total history'), injecting social history and 'mentalities' (especially through under-exploited documents and archives for the medieval and early modern periods) as well as engaging with landscapes (including seascapes).[6] Braudel, in particular, elevated the sea, and sea routes, into historical actors, an inspirational if still metaphorical perspective. As with his evocative model of three scales of periodicity—*événements* (events),[7] *conjonctures* (series of large-scale events with common features), and perhaps most helpfully the *longue durée* (semi-permanent characteristics of society or the environment)—it has been necessary to resile from these schemes to some extent (as he himself did), though his grand ideas continue to enthuse field archaeologists in Mediterranean lands.[8] But ancient Mediterranean history no longer ignores the land, the sea, and the atmosphere even if with Peregrine Horden and Nicholas Purcell we accept that it is humankind, not the Earth, that is the agent of change and takes opportunities presented by Nature. The last two authors have also established certain key concepts as crucial, such as 'connectivity' and 'micro-ecology' (or 'micro-environment').[9] For the student of ancient geography, a striking feature of the ancient texts is how these features are very often presented as of secondary importance behind human achievements, history, and contingent circumstances.

An interesting special case in modern geographical practice is also relevant to the present work: 'humanistic geography' (particularly associated with Yi-Fu Tuan)[10]

---

[6] Febvre 1925 (English trans.) is still useful for thinking about the 'geographical history' of the Mediterranean. Braudel is chiefly known to classicists for his study of the Mediterranean world in the C16 AD, especially the first part on the *longue durée* (Engl. trans. Braudel 1972, i. 23–352).

[7] Spelled thus in his day; now *évènements*.

[8] On the *Annales* 'school' (named after its journal, *Annales: économies, sociétés, cultures* or *Annales ESC*), see e.g. the opposed views of Trevor-Roper 1972 (enthusiastic) and Hexter 1972 (critical), in the year when Braudel's most famous book was reissued in English; later, Bintliff 1991; Knapp 1992; and from an historical point of view Arnold 2000, 94–109.

[9] The epoch-making response of Horden and Purcell 2000 was at one time to be entitled 'Beyond Braudel'. For a reappraisal of the authors' work, see the chapters in Harris 2005, including one by Horden and Purcell; and their further thoughts, e.g. Horden and Purcell 2006; Horden and Purcell 2020, upon which I have not yet had an opportunity to reflect. Mathieu 2017 finds Braudel's assessment of the Alps in need of revision.

[10] See Tuan 1974a; Tuan 1974b (2nd edn, Tuan 1990); Tuan 1975; and esp. Tuan 1977. For recent overviews of humanistic geography, see P. C. Adams 2017; Seamon 2015.

investigates how people endow environments with meaning, in the interest of a better understanding of our relationship with space and place. The present book, likewise, aims to help us listen to some rarely heard voices, and to sharpen our hearing as we do so. It would be easy to view each of our writers through a 21st-century lens, for example post-colonial theory—to see Greek geographical writing as largely tainted with the ancient equivalent of imperialism or Orientalism; to see all investigation and exploration as acquisitive or aggressive—but this would ignore most of the picture.[11] How would such a view explain, for example, 15 Agatharchides' stinging criticism of the effects of Ptolemaic rule on the native peoples of East Africa, or 30 Dionysios of Byzantion's admiration of his homeland—his clear 'sense of place'?[12] Several authors reflect on the Greek homeland, for example 9 Dikaiarchos with his measurements of mountain heights and 11 Herakleides Kritikos' sketches of central Greek communities (not forgetting the *Catalogue of Ships* in the Prologue).

Modern scholars approaching the ancient geographers have tended to see their works chiefly in terms of either the advancement of knowledge, to which I have already referred, or the Greeks' inherent curiosity about the world beyond the familiar.[13] In the *longue durée*, one clear pattern is the steady increase in the understanding of what was previously more sketchily known, combined with a widening of horizons, as first Greek and then Roman traders interacted more intensively with ever more distant communities, especially in northern Europe, eastern Africa, and southern Asia—and, of course, *vice versa*. Indeed, the earliest of our authors after Homer, 1 Aristeas of Prokonnesos, already reflects an expanding Greek diaspora: he came from a Milesian colony in the Propontis (*Sea of Marmara*) and travelled north of the Black Sea.

One viewpoint draws a contrast between Greek commercial motivations for an interest in geography on the one hand, and Roman militaristic ones on the other;[14] it is a fair point to make about the genesis and nature of some of their respective geographical writings, but it should not be extended to the two cultures in general—neither of which, in any case, was monolithic. Furthermore, earlier stimuli to expanding awareness of lands beyond the eastern Mediterranean are also identified by ancient writers: first, the creation of the Persian empire (which had, indeed, a direct impact through the royal patronage that led to 2 Skylax's voyage; indirectly in Ktesias' work, see §VI. 2. d);[15] second, Alexander's conquests; third, the completion of Roman domination as the latest or final turning-point in geographical knowledge.[16] All three are mentioned in 34 Markianos' preface to Pseudo-Skylax (at §2).

---

[11] Cf. the cautions of McPhail 2016, e.g. 215–20.   [12] On 'sense of place', see Seamon 2022.
[13] Thus Dueck 2012, 123 (necessity plus curiosity). The progression of knowledge is the dominant theme of Roller 2015.
[14] The Greek–Roman contrast is drawn in terms of trade versus war by Dueck 2012, 17–18.
[15] On early Near Eastern and Egyptian patronage of exploration, see Kaplan 2008, 29–34.
[16] See e.g. Erat. 13; Markianos' preface to Menippos, §3. For the impact of Alexander's expedition on geography, see Gehrke 2016; Bucciantini 2016. Pliny celebrates how Roman arms have made new lands accessible (see Pyth. 22; Juba 4).

Ancient geography is certainly bound up with expanding horizons. Some works undoubtedly reflect the philosophical, scientific, and geopolitical situations in which they were created. This is not always a matter of ideology, however: it may simply mirror the limits of knowledge at a given time. The reign of Augustus, the first 'emperor' of Rome (more accurately *princeps* or 'first man'; r. 27 BC–AD 14), pivotal in so many ways, provides not only a bounty of geographical writing but also examples of both these phenomena: it has often been commented that Strabo's geography, begun under Augustus and completed under his successor, Tiberius, embodies a sense that Greek and Roman knowledge and power now encompassed the whole known world in some sense, even if in reality imperial control did not yet do so.[17]

II. 2. TAKING AND GIVING: GEOGRAPHY IN GREEK SOCIETY

We must beware of slipping into a kind of points-scoring competition, grading texts only on the basis of what they have contributed to current knowledge or later understanding, or attributing a wide range of action and writing to *mentalités* alone. We can aim higher by going deeper, to consider the very varied social contexts of writing in which geographical texts arose.

In antiquity, although most of the subjects and sub-disciplines mentioned above did not exist—indeed, few subjects of study were formally defined at all before the hellenistic period (the last three centuries BC)—geographical writers tended to draw simultaneously upon what we would call (*a*) the earth sciences as well as cosmology, astronomy, and mathematics, and (*b*) history, legend, and mythology, as well as (*c*) detailed description of population groups or 'nations' (often called *ethnē*, the plural of *ethnos*) and their customs and economies.[18] A given author might combine these elements in different proportions or focus exclusively on two or even one. Yet scholars persist in classifying the geographers: the hundred-odd authors covered by the Jacoby V project in progress (see §VII. 3 below), for example, are divided into 'descriptive geography', 'mathematical geography', and 'exploration'.[19] To what extent are these modern constructs either valid or operable?[20] Why count Polybios as a mathematical geographer and not an explorer? Or Hipparchos as only a mathematical geographer and not also a descriptive? For that matter, why does the shadowy Pausanias of Damascus (if he is real) appear only in the historiographical parts of 'Jacoby'?[21]

The interface with historiography is often crucial. In all but its purely mathematical aspects, Greek geography shows awareness of the past of the places it describes, and may be said to have developed out of not only cosmology (eternal structures of the

---

[17] This is the main message of Nicolet 1988, trans. as Nicolet 1991. On Strabo generally, see the references under section III below. See also Dueck 2012, 43–4.

[18] Cf. Talbert 2012b: 'the bounds of geography as a discipline always remained loose [. . .] no distinct format or style came to be prescribed for contributions made to it'.

[19] Gehrke n.d.   [20] For similar observations, see Dan, Crom, *et al.* 2016, 574.

[21] See *FGrH* 854.

world and its heavenly location) but also mythology.[22] As well as his more geographical work (whose title, if any, is uncertain), 3 Hekataios wrote *Genealogies* focusing on the history and foundations of existing communities. Even leaving aside historians such as Herodotos, whose main business was naturally long-ago and recent events, many geographical writers had one eye firmly on the past. Then, even more than now, history and geography were inseparable.[23] Conversely, geography and geographical knowledge were used by other domains: for example, an awareness of hydrological and climatic environments informs discussion of medical prognoses in 5 *Airs, Waters, and Places*.

As already noted, the different social milieux in which people wrote must be considered. Much of the preserved, or quoted, writing reflects elite culture and was created by educated men from the leisured, politically active levels of society; such is probably the case with, for example, 3 Hekataios and 4 Hanno (if real). Some writers foreground their status as members of a *polis* (city-state), such as 6 Eudoxos of Knidos, 8 Pytheas, 11 Herakleides Kritikos, 16 Hipparchos, and 18 Artemidoros. Others were in royal or imperial service, like 2 Skylax, 10 Timosthenes, 27 Arrian, and perhaps the authors of 31 the *Stadiasmos* and 36 the Pseudo-Arrianic *Euxine*. Some, perhaps enjoying the birth-given advantages of leisure and self-supporting resources, depended upon patronage, as may have been the case with 12 Eratosthenes, 15 Agatharchides, the author of 17 the *Nikomedean Periodos*, and 34 Markianos. Patronage may extend to the private academy within a *polis* context, as seems to be the case with 7 Pseudo-Skylax and 9 Dikaiarchos. Occasionally we find texts directly related to a profession, such as 5 *Airs, Waters, and Places*, 25 *Circumnavigation of the Erythraian Sea*, and probably 33 *Expositio*. Any of these may spread over into seemingly autonomous scholarship with no obviously utilitarian purpose, like the efforts of 21 Menippos, 27 Arrian, and 34 Markianos to compile collections of geographical writings; likewise 29 Agathemeros and the authors of the later prefaces that were added to the corpus of geographical writings first assembled by Arrian (33 *Hypotyposis* and the much later text known as *Diagnosis*; for the last, and for the corpus, see §VIII. 2. a); and of course into purely literary undertakings like the works of poets (17 the *Nikomedean Periodos*, 20 Dionysios son of Kalliphon, 28 Dionysios Periegetes, and 32 Avienus). The process of conceptualizing geography was characteristic of the intellectual life of educated Greeks, that is, mostly male citizens—though one female geographer of hellenistic date, Hestiaia, is known (§VI. 4. c).[24] Geographical writings represent attempts to categorize, and sometimes to theorize about, observed phenomena at the local, regional, global, or cosmic level as they were encountered, and increasingly widely explored, by the citizen communities of archaic to hellenistic Greece, and then of provincial societies under the Roman empire.

---

[22] I am grateful to Yi-Fu Tuan for discussion of this point.   [23] Clarke 1999, ch. 1.
[24] On the absence of 'professional' geographers in antiquity, see Dan, Crom, *et al.* 2016, 574.

Despite these elite features, geographical writings also had their roots in a variety of real experiences specific to different social groups: from labourers with narrow horizons to soldiers, traders, commanders, and intellectuals whose lives took them into wider geographical areas; increasingly wide, indeed, over the course of the thirteen hundred years covered by these texts. The direct evidence for 'popular' ideas about geography is limited, but indirect evidence abounds: for example, in 'administrative and legal texts [. . .] Roman military diplomas and many other inscriptions, sundials, *tesserae*,[25] and a range of further sources. Works of literary imagination may also provide such evidence, just as Aeschylus in his tragedies felt able to refer without explanation to ideas about remote parts of Europe and western Asia.[26] Poets referring to exotic geographical information did not require detailed knowledge on the part of an audience, any more than they aimed to impart detailed knowledge,[27] but they presumed mental schemata of the general form of the wider world.[28] Philosophical dialogues such as Xenophon's *Oikonomikos* (*Estate Manager*), read against the grain,[29] reveal unstated assumptions about the organization of activity and space across a landscape. We shall return in §III. 2. c to the different 'levels' of geographical understanding and where our texts lie within that hierarchy.

Works can thus be grouped according to the motives we impute to the writer, which may account for the underlying research (or selection of information) and the desire to communicate it. Among possible motives that may be envisaged are the following, though the distinctions and boundaries between motives are often flexible: communicating new 'scientific' data; expounding a new theory or refining an existing one; applying a theory to one's own observational data; communicating one's own observational data; communicating such data collected from previous writers rather than through autopsy; updating earlier writings; instructing or guiding about geography; instructing or guiding about life; meeting a public interest; communicating with another person 'privately'; exploring and expressing local identities (e.g. foundation legends); fulfilling the aims of one's state or one's employer; seeking or responding to patronage; promoting professional development; promoting commerce; advancing a political view; displaying literary skill; or entertaining. As we shall see in §III. 2. c, these may broadly be mapped onto different modes or 'levels' of understanding of 'geography'. Among the writers selected for these volumes, the commonest motivations we can attribute to authors for writing and dissemination are probably the desire to display new knowledge, and the desire or need to fulfil the wishes of a state, employer, or patron. On this basis, it seems simplistic to classify authors into the three basic categories mentioned above; and this finding will bear upon our discussion of 'genre' and its visibility in this body of work.

---

[25] As recommended by Talbert 2012b.   [26] Roller 2015, 62–3; Dueck 2012, 119–20.
[27] Dueck 2012, 31–4.   [28] For mental schemata, cf. Tuan 1975.
[29] For 'reading against the grain', see Arnold 2000, 102–4.

III. THE CHARACTER OF ANCIENT
GEOGRAPHICAL WRITING

Having briefly surveyed the field of ancient geographical writers, we may turn to the content and form of their works.[30]

III. 1. MODES OF ORGANIZATION

It should be noted that geographical writing down to the Late Antique period was nearly all in Greek.[31] Having developed the field in the classical and early hellenistic periods (and apparently effected the translation of a Carthaginian source into Greek), educated Greeks, or Hellenes, continued to provide most of the impetus for the continual revision and enlargement of the subject. We need not psychologize this in terms of Roman reluctance to engage with the subject, or their greater concern with practical than with theoretical matters; in any case, the majority of Greek geographical writing was descriptive or/and practical in tenor. It was simply that elite Romans, from the middle Republic (say, 250–100 BC) onwards, read Greek as readily as Latin, so that for them language was no barrier; and that most regions of strategic interest to Rome at that time were in the central and eastern Mediterranean, where the 'official language' of a city was usually Greek.

By the late Republic, when the Romans encountered non-Greek-speakers, they did begin to describe them in Latin, as Julius Caesar did in his *Gallic War* memoirs in the 50s BC. Under the early Principate, Tacitus immortalized the British peoples in a tribute to his father-in-law Agricola (AD 40–93), a former governor of Britain, and then portrayed the Germanic peoples in his *Germania*, admittedly derivative rather than based on eye-witness observation.[32] The same century also saw a Latin overview of world geography by Pomponius Mela (§VI. 1. b)—the first 'Roman geographer' properly speaking—and a Latin compendium of geographical information by Pliny the Elder (§VI. 1. c). Nor should we neglect the work of the Roman land surveyors, whose techniques for modifying landscapes, developed and refined from Republican times onwards, were embodied in extensive technical treatises in Latin during Imperial and Late Antique times.[33] In terms of geographical writings proper, however, the authors of those centuries were still mostly composing in Greek, with exceptions such as the poet **32** Avien(i)us (who is, however, reworking Greek writing) and the much less literary author of **33** *Expositio*.

---

[30] On the history of the study of ancient geography, see Koelsch 2013 (but note the cautions of Talbert 2015).

[31] On Greek domination of the field, see Dueck 2012, 17–19.

[32] On the *Germania* in relation to earlier geography writing and as reacting against the mythic and fantastical, see Jessica Lightfoot 2020b.

[33] See especially J. B. Campbell 1996; 2000.

Four category terms commonly applied to geographical writings—by both ancient writers and modern scholars—may here be introduced (they are also in the Glossary). Whether these terms were present in the minds of writers, and whether they constituted 'genres' in the sense of templates for organizing one's writing in certain ways, is considered in §III. 2 below. It is important to note that ancient writings, particularly before the rise of scholarship in the 3rd century BC, may not have had formal or stable titles. (Indeed, what appear to be multiple works by the same author with different titles may sometimes be one and the same work.)[34]

a. Gēs periodos

Some extant or lost works are referred to, at least after their date of writing, as a *gēs periodos* (or *periodos gēs*), a 'way (*periodos*) round the Earth (*gē*)' or, more comprehensibly, a 'circuit of the Earth'. Hekataios' book (3), variously referred to as *Periodos ges* or *Periegesis* (for the latter term, see (*c*) below), adopted a clockwise organization beginning in western Europe, a structure followed by many later geographical works, though not all. *Periodos* is also the term used by Herodotos for the map supposedly displayed by Aristagoras around 499 BC (see §V. 2 below). The application of the category term *gēs periodos* probably indicates that a written work attempted to depict, in greater or lesser detail, the whole inhabited world, relative to how much was known of distant lands at a given time. It might focus on settled areas, or might include inland regions too. *Periodos* can also be qualified with a regional name, as in 'the *periodos* of Asia'.

b. Periplous and paraplous

A second term, *periplous*,[35] is applied, as a title or as a descriptive term, to a wide range of geographical writings.[36] It literally means 'sailing (*plous*) round (*peri-*)' or 'circumnavigation', and denotes the description of an (actual or virtual) sea journey along, or round, the coasts of a land mass. A third, related term is *paraplous*, a 'sailing beside (*para-*)' or 'coastal sailing'; in some texts it denotes a section within a *periplous* giving the length of a particular region's coast.[37] (Two other terms, formed, like *periplous* and *paraplous*, from the noun *plous*, a 'sailing' or 'voyage', are *anaplous* and *diaplous*, both explained in the Glossary.)

Periplous does not necessarily, or even usually, denote the record of an actual sea journey; more often it means a written enumeration of places in coastal sequence, whether with the aim of providing guidance to future navigators (or their financial or military backers), as in **27** Arrian's *Periplous of the Euxeinos Pontos*, or of measuring

---

[34] On the uneven evolution of fixed titles for books, see Castelli 2020, who distinguishes Ar and Cl verse from prose and argues that Xenophon (not only in his histories but also in his wider oeuvre) and Plato mark a turning-point (see e.g. summary of conclusions, at 321).

[35] Plural περίπλοι–*periploi* (Latin *peripli*).

[36] See e.g. introductions to Chs 2, 4, 7, 10, 13–14, 21, 25, 27, 31, 34, and 36.

[37] Other early occurrences of the word *periplous* refer to specific actual or potential journeys (e.g. Hdt. 6. 95; Thuc. 2. 80. 1; Xen. *Hell.* 6. 2. 27) and a tactical manoeuvre in a naval battle (Thuc. 7. 36 etc.). See e.g. Shipley 2021a.

summative long distances between ports and landmarks, as in 7 Ps.-Skylax, or of offering a stirring narrative of exploration, as may be the case with 4 Hanno.[38]

Such a textual narrative, or quasi-narrative, typically contains a list of cities and landmarks, together with indications of sailing times and/or distances. A *periplous* could be comprehensive in some sense, like 7 Ps.-Skylax's retrospectively named *Periplous of the Oikoumene* ('circumnavigation of the inhabited (world)') or 34 Markianos' self-designated *Periplous of the Outer Sea*; or regional, like 4 Hanno's real or imaginary journey along Morocco and beyond. As the label suggests, this kind of writing would focus on the coast at the expense of the interior. In explanation of the way Ps.-Skylax's narration of his coastal sequence changes its character at a number of points, it has been suggested that he is partly drawing on other *periploi* that described the coasts of particular regions of the Mediterranean and Black Sea. On this view, *periploi* of the latter kind—whose existence can only be assumed—will originally have been purely functional documents designed to assist the planning of voyages. They were not necessarily used by sea-captains, who even if literate would surely need no such outline information for places they had visited before,[39] as their experience would tell them how to construct a plan for a long-distance voyage from a succession of intermediate stages; while for journeys to places to which they had not previously travelled they could consult other sailors or local pilots in the destination region. Such regional *periploi* were perhaps maintained, rather, by merchants and financiers,[40] or conceivably kept in the archives of a city-state or its ruler.

Thus a distinction can be drawn between (*a*) functional *periploi*, the existence of many of which we infer but whose only surviving instances are, perhaps, the incomplete text of 4 Hanno (if it is genuine) and Roman-period works such as 25 *Circumnavigation of the Erythraian Sea*, 27 Arrian's *Euxine* (and its late antique 'second edition', 36), and 31 the *Stadiasmos*; (*b*) other works that take on the mantle of the *periplous* format but with very different aims, either (i) broadly scientific and academic or (ii) more literary. One example of the more scientific type is 7 Ps.-Skylax, which (as argued in the relevant chapter) is an academic exercise in world-construction rather than a work related to actual travel. This may be why the author occasionally departs from the coast to mention features of the interior, such as towns in Laconia and Arkadia (§45, §46. 2) or the overall shape of Egypt (§106. 3), even though one of his overriding aims is to calculate the length of the coasts of the inner seas. Artemidoros and Markianos performed similar exercises. Texts of a primarily literary character include 17 the *Nikomedean Periodos*, 20 Dionysios son of Kalliphon, and 28 Dionysios Periegetes (with Avienus' Latin reworking of it, not in this collection). Arrian's *Periplous* (27), already noted above as a functional *periplous*, was addressed to Hadrian and, obviously,

---

[38] On the 'corpus' of *periploi*, see González Ponce 2008b, 17–48.

[39] For a similar view, see Kaplan 2008, 28.

[40] For Greek nautical writings as more probably of use to 'geographers, travelers, and merchants' than to sailors as such, see Davis 2009, 196–7.

published later, and was surely seen by its author as a literary achievement. Other works combining both aspects may include that of 21 Menippos.

In general, it appears that, at least down to the classical period, the fact that a more functional work of type (*a*) may have been called a *periplous*, then or later, does not entail that its author had in mind, in advance of putting pen to paper, a particular way of organizing his material. Rather, the appellation is bestowed with hindsight. The 'coastal sailing' format, in essence, was simply dictated by the needs of the material, where *periploi* were designed to be consulted by people planning voyages. Where a *periplous* was non-functional (*b*), the author adopted the already conventional places-and-distances sequence for either (i) scientific or (ii) literary reasons, and in these cases it may be meaningful to speak of the *periplous* format as a model or 'genre' (see §III. 2 below).

c. Periēgēsis

A fourth term, *periēgēsis*, a 'guiding round' or more colloquially a guided tour, tends to imply an account of one or more specified regions which includes both coastal and inland areas. Originally applied to guidebooks for visitors to major religious sanctuaries, perhaps in the 3rd or 2nd century BC,[41] it could still be used literally, as by Strabo,[42] but was transferred in the Hadrianic era (in its noun form, *periēgētēs*, 'guide'), to the poet 28 Dionysios of Alexandria, known today as Dionysios Periegetes; the sobriquet captures how he has a totalizing or holistic view of the *oikoumenē* similar to that of his near-contemporary Pausanias of Magnesia, author of the extant *Periegesis of Hellas*.

∗∗∗

The terms *periodos*, *periplous* (with *paraplous*), and *periēgēsis* are usually applied to texts retrospectively, and some works are easier to classify in this simple way than others.[43] They helpfully bring out recurrent features of these writings, and thus indirectly highlight the differences between them, to which we shall return; but, as already noted, they should not be seen as strictly separate templates or models (see further §III. 2). They also touch on the possible relationship between cartography and text, and whether writers designed their text to be read alongside a map (discussed further in §V).

d. Chōrographia

We have distinguished between (relatively) comprehensive and partial, or regional, geographies. A key term that to some extent cuts across others above is *chōrographia* ('chorography', lit. 'land- or territory-writing'), formed from *chōra*, meaning 'land' in general or the territory of a city. Its noun form, *chōrographos* ('chorographer'), first occurs in Strabo, who supposes that in a world geography one man may be the

---

[41] Marcotte 2000b, lxii–lxxiii.

[42] e.g. 5. 2. 1, C218, stating that the region of Liguria has 'nothing worth a guided tour'.

[43] On these three categories, see the helpful discussions of Marcotte 2000b, lv–lxxii; Dueck 2012, 6–10.

chōrographos for one region, another man for another.[44] The earliest definite use of the term *chōrographia* is earlier, in a Cretan inscription of 139 BC, where it denotes a local survey of the frontiers between two cities.[45] Around the same time, in the mid-2nd century BC, Polybios may have used the term in his *Histories*, if an apparently verbatim quotation by Strabo is accurate,[46] in which the historian is alleged to have used it to mean the general description of a specific region including localities and distances.[47] The quotation is usually assigned to book 34, one of the last 'decade' of books in Polybios' *Histories*, thought to have been completed after 129 BC;[48] we shall see later (§VI. 2. g) that he did not necessarily gather all his geographical material into that book; but it remains possible that, if he did use the term, he did so at a date later than that of the Cretan inscription. Either way, by the last quarter of the 2nd century *chōrographia* had both a narrower and a broader sense. Elsewhere Strabo uses an adjectival form of the word, *chōrographikos*, coupled with *pinax*, 'tablet', to refer to a hypothetical depiction of the whole world in map or data-table form.[49] Once again, *chōrographia* and its cognates seem like class terms that have been generalized from a set of instances, rather than 'genre' terms defined *a priori* and used as templates for writing.

III. 2. DIVERSITY AND GENRE

While a simple division of works into exploratory, mathematical, and descriptive is no longer satisfying, we can identify a valid pattern of differential interest in Greek geographical writings during the later centuries of our period. In general, the more descriptive works are likelier to survive than the more mathematical or theoretical, owing to the selective interests of Roman and late Roman writers.[50]

a. Issues of Genre

The beginnings of genre classification appear in the 4th century BC, in Plato's philosophical dialogues.[51] In one work he distinguishes different kinds of poetry as tragedy,

---

[44] Strabo 1. 1. 16, C9. Strabo also refers repeatedly to 'the Chorographer' as a source; that writer's identity is debated (Diller 1958, 532; Roller 2015, 167).

[45] *Syll.*[3] 685, an arbitration between Cretan city-states concerning disputed territory: l. 71, καθότι καὶ διὰ τῶν ἐπιδεικνυμένων ἡμῖν χ[ωρο]γραφιῶν εὐσύνοπτον ἦ[ν], 'as was also evident from the *chōrographiai* displayed to us'.

[46] Strabo 10. 3. 5, C465 = Polyb. 34. 1. 15 = Artem. 81 and Pos. 6 below: 'we will show things as they are, concerning both the position of places and the distances between them, for this is most suitable for chorography' (trans. Roller).

[47] Cf. also Strabo 2. 4. 1, C104 = Polyb. 34. 5. 1 = Pyth. 6 and Erat. 18 below: 'Polybios says that in his European chorography he omits those from antiquity in favour of those who refute them' (trans. Roller).

[48] Walbank 1980, 43 = Walbank 2002, 195–6.   [49] Strabo 2. 5. 17, C120.

[50] Marcotte 2000b, lix.

[51] See the important remarks of Dover 1983, 60–1: genre may have influenced historiographers in C4, but not yet in C5 when writers were pioneers; he warns that exaggerated ideas of the importance of genre to writers 'may promote hasty judgment on matters remote from poetry, especially when there is a temptation to formulate sweeping rules of genre'. Against the over-rigid use of 'genre', see Conte and

comedy, and dithyramb (a lyric myth-narrative, or a hymn to Dionysos).[52] Later he divides music into hymns, dirges (*thrēnoi*), paeans, dithyrambs, and nomes (*nomoi*, a kind of song; cf. **10** Timosthenes, extract 8). Genre as an analytical concept seems to have been further developed by Aristotle in the *Poetics*, then elaborated by poets and scholars in the hellenistic period as a way of exploring relationships between different kinds of poetic text—above all epic, tragedy, and comedy—rather than between other kinds of writing,[53] though it was extended over time to other forms of verse such as didactic and personal poetry. Greek poetic genres comprised epic, elegy, tragedy, comedy, mime, hymn, iambus (typically humorous, satirical, or political), *epinikion* (victory hymn), *eidyllion* (idyll, typically pastoral), and *epyllion* (little epic).[54] But none of our geographical poems (other than, obviously, Homer's Catalogue), even the iambic poems (**17** the *Nikomedean Periodos* and **20** Dionysios son of Kalliphon, both in comic iambics), would fit any of these; if anything, categories such as *gēs periodos* and *periēgēsis*, normally used for prose works, would be more appropriate though, as has been noted above, inadequate. The main prose genres defined in antiquity were *logos* (story, tale, oration), *historia* (enquiry), and *dialogos* (philosophical dialogue); but again, it would be terms with geographical import that would be used, if any can, to define our prose geographical texts. The attempt to pin them down seems unlikely to succeed.

The key feature of generic composition in its full flowering is the conscious imitation of and variation upon earlier models that a sensitive reader is expected to detect and appreciate. On this measure, it may be doubted whether any of the categories of geographical writing, other than the philosophical (**24** Ps.-Aristotle) and poetic (**1** Aristeas; **17** the *Nikomedean Periodos*; **20** Dionysios son of Kalliphon; **28** Dionysios Periegetes; **32** Avienus), have the potential to fulfil high literary expectations; while it may be equally doubted that the more functional kinds of *periplous* are 'literary' products at all, or fall within the ambit of genre theory as such. The poetic works that adopt a *periplous* format may well have more 'generic' features—necessarily so in poems such as the *Nikomedean Periodos* and those by Dionysios son of Kalliphon and Dionysios Periegetes, who are calling the reader to compare them with earlier poets as well as with prose geography. The salient characteristics of what came to be called *gēs periodoi* and *periēgēseis*, too, are perhaps slightly more genre-like than those of literary prose in *periplous* format.[55] Moreover, certain literary qualities may be seen in chorographic accounts of regions, such as the geographical and ethnographic passages of **15**

Most 1996 ('Much confusion has been caused in modern times both by attempts to hypostasize genres, attributing to them an existence independent of the particular literary works, and by the opposed overreaction, denying the very existence of genres'); Shipley 2011, 20–1 ~ Shipley 2019, 22; Shipley 2012, 134–5; but esp. Dan, Crom, *et al.* 2016, 574–7 *passim*, 582.

[52] *Republic* 3. 394 b–c.   [53] See in general the useful discussion by Huß and Huß 2006.
[54] Latin scholars and poets adopted these, adding a few home-grown ones such as *satura*, 'satire'.
[55] On the relevance of genre to geographical poems, see Dueck 2012, 28–31.

Agatharchides on north-east Africa;[56] possibly the humorous sketch of central Greece by 11 Herakleides Kritikos in the previous century; certainly, one supposes, in the *Hellados Periegesis* of Pausanias of Magnesia. Again, however, each geographical work has a plurality of features, and there is no formulaic repetition in the ways in which material is organized. On the other hand, there is a marked tendency among geographical writers, whether in primarily geographical works or others such as histories, to interpret landscape and seascapes from a political point of view,[57] rather than to be governed by some sense of a template that dictates choices or must be consciously departed from.

For a strange example of formulaic composition, one may look at 26 Ps.-Plutarch, where each of the twenty-five river stories begins, develops, and concludes in almost identical fashion, to the point of tedium. By contrast, 27 Arrian's *periplous* has a unique style of opening: an address to the emperor, followed by an account of the restoration of a monument.

b. Explanations of Diversity

It is the oft-observed diversity of presentation in these sources, and the lack of any uniform way of representing space and movement,[58] that catch the eye: whether in terms of the sequencing of sections, or of the linguistic register employed. In large part, the evolution of geographical prose is dictated by the expansion of knowledge into new regions rather than by any literary desire to display adherence to a schema of style or organization or departure from it.[59] If the above categories are not to be taken as formal models requiring either a standard approach to the structuring of material or the adoption of stylistic features, then we could relax the denotation of the term 'genre'—often applied to Greek geographical writing in general, or to one of the above categories in particular—down to the level of a simple 'family resemblance' between different kinds of work, largely dictated by the content—whose selection and organization seems markedly lacking in consistency. This would be particularly applicable to the claimed 'periplographic genre'.[60] Content alone does not make a genre; it is a matter of intended readership.[61]

c. Common Sense Geography

A more helpful perspective assesses authors according to the level of understanding they (*a*) display, (*b*) expect readers to recognize, and (*c*) wish to promote. The notion of three levels of understanding has been developed by Dan, Geus, Thiering, and others in

---

[56] See Roller 2015, 113: Agatharchides probably summarized work of earlier writers such as Philon and Timosthenes, though R. rightly says A.'s work is mainly historical (cf. also his p. 112 on Philon's expedition and A.'s discussion of topaz). On A.'s aims and sources, see also Marcotte 2016, 166–73.

[57] Bianchetti 2013.   [58] Rightly emphasized by Dueck 2012, 9, 66–7.

[59] Cf. Roller 2015, 78–80.

[60] The notion of the *genere periplografico* continues to influence treatments of the geographers, as in Brillante 2020, 44; 60 *bis*; see also Shipley 2023.

[61] A defining feature of *periploi* may, in fact, be that they were usually compiled from older works: Arnaud 2017b, 726–7.

several publications,[62] recognizing that (i) the most scientific, 'fully reasoned' framing of material (also 'intellectual' or 'abstract')[63] occurs but rarely in antiquity (for example with Ptolemy of Alexandria in the 2nd century AD), while (ii) the unscientific, 'intuitive' (also 'naïve', 'concrete', or 'practical') is equally uncommon in literary works but may appear in everyday documents and itineraries and presumably appeared in forms never written down, serving well the professional groups such as guides, merchants, and translators. Between these poles lies (iii) the main focus of our texts, 'common sense geography' (also 'scholarly', 'canonical', 'traditional'), designed to satisfy educated readers: 'common sense' not connoting 'unexamined' or 'inconsistent', but in the sense which illuminates the actual social roles of literature. Scholarly geographical texts, then, hardly come close to the modern definition of science, in which we expect the development and consistent application of a theory across all relevant data, the open acknowledgement of sources, the rational (especially numerical or statistical) comparison and evaluation of contradictory data, and the testing of hypotheses against observation or experiment. Even Ptolemy does not exemplify these four criteria.

Hence we can—with greater confidence thanks to the work of these specialists—lay down certain 'rules of engagement' with our texts, such as the following. (i) Few of them fulfilled an indispensable practical need, even though all but the most abstract contained information that was derived ultimately from original primary data (e.g. mariners' experience or the observation of the author themselves). (ii) They need not be separated into descriptive, mathematical, and exploratory. (iii) Neither should we impose genre constraints, as if, for example, authors had to follow templates designated *periodos, periēgēsis, periplous, chōrographia*, etc.; though it remains true that given passages within a text, or even a text as a whole, may reflect one or more of these in a varying balance, or may be chiefly characterized by one in particular.

Apart from widening horizons—more accurate knowledge of southern Asia and China, for example, emerging from the fog of ignorance during the Roman Imperial period, as seen in **25** *Circumnavigation of the Erythraian Sea* and **34** Markianos and reflected in the compendious dataset collected by Ptolemy from the work of Marinus—a number of other *longue durée* changes can be seen. On a simple level, works written in the era of Roman supremacy reflect, unsurprisingly, the assumption that Rome is all-powerful and is here to stay. Yet neither Greek nor Roman writers consistently denigrate the Others in their world, in the way that we have become accustomed to assume in the past generation.[64] While there are misrepresentations, simplifications, inventions, and prejudices, as well as concoctions of fantasy unrelieved by contact with reality, Greek historians and geographers, hellenistic poets, and Roman aristocrats often express a boundless fascination with other cultures and a desire to explain

[62] See esp. Geus and Thiering 2014 and (more developed) Dan, Crom, *et al.* 2016.
[63] In the parentheses I collect a number of adjectives used by those authors to characterize each of the three levels.
[64] For a countervailing caution, see McPhail 2016.

them in detail to others. Not all authors' accounts may approximate to the notion of the 'noble savage' as does **15** Agatharchides' of the Ichthyophagoi (Fish-eaters), who in his depiction (§49) are happily immune to the ambition and luxury that distract the rest of us from the good life; often foreign peoples are admired for their sense of justice, their good behaviour, their truthfulness, and so on. The more the Mediterranean peoples got to know about peoples beyond their world, the more a simplistic or crude division between 'us' and 'them' was broken down in the face of the facts. Greek and Roman writers may be largely ethnocentric in their assumption that their own civilization is superior (and which culture is not?), but they do not suppose that those of different ethnicity, if not already civilized, are incapable of becoming so in spite of the deterministic qualities of their places of residence.[65]

III. 3. RECURRENT TOPICS

Still there remain areas in which Greek writers and thinkers seem to have been motivated by a 'pure' desire to be the first finder of something, to discover or create new data and to disseminate it. This, of course, was bound up with their own social standing, acknowledged credentials, and self-evaluation as well as their performative roles in society.

The provision of information that may be useful to navigators, or to those in authority devising and launching voyages, is certainly a recurrent feature of some of our texts. Not only land and sea distances (§IV below), but also stopping-points and landmarks, form part of the texture of both 'functional' and 'literary' *periploi* (for this distinction, see §III. 1. b). In the hellenistic and Roman periods, not only harbours, anchorages of different kinds (see §X and the Glossary), and settlements but also towers (*pyrgoi*) appear in coastal enumerations (see (j) below).

a. The Earth

Reflecting the origins of Greek geographical thinking in early Ionian cosmology, writers throughout the millennium covered in this collection return again and again to the theme of the overall shape and size of the Earth. The realization that the Earth is round came early and was not abandoned even during the Christian era (despite the popular belief today that this was so), though there was room for uncertainty as late as the mid-4th century BC, when Aristotle shows awareness of both the flat-Earth and the round-Earth theory.[66] As we noted earlier (§VI. 1. f), some Christian writers rejected a spherical Earth, but still in the Carolingian period the ruler might be depicted holding an orb representing the Earth.[67]

---

[65] Cf. Dueck 2012, 88–9.

[66] *De Caelo*, 2. 13, and *Mete.* 2. 7, respectively. On these notions, see Dueck 2012 69–70; Roller 2015, 28–30; and §VI. 1 n. 239 below.

[67] Cf. the C9 equestrian sculpture of Charlemagne or Charles the Bald (Musée du Louvre OA 8260, https://collections.louvre.fr/en/ark:/53355/cl010099888). Similarly, J. B. Russell 1991 argues that most

The attempt to estimate or calculate the sphere's circumference may have begun, likewise, with Plato's associate Archytas of Taras, a Pythagorean,[68] and been taken up by Aristotle, who posits 400,000 stades (*c.*50,000 mi, *c.*80,000 km),[69] twice the actual figure but not an absurd estimate given the unavailability of accurate data. Experiments to refine the figure followed within a century, conducted by, probably, 9 Dikaiarchos and then 12 Eratosthenes; the issue was further broached by 16 Hipparchos, 19 Poseidonios, 34 Markianos, and the author of 35 the late antique *Hypotyposis*.

b. The Oikoumenē

The dimensions and shape of the *oikoumenē*, the 'inhabited' portion of the Earth's surface, were a matter of prolonged debate. The term may have been introduced by Aristotle,[70] though the participial phrase 'the (*part of the*) Earth inhabited by us' occurs in an apparent quotation from the 5th-century philosopher Xenophanes.[71] Different constructions were given successively by Aristotle (*Meteorologika* 2. 5, 362b 13, etc.), 9 Dikaiarchos, 12 Eratosthenes, 16 Hipparchos, 19 Poseidonios, and others (see index s.v. *oikoumenē*) but no consensus was reached, so that Ptolemy could even make it extend over 180 degrees of longitude, a vast over-estimate: China, the most easterly land then known to Mediterranean writers, extends no further than about 150 degrees east of the Canary Islands, where Ptolemy placed his zero longitude.[72]

c. Latitude

It was relatively easy to establish the latitude of a place once a baseline was defined. The earlier manner of expressing what we call latitude in terms of the length of the day at the two equinoxes is seen in 8 Pytheas, who observed the changes in the elevation of the sun as he travelled in northern European latitudes. Latitude still appears to have been described in terms of hours by 12 Eratosthenes, 16 Hipparchos, and 19 Poseidonios. (This, incidentally, implies the adoption of a 'mean' or standard length for the hour.) 9 Dikaiarchos, however, had devised a central parallel running the length of the Mediterranean and on to the Himalayas; defined as a series of straight lines between known places, but slightly irregular, this was used as the line of zero latitude until Eratosthenes devised a straighter version; later it was replaced by the equator.[73]

d. Longitude

Longitude was much harder to calculate. The notion of parallel meridians existed early: in the 3rd century BC, for example, 12 Eratosthenes added a line from Alexandria through Rhodes to the river Borysthenes.[74] Given the assumption that the Earth

people in the Middle Ages believed the Earth was a globe.

---

[68] Roller 2015, 75.   [69] Roller 2015, 75.   [70] Roller 2015, 77.
[71] Fr. 41a in Diels and Kranz 1959–60, for which the source is Aëtios (C1 AD). This is sometimes wrongly taken as evidence that the noun 'the *oikoumenē*' was used by Xenophanes.
[72] Details in Dueck 2012, 75–6; Roller 2015, 74–5. On the impact of mathematical geography on conceptions of world space, see Aujac 2020a.
[73] Dueck 2012, 95–6.   [74] Erat. 28 §7.

was a sphere of known circumference, it was certainly possible to equate west–east distances—though these might themselves be no more than distances calculated trigonometrically from the lengths of other lines not running west–east—with degrees of longitude, adjusting for latitude.[75] In the next century, **16** Hipparchos recognized that this was a haphazard method given the then state of knowledge,[76] and that sufficiently accurate lunar eclipse data (that is, the same eclipse observed at different times of day in places at different longitudes) could give finer resolution.[77] Even by Ptolemy's time, however, longitude was still largely based on distance reckoning.

e. Measurement

The attempt to measure local phenomena accurately, other than simple land distances (on which see §IV), developed only to a limited extent, but occasional references may be the tip of the iceberg. Mountains were always, like the sea (h–j below), a locus of important meaning—for the sacred, as well as for ethnic boundary maintenance—as well as landmarks for navigation by land;[78] **9** Dikaiarchos seems to have made something of a specialism of measuring their heights by triangulation.[79] In the opposite direction, we have at least one reference implying that by the 1st century BC attempts had been made to measure the depth of the open sea, perhaps using chains, even down to a mile.[80]

f. Zones

A corollary of latitude was the development of climatic zones,[81] a schema we still use today when we distinguish equatorial (or torrid), temperate, and polar (or frigid) zones of the Earth. Again, the basic idea originated with the early philosophers and their *a priori* cosmological speculations, appearing in the mid- to late Classical period in **5** the Hippocratic *Airs, Waters, and Places*, in Eudoxos of Knidos,[82] and then in Aristotle's *Politics* (late 4th century),[83] to be refined later by **12** Eratosthenes, Polybios, **19** Poseidonios, and Strabo. The term *klima* originally meant 'inclination', specifically the latitude of a point on the Earth's sphere, and was naturally transferred to its climate and habitability. The number of the zones was not always five: Polybios posited six, and

---

[75] One degree of longitude covers *c.*69 mi (*c.*111 km) at the equator, but increasingly less at latitudes N or S of it, as parallels of longitude converge towards the poles.

[76] On latitude and longitude, see Dueck 2012, 92–7.

[77] Unlike a solar eclipse, a lunar eclipse is observed simultaneously from anywhere on the side of the Earth facing the Moon, normally at night (though occasionally just before sunset or just after sunrise). Observers at different longitudes will experience the event as occurring at a different 'local time', that is, according to their local timepieces, and with the Moon at a different place in the sky (a different elevation above the horizon, and/or a different azimuth or compass bearing).

[78] See Wiznura and Williamson 2018–20 on mountains' meanings and inter-visibility; on the latter, also Mauro and Durastante 2022. On the conceptualization of local and regional frontiers, see papers in H. Berthelot, Boiché *et al.* 2016.

[79] Keyser 2000, 353–61.

[80] See Pos. 35 (from Strabo). Oleson 2008, 128–9, confirms that the sea in the area specified is of approximately the right depth. Arist. *Mete.* 1. 13, 351a 11–13 refers to a part of the Black Sea too deep to measure (cf. Pliny 2. cv. 224); at 2. 1, 354a 19–22, he compares the depths of different seas.

[81] See further Dueck 2012, 85–6.   [82] Roller 2018, 144.   [83] Arist. *Pol.* 7. 6.

his own voyage round West Africa led him to confirm Eratosthenes' hypothesis that not all places in the equatorial zone are hot.[84]

g. Continental Divisions

A favourite subject of geographical discussion was the number and boundaries of the continents in the *oikoumenē*.[85] Herodotos (4. 45) is aware that some thinkers divide Europe from Asia at the river Tanaïs (*Don*) flowing into the northern Black Sea, others at the Phasis further east (probably the *Rioni* in modern Georgia).[86] He also parodies the debate about where to divide Asia from Libyē (our Africa), arguing by *reductio ad absurdum* that the Delta should be accounted a continent in its own right.[87] Some authors, both earlier and later than Herodotos, made Asia include Libyē; others adopted the eventual consensus view that Libyē was its own continent.[88] In some discussions, we encounter the view that continents were divided by isthmuses.[89] By Strabo's time it was also possible to think of major mountain ranges as separating distinct units of the world.[90] Those writers who chose a clockwise circuit of the Black Sea may have done so because they wanted to organize their data by continent. A persistent illusion seems to have been that Libyē (Africa) was joined to eastern Asia by a continuous tract of land enclosing the sea south of India and China.

h. The Outer Ocean

The attempt to reach a firm conclusion about the continents was bound up with debates about the situation of the *oikoumenē* within a possible outer Ocean.[91] **19** Poseidonios devoted an entire treatise to the Ocean,[92] while several authors attempted to account for one of its most characteristic features, unfamiliar to inhabitants of Mediterranean lands: the tides, of which various observations were made (e.g. **9** Pytheas, extract 9) and various theories advanced.[93] By the 1st century AD, practical experience in the Indian Ocean allowed the author of **25** *Circumnavigation of the Erythraian Sea* (§45) simply to link the highest tides to the days around the new moon and full moon. Debate subsisted about whether bodies of water such as the Caspian were inland seas or gulfs of the Ocean, sometimes called Atlantic, as in **24** *De mundo*.[94]

---

[84] Erat. 28 in Ch. 11 below, from Strabo 2. 3. 2, C97; also designated Polyb. 34. 1. 16. See Roller 2015, 138. The notion that one's latitudinal zone determines one's fate reappears in a Syriac work (showing Greek influence) of *c.* AD 200, the *Book of the Laws of the Countries* (or *On Fate*) by Bardaisan (Bardesanes).

[85] See in general Dueck 2012, 79–80; Roller 2015, 50–1, 62, 192, etc.

[86] Though see the brilliant admonitions of Dan 2016: the identification of the Phasis was a matter of contention.

[87] Hdt. 2. 15–16.

[88] The Index may guide the reader to many passages.

[89] Pajón Leyra and Bartoš 2020, 103–12.   [89] Marcone 2020.

[91] Roller 2015, 21. The present volumes will employ Ocean, capitalized, for the outer sea alone.

[92] On Poseidonios, see in general Roller 2015, 145–9.

[93] See Index; also Dueck 2012, 43; Shipley 2012, 127; Roller 2015, 21, 89, 97, 135, 147.

[94] Pajón Leyra and Bartoš 2020, 92–4 and 96–102.

j. The Sea

The sea in general was a focus of intense cultural and practical interest, and naturally played an important role in community identity;[95] a late antique author, almost pre-figuring *Annales* history (see §II. 1), could claim that while the coast was a corrupting force the sea was a civilizing one.[96] The sea could be a metaphor for many things, including poetry.[97] Communities and states endeavoured to control the 'watery world' of seas and rivers;[98] recent work has clarified the sophistication of networks of trade ports as well as the co-existence of *cabotage* (a French term for coastal harbour-hopping by ships with mixed cargoes) with direct trans-maritime sailing routes.[99] Aids to navigation contributed to this. Evidence for 'day-marks' of various forms—such as prominent sanctuaries or funerary monuments, towers,[100] and various means of indicating harbour entrances and navigable channels; together with nocturnal guide-points such as lighthouses, upland beacons, and the like—represents a new field of research that forces us to conceive of the coast as seen from the sea rather than the converse.[101]

k. Extremities and Limits

Like the Ocean, other extremities of the world were a refrain throughout much of Greek geographical literature, and indeed early mythology, and were bound up with exploration and military campaigning.[102] Geography could even be manipulated to serve commanders' ambitions, enabling them to claim to have reached the limits;[103] Alexander's entourage even defined a new location for the Caucasus to exaggerate his achievements.[104] The circumnavigation of Africa had been an ambition of the Persian kings (Herodotos 4. 42–4; see also §VI. 2. a; §VII. 1. a);[105] likewise the search for the source, or sources, of the Nile,[106] which was sometimes thought to flow into Africa

---

[95] Ayodeji 2009.   [96] Marshall 2000, citing Synesios' *Letters*, 5 and 148.   [97] Harrison 2007.
[98] Respectively, Irby 2021; J. B. Campbell 2012. See also Purcell 1996.
[99] See Arnaud 2014, centred on Massalia (*Marseille*); on Indian Ocean trade, De Romanis 2020.
[100] e.g. the tower of the Salakeinoi, also in the Artemidoros Papyrus, col. iv; Artemidoros 48 (Straton's tower); Ps.-Skyl. §111. 3 (3 towers on *Lampedusa*, whose Greek name Lampas means 'torch'); Dion. Byz. §§12, 77 *ter* (with display of torches), §88–9 (tower of Medea); *Stadiasmos* §§13, 38–9 ('Antipyr-gos', suggesting a *pyrgos* nearby), 41, 78, 96, 100–2, 124, 185, 237–8, 345, and 349. One might think also of the beacon-towers of Ps.-Aristotle §6. 3. The 'tower of Menestheus' in the Art. Pap. (col. iv) has even been taken for a lighthouse (Luppe 2008, 689), a role it is tempting to ascribe to other *pyrgoi*. The tower on the R. Phasis at Arr. §9. 4 is less plausible as a lighthouse; and any of these may be mentioned as a landmark for navigators rather than specifically a lighthouse or the site of a beacon.
[101] See the ground-breaking paper of Arnaud 2020.
[102] Edges of the world: Dueck 2012, 21–7, e.g. Odysseus, Herakles, Argonauts; Roller 2015, 9–12. Leaders' ambitions: Dueck 2012, 12–16, 55–6, 115; Roller 2015, 90–102.
[103] Roller 2015, 95–6, 102–4.   [104] See e.g. Erat. 20, 23; Bianchetti 1998, 35–7.
[105] Dueck 2012, 53–4; Roller 2015, 24–5, 100.
[106] Dueck 2012, 89; Roller 2015, 158, 182–5; cf. 38, 45, 97.

from the west and out again at Egypt.[107] The identification of its course, and source(s), makes several appearances in these volumes (e.g. **3** Hekataios 17; **24** Ps.-Aristotle §3; and notably **22** Juba 4 and 16), as does the attempt to account for its annual flood (**9** Dikaiarchos 14; **12** Eratosthenes 115; **19** Poseidonios 10; **35** *Hypotyposis* §31), which was also the subject of mythology (**26** Ps.-Plutarch 16). In the far north-west of the *oikoumenē*, Pytheas' report about Thoule (**8** Pytheas 6), treated scornfully by Polybios, provided geographers with a limiting meridian with which to define the western limit of the *oikoumenē* (e.g. **12** Eratosthenes 25–6; **34** Markianos, *Periplous* 1. 6). Debate about the identification of Thoule continues to this day.[108]

l. Particular Seas and Regions

Certain seas[109] and outlying regions recur as focuses of interest and of the generation of alternative presentations. Iberia, the Carthaginian west, the Black Sea,[110] the Indian Ocean (though the advance of time did not always mean an advance in accuracy),[111] Aithiopia 'beyond Egypt',[112] 'Indike' (mostly referring to the north-west of the Indian subcontinent), Skythia (a fluid concept), and the peoples, flora, and fauna of those regions, all occur regularly (see Index); less often the peoples of northern Europe.[113] More intriguingly, the Caspian and its relationship to the outer Ocean are mentioned with surprising frequency, though no accurate conclusion was ever reached.[114] The extent of the Caucasus, its possible role as a continental boundary, and the origin of its name were debated.[115] The far east appears later than other remote regions, especially as knowledge grows through the Imperial period (i.a. **25** *Circumnavigation of the Erythraian Sea*, **34** Markianos).

m. Marvels and Wonders

Reports from, or purportedly from, the remote parts of the world could be enlivened with reports of unusual plants and creatures or marvels of many kinds, be they credible

---

[107] On variants of, and ancient resistance to, this persistent tradition, see Merrills 2017, 44–8.

[108] Among recent studies, see McPhail 2014, favouring N. Norway; Breeze and Wilkins 2018, arguing that Agricola mis-identified the Shetland Is. as Thoule, as did Ptolemy. (But Roller 2015, 186, believes Agricola saw Orkney.)

[109] On the progression of factual knowledge about the various divisions of the outer sea, see Janni 2016.

[110] Olshausen 2016 gives an overview of the development of geographical thinking about the Black Sea, with a focus on the late Hl and Roman periods.

[111] Janni 2016, 41–2, notes that the conception of the Indian Ocean as a closed sea became standard only with the work of Ptolemy.

[112] Confusion of Aithiopia and India: Schneider 2016. Land 'bridge' from either E. or W. Africa to India: acknowledged as a possibility by Polyb. 3. 38. 1; accepted by Ptol. 7. 3. 6; 7. 5. 2; cf. Romm 1992, 82; Panchenko 2003, 280–1.

[113] See Dueck 2012, 33–4, on its remote peoples; first named in C5; Roller 2015, 12, dates their first mentions to C5.

[114] Roller 2015, 96, 102–4.   [115] Roller 2015, 95.

or not.[116] 'Paradoxography', the reporting of strange phenomena, is a strong thread through ancient literature.[117] In the 5th century BC, the Athenian playwright Aeschylus, described by Roller as 'the first popularizer of geographical data',[118] presented his audience in his fragmentary tragedy *Prometheus Unbound* with a reference to a plain in southern France where rocks moved of their own accord[119] (one recalls the jumping and other miraculous stones of 26 Ps.-Plutarch). Ktesias (see §VI. 2. d) says he will limit himself to reliably reported wonders, which does not make all of them more credible to us:

> Ktesias says that in writing and narrating these things he is writing the purest truth.[120] He adds that he writes some of them after seeing them for himself, and others after learning about them from the very people who saw them; but that he has left out many of these, and others that are more amazing (*thaumasiōtera*), so as not to appear, to those who have not seen them, to be composing unreliable things. Among them (*the things he tells*) are these: . . .
>
> Photios, *Bibliotheke*, cod. 72. 49b 39–50a 4[121]

While 12 Eratosthenes (17) is sceptical of reports of extraordinary human-like beings, the author of 25 *Circumnavigation of the Erythraian Sea*, though his primary interest is trade, is fond of mentioning *paradoxa*, 'wonders'. Magical waters and herbs are a favourite of 26 Ps.-Plutarch; 11 Herakleides Kritikos, too, mentions medicinal herbs (2. 3–4). Close to marvels are precious minerals and ores, such as those mentioned by 15 Agatharchides, or the 'archaeological' remains connected with the ship *Argo* in 27 Arrian's *Periplous* (9. 2). Giant or poisonous snakes occur in various authors (see Index).

n. The Notion of Homeland

Conversely, the positive value placed on one's homeland is not often reflected in the statements made about the superiority of one particular region over others. Not many authors enthuse about their home country as much as does 30 Dionysios of Byzantion, but several speak of one region as privileged above others. For Herodotos (1. 142), it is Ionia that is neither too cold nor too hot, neither too moist nor too dry. A similar claim is made at considerable length for Asia (perhaps meaning Asia Minor) by the Hippocratic author of 5 *Airs, Waters, and Places* (§12)—surprising only if one has fallen into the error of thinking that Greeks in the Classical period thought of the Orient only in terms of an alien and inferior 'other'. For the contemporary historian Xenophon, it is true—admittedly in a pamphlet intended to be read by his fellow countrymen—it

---

[116] On distant marvels, see Jessica Lightfoot 2021, ch. 6 (pp. 138–73).

[117] See Concordance, e.g. for citations of Apollonios Paradoxographos; and in general Chapter 26 on Ps.-Plutarch.

[118] Roller 2015, 63.   [119] Aeschylus, fr. 199 = Strabo 4. 1. 7, C182; Roller 2015, 62–3.

[120] *t'alēthestata*, lit. 'the truest (*things*).   [121] My translation.

is their own city of Athens that, one might think, lies at the centre of Greece and the world because of its key position for travel and trade (*Poroi*, 1. 6). For Aristotle, Europeans are spirited but Asians intelligent, while Greece (Hellas), situated on the border between them, combines both virtues (*Politics*, 7. 6).[122]

Predictably, once Roman power is widespread, the focus changes. For the civil engineer Vitruvius, writing in Latin in the second half of the last century BC—most likely in the 20s, during the early phase of the Augustan regime—it is Italy that benefits most from a central location: 'and so she repels the bravery of the barbarians by intelligent plans, the schemes of the southerners by a strong hand'.[123] A generation later, Strabo gives similar praise to Europe (2. 5. 26) and specifically to Italy (6. 4. 1).[124] Likewise, Pliny ends his massive *Natural History* with a tumultuous passage (37. lxxvii. 201–lxxviii. 204) in praise of Nature and her greatest treasures, which begins with the famous *laus Italiae*, 'praise of Italy':

> lxxvii. (201) And so, all Nature's work being now completed, it will be appropriate to make some sort of judgement of the things and the lands themselves.
>
> Therefore, in all the world (*orbis*), wherever the convexity of heaven (*caelum*) turns, the most beautiful of all (*lands*) in terms of those things that rightly gain the preeminent place in Nature is Italy: queen and second mother to the world (*mundus*), with her men and women, her commanders and soldiers, her slave forces; with the distinction of her arts, the renown of her talents; then again, with her position, the healthfulness and moderation of her sky (*caelum*),[125] her accessibility to every nation, her shores rich in harbours, the winds' kindly breath—all of which attach to her by reason of her situation—that of (*a land*) running out in the most beneficial direction, midway between sunrise and sunset[126]—and by reason of her bounty of water, the healthfulness of her woods, the connexions of her mountains,[127] the tameness of her wild beasts, the fertility of her soil, and the lavishness of her food supply.
>
> (202) Whatever a life ought not to lack is nowhere more excellent: crops, wine, olive oil, wool, flax, clothing, and young cattle. People do not even rate any horses more highly in the chariot-racing schools of our land. She yielded to no lands in her mines of gold, silver, copper, and iron, for as long it was permitted to work them; and now, pregnant (*with those*) inside herself,[128] she pours forth, by way of unstinting dowry, the multitude of essences and of the tastes of crops and fruits.[129]

---

[122] Dueck 2012, 87, cf. 89–90.

[123] 6. 1. 11, *itaque consiliis refringit barbarorum virtutes, forti manu meridianorum cogitationes*; my translation. For Vitruvius' take on geographical sources, both visual and written, see Merrills 2017, 39–50.

[124] Cf. Dueck 2012, 13.   [125] i.e. her atmosphere, climate.

[126] We, too, tend to think of Italy as projecting S from mainland Europe, yet the peninsula's axis and main coasts run almost exactly NW–SE, so that it might be said to have N and S coasts as much as W and E. However, the projecting 'toe' of Calabria means that (e.g.) Reggio is *c.* SSE of Venice, while Palermo in Sicily is almost exactly S of Venice.

[127] i.e. mountain passes.   [128] i.e. with the ores unmined.

[129] My translation.

Geography in this respect naturally follows the flag, just as down to the mid-20th century it was northern Europe, or sometimes specifically Britain, whose environment, according to school textbooks in English, possessed the necessary blend of energizing and challenging qualities to condition its peoples for success.[130]

III. 4. CHANGE AND INSTABILITY

a. The Theory of Change

Although much geographical discourse looks to the distant past in the form of myths about the heroic age, or memories of city foundations[131]—just as Strabo is at pains to uphold the geographical wisdom of Homer—geographical writers are often aware that even communities with deep roots in the past are subject to uncertainty and change in both the physical world and the human. The instability of things is a theme of the earliest philosophy: Herakleitos of Ephesos (c.500 BC) says that 'everything is flux'.[132] Plato's Atlantis myth (in his dialogues *Timaeus* and *Critias*) envisages the disappearance of land masses. The impermanence of all things on Earth was a topic familiar to Roman philosophers and moralists, such as Seneca the Younger in his tragedy *Medea* (lines 369–79, quoted as an epigraph to Part Five of this work).[133]

b. Violent Nature

Historians and geographers, too, were well aware of the violence of nature, not least from events in their own era such as the notorious earthquake at Sparta in the 460s[134] and the collapse into the sea of the *polis* (city-state) of Helike in Achaia (northern Peloponnese) in the year 373/2.[135] More than one author offers a catalogue of different types of natural disasters, such as **12** Eratosthenes in a notable passage of Strabo,[136] who adds examples such as the volcanic eruption on the peninsula of Methana in the north-eastern Peloponnese during the mid-3rd century.[137] **24** Pseudo-Aristotle (§6) offers a torrential passage outlining the dangers from earthquake, inundation, storms, lightning, and vulcanism.[138] Other volcanic events are not infrequently mentioned. **4** Hanno and Polybios may have seen Mt Cameroon. **8** Pytheas described the volcanic Aiolides islands (*Lipari*) north of Sicily (27). Alterations to land masses were a topic of

---

[130] On Greeks versus 'barbarians', and the central ideal location of an ideal country, see Dueck 2012, 87, 89–90.

[131] e.g. Hekat. 26; Ps.-Skyl. §67. 2; also the 'foundation' of Hellas, HK fr. 3 §2.

[132] Plato, *Cratylus*, 401d 5, 402a 8, cf. 439d 4.   [133] Dueck 2012, 78–9.

[134] Thuc. 1. 101. 2; Plutarch, *Kimon*, 16. Collapse of a school in Chios, possibly the result of earthquake: Hdt. 6. 27.

[135] See e.g. Lafond 1998; Katsonopoulou 2016; Koukouvelas, Piper *et al.* 2020. On representations of earthquakes in written sources, see Waldherr 1997.

[136] Erat. 13–14 = Strabo 1. 3. 3–4, C49–50; 1. 3. 11–15, C54–7.

[137] Paus. 2. 34. 1 (reign of Antigonos II Gonatas); Strabo 1. 3. 18, C59, where 'Methone' is an obvious error for 'Methana'.

[138] Ammianus Marcellinus 17. 7 posits that earthquakes were caused by fluid movements in subterranean vacuities, which suggests the influence of the tradition we see in Ps.-Aristotle.

interest to both Theophrastos, Aristotle's successor as head of the Lyceum or Peripatos in Athens, and his own successor, Straton.[139] **19** Poseidonios recorded eruptions (44) as well as an apparent tsunami that occurred in his own lifetime (41).[140] Natural catastrophes could, however, be in the distant past: in the 2nd century BC, the Roman historian Gaius Acilius believed that an inundation had divided Sicily from Italy,[141] while Strabo refers to the fracturing of a peak of Mt Taÿgetos, between Laconia and Messenia, in terms that point to remote antiquity.[142]

c. Benign Change

Sudden change need not be negative: Straton and others expressed the view that the Mediterranean filled up when the waters of the Atlantic burst in,[143] Herodotos (2. 12) notes shells in upland Egypt and discusses erosion and deposition.[144] The late antique *Hypotyposis* (35) assumes without discussion that the Mediterranean is supplied with water by the western Ocean (§§45–6); it is, in fact, the case that at the surface the main current through the Straits is eastward, though this is counterbalanced by an underwater westward current, obviously unknown in antiquity.[145] An awareness of differing sea levels allegedly led to the abandonment of Ptolemy II of Egypt's attempt to dig a canal from the Red Sea to the Nile, in a precautionary measure against unwelcome change.[146] Similar observations accompany plans to create a canal at Corinth.[147]

d. Long-term Change

As well as short-term catastrophes, geographical writers were aware of long-term change, which indicates not only their sophistication but also the continual sharing of information across the world accessible to the Greeks. The 5th-century BC historian Xanthos of Lydia inferred from the existence of shells within rocks far inland that an area had once been a sea.[148] Alluviation, the removal of soil by a river and its deposition downstream or out at sea, is regularly noted: 7 Ps.-Skylax records islands off Akarnania becoming part of the mainland;[149] Diodoros (following **15** Agatharchides or **18** Artemidoros?) discusses the formation of the Nile Delta;[150] and Hestiaia, as we saw, researched the changing topography of the Trojan plain (§VI. 4. c).

---

[139] Roller 2015, 108; Strabo 1. 3. 3–5, C48–51 = Erat. 13.
[140] For other possible tsunamis, see Thucydides 3. 89; Pliny the Younger, *Letters*, 6. 20; Tacitus, *Annals* 3. 89; Ammianus Marcellinus 26. 18–19 (with Kelly 2004). Similar events have been detected or inferred at various coastal sites, e.g. Ostia (Tuck 2018); Cádiz (Álvarez Martí-Aguilar 2017a; Álvarez Martí-Aguilar 2017b); Jutland (Strabo 2. 3. 6, C102; with Compatangelo-Soussignan 2016); Olympia (Vött 2011; Vött 2013); Caesarea Maritima (Dey and Goodman-Tchernov 2010); and at the S end of the Thracian Bosporos, as an explanation of the name of the 'Clashing Rocks' as its N entrance (Şengör 2002).
[141] *BNJ* 813 F 3, from a late paradoxographer; Pomponius Mela 2. 115; cf. Dueck 2012, 79.
[142] Strabo 8. 5. 7, C367.   [143] Roller 2015, 108. Cf. Erat. 10.   [144] Roller 2018, 129.
[145] See e.g. Sannino, Pratt, and Carillo 2009; Sánchez-Román, García-Lafuente *et al.* 2012, 9.
[146] Juba 23.   [147] See Erat. 14 §11 on King Demetrios' attempt.
[148] Erat. 13 (from Strabo).   [149] §34. 3; previously noted by Thucydides 2. 102. 2–4.
[150] Diod. 3. 3. 2–3; noted earlier by Herodotos at 2. 15.

e. Climatic Instability

Instability is also reflected in the unpredictability of climate (the author of 5 *Airs, Waters, and Places* is aware that seasons in different years can have different characters), the strength and direction of winds (a particular concern for sailors; hence the interest in classifying the 'wind rose', see §VI. 2. f–g below, under Aristotle and Polybios, as well as 10 Timosthenes 3 and 18), and unfamiliar phenomena outside the Mediterranean and Black Sea, above all the tides, which could trap the unwary and for which alternative explanations abounded (see Index s.v. tides, for many references in these volumes).

f. Change in Society

Change, finally, could also be manifested in the human environment, though this is naturally less in evidence in our sources than in historical writings. The most striking discussions of changing political and economic circumstances that we find in geographical sources are in 25 *Circumnavigation of the Erythraian Sea* and 27 Arrian, who even name living rulers of non-Greek peoples, apparently in order to provide vital information to those planning trade voyages or military interventions. Equally striking is 15 Agatharchides' savage criticism of the effects of Ptolemaic rule on the native peoples of the gold-mining area of East Africa.

IV. DISTANCE

Like many other peoples, the Greeks and Romans based shorter measures on parts of the body, longer ones on how they interacted with space: for example, the pace (or double pace) and multiples thereof.[151] The countless distances recorded in historical and geographical sources, however, are not all of equal reliability. (See the list of 'Units of measure' following the Glossary.)

IV. 1. LAND DISTANCES

> The ancients certainly did not trouble themselves about exact measurements based on fixed standards with carefully worked out equivalents for the various systems in the modern manner.
>
> Dicks 1960, 45

Unfortunately, Dicks's caution holds true for Greek authors, even in the Roman periods. We have already encountered (at §III. 3. a) the standard Greek distance measurement, the *stadion* (plural *stadia*), a word originally meaning 'running-track'; the origin of our 'stadium' but normally Englished as 'stade'. A running-track, in a *polis* (city-state) or at a major cult site such as Olympia or Delphi, is thought to have been standardly 3

---

[151] Dilke 1987f, 23; and now Rubincam 2021, 44.

plethra long (1 *plethron* = *c*.100 feet); athletes normally ran from one end to the other and back again, making the length of a race 600 feet. The actual lengths of such tracks, when doubled, yield distances of somewhat under 200 m. But how long was a foot? There was, of course, no standardized value for that; *a fortiori*, not for the *stadion* either (see 'Units of Measurement' in the Glossary). Therein lies the fundamental issue identified by Dicks.[152] The Glossary testifies to the variation in its length—according, that is, to modern scholars' reckoning, for units of length were not standardized but varied from one state to another. Nevertheless, as early as the 5th century BC, as we see from Herodotos (quoted at §VI. 2. a), the stade was a standard measure of distance in geographical writing. Statements such as his express a rhetorical claim to authority, but scarcely a claim to scientific accuracy: his readers and listeners knew this, but wanted to be taken on an imaginary journey.

Dicks's caution must be qualified—he does not need to do so himself, since in the passage quoted he is dealing with **16** Hipparchos and the 2nd century BC—by the observation that, from the mid-republican period, Roman surveyors applied a standard mile of *c*.4,850.7 feet (*c*.1,478.5 m)[153]—about 9 per cent shorter than a modern mile—to their expanding road system, such as when erecting milestones and calculating distances between centres. The word 'mile' comes from *mille passūs*, 'one thousand paces', or *mille passuum*, 'a thousand of paces'—that is, double paces—the plural, 'miles', being *milia passuum*, 'thousands of paces'.[154] The distance was probably measured, however, not by paces but with ropes, staves, or chains. Those methods were, of course, possible long before the Roman periods, and Greek surveyors already used sighting instruments in the archaic period, while in Pharaonic Egypt the surveying of parcels of land was established practice. In an un-measured landscape while one was on the move, however, it might be necessary to employ *bēmatistai* or 'pacers' to count the steps (*bēmata*) taken, as Alexander did on his expedition into Egypt and Asia.[155] Pacers might try to standardize the length of their stride, but scientific accuracy was impossible—and unnecessary.[156]

Other land-based units included the Persian *farsang* (*parasangēs* in Greek, 'parasang' in English; variously defined as between 30 and 120 stades),[157] used particularly by Xenophon (§VI. 2. c); and the Egyptian *schoinos* (lit. 'line', 'rope'), used especially by **23** Isidoros. Strabo and Pliny explicitly discuss different stade values for the *schoinos*, the former even remarking that at a certain point along the Nile 'the 60-stade *schoinoi*

---

[152] And earlier by Diller 1949, cited by Roller 2010, 271. On the absence of standardization in the Greek world, see now Rubincam 2021, 42–6.
[153] Estimates vary; I take the figure in metres from Dilke 1987f, 27.
[154] Often abbreviated to 'p.' in the manuscripts of Pliny the Elder, quoted often in these volumes.
[155] Dueck 2012, 115.
[156] Arnaud 1993 remains a fundamental discussion of maritime distances in Greek and Roman sources.
[157] Roller 2014, 33.

begin'.[158] The author of 35 *Hypotyposis* feels obliged to define that he is working with a *schoinos* of 30 stades (§2). These authors cannot, of course, tell us how long their stade is, other than a particular fraction of a Roman mile. The Bordeaux Pilgrim (mid-4th c. AD) uses *leugae*, 'leagues', in the first part of his journey as far as Tolosa; the *leuga* (also *leuca*) is defined as a 'Gallic mile' of 1,500 (double) paces or 3 Roman miles.[159]

IV. 2. SEA DISTANCES

Sea distances are another matter. Herodotos (e.g. 4. 85–6, quoted at §VI. 2. a) offers the first preserved attempt to systematize long sea distances, converting days and nights of sailing at the rates of 70,000 *orguiai* ('fathoms' is the nearest English equivalent)[160] in a 'long day' and 60,000 in a night. Remarkably, he prefaces his numbers with no fewer than three qualifiers—'on the whole (*epipan*) roughly (*malista*) something like (*kēi*)'—and as for the dimensions of the Black Sea that his calculations produce, they are 'made to conform to an aesthetic pattern'.[161] He makes 100 *orguiai* equal to 1 stade (§IV. 1 above). Again, it is not so much a claim of 'scientific' accuracy as a rhetorical device to stimulate his readers' and listeners' imagination.

Herodotos does not explain why a ship should travel less far, or more slowly, by night. Is he thinking of a typical day-and-night period, during the sailing season of around nine months, when day is *usually* longer than night (other, that is, than just before the spring equinox or just after the autumn equinox), and is also *on average* longer than night? Ancient writers did not, however, work with averages as we do;[162] though 34 Markianos comes close to it when he writes of how he will handle discrepant data (*Periplous*, 2. 5). Is Herodotos, then, allowing for twilight, which makes the period of effective daylight longer than the period when the Sun is below the horizon, even around the equinoxes when day and night are technically equal?[163] Whatever may be the case, he is surely thinking of good sailing conditions.[164] We cannot offer here a full discussion of these and related problems: merely warn the reader that sea distances, even when presented to two or three significant figures in a text, cannot be accurately

---

[158] Strabo 17. 1. 24, C803–4 = Artem. 100 below; 17. 1. 41; Pliny 12. xxx. 53 = Erat. 36.

[159] See the opening of *Itinerarium Burdigalense* in Geyer, Cuntz, *et al.* 1965, 1. The unit is called *leuca* by Amm. Marc. 15. 11. 17 and other late authors.

[160] 1 fathom, colloquially 2 yards = 6 feet, is one-thousandth of a UK nautical mile, traditionally 6,080 feet (1,853.184 m); thus 6.08 feet = 6 feet 0.96 inches ≈ *c*.1.853 m (1 foot ≈ 30.48 cm). The nautical mile is now, however, internationally defined as exactly 1,852 m (*c*.6,076.12 feet), about 15 per cent longer than an English mile.

[161] Rubincam 2021, 57–8 (quotation at 58).

[162] Geus 2014. My late father, D. R. Shipley, RNVR, was taught in the Fleet Air Arm to take readings with a sextant. The prescribed procedure, I believe, was to take three readings and average the two that were closest together, ignoring the third.

[163] Nautical twilight is defined nowadays as beginning when the Sun reaches 12° below the horizon (astronomical twilight is 18°, civil twilight just 6°).

[164] Arnaud 1993, 227, suggests that Greek sources were usually thinking of journeys under sail and in favourable conditions.

converted into 'true' measurements equivalent to those derived from mapmakers' use in the early modern era of the compass, sextant, and chronometer (without the last of which accurate determination of longitude was impossible); or more recently of the Global Positioning System (GPS).

Yet Herodotos is applying land-based measurements to the sea. How is that possible? The answer is simple: it is not possible, or not directly. Ancient ships had no spinning 'logs' to measure the distance they had traversed through a body of water, and none of the locational instruments we have mentioned. All such statements are an attempt to communicate to readers who are familiar with land measurements and who wish to feel in command of 'accurate' facts, or who are thinking about a potential journey in the context of others and wishing to compare them—perhaps even adopting a cartographic perspective—or who need to make plans for sea voyages while feeling more or less in control of the facts. Above all, Herodotos—like other authors—wishes to give a *demonstration* (a word he uses in the first sentence of his *Histories*) of the results of his research and prove his authority.

So although Herodotos' figure of 11,100 stades for the length of the Black Sea is beset with uncertainties, does it matter? In practice it could not possibly matter whether the 'true' distance was 11,100 or 11,200 or even 10,000 or 12,000 stades; all that mattered was how many days and nights it would take. Writers themselves were probably aware of the imprecision of their data; otherwise, why are nearly all stade distances, apart from some of the shortest, rounded to the nearest 10 or 100?

IV. 3. HANDLING OF UNRELIABLE DATA

An illuminating comparison is available within the *periplous* of 7 Pseudo-Skylax, who typically gives very long distances to the nearest 100 stades (e.g. each side of Sicily is *c.*1,500 stades, §13. 4), medium-length coastal transects to the nearest 10 (e.g. the island of Istris is 210 × 120 stades, §21. 2; the coast of Troizen is 30 stades, §52. 1), but some local distances as a number that is not a multiple of 10 (e.g. the strait of Messina is 12 stades wide, §13. 1; certain Adriatic islets are 2 stades or a little more apart, §23. 2). The revealing exception is his section on Attica, the three parts of whose coast are said to measure 1,140, 490, and 650 stades respectively (§57. 2); while they are multiples of 10, they are unusually precise for such long distances, and may derive from accurate land-based measurement of coastal roads.[165]

Some writers were aware of these problems. Noting the differences between distances between the same places as given by different writers, 34 Markianos, around AD 400, is well aware that ships travel at different speeds and that while some journeys

---

[165] Shipley 2010. On the prevalence of 'round numbers' in distances given by ancient Greek historians, see now Rubincam 2021, 53.

hug the coast, others cut across bays from cape to cape.[166] A century later, Julian of Ascalon asserts that Eratosthenes and Strabo operated with a mile of 8¼ stades, while in his own day the standard factor is 7½.[167] He is not quite correct: Strabo says the usual factor is 8 but that Polybios uses 8⅓.[168] As the Roman mile was $c.$1,481 m,[169] these various values imply a stade between $c.$177.7 and $c.$197.5 m, the most usual factor of one-eighth of a mile[170] implying $c.$185.1 m.

V. SPACE AND CARTOGRAPHY

It is a natural question, in considering ancient geography, whether any of the authors provided maps to go with their texts. The following discussion aims to show why maps were rarely integral to our texts: the words were independent of any accompanying map.

V. 1. USE OF MAPS

Much has been written in recent years about the question of how widely, if at all, maps were used in antiquity before the Roman Imperial period. Obviously there was no equivalent of today's printed maps and atlases accessible by all, let alone the online geographical data now available with any digital device. One problem with the scant evidence is that the words for a map—*pinax* in Greek, *tabula* in Latin—essentially mean nothing more precise than a hard surface with either writing or images upon it; they can thus refer to paintings, written documents for display, and probably even lists and catalogues (including such information transferred to a handwritten medium).

At the outset, it must be acknowledged that no single Greek or Roman map survives directly from before the medieval period, with the possible exception of the some-what mystifying sketch on the Artemidoros Papyrus of early Imperial date (Chapter 18 below, no. 167). Maps for public display are not attested for the hellenistic period, though they may possibly be for the Roman Republic. The debate about the extent to which people, even later than those periods, were familiar with physical maps—while it establishes that those maps that were made were made to high standards—does not alter the picture of a world in which portable maps were not a feature of everyday life, publicly displayed maps a rarity.

---

[166] See his *Periplous*, §1. 2, Ch. 34 below, to which he cross-refers from his preface to Menippos, Ch. 21 below, §5. For praise of his analysis, see Arnaud 1993, 226.

[167] Pos. 17 below.   [168] Strabo 7. 7. 4, C322.

[169] Rathmann 2006. For comparison, the modern English and US mile (abbreviated mi) is 1,760 yards = 5,280 feet = 1,609.344 m.

[170] Pothecary 1995, 67.

V. 2. INVENTION

The first map of the *oikoumenē* is credited to Anaximandros of Miletos (6th century BC), followed soon after by **3** Hekataios.[171] Herodotos may have the latter in mind when he criticizes the flights of fancy indulged in by people who make maps, 'who not only draw Ocean flowing round the Earth, which is circular as if compass-drawn, but make Asia equal to Europe' (4. 36).[172] He tells the story that he heard from the Lakedaimonians—presumably the Spartans themselves—of how Aristagoras of Miletos came to them to seek military assistance in 499 (5. 49), employing as a visual aid 'a bronze tablet (*pinax*) on which had been incised a circuit (*periodos*) of all the Earth, all the seas, and all the rivers' (perhaps just the locations of their mouths), as well as the peoples of western Asia and at least one of the Persian royal capitals, presumably with their names. It is clear that by the late 5th century or earlier maps could be made for special purposes, or at least be imagined being made; there is no evidence that they were regularly made. Indeed, the famous scene in Aristophanes' comic drama *Clouds* (423 BC), in which a pupil of the philosopher Sokrates displays a map and is confronted with sceptical mockery by an ordinary citizen, is clear evidence that the Athenian audience were also able to laugh at a representation of someone who betrayed his ignorance of two-dimensional maps—thereby demonstrating that the audience in general did understand them.[173]

V. 3. MAPS IN CLASSICAL AND HELLENISTIC WRITING

Subsequently, in the 4th century, we may infer the possible creation of maps by **6** Eudoxos of Knidos (see introduction to the relevant chapter). We know that diagrams could accompany technical writing by this time, too, for Aristotle refers in his *Meteorologika* (2. 6; appendix to Chapter 10 below) to an accompanying drawing of wind directions, in a passage that begins:

> Concerning their (*the winds'*) positions, one must consider the words by using the diagram (*hypographē*) at the same time. In it has been drawn the circle of the horizon, so that it is intelligible; for which reason it is round. . . . Let the point marked *A* be the equinoctial sunset (*due west*), and let the point marked *B* be the location opposite this, the equinoctial sunrise.

> (363a 25–363b 1)[174]

---

[171] See Hekat. 5 = Erat. 2; cf. Hek. 9–10. On the earliest Greek maps, see Roller 2015, 28. For a detailed consideration of A.'s *pinax*, see Panchenko 2013. Rossetti 2020 seeks to restore A.'s making the whole world 'legible' by his fellow-citizens to the prime position among his achievements.

[172] My translation.   [173] See the illuminating discussion by Dan, Crom, *et al.* 2016, 571–4.

[174] My translation.

The work of his younger colleague 9 Dikaiarchos included, or was accompanied by, what Cicero calls *tabulae*,[175] which may mean he attached maps to his work; but we have no direct quotation to confirm how he himself referred to them. The 3rd-century AD philosopher Diogenes Laërtios claims (5. 51) to have seen the testament of Theophrastos, Aristotle's successor as head of the Peripatos, in which the philosopher stipulated that 'the tables (*pinakes*) in which are the circuits of the Earth (*gēs periodoi*) shall be set up in the lower stoa'.

For the hellenistic period, Strabo quotes 16 Hipparchos as referring to 'the ancient maps (*pinakes*)' on which the line from the Pillars of Herakles to Kilikia is 'crooked' (*loxos*), i.e. at an oblique angle to a parallel of latitude.[176] This proves that Hipparchos knew of cartographic, or at least diagrammatic, two-dimensional representations of lines of latitude, but not necessarily a map of the Mediterranean as such; nor does it prove that his work included such a diagram or map. As we have noted, if the text on the Artemidoros Papyrus is genuine it suggests that the said author meant his readers to adopt a cartographic perspective, with all that that implies about the possibility of imagining non-linear and alternative journeys.

V. 4. ROMAN MAPS

Some of the evidence for display maps in the Roman Republican period is vague. At Rome in 174 BC, for example, the military commander Tiberius Sempronius Gracchus endowed a temple with a '*tabula*' depicting Sardinia to commemorate a military campaign (Livy 41. 28. 8–10); but beyond the fact that it 'had the form of the island of Sardinia' (*Sardiniae insulae forma erat*) and that 'pictures of battles were painted on it' (*in ea simulacra pugnarum picta*) we know nothing of the extent to which it would be recognizable as a map today. Equally inconclusive is the statement by Varro (116–27 BC) that he saw 'Italy painted on a wall' (*in pariete pictam Italiam*) in a temple of Tellus (the personification of the cultivable Earth; *De re rustica*, 1. 2. 1, written *c*.59–27 BC);[177] again, this does not allow us to say anything about cartography (and the painting may have been of Italia personified).[178]

From the beginning of the Principate, Marcus Vipsanius Agrippa (d. 12 BC), Augustus' son-in-law and close associate in power, is cited more than fifty times by Pliny the Elder for geographical information.[179] Pliny tells us that before he died Agrippa 'had been about to place a circle of the lands' (*orbis terrarum*) before the public with the support of Augustus, who completed the portico 'which enclosed it in accordance with

---

[175] Dikaiarchos 1 = Cicero, *To Atticus*, 6. 2. 3.

[176] Erat. 50 = Hipparch. 24; cf. Erat. 52 = Hipparch. 29 §34; Hipparch. 22, 26, 31 §38.

[177] For the dates, see Sallmann 2006. For the problem of defining Tellus exactly, see Phillips 2006.

[178] On these visual representations from the late Republic and early Principate, and modern attempts to understand them, see Merrills 2017, 27–36.

[179] In the present volumes for the length of Africa (Pliny 5. vi. 40 = Artem. 5) and the limits of Characene (6. 136–41 = Juba 21).

the purpose and expositions (*commentarii*) of Marcus Agrippa' (3. 2. 17).[180] Opinion is divided as to whether these 'expositions' comprised only a prose work or a map as well.[181] A recent detailed study suggests that we cannot know whether Agrippa's work, whichever was its form, was displayed in a permanent material such as stone or bronze or only as a set of perishable documents; and judges the undertaking not a work of Augustan imperial propaganda, as some have suggested, but a digest of existing knowledge.[182] Another study, however, while acknowledging that the work celebrated Roman (and Augustan) imperial achievements, argues against the view that it, and similar creations, were meant as official, authoritative repositories of validated geographical data to be quarried by scholars and others.[183]

From the Imperial period we begin to have two-dimensional maps of localities incised on stone, such as the cadastral map of surveyed landholdings at Arausio (*Orange*) from Vespasian's reign (late 1st century AD), or the Forma Urbis Romae, a plan of Rome, from the time of the emperor Septimius Severus (early 3rd century AD).[184] Yet it is uncertain whether even Ptolemy's *Geography* from the 2nd century, which consists entirely of coordinates compiled to enable the drawing of a world map—compiled, in all probability, by measurements taken from existing maps—was itself accompanied by maps exemplifying his principles until its medieval copies were created. Ptolemy's near-contemporary **29** Agathemeros appears to adopt a cartographic viewpoint, but it is unclear whether his *hypotypōsis* (outline) of geography was endowed with its own map. It would not be surprising if it were not, given that there was no consistent tradition of cartographic representation in public works of art in early Imperial Rome.[185]

V. 5. LATE ANTIQUE MAPS

The 4th- or 5th-century Peutinger Map (§VI. 1. f), surviving in a 13th-century copy, has convincingly been read as a high-end work of art, but debate surrounds its purpose: to assemble useful knowledge, or to celebrate the Roman empire and its power? Indeed, the map itself may be taken as evidence of a vast pre-existing repository of practical data.[186] What seems certain is that 'no one was ever seriously expected to plan a long

---

[180] My translation.

[181] Roller 2015, 166–7, accepts the map; Brodersen 2012, 108–9, doubts it.

[182] Arnaud 2007–8 (outline in Arnaud 2016); cf. Talbert 2010, 135–6, against the view that Agrippa's work directly influenced the *Tabula Peutingeriana*. For the map as propaganda, see Nicolet 1988 (trans. as Nicolet 1991).

[183] e.g. Merrills 2017, 7–11. Indeed, Merrills argues (e.g. 11–15, 296–7) that public notions of geography in Roman times were essentially contested, varying according to the position and role of the spectator (or reader); there were alternative, 'discordant or subversive geographies' (14).

[184] Arausio cadaster, Forma Urbis Romae: Brodersen 2012, 102–3. Another example is the maps of the whole of the known world created at Autun (Augustodunum), rebuilt under the Tetrarchs and commemorating the victorious campaigns of past emperors: Eumenius, *For the Restoration of the Schools*, 19–21, trans. in Nixon and Rodgers 1994, 171–7.

[185] See Merrills 2017, 27–68 (ch. 1), esp. 65–8.

[186] See the emphasis on practicality in Purcell 2010, reviewing Talbert.

journey or a military campaign from this map'.[187] These and other impressive examples of extant or attested maps can be assembled from the Imperial and late antique periods,[188] and it has been noted that the original of the Peutinger Map was itself the heir to a long development through hellenistic times (the rendering of land masses has been shown to inherit hellenistic conceptions)';[189] but still this does not amount to evidence that maps were in everyday use or frequently displayed in public.

Returning to our texts: by the late antique period, both **34** Markianos and **35** the *Hypotyposis* (another outline of geography) do appear to be referring to maps, though not necessarily maps devised for the immediate purpose. The more mathematical approach, however, developed by **6** Eudoxos of Knidos, **8** Pytheas, and **12** Eratosthenes, and fully embodied in Ptolemy's work, gave way to a more descriptive form of writing, seen for example in Markianos.[190]

V. 6. MAPS IN SOCIETY

In sum, the evidence for ancient cartography depends on frustratingly disconnected pieces of evidence;[191] but does this mean a great deal has been lost without trace, or that there never was much to preserve? It has reasonably been doubted whether cartography as such was a professional specialism: maps alongside texts essentially repeated the information given in those texts.[192] No source tells us that maps were a feature of practical life—maps, that is, that were used by military commanders on campaign, by traders or other travellers, and so on. Such persons probably needed no maps but relied on experience and local advice.[193] Neither did they need texts. The more functional kinds of text—some surviving from the Roman and late Roman periods (**23** Isidoros, **27** Arrian, **31** the *Stadiasmos*, and **36** the Pseudo-Arrianic *Euxine*; perhaps also **25** *Circumnavigation of the Erythraian Sea*) but rarely from earlier times (perhaps **10** Timosthenes)—are still literary, still embodiments of the 'Common Sense Geography' discussed earlier. Their functionality may have extended to planning and policy-making, but not to delivery. (Other kinds of writing or documentation, now invisible to us but more connected to practical action, may have lain behind compilations such as **7** Ps.-Skylax.)[194] Texts without maps, such as lists of places and distances, or the functional *periploi* we have imagined, may have sufficed for the needs of merchants, magistrates, and monarchs.[195]

The maps we hear of were rarely public display pieces, much more commonly figures drawn by (or for) thinkers who also wrote books; examples of the latter clearly existed as early as the late archaic period. The rather puzzling drawing on the Artemidoros

---

[187] Talbert 2010, 7.
[188] See e.g. Talbert 2012b, commenting on Brodersen's chapter on cartography in Dueck 2012.
[189] Rathmann 2013b.   [190] Bianchetti 2008, esp. 50–2.
[191] Marcotte 2010, 356 (quoted at Chapter 18 n. 24 below).
[192] Dan, Crom, *et al.* 2016, 575–6.   [193] Cf. Shipley 2006.   [194] Shipley 2019, 13.
[195] Brodersen 2012, 109.

Papyrus, probably unfinished, may be the only surviving example (and one which, in its existing form, post-dates the presumed author by more than a century: see Chapter 18, introduction). The text on the papyrus (column iv) also appears to refer to a *peri-graphē* ('description') of Iberia indicating its shape, which is probably not a reference to the map we have but to a separate graphic representation, actual or conceived.

V. 7. THE CARTOGRAPHIC PERSPECTIVE

Many texts adopt a cartographic perspective, either communicated in words alone or with an eye on some accompanying graphic depiction, perhaps of rather simple form. This shows that two-dimensional representations of geographic space were readily conceived, but is also compatible with the notion that fully designed maps were seen only rarely. One feature of such texts is the habit of describing large land masses using geometrical shapes to help the imagination, Sicily for example being called a triangle (e.g. 7 Ps.-Skylax §13. 4). Such schematic observations are, of course, possible without the aid of manned flight or even a view from a mountain top—it would be obvious to a sailor[196]—but the habit of describing areas of the Earth's surface in this way suggests that, for the social groups who were aware of written literature, assuming a bird's-eye view in imagination was a familiar move. The example from Aristophanes cited above, moreover, shows that this awareness need not have been restricted to those who could read books. A more sophisticated example of the phenomenon is seen when 12 Era-tosthenes, from a cartographic perspective, describes the *oikoumenē* as shaped like a cloak (29 §6; 57) or divides it into 'sealstones' (*sphragides*, 52 §§22–36; 73 §5); or when 16 Hipparchos refers to perpendicular lines and right angles (e.g. 28).

V. 8. MENTAL MAPPING

Most of our texts work independently of graphic representation, and use language to help readers create a virtual, or interior, 'journey' in the imagination.[197] Such 'verbal mapping' and the 'mental mapping' that accompanies it are, indeed, inherent features of any geographical description in words. A particular aspect of 'mental travel' is 'hod-ological space',[198] the notion that the ancients, like us, often described geographical space in linear rather than two-dimensional terms: from *A* one goes to *B*, and from there to *C*, even when there might be a shorter route direct from *A* to *C* (as in the old joke whose punch line is 'if I were going there, I wouldn't start from here'). It does

[196] On the use of geometrical figures in geography, see Dueck 2009.

[197] On verbal mapping and mental travel in Greek geography, see the fundamental work of Janni 1984; also Arnaud 1989; Talbert 1989; Sundwall 1996; Dueck 2012, 50, cf. 85; Talbert 2013; Dueck 2016); Podossinov 2016. For the 'mental map' in geography in general, see Trowbridge 1913; Gould 1972; and esp. Tuan 1975, who prefers 'schemata'.

[198] Invented by a psychologist (Lewin 1934), and aired with reference to ancient geography in a review (Janni 1982), it is explored in detail by Janni 1984, 75–158, esp. 75–90. On Roman 'subjective geography', see Bekker-Nielsen 1988.

not betoken a lack of sophistication: it is a natural feature of the verbal description of any route from the viewpoint of actual experience, and is unavoidable when one wishes to describe a journey usefully. Few texts, however, are purely one-dimensional: 7 Ps.-Skylax, for example, punctuates his coastal narrative (a narrative of merely virtual travel) with transverse crossings, such as from Sardinia to Africa (§7). Authors do not necessarily limit themselves to describing linear movement; they may present alternative possible voyages that allow readers, so to speak, to give rein to their two-dimensional imagination.[199] Greek geographical texts do, in fact, adopt a wider variety of perspectives than just the 'hodological'—such as the bird's-eye (or indeed god's-eye) or cartographic view, whether real or imaginary[200]—depending on the purpose for which a particular geographical exposition is being created.[201]

Thus we are brought back to the point made in §III. 2. c, that what we have in most of our texts is neither 'fully reasoned' nor 'intuitive', but—because they are what they are, which is written text—embodies the 'Common Sense Geography' of a reasonably well-informed reader.

VI. THE RANGE OF ANCIENT GEOGRAPHICAL WRITING

VI. 1. EXTANT PROSE GEOGRAPHIES

No single volume (or even two) could contain all ancient geographical writing. In particular, this book cannot encompass the five lengthy surviving works outlined below, including two in Latin which give important context to the Greek sources. All five are from the first two centuries AD and are readily available in translation (all but one in English). Many extracts from Strabo and Pliny will be found in the first twenty-three chapters of this collection.

Discussion of these five works, in chronological order, is followed by a short review of late Roman and Christian geography giving context to the last five works in the present volumes (32–6), which belong to the 4th to 6th centuries AD.

a. Strabo

The earliest of the 'major' geographers, and for the history of geography by far the most important in the surviving evidence, is Strabo (Strabōn, c.60 BC–AD 25) from Amaseia in the Black Sea. Around AD 20, having earlier written a universal history (*BNJ²* 91), he

---

[199] Cf. Canter 1977, 51, quoted by Janni 1984, 157 n. 234: like verbal descriptions of routes that allow for the possibility of two-dimensional, not only one-dimensional, movement, maps 'provide the potential for the discovery of relationships not explicitly intended'.

[200] Poiss 2014; also Dan, Crom, *et al.* 2016, 572, 579, etc.

[201] For the need to nuance the idea of hodological space, see Merrills 2017, 203–6.

completed his *Geographia* covering the entire known world in 17 books,[202] one of the largest books we have from antiquity (around half a million words in translation).[203] Although not awarded a chapter in these volumes—his text even without annotations would treble its length—Strabo is ubiquitous: quoted over 260 times, more than a quarter of all the extracts, and sometimes at considerable length (though some extracts overlap), because he is the main source for several lost writers whose works he continually cites (not all at first hand) and discusses. Notable among these are **3** Hekataios, **8** Pytheas, **12** Eratosthenes, **16** Hipparchos, **18** Artemidoros, and **19** Poseidonios, though Strabo's rapid and allusive style sometimes leaves it unclear where paraphrases of these authors begin and end. He also occasionally cites **1** Aristeas, **2** (or **7**) Skylax, **6** Eudoxos of Knidos, **9** Dikaiarchos, **10** Timosthenes, and **15** Agatharchides (whom he probably consulted via Artemidoros),[204] and several times mentions **22** Juba though as a statesman, not a writer. Notable by their absence are **11** Herakleides Kritikos, **13** Mnaseas, **14** Skymnos, the unknown author of **17** the *Nikomedean Periodos*, **20** Dionysios son of Kalliphon, and **23** Isidoros, to all of whom Strabo presumably did not have access. Other material in Strabo, remaining unattributed, probably derives from other lost writers.

After a theoretical introduction and an account of the previous development of geography (books 1–2), he organizes his account of the known world by beginning, as many ancient writers did, in the far west of Europe and proceeding as far as Sicily (books 3–6) before covering northern Europe and the Greek homeland in five books

---

[202] General comments on Strabo: Dueck 2012, 43–5 and *passim* (see index); Roller 2015, 167–70; fuller overview in Prontera 2016. The best Greek text is now Radt 2001–11 (10 vols). The translation by Roller 2014, with separate commentary (Roller 2018), includes a full reconstruction of S.'s life (pp. 1–16) and replaces the Loeb (H. L. Jones 1917–32), rendered out of date by the publication of a palimpsest preserving various superior readings (Aly 1956). The 'Budé' series (Collection des universités de France) published by Les Belles Lettres (under the auspices of the Association Guillaume Budé) contains the majority of the 17 books (not yet 13–14 and 16) with Greek text and facing French translation. Other important studies include Clarke 1999, esp. chs 1 and 4; Dueck 2000; Dueck, Lindsay, and Pothecary 2005; Dueck 2017.

[203] Book 7 is incomplete, partly reconstructed from fragments.

[204] Among special cases are (1) the several short passages naming elephant-hunting stations in Upper Egypt, dispersed through Strabo 16. 4. 8–14, C770–4. These were clearly drawn from Artemidoros but were probably derived by him from Agatharchides, whom S. appears to have known only through Art. Since this information does not occur in the paraphrases (by Diodoros and Photios) of book 5 of Ag.'s *On the Erythraian Sea*, it may be that Art. took it from books 1–4 of that work or from another of Ag.'s historical writings. In this case the decision has been made to include Strabo 16. 4. 5–20, C769–79, in the chapter on Art. (as no. 98), while including the short elephant-station passages (parts of 16. 4. 5–15) in the chapter on Ag. (as no. 4).   (2) Another special case is Strabo 17. 2, C821–4, a fairly short chapter on the customs, flora, and fauna of Meroë and Egypt; this is included under Art. (as 44 *a*), accompanied by D.'s parallel passage (3. 5–11; no. 44 *b*) where, though D. consulted both Art. and Ag. directly, we cannot distinguish the two threads clearly.   (3) Finally, Diod. 1. 32–41 on the Nile has not been included, as it probably derives from Ag.'s historical works *On Asia* and *On Europe*, not from his more geographical (albeit still partly historical) work *On the Erythraian Sea*, which is the focus of Ch. 15. (I am grateful here, as elsewhere, to Stanley Burstein for his expert advice.)

(7–11), Asia Minor and Cyprus in three (12–14), and the far east, Egypt, and Libya (that is, North Africa), in the last three (15–17).

Invaluable as Strabo is to us, he does not appear to have published his work, with the result that it is rarely cited before the late antique period. (Only six papyrus fragments are known, all from the 2nd and 3rd centuries AD and from Oxyrhynchos, suggesting that no copy reached Alexandria before the early 2nd century.)[205] Throughout the work the author, whose family was distinguished in the service of the Pontic kings and survived their conquest by the Romans, upholds the value and intelligence of Homer as a geographer and gives detailed critiques of earlier geographers, while at times making plain his admiration for Augustus and contextualizing world geography within a Roman frame of governance. Though reasonably widely travelled he does not, as a modern geographer might, build pictures of regions, their societies, or their economies on the back of contemporary evidence, but relies on support from any available earlier writers—from the 2nd century BC back to the Attic tragedians and then, of course, Homer—to characterize the regions to which they refer and give them historical depth.[206]

b. Pomponius Mela

The first Latin work devoted exclusively to geography, Pomponius Mela's *De chorographia* was written during the reign of the emperor Claudius (AD 41–54) and is a somewhat popularizing work, perhaps intended to celebrate the conquest of Britain.[207] The *chorographia* of the title usually refers to a detailed account of a particular region, but in this case to a world geography. Lesser in scale than the other works described in this section (at under 18,000 words), it comprises three short books: the first two a circuit—unusually arranged anti-clockwise from North Africa to Iberia, then the Mediterranean islands—the third covering the coasts of the outer Ocean, where it provides some unique material. Though aware of Greek geographers, Mela rarely names his authorities and so is cited rarely in the present volumes;[208] he is unaware of the recent work of Strabo.

c. Pliny the Elder

Of very slightly later date is Pliny the Elder (Gaius Plinius Secundus, AD 23–79), a Roman aristocrat who perished in the eruption of Vesuvius and is best known for his compendious *Natural History*. Though quoted some 130 times in these volumes (most often as a source for **18** Artemidoros, **22** Juba, and **23** Isidoros), he is much more than a

---

[205] Hatzilambrou 2022, §5.

[206] On S.'s conceptualization of his geographical work, and on how he 'mak[es] it 3-D in terms of the time–space matrix', see Clarke 1999, esp. ch. 5, 'Strabo and time' (pp. 245–93); quotation from Clarke 2020, 195.

[207] General discussions of Mela: Roller 2015, 187–9; Irby 2020. Text: Brodersen 1994b (with German trans.); Silberman 1988 ('Budé' edition with French trans.). English trans.: Romer 1998.

[208] See Hipparchos 20.

geographer. Of his 37 books, the first contains his introduction, a detailed table of contents, and lists of the numerous authors cited in each of the remaining books; several extracts from these lists appear in the present volumes. Books 3–6 (over 80,000 words in English translation) contain the fullest account of world geography that survives in Latin.[209] Designed as a gathering in of, and celebration of, Roman power through the compilation of material from a vast array of earlier writers, they nevertheless embody contradictions in their subject matter without an attempt to establish an authoritative version: for example, of the location of the Nile's source.[210]

Like Strabo (whose work he appears not to have seen), Pliny organizes his world topographically and frames it in terms of the Roman empire and its provinces; beginning with the western Mediterranean and moving via the eastern to Africa and finally Asia. He tends to cover regions rapidly and in limited detail, instead providing copious and frequently uninterrupted lists of place-names, many recorded nowhere else (their spelling often varies between different manuscripts); but a valuable feature is the distances in miles that he frequently records, sometimes even giving alternative values from different sources. Unlike earlier authors, Pliny shows awareness of communications with the interior beyond a coast reached via navigable rivers, as well as of the natural features of each region and in some cases the ethnography of the peoples who lived there.

There are three ways of numbering chapters within Pliny's 37 books. (1) The first derives from the author's own tables of topics in book 1, and represents the coarsest mesh, each book being divided into only a few score chapters. In the present volumes, these numbers are given in lower-case roman numerals. (2) The excellent 19th-century edition by Mayhoff uses a different numeration, not much used today as it tends not to give much greater resolution than the original; these are not used in the following chapters.[211] (3) Most commonly used today is the finest-grained set of subdivisions, in which some books comprise over two hundred chapters, allowing specific passages to be located more quickly. In the present volumes, the last are given as arabic numbers.

---

[209] On Pliny's place in the geographical tradition, see Brodersen 2016b, esp. 298–302 (his work eclipsed by that of Solinus from C3e AD, the latter heavily reliant upon it; unjustly neglected today). The MS tradition is chaotic. The 10-volume Loeb edition by H. Rackham *et al.*, esp. vol. 2 (1942) containing books 3–7, is sorely in need of modernization and renders many distances differently from other editions. A new translation of books 1–6, with geographical passages of books 7–37 (Turner and Talbert 2022; methodology described in Talbert 2020) appeared after the present volumes went to press. A commentary on those books is being prepared by D. W. Roller. Revised texts of 3–4 but only parts of 5–6 are available in the 'Budé' series, with facing French translation (3, Zehnacker 2004; 4, Zehnacker and Silberman 2017; **5.** i. 1–viii. 46, Desanges 1980; **6.** xxii. 66–xxvi. 106 and xxxiii. 163–xxxix. 220 (end): André and Filliozat 1980 and Desanges 2008). All of books 3–6 appear in the outstanding, and now complete, Artemis & Winkler series with facing German translation (3–4, Winkler 2002; 5, Winkler 1993; 6, Brodersen 1996). Many important studies have appeared in recent years, including Beagon 1992; Healy 1999; Morello and Gibson 2003; Carey 2004; Beagon 2005; Doody 2010; and Gibson and Morello 2011. Most concerned with the geographical books, perhaps, is T. Murphy 2004.

[210] Merrills 2017, 279–90.

[211] See Mayhoff 1875–97. It occurs, for example, in Dicks's edition of Hipparchos' geographical fragments (Dicks 1960).

Thus references to the *Natural History* (after book 1) take forms such as '4. xiii. 94' (book, traditional chapter, modern short chapter).[212]

d. Pausanias

The author known as Pausanias, whose identity and origin (Magnesia in Asia Minor?) are by no means certain, wrote a *Periegesis* (*Guided Tour*) *of Hellas* in the mid-2nd century AD.[213] Occupying some 270,000 words in English translation, the work covers the southern Greek mainland in ten books, arranged by region: in book 1 Attica (almost entirely Athens), in books 2–8 the Peloponnese (in a clockwise spiral from Argolis, ending in Arkadia), then in 9 and 10 Lokris and Phokis, respectively, in central Greece. The work concludes with the key sanctuary of Delphi.

Though mentioned several times by authors of whom extracts appear below,[214] Pausanias is less important for our purposes as he rarely names geographers as sources. Though writing under the Antonine emperors, he makes many historical digressions that mostly ignore the recent, Roman-dominated past from about the mid-2nd century BC onwards. Instead, he presents us with a world deeply immersed in myth and Hellenic history: for his main interest is in the already ancient monuments, large and small, through which a landscape of cultic networks was constructed that embraces cities (*poleis*, formerly city-states) together with the sacred spots in their territories and along their country roads. In modern times his text has been an indispensable source for attempts to identify archaeological remains with named ancient locations.

Pausanias is representative of the intellectual movement known as the Second Sophistic, in which Romans and Greeks of the 2nd century AD set about reviving, recreating, and even imitating the art, literature, and even diction of a Greek past of which 5th- and 4th-century BC Athens was selectively made the archetype. This cultural milieu was important for the preservation and elaboration of Greek geographical writings, as we shall see when we discuss Arrian (§VI. 2. h).

e. Ptolemy and Marinos

At around the same epoch, Ptolemy of Alexandria (Klaudios Ptolemaios, *c.* AD 110–70), fundamentally a mathematician, was writing monumental works on astronomy and astrology and, most relevantly for present purposes, a *Geōgraphikē hyphēgēsis* (*Geographical Introduction*).[215] Though usually quarried today for individual place-names

---

[212] I am grateful to Mary Beagon for advice on this point.

[213] Major studies of Paus. include Arafat 1996; Habicht 1998; Hutton 2005; Pretzler 2007; see also the essays in Alcock, Cherry, and Elsner 2001. As well as a Loeb translation and a Penguin Classics version with detailed, if sometimes idiosyncratic, notes (Levi 1971), most of the ten books have a 'Budé' edition with detailed topographical commentary. The standard Greek text is Rocha-Pereira 1989–90.

[214] Skylax §12; Hekat. 27; Erat. 127; Artem. 133.

[215] General remarks on Ptol.: Roller 2015, 196–200. Fuller overview: Aujac 2016, esp. 317–21. New Greek text: Stückelberger and Graßhoff 2006 (2 vols., with German trans.). The theoretical sections (all of book 1; parts of books 2, 7, and 8) are excellently translated by Berggren and Jones 2000. The translation by Stevenson 1932, reprinted 1991, is unreliable and partly based on the Latin version in C.

and their locations, the overall character and aims of the work need consideration. This is not a world geography as such—Ptolemy shows little interest in the wider concerns of his predecessors[216]—but a prescription and dataset for the design of a world map. Beginning with a discussion of cartography (book 1), it is accompanied in some of the medieval manuscripts by a remarkable series of maps of the known world (making up the eighth and final book), constructed on the basis of the instructions in the text, though it is uncertain whether the original work included these.

Alongside important general and theoretical discussions, the work is largely made up (books 2–7) of tabulated coordinates of latitude and longitude, measured from the Equator and the 'Fortunate Isles' (*Canaries*) respectively, for some 8,000 places from West Africa to South-East Asia, comprising natural features as well as settlements, many of which are unattested elsewhere, but often without any detail. Coordinates are given to the nearest twelfth of a degree, expressed not in minutes of arc (sixtieths of a degree) as today, but in forms such as 'one-half' (i.e. 30′) and 'one-third' (20′), and composites such as 'one-third plus one-quarter' (35′) and 'one-third plus one-sixth' (40′); examples may be seen in the present volumes.[217] The tabulated data are interspersed with brief textual overviews in the manner of earlier geographers, as here:

> Position of the island of Crete. Crete is bounded on the west by the Adriatic open-sea (*pelagos*), on the north by the Cretan open-sea, on the south by the Libyan open-sea, and on the east by the Karpathian open-sea. And its coast has a description of the following kind:
>
> Description of the western side: Korykos, cape and city, $52^1/_{12}°$, $34^2/_3°$. Phalasarna $52^1/_3°$, $34^2/_3°$. Chersonesos $52^1/_2°$, $34^7/_{12}°$. Rhamnous, harbour, $52^1/_2°$, $34^1/_2°$. Inachorion, $52^7/_{12}°$, $34^1/_3°$. Kriou Metopon Point, $52^7/_{12}°$, $34^1/_6°$.
>
> (3. 17. 1–2)

Ptolemy cites no authorities earlier than Hipparchos, but the *Geographia* is remarkable for its comprehensiveness, demonstrating how knowledge of places away from the Mediterranean had increased since Classical times. It relies heavily on data collected by Marinos of Tyre, perhaps to be identified with Lucius Iulius Marinus Caecilius Simplex, suffect (substitute) consul of Rome in AD 101.[218] Marinos' work is known only through Ptolemy's criticisms—of his estimate of the size of the *oikoumenē*, and of his map projection (similar to Mercator's later, with lines of longitude drawn parallel to one another)—but he was clearly an innovator who sought to improve cartography and drew upon Roman administrative sources unavailable to most writers.

W. L. Müller 1883. That of 2. 1–6. 11 by B. Kiesling on the ToposText website is based on Müller and the earlier Greek of Nobbe 1843–5, not on Stückelberger–Graßhoff, so that coordinates and chapter numbers sometimes differ.

---

[216] Geus 2017, 13.

[217] e.g. Hipparch. 40 §42 (from Strabo) and 44 (from Ptolemy himself); *Hypotyposis* §39.

[218] Geus 2017. For a brief appraisal of Marinos, see Dueck 2008a.

Unfortunately, while sound calculations of latitude had been attained relatively easily since the 4th century BC, longitude was another matter given the absence of accurate distance measurement and reliable timepieces (§III. 3. c–d). Some of Ptolemy's coordinates are therefore based on estimates of distances, necessarily unreliable.

f. Latin and Christian Traditions

Down to the Imperial period (conventionally the first three centuries AD), nearly all geographical writing is in Greek, Mela (at *b* above) being one literary exception. Latin texts may have begun with the geographical compilation by Augustus' colleague Agrippa, though its precise nature is debated (see §V). The following paragraphs give pointers to some key geographical writings of the 4th to 7th centuries, to give context to Chapters 32–6.

Following the example of compilations such as the *Anagraphē stathmōn* used by 12 Eratosthenes[219] and similar writers of hellenistic date,[220] as well as 23 Isidoros in the Augustan era and possibly the original of 31 *Stadiasmos* at a similar date, Latin texts begin to appear which listed places and distances, either on land or at sea.[221] Presumably they had practical and administrative purposes.[222] One of the most detailed is the *Antonine Itinerary* from around the reign of Diocletian (AD 284–305), perhaps based on an original of about a century earlier.[223] It lists over two hundred stopping-places along seventeen routes across the Roman empire, but its information is often problematic. The same era—or alternatively the early 5th century—saw the creation of the lost original that underlies the Peutinger Map (conventionally 'Tabula Peutingeriana'), whose surviving copy was made centuries later, just before or just after 1200. The extant version, comprising eleven vellum sheets pasted together, nearly 23 feet (7 m) long but just 13 inches (33 cm) high, shows the main roads and stopping-places of the Roman empire compressed into this long rectangle; perhaps for display on the internal wall of a building. Recent study suggests that the cartographic design of the land masses reflects a hellenistic, even 3rd-century BC, understanding of the *oikoumenē*, though the Roman-period data were successively updated until the 5th century AD[224] (see further §V. 4).

---

[219] Strabo 2. 1. 7, C69 = Erat. 49.   [220] Strabo 15. 2. 8–9, C723–4 = Erat. 81 §8.

[221] On maritime itineraries, see the detailed study by Salway 2004.

[222] For an objection to the view that compendium-style texts are necessarily ideological, see Marcotte 2000b, lxx.

[223] For general information on this and other *itineraria*, see generally K. Kessler and Burian 2006; see also Dueck 2012, 59–61. For the Antonine Itinerary, see Cuntz 1929; Talbert 2007. The entries at *ODLA* 1085–7 on (to reorder them by date) the 'Notitia Galliarum' (C4), 'Notitia Urbis Romae' (C4s) 'Notitia Dignitatum' (c.395–408), 'Notitia Urbis Constantinopolitanae' (C5f), 'Notitia Antiochena' (C6l), and 'Notitiae Episcopatuum' (C7) illustrate the range of texts variously listing place-names, administrative areas, dioceses, areas within major cities, etc.

[224] Alternatively, the map was first created *c.*435: (Rathmann 2016b, 353 n. 63, disputing the Diocletianic–Tetrarchic date of Talbert 2010, 133–6). See also Rathmann 2011–12; Rathmann 2013a; Rathmann 2013b; Rathmann 2016b; and the successive editions of the authoritative republication: [1]Rathmann 2016a ~ [2]Rathmann 2017 ~ [3]Rathmann 2018, with images at https://tp-online.ku.de/index_en.php [last accessed 23 January 2023]. (For additional images accompanying Talbert's study, see https://peutinger.atlantides.org/map-a/ or at www.cambridge.org/us/talbert/.)

Papyri from the 320s AD record the practicalities of one man's journey from Egypt to Antioch and back.[225] On a more literary plane, a personal if intellectualized appreciation of landscape is seen in Ausonius' highly literary poem *Moselle* (from about the 380s), which begins as a journey narrative but is chiefly dedicated to lauding the life in and around that river in north-eastern Gaul.[226] In conceptual terms the world had shrunk; the remarkable 4th-century silver cups from Vicarello near Rome, for example, list place-names and distances from Gades to Rome,[227] echoing the epigram by Metrodoros (*c.*250–300) that follows Chapter 36.[228] A sense of pride in Rome's achievements combined with melancholy reflections on the present state of things pervades Rutilius Namatianus' poem *On His Return*, describing his sea voyage to Gaul around 417, only a few years after the sack of Rome by the Visigoths.[229]

Although the present volumes include works in the classical tradition down to the 6th century AD, it does not pretend to document the transition to a Christian world-view, of which there are no obvious traces in the last five chapters—even in 34 Markianos, who was probably working in Constantinople. Nevertheless, it is worth noting that an alternative view of world geography and history was emerging after the official adoption of Christianity as the religion of the Roman empire in the early 4th century. We do not know the contents of the lost *Hodoeporicum* by the Christian author Lactantius, narrating a journey from Africa to Nikomedeia before *c.*325.[230] Before 331, however, Eusebios, bishop of Caesarea (in the province of Syria Palaestina), in his *Onomastikon* (more fully *On the Place-names in the Holy Scripture*), produced a selective, alphabetized gazetteer of places in the Holy Land.[231] Around the same time, we begin to see narratives of pilgrimage to the Near East,[232] such as the *Itinerarium Burdigalense* dated to 333, which includes details of residential stopping-points on a journey from Burdigala (*Bordeaux*) via the Balkans to Jerusalem, returning by Constantinople and Milan;[233] or some time later the partially preserved account by Egeria (or Aetheria) of her three-year pilgrimage from France or Spain to the Holy Land, a few years before or after 400.[234] Pilgrimage to the Holy Land remains a feature in later generations, as in the early 6th-century journey of one Theodosius recorded in Latin and drawing upon earlier itineraries.[235]

---

[225] *ODLA* 1487–8 s.v. Theophanes of Hermopolis.
[226] *ODLA* 182–3 s.v. Ausonius; Evelyn-White 1919, 225–63.
[227] *ODLA* 798 s.v. itineraries; M. Schmidt 2011.　　[228] *Anthologia Graeca*, 14. 121.
[229] *ODLA* 1314 s.v. Rutilius Namatianus; Duff and Duff 1934, 753–829 ~ iid. 1982, ii. 753–829. For recent work, see Wolff 2020.
[230] *ODLA* 872–3 s.v. Lactantius, at 873.
[231] Klostermann 1904 (Greek at 2–176; Jerome's Latin version on facing pp. 3–177). See Stenger 2013 (on the construction by E. of an artificial 'reality').
[232] On *itineraria*, see generally Hunt 2004.
[233] Geyer, Cuntz, *et al.* 1965, xviii and 1–26; Elsner 2000.
[234] Dated 381–4 (*ODB* 679); either 395–8 or 415–18, K. Kessler and Burian 2006. For the text, see e.g. Wilkinson 1999 (his 3rd edition, with Engl. trans.); Brodersen 2016a (text, German trans.); McGowan and Bradshaw 2018; Bradshaw 2020.
[235] Geyer, Cuntz, *et al.* 1965, 113–25.

Between the 5th and 8th centuries, geographers began to adapt to a Christian world, resorting to new expositions of geography to explain the changing world in which they lived.[236] Among the most famous such work is Orosius' *History against the Pagans*, probably completed in 417, in which the prologue outlines world geography, setting the trend for geographical exposition that was not an add-on but integral to historical narrative. Nevertheless, the Christian agenda is not always visible: in the early 6th century a certain Hierokles (of whom nothing is known), in the service of the Byzantine empire, wrote the laconic *Synekdemos* ('travel companion'), an index of the provinces and towns of the empire. It was used later by the scholar–emperor Constantine VII Porphyrogennetos (r. 913–59) as a basis for his work on the imperial provinces (*Peri tōn thematōn*; in Latin *De thematibus*), cited several times in these volumes (see Concordance). Hierokles' list is partly based on earlier material and preserves valuable information about the eastern Roman provinces.[237] Of explicitly Christian intent, on the other hand, is the surviving *Christian Topography* in twelve books by Kosmas Indikopleustes (the sobriquet meaning 'sailor to India', or perhaps 'sailor on the Indian sea'), a merchant from Alexandria who compiled a world geography between 535 and 547.[238] Almost uniquely among ancient and medieval writers, he argues from Biblical evidence that the Earth is a flat disk, an idea that gained no traction in medieval times—contrary to popular belief today.[239] In other respects, his geography, though little circulated other than in Slavic nations,[240] was valuable for its information on the natural species of India and Sri Lanka, as well as on trade and Christian calendars. One of the culminating texts of this period is the *Anonymi Cosmographia* or *Ravenna Cosmography* of around 700, listing places all the way from India to Ireland.[241] Greek and Roman geography continued to be exploited and refashioned for the purposes of each generation.

VI. 2. GEOGRAPHY WITHIN HISTORICAL AND PHILOSOPHICAL PROSE

Geography, apart from the mathematical kind seen in Ptolemy, is almost impossible to write without an awareness of the processes subject to time: the creation and disappearance of settlements, the evolution of a tradition of knowledge, changes in the natural landscape, and so on. Equally, it is virtually impossible to write history without

---

[236] On Orosius and his successors, see Merrills 2005.

[237] Summarized in the dedicated map 102 in *Barr*. Edition: Honigmann 1939.

[238] Date from Lozowsky 2008. Edition: Wolska-Conus 1968–73. Overview: Brodersen 2006. Positive reassessment: J. C. Anderson 2013.

[239] For a refutation of the misconception—still widespread today—that people in the Middle Ages believed the Earth to be flat, see J. B. Russell 1991. Another exception, however, is the early Christian author Lactantius (*c.*250–325), who at *Divine Institutes* 3. 24 attacks the notions of a spherical Earth and Antipodes (inhabited lands opposite our own). For other C4 AD questioning of sphericity, see Gleede 2021.

[240] Lozowsky 2008.   [241] Cuntz and Schnetz 1940.

the spatial element—a particular feature of many of the works already mentioned, such as Strabo and Pausanias in their accounts of the Peloponnese, where their own present time is subordinated to the task of endowing rural and urban landscapes with historical and mythological depth.[242]

Accordingly, much of the most valuable geographical information from antiquity is included not in the works of 'geographers' but in those of historians who make extensive use of geography and often theorize about it. No attempt is made, either in the present volumes or in this Introduction, to cover all the major historians and other authors who present geographical information, but several of the main authors deserve a closer look, and readers who wish to know more about ancient geography will want to consult them directly.

a. Herodotos

Pre-eminent among those who survive, whether completely or in substantial part, and who devote parts of their historical work to geographical material, is Herodotos of Halikarnassos. Like Homer, indeed, he was central to the ancient writers' conceptions of both history and geography.[243] A selection of his *Histories* that aimed to represent his geographical output would have to include the greater part of his book, but he is at his most geographical and ethnographic in the accounts of Persia (1. 130–40; 3. 89–96; and elsewhere), Egypt (book 2 generally), the peripheral lands of Asia and northern Europe (3. 97–117), Libyē (North Africa; 4. 168–99), Thrace (5. 3–10), and the description of Skythia and its peoples (most of 4. 1–144). The last includes a remarkable passage where he theorizes about the dimensions of the Black Sea (see Glossary for the units of measurement, and §IV for further discussion of this passage):

> 4. 85. (2) Of all open-seas (*pelagea*)[244] that exist, it is the most wonderful. Its length is 11,100 stades,[245] and its breadth where it has its widest part is 3,300 stades.   (3) The mouth of this open sea is 4 stades in breadth, and the length of the mouth—the neck, which is called the Bosporos, at which in fact the bridge was put across—occupies 120 stades; and the Bosporos extends into the Propontis.   (4) The Propontis, being 500 stades in breadth and 1,400 in length, issues into the Hellespont, which at its narrowest parts is of 7 stades, and in length 400. . . .
>
> 86. (1) These things have been measured as follows. Generally a ship completes, on the whole, roughly something like 70,000 fathoms (*orguiai*) in a long day, but by night 60,000.   (2) Now to Phasis from the mouth—for this is the longest (*dimension*) of the

---

[242] For this theme, see esp. Clarke 1999, ch. 1.

[243] General remarks on Hdt.'s geography: Roller 2015, 64–7.

[244] The Ionic dialect form of *pelagē*.

[245] This and the other quantities in the passage have been simplified from their more discursive forms in the Greek text. This, for example, is 'a hundred, a thousand, and a myriad (*ten thousand*) stades'; the next 'three hundred and three thousand stades'; and so on.

Pontos—is a voyage of 9 days and 8 nights. These are turned into 1,110,000 fathoms,[246] and from these fathoms come 11,100 stades. (3) To Themiskyra on the river Thermodon from Sindike—for this place is where the widest (*dimension*) of the Pontos is—a voyage of 3 days and 2 nights, and these are turned into 330,000 fathoms or 3,300 stades.[247]

Many counterparts of such calculations will be seen in the texts making up the present volumes. Herodotos also gives us some of the most famous aphorisms in the field of geography. He praises Ionia in western Asia Minor for its perfect air and climate, which he explains by its position between hot countries and cold, between dry and moist (1. 142). In the final sentence of the work (9. 122), he suggests that environment determines society: after debating with Cyrus, founder of their empire, the Persian nobles 'chose to rule while inhabiting an unpleasant land rather than to sow a plain and be slaves to others'.[248] These ideas chime with others expressed in the present volumes, notably in the Hippocratic *Airs, Waters, and Places* (5).

b. Thucydides

The late 5th-century Athenian historian Thucydides keeps geographical discussion to a minimum in his work, one exception being his digression on alluviation by the Acheloös river (2. 102. 2–4),[249] which is echoed in later sources such as 7 Pseudo-Skylax (§34. 3).

c. Xenophon

In contrast to Thucydides, the soldier and prolific author Xenophon of Athens, whose general history *Hellenika* continues the history of Thucydides where it breaks off, often presents geographical information in this and his other writings. Most characteristic in this respect is his *Anabasis* (*Journey Inland*),[250] which tells of Cyrus the Younger's revolt within Persia around 400–399 BC. After the defeat of the expedition in Mesopotamia, Xenophon himself led the Ten Thousand, a Greek mercenary army (or rather the survivors),[251] on their hazardous return to Trapezous on the Black Sea coast of Asia Minor (book 4) and thence to the fringes of the Aegean (book 7). Books 1 and 4 are particularly rich in distances; book 4—the army passing through Armenia—is also plentiful in ethnographic observation that betokens a genuine curiosity but also the patronizing attitude of well-armed, aristocratic Greeks towards 'barbarian' populations:

---

[246] 'Eleven myriads and a hundred of fathoms' in Hdt.'s Greek; and similarly with the other measurements.

[247] My translation.

[248] My translation. Possibly a veiled warning to the Athenians during the acme of their empire: Xian 2020.

[249] Dueck 2012, 37–8.

[250] For general comments on the geography of *Anab.*, see Roller 2015, 69–71. Dan 2014 shows the importance of *Anab.* as evidence of different models of ancient geographical thinking.

[251] Numbering only 8,600 at one later stage: *Anab.* 5. 3. 3.

4. 4. (1) When they had crossed (*the river*), they formed up around the middle of the day and travelled through Armenia, all level plain and gentle hills, for not less than 5 parasangs;[252] for there were no villages (*kōmai*) close to the river on account of the wars (*of the Armenians*) against the Kardouchoi.   (2) The village they reached was large and had a palace for the satrap, and upon most of the houses there were towers; there were abundant supplies.   (3) From there they travelled two stages, 10 parasangs, until they had passed the sources of the river Tigris. From there they travelled three stages, 15 parasangs, to reach the river Teleboas. This was beautiful but not large, and there were many villages around the river.   (4) This locality was called Westward Armenia. . . .

(7) From there they travelled three stages through the plain, 15 parasangs . . . and came to palace buildings with many villages round about, full of plentiful supplies.   (8) While they were encamped there, a heavy snowfall occurs at night,[253] and at dawn they decided to billet the rank-and-file soldiers and the generals among the villages: for they could see no enemy and it seemed to be safe on account of the quantity of snow.   (9) There they had a full range of good supplies: sacrificial animals, grain, fragrant old wines, raisins, and pulses of all kinds. But some of those who wandered away from the camp were saying that they had seen many fires shining in the night.   (10) So the generals decided it was unsafe to stay apart and that they should regather the army; so they assembled, also because it appeared that the sky was clearing.   (11) But as they were passing the night there, there falls a vast amount of snow, so that it covered over both the weapons and the men as they lay. The snow also impeded the transport animals; and there was great reluctance (*among the men*) to stand up, as the snow that fell upon them was warm, to the extent that it did not fall off.   (12) But when Xenophon steeled himself to get up, though unclad,[254] and began chopping firewood, some other man soon got up, took it (*the axe*) off him, and began chopping; and from that moment others, too, got up, made a fire, and began anointing themselves;   (13) for a lot of ointment could be found there, which they used instead of olive oil; it was made of pig-fat, sesame, almonds—the bitter kind—and terebinth. Myrrh made from the same items was also found.[255]

This and similar passages are some of the most remarkable in Classical literature for their vivid observation of physical experiences and their, all too self-revealing, eye-witness perspective. Xenophon is also noteworthy as the first historian to describe locations while focalizing orientations from the point of view of the reported observers:[256]

4. 8. (1) On the first day they came to the river which divided the land of the Makrones and that of the Skythenoi.   (2) They had *over their right hands* a locality of the most difficult kind, and *on the left* another river into which the boundary river flowed, and this they had to cross.[257]

---

[252] For this unit of distance, see §IV. 1 above.
[253] Xenophon switches into the 'historic present' momentarily, as again below.
[254] Lit. 'naked', i.e. without a cloak or other outer garment.   [255] My translation.
[256] Huitink 2019.   [257] My translation.

d. Ktesias

Sometimes regarded as a geographical author, Xenophon's contemporary Ktesias of Knidos (*BNJ* 688)[258] was a Greek doctor who spent much of his life in the service of the Persian kings.[259] He personally tended the wounds which Artaxerxes II sustained at the battle of Cunaxa against Cyrus the Younger. Author of a largely historical *Persika* (*Persian Matters*) and other works, Ktesias set an influential precedent by writing a book about a single region remote from the Greek world in his *Indika* (*Indian Matters*), whose coverage is mainly restricted to the north-west of the subcontinent.[260] The surviving fragments include a summary (fr. 45) made for Photios (*Bibliotheke*, codex 72)[261] that occupies a dozen pages in a modern edition; the other seven (frs 46–52) actually comprise nearly fifty extracts, nearly half of them from Pliny (§VI. 1. c above) and Aelian (late 2nd–3rd century AD). The work is based, however, on reports from travellers to the Persian court, not on personal observation. Moreover, it is only marginally geographical, concentrating instead on wonders, climate, flora, minerals, drugs, poisons, customs, diet—and above all on wondrous creatures wild and domestic, real and unreal. Indeed, recent work has characterized Ktesias' work as situated between fact and fiction, the author as 'an innovator in the genre of romance writing'.[262] Several citations of Ktesias will, however, be found in the present volumes (see Concordance). Among his other topographical observations are that the river Indus varies from 40 to 200 stades (*c*.5–25 mi, *c*.8–40 km) wide, that the population of Indike almost exceeds that of the rest of the inhabited world,[263] and that territorially Indike makes up half of Asia.[264]

e. Ephoros

Ephoros of Kyme (*FGrH* 70), a slightly later contemporary of Xenophon, wrote an influential history which is largely lost though known in part through its adaptation by Diodoros of Sicily (1st century BC). He organized his material thematically, confined geographical material to particular books (his fourth and fifth), and introduced astronomical data into the discussion of locations:[265]

> Ephoros also reveals the ancient opinion about Aithiopia, for in his treatise *On Europe* he says—dividing the regions of the heavens and Earth into four parts—that the Indians will be towards the Apeliotes (*east wind*), the Aithiopes towards the Notos (*south wind*), the Kelts towards the sunset (*dysis*), and the Skythians towards the north wind

---

[258] The standard Greek text of Ktesias' works is that of Lenfant 2004, in the 'Budé' series with facing French translation.

[259] General overview: Dueck 2012, 38–9; Roller 2015, 68–9.

[260] Translations of *Persika*: Llewellyn-Jones and Robson 2009; Stronk 2010. Of *Indika*: Nichols 2011, 47–81.

[261] For Photios, see *k* below.

[262] Waters 2020, quoted in the review by Bichler 2021.   [263] Both in fr. 45 = Photios 72. 45a 21–5.

[264] Fr. 49a = Arrian, *Indike*, 3. 6.   [265] General remarks: Roller 2015, 81–3.

(*borrhas anemos*).[266] He adds that Aithiopia and Skythia are the larger, for he says it seems that the Aithiopian peoples extend from the winter sunrise as far as the sunset, and Skythia lies directly opposite them.

(Strabo 1. 2. 28, C34, trans. Roller, lightly adapted)

This particular discussion was clearly known to Aristotle when he wrote about the winds (see next subsection), and his organization of geographical material within an account of history was influential upon Polybios (below).[267]

f. Aristotle

The philosopher and natural scientist Aristotle's most geographical work[268] is the *Meteorologika* or *Mid-air Matters*, which includes a lengthy discussion of winds, here printed as an appendix to 10 Timosthenes (no. 38). The passage clearly echoes Ephoros (above) and prefigures the more elaborate 'wind rose' offered by Timosthenes in which he, again like Ephoros (quoted by Strabo; see the preceding subsection), identifies the locations of different nations by the directions from which the winds blow.

g. Polybios

The Arkadian historian and traveller Polybios of Megalopolis wrote in the mid-2nd century BC.[269] In important respects, his approach to geographical material followed precedents set by Ephoros (above). In his own *Histories* Polybios, too, reserved many (not all) of his treatments of geography for the now lost book 34, whose reconstructed fragments comprise some 6,000 words, largely taken from Strabo, who names him more than fifty times.

Having been a commander in the Achaean league and seen it defeated by Rome in 146, Polybios (*c.*200–*c.*118) is best known as the historian who, from a position of personal friendship with leading Romans, documented Rome's takeover of the Greek homeland. In and after his own time, however, he was equally admired as an explorer who travelled north from the strait of Gibraltar at least part-way towards the British Isles, and south at least as far as the river Lixos in Morocco.[270] His book *On the Inhabited Parts of the Earth under the Equator* (that is, the celestial equator) is lost, but

---

[266] For the use of winds as indicating direction, see the next subsection (on Aristotle) and §X. 3. b below. For the distribution of remote peoples according to the wind that blows from their region, cf. Timosthenes 18 (Agathemeros ii. 7).

[267] For the ancient confusion between Aithiopia and India, see Schneider 2004.

[268] Roller 2015, 76.

[269] For Polyb.'s career and writings, see the brilliant outline by Derow 2012; more fully, Walbank 1948; Walbank 1972, 117–29. General remarks on Polyb.'s geography: Roller 2015, 137–9; fuller discussion in Clarke 1999, ch. 2; Bianchetti 2005; Ercolani and Nicolai 2011 (in Jacoby V). The revised Loeb (Paton, Walbank, and Habicht 2010–12) gives Greek text and English trans.; the 'Budé' series Greek and facing French has reached book 16. The classic historical commentary is by Walbank 1957–79.

[270] On P.'s voyage, see Desanges 1978, 121–47. Eichel and Todd 1976 argue from timed events in P.'s life, and from navigational considerations, that P. cannot have travelled further than the Lixos (*Wadi Dra'a*), and therefore not as far as Mt Cameroon as some have suggested (e.g. Roller 2015, 137–8), which would have required a further voyage of at least 3,500 miles (5,600 km).

he may have been responsible for the translation into Greek of Hanno's account of a voyage round West Africa (Chapter 4). He also challenged the view of Eratosthenes that the *oikoumenē* known to us was entirely north of the Equator.[271] Referring to his own 'voyages' (3. 59), he says he undertook them primarily to collect data in order to correct the errors of earlier writers (which begs the question how he knew that they were errors before he set out). In short, Polybios seems anxious to demonstrate that he is now the true revealer of the far West.[272]

Unfortunately, Polybios is also responsible for the denigration of 8 Pytheas' reputation; yet his extreme scepticism suggests he did not himself reach Britain. Book 34 was not the sole repository of geographical material:[273] Polybios' personal experience of the Alps allowed him to criticize earlier historians of Hannibal's invasion of Italy:

> 3. 39. (6) To the city (*polis*) of New (*Carthage*) from the Pillars (*strait of Gibraltar*), from where Hannibal started out for Italy, comes to 3,000 (*stades*). (7) From this to the river Iber (*Ebro*) is 2,600 stades; and from the Iber to Emporion 1,600. (8) Then from there to the crossing of the Rhodanos (*Rhône*) around 1,600—for these places have now been paced and carefully marked every 8 stades by the Romans.[274] (9) From the crossing of the Rhodanos, for those travelling right beside the river in the direction of its sources, as far as the ascent of the Alps (*that leads*) into Italy, 1,400. (10) The remaining ascents of the Alps (*are*) about 200; having crossed those, he intended to arrive at the plains around the river Pados (*Po*) in Italy. (11) Thus the total number of stades from New (*Carthage*) that he had to pass through was around 9,000. . . .
>
> 47. (9) By supposing that the precipitous and rugged character of the Alpine mountains was such that not merely horse and infantry, and elephants with them, but not even light-armed foot-soldiers, could easily pass through—and by portraying to us the desert nature of the localities as such that, unless a god or some hero encountered Hannibal's company and pointed the way, they would have got lost and been wiped out—they (*certain historians*) undoubtedly fall into both of the aforementioned errors.
>
> 48. (10) . . . So, in contradiction to what these men write, Hannibal managed his plans very practically. (11) For he had discovered accurately the prosperity of the land into which he planned to come down, and the alienation of the mass of the people from the Romans. In face of the intervening difficulties, he used as guides and explorers local men who were likely to share those very people's hopes. (12) We state our views on these matters with confidence, as we have enquired about the events from the very men who were present at those times, have observed the localities, and have ourselves performed the journey through the Alps in order to understand and observe.[275]

For Polybios here, geography is here at the service of history.

---

[271] Arnaud 2007–8, 217.   [272] Cf. Cruz Andreotti 2016, 280.   [273] Clarke 1999, 77–9, 104.
[274] These 15 words are accepted as genuine by Walbank 1957–79, i. 373. They are assumed to be a late addition to the text by Polybios himself, as they must postdate the completion of the Via Domitia in 118 (Paton, Walbank, and Habicht 2010 ad loc.).
[275] My translation. I follow the Greek text of the revised Loeb edition, Paton, Walbank, and Habicht 2010.

h. Arrian

Besides the *Circumnavigation of the Black Sea* (27), Arrian (Lucius Flavius Arrianus, early 2nd century AD) wrote many other extant works in Greek. His *Anabasis of Alexander*[276] is the best account of Alexander the Great that we have, despite being written over four hundred years after the lifetime of its subject. The eighth and last book has something of the character of an appendix and is known by a separate title, *Indikē*,[277] the Greek name for all of the Indian subcontinent (and sometimes beyond, to the east). Before narrating the return journey of Alexander's fleet from the mouth of the Indus to the Persian gulf, Arrian supplies extensive information about Indian peoples (including the caste system, §§11–12) and about elephants and other animals (§§13–16). In the last part (§§18–42), he details the voyage on the basis of the detailed and dramatic account by Alexander's admiral Nearchos (*FGrH* 133), which complemented more factual observations by the chief pilot, Onesikritos (*BNJ* 134).[278] Distances are often given, and the text is enriched from Arrian's own knowledge of trade in the Persian gulf,[279] so that the book forms a useful complement to the slightly earlier *Circumnavigation of the Erythraian Sea* (25).

Arrian is a representative of the Second Sophistic, a cultural milieu of great importance for the codification and preservation of Greek written culture (see introduction to Chapter 27). He himself played a crucial role, compiling the first of the two principal corpora of geographers, to which the prefatory essay by **29** Agathemeros was probably added either at the time or not long after.[280]

j. Stephanos of Byzantion

A source not to be considered geographical in the usual sense, but invaluable for the present book, is the *Ethnika* of Stephanos of Byzantion,[281] a work of over fifty volumes written in about the mid-6th century AD but surviving only in late medieval copies of an abridgement by one Hermolaos.[282] Of the original text in its full form only a few pages are preserved (in an 11th-century manuscript), containing fourteen entries from the end of the section on the letter delta, plus a few entries taken over into Constantine Porphyrogennetos's *De administrando imperio* and *De thematibus*; these indicate

[276] Revised Loeb translation of Arrian with Greek text: Brunt 1976–83. Recent translation, incl. *Indike*: M. Hammond 2013.

[277] General comments on Arrian: Dueck 2012, 55–6; Roller 2015, 98–9.

[278] On this voyage, see Bucciantini 2016, characterizing them differently: Nearchos as the rationalist, Onesikritos as the lover of marvels (p. 109). Testimonia and fragments: Whitby 2011; Bichler 2018. See also Winiarczyk 2007; S. Müller 2011; Mariotta 2017; on Alexander and the Ocean, Gómez Espelosín 2021.

[279] On Nearchos' treatment of distances, see Bucciantini 2013.

[280] On the Second Sophistic, see the seminal paper by Bowie 1970; more recently, chapters in Richter and Johnson 2017.

[281] Superb new edition with German trans.: Billerbeck 2006–17. There is as yet no English trans.

[282] Dated after 527 and before 573 by Billerbeck 2006–17, i, page 3*. Hermolaos wrote under either Justinian I (r. 525–65) or Justinian II (r. 685–95 and 705–11; *ODLA* 1416 s.v. Stephanus of Byzantion; cf. *PLRE* ii s.v. Stephanus 24).

that the entries were originally several times longer than their abridgements. This encyclopaedic work contains over 3,600 alphabetized entries, each beginning with a place-name or the name of a people, followed by an explanation of its origin and often giving alternative forms such as a city's *ethnikon* (the surname, as it were, that could be appended to a citizen's name). Despite the extreme truncation, the surviving digest is an unparalleled repertory of topographic information, often derived from Classical and hellenistic authors whom Stephanos names. Quotations from him make up over one-fifth of the extracts in the present volumes (222 in all), mainly for the lost works of 3 Hekataios, 18 Artemidoros, and 34 Markianos. Examples of the typical layout of an entry will be found in those chapters.

k. Photios

Born around 810 and serving twice as patriarch of Constantinople between 858 and 896, Photios I (St Photios in the Orthodox church) compiled or commissioned, at an uncertain point in his life, a *Bibliotheke* (*Library*) composed of descriptions of varying fullness of a wide range of older books including many from the Classical and Hellenistic periods. These précis are in numbered 'codices', of which for present purposes the most important are Nos 213 and 250 summarizing work by 15 Agatharchides. His *Lexikon* is also an important source, cited four times in these volumes, three times for 13 Mnaseas (see Concordance).[283]

l. Suda (Soudas, Suidas)

A certain amount of information about ancient geography is found in a Byzantine encyclopaedia of over 30,000 entries, composed around the year 1000, which draws on earlier compilations and preserves copious information from classical and hellenistic Greece, often accurately. The text begins with a list of the eleven compilers of the work, but it is always known by its title 'the *Souda*' (Latin *Suda*).[284] Many biographical entries on ancient writers are reproduced as 'testimonia' in collections of fragments such as *FGrH* and *BNJ*, though not all testimonia are included in the present volumes; unfortunately, some of them embody confusion between different authors of the same name, or the misattribution of certain works (e.g. 2 Skylax of Karyanda, 13).[285]

***

Other prose writings from which geographical fragments are drawn are named in the Time-line.

---

[283] On the *Bibliotheke*, see *ODB* 288 s.v. Bibliotheca; on the *Lexikon*, *ODB* 1669–70 s.v. Photios.

[284] The name is thought to derive from the Arabic for 'fence' or 'moat'—knowledge as a safe haven?—but was once misunderstood as a personal name, Souidas. See *ODB* 1930–1 s.v. Suda.

[285] The standard edition is Adler 1928–38. The whole work has been collaboratively translated at the *Suda on Line* website, www.cs.uky.edu/~raphael/sol/sol-html/ (1998–2014, with revisions continuing).

VI. 3. GEOGRAPHY IN EXTANT POETRY

Though the book includes the surviving portions of several shorter poems (Chapters 1, 17, 20, 28, and 32), it does not include epics that build their narrative around geography and travel. An exception is made, however, for the Homeric *Catalogue of Ships* from *Iliad* book 2, which forms the Prologue and was central to the understanding of many of the authors represented. Much geographical writing was at least in part a response to Homer. Striking examples can be seen in Strabo's descriptions of the Peloponnese (in his 8th book), whose western and southern parts he may not have visited and where much of the long section on Eleia (8. 3) engages with long-standing debates about the relationship between Homer's references to the towns of the region and the actual landscape.[286]

The other notably geographical epic was the *Argonautika* of the 3rd-century poet Apollonios of Rhodes,[287] readily available elsewhere in English translation. Apollonios, who wrote at Alexandria, was clearly well informed about geography, particularly that of the Black Sea where much of the action of the story of Jason and the Argonauts takes place. It is not surprising, therefore, that the scholia (ancient commentaries) on the poem are quoted over thirty times in the present volumes.[288]

VI. 4. FRAGMENTARY GEOGRAPHERS BEYOND THESE VOLUMES

As noted in §VII. 3, some fragmentary geographical authors, or authors who are only the subject of testimonia, are not the subject of a chapter in these volumes: partly for lack of material, partly because this book aims, in general, to provide *readable* (while also rigorous) translations rather than overload the pages and notes with technicalities.[289] Some whose other work survives extensively, such as Arrian and Polybios, are included in *FGrH* v in respect of their specifically geographical works.

Some authors not included in the present volumes who are known, perhaps, from a laconic entry in the *Suda*, one or two 'testimonia', and at most a few 'fragments' in the form of citations or paraphrases, are worthwhile to introduce. Among them are figures whose work was highly influential and whose loss is therefore particularly regretted. They are arranged below by period.

---

[286] On Strabo's use of earlier literary sources as proxies for information on the resources of the Peloponnese, see Baladié 1980, 167–95.

[287] On the Argonauts myth within a geographical perspective, see Dueck 2012, 26–7; Roller 2015, 9–12, also 61, 134.

[288] Scholia on Apollonios of Rhodes: Hekat. 16–18, 23, 29; Ps.-Skylax T 1–2; Pytheas 27; Tim. 31–6; Erat. 108–13; Mnaseas 17–20, 30, 36, 45; Skymnos 7–9; Artem. 8, 162–5; see also introductions to Ps.-Plutarch and Dionysios Periegetes. They have been checked against Wendel 1935. On Ap. Rhod. as a geographer, see Meyer 2008.

[289] Some 70 of those in *BNJ* and *FGrH* v are not included in the present volumes (see TABLE I.1), though some are named in extracts under other authors (see Concordances and Index).

a. Archaic

One intriguing but shadowy figure is Euthymenes of Massalia (*FGrH* 2207), who made a voyage south from the strait of Gibraltar, perhaps in the second half of the 6th century BC, and probably wrote an account in *periplous* form, though some of the ancients doubted (as some scholars do today) that the text that was then extant under his name was genuine. He was known to Ephoros (the only definite dating criterion we have), from whom all later citations may derive; they are all in the Roman and later periods,[290] and include 34 Markianos in the preface to his epitome of 21 Menippos.[291] If the text was genuine, then already in the archaic period the cause of the Nile's flood was a topic of interest for Euthymenes, which may suggest that like later authors he looked for the river's source in the far west (cf. §III. 3. k).

Another citizen of Massalia is hypothesized to have travelled in the opposite direction and written the so-called 'Massaliote *periplous*' whose existence seems implied by 32 Avienus in his *Ora maritima* (see introduction to that chapter).[292]

Still in the West, we hear of a Carthaginian named Himilco, probably a contemporary of Euthymenes, who also appears several times in Avienus. He travelled to the northern Atlantic and possibly to the Sargasso sea.[293]

A Skythian named Anacharsis is described by Herodotos (4. 76–7, cf. 46) as travelling widely, including to Sparta, returning via Kyzikos, and attempting to introduce the cult of the Mother of the Gods into his homeland, at the cost of his life. Letters and gnomic sayings were attributed to him—both in classical to Roman sources and in various late collections of such aphorisms—but he remains a mystifying persona. Elements of shamanism have been detected in his story, like that of 1 Aristeas, but unconvincingly.[294]

b. Classical

One of the most notable fragmentary geographers, but very ill served by the tradition, is Phileas of Athens (*FGrH* 2038), probably active in the late 5th century BC.[295] He is

---

[290] The earliest references are Aelius Aristeides 36. 85–95, citing Ephoros; Seneca *NQ* 4a. 2. 22. General comments: Dueck 2012, 52; Roller 2015, 44–5. The few testimonia and fragments are brought together, with Spanish trans., by González Ponce 2008b, 179–91; see also *FGrH* 2207 = González Ponce 2013a (with German trans.).

[291] Cf. also the introduction to 32 Avienus.

[292] Dueck 2012, 52; Roller 2015, 38; Keyser 2008a notes specific citations and the suggestion by some that the Massaliote (or 'Massiliot') *Periplous* dated from C4f. For Pytheas' predecessors in the Atlantic, see Bianchetti 1998, 47–52.

[293] González Ponce 2019b. Himilco will appear as *FGrH* 2210.

[294] His *apophthegmata* (sayings): Kindstrand 1981 (sources listed at 100 n. 7 include Diogenes Laërtios). Letters (most or all of Hl date): Reuters 1957; Reuters 1963. For references to Anacharsis, see introduction to 1 Aristeas; *Nik.* fr. 17 = *Eux.* 78.

[295] For the fragments of Phileas, see González Ponce 2008b, 193–213 (with Spanish trans.); *FGrH* 2038 = González Ponce 2013b (with German trans.). There are only 5 minimal testimonia in *FGrH*, plus 13 fragments including those mentioned here. The earliest witness is Dionysios son of Kalliphon (see next n.; C1), the next earliest Harpokration (C2 AD). In F 4 (schol. Euripides, *Andromache* 1), Phileas is cited before Theopompos (378/7–after 320) and refers to Thebai in Thessaly. In F 5 (Har-

the only known Athenian to have written a *periplous* ('circumnavigation'), which may have covered both Europe and Asia–Libyē after the model of 3 Hekataios, but did not necessarily embody the results of autopsy. He is cited several times for the forms of town names and some locations of towns, occasionally for foundation legends; and seems to have covered inland places as well as coasts, though the evidence is minimal. His work was read throughout antiquity, though not cited often, and may have been used by a number of our authors as an authority for the limits of 'continuous Hellas'.[296]

Damastes of Sigeion (*FGrH* 2012), also probably 5th-century BC, is mentioned a number of times by authors in the present volumes, but is little known.[297] He is credited with, among other writings, a *periplous* as well as a *Peri ethnōn* (roughly *On Nations*), which extended to the Hyperboreans beyond the Black Sea and thus may have covered all known lands. If a report by a much later author is correct, he was the first Greek writer to mention Rome.[298]

A certain Zenothemis (*FGrH* 2054), of the 4th or 3rd century BC, may have been the first author of a *periplous*-style poem.[299]

c. Hellenistic

An anonymous 3rd-century BC description of the Piraeus preserved on papyrus will be found in the appendix to 11 Herakleides Kritikos.

A possible author of note is the supposed 2nd-century BC historian Pausanias of Damascus or Antioch (*FGrH* 854), who has been suggested as the author of the *Nikomedean Periodos* (17); but this has been challenged, and the very existence of a Pausanias of Damascus has been questioned (see introduction to that chapter).

A major scholar of the later 2nd century, Apollodoros of Athens, wrote books on the gods, comedy, poetry, and linguistic matters, but most relevantly on chronology: his *Chronika* began from the death of Alexander, where Eratosthenes' chronological work had left off, and was written in iambic trimeters.[300] His attested work *Peri ges* (*On the Earth*) 'in comic iambics' may in fact be the *Nikomedean Periodos*;[301] if so, this was his one direct venture into geography, for though he also wrote a colossal work of 12

---

pokration s.v. Thermopylai), P. explains another place-name in Thessaly. He is also cited (F 8 = Steph. Byz. α 317 Antheia) for the earlier name of Apollonia Pontike in the Black Sea; Ps.-Skylax already knows the new name in the 330s. So P.'s active period looks no later than C4m.

---

[296] HK §3, though not naming Phileas; Dionysios son of Kalliphon, ll. 32–8 = *FGrH* 2038 F 2; Markianos, in his preface to Menippos, §2 = T 2; Avienus 42 and 695–6 = T 1 and T 3a. Cf. Shipley 2019, 17, 118, 129, 145–6 with Ps.-Skyl. §§33. 2 and 65. 2, though Phileas is not named there and it is possible that PS rather than Phileas invented the notion of 'continuous Hellas'.

[297] See Hekat. 9 and 13; Ps.-Skyl. F 4 = Avien. 370–4; Tim. 11; Erat. 12 and 76; Agathem. i. 1; Avien. 45. The remaining evidence for Damastes is collected by González Ponce 2008b, 215–31. Mentioned: Dueck 2012, 55.

[298] Roller 2015, 136 n. 3, citing Dionysios of Halikarnassos (of Augustan date), *Roman Antiquities*, 1. 72.

[299] Hanigan 2022.   [300] On Apollodoros, see the full outline by Montanari 2006a.

[301] For the fragments of the *Peri ges* (all from Steph. Byz.), see Marcotte 2000b, 265–70, with Chapter 17 below, nn. 4 and 8.

books on Homer's *Catalogue of Ships* it is thought that his interest in it was primarily philological rather than geographical.

It may be appropriate to mention here an explorer who is not known to have left any written records, but about whose voyage a great deal is written.[302] Eudoxos of Kyzikos is said by Strabo, citing **19** Poseidonios,[303] to have made a voyage to India under Ptolemy VIII of Egypt; then another after the king's death in 116 during which he was carried by unfavourable winds all the way round to West Africa; later he travelled to Gadeira (*Cádiz*), from where he made two attempts to circumnavigate Libyē (Africa), from the second of which he never returned. Strabo criticizes Poseidonios' credulity about much of the story. If it is an historical voyage, then despite his ultimate failure and probable lack of literary output Eudoxos of Kyzikos can be credited with the discovery of the Cape Verde Islands. His pioneering voyage to the west coast of India was followed up by one Hippalos, who is said to have discovered how to time voyages to best advantage using the monsoon winds (**25** *Circumnavigation of the Erythraian Sea*, introduction and §57); these winds as such were, however, already known to Alexander's admiral Nearchos.[304] Scholars differ in how much of the story they accept, but Ptolemaic interest in India is real, while the circumnavigation of Libyē and the existence of an outer Ocean encircling the *oikoumenē* were long-standing subjects of debate among Greek writers (see §III. 3. g–h).

Beyond extant poetry, it is worth remembering that Eratosthenes expounded some of his geographical theory, such as about the climatic (latitudinal) zones of the Earth, in verse form.[305]

Finally, a particularly intriguing lost author is Hestiaia of Alexandria, the only known female geographer from Greek and Roman antiquity.[306] All we know about her work is a single mention in Strabo, who says the 2nd-century BC scholar Demetrios of Skepsis (*FGrH* 2013) cited her on a question of Homeric topography (some words are missing in Strabo's text):

> Demetrios invokes as witness the Alexandrian Hestiaia, who wrote about the *Iliad* of Homer. She investigated whether the (*Trojan*) war occurred in the area of the present

---

[302] *FGrH* 2206 = Albaladejo Vivero 2011. See also Dueck 2012, 57; Habicht 2013; Roller 2015, 141–2, 146–7. There are three designated fragments in *FGrH* 2206, but no evidence that E. wrote anything. F 1 a/b/c are three versions of the statement that before the coming of E. there were peoples ignorant of the use of fire (Mela 3. 92; indirectly Pliny 6. xxxv. 188; Solinus 30. 14), which plausibly refer to E. of Kyzikos but cite no written account; F 2 = our Eudoxos of Knidos 75 and Tim. 17, where Pliny's *tradidit* ('handed down') fits better a man who left writings; F 3 = our Eudoxos of Knidos 31, again without reference to any writing.

[303] Strabo 2. 3. 4–5, C98–102 = Poseidonios 2 below.

[304] See *PME* (Ch. 25 below), n. 24 to introduction. A different view is that Nearchos' and Onesikritos' route was used until the discovery of the monsoon (Roller 2015, 99).

[305] For example, in his *Hermes*, which fragments such as *P. Oxy.* 42. 3000 suggest comprised *c.*1,600 lines (Bulloch 1985, 604–5).

[306] Not in *FGrH*, *BNJ*, or *FGrH* iv–v. See Ippolito 2006, noting that Eustathios (*Il.*, vol. i, p. 430. ll. 24–6, on *Il.* 1. 530; i, p. 606, ll. 23–4 on *Il.* 3. 64) appears to repeat Strabo though also giving a variant form of her name, Histiaia.

city (*polis*) [—] and the plain of Troy which, so the poet states, lies between the city and the sea: for the (*plain*) visible in front of the present city is an accumulation from the rivers and occurred later.

(Strabo 13. 1. 36, C599)[307]

The passage appears to imply that Hestiaia had visited the spot herself, which may suggest that her home city was Alexandria in the Troad rather than Alexandria-by-Egypt. Although women of citizen family began to wield more economic and political power in Greek cities in the hellenistic period, they are named as authors surprisingly rarely.

VII. SCOPE OF THE VOLUMES

VII. 1. THE TEXTS

The present book is designed to be *read*. That is not meant as a trivial remark. The arrangement of material has been chosen to promote continuity and not overload chapters with detailed scholarly discussion (though some technicalities are unavoidable). This part of the Introduction is designed to orientate readers who may be unfamiliar with ancient texts beyond the standard historical and literary authors commonly studied at school and university. It may be read in combination with the Time-line that follows §XI. The following remarks on individual authors and texts are arranged into a number of broad themes, for ease of understanding, but it is important to emphasize that those investigative categories are neither hermetically separate nor mutually exclusive. Many of the authors and texts would fit into more than one.

a. 'Exploration' Texts

Some of the chapters contain accounts of actual expeditions. The three earliest take us to the margins of the inhabited world (*oikoumenē*) as it was known to the Greeks. Such is the case with the earliest author, Aristeas (1), whose little-known poem in Homeric metre recounted his travels beyond the Greek fringes of the Black Sea and reflect his society's deep interest in both Greek and non-Greek religious practice. The next, Skylax (2), travelled the Indian subcontinent on behalf of the king of Persia. The short, puzzling text transmitted under the name of Hanno (4)—possibly translated from Punic; but possibly fictional, and possibly of hellenistic rather than early Classical date—purports to narrate, partly in the first person, a Carthaginian expedition down the coast of Morocco, perhaps as far as Cameroon.

We should not see this in terms of 'One small step for a man'. Most or all of these travellers and their successors are unlikely to have been the first of their compatriots ever to explore a given foreign region: they undoubtedly followed in the wake of previous voyagers, above all traders. (The present tense is used for those authors of whom

---

[307] My translation.

we have substantially continuous text, the past for those we know largely or solely through 'fragments'.) Other authors mentioned below certainly travelled, as did some mentioned in part VI of this Introduction.

b. 'Scientific' Texts

By the Classical period, broadly scientific aims begin to come to the fore. Some authors, even if they personally travelled widely using established routes, framed their observations as a contribution to abstract ratiocination about the nature of the world. Thus **3** Hekataios, the first Greek known to have written not only historical works but a comprehensive geography of Europe and Asia (at least, the parts the Greeks knew well, and including the far west), was part of the so-called Ionian Renaissance in which leading men strove to systematize knowledge and discover explanations for the workings of the cosmos and the Earth. Hekataios may have been the first writer to create a map to accompany geographical writing—not to help him travel, but to illuminate his text. Next, **5** *Airs, Waters, and Places*, while short on concrete detail, presumes a knowledge and an understanding gained by well-travelled doctors, and claims to show how climate, hydrology, and geology (to use modern terms) explain cultural and social differences between Europeans and Asians—but also, importantly, variations within those continents. Another much-travelled man, **6** Eudoxos of Knidos,[308] may have given a richer account of the central Mediterranean and easterly regions than Hekataios, but was best known as a mathematician and astronomer who applied geometrical frameworks to the description of the *oikoumenē*.

The Mediterranean and Black Sea gazetteer of **7** Pseudo-Skylax, enumerating regions, peoples, and coastal distances while calculating total lengths of the continental coasts, is a desk-based study that draws upon previous writings but also probably uses oral informants and possibly administrative records. It sits within the scientific context of Aristotle's new Lyceum or Peripatos at Athens: verbal similarities hint (but cannot prove) that it may be an early work by one of the founder's younger associates, **9** Dikaiarchos, who had a strong interest—building upon Eudoxos' work—in establishing accurate dimensions for the known continents and seas. Potentially connected to this Athenian intellectual enterprise, and certainly informed about contemporary scientific developments, is **8** Pytheas, who filled a gap that Ps.-Skylax had effectively left, by exploring the coasts and islands of the North Atlantic, but put his descriptive observations at the service of a refined methodology of calculating latitude, again based on Eudoxos' principles.

By the 3rd century BC, with the rise of the Mouseion ('shrine of the Muses', a research institute) and Library at Alexandria, scientific and mathematical aspects are elaborated with rigour, though there is no geographic 'profession' since the main

---

[308] Cited with his city-ethnic to distinguish him from the later explorer Eudoxos of Kyzikos (C2 BC), of whom we have no trace of writing.

authors were polymaths working in various 'subjects'. 12 Eratosthenes and, from the 2nd century, 16 Hipparchos, both known to us largely through Strabo, took the cartographic schemes of their predecessors and developed their rigour, though not without sparking fierce debates. Equally polymathic in the 1st century BC is 19 Poseidonios, another widely travelled man who blended all the above aspects of geography—physical, cultural, biological, observational, mathematical, theoretical—into a sophisticated synthesis that provided firmer philosophical underpinnings for the whole geographical enterprise.

c. Descriptive Texts: Science, Utility, Rhetoric

Many works cited above contain, or contained, extensive records of observed phenomena. The descriptive tradition continues in the hellenistic and Roman periods, but authors' aims vary widely.

Some in the hellenistic era seem to have aspired to imitate or develop the Hekataian model for its own sake, or for literary ends and their own reputation, like 13 Mnaseas with his apparent interest in the historical and mythological backgrounds of Greek cities; 14 Skymnos, author of a barely attested geography in at least ten books which seems to be another variant on the Hekataios model; and 18 Artemidoros with his oft-cited universal portrayal of the *oikoumenē* that was evidently rich in observation but also in useful details of local distances. Writers of this kind do not appear to have placed a high premium on methodological innovation, rather on arousing the reader's interest through dense description and the deployment of inherently fascinating detail.

Others seem to have leant, like 7 Ps.-Skylax, towards the cataloguing mentality and evince practical utility in their texts. One such was 10 Timosthenes, a high-ranking officer of the ruling Macedonian dynasty of Egypt, with his compilation of information about harbours. At the end of the hellenistic period, as Roman power began to reach its furthest extent, 21 Menippos and 23 Isidoros offer functional lists of places and distances, coastal and inland respectively. The four surviving sections of 31 the *Stadiasmos*, perhaps based on data from the era of the Roman Principate but reworked a couple of centuries later, likewise combine detailed coastal enumeration with purportedly current information about the facilities available at certain harbours. Still in the 1st century AD, 25 *Circumnavigation of the Erythraian Sea*, seemingly motivated by a desire to promote and facilitate sea trade across the Indian Ocean, offers a discursive picture of that region, informed by detailed observation including local political circumstances at the time of writing. A much later work seemingly also has a commercial character: the puzzling text known as 33 *Expositio*, surviving in Latin but possibly translated from a Greek original; it is unusual in being Romanocentric, uncritical, and vague about its aims, though informative about commercial realities—perhaps a document for private use?

d. Didactic Texts

Several texts from the Imperial centuries revert to the scientific tone. Three of them have an ostensibly didactic (instructional) aim and were successively placed at the front of one of the two great collections of geographical writings—the one probably created by Arrian—that saved many of these works from oblivion. The first two are the outline (*hypotypōsis*) of geography by **29** Agathemeros in the 2nd century AD, and **35** the *Hypotyposis*, similarly entitled but anonymous, from the 6th century, which aims to update the readers of the collection with what was learned from Ptolemy (whose work was evidently not yet published when Agathemeros wrote). The third, not included in the present work because it relates almost entirely to Ptolemy and is probably much later than the others (perhaps as late as the 9th century), is the so-called *Diagnosis* ('determination') *of Geography* (see §VIII. 2. a).

The most important late antique geographer, one with descriptive, scientific, and even didactic aims, is **34** Markianos, who not only collects earlier geographical texts—forming the second great 'corpus' (collection) of treatises, probably on the basis of a nucleus gathered by **21** Menippos[309]—but also edits and critiques several of them (including Ps.-Skylax, Artemidoros, and Menippos), expounding an intelligent geographical methodology which he then exemplifies in his own detailed, cartographically informed accounts of the oceanic coasts of Asia and Europe.

e. Further Literary Motives

Particular regions of the world may also be selected for descriptive accounts, whose cultural, scientific, or rhetorical motives vary. Focused on the writer's present day like the six works last mentioned, partly functional (*qua* administrative) but with literary aspirations, is the unusual treatise by Arrian on the Black Sea (**27**), comparable to that of Timosthenes in being a state-commissioned work. Formally a report to the emperor Hadrian on the state of Roman naval dispositions in the eastern Euxine, it is interwoven with literary evocations of particular places and a somewhat inadequate attempt to complete the circuit on the basis of earlier sources. Its much later 'second edition', **36** the Pseudo-Arrianic *Euxine*, updates Arrian's information for the 6th century.

The sketch of communities in central Greece by **11** Herakleides Kritikos (fr. 1) seems designed to raise a laugh, whereas **15** Agatharchides' detailed ethnographic observations of North-East Africa, situated within a work of history rather than pure geography, at times come close to polemic with their disillusioned accounts of the dire effects of Ptolemaic rule on some of the native peoples; equally—as befits a moral history—they explore the lessons that the 'simple life' could teach jaded elite readers. **22** Juba of Mauretania, a client king under Augustus and one of the highest-achieving scholars of his age, may have intended his compendious documentation of the wealth of North Africa's natural and geological history to promote the standing of his kingdom and

---

[309] For Menippos' role, see Marcotte 2000b, cxxii.

its people. From the first half of the 2nd century AD—an era of very active outputs in Greek literature more widely, and equally in geography—we have **30** Dionysios of Byzantion's enthusiastic depiction of the beauties and historical-mythological depth of his home region, the Thracian Bosporos.

The unknown Pseudo-Aristotle, in the rhetorically powerful *On the Cosmos* (**24**), puts scientific geography and cosmology to philosophical, indeed theological, use to substantiate a late hellenistic version of Aristotelianism. By contrast, a unique and curious work, the Pseudo-Plutarchean *On the Names of Rivers and Mountains and the Things Found in Them* (**26**), is the only surviving text ostensibly dedicated to particular categories of geographical data. Other such works do not survive; but it is probable they were not like this one, for the author not only follows a rigid template for each chapter on a famous river, but foregrounds the fantastical in offering bizarre explanations of rivers' names, repetitiously based on mythical accounts of rape, revenge, and suicide, interspersed with magical herbs and stones from different environments. He even invents imaginary source authors to whom he attributes much of his 'information'. What kind of readership relished such material is uncertain.

Finally, we come to a group of verse texts which—unlike the early, oral-influenced hexameters of Homer (in the Prologue) and Aristeas (**1**)—draw upon geographical writings to show their literary sophistication and skill. Each begins with an address: to a patron in the case of the coastal tour of the inner seas in **17** the *Nikomedean Periodos*; to a friend in the cases of **20** Dionysios son of Kalliphon's sketch of Old Greece, **28** Dionysios Periegetes' evocation of the known world, and **32** the late Latin poet Avienus, who also wrote an expanded version of Dionysios Periegetes. (Only the third of these four is complete.) Avienus' *Ora maritima* is of particular interest as it preserves material from lost Greek texts, and one Carthaginian, from the archaic and Classical periods that dealt with the far west of the *oikoumenē*. Thus it brings us back again to exploration.

VII. 2. PRESERVATION OF CONTINUOUS TEXTS

Until the introduction of mechanical printing into Europe in the third quarter of the 15th century, laborious copying by hand was the only way in which Greek and Latin texts could be preserved or shared—except in the rare cases when they were inscribed on imperishable materials. Of the 37 texts in this collection, all of which were composed between about 700 BC and AD 600, only a few (see §VIII. 1) survive as part of a 'manuscript tradition' to which, if there are multiple copies with variations between them, we can apply the techniques of 'textual criticism': comparing versions from different times and places in order to establish the most reliable form of the text. Some geographical works have barely avoided the sad fate of nearly all classical writing, surviving in just one or two copies; among these, fifteen belong to one of two damaged collections or 'corpora' of geographical texts (one surviving in a single copy, the other in two; details in §VIII. 2; in a couple of cases we have additional copies made from these, but they normally have no independent value as evidence and add little or nothing to our knowledge of the texts).

VII. 3. 'FRAGMENTS' AND 'TESTIMONIA'

Other texts (chiefly those in Chapters 1–3, 6, 8–10, 12–14, 16, 18–19, and 22–3), none of them later than the Augustan period, have been compiled in the present volumes from what are commonly called either 'fragments' (texts deemed to preserve the actual words of an author) or 'testimonia' (texts giving other information about the author).[310] A 'fragment' may be literally a physical chunk of inscribed material (a broken inscription, a torn papyrus), but in this context the term more commonly refers to a quotation, paraphrase, or citation of the text of an earlier author by a later. The confidence with which the later author's words can be linked with the earlier will vary with both content and context. A 'testimonium' is a reference to an author by a later writer which gives us information about that author, or their works, without necessarily supplying material that we can attribute to the earlier writer's actual text. The same passage in the later author may, of course, do double duty as both fragment and testimonium. In these volumes, however, the distinction between fragments and testimonia is often set aside so that extracts can, where possible, be arranged simply in date order (as explained in §IX below).

One of the most monumental scholarly works of the modern era, which perhaps more than any other exemplifies the skilful deployment of 'fragment' and 'testimonium', is Felix Jacoby's unfinished *Fragmente der griechischen Historiker* ('fragments of the Greek historians') or *FGrH* i–iii, published in 16 volumes between 1923 and 1958, mainly in German, though some of the commentaries are in English. The project was intended to cover nearly nine hundred sources (nos 1–856 with some additions denoted by suffixes a, b, and c), often anonymous and including non-literary authorities such as inscribed chronologies.[311]

FGrH i–iii is now being completed and revised as *Brill's New Jacoby* (BNJ, in English; so far only online),[312] which uses the same author numbers as Jacoby (as well as retaining his numbering of testimonia and fragments) but offers revised Greek texts with new English translations and commentaries (including commentaries on 248 authors Jacoby did not live to complete). Although BNJ is still in progress, some 260 authors have already appeared in a second edition (BNJ²), including seven who appear in the present volumes.[313] The fourth part of Jacoby's work is being continued, according to his design, by *FGrH* iv (in English), which will cover authors 1000 to 1787.[314]

---

[310] On the problems surrounding the concept of 'fragment', see Coo and Finglass 2020, 3–5.

[311] Jacoby 1923–58, comprising 708 authors.

[312] Worthington 2007–.

[313] BNJ² 35 Aristeas, 91 Strabo, 275 Juba, 369a Herakleides Kritikos, 438 Artemidoros (his historical work), 709 Skylax of Karyanda, and 781 Isidoros.

[314] Bollansée and Schepens 1998– (fascicles 1, 3, and 7 printed); continued online by Schorn 2011–.

For geographical writing, Jacoby's project is being continued in *FGrH* v or 'Jacoby V' under the editorship of H.-J. Gehrke and F. Maier. Works are arranged in three thematic series (nos 2001–54, 2101–18, and 2201–20, plus five denoted by letter suffixes).[315] It will include all the 'minor' and fragmentary geographers,[316] each with revised Greek or Latin text plus commentary and translation (in English, German, French, or Italian). Alongside the recent studies of specific authors cited throughout the present volumes, as a corpus *FGrH* v will replace Carl (or Karl, or Charles, or Carolus) Müller's *Geographi Graeci minores* from the mid-19th century, still an invaluable source of data, pending the completion of *FGrH* v, but still often misguidedly cited as if its Greek and Latin texts are standard.[317]

All of the Jacoby family adopt the formal distinction between fragments (designated with F and a number) and testimonia (T plus number), some extracts appearing twice as described above. The sequencing of extracts is heuristic rather than chronological, typically beginning with a listing of an author's works from a source such as the *Suda* rather than with the earliest fragment or testimonium.

The TABLE I.1 lists the geographical texts that appear in the Jacoby family of works, indicating those in the present volumes by bold type and their chapter number.[318] The Concordance at the end of the book allows readers to cross-refer to *BNJ* and *FGrH* iv–v.

VII. 4. ANONYMOUS AND PSEUDONYMOUS TEXTS

Three of the continuous texts in the present volumes are anonymous (17 the *Nikomedean Periodos*, 33 *Expositio*, 35 *Hypotyposis*). The *Nikomedean Periodos*, however, is commonly referred to as 'Pseudo-Skymnos'; this is misleading, as nothing in the manuscript tradition links it to the real Skymnos of Chios (14) and the only connexion is that an early modern scholar suggested him as the author. The proposal was refuted before very long, but has lingered on in scholarship, with the prefix 'Pseudo-' added, in the absence of a conclusive attribution (see introduction to 17). This gives the false impression that the work is pseudonymous—falsely attributed to a known author.

---

[315] Gehrke and Meier 2011–.

[316] Though not the Homeric Catalogue (Prologue to the present volumes), 5 *AWP* or 24 Ps.-Aristotle, *De mundo*. Of the texts in the present volumes, four are in *FGrH* i–iv (and therefore in its successor, *BNJ*) but not in *FGrH* v, while seven are in both (see TABLE I.1).

[317] *GGM*; further texts in *FHG* v. The parallel Roman successor to Müller's *GGM*, Riese 1878, should be noted.

[318] In the present volumes, serial numbers of authors who appear in *FGrH* i–iii are preceded by *BNJ* (or *BNJ²*) rather than by *FGrH*. Only those in *FGrH* iv and v have *FGrH* numbers, apart from a few in *FGrH* i–iii who have not yet appeared in *BNJ*. A fuller list of 236 geographical authors, including the non-fragmentary, may be found in the *Encyclopedia of Ancient Natural Scientists* (*EANS*; Keyser and Irby-Massie 2008, 999–1002). This includes both Greek and Latin authors as well as authors whose primary identity is not that of geographer but, for example, historian or encyclopaedist.

TABLE I.1. Geographical authors in the Jacoby 'family' of works. (Some names modified or simplified.)

BNJ (^{2} = 2nd edition)		
1 **Hekataios** (3)	241 **Eratosthenes** (12) (also 2109)	438^2 **Artemidoros** (also 2008)
35^2 **Aristeas** (1)	275^2 **Juba** (22)	709^2 **Skylax** (2) (also 1000 for historical writing)
86 **Agatharchides** (15) (also 2001)	369 *P. Hawara* 80–81 (appendix to **11**)	781^2 **Isidoros** (23)
91^2 Strabo (for his *History*)	369a^2 **Herakleides Kritikos** (**11**) (also 2022)	854 Pausanias of Damascus

FGrH iv		
1000 **Skylax** (2) (also 709)	1400 **Dikaiarchos** (9) (also 2015)	

FGrH v		
2001–54 *Descriptive geography* (55)		
‡2001 **Agatharchides** (15) (also 86)	‡2019 **Dionysios Periegetes** (28)	2037 *Anonymi Periplus Ponti Euxini* (36)
‡2002 Alexandros of Ephesos	‡2020 *Expositio* (L) (33)	2038 Phileas
2003 Apellas of Kyrene	2021 *Hypotyposis* (35)	2039 Philemon
2004 Apollonides	2021a *Pinax* (table of contents) to corpus A	‡2040 **Pseudo-Plutarch** (26)
2005 Athenagoras son of Arimnestos	2022 **Herakleides Kritikos** (**11**) (also 369a)	‡2041 **Poseidonios** (19)
2006 Aristeides of Miletos (?)	2023 **Iunior Philosophus** (L) (33)	‡2042 Priscianus
‡2007 **Arrian** (27)	2024 Kleoboulos	2043 Promathos of Samos
‡2008 **Artemidoros** (18) (also 438)	‡2025 Kleon of Syracuse	2044 Protagoras
2009 **Avienus** (L) (32)	2026 Knossos	2045 Simmeas
2010 Bakoris of Rhodes	‡2027 **Markianos** (35)	2046 **Pseudo-Skylax** (7)
2011 Botthaios	‡2028 Menekrates of Elaia (in Argolis)	2047 **Skymnos** (14)
‡2012 Damastes of Sigeion	‡2029 **Menippos** (21)	2048 *Nikomedean Periodos* ('Pseudo-Skymnos') (17)
2013 Demetrios of Skepsis	2030 Menogenes	‡2049 *Stadiasmos* (31)
2014 Demokles of Phygela	‡2031 **Mnaseas** (13)	2050 Timagetos

‡2015 **Dikaiarchos (9)** (also 1400)	2032 Nikagoras of Cyprus	2051 **Timosthenes (10)**
2015a Diogenianos	2033 Ophelas	‡2052 Timotheos
2016 Diognetos	2034 Pausimachos of Samos	‡2053 Xenophon of Lampsakos
‡2017 **Dionysios of Byzantion (30)**	‡2035 *Perimetros tou Pontou* (appendix to **36**)	2054 Zenothemis
‡2018 **Dionysios son of Kalliphon (20)**	2036 *Periplus maris Erythraei* (**25**)	

2101–18 Mathematical geography (**20**)		
‡2101 Achilles Tatius	2108 Dionysodoros of Melos	2115 Oinopides of Chios
2102 **Agathemeros (29)**	‡2109 **Eratosthenes (12)** (also 241)	2116 Pappos of Alexandria
2103 Anaximandros of Miletos	‡2110 **Eudoxos of Knidos (6)**	2117 Polybios
2104 Anaximenes of Miletos	‡2111 Euktemon of Athens (?)	2118 Serapion of Antioch
2105 Bion of Abdera	‡2112 **Hipparchos (16)**	‡2118a Geminos
‡2106 Demokritos of Abdera	2113 Krates of Mallos	‡2118b Kleomedes
2107 *Diagnosis*	2114 Marinos of Tyre	

2201–20 Explorations (**21**)		
2201 Alexandros of Myndos (?)	2207 Euthymenes of Massalia	2214 Pythagoras
2201a Anaxikrates	2208 **Hanno (4)**	‡2215 **Pytheas (8)**
2202 Archias of Pella	2209 Hieron of Soloi	2216 Sataspes
2203 Diodoros of Samos	‡2210 Himilco	‡2217 Septimius Flaccus (L)
2204 Diogenes	2211 Hippalos	2218 Simmias or Simias
2205 Dioskoros	‡2212 Iulius Maternus (L)	2219 unknown travellers in India
2206 Eudoxos of Kyzikos	2213 Maës Titianos	2220 Theophilos

‡ = not yet published (as at summer 2021).
(L) = Latin text.
Bold = included in present volumes (with chapter no.).

In one case (**5** *Airs, Waters, and Places*) the attribution to Hippokrates is possibly correct but uncertain. Six further chapter titles begin with 'Pseudo-' (a prefix often abbreviated to 'Ps.-'), indicating that while a text is preserved under an author's name the attribution is considered incorrect: **7** Pseudo-Skylax, **24** Pseudo-Aristotle, both **25** and **36** Pseudo-Arrian, **26** Pseudo-Plutarch, and **31** Pseudo-Hippolytos. Four of these texts can be shown to have been written later than the lifetime of their supposed author, two earlier.

VII. 5. FORMS OF WRITING

The 36 texts in the volumes (or 37 if we include the prologue, taken from Homer's *Iliad*) are arranged in chronological order. They comprise several different forms of writing and span roughly 1,300 years, from the early archaic period of Greece to the 'later Roman empire' (the said 'empire' includes the eastern part centred on Byzantion, later Constantinople), also known as the 'late antique period' (4th–6th centuries AD). Using the conventional dates of the texts, there are 3 archaic texts (1–3), 5 classical (4–8), 12 hellenistic (9–20),[319] 11 Roman (21–31), and 5 late Roman (32–6). Unless 4 Hanno, preserved in Greek, is a translation of a Punic writing, all are, or were originally, in Greek other than two late Roman texts (32, Latin; 33, Latin but possibly translated from another language). The majority, 21 or more texts (10–30; possibly 9, 31), were written between the 3rd century BC and the 2nd century AD, the five hundred years during which geography can be said to have developed as a fully-fledged science.

The state of preservation of these texts is highly discouraging: a rapid review will show that pre-Roman texts are much less likely to survive. Likewise, of the few surviving geographical works in either language (§VI. 1 above), none is earlier than the Augustan period.

a. Prose

The great majority of our authors, 31 in number, wrote in prose: 30 in Greek (if we include 4 Hanno) and 1 in Latin (32, the author of the *Expositio*).[320] For 18 of them, mostly Roman and late antique, we possess some 'readable', continuous text, whether an incomplete version, abridgement, close paraphrase, or Latin translation:

  3 classical (*c*.500–*c*.300 BC): **4** Hanno; **5** *Airs, Waters, and Places*; **7** Pseudo-Skylax

  3 hellenistic (*c*.300–*c*.1 BC): **11** Herakleides Kritikos; **15** Agatharchides; **21** Menippos

  8 Roman (AD *c*.1–*c*.300): **23** Isidoros; **24** Pseudo-Aristotle, *On the World* (*De mundo*); **25** *Circumnavigation of the Erythraian Sea*; **26** Pseudo-Plutarch; **27** Arrian; **29** Agathemeros; **30** Dionysios of Byzantion (Greek, but part preserved only in Latin); **31** *Stadiasmos*

  4 late antique (AD *c*.300–*c*.600): **33** *Expositio* (Latin, but perhaps from a non-Latin original); **34** *Hypotyposis*; **35** Markianos; **36** the Pseudo-Arrianic *Euxine*

The remaining 13 prose authors, none of whom is later than the early 1st century AD, are preserved only through fragments and testimonia (as defined above):

  2 archaic: **2** Skylax; **3** Hekataios

  2 classical: **6** Eudoxos of Knidos; **8** Pytheas

---

[319] Taking 'hellenistic' to mean 323–30 BC.
[320] Juba II of Mauretania (Ch. 22 below, no. 20a) wrote in both Greek and Latin, though his main geographical works were in Greek.

8 hellenistic: **9** Dikaiarchos; **10** Timosthenes; **12** Eratosthenes; **13** Mnaseas; **14** Skymnos; **16** Hipparchos; **18** Artemidoros; **19** Poseidonios

1 Roman: **22** Juba

b. Verse

Besides Homer in the Prologue, there are in the present volumes 5 verse texts (4 Greek, 1 Latin), of which the first is fragmentary but the rest either complete or preserved in substantial, continuous passages:

1 archaic: **1** Aristeas

2 hellenistic: **17** *Nikomedean Periodos*; **20** Dionysios son of Kalliphon

1 Roman: **28** Dionysios Periegetes

1 late Roman: **32** Avienus, *Ora maritima* (Latin)

Once again, the preservation of dedicated geographical writings is strongly biased: in this case, to works later than 150 BC.

VIII. TRANSMISSION

VIII. 1. TEXTS SURVIVING (OR ONCE SURVIVING) WITHIN A MANUSCRIPT TRADITION

As we have seen, 14 of the 36 works in the present volumes (leaving aside the Prologue from the *Iliad*) may be described as 'fragmentary': lost, but partly preserved in short quotations, paraphrases, or citations in later authors' works, often of late antique or early medieval date. These are discussed in §VIII. 3 below, along with a fifteenth, the special case of Agatharchides.

As noted earlier, hardly any of our texts are preserved, in part or in whole, in extant manuscripts. Only three belong to a manuscript tradition in the conventional sense:

5 *Airs, Waters, and Places* is found in 11 manuscripts as part of the Hippocratic corpus of medical texts;

24 Ps.-Aristotle, *De mundo* is preserved (not always complete) in 95 manuscripts;

27 Dionysios Periegetes survives in over 110 medieval manuscripts (and several dozen later ones), for the work was highly popular from the 13th century on.

The remaining eighteen works in this book exist in whole or part, but have survived by a process that might be described as little short of miraculous. One work, the *Stadiasmos* (**31**), is preserved in a single manuscript of the 10th or 11th century. Fifteen survive in one or both of two priceless compilations of geographical works, created in Roman and late antique times and then recopied; one of these two collections survives in a single main manuscript, the other in just two manuscripts (there are a few partial derivative manuscripts in each case). These are discussed in §VIII. 2 below.

Finally, two works are known, in whole or in part, only because they survived in manuscript form just long enough to be printed in the early modern period before disappearing:

32 Avienus' *Ora maritima* is known only from the first printed edition of 1488;

33 the *Expositio* was in a Latin manuscript of unknown date, now lost, while Iunior Philosophus' summary of the same work is extant in a 12th-century manuscript.

VIII. 2. TEXTS IN THE TWO GEOGRAPHICAL CORPORA

As noted above, fifteen works depend for their existence almost entirely on just three medieval manuscripts representing two original 'corpora' or compilations (see TABLE I.1), both now preserved incompletely. In some cases, what is (or was) contained in these was not the original geographical treatise but an 'epitome' (digest, précis), such as Markianos' epitomes of Artemidoros and Menippos.

(a) The Arrianic Corpus

Eight of our works belong to a corpus (collection) of geographers whose core—at least four works—was evidently put together by Arrian in the first half of the 2nd century AD: in date order **4** Hanno, **25** *PME*, **26** Ps.-Plutarch, and **27** Arrian's own *Periplous*. Prefatory treatises were later added (**29** Agathemeros, with **35** *Hypotyposis* in front of it), as were **30** Dionysios of Byzantion, **36** the Pseudo-Arrianic *Euxine* (a late antique revision of Arrian's *Periplous*, placed immediately before his original), and finally the very late *Diagnosis*, a didactic treatise of some 2,500 words on Ptolemaic geodesy (9th century? not in the present book), which was placed before the *Hypotyposis* and Agathemeros.

Two versions of this corpus are extant:

A. THE HEIDELBERG CODEX

Six of the above eight works (in date order **4** Hanno, **25** *PME*, **26** Ps.-Plutarch, and **27** Arrian, plus the post-Arrianic **35** *Hypotyposis* and **36** the Pseudo-Arrianic *Euxine*)[321] survive in a parchment manuscript in Heidelberg (codex Palatinus Heidelbergensis 398), dated to the last quarter of the 9th century and known to geographical scholarship as A.[322] Its folios (of which there are images in the chapters just mentioned) measure some 9¾ inches tall and 6¾ inches wide (25 × 17 cm) with a text width of just *c.*4¼ inches (*c.*11 cm) accommodating 30–40 letters in a rather formal script.[323] It also contains extensive

---

[321] The order of the minor works in A is *Eux.*, Arr., *PME*, Hanno, and Ps.-Plutarch, with other works intervening (listed at the start of Chapter 26 below). Details of A: Marcotte 2000b, xx and lxxxviii–c (present and lost contents of A listed at xc–xciii).

[322] Diktyon no. 32479. Date and images at https://digi.ub.uni-heidelberg.de/diglit/cpgraec398 [last accessed 24 January 2023].

[323] Diller 1952, 3, 5.

Chrestomatheiai ('exemplary lessons') from Strabo, together with fifteen non-geographical texts (listed in the introduction to Chapter 26 below). Extracts from this codex were among the earliest printed texts of Greek geographers, such as in Gelen's pioneering 1533 edition of Arrian, Hanno, *PME*, and Ps.-Plutarch, as well as the *Chrestomatheiai*.[324]

B. THE VATOPEDI CODEX

The six above authors from A that are translated in the present volumes also survive, together with **29** Agathemeros, **30** Dionysios of Byzantion, and the *Diagnosis*, in a 14th-century manuscript copied from A and known as B (codex Vatopedinus 655), which also includes an illustrated Ptolemy.[325] Its large pages of *c*.13¾ × 9¾ inches (*c*.35 × 25 cm;[326] again, illustrated in the chapters just mentioned) have a text width of *c*.7½ inches (*c*.19 cm) accommodating some 90 characters in a close, rather irregular script. Nearly all of B is still at the *Vatopédi* monastery on Mt Athos, but 30 folios of critical importance for geography were stolen in the 19th century, of which 21 are in London (British Library MS Add. 19391)[327] and 9 in Paris (Parisinus supplément grec 443a).[328] Notably, the manuscript includes several circular diagrams within the late *Diagnosis* illustrating zones of latitude, the structure of the Earth, and so on, that surely derive from its original (9th-century?) version.

Thus, of the geographical works in the present volumes, eight survive only in A or B (some in both); of these, the Pseudo-Arrianic *Euxine* alone survives elsewhere (other than a few derivative transcripts of little or no independent worth).[329]

(b) The Menippos–Markianos Corpus

We also have the majority of a second corpus, evidently put together by Markianos of Herakleia around AD 400—probably on foundations laid by Menippos[330]—to remedy gaps in Arrian's collection.

[324] Gelenius 1533; Diller 1952, 48 no. 2. A Latin Strabo was printed at Rome as early as 1469, followed in 1471 by an edition of Pomponius Mela at Milan. Other geographical works included a Latin Ptolemy at Vicenza in 1475, and Avienus' *Descriptio orbis terrae* and *Ora maritima* in 1488 at Venice (in Pisanus 1488). (Data from 'Incunabula Short Title Catalogue', British Library, last accessed 26 January 2022.) The MS of the *OM* is now lost, making this *incunabulum* the sole independent evidence for the text (see Ch. 32 below).

[325] Details of B: Diller 1937; Diller 1952, 11–14; Marcotte 2000b, xx and c–cviii (contents, cii–ciii). Its contents are also listed in the introduction to Ch. 26 below. The original order of the relevant works in B, as reconstructed by Diller 1952, 11, was *Diagnosis*, **33** *Hypotyposis*, **28** Agathemeros, **29** Dionysios of Byzantion, **35** *Eux.*, **27** Arr., **24** *PME*, **4** Hanno, and **25** Ps.-Plutarch, with other works intervening. On *Diagn.* see Diller 1943; Altomare 2013, 29–30; Mittenhuber 2011a.

[326] Diller 1952, 10.

[327] Diktyon no. 38967. Images at www.bl.uk/manuscripts/FullDisplay.aspx?ref=Add_MS_19391 [last accessed 24 January 2023].

[328] Diktyon no. 53176. Images at https://gallica.bnf.fr/ark:/12148/btv1b11004972g?rk=21459 [last accessed 24 January 2023]. The most important direct copy of B, known as C, is Cambridge, University Library Gg. II 33 (dated C16); images at https://cudl.lib.cam.ac.uk/view/MS-GG-00002-00033/249 and the four pp. following.

[329] In Vaticanus gr. 143 (known as V; early C14) and Vindobonensis theol. fr. 203 (W; late C14), with extracts elsewhere. Marcotte 2000b, xciii, cxiv, cxvi.

[330] Marcotte 2000b, cxxii.

TABLE I.2. Contents of the three principal MSS relevant to the present volumes (B follows the reconstruction by Diller 1952, 11). ᵣ = recto (right-hand page), ᵛ = verso (left-hand page). Subscript numbers are lines of a MS (not specified where the beginning or end of work occupies a whole page).

ch. no.		Corpus A (Arrian)		Corpus D (Menippos–Marcian)
		codex A	codex B	codex D
		Palatinus Heidelbergensis Graecus 398 (C9 AD)	Athous Vatopedinus 655 + Londiniensis add. 19391 + Parisinus suppl. fr. 443a (C15 AD)	Parisinus supplément grec 443 (C13 AD)
		see Marcotte 2000b, xci–xciii	*see Marcotte 2000b, c–ciii*	*see Marcotte 2000b, lxxviii–lxxix*
—	*Diagnosis*	(lost)	Par. 10ʳ (stood first)	
35	*Hypotyposis*	(lost)	Lond. 1ʳ₁₀–3ʳ₁₀	
29	Agathemeros	(lost)	Lond. 3ʳ₁₀–3ᵛ + Par. 2ʳ₁₋₄	
30	Dionysios of Byzantion	(lost)	Par. 2ʳ₂₃–3ᵛ + Lond. 4ʳ₁₋₃₃	
36	Ps.-Arrian, *Periplous of the Euxine* ('*Eux.*')	(beginning lost) 11ʳ–16ᵛ	Lond. 4ʳ₃₅–7ᵛ₈	
27	Arrian, *Periplous of the Euxine*	30ᵛ–40ʳ	Lond. 7ᵛ₉–9ʳ₄₃	
25	Ps.-Arrian, *Circumnavigation of the Erythraian Sea* (*PME*)	40ᵛ–54ᵛ	Lond. 9ʳ₄₄–12ʳ₄₂	
4	Hanno	55ʳ–56ʳ	Lond. 12ʳ₄₄–12ᵛ₂₅	
26	Ps.-Plutarch, *De fluviis*	157ʳ–173ʳ	Par. 6ᵛ₂₁–9ᵛ	
34	Markianos, *Periplous of the Outer Sea*			1₁–49₃ (beginning & end lost)
21/34	Menippos (Markianos' preface)			49₃–56₁₅ preface
21/34	Menippos (Markianos' epitome)			56₁₅–60₂₂ epitome (end lost)
7	Ps.-Skylax			62₁–106₁₁

—	[end title 'Athenaios, *Poleōn skōmmata kai hodoi*, without text]			106_{11-12}
23	Isidoros of Charax			$106_{13}-111_{10}$
20	⟨Dionysios son of Kalliphon, lines 1–109b⟩			$111_{10}-114_{13}$
11	⟨Herakleides Kritikos frs 1 + 3⟩			$114_{13}-123_{19}$
20	⟨Dionysios son of Kalliphon, lines 110–50⟩			$123_{20}-124_{25}$
—	[end title 'Dikaiarchos, *Anagraphē of Hellas*', referring to previous 3 items as 1]			124_{26}
17	*Nikomedean Periodos*, a.k.a. 'Ps.-Skymnos'			125_1-143_{26} (end lost)

D. *THE PARIS CODEX*[331]

This mid-13th-century manuscript was written in the Cyprus–Palestine area and is now in Paris (Parisinus supplément grec 443). For present purposes it is known as D. Painstakingly crafted (as personal inspection of the penmanship will convince anyone) by a copyist who was meticulous but appears not to have known enough Greek to correct obvious errors, it has narrow pages of *c.*6¾ × 4¾ inches (17 × 12 cm), with lines around 4 inches (11 cm) long accommodating some 35 letters (though very variable).[332] It has 143 pages but has lost at least 4 of its original 13 or more quaternions[333] (nos 1–2, 6, and at least one after no. 12), yet still contains a further seven of our authors; not all complete; some misattributed. Rearranged in date order, these are 7 Ps.-Skylax, 11 Herakleides Kritikos, 17 *Nikomedean Periodos*, 20 Dionysios son of Kalliphon, 21 Markianos' preface to and abridgement of Menippos, 23 Isidoros, and 34 Markianos' own *Periplous of the Outer Sea*.[334] (Portions of the manuscript are illustrated in the relevant chapters below.)

Markianos supplemented his collection of at least five earlier texts with several of his own writings: namely, his *Epitome of Artemidoros* (now missing from the beginning of the codex), his *Periplous* (34, partly lost in missing quaternions), and his *Epitome of Menippos* (21, incomplete for the same reason) together with his preface to it. He also added an introductory note to Ps.-Skylax. The learned Byzantine emperor Constantine VII Porphyrogennetos (r. 913–59) consulted an earlier copy of D; the

[331] Diktyon no. 53175.   [332] Described by Marcotte 2000b, lxxvii.
[333] A 'quaternion' is a sequence of 16 pages formed by sewing together four sheets, each folded double.
[334] Images at https://gallica.bnf.fr/ark:/12148/btv1b11000074k [last accessed 24 January 2023].

copy we have is poor (the text of Ps.-Skylax is notoriously confused) and was evidently transcribed from an inferior copy.[335] About half of the *Nikomedean Periodos* is lost from the end of the codex, where its author will have been named (see Chapter 17, introduction).[336]

Other than in three later copies of D, not all complete,[337] none of the works in D survives elsewhere, apart from Isidoros.[338]

VIII. 3. PRINCIPAL SOURCES OF EXTRACTS

The work of one author, Agatharchides, specifically his *On the Erythraian Sea* (15), though not extant, has been fortunate in that long passages from two of its five books are paraphrased by Diodoros Siculus (1st century BC), less fully by Strabo (early 1st century AD, drawing on earlier paraphrases), and most importantly in a detailed and demonstrably reliable summary made directly from the original work for the head of the Orthodox Church in the East, St Photios (9th century).

As noted earlier (§VII. 3), fourteen further texts (all but one in prose) are fragmentary in the normal sense: assembled from citations, paraphrases, and occasional quotations in later authors. (All these classes of evidence are generally called 'extracts' in the present book.) In date order, they are 1 Aristeas, 2 Skylax, 3 Hekataios, 6 Eudoxos of Knidos, 8 Pytheas, 9 Dikaiarchos, 10 Timosthenes, 12 Eratosthenes, 13 Mnaseas, 14 Skymnos, 16 Hipparchos, 18 Artemidoros, 19 Poseidonios, and 22 Juba. Other texts, among the category of those wholly or partly extant, are supplemented by additional extracts.[339] The mode of preservation of these multifarious elements is that of their respective 'source-authors', and thus is due to medieval manuscripts (and two papyri).[340]

Two-thirds of these extracts, which number well over nine hundred,[341] come from just three ancient authors, all of Roman date though two of them wrote in Greek. (*a*) The most important source of extracts, Strabo's *Geography* (quoted some three hundred times in the present volumes), survives in about thirty manuscripts, of which the best are from the 10th and the 13th century, supplemented by a 5th-century palimpsest discovered in the 19th century and fully published in 1956–7.[342] (*b*) Strabo's younger contemporary Pliny the Elder, who appears over 130 times, is better served: parts of

---

[335] Details of D: Marcotte 2000b, lxvii–lxxxiv; Brillante 2020, 213–19.

[336] Morellus 1606.

[337] Monacensis gr. 566 (*m*, in Munich; *c*.1500), incomplete; Palatinus Vaticanus gr. 142 (*v*, in Vatican; C15 AD), copied from D and *m*; and Scaligeranus 32 (*Scal.*, in Leiden, made by Scaliger *c*.1570), selective. See Marcotte 2000b, lxxxiv–lxxxvii.

[338] Isidoros is also in cod. Parisinus graecus 571 (known as 'E'), currently dated C15 in Pinakes but late C13 by Diller 1952, 30, which also contains fr. 2 of HK (see Ch. 11, introduction).

[339] Generally the present work reports such additional material, including many 'testimonia', only selectively.

[340] See the appendix to HK (Ch. 11 below, no. 5), and Artem. 168, the 'Artemidoros Papyrus'.

[341] Sometimes the same 'extract' does duty in more than one chapter.

[342] Roller 2014, 28. For an overview of the discovery and study of the Strabo palimpsest, see Diller 1958.

his *Natural History* in Latin are extant in several late antique palimpsests, though this does not include the four books (3–6) in which he focuses on geography; the latter are contained in several complete or near-complete manuscripts of the 8th to 10th centuries; there are many later copies.[343] A new translation of the geographical books is in preparation.[344] (*c*) The third plentiful source of 'fragments' is Stephanos of Byzantion's *Ethnika* (see §VI. 2. j), quoted well over two hundred times in the present collection. The extant summary of his book is preserved in eight principal manuscripts of the 15th and 16th centuries and various derivative copies; a short passage of the unabridged work survives in an 11th-century manuscript.[345]

IX. ORGANIZATION OF THE VOLUMES

As noted earlier, an overriding aim of this book and its organization is to make hitherto recherché texts more accessible. Accordingly, for texts of which at least some continuous writing survives, not all supplementary paraphrases, quotations, and citations in later authors have necessarily been printed; a selection has sometimes been made of the evidence accompanying the continuous prose or verse. For the same reason, where an issue relating to an author's work has been aired in a chapter's introduction—if possible with a numerical pointer to the relevant extracts or sections—there is not necessarily a duplicate reference back from extract to introduction.

For some of those texts that have been reconstituted entirely from later citations and quotations, the complete set of data has been presented; an example is Artemidoros, where the last 'corpus' was compiled in 1856 and of whom there has never before been a systematic modern translation. For others, such as Hekataios, a representative selection has been made, typically omitting some of the minor citations or testimonia. Where an author had expertise in other areas besides geography (as did Hekataios and Poseidonios), a full selection has been offered, focused on geographical material. In each case, the numbers in one or more standard corpora are included in the Concordance at the end of the book, to allow the reader to assess any other evidence supporting that collected here.

In some of the texts that are wholly or partly reliant on secondary material, the customary division between 'testimonia' and 'fragments'—appropriate for a comprehensive scholarly edition such as those by Jacoby (*FGrH* i–iii) and his successors (in *BNJ* and *FGrH* iv–v)—has usually been eschewed in favour of chronological sequence, either maintained over the whole set of extracts or within each written work, or numbered book of a work, by the author in question. In such cases, the earliest attestation stands first and the latest last. Multiple extracts from the same source-author are ordered by

---

[343] Reynolds 1983, 307–16.   [344] Described by Talbert 2020.
[345] Billerbeck 2006–17, vol. i, pp. 5*–16*.

book, chapter, or line number, as applicable.[346] This arrangement avoids forcing the reader into the editor's way of thinking, and has the additional merit that closely related, even adjacent, passages of a given source text are kept together, helping the reader appreciate better the secondary author's response to the earlier. This is particularly important in the case of Strabo, extracts from whose *Geography* make up several tens of thousands of words in Volume One; in other editions of the geographical authors, those passages have often been carved into disconnected chunks on the basis of a thematic or other principle of organization (while some passages have even appeared twice, once as 'testimonium' and once as 'fragment'). Conventionally, too, in collections of the testimonia and fragments of an author, any available entry in an ancient encyclopaedia that lists his works (e.g. in a compendium such as the *Suda*) is printed first as a starting-point for discussion. In the present arrangement, by contrast, sources are placed in date order, and thus the reader will be made aware that these lists are not only frequently unreliable but the product of centuries of ancient reflection, and possibly growing confusion.

Chapter headings represent a compromise between accuracy and familiarity, varying in what information they contain and whether a work's title is translated or not.

The 'Selected further reading' section at the end of each chapter (like that at the end of this Introduction) is not a complete list of editions or scholarly treatments, but is highly selective. English-language scholarship has been included whenever possible. Critical editions (i.e. with at least a revised original text and usually an *apparatus criticus* or the equivalent) are marked with an asterisk (*).

Similarly, the main Index is designed to aid the readability of the volumes. Topics are given 'reference locators' that are not page numbers but the numbers of individual extracts, or text positions within a continuous text, which will guide the reader more quickly to the correct place. For fragmentary authors (or fragmentary material accompanying continuous passages of text), the serial numbers of extracts are those devised for this book; their locations in original sources will be found in the Concordances at the end of the work and in the Index, which uses chapter, section, or extract numbers, not page numbers. In these sections of 'endmatter', an author's name or a source's title is abbreviated to two or three letters (see table in List of Abbreviations, above).

X. THE TRANSLATOR'S ART

X. 1. GENERAL

In a collection of translations by more than a dozen hands, total consistency is an unrealistic aim, and perhaps undesirable given the multifarious cultural and chronological contexts in which our texts sit. Translations have been standardized for UK English and to some extent idiom, as well as for the styles of transliteration and name forms set out below.

---

[346] Where the translator prefers another arrangement, however, this has been respected.

A special word about the translation of entries from Stephanos of Byzantion and other encyclopaedic works (Harpokration, Hesychios, and the *Suda*), in particular their citations of other texts with locations or implied titles, and sometimes with book numbers. In Greek the book numbers (i.e. letters, such as α, β, γ, and so on) stand for ordinal adjectives such as '1st', '2nd', '3rd', but the number is not always preceded by the definite article ('the') and the term 'book' is not always specified. The word order also varies. I have standardized such entries to reflect, as far as possible, the exact wording and the twelve different ways in which such citations of earlier works can be expressed: for example, 'in (*the*) 4th (*book*) of . . .' or 'Eudoxos of Knidos, 2nd (*book*)'.

For the Greek vowel upsilon, transliterations use mainly *y* unless it is part of a diphthong: thus *kynara*, *hyphormos* but in diphthongs *au*, *eu*, or *ou* as is standard practice. Occasionally upsilon is *u* when a vowel follows, e.g. *orguiai* (rather than *orgyiai*), Oguion, *duo* (rather than *dyo*), *anuei*, 'Paktuic', 'Bituis'; but the *y* is retained in 'Syene' as the form is traditional, in words like *myops* (related to 'myopia'), towns like Sikyon, and in 'Polyidos' because *poly-* is a prefix.

In the translations, an obelos or dagger † stands after a single problematic word or number. Where it stands before a word or number, it is the first of a pair enclosing two or more words.

Within a translation, words in round parentheses are one of the following (unless otherwise specified):

an insertion to supply words necessary to the sense, e.g. '(*he says*)'

an explanation of a transliteration, e.g. 'Polichnion (*Little Town*)'

a transliteration to explain a translated word or name, e.g. 'horse-eating (*hippophaga*)'

a flagging up to show which technical term is being translated, e.g. 'main (*pontos*)' or 'open sea (*pelagos*)'

X. 2. NAMES

Conventional modern forms are used for the most familiar Greek names, such as Aeschylus, Adriatic, Alexander, Alexandria (rather than Alexandreia), Athens, Atlantic, Caspian, Egypt, Homer, Indians, Nile, Phrygia, Roman, Rome, Sicily, Thucydides. 'Macedonia' is used with no implications about modern political geography.

Some familiar names, however, are made more Greek-like if they are judged unlikely to confuse the reader: e.g. Achaia(n) (except for 'Achaean league'), Anaximandros, Dionysios, Gallia, Hekataios, Herodotos, Indos, Keltoi, Kilikia, Poseidonios, Skythia.

Note that ancient 'Mauretania' is a region further east than modern 'Mauritania'.

Where, however, a familiar modern name refers, or may refer, to a distinctly different area from its ancient counterpart, a Greek-like form is preferred if the original is in Greek: e.g. Aithiopia, Aithiopian, Indike, Libyē (rather than Ethiopia, Ethiopian, India, Libya). This also applies when the translator desires to avoid conflating Greek and Roman forms: thus Akytania and Narbonesia will normally be retained (not converted to Aquitania and Narbonensis).

These practices may vary in the case of poetry; Dionysios Periegetes, for example, uses different forms of the term 'Tyrrhenic'.

In Latin authors, however—most frequently Pliny the Elder—Latin forms of names are generally preserved, e.g. Aethiopia, India, Libya.

In some passages, especially where a text depends on limited manuscript evidence (such as *Stadiasmos* or *Markianos*), inconsistent spellings of names are preserved.

Except in capitalized titles of books, in order to reduce the density of capital letters on the pages, the present volumes follow the revisers of the Loeb translation of Pliny books 3–6[347] (and some nautical handbooks or 'pilots') in not capitalizing 'sea' or related English terms (such as 'ocean') when they are part of a place-name (Erythraian sea, Mediterranean sea), unless the distinguishing element is a common adjective and could not stand on its own as the name (Red Sea, Black Sea, Great Sea, etc.) and where the modern name begins with 'Sea' (Sea of Azov, Sea of Marmara, etc.). The outer ocean, not otherwise qualified, is always 'Ocean', but its divisions use 'ocean', as in Atlantic ocean, Hibernian ocean, etc., except for the Indian Ocean (the first word again being undetachable), discussed further below.

Modern place-names are usually in italics, e.g. *Weser*, other than the most familiar (e.g. Athens, as above), large land masses (e.g. Iberia, Jutland), major bodies of water (e.g. Atlantic, Black Sea, Mediterranean, Sea of Marmara), major islands (e.g. Cyprus, Ireland), and modern states (e.g. Morocco), though all these are italicized when they stand in parentheses as explanatory comments within a translation. Modern place-names added to a translation are usually placed in italics within parentheses unless inconveniently long, but in poetry—especially Homer, the *Nikomedean Periodos*, Dionysios son of Kalliphon, Dionysios Periegetes, and Avienus—they are usually relegated to footnotes to avoid disrupting the verse layout and the metre to which the translations approximate, usually the English iambic pentameter. In transliterating Modern Greek place-names, the stress is sometimes indicated by an acute accent (e.g. *Kastellórizo*).

Variation in the original text between Euxeinos, Pontos, and Euxeinos Pontos is normally respected.

The modern Red Sea and the adjacent area of the Indian Ocean pose a particular problem. The Greek name *Erythra thalassa*—literally either 'red sea' or, as per the explanation offered by Agatharchides and others, 'sea of Erythras' (a man in legend)—denotes a wider area than the modern Red Sea, 'not just the gulf sandwiched between the Egyptian and Arabian coasts, but also the area extending from the Horn of Africa in the west to Cape Comorin and the Bay of Bengal in the east', thus including the western and northern Indian Ocean.[348] Accordingly, 'Erythraian sea' is normally used to translate the Greek term. But the Latin *Rubrum mare* is translated 'Red Sea'.

---

[347] Talbert 2020.   [348] Marcotte 2016, 163 (quotation); Marcotte 2021, 103.

Final 'ē' in Greek and Latin names (e.g. Dyme, Mytilene, Thoule) and certain other terms (e.g. *oikoumenē*) is not silent but sounded (except in traditional English forms such as Crete, Peloponnese, Rome); thus Kerne has two syllables, Syene three. It is usually a long vowel (η, eta), but in order not to complicate the text or hinder electronic searches the macron (as in ē) is not normally employed here. An exception may be made in transliterations of Greek terms or phrases (e.g. *en epitomēi*), especially in the Glossary; or to avoid ambiguity (e.g. Sidē, Kanē; *mesēmbria* as opposed to the city of Mesembria; *anatolē* as opposed to the modern personal name); or to separate two vowels (e.g. Libyē), though a diaeresis is sometimes used instead (Meroë).

Macrons are selectively applied to *o* to distinguish the long vowel omega (ω, as in *ēōs*), from the short omicron (o), but not normally in titles of actual works. Note that the Ionian gulf (southern Adriatic), usually Ἰόνιος κόλπος–*Iŏnios kolpos*, has a short first *o* (omicron) though it is named after the mythical woman Iō (Ἰώ, with a long *ō*), daughter of Inachos, who swam across it. It is etymologically distinct from the Ionians (Ἴωνες–*Iōnes*), their male mythical ancestor Iōn (Ἴων), and their homeland of Iōnia (Ἰωνία) in western Asia Minor, all of which have a long *ō* (omega). The distinction, however, will not normally be indicated typographically.

X. 3. TECHNICAL TERMS

Certain clusters of technical terms are difficult to equate with clusters of English terms on a systematic basis. I explore some of the issues in detail elsewhere,[349] advocating the following policies.

a. Bodies of Water

The dearth of distinguishing terms in English necessitates the use of unfamiliar words such as 'roadstead' and 'main', and the careful handling of 'open sea':

> harbours, etc.: *limēn* 'harbour'; *salos* 'roadstead' (in the sense of safe open water close to shore); *hormos* 'anchorage' (with or without manmade installations); *hyphormos* 'minor anchorage'

> bodies of water: *thalassa* 'sea'; *pelagos* 'open sea' (or 'open-sea' if a place-name precedes it, e.g. 'Tyrrhenic open-sea'); *pontos* 'main'; *ōkeanos* always 'Ocean'

b. Directions

Greek has no distinct set of 'compass directions' as English has north, east, south, and west, but uses eight or nine terms which can also be used with literal meanings denoting specific winds,[350] astronomical phenomena, or times of day:

---

[349] Shipley 2021b.
[350] On wind roses and stellar navigation, see the judicious analysis by Davis 2009, 90–119 and 120–57 respectively.

north: (1) *boreas* 'north wind'; (2) *arktos* 'bear' (or the plural *arktoi*), referring to the circumpolar constellation(s) Ursa Minor and/or Ursa Major

east: (1) *ēōs* 'dawn'; (2) *anatolē* 'rising' (of the sun)

south: (1) *notos* 'south wind'; (2) *mesēmbria* 'midday'

west: (1) *hespera* 'evening'; (2) *dysis* (pl. *dyseis*), lit. 'sinking(s)', 'setting(s)' (of the sun); *dysmē*, pl. *dysmai*, with same meaning; (3) rarely *zephyros* 'west wind'

A translator will wonder whether to translate these Greek terms literally (e.g. 'north wind') or metonymically ('north'), especially when a modifier is added, as in *pros hēliou anatolas* (literally 'towards the risings of the sun', meaning the east) or *pros cheimerinas dyseis* ('towards the winter settings', meaning the south-west). The policy normally followed in this book is as follows:

single words used metonymically are rendered as simple directions: e.g. *boreas*, 'north' (not 'north wind'); *ēōs*, 'east' (not 'dawn')

multi-word expressions are translated so as to reflect the original senses of the words and their syntactical relationship: e.g. *boreas anemos*, 'north wind'; *hēliou dysmai*, 'settings of the sun'

phrases with astronomical modifiers are translated literally: e.g. *isēmerinē anatolē*, 'equinoctial' (literally 'equidiurnal'; see below) 'sunrise', meaning due east; *therinai dyseis*, 'summer sunsets' (incorporating the implied sun—not simply 'equinoctial rising' or 'summer risings')

names of winds, except when used as simple direction markers (as above), are kept as names, e.g. 'Euros' (not converted into directional expressions, e.g. 'the east-south-easterly wind') with any necessary explanation appended in italics in parentheses, such as '(*SE wind*)'

For names of further winds, see **10** Timosthenes and the appendix to Chapter 10 (from Aristotle), as well as the index s.v. 'winds'.

Note that the Greek for 'equinoctial', which means 'with night equal (*to day*)', is *isēmerinos*, which inverts the sense, meaning 'with day equal (*to night*)' or 'equidiurnal'. In the present volumes, however, *isēmerinos* is translated as 'equinoctial'.[351]

c. Terms for Communities

A number of terms in Greek are difficult to equate with any one English word. One such is *ethnos* (ἔθνος), a full definition of which might be 'a community, usually linked to a locality or region, that believes it is united by kinship, religion, and language'. Earlier scholars often used 'tribe' (but for various reasons the word is out of vogue among archaeologists, partly for its connotations of primitiveness), or 'people' (but we should reserve that for *dēmos* in the sense of a political body of citizens, or sometimes

---

[351] It occurs in Chs 8, 10, 12, 16–17, 19, 24, and 29.

the common people among them), or 'ethnic community' (but that is too heavy a translation for a single word, and carries technical implications in modern social science that may not be relevant to antiquity). With some hesitation, the choice is made here to use 'nation' for *ethnos*. This is not to imply any similarities between an ancient *ethnos* (plural *ethnē*) and modern nation-states, but is chosen specifically for its association with *territory*. *Ethnos* is a scalable term: the Hellenic *ethnos* comprises all Hellenes (Greeks); the inhabitants of a region, such as Arkadia, can be called an *ethnos* even if they live in city-states; the people of a city-state, too, can be referred to as an *ethnos* and their 'city surname' is an *ethnikon*. 'Nation', likewise, can be adjusted to any of these scales.

A potentially more fraught term is *genos* (γένος), another word for a supposedly kin-based community though also scalable down to below the level of a *polis*, when it can approximate to 'clan', as well as up to the widest scope. Here, when it refers to the population of a wide area such as a region, it is normally translated by 'race' within translations, though 'people' in accompanying material. As with *ethnos*, there is no intention of asserting that a social group in the ancient world that some source calls a *genos* was, *in reality*, an instance of the, no longer credible, modern notion of a race as a social group with the same genetic inheritance that endows each member with similar characteristics, for example of intelligence or behaviour. Although archaeology and the study of ancient DNA today show that there is no such thing as a genetically or 'racially' unitary human population, the choice of 'race' reflects the fact that the Greeks *did* see social groups in this way.

The less common term *phylon* (φῦλον), another word expressing genetic kinship is translated 'tribe' in Chapter 28 (Dionysios Periegetes), where the context is poetic.

X. 4. TREATMENT OF ACROSTICS

A special feature of two verse texts, Dionysios son of Kalliphon and Dionysios Periegetes, is the use of the acrostic, when the poet makes the first letter of successive lines spell out a name or word. The translators of these two texts have replicated the acrostics in English by making the first letter of each line bold.

XI. SELECTED FURTHER READING

The footnotes to the foregoing sections will guide the reader to further reading on specific topics. The material below has been assembled with a certain emphasis on Anglophone scholarship.

In these and other 'further reading' sections, series titles are included only selectively; the same applies to the 'Works Cited' section at the end of the volume.

XI. 1. SYNTHESES AND SURVEYS

For more general approaches, this Introduction has also made systematic reference to the two best recent surveys of ancient geography (as opposed to Mediterranean history) in English, by Dueck (with Brodersen) and Roller. The reader may use these to extend the outline discussion of particular authors and topics in the present Introduction and the succeeding chapters; often these works complement each other, with thematic organization being a strength of Dueck's volume, rich detail of diachronic coverage and context a feature of Roller's longer work. Another good starting-point is Rihll's chapter in her *Greece & Rome New Surveys* volume, while Kaplan interestingly sets geography down to *c.*350 BC in the context of Egyptian and Near Eastern science, Homer, and the Presocratics.

For those wanting to dig deeper, the twenty-one chapters of the *Brill Companion to Ancient Geography* (cited often in the present volumes) explore a stimulating range of specific topics rather than being a comprehensive guide. More selectively, the recent *New Directions* volume from the (American) Association of Ancient Historians, edited by Roller, offers case studies to exemplify where the subject has got to and where it is going.

Some older syntheses are still of value, such as the compendious treatments by Bunbury and Thomson, though of course only a starting-point.

It is worth singling out a few important studies from recent years that have not been cited previously in this Introduction, but which crucially underpin all recent thinking. I have in mind the volume edited by Podossinov on the periphery of the world; the volume edited by Geus and Thiering on 'common sense geography'; three monographs by Merrills on Roman and late antique geography; and those by Clarke on hellenistic thinkers and on Herodotos. A volume edited by Raaflaub and Talbert sets Greco-Roman geographical thought in its world context.

Bianchetti, S., Cataudella, M. R., and Gehrke, H.-J. (eds 2016), *Brill's Companion to Ancient Geography: The Inhabited World in Greek and Roman Tradition*. Leiden–Boston.

Bunbury, E. H. (1883), *A History of Ancient Geography*, 2nd edn (and later). 2 vols. London. Repr. New York, 1932; 1959.

Clarke, K. (1999), *Between Geography and History: Hellenistic Constructions of the Roman World*. Oxford.

—— (2018), *Shaping the Geography of Empire: Man and Nature in Herodotus' Histories*. Oxford.

Dueck, D. (2012), with K. Brodersen, *Geography in Classical Antiquity*. Cambridge.

Geus, K., and Thiering, M. (eds 2014), *Features of Common Sense Geography: Implicit Knowledge Structures in Ancient Geographical Texts*. Berlin.

Kaplan, P. G. (2018), 'Early Greek geography', in P. T. Keyser and J. Scarborough (eds), *Oxford Handbook of Science and Medicine in the Classical World* (Oxford), 195–213.

Merrills, A. H. (2005), *History and Geography in Late Antiquity*. Cambridge.

—— (2017), *Roman Geographies of the Nile: From the Late Republic to the Early Empire*. Cambridge–New York.

—— (forthcoming 2023), *War, Rebellion and Epic in Byzantine North Africa: A Study of Corippus Iohannis*. Cambridge.

Podossinov, A. V. (ed. 2014), *The Periphery of the Classical World in Ancient Geography and Cartography*. Leuven.

Raaflaub, K. A., and Talbert, R. J. A. (eds 2010), *Geography and Ethnography: Perceptions of the World in Pre-modern Societies*. Malden, Mass.–Oxford–Chichester.

Rihll, T. E. (1999), *Greek Science*. Oxford.

Roller, D. W. (2015), *Ancient Geography: The Discovery of the World in Classical Greece and Rome*. London–New York.

—— (ed. 2020), *New Directions in the Study of Ancient Geography*. Sarasota.

Thomson, J. O. (1948), *A History of Ancient Geography*. Cambridge.

XI. 2. KEY ANCIENT SOURCES

The Jacoby project and its continuations *BNJ* and *FGrH* v (or 'Jacoby V') will cover the entirety of Greek geographical writing, other than the major surviving authors (Strabo, Pausanias, and Ptolemy) and the many passages of geographical discussion contained within Greek historians who survive extensively (such as Herodotos and Polybios). (See §VII. 3 above for the Jacoby 'family'.) They replace Müller's brilliant *Geographi Graeci minores* and *Fragmenta historicorum Graecorum* (§VII. 3 above). Almost all editions of texts before Müller can be regarded as superseded, though a few close in time to *FHG* and *GGM* offer better texts, albeit without the immense weight of documentation he presents.[352]

A particular landmark in the study of several of the geographers (particularly the Pseudo-Arrianic *Euxine*, Menippos, Markianos, and the *Nikomedean Periodos*) is the work of Aubrey Diller on the manuscript tradition (especially of the Menippos–Markianos corpus), which has ramifications far beyond those texts.[353]

Already cited above, but fundamental for anyone contemplating Greek geography down to the age of Augustus and Tiberius, are Roller's monumental yet accessible translation of Strabo together with his equally expansive historical and topographical commentary. Major studies of Pausanias and Ptolemy are cited in §VI above; a selection of editions of major sources of fragments is listed after Chapter 36 of the present volumes.

---

[352] e.g. B. Fabricius 1848 (real name H. T. Dittrich) on Ps.-Skylax and Stiehle 1856 on Artemidoros. On Müller's apparently self-effacing career, see Talbert 1994, 129 (repr. as Talbert 2019a, p. 22); also Talbert 2019c, 9.

[353] Diller 1952; it also includes an annotated bibliography of 452 works of scholarship from C15 to 1948 (pp. 38–99; addenda, 177–9).

Other translations, besides those cited in this Introduction or in chapter introductions below, include a selection of four texts in Spanish in a miniature format by Garzón Díaz, and the first volume of what promises to be an epoch-making series of all *Periploi* by González Ponce (cited in the next subsection).

Useful sketches (if variable in depth) of authors and texts (including those not the subject of a chapter in the present volumes), together with further bibliography, can be found in Keyser and Irby-Massie's encyclopaedia as well as in standard Classical dictionaries, of which three are listed here.

Bagnall, R. S. (ed. 2012), *The Encyclopedia of Ancient History*. 13 vols. Malden, Mass.–Chichester.

Garzón Díaz, J. (2008), *Geógrafos griegos: Escílax de Carianda; Hannón de Cartago; Heraclides crético; Dionisio, hijo de Califonte*. Oviedo.

Gehrke, H.-J., and Meier, F. (eds 2011–), *Fragmente der griechischen Historiker*, v (Leiden).

Hornblower, S., and Spawforth, A. J. S., with E. Eidinow (eds 2012), *The Oxford Classical Dictionary*, 4th edn. Oxford–New York.

Keyser, P. T., and Irby-Massie, G. L. (2008), *The Encyclopedia of Ancient Natural Scientists: The Greek Tradition and its Many Heirs*. London–New York.

Müller, C. W. L. (1841–70), *Fragmenta historicorum Graecorum* (*FHG*). 5 vols. Paris.

—— (1855–61), *Geographi Graeci minores* (*GGM*). 3 vols. Paris. Repr. Hildesheim, 1965; 1990. [No longer standard, and prone to over-emend the texts, but a vast repertory of invaluable data. Includes Latin translations; vol. iii is maps. Some chapters superseded in vol. v of *FHG* (above).]

Roller, D. W. (2014), *The Geography of Strabo: An English Translation, with Introduction and Notes*. Cambridge.

—— (2018), *A Historical and Topographical Guide to the Geography of Strabo*. Cambridge–New York.

Shipley, D. G. J., Vanderspoel, J., Mattingly, D. J., and Foxhall, L. (eds 2006), *The Cambridge Dictionary of Classical Civilization*. Cambridge.

XI. 3. SPECIALIST STUDIES

Beyond the geographical texts, notable syntheses and theoretical treatments of Mediterranean geographical history include the highly influential works of Horden and Purcell (a sequel is awaited; note important reflections in Harris's volume), Abulafia, and Kinneging. There are interesting chapters on landscape thinking in the Leicester–Nottingham volume edited by Shipley and Salmon, and on travel in two co-edited by Adams. Of surpassing range are the multilingual collections of studies in the *Geographica historica* series (1976–); among recent volumes moving beyond descriptive geography or particular regions, one may note those edited by Olshausen and Sauer on mobility, Bekker-Nielsen and Gertwagen on eco-history, Cordovana and Chiai on pollution, and Schliephake *et al.* on sustainability. The recent volume edited by Dierksmeier and others contains important papers on islands as a geographical category.

Major journals relevant to ancient geography include *Orbis terrarum* (1995–) and, for cartography, *Imago mundi* (1935–).

The collected papers of Prontera are an important landmark, as is the first instalment of González Ponce's collection of *periploi*. A particular focus on navigation and the maritime experience has benefited from important studies in recent years, notably those of Arnaud and Kowalski, as well as Roller's volume on exploration of the Atlantic. On ancient topographical measurement, much work through the Topoi project in Berlin's Freie Universität has appeared in important collaborative volumes on the understanding of space. The copious supply of archaeological and geographical work on Iberia is reflected in co-authored volumes, mainly in Spanish and Portuguese.[354]

Abulafia, D. (ed. 2004), *The Mediterranean in History*. London.

—— (2011), *The Great Sea: A Human History of the Mediterranean*. Oxford.

Adams, C. E. P., and Laurence, R. (eds 2001), *Travel and Geography in the Roman Empire*. London–New York.

—— and Roy, J. (eds 2007), *Travel, Geography and Culture in Ancient Greece, Egypt and the Near East*. Oxford.

Arnaud, P. (2005), *Les Routes de la navigation antique: itinéraires en Méditerranée*. Paris.

Bekker-Nielsen, T., and Gertwagen, R. (eds 2016), *The Inland Seas: Towards an Ecohistory of the Mediterranean and the Black Sea*. Stuttgart.

Buisseret, D. (ed. 2007), *The Oxford Companion to World Exploration*. 2 vols. Oxford.

Cordovana, O. D., and Chiai, G. F. (eds 2017), *Pollution and the Environment in Ancient Life and Thought*. Stuttgart.

Dierksmeier, L., et al. (eds 2021), *European Islands between Isolated and Connected Worlds: Interdisciplinary Long-term Perspectives*. Tübingen.

Geus, K., and Rathmann, M. (eds 2013), *Vermessung der Oikoumene*. Berlin–Boston.

—— and M. Thiering (eds 2014), *Features of Common Sense Geography: Implicit Knowledge Structures in Ancient Geographical Texts*. Berlin.

González Ponce, F. J. (2008), *Periplo de Hanón y autores de los siglos VI y V a.C.* Zaragoza.

Harley, J. B., and Woodward, D. (eds 1987), *The History of Cartography*, i: *Cartography in Prehistoric, Ancient, and Medieval Europe and the Mediterranean*. Chicago–London.

Harris, W. V. (ed. 2005), *Rethinking the Mediterranean*. Oxford.

Horden, P., and Purcell, N. (2000), *The Corrupting Sea*. Oxford–Malden, Mass.

Kinneging, A. A. M. (2009), *The Geography of Good and Evil: Philosophical Investigations*. (Trans. I. Hardy.) Wilmington, Del.

Kowalski, J.-M. (2012), *Navigation et géographie dans l'antiquité gréco-romaine: la terre vue de la mer*. Paris. [With review in English by Roller in *BMCR* 2013.01.07.]

Olshausen, E., and Sauer, V. (eds 2014), *Mobilität in den Kulturen der antiken Mittelmeerwelt*. Stuttgart.

Prontera, F. (2011), *Geografia e storia nella Grecia antica*. Florence.

---

[354] e.g. Cruz Andreotti, Le Roux, and Moret 2006; Cruz Andreotti, Le Roux, and Moret 2007; Álvarez Delgado, Mederos Martín, and Escribano Cobo 2015; Ferrer Albelda 2019.

Rathmann, M. (ed. 2007), *Wahrnehmung und Erfassung geographischer Räume in der Antike*. Mainz am Rhein.

Roller, D. W. (2006), *Through the Pillars of Herakles: Greco-Roman Exploration of the Atlantic*. London–New York.

Schliephake, C., Sojc, N., and Weber, G. (eds 2020), *Nachhaltigkeit in der Antike: Diskurse, Praktiken, Perspektiven*. Stuttgart.

Shipley, D. G. J., and Salmon, J. B. (eds 1996), *Human Landscapes in Classical Antiquity: Environment and Culture*. London–New York.

XI. 4. CARTOGRAPHY AND ATLASES

No serious research on the ancient Mediterranean is now possible without consulting the *Barrington Atlas* and its *Directory*, both achievements of the Ancient World Mapping Center at the University of North Carolina, Chapel Hill; data from the atlas can be accessed at the interactive Antiquity À-la-carte and Pleiades websites.[355] The online atlas forming part of *Brill's New Pauly* (ed. Salazar, below) includes clear thematic and period maps. Among a variety of other online resources, the growing ToposText database edited by Brady Kiesling links online mapping to translated ancient texts.[356]

On ancient cartography, Dilke's classic contributions are complemented by Talbert's study of the Peutinger Map (cited in §V. 5), his 2012 edited volume, and his collected papers on the history of modern atlases of antiquity.

Dilke, O. A. W. (1985), *Greek and Roman Maps*. London/Ithaca.

—— (1987a), 'Cartography in the ancient world: a conclusion', in J. B. Harley and D. Woodward (eds), *The History of Cartography*, i (Chicago–London), 276–9.

—— (1987b), 'Cartography in the ancient world: an introduction', ibid. 105–6.

—— (1987c), 'Cartography in the Byzantine empire', ibid. 258–75.

—— (1987d), 'Itineraries and geographical maps in the early and late Roman empires', ibid. 234–57.

—— (1987e), 'Maps in the service of the state: Roman cartography to the end of the Augustan era', ibid. 201–11.

—— (1987g), 'Roman large-scale mapping in the early empire', ibid. 212–33.

—— (1987h), 'The culmination of Greek cartography in Ptolemy', ibid. 177–200.

Salazar, C. F., Wittke, A., Olshausen, E., and Szydlak, R. (eds 2010), *Historical Atlas of the Ancient World* (Brill's New Pauly Supplements, 1. 3). Leiden.

Talbert, R. J. A. (ed. 2000), *Barrington Atlas of the Greek and Roman World*. Princeton–Oxford.

---

[355] See https://pleiades.stoa.org/ [last accessed 24 January 2023].
[356] See https://topostext.org/ [last accessed 24 January 2023].

—— (ed. 2000), *Map-by-map Directory: To accompany Barrington Atlas of the Greek and Roman World*. 2 vols. Princeton–Oxford. [http://mail.nysoclib.org/Digital_Archives/ebooks/Barrington_Atlas/] (map-by-map chapters, also BATL-GAZ.PDF, the complete *Directory*).

—— (ed. 2012) *Ancient Perspectives: Maps and their Place in Mesopotamia, Egypt, Greece, and Rome*. Chicago.

—— (2019), *Challenges of Mapping the Classical World*. Abingdon–New York. [Collected papers.]

TIME-LINE

D. Graham J. Shipley

Includes authors and texts that are the subjects of chapters, together with a selection of others including the extant 'major' geographers, other important surviving authors who convey geographical information, some 'minor' geographers not made the subjects of chapters, and a few key military-political and cultural events.

§   Latin work
v.   voyaged
w. wrote

		Geographical source		Other source		Events
300	282–246	10 Timosthenes of Rhodes	c.295–c.246	Apollonios of Rhodes	C3e	foundation of Mouseion and Library at Alexandria
	279–239	11 Herakleides Kritikos	c.287–c.212	Archimedes of Syracuse	261	Pergamon becomes independent state
	c.276–195	12 Eratosthenes of Kyrene	C3	Ps.-Aristotle, *On Miraculous Things Heard?*	241	Sicily becomes Roman province
	C3?	Hestiaia of Alexandria	c.240	Pseudo-Antigonos		
	C3d	13 Mnaseas of Patara	c.247–197	Antigonos of Karystos	197	two Roman provinces created in Spain
200	C2e	14 Skymnos	C2	Apollonios Paradoxographos Krates of Mallos	167	end of Macedonian kingdom
	c.145	15 Agatharchides	C2	Aristoboulos of Alexandria	146	Romans destroy Carthage & Corinth
	w.162–128	16 Hipparchos of Nikaia	c.200–118	Polybios of Megalopolis (major source for Pytheas)	133	end of kingdom of Pergamon
	v.118–c.100	Eudoxos of Kyzikos	C2l	Ecclesiasticus (Sirach) translated		
	C2l/C1e	17 *Nikomedean Periodos* [*vulgo* 'Ps.-Skymnos']	C2l	Apollodoros of Athens		
	fl.104–100	18 Artemidoros of Ephesos				
100	C1f	19 Poseidonios of Apameia	C1f	Alexander Polyhistor		
	c.135–c.51		c.135–c.51	Geminos		
	C1e–C1m	20 Dionysios son of Kalliphon	106–43	$ Cicero	86	Sulla sacks Athens, ends democracy

§ Latin work   v. voyaged   w. wrote

		Geographical source		Other source		Events
	64–12	Marcus Vipsanius Agrippa	c.63 BC–AD 10	Didymos 'Chalkenteros,' grammarian	58–54	Julius Caesar conquers Gaul, briefly invades Britain 55–54
			fl. 60–30	Diodoros of Sicily (major source for i.a. Agatharchides, Artemidoros.)	30	Egypt becomes Roman province
	fl. c.26/5	21 Menippos of Pergamon (assembles the corpus later augmented by Markianos)	c.60–after 7	Dionysios of Halikarnassos	27	S. Greece becomes province of Achaia
BC	c.27/6 BC–AD 23–4	22 Juba II of Mauretania			26/5	voyage of Gallus
AD	c.1–14	23 Isidoros of Charax			AD 14	death of Octavian Augustus
	c.1–c.25	Strabo of Amaseia (main source for i.a. Eratosthenes, Hipparchos, Artemidoros, Poseidonios)				
	C1e–C1m?	24 Ps.-Aristotle, On the Cosmos (De mundo)	C1	Aëtios		
	w. 41–54	§ Pomponius Mela	c. C1	Ps.-Longinus, On the Sublime	C1	career of Apollonios of Tyana
	c.23–79 D.	§ Pliny the Elder (major source for i.a. Pytheas, Eratosthenes, Artemidoros, Juba, Isidoros)	c.40–90	Pedanius Dioskorides	43	Claudius invades Britain
	C1m–C1l	25 *Periplus maris Erythraei*	c.4 BC–AD 65	Seneca the Younger		

§ Latin work v. voyaged w. wrote

	Geographical source		Other source		Events
		C1/C2	Josephus	37–c.100	
100	**26 Ps.-Plutarch, On Rivers**				
	Marinos of Tyre	c.70–130	Kleomedes	C1 BC? C1/2/3 AD?	
	Ptolemy of Alexandria	c.110–70	Plutarch of Chaironeia	46–after 119	
	27 Arrian of Nikomedeia, *Periplous of the Euxine*; assembles geographical corpus (see manuscripts 'A' and 'B' below)	w. c.131–5	Theon of Smyrna	d. c. AD 135	
	28 Dionysios Periegetes	117–38	Diogenianus Zenobios	fl. 117–38	
	29 Agathemeros son of Orthon	C2b	Achilles Tatius Aelius Aristeides (b. 117) Herodian (grammarian) Harpokration original of *Vita Arati*	C2	
	Pausanias (of Magnesia?)	C2m	Lucian of Samosata	115–125 to c.190	
			Galen (Klaudios Galenos)	129 to c.200/c.216	
	30 Dionysios of Byzantion	c. C2m	Clement of Alexandria	c.150–c.215	
			Sextus Empiricus	c.160–c.210	siege of Byzantion by troops loyal to Septimius Severus 197–200
			Maximus of Tyre	C2l	
200	§ original of *Antonine Itinerary*	198–207	Athenaios of Alexandria	c. C2l–C3e	

§ Latin work   v. voyaged   w. wrote

	Geographical source		Other source		Events
		c.170–240	Herodian of Antioch		
		c.175–235	Aelian		
		C3f	Philostratos of Athens		
		C3	Diogenes Laërtios		
C3s?	31 **Stadiasmos**	234–305	Porphyrios of Tyre		
		c.240–c.325	Iamblichos of Chalkis (in Koile Syria)		
300		c.250–c.325	§ Lactantius		
c.284–c.305 Talbert (c.425 Rathmann)	§ original of *Tabula Peutingeriana?*	fl. 297–303	§ Arnobius		
		c.300	§ Solinus		
		c.322/3	Theophanes of Hermpolis		
		pre-331	Eusebios of Caesarea, *Onomastikon*	324	foundation of Constantinople
333	§ *Itinerarium Hierosolymitanum sive Burdigalense*	C4?	Ammonius Grammaticus		
		C4?	§ Vicarello cups		
C4m	32 § **Avienus**	c.310–c.395	§ Ausonius		
C4m	33 § ***Expositio* and Iunior Philosophus**	c.330–c.390/400	§ Ammianus Marcellinus		
		c.335–c.405	Theon of Alexandria		
		C4s	*Catalogus codicum astrologorum Graecorum*		

§ Latin work   v. voyaged   w. wrote

		Geographical source		Other source	Events
	v. 381–4	§ Egeria, *Itinerarium Egeriae*	c.370–c.413 NP	Synesius	
			c.400 BNP	§ Servius	
400	400	**34 Markianos of Herakleia**	v. c.417	§ Rutilius Namatianus	
	c.425? (or	§ original of *Tabula Peutingeriana*?	417	§ Orosius, *Against the Pagans*	
	c.284–c.305)		C5	Stobaeus	
			c.420 / c.470s	Martianus Capella	
			412–485	Proclus	
500	C5/C6	**35 Hypotyposis**	C5/C6	Hesychios of Alexandria	
			C5–C6	§ Fulgentius	
			C5/C6	Julian of Askalon	
			C6e	§ Theodosius (pilgrim)	
	C6e	Hierokles, *Synekdemos*	fl. 529–32	Priscianus Lydus (Priskianos ho Lydos)	
	535–47	Kosmas Indikopleustes	C6	Priscianus Caesariensis	
	C6	**Stephanos of Byzantion**	C6	Ioannes Lydus (Ioannes ho Lydos)	
	C6s or later	**36 Ps.-Arrian, *Periplous of the Euxine***			
600					

§ Latin work   v. voyaged   w. wrote

		Geographical source		Other source		Events
700	C6–C10	surviving epitome of Stephanos of Byzantion	c.700	§ *Ravenna Cosmography*		
800	C9 or earlier	*Diagnōsis en epitomēi tēs en tēi sphairai geōgraphias*				
	C9	**Heidelberg Codex ('A')**	c.810–c.893	Photios I, patriarch of Constantinople		
			C9	*Epimerismoi Homerikoi*		
900			r. 945–59	reign of Constantine VII Porphyrogennetos, Byzantine emperor		
1000			C10 (C10s?)	*Suda*		
			c.1035–c.1110	Symeon Seth		
1100	C12	§ MS of Iunior Philosophus	c.1110–1138	Isaac Tzetzes		
			c.1110–c.1185	Ioannes Tzetzes		
			c.1115–c.1195	Eustathios of Thessalonike		
1200	c.1280	**Codex Parisinus supplement grec 443 ('D')**	1197–1272 [but the work a later forgery]	Nikephoros Blemmydes		
1300	C14	Vatopedi Codex ('B')				
1400	C14/C15	*Anametrēsis* (see Eratosthenes 41 and appendix to Chapter 36 below)			1453	Constantinople falls to Ottomans

§ Latin work   v. voyaged   w. wrote

	Geographical source	Other source	Events
		Printed editions	
		1475 Angelus's Latin Ptolemy	
		1488 Pisanus's Avienus, *Ora maritima*	
1500	1520–82 § Natalis Comes (Natale Conti)		
		1533 Gelen publishes Arrian's *Euxine*, Hanno, *PME*, Ps.-Plutarch, etc.	
		1561 Gyllius (Gilles)'s Dionysios of Byzantion	
1600		1600 Hoeschel's Markianos, Ps.-Skylax, etc.	
		1639 Isaac Vos's Ps.-Skylax	
		1689–90 Michelot and Therin's map of Mediterranean	
1700		1697 Gronov's corpus	
		1698–1712 Hudson's corpus	
		1715 Michelot's *Mediterranean Pilot* Englished	
1800		1826–31 Gail's corpus	
		1839 E. Miller publishes content of MS 'D'	
		1841–70 Müller's *FHG*	

§ Latin work   v. voyaged   w. wrote

Geographical source	Other source	Events
	Müller's *GGM* (1855–61)	
	Smith's *Atlas* (designed by Müller) (1872–4)	
1900	Jacoby's *FGrH* i–iv (1923–58)	
	Aly begins to publish Strabo palimpsest[1] (1927)	
	Diller's *Tradition* (1952)	
2000	Talbert's *Barrington Atlas* (2000)	
	FGrH v ('Jacoby V') (2011–)	

1 See Aly 1956; Aly 1957.

PROLOGUE

THE HOMERIC CATALOGUE OF SHIPS (*ILIAD*, 2. 484–760)

(8TH/7TH C. BC)

D. Graham J. Shipley

INTRODUCTION

The so-called Catalogue of Ships in the second book of Homer's *Iliad* enumerates the Achaian contingents at the siege of Troy.[1] It may stand as an epigraph to these volumes because it is evidence that the early Greeks conceived their homeland as comprising ethnic regions containing nucleated settlements. These regions and most of the towns remained, with limited changes, important definers of identity for free Greek males and their families for a millennium afterwards. Indeed, many of the regions and towns had their origins long before the Homeric poems were written down, generally thought to be in the second half of the 8th century BC or the early 7th. Perhaps, like the writings in some later chapters, the Catalogue draws upon oral and written sources from more than one of those periods—or all of them.[2]

It has long been debated whether the geography portrayed here reflects the end of the Bronze Age and the Mycenaean palace system,[3] the succeeding 'Dark Age' (roughly 1100–800 BC) when a new societal organization was coming into being,[4] or the world of already developed *poleis* (city-states).[5] There are, however, important absences— most conspicuously, the hero Patroklos from Opous in Lokris (here named Opoëis)— as well as possible interpolations or elaborations in the historical period (Athens being one such case), while the selection of places (e.g. the presence of only three Aegean islands) makes the Catalogue hard to map onto any one period. As Map 0.1 shows, the fullest knowledge on display is of the Peloponnese and mainland Greece, especially the region with which the passage ends, Thessaly, though it is not given that name even though the 'sons of Thessalos' have just been named as rulers of islands (679).

Homer's poems, especially the *Odyssey* with its narration of Odysseus' wanderings and the travels of Telemachos, served as a frame of reference for much later geographical as well as historical writing.[6] The distinction between sure and unsure knowledge is

---

[1] Another, shorter and much less detailed 'catalogue' follows (at ll. 816–77), describing the Trojans' allies from Asia Minor. I have not seen Kirk 2021 or Visser 2021.
[2] Kelder 2017.   [3] As argued by Page 1959.
[4] The view of Hope Simpson and Lazenby 1970.   [5] J. K. Anderson 1995.
[6] Roller 2015, 13–19. See e.g. Cicero, quoted below as Dikaiarchos 1; Strabo, as Hipparchos 17.

worth noting: the world of the *Odyssey* spans the familiar regions of Asia Minor, the Aegean, mainland Greece, Crete, and the Adriatic, but with the last we are already into territory that is more framed by legend than by experience. Homer is aware, more dimly still, of such distant folk as the Aithiopes and of the distant North and West.[7]

The passage abounds in words such as 'those who owned', 'held', and 'dwelt', signifying the possession of territory by a people, as distinct from the role of a single man (sometimes more than one) to 'rule', 'lead', and 'command' as well as 'bring', implying the power to organize those people and direct the ships.[8] These notions of occupancy as well as rulership, too, permeated the topographical structuring of the landscape of Greece in later writings.

SELECTED FURTHER READING

Anderson, J. K. (1995), 'The Geometric catalogue of ships', in J. B. Carter and S. P. Morris (eds), *The Ages of Homer: A Tribute to Emily Townsend Vermeule* (Austin, Tex.), 181–91.

Dickinson, O. T. P. K. (2011), 'Catalogue of Ships', in M. Finkelberg (ed.), *The Homer Encyclopedia*, i (Chichester), 150–5.

Hope Simpson, R., and Lazenby, J. F. (1970), *The Catalogue of Ships in Homer's Iliad*. Oxford.

Kelder, J. (2017), 'Catalogue of Ships', in R. S. Bagnall (ed.), *Encyclopedia of Ancient History* (Malden, Mass.).

McLeod, W. (1970), review of R. Hope Simpson and J. F. Lazenby, *The Catalogue of Ships in Homer's Iliad*. In *Phoenix*, 24: 256–60.

TEXT

Headings are added.

> Tell me now, Muses, who hold your dwellings on Olympos—
> for you are goddesses, you are present, you know all things,
> but we hear only a rumour and know nothing—
> who the leaders and chiefs of the Danaoi were.
> I could not narrate or commemorate the multitude
> even if I had ten tongues and ten mouths
> 490 and an indomitable voice, and there was a bronze heart in me,
> unless you, Olympian Muses, daughters of Zeus
> the aegis-bearer, recall how many came to be under Ilion.
> So instead I will say the rulers and the entirety of ships.

---

[7] Dueck 2012, 20–2.

[8] The translation distinguishes these terms, using 'own' for the verb *nemomai* (with 'own land about' for *amphinemomai*), 'hold' for *echō*, and 'dwell' for *naiō*; 'rule' for *archō* and related words, 'lead' for *hēgeomai* (but 'commander' and 'command' for the more weighty *hēgemōn* and *hēgemoneuō*), and 'bring' for *agō*.

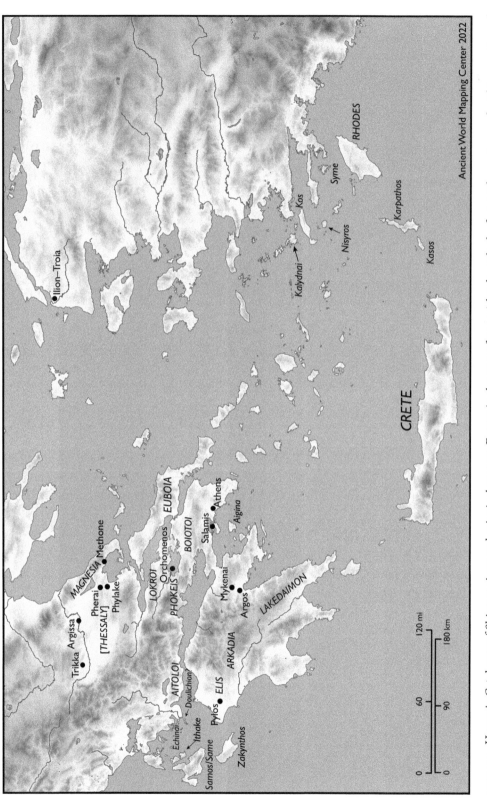

MAP 0.1. Homeric Catalogue of Ships: regions and principal centres. Except in the case of some islands, only the first settlement named within a section of the poem, referring to one contingent of men and ships, is listed (e.g. Mykenai, Pylos).

Ancient World Mapping Center 2022

Eastern Central Greece

The Boiotians were ruled by Peneleōs and Leïtos,
with Arkesilaos, Prothoēnor, and Klonios:
those who owned Hyriē and rocky Aulis,
Schoinos, Skolos, and Eteonos with the mountain spurs,
Thespeia, Graia, and broad-spaced Mykalessos,
and who owned land about Harma, Eilesion, and Erythrai,
500   who held Eleōn, Hyle, and Peteōn,
Okalea, and Medeōn, a well-built town,
Kopai, Eutresis, and Thisbe with many doves,
Koroneia and grassy Haliartos,
who held Plataia, who owned Glisas,
who held Hypothebai, a well-built town,
Onchestos the wonderful sacred grove of Poseidon,
who held Arne of many vines, and Mideia,
divine Nisa, and Anthedon the outermost.
Of these there came fifty ships, but in each
510   embarked a hundred and twenty youths from the Boiotians.
          Those who dwelt in Aspledon and Minyan Orchomenos
were ruled by Askalaphos and Ialmenos, sons of Ares,
borne by Astyoche in the house of Aktor son of Azeus,
a modest maiden who ascended to the upper floor
for mighty Ares, and he lay with her in secret.
Thirty hollow ships lined up with them.
          But the Phokians were ruled by Schedios and Epistrophos,
sons of great-spirited Iphitos son of Naubolos:
those who held Kyparissos and rocky Python,
520   sacred Krisa, Daulis, and Panopeus,
who owned land about Anemoreia and Hyampolis,
who dwelt beside the divine river Kephisos,
who held Lilaia at the spring of Kephisos.
There followed with them forty dark ships.
These men directed and placed the lines of Phokians,
but arrayed them close on the left of the Boiotians.
          The Lokrians were commanded by Oileus' son, swift Aias[9]
the Lesser—not at all as great as Telamonios Aias,
but much lesser: his linen corselet was slight,
530   but with his spear he surpassed the Panellenes[10] and Achaioi—

[9] Ajax.
[10] i.e. 'all the Hellenes'. Apart from l. 684 below, this is the only place where the *Iliad* refers to the allies attacking Troy as Hellenes; elsewhere they are normally called Achaioi or Danaoi.

those who owned Kynos, Opoëis, Kalliaros,
Bessa, Skarphe, and lovely Augeiai,
Tarphe and Thronios around the streams of Boagrios.
There followed with him forty dark ships
of the Lokrians who dwell beyond sacred Euboia.

    Those force-breathing Abantes who held Euboia,
Chalkis, Eretria, and Histiaia with its many vines,
Kerinthos on the sea, the lofty town of Dion,
those who held Karystos, those who dwelt in Styra—

540   these were led by Elephenor, offshoot of Ares,
son of Chalkodon, ruler of the great-spirited Abantes.
Following with him were the swift Abantes, long-haired behind,
spearmen eager to break with outstretched ash
the breastplates round the chests of the enemies.
There followed with him forty dark ships.

    Those who held Athenai, a well-built town,
country (*dēmos*)[11] of great-hearted Erechtheus, whom once Athena
nurtured, daughter of Zeus, and grain-giving plough-soil bore him—
she set him in Athens in her rich temple,

550   where he is appeased with bulls and rams
by Athenian youths as the years roll round—
these were commanded by Peteoös' son, Menestheus;
never yet was born a man on Earth like him
for ordering horses and shielded men—
Nestor alone competed with him, who of course was elder-born.
There followed with him fifty dark ships.

    Aias from Salamis brought twelve ships,
bringing them to set them where the ranks of Athenians were set.

The Peloponnese

Those who held Argos and Tiryns with its walls,
560   Hermione and Asine holding to the deep gulf,
Troizen, Eiones, and Epidauros with its vines,
those youths of the Achaioi who held Aigina and Mases—
these were commanded by Diomedes good at the war-cry
and Sthenelos the dear son of high-famed Kapaneus.

---

[11] In Homer, *dēmos* often refers either to 'the people' but also to a 'district, region, land' (*CGL*). For Cl historians, it usually means 'the people' in a political sense, but the spatial sense is preserved when it is used to mean a parish of Athens (anglicized as 'deme').

With them came a third, Euryalos, a godlike fellow,
son of lord Mekisteus son of Talaos.
All were led by Diomedes good at the war-cry.
There followed with them eighty dark ships.
    Those who held Mykenai, a well-built town,
570   wealthy Corinth and well-built Kleonai,
and owned Orneiai and lovely Araithyrea
and Sikyon, where Adrestos was first king,
who held Hyperesia, steep Gonoëssa,
and Pellene, and owned land about Aigion
and all along the Aigialos[12] and around broad Helike—
one hundred ships of theirs were ruled by mighty Agamemnon
son of Atreus; there followed with him folk (*laoi*) highest in number
and quality, and among them he donned his flashing bronze,
glorying in it, and among all the heroes he was most resplendent,
580   since he was best and brought by far the most numerous folk.
    Those who held hollow Lakedaimon with its ravines,
and Pharis, Sparta, and Messe with its many doves,
and owned Bryseiai and lovely Augeiai,
who held Amyklai, and Helos the town on the sea,
who held Laas, who owned land about Oitylos—
their ships were ruled by Menelaos good at the war-cry,
sixty in number, and they were arrayed separately.
Among them he went, trusting in his eagerness
and urging them to war; above all of them was his spirit set
590   on getting payment from Helen for his labours and his griefs.
    Those who owned Pylos[13] and lovely Arene,
and dwelt in Thryon, ford of the Alpheios, and well-built Aipy
and Kyparissēëis and Amphigeneia
and Pteleon and Helos and Dorion—where the Muses,
meeting Thamyris the Thracian, put a stop to his song
as he went from Oichalia, from (*the home of*) Eurytos of Oichalia;
for he undertook in a prayer to be victorious even if the very
Muses should sing, the daughters of Zeus aegis-holder;
but they, enraged, rendered him lame but also took away

[12] The coast of Achaia.
[13] Ancient authors debated whether Nestor's Pylos was (*a*) this one, 'Eleian Pylos', inland in the NW Peloponnese (Strabo 8. 2. 1, C336; 8. 2. 7, C339; etc.), as the reference to the R. Alpheios in the next line dictates; (*b*) 'Triphylian, Lepreatic, or Arkadian Pylos' by the coast (8. 3. 14, C343–4), or (*c*) 'Messenian Pylos' (8. 4. 2, C359, where the Bronze Age palace has been excavated and the Athenians captured the Spartans in 425 BC). Cf. Dickinson 2011, e.g. p. 4. Since the rest of this passage concerns the region of Messenia (unnamed), there is some confusion whichever way we take it.

600   his divine song and the memory of his lyre-playing—
these were led by Nestor, Gerenian horseman.
Ninety hollow ships lined up with him.
    Those who held Arkadia under Kyllene's steep mountain
beside Aipytos' tomb, where close-fighting men are found,
those who owned Pheneos and Orchomenos with its many sheep,
Rhipe, Stratia, and windy Enispe,
and held Tegea and lovely Mantinea,
and held Stymphalos and owned Parrhasia—
their ships were ruled by Ankaios' son, mighty Agapenor,

610   sixty in number, and in each of the ships
many Arkadian men embarked, who knew about war-making;
for Agamemnon himself, lord of men, gave them
well-benched ships to cross upon the wine-coloured main (*pontos*),[14]
the son of Atreus, since matters of the sea were no concern of theirs.
    Now those who dwelt in Bouprasion and glorious Elis,
all the land that Hyrmine, remote Myrsinos,
the rock Olen, and Alesion enclose—
these had four rulers, and each man was followed by
ten swift ships, and many Epeioi embarked in them.

620   Some were led by two men, Amphimachos and Thalpios,
one son of Kteatos and one of Eurytos, Aktor's kin both;
others were ruled by Amarynkeus' son Diores;
the fourth part were ruled by godlike Polyxeinos,
son of the lord Agasthenes son of Augeias.

Western Central Greece and Islands

    Those from Doulichion and the sacred isles of
Echinai, which lie beyond the salt sea, facing Elis—
they were commanded by Meges, Phyleus' son, a match for Ares,
sired by the horseman dear to Zeus, Phyleus,
who once emigrated to Doulichion in wrath at his father.

630   There followed with him forty dark ships.
    But Odysseus brought the great-spirited Kephallenians,
and those who held Ithaca and leaf-shaking Neritos
and owned Krokyleia and rugged Aigilips,
who held Zakynthos, who owned land about Samos,

---

[14] Homer's customary epithet for the sea, *oinops*—literally 'having the appearance of wine' (*CGL* s.v., suggesting 'wine-coloured' and 'wine-dark'), rather than 'wine-faced'—probably connotes darkness rather than any purplish or reddish colour.

who held the mainland and owned the land opposite.
These were ruled by Odysseus, a match for Zeus in cunning.
There followed with him twelve red-cheeked ships.
    The Aitolians were led by Thoas son of Andraimon,
those who owned Pleuron, Olenos, Pylene,
640   Chalkis by the shore, and rocky Kalydon;
for the sons of great-hearted Oineus were no more,
nor was he himself any more, and fair-haired Meleagros died—
to him (*Thoas*) was the command given to be lord of the Aitolians.
There followed with him forty dark ships.

Crete and Aegean Islands

The Cretans were commanded by Idomeneus famed for his spear,
those who held Knosos and Gortyn with its walls,
Lyktos, Miletos, and shining white Lykastos,
Phaistos and Rhytion, well-peopled cities,
and other men who owned land about hundred-citied Crete—
650   these were commanded by Idomeneus of spear fame
and by Meriones, a match for man-slaying Enyalios.[15]
There followed with them eighty dark ships.
    Tlepolemos, Herakles' son, a large, fine man,
brought nine ships from Rhodes and the proud Rhodians,
those who owned land about Rhodes, arranged three ways
in Lindos, Ialysos, and shining white Kameiros.
These were commanded by Tlepolemos of spear fame,
whom Astyocheia bore by the violence of Herakles,
she whom he brought from Ephyra and the river Selleëis
660   after sacking many towns of Zeus-born, vigorous men.
So when Tlepolemos was reared in the well-fitted hall,
straightway he killed the dear uncle of his own father,
an ageing man, Likymnios, offshoot of Ares;
at once he fitted ships, and gathering a great folk went fleeing
upon the main (*pontos*), threatened by the other sons
(*born*) by the violence of Herakles.
But by wandering he came to Rhodes, suffering agonies,
and they settled by tribe three ways, and became dear
to Zeus, who is lord over gods and humans
670   and poured divine wealth over them, the son of Kronos.
    Nireus now brought three fine ships from Syme,

[15] i.e. Ares.

Nireus son of Aglaia and lord Charopos,
Nireus, who came as the handsomest man under Ilion
among the other Danaoi, after the excellent son of Peleus—
but he was feeble, and scant folk followed him.
  Those who held Nisyros, Krapathos,[16] Kasos,
and Kos the city of Eurypylos, and the Kalydnai isles[17]—
these were led by two men, Pheidippos and Antiphos,
two sons of Lord Thessalos, Herakles' son.
680 Thirty hollow ships lined up with them.

Thessaly

Now all the men who dwelt in Pelasgian Argos,[18]
those who owned Halos, Alope, and Trachis,
who held Phthia and Hellas where beautiful women live—
they were called Myrmidones, Hellenes, and Achaioi—
fifty ships of theirs had Achilles as ruler.
But they cared not for the cacophony of war,
for none there was that might lead them into ranks:
for glorious, swift-footed Achilles was lying at the ships,
angry about the lovely haired maiden Briseïs,
690 whom he seized at Lyrnessos after great toil,
sacking all of Lyrnessos and the walls of Thebe,
when he cast down spear-wielding Mynes and Epistrophos
the sons of lord Euenos, Selepos' son.
He lay in grief for her—but he would soon get up again.
  Those who held Phylake, and flowery Pyrasos
the sanctuary of Demeter, and Iton mother of sheep,
and Antron by the shore, and grass-bedded Pteleon—
these were commanded by warlike Protesilaos
when alive: but now the dark earth held him under.
700 His wife, now with scarred cheeks, had been left at Phylake,
his house was half-done, and a Dardanian man killed him
as he leapt off the ship by far the first of the Achaioi.
They were not unruled even so, though they missed their ruler:
for they were drawn up by Podarkes, offshoot of Ares,
son of Iphiklos of many sheep, the son of Phylakos,
the very brother of great-spirited Protesilaos,

---

[16] Karpathos.
[17] Kalymnos and its neighbouring islets, principally Telendos (*Barr.* 61 D3–E4).
[18] A town or district within Thessaly; its location is uncertain.

younger by birth, but the firstborn was better,
the warlike hero Protesilaos; still, the folk in no way
lacked a leader, while they missed him, a fine man.

710   There followed with him (*Podarkes*) forty dark ships.

      Those who owned Pherai beside the lake of Boibeïs,
and Boibe, Glaphyrai, and well-built Iaolkos—
eleven ships of theirs were ruled by a dear son of Admetos,
Eumelos, whom Alkestis bore, glorious among women,
finest in beauty of the daughters of Peleus.

      Those who owned Methone and Thaumakia,
and held Meliboia and rugged Olizon:
their ships were ruled by Philoktetes, well-skilled in bows,
seven in number, and in each ship fifty rowers

720 embarked, well-skilled in bows for violent fighting.
He, however, lay on an island suffering mighty agonies,
at beautiful Lemnos, where the sons of the Achaians left him,
labouring under an evil wound from a baleful water-snake.
There he lay in his grief; but soon the Argives would remember
the lord Philoktetes beside their ships.
They were not unruled even so, though they missed their ruler:
but Medon drew them up, illegitimate son of Oileus,
whom Rhene bore to Oileus sacker of cities.

      Those who held Trikka and rock-strewn Ithome,

730 who held Oichalia the city of Eurytos of Oichalia—
these were led by two good sons of Asklepios
the healer, Podaleirios and Machaon.
Thirty hollow ships lined up with them.

      Those who held Ormenios, and the spring of Hypereia,
who held Asterios and the white summits of Titanos—
these were ruled by Eurypylos, wonderful son of Euaimon.
There followed with him forty dark ships.

      Those who held Argissa, who owned Gyrtone,
Orthe, and the city of Elone, and white Oloössōn—

740 these were commanded by Polypoites strong in war,
son of Peirithoös whom immortal Zeus sired;
but he was born to Peirithoös by renowned Hippodameia
on that day when he got recompense from the shaggy creatures,
ousted them from Pelion and drove them to the Aithikes—
not on his own, but with him was Leonteus, offshoot of Ares,
son of high-spirited Koronos son of Kaineus.
There followed with them forty dark ships.

Gouneus from Kyphos brought two and twenty ships.
There followed him the Eniēnes and the Perrhaiboi strong in war,
750   who set their houses around Dodona, harsh in winter,[19]
and those who owned land about longed-for Titaressos,
which sends forth its streaming water into the Peneios:
but it is not mixed in with the silver-eddied Peneios,
but flows on top of it like olive oil;
for it is a branch of the water of Styx, dread river of oath.

The Magnesians were ruled by Prothoös son of Tenthredon;
around the Peneios and leaf-shaking Pelion
they dwelt. They were commanded by swift Prothoös.
There followed with him forty dark ships.
760   These, then, were the leaders and chiefs of the Danaoi.

---

[19] Dodona, the famous oracular sanctuary, is not in Thessaly but further W, in Epeiros.

PART ONE
ARCHAIC PERIOD

(C.700–C.490 BC)

Then take a well-fitted oar and go away
until you come to those that know not the sea (*thalassa*),
where men eat not their food admixed with salt,
nor even know of the ships with purple cheeks
or well-fitted oars that serve a ship for wings.
I tell you a sign most plain that shall not elude you:
whenever another man of the road meets you
and says you've a winnowing-fan on your radiant shoulder,
plant then and there your well-fitted oar in the ground,
enact fine holy offerings to Lord Poseidon—
a ram, a bull, a boar that mounts the sows—
then set your steps home and enact the holy sacrifices
to the undying gods who hold wide Heaven,
all of them, in due order.

Homer, *Odyssey* 11. 121–34 (my translation)

The lord, who leads the Spartan host,
    Stands with a little maid,
To greet a stranger from the coast
    Who comes to seek his aid.
What brings the guest? a disk of brass
    With curious lines engraven:
What mean the lines? stream, road, and pass,
    Forest, and town, and haven.

William Cory (1823–92), *The Daughter of Cleomenes*

1

ARISTEAS OF PROKONNESOS

(ARCHAIC PERIOD)

David C. Braund

INTRODUCTION

The remarkable Aristeas came from Prokonnesos, an island colony near the southern shore of the Propontis (now the Sea of Marmara), the gateway to the Pontos, the Black Sea.[1] He belonged to a prominent family of his community, which claimed to have been founded from Miletos: we may suppose his inherited wealth and sense of aristocracy. He lived in the archaic period (*c.*750–490 BC), but his more precise dates are very uncertain: our information is inadequate, and scholarly struggles have not improved upon our ignorance.[2] His rather idiosyncratic importance among Greek geographers demands explanation. It centres upon his account of the far north, beyond the north coast of the Black Sea, presented in a work called the *Arimaspeia*.

This *Arimaspeia* was a poem in epic hexameters. The *Suda* (5 below) tells us that it consisted of three books, which would suggest a length between perhaps 2,000 and 3,000 verses. A link with Homer was suggested in antiquity: the *Iliad* had included a little about the north, while comparisons with Homer's *Odyssey* were easily made.[3] For the *Arimaspeia* centred upon Aristeas' journeying in strange parts and the remarkable phenomena he found there, including even the Arimaspians, whose single eye evoked the Cyclopes.[4] The range of the poem (and so the extent of these travels) remains unclear, but Aristeas had travelled for many years (as Odysseus, albeit rather fewer), and three books of poetry were filled with his account, and perhaps a sense of epic grandeur. The poem seems, therefore, to have entailed much more than the Arimaspians and their neighbours. The poem's title (which need not be Aristeas') probably indicates its prime interest for most ancient readers. The one-eyed Arimaspians lay at the very limit of Aristeas' reported travels: he knew them only from their neighbours, the Issedones, and chose not to venture into their lands, a world of conflict and terror. For the Issedones told him (the poem said) that the Arimaspians were engaged in an on-going struggle with griffins over gold there. However, to reach the Issedones was an extraordinary feat in itself. To seek to go further, even with the divine support of

---

[1] For discussion on points of language and detail beyond the scope of our present concerns, see especially Bolton 1962; Dowden 2016; and Dan 2008. There is ample room for disagreement.
[2] See below on *Suda*.   [3] Further, S. R. West 2004.   [4] e.g. Strabo 1. 2. 10, C21 (T 7 Bolton).

Apollo, such as Aristeas claimed, was to test the very limits of what mortal humans might achieve, or be allowed to achieve. While the Arimaspian lands were horrendously dangerous, the world of the Hyperboreans beyond them was closed to all but the gods and the most outstanding of heroes, such as Herakles and Perseus.[5] Theirs was a land remarkable for its utopian lifestyle and balmy climate, the far side (Greek *hyper-*) of Boreas, the north wind, himself a superhuman force rich in mythology among Greeks as far afield as Athens.[6] The sacred nature of the Hyperboreans and their special world was confirmed in Greek culture not only by location (outside the weather system of the *oikoumenē* and far from the travails of mortals), but also by its impenetrability. Exceptional contacts were the source of cult aetiologies, as on Delos and at Olympia. Accordingly, Aristeas' failure to reach the Hyperboreans was almost inevitable from the first, and served to confirm their important isolation from Greeks and their geographical experience. If Apollo himself had ever sought to bring the poet into this most special of worlds, he was dissuaded, at least in Aristeas' lifetime. Meanwhile, we should reflect upon the wealth of key Greek traditions in which Hyperboreans played a major role, for their existence warns against any notion that tales of the far north and beyond all somehow sprouted from Aristeas' poetry.[7]

Aristeas was a geographer in the sense that extensive travels were central to his biography and writing, with reports of the peoples, places, customs, and events that might be found in distant parts, or were at least discussed there. Most of what we hear of him and his work concerns the far north, from the approaches to the Black Sea to the mysterious realms of one-eyed warriors (Arimaspians), gold-guarding griffins, and the Hyperborean utopia. However, Aristeas had a much broader significance around the Greek world, as is indicated by his special importance in southern Italy, where the Greeks of Metapontion even erected a statue of him at the centre of their city, next to that of Apollo, his particular patron deity. In that sense, he was part of a Greek colonial culture which stretched around the vast periphery, where pioneering Hellenism encountered other peoples, with their own particular beliefs and local traditions. We shall see how Aristeas' mysticism has a special connection with such colonial processes to the north and west, as also elsewhere in the Greek world.

While Aristeas' contribution to geography was important for Greeks, his mystical aspects were still more astonishing. Strange far-off regions certainly fascinated, but Aristeas' apparent ability to touch the divine entailed a series of fundamental human questions about life and death, the body and the soul, and the relationship between

---

[5] Herodotos 4. 36 shows impatience (minimized by Romm 1989) with tales of Hyperboreans, which were numerous, and included the fantastical Abaris (see Zhmud 2016). On occasion the Arimaspians might be included among them: so Kallimachos, according to Steph. Byz. υ 47 Hyperboreoi (*BNJ*² 35 F 9).

[6] Further, Calame 2011.

[7] Further, Romm 1989. Hdt. 4. 33–5 shows the complex contexts of the Hyperboreans of Delos, which demanded his respect, if not belief.

mankind and the gods. Accordingly, we may readily understand why both ancient and modern writers have tended to focus more on his mysticism than on his geography. At the same time, these two parts of his endeavours have never sat easily together. For both his fantastical geography and his mysticism raise large questions of truth and fiction, and these become still more problematic when geography and mysticism are taken together, as tends to happen with Aristeas. For Aristeas' mysticism was embedded in his geography, and *vice versa*. As the late 5th-century historian Herodotos (1 below, §§13, 15) makes very clear, Aristeas was said to have travelled in the company of Apollo, at least sometimes as a bird. His soul was said to be able to leave his body and return to it once more.[8] And yet—as mysticism demands—the details seem not to have been very clear even in antiquity. For example, despite suggestions that he visited the far north in the form of a disembodied soul, or a bird (attested only in Italy) or other creature, his miraculous departure for the north, as told in his native Prokonnesos, suggests that he started the lengthy journey of many years in human form. Moreover, Herodotos' evident respect for his account (revealed not least in the sheer space he gives to Aristeas) encourages the inference that Aristeas had presented his journeying in at least a sober manner. Where Herodotos expresses disbelief in tales of Arimaspians sending griffins' gold southwards,[9] he does not attribute the notion to Aristeas, whether through respect or because the poet never said as much. As often with Aristeas, a large part of our difficulty in these key details results from the fact that we have only a few lines that may have been written by Aristeas himself (2 and 6). The rest is a noisy assemblage of stories, hypotheses, and imagination, whose foundations are at least unclear for the most part, and which of course entail considerable inconsistencies.

While various claims have been made by modern scholars about the amount in Herodotos' account of the north that comes from Aristeas, these are highly speculative. It is certainly true that Aristeas' *Arimaspeia* became a key work for Greeks who considered these northern regions, but we may be sure that there were other sources of information besides. Herodotos says as much, when he tells of Skythians bringing down to the Black Sea stories they have had from the Issedones, whom Aristeas also claimed as principal informants (Herodotos 4. 27). The fact that Alkman could include the Issedones in public poetry in Sparta around 600 BC also suggests a broader awareness of the region, aside from the writings of Aristeas, especially in view of his different spelling of their name and the other details of the region to which he alludes.[10] For all his undoubted importance, Aristeas cannot plausibly be considered the only, or even the principal, source of fact and fiction for this enormous northern

---

[8] Further, Seaford 2009. For recent reflections on Hdt.'s use of Aristeas, see Gagné 2020.

[9] Hdt. 3. 116, where the existence of especially large amounts of gold in the far north is accepted. Cf. Hdt. 4. 32 for probable rejection of A.'s version of what Issedonians say, where the poet is also not named.

[10] See Zaikov 2004; cf. Ferrari 2008.

world, where Greeks had begun to explore and settle from early archaic times. Of course, we are in no position to speculate about how much of this kind of material was written down or when.[11] However, this pool of knowledge would account for Aristeas' ability to create a work on the north which seemed worthwhile to Herodotos. However far the author of the *Arimaspeia* had actually travelled from Prokonnesos, there was sufficient knowledge and storytelling in the Black Sea world to provide content for his poem.

Later Greek writers took a range of views about Aristeas and his work. The geographer Strabo is especially interesting, giving a view from the beginning of the 1st century AD. He does not say a great deal about Aristeas, but shows him a measure of respect.[12] Especially so, when he even chooses to report (without comment) that some authorities regarded Aristeas as the teacher of Homer himself.[13] For Strabo, Homer was the first geographer, and a great one. Strabo is at pains to defend Homer's geographical observations against his critics at every turn. The fact that Strabo even mentions Aristeas as Homer's teacher demonstrates a respect for the mystical Prokonnesian. By contrast, in the following century, the sophist Maximus of Tyre takes a harsher view (3–4). He brackets Aristeas with poets who write in riddles and couch their great claims in incoherent verbiage. In his critical perspective Aristeas was a charlatan in large part, because he invented mystical tales to obscure the fact that he had no philosophical training. Aristeas' appeal to the divine and the wondrous, as Maximus sees it, was a clumsy stratagem by which he could gain some authority for his nonsense. We simply cannot know how much of Aristeas' work either of these later authors had read. However, Strabo offers a little detail at least, while Maximus' criticisms did not require direct knowledge of Aristeas' text. It may be that the more sympathetic of the two had read a little more. At any rate, a picturesque vignette by Aulus Gellius (Maximus' younger contemporary) should not be pressed as evidence for Aristeas' rarity among bibliophiles of the early Roman empire, not least because (even if we take his account literally) his is a tale about the cheap price of books as much as their obscurity. A few decades earlier the elder Pliny seems to have had a copy of Aristeas' work, while later still the *Suda* clearly knew much more than we do about his works and traditions of his life, including an alternative identification of his father that is otherwise unknown to us.[14]

Closer to home, in Prokonnesos and the other Milesian settlements on the mainland nearby, Aristeas was a local hero. His birthplace had other claims to fame,

---

[11] Among important hints at other traditions, see notably the scholion on Pindar, *Olympian* 3. 38c. On Alkman and Hekataios of Miletos, see Strabo 7. 3. 6, C299, with Steph. Byz. s.v. Issedones.

[12] For example, Strabo 7. 3. 6, C299, omits him from the list of ignorant purveyors of tall tales about the north, which includes Hesiod (cf. fr. 150 M.–W.) and the Aeschylean Prometheus trilogy.

[13] On A. and Homer, Strabo 14. 1. 18, C639 (T 26 Bolton), with Jane L. Lightfoot 2017; cf. 1. 2. 10 (T 7 Bolton), Arimaspians; Strabo saw Homer as the first geographer proper, Strabo 1. 1. 11, C7.

[14] Aulus Gellius, *Attic Nights*, 9. 4 (*BNJ*[3] 35 T 7a/F 3a; T 9 Bolton); Pliny 7. ii. 9–12 (*BNJ*[2] 35 F 3b).

including the provision of high-quality marble for the Black Sea Greeks and others.[15] That marble supply was one among many vectors northwards from Aristeas' homeland. At a supernatural level, among other deities,[16] Apollo was of prime significance there, which was consonant with Aristeas' claim to a special connection with the god. While Apollo was regularly central to traditions of Greek colonial settlement, the occasional coinage of Prokonnesos boasted Apollo's portrait. An inscription from Miletos shows us how Greeks of the Propontis might revel in the notion that the god had joined with them in conquering any barbarians who tried to resist the establishment of Greek communities there, for Apollo was a warrior as well as a singer of poetry.[17] The god was also a source of prophecy and a purveyor of special knowledge about unknown regions, especially through his oracles, notably at Didyma, near Miletos, in a temple decorated with griffins.[18] There is important context here for Aristeas' poem and the geography it presents, all rooted in the patronage and intervention of Apollo himself, it was said. When Aristeas seemed to have appeared in southern Italy, with claims about Apollo and instructions for the Metapontines, the whole matter was taken to Apollo at Delphi, whose oracle was at least as renowned as its counterpart at Didyma, and far more so for the Greeks of the mainland and the western colonies. Meanwhile, on the north coast of the Black Sea itself, Herodotos perceived the Milesian colony of Olbia as a cardinal location, the gateway to Skythia and points further north.[19] Apollo Boreas was clearly significant there, while the city's cult of Kybele was said to have been brought from Kyzikos by a Skythian, Anacharsis, who had returned from the Greek world. The important cult of Aphrodite in Olbia may well have been brought from Artake near Kyzikos,[20] which also features in Herodotos' report of traditions about Aristeas. As indicated above, there is inevitable uncertainty about the extent of Aristeas' impact on the details and substance of Herodotos' account of Skythia and beyond. However, we may observe the larger point that there was in reality a conceptual mapping of the region, which led from the Propontis to Olbia, and it is hard to avoid the suspicion that Aristeas' account had shared in that geographical outlook and orientation. It is a pity that Herodotos does not happen to tell us what was said about Aristeas in Olbia. We may be sure enough, even so, that his poem was very familiar to Greeks of the northern Black Sea in particular, who shared in the general Greek interest in Hyperboreans, griffins, and the rest, and who certainly had a special regional interest in them, including notions about the sources of gold that reached them, as it seemed (Hdt. 3. 116),[21] from the strange environment of the distant north, familiar to Apollo. We may note the origins of key works about that world, including the Hyperborean accounts by Hekataios of Thracian Abdera and Herakleides Pontikos of Herakleia Pontike.

---

[15] In general, Hasluck 1909.
[16] Especially Kybele, see Paus. 8. 46. 2 with Hdt. 4. 76.
[17] Further, Giovannini 1993, 278, on *Delphinion* 155.   [18] In general, Fontenrose 1988.
[19] See Braund and Kryzhitskiy 2007.   [20] Braund 2020.   [19] *BNJ*[2] 35 F 6a.

A concomitant geographical consideration is the popularity of forms of Pythagoreanism and Orphism in this Thraceward region, as also among the western colonies of Sicily and southern Italy.[22] We see elements of this among the Getai above the Danube delta, and in Olbia itself. Herodotos (4. 95) reports a colonialist version of these traditions, whereby Greeks of the region mocked their Getan neighbours as unsophisticated, claiming that their local deity, Zalmoxis, was in fact a crafty slave of the 6th-century philosopher Pythagoras of Samos (later of Kroton in southern Italy), who had tricked them into believing in his ability to overcome death.[23] We may well suspect that these notions in fact arose from cultural contacts in which the similarities between Greek Pythagoreanism and local belief in Zalmoxis were observed. Herodotos refrains from decisive comment, but shows a measure of respect for local practice, as usual. For him Pythagoreanism itself had a complex cultural history, while he must also have been aware that many Greeks responded to its tenets and associated stories with mockery in any case.[24]

Over the centuries Aristeas and his work have been approached and understood in quite different ways. The importance of the *Arimaspeia* for Greek conceptions of the distant north, especially as mediated by Herodotos, has even encouraged sober scholars to claim significant links between Aristeas and the practices of shamans and the like, usually located to the distant east in Siberia. The roots of these modern notions lie in diffusionism and a willingness to replace geographical study of the extent of Russia with vague notions of migrating nomads.[25] The fact that Herodotos says almost nothing of shamanic practices and makes no attempt to connect Aristeas with such medicine-men should at least constitute a warning against this kind of scholarly fantasy. More obviously conclusive, however, is Aristeas' place among the many wonder-workers associated with Pythagoras and often enough, like Pythagoras himself, with Apollo and extensive travelling. Accordingly, while there is no sign of disembodied souls in Herodotos' long account of Skythians, for example, we find such ideas close to the Danube among the Getai, on the western periphery in Italy and Sicily, and elsewhere in and around the Greek world.[26] It is neither a surprise nor a mistake that southern Italy was brought directly into the tale of the fuller's shop told by Herodotos, with Kroton replacing Kyzikos.[27] And it was much easier for Greeks to find what may be called 'shamanism' in their own cultures, without recourse to distant peoples far beyond their experience.

---

[22] Further, Zhmud 2016, observing that Pythagoras' extensive travels did not include the Black Sea world and the north beyond (where Orpheus travelled, as others: Dio Chrys. 36. 1). On material similarities, Petersen 2011. On Pythagoreanism (or Orphism) in Thrace and elsewhere, see Bernabé 2016.

[23] Hdt. 4. 95; cf. Zhmud 2016.

[24] Egyptian connections: Hdt. 2. 124; cf. 49; 81. Comedy: Ogden 2006.

[25] Meuli 1935 bears much of the responsibility for this. Bolton 1962 sees the weakness of such arguments, but for other vain reasons argues that Hdt.'s north is somehow the east.

[26] For bibliography and judicious brevity on all this, see Ogden 2001, 116–17.

[27] Plutarch, *Romulus*, 28. 4 (T 16 Bolton); cf. Dan 2008 on Aristeios.

We do better to locate Aristeas' mystical tendencies with Pythagoreans than with imagined shamans, unknown even to Herodotos. His ideas and his geography, insofar as we can know them, belong firmly to the Greek world and especially its colonial periphery, perhaps most importantly among the Milesian colonists towards Thrace. On that view he was very much a man of Prokonnesos and we may appreciate how and why his mysticism could have been accepted and valued there, as Herodotos indicates. There is nothing in the *Arimaspeia* that has come from the far north or from Siberia: the griffins sometimes shown in Siberian art are now thought to have come from Greek culture, or perhaps from the Achaemenid melting-pot of cultures.[28] Meanwhile, we have seen that Aristeas fits well enough among the poets and poetical philosophers of the archaic Greek world, including the elusive Homer himself. Herodotos' respect for Aristeas and Strabo's tolerance of him, at least, make much more sense when we understand him and his work as quite different from the bizarre nonsense of others—for example, tales of Hyperborean Abaris (whom Herodotos dismisses, 4. 36). This was an aristocrat of a Greek state, valued and authenticated by his own community and its neighbours, whose devotion to Apollo was to be reckoned with. Insofar as his geography accorded with other information about the north, it was to be taken seriously, and emended or doubted where it did not. With regard to the north, this special Prokonnesian was well placed to have knowledge without even leaving his island, while his broadly Pythagorean biography, his claimed bond with Apollo, and more generally perhaps his *bona fides* as an esteemed author of the colonial periphery brought him special importance across Greek culture and particularly among the Greeks of the west, with their own lines to Pythagoras and Apollo.

For clarity's sake, passages which do not contribute directly to our understanding of Aristeas and his work have not been translated below, though they are cited above where appropriate.

SELECTED FURTHER READING

*Bolton, J. D. P. (1962), *Aristeas of Proconnesus*. Oxford.
*Dowden, K. (2016), 'Aristeas (35)', in *BNJ²*.
Hadas, M. (1935), 'Utopian sources in Herodotos', *Classical Philology*, 30: 113–21.
Szpakowska, K. (ed. 2006), *Through a Glass Darkly: Magic, Dreams and Prophecy in Ancient Egypt*. Swansea.
West, S. R. (2004), 'Herodotus on Aristeas', in C. J. Tuplin (ed.), *Pontus and the Outside World: Studies in Black Sea History, Historiography, and Archaeology* (Leiden–Boston), 43–67.

---

[28] On Siberian and Milesian griffins, see Braund 2019b with bibliography. On griffins in Greek culture, see also Arnott 2007, 90. In general, Bremmer 2002.

TEXTS

1 Herodotos 4. 13–16[29]

13. (1) Aristeas, son of Kaÿstrobios,[30] a man of Prokonnesos,[31] said, composing his epic, that he reached the Issedones,[32] possessed by Phoibos Apollo,[33] and that above the Issedones dwell the Arimaspoi, one-eyed men, and that above them dwell the gold-guarding griffins, and above them the Hyperboreans, dwelling on the coast of the sea.[34] (2) And that all these, except the Hyperboreans, beginning with the Arimaspoi, always attack their neighbours, and the Issedones are pushed out of their land by the Arimaspoi, and the Skythians by the Issedones,[35] and that the Kimmerioi dwelling on the southern sea abandoned their land,[36] under pressure from the Skythians. So Aristeas does not agree at all with the Skythians about this land.[37]

14. (1) Whence was Aristeas, who said these things, I have stated. The story I heard about him in Prokonnesos and Kyzikos, I shall tell. For they say that Aristeas, being of a family inferior to none of the townsmen, went into a fuller's shop[38] in Prokonnesos and died, and that the fuller locked his workshop and went to inform the relations of the deceased. (2) However, as the story of Aristeas' death spread about the city, a man of Kyzikos who had come from the town of Artake[39] argued with those who told the story, saying that he had encountered Aristeas heading for Kyzikos and

[29] Herodotos the historian completed his work around 425 BC. He provides our longest and best-informed account of Aristeas' reputation, with a general idea of the content of the *Arimaspeia*, which he incorporates into his own account of the north (not uncritically: see introduction to chapter).

[30] See *Suda* s.v. Aristeas (T 11 Bolton).

[31] On the places named, see introduction to chapter.

[32] The Issedones were the limit of A.'s claimed travels, but he was by no means the only source on them and their stories, as Hdt. 4. 27 and 32 makes clear, tracing the passage of knowledge from them via Skythians to Greeks. Hdt.'s concomitant Skythian etymology of 'Arimaspians' is probably no better than most ancient etymologies, though we may ask why he found it plausible.

[33] On his seizure by Apollo, see introduction to chapter. The Greek word *phoibolamptos* does not scan, but we need not suppose that Hdt. has changed the substance of Aristeas' verse, whose contents are clearly summarized in this paragraph in large part. The idea could be expressed without the compound term itself, as we see at Hdt. 4. 76. 4 on Dionysiac possession. A.'s form remains obscure, whether he was a man, a bird (below), a disembodied soul, or something else.

[34] On this geography, see introduction to chapter.

[35] Herodotos (below) takes this to support his own analysis of Skythian origins.

[36] Hdt. 4. 11–12 has related their expulsion from the N coast of the Black Sea, the monuments and toponyms that they left there, and their subsequent activities in Asia Minor below. The importance of the Kimmerians in traditions of origins there is clear, but the historicity of this Kimmerian invasion from the north remains very obscure (cf. already Hdt. 1. 103–6). Ivantchik 1993 is more optimistic.

[37] Hdt. 4. 5–7 says how the Skythians claimed to be autochthonous on the northern Black Sea. At 4. 8–10 he relates local Greek claims that Skythians were descended from Herakles and a local deity of the place, without supporting them. These autochthonous traditions undermine much of the argument of Hartog 1988: see Braund 2004.

[38] The location of this miracle suggests cleansing, such as a soul might achieve by leaving its body (cf. Bremmer 1983; Seaford 2009), but (as Hdt. reports the story) A.'s body also left the locked shop as well as his soul.

[39] The identity of this key individual is left obscure. On the locations named, see introduction to chapter.

had even spoken with him. And while this man insistently disputed the matter, the relations of the deceased went to the fuller's shop with the things needed for those who pass away.   (3) But when they opened the building Aristeas was not to be seen, dead or alive. And they say that in the seventh year he appeared in Prokonnesos and composed the verses that are now called by the Greeks the *Arimaspeia*, and then disappeared a second time.[40]

15. (1) That is what those cities say. I know the following, which befell the Metapontinoi in Italy 240 years after the second disappearance of Aristeas,[41] as I found by making a comparison in Prokonnesos and Metapontion.   (2) The Metapontinoi say that Aristeas himself appeared in their land and instructed them to establish an altar of Apollo and to set up beside it a statue bearing the name of Aristeas of Prokonnesos: for Apollo, he said, had come to the land of the Metapontinoi, alone of the Italians, and he himself had followed him, now being Aristeas, but at that time, when he followed the god, he was a raven.[42]   (3) And the Metapontinoi say that after saying that, he disappeared, and that they sent to Delphi and asked the god what this apparition of a person might be. And that the Pythia instructed them to obey the apparition, and said that obedience would be to their benefit. And that, after receiving that reply, they carried out the instructions.   (4) And now the statue stands with the name of Aristeas by the image of Apollo himself, and laurel trees[43] stand around it. The image is located in the marketplace. Let that suffice about Aristeas.

16. (1) As for the part of the Earth about which the present account has begun to tell, no one knows for sure what is beyond it. For I can discover no one who claims to know it as an eye-witness. For not even Aristeas, whom I have just mentioned, said in those verses of his that he had gone further than the Issedones. Rather, he said that he wrote of things beyond from hearsay, and that it was the Issedones who spoke of them.   (2) However, as far as we can proceed for sure by hearsay, all will be told.

---

[40] The length of his absence might suggest the extent of the travels which informed the poem he wrote upon his return. His second absence was spent with Apollo in Italy, at least in part, as we soon learn. We are not told that he ever returned to Prokonnesos, though that may have been imagined.

[41] Hdt. therefore places A. as early as C8l, though we need not agree with him. Textual emendation is not required: see Dowden ad loc., who proceeds to quote Tatian, *To the Greeks*, 41 (C2 AD; *BNJ*³ 35 T 3; T 27 Bolton), who makes Aristeas at least that early; cf. also Dion. Hal. *On Thucydides* 23. 4–6 (*BNJ*³ 35 T 5; T 10 Bolton); Strabo 14. 1. 18, C639, Aristeas as teacher of Homer (*BNJ*² 35 T 4; T 26 Bolton).

[42] *Korax*, as all corvids: they were associated with Apollo and tales of metamorphosis, for they can mimic human speech (cf. Pliny 10. lx. 121–3) and were known for their longevity, with prophetic abilities: see Arnott 2007, 163–6. As Apollo's envoy, see already Hesiod fr. 60 in Merkelbach and West 1967, with Dettori 2006.

[43] The tree of Apollo, apparently here made of bronze and capable of giving oracles: Athenaios 13. 605c (T 18 Bolton), specifying a single laurel, as we have on the civic coinage of C5 (Head 1911, 76).

2 Pseudo-Longinos, *On the Sublime*, 10. 4[44]

For the poet of the *Arimaspeia* thinks the following fear-filled:

> A wonder for us[45] is also this, great in our minds.
> men inhabit water, away from land in open seas (*pelagē*)
> wretched persons are they, for theirs are sorry tasks:
> they have their eyes among the stars[46] and their souls on the main (*pontos*).
> often raising their dear hands to the gods
> they pray, their entrails tossing evilly.

I think it clear to all how these words hold more flourish than fear.

3 Maximus of Tyre, *Dissertation* 10. 2

A Prokonnesian man's body lay alive but feeble and very close to death. The soul had left the body, and was wandering in the upper air like a bird, gazing on all below—earth and sea and rivers and cities and tribes of men and sufferings and natures of every kind. And when it re-entered the body and restored it, as if using a tool, it held forth on what it had seen and heard, various things in various contexts.[47]

4 Maximus of Tyre, *Dissertation* 38. 3

A man named Aristeas was born in Prokonnesos, a philosopher.[48] However, his wisdom was not acknowledged at first, because he had no teacher of wisdom to show. Accordingly, he devised a story to counter people's disbelief. He used to say that his soul left his body and flew up straight into the upper air, roving the Earth, both Greece and *barbaricum*, and all the islands, and rivers, and mountains, and that the end of this roving was the land of the Hyperboreans. And that his soul had surveyed all the social customs and practices and the natures of places and the changes of the airs and the effusions of the sea and the estuaries of the rivers. And that his soul gained a much clearer vision of the heavens than that from below. By saying these things, Aristeas became more plausible than Anaxagoras or than Xenophanes, or anyone else who

---

[44] The author is unknown, but his work is dated to C1 AD. It is a treatise on style, good and bad, which presents its arguments through examples. Here a fragment of the *Arimaspeia* has not had an appropriate impact, in the critic's view, especially when set beside a Homeric passage on a similar subject.

[45] We seem to have the voice of someone amazed at human willingness to sail the open sea: further, Bowra 1956. Distaste for seafaring is a key trope in Greek culture: further Beaulieu 2016; on Hesiod's outlook, see Griffith 1983, esp. 61.

[46] Navigating by the stars, yet with an experience that is far from heavenly.

[47] In this extract and 4 below, the sophist Maximus groups A. with authors, such as Pythagoras and Epimenides, who told wondrous tales and claimed special links to the divine. He presents him as a charlatan who sought belief by claiming to have journeyed in the form of a disembodied soul, flying above the earth and gaining knowledge by observing everything above and below. However, it is not clear that M. has troubled to read the *Arimaspeia*, so that he may rely on a general notion of A. and his poem which may well not be reliable. He gives no detail about its contents, while the respectful Hdt. (1 above) reports a version that the body too had left (see introduction to chapter).

[48] Maximus calls him a 'philosopher' with reservations and irony. He draws a sharp distinction between the enigmatic mythologizing of poets like A. and the clear, comprehensible argumentation of true philosophers (cf. 3 above).

interprets how existence is. For mankind did not yet know clearly the roving of the soul, nor with what eyes it sees things, but simply thought that the soul must journey about if it is to pronounce the greatest truths for each thing.[49]

5 *Suda* α 3900[50]

Aristeas: (*son*) of Democharis[51] or Kaÿstrobios,[52] Prokonnesian epic poet: wrote the poem called the *Arimaspeia*. It is an account of the Hyperborean[53] Arimaspoi, three books. They say that his soul came and went as he wished. He was born in the time of Kroisos (*Croesus*) and Kyros (*Cyrus*) in the 58th (?) Olympiad.[54] He also wrote a prose *Theogony* of 1,000 lines.

6 Tzetzes (Ioannes), *Chiliades*, 7. 678–84[55]

> And Aristeas says in the *Arimaspeia*:
> 'Issedoi glorying in (*their*) flowing locks',
> 680   and that there are humans beyond, neighbours,
> towards the north wind, many and very fine warriors,
> rich in horses, flocks of sheep, and herds of cattle.
> each has a single eye in a comely forehead,
> shaggy-haired,[56] the sturdiest of all men.

[49] See n. on 3 above.

[50] The *Suda*, sometimes called Suidas, is an encyclopaedic lexicon compiled in Byzantion around C10 AD. Its masses of information, variable in quality, are arranged alphabetically by subject.

[51] Unknown elsewhere, indicating how much of the tradition on Aristeas may have been lost.

[52] The name (also at Hdt. 4. 13. 1) evokes a Lydian river, though its use in A.'s family tells us little.

[53] On occasional coalescence of Arimaspians and Hyperboreans, see introduction. It is hard to see how they could be brought together, for—usually—Hyperboreans lived a utopian lifestyle, while Arimaspians fought endlessly with griffins. Possibly it was enough that the latter also might be placed 'beyond the north wind', the literal meaning of the Greek name 'Hyperborean'.

[54] The 58th Olympiad (548–545) follows emendation of the text from '8th' (748–745) to coincide with Croesus and Cyrus, but the date need not be seen as at all precise, while *Suda* may mean either birth or *floruit*. We have no grounds for confidence in any precise date, despite much scholarly effort.

[55] John (Ioannes) Tzetzes, a Byzantine writer of C12 AD, claims to have read some verses of Aristeas. He knew also of other relevant texts, not only Hdt. but Zenothemis and Pherenikos, obscure Hl authors. The second line, where the metre changes from T.'s decapentesyllables to hexameters, seems to be a quotation from the *Arimaspeia*, while the rest (680–4, where the Greek text is problematic: see Dowden 2016 ad loc.) could well be a summary, again in hexameters, of what Aristeas wrote, here compressed in T.'s verse abridgment.

[56] The long hair of the Issedones is distinguished from the more woolly hair of the Arimaspians.

2

SKYLAX OF KARYANDA

(ACTIVE C.520–C.518 BC)

D. Graham J. Shipley

INTRODUCTION

Writing in the second half of the 5th century BC, Herodotos (4. 44; 1 below) describes how King Darius of Persia organized an expedition into India under one Skylax,[1] a citizen of Karyanda in the semi-Hellenic region of Karia, to whom the *Suda* (13) attributes four writings, one of which should be the lost prose narrative of his long voyage.[2] The testimonia and fragments selected here are those relevant to this, the historical Skylax;[3] the surviving 4th-century *Periplous* (*Circumnavigation*) must be detached from his name, and its author is known as Pseudo-Skylax (see Chapter 7).

Beyond that, however, matters are not simple. Of the *Suda*'s attributions, the fourth, the criticism of Polybios, must, if genuine, be the work of the 1st-century BC Skylax of Karyanda whom Cicero mentions (*De divinatione*, 2. 42), and who is more likely to have been a 'mathematician and musician' than his archaic-period counterpart. It is uncertain who wrote the second work, about a king of Mylasa, though recent opinion assigns it to the earlier Skylax.[4] The first and third works, *Periplous of Places outside the Pillars of Herakles* and *Circuit of the Earth*, must now be considered.

Sources including Aristotle (2) cite 'Skylax' or 'Skylax of Karyanda' for information about India, others for the Greek world. The 'outside' in the title of the *Suda*'s first work could refer to the far west, but no evidence links the Herodotean Skylax with the Atlantic, while in the pseudonymous *Periplous* only the last few pages refer to the coast of that ocean. Some editors change 'outside' to 'inside' to make the reference fit the surviving *periplous*; but 'outside' is also consistent with a voyage in the seas and oceans east of Africa—one reason is that 'Libyē' or Africa was thought to be much smaller than it really is—and the surviving *Periplous* does not venture east of the Levant; so

---

[1] Σκύλαξ, literally 'puppy' or 'cub'; often rendered today in its Latin form, 'Scylax'; also Skulax (*EANS*), Skilaks (Serbian, Croatian), Skylaks (Polish), Scilace (Italian), Escílax (Spanish), etc.

[2] For a more extended discussion of the *Suda* entry, see Shipley 2019, 4–8. The evidence for Skylax is summarized by Dueck 2012, 10 and 53–4, who notes the Persian context.

[3] For an alternative reconstruction with facing Spanish trans. and notes, see González Ponce 2008b, 155–77.

[4] Schepens 1998. See also Kaplan 2009 ~ Kaplan 2019.

Suda's first work could be the real Skylax's record of his Indian explorations. The title of the third, *Circuit of the Earth*, could refer to either work or to neither, but perhaps suits approximately enough the surviving *periplous*.

The most judicious reconstruction assigns the *Periplous of Places outside the Pillars of Herakles* to Herodotos' Skylax; and recent scholarship has made a case that in this work he wrote only about the East, not the Mediterranean or the West. It has been argued persuasively that Philostratos of Athens (first half of the 3rd century AD) drew upon Skylax, directly or indirectly, for his partly fictionalized account of the wandering sophist Apollonios of Tyana (early 1st century AD) and his journey into India.[5] This suggestion rests upon four supports. First, the one explicit citation of Skylax by Philostratos (8)—a rare enough example. Second, Philostratos' comparisons of passenger boats on the sea-coast to those of the Etruscans (*Life of Apollonios*, 3. 50) and of Taxila to Nineveh (2. 20), both of which are anachronistic and suggest an archaic source. Third, but only suggestively, the repeated relating of phenomena in the East to those of the Greek world: the Caucasus ending as far west as Karia (2. 2. 1); the comparison of the vegetation of Mt Nysa with that of Mt Tmolos in Lydia (2. 8); of the breadth of the river Hyphasis to that of the Istros (3. 1); of small vines in the Ganges valley to those of Lydia and Maionia (3. 5. 2); of the diet of flocks in the land of the Fish-eaters to that in Karia (3. 55); the mention of the Karmanoi not salting their fish as is done in the Pontos (3. 55 again); the comparison of the rocks at the Nile Cataract to Mt Tmolos (6. 23); and of the rapids to the rivers Marsyas and Maeander (6. 26). Finally, and more tentatively still, the presence of hippopotamuses in the Nile (plausibly from our Skylax)[6] and the ruined character of Egyptian Thebes, destroyed by the Persian king Kambyses in the late 6th century BC (6. 4).

All this allows us to infer the scope and themes of Skylax's work. If the comparisons noted above are correctly identified as his, it is striking that nearly all of them refer to Asia Minor, which may have been a major focus of the *Circuit of the Earth*. For the *Periplous of Places outside the Pillars of Herakles*, they allow us to characterize his route from Babylon to the east side of India, possibly as far as Taprobane (Sri Lanka),[7] and the date of his journey: Panchenko places his arrival at Babylon in 520, and his departure from there in summer 518.[8] Skylax may reappear in Herodotos' account of the Ionian Revolt some twenty years later, in which a captain of this name is maltreated by the Persian commander Megabates (5. 33); the identification is possible, though this second Skylax is said to be a citizen of Myndos, another Karian city, rather than Karyanda. Be that as it may, the record of the voyage to India was a 'first' as far as the Greeks were concerned, and its impact upon Greek awareness of the Indian Ocean was far more extensive than was the impact of the

---

[5] Panchenko 1998; Panchenko 2002; Panchenko 2003.   [6] Panchenko 1998, 230.
[7] For details, Panchenko 2002, 9, citing a further eight passages from books 2–3 of *VA*. For Taprobane, see Ch. 34 Markianos 1, §§35–6.
[8] Panchenko 2002, 10–11.

later, desk-based treatise incorrectly preserved under Skylax's name. Although the work may not have been widely circulated,[9] it was well enough known to be cited several times.

SELECTED FURTHER READING

Brillante, S. (2020), *Il Periplo di Pseudo-Scilace: l'oggettività del potere*. Hildesheim–Zürich–New York. [Appeared too late to be taken into account fully.]

*González Ponce, F. J. (2008), *Periplo de Hanón y autores de los siglos VI y V a.C.* Zaragoza. [Pp. 155–77.]

*Kaplan, P. (2019), 'Skylax of Karyanda (709)', in *BNJ²*.

Panchenko, D. V. (1998), 'Scylax' circumnavigation of India and its interpretation in early Greek geography, ethnography and cosmography, I', *Hyperboreus*, 4. 2: 211–42.

—— (2002), 'Scylax in Philostratus' Life of Apollonius of Tyana', *Hyperboreus*, 8. 1: 5–12.

—— (2003), 'Scylax' circumnavigation of India and its interpretation in early Greek geography, ethnography and cosmography, II', *Hyperboreus*, 9. 2: 274–94.

*Schepens, G. (1998), '1000 (= 709) Skylax of Karyanda', in *FGrH* iv A 1, 2–24.

Shipley, D. G. J. (2019), *Pseudo-Skylax's Periplous: The Circumnavigation of the Inhabited World*, 2nd edn. Liverpool. [Esp. introduction.]

—— (2021), 'Scylax (Σκύλαξ, ὁ) of Caryanda', in C. A. Baron (ed.), *The Herodotus Encyclopedia*, iii (Hoboken), 1300–1.

TEXTS

1   Herodotos 4. 44: *Skylax's voyage*

The greater part of Asia was discovered by Darius. As the Indos river is the only other river (*besides the Nile*) that supports crocodiles, wishing to know where this river discharges into the sea he sent a number of men in boats whom he trusted to tell the truth; and among them Skylax, a man of Karyanda.[10]   (2) Starting from the city of Kaspatyros and the Paktuic land, they sailed by river towards the dawn and the risings of the sun (*pros ēō te kai hēliou anatolas*) into the sea;[11] and sailing through the sea towards the west they arrived in the thirtieth month at that place from which the king of the Egyptians sent off the Phoenicians I mentioned earlier to circumnavigate Libyē.[12]   (3) After these men had made their circumnavigation, Darius both overthrew

---

[9] Roller 2015, 47–8.

[10] It is often assumed that Skylax led the expedition; it may be so, but Herodotos does not say so.

[11] If Panchenko 1998 (modified by Panchenko 2003) is right, they travelled down the Ganges rather than the Indus, and went on to Sri Lanka. S. R. West 2012 notes that this was proposed by Blakesey 1854, i. 463 n. 138, and Myres 1953, 39–40; she doubts it, as Persian conquests were less extensive than suggested, but it may be questioned whether the idea depends on this: Hdt.'s informants may have exaggerated.

[12] See Hdt. 4. 42 for the story of the pharaoh Necho launching a circumnavigation of Africa.

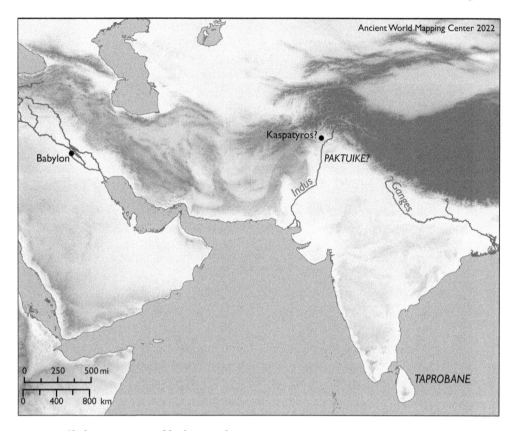

Ancient World Mapping Center 2022

MAP 2.1. Skylax: area covered by his travels.

the Indians and exploited this sea. Thus all of Asia, except the parts towards the rising sun, has been found to be of a similar nature to Libyē.[13]

2   Aristotle, *Politics,* 7. 13. 1, 1332b 12–27: *Kings in India*
Since each civic association is made up of rulers and the ruled, let us consider this: whether the rulers and ruled must be different men, or the same for life; for it is clear that education, too, must be consistent with this distinction. So if one group were as markedly different from the other as we believe the gods and the heroes are different from humans—having, first, vast superiority of body; second, of soul—so that the pre-eminence of the rulers were indubitable and evident to the ruled, then clearly it would be better that the same men should always rule and the same always be ruled, once for all. But since this is not easy to grasp, nor is it possible for the kings to be so different from the ruled as Skylax says is the case among the Indians,[14] it is evident that for many reasons it is essential that all alike should periodically associate in ruling and being ruled.

[13] A passing reference to Hdt.'s passage is at Strabo 2. 3. 4, C98; see Poseidonios 2 below.
[14] Skylax stresses the vast social distance between kings and subjects in India.

3 Strabo 12. 4. 8, C566: *Bithynia*
That Bithynia is settled by the Mysians is attested first by Skylax of Karyanda, who says that around Lake Askania dwell Phrygians and Mysians.[15]

4 Strabo 13. 1. 4, C583: *the Troad*
'the Troad . . . but Skylax of Karyanda begins from Abydos'.[16]

5 Strabo 14. 2. 20, C658: *Karyanda*
In between (*Myndos and Bargylia*) is Karyanda: a lake, an island, ⟨and a city⟩ of the same name settled by the Karyandeis (*men of Karyanda*). From here came Skylax, the ancient writer.

6 Harpokration s.v. *hypo gēn oikountes*: *Dwellers underground*
'Living underground': ⟨Antiphon in the *On Concord*.⟩ He might be referring to the people called Trogodytai by Skylax in his *Periplous*,[17] and the people named Katoudaioi by Hesiod in (*the*) 3rd (*book*) of *Catalogue*.

7 Athenaios 2. 82, 70a–c: *The artichoke (in India?)*
kynara (*artichoke*): . . . Hekataios of Miletos in his *Periegesis of Asia* . . . also says the *kynara* grows around the river Indos. And (*either*) Skylax or Polemon[18] writes, 'The land is damp from springs and channels, and in the mountains grow *kynara* and other plants'. Also in the following words: 'From here the mountain extended on this side and that side of the river Indos, high and thick with wild vegetation and the thistle-*kynara*'.[19]

8 Philostratos, *Life of Apollonios*, 3. 47: *Bizarre peoples*
(*Iarchas, Apollonios' interlocutor, said that*) the Pygmaioi lived underground and were situated beyond the Ganges, living in the way that everyone has reported; but that the people (*called*) Skiapodes (*Shadowfoots*), or Makrokephaloi (*Longheads*), or whatever the compositions of Skylax have celebrated, lived nowhere else on Earth, nor even among the Indians.

9 Markianos, *Preface to Pseudo-Skylax*[20]
(1) Skylax of Karyanda is a very ancient man; and since most of the places in the inhabited world of ours, and in the sea within the Pillars of Herakles, were still unknown to the majority of people, he undertook to write up a voyage round

---

[15] As Ps.-Skylax does not mention L. Askania or the Phrygians, Strabo must be citing the archaic Skylax of Karyanda (SK).

[16] The *Periplous* of Ps.-Skylax does begin with the Troad immediately *after* Abydos (§§94–5); the same appears to have been true of SK.

[17] This must be SK, as the C4 *periplous* does not include E. Africa or name the Trogodytai.

[18] Polemon of Ilion (active in C2e) was a writer of *periēgēseis*.

[19] For the *kynara*, see also Hekataios 87–9.

[20] Markianos' preface stands before the text we know as Pseudo-Skylax (Ch. 7 below), which in the principal MS has its author named as Skylax of Karyanda. M. is aware of Herodotos' report about the real Skylax, and correctly places Skylax in the period before Alexander and links him to Darius (evidently Darius I/II of Persia in C6l–C5e).

the inhabited world. (2) For all the places of the eastern land Alexander the Macedonian made familiar to humankind, while the parts belonging to the western nations (*were made so*) by the bravery of the Romans, which seized them in warfare. . . .[21] (6) Ailios Dios, in the 1st book of *On Alexandria*, says that Skylax addressed his invention to Darius.

10   Markianos, *Epitome of Menippos*, 2:[22] *Sea distances*
I write these things having encountered many circumnavigations. . . . For those who seem to have researched these matters with reasoning[23] are [. . . *list of names* . . .]. Then again there are Skylax of Karyanda[24] and Botthaios:[25] for both of these men used the daily sailings, not the stades, to show the sea distances.

11   Stephanos of Byzantion κ 102: *Karyanda*
Karyanda: a city and a lake of the same name, near Myndos and Kos. Hekataios refers to it as Karyanda. . . . From here came Skylax the ancient prose-writer.

12   Constantine Porphyrogennetos, *De thematibus*, 1. 2: *Scope of Skylax's work*
. . . the *thema* (*province*) called the Armeniakon . . . neither does Strabo mention such a nomenclature . . ., nor even Skylax the Karyandene.[26]

13   Suda σ 710: *Skylax's writings*
Skylax of Karyanda: Karyanda is a city in Karia near Halikarnassos. Mathematician and man of letters. (*Wrote*) (1) *Circumnavigation (Periplous) of Places outside the Pillars of Herakles*; (2) *The History of Herakleides King of the Mylasians*; (3) *Circuit of the Earth*; (4) *Response to the History of Polybios*.[27]

14   Tzetzes (Ioannes), *Chiliades*, 7. 621–36: *Bizarre peoples*

> There is a certain book of the Karyandaian Skylax
> which writes that around India people are born
> whom they call Skiapodes, also the Otoliknoi.
> The Skiapodes have extremely wide feet,
> and at the midday time they fall to the ground
> and raise up their feet to make shade for themselves.
> The Otoliknoi, possessing huge ears,
> likewise shade themselves in the manner of parasols.

---

[21] For §§3–5, see under Ps.-Skylax, Ch. 7 below, B 6.
[22] For full text, see Ch. 21 no. 6.
[23] *meta logōn*, lit. 'with words', with 'accounts', or 'with reasons'.
[24] M. is, of course, comparing the text of what we call Ps.-Skylax against other *periploi*, but this passage confirms that late antique scholars were aware that Skylax of Karyanda wrote a *periplous*. Nothing is known of the units of distance employed by SK; it is PS who sometimes uses days and nights of sailing (but M. has forgotten that PS also gives many distances in stades).
[25] Nenci 1953 emends to 'Hekataios'; followed by Orth 2011a.
[26] This form of the *ethnikon* is otherwise unattested. On this passage, see further Ch. 17 (*Nik.*), n. 14.
[27] See introduction to chapter.

Skylax also writes ten thousand other things,

630 about Monophthalmoi (*One-eyed Folk*) and Henotiktontes (*Single-birthers*)[28]
and monsters and ten thousand other sights.
These things he declares true, in no way fabricated.
From lack of experience, I believe these things false;
but ten thousand others say they belong among true things,
that one sees such things, and yet more novel, in real life;
thus Ktesias and Iamboulos . . . [*list of authors continues*]

---

[28] Some scholars (see Kaplan 2019 on his F 7b) alter this to Enotokoitai (*Sleep-in-Ears*), cf.
Eratosthenes 17 (from Strabo), but for the idea of giving birth but once in a lifetime see Hdt. 3. 108. 4
(referring to lionesses).

3

HEKATAIOS OF MILETOS

(LATE 6TH–EARLY 5TH C. BC)

Selection of geographical testimonia and fragments

D. Graham J. Shipley

INTRODUCTION

Only the basic outline of Hekataios' life is known, though the sources indicate that he was born in the mid-6th century BC and lived into the first quarter of the 5th. He was an established figure by the time of the Ionian revolt of 499–494, when he attempted to discourage the leaders of the cities from rebelling against the Persians (Herodotos 5. 36) and later urged the defeated commanders to create a base on the island of Leros (5. 125). No evidence for him survives from his own lifetime, however, and his prose work describing all the lands in Europe and Asia that were accessible to the Greeks survives only in hundreds of 'fragments': that is, quotations, summaries, or citations by later writers. A representative (though generous) selection is offered here, focused on his geographical writing in order to indicate its scope and character.[1]

'Geography' is, of course, a term from a later period; and ancient books did not necessarily have specific or fixed titles such as we now expect. Hekataios' known works appear to have numbered just two, reported under various names: one as *Genealogiai* or *Historiai*, the other as *Periegesis* (*Guided Tour*) or *Periodos ges* (*Circuit of the Earth*).[2] Even leaving aside occasional doubts about authorship (expressed below by authors as learned as Arrian, **92**, and Athenaios, **12**), it is uncertain which of the two was the earlier;[3] both display the intellectual curiosity and rigour (especially in dealing with the physical world) that characterize the early Ionian philosophers, a group centred upon Miletos. Such was their dominance of the intellectual tradition that their Ionic dialect, in which Hekataios wrote, became the norm for prose writers until Attic became dominant. Hekataios will have learned much from the examples of Thales and his pupil Anaximandros; the latter was believed to have created the first map, upon which

---

[1] Roughly one-quarter of the known material is included below, out of Jacoby and Pownall's 398 testimonia and fragments (many subdivided and containing several related texts). Pownall 2013 includes English translations of the full set.

[2] On the *Genealogiai*, see the comprehensive collection of testimonia and fragments by Fowler 2000, 110–46, esp. 110–40; (commentary in Fowler 2013, 658–81).

[3] Pownall 2013, 'Biographical essay' section. Overview of H.: Roller 2015, 49–55.

Hekataios improved (5, 9–10), though Strabo (5) perhaps means us to understand that, unlike Anaximandros, Hekataios' writings were not themselves accompanied by a map.

One of the legacies of the Ionian philosophers was the determination to systematize the world. This may account for Hekataios' oft-quoted statement, from the opening of the *Genealogiai*, that 'the stories (*logoi*) of the Hellenes are numerous and risible, as they seem to me'.[4] Implicit therein is the exposing of contradiction and inconsistency between different versions, and a claim to authority in establishing truth and advancing understanding. Hence we see the beginnings of a systematic construction of the form of the Earth (e.g. 17, cf. 58 on the far north), explanations of the divine genealogy of the parts of the cosmos (26), a definition of the Sun's physical nature (8), and reckonings of the size of the Black Sea and adjacent bodies of water (59–60). Hekataios may have pronounced on etymology (e.g. 47, 76, 80) and changes of place-name (81), though in the latter case it is not always possible to be sure on the basis of Stephanos' laconic lemmata. He entered into debates, presumably already under way, about disputed locations (e.g. 73–4, 76) and we see hints of a desire to correct his predecessors (e.g. 42 on the rivers of Akarnania). In so doing, he established a set of precedents for the organization of geographical material.

The 111 extracts below illustrate a remarkably wide-ranging blend of mythological history, genealogy, linguistics, etymology, ethnography, and natural history. In some extracts (e.g. 35, 41, 43–4, 56, 79), we appear to have a bald enumeration of places in coastal or topographical sequence; but neither work as a whole was a mere *periplous* or coastal 'voyage', for they covered inland areas of Europe and Asia, insofar as information was available.[5] It is evident that Hekataios enlivened his topographical narrative with details such as customs, including diet and dress (e.g. 28, 47, 57, 84, 100–1, 104), the local flora (33, 87–9), and domesticated animals (37).

Equally characteristic is his concern to relate Homer's poems to current geography (implied, perhaps, in 66–7). Homer himself had set an example by combining space and history: the Catalogue of Ships, for example, includes within its regionally ordered account of the Greek homeland the story of Thamyris' meeting with the Muses at Dorion (*Il.* 2. 594–600; see Prologue to the present volumes). The Trojan war, unsurprisingly, lies behind several of Hekataios' discussions (e.g. 66–7).[6] A wider interest in mythology (e.g. 15, 22, 25, 27) and the legendary origins of names (e.g. 72, 75, 77–8, 96–7, 111) is also a marked feature. Recurrent figures include Herakles (22, 24–5, perhaps 29) and the Argonauts (17–18, 21, and possibly 16, 23, and 29).

Later writers indicate their approval of Hekataios' wide knowledge and reliability. He was believed to have travelled widely (e.g. 9), and the very specific data he includes are evidence of detailed research, whether conducted on the spot or through oral and written sources. Repeatedly we encounter rivers of both continental importance

---

[4] Pseudo-Demetrios (C3 BC), Περὶ ἑρμηνείας (*De elocutione, On Style*), 12 (Roberts 1902, 74–5) = *BNJ* 1 F 1a (Pownall 2013; my translation).

[5] If the name 'Botthaios' in Markianos, *Epitome of Menippos*, 2 (Ch. 34, section C, no. 41 with n. 174), conceals that of Hekataios, the latter expressed distances in days' sailing.

[6] Also perhaps 30, Bellerophon being the grandfather of Sarpedon and Glaukos.

(17–18, 42, 58, 61, 89, 91–2, 99) and local (23–4, 35, 37–8, 61, 67, 72, 75–6), lakes (48, 50, 61, 110), capes (68), mountains (40, 71, 74, 87), and enumerations of cities on islands with more than one *polis* (52, 54).[7]

The indications above are enough to substantiate Hekataios' legacy. Particularly influential upon geographical writers such as Phileas (Introduction, §VI. 4. b) and Eudoxos of Knidos (Chapter 6 below) were the 'global' scope of the *Periegesis*; the division, perhaps original, of the known world into continents—first Europe, then Asia including 'Libyē' (Africa); its topographical organization, beginning in the far west and indicating when places follow one another in a clockwise progress (cf. e.g. 35, 107); and the emphasis upon 'nations and cities' (usually Greek city-states, *poleis*) as the building-blocks of the mental journey (3). Not partaking of the highly standardized use of the word *polis* in Classical times,[8] he applies the term to non-Greek cities as well as Hellenic,[9] which suggests something more than discrimination between Hellenic and the non-Hellenic spheres: a desire to unify the data.

Extracts are here assigned, when possible, to one or the other work of Hekataios', according to Pownall's edition,[10] then by book number within that work, then by section or theme within a book (if any). In parts I (general texts) and II (the *Historiai* or *Genealogiai*), extracts are ordered by date within each section or subsection; in part III (the *Periegesis* or *Periodos ges*) they are sequenced topographically. Many extracts are simply jejune entries from the surviving 10th-century epitome (précis) of Stephanos of Byzantion's 6th-century *Ethnika*, which occasionally include what are evidently verbatim quotations from Hekataios.[11] A selection from those entries has been made here, in order to illustrate the range of Hekataios' geographical and thematic coverage.

SELECTED FURTHER READING

Bertelli, L. (2001), 'Hecataeus: from genealogy to historiography', in N. Luraghi (ed.), *The Historian's Craft in the Age of Herodotus* (Oxford), 67–94.

Braun, T. F. R. G. (2004), 'Hecataeus' knowledge of the western Mediterranean', in K. Lomas (ed.), *Greek Identity in the Western Mediterranean: Papers in honour of Professor B. B. Shefton* (Leiden), 287–347.

Burstein, S. M. (2009), 'Hecataeus of Miletus and the Greek encounter with Egypt', *Ancient West and East*, 8: 133–46.

Fowler, R. L. (2000), *Early Greek Mythography*, i: *Texts*. Oxford.

—— (2001), 'Early historiē and literacy', in N. Luraghi (ed.), *The Historian's Craft in the Age of Herodotus* (Oxford), 95–115.

—— (2013), *Early Greek Mythography*, ii: *Commentary*. Oxford.

*Pownall, F. (2013), 'Hekataios of Miletos (1)', in *BNJ*.

---

[7] On such islands, see Reger 1997.   [8] On H.'s use of *polis*, see Hansen 1997.

[9] The many examples below include 24, 29, 34–5, 62, 64, 83, 85, 94–5, 105–7, and 109.

[10] Pownall 2013, who follows the numbering of Jacoby in *FGrH* 1.

[11] For the practice of epitomization, see Introduction, §VIII. 3 init.

Thomas, R. (2006), 'The intellectual milieu of Herodotus', in C. Dewald and J. M. Marincola (eds), *The Cambridge Companion to Herodotus* (Cambridge), 60–75.

West, S. R. (1991), 'Herodotus' portrait of Hecataeus', *Journal of Hellenic Studies*, 111: 144–60.

A. GENERAL TEXTS

In date order.

1 Herodotos 2. 143. 1: *Hekataios' travels*
And earlier, after Hekataios the prose writer (*logopoios*), while at (*Egyptian*) Thebes, set out his own ancestry and linked his family line to the sixteenth (*ancestor*), a god, the priests of Zeus treated him in the same way as they did me, though I had not set out my ancestry.

2 Agatharchides §65: *Early geographers*
The whole inhabited world, as he (*Agatharchides*) says, being encircled in four parts—I mean east, west, north, and south—the westerly parts have been covered by Lykos and Timaios, the easterly by Hekataios and Basilis, the northerly by Diophantos and Demetrios, and the southerly—a burdensome task, he says, which is the truth—by ourselves.[12]

3 Dionysios of Halikarnassos, *On Thucydides*, 5: *Hekataios' style*
As I am about to begin my writing about Thucydides, I wish to say a few things about the other writers: both those older than he and those who lived around the same time as him. From this will be evident both this man's design, by using which he distinguished himself from those before him, and his power.   (2) For the ancient writers were numerous and were born in many places before the Peloponnesian war; among them are . . . Hekataios of Miletos . . .

(3) These men used a similar design as regards the selection of topics and had quite similar powers to one another. Some composed Hellenic histories, others barbarian. They did not weave these into each other, but divided their material by nations and cities, presenting them separately from one another. They maintained the same goal: to present for common knowledge any memories preserved by local people in their several nations or cities, including written accounts either in sanctuaries or in public places; (*they retailed them*) in the form in which they had received them, neither adding anything to them nor subtracting from them. Among these were various myths that have been believed for ages since, as well as certain theatrical reversals of fortune that seem full of nonsense to people of today.   (4) They all adopted, for the most part, the same diction—those of them that chose the same form of dialect—namely a clear, accessible, clean, concise style appropriate to the material and exhibiting no

---

[12] Pownall 2013, on T 14, argues (against Fowler 2000, 115), that the eastward emphasis of this quotation suggests it refers to H. of Miletos rather than H. of Abdera.

technical intricacy. There occurs in their works, nevertheless, a certain suitability and grace—more so in some than in others—because of which their writings still survive.[13]

4 Strabo 1. 1. 1, C1: *Pioneers of geography*
We consider that geography is part of the business of a philosopher, if anything is. . . . For the first men bold enough to grasp it were such as Homer, Anaximandros of Miletos, Hekataios—his (*fellow*) citizen, as Eratosthenes also says—as well as Demokritos, Eudoxos, Dikaiarchos, Ephoros, and several others; and those who came after them, Eratosthenes, Polybios, and Poseidonios, were still philosophers (*practising geography*).

5 Strabo 1. 1. 11, C7: *Homer's geographical successors*
What I have said may now be taken as evidence that Homer was the pioneer[14] of geography (*geōgraphia*). Those who followed him are conspicuously notable as men and as adherents of philosophy. The first two of them, after Homer, are said by Eratosthenes to have been Anaximandros, a close associate and fellow-citizen of Thales, and Hekataios of Miletos. (*He says that*) the former was the first to publish a geographical map (*pinax*),[15] while the latter left a treatise (*gramma*)[16] which is inferred from his other writing (*graphē*) to be his.

6 Strabo 7. 3. 6, C298–9: *Homer's knowledge of distant places*
What Apollodoros[17] has said in his preface to book 2 of *On Ships* (*i.e. the Homeric catalogue*) could only in the slightest degree be asserted. For he praises Eratosthenes for saying that Homer and other early writers knew about Greek (*places*) but were seriously lacking in experience of those further off. . . . From these authors he goes on to those who talk about the Rhipaia mountains[18] . . . and the city of Kimmeris in Hekataios.[19]

7 Pliny, *Natural History*, 1. 4–6 and 18: *Pliny's sources*
In the 4th book are contained places, peoples, seas, towns, harbours, mountains, rivers, measurements, and peoples who exist or who existed . . . from these authors: . . . foreign (*i.e. non-Roman*): Polybius, Hecataeus . . .

---

[13] *BNJ* 1 F 17b, §23 of the same passage by Dionysios, largely duplicates the above but also specifies that authors earlier than Thucydides wrote in either Attic or Ionic Greek. The latter was H.'s native dialect.

[14] Lit. 'began (ἦρξεν–*ērxen*) geography'.

[15] Cf. **9–10**. On the meanings of *pinax*, see the Introduction, §V, and the Glossary.

[16] Lit. 'a writing', i.e. a written thing rather than the act or process of writing.

[17] *BNJ* 244 F 157a. Apollodoros of Athens (C2l) wrote a commentary on the Homeric *Catalogue of Ships*.

[18] A semi-legendary mountain range bounding the N of the *oikoumenē*; see e.g. Podossinov 2019.

[19] Possibly Hekataios of Abdera (C4l), *BNJ* 264 F 8, rather than our H. The historical Kimmerioi (under various names) were believed to have invaded Asia Minor in C7 (Hdt. 1. 6, 16, etc.), perhaps from an area N of the Black Sea; but Homer (*Od.* 11. 14) had located them beyond Okeanos. Their city was probably a Greek fiction.

In the 5th book are contained places, peoples, seas, towns, harbours, mountains, rivers, measurements, and peoples who exist or who existed . . . from these authors: . . . foreign: King Juba, Hecataeus . . .

In the 6th book . . . (*the same*).

In the 18th book are contained the natures of fruits . . . from these authors: . . . foreign: . . . Hecataeus . . .

8 Aëtios, *De placitis* 2. 20. 6: *Hekataios' cosmology*
Herakleitos and Hekataios (*say*) that the Sun is the intelligent, kindled object that comes from the sea.

9 Agathemeros i. 1: *Hekataios' map*[20]
Anaximandros of Miletos, a pupil of Thales, was the first man bold enough to draw the inhabited world on a map (*pinax*).[21] After him Hekataios of Miletos, a much-travelled man, examined the matter thoroughly to the extent that it was a cause of wonder . . .

10 scholion to Dionysios Periegetes, p. 428, col. i, ll. 7–9: *Hekataios' map*
Who were the first men to draw (*graphein*) the *oikoumenē* on a map (*pinax*)?[22] First Anaximandros, second Hekataios of Miletos, third Demokritos the pupil of Thales,[23] and fourth Eudoxos. . . .

11 Athenaios 2. 82, 70a–b: *Hekataios' book on Asia*
Hekataios of Miletos (*says this*) in his *Periegesis of Asia*—if it is a genuine book of that writer, for Kallimachos records it as the work of Nesiotes.

12 Athenaios 9. 79, 410e: *Hekataios' book on Asia*
As Hekataios, too, shows, in the (*periegesis*) entitled *Asia*, or whoever wrote the *Periegeseis*.

13 Avienus, *Ora maritima*, 32–42: *Avienus' sources*

> You asked, if you remember, what the region
> of the Maeotic sea is. I knew that Sallust
> had reported this, and I could not deny that his words
> are accepted by everyone to be of settled
> authority. So, to his famous description,
> where that writer, adept with his pen and truthful,
> set out in elegant words the pattern and appearance
> of those places almost as though they were

40 > before our sight, I have added many things
> taken from the commentaries of very many authors.
> Obviously, Hecataeus the Milesian will be found there . . .

---

[20] See nn. to Agathemeros i. 1 in Ch. 29 below.   [21] Cf. n. to **5**.   [22] See **5, 9**.
[23] Pownall observes that this is probably an error: for Demokritos as author of a work on geography, see **4**.

14   Suda ε 360: *Hekataios' biography*
Hekataios son of Hegesandros, from Miletos: He was born in the time of Darius who ruled (*Persia*) after Kambyses, . . . in the 65th Olympiad (*520–516 BC*). History writer. Herodotos of Halikarnassos has benefited from his work, being younger. . . . He was the first person to write history in prose, though Pherekydes was the first to write a composition (*in prose*), for those of Akousilaos are not genuine.

B. HISTORIES OR GENEALOGIES

Extracts are arranged by date within each section or subsection.

BOOK 1

15   scholion to Homer, *Odyssey,* 10. 139: *On mythology*
'Both were born of light-bringing Helios and from their mother, Persē, whom Okeanos bore as child': Persē is the daughter of Okeanos and wife of Helios. From Helios and Persē (*came*) Aiētes and Circe; though Hesiod and Hekataios call her Perseïs.

16   scholion A to Apollonios of Rhodes 1. 551: *The ship Argo*
'The work of Athena Itonis': there is a sanctuary of Itonian Athena at Koroneia in Boiotia; but Apollonios would not speak of Athena in relation to the building of *Argo* by her surname at Koroneia, but rather by that from Thessalian Itonia, about which Hekataios speaks in the 1st (*book*) of his *Histories*.

17   scholion B to Apollonios of Rhodes 4. 257–62: *The Argonauts' route*
Herodoros in his *Argonauts* says that they (*the Argonauts*) came back through the same sea through which they came to Kolchis. But Hekataios of Miletos (*says*) that from the Phasis they went through to the Ocean, then from there into the Nile, and thence into our sea.

18   scholion B to Apollonios of Rhodes 4. 282–91: *The Argonauts' route*
Hesiod says they (*the Argonauts*) sailed in along the Phasis; but Hekataios [—] . . . ⟨Artemidoros, however,⟩ criticizes him, reporting that the Phasis does not discharge into the sea; nor did they sail along the Tanaïs, but via the same voyage as before, as Sophokles reports in his *Skythians* and Kallimachos [—] . . . (*says*) some of them, after sailing into the Adriatic, did not find the Argonauts, while others (*sailed*) between the Kyanean rocks to Kerkyra, where they were at the time. The Istros comes down from the Hyperboreans, and when it reaches the locality between Skythia and Thrace it splits into two; one part of it discharges into the Euxeinos Pontos, the other into the Tyrrhenic (*Etruscan*) sea.[24]

---

[24] Wendel adopts a suggested emendation to 'Trinakrian sea', i.e. Sicilian.

19   Stephanos of Byzantion α 288: *A Dorian city*
Amphanai: a Dorian city. Hekataios, in (*the*) 1st (*book*) of *Genealogies*.

20   Stephanos of Byzantion ο 25: *A city belonging to Argos*
Oinē: a city of (*i.e. belonging to*) Argos. Hekataios, *Histories*, 1st (*book*).[25]

21   Stephanos of Byzantion φ 12: *Part of the story of the Argonauts*
Phalanna: a city in Perrhaibia, (*named*) after Phalanna daughter of Tyro.[26] . . . Hekataios, *Histories*, 1st (*book*), calls her Hippia.

BOOK 2

22   Strabo 8. 3. 9, C341: *Herakles' labours*
Hekataios of Miletos says the Eleians are not the same people as the Epeians; at least, (*he says*) the Epeians marched with Herakles against Augeas and destroyed Augeas and Elis with him. He says Dyme is both Epeian and Achaian.

23   scholion to Apollonios of Rhodes 2. 998–1000: *North-east Europe*
'Lykastiai': ⟨Lykastos⟩ is a place in Leukosyria, after which he (*Apollonios Rhodios*) called the Amazons Lykastiai. He also calls them Chadesiai, as does Hekataios, from the (*river*) Chadesios.

24   Stephanos of Byzantion χ 2: *Herakles' labours*
Chadisia: a city of the Leukosyroi (*White Syrians*). Hekataios, *Genealogies*, 2nd (*book*): 'the plain (*called*) Themiskyre extends from Chadisiē to (*the river*) Thermodon'.

25   Stephanos of Byzantion ψ 21: *Herakles' labours in Arkadia*
Psophis: a city in Arkadia. It has been given its name after Psophis daughter of Lykaon, by whom they say the city was founded in olden times; or after Psophis daughter of Eryx. There is another city of Psophis in Akarnania, known as Palaia (*Old*) [—].[27] There is also a third in Achaia. The citizen should have been a Psophites . . . but it (*the ethnic*) comes from the genitive, like Arkadios from Arkas, and Aulidios from Aulis: thus Psophidios from Psophidos. Hekataios, *Genealogies*, 2nd (*book*): 'there was a boar on the mountain, and it did great harm to the Psophidioi'.

26   Natalis Comes, *Mythologiae*, 7. 2: *River myths*
Alkaios perceived him (*Acheloös*) to be the son of Ocean and Earth, and Hecataeus said of Sun and Earth.[28]

---

[25] This extract is chosen as a typical 'minimal' entry in Steph. Byz.
[26] Mother of Pelias king of Iolkos, who sent Jason and the Argonauts to the Black Sea (Pownall).
[27] Fowler follows Meineke in supposing that a name has dropped out.
[28] Natalis Comes (Natale Conti, 1520–82) wrote an influential and oft-reprinted compendium of ancient mythology interpreted allegorically. In this and the next extract, he may be drawing on

27   Natalis Comes, *Mythologiae*, 9. 9: *Herakles' labours?*
This (*that Callisto became the constellation Ursa Major*) is what Pausanias wrote in his *Arcadica*.[29] . . . He also says she was shot with arrows to gratify Juno (*Hera*) even though Dia, mother of Dryops, was also a daughter of his, as Hecataeus has written.[30]

BOOK 3

28   Athenaios 4. 31, 148f: *The Arkadian diet*
Portraying an Arkadian meal, the Milesian Hekataios, in (*the*) 3rd (*book*) of the *Genealogies*, says it was 'barley-cakes and pig flesh'.

BOOK 4

29   scholion c to Apollonios of Rhodes 2. 946–54: *The Amazons*
'Next Sinope': . . . The Teian Andron (*from Teos*) says that one of the Amazons, fleeing to the Pontos, married the king of those places and, after drinking a very large quantity of wine, was named Sanape, since drunkards are called *sanapai* among the Thracians, whose dialect the Amazons also use; ⟨and⟩ the city was called ⟨Sanape⟩ and then by deformation Sinope. The drunken Amazon came to Lytidas from ⟨this⟩ city, as Hekataios says.

30   Stephanos of Byzantion µ 126: *A city's foundation*
Melia: a city in Karia.[31] Hekataios, *Genealogies*, 4th (*book*). The ethnic is Meliëus.

31   Stephanos of Byzantion µ 227: *A city*
Mygissos: a city in Karia. Hekataios, 4th (*book*) of *Genealogies*. The ethnic is Mygissios; there is also Athena Mygissia and (*Athena*) Mysigais.

32   Stephanos of Byzantion τ 178: *Names of the Lykians*
Tremile: Lykia used to be called by this name.[32] The inhabitants are Tremileis, after Tremiles, as Panyasis says . . . (*his verses are quoted*). Alexandros (*Polyhistor*), 2nd (*book*), says, 'But when ⟨Tremiles⟩ died, Bellerophon renamed the Tremileis Lykians'. Hekataios calls them Tremilai in (*the*) 4th (*book*) of *Genealogies*.

---

manuscript sources now lost to us, perhaps of post-Cl works which were themselves compilations of nuggets going back to H.'s day. Although we cannot rely unconditionally on Conti—who certainly fabricated and manipulated evidence (see e.g. Gysembergh 2020, 3–4, and earlier studies cited there, especially Mulryan and Brown 2006, xvi)—the subjects are typical of H. (Pownall).

---

[29] i.e. book 8 of the *Periegesis of Hellas*.

[30] This extract is chosen to illustrate H.'s interest in verifying the details of myths.

[31] Later sources place Melia or Meliē in Ionia; according to tradition, it was destroyed by the other Ionians *c.*700 BC (Shipley 1987, 29–31).

[32] Hdt. tells of this change of name at 1. 171. 3; 7. 92.

C. PERIEGESIS (GUIDED TOUR) OR PERIODOS GES (CIRCUIT OF THE EARTH)

Arranged topographically within each region, retaining the order in *BNJ* with a few exceptions.

BOOK 1: EUROPE

33 Harpokration s.v. *rhodōniá: Flower names*
'Rose-bed': . . . a rose-bed (*rhodōniá*) is a planting of roses (*rhoda*), as a violet-bed (*iōniá*) is one of violets (*ía*), as Hekataios shows in (*the*) 1st (*book*) of *Periegesis*.[33]

Iberia

34 Stephanos of Byzantion ε 55: *Iberia?*
Elibyrge:[34] a city of (*i.e. belonging to*) Tartessos. Hekataios, *Europe*. The ethnic is Elibyrgios.

35 Stephanos of Byzantion υ 30: *Iberia*
Hyops: a city in Iberia, on a peninsula. Hekataios, *Europe*: 'After (*this is*) the city of Hyops, and after (*it*) the river of Lesyros.'[35] The ethnic is Hyopios, from the genitive.

ITALY

36 Stephanos of Byzantion κ 138: *Italia*
Kaulonia: a city in Italia, which Hekataios calls Aulonia because it lies in the middle of an *aulōn* (*defile*). From the *aulōn* it was later renamed Kaulonia, just as Metapontion (*was renamed*) after the hero Metabos, Epitauros (*was renamed*) Epidauros, and Plazomenai Klazomenai.[36]

37 Stephanos of Byzantion α 65: *The Adriatic*
Adria: a city; also beside it the Adrias (*Adriatic*) gulf, and a river similarly (*named*), as Hekataios (*says*). The land is good for cattle, so much so that they give birth twice each year and bear twins, and often even three and four calves; occasionally even five and more. And the chickens lay twice a day, yet are smaller in size than all other (*domesticated*) birds.[37]

---

[33] H. probably referred to these flowers in relation to the names of the island of Rhodes and of the Ionians.

[34] Possibly mod. *Granada* (Pownall).

[35] These places are unknown; the quotation suggests that his work at least partly consisted of a bare enumeration of places in sequence (Pownall).

[36] Kaulonia was in fact probably named after the hero Kaulon (Billerbeck iii. 69 n. 193).

[37] This and other such entries are chosen because the additional comments preserved by Steph. are assumed to represent information imparted by H., unless another author is named.

THE GREEK MAINLAND

We follow '*periplous* order', though Hekataios appears to have described the Adriatic coast from south to north (see **41**).

38   Strabo 7. 5. 8, C316: *The river Aōos*
The Aōos, on which is the city of Apollonia (*in the Adriatic*) . . . But Hekataios calls the Aōos 'Aias', and says that from the same spot, around Lakmos, or rather from the same inner location, the Inachos flows south to Argos and the Aias west towards the Adriatic.

39   Stephanos of Byzantion χ 22: *A region in Epeiros*
Chaonia: the central part of Epeiros. . . . Hekataios, *Europe*: 'the Kirrhaios gulf[38] and the plain in Chaonike'.

40   Stephanos of Byzantion δ 52: *A nation in Epeiros*
Dexaroi: a nation (*ethnos*) belonging to the Chaones, neighbours of the Encheleai. Hekataios, *Europe*: 'they live under the Ameros mountain'.[39]

41   Stephanos of Byzantion ω 15: *A city in Epeiros*
Orikos: a city in the Ionian gulf. Hekataios, in the *Europe*, calls Orikos a harbour in Epeiros: 'after (*this is*) the city of Bouthrotos, and after (*this*) the harbour of Orikos'.[40]

42   Strabo 6. 2. 4, C271: *River Inachos in Akarnania*
Numerous rivers run under the Earth in many parts of the Earth, but none over such a distance (*as the Alpheios is supposed to do*). Supposing this were possible, at any rate the things mentioned above are impossible, just like the myth of the Inachos . . . Hekataios is better (*than Sophokles*): he says the Inachos in (*the land of*) the Amphilochians, which flows from Lakmos from where the Aias also flows, is not the same as the one in the Argolid, but was named after Amphilochos, who also gave his name to the city of 'Amphilochian' Argos (*in Akarnania*). He says this discharges into the Acheloös, while the Aias flows west to Apollonia.

43   Stephanos of Byzantion χ 7: *A city in Western Lokris*
Chalaion: a city of the Lokroi. Hekataios, *Europe*: 'after (*this are*) the Lokroi; and in (*their territory*) the city of Chalaion; also in it is the city of Oianthe'.[41]

44   Stephanos of Byzantion χ 6: *A city in Boiotia*
Chaironeia: a city beside the frontiers of Phokis. Hekataios, *Europe*: 'in (*this territory is*), first, the city of Chaironeia'. It is named after Chairon.[42]

45   Stephanos of Byzantion γ 68: *Two cities in Boiotia*

---

[38] This is in another part of Greece: below Delphi, on the gulf of Corinth.
[39] The last words may be a quotation from H.
[40] This shows that H. narrated the Adriatic coast from S to N (Pownall).
[41] Another example of topographically organized enumeration.
[42] Son of Apollo and Thero (Pownall). See also preceding note.

Gephyra: a city in Boiotia. Some say the Tanagraioi are the same people, as (*do*) Strabo and Hekataios. From it Deo (*Demeter*) is (*called*) Gephyraia.[43]

46 Stephanos of Byzantion χ 17: *Chalkis in Euboia*
Chalkis: a city on Euboia. Hekataios, *Europe*: 'Chalkis is a city which formerly was designated Euboia'. It was called after Kombe, called Chalkis, a daughter of Asopos.[44] Some Chalkidians say it was called this because copper-working (*chalkourgeia*) first appeared among these people.

THRACE AND THE AEGEAN

47 Athenaios 10. 67, 447d: *Paionian beer*
Hekataios . . ., in his *Periodos of Europe*, says the Paiones drink 'beer made from barley groats, and *parabiē* made from millet grains with inula'.[45]

48 Stephanos of Byzantion χ 8: *A city in 'Thrace'*
Chalastra: a city in Thrace, close to the Thermaios gulf. Hekataios, *Europe*: 'in it (*the gulf*) is Therme, (*a city*) of Hellenes; and in (*it is also*) Chalastre, a city of (*the*) Thracians'.[46] . . . It has been named after Chalastre. There is also a lake which has the same name as the city.

49 Herodian, *General Prosody* **book 5 fr. 34 Hunger:**[47] *A river in Chalkidike*
These (*words ending in -óös*) we pronounce as paroxytone (*with acute accent on penultimate syllable*): I refer to *haplóös* 'single', *diplóös* 'double', *triplóös* 'triple', and any others of this kind. . . . But proper names, though they are rarely found, are proparoxytone (*with acute on antepenultimate syllable*), as with Síngoös, which is a river; so Hekataios, *Periegesis of Europe*.

50 Stephanos of Byzantion μ 81: *Maroneia in Thrace*
Maroneia: a city in Kikonia beside the peninsula in Thrace (*Thracian Chersonese*):[48] 'in (*it is*) the lake of Ismaris; in (*it is also*) the city of Maroneia'.[49]

51 Stephanos of Byzantion χ 40: *Cities named Cherronesos*
Cherronesos: a city on the peninsula beside Knidos. . . . There is a second city of Cherronesos in Thrace, of which Hekataios (*says*) in *Europe*, 'among them is the city of Cherronesos on the isthmus of the peninsula (*cherronēsos*)'.[50] They call the

---

[43] This fragment may be from the *Genealogiai* or from the *Periegesis* (Pownall).

[44] The Asopos is a river in Boiotia.

[45] Paionia is to the N and W of Macedonia. The word *parabiē* appears to be a *hapax* (a word found nowhere else).

[46] Chalastra is W of Thessalonike and the Chalkidike peninsula. Its attribution to Thrace perhaps reflects the early date of the information, before Macedonian control of this coast was established.

[47] A new fragment of Herodian, not in Lentz's edition: see *BNJ* 1 F 145a; Mette 1978, 6; first published by Hunger 1967, 10.

[48] Maroneia is in fact some 50 mi (80 km) NW of the Thracian Chersonese (*Gallipoli* peninsula).

[49] This is inferred to be a quotation from H. on the basis of its wording.

[50] Situated on the Thracian Chersonese (*Gallipoli* peninsula), the town was more correctly known as

citizen a Cherronesios: 'sharing a border with[51] the Apsinthioi to the south are the ⟨Cherronesioi⟩'.

52   Stephanos of Byzantion λ 46: *Lemnos*
Lemnos: an island next to Thrace, possessing two cities, Hephaistia and Myrina, as Hekataios (*says in*) *Europe*. (*Named*) after the so-called Great Goddess, whom they refer to as Lemnos. Virgins (*it is said*) are also sacrificed to her.

53   Stephanos of Byzantion τ 91: *Tenedos*
Tenedos: an island in the Sporades; (*or*) as Hekataios (*says*), in the Hellespont. (*Named*) after Tennes and Amphithea or Hemithea, Kyknos' children; as it were, Tennou Hedos (*Tennēs' Seat*). It was called Leukophrys (*White Brow*).

54   Stephanos of Byzantion μ 262: *Mytilene on Lesbos*
Mytilene: city on Lesbos, the largest. Hekataios, *Europe*. (*Named*) after Mytilene, daughter of Makar or of Pelops; but others say Mytiles was the founder, and others (*that it was named*) after Myton son of Poseidon and Mytilene; hence Kallimachos in the 4th (*book*) calls Lesbos Mytonis, while Parthenios says women of Lesbos are Mytonides.

55   Stephanos of Byzantion χ 44: *Chios*
Chios: the most renowned island of the Ionians, also possessing a city of the same name. Hekataios, *Europe*: 'Chios (*is*) by Erythrai; on (*it is*) the city of Chios'. (*Named*) after Chios son of Okeanos; or after the plentiful snow (*chiōn*) occurring there; or after a nymph, Chione.

56   Herodian, *On the Unique Word* 2. 31. 26 (937. 10–11 Lentz): *A city in the western Black Sea (?)*
Boryza: a Persian city, as Hekataios (*says*) in his *Periegesis of Europe*: 'after (*this is*) Boryza, a city of the Persians; and after (*this is*) Thynias'.[52]

57   Stephanos of Byzantion μ 119: *The Melanchlainoi and others in Skythia*
Melanchlainoi (*Black-cloaks*): a Skythian nation. Hekataios, *Europe*: 'they are called after what they wear, as the Hippemolgoi (*are called*) in relation to the milking of mares, and the Mossynoikoi (*Hut-dwellers*) in relation to their houses'.[53]

Agora, at least later.

[51] 'Sharing a border with' is *homoureousi*, an Ionic dialect form evidently quoted from H. directly.
[52] Boryza may be a foundation of Darius during his Skythian campaign of 513 BC, which would indicate that H. wrote later; Thynias was a name of the S coast of the Black Sea (Pownall).
[53] Evidently presented by Stephanos as a direct quotation from H. H. evidently located other Skythians in Asia: see **58**.

BOOK 2: ASIA

THE FAR NORTH

58   Pliny, *Natural History,* 4. xiii. 94

The remaining shores are obscure, (*but*) the northern Ocean is assured by report.[54] Hecataeus calls it Amalcius beyond the river Parapanisos, where it washes (*the coast of*) Scythia.[55] This name, in the language of that nation, signifies 'frozen'.

BLACK SEA

We follow a clockwise circuit.

59   *Epimerismoi Homerikoi* s.v. *memetreatai:*[56] *Size of the Black Sea*

'Have been measured': this is in Ionic. ... *memetrēntai* (*becomes*) *memetreatai* in Hekataios: 'So the Bosporos and the Pontos, and in the same way the Hellespont, have been measured in the same way by me'.[57]

60   Ammianus Marcellinus 22. 8. 10–13: *Size and shape of the Black Sea*

(10) Its (*the Black Sea's*) total coastal navigation, as if it were an insular circuit, has been measured as 23,000 stades, as Eratosthenes declares and also Hecataeus, Ptolemy, and other most detailed investigators of this sort of knowledge. It is formed into the appearance of a Skythian bow when strung, on which all of geography concurs.... (13) But the two outermost points of the bow, (*one*) on each side, are represented by the two Bospori, placed in opposite regions to one another, namely the Thracian and the Cimmerian.

61   Pseudo-Arrian, *Circumnavigation of the Black Sea,* 78: *Lake Maiotis*[58]

Taking its name from the Maiotai, 'lying next is the Maiotis lake'[59] into which the Tanaïs (*Don*), 'taking the current from the river Araxes, is mingled, as Hekataios of Teos (?) said, | or, as Ephoros reports, from a certain lake | whose limit is unstated. It (*the Tanaïs*) debouches, | with double-mouthed stream, into the so-called Maiotis | and (*then*) into the Kimmerian Bosporos'.

---

[54] Following Zehnacker and Silberman 2017, 71, who punctuate after *incerta* and print *oceanus* (not *Oceani* as in Winkler 2002, 180).

[55] The source may be H. of Abdera (cf. n. 12 above), who wrote *On the Hyperboreans* (Zehnacker and Silberman 2017, 317); but Pownall 2013 comments that H. of Miletos also wrote about the far north.

[56] This C9 AD compilation of grammatical examples (*epimerismoi* means 'parsings') from Homer probably draws on lost work by Herodian (C2 AD) and others (Cramer 1835, vol. i, p. iv); Dickey 2011. The present extract is at Cramer 1835, 287; Dyck 1995, 509 (μ 86).

[57] A direct quotation from Hdt. 4. 86. H. probably expressed the dimensions of the Black Sea in days (or days and nights) of sailing (Pownall).

[58] Possibly from H. of Abdera rather than H. of Miletos (Pownall).

[59] The words in quotation marks are metrical lines (or parts thereof) attributed to the lost second half of the *Nikomedean Periodos* (Ch. 17), incorporated in his text by the author of the Pseudo-Arrianic *Periplous of the Euxine* (Ch. 36 below). A vertical line | indicates the end of a line of verse.

62 **Stephanos of Byzantion** ε 123: *A city on the Kimmerian Bosporos*
Hermonassa (*Taman*): a small island bearing a city, in the Kimmerian Bosporos.[60] . . .
But Menippos in (*the*) *periplous* of the two Pontoi (*describes it as*) a settlement (*chōrion*)
belonging to Trapezous. But Hekataios and Theopompos describe it as a city (*polis*).

63 **Stephanos of Byzantion** χ 47: *A nation of the SE (?) Black Sea*
Choi: a nation near the Becheiroi. Hekataios, in *Asia*: 'up to this point it is the Becheirike
(*territory*); they are succeeded by the Choi'. And again: 'the Choi extend as far as these
people'. And again, 'Towards the rising sun, the Byzeres share a border with the Choi'.[61]

64 **Stephanos of Byzantion** χ 48: *A nation of the southern Black Sea*
Choirades: a city of the Mossynoikoi. Hekataios, *Europe*: 'Towards the rising sun, the
Mossynoikoi share a border with the Tibarenoi.[62] Among them is the city of Choirades'.

65 **Stephanos of Byzantion** χ 19: *A nation of the SW Black Sea*
Chalybes: a nation beside the Pontos, on the river Thermodon. . . . The Chalybes also
(*occur*) in Hekataios: 'To the south the Armenioi share a border with the Chalyboi'
(*sic*).[63]

66 **Strabo** 12. 3. 25, C552–3: *The city of Amisos and the Trojan war*
But such a view cannot be stated for all the ancients, as if all agreed that no community
from the area beyond the Halys took part in the Trojan war. . . . Apollodoros (*of Athens*)
himself presents the statement of Zenodotos, who notes (*the line*) 'From Eneta from
where the race of wild mules comes',[64] and says Hekataios of Miletos accepted (*that the
city was*) Amisos.

ASIA MINOR

67 **Strabo** 12. 3. 22, C550–1: *Places in NW Asia Minor*
The man from Skepsis (*i.e. Demetrios*) neither accepts this man's (*Ephoros'*) opinion,
it appears, nor that of people who understand the Halizones as living in the Pallene
area. . . . Similarly, he seriously doubts how one could think an alliance with the Trojans
might have been made by the nomads beyond the Borysthenes.

He particularly praises the opinion of Hekataios of Miletos and Menekrates of
Elaia, an associate of Xenokrates, as well as that of Palaiphatos. The first of these, in
his *Periodos ges*, says, 'After the city of Alazia is the river Odrysses, ⟨which⟩, flowing
through the plain of Mygdon⟨i⟩a from the west, out of Lake Daskylitis, discharges into
the Rhyndakos'.[65] He says Alazia is now deserted, though many villages are inhabited
by the Alazones and the Odrysses flows through these. . . .

What, then, is the value in praising the opinions of these men? Not only do they
alter the ancient text, but they omit to point out the silver mines, or where in the

---

[60] On its E shore, and thus in Asia if the R. Tanaïs is the limit of Europe.
[61] See n. 37.   [62] See n. 37.   [63] For 'share a border with', *homoureousi*, cf. 51.
[64] *Il.* 2. 852, altered.   [65] These places are in Phrygia, S of the Propontis.

Myrleatis Alope is, or (*say*) that the men who had come to Ilion were from far away—even supposing anywhere called Alope or Alazia existed.[66]

68   Stephanos of Byzantion α 4: *A place in the Hellespont*
Abarnos: a city, territory, ⟨and⟩ cape in the territory of Parion. . . . Hekataios of Miletos, in *Periegesis of Asia*, says that it is a cape belonging to Lampsakos.

69   Stephanos of Byzantion μ 249: *A place in the Troad*
Myrikous: a city in the Troad, opposite Tenedos and Lesbos. Hekataios: 'to Myrikoëis in the territory of Troia (*Troy*)'.

70   Stephanos of Byzantion α 245: *The other name of Kyme*
Amazoneion: . . . this was also the name of Kyme, where the Amazons used to live. But Hekataios in the *Aiolika* writes the name with the iota (*i.e. Amazonion*).

71   Stephanos of Byzantion κ 313: *Mount Korykos in Ionia*
Korykos: . . . There is also a mountain called Korykos, a masculine (*name*), a high one near Teos and Erythrai in Ionia, as Hekataios (*says*) in *Asia*.[67]

72   Stephanos of Byzantion μ 125: *The Meleteios gulf*
Meleteios kolpos: the Smyrnaian gulf was (*so*) called from the river Meles, as Hekataios (*says*) in *Aiolika*.

73   Herodian, *On the Unique Word* 1. 13. 19–20 (920. 7–8 Lentz): *Koloura near Priene*
Koloura: it is the name of a city. Thus Hekataios: 'and I think (*it is*) most likely by Koloura, where the Prieneans had their home'.

74   Strabo 14. 1. 8, C635: *The Latmian gulf*
Next is the Latmic gulf, in which lies the so-called Herakleia-under-Latmos, a small city with a minor anchorage (*hyphormos*). Formerly it was called Latmos, using the same name as that of the mountain lying above it. Hekataios indicates this, as he believes it is the same as the mountain called Phtheirai by the poet;[68] for he says the mountain of the Phtheirai lies above Latmos.

75   Stephanos of Byzantion ξ 2: *Xanthos in Lykia*
Xanthos: a city in Lykia. Hekataios, *Asia*: 'beside which issues the river Xanthos'. It was called after Xanthos of Egypt or Crete, the founder.

76   Stephanos of Byzantion ι 29: *Idyros in Pamphylia*
Idyros: a city and a river in Pamphylia, Hekataios. It is also 'Idyrís', oxytone (*i.e. with acute accent on last syllable*).

---

[66] Mygdonia is, according to Pownall here, 'in Hellespontine Phrygia'.
[67] A place named Korykos was in the territory of Erythrai in C5l (Thuc. 8. 33. 2). Cf. **80** for H.'s possible mention of another Korykos, from the same entry in Steph. Byz., but in Kilikia.
[68] *Il.* 2. 868.

77   Stephanos of Byzantion ν 3: *Nagidos in Kilikia or Pamphylia*
Nagidos: a city between Kilikia and Pamphylia.[69] Hekataios, *Asia*: 'and after (*it is*) the city of Na⟨gi⟩dos, (*named*) after Nagidos the helmsman; and the island of Nagidoussa'.

78   Stephanos of Byzantion σ 143: *Sidē in Pamphylia*
Sidē: a city in Pamphylia, as Hekataios (*says in*) *Asia*. It has been called after Sidē, the daughter of Tauros and wife of Kimolos after whom the island (*Kimolos*) is named.

79   Stephanos of Byzantion χ 24: *Charadros in Kilikia*
Charadros: a harbour and dependent harbour in Kilikia. Hekataios, *Asia*: 'and after (*it is*) the river Charadros'.

80   Stephanos of Byzantion κ 313: *Korykos in Kilikia*
Korykos: a city in Kilikia. . . . But Hekataios† calls the city Korykeia.[70]

PERSIAN EMPIRE

81   Stephanos of Byzantion δ 150: *Doros in Phoinike*
Doros: a city in Phoinike. Hekataios, *Asia*: 'and after (*it is*) the former Doros; it is now called Dora'.

82   Stephanos of Byzantion κ 287: *Kyrē in the Persian gulf*
Kyrē: an island in the Persian main (*pontos*). Hekataios in *Periegesis*, 2nd (*book*).

83   Stephanos of Byzantion π 49: *A Persian people*
Parikane: a Persian city. Hekataios, *Asia*: 'among these (*people*) is a city, Parikane by name'. The *ethnikon* is Parikanioi. They are also called Parikanoi.[71]

84   Harpokration s.v. *kypassis: A Persian garment*
kypassis: . . . Those who write about languages say that the *kypassis* is a kind of *chitōn* (*tunic*); some say it is women's wear, others men's. It is mentioned by Hipponax, and by Hekataios in *Periodos of Europe*,[72] who says, 'For clothing the Kissioi wear Persian *kypasseis*'.

85   Stephanos of Byzantion υ 57: *A city of the Matienoi (in western Asia)*
Hyope: a city of the Matienoi, adjacent to the Gordioi.[73] Hekataios, *Asia*: 'in (*it is*) the city of Hyope. The people wear clothing such as the Paphlagonians wear'.

---

[69] Ps.-Skylax §102. 1 locates it in Kilikia.

[70] The text (from the same entry as **71**, referring to Ionia) is not certain, H.'s name depending on an emendation of ἐκεῖ–*ekei* ('there') not adopted by Billerbeck, who understands 'There they refer to it as Korykeia'. The MSS vary between 'refers' (φησι) and 'refer' (φασι).

[71] Probably the people in Media called Parikanioi by Hdt. 3. 92. 1.

[72] Pownall in *BNJ* 1 F 284, following Jacoby, adopts the emendation 'Asia' in place of 'Europe', perhaps rightly.

[73] Hdt. mentions these Matienoi at 3. 94. 1; they lived N of Media (Pownall).

86   Stephanos of Byzantion μ 232: *The Mykoi*
Mykoi: a nation about which Hekataios in *Asia* (*says*), 'from the Mykoi to the river Araxes'.[74]

87   Athenaios 2. 82, 70a: *The cardoon (or artichoke) found beside the Caspian sea*
kinara: . . . Hekataios of Miletos, in *Periegesis of Asia*, . . . speaks thus: 'around the sea called Hyrkanian are high mountains, thickly wooded, and on the mountains (*is the*) *kynara* (*sic*) thorn'.[75]

88   Athenaios 2. 82, 70b: *The cardoon found in Chorasmia*
And (*Hekataios says*) the following: 'Towards the rising sun from the Parthians, the Chorasmians occupy the land. They have both plains and mountains; and in the mountains are wild trees, the *kynara* thorn, willow, and tamarisk'.[76]

INDIA

89   Athenaios 2. 82, 70b: *The cardoon found beside the Indos*
He (*Hekataios*) also says the *kynara* occurs in the area of the river Indos.[77]

90   Stephanos of Byzantion γ 31: *The Gandarai of India*
Gandarai: a nation of Indians. Hekataios, *Asia*. They are also called Gandarioi in his work, and the land Gandarike.

91   Stephanos of Byzantion ω 13: *The Opiai of India*
Opiai: an Indian nation. Hekataios, *Asia*: 'among them live people along the river Indos, the Opiai; and in (*their land is*) a royal fortress. The Opiai (*extend*) up to this point; but beyond these is a desert up to the Indians.'

EGYPT

92   Arrian, *Anabasis of Alexander*, 5. 6. 5: *Importance of the Nile*
The prose writers (*logopoioi*) Herodotos and Hekataios—whether or not the writings concerning the Egyptian land are by someone other than Hekataios—call Egypt 'the gift of the Nile'. That this is the case has been demonstrated by Herodotos using evidence that is far from obscure.

93   Stephanos of Byzantion φ 8: *A village in Egypt*
Phakoussa: a village between Egypt and the Erythraian sea.[78] . . . But Hekataios refers to it as Phakoussai and (*in the dative case*) Phakoussais.[79] There are also Phakoussai islands and Phakaioi.

---

[74] The Mykoi lived around the straits of *Hormuz* (Pownall).
[75] The *kinara* or *kynara* was probably the cardoon or wild artichoke (Pownall). Continued by **88–9**. Cf. Skylax of Karyanda 7.
[76] Follows **87**; continued by **89**.   [77] Follows **87–8**.
[78] The western Indian Ocean plus the mod. *Red Sea*.
[79] Phakousa is at the S point of the Delta (Pownall).

94 **Stephanos of Byzantion** α 79: *A province and city in Egypt*
Atharrhabis: a city in Egypt . . . But Hekataios, in (*the*) 2nd (*book*) of *Periegesis*, (*writes it*) using one rho and a mu: 'the Atharambites province and the city of Atharambe'.

95 **Stephanos of Byzantion** χ 39: *An island in the Delta*
Chemmis: a city in Egypt. . . . There is also an island of Chembis, with a beta, among the Boutoi, as Hekataios (*says*) in *Periegesis of Egypt*: 'among the Boutoi, near the sanctuary of Leto, is an island, Chembis by name, sacred to Apollo; the island is free-floating, sails upon the water, and moves around'.

96 **Herodian,** *On the Unique Word* 2. 36. 29–31 (942. 11–13 Lentz): *On the name Pharos*
pharos: . . . a masculine noun, for this is how the steersman of Menelaos was called. But there is also a feminine, applied to the island which took its name from him, as Hekataios says.

97 Aelius Aristeides, *Oration* 36. 108: *On the name Kanobos*
Indeed, Kanobos is the name of Menelaos' helmsman, both as Hekataios the prose writer (*logopoios*) says and also as common opinion (*has it*); as he died near this locality, his name remains.

98 **Stephanos of Byzantion** ε 43: *An Egyptian locality*
Heleneios: a locality by Kanobos. Hekataios, *Periegesis of Libyē*.

99 **Stephanos of Byzantion** ε 179: *On names of islands in the Nile*
Ephesos: . . . There is also an island of Ephesos in the Nile, also a Chios, a Lesbos, a Cyprus, a Samos, and others; as Hekataios (*says*).

100 **Athenaios** 10. 67, 447c: *Egyptian bread and drink*
Hekataios in book 2 of his *Periegesis*, speaking of how the Egyptians are bread-eaters, offers this: 'they grind barley groats to make their drink'.[80]

101 **Athenaios** 10. 13, 418e: *Egyptian bread*
Hekataios says the Egyptians are bread-eaters, as they eat *kyllēstiai* (*sourdough bread*) and grind barley groats to make a drink.[81]

102 **Stephanos of Byzantion** υ 49: *Aithiopian islands*
Hysaëis: a small island and a large one (*belonging to*) the Aithiopes. Hekataios, *Periegesis of Egypt*.

103 **Stephanos of Byzantion** σ 204: *The Aithiopian Skiapodes*
Skiapodes (*Shadowfoots*): an Aithiopian nation, as Hekataios (*says*) in *Periegesis of Egypt*.

---

[80] See n. to **101**.
[81] Cf. **100**. Athenaios has discussed *kyllastis* (*sic*), 'sourdough bread', a few pages earlier (3. 114c = Hekat. F 322 Pownall), referring to *kyllastis* (cf. Hdt. 2. 77. 4).

104 Athenaios 9. 79, 410e: *An item of headwear*

Sappho: . . . she says *cheirōmaktra* are an ornament for the head, just as Hekataios, or the composer of the *periēgēseis*, demonstrates in the *Asia*: 'women have *cheirōmaktra* on their head'.[82]

REMAINDER OF LIBYĒ

105 Stephanos of Byzantion μ 86: *A city in Libyē*

Maskotos: a city in Libyē. Hekataios, *Periegesis*, ⟨2nd⟩ (*book*). It is near Hesperides.

106 Stephanos of Byzantion φ 86: *Phoenician islands off Carthage*

Phoinikoussai: two islands in the Libyan gulf, by Carthage, as Hekataios (*says in*) *Periegesis of Libyē*. . . . There is also a city of the Phoenicians (*who live*) in Syria, Phoinikoussai, as the same (*author*) says in *Asia*.

107 Stephanos of Byzantion μ 108: *A city in Libyē*

Megasa: similar to 'Gerasa'; a city in Libyē. Hekataios, *Periegesis of Asia*: 'next after it come grain-eaters and ploughmen'.[83]

108 Stephanos of Byzantion κ 246: *An Ionian city in Libyē*

Kybos: a city of the Ionians, in the Phoenicians' Libyē. Hekataios, *Periegesis* of it (*the region*): 'and the harbour of [—] ⟨and Hip⟩pou Akra (*Cape Horse*), and Kybō' (*sic*).

109 Stephanos of Byzantion θ 60: *An island near the strait of Gibraltar*

Thrinke: a city in the area of the Pillars. Hekataios, *Asia*.

110 Herodian, *On the Unique Word* 2. 31. 25–6 (937. 9–10 Lentz): *A lake in Libyē beyond the Pillars*

Douriza: a lake beside the river Liza.[84] Hekataios, *Periegesis of Asia*: 'the lake, Douriza by name'.

111 Stephanos of Byzantion μ 131: *A city in western Libyē*

Melissa (*Bee*): a city of the Libyans.[85] Hekataios, *Asia*. The founder is Melissaios, the land Melissaia.

---

[82] This may refer to Egypt: at Hdt. 2. 122, Rhampsinitos, mythical king of Egypt, dices with Demeter and wins a golden *cheirŏnaktron* (printed thus, with short *o*, by N. G. Wilson 2015b), probably the same as a pharaoh's head-dress (Pownall). At Hdt. 4. 64. 2, the Skythians use softened human scalps as *cheirōmaktra* (*sic* Wilson) and stitch them together into articles of clothing. Among the Medes, the word meant a napkin for wiping the hands (Xenophon, *Cyropaedia*, 1. 3. 5).

[83] As Pownall notes (citing Jacoby and others), this is one of the extracts that shows H. proceeded westwards in his account of Libyē.

[84] The Liza is the same as the Lixos (e.g. Ps.-Skyl. §112. 4).

[85] Mentioned by Hanno §5 as having been founded by Carthaginians; but 'Melissaios' is a Greek name.

PART TWO
CLASSICAL PERIOD

∽

(c. 500–323 BC)

Here are we who once left the Aegean's deep-roaring swell.
Now we lie in the midmost spot in the plain of Ekbatana.
Farewell, once-famous fatherland, Eretria. Farewell, Athens,
neighbours to Euboia! Farewell, beloved sea (*thalassa*)!

Plato, *Anthologia Graeca*, 7. 256 (my translation)

4

HANNO OF CARTHAGE

(5TH C. BC?)

Richard J. A. Talbert and D. Graham J. Shipley

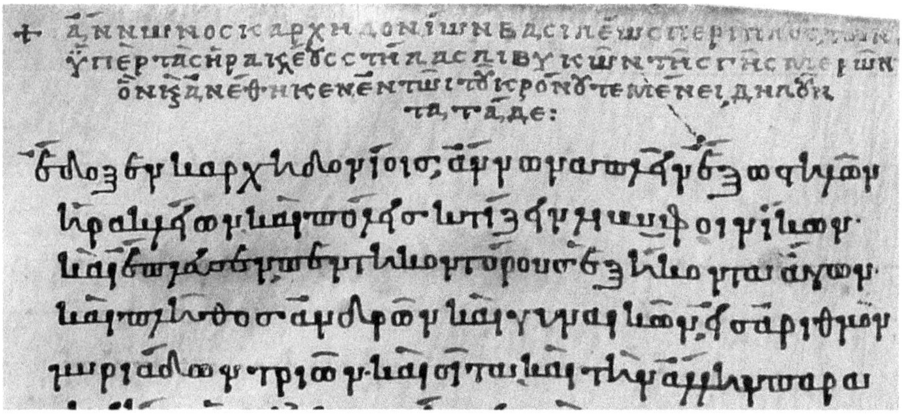

FIG. 4.1. Opening of the text of Hanno, fo. 55ʳ (detail)

INTRODUCTION

A Carthaginian named Hanno (otherwise unidentifiable) evidently wrote—in Punic presumably[1]—an account of a voyage beyond the Pillars of Herakles, of which the 9th-century manuscript A (see Introduction, §VIII) preserves the earliest extant version in Greek (fos. 55ʳ–56ʳ), possibly 'improved' by a translator. A later copy survives in the London pages of manuscript B (fos. 12ʳ–12ᵛ). It has been suggested that the work may have been commissioned by Polybios from material found in the archives of Carthage after its defeat by the Romans in 146 BC.[2] If so, one or more similar accounts of such a voyage—perhaps different versions of the present text—may well have existed earlier, one of which may underlie the so-called *periplous* of Ps.-Skylax compiled in the 330s BC (Chapter 7 below, §112. 4–5).[3] A roughly contemporary source (B. 1) preserves a possible trace of Hanno's name in African geography, and the '*periplous* of Hanno' is cited in a collection of anecdotal scraps about marvels preserved with Aristotle's

---

[1] Blomqvist 1979 dates the voyage to C5 and argues for a non-Greek original.
[2] Roller 2015, 60 (cf. 137 for Polyb.'s despatch to Kerne).
[3] Hdt.'s account of Carthaginian trading beyond the Pillars of Herakles (4. 196) also resembles Ps.-Skylax §112. 7, but is less detailed.

works (2), at least part of which goes back to the 3rd century BC. The text in the form in which we have it was available in the era of Augustus, when Juba devoted a study to it (8 = Chapter 22 below, no. 2); this was perhaps the source for Pomponius Mela's paraphrase written soon afterwards, in which the issue of its credibility surfaces (3). The presumed Punic original, however, has been variously dated between the 5th and 1st centuries BC, and remains the subject of controversy in most other respects too.[4]

The text, in which several disjointed passages may indicate omissions,[5] opens in the form of a third-person record (A §1), but continues thereafter as a narrative in the first person plural, with a curious mix of detail and vagueness. Its accuracy is called into question at the outset, when it is implied that each of the ships in Hanno's expedition carried 500 people. Despite persistent efforts, attempts to plot on a modern map the places and physical features mentioned have so far achieved minimal consensus,[6] not least about the stated journey times, which scholars sometimes amend and reconstruct differently to fit their theories. This said, Kerne (§§8–10) might be an island near *Essaouira* in Morocco (but see note on §9 below),[7] and Theon Ochema (§16) the volcano Mount Cameroon. If genuine, the voyage may have been made in part to identify possibilities for trade.[8] However, the many 'marvellous' elements in the narrative, along with the absence of remains for most of the settlements supposedly founded, have fuelled suspicions that this account is really a Greek creation (not a translation from Punic), and fiction rather than a factual record.[9]

Nevertheless it had a legacy, and it or a version of it is referred to by several Greek and Latin authors: Juba, as we have seen, wrote a treatise about it (B. 8), drawn upon by Mela (3); Pliny the Elder cites it several times a little later (4–6);[10] and Arrian paraphrases it in language that partly echoes our Greek text (7), though the directions and length of stages on the voyage are no clearer than in the text we have (and his '35 days' exceeds the total of sailing times in our text, which is 32½ or 33½ unless we alter the text).[11] Around AD 400, Markianos read the *periplous* (9), probably in the collection of geographers compiled by Arrian himself (cf. Introduction, §VIII. 2. b).[12]

The text translated is that of González Ponce in Jacoby V.[13] The divisions between sections (numbered in the translation) are marked in manuscript A itself.

---

[4] For discussion of the work, see Roller 2006, 29–43; Roller 2015, 56–9. Among many detailed treatments, see e.g. Desanges 1978, 39–85; González Ponce 2008b, 75–151 (Greek text, Spanish trans.); González Ponce 2011 (Greek text, German trans. and commentary).

[5] Roller 2006, 31, 33, cf. 131–2 (the gaps indicated by Roller are adopted here).

[6] For one representation, see route 4 on the excellent map entitled 'Exploration in the ancient world' in Olshausen 2010.

[7] *Barr.* 1a C2 Cerne. For discussion of all places and physical features, see Roller 2006, 34–41.

[8] Roller 2006, 42. Roller 2015, 56, also views the Hanno narrative as genuine.

[9] Desanges 1978, 83, argues that the text we have cannot be earlier than C2m (the era of Polybios), and (84–5) that it is composite and corrupt.

[10] Cf. also Pliny 2. cx. 237; 6. xxxv. 197.

[11] Roller 2006, 33.

[12] On Markianos, see Chapter 34.

[13] González Ponce 2011.

SELECTED FURTHER READING

Bayer, K. (1993), 'Der Fahrtenbericht des Hanno', in G. Winkler (ed.), *C. Plinius Secundus d. Ä., Naturkunde, lateinisch–deutsch, Buch V: Geographie. Afrika und Asien* (Sammlung Tusculum; Munich), 337–53.

Bosak-Schroeder, C. (2019), 'Making specimens in the Periplus of Hanno and its imperial tradition', *American Journal of Philology*, 140. 1: 67–100.

Brodersen, K. (2001), 'Savage's savages: how the gorilla became a savage beast because of Hanno's Periplus', in K. Geus and K. Zimmermann (eds), *Punica—Libyca—Ptolemaica: Festschrift für Werner Huß* (Leuven), 87–98; repr. in K. Brodersen, *Classics outside Classics* (Heidelberg, 2015), ch. 5.

Desanges, J. (1983), 'Des interprètes chez les "Gorilles": réflexion sur un artifice dans le Périple d'Hannon', in *Atti del I congresso internazionale di studi Fenici e Punici, 1981*, i (Rome), 267–75.

Domínguez Monedero, A. J. (2010), 'El viaje de Hanón de Cartago y los mecanismos de exploración fenicios', in F. Marco Simón *et al.* (eds), *Viajeros, peregrinos y aventureros en el mundo antiguo* (Barcelona), 77–93.

González Ponce, F. J. (2008a), 'Los huidizos gorilas de Hanón y la tradición helenística sobre la zoología fabulosa de la India', in J. M. Candau Morón *et al.* (eds), *Libyae lustrare extrema: realidad y literatura en la visión grecorromana de África. Hommaje al Prof. Jehan Desanges* (Seville), 291–304.

*——— (2008b), *Periplo de Hanón y autores de los siglos VI y V a.C.* Zaragoza. [Esp. pp. 79–151.]

*——— (2011), 'Hanno von Karthago (2208)', in *FGrH* v.

Huß, W. (1993), 'Das afrikanische Unternehmen des Hanno', in G. Winkler (ed.), *C. Plinius Secundus d. Ä., Naturkunde, lateinisch–deutsch, Buch V: Geographie. Afrika und Asien* (Sammlung Tusculum; Munich), 354–63.

Oikonomides, A. N., and Miller, M. C. J. (1995), *Hanno the Carthaginian, Periplus or Circumnavigation [of Africa]*, 3rd edn. Chicago.

Ramin, J. (1976), *Le Périple d'Hannon—The Periplus of Hanno.* Oxford.

Roller, D. W. (2006), *Through the Pillars of Herakles: Greco-Roman Exploration of the Atlantic.* London–New York. [Text, trans. at 129–32.]

A. *CIRCUMNAVIGATION* (*PERIPLOUS*)

Headings are added.

Launch of the Expedition

1. Circumnavigation (*Periplous*) by Hanno, king (*basileus*)[14] of the Carthaginians, to the Libyan parts of the Earth beyond the Pillars of Herakles, (*a record*) which he also set up in the sanctuary of Kronos, revealing what follows.

The Carthaginians resolved that Hanno should sail out from the Pillars of Herakles and establish cities of Libyphoinikes; and he sailed off at the head of 60 penteconters;

---

[14] Whether or not this text was translated from a Punic original, the term 'king' need not mean (sole) ruler: *basileus* in Greek is a title that can be held by many men at the same time, and may approximate to 'nobleman'.

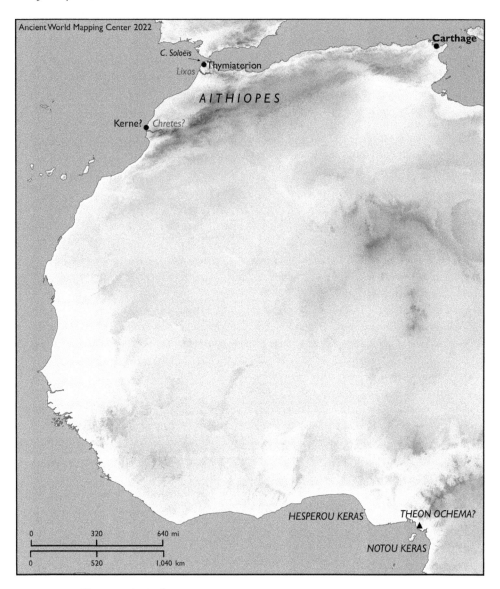

MAP 4.1. Hanno: principal stages.

and (*with him*) was a mass of men and women numbering 30,000, as well as provisions and other resources. [—]

Into the Atlantic

2. 'So, after putting to sea, we passed the Pillars and sailed for a two-day voyage beyond, (*then*) established the first city, which we named Thymiaterion (*Incense-burner*);[15] below it there was an extensive plain.

---

[15] Possible locations: Roller 2006, 34–5. Several of the place-names in the following passage also

3. 'And next, after putting to sea and heading west, we came to the Libyan cape Soloëis (*C. Spartel*), one overgrown with trees.   4. After erecting a shrine to Poseidon there, we made once more for the rising sun (*i.e. eastwards*) for half a day until we were conveyed into a lake lying close to the sea and full of many tall reeds; elephants were there too, along with numerous other beasts feeding.   5. Proceeding beyond the lake for about a day's voyage, we founded cities by the sea called Karikon Teichos (*Karian Fort*), Gytta, Akra (*Cape*), Melitta (*Bee*), and Arambys.

6. 'And putting to sea from there we came to a great river, Lixos, flowing from Libyē. Pasturing flocks beside it were nomadic Lixitai people, among whom we stayed long enough to become friendly.[16]   7. Above them, unwelcoming Aithiopes were living, inhabitants of a land full of wild beasts and ruptured by a mass of mountains. From these, they say, the Lixos flows, and amid the mountains dwell oddly built Trogodyte people who, the Lixitai stated, outrun racehorses.

8. 'Taking interpreters from them (*the Lixitai*), we sailed south past the desert for two days [—] and from there a day's run back towards the rising sun; and then far into some bay we found a small island five stades in circumference. We established a settlement there and named it Kerne. From the voyage we reckoned that its location is right opposite Carthage, because the voyage from Carthage to the Pillars gave the impression of matching that from there to Kerne.[17]

Diversion Up-river

9. 'Thereafter we reached a lake by sailing up a certain large river, the Chre⟨me⟩tes;[18] the lake had three islands, ones larger than Kerne. After pressing on for a day's sail from these, we reached the furthest part of the lake, overhung by really great mountains full of wild people wearing animal skins who kept us away by hurling rocks and prevented our landing.

10. 'Sailing on from there, we came to another river, large and wide and full of crocodiles and hippopotamuses; so we reversed course from there and made our way back to Kerne.

Beyond Kerne

11. 'From there we sailed south for twelve days, advancing past territory all inhabited by Aithiopes who fled from us without even waiting. Their language was unintelligible, even to the Lixitai who were with us.   12. On the last day we came to anchor by some large, thickly covered mountains; the wood of the trees was sweet-scented and

---

occur at Ps.-Skyl. §112. 4–5, though that author appears to use a different source from the present one (or a different version of this); see Shipley 2019, 214–17.

[16] 'Hanno' does not say that the expedition founded a settlement on the Lixos; but the town existed from C8, with separate Phoenician (800–500) and Punic (500–200) phases distinguished, becoming prosperous in Roman times, when Juba II may have built a palace there (Aranegui and Mar 2009).

[17] Proposed locations are widely separated: Roller 2006, 37.

[18] Chretes in the MSS; González Ponce emends on the basis of Arist. *Mete.* 1. 13, 350b 12–13, following Müller and other editors.

its colouring varied.   13. After sailing round (*peripleusantes*) here for two days we found ourselves in an immense expanse of sea, with the land either side of it a plain where at night we saw fire—sometimes more, sometimes less—rising everywhere at intervals.[19]

14. 'After taking on water there, we sailed on past land for five days until we came to a great bay which the interpreters said was called Hesperou Keras (*Horn of the West*).[20] Within it was a large island, and on the island a saltwater (*thalassōdēs*) lake; in this was another island where on landing we could see nothing by day but forest, though at night there were many fires burning,[21] and we heard the sound of pipes as well as cymbals and drums beating and a huge amount of shouting. So we were gripped by fear, and the diviners kept urging us to leave the island.

15. 'We quickly sailed out and passed by country that was on fire and filled with incense; ⟨vast⟩[22] fiery streams were pouring down from there into the sea; heat made the ground impassable.   16. So in terror we quickly sailed away from there. Moving on for four days we saw that at night flames filled the land. There was some tall fire at the centre, larger than the others and seeming to reach the stars; by day it was visibly a very large mountain called Theon Ochema (*Chariot of the Gods*).[23]

17. 'From there on the third day we sailed past fiery streams and reached a bay said to be Notou Keras (*Horn of the South*).[24]   18. Far into it there was an island like the first, with a lake; and on this there was another island full of savage people; these were predominantly women with shaggy bodies, called Gorillai[25] by the interpreters. Our efforts to chase and capture the men failed; rather, they all escaped by climbing precipices and fending us off with rocks. But (*we did take*) three women, who bit and scratched their captors and resisted following them; but we killed and flayed these, and brought the skins to Carthage. [—]

'We did not sail any further because our provisions had run out.'

---

[19] Cf. B. 2 below.   [20] 'Horn' in the sense of an inlet of the sea.

[21] We are to understand these as manmade fires, rather than the volcanic activity described in the next two sections.

[22] Reading μες⟨στοί· μέγιστ⟩οι with González Ponce.

[23] Often thought to be Mt *Cameroon* or *Fako*, where the 1,000-mile long 'Cameroon Line' of volcanoes crosses the coast at the *Bight of Bonny*. On this area, see Roller 2006, 39–40. The total of 23 days from Kerne so far enumerated, at a notional 500 stades' sailing per day (cf. Ps.-Skyl. §69), or *c*.57 mi or *c*.92.5 km, would make *c*.1,400 mi (*c*.2,300 km).

[24] Again, 'horn' meaning an inlet. The inlets of §§14 and 17 may, however, be the same: Roller 2006, 38–9.

[25] This passage has been highly influential: first on Roman-period perceptions of barbarians and wild animals (see Bosak-Schroeder 2019), then on the naming of the gorilla in C19 (Roller 2006, 41). Many interpretations have been offered, which space precludes citing in their entirety. Ironically, though the MS clearly reads *gorillas* (printed correctly by Gelenius 1533, 40), this may be the result of miscopying (at an early medieval date when MSS were written in uncial capitals) of *gorgades*, equivalent to 'Gorgons'; ΓΟΡΓΑΔΑΣ hypothetically becoming ΓΟΡΙΛΛΑΣ (cf. Desanges 1983; Brodersen 2001 ~ Brodersen 2015). This suggestion receives support from the fact that Pliny names the Gorgades at B. 6 below. At any rate, the beings reported in the text are likely to have been apes, not humans.

B. OTHER TEXTS

1   Palaiphatos, *On Incredible Tales,* 31: *Kerne*
The people of Kerne are Aithiopes by race, but inhabit the island of Kerne outside the
Pillars of Herakles, and cultivate (*the land of*) Libyē beside the river Annōn†[26] on a
straight line from Carthage; and are extremely golden (*i.e. rich in gold*).

2   Pseudo-Aristotle, *On Miraculous Things Heard,* §37, 833a 9–12: *Volcanoes*
It is also said that the places outside the Pillars of Herakles are on fire, some permanently and others only at night, as the *Circumnavigation* by Hanno records.[27]

3   Pomponius Mela 3. 89–99: *Hanno's voyage*
For a considerable time it was doubtful whether there was any open sea (*pelagus*)
beyond (*as one sailed east round western Africa*) and whether the Earth had an outer
circuit, or whether the seas were consumed and Africa extended without end. (90) But
Hanno the Carthaginian, sent exploring by his people, after exiting by the mouth of
the Ocean sailed round a great part of it and had reported in his memoir that (*Africa*)
was inadequate not in sea (*mare*) but in human society.[28] . . .

(93) Beyond these people a great curve of the shore encloses a great island, in which
they tell that only women exist, hairy over their whole body and reproducing spontaneously without any intercourse with males. Their customs are (*said to be*) so harsh and savage that some of them resist restraint and can scarcely be held by chains. Hanno reported
this, and has been believed because he had brought back their skins, removed after they
were killed. (94) Beyond this bay is a high mountain, Theon ⟨Ochema⟩ as the Greeks call
it, which blazes with perpetual flames. (95) Beyond the mountain is a green hill extending
over a long stretch by long shores, from which are viewed the plains, opening further than
can be perceived, of the ⟨Goat⟩-Pans and Satyrs. This is why the opinion of the matter has
been given credence: although there is nothing cultivated in these (*plains*), no residences
of inhabitants, no tracks left, a solitude vast by day and vaster silence, by night numerous
flames flash forth and are displayed like those of a far-flung (*army*) camp, cymbals and
drums sound, and pipes louder than human ones are heard. . . .

(99) Opposite them[29] are the Gorgades islands, once the home, they say, of the
Gorgons. The lands themselves[30] end in the promontory which possesses the name of
Hesperu Ceras.

---

[26] A similar name in this general area is the river Anides, but it appears to be too far N (Ps.-Skyl.
§112. 3 *bis* with Shipley 2019, 209–11, 213–14). More likely another name has been supplanted by that
of Hanno himself.

[27] Savino 1991 shows that the second half of this work is probably from the Roman period; but the
anecdotes about Agathokles of Syracuse (d. 289; *Mir. ausc.* 110, 840b 18–24) and Kleonymos of Sparta
(d. 272; 78, 835b 33–836 a6) give a *terminus post quem* for at least part of the work (Wenskus and Daston 2006a ~ Wenskus and Daston 2006b, German version; both containing misprinted dates).

[28] We follow the interpretation of Romer 1998, 126. This passage clearly draws, directly or otherwise,
on Hanno; but Mela does not name the islands where the hairy women live. Contrast Pliny at 6 below.

[29] The Catoblepae, wild animals whose glance is deadly (§98).

[30] i.e. the mainland of Libya.

4   Pliny, *Natural History,* 2. lxvii. 169: *Hanno's voyage*
When the power of Carthage was at its height, Hanno sailed round from Gades to the confines of Arabia and published this voyage in a written work, just as in the same period Himilco was sent to gain knowledge of the outer parts of Europe.

5   Pliny, *Natural History,* 5. i. 8: *Hanno's voyage*
There existed, too, the memoirs of Hanno, leader of the Carthaginians, who, at a time when the power of the Punic state was at its height, was instructed to explore the circumference (*ambitus*) of Africa. Relying on him, several of the Greek authors and our own have reported many things that are surely imaginary, including the founding of many cities by him, of which no memory and no trace exists.

6   Pliny, *Natural History,* 6. xxxvi. 200: *Gorgades, Gorgons, and gorillas (?)*
Opposite this promontory,[31] too, are said to lie the Gorgades islands, once the home of the Gorgons. According to Xenophon of Lampsacus they are two days' sail from the mainland. Hanno, the commander of the Poeni (*Carthaginians*), got into them and reported hairy bodies of women whose men had escaped through their agility. He placed the skins of two Gorgades in the temple of Juno[32] for the purpose of proof and as a wonder; they were viewed up to the time when Carthage was captured.[33]

7   Arrian, *Indike,* 43. 11–12: *Hanno's voyage*
And Hanno the Libyan, from Carthage, sailed out beyond the Pillars of Herakles into the Outer Main (*pontos*), keeping Libyē on the left; and his voyage was right towards the rising sun for the whole 35 days; and when he turned round to the south, he met with many difficulties: lack of water, blazing heat, and streams of fire debouching into the main.

8   Athenaios 3. 25, 83c: *Juba's book on Hanno*
Demokritos said, 'if Iobas (*Juba*) says any of these things (*about the citron fruit in Libyē*), say farewell to his Libyan books and even his *Wanderings of Hanno*; but I say this name does not exist among the old (*writers*)'.

9   Markianos, *Epitome of Menippos,* 2: *Hanno as a source*
I write this having encountered many *periploi* and having spent a lot of time acquiring knowledge of these topics. . . . Those who in my view have investigated these matters intelligently are . . . Then there are Apelles of Kyrene, Euthymenes of Massilia, Phileas of Athens, Androsthenes of Thasos, Kleon of Sicily, Eudoxos of Rhodes,[34] and Hanno of Carthage.

---

[31] *Hesperu Ceras* (a transliteration from the Greek), 'Horn of the West'. Cf. Mela 3. 99 at 3 §99 above.
[32] i.e. the goddess Tinnit (Draycott 2010, 212).
[33] Pliny's Latin predecessor Mela (see 3 §99 above) says of the Gorgades Is. only that their inhabitants are said to have been the Gorgons; what he tells us about the hairy women is at a separate location.
[34] Presumably Eudoxos of Knidos is meant.

5

HIPPOKRATES OF KOS (?), *AIRS, WATERS, AND PLACES*

(*'AWP'*)

(C. LATE 5TH C. BC)

D. Graham J. Shipley

INTRODUCTION

The inclusion, in a collection of Greek geographical writings, of this ostensibly medical text—preserved in the collection of works attributed to the doctor Hippokrates of Kos (*c.*470–*c.*400 BC), and evidently written during or soon after his lifetime—may cause some initial surprise. The largely theoretical exposition purports, however, to show how wind, water, and climate influence human types and societies, as well as their medical susceptibilities, in different regions, particularly in Asia (including Egypt) as distinct from Europe, but also in specific parts of those continents. Only a few passages, however, are enriched with specific examples of peoples and their character. The chief points of geographical interest within the *Airs, Waters, and Places* (*Peri aërōn hydatōn topōn*) are compelling: first, the systematic treatment of the winds that blow from each of the eight cardinal and ordinal points of the compass, and their respective impacts upon health; second, the exposition of strong characterizations of peoples in different continents and their physical tendencies, which easily shades over into their moral and political qualities. The treatise thus depends closely on the development of both geographical and medico-scientific knowledge in the Greek world around the late 5th century.

The ostensible justification for the approach adopted by the author is the expectation, implicit but clear at the outset, that a doctor will be a travelling practitioner (§1. 3). He must therefore be acquainted with the prevalent winds in the place where he practises, and with their predictable effects (§§3–6); with the ground-waters and the waters deriving from precipitation (§§7–9); and with the effects of the changing seasons upon the body (§§10–11). In the second half of the treatise (§§12–24), the author refocuses upon the specific conditions in Asia and Europe and the contrasting moral and political traits they promote. His division between the continents at Lake Maiotis (*Sea of Azov*) differs from that adopted by Herodotos (4. 45), who worked with the river Phasis (probably the *Rioni*) as the boundary though allowing the Tanaïs, *Don*, as an alternative.[1] It requires him, as we shall see, to divide the Skythians between Europe and Asia; if the Phasis were the boundary, all Skythians would be European.

The author presumes that a given community's members will display common traits; a rhetorical move perhaps designed to confer scientific authority. The division between continents, indeed, is not uniform. At first, the author does not appear to be particularly Eurocentric or Orientalizing, as Asia is initially allowed some positive qualities (§12. 2–5) and its best portion (unnamed in the passage, though its end may be missing) occupies the central position in the world that allows it to avoid the extremes of temperature and humidity to either side (§12. 4). Herodotos, writing around the same time as the author of *AWP* or a little earlier, attributes a similar combination of advantages to Ionia (1. 142), which is in Asia; Xenophon would later do the same for Athens (specifically with reference to hot and cold, and to its situation between two seas: *Poroi*, 1. 6–7); Aristotle would apply the same model to 'the race of the Hellenes', ignoring its far-flung geographic spread (*Politics*, 7. 7); much later, Vitruvius would claim for Italy the same advantage of balanced centrality (1. 6. 11). On the downside, however, we soon learn that Asians lack those sterling qualities that a more challenging climate fosters; not least in their tendency towards autocratic systems in which the citizen's interests are not served (16. 3–5). Medicine seems here subordinated to politics; but while the term 'Asians' (*Asianoi*) appears first in this work, it is employed in support of an environmental theory, not as a pejorative ideological construct.[2]

The author's selection of case studies within Asia and Europe is extremely limited, though the passage on Egypt and Libyē (which seem to be treated as parts of Asia, as they were by Hekataios: Ch. 3 above) is missing. First he focuses on the peoples east of the Black Sea (§§13–15), and then—after a theoretical passage on the moral character of Asians in general (§16), with no distinction stated between Greeks and non-Greeks—he turns to those Skythians called the Sauromatai, who are located in Europe (§17).[3] These he appears to want to contrast with the other Skythians in Asia (§§18–22), though the comparison is not well framed since we are told only one thing about the Sauromatai: their women are warriors (§17). About the other Skythians we learn, it is true, that their women are lazy (§21. 2), but the author's chief aim seems to be to demonstrate that the combination of the women's flabbiness and the damage caused to the men by horse-riding leads to a failure to reproduce. Much of this passage could, in fact, be read as applying to Skythians in both continents. Indeed, the author eventually insists (§21. 8–10) that there are variations among Skythians which are attributable to social class.[4]

---

[1] For the various ancient identifications of the Phasis, which finally settled on the *Rioni* in mod. Georgia, see Dan 2016.

[2] See Lenfant 2017.

[3] Hdt. 4. 21, however (and later in book 4), locates them E of the Tanaïs.

[4] Chiai 2021 argues that *AWP*'s presentation of the Skythians is more negative than that of Herodotos.

There follows a theoretical passage on Europeans (§§23. 1–24. 6), which first homogenizes them but then recognizes their diversity, somewhat undermining the schematic continental polarity the text has set up. The treatise concludes, however, by reverting to the lazy Asia–energetic Europe polarity. The author, once again, seems to regard politics as the thing most important to understand. It is, perhaps, over-simplistic to read into the text a Greek–Persian polarization;[5] more precisely, perhaps, the work may reflect Athenians' belief in their superiority.[6]

The translation is based on the Greek of Jouanna's edition.[7]

SELECTED FURTHER READING

Irwin, E. (2015), 'Imperialism, ethics and the popularization of medical theory in later fifth-century Athens: Airs, Waters, Places', Ἀριάδνη, 22: 57–92.

*Jouanna, J. (1996), *Hippocrate, Airs, eaux, lieux*. Paris. ['Budé' edition.]

Lateiner, D. (1986), 'Early Greek medical writers and Herodotus', *Antichthon*, 20: 1–20.

Lenfant, D. (2017), 'Les "Asiatiques" du traité hippocratique Airs, Eaux, Lieux ont-ils été les premiers "Orientaux"?', *Archimède*, 4: 19–25.

Lloyd, G. E. R. (1978) with J. Chadwick *et al.*, *Hippocratic Writings*. Harmondsworth. [Esp. introduction.]

*Potter, P. (2022), *Hippocrates, Ancient Medicine; Airs, Waters, Places; Epidemics 1 and 3; The Oath; Precepts; Nutriment*. [Loeb edition.] 2nd edn. Cambridge, Mass. [Appeared after the present work went to press.]

Raaflaub, K. A. (2002), 'Philosophy, science, politics: Herodotus and the intellectual trends of his time', in E. J. Bakker *et al.* (eds), *Brill's Companion to Herodotus* (Leiden), 149–86.

Thomas, R. (2000), *Herodotus in Context: Ethnography, Science and the Art of Persuasion*. Cambridge. [Esp. ch. 3 (75–101).]

TEXT

Headings are added.

CLIMATE AND HEALTH

Introduction

1. Whoever wishes to study medicine correctly must do as follows. First, one must consider the seasons of the year and what each one is capable of causing. For they in no way resemble each other, but differ greatly both in themselves and in their changes. (2) Next, one must consider the winds, both hot and cold; especially those common to all peoples, next those existing locally in each land.[8] It is also necessary

---

[5] As Thomas 2000, 90–4, rightly cautions.   [6] Irwin 2015.

[7] Jouanna 1996. Chapter divisions vary slightly between editions; I follow Jouanna.

[8] On the classification of winds, see esp. Timosthenes 3 and 18.

to consider the capacities of the waters: for just as they differ in the mouth and in the balance (*i.e. weighing-scales*), so the power of each differs greatly.   (3) Thus, when one arrives in a city of which one has no experience, one must analyse its location and how it lies with reference to both the airs and the risings of the sun.[9] For a situation inclining towards the north has a different capacity from one facing the south, the rising sun, or the setting (*sun*).   (4) One must consider these things as best one may, as well as how the people fare in the matter of waters, and whether they use marshy, soft water, hard water from high, rocky places, or salty and alkaline.   (5) Also the earth: whether it is bare and waterless or thickly covered and well-watered, and whether it is in a hollow and airless or elevated and cold. Also the way of life that the people enjoy: whether they are heavy drinkers, enjoy their lunch, and are untoiling; or are lovers of exercise and hard work, appreciating food but abstaining from drink.

2. One must consider all matters from this starting-point. For if one knew these things well, or indeed all of them—or, if not, at least the majority—then, on arriving in a city of which one had no experience, one would not be unaware of the local diseases or what the nature of people's inner organs may be.[10] Thus one will not be in doubt as to the treatment of diseases, or commit errors; things which are likely to happen if one does not make one's initial analysis in the knowledge of those matters.   (2) As time and the year move on, one could then state how many diseases are likely to grip the city in summer or winter, and how many each person is at risk of getting because of changes in lifestyle. For knowing the changes of the seasons, the (*heliacal*) risings and settings of the stars,[11] and how each of these occurs, one would know in advance what sort of year is going to occur. Thus, by investigating and being aware of the right times in advance, one could have full knowledge of each aspect, achieve health in the majority of cases, and move in the right direction in one's art to no small degree.   (3) If one thought that these things were meteorological matters, and did not alter this opinion, one would learn that astronomy does not make a minor contribution to medicine, but a very large one. For in accord with the seasons, both diseases and people's inner organs undergo change.

[9] Although 'the rising sun' and similar phrases had been used to mean the east by earlier authors such as Hekataios (62–3, 86 above) and Hanno if he is genuine (§§4, 8)—as the Hippocratic author himself does in the following words—he seems here to use the phrase 'risings of the sun' to refer to the daily round of the Sun's positions as a whole. On the translation of such direction terms, see the Introduction, §X. 3. b.

[10] The word translated 'inner organs' here and many times below is κοιλίαι (*koiliai*), literally 'cavities'. Jouanna 1996, 258 n. 8 (to p. 189 and §2. 3), explains that the author distinguishes an upper and a lower cavity in the body (cf. 4. 2; 7. 3), whose nature varies with the seasons (see 10. 3 and 9).

[11] The heliacal rising of a star refers to the date on which it is first visible before sunrise after the sun (*hēlios*), in its eastward movement, has passed through the part of the sky where the star is located. Greek writers were aware of this phenomenon already before 700 BC: Hesiod, *Works and Days*, 383, uses the rising of the Pleiades as a calendrical marker.

Effects of Winds

3. I shall now state clearly how one should examine and test each of the above-mentioned matters. That city which lies facing the hot winds—namely, those between the winter rising of the sun (*south-east*) and its winter settings (*south-west*)—and has those winds as its companions while having protection from northerly winds, this city has copious water but quite salty; it necessarily rises at a high level and is hot in summer, cold in winter.   (2) The people are bound to have moist heads full of phlegm; their inner organs are frequently disturbed by the downward flow of phlegm from the head. The physique of the majority of them will be rather slack; they will not be good eaters and drinkers, for any that have weak heads cannot be good drinkers since a hangover is worse for them.   (3) The following diseases will occur locally. First, the women will be prone to illness and discharges. Next, many will be infertile by reason of disease, not by nature, and will frequently miscarry. The children will be afflicted by spasms and asthma, and by what is thought to cause 'the child' or 'the holy disease' (*epilepsy*). The men will be afflicted by dysentery, diarrhoea, long-lasting chills and fevers in winter, nocturnal blisters, and haemorrhoids in the fundament.   (4) But cases of pleurisy, pneumonia, severe fever, and other diseases regarded as acute do not occur often; for these diseases cannot gain power where the inner organs are moist. Eye diseases occur, moist but not serious; they last a short time unless a communal disease takes hold as a result of a pronounced change. When people pass fifty years, discharges of catarrh from the brain partially paralyse them whenever they are sunstruck or get cold. These are their local diseases; but apart from these they will also suffer if a communal disease takes hold as a result of changes in the seasons.

4. Such cities as lie in the opposite direction, facing the cold winds, those between the summer settings of the sun (*north-west*) and its summer rising (*north-east*), and have these winds for their local ones while having protection from the south wind and the hot winds—this is how it is with these cities.   (2) First, their waters are mostly hard and cold, as well as sweet.[12] The people are bound to be taut and lean, and the majority will have alkaline inner organs, hard in the lower parts and with an easy flow in the upper. They will be bilious rather than phlegmatic. They have healthy, tough heads, with lesions for the most part.   (3) The following diseases are epidemic. (*There are*) many cases of pleurisy and the diseases regarded as acute; people are bound to be in such a condition whenever their inner organs are hard. Many will have abscesses for any number of reasons; the cause of this is the tension of the body and the hardness of the internal organs. For dryness, and the coldness of the water, cause lesions to form. Persons of such constitutions are necessarily good eaters but not heavy drinkers; for it is not possible for people to be both heavy feeders and heavy drinkers. In time, eye inflammations will occur and become hard and powerful; the eyes will soon rupture. In summer, young persons under thirty will have severe nosebleeds; and the so-called

---

[12] i.e. 'fresh' in the UK English sense, the opposite of 'brackish' (salty).

'holy diseases', while scarce, are severe. But it is likely that these people will be more long-lived than others. Their ulcers will not take a phlegmatic form or become malignant. Their characters, however, are more wild than mild.   (4) Among the men, such are the local diseases; and apart from those, they will suffer if something universal takes hold because of a change in the seasons. Among the women, first, many become barren owing to the waters being hard, alkaline, and cold; for their monthly discharges do not recur properly, but are few and poor. Next, they give birth with difficulty, and do not miscarry much. When they do give birth, they are incapable of feeding the children: for the milk dries up because of the hardness and alkalinity of the waters. Consumption often occurs after births, for the violent process involves tears and spasms.   (5) Dropsy of the testicles occurs often in children when they are young; then, as their age increases, they disappear. In this city, people reach adulthood late.

Concerning hot winds, cold winds, and these cities, the case is as described above.

5. Such cities as lie facing the winds between the summer risings of the sun (*north-east*) and the winter ones (*south-east*), and such as lie in the opposite sense to these, for them the situation is as follows.   (2) Such as lie facing the risings of the sun are likely to be healthier than those turned towards the north and those (*turned*) towards the hot winds, even if (*only*) a stade[13] lies between them.   (3) First, the heat and cold are more moderate. Next, such waters as face the risings of the sun are bound to be transparent, sweet-smelling, and soft, and mists do not arise in this city; for the rising sun restrains them as it rises and shines down upon them. For on each occasion this dawn air persists for a long time.   (4) People's bodies are of good colour and rather blooming, unless some disease prevents it. The people have clear voices and are better in mood and understanding than those to the north, just as all growing things there are better.   (5) A city with this situation is exactly like the spring in terms of the moderate heat and cold. The diseases are inferior and weaker, but are like the diseases that occur in cities turned towards the hot winds. Women there are very fertile and give birth easily.

Such is the case concerning these things.

6. Such cities, however, as lie facing the west, and have protection from the winds blowing from the east, have both the hot winds and the cold northerlies flowing past them. These cities are bound to lie in a very diseased location.   (2) First, the waters are not clear; the reason is that the dawn air takes them over for the most part, and being mingled with water it removes the clarity, for the sun does not shine upon it until it rises high. In summer, cold breezes blow at dawn and dews fall. As for other times, the sinking sun bakes the people intensely,   (3) which is why they are likely to be both lacking in good colour and weak, and to experience all the aforesaid diseases; none is distinctive to them. It is likely that they will have deep, hoarse voices because of the air, because it mostly has an uncleansed, moist character there; for neither is it

---

[13] Roughly an English furlong; for the meaning of *stadion*, see the Glossary.

forcibly expelled by the northerly (*winds*)—for those winds do not occur often—and the ones that do occur in these (*cities*) and relate to the place are extremely watery, since winds from the west are of that kind. (4) Such a location for a city is exactly like the autumn in terms of changes during the day, because there is a great separation between the situation early in the morning and in the afternoon.

Such is the case concerning winds, both suitable and unsuitable.

Effects of Waters

7. As for the remaining waters, however, I wish to recount which are diseased and which most healthy, and what evils are likely to arise from water and what good things. For it (*water*) contributes a large proportion of health.

(2) So such waters as are marshy, standing, and swampy are bound to be hot in summer, become thick, and have a smell, seeing that they are not flowing out. Instead, new rainwater is always being engendered and, as the sun burns it, it is bound to have a bad colour and be poor and bilious. In winter, they will be frozen, cold, and stained by snow and ice, so that they are extremely full of phlegm and hoarseness. (3) Those who drink these waters will always have large, closed spleens; their stomachs will be hard, thin, and hot; their shoulders, collarbone, and face attenuated; for the flesh is consumed and goes into the spleen, which is why they are gaunt. Such people will be heavy eaters and thirsty. They will have very dry, hot inner organs in both the upper and the lower parts, so that they will require more powerful medicines. This disease is their constant companion in summer and winter. (4) In addition, cases of dropsy are very numerous and very often fatal. For in summer many cases of dysentery assail them, also diarrhoea and chronic fevers with a four-day cycle. These diseases, being prolonged, render such physiques open to dropsy and cause death. These things occur in summer. (5) In winter, younger persons suffer pneumonia and diseases causing madness, while the older ones suffer severe fever because of the hardness of their inner organs. (6) Among women, swellings and white phlegm occur; they can hardly conceive, and give birth with difficulty: their babies are large and swollen. Next, at the nursing stage, they become emaciated and poor. Women's discharges do not occur normally after birth. (7) Among small children, hernias notably occur, while men suffer varicose veins and ulcers on their legs, so that with such physiques they cannot be long-lived, but grow old before their time comes. (8) Moreover, the women appear to have conceived, and when birth occurs the swelling of the stomach disappears; this occurs when wombs suffer from dropsy. (9) Such waters I regard as being extremely bad for all purposes.

The second worst would be those that have their sources in rocks—for they are bound to be hard—or in ground where there are hot waters or where iron, copper, silver, gold, sulphur, alum, bitumen, or soda occurs; for all these are created by the violence of heat. So it is not possible for good waters to arise from such ground, but only hard, feverish waters, difficult to pass and inhibiting evacuation (*of the bowel*).

(10) The best waters are such as flow from elevated locations and earthy hills. For they are sweet, white, and capable of carrying only a little wine. In winter they become hot, in summer cold; they will be from very deep sources. I praise especially waters whose streams break forth in the direction of the risings of the sun, and more so the summer ones; for they are bound to be clearer, sweet-smelling, and light.　(11) All those that are salty, alkaline, and hard are not good to drink. There are some physiques and some diseases for which the drinking of such waters is appropriate, about which I shall explain directly. Such is the case concerning these things.

Those (*waters*) whose springs face towards the east are best of all. Second best are those between the summer risings (*north-east*) and settings (*north-west*) of the sun, though more so those facing the sunrise. Third best are those between the summer and winter sunsets (*north-west and south-west*). Worst of all are those facing south between winter sunrise (*south-east*) and sunset (*south-west*). These are very poor in southerly winds, but better in northerlies.　(12) They must be used as follows: a man who is healthy and strong should not distinguish waters, but always drink what is to hand; but he who, because of a disease, wishes to drink the most appropriate water may best achieve health by doing as follows. For those who have hard inner organs, prone to become heated, the sweetest, lightest, clearest waters are beneficial; for those whose bellies are soft, moist, and full of phlegm, the hardest, most alkaline, and rather salty waters, since in this way they could best be dried up;　(13) for those waters that are best for cooking and softening are especially likely to loosen the inner organs and liquefy them, while those that are alkaline, hard, and least good for cooking will compact the inner organs and dry them out. Yet people are deceived about salt waters because of their lack of experience. Brackish waters are believed to be laxative; but they are quite the opposite as regards evacuation, since they are alkaline and not suitable for cooking, so that the inner organs are constricted by them rather than liquefied.

Such is the case concerning waters from springs.

8. Concerning rainwaters, however, and such as come from snow, I shall tell how things are.

(2) Rainwaters are very light and very sweet, also very thin and bright. For at the beginning the sun lifts and draws up the finest, lightest part of the water;　(3) salts make this obvious, for the salty part of the water is left behind by reason of its size and weight, and becomes salts, while the sun draws up the finest part by reason of its lightness. It lifts this part not only from swamp waters but also from the sea and from all things in which some moisture is contained; and it is contained in all things.　(4) Even from humans themselves it draws the finest, lightest part of the juice. There is a very substantial proof: for when a person walks or sits in the sunshine wearing a cloak, whatever parts of his flesh the sun shines upon will not sweat, for the sun draws up the visible part of the sweat; but whatever parts are shaded under the cloak, or some other garment, do sweat, for (*the moisture*) is lifted out by the sun and forced out but is preserved by its covering, so that it does not disappear under the influence of the sun. But when the person moves into the shade, the whole body alike

turns sweaty, for the sun no longer shines upon it. (5) For the same reason, these waters turn foul most quickly of all, and rainwater has an unpleasant odour, because it has been brought together from very many things and mixed, and thus turns foul most quickly. (6) In addition, whenever it is drawn and borne aloft, being carried about and mingled into the air, the muddy, nocturnal part is removed, is displaced, and becomes vapour and mist, while the brightest, lightest part of it is left behind and becomes sweet as it is burned and cooked by the sun; indeed, all things that are cooked always become sweet. (7) Therefore, while it is scattered and has not yet condensed, it is borne aloft; but whenever it gathers somewhere and is compacted into one place by winds that suddenly blow against one another, it is broken apart wherever it happens to be most compacted. For this is more likely to happen whenever the clouds, receiving their constitution from the wind, being impelled, and travelling on, suddenly collide with a contrary wind and with other clouds. Then the first of them are compacted while those behind are borne on and thus made thick and dark and compacted into one place; and by reason of their weight they break apart and showers occur. (8) These (*waters*) are most likely best: but they require to be heated and have their foul part removed, otherwise they have an unpleasant odour and in those that drink them a sore throat, coughs, and loss of voice is caused.

(9) Those (*waters*) that come from snow and ice are all unpleasant. For whenever it has once been frozen, it never settles into its old nature but the bright, light, sweet part of it congeals and disappears, while the muddiest, most stagnant part is left behind. (10) You may know it thus: if you wish, when it is winter, pour water into a vessel and put it in the open air so that it may freeze hard. Then, next day, carry it into a shelter where the ice may easily melt; when it is dissolved, measure the water and you will find there is much less of it. (11) This is a proof that during freezing the lightest, finest part disappears and is dried up, but not, of course, the heaviest and coarsest; for it could not do so. By this, then, I believe that these waters—those from snow and ice and those that go with them—are the most unpleasant for all uses.

Such is the case concerning rainwaters and water from snow and ice.

9. People get the stones most of all, however, or are attacked by nephritis, strangury, and sciatica, and suffer ruptures, where they drink exceedingly numerous varieties of water, or water from great rivers into which other rivers discharge, or from a lake into which many varied streams enter; likewise people who use imported water brought over a long distance and not from nearby. (2) For it is impossible for one water to resemble another. Instead, some will be sweet, some salty and containing alum, while others will flow from hot springs. Mixed together in the same (*place*), these waters will dispute with each other and the strongest will always win; but the same one is not always strong: rather, sometimes one and sometimes another. For the north wind gives strength to one (*water*), the south wind to another, and concerning the others the story is the same. So with such waters it is bound to be the case that mud and sand are deposited in vessels, and the aforementioned diseases are caused by them if they are drunk out of; (3) though not for all people, as I shall tell next.

Those whose inner organs have a good flow and are healthy, whose bladder is not fevered, and the neck of whose bladder is not excessively constricted urinate easily, and nothing is compacted within the bladder. (4) Those, however, whose inner organs are fevered are bound to have a bladder in that condition. For whenever it is warmed more than is natural, its neck has become inflamed; and whenever it is in this condition it does not release the urine but cooks and burns it within itself. Then the thinnest and cleanest part of it passes through and is discharged as urine, but the coarsest, muddiest part is compacted and solidifies. Small at first, it afterwards grows larger; for being rolled about by the urine it attaches to itself whatever collects in a coarse form, and thus is increased and petrified; and when one urinates, it is pushed by the urine and prevents urination, causing severe pain. Hence children suffering from the stone rub their genitals and manipulate them, as it seems to them that the reason for the (*failure to*) urinate is to be found there. (5) The proof that this is the case is that those suffering from the stone pass water that is very bright, because the coarsest, muddiest part of it stays behind and is compacted. Most cases of the stone come about in this way; but limestone is also produced from milk if it is not hygienic but excessively hot and bilious, for it thoroughly warms the inner organs and bladder so that the urine is overheated and takes on the same condition. I say that it is better to give children wine only if it is very dilute, for it overheats and dries up the veins to a lesser degree. (6) Stones do not occur in the same way among females, for the urethra leading from their bladder is short and wide, so that the urine is easily forced out. Nor does the female rub the genital area with her hand as the male does, nor squeeze the urethra: for females have an opening into the genitals, while males do not have a direct opening and their urethras are not wide. They also drink more than boys do.

Such is the case concerning these matters, or very close to it.

Effects of the Seasons

10. Concerning the seasons, however, by pondering the following information one may discern what sort of year it will be, whether diseased or healthy. (2) For if the signs occur correctly at the rising and setting of stars, if rains occur in autumn and the winter is mild, neither too fine nor exceeding the proper degree of cold, and if timely rains occur in spring, then it is likely that the year will be very healthy.

(3) But if winter brings drought and northerly winds but spring brings showers and southerlies, then the summer is bound to be feverish and cause eye disease and dysentery. For whenever the stifling heat occurs suddenly while the earth is moist because of the spring rains and the south wind, the heat is bound to be double by reason of the rain-soaked, warm earth and the burning sun. Then, while people's inner organs are not solid and their brain not dried out—for it is impossible, during such a spring, for the body and the flesh not to go soft—then the most acute fevers befall everyone, especially phlegmatic persons. It is likely, too, that dysentery will occur among women and people with the moistest bodies. (4) If, at the rising of the Dog

(*Sirius*),[14] rain and stormy weather should occur and the Etesians should blow, there is some hope (*of the disease*) stopping and the autumn being healthy. If not, there is a danger of deaths occurring among children and women, though least often among the old; and that the survivors may go on to get quartan fevers, and after quartan fevers dropsy.

(5) If, however, winter brings southerly winds with rain and fine weather and spring brings northerlies with drought and wintry weather, then first those women that are with child and whose birth is due towards spring are likely to suffer a miscarriage, while those that do give birth will bear weakly, diseased children so that they either die immediately or survive but are thin, weak, and diseased. That is what these (*conditions*) do to women.   (6) To others (*they bring*) dysentery and dry eye disease; to some, discharges from the head running into the lung. It is likely that dysentery will occur among phlegmatic persons and women, as the phlegm flows down from the brain on account of the moistness of their nature; among the bilious, dry eye disease will occur on account of the warmth and dryness of their flesh; among the old, discharges on account of their slenderness and the attenuation of their veins, so that some will die suddenly while others become paralysed on the right side.   (7) Whenever, the winter having southerly winds and warmth, neither the body nor the veins become solid, and then a northerly, dry, cold spring follows, the brain—at the moment when it should have been softening and being cleansed by a head-cold and a sore throat—is at this very time made firm and solidified, so that when suddenly summer follows with heat and burning and the great change occurs, these diseases will attack people.   (8) Those cities that lie in a good relation to the sun and winds and employ good waters will feel such changes less. Those that employ marshy, swampy waters and lie in a bad relation to the winds and sun will feel them more.

(9) If summer be dry, the diseases stop more quickly; if rainy, they become long-lasting. There is a danger that cancers will be generated from all sorts of causes if an ulcer is generated. Lientery[15] and dropsy occur among those recovering from such disease, for their inner organs are not easily dried up.

(10) If summer be rainy and southerly and autumn too, the winter is bound to be diseased and it is likely that among the phlegmatic and persons older than forty years burning fevers will occur; among the bilious, pleuritis and pneumonia.

(11) If summer be dry and northerly and autumn rainy and southerly, it is likely that in the winter headaches and gangrene of the brain will occur, along with coughs, sore throats, and head-colds, and in some persons consumption.

---

[14] i.e. in the hottest part of the summer. The heliacal rising of Sirius (α Canis Majoris) takes place in late July–early August.
[15] A form of diarrhoea.

(12) If it (*the summer*) were northerly and waterless, with no rain following either (*the rising of*) the Dog or that of Arcturus,[16] it could be particularly advantageous for those of a phlegmatic nature, and also for moist persons and women. To bilious persons, however, these conditions are highly inimical, for they become extremely dried up and dry eye diseases occur among them, as well as acute and chronic fevers and in some cases episodes of melancholy. This is because the wettest and moistest part of the bile is consumed, while the thickest and bitterest is left behind, and that of the blood for the same reason; and from these substances those diseases arise in such people. All these things are beneficial to phlegmatic persons, for they are dried out and arrive at winter not flabby but dried up.

11. By thinking and reflecting in this way, one could foresee the majority of what will result from the changes. One must especially guard against the greatest changes of seasons, and neither give medicine unnecessarily nor practise any cautery or surgery upon the inner organs, before a period of ten or more days has passed.   (2) The greatest and most dangerous changes are the following: both solstices, especially the summer one; both equinoxes are so regarded as well, especially the autumn one. One must guard against the risings of stars, especially the Dog, next Arcturus, and then the setting of the Pleiades;[17] for the outcomes of illnesses are decided in these days particularly: some cause death, others decline, and all the others evolve into another form and another constitution.

Such is the case concerning these things.

CLIMATE AND CHARACTER

12. But now I wish to tell of the extent to which Asia and Europe differ from one another in all respects, and show in what respect the appearances of the nations are distinct and in no way similar to one another. It would be a long tale to recount them all, but I shall tell it how it seems to me concerning the greatest and the majority of differences.

Effects of Conditions in Asia

(2) I say that Asia differs a great deal from Europe in the natures of all things that grow from the ground and of people. For everything grows to a much greater beauty and size in Asia. (*That*) land is more civilized (*than this*), and the characters of the people are milder and better-tempered.   (3) The cause of these things is the mixture of the seasons: it lies midway between the (*sc. solstitial*) risings of the sun (*north-east and south-east*), and towards the east; and is further from the cold. Conditions promote growth and civilization most of all when nothing is forcefully prevalent and equality

---

[16] The heliacal rising of Arcturus (α Boötis) marked the beginning of autumn (Jouanna 1996, 219 n. 1).
[17] For the Dog Star, see n. 14; for Arcturus, n. 16. The Pleiades' heliacal setting signified the start of winter (Jouanna 1996, 219 n. 1).

of all things is dominant.   (4) But things are not everywhere similar across Asia; still, the part of the region that lies midway between the hot and cold is the most fruitful, has the most trees, has the best climate, and enjoys the best waters both from heaven and out of the earth. For it is neither burned up by the heat nor dried out by dryness and drought; nor is it ravaged by cold, nor is it damp and soaked by numerous rains and snow.[18]   (5) It is likely that many seasonal crops will grow, both those from seeds and those plants that the earth itself brings forth, whose fruits people use by taming the wild ones and transplanting them into an appropriate place. The flocks reared there are likely to thrive, and especially to give birth to very sturdy offspring and bring them up to be very beautiful. The people will be well fed, very beautiful in form, very great in size, and hardly varying at all in form and size.   (6) It is likely that the region will be closest to spring in terms of its nature and the moderate character of its seasons. Bravery, perseverance, hard work, and spiritedness could not arise in a place of this nature [—].

Effects of Conditions in Egypt and Libyē

[*The passage on Egypt and Libyē is missing.*] (7) [—] on the part of either the native or the alien, but pleasure is bound to prevail; for which reason a multiplicity of forms exists among the wild animals.

Such is the case concerning the Egyptians and Libyans, it seems to me.

Asians around the Black Sea

13. Concerning those to the right of the summer risings of the sun (*the north-east*), as far as Lake Maiotis (*Sea of Azov*)—for this is the boundary of Europe and Asia— the case is as follows.   (2) These nations in this direction differ from one another more than the preceding ones because of the changes of seasons and the nature of the land.   (3) What is true for the earth is likewise true for other people. For where the seasons make the greatest and most frequent changes, there the land, too, is wildest and most uneven, and you will find that there are very numerous and wooded mountains, as well as plains and meadows. But where the seasons do not change greatly, for those people the land is very uniform.   (4) The same is the case for humans, if one is willing to consider it. For some (*physical*) natures are similar to tree-clad, well-watered mountains; others to light, waterless (*places*); others to rather grassy or marshy (*places*); and others to a plain or to bare, dry earth.   (5) For the seasons that alter the nature of a form are various; and if they vary greatly among themselves, a greater number of differences arise in the shapes also.

14. I shall leave aside those nations that differ a little, but about those that differ greatly, either in nature or custom, I shall tell how it is.

---

[18] For similar claims in ancient authors that a region is medially and ideally located, see the Introduction, §III. 3. n.

First about the Makrokephaloi (*Longheads*),[19]   (2) because there is no other nation but this that has heads like theirs: for, in the beginning, custom was the most important reason for the length of their head, but now nature too contributes to custom. For they regard as most noble those that have the longest head.   (3) The situation about the custom is this: as soon as a child is born they use their hands to reshape its head, which is still soft—the child, too, is soft and pliable—and force it to grow by applying a band and appropriate devices. By these the sphericity of the head is deformed but the length increases. Thus, in the beginning, the custom caused such a nature to take on this character;   (4) but with the progress of time it happened by nature, so that custom no longer compelled it. For the seed comes from everywhere in the body: a healthy one from the healthy parts, diseased from the diseased. So if, in general, bald offspring come from bald people, grey-eyed from grey-eyed, crooked from deformed, and the story is the same with the rest of the shape, what stands in the way of a long-headed child being born of a long-headed person?   (5) Now, however, they do not occur in the same way as before, for the custom has less power because of intercourse with (*other*) people.

Such is the case concerning these people, it seems to me.

15. Concerning those in Phasis,[20] however, that land is marshy, hot, watery, and wooded, and many powerful rains occur there in all seasons. People's life is lived in the marshes; their houses are of wood and reed and have been contrived amid the waters. They do not use walking much in their city and trading-place, but sail up and down in boats made of a single log, for there are many canals. They drink waters that are hot, stagnant, putrefied by the sun, and increased by the rains. The Phasis itself is the most stagnant of all rivers and flows most gently. The crops produced there are all weak, effeminate, and incomplete because of the great quantity of water; for this reason, too, they do not ripen. A great deal of mist covers the land, coming off the waters.   (2) From these causes, indeed, the Phasienoi have bodily shapes that diverge from other people: for in stature they are great, in thickness excessively stout, with no visible joint or vein. They have a colour that is slightly yellow as if they were seized with dropsy. They speak the most deeply of all people, using air that is not clear but damp and murky. As for enduring hardship, they have become rather indolent in body.   (3) The seasons do not change much towards either heat or cold; the winds for the most part are southerly except for a single local breeze: this sometimes blows forcefully, harshly, and hot, and they name this wind *kenchrōn* (*Millet Seed*). The north wind does not often occur; when it does blow, it is feeble and weak.

Such is the case concerning the difference of nature and shape among people in Asia.

---

[19] This people, possibly to be connected with the Makrones attested in other evidence, lived inland from the SE coast of the Black Sea, Xen. *Anab.* 4. 8. 22.

[20] See n. 1.

16. Concerning the lack of spirit and manliness among the people, however, the fact that, compared with Europeans, Asians are extremely unwarlike and tamer is chiefly due to the seasons, which make smaller changes towards either the hot or the cold, but are similar.   (2) For violent upsets of mind or a powerful change in body do not occur, such as would be likely to make the mood become wild, full of recklessness, and passionate rather than resting in the same state. For of all things it is changes that always stimulate the mind of people and will not let it remain calm.   (3) It seems to me that it is from these causes that the Asian race is without strength, and even more because of their customs: for most parts of Asia are ruled by kings. Where people are not in charge of themselves or independent, but have masters, the thinking among them is not about how to study warfare but about how not to appear ready for fighting;   (4) for the dangers are not the same. The former are likely to serve in the army, endure hardship, and die under compulsion on behalf of their masters and be away from their children, their wives, and their other associates. For all the useful and brave actions they may perform, it is their masters who are increased by them and thrive; they themselves reap dangers and deaths. In addition, the land of this kind of people is bound to be made empty by enemies and indolence, so that even if one is born brave and courageous one's mind will be diverted by custom.   (5) The weighty proof of these things is this: those Hellenes or barbarians in Asia that do not have masters, but are independent and endure hardship for their own benefit, are the most ready of all to fight. They face dangers on their own responsibility; they themselves win the rewards for bravery, just as they suffer the penalty for cowardice. You will also find the Asians varying among themselves, some being better, others more lightweight. It is the changes in the seasons that are responsible for this, as has been stated by me earlier.

Such is the case concerning those in Asia.

Sauromatai and Other Skythians in Europe and Asia

17. In Europe, however, there is a Skythian nation that lives around Lake Maiotis and differs from the other nations. They are called the Sauromatai.   (2) Their women raise horses, shoot bows, throw javelins from their horses, and fight against their enemies as long as they are virgins. They do not lose their virginity until they kill three of the enemy; they do not cohabit before the time when they make the sacrifices according to the law. She who takes a man to herself ceases to ride until obliged by the need for a communal expedition.   (3) They lack the right breast; for while they are still infants their mothers take a bronze implement crafted for the purpose, make it very hot, place it on the right breast and sear it so that its growth is stunted and all the power and mass come out in the right shoulder and arm.

18. Concerning the shape of the other Skythians, the reason why they resemble themselves but in no way (*resemble*) other people is the same as in the case of the Egyptians, except that the latter are constrained by heat, the former by cold.   (2) The

so-called desert[21] of the Skythians is a plain that is like a meadow and elevated, but lacks trees and is moderately well watered; for it has great rivers which channel the water off the plains. Here, too, live the Skythians called Nomades (*Pasturers*); the reason is that there are no houses and they live in waggons instead.   (3) The smallest waggons are four-wheeled while others are six-wheeled; they have been protected with felt and crafted like houses; some are single-(*roomed*), others triple. They remain dry in the face of water, snow, and winds. Some waggons have two pairs of oxen without horns to draw them, others three; the reason they have no horns is the cold.   (4) The women live in these waggons; the men are carried on horseback; the sheep they possess follow behind, along with the oxen and horses. They stay in the same spot for as long as the grazing supports the animals; when it no longer does, they relocate to another land. They themselves eat boiled meat and drink the milk of horses, and they eat *hippakē*, that is, 'horse cheese'.

Such is the case concerning their lifestyle and customs.

19. Concerning the seasons and their shape, however, the Skythian race has diverged much from the rest of humanity; it is very uniform like the Egyptian race, and has very few offspring. The land, too, is very unproductive of wild animals, in terms of both size and numbers.   (2) For it lies under the very Bears (*Ursa Minor and Ursa Major*) and the Rhipaian mountains from which the north wind blows. The sun comes closest in the final stage, when it comes to its summer circuit; at that point it warms (*the land*) for a little time, but not strongly. The winds that blow from the hot places do not come there, unless occasionally and in a weak form; but from the north there continually blow winds that are chilled by snow, ice, and many waters; these winds never leave the mountains, which as a result are uninhabited. By day a great deal of mist fills the plains, and this is where they live, so that it is always winter, but summer only for a few days and scarcely then. For the plains are lofty and bare, and not fringed with mountains except in this direction, to the north.   (3) In this region the wild animals do not grow big but are able to shelter underground; for the winter and the bareness of the land restrict them, because there is no shelter or cover.   (4) For the changes of the seasons are not great or powerful, but are uniform with one another and bring little change. For this reason, they (*the people*) are similar to one another in bodily form; they always use similar food, and the same clothing in summer and winter; they draw in watery, thick air, drink waters from snow and ice, and have no endurance, for it is impossible for the body or soul to endure hardship where there are no powerful changes.   (5) By reason of these compelling factors, their bodily forms are thick, fleshy, without (*visible*) joints, moist, and lacking in tone. Their inner organs lower down are the moistest of any; for it is impossible for the belly to dry up in such a land, natural condition, climate, and disposition of the seasons. Instead, their flesh will be eternally fatty and smooth and their bodies like one another, males to males

---

[21] *erēmiē*, 'empty land', referring to the steppe region N of the Black Sea (Jouanna 1996, 323 n. 4).

and females to females. For since the seasons are similar there is no damage or deterioration in the formation of the seed, unless it meet with some violent constraint or disease.

20. I shall present a great proof of their moistness. For you will find that the greater part of the Skythians, and all of them that are Nomades, are branded on the shoulders, arms, wrists, chests, and loins, for no other reason than the moistness of their nature and their softness. For they cannot draw bows or apply their weight to a javelin by reason of their moistness and lack of tone; but when they have been branded, most of the moisture is dried out from their joints and they become better toned, better fed, and better articulated in their bodies, (2) which grow crooked[22] and broad: first because they are not swaddled as (*children are*) in Egypt, a custom they avoid because of horse-riding, so that they may have a good seat; next, because of their habit of sitting: for the males, as long as they are unable to ride a horse, spend most of their time sitting in the waggon and make little use of walking owing to all the relocations and journeys. The females are fluid in bodily form to an astonishing degree, and slow. The race is red-skinned because of the cold, not because the sun is sharp; their whiteness is scorched by the cold and becomes red.

21. It is impossible for such a nature to produce many offspring; nor is there much desire among the men for intercourse because of the moistness of their nature and the softness and coldness of their inner organs, which make a man unlikely to be lustful. Moreover, being continually shaken by their horses they become too weak for intercourse. Such are the causes that occur in men. (2) For the women it is the fatness and moistness of their flesh; for their womb is unable to capture the seed, nor does the monthly cleansing occur among them as it ought to, but too little and too late: the mouth of the womb is blocked by fat and does not accept the seed. These women are incapable of enduring hardship; they are fat, and their inner organs are cold and soft. (3) These are the compelling causes why the Skythian race is not prolific. The slave-women provide a strong proof of this: they barely come to a man before they are with child, because of their endurance and the spareness of their flesh.

22. In addition, a large number of men among the Skythians become like eunuchs, do the work of women, and speak as women do. Such men are called Anarieis.[23] (2) The local people attribute the cause to a god; they both worship these men and bow down to them, each of them fearing for themselves. (3) I myself believe that these conditions are divine as are all others, none being more divine or more human than another: all are alike, all divine. Each condition of this sort has its own nature, and none occurs without its nature. (4) How this condition arises, as it seems to me, I shall state. During horse-riding, rheumatism affects them, since they are always holding onto the horse with their legs; then they become lame and their hips get ulcers, if they are affected severely. (5) But they cure themselves in the following way: at the

---

[22] Reading ῥοικά 'crooked' rather than ῥοϊκά 'fluid' (Jouanna 1996, 236 n. 3).
[23] Cf. the Skythian Enareës, Hdt. 1. 105. 4 (Jouanna 1996, 337, end of n. 3).

onset of the disease they cut the vein behind each ear; and when the blood has flowed out, sleep takes them because they are weak, and they lie down. Later they awake, some cured and others not.   (6) It seems to me that the seed is destroyed by this treatment; for there are veins beside the ear which, if one cuts them, the persons who are cut become infertile. It seems to me that it is these veins they are cutting.   (7) When subsequently they come into contact with a woman and are unable to use their body, at first they do not think about it but say nothing; but when they attempt the same thing two or three times, or more often, and nothing turns out differently, they think they have sinned against God, to whom they attribute the cause, and dress in women's clothing, recognizing their lack of manhood. They act as women and work with the women in the work that women do.

(8) This is a thing that the rich Skythians suffer: not the lowest sort but those who are most noble and have the greatest power, because of their horse-riding; the poor suffer it less because they do not ride.   (9) Yet if this disease were more divine than others it ought not to assail the most high-born Skythians or the rich only, but all men alike, and mostly those with few possessions. The gods ought to enjoy being honoured and admired by people, and return favours in return;   (10) for the rich probably make many sacrifices to the gods and make dedications from their extensive wealth and honours. The poor do less of this because they have nothing, and consequently hold it against the gods that they do not give them wealth. As a result, the people with few possessions pay the penalty for such offences more than the rich.   (11) In fact, as I said earlier, these diseases are just as much divine as others, and each occurs according to its nature. A disease of this sort occurs among the Skythians from a cause of the sort which I have stated.   (12) The same holds likewise among the rest of mankind; for wherever people ride often and continually, very many are seized with rheumatism, sciatica, and gout and are hardly lustful at all.   (13) This is a feature of the Skythians, the most eunuch-like of people, for the aforementioned reasons and also because they always wear trousers and are on horseback much of the time, so that they cannot touch their private parts with their hand and, owing to the cold and their exertions, forget about desire and intercourse, enjoying no excitement before they come to manhood.

Such is the case concerning the race of the Skythians.

Effects of Conditions in Europe

23. The rest of the (*human*) race in Europe, however, is varied among itself both in size and shape because of the changes of the seasons, which are great and frequent. There are periods of powerful heat, severe winters, many rains and then long-lasting droughts and winds; all these things cause many and various changes, from which one can learn that the process of generation is different as regards the formation of the seed, and is not the same in the same (*seed*) in summer and winter, or in rain and drought.   (2) This, I believe, is why the bodily forms of Europeans have diverged more than those of Asians, and why their sizes are extremely variable from one to another within each city. For more

damage takes place in the seed during its formation in changes of seasons that are frequent than in seasons that are alike and similar.   (3) Concerning characters, the reason is the same: wildness, intractability, and high spirits arise in such a (*climatic*) nature, for when frequent, violent upsets of mind occur they instil wildness and erase tameness and calmness. Therefore I regard those inhabiting Europe as more courageous than those in Asia; for when things are always much the same laziness is found, while when things keep changing we find endurance of body and soul. From quietness and laziness cowardice grows; from endurance and toil, bravery.   (4) For this reason those living in Europe are readier for fighting; and also because of their customs, since they are not ruled by kings as Asians are. For when men are ruled by kings they are bound to be most cowardly; this has been stated by me earlier. For their souls have been enslaved and they do not want to take risks willingly on behalf of another's power; but those that are independent, since they choose danger on their own account and not because of others, show a willing spirit and go into the place of fear, since they themselves carry off the prizes of victory. Thus customs create courage in no small measure. In a total and overall sense this is the case concerning Europe and Asia.

24. In Europe, too, there are tribes that differ one from another in size, shape, and manliness. The respects in which they diverge are the same as have also been mentioned above, but I will state them more clearly.   (2) Those that live in a mountainous, rough, high, and well-watered region, and to whom changes of seasons happen that vary greatly, will probably have bodily forms that are large and well formed in respect of endurance and manliness; such natures also have more than a little wildness and fierceness in them.   (3) Those that live in hollow places which are like meadows and are airless, and who experience a larger proportion of hot winds than cold, and use hot waters, could scarcely be large or straight but rather formed for breadth, fleshy, dark-haired, and themselves dark rather than whitish, phlegmatic rather than bilious. Both manliness and endurance could not exist in their soul naturally in the same way, though the application of law could generate them insofar as the characteristic was not present.   (4) If there were rivers in the land that drained away from the land the stagnant water and the rainwater, these people could be healthier and flexible; but if there were no rivers and the water they drank was swampy, stagnant, and marshy, these bodily forms would be bound to be round-bellied and diseased in the spleen.   (5) Those that live in an elevated land, windy and well-watered, would be large in bodily form and similar to one another; but their minds would be less manly and tamer. Those that are in a well-tempered place, and use plentiful water of good quality, will have good body-shapes and character, and will be well-built and similar to one another.   (6) Those in thin, waterless, and bare places, extreme in their changes of seasons—in such a land their bodily forms would probably be hard, well-toned, and more blond-haired than dark; in their character and moods they would be strong-willed and opinionated. For wherever the changes of the seasons are most frequent and differ most among themselves, there you will find bodily forms, character, and natures differing the most.

CONCLUSION

(7) These are the greatest variations of nature; next come the land in which one is brought up, and the waters.   (8) For you will find, for the most part, that the forms of the people and their ways follow the nature of the land. For wherever the earth is rich, soft, and well watered and the waters are very high, so that they are hot in summer and cold in winter, and lie in a good relation to the seasons, here people are fleshy, lacking in (*visible*) joints, watery, short of endurance, and all in all poor in spirit. Laziness and sleepiness are there to be seen among them; they are thick-limbed when it comes to skills; not refined or sharp-witted.   (9) Where the land is bare, waterless, rough, oppressed by winter, and wholly burned by the sun, here you might see people who are hard, spare, well-articulated, well-toned, and thick-haired; the spur to labour will be intense in such a nature, as will wakefulness; their character and moods will be strong-willed and opinionated, partaking of wildness more than tameness; they will be sharper in skills, more intelligent, and superior in matters of war.

The things growing in the earth will all follow the earth. The most opposed natures and bodily forms have this character.   (10) If you judge by these things in order to consider other matters, you will not go wrong.

6

EUDOXOS OF KNIDOS

(391/0–338/7 BC)

D. Graham J. Shipley

INTRODUCTION

Eudoxos of Knidos has perhaps not received due credit for his contributions to Greek geography,[1] particularly in respect of the mathematical and astronomical frameworks that can be used to investigate the Earth-bound *oikoumenē*. While it is less clear that his organization or observational descriptions were innovative, his *Circuit of the World* clearly offered a novel and vivid portrayal, beyond that of Hekataios a century earlier, of the character and life of communities around the known world, as the relative frequency with which he is cited may suggest.

Eudoxos' primary formation was as a mathematician. His date of birth is disputed, but was most likely 391/0.[2] His life is reasonably well known from a memoir of some 800 words in Diogenes Laërtios' *Lives of Eminent Philosophers*,[3] though it ends with a bizarre poem in galliambics by Diogenes himself, telling how in Egypt the Apis bull warned Eudoxos of his imminent death (but unless Eudoxos returned to Egypt a second time, his death was delayed until his 53rd year). Originally from Knidos in Karia (a partly Hellenic region of south-western Asia Minor), Eudoxos studied briefly at Athens (attending Plato's teaching) in the early 360s, then visited Egypt for 16 months, where he gathered information for his astronomical works and wrote his *Oktaëtēris* (*Eight-year Cycle*). Later he founded an academy in Kyzikos, resided with Maussollos the governor of Karia, returned to Athens, and finally retired to his home city. In common with many educated members of Greek elites who wrote literary works, Eudoxos is credited with participation in public affairs; at any rate, Diogenes Laërtios says he was honoured with a decree at Knidos and became famous for 'writing laws for his own fellow-citizens' (8. viii. 88).

Like Aristotle and other leading post-Platonic figures, Eudoxos was a master of different disciplines, writing for example on geometry (including the theory of proportions), computation, the method of exhaustion (for calculating areas and volumes

---

[1] E. does not feature in the index to Dueck 2012. General sketch: Folkerts 2006.
[2] Lasserre 1966, 137–9, examines the conflicting evidence in detail.
[3] D. L. 8. viii. 86–91 = fr. 7 Lasserre.

not bounded by straight lines), the spherical divisions of the heavens (zodiac, equator, tropics, etc.; cf. **23** below), the positions and definitions of the constellations (work known mainly through its much later use by Aratos, Hipparchos, and Vitruvius), the apparent movements of heavenly bodies (based on the long-to-endure model of concentric spheres), the annual periods of invisibility of zodiacal stars in the sun's glow (influential upon later calendrical works), the theory of pleasure and of colour—and a geographical work in seven books, systematically enumerating the inhabited world. It is in relation to this last that Strabo (10. 3. 5, C465) quotes Polybios as saying that while Eudoxos 'did well in respect of Hellenic things, Ephoros gave the best account of foundations (*ktiseis*)' (sc. of cities; cf. **70**), 'kinship relations (*syngeneiai*), relocations (*metanastaseis*), and colony-leaders (*archēgetai*)', which probably implies that Eudoxos, too, covered exactly those and other historical matters within his geography.

This last work is consistently cited as *Ges periodos* (or simply *Periodos*), meaning a description of the *oikoumenē* (the inhabited portion of the Earth) that was not limited to its coasts but extended inland. The work is lost, but most of the identified 'fragments' or quotations from it are presented below (apart from certain passages focused on myth and philosophy). It was clearly influenced in form and content by Hekataios (Chapter 3 above); we could probably also identify the influence of Phileas of Athens (see Introduction, §VI. 4. b) if we knew more about the latter's work. It was also, however, informed by new 4th-century thinking about the layout of the Earth (e.g. **4**). Eudoxos' work may have been accompanied by a map,[4] for he referred to an imaginary line from the western end of the gulf of Corinth to Cape Sounion in Attica (see **48**); this may have been part of a conceived central parallel of latitude intended as a frame of reference for the whole *oikoumenē*,[5] but was perhaps rather a first step in that direction, followed up for example by Dikaiarchos (Chapter 9 below).

Unlike the work of Hekataios, with its trend-setting clockwise progress round the *oikoumenē*, the first six books of the *Ges periodos* begin with the east and north-east of the world and follow an approximately anti-clockwise sequence. Book 1, judging by the extracts explicitly linked to it (**12–13, 15–21**), focused on the east and north-east (including Eudoxos' own homeland of Asia Minor, the lands east of the Black Sea, and the Levant). Book 2 (cited in **24, 29**) was on Egypt; book 3 perhaps covered the south-east of the *oikoumenē* including India and Persia; book 4 (see **36** (?), **37–40, 42, 44**) the north, from Skythia to Macedonia; book 5 (cited only in **53**) central Greece; book 6 (see **55** (?), **58, 60–6, 68**) the Peloponnese as well as the lands facing it in Italy (not just the south, but as far north as Spina in the Po valley), Sicily and to the south Libyē. Book 7 (cited only in **77–8**) may have been specifically dedicated to islands, though the only fragment attributed to it refers to the Aeolian Isles north of Sicily, so a western focus continuing that of book 6 is also possible; the other fragments attributed to book 7 by Lasserre may, alternatively, be derived from appropriate places in books 1–6. Other works treat islands as a special class of places (see Index); there are

---

[4] Gysembergh 2016, 31–2.   [5] As suggested by Lasserre 1966, 259.

even lists of 'greatest islands', such as that appended to the *Periplous* of Pseudo-Skylax (Chapter 7 below).[6]

Eudoxos' coverage of the *oikoumenē* was thus most detailed for the parts most immediately accessible to Greeks; less so to the west of Carthage and Italy and, like authors before Pytheas, eschewing everything north of Italy. His own travels may have been limited to the eastern Mediterranean and adjacent lands.

It is plain that Eudoxos was held in high repute in after times (1) and regarded as a standard author (3–4) who, moreover, wrote good Greek (2). His geographical work was available down to the Byzantine period (5). His presentation of material has much in common with that of Hekataios (Chapter 3 above), such as the recording of place-names (e.g. 38–9, 41, 52, 62), the enumeration of *poleis* (e.g. 52, 61, 66–7) and non-*polis* settlements (64), and the attribution of places to regions (10, 42, 61–2, 66–7, 74). Like Hekataios, too, he enlivened his survey with quite detailed topographical information, for example about cities' locations (56), capes or sea straits (34, 42, 44, 48), and islands both famous and obscure (29; possibly the whole of book 7); Strabo's passage on the form of the Saronic gulf (48) is particularly striking. Like earlier geographers, he modified his predecessors' theories (4) and entered into debates over topography (25, 59) and changing place-names (41).[7] Like other Classical geographers, he shows a strong interest in foreign peoples (e.g. 15–16, 18–21, 35–6, 39–40, 55, 63, 65, 68), their customs (12, 15–16, 20, 24), languages (16, 65), religious cults (13, 24–6, 36), and even their productive economy (17 (?), 21, 27, 55, 58, 63). His interest in a proverb (11) may have arisen from a particular locale as well as reflecting his philosophical inclinations. We may infer that he was proud of his home city (14), and that he noted famous men from there and elsewhere (37, 78). Certainly, like other geographers, he placed great emphasis on historical depth, as the Polybios passage quoted above implies: we have examples of his discussions of foundation myths (70) and mythology (11, 13, 69), as well as of local events relevant to wider history (53), the characters of local communities (49, 79), and of course calendars (28).

The influence of contemporary climate theory may be inferred (23, 30) and one may suppose that Eudoxos knew the Hippocratic *Airs, Waters, and Places* (Chapter 5 above). He recorded an explanation for the coldness of Boiotian Askra in winter (51), and clearly had a strong interest in hydrology: he discussed the name of the spring at Delphi (50); the river system of Macedonia (45), the behaviour of wells at one city (7); outflows of fresh water within the sea (71); the behaviour of the Nile, already a favourite topic of geographical writers (7, 26, 30); the effects of drinking certain waters, whether beneficial (46) or adverse (57, 60); springs with strange properties (47, 73, 76); petrifying streams (72); alien substances found in lakes or the sea (32,[8] 54); and a spring in the Black Sea where small crocodiles occurred (33). Some of these obser-

---

[6] On insularity in the Mediterranean generally, see the valuable collection of papers in Ampolo and Michelini 2009, esp. pp. 3–346.

[7] His recording of names which later scholars found interesting as alternative forms was presumably not a conscious strategy: see e.g. 19, 35, 38–9, 43, 45, 52–3, 62.

[8] Also mentioned at *AWP* 7. 9.

vations (not necessarily all from autopsy) shade over into the recording of wondrous phenomena, such as the occurrence of fish in the ground (9), remarkable geological formations (6, 22), minerals and stones (8, 16, 21), creatures both unusual (29, 33 again, 58) and domesticated (27), and unusual human physiques (31).

Although surviving only in extracts, the wide-ranging influence of Eudoxos' work upon succeeding generations and centuries was comparable to that of the greatest geographical observers and theoreticians, including several represented by their geographical writings in this book, such as Eratosthenes, Hipparchos, and Poseidonios.

This selection of fragments includes most of those assigned to the *Ges periodos* by Lasserre, whose text is followed except where otherwise indicated.[9] Fragments printed in small type by Lasserre, which do not name Eudoxos, are not selected below. Those containing a book number are interleaved with those that Lasserre in his commentary assigns to a particular book.

Extracts are ordered by date within each section (with scholia at the end of the section).[10]

SELECTED FURTHER READING

Cataudella, M. R. (2016), 'Some scientific approaches: Eudoxus of Cnidus and Dicaearchus of Messene', in S. Bianchetti *et al.* (eds), *Brill's Companion to Ancient Geography: The Inhabited World in Greek and Roman Tradition* (Leiden–Boston), 115–31.

Folkerts, M. (2006), 'Eudoxus [1] of Cnidus', in H. Cancik *et al.* (eds), *Brill's New Pauly* (Leiden).

*Lasserre, F. (1966), *Die Fragmente des Eudoxos von Knidos: herausgegeben, übersetzt und kommentiert.* Berlin.

Mendell, H. (2008), 'Eudoxos of Knidos (ca 365–340 BCE)', *Encyclopedia of Ancient Natural Scientists* 310–13. [Mostly on E.'s mathematics.]

Roller, D. W. (2015), *Ancient Geography: The Discovery of the World in Classical Greece and Rome* (London–New York), 75–6.

TEXTS

TESTIMONIA

1 Strabo 1. 1. 1, C1: *Pioneers of geography*
We consider that geography is part of the business of a philosopher, if anything is. . . . For the first men bold enough to grasp it were such as Homer, Anaximandros of Miletos,

---

[9] Lasserre 1966, pp. 96–126 frs 272–372. Source texts have been checked, and some entries revised accordingly. I have not seen the new corpus of all E.'s fragments in the unpublished thesis of Gysembergh 2015.

[10] e.g. Musso 1986.

Hekataios—his (*fellow*) citizen, as Eratosthenes also says—as well as Demokritos, Eudoxos, Dikaiarchos, Ephoros, and several others . . .

2 Plutarch, *That it is Not Possible to Live Contentedly while Following Epicurus,* 10 (*Moralia,* 1093b–c): *Eudoxos' literary style*
When narrative (*historia*) and exposition has nothing grievous or harmful (*in it*) and adopts a style possessing power and grace to describe fine, great deeds—as in the *Persika* (*Persian Affairs*) of Herodotos and the *Hellenika* (*Greek Affairs*) of Xenophon[11] . . . or the *Periodoi* which Eudoxos wrote, or the *Foundations* and *Constitutions* by Aristotle, or the biographies of men by Aristoxenos—not only is there a great element of giving pleasure, but it is pure and never to be regretted.

3 Agathemeros i. 1: *Eudoxos' geographical work*
Then Demokritos, Eudoxos, and certain others created circuits of the Earth (*gēs periodoi*) and circumnavigations.

4 Agathemeros i. 2: *Eudoxos' view of the form of the oikoumenē*
The old writers drew the inhabited world as round, and believed that Hellas lay in the middle, with Delphi in the middle of Hellas as it contained the navel of the Earth. But Demokritos, a man of great experience, was the first to perceive that the Earth (*i.e. the inhabited part*) is oblong, with a length one and a half times its breadth. Dikaiarchos the Peripatetic agreed with this; but Eudoxos (*made*) the length double the breadth,[12] Eratosthenes more than double . . .

5 Tzetzes (Ioannes), *Chiliades* 7. 633 8: *Survival of Eudoxos' text*

633 From lack of experience, I believe these things[13] false;
    but ten thousand others say they belong among true things,
    that one sees such things, and yet more novel, in real life;
636 thus Ktesias and Iamboulos . . .
638 . . . and Eudoxos . . .

BOOK 1

6 Pseudo-Antigonos of Karystos, *Collection of Marvellous Stories,* 123: *Examples of large caverns*
And in many places, it seems, are the category of clefts (*barathroi*) and Charonian caverns (*charonia*), such as the so-called Kimmeros[14]—the hole in Phrygia, as Eudoxos says—and the pit in Latmos.[15]

---

[11] Another version of the passage gives the *Hellenika* to Herodotos and the *Persika* to Xenophon.
[12] E. was, of course, writing earlier than Dikaiarchos (Ch. 9 below).
[13] i.e. things said by Skylax, cf. Skylax 14 above.
[14] So Eleftheriou, following Musso and Giannini; Lasserre reads 'Kimbros'.
[15] Ps.-Antigonos can be dated *c.*240 BC and was a contemporary of Antigonos of Karystos, to whom the *Collection* might otherwise be attributed (Eleftheriou 2018, 14–16, cf. 310–11).

7 Pseudo-Antigonos of Karystos, *Collection of Marvellous Stories,* 162: *Properties of wells in Pythopolis*
And (*Kallimachos states*) that Eudoxos says, regarding the wells in Pythopolis,[16] that they behave similarly to the Nile: for in summer they are filled over the rim, but in winter they stop short[17] to the extent that it is not easy even to dip (*a vessel*) in.

8 Pseudo-Aristotle, *On Miraculous Things Heard,* §173, 847a 5–7: *A magical mineral in Asia Minor*
In Mount Berekynthion is said to occur the stone called *machaira* (*knife*). If ever someone finds it while the mystery rites of Hekate are being celebrated, he goes mad, so Eudoxos says.[18]

9 Strabo 12. 3. 42, C562–3: *Fish in the ground*
Eudoxos, while saying that fish are excavated in dry places in Paphlagonia, does not specify the locality; and he states that (*they are found*) in wet places around the Askanian lake below Kios, saying nothing clear.

10 Strabo 13. 1. 4, C582: *Limits of the Troad*
Indeed, regarding the localities on the Propontis, Homer places the beginning of the Troad at the (*river*) Aisepos, but Eudoxos (*begins it*) at Priapos and Artake—the settlement (*chōrion*) on the island of the people of Kyzikos that lies facing Priapos—and thus contracting its limits.

11 Zenobios, *Proverbs* 5. 56:[19] *Myth and history*
'A quail saved mighty Herakles': this (*proverb*) is not in any of the ancient (*writers*). It is said about those who are saved from things they had no hope of (*surviving*). For Eudoxos (*says*) that Herakles of Tyre was destroyed by Typhon, but Iolaos, doing everything he could to revive the hero, burned up a quail, something Herakles used to enjoy when alive, and from this smoke Herakles was brought back to life.

12 Sextus Empiricus, *Outlines of Pyrrhonism,* 1. 152: *Customs of the Massagetai*
Among us, too, adultery is forbidden, but among the Massagetai (*women*) it has been handed down by custom as indifferent, as Eudoxos of Knidos records in the 1st (*book*) of the *Periodos*.

13 Athenaios 9. 47, 392d–e: *Phoenician worship of Herakles*
Eudoxos of Knidos, in the 1st (*book*) of *Ges periodos,* says that the Phoenicians sacrifice quails to Herakles because Herakles, son of Asteria and Zeus, when travelling to Libyē,

---

[16] A city in Mysia or Bithynia in NW Asia Minor.
[17] Lasserre omits 'stop short' (*ekleipein*) without comment, probably by a misprint.
[18] Cf. Ps.-Plutarch, §5 (Ch. 26 below).
[19] A very slightly different version is in Diogenianos (a contemporary of Z.), *Proverbs* 3. 49. See also 13.

was killed by Typhon, but when Iolaos brought him a quail he caught the scent of it and was brought back to life.[20]

14   Diogenes Laërtios, *Lives of the Philosophers,* 8. viii *(Eudoxos),* 90: *Eudoxos' namesake*
We also find another doctor *(called Eudoxos)* from Knidos, about whom Eudoxos in his *Ges periodos* states that he always recommended that the limbs should be moved in every kind of exercise, but also the senses similarly.

15   Diogenes Laërtios, *Lives of the Philosophers,* 9. xi *(Pyrrhon),* 83: *Customs of the Massagetai*
And the Massagetai, as Eudoxos too says in the 1st *(book)* of the *Periodos,* hold their women in common; but the Hellenes do not.

16   Stephanos of Byzantion α 437
Armenia: . . . The inhabitants are Armenioi, as Eudoxos *(says in the)* 1st *(book)* of *Ges periodos*: 'The Armenioi by race are from Phrygia, and in their speech they adopt the Phrygian fashion in many respects. They produce the stone that shapes and pierces sealstones.'

17   Stephanos of Byzantion α 476
Askalon: a city in Syria, beside Judaea. . . . In Eudoxos *(the ethnikon is written)* with *ai* in the 1st *(book)* ⟨of *Ges periodos*: [—] Askalonaioi [—]⟩ 'and the city where they say onions were first grown'.

18   Stephanos of Byzantion μ 212
Mossynoikoi: A nation *(ethnos),* about whom Eudoxos *(writes)* in *(the)* 1st *(book)* of *Ges periodos.*

19   Stephanos of Byzantion σ 327
Syrmatai: the Sauromatai, as Eudoxos *(says in the)* 1st *(book)*: 'That the Syrmatai occupy the river of the Tanaïs.'[21]

20   Stephanos of Byzantion χ 1
Chabarenoi: A nation. Eudoxos, 1st *(book)* of *Ges periodos*: 'For those living round about the Chalybes are named Chabarenoi, and if ever they become masters of foreign women they eat ⟨their⟩ breasts raw and feast upon the children.'

21   Stephanos of Byzantion χ 19
Chalybes: A nation around the Pontos, upon the river Thermodon, about whom Eudoxos in *(the)* 1st *(book says)*: 'From the land of the Chalybes *(comes)* the iron that is recommended *(to put)* round openings.'

---

[20] See also **11.**
[21] This form of the name occurs only here and in Ps.-Skylax §68. 5; see the n. there.

BOOK 1 OR 3

22 **Strabo** 11. 7. 5, C510: *Sea caves in the Caspian*
This, too, belongs to the marvels (*paradoxa*) in Hyrkania recorded by Eudoxos and others: that certain promontories project into the sea and have caves underneath them. Between these and the sea lies a low shore, while from the crags above rivers flow with such force that when they make contact with the promontories they shoot out their water into the sea, keeping the shore unwetted, which is thus passable for armies, sheltered from the stream. The local people often come down to the spot to enjoy feasts and sacrifices, and sometimes lie down under the caves; at other times they enjoy the sun right under the stream, each taking pleasure in their own way, with the sea on one side and the beach on the other, which is covered with flowers because of the moisture.

BOOK 2

23 **Aëtios,** *De placitis* 4. 1. 7: *Seasonal rains in Africa*
Eudoxos states that the priests say the showers of rain (*are*) according to the reciprocal replacement of the seasons: for whenever it is summer for us living under the summer tropic (*Tropic of Cancer*), at that time for those dwelling opposite under the winter tropic (*Topic of Capricorn*) it is winter, and from their region the water, now at its highest level, bursts out.

24 **Plutarch,** *On Isis and Osiris* 6 (*Moralia* 353a–c): *Egyptian priests as a source*
In Helioupolis (*Sun City*) the servants do not bring wine into the sanctuary at all, believing it unfitting to drink in the daytime when the lord and king observes them. Others use it, but not much. They observe many holy periods without wine, during which they spend their time practising philosophy, and learning and teaching divine matters. The kings also used to drink (*wine*) measured according to the sacred writings, as Hekataios has recorded, since they are priests. They began drinking it from the time of Psammetichos; previously they used not to drink wine or pour libations with it as a thing dear to the gods, but (*believed it to be*) the blood of those who once fought against the gods, from whom they think vines grew after they fell down and were mixed with the Earth; they consider that this is why it drives men out of their senses and paralysed, because they are replete with the blood of their ancestors. Eudoxos states in the 2nd (*book*) of the *Periodos* that these things are told in this fashion by the priests.[22]

25 **Plutarch,** *On Isis and Osiris* 21 (*Moralia* 359c): *Religiously significant place-names in Egypt*
But Eudoxos (*says*) that many tombs (*of Osiris*) are found in Egypt, but that his body lies at Bousiris, for this was the homeland of Osiris; and that (*the place-name*) Taphosiris needs no explanation, for the very name expresses 'Tomb of Osiris'.

---

[22] This is part of a long passage of the same work which probably makes use of Eudoxos.

26   Plutarch, *On Isis and Osiris* 64 (*Moralia* 377a): *Inadequacy of religious explanation*
But we shall also rebut Eudoxos in his disbelief and uncertainty over how not Demeter but Isis partakes in the overseeing of matters of desire (*erōtika*), and (*his view that*) Dionysos can neither cause the Nile to rise nor rule the dead.

27   Aelian, *On the Nature of Animals*, 10. 16: *Egyptian treatment of domesticates*
Eudoxos says that the Egyptians spare sows and do not sacrifice them, because after the wheat is sown they bring along herds of them; the sows tread on (*the seed*) and drive it into the moist earth so that it may remain live and not be consumed by birds.

28   Proclus, *On the Timaeus*, 1. 31f (on Plato, *Timaeus* 22b): *Egyptian calendar*
If what Eudoxos says is true, that the Egyptians used to call the month a year, the enumeration of these large numbers of years would have nothing miraculous about it.

29   Stephanos of Byzantion α 472
Asdynis: an island in the lake of Moiris.[23] Eudoxos, 2nd (*book*): 'And they used to be seized in Asdynis, the island'.

30   scholia EHPQT to Homer, *Odyssey* 4. 477: *Explaining the rise of the Nile*
While many things are said about the voyage up the Nile, Homer is the first to state the truest explanation, describing it as *diipetēs* ('heaven-fallen') because it is filled up from the incessant and heavy summer rains in Aithiopia, as both Aristotle and Eudoxos (*say*), stating that they learned these things from the priests in Egypt.

BOOK 3

31   Pliny, *Natural History*, 7. ii. 24: *Human proportions in southern India*
Eudoxus (*says*) that in the southern parts of India the men's feet are a cubit long, while the women's are so small that they are called Sparrowfoots.

BOOK 4

32   Pseudo-Antigonos of Karystos, *Collection of Marvellous Stories*, 129: *Bitumen in the sea*
He (*Kallimachos*) says that Eudoxos records that in the sea of Thrace by Hieron Oros (*Sacred Mountain*) bitumen (*asphaltos*) floats on the water at certain times.

33   Pseudo-Antigonos of Karystos, *Collection of Marvellous Stories*, 147: *Crocodiles in the Black Sea*
(*Kallimachos says*) that Eudoxos records that the one (*sc.* spring) at Kalchedon ⟨has⟩ small crocodiles in it, similar to those in Egypt.

---

[23] A lake in the *Fayum* oasis region of NW Egypt.

34 Strabo 7 fr. 21a: *NE Aegean*
Next is Cape Sarpedon; next the Chersonesos called Thracian, forming the Propontis, the Melas (*Black*) gulf, and the Hellespont. For the cape projects to the south-east (*euronotos*), connecting Europe to Asia with a 7-stade strait by Abydos and Sestos. It holds the Propontis on its left, but on its right the Melas gulf, so called from the (*river*) Melas that issues into it, as Herodotos and Eudoxos (*say*).

35 Strabo 12. 3. 21, C550: *Disputed emendations in Skythia*
Some write the text (*of Iliad* 2. 856–7) differently, with 'Alazones', others with 'Amazons'; or make 'from Alybe' into 'from Alope' ⟨or⟩ 'from Alobe', claiming that the Skythians beyond the Borysthenes are Alazones, Kallipides, and other such names that Hellanikos, Herodotos, and Eudoxos have wittered on to us about.

36 Clement of Alexandria, *Protreptikos* (*Exhortation to the Greeks*) 5. 64. 5: *Skythian customs*
Wherefore, indeed, it seems to me, many peoples appear simply to plant their sword (*in the ground*) and sacrifice (*to it*) as if to Ares. This is a custom of the Skythians, as Eudoxos says in the 4th (?) (*book*) of *Ges periodos*.[24]

37 Stephanos of Byzantion α 6
Abdera: . . . Eudoxos makes mention of 'Abderites' (*the ethnikon*) in (*the*) 4th (*book*) of *Periodoi* (*Circuits*) . . . Very many Abderitai are depicted by the tablet-painters (*pinakographoi*): Nikainetos the epic poet; also Protagoras, whom Eudoxos records as having made the weaker and stronger argument (*the same*) and to have taught his pupils to censure and (*then*) blame the same man.[25]

38 Stephanos of Byzantion κ 26
Kale Akte: a city of the Sikeloi. Eudoxos, 4th (*book*) of *Ges periodos*. It is ⟨like⟩ Megale Kome, and so the derivation (*of the ethnikon*) is from both (*parts*): Megalokometes, (*or*) Kalaktites and Kaloaktites with iota (*before the termination*).[26]

39 Stephanos of Byzantion σ 174
Sintia: a city in Macedonia, by Thrace, as Eudoxos (*says*) in (*the*) 4th (*book*) of *Ges periodos*. The inhabitants are Sintoi, oxytone (*with the accent on the last syllable*).

40 Stephanos of Byzantion σ 229
Skymniadai: a nation accompanying the Getai. Eudoxos, 4th (*book*) of *Ges periodos*: 'Skymniadai and Getai'.

---

[24] Lasserre 1966, 111, cf. 257, alters 'second' to 'fourth'. Book 2 dealt with Egypt, while other parts of book 4 covered the NE parts of the world. Butterworth 1919, 146 (who numbers the passage 5. 56), and Marcovich 1995, 98, retain 'second' (and also read *Ges periodos*, which I have adopted).

[25] I follow Billerbeck's understanding of these words.

[26] I follow Billerbeck in rendering this extract. Lasserre, however, doubts that the book number is correct, and his text implies the translation 'It is a large village (*kōmē*).'

41 Stephanos of Byzantion φ 77
Phlegra: a city in Thrace, which Eudoxos says was afterwards called Pallene.

42 Stephanos of Byzantion χ 17
Chalkis: a city in Euboia.... There is also another Chalkis in Athos, as Eudoxos (*says*), 4th (*book*): 'And after Athos as far as Pallene, which on the other side has created a deep, wide gulf with the name of Chalkis'.

43 Photios, *Lexikon* s.v. Haimon: *Correct gender of the name of a mountain*
The mountain is neuter, as Hekataios (*of Miletos*) consistently (*says*), as do Dionysios (*of Miletos*), Hellanikos in (*the*) 1st (*book*) of *Atthis,* Timaios, and Eudoxos.[27]

44 scholion to Apollonios of Rhodes 1. 922: *The Melas gulf*
'through the depths of Melas': 'Melas Pontos' (*Dark Main*) is its name, as Eudoxos records in the 4th (*book*) of the *Ges periodos*. Behind it, he says, is the Sarpedonian rock.[28]

45 scholia HQT to Homer, *Odyssey*, 11. 239: *Hydrology of Macedonia*
'who is by far the most beautiful of rivers':... 'The Axios, whose finest water pours over the Earth (*aian*)':[29] Eudoxos cites the line without the nu: 'The Axios, where Aia pours on its finest water'. For while many violent rivers discharge into the Axios, the spring of Aia sends forth the clearest water.

BOOK 5

46 Pseudo-Antigonos of Karystos, *Collection of Marvellous Stories*, 138: *A curative spring in Thessaly*
Eudoxos says the (*spring of*) Ophioussa at Halos stops leprosy.

47 Pseudo-Antigonos of Karystos, *Collection of Marvellous Stories*, 148: *A magical spring in Athamania*
Also (*Kallimachos says that Eudoxos records*) that in Athamania[30] there is a sanctuary of the Nymphs in which the spring has water that is inexpressibly cold but heats anything you place over it; and if one brings to it a dry stick or something else of that sort, it burns with a flame.

48 Strabo 9. 1. 1–2, C390–1: *Topography of the area between Attica and the Peloponnese*
(1) ... Eudoxos states that, if one were to imagine a straight line extending in an easterly direction from the Keraunia mountains to Sounion, the extremity of Attica, one would leave on one's right the whole Peloponnese to the south, but on one's left and to the

---

[27] Yet the name is usually given as Haimos, masculine.
[28] The Melas kolpos is the bay on the W side of the Thracian Chersonese (*Gallipoli* peninsula).
[29] A version of *Il.* 21. 158. (Lasserre cites this as a scholion on that passage of the *Iliad*, but it is one on the *Odyssey* quoting that line of the *Iliad*.)
[30] Part of Thessaly.

north the continuous coast from the Keraunian mountains as far as the Krisaian gulf, the Megarid, and the totality of Attica; and that he does not think that the narrow beach from Sounion to the Isthmus would form a gulf—for it only has a slight curvature—without the addition of the places in the Peloponnese connected to the Isthmus and lying along the Hermionic gulf and the Akte.[31] Similarly, neither would the (*beach*) from the Keraunian mountains to the Corinthian gulf, by its nature, have so great a curvature as to be hollowed out like a gulf, but that Rhion and Antirrhion, converging upon a narrow place, form this shape. Likewise with the places around the head of the Krisaian gulf, in which it comes about that the Krisaian sea terminates.   (2) As Eudoxos has said so—a man who was a mathematician with experience of shapes and latitudes, and with knowledge of these places—one must understand this side of Attica, with the Megarid, from Sounion to the Isthmus, is concave but only to a small degree.

49 **Strabo** 9. 2. 35, C413: *Askra in Boiotia*
Zenodotos writes[32] 'they held Askre rich in grapes', and does not appear to have encountered the things said by Hesiod about his homeland,[33] or by Eudoxos, who speaks much less well of Askre.

50 **Plutarch,** *The Oracles at Delphi No Longer Given in Verse*, 17 (*Moralia*, 402d): *Nomenclature of the Kastalian spring*
(*In light of Simonides' lines about the sanctuary of the Muses and the water of Kastalia at Delphi*), Eudoxos was therefore incorrect to believe those who informed him that this was called the water of Styx.[34]

51 **Proclus,** *On Hesiod, Works and Days*, 640: *Askra in Boiotia*
So Eudoxos says that the place (*Askra*) is sunless in winter because of the mountain at Helikon—this is in Boiotia—and burns in the summer.[35]

52 **Stephanos of Byzantion** κ 119
Kastanaia: Eudoxos says this with a theta.[36]

53 **Stephanos of Byzantion** π 176
Plataiai: a city in Boiotia. . . . Eudoxos, ⟨5th⟩ (*book*) of *Ges periodos*, (*gives it*) in the plural: 'That Plataiai [—] by possessing the tombs and trophies[37] of good men who liberated Hellas and enslaved the royal army.'

---

[31] i.e. the Argolid.   [32] In his edition of *Iliad* 2. 507. For Askra, cf. **51**.
[33] *Works and Days*, 639–40.   [34] The river of the underworld.   [35] Cf. **49**.
[36] i.e. as Kasthanaia, which is the correct form, or Kasthanaie in Hdt.'s dialect (see Hansen and Nielsen 2004, no. 450).
[37] In the sense of battlefield memorials. The reference is to the battle of Plataiai (479 BC) in which the Greek land army defeated the Persians.

BOOK 6

54 **Pseudo-Antigonos of Karystos,** *Collection of Marvellous Stories,* 153: *Pitch from a lake*
He (*Kallimachos*) says Eudoxos records that from the lake in Zakynthos pitch (*pissa*) is brought up, even though the lake produces fish; and that whatever you throw into this (*lake*) resurfaces in the sea, though a distance of 4 stades lies between them.

55 **Apollonios Paradoxographos,** *Stories about Wonders,* 38: *The Gyzantes of Libyē*
Eudoxos of Knidos, in the ⟨6th⟩ (*book*) of *Ges periodos*, says there is a certain nation, across most of Libyē, lying above the Syrteis and Karchedon (*Carthage*) and to the east, who are called (*the*) Gyzantes. They pursue the craft of gathering the flowers of those places and making honey in such quantity and of such quality that it becomes like that produced by bees.[38]

56 **Strabo** 8. 6. 21, C378–9: *Relation of Acrocorinth to Corinth*
It comes about that the situation of the city, from what Hieronymos (*of Kardia*) has said, and Eudoxos and others, we ourselves saw when it had lately been restored by the Romans, is of the following kind: a mountain having a perpendicular height of about 3½ stades, and an ascent of about 30,[39] terminates in a pointed summit and is called Acrocorinth. Its northward part is the steepest, under which lies the city upon a trapezoidal, level site beside the very root of Acrocorinth.

57 **Pliny,** *Natural History,* 31. xiii. 16: *An Arkadian lake*
Eudoxus says that wine becomes distasteful to those who have drunk from Lake Clitorion.[40]

58 **Athenaios** 7. 31, 288c: *Giant eels at Sikyon*
And Eudoxos, in the sixth book of *Ges periodos*, says that many conger eels the size of a man are caught at Sikyon, some of which even have to be carried by waggon.

59 **Stephanos of Byzantion** α 21
Agathe (*Good; Agde*): a city of the Ligyes (*Ligurians*) or Keltoi. . . . There is also another city, as Philon says, belonging to the Ligystioi (*Ligurians*), upon Lake Ligystia; but perhaps it is the same as the first, as Eudoxos says.

60 **Stephanos of Byzantion** α 71
Azania: a part of Arkadia. . . . It is also called Azenia; and Eudoxos in (*the*) 6th (*book*) of *Ges periodos* says: 'There is a spring in Azenia that causes those who taste the water

---

[38] Cf. **63**, with discussion of the names by Gysembergh 2016, 39–41.
[39] E. did not necessarily measure the height himself; it may derive from the slightly later Dikaiarchos (see introduction to Ch. 9 below, with n. 12 there). '30 stades' refers to the journey to the summit.
[40] In the territory of Kleitor in Arkadia. Cf. **60.**

to be unable to bear even the smell of ⟨wine⟩.[41] They say that Melampous, when he was purifying the daughters of Proitos, threw the sweepings into it.[42]

61 Stephanos of Byzantion α 108
Aigion: a city in Achaia, as Eudoxos (*says*) in (*the*) 6th (*book*).

62 Stephanos of Byzantion α 475
Asine: a Laconian city, (*named*) after Asine daughter of Lakedaimon. A second in Messene, beside the Laconian, settled by Argives. A third in Cyprus. A fourth in Kilikia. The *ethnikon* is Asinaios, also Asineus as Eudoxos (*says*) in (*the*) 6th (*book*) of *Ges periodos*.[43]

63 Stephanos of Byzantion ζ 30
Zygantis: a city in Libyē. . . . The citizens are (*called*) Zygantes, and they gather flowers to make honey that is in no way inferior to the honey made by bees, as Eudoxos of Knidos (*says*) in (*the*) 6th (*book*) of *Ges periodos*.[44]

64 Stephanos of Byzantion κ 211
Kremmyon: a village in Corinth. Eudoxos, 6th (*book*) of *Ges periodos*.

65 Stephanos of Byzantion ο 79
Opikoi: a nation in Italia.[45] Eudoxos, 6th (*book*) of *Ges periodos*: 'They mingled their languages'.

66 Stephanos of Byzantion σ 227
Skylletion: a city in Sicily, as Eudoxos (*says*), 6th (*book*).

67 Stephanos of Byzantion σ 263
Spina: a town in Italia, as Eudoxos and Artemidoros (*say*).

68 Stephanos of Byzantion φ 46
Phelessaioi: a nation bordering on the Ombrikoi (*Umbrians*), by Iapygia, as Eudoxos (*says*), 6th (*book*).

69 scholion B to Apollonios of Rhodes 4. 263–4: *Arkadian autochthony*
The Arkadians appear to have been born before the Moon, as Eudoxos also says in the *Periodos*.[46]

---

[41] Cf. 57.
[42] The seer Melampous cured the daughters of Proitos (king of Argos) of their madness in the sanctuary of Artemis at Arkadian Lousoi (Paus. 8. 18. 8).
[43] Since his 6th book is cited, E. probably referred to one of the first two cities of this name; Lasserre inclines towards the Messenian one.
[44] Cf. 55.   [45] Identified with the Oscans.
[46] For more of this extract, see Mnaseas 24; Dueck 2020.

70   scholion to Euripides, *Trojan Women*, 221: *Foundation of Carthage*
Karchedon (*Carthage*) is a city in Libyē. Eudoxos of Knidos ⟨says⟩ that a little before
the Trojan matters (*i.e. Trojan war*) the people of Tyre sent a colony to it; the leaders
were Azaros and Karchedon, from whom the city also took its name.

BOOK 7

71   Pseudo-Antigonos of Karystos, *Collection of Marvellous Stories*, 129: *Freshwater
springs within salt sea*
Also (*Kallimachos says that Eudoxos reports*) that the one (*the sea*) off the Chelidoniai
(*islands*) contains freshwater springs over a wide area.[47]

72   Pseudo-Antigonos of Karystos, *Collection of Marvellous Stories*, 161: *A petrifying
spring on Kos*
(*According to Kallimachos, Eudoxos says*) that there is also among the people of Kos
another small stream which turns into stone all the channels through which it flows.[48]

73   Pseudo-Antigonos of Karystos, *Collection of Marvellous Stories*, 163: *Europa's
spring on Crete*
Also about the small watercourse in Crete where those who sit over it, when it is rainy,
remain unwetted, that the tradition has been handed down to the Cretans that Eurōpē
washed from it after she had intercourse with Zeus.[49]

74   Strabo 10. 4. 2, C474: *Location of Crete*
And now let us speak first of Crete. Eudoxos says it is set in the Aegean; but this is not
so. . . .

75   Pliny, *Natural History*, 6. xxxvi. 198: *Islands in the Indian Ocean: Numbers of islands in the Erythraean sea*
That there are very many islands in the whole of this sea (*the Erythraean*) is reported
by Ephorus, and also by Eudoxus[50] and Timosthenes.

76   Pliny, *Natural History*, 31. ix. 13: *Magical springs in Euboia*
Eudicus (*i.e. Eudoxus?*) reports that in the territory of Hestiaia there are two springs:
Cerona, where sheep drinking from it turn black, and Nelea,[51] where they turn white.
If they drink from both, they become variegated.

---

[47] These islands are off Lykia. This extract follows **32**.

[48] The text continues: 'The following is omitted by Eudoxos and Kallimachos: that the people of Kos
built their theatre by quarrying stones out of this water, so strongly petrified is any sort of object.' **7** and
73 then follow.

[49] This follows **72** and **7**.

[50] More likely to be E. of Knidos than E. of Kyzikos, the C2 explorer, since the latter is not known to
have written anything (see Introduction, §VI. 4. c).

[51] Lasserre prints 'Melea', but Strabo 10. 1. 14, C449, calls the rivers Kereus and Neleus (König 1994,
94).

77 **Harpokration** s.v. Lipara: *One of the Aeolian islands*
Lipara: . . . One of the so-called Islands of Aiolos near Sicily is Lipara, as Eudoxos (*says*) in (*the*) 7th (*book*) of *Periodos*.

78 **Porphyry,** *Life of Pythagoras, 7: Pythagoras' habits*
(*They say*) that generally many folk recognize these things because they were written down in his (*Pythagoras'*) *Hypomnemata*,[52] but that the remainder of his practices are less well known—except that Eudoxos, in the 7th (*book*) of *Ges periodos*, says that he adopted such great purity, and avoidance in relation to both killing and killers, that he not only abstained from (*eating*) animate things but even avoided associating with butchers and huntsmen.

79 **Hesychios** s.v. *bous Kyprios: A pejorative epithet for Cypriots*
Cyprian ox: dung-eating, useless, unclean. It signifies the exceptionality of the people of Cyprus. Also Eudoxos relates that they eat dung.

---

[52] Containing the root meaning 'memory', this is a term with a wide range of meanings, e.g. 'records', 'memoranda', 'memoirs', 'treatises' (Montanari 2006b).

7

PSEUDO-SKYLAX

(WRITTEN 338–335 BC)

D. Graham J. Shipley

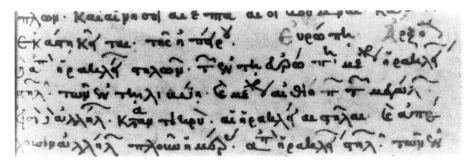

FIG. 7.1. Opening of the text of Ps.-Skylax, p. 62 (detail).

INTRODUCTION

The Greek prose work known as the *Periplous* of Pseudo-Skylax (often abbreviated to 'Ps.-Skylax') is not a work of travel, but a gazetteer of the inhabited coasts of the seas best known to the Greeks. Beginning at Gibraltar, its 'route' proceeds eastwards (like Hekataios: see Chapter 3 above) along the north shore of the Mediterranean (crossing over itself while completing a clockwise circuit of Sicily), circles the Black Sea clockwise (as Hekataios probably had), continues along the western and southern coasts of Asia Minor, and concludes with a less detailed enumeration of the Levant, Egypt, and North Africa. The final paragraphs take the reader beyond Gibraltar and some way (just how far is debatable) down the west coast of Morocco.[1] It does not, however, venture further round Africa, or north into the Atlantic waters of Europe, or (at the other end of the *oikoumenē* or inhabited world) into the Red Sea or Indian Ocean. A passage at the end of the text (§§113–14), obviously tacked on and not necessarily contemporary with the work, lists certain open-sea distances in the Aegean, followed by a list of the twenty supposedly largest islands. The author makes no mention of north-western Europe, the Caspian, or the seas east of Africa even though these were, in some degree, known to many of the writers in the present volumes. Neither does he mention the interior parts of its regions, unlike, for example, Hekataios.

---

[1] On the NW African section, cf. Roller 2015, 56–7, 60.

The text is preserved in a single mid-13th-century manuscript, generally known as 'D' for the purposes of research on the Greek geographers,[2] which also contains, sometimes in their sole copies, a variety of other Greek geographical texts. Source B. 6 below is the preface from this text, evidently by the late 4th- to early 5th-century AD scholar Markianos of Herakleia, which calls the work a *periplous* (circumnavigation) of the *oikoumenē* (inhabited world) and assumes that its author is the Skylax of Karyanda whose voyage to India, undertaken at the behest of King Darius around 520 BC, is noted by Herodotos (4. 44; see Skylax 2 in Chapter 2 above).

Markianos astutely notes that the *periplous* must antedate Alexander the Great's conquest of western Asia; but closer observation of the text shows that in its original form it cannot have been written many years before those events, since a number of the circumstances it mentions were not the case before the 4th century BC;[3] equally, however, certain details within the account had become untrue before that time. The most logical view is that the *periplous* is a work of desk-based research, probably compiled at Athens[4] in the early or mid-330s—perhaps specifically between 338 or 337[5] and 335[6]—and drawing upon a variety of sources for different regions: some recent and some outdated, some specific to individual regions or groups of regions, and in all probability some oral or administrative; all now lost to us.[7] It bears the

---

[2] Parisinus supplément grec 443, folios 62. 1–106. 11. A small number of derivative MS copies of the *periplous*, from the early generations after the invention of printing, have no independent authority.

[3] This view of the date of Pseudo-Skylax (PS) is that of Shipley 2019 (2nd edition of Shipley 2011), and ultimately that of *GGM* i. 15–96, though (*a*) Müller believes there were substantial Byzantine-period alterations, an unnecessary complication; (*b*) a significant scholarly tradition (its chief representative Peretti 1979) insists that the preserved *periplous* is at its core a C6l work by the said Skylax of Karyanda (SK), periodically overlaid with factual updates. This is extremely unlikely; it rests on the premises that (*a*) Skylax travelled round the Mediterranean and Black Sea and (*b*) the work was designed to be of practical use to navigators; neither has a foundation in evidence. See also Ch. 2, introduction. (There is no evidence to confirm the assertion by Dueck 2012, 54, that the C4 work was 'composed under the name' of the earlier Skylax of Karyanda, for whom see Ch. 2 above.)

[4] For Brillante 2020, 5–7, the author must be Athenian since he uses the first person in relation to the Saronic gulf (§40) and shows local knowledge (§§56; 57. 1; 67. 2; 112. 10). He may also display pro-Athenian attitudes regarding Athenian colonies on Crete (§47. 2, cf. Marcotte 1986, 168–9) and in calling Elea a colony of Thourioi (§12). Such postures could surely be adopted equally by a resident foreigner addressing an audience there (whether all-Athenian or mixed).

[5] The work should not antedate Aitolian possession of Naupaktos (§35), which should date from soon after his victory at Chaironeia in 338. It is unlikely to be much later than the assignment of coastal towns in Messenia to Lakedaimonian control (§§45–46. 1), from which Philip is assumed to have removed them at the same period.

[6] Brillante 2020, 25–7, regards the mention of Thebes (§59) despite its destruction by Alexander in 335 as inconclusive as evidence that PS wrote earlier, since Mykenai and Tiryns (named at §49) had been abolished as *poleis* (city-states) in C5m; but M., at least, existed later as a non-*polis* settlement (Piérart 2004, 311–12 no. 353) and both may be included as well-known landmarks and Homeric towns; alternatively, as with Sicilian Naxos (§13. 3), PS may be using older lists (Shipley 2019, 134). The destruction of Thebes, by contrast, was a momentous event hardly likely to be ignored by an author active soon afterwards. B. accepts, however, the inference by Markianos, in his preface to the work, that the *periplous* takes no account of Alexander's conquests.

[7] Naturally, PS's information, though largely second-hand, rested ultimately on the actual experience of mariners; cf. Mauro 2021; Mauro 2022b.

hallmarks of Aristotle's college known as the Peripatos or Lyceum, founded at Athens in 335, and has strong similarities in some passages to the known fragments and testimonia of Aristotle's associate Dikaiarchos of Messana (Chapter 9 below); it may conceivably be an early work of his, but it is difficult to make a case for his having been active as early as the mid-330s.[8] The distinctive feature that assimilates the work—though not necessarily all the elements which it draws upon—to the Peripatos is the attempt to calculate summative, large-scale distances and dimensions across the known world, such as the 153 days' circuit of the coast of Europe from Gibraltar to the Don (§69), the 87 of Asia (§106. 4), and the 54 of North Africa (§111. 8). Consistently, he also totals up the extension of his 'voyage' past Gibraltar at 12 days (§112. 5). The 'partitions' across the Aegean (§113. 1–2), part of the intrusive endmatter mentioned above, further recall Dikaiarchos, who devised a central line of latitude running from Gibraltar to the Himalayas (see Chapter 9, introduction and no. 10).

As well as measuring the world on a grand scale, the unknown author follows others in dividing it into three continents, whose divisions he places at the Tanaïs (*Don*) and the Nile. He marks the beginning and end of two super-regions, the Peloponnese and the Cyclades. Otherwise he is at pains to produce a seamless chain of regions, each conceived as a 'nation' (*ethnos*), a term that sometimes almost becomes spatial.[9] With certain exceptions such as the Cycladic archipelago with its many small islands, each is defined by the name of its people and the length of the voyage along its coast. These distances are stated variously in days' and nights' sailing (the smallest divisions being thirds and quarters of a day) and in stades (*stadia*); most of the latter data presumably calculated by converting from time measurements, though in some cases where greater precision is offered (e.g. Attica, §57. 2) they may be the result of direct land-based measurement by surveyors or by bematists (*bēmatistai*) like those whom Alexander took on his expedition: professional 'pacers' whose task was to record lengthy distances.[10]

Within each region, too, Ps.-Skylax purports to enumerate its cities (*poleis*), though the repeated promise is sometimes delivered in the form of a mixed list of cities and natural features such as rivers and capes. The term *polis*, strictly 'city-state', is applied to urban communities both within and outside the area the author designates as 'continuous Hellas' (the term is used at §33. 2 and §65. 2), which runs from Ambrakia in north-west Greece to the river Peneios on the east coast where Thessaly meets

---

[8] Shipley 2012. Brillante 2020, 43–4, misrepresents my view in that paper: I do not urge or assume the identification of the author with Dikaiarchos, merely raise the possibility and at the same time the difficulty in accepting it. He is correct, of course, to point out (44) that PS's work reflects more widely the culture of educated Athenian society.

[9] On the difficulties of translating this term, see the Introduction, §X. 3. c.

[10] See Bearzot 2020. Russo 2013, however, points out that the term *bēmatistēs* occurs only in Ktesias F 54 Jacoby, from Athenaios 10. 59, 442b, and doubts whether the method was widespread.

Macedonia.[11] Outside 'continuous Hellas' Ps.-Skylax distinguishes 'Hellenic cities' from others, implicitly made up of non-Greeks. By placing Crete and the Cyclades within his description of continuous Hellas, the author admits them to the reserved status; but logically he cannot do so in the case of East Greece, since Thrace intervenes. More controversially, Macedonia is also firmly placed in what might be termed 'discontinuous Hellas', the plethora of its towns being designated Hellenic. In the latter case, the distinction is surely political, excluding the Macedonians from the catalogue of Hellenic peoples despite the presence of many 'colonial' Greek communities on the coasts. As such, it may reflect the geopolitics of the time when it was composed, in the third quarter of the 4th century BC.[12]

As the earliest surviving Greek work framed entirely in terms of geography, the work may be regarded as pioneering. It is not, however, primarily a literary work. While there are structuring devices such as the language of digression (phrases like 'I return again to the mainland from which I departed' are frequent), the language, while exhibiting some variation in word order, is often severely functional; the syntax frequently jejune; verbs regularly absent. Points of 'colour' are occasionally inserted, such as information about tides that occur both outside the Mediterranean (§1) and even within it (§110. 8), or the occurrence of spontaneously ignited methane exhalations in Lykia (§100. 1); but they are so occasional and unsystematic that they seem like chance information that was (as indeed we know in some cases) circulating among the members of the Peripatos.

The material draws little from its predecessors as far as we can tell, except that the principle of organization by area and people may have been learned from the 4th-century historian Ephoros of Kyme.[13] Even the passage on north-west Africa is less similar to Hanno's account of a voyage than might at first sight appear. Ps.-Skylax retails some information from Herodotos (e.g. the mistake about the narrow 'isthmus' of Asia Minor at §102. 2, cf. Herodotos 2. 34), in places he has more detail to offer (e.g. on the Black Sea). Other information may have come to him from Hekataios, Phileas of Athens (see Introduction, §VI. 4. b), and Herodoros of Herakleia (a late 5th-century mythographer).[14]

Despite its innovativeness, the *periplous* seems to have had little impact, unless upon the work of Dikaiarchos in the following decades. Two passages in Dionysios son of Kalliphon's incomplete poem imitate our author's presentation (lines 27–34, 110–25; see Chapter 20 below), showing that it was known in the 1st century BC. The few citations, apparent or explicit, in other authors may be read in the fragments that stand before the main *periplous* below. It was rarely read, it seems; this may have contributed

---

[11] On the notion of 'continuous Hellas', see Brillante 2020, 159.
[12] On the term *polis* in PS, see Flensted-Jensen and Hansen 1996 ~ Flensted-Jensen and Hansen 2007. On the influence of C4 geopolitics on PS, see the useful discussion by Brillante 2020, 61–85.
[13] Drews 1963, 250–1.   [14] Brillante 2020, 153–9.

to the woeful state of the text preserved down to the 13th century—described by the pioneering textual critic Richard Bentley, four centuries later, as 'one of the most corrupted Books in the world'[15]—and certainly accounts for the absence of multiple versions that we could check against one another, as well as for the relative lack of attention paid to the book by scholarship.[16]

The present translation is a revision of that in my earlier book,[17] with paragraphing and syntax simplified and certain details of terminology revised. Modern place-names are given selectively, and not usually in order simply to identify an archaeological site. Italics *outside* parentheses indicate uncertain words (not merely restored or conjectural) or sense. Headings within the translation of the *periplous* are added by the translator. Omitted altogether are the names of peoples or regions with which sections of the text begin in the manuscript; these were added during transmission, perhaps by Markianos. The testimonia are presented in date order.

SELECTED FURTHER READING

*Brillante, S. (2017), 'Pseudo-Scylax: édition, traduction et commentaire', Ph.D. thesis. Università di Studi di Bari/Université de Reims Champagne-Ardennes. [Revised Greek text does not include the Black Sea sections.]

—— (2020), *Il Periplo di Pseudo-Scilace: l'oggettività del potere.* Hildesheim–Zürich–New York. [Appeared too late to be taken into account fully; see, however, Shipley 2023.]

*Counillon, P. (2004), *Pseudo-Skylax, Le Périple du Pont-Euxin: texte, traduction, commentaire philologique et historique.* Bordeaux.

Matijašić, I. (2016), 'Scylax of Caryanda, Pseudo-Scylax, and the Paris Periplus: reconsidering the ancient tradition of a geographical text', *Mare Nostrum*, 7: 1–19.

Mauro, C. M. (2022), 'The Periplus of Pseudo-Skylax and its relationship with earlier nautical knowledge', *The Mariner's Mirror*, 108. 1 (Feb.): 6–30.

Shipley, D. G. J. (2012), 'Pseudo-Skylax and the natural philosophers', *Journal of Hellenic Studies*, 132: 121–38.

*—— (2017), 'Pseudo-Skylax (2046)', in *FGrH* v.

*—— (2019), *Pseudo-Skylax's Periplous: The Circumnavigation of the Inhabited World*, 2nd edn. Liverpool.

—— (2023), 'Rules of engagement with Greek geographical writing', *Histos*, 17: xxii–xl.

---

[15] Bentley 1699, 327.

[16] This is not to minimize the enormous contribution of recent Francophone scholarship, such as the sound assessment of the Black Sea chapters by Counillon 2004 and various earlier and later papers by him. The thesis of Brillante 2017, supervised by D. Marcotte (himself the author of a crucial reappraisal, Marcotte 1986), covers all of the work bar the Black Sea; his book, Brillante 2020, is the fullest attempt so far to understand the work in the widest possible context of Greek society and intellectual culture.

[17] Shipley 2011, revised as Shipley 2019; that in Shipley 2017 is in German, courtesy of Dr J. Nikolaus. Both works contain the revised Greek text.

A. *PERIPLOUS* OF THE INHABITED WORLD

Codex Parisinus supplément grec 443, pp. 62. 1–106. 11

For reasons of space, I have not usually noted when a place has no certain or agreed location, or where alternative locations have been proposed with no resolution. Details may be found in the commentary in Shipley 2019.

When a gloss in parentheses is preceded by 'or', the following name is an alternative ancient one.

Headings are added. (The region or people names at the start of each section are omitted as a later addition to the text, perhaps by Markianos.)

EUROPE

1. And I shall begin from the Pillars of Herakles in Europe (*and go*) as far as the Pillars of Herakles in Libyē, and as far as the Great Aithiopes. The Pillars of Herakles are directly facing one another, and they are a day's voyage from one another.

Pillars of Herakles to South Italy

Past the Pillars of Herakles in Europe are many trading-places of the Carthaginians (*Karchēdonioi*), and mud and high tides and shoals.

2. In Europe the first (*people*) are the Iberes, a nation in Iberia, with the river Iber.[18] Two islands come next here, which have the name Gadeira (*Cádiz*). One of these two has a city that is a day's voyage distant from the Pillars of Herakles. Then a trading-place (*emporion*) ⟨and⟩ city, which has the name *Emporion* (*Empúries*), a Hellenic city; and these people are colonists from the Massaliotai (*men of Marseille*). Coastal sailing of Iberia: 7 days and 7 nights.

3. Past the Iberes there follow the Ligyes (*Ligurians*) and Iberes mixed, as far as the river Rhodanos (*Rhône*). Coastal sailing of the Ligyes from Emporion as far as the Rhodanos river: 2 days and 1 night.

4. Past the Rhodanos river there follow the Ligyes as far as Antion (*Antibes*). In this territory there is a Hellenic city, Massalia (*Marseille*), with a harbour, ⟨Olbia, and Antion with a harbour⟩. These cities are colonists from Massalia. The coastal sailing of this (*territory*), from the Rhodanos river as far as Antion, is 2 (?) days and 2 (?) nights.

From the Pillars of Herakles as far as Antion, all this territory has good harbours.

5. Past Antion are the Tyrrhenoi (*Etruscans*), a nation, as far as Rome, a city. Coastal sailing: 4 days and 4 nights.

6. By Tyrrhenia lies the island of Kyrnos (*Corsica*). From Tyrrhenia the voyage to Kyrnos is 1½ days. There is an island in the middle of this voyage, which is inhabited and which has the name Aithalia (*Elba*); and many other deserted islands.

---

[18] Probably the *Tinto* rather than the *Ebro*.

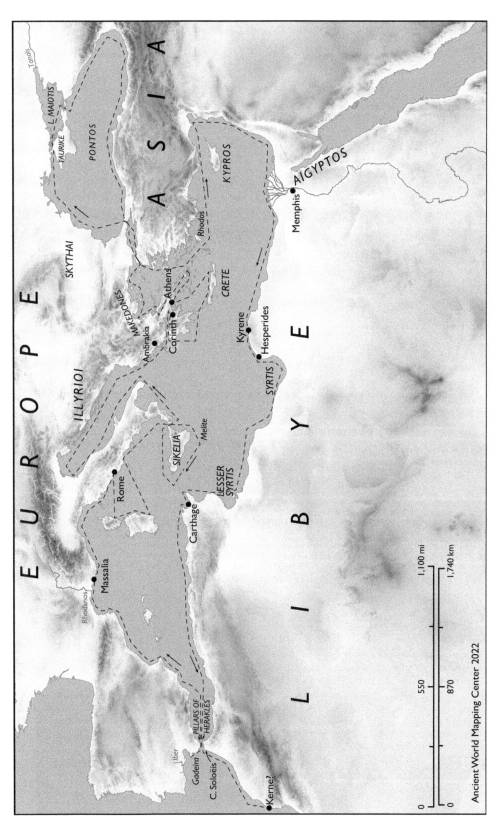

MAP 7.1. Pseudo-Skylax: general map. Broken line and arrows indicate direction of narrative. For more details, see maps in Shipley 2011 ~ 2019.

Ancient World Mapping Center 2022

7. From Kyrnos island to Sardo island (*Sardinia*): a voyage of one-third of a day, and there is a deserted island in between.

From Sardo to Libyē: a voyage of a day and a night.

To Sikelia (*Sicily*) from Sardo: a voyage of 2 days and 1 night.

I return again onto the mainland, from where I turned away to Kyrnos.

8. After Tyrrhenia there follow the Latinoi as far as the Kirkaion. Also the monument of Elpenor belongs to the Latinoi. Coastal sailing of the Latinoi:[19] a day and a night.

9. After the Latinoi there follow the Olsoi (*Volsci*). Coastal sailing of the Olsoi: 1 day.

10. After the Olsoi there follow the Kampanoi (*Campanians*). There are these Hellenic cities in Kampania: Kyme (*Cumae*), Neapolis (*Naples*). By these is Pithekoussa (*Ischia*) island with a Hellenic city. The coastal sailing of Kampania is 1 day.

11. After the Kampanoi there follow the Saunitai (*Samnites*). The coastal sailing of the Saunitai is half a day.

12. After the Saunitai there follow the Leukanoi (*Lucanians*) as far as Thouria.[20] The voyage beside Leukania (*Lucania*) is 6 days and 6 nights.

Leukania is a headland. In this there are Hellenic cities as follows: Poseidonia (*Paestum*) with Elea; ⟨Laos⟩, a colony of the Thourioi; Pandosia; Plateëis[21]; Terina; Hipponion; Mesma; and Rhegion (*Reggio di Calabria*), a promontory with a city.

13. (1) By Rhegion is Sikelia island (*Sicily*), 12 stades distant from Europe *to* Pelorias (*Faro*) from Rhegion.[22] (2) In Sikelia are the following barbarian[23] nations: Elymoi, Sikanoi, Sikeloi, Phoenicians, and Trojans.[24] Now these people are barbarians, but Hellenes also live here. The promontory of Sikelia is Peloria. (3) Past Pelorias there are Hellenic cities as follows:[25] Messene (*Messana*) with a harbour, Tauromenion, Naxos,[26] Katane (*Catania*), Leontinoi (*Lentini*)—and to Leontinoi along the Terias river is a voyage upstream of 20 stades—the Symaithos river with a city, Megaris, and a harbour, Xiphoneios. Following Megaris is the city of Syrakousai (*Syracuse*), with two harbours in it, one of these inside a fort and the other outside. After this is the city of Heloron, and Pachynos, a promontory. Past Pachynos are the following Hellenic

---

[19] The region of Latium is meant.   [20] We reach Thouria at §13. 5.

[21] Rather than Müller's emendation 'Klampeteia'; see Brillante 2020, 39.

[22] If the text is sound, PS wrongly says the shortest crossing is from Rhegion, actually 6 mi (10 km) from Sicily.

[23] PS uses this term only here and at 22. 2 (twice), 81, and 103.

[24] The list of peoples in Sicily is more characteristic of C5 sources. Thucydides (6. 2) regards the Elymoi as of Trojan descent, but PS mentions 'Troës' separately. 'Phoinikes' was an out-of-date term by C4m, and again suggests the use of an earlier source; the well-known Phoenician cities of Motya, Panormos (*Palermo*), and Soloëis are absent.

[25] In this passage alone, PS keeps the coast on his right hand and thus circles Sicily clockwise, crossing his own 'route' at §13. 5. This surprising choice may reflect the use of an earlier *periplous* of the island, as may the temporary switch from days' and nights' sailing to measurements in stades.

[26] This Naxos had been destroyed by Dionysios I of Syracuse in 403; there is some C4 archaeology (Fischer-Hansen, Nielsen, and Ampolo 2004, 219), but N. was probably no longer regarded as a *polis*. Again PS's information is out of date.

cities: Kamarina, Gela, Akragas (*Agrigento*), Selinous, and Lilybaion, a promontory. Past Lilybaion there is a Hellenic city, Himera.[27]   (4) Sikelia is triangular:[28] and each limb of it is approximately 1,500 (?) stades. *After Himera* city is Lipara island (*Lipari*); and a Hellenic city, Mylai, with a harbour. There is from Mylai up to Lipara island a voyage of half a day.

(5) I return again onto the mainland, from where I turned away. For past Rhegion the cities are as follows: Lokroi, Kaulonia, Kroton; Lakinion, a sanctuary of Hera; Kalypso's Island, in which Odysseus dwelt with Kalypso; the river Krathis; Sybaris;[29] and Thouria, a city. These are the Hellenes in Leukania.

14. After Leukania are the Iapyges, a nation, as far as the Hyrion mountain in the Adrias (*Adriatic*) gulf. Coastal sailing beside Iapygia: 6 days and 6 nights. In Iapygia live Hellenes, and the cities are as follows: Herakleion;[30] Metapontion (*Metaponto*); Taras (*Taranto*), with a harbour; and Hydrous (*Otranto*) upon the mouth of the Adrias or Ionios (*Ionian*) gulf.

The Adriatic

15. After the Iapyges, past *Hyrion* are the Daunitai,[31] a nation. In this nation are the following tongues: *Alphaternioi*, Opikoi, *Karakones*, Boreontinoi, and Peuketieis,[32] extending from the Tyrrhenic open-sea (*pelagos*) to the Adrias.[33] Coastal sailing of the Daunitid territory: 2 days and 1 night.

16. After the Daunitai is the nation of the Ombrikoi (*Umbrians*), and among them is a city, Ankon (*Ancona*). This nation worships Diomedes, having received benefaction from him: and there is a sanctuary of him.[34] The coastal sailing of Ombrike is 2 days and 1 night.

17. After the Ombric (*nation?*) are the Tyrrhenoi (*Etruscans*).[35] These people extend from the Tyrrhenic open-sea (*pelagos*) to the Adrias *gulf*: and there is a Hellenic city among them, ⟨Spina,⟩ with a river: and the voyage upstream to the city along the river

[27] Destroyed by the Carthaginians in 409/8, and superseded by Thermai Himeraiai.

[28] This statement does not require us to suppose that the author was using a map (on cartography, see Introduction, §V). On the use of geometrical schemata, see Dueck 2005.

[29] Sybaris, famously sacked by the people of Kroton before 500, was still a dependent *polis* of that centre until C5m. When the Panhellenic colony of Thouria was founded nearby in the 440s, the remaining Sybarites occupied a new site (unlocated) which was itself destroyed by the Bruttians after 356 (Diod. 12. 22. 1). Again, therefore, PS (writing in the 330s) uses out-of-date evidence.

[30] Founded 433/2 at *Policoro*; one of the many proofs that the text as we have it is Cl, not Ar.

[31] Daunia is N. Apulia.

[32] The list, including the Alfaterni and Opici from the W coast of Italy, appears to be a catalogue of Samnites rather than Daunians. The 'Karakones' may be the people whose Latin name was Carecini or Carrecini; the 'Boreontini' the Frentani; the 'Peuketieis' are elsewhere Peuketianteis or Picentes.

[33] Here begins the earliest detailed account of the Adriatic, though the information for its E side is fuller, perhaps suggesting a change of source at §21. 1 though the W side was admittedly short of trading-places of interest to Greeks.

[34] The Homeric hero was a major figure in Adriatic cults; see e.g. M. P. Castiglioni 2008; Zweifel 2012.

[35] First met at §5 above.

is about 20 stades. ⟨The coastal sailing of the Tyrrhenoi is 1 day⟩ from —, a city: and it is a road (*journey*) of 3 days.

18. After the Tyrrhenoi are the Keltoi (*Celts*), a nation, left behind from the expedition,[36] upon a narrow front as far as the Adrias, ⟨extending from the outer sea as far as to the Adrias gulf⟩.[37] Here is the inner end of the Adrias gulf.

19. After the Keltoi are the Enetoi (*Veneti*), a nation, and the river Eridanos (*Po*) among them. The coastal sailing of the *Enetoi* in a direct line is 1 day.

20. After the Enetoi are the nation of the Istroi,[38] and the river Istros (*Danube*). This river also discharges into the Pontos in *a scattered bed*, as ⟨the Neilos (*Nile*) does⟩ into Egypt.[39] The coastal sailing of the territory of the Istroi: a day and a night.

21. (1) After the Istroi are the Libyrnoi, a nation. In this nation there are cities beside the sea, *Arsias, Dassatika, Senites,* Apsyrta, Loupsoi, Ortopeletai, and *Heginoi*. These people are ruled by women;[40] and the women are (*wives*) of free men, but mingle with their own slaves and with the men of the nearby lands.   (2) By this territory are the following islands whose names I am able to state—and there are also many others unnamed—Istris island (*Krk*), 210 stades (*in length*) and 120 in width; the *Elektrides* ('*Amber Is.*'); the Mentorides;[41] and these islands are great. The Kataibates river (*Krka?*). Coastal sailing of the Libyrnid territory: 2 days.

22. (1) After the Libyrnoi are the Illyrioi (*Illyrians*), a nation, and the Illyrioi live beside the sea as far as Chaonia by Kerkyra (*Corfù*), the island of Alkinoös.[42] There is a Hellenic city here, which has the name Herakleia, with a harbour.   (2) The barbarians called Lotophagoi (*Lotus-eaters*) are the following: *Iadasinoi*,[43] Boulinoi, and *Hylloi*; with the Boulinoi the Hylloi are coterminous. These people say Hyllos son of Herakles settled them; and they are barbarians. They are settled in a peninsula a little smaller than the Peloponnese.[44]   (3) Past the peninsula ⟨is — island⟩ *beside a straight mouth*; the Boulinoi live beside this. The Boulinoi are an Illyric nation.[45] There is a coastal sailing of the territory of the Boulinoi, a long day up to the Nestos (*Cetina*) river.

---

[36] Perhaps that of c.390 in which Rome was captured. The region is named Gallia Cisalpina in Latin.

[37] These words transposed from §17.

[38] In the *Istria* peninsula.

[39] PS is under the impression that it emerges both in the Black Sea and in the Adriatic.

[40] Like the Gynaikokratoumenoi of §70.

[41] Probably the archipelagos off *Zadar* and *Šibenik*, including *Pag* (anc. Cissa). This and the next few chapters are one of the hardest passages of PS, with many identifications under debate. For the Mentorides as Liburnian, see Pliny 3. xxv. 139.

[42] King of the island in the *Odyssey*.   [43] Probably from anc. Idassa.

[44] A mistake (unlikely to be caused by the group of islands giving the appearance of a mainland promontory, as suggested by Counillon 2007, 23). The size of the peninsula is also exaggerated, though not by so much, at Pliny 3. xxvi. 141, where it is 'Diomedes's Cape' or Hyllis and has a circumference of 100 miles; it probably extends from *Grebaštica* (S of Šibenik) to *Marina* (near *Trogir*, anc. Tragurium). On the peninsula, see Čače 2015, 17–19. For the 'barbarized' Hylloi, see Eratosthenes 42 = *Nikomedean Periodos*, 405–12.

[45] In the Peutinger Map the Bulini are located NW of Salona. Bouline is a *polis* at Artemidoros 133 (from Steph. Byz.).

23. (1) Past the Nestos there is a gulf-shaped voyage. All this gulf is called Manios.[46] The coastal sailing is 1 day. (2) There are in this gulf the islands of *Tragyras*,[47] *Brattia* (*Brač*), and Olynta (*Šolta*). These are 2 stades distant from one another or a little more, by Pharos and Issa. For here is the island of Pharos (*Hvar*) ⟨with⟩ a Hellenic city, and Issa (*Vis*) island; and these are Hellenic cities. (3) Before voyaging along the coast up to the Naron (*Neretva*) river, a lot of territory extends markedly into the sea.[48] There is an island near the coastal territory, which has the name Melite (*Mljet*), and a second island near this, which has the name Kerkyra Melaina ('*Black Corcyra*'; *Korčula*): and this island *projects* very far *with one* of its promontories from the coastal territory, and with the other promontory it comes down to the Naron river. From Melite it is 20 stades distant, and from the coastal territory it is 8 stades distant.

24. (1) Past the Nestoi is the Naron river: and the voyage into the *Naron* is not narrow, and even a trireme sails into it, and boats do so into the upper trading-place, 80 stades distant from the sea. These people are a nation of the Illyrioi, the Manioi. There is a lake inland from the trading-place, a great one,[49] and the lake extends to the Autariatai,[50] an Illyric nation. There is an island in the lake 120 stades (*long*), and this island is extremely good for farming. From this lake the Naron river flows away. (2) From the Naron up to the *Arion* river is a day's voyage.

From the Arion ⟨up to the Rhizous⟩ river: a voyage of half a day.

Kadmos' and Harmonia's stones are here, and a sanctuary above the *Rhizous* river.[51] From the *Rhizous* river the voyage is to Bouthoë (*Budva*) and the trading-place.

25. A nation belonging to the Illyrioi are the Encheleis, following the Rhizous.[52] Out of Bouthoë to Epidamnos, a Hellenic city: a voyage of a day and a night, and a road (*journey*) of 3 days.

26. (1) Belonging to the Taulantioi is the Illyric nation in which is Epidamnos (*Dürres*); and a river flows beside the city, which has the name Palamnos. Out of Epidamnos to Apollonia (*Pojan*), a Hellenic city: a road (*journey*) of 2 days.

Apollonia is 50 stades distant from the sea,[53] and the river Aias (or *Aoös; Vijosë, Vjosë*) flows beside the city. From Apollonia into Amantia is 320 stades. The Aias river flows from the Pindos mountain beside Apollonia. (2) [—] towards Orikos (*Orikumi*), rather more into the *gulf*. Some 90 stades of the Orikia come down to the sea, and

---

[46] *Neretvanski Canal* (Čače 1999).   [47] 'Proteras' in the MS.
[48] The *Pelješac* peninsula.   [49] Most likely *Hutovo Blato*; see Šašel Kos 2013.
[50] First mentioned here, though an historical fragment contemporary with PS (*c*.350–310 BC; preserved on papyrus, *P. Oxy.* 4. 681) reveals them to be a dominant force in their region; the original may have been consulted by Strabo 7. 5. 11, C317–18. See Pajón Leyra 2021. For the C4l rain of frogs in their land, see Agatharchides §60 a–b (from Photios and Diodoros), B 7 (Aelian); Appian, *Illyrike* 4. 8; Šašel Kos 2005, 190–5, esp. 190–3.
[51] *Arionos* in the MS. Cf. *Rison* in Montenegro.
[52] On the Encheleis and their relationship to similarly named peoples, see Proeva 2021 (updating Proeva 1993).
[53] The author switches back to distances in stades.

60 stades of the Amantia.[54]   (3) Sharing a border with the *Amantes* in the interior are the Atintanes above the Orikia[55] and *Karia* as far as *Idonia*. In the *Kastid*[56] territory is said to be a plain ⟨which has⟩ the name Erytheia. Here Geryones is said to live and to pasture his oxen.[57] By these places are the Keraunia (*Cikes*) mountains on the mainland, and there is an island beside these places, a small one, which has the name Sason (*Sazani*). From here to Orikos, a city, is a coastal sailing of one-third of a day.

27. (1) The Orikoi are settled within the Amantian territory. These people are Illyrioi as far as here, past the Boulinoi.   (2) The mouth of the Ionios gulf is from the Keraunia mountains as far as Cape Iapygia. Up to Hydroëis, a city which is in Iapygia, from the Keraunia (*mountains*) the stades of the voyage across are about 500, ⟨which⟩ is the mouth of the gulf: and the places inside are the Ionios.

There are many harbours in the Adrias (*Adriatic*): and (*the*) Adrias is the same thing as (*the*) Ionios.[58]

28. After the Illyrioi are the Chaones.[59] Chaonia has good harbours: and the Chaones live in separate villages.[60] The coastal sailing of Chaonia is a half a day.

29. By Chaonia is the island of Korkyra (*Corfù*), and a Hellenic city in it, with three harbours by the city; one of these is enclosed (*kleistos*).[61] Korkyra belongs also to Thesprotia more than it does to Chaonia. I return again onto the mainland, from where I turned away.

30. After Chaonia are the Thesprotoi, a nation. These people, too, live in separate villages: and this territory also has good harbours. Here there is a harbour, which has the name Elaia. Into this harbour the river Acheron discharges: and there is a lake, Acherousia, out of which the Acheron river flows. The coastal sailing of Thesprotia: half a day.

31. After Thesprotia is Kassopia, a nation. These people, too, live in separate villages. These people live alongside as far as into the Anaktoric gulf. The coastal sailing of the territory of the Kassopoi is a half a day. The Anaktoric gulf is a little less than 120 stades from its mouth as far as the inner end. The mouth is 4 stades in width.

---

[54] i.e. the territory of the *polis* of Amantia.   [55] The territory of Orikos.

[56] Or 'Kestris', cf. *Barr.* 52 B2 Kestria. The order of places is confusing around this point; the author makes a 'flash-forward' to the Keraunia Mts, follows them back NW towards the coast, and then has to jump back to Sason. Possibly this indicates a local source arranged from S to N.

[57] Herakles seized the cattle of Geryon(es).

[58] This odd generalization is evidently meant to round off the Adriatic.

[59] We enter Epeiros (not named), where PS names only the most powerful peoples (§§28, 30–3). By the 330s, the Molossians were dominant within an increasingly unified Epeiros.

[60] Though PS omits the towns in this passage (such as the new *polis* of Kassope), this is not necessarily a claim that people did not live in *poleis* (city-states): *kōmē*, conventionally translated 'village', is a size category, not a political term (Hansen 1995; Hansen and Nielsen 2004, 74–9).

[61] Counillon 1998b argues that 'closed' or 'enclosed' harbours are naval bases that can be sealed in an emergency; Mauro and Gambash 2020, however, suggests that in PS the phrase denotes a harbour with a narrow entrance. See also Mauro 2022a for *kleistos* as a multivalent term.

32. After Kassopia are the Molottoi, a nation. These people live in separate villages: and they come down only a little here to the sea, but over a large extent into the interior. The coastal sailing of the Molottian territory is 40 stades.

Continuous Hellas

MAINLAND GREECE (WEST)

33. (1) After Molottia is Ambrakia (*Árta*), a Hellenic city: and this is 80 stades distant from the sea. There is also upon the sea a fort with an enclosed harbour.

(2) From here Hellas begins to be continuous as far as the Peneios river and Homolion,[62] a city in Magnesia, which is beside the river. The coastal sailing of Ambrakia: 120 stades.

34. (1) After Ambrakia is Akarnania, a nation; and the first city on this spot is Argos the Amphilochic, and Euripos, and *Thyrrheion* in the *federal state*. Outside the *Ambrakic* gulf are the following ⟨cities⟩: Anaktorion with a harbour; Akte; and the city of Leukas with a harbour: this city stands forth upon the Leukatas, which is a promontory ⟨visible⟩ from afar ⟨in⟩ the sea. This city was previously also named Epileukadioi. The Akarnanes, having fought a civil war, took out of Corinth 1,000 new settlers; and the new settlers, after killing *these people*, hold their territory themselves. This territory (*i.e. Leukas*) is now an island, having been cut off at the isthmus with a ditch.[63] After these places is the city of Phara; and by these places there is the island of Ithaca, with a city and a harbour. After these places the island of Kephalenia. (2) I return again onto the mainland, from where I departed.

After these places the city of Alyzia, and by this the island of Karnos, and the city of Astakos with a harbour, and the river Acheloös, and Oiniadai, a city: and to this there is a voyage upstream along the Acheloös. There are also other cities of Akarnanes in the interior.[64] The coastal sailing of Akarnania is 2 days. (3) All of Akarnania has good harbours: and by these places many islands lie alongside, which the Acheloös is making into mainland by silting them up. The islands are called Echinades: and they are deserted.

35. After Akarnania is Aitolia, a nation, and in it the cities are as follows: Kalydon, Halikarna, and Molykreia: and the Delphic gulf (*gulf of Corinth*): and the mouth of this gulf is 10 stades, and upon it is a sanctuary; and Naupaktos, a city: and after it (*sc. Naupaktos*) the Aitoloi have many other cities in the interior. The coastal sailing of Aitolia is 1 day.

---

[62] Homolion is not mentioned under Magnesia (§65. 1 below). In the passage on the Greek mainland that begins here, PS ceases to specify whether a *polis* is 'Hellenic'. Despite the plethora of *poleis* here, he includes fewer enlivening details other than the details of civil war in Leukas (in this section) and Homer's burial-place (§58. 2) and certain sanctuaries and rivers. For 'continuous Hellas', cf. Herakleides Kritikos fr. 3 §8; Dionysios son of Kalliphon, 31–4; and introduction to chapter.

[63] This is the longest historical comment in the treatise.

[64] A rare mention of an inland place (cf. §26. 3 and §32 above); PS names inland places regularly only from §43 to §66. 5.

Aitolia stretches along all of Lokris from the interior as far as the Ainianeis.[65]

36. After the Aitoloi (*Aitolians*) are the Lokroi (*Lokrians*), a nation, in whom are *the* people called Ozolai[66] and the following cities: Euanthis, Amphissa. These people also have cities in the interior. The coastal sailing of the territory of the Lokroi is half a day.

37. After the Lokroi are the nation of the Phokeis (*Phokians*) by the Kirrhaion plain; and the sanctuary of Apollo, and Delphi, a city,[67] and Antikyra, a city, where the best hellebore[68] treatments take place. The coastal sailing of the territory of the Phokeis: half a day.

38. After the Phokeis are the Boiotoi (*Boiotians*), a nation, and the following cities: Korsiai, Siphai with a harbour, and *Eutresis* with a fort of the Boiotoi. The coastal sailing of Boiotia: half a day ⟨or⟩ less.[69]

39. After the Boiotoi are the Megareis (*Megarians*), a nation, and the following cities: Aigosthena; Pegai, a fort; Geraneia; and A⟨igei⟩ros. The coastal sailing of the territory of the Megareis: 100 stades.

PELOPONNESE (FIRST PART)

40. After the Megareis are Corinth, a city with a sanctuary, *Lechaion*,[70] and the Isthmus. Now from here begins the Peloponnesos. From the sea the road towards the sea on our side,[71] through the isthmus, is 40 stades. These places are all gulf-shaped. The coastal sailing of the territory of the Corinthians: half a day.[72]

41. After Korinthos is Sikyon, a city. Of this the coastal sailing: 120 stades.

42. After Sikyon the Achaians, a nation, and among them the cities are as follows: Pellene, Aigeira, Aigai, Aigion, and Rhypes; and outside Rhion (*are*) Patrai and Dyme.[73] The coastal sailing of the Achaian territory: 700 stades.

43. After the Achaioi is Elis,[74] a nation, and in it the following cities: Kyllene with a harbour; and the river Alpheios: and there is also another union of cities, Elis, in the interior. By this territory is the island of Zakynthos, in which there is both a city and a harbour. The coastal sailing of the territory of the Eleians right up to the ⟨boundaries⟩ of the Lepreatai: 700 stades.

44. After Elis is Arkadia, a nation. Arkadia comes down to the sea at Lepreon out of the interior.[75] Their cities in the interior are the following: ⟨Megale Polis⟩ (*Megalopolis*),

---

[65] Whom we meet again at §62. 2.   [66] This refers to Ozolian, or Western, Lokris.
[67] PS, more interested in cities than in Panhellenic cults, does not mention the oracular sanctuary of Apollo.
[68] A herbal medication for administering purges.
[69] This is the W coast of Boiotia, on the gulf of Corinth; for the other, see §59.
[70] Corinth's port on the gulf of Corinth; answered by Kenchreiai at §55.
[71] The writer adopts a standpoint from the Aegean, probably from Athens.
[72] Like Boiotia, Korinthia has two coasts, reappearing at §55.
[73] An incomplete list of the, conventionally twelve, *poleis* of Achaia, even allowing for the destruction of Boura and Helike by seismic activity in 373 (the latter soon rebuilt).
[74] Elis here refers to the region also called Eleia, with the *polis* of Elis inland representing a synoecism of different communities created in 471.
[75] And thus qualifies for inclusion in PS's gazetteer of settled coastal lands. Cf. Dikaiarchos 1 below

Tegea, Mantineia, Heraia, Orchomenos, and Stymphalos. There are also other cities. The coastal sailing of the territory of the Lepreatai: 100 stades.

45. After Arkadia is the nation of Messene,[76] and in it the following cities: Kyparissos, 7 stades distant from the sea; ⟨Prote island with a harbour⟩; Ithome in the interior, 80 stades distant from the sea. The coastal sailing of the Messenian territory: 300 stades.

46. (1) ⟨After Messene is⟩ Lakedaimon,[77] a nation, and in it the cities are the following: Asine; Mothone; Achilleios, a harbour, and back-to-back with this Psamathous, a harbour.[78] In the middle of both these, projecting into the sea, is a sanctuary of Poseidon, Tainaros; Las, a city with a harbour; Gytheion, in which is a shipyard with a fort; the river Eurotas; Boia, a city; and Malea, a cape. By this (*cape*) lies Kythera island, with a city and a harbour. By this is Crete island.   (2) After this aforementioned cape Malea are Side, a city with a harbour; Epidauros,[79] a city with a harbour; Prasia, a city with a harbour; and *Anthana*, a city with a harbour. There are also many other cities of the Lakedaimonians. In the interior is Sparta, and many others. The coastal sailing of the territory of the Lakedaimonians: 3 days.

CRETE AND CYCLADES

47. By Lakedaimon lies the island of Crete: for Lakedaimon lies closest to it of (*all*) Europe. The voyage across from Lakedaimon as far as to the promontory of Crete upon which is the city of Phalasarna: a day's run.

Past Phalasarna is Kriou Metopon ('*Ram's Brow*'; *C. Krios*) promontory. Towards the south wind there is the voyage to Libyē, and up to the *Azirides* of Chersonesos, those of the Kyrenaioi (*Cyrenaeans*): the voyage of a day and a night.

(2) Crete is 2,500 stades long, and narrow, and extends from the settings of the sun towards the risings of the sun.[80] There live in Crete Hellenes, some of them colonists from the Lakedaimonians, others from the Argives, others from the Athenians, others from the rest of Hellas from wherever it chanced. Some of them are aborigines. (*There are*) many cities in Crete.   (3) ⟨After Koryk⟩os promontory the first city towards the setting sun is the aforementioned Phalasarna with an enclosed harbour.

---

for debate about whether Arkadia was landlocked. Lepreon was the main *polis* in the small region of Triphylia on the W coast; the cities of Triphylia joined the Arkadian league soon after it was founded in the 360s.

---

[76] The correct name of the region after its liberation from Spartan rule in the 360s, only later replaced by the conventional 'Messenia', lit. 'territory of Messene'—the latter, as a *polis*, being initially called Ithome.

[77] 'Laconia' in English; the area comprising the territories of the Spartans and of their dependent cities, only a few which are named here.

[78] Achilleios and Psamathous are on opposite sides of the *Máni* peninsula where it narrows to a point.

[79] Sometimes called Epidauros Limera, as distinct from Epidauros in the Argolid (§50).

[80] The remarkable description of Crete does not form a *periplous* or coastal circuit, but begins in the W and travels E while zigzagging between the N and S coasts. Once again, a distinct local source may be being used.

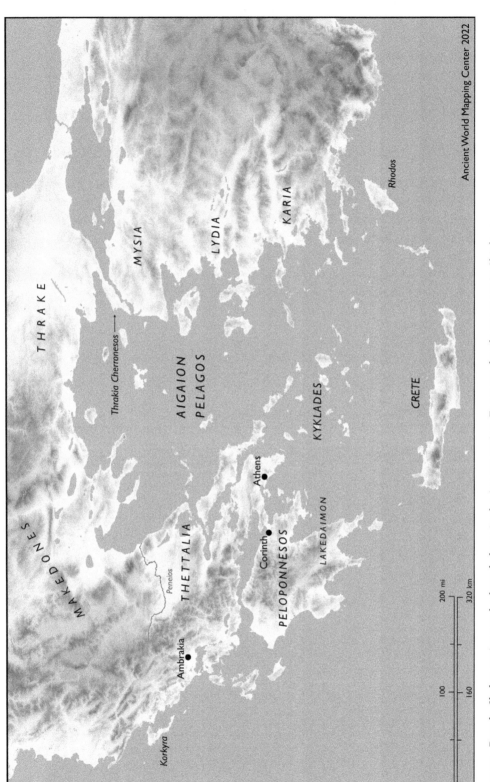

MAP 7.2. Pseudo-Skylax: regions and selected places in the Aegean region. For more details, see maps in Shipley 2011 ~ 2019.

(*Then*) Polyrrhenia,[81] and it extends from the north towards the south. Diktynnaion, a sanctuary of Artemis, towards the north wind, belonging to the Pergamia territory. Towards the south Hyrtakina. Kydonia with an enclosed harbour towards the north. In the interior Elyros, a city. Towards the south Lissa, a city with a harbour beside Kriou Metopon. Towards the north wi⟨nd⟩ the Apteraian territory. Then the Lampaia,[82] and this extends on both sides, and the river Mesapos is in it.   (4) After this *Mount Ida*, with Eleuthernai towards the north. Towards the south Sybrita with a harbour towards the south, Phaistos.[83] Towards the north Oaxos and Knossos. Towards the south Gortyna. Rhaukos ⟨in the interior⟩, and in the interior Lyktos, and this extends on both sides. ⟨Towards the north wind Mount Kadistos with a harbour in it, (*namely*) Olous, and all . . .⟩ Prasos; it extends on both sides. *Itanos*, the promontory of Crete towards the rising sun. There are also other cities in Crete: and it is said to be hundred-citied.

48. The following are the Cyclades by the Lakedaimonian territory that are inhabited: Melos with a harbour, and by this Kimolos, and by this *Pholegandros*, and by this Sikinos, *an island* and a city. By this Thera, by this Anaphe, and by this Astypalaia.[84]

I return again onto the mainland, from where I turned away.

PELOPONNESE (SECOND PART)

49. After Lakedaimon is the city of Argos, and in it Nauplia,[85] a city with a harbour: and in the interior Kleonai, Mykenai, and Tiryns. Coastal sailing of the Argeian territory in a circle, for it is a gulf, called the Argolic: 150 stades.

50. (1) After Argos is the Epidaurian territory:[86] for it comes down to this gulf for 30 stades.[87]   (2) After the Epidaurian territory is the Halia[88] with a harbour. This is upon the mouth of the Argolic gulf. The voyage round this is 100 stades.

51. (1) After this is Hermion, a city, with a harbour. The voyage round this is 80 stades.   (2) After Hermion is Skyllaion, the promontory of the gulf towards the Isthmus: and Skyllaion belongs to Troizenia.[89] Directly facing it is Sounion, the promontory of the territory of the Athenians. By this is the island of Belbina with a city.[90]   (3) Of this gulf, from this mouth inwards to the Isthmus, there are 740 stades. This gulf itself is very straight at the mouth.

---

[81] i.e. the territory of the *polis* of Polyrrhen.

[82] i.e. the territory of Lappa, also called Lampe, Lampai.

[83] Phaistos is in fact 3 mi (5 km) inland.

[84] These are the southern, Dorian Cyclades, on a sea route to Rhodes; the Ionian appear at §58.

[85] Nauplia and Argos were separate cities, but the language reflects the domination exerted by Argos over all the *poleis* of the Argolid.

[86] Or 'the territory (*that is*) Epidauros', if one accepts that standardization with §50. 2 is not essential (Brillante 2020, 94 & n.).

[87] Its coast on the other face of the Argolid is at §54.

[88] The territory of the *polis* of Halieis.   [89] The territory of the *polis* of Troizen (§52).

[90] *Ágios Geórgios* islet, midway between C. Skyllaion and C. Sounion.

52. (1) After Hermion is Troizen, a city with a harbour. The coastal sailing of it is 30 stades.   (2) After these places is the island of Kalauria, with a city and a harbour. The coastal sailing of it is 300 (?) stades.

53. By this is the island and city of Aigina with two harbours. I return again onto the mainland, from where I turned away.

54. After Troizenia is the city of Epidauros with a harbour. The coastal sailing of the Epidaurian territory: 30 (*i.e. 130*) stades.

55. After Epidauros is the territory of the Corinthians, ⟨the part⟩ towards the east; the fort of Kenchreiai;[91] and the Isthmus, where there is a sanctuary of Poseidon.

Here the Peloponnesos ends.

MAINLAND GREECE (EAST)

The Korinthioi also have territory outside the Isthmus, and the fort of Sidous, and the other fort, Kremmyon. The coastal sailing of the territory of the Korinthioi as far as the bounds of the Megarians: 300 stades.

56. Past the territory of the Korinthioi is Megara, a city with a harbour, and Nisaia, a fort. The coastal sailing of the territory of the Megareis as far as Iapis, for this is a boundary of the territory of the Athenians: 140 stades.

57. (1) After the Megareis are cities[92] of the Athenians. The first (*place*) in Attica is Eleusis, where there is a sanctuary of Demeter and a fort. By this is Salamis, an island with a city and a harbour. Next the Peiraieus and the Legs (*Long Walls*) and Athens. The Peiraieus has 3 harbours.   (2) (*Then*) Anaphlystos, a fort with a harbour; Sounion, a promontory with a fort; a sanctuary of Poseidon; Thorikos, a fort with two harbours; Rhamnous, a fort. There are also many other harbours in Attica.

Voyage round the territory of the Athenians: 1,140 stades. From the Iapid territory up to Sounion: 490 stades. From Sounion as far as the boundaries of the Boiotians: 650 stades.[93]

58. (1) By Attica are the islands called Cyclades,[94] and the following cities in the islands: Keos—this one is four-citied: ⟨Poieëssa, a city⟩ with a harbour; Koressia, Ioulis, and Karthaia—Helene; Kythnos island, with a city; Seriphos island, with a city and a harbour; Siphnos; Paros with two harbours, one of which is enclosed; Naxos; Delos; Rhene (*or Rhenaia/-eia*); Syros; Mykonos—this one is two-citied; Tenos with a harbour; and Andros with a harbour. Now these are the Cyclades islands.[95]   (2) But

---

[91] Corinth's port on the Saronic gulf, answering Lechaion at §40.

[92] Not a slip: Salamis was a separate *polis* from Athens (as PS says below). He does not name the major inland demes of Attica but only some of the major coastal ones, even though they are not *poleis* in their own right, unlike Salamis or the towns in Lakedaimon (§46). This over-representation of Attic settlements fits a writer working out of Athens.

[93] These distances, unusually precise for such long transects, may be based on land measurement: Shipley 2010.

[94] Introduced as if for the first time, but see §48. These are the northern and central Cyclades, the Ionian ones.

[95] Cf. the list at Artemidoros 83 (from Strabo).

under these are the following other islands towards the south: Ios with a harbour—in this (*island*) Homer is buried; Amorgos—this one is three-cited—with a harbour; and Ikaros—two-cited.

(3) After Andros is Euboia island[96]—this one is four-cited: there are in it Karystos, Eretria with a harbour, Chalkis with a harbour, Hestiaia with a harbour. Euboia from (*the sanctuary of*) Zeus Kenaios up to Geraistos, Poseidon's sanctuary, has 1,350 stades; and in width Euboia is narrow.

(4) In the Aegean open-sea (*pelagos*) are the following islands: by Eretria Skyros, with a city; Ikos—this one is two-cited; Peparethos—this one is three-cited—with a harbour; Skiathos—this one is two-cited—with a harbour. After these places I return again onto the mainland, from where I turned away.

59. After Athens are the Boiotians, a nation: for these people come down to this sea *as well (as the other)*.[97] In it the first (*place*) is a sanctuary, Delion; Aulis, a sanctuary; Euripos, a fort; Anthedon, a fort; Thebes; Thespiai; and Orchomenos in the interior. There are also other cities.[98] The coastal sailing of the Boiotian territory from Delion as far as the bounds of the Lokrians: 250 stades.

60. After the Boiotoi are the Lokroi,[99] a nation. By Euboia they have the following cities: Larymna, Kynos, Opous, and Alope; and the Lokroi also have many others. The coastal sailing of their territory: 200 stades.

61. After the Lokroi are the Phokians:[100] for these people, too, extend to this sea. They have the following cities: *Thronion*, Knemis, Elateia, and Panopeus. They have also other cities in the interior. The coastal sailing of the territory of the Phokeis is 200 stades.

62. (1) After the Phokeis are the Melieis and the Melieus gulf.[101] In this gulf are the people called Limodorieis,[102] the following: Erineos, Boion, and Kytinion. Here are Thermopylai, Trachis, Oite, Herakleia, and the Spercheios river. (2) After the Melieis ⟨are the Malieis⟩, a nation. The Malieis have as their first city Lamia, and as the last Echinos: and the Malieis also have other cities, as far as where the gulf reaches. Against the territory of the Malieis live the Ainianes, above from the interior. Through them flows the Spercheios river.

63. Outside the Maliaios gulf are the Achaioi Phthiotai, a nation: and they are also in the Pagasetic gulf, on the left as one sails in, to about halfway up the gulf. The cities

---

[96] We have left the Cyclades.   [97] For the W coast of Boiotia, see §38.

[98] PS has named all the important coastal *poleis* of Boiotia.

[99] i.e. the Eastern or Opountian Lokrians (cf. §36).

[100] In the region of Phokis.

[101] PS begins to enumerate the nine 'junior' districts of Thessaly, as opposed to the four dominant *tetrades* of Pelasgiotis, Achaia Phthiotis, Thessaliotis, and Histiaiotis. The Melieis occupy the region of Malis or Melis; but the passage is confused, this region apparently occurring twice.

[102] PS oddly uses this jocular name ('Starving Dorians') instead of *Dōrieis*, perhaps having in mind the proverbial statement that the Dorians emigrated from the Peloponnese during a famine (Ps.-Plutarch, *Proverbs the Alexandrians Used*, 1. 34). Both names perhaps originally stood in the text, one being omitted in copying.

belonging to the Achaioi are the following: Antrones, Larissa, Melitaia, Demetrion, and Thebai: and the Achaioi also have other cities in the interior.

64. (1) After the Achaians Thettalia (*Thessaly*) comes down to the sea out of the interior on a narrow front to the Pagasetic gulf, 30 *stadioi*. Belonging to Thettalia there are the following cities upon the sea: Amphenai, Pagasai, and in the interior Pherai, Larissa, Pharsalos, Kierion, Pelinnaion, Skotousa, and Krannon. There are also other cities of the Thettaloi in the interior. Thettalia stretches along in the interior above the Ainianes, Dolopes, Malieis, Achaioi, and Magnetes, as far as Tempe. (2) The Pagasetic gulf's length is, from the mouth to the inner end of Pagasai, a voyage before the midday meal. The mouth of it is 5 stades. In the Pagasetic gulf is the island of Kikynethos, with a city.

65. (1) ⟨After Thettalia⟩ there is the nation of the Magnetes (*Magnesians*) beside the sea, and the following cities: Iolkos, Methone, Korakai, Spalauthra, Olizon, and Tisai, a harbour. Outside the gulf of Pagasai are Meliboia, Rhizous, Eurymenai, and Amyros. Against them in the interior live the nation of the Perrhaiboi, Hellenes.

(2) As far as here from Ambrakia Hellas is continuous:[103] and probably also ⟨the⟩ seaward parts (*of Magnesia*) are similarly ⟨in⟩ Hellas.

Macedonia to Northern Black Sea

66. (1) Past the Peneios river are the Makedones (*Macedonians*), a nation, and the gulf of Therma. (2) The first city of Macedonia is Herakleion; (*then*) Dion; Pydna, a Hellenic city;[104] Methone, a Hellenic city, with the Haliakmon river; Aloros, a city with the river Loudias; Pella, a city with a royal seat (*basileion*) in it, and there is a voyage upstream to it up the Loudias; (*then*) the Axios river; the Echedoros river; Therme, a city; and Aineia, Hellenic.

(3) (*Then*) Pallene,[105] a long cape stretching up into the open sea (*pelagos*), and the following Hellenic cities in Pallene: Potidaia, forming a barrier across the isthmus in the middle, Mende, Aphytis, Thrambeïs, Skione, and Kanastraion the sacred promontory of Pallene. (4) Outside the isthmus the following cities: Olynthos, Hellenic; Mekyberna, Hellenic; Sermylia, Hellenic, with the Sermylic gulf; and Torone, a Hellenic city with a harbour. Dion, Hellenic; Thyssos, Hellenic; Kleonai, Hellenic; Athos Mountain; Akrothoöi, Hellenic; Charadrous, Hellenic; Olophyxos, Hellenic; Akanthos, Hellenic; and Alapta, Hellenic. Arethousa, Hellenic; Lake Bolbe; and Apollonia, Hellenic. (5) There are also many others belonging to Macedonia in the interior. It is gulf-shaped. The coastal sailing round the gulfs: 2 days.

After Macedonia is the Strymon river; this bounds Macedonia and Thrace.

---

[103] PS here omits Homolion, which he specified at §33. 2 as the limit of continuous Hellas, and postpones mention of the R. Peneios to §66. 1.

[104] Having left 'continuous Hellas', PS resumes his habit of specifying whether cities are 'Hellenic'. At §66. 5, he also resumes giving distances in sailing times.

[105] Pallene is the first of the three promontories of Chalkidike (not named), where 1 in 16 of all known Greek *poleis* are located. The second promontory, Sithonia, is not named. The third is Athos (§66. 4).

67. (1) Thrace extends from the Strymon river as far as the Istros river in the Euxeinos Pontos (*Black Sea*). There are in Thrace the following Hellenic cities: Amphipolis, Phagres, Galepsos, Oisyme, and other trading-places of the Thasians. By these places is Thasos island with a city and two harbours; of these, one is enclosed.

(2) I return again to the point from where I turned away. Neapolis, by this; Daton, a Hellenic city, which Kallistratos of Athens founded;[106] the river Nestos; Abdera, a city; and Koudetos river with the cities of Dikaia and Maroneia.   (3) By these places is Samothrake ⟨island⟩, with a harbour. By this on the mainland are the trading-places of Drys, Zone, and Douriskos. The river Hebros (*Evros, Meriç*) with a fort upon it, (*namely*) Ainos, a city with a harbour. Forts of the Ainioi in Thrace; the Melas (*Saros*) gulf; the Melas river; Deris, a trading-place;[107] Kobrys, a trading-place of the Kardianoi (*people of Kardia*); and another, Kypasis.   (4) By the Melas gulf is Imbros island, with a city; and Lemnos island, with a harbour.

(5) I return again onto the mainland, from where I turned away. After the Melas gulf is the Thrakia Cherronesos,[108] and in it are the following cities: Kardia, Ide, Paion, Alopekonnesos, Araplos, Elaious, Madytos, and Sestos upon the mouth of the Propontis (*Sea of Marmara*), ⟨which⟩ is 6 stades (*wide*).[109] Within Aigos Potamos are Kressa, Krithote, and Paktyë.   (6) As far as here it is the Thrakian Chersonesos. Out of Paktyë to Kardia through the neck on foot is 40 stades, out of the sea into the sea; and there is a city in the middle, which has the name Agora (*'Market-place'*).[110] The length of the Chersonesos out of Kardia to Elaious—for here it is longest: 400 stades.

(7) After the Chersonesos are Thracian forts as follows: first Leuke Akte, (*then*) Teiristasis, Herakleia, Ganos, Ganiai, and Neon Teichos; Perinthos, a city[111] with a harbour; Daminon Teichos; and Selymbria, a city with a harbour. From this up to the mouth of the Pontos there are 500 stades.   (8) The place is called Anaplous (*'Voyage Upstream'*)[112] along the Bosporos until you come to Hieron (*Sanctuary*). From Hieron it is the mouth of the Pontos, 7 stades in width.

(9) There are in the Pontos the following Hellenic cities in Thrace:[113] Apollonia (*Sozopol*), Mesēmbria (*Nesebur*), Odesos Polis (*Varna*), Kallatis (*Mangalia*), ⟨Tomis (?),[114] Istros,⟩ and the river Istros.   (10) The coastal sailing of Thrace from the Strymon river as far as Sestos: 2 days and 2 nights.

---

[106] An Athenian general of the 370s and 360s, in exile at the time. PS, here and elsewhere, overplays Athens' historical role (Brillante 2020, 5–7; 69–70).

[107] But also recognized as a *polis*, unlike Kobrys and Kypasis that follow.

[108] The *Gallipoli* peninsula.   [109] PS does not name the Hellespont as such.

[110] Also known as Chersonesos.   [111] Unlike the preceding five settlements.

[112] Cf. Dionysios of Byzantion's *Anaplous* (Ch. 30). The omission of Byzantion and the Bosporan towns may reflect MS error or inept source blending; maybe Markianos excised them because Menippos's description (Ch. 21), also in his corpus, was fuller (Brillante 2020, 196–7).

[113] PS adopts a clockwise circuit of the Pontos, unlike several late authors.

[114] A suggestion not in Shipley 2019. The MS reads Καλλάβις (Kallabis) for Kallatis; in medieval scripts, some forms of β and μ can be confused (i.e. 'Kallatis Tomis' may have become 'Kallamis' and then 'Kallabis'). (I thank Richard Janko for discussion of this passage.)

From Sestos as far as the mouth of the Pontos: 2 days and 2 nights.

From the mouth as far as the Istros river: 3 days and 3 nights.

The total voyage round, from Thrace and the river Strymon as far as the Istros river: 8 days and 8 nights.

68. (1) After Thrace are the Skythai, a nation, and among them the following Hellenic cities: the Tyras (*Dniester*) river; Nikonion, a city; and Ophiousa, a city. (2) Against the Skythike the Tauroi, a nation, occupy a promontory of the mainland: and the promontory is (*projecting*) into the sea. In the Taurike[115] live Hellenes ⟨and their *poleis* are the following⟩: Chersonesos (*Cherson*), a trading-place; Kriou Metopon ('Ram's Brow'; C. *Sarych*), a promontory of the Taurike. (3) After these places are the Skythai again, and the following Hellenic cities in it (*sc. Skythia*): Theudosia (*Feodosiya*), Kytaia with Nymphaion, Pantikapaion (*Kerch*), and Myrmekion. Coastal sailing direct from (*the*) Istros up to Kriou Metopon: 3 days and 3 nights; and that beside land is double, for it is a gulf.

(4) In this gulf there is an island—and the island is deserted—which has the name Leuke, sacred to Achilles.[116] From Kriou Metopon is a voyage to Pantikapaion of a day and a night: and from Pantikapaion up to the mouth of the Maiotis lake (*Sea of Azov*) is 20 stades.

(5) The Maiotis lake is said to amount to half of the Pontos.[117] In the Maiotis lake, as one sails directly in, on the left are Skythai: for there come down out of the outside sea, above the Taurike, to the Maiotis lake the Syrmatai, a nation.[118] The river Tanaïs (*Don*) bounds Asia and Europe.

Length of Europe

69. From the Pillars of Herakles in Europe, as one sails round the gulfs beside land—if, for as many nights as have been written (*above*), one reckons days in place of these; and, where stades are written, in place of the 500 stades *a day of a man sailing*—the coastal sailing of Europe becomes **153 days**.

The greatest rivers in Europe are the Tanaïs, the Istros, and the Rhodanos.

ASIA

Southern Black Sea

70. Past the Tanaïs river, Asia begins. The first nation of it is, in the Pontos, the Sauromatai. To the Sauromatai belongs the nation of the Gynaikokratoumenoi.[119]

---

[115] Territory of the Tauroi; in full Taurike Chersonesos, the *Crimea*.

[116] Cf. Arrian §§21–3 (Ch. 27 below); Dion. Peri. 541–8; *Eux.* §§87, 93–5, 97. This is *Zmiinyi*, 'Snake Island', made famous by the war of 2022.

[117] The size of the Sea of Azov is over-estimated (cf. Bianchetti 1998, 32), as it is by Ptolemy, *Geography* 7. 5. 10; *Eux.* §44. It is a false view if their areas are considered, but more reasonable in terms of their coastal lengths.

[118] See n. on Eudoxos of Knidos 19. PS distinguishes the Syrmatai W of the Tanaïs from the Sauromatai to its E (§70); see Marcotte 2000b, 141 n. 15; 251–2.

[119] Cf. §21. 1.

71. After the Gynaikokratoumenoi there follow the Maiotai.

72. After the Maiotai are the Sindoi, a nation: for these people extend also to the outside of the lake, and there are Hellenic cities among them, the following: Phanagorou Polis (*or Phanagoria*); Kepoi (*'Gardens'*); Sindikos, a harbour; and Patous.

73. After Sindikos harbour are the Kerketai ⟨or rather Toretai⟩, a nation, 74. and a Hellenic city, Torikos, with a harbour. 75. After the Toretai are the Achaioi, a nation. 76. After the Achaioi are the Heniochoi (*'Charioteers'*), a nation. 77. ⟨After the Heniochoi are the Koraxoi, a nation.⟩ 78. After the Koraxoi is Korike, a nation. 79. After Korike are the Melanchlainoi (*'Black-cloaks'*), a nation, and among them the river Metasoris, and the Aigipios river. 80. After the Melanchlainoi is Gelon.

81. After these are the Kolchoi, a nation, with Dioskourias (*Sukhumi*),[120] a city; Gyenos, a Hellenic city,[121] with the Gyenos river and the Chirobos river; the Chorsos river, the Arios river, and the Phasis river (*Rioni?*) with Phasis, a Hellenic city; and there is an upstream voyage up the river of 180 stades to the city of Aia, a great barbarian one, where Medea was from.[122] Here are the Rhis river, the Isis river, Lēstōn Potamos, and the Apsaros (*Tchoroikhi?*) river.

82. After the Kolchoi are the Bouseres, a nation; the river of the Daraanoi; and the Arion (*Abu*) river.

83. After the Bouseres are the Ekecheirieis (*'Truce-makers'?*),[123] a nation; the river Pordanis; the Arabis river; Limne, a city; and Hodeinios, a Hellenic city.[124]

84. After the Ekecheirieis are the Becheires, a nation;[125] Becheirikos, a harbour; and Becheiras, a Hellenic city.

85. After the Becheires are the Makrokephaloi (*'Long-heads'*),[126] a nation; Psōrōn Limen (*'Itching Harbour'; Araklıçarşısı*); and Trapezous (*Trabzon*), a Hellenic city.[127]

86. After the Makrokephaloi are the Mossynoikoi (*'Hut-dwellers'*), a nation, with Zephyrios Limen (*'West-wind Harbour'; Zefre*); Choirades, a Hellenic city; and Ares' Island (*Giresun Adası*). These people occupy mountains.

87. After the Mossyn⟨oik⟩oi is the nation of the Tibarenoi.

88. After the Tibarenoi are the Chalybes, a nation; Genesintis,[128] an enclosed harbour;[129] Ameneia, a Hellenic city; and Iasonia (*Yasun Burnu*), a cape and Hellenic city.

89. After the Chalybes is Assyria, a nation; the river Thermodon; a Hellenic city, Themiskyra; the Lykastos river (*Merd Irmağı*), with a Hellenic city; the Halys river

---

[120] Later Sebastopolis, a major node in Arrian's *Periplous* (Ch. 27 below).

[121] The first of six alleged Hellenic *poleis* between Kolchis and Trapezous, the largest number reported before Roman times. On Gyenos, see Braund 2021.

[122] In the myth, Medea was a Kolchian princess.

[123] Only here and at *Eux.* §42. 1, where they are said to be former inhabitants.

[124] The last four locations are probably Arrian's Prytanis, Zagatis, Athene, and Adienos.

[125] Again *Eux.* §38 indicates relocations of peoples in the intervening 700 years.

[126] Cf. *AWP* §14. 1–5; Makrones in e.g. *Nik.* fr. 21; *Eux.* §38.

[127] PS omits the cities of Kerasous (Xen. *Anab.* 5. 3–7) and Kotyora (ibid. 5. 5, etc.), which existed in C4.

[128] The E tip of C. Iasonia.   [129] i.e. a secure naval harbour (Counillon 1998a).

(*Kızıl Irmak*) and Karoussa (*Gerze*), a Hellenic city; Sinope (*Sinop*), a Hellenic city; Kerasous, a Hellenic city with the Ocherainos river (*Kara Su*); Harmene (*Akliman*), a Hellenic city with a harbour; and Tetrakis, a Hellenic city.

90. After Assyria is Paphlagonia, a nation. In it is Stephane (*Istifan*), a harbour ⟨and a Hellenic ci⟩ty; Koloussa (*Güllüsü*), a Hellenic city; Kinolis (*Ginoğlu*), a Hellenic city; Karambis (*Fakas?*), a Hellenic city; Kytoris, a Hellenic city; Sesamos (*Amasra*), a Hellenic city with the Parthenios river; and Tieion (*Hisarönü*), a Hellenic city, with the harbour of Psylla (*Çatal Ağzı*) and the river Kallichoros (*Ilık Su*).

91. After Paphlagonia are the Mariandynoi, a nation. Here is the city of Herakleia (*Ereğli*), Hellenic, with the river Lykos (*Gülünç Su*) and another river, the Hypios (*Büyük Melen Su, Akarsu*).

92. (1) After the Mariandynoi are the Bithynoi Thracians, a nation; the river Sagarios; another river, Artones (*Şile*); the island of Thynias—and men of Herakleia (C. *İğneada*) live on it—and the river Rhebas (*Rıva Deresi*). Then directly (*after*) are the Strait and the aforesaid Hieron[130] in the mouth of the Pontos, and after this the city of Kalchedon outside Thrace, after which is the Olbian gulf (*or gulf of Astakos; İzmit Körfezi*). Coastal sailing from the Mariandynoi as far as the inner end of the Olbian gulf—for so great is the Thrace of the Bithynoi: 3 days.

(2) From the mouth of the Pontos as far as the mouth of the Maiotis lake, the voyage is of similar size, both that along Europe and that along Asia.[131]

Mysia to Cyprus

93. After Thrace is Mysia, a nation.[132] It is the left side of the Olbian gulf as one sails out into the Kian gulf as far as Kios. Mysia is a headland. The Hellenic cities in it are as follows: Olbia with a harbour; Kallipolis with a harbour; the promontory of the Kian gulf; and on the left Kios, a city, and the Kios river. The coastal sailing of Mysia to Kios: 1 day.

94. After Mysia is Phrygia, a nation, and the following Hellenic cities: Myrleia with the Rhyndakos river, and upon it Besbikos island; the city of Plakia; Kyzikos (*Kelkiz Kale*) in the middle,[133] forming a barrier across the isthmus; and within the isthmus Artake (*Erdek*). By this is an island and city of Prokonnesos (*Marmara I.*), and a second island, with good harbours, Elaphonnesos (*Ekinlik Adası*): and Prokonnesioi farm it. On the mainland is the city of Priapos (*Karabiğa*); (*then*) Parion (*Kemer*), Lampsakos (*Lepseki*), Perkote, and Abydos (*Maltepe*); and this is the mouth of the Propontis by Sestos.

95. From here Troas (*the Troad*) begins, and the Hellenic cities in it are as follows: Dardanos, Rhoiteion (*Baba Kale*), and Ilion—and it is 25 stades distant from the sea—with the river Skamandros (*Menderes Çay*) in it. An island lies by these places,

---

[130] See §67. 8.
[131] This sentence may come from a *periplous* organized in the reverse direction.
[132] From this point, PS builds in more mythological and historical points of interest.
[133] See the emendation by Lucarini 2021.

Tenedos (*Bozcaada*), with a harbour, where Kleostratos the astronomer is from.[134] On the mainland Sige (*Yenişehir*), Achilleion (*Beşika Burnu*), Krateres Achaiōn (*Hantepe*), Kolonai (*Beşiktepe*), Larissa (*Limantepe*), and Hamaxitos (*Beşiktepe/Gulpınar*) with a sanctuary of Apollo, where Chryses served as priest.[135]

96. From here it is called the Aiolis territory. The Aiolid cities in it, upon the sea, are as follows: ⟨Assos (*Beryamkale*) (and/or) Gargara (and) Antandros (*Devren/Avcılar*); and in the interior as follows:⟩ Kebren (*Fuğla Tepe/Çal Dağ*), Skepsis (*Kurşunlu Tepe*), Neandreia (*Çığrı Dağ*), and Pityeia. Coastal sailing of Phrygia from Mysia as far as Antandros: [—].

97. By these places is an Aiolid island, Lesbos, with five cities in it, the following: Methymna (*Míthymna*), Antissa (*Skalochóri/Obriókastro*), Eresos (*Skála*), Pyrrha (*Megáli Límni*) with a harbour, and Mytilene (*Mytilíni*) with two harbours. By this there is an island with a city: and the name that this has is Pordoselene (*Alibey Adası*). I return again onto the mainland, from where I turned away onto the islands.

98. (1) Past Antandros and downwards from *Aiolis, this* territory *too* was previously Mysia as far as Teuthrania (*Kalerga*), but is now Lydia; and the Mysoi migrated up into the mainland. (2) There are the following Hellenic cities in it and in Lydia: Astyra (*Kilisetepe Kaplıcaları?*), where there is the sanctuary ⟨of Artemis, and⟩ Adramyttion (*Karataş/Ören*). ⟨After Adramyttion⟩ the territory is Lesbian; and above this is the territory of the Chians and the city of Atarneus (*Kale Tepe*): and below these places, upon the sea, the ⟨city and⟩ harbour of Pitane (*Çandarlı*) with the river Kaïkos.[136] After Pitane are Elaia (*Kazıkbağları*), Gryneion (*Termaşalık Burnu*), and Achaiōn Limen ('*Achaians' Harbour*'): in this the Achaians are said to have taken counsel against Telephos,[137] whether to march or to depart; the city of Myrina with a harbour; Kyme (*Nemrut Limanı*) with a harbour—and above Kyme in the interior is a Hellenic city, Aigai (*Nemrut Kale*)—and Leukai (*Üçtepeler*) with harbours; Smyrna (*İzmir*), in which Homer was; Phokaia[138] (*Foça*) with a harbour and the Hermos river (*Gediz Çay*); Klazomenai (*Klazumen*) with a harbour; and Erythrai (*Ildır*) with a harbour. By these is the island of Chios with a harbour.

(3) I return again onto the mainland. *Airai* (or *Gerraidai; Sığacık Liman*), a city with a harbour; Teos (*Sığacık*), a city with a harbour; Lebedos; Kolophon in the interior; Notion ('*South Wind City*') with a harbour; the sanctuary of Apollo Klarios; the Kaÿstros river (*Küçük Menderes*); Ephesos with a harbour; Marathesion (*Ambar Tepe*) with, on the mainland, Magnesia, a Hellenic city; Anaia (*Kadikalesi*), Panionion,[139]

---

[134] PS, unusually, mentions an historical figure: Kleostratos (possibly C6l) is credited with defining the zodiac.

[135] The priest of Apollo whose daughter Agamemnon seizes, *Iliad* book 1.

[136] We enter S. Aiolis; PS omits most of the towns.

[137] King of Mysia, healed by Achilles, in the Trojan war legend.

[138] PS omits to name the famous region of Ionia.

[139] The former common sanctuary of the archaic Ionian league.

Erasistratios, Charadrous, Phokaia, Akadamis,[140] and Mykale (*C. Samsun Dağı*)— these places are in the territory of the Samians. In front of Mykale is Samos island, with a city and an enclosed harbour. This island is not lesser than Chios.

(4) I return again onto the mainland, from where I turned away. Upon Mykale is the city of Priene, with two harbours, of which the one is enclosed: then the river Maiandros (*Maeander; Menderes*). The coastal sailing of Mysia and Lydia, from Astyra as far as the Maiandros river: 2 days and 1 night.

99. (1) After Lydia is Karia, a nation, and in it the following Hellenic cities: Herakleia (*Kapıkırı*);[141] then Miletos;[142] then Myndos (*Gümüslük*) with a harbour; Halikarnassos (*Bodrum*) with an enclosed harbour and another harbour around the island (*Arkonnesos; Kara Ada*), and a river; Kalymna island; Karyanda island (*Salih Adası*), with a city and harbour—these people are Karians. The island of Kos, with a city and an enclosed harbour. By these places is the Keramiac gulf of Karia, and the island of Nisyros, with a harbour.

(2) I return again onto the mainland. A sacred promontory ⟨of Knidos⟩, Triopion (*Deveboynu Burun*); Knidos (*Tekir*), a Hellenic city, with the territory of the Rhodians on the mainland; Kaunos (*Dalyan*), a Karic city with an enclosed harbour; Kragos, a promontory.[143]

(3) By this is ⟨Rhodos⟩ (*Rhodes*) island, ⟨with a city: and⟩ an ancient triple city in it, namely the following cities: Ialysos, Lindos, and Kameiros.[144] Beside Rhodos the following islands are inhabited: Chalkeia (*Chálki*), Telos (*Tílos*), Kasos, and Karpathos—this one is three-citied. The coastal sailing of Karia, from the Maiandros river up to *Kragos*,[145] which is (*the*) promontory of Karia: 2 days.

I return again onto the mainland, from where I turned away.

100. (1) Past Karia is Lykia, a nation: and the Lykioi have the following cities: Telmissos (*Telmessos; Fethiye*)[146] with a harbour and the river Xanthos, through which is a voyage upstream to ⟨Xanthos (*Kınık*), a city⟩; Patara (*Gelemiş*), a city, and it has a harbour; Phellos (*Çukurbağ*), a city with a harbour—by these places is an island of the Rhodioi, Megiste (*Kastellórizo*); and Limyra, a city, to which the voyage upstream is along the river. Then Gagaia (*Yenice*), a city; then Chelidoniai (*Beş Adalar*),[147] a promontory with two islands; Dionysias island (*or Krambousa; Sulu Ada*); and the promontory and harbour of Siderous (*Adrasan Burnu*). Above this is a sanctuary of

---

[140] These four places are unlocated.   [141] Called Latmos until about the time of composition.

[142] The southernmost Ionian *polis*.

[143] Mentioned again (if the text is correct) in the next paragraph.

[144] These were synoikized in 408/7 to form the new *polis* of Rhodos, but remained in existence.

[145] Müller suggests 'Kryassos', but see n. on *Stadiasmos* §259 (Ch. 30 below).

[146] Telmessos in SW Lykia, one of three similarly named places in the region (a fourth is just over the frontier into Pamphylia); Lykian only *c*.400–*c*.360 and again from 333. As PS elsewhere knows nothing of Alexander's reign, we must assume he is using slightly out-of-date information.

[147] The Turkish name means 'five islands'.

Hephaistos in the mountain, and a lot of spontaneous fire burns out of the ground and is never extinguished.[148]

(2) If you go forward higher from the sea there is [—], (*then*) Phaselis (*Tekirova*), a city with a harbour—and this is a gulf; and Idyros (*Kemer?*), a city; the island of Lyrnateia (*Reşat Ada*); Olbia (*Koruma*); Magydos (*Lara Manastır*) with the river Katarraktes (*Düden Çay*); and Perge (*Aksu*), a city with a sanctuary of Artemis. In a direct line the coastal sailing of Lykia from [—] is a day and a night, for it is gulf-shaped: and that beside land is double this.

101. (1) After Lykia is Pamphylia, a nation, and in it the following cities: Aspendos, a city—to this the voyage upstream takes place along the river, and the river is the Eurymedon; then the city of Sylleion (*Asar Köy*); and another city, Side (*Selimiye*), a colony of the Kymaioi, with a harbour. Coastal sailing of Pamphylia from Perge: half a day.

(2) There are also other cities of Pamphylia: Kibyra (*Kara Burun*), then Korakesion (*Alanya*).

102. (1) After Pamphylia is Kilikia, a nation, and in it the following cities: Selinous (*Kale Tepe*); Charadrous (*Yakacık*), a city with a harbour; Anemourion (*Belkis*), a cape with a city; and Nagidos (*Bozyazı*), a city, and it has an island. Towards *Setos* (*Softa Kalesi*) are *the harbours* Poseideion (*Kızıl Burun*); Salon; Myous (*Yenikaş*); Kelenderis (*Aydıncık*), a city with the harbour of Aphrodisios and another harbour; Holmoi (*Taşucu*), a Hellenic city with ⟨a harbour⟩; Sarpedon (*İncekum Burnu*), a deserted city with a river; Soloi (*Viranşehir*), a Hellenic city; Zephyrion (*Mersin*), a city; the river Pyramos (*Ceyhan Nehri*) and the city of Mallos, to which the voyage upstream is along the river; the trading-place of *Amane* with a harbour; Myriandos Phoinikōn (*of the Phoenicians*); and Thapsakos, a river. Coastal sailing of Kilikia from the bounds of Pamphylia as far as the Thapsakos river (*Orontes?*): 3 days and 2 nights.

(2) Out of Sinope in the Pontos, through the mainland and Kilikia to Soloi, the road from sea to sea is 5 days.[149]

103. By Kilikia is the island of Kypros, and in it the following cities.[150] Salamis, Hellenic, with an enclosed winter harbour;[151] Karpaseia (*Rizokarpaso*); Keryneia (*Kyrenia*); Lepethis[152] Phoinikōn (*of the Phoenicians*); Soloi—this too has a winter harbour; Marion, Hellenic; and Amathous—they are aborigines; all these have deserted harbours.[153] There are also other cities in the interior (*that are*) barbarian. I return again onto the mainland, from where I turned away.

---

[148] At *Yanar Taş*, 'Flaming Rock'; possibly anc. Chimaira (but see Bean 1979, 138), cf. Ps.-Arist. *Mir. ausc.* 127, 842b 25–6, a source that in part dates to C3. For the geology, see Hosgormez, Etiope, and Yalçin 2008.

[149] A great under-estimate, presumably derived from Hdt. 2. 34, though a simple emendation makes the distance 15 days. On the 'isthmus' of Asia Minor, cf. Artem. 95 (Strabo 14. 5. 22, C677); *Nik.* fr. 29 ~ *Eux.* §27.

[150] PS makes an anti-clockwise tour, beginning in the E. The terms used for harbours indicate a specialized source; it omits several cities in the S and reflects Athenian interest in the N and W in the era of the powerful Euagoras I of Salamis (r. 411–374/3; Counillon 1998b).

[151] i.e. a secure naval base.   [152] Usually 'Lapethos'.   [153] i.e. undefended.

Syria–Phoenicia to Egypt

104. (1) There is after Kilikia the nation of the Syroi.[154] In Syria there live, in the seaward part, the Phoenicians, a nation, upon a narrow front less than up to 40 stades from the sea, and in some places not even up to 10 stades in width.

(2) Past the Thapsakos river is Tripolis Phoinikōn (*of the Phoenicians*).[155] Arados (*Rouad*) island with a harbour, a royal seat (*basileia*) of Tyros (*Tyre; Šur*) with a harbour roughly 8 stades from the land. In the peninsula is a second city of Tripolis (*Tarabulus*): this belongs to Arados, Tyros, and Sidon; in the same place are three cities, and each has its own circuit of the enclosure wall. A mountain, Theou Prosopon (*'God's Face'; Ras Shaqqa*); Trieres (*El Heri/Batrun*), ⟨a city⟩ with a harbour; Berytos (*Beirut*), a city with a harbour; ⟨the river⟩ Bostrenos; Porphyreōn (*Khan Nebi Yulas/ Nabe Yūnəs*), a city; ⟨Leontōn Polis ('*Lionstown*'; *Wādī as-Sekke?*);⟩ Sidon, a city with an enclosed harbour; and Ornithōn Polis ('*Birdstown*'; *Adlun?*). Belonging to the Sidonioi is (*the area*) from Leontōn Polis as far as Ornithōn Polis.

(3) Belonging to the Tyrioi is the city of Sarapta (*Sarafend*). The city of Tyros, with a harbour within a fort; and this island is a royal seat of the Tyrioi, and is 3 stades distant from the *sea*. Palaityros (*Ras el-'Ain*), a city; and a river flows through the middle. A city of the Tyrioi, ⟨Ekdippa⟩ (*Achziv*), with a river; Ake (*Akko*), a city; Exope, a city of the Ty⟨rioi; Karmelos (*Mt Carmel*)⟩, a mountain sacred to Zeus; Arados (*'Atlit*), a city of the Sidonioi; ⟨Magdolos (*Wādī al-Maġāra?*), a city⟩ and river of the Tyrioi; Doros (*Dor*), a city of the Sidonioi; and ⟨Ioppe (*Jaffa*), a city;⟩ they say it was here that Androm⟨eda⟩ was ⟨ex⟩posed ⟨to the monster. Aska⟩lon, a city of the Tyrioi and a royal seat; her⟨e is the boundary of Koile⟩ ('*Hollow*') Syria. Coastal sailing of Koile Syria ⟨from the Thapsakos river as far as⟩ Askalon: 2,700 stades.

105. (1) ⟨After Syria are the Arabes,⟩ a nation, horse-riding herders ⟨and having pastures of all kinds of ani⟩mals: sheep and goats [—] and camels; and thi⟨s⟩ is [—] is for the most part w⟨aterless⟩ [—] Egypt [—] in it a gul⟨f⟩[156] [—] is out of the E⟨rythraian sea⟩ [—] ⟨ou⟩ter se⟨a⟩ [—] ⟨s⟩ea [—] and [—] k [—— (*gap of c.35 words*) ——] ⟨The coastal sailing of [—]⟩. (2) [—] and of ⟨A⟩rabia itself, from the bounds of Syria as far as the mouth of the ⟨Nile i⟩n Pelousion (*Tell el-Farama*), for this is the boundary of Arabia: 1,300 stades. ⟨They say A⟩rabia belongs to Egypt as far as the Nile next to the Ara⟨bian gulf⟩ (*mod. Red Sea*) [—] the Egyptians; and they bring tribute (*to*) Aigy⟨pt⟩[—] always to the Arabes.

106. (1) ⟨After Arabia is⟩ the nation of ⟨Aigyptos (*Egypt*)⟩; and the cities in it are ⟨the following: Pelousion, a city with a harbour⟩ and a royal seat, where the mouth ⟨of

---

[154] Syria and Phoenicia are strongly characterized in terms of geography, and have a different complexion from largely pastoral Arabia. PS names no further Hellenic cities until §108. 3 Kyrene; so his aims are not limited to expounding the extent of Greek settlement; rather, his view is 'global' (within the Mediterranean and Black Sea).

[155] The cities of Karnos, Enydra, and Marathos opposite Arados.

[156] Here PS will have named one or both arms of the mod. *Red Sea*.

the river Nile, the Pelousiac, lies⟩ first, Arabia's ⟨boundary. Second, the Tanitic,¹⁵⁷ and a roy⟩al ⟨city⟩. Third, the ⟨Mendesian with Mendes, a city. Fourth, the Phatniti⟩c.¹⁵⁸ Fifth, the Sebenny⟨tic, with Sebennytos, a city; Boutos, a lake (*Kom el-Farain*), wh⟩ere there is a city and a ro⟨yal seat. Sixth, the Bolbitic, with a roy⟩al ⟨city⟩. Seventh, ⟨the Kanopic, with Thonis (*Aboukir*), a city. After these places a lake⟩ which has the name ⟨Mareia (*Mariout*). This lake is already i⟩n Libyē [—] and it [—] council [—] e [—] (*gap of about 60 words*) [—] ⟨the Canobic [—] the Sebennytic [—]⟩

(2) [—] the other the Pelousiac.¹⁵⁹ Again it is split apart: and the Sebennytic (*goes*) on the one hand into the Mendesian, on the other hand into the sea. From the Mendesian (*the river goes*) into the Phatnitic mouth; and from the Pelousian into the Tanitic mouth. The one from Kanopos (*goes*) as far as the Sebennytic lake, and the Bolbitine mouth flows out of the lake. Mostly the seaward parts of Egypt are lakes and marshes.

(3) Egypt has the following shape: similar to an axe.¹⁶⁰ For it is broad by the sea, narrower in the interior, and by Memphis is the narrowest part; and next, as one goes into the interior from Memphis, wider; and wider by the uppermost part. The part of Egypt above Memphis is the most substantial compared with the part beside the sea. The Kanopic mouth bounds Asia and Libyē. The coastal sailing of Egyptians from the Pelousian mouth is 1,300 stades.

Length of Asia

(4) The voyage round Asia—for it is convex in shape—as one reckons in the same manner that has been described for Europe, is **87 days.**¹⁶¹

(5) Upon the Kanopic mouth there is a deserted island, which has the name Kanopos; and on it there are monuments, the tomb of the ship-captain of Menelaos¹⁶² from Troy, who had the name Kanopos. Both the Egyptians and the neighbours to these places say that Pelousios came to Kasion, and Kanopos came to the island where the memorial of the ship-captain is.

LIBYĒ

Non-Carthaginian Libyē

107. (1) Libyē begins from the Kanopic mouth of the Nile.¹⁶³ A nation of the Libyans, the Adyrmachidai. Out of Thonis the voyage to Pharos, a deserted island¹⁶⁴—and it has good harbours and no water—is 150 stades.

---

¹⁵⁷ 'Saitic', Hdt. 2. 17.　　　¹⁵⁸ 'Boukolikon', Hdt. 2. 17.
¹⁵⁹ PS clearly described here the division of the Nile below Memphis.
¹⁶⁰ i.e. a double-headed axe: narrowing to Memphis, then widening further S.
¹⁶¹ PS thus ends Asia and begins Libyē at the W apex of the Delta, specifically at L. Mareia (§106. 1).
¹⁶² King of Sparta and husband of Helen of Troy.
¹⁶³ As far as Cyrenaica, PS's passage on N. Africa is rich in harbours and distances; thereafter more plentiful in ethnographic detail. Beyond Carthage and the unwelcoming coast of mod. Algeria, it seems to benefit from Carthaginian sources. For the understanding of this passage, I have drawn particularly on Peretti 1979, 345–417; Desanges 1978, 87–120; Lipiński 2003, 337–434.
¹⁶⁴ Later the site of Alexandria's lighthouse.

In Pharos are many harbours. They draw water out of the Mareia lake, for it is drinkable. The voyage upstream out of Pharos to the lake is short. There is also Chersonesos (*Marabit?*) with a harbour. The coastal sailing has 200 stades.

(2) Past Chersonesos is the Plinthinos gulf.[165] The mouth of the Plinthinos gulf to Leuke Akte (*'White Headland'; Ras el-Abiad*): a voyage of a day and a night; and that to the inner end of the Plinthinos gulf twice as much; and it is surrounded by inhabitants in a circle.

From Leuke Akte to Laodamanteios, a harbour: a voyage of half a day.

From Laodamanteios harbour to Paraitonios (*Marsa Matruh*), a harbour: a voyage of half a day.

(3) There follows Apis (*Zawiet Umm el-Rakham*), a city. So as far as here the Egyptians rule.

108. (1) Past Apis is a nation of the Libyes, the Marmaridai, as far as Hesperides. From Apis up to Tyndareioi Skopeloi: a voyage of a day.

From Tyndareioi Skopeloi (*Ishaila*) to Plynoi (*or Katabathmos; Sollum*), a harbour: a voyage of a day.

Out of Plynoi to Petras the Great (*Bardia*): a voyage of half a day.

Out of Petras to Menelaos (*Marsa Ahora?*): a voyage of a day.

Out of Menelaos to Kyrthaneion (*Marsa el-Afarid?*): a voyage of a day.

Past Kyrthaneion is Antipygos (*Tobruk*), a harbour: a voyage of half a day.

Past Antipygos is Petras the Small (*Marsa Tarfaia*), a harbour: a voyage of a half a day.

Past Petras ⟨the⟩ Small is Chersonesos (*Ras et-Tin*) and *Azirides* (*Wadi el-Chalig*), a harbour—these places are in the territory of the Kyrenaians—a voyage of a day.

(2) In the middle of Petras and Chersonesos are the islands of Aëdonia (*Geziret el-Maracheb*) and Plateiai (*C. Bomba*). There are minor anchorages (*hyphormoi*) under them. From here the silphium begins to grow in fields:[166] and it stretches along from Chersonesos through the interior as far as (*the city of*) Hesperides, nearly 1,500† stades beside the land. (*Then*) Aphrodisias island (*Geziret Chersa*), a minor anchorage; Naustathmos (*'Ship-station'; Marsa Hilal*), a harbour. Voyage from Chersonesos: 1 day.

From Naustathmos to the harbour of Kyrene (*Ain Shahat/Grennah*): 100 stades.

Out of the harbour to Kyrene: 80 stades.

(3) Kyrene is in the interior. These are all-weather harbours. There are other refuges under islets, and there are minor anchorages and many headlands in the territory between. Out of the harbour of Kyrene as far as the harbour by Barke (*el-Merg*), 500 stades. The city of the Barkaioi is 100 stades distant from the sea. Out of the harbour by Barke up to Hesperides, 620 stades.

---

[165] The W frontier of Egypt, Hdt. 2. 6.

[166] The silphium plant produced a valuable resin; its export contributed to the wealth of Cyrene. It may not, after all, be extinct (Gresco 2022).

(4) Out of Kyrene there are harbours, and there are the following *divided locali-ties* as far as Hesperides: Phykous, a gulf;[167] and inland here is the garden of the Hes-perides.[168] It is a place 18 fathoms deep, sheer in a circle, having nowhere a descent; and it is 2 stades every way, not less, width and length. This is shaded with trees wo-ven into one another as densely as possible. The trees are lotus (*and*) fruit-trees of all kinds: pomegranate-trees, pear-trees, arbutus fruits, mulberries, vines, myrtles, bay-trees, ivy, olive-trees, wild olive-trees, almond-trees, and nut-trees.   (5) Among the localities that have not been mentioned is, by the garden, Ampelos (*'Vine'*); Apios (*'Pear'*)—it is 30 stades distant; Chersonesos; very many gardens; Zenertis; Taucheira (*Tocra*); *Bakalou* Kome; Hesperides,[169] a city with a harbour; and a river after[170] the city, the *Encheleios* (*'Eel River'*). By these localities, past the Chersonesoi of the *Azirides*, some are of the Kyrenaioi and others of the Barkaioi as far as Hesperides.

109. (1) Past Hesperides there is a great gulf, which has the name Syrtis (*gulf of Sidra*), and, so to say, as one guesses approximately, (*a length*) of some 5,000 stades. In width it is, from Hesperides to Neapolis (*Lepcis Magna*) on the other side, a voyage of 3 days and 3 nights.

(2) There live around it a nation of the Libyes, the Nasamones,[171] as far as the inner end on the left. After these there follows a nation of the Libyes beside the Syrtis, as far as the mouth of the Syrtis, (*namely*) the Makai.

(3) As one sails into the Syrtis from Hesperides, the first (*place*) is Herakleioi Thines (*'Herakles' Banks'*); there follow after these Drepanon (*'Sickle'; Ras Carcura?*), the three islands of Pontiai (*'Marine Is.'?*), then after these the so-called Leukai (*'White' Is.*). In the most hollow part of the Syrtis, in the inner end, is Philainou Bomoi (*'Philainos' Altars'*), a dependent harbour; *the grove of Ammon* (*Maaten Bescer?*) [—] of the Syrtis. From this, living beside the Syrtis, the Makai winter by the sea, shutting away their animals; and in the summer, with the waters receding, they drive away their animals up into the interior with themselves.

(4) After the Syrtis there is a fine locality and a city, which has the name Kinyps;[172] and it is deserted. From Neapolis into the Syrtis it is 80 (?) stades distant:[173] and under it is the river Kinyps, and below it is an island towards the river.

(5) The depth of the Syrtis inside Hesperides towards Philainou Bomoi, to the in-ner end of the gulf: a voyage of 3 days and ⟨2⟩ nights.

Width from Kinyps river towards the Leukai islands: a voyage of 4 days and 4 nights.

---

[167] The town of Phykous is *Zaviet el-Hamama*.

[168] Possibly in limestone depressions at *Coefia*: G. D. B. Jones and Little 1971, 78–9, with 66 fig. 4 and pl. 8. 2. The home of the Hesperid nymphs, it appears to have changed location as Greek knowledge of the far west grew. Some of the species named are suited to different altitudes.

[169] Normally called Euesperides, near the later Berenike (*Benghazi*).   [170] Or 'at' (*epi*).

[171] Transhumant pastoralists according to Hdt. 2. 32; 4. 172.

[172] A short-lived Spartan colony of C6l (Hdt. 5. 42), near *Wadi Caam/Ki'am*.

[173] We have not yet reached Neapolis; possibly PS is using a W–E *periplous*.

Carthaginian Libyē

110. (1) Beside the places outside the Syrtis live the Lotophagoi (*Lotus-eating*) Libyes, a nation, as far as the mouth of the other Syrtis (*gulf of Gabès*). These people use lotus as food and drink. Past Neapolis (*Lepcis Magna*), in the territory of the Carthaginians,[174] is *Gaphara*, a city. Of this (*territory*), coastal sailing: 1 day from Neapolis.

(2) Past *Gaphara* is Abrotonon (*Sabrata*), a city with a harbour. Of this, the coastal sailing: 1 day.

(3) Past Abrotonon is Taricheiai (*Saltings; Henchir el-Mdeina?*),[175] a city with a harbour. The coastal sailing from Abrotonon: 1 day.

(4) By these places there is an island, which has the name Bracheion,[176] after the Lotophagoi (*and*) by Taricheiai. This island is 300 stades (*long*) and a little less in width. It is about 3 stades distant from the mainland. In the island grows a lotus which they eat, and another from which they make wine. The fruit of the lotus is in size as big as an arbutus fruit. They make much oil out of wild olive-trees. The island bears much produce, namely wheat and barley. The island has good earth. Voyage from Taricheiai to the island: 1 day.

(5) After the island is *Gichthis* (*Bou Grara*), a city. From the island to *Gichthis*: voyage of half a day.

(6) [— ⟨to Eschides⟩[177] —] From *Eschides* ⟨to Neapolis⟩:[178] voyage of a day.

(7) An island is at hand by it, deserted. After this is Karkinitis[179] (*Gharbi*), an island with a city; and by this is Thapsos. Coastal sailing from this to Thapsos: a day and a half.

From Thapsos ⟨to Leptis the Small is a voyage of [—].

From Leptis to Adrymes (*Hadrumetum*) is a voyage of [—].

(8) Past Leptis⟩ the Small (*Lepti Minus*) and Adrymes (*Hadrumetum*) there is a great gulf inside, in which is the Small Syrtis (*gulf of Gabès*),[180] called Karkinitis, much more dangerous and harder to sail than the other Syrtis; its circumference is 2,000 stades. In this Syrtis stands the so-called island of the Triton ⟨with a lake⟩ (*Chott el Jérid*) and the river Triton, and just here there is a sanctuary of Athena Tritonis. The lake has a small mouth, and in the mouth an island is at hand; and whenever there is an ebb tide, sometimes the lake does not allow a voyage in *for* ⟨ships, as it⟩ *appears*. This lake is great, having a circumference of about 1,000 stades.

(9) Libyes live around it, the Gyzantes,[181] a nation, and a city beyond (*the lake*) towards the settings of the sun; for these *Gyzantes* Libyes are said to be all fair-haired

---

[174] PS marks the beginning of Carthaginian territory.
[175] One of a number of places with this name on the N. African coast, where fish was processed.
[176] Also known as Meninx, Lotophagitis, and Girba (*Gerba*).
[177] In the Lesser Syrtis, not named here in the extant text (cf. §110. 8).
[178] Not Lepcis Magna (above) but Makomades/Iunci (*Bordj Younga*). Also distinct from Neapolis–Nabeul at §110. 8.
[179] Cf. Karkinitis, Agathemeros v. 21.
[180] The sequence is wrong: PS jumps back to places which belong between §110. 5 and §110. 6.
[181] The name occurs in various forms, possibly related to Latin *Byzacium*.

and very beautiful. This territory is excellent and very productive, and among them there are animals both very large and very numerous; and they themselves are very rich and very beautiful.

(10) After this Syrtis is Neapolis (*Nabeul*).[182] The coastal sailing from Adrymes up to Neapolis is a day.

After Neapolis is Hermaia (*Cap Bon/Ras Addar*), a cape with a city. The coastal sailing from Neapolis to Hermaia is a day and a half. From Nea⟨polis⟩ to the isthmus is 180 stades on foot towards the other sea, towards Carthage. It is a headland, through which is (*the*) isthmus. [—] ⟨river⟩ [—] Coastal sailing from the river, from here to Carthage: a half of a day.

The territory of the Carthaginians is in a gulf.

111. (1) After the isthmus is Carthage, a city of the Phoenicians with a harbour. Coastal sailing from Hermaia: half a day to Carthage.

(2) Islets are at hand upon Hermaia Cape, Pontia (*'Marine'?*) island and Kosyros (*Pantelleria*). The voyage from Hermaia up to Kosyros: a day.

(3) Past Hermaia Cape towards the rising sun, *a long way* from Hermaia, are three small islands by this place, inhabited by Carthaginians: Melite (*Malta*), a city with a harbour; Gaulos (*Gozo*), a city; Lampas (*Lampedusa*)—this one has two or three towers. Past Kosyros up to Lilybaion, the promontory of Sikelia (*Sicily*): a voyage of 1 day.

(4) After Carthage is Ityke (*Utica*), a city with a harbour. The coastal sailing from Carthage to Ityke: 1 day.

(5) From Ityke to Hippou Akra (*'Cape Horse'*): ⟨a voyage of 1 day⟩. Hippou ⟨Akra⟩, a city,[183] and after it there is a lake, and islands in the lake, and around the lake the following cities in the islands: Psegas (*Ras Ben-Sekka*), a city, and right by it many Naxian islands (*Cani Is.?*): Pithekousai with a harbour; opposite it Kalathe island (*La Galite/Zalita*), and a city in the island, Euboia. Thapsa (*or Rusicade; Ras Skikda*) with a city and a harbour; Igilgilis (*Jijel*), a city with a harbour; Sida, a city; Iomnion (*Tigzirt*), a cape; a city with a harbour; Hebdomos, a city with a harbour; Akion island, and a city with a harbour is upon it; Psamathos (*'Sand'*) island; a city with a harbour, and a gulf; and in the gulf is Bartas, an island with a harbour; Chalka, a city in the river; Arylon, a city; Mes, a city with a harbour; Sige (*Takembrit*), a city in the river, and before the river is the island of Akra (*Rachgoun*); a great city ⟨with⟩ a harbour; Akros, the city and the gulf in it; and a deserted island, Drinaupa by name.

(6) The Pillar of Herakles in Libyē (*Monte Acho?*). Cape Abilyke (*Ğebel Mūsā*), ⟨and⟩ a city in a river, and opposite it the Gadeira islands. From Carthage in this direction, up to the Pillars of Herakles, with the best sailing the coastal sailing is 7 days and 7 nights.

---

[182] Correct geographical order is restored.   [183] Later Hippo Diarrhytus (*Bizerte, Banzart*).

(7) These islands are beside Europe; one of these two has a city: and the Pillars of Herakles are by these, the one in Libyē low, the one in Europe high. These are capes directly facing one another; and these a day's voyage apart from one another.

Length of Libyē

(8) The coastal sailing of Libyē from Egypt, *(from)* the Kanopic mouth as far as the Pillars of Herakles, the reckoning being put in the same terms as has been written in Asia and Europe, as one sails round in a circle along the gulfs: **50 (?) and 4 days.**[184]

(9) As many townships or trading-places as have been described in Libyē, from the Syrtis beside Hesperides as far as the Pillars of Herakles in Libyē, all belong to the Carthaginians.

Beyond the Pillars of Herakles

112. (1) After the Pillars of Herakles, as one sails to the outside holding Libyē on the left, there is a great gulf as far as Cape Hermaia. For here, too, is a Cape Hermaia. By the middle of the gulf lies Pontiōn (*'Marine'?*), a place with a city. Around the city lies a great lake, and in this lake lie many islands. Around the lake grows reed, also galingale, wool-tufted reed, and rush. The Meleagrid birds are here, and nowhere else unless they are exported from here.[185] This lake has the name Kephisias, and the gulf (*has the name*) Kotes, and it is between the Pillars of Herakles and Cape Hermaia.

(2) Past Cape Hermaia there extend great reefs from Libyē up to Europe, not projecting above the water: and it washes over them in places. The reef extends up to the other cape of Europe directly facing it: and this cape has the name Hieron (*Sacred*) Promontory.[186]   (3) Past Cape Hermaia is the river Anides: and this discharges into a great lake. After Anides there is another great river, the Lixos, and a city of the Phoenicians, Lixos;[187] and there is a second city of the Libyes beyond the river, with a harbour.

(4)[188] After Lixos is the Krabis river[189] with a harbour and a city of the Phoenicians, Thymiateria (*'Incense-burner'*) by name.[190] From Thymiateria ⟨is a voyage⟩ to Soloësa Cape (*C. Spartel?*), which projects somewhat into the main (*pontos*). Out of all Libyē

---

[184] PS gives the length of Libyē only as far as the Pillars, an indication that his overriding scheme is governed by the dimensions of the Mediterranean and Black Sea coasts alone. Perhaps he includes part of NW Africa only because he happens to have the information at his disposal.

[185] Probably guinea fowl; see Index for other sources placing them in both NW and E. Africa; also Panchenko 2003, 278, 283, detecting a link between their claimed distribution and the notion of a land bridge between India and W. Africa.

[186] C. *St Vincent* or possibly C. *Trafalgar*.   [187] Cf. Hanno §§6–7 and n. there.

[188] This paragraph probably refers to the area already described at §111. 6. There are widely divergent reconstructions of the relationship between this passage and places on the ground; probably there has been dislocation, causing some repetition. I follow *GGM* i. 91 and Lipiński 2003, 337–434, though not in moving the text to an earlier position: the dislocation may be original, perhaps the result of blending multiple sources. Despite Roller 2006, 19, if PS is using the first part of Hanno it is probably only indirectly; both may be using different sources. They do not, however, differ vastly about the distance from the Pillars or C. Soloëis to Kerne, surely within Morocco—perhaps at *Mogador* I. in the bay of *Essaouira*—even if the rest of Hanno's journey took him far beyond, even perhaps to Mt *Cameroon*.

[189] Cf. Mnaseas 44 for R. Krathis.   [190] Cf. Hanno §2.

this territory is the most renowned and sacred. Upon the promontory of the cape there is a magnificent altar of Poseidon. On the altar are carved human statues, lions, and dolphins; they say Daidalos made them.

(5) Past Soloëis Cape (*C. Spartel*) there is a river, which has the name Xion. Around this river live the Sacred Aithiopes. By these places there is an island, which has the name Kerne.[191] The coastal sailing from the Pillars of Herakles up to Hermaia Cape: 2 days.

From Cape Hermaia to Cape Soloëis, coastal sailing: 3 days.

From Soloëis to Kerne, coastal sailing: 7 days.

The total of this coastal sailing is, from the Pillars of Herakles to Kerne island, 12 days.

(6) The places beyond Kerne island are sailable no further because of the shallowness of the sea and (*because of*) mud and seaweed.[192] The seaweed is the breadth of a hand and is sharp on top, so that it stabs.

(7) The traders are Phoenicians; but whenever they arrive at the island of Kerne, they anchor the round-ships (*gauloi*),[193] having made tents on Kerne for themselves; but taking out the cargo they themselves transport it to the mainland in small boats (*ploia*). (8) There are Aithiopes towards the mainland; and it is these Aithiopes for whom they set out (*their wares*). They sell (*them*) for skins of deer and lions and leopards, and skins and teeth of elephants and (*skins*) of domestic animals. (9) The Aithiopes use for adornment [—] pricked with decoration, and for drinking-vessels bowls of ivory; and their women use for adornment bracelets of ivory; and they also use ivory decoration on their horses. These Aithiopes are the largest of all the humans of whom we know, larger than four cubits (*pēcheis*),[194] and some of them are even five cubits, and they are beard-wearing and long-haired; and these people are the most beautiful of all humans, and there rules over them whoever is tallest. They are also horsemen and javelin-men and archers, and use their weapons fire-hardened.[195] (10) The Phoenicians (*that are*) traders import to them perfumed oil, Egyptian stone, *other mined* (*ones*), Attic tile and pitchers: for the artefacts are on sale at the festival of the Choës.[196] (11) These Aithiopes are meat-eating milk-drinkers, and make much wine from vines: and the Phoenicians themselves also bring this. They also have a great city, to which the Phoenicians, the traders, sail in.

---

[191] Polybios 34. 15. 9 (from Pliny 6. xxxvi. 199) stated, apparently from autopsy, that 'Cerne' was 8 mi offshore. Strabo 1. 3. 2, C47–8, says it (presumably the trading-place) is no longer visible.

[192] Possibly fabricated claims by travellers trying to conceal their ignorance, or locals aiming to monopolize trade.

[193] Round-built boats or merchant vessels as opposed to warships.

[194] A cubit, the distance from elbow to middle finger, is around 1 ft 6 in (*c.*45 cm).

[195] Cf. the fire-hardened arrows of Aithiopes at Agatharch. §53b; Artem. 44.

[196] On this passage and Phoenician trade in the far west, see Gill 1988.

(12) Some say that these Aithiopes stretch along inhabiting continuously from here to Egypt, and that this sea is continuous, and that Libyē is a headland.[197]

ENDMATTER

These two passages are probably additions to the original.[198]

113. (1) Partition through the sea ⟨from⟩ Europe to Asia, fairly direct in a straight fashion; the partition begins from the Euripos by Chalkis, and up to Geraistos it is 850 stades.

> From Geraistos up to the Paionion in Andros, 80 stades.
>
> Andros itself up to the Aulon, 280 stades.
>
> Voyage across the Aulon to Tenos, 12 stades.
>
> Tenos itself up to the promontory by Rhenaia, 150 stades.
>
> The voyage across to Rhenaia, 40 stades.
>
> Rhenaia itself and the voyage across to Mykonos, 40 stades.
>
> From Mykonos the voyage across up to the Melantioi Skopeloi, a little less than a voyage before the midday meal, is 40 stades.
>
> From the Melantioi Rocks, a voyage to Ikaros before the midday meal.
>
> Ikaros itself, 300 stades lengthwise.
>
> From Ikaros, a voyage to Samos before the midday meal.
>
> Samos itself, 200 stades.
>
> Out of Samos to Mykale, 7 stades of the voyage across.
>
> The whole, if they sail out of Samos with the finest sailing, 2,370 stades, without reckoning in addition the voyage ⟨out of Mykale to Samos⟩.

(2) Another partition, straight in a direct fashion.

> ⟨From Malea⟩ as far as Kythera, ⟨1⟩30 stades.
>
> Length of Kythera itself, 100 stades.
>
> To Aigilia, a voyage before the midday meal.
>
> ⟨Length of Aigilia itself, 50 stades.
>
> From Aigilia to Crete, a voyage before the midday meal.⟩
>
> Length of Crete itself, 2,500 stades.
>
> From Crete to Karpathos, 100† stades.
>
> Length of Karpathos itself, 100 stades.
>
> To Rhodos from Karpathos, a voyage of 100 stades.
>
> Length of Rhodos itself, 600 stades.
>
> From Rhodos to Asia, 100 stades.
>
> The partition of the voyage across is 4,270 stades.

---

[197] i.e. it can be circumnavigated.

[198] Though clearly not directly related to the *periplous* above, these passages may still be Cl in date and perhaps, like the *periplous*, related to the work of the scholars in the Peripatos (Lyceum), such as Dikaiarchos.

114. Sizes of islands. Greatest Sardo (*Sardinia*), second Sikelia (*Sicily*), third Crete, fourth Cyprus, fifth Euboia, sixth Kyrnos (*Corsica*), seventh Lesbos, eighth Rhodos, ninth Chios, tenth Samos, eleventh Korkyra, twelfth Kasos†,[199] thirteenth Kephallenia, fourteenth Naxos, fifteenth Kos, sixteenth Zakynthos, seventeenth Lemnos, eighteenth Aigina, nineteenth Imbros, twentieth Thasos.

B. OTHER TEXTS

For the *Suda's* entry on Skylax of Karyanda, see Chapter 2 above, no. 13.

1   Strabo 13. 1. 4, C583
'the Troad . . . but Skylax of Karyanda begins from Abydos'.[200]

2   scholion A to Apollonios of Rhodes, 1. 1177–8
'Kianian': (*These lines refer*) by circumlocution to Kios. It is a city in Mysia. . . . And there is a river, named thus, flowing beside the city, which Skylax of Karyanda mentions.

3   scholion to Apollonios of Rhodes 4. 1215
Skylax says the Nestaioi are an Illyric nation: 'from these there is a coastal sailing into the gulf [— *distance missing?* —]'.

4   Avienus, *Ora maritima*, 32–44

32	You asked, if you remember, what the region
	of the Maeotic sea is. . . .
36	. . . So, to his (*Sallust's*) famous description . . .
40	. . . I have added many things
	taken from the commentaries of very many authors.
	Obviously, Hecataeus the Milesian will be found there,
	Hellanicus of Lesbos, and Phileas
	the Athenian, Scylax of Caryanda . . .

5   Avienus, *Ora maritima*, 370–4

370	But as to the heaving waves that flow between
	the Pillars, Damastes[201] says they are scarcely
	seven stades across. Scylax of Caryanda maintains
	that the flood flowing between the Pillars
	is as wide as the swell of the Bosphorus.

---

[199] A clear error in view of the size of Kasos; probably either Ikaria or Karpathos should stand here.
[200] This is true of the *periplous* of PS; it may have been true of Skylax of Karyanda as well.
[201] Damastes of Sigeion; see Introduction, §VI. 4. b.

6 Markianos, *Preface to Pseudo-Skylax*

(1) Skylax of Karyanda is a very ancient man; and since most of the places in the inhabited world of ours, and in the sea within the Pillars of Herakles, were still unknown to the majority of people, he undertook to write up a voyage round the inhabited world. (2) For all the parts of the eastern world were made familiar to humankind by Alexander the Macedonian, while the parts belonging to the western nations (*were made so*) by the bravery of the Romans, which seized them in warfare.[202]

(3) For the aforementioned reasons Skylax did not succeed in attaining exact knowledge of all places, but sailed round very many parts both well and appropriately, for example the Ionios or Adrias gulf, and, what is more, Attica and all of the Peloponnese with the nations that lived in it, and also representing clearly other parts of the sea, with the people who lived by it. (4) He himself seems somehow to have made brevity of expression a kind of defence for his ignorance of the great majority of places, wishing those who encountered (*his book*) either to seek out, or to know, most things through very few places.

(5) Clear evidence of the antiquity of the man is that he knows neither Alexander, king of the Macedonians, nor the time a little before him.[203] So one would not be wrong to think it worthy of admiration that the man was able to reach most places. (6) Ailios Dios, in the 1st book of *On Alexandria*, says that Skylax addressed his invention to Darius.

7 Constantine Porphyrogennetos, *De thematibus*, 1. 2

. . . the *thema* (*province*) called the Armeniakon . . . neither does Strabo mention such a nomenclature . . ., nor even Skylax the Karyandene.[204]

---

[202] Has M. forgotten that according to Hdt. 4. 44 (see Skylax of Karyanda 1 in Ch. 2 above) Darius discovered the East?

[203] It is unclear why Markianos adds the last few words, given that he believes the author to be Skylax, a contemporary of King Darius (r. 522–486) and thus living at least 150 years before Alexander's accession.

[204] On this passage, see further Ch. 2 n. 26; Ch. 17, introduction, n. 14.

8

PYTHEAS OF MASSALIA

(ACTIVE C.330–C.320 BC)

D. Graham J. Shipley

INTRODUCTION

Pytheas is probably the only Greek geographer to have a public profile today in the English-speaking world,[1] as the first Mediterranean traveller known to have reached the British Isles, and the first Greek or Roman author to describe them. Beyond that, he made a profoundly innovative contribution to scientific geography by applying the mathematical discoveries of Eudoxos and others to the lands along the North Atlantic.

The titles of his works, as reported by Geminos (**15** below) and a scholiast on Apollonios of Rhodes (**27**), are *On the Ocean* (*Peri Ōkeanou*) and *Circuit of the Earth* (*Periodos gēs*) respectively; but they were one and the same, and neither need imply a more general treatment of the coasts of the outer Ocean, since nearly all our evidence about Pytheas concerns the coasts of the North Atlantic and its offshore islands.[2]

In antiquity, however, his reputation was more contested. While Strabo, early in the 1st century AD, reports that Aristotle's younger colleague Dikaiarchos approved of Pytheas' notions (**6** §2), readers of the fragments of Polybios' 34th book (specifically the chapters now numbered 5 and 10) encounter stinging criticisms of the Massaliote by the historian from Megalopolis. What may not be immediately apparent to most who read those passages attributed to Polybios (**6, 11**) is that they, too, are from Strabo, who merely summarizes sections of Polybios' text not preserved elsewhere. These, and the other ten passages in which Strabo mentions Pytheas' work, do not add up to much more than a tantalizing, quite possibly unrepresentative sample of what it may have looked like.

The only attestation of Pytheas earlier than Strabo's, however, is a positive one. In the 2nd century BC, Hipparchos (**1**) cites him in support of a correction to Eudoxos of Knidos (Chapter 6 above). This is also evidence for Pytheas' earliest possible date,

---

[1] As witness the oft-reprinted book of Cunliffe 2001 (2nd edn Cunliffe 2002), and the fictional account by Corda 2019. On Pytheas' record, see Dueck 2012, 56–7; Roller 2015, 84–90; also Roller 2006, 57–91 (ch. 4).

[2] The exceptions are his discussion of the Aiolian islands N of Sicily (**27**) and the odd statement that his journey back from Brettanike took him from Gadeira to the R. Tanaïs (*Don*) (**6** §1), which possibly indicates a second voyage from the Mediterranean into the Black Sea; it is very unlikely that he travelled overland from the North Sea to that region (Roseman 1994, iv n. 2).

since Eudoxos had published his *Ges periodos* (*Circuit of the Earth*) by 342.[3] Strabo also says (**6**) that Dikaiarchos did not believe Pytheas on a particular point, which means that Pytheas' voyage took place no later than the years *c.*325–*c.*300, when Dikaiarchos appears to have been writing.[4]

Strabo probably consulted Pytheas' work only indirectly through other authors, and does not always make clear whom he is quoting at any given moment.[5] Nevertheless it is clear that Polybios was the most hostile among those sources, perhaps because he had himself travelled outside the Pillars of Herakles (in 151/0 and again in 146) and wished to be regarded as the pioneer of exploration in the north-eastern Atlantic and the authoritative expert.[6]

Despite criticism by Polybios and Strabo, as well as by Artemidoros (**9**)—who, according to Strabo, attested that Eratosthenes was led into error by his reliance on Pytheas—the Massaliote was taken seriously by eminent geographers in the century after his lifetime, both those already named and Timaios of Tauromenion (**23–4**). His later impact can be detected in Skymnos (**6**; cf. Skymnos 5, including a possible observation on the flora of Great Britain), Poseidonios (**5–6**), Geminos (**15**), and Kleomedes (**26**), by whose time north-western Europe was much better known to the Greeks and Romans; and possibly in Avienus.[7] Given that ancient views about Pytheas were mixed, we can only form our own view by looking at what he did, and assessing how successful he was, before attempting to divine his aims.

His journey will have lasted at least a few months and evidently spanned a winter solstice (**4**); his reports of phenomena around the summer solstice (e.g. **4, 15, 19**) may have been second-hand. Since some of his travel times seem long to Strabo, he was perhaps conveyed in slow merchant ships.[8] His route has usually been reconstructed as passing through the strait of Gibraltar, rounding Iberia and Brittany, and sailing up the west side of Great Britain before reaching Thoule (of which more below), returning down the east coast of Great Britain, then along the European coast, and presumably retracing his course to Gibraltar.[9] There is an alternative view, however, that he travelled overland from his home in Massalia up the *Rhône* and *Saône*, and then down the *Seine*, a route which has been speculatively linked to the tin trade;[10] but if he genuinely saw Gadeira (**2, 9**) and Brittany (Ouxisame, **3**, is probably *Ushant, Île de Ouessant*), the

---

[3] Gärtner 2006.

[4] On P.'s date, see Roller 2006, 61, 64–6; Pajón Leyra and Bartoš 2020, 85–9, suggesting that his work was well known from *c.*315 though his travels may have taken place before Aristotle's death in 322. On Dikaiarchos' dates, see Shipley 2012, 132–4. Gärtner 2006 argues for a *terminus ante quem* of 309–306, but that case is an unnecessary concoction (Shipley 2012, 133 and n. 135).

[5] Roller 2008a (conference abstract).   [6] Walbank 1972, 126–7.

[7] Bianchetti 1998, 47–52, argues that any influence of P.'s work on Avienus' *Ora maritima* was indirect.

[8] Roseman 1994, 5–6.

[9] Bianchetti 1998, 60–1; Gärtner 2006. Roseman 1994, 3, cautions that radical changes in the coasts and islands of northern Europe may make certain reconstruction impossible.

[10] Ellmers 2010 believes that the Vix Krater, found near the sources of the Seine, reflects Greek interest in the route to Cornwall.

sea journey is likelier.[11] Strabo gives no reasons why we should doubt Pytheas' account of Ouxisame and nearby places (**2**). A further alternative is that Pytheas took a direct oceanic route in one direction (perhaps on the outward voyage) and a coastal in the other.[12]

Pytheas clearly claimed to have travelled all over Great Britain (**6** §1) and beyond it to Thoule (see further below). The 'sea lung' phenomenon was perhaps half-thawed sea ice, and even Strabo does not dispute Polybios' report that Pytheas was speaking from autopsy. It is not clear what precisely Dikaiarchos found to disagree with. More transparent is Polybios' apparently snobbish dismissal of 'a private individual and poor' as a witness; wealthy or not—perhaps Polybios scorned him as a man 'in trade'—it is far likelier that Pytheas was, if not from his earliest years at least by now, an educated citizen of Massalia. We do not know why Strabo was at pains to undermine Pytheas' credibility, but the fact that he resorts to quoting sarcastic comments by Eratosthenes, rather than proving his point with facts as he so often does, must lead to a suspicion of bias. Geminos, after all, not long before (or perhaps not long after) Strabo's day, accepted Pytheas' account of short northern nights (**15** §9). Pliny, almost certainly unaware of Strabo's strictures,[13] did not hesitate to cite Pytheas (esp. **19–20**).

Precursors have been noted. One is the reputed journey of Midakritos (possibly from Phokaia or Massalia) and his discovery of the Kassiterides (*Tin Islands*), somewhere in the vicinity of Britain, perhaps around 500 BC.[14] Another is the rarely mentioned, but seemingly authentic, voyage at a similar date by Euthymenes of Massalia, though he seems only to have travelled down the African coast, not to the north. Finally, the so-called Massaliote *periplous*, if it is real, will have involved another citizen of Massalia in a journey into the North Atlantic.[15] But Pytheas' scientific achievement is of a different order.

His activities were, in fact, remarkable. His interests, and his most concrete contributions to knowledge, include long-distance mensuration, such as the circuit of Britain (**2** §3, **6** §1), and the lunar theory of the tides, a frequent interest of geographers;[16] he may have been the first observer to link tides, correctly, to the Moon's phases (**25**). We have only scraps of his ethnographic observations, and only hints of his knowledge of trade,[17] but somewhat more about his work on geodesy. He was the first person to attempt the reckoning of latitudes in the north-west of the *oikoumenē* (**3**), building upon the geodesy of Eudoxos, whom he corrected about the polar stars. Both Dikaiarchos and Aristotle (*On the Heavens*, 2. 14, 297b 31–298a 9) discuss how people at different

---

[11] Bianchetti 1998, 52–4.   [12] Bianchetti 2019.

[13] Roseman 1994, 11: Strabo's work was not known to Mela, Pliny (who never cites S. in his compendious tables of contents), Tacitus, or Ptolemy; and perhaps not widely known until C6 AD.

[14] Roller 2015, 43–4. The only source is Pliny 7. lvii. 197.

[15] On the last two, see Introduction, §VI. 4. a.

[16] See i.a., in these volumes, Dik. 14, from Stobaeus; Erat. 14, from Strabo; Agatharch. 32a–c, 85a–b, 109–10; Pos. 33–4, 36–8, 69 §1, from Strabo, also 46; Ps.-Arist. 4; *PME* §§45–6; *Hyp.* 33.

[17] On this aspect, see Roseman 1994, 2.

latitudes see a different subset of constellations (**30**): Aristotle in order to demonstrate the sphericity of the Earth, Pytheas in order to establish the latitudes of specific places. Fixing the latitude of Massalia (**2–3, 7** §8), however, need not have been achieved during his famous voyage. Even Strabo concedes (**13**) that Pytheas was careful with astronomical data and mathematical calculation.

The writings of Aristotle, who died in 322, show no knowledge of those ideas of Pytheas that contradict his own: for example, about the causes of tides or the northern limit of the habitable zone;[18] this is further evidence that Pytheas' explorations, or at least his writing, should be dated no earlier than the mid-320s. It seems, however, that he was, or became, part of the wider Hellenic intellectual diaspora, given his evident knowledge of Eudoxos' work and because his interests so closely match those of scientists like Dikaiarchos and the so-called Ps.-Skylax (if the latter is not himself Dikaiarchos). We must assume he was in regular contact with developments at Athens, including at Aristotle's Lyceum (Peripatos), either by correspondence or as a result of personal visits.[19] He will very likely have been aware of Ps.-Skylax; perhaps even motivated to travel to the far north to make good the lack of coverage of that region in that text. (The suggestion that he may have been sent there by Alexander, however, is excessively speculative.)[20]

As further evidence of his intellectual context, it appears Pytheas was well aware that his account of the North, especially Thoule, resonated with Homer's story of the Laistrygonians, who live where 'the ways of night and day are close (*to one another*)' (*Odyssey* 10. 86), which the later scholar Krates of Mallos (2nd century BC) interpreted in terms of the Arctic Circle.[21] All this strengthens the idea that, whether rich or not, Pytheas was well educated.

Some of Strabo's strictures are justified. The exaggerated size of Lake Maiotis (*Sea of Azov*), implied by a reported error in latitude committed by Pytheas (**7**), is found in other authors,[22] such as indeed the aforementioned Ps.-Skylax (§68. 5). Pytheas may also have over-estimated the length of Great Britain; certainly he thought it was triangular, with its Europe-facing side running SW–NE and an obtuse angle pointing north-west, Ireland to its N, and Thoule six days north of its northernmost point (which fits no proposed location: if the days are right, the direction must be wrong, and *vice versa*). Such apparent mistakes are understandable given that he is the first

---

[18] Bianchetti 1998, 29.

[19] Pajón Leyra and Bartoš 2020, 89, are sceptical; but rightly observe that this possibility is not evidence in favour of attributing the *De mundo* (Ch. 24 below) to Aristotle. Roller 2006, 64, notes attested connexions between Massalia and Athens in C4m, and argues for P. as a possible source of information for Aristotle's *Constitution of the Massalians* and other works, though the *Ocean* was probably not written early enough to be available to A.

[20] Bianchetti 1998, 30–2, and Pajón Leyra and Bartoš 2020, 86–7, doubt this suggestion, made by Dion 1977.

[21] Bilić 2012; for P. as a literary author, see further Bilič 2020. On the Laistrygonians, also the Kimmerians who live in the dark, see Roller 2015, 19–21.

[22] Bianchetti 1998, 32.

Greek writer known to have visited this region—even Strabo concedes that he was meticulous in his observations of celestial phenomena (13)—and are less important than the fact that he attempted to make new discoveries, and succeeded.

There remains the perennial question of the mysterious land, or island, of Thoule, which survives in the English expression 'Ultima Thule'.[23] After Kerne (see e.g. Hanno §§8–10; Pseudo-Skylax §112. 7), it is perhaps the most sought-after yet wandering ancient landmark, identified at one time or another with all of the islands north-west and north of Britain, or even—and perhaps more credibly—with Norway or Finland.[24] It should be noted that none of the evidence for Pytheas actually says that he claimed to have been there, only that he reported its existence (Kleomedes, **26,** can only tell us that *others* say Pytheas visited it) and that he travelled out of sight of the British Isles (**6** §1). The negative portrayal of Pytheas' work by Polybios (rather than the rarely read Strabo) may account for the disappearance of his writings—that is, the failure to re-copy them in the Roman period—and the recasting of Thoule as an imaginary, even utopian land.[25]

Extracts are ordered by date in order to give a sense of how our understanding of Pytheas has been constructed. Those from Strabo are adapted from Roller's translation, except for passages within raised points (·), which are translated by me.

SELECTED FURTHER READING

*Bianchetti, S. (1998), *Pitea di Massalia, L'Oceano*. Pisa.

—— (2015), 'Il "Grande Nord" tra scienza e letteratura fantastica da Pitea a Antonio Diogene', *Orbis Terrarum*, 13: 11–31.

Bilič, T. (2020), 'Pytheas and Hecataeus: visions of the north in the late fourth century BC', *Greek, Roman and Byzantine Studies*, 60. 4: 574–93.

Breeze, D. J., and Wilkins, A. (2018), 'Pytheas, Tacitus and Thule', *Britannia*, 49: 303–8.

Cunliffe, B. (2002), *The Extraordinary Voyage of Pytheas the Greek: The Man who Discovered Britain*, 2nd edn. London.

McPhail, C. (2014), 'Pytheas of Massalia's route of travel', *Phoenix*, 68. 3: 247–57.

Roller, D. W. (2006), *Through the Pillars of Herakles: Greco-Roman Exploration of the Atlantic*. London–New York. [Esp. ch. 4 (pp. 57–91).]

*Roseman, C. H. (1994), *Pytheas of Massalia, On the Ocean*. Chicago.

---

[23] 'a distant unknown region; the extreme limit of travel and discovery', *COD*[12].

[24] Wijsman 1998 (followed by Dueck 2012, 56) argues that Thule is Iceland or Shetland, as indeed 7 §8 below would imply at first sight. Breeze and Wilkins 2018 suggest that Tacitus' implied identification of *Thule* with Shetland (*Agricola*, 10; cf. Roller 2015, 186 & n.) is mistaken. One might follow Bianchetti 1998, 63–4, and McPhail 2014, who argue for a location in Norway, if one were to set aside Strabo's assertion that P. made Thoule an island.

[25] Gärtner 2006.

TEXTS

1   Hipparchos, *On Aratos and Eudoxos,* 1. 4. 1: *The North Pole*
Eudoxos (*of Knidos*)[26] displays ignorance about the North Pole when he says, 'There
is a particular star that remains always in the same location; this star is the pole of the
heavens'. For it is not the case that a single star lies at the pole: rather, it is an empty
place with three stars lying beside it, together with which the point representing the
pole encloses an almost rectangular shape, just as Pytheas of Massalia says.[27]

2   Strabo 1. 4. 2–5, C62–4: *Dimensions of the oikoumenē*
(2) In determining the width of the inhabited world, he (*Eratosthenes*) says that from
Meroë[28] it is 10,000 stades along its meridian[29] to Alexandria, and from there to the
Hellespont about 8,100, then 5,000 to the Borysthenes (*R. Dnieper*), and then to the
parallel[30] that runs through Thoule—which Pytheas says is six days' sail north of Brettanike (*Great Britain*)[31] and is near the Frozen Sea[32]—an additional 11,500. Moreover, if
we add 3,400 more beyond Meroë, so that we include the Egyptian island (*there*), the
Kinnamomophoros (*Cinnamon-bearing Land*), and Taprobane (*Sri Lanka*), we have
38,000 stades.

(3) Let the other distances be granted to him because there is sufficient agreement.
Yet would any sensible person grant him the one from the Borysthenes to the circle
of Thoule? For the one who records Thoule, Pytheas, has been established as a man
of the greatest falsehoods, since those who have seen Brettanike and Ierne (*Ireland*)
have nothing to say about Thoule, although mentioning other islands—the small
ones around Brettanike.[33] Brettanike extends alongside Keltike (*Gaul*) for about an
equal distance, no greater than 5,000 stades, its boundaries marked off by the boundaries that lie opposite. The eastern extremities lie opposite the eastern extremities of
the other, the western (*opposite*) the western. The eastern are near enough to each
other that one may look across from Kantion[34] to the mouth of the Rhenos (*Rhine*).
Yet he (*Pytheas*) declares that the extent of the island is more than 20,000 stades[35]
and says that Kantion is several days' sail from Keltike. Concerning the Ostidaioi and

---

[26] See Ch. 6 above.

[27] A good example of P.'s reliability. Because of precession, what we call the Pole Star (α Ursae Mino-
ris) was not close to the celestial pole in antiquity.

[28] Meroë on the Nile (in mod. Sudan; *c.*16° 56′ N), one of the most remote destinations in Greco-Roman travel, became a standard baseline for latitude, mentioned by many authors (see Index). Thought
to be due S of Alexandria, it was actually *c.*3½° further E.

[29] i.e. line of longitude.   [30] sc. of latitude.

[31] Strabo's spelling of this and related names sometimes uses an initial B, sometimes a P.

[32] For Thoule, see chapter introduction.

[33] Their silence would not be surprising if Thoule was indeed six days' sail from Great Britain (above).

[34] Probably *South Foreland* in Kent.

[35] About 2,500 mi (*c.*4,000 km). P. may have been referring to the circumnavigation of Great Britain,
not its length. There can be no definitive value for the coastline of a land mass, as it depends on the
resolution desired (Mandelbrot 1967); but the figure above coheres well with empirical guidance for
those planning to tour the coastline on water or land (e.g. Rae 2016, 'around 2,000 miles').

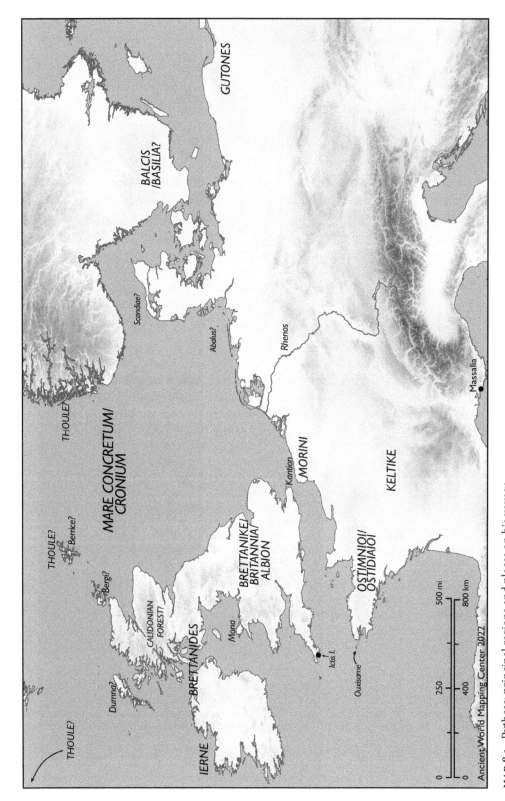

MAP 8.1. Pytheas: principal regions and places on his voyage.

what is beyond the Rhenos as far as Skythia, anyone who has told such falsehoods about known places would hardly be able to tell the truth about places unknown to everyone.

(4) ·That the parallel (*of latitude*) through the Borysthenes[36] is the same as that through Brettanike is conjectured by Hipparchos and others, from the fact that the one through Byzantion is the same as that through Massalia. For the ratio stated by Pytheas between the gnomon and its shadow at Massalia is the same as that which Hipparchos says he has found at Byzantion at the identical season.·[37] Yet from Massalia to the middle of Brettanike is no more than 5,000 stades. Moreover, if one were to proceed no more than 4,000 from the middle of Brettanike you would find (*a region*) only somewhat inhabitable—this would be around Ierne—and it would no longer be inhabitable further on, to where he removes Thoule. By what guesswork he could say that from (*the parallel*) through Thoule to that through the Borysthenes is 11,500 (*stades*) I cannot see.

(5) . . . Then it is still necessary to add the bulge of Europe outside the Pillars of Herakles, set against the Iberians and sloping to the west—no less than 3,000 stades—as well as all the promontories, especially that of the Ostidaioi (*which is called Kabaion*), and the surrounding islands, the farthest of which, Ouxisame (*Ushant*), Pytheas says is three days' sail away. After mentioning these final places, which in their extent add nothing to its length, he adds the districts around the promontories, that of the Ostidaioi and Ouxisame and the islands of which he speaks. All these places are towards the north and are in Keltike, not Iberike, or rather they are fantasies of Pytheas.

3 Strabo 2. 1. 12, C71–2: *Latitude of Byzantion*
·First of all, if the same parallel passes through Byzantion as through Massalia—just as Hipparchos has stated, relying upon Pytheas—and if the same meridian passes through Byzantion as through the Borysthenes,[38] a fact that Hipparchos declares to be true; and if he also declares that the distance from Byzantion to the Borysthenes is 3,700 stades: thus the distance would be the same from Massalia to the parallel through the Borysthenes, which would also run through the Ocean-facing part of Keltike. For as people travel roughly this far they meet the Ocean.·

4 Strabo 2. 1. 18, C75: *Northerly latitudes in the British Isles*
·Hipparchos, anyhow, says that at the Borysthenes and in Keltike, during all the nights of summer, the sun is partially lit up (*sic*) as it moves in a contrary direction

---

[36] Its mouth is at *c.*46° N; the SE corner of Great Britain at *c.*51° N.

[37] That is, they were at the same latitude. The ratio of the gnomon to its shadow at midday 'at the same time'—i.e. on the same day of the year, presumably the summer solstice—gave the angle from which a place's latitude could be securely established. Byzantion was in fact at 41° 0′ N, Massalia at 43° 17′ N.

[38] In fact, Byzantion was at *c.*29° E, the mouth of the Borysthenes at *c.*32° E.

from setting to rising; and that at the winter solstice the sun rises at most 9 cubits (*pēcheis; i.e. 18°*).[39] Among the people that are at a distance of 6,300 from Massalia—whom he (*Hipparchos*) understands still to be Keltoi, but who I think are Brettanoi, 2,500 stades further north than Keltike—this occurrence is much more notable. In the winter days the sun rises at most 6 cubits (*12°*),[40] but only 4 (*8°*) for the people at a distance of 9,100 stades from Massalia, and less than 3 (*6°*) for the people beyond them. According to our account these people would be far further north than Ierne (*Hibernia, i.e. Ireland*). But he (*Hipparchos*), relying on Pytheas, locates this inhabited region among places further south than Brettanike, and says that there the longest day is 19 equinoctial hours,[41] but 18 where the sun rises 4 cubits.[42] He says they lie at a distance of 9,100 stades from Massalia. So the southernmost Brettanoi are further north than they.·

5   Strabo 2. 3. 5, C102: *Unreliability of Pytheas*
This (*the account of Eudoxos of Kyzikos*) is not so far from the fabrications of Pytheas, Euhemeros,[43] and Antiphanes. They can be pardoned, however, since this is what they practise, like conjurors, but how can he (*Poseidonios*), who is precise and a scholar, essentially the first contender, be pardoned? He does not do this well.

6   Strabo 2. 4. 1–2, C104: *Polybios' criticisms of Pytheas*
(1) ·Polybios,[44] in describing the land of (*chōrographōn*) Europe,[45] says that he leaves aside the old (*writers*) but examines those who criticize them: Dikaiarchos, Eratosthenes—the latest who had practised geography—and Pytheas, by whom he says many were led astray.· (*Polybios says that*) he (*Pytheas*) asserted that he travelled over the whole of Brettanike that was accessible, reporting that the circumference of the island was more than 40,000 (*stades*),[46] and also recorded matters about Thoule and those places where there was no longer any land in existence—and neither sea nor air—but something compounded from these, resembling a sea lung in which, he (*Pytheas*) says, the earth, sea, and everything are suspended, as if it were a bonding for the whole, accessible neither by foot nor by ship.[47] He himself saw the lung but tells the rest from hearsay. That, then, is the report of Pytheas, and he adds that when

---

[39] 1 cubit = *c.*1 ft 6 in (*c.*45 cm), but in astronomy it represented 2° (Dicks 1960, 185). An elevation of the Sun of 18° at the winter solstice implies a latitude of *c.*50° N, roughly that of NE France.

[40] This would be the case at a latitude of *c.*56° N, approx. that of Edinburgh.

[41] Lit. 'equidiurnal hours'; for this term, see Introduction, §X. 3. b fin. Standard mean hours, as in modern clocks, each $^1/_{12}$ of the daylight period at spring or autumn equinox when day and night are equal in length. The longest day (i.e. at summer solstice), measured in equinoctial hours, is a standard expression of geographical latitude in ancient Greek authors. It increases towards the poles.

[42] For latitude expressed in terms of the length of the longest day, see n. on **4**.

[43] Eu(h)emeros (*BNJ* 63; *c.* C4l) wrote philosophical works set in an imaginary society.

[44] Polyb. 34. 5. 1–6; see Walbank 1972, 587–90.

[45] *Chōrographia*: a written account of a particular region or regions (from *chōra*, 'land').

[46] *c.*5,000 mi (*c.*8,000 km), about double the practical distance. See n. on **2** §3 above.

[47] See chapter introduction.

he returned from there he went along the entire ocean coast of Europe from Gadeira to the Tanaïs.

(2) Now Polybios[48] says that this is unbelievable: how could someone who was a private individual and poor have gone such distances by ship and foot? Eratosthenes was at a loss whether to believe these things, but nevertheless believed him (*Pytheas*) about Brettanike and the regions of Gadeira and Iberia. ·He (*Eratosthenes*) says it is much better to believe the Messanian (*Euhemeros*) than him (*Pytheas*);[49] for the former says he sailed to a single land, Panchaia, while Pytheas says he has observed all the northward part of Europe even as far as the end of the world. No one would believe even Hermes if he said that! Eratosthenes (*says Polybios*) calls Euhemeros a Bergaian[50] and believes Pytheas, yet not even Dikaiarchos believed those things—though 'not even Dikaiarchos believed' is laughable: as if it were appropriate for Eratosthenes to use that man as a standard upon whom he himself heaps so many criticisms!

With respect to the western and northern parts of Europe, I have already reported Eratosthenes' ignorance.[51] While we should forgive him and Dikaiarchos, since they had not observed those places, who could forgive Polybios and Poseidonios? Polybios is the one who calls those writers' conclusions about distances in those and many other places 'folk judgements', yet he does not elucidate the things for which he criticizes those writers.·

7   **Strabo** 2. 5. 7–8, C114–15: *Pytheas' errors about northern latitudes*
(7) The Rhoxolanoi, the farthest of the known Skythians, live beyond the Borysthenes, although they are further south than the remote peoples we know about north of Brettanike. The area lying beyond immediately becomes uninhabitable because of the cold. Further to the south of them are the Sauromatai beyond the Maiotis (*Sea of Azov*) and the Skythians as far as the eastern Skythians.

(8) Now Pytheas of Massalia says that the region around Thoule, the most northerly of the Brettanides (*British Isles*),[52] is the farthest, and that the circle of the summer tropic is the same as the arctic circle.[53] I have learned nothing about this from anyone else: whether there is a certain island called Thoule, or whether there is habitation up to where the summer tropic becomes the arctic. I believe that the northern boundary of the inhabited world is much further to the south. Nothing is described beyond Ierne, which lies to the north of Brettanike and near to it, where men are

---

[48] Polyb. 34. 5. 7–6. 10.   [49] See n. on **5**.
[50] Antiphanes of Berga was a C4 writer of *Unbelievable Things*.   [51] At 2. 1. 41.
[52] See introduction to chapter.
[53] The Arctic Circle is defined nowadays, for all of the Earth, as the parallel of latitude (*c.*66½° N, passing through N. Norway for example) beyond which 24-hour darkness occurs (on at least one day) around the winter solstice and 24-hour daylight around the summer solstice. But Greek geographers sometimes use the term in a local sense, to mean the imaginary celestial circle enclosing all stars that are circumpolar (i.e. always above the horizon) in a given locality; it thus varies with latitude. Cf. Dicks 1960, 165–6; more briefly, Roseman 1994, 57–8. The 'summer tropic' or Tropic of Cancer marks the northernmost annual position of the Sun (*c.*23½° N), and coincides with the variable celestial arctic circle in places at latitude *c.*66½° N.

totally wild and live badly because of the cold, and thus I believe that the boundary is to be placed there.

·Given that the parallel through Byzantion goes roughly through Massalia, as Hipparchos says, relying upon Pytheas—for he says that at Byzantion the ratio of the gnomon to its shadow is the same as Pytheas says it is in Massalia·—and with the one running through the Borysthenes about 3,800 from there, considering the distance from Massalia, the circle through the Borysthenes would fall somewhere in Brettanike. But Pytheas, who misleads men everywhere, is in error here. That the line from the Pillars to the region of the Strait, and to Athens and Rhodes, lies on the same parallel, is agreed by many.

8   Strabo 2. 5. 43, C136: *The far north*
There the Sun is carried above the Earth through the entire revolution of the cosmos, and it is clear that the shadow will be carried in a circle round the gnomon. This is why he (*Poseidonios*) called them (*people in the far north*) Periskioi (*Shadow-abouts*),[54] although they do not exist in regard to geography. That region is uninhabitable because of cold, as we have already said in the comments against Pytheas. Thus one should not consider the size of this uninhabitable region, beyond the fact that those who have the tropic as arctic circle fall below the circle delineated by the pole of the zodiac, according to the revolution of the cosmos, assuming that the distance between the equator and the tropic is four-sixtieths of the greatest circle.[55]

9   Strabo 3. 2. 11, C148: *Pytheas' errors about Iberia*
Eratosthenes says that the territory adjoining Kalpe is called Tartessis (*sic*), and that Erytheia is the Fortunate Island. Artemidoros contradicts him and says that this is a falsehood by him: just as it is that the distance from Gadeira to the Sacred Promontory is a five-day sail, although it is no more than 1,700 stades; that the tides terminate at that point, although they exist around the circuit of the entire inhabited world; that the northerly part of Iberia is an easier means of access to Keltike than sailing by the Ocean, and everything else that he (*Eratosthenes*) said while relying on Pytheas, because of the latter's false pretensions.

10   Strabo 3. 4. 4, C157–8: *Homer and Pytheas*
But they (*Homer's critics*) do not propose defending, correcting, or doing anything else about what the former (*Homer's followers*) have said: neither the grammarians nor those clever at scientific matters have any confidence. But to me it seems possible to defend much of what they said and to correct many other things, especially where Pytheas has led astray those who believed him, because of their ignorance of places in the west or those towards the north along the Ocean.

---

[54] From *peri*- 'around' + *skia* 'shadow'. During perpetual summer daylight, the gnomon will cast its revolving shadow continuously for 24 hours (if the sky is clear).
[55] i.e. 24°; it is actually *c*.23½°.

11   Strabo 4. 2. 1, C190: *Polybios' criticism of Pytheas*

The Ligeir (*Loire*), however, empties between the Piktones and Namnetai. Formerly there was a trading-place called Korbilon[56] on this river, about which Polybios has said[57]—remembering the mythic stories of Pytheas—that the Massaliotai who were associated with Scipio, when questioned by Scipio about Brettanike, were unable to say anything worth recording, nor were any of those from Narbon or those from Korbilon, although these were the most important cities in that region. Pytheas was bold enough to tell these falsehoods.

12   Strabo 4. 4. 1, C195: *Brittany*

The Osismioi[58] are those whom Pytheas calls the Ōstidaioi, living on a promontory (*Brittany*) that projects very far into the Ocean, although not as far as he and those who have trusted him say.

13   Strabo 4. 5. 5, C201: *Thoule*

Concerning Thoule the record is even more indistinct because of its remoteness, for it is situated the farthest north of all known named (*places*). What Pytheas has said about it—as well as other places there—has been fabricated, as is clear from regions that are known. Most of them he has reported falsely about, as has been said previously,[59] and thus he is clearly speaking falsely about remote places. Yet it would seem that he used the facts adequately concerning celestial phenomena and mathematical speculation.

14   Strabo 7. 3. 1, C295: *Pytheas' errors about the far north*

Because of ignorance of these places, consideration is given to those creating stories about the Rhipaia mountains and the Hyperboreans, and what Pytheas of Massalia falsely reported about the territory along the Ocean (*parōkeanitis*), using as a screen his knowledge about the heavens and mathematics. Such (*people*) are to be dismissed.

15   Geminos, *Introduction to the Phenomena*, 6. 8–9: *Lengths of day in the north*

In Rhodes the greatest day is one of 14 equinoctial hours, but around Rome the greatest day is one of 15 equinoctial hours. For those dwelling further north than the Propontis the greatest day becomes one of 16 equinoctial hours, and for those still further north the greatest day becomes one of 17 and 18 hours.

(9) Pytheas of Massalia, indeed, seems to have been in these places; at least, he says, in the work *On the Ocean* which he composed, that 'the barbarians used to show us where the Sun sleeps; for around these places it was the case that the night became an extremely short one, 2 hours for some people and 3 for others, so that after sunset there was a short interval and straightaway the sun rose'.[60]

---

[56] Unlocated.   [57] Polyb. 34. 10. 6–7.
[58] The ethnonym is corrupt in the MS; see Roller 2018, 196, for various suggestions.
[59] At 1. 4. 3.   [60] The past tense is because P. was recalling his own voyage.

16   Pliny, *Natural History*, 1. 2
In the 2nd book are contained . . . where the days are longest and where shortest . . . for what reason the tides of the sea advance and recede; where the tides do the same to an exceptional degree . . . from these authors . . . foreign (*i.e. non-Roman*): . . . Pytheas . . .

17   Pliny, *Natural History*, 1. 4: *Pliny's sources*
In the 4th book are contained places, peoples, seas, towns, harbours, mountains, rivers, measurements, and peoples who exist or who existed . . . in the islands of the Pontus, in Germania, in the 96 islands of the Gallic ocean, among which are Britannia . . . from these authors: . . . foreign (*i.e. non-Roman*): . . . Pytheas . . .

18   Pliny, *Natural History*, 1. 37: *Pliny's sources*
In the 37th book are contained . . . amber; what lies authors have told about it; its seven kinds . . . from these authors: . . . foreign (*i.e. non-Roman*): . . . Pytheas . . .

19   Pliny, *Natural History*, 2. lxxvii. 186–7: *Short nights in the far north*
(186) Thus it is that, as, by the varying increase in light, at Meroë the longest day amounts to 12 equinoctial hours and eight parts (*i.e. eight-ninths*) of one hour; at Alexandria, however, 14 hours; in Italy 15; in Britannia 17, where in summer the bright nights demonstrate without doubt what reason requires us to believe: that over the solstice days, as the Sun moves nearer to the top of the world, the parts of the Earth that are subject to a narrow course of the light have continuous days in six months of each year, and likewise nights when it (*the Sun*) has moved in the opposite direction for the winter. (187) That this occurs on the island of Thyle (*Thoule*) is written by Pytheas of Massilia, as it lies six days' sailing northwards from Britannia. They declare that it also occurs in Mona (*Anglesey, Ynys Môn*), which is around 200 (*miles*) from Camalodunum (*Colchester*),[61] a town in Britannia.

20   Pliny, *Natural History*, 2. xcix. 217: *Height of the tides around Britain*
In the Ocean, all the tides cover and uncover wider areas than in the remainder of the sea. This may be because in its totality it is more animated over the entirety than over a part; or because the open vastness feels more strongly the force of the star (*i.e. the Sun*) as it moves, while narrow places deflect the same. This is the reason why neither lakes nor rivers are similarly stirred. Pytheas of Massilia is the authority for the statement that over Britannia the tides swell to 80 cubits on each occasion.[62]

---

[61] Normally 'Camulodunum'.   [62] This is excessive, equal to *c*.120 ft or *c*.35 m.

21 **Pliny,** *Natural History,* 4. xiii. 95: *The island of Basilia*
Xenophon of Lampsacus reports that (*in the northern ocean*), three days' sailing from the shore of the Scythae, is an island of vast size, Balcia.[63] Pytheas names the same island Basilia (*King's I.*).[64]

22 **Pliny,** *Natural History,* 4. xvi. 102: *Great Britain*
Opposite this location the island of Britannia, renowned in Greek histories and our own, lies between north and west opposite Germany, Gallia, and Hispania—by far the largest parts of Europe—at a great distance. Its own name was Albion when all those (*islands*) of which we shall shortly speak were called Britanniae. This one is off the Gesoriac shore of the Morini people, by the closest crossing 50 (*miles*). Pytheas and Isidorus report that in its circuit it extends 4,875 (*miles*). In the past thirty years, Roman arms have been increasing (*our*) acquaintance with it, but not beyond the neighbourhood of the Calidonian (*sic*) forest.

23 **Pliny,** *Natural History,* 4. xvi. 104: *Thoule and other islands of the far north*
The last among all those they note is Tyle (*i.e. Thoule*), in which, as we have stated, there are no nights at the solstice, when the Sun is passing through the sign of Cancer; and contrariwise no days during winter. Certain people believe this happens in six months of each year without interruption.

The historian Timaeus says that six nights' sail from Britannia inwards is the island of Ictis,[65] in which white lead (*i.e. tin*) occurs; the Britanni are said to sail to it in wicker boats covered with leather.[66] Some refer to others: the Scandiae, Dumna, the Bergi, and largest of all Berrice from which (*they say*) the voyage to Tyle is made.[67] One day's sail from Tyle, the Mare Concretum (*Solid Sea, i.e. frozen*) is called by some Cronium.[68]

24 **Pliny,** *Natural History,* 37. xi. 35–6: *Amber in the northern Ocean*
(35) Sotacus believed that in Britannia it (*amber*) flowed from rocks which he called *electrides*. Pytheas (*believed*) that a salt-marsh of the ocean was inhabited by the

---

[63] Winkler 2002 follows one MS that reads *Baltia*; Zehnacker and Silberman 2017 prefer the majority reading. Whatever the name, W.'s identification of the place (p. 424) as S. Sweden is plausible, though if it is identical with Abalus (**24** below) it would be the islet of *Heligoland*.

[64] Somewhere in the Baltic? Not necessarily an island (though *Sjælland*, Zealand in English, comes to mind); it could be a peninsula (e.g. *Jutland*) or part of the mainland.

[65] The MSS read *Mictis* (in the accusative form *Mictim*), clearly distinct from *Vectis*, the Isle of Wight, mentioned just above by Pliny (4. xvi .103). Editors correct the name to *Ictis*, following Diod. 5. 22. 2 (Ἴκτιν). It will be one of the islands off S. England or Cornwall; possibly *St Michael's Mount* (Cunliffe 1983).

[66] i.e. coracles.

[67] Zehnacker and Silberman 2017, 336, following Winkler 2002, 434, identify Scandiae as 'les îles danoises'; Dumna as *Lewis*; the Bergi as *Hoy* or *South Ronaldsay* in the Orkney Is. (the plural may suggest both); and Berrice tentatively as *Mainland* in the Shetland Is.

[68] The extract does not name P., but much of the information probably derives from him (Roseman 1994, 92). Zehnacker and Silberman 2017, 319, identify Cronium as the area of the Atlantic off Norway.

Gutones,[69] a nation in Germania, (*the marsh*) being called Metuonis and extending for 6,000 stades; and that a day's sailing from this lay the island of Abalus,[70] from which during spring it (*amber*) was borne by the flood-tides and was a secretion of the Mare Concretum (*Solid Sea*); and that the inhabitants used it in place of firewood and sold it to their nearest neighbours, the Teutoni. (36) Timaeus also believed him but called the island Basilia.[71]

25   Aëtios, *De placitis* 3. 17. 3: *Causes of the tides*
How the ebb tide and high tide happen: . . . Pytheas of Massalia attributes the causes of both of these to the waxing and waning of the Moon.[72]

26   Kleomedes, *Meteora* (*Caelestia*), 1. 4. 208–10: *Perpetual daylight at Thoule*
In the area of the island called Thoule, to which they say the philosopher Pytheas of Massalia went, the story is that all of the summer (*circle*) is above ground, this also being the arctic (*circle*) for them.[73]

27   scholion A to Apollonios of Rhodes 4. 761–5: *The volcanic Aiolian islands*
'Where the anvils of Hephaistos lie': The islands of Aiolos (*Lipari/Isole Eolie*) number seven. Of these, the one called Lipara or Strongyle (*Stromboli*) is where Hephaistos seems to spend time and where the roaring of fire and the sound of hammers are heard. In olden times it was said that he who desired shining iron would bring it there and, on the next day, take away a sword or whatever he wanted made, and would hand over the price. These things are told by Pytheas in his *Periodos ges*; he also says the sea boils there. The seven islands of Aiolos are these: Strongyle, Euonymos, Lipara, Hiera, Didyme, Erikodes, and Phoinikodes.

28   Markianos of Herakleia, *Epitome of Menippos*, 2: *Pytheas as a source for Markianos*[74]
Those who in my view have investigated these matters (*the details of periploi*) with careful attention are: Timosthenes of Rhodes, chief helmsman of Ptolemy II, and after him Eratosthenes, whom the officials of the Museum (*at Alexandria*) called Beta; in addition to these: Pytheas of Massalia, and Isidoros of Charax . . .

---

[69] Or Guiones; Gothones in Tacitus, *Germania*. 44. 1. König 2007, 151, locates them on the *Vistula*; their salt-marsh must have been in the *Gdańsk* area, though its stated size (c.750 mi, c.1,200 km) is impossibly large.

[70] Marked in *Barr.* as *Heligoland*; possibly the same as *Balcia/Baltia* in **21.**

[71] In **21** it is P. who calls an island Basilia.

[72] P. does not attribute high tide to the full moon and low tide to the new moon, but may be thinking (correctly) of 'spring tides' at both these phases and 'neap' tides at the quarters; his view has perhaps been summarized in too compressed a fashion (*contra*, Dicks 1960, 115).

[73] Cf. n. 53 above (on arctic circles).   [74] Trans. Campbell (see Ch. 34 below, no. 41).

29 Martianus Capella, *On the Marriage of Philology and Mercury,* 6. 595: *Perpetual daylight at Thoule*

This is why in Meroë the longest day comprises 12 equinoctial hours and two-thirds of the next; at Alexandria 14; in Italia 15; in Britannia 17. (*This is*), indeed, at the solstitial time, when the Sun, carried to the top of the heavens, illuminates the lands laid out below in a succession of uninterrupted day; similarly, in its winter descent it makes people tremble at the night lasting half a year. Pytheas of Massilia declared that this was discovered in the island of Tyle (*Thoule*). Unless I am mistaken, it is declared that on the evidence of these differences of times the Earth is considered to be spherical and to have rotary movements.

30 Martianus Capella, *On the Marriage of Philology and Mercury,* 6. 608–9: *Stars visible in the polar regions*

(*Preceded by a passage on the polar regions.*) (608) Furthermore, the fixed stars are seen in six months; likewise, in six months they do not appear, and the circle of rising is for these people the equinoctial (*circle*). They (*the polar regions*) see six signs of the zodiac at a time; finally, days and nights last six months, so that for each of them the poles and the ends of the (*Earth's*) axis are seen overhead. But the former (*region*) does not know the other parts lit by the glow of the Septentrio (*Seven Oxen, i.e. Ursa Major*), the latter those lit by the glow of the star of Canopus. (609) The most learned Pytheas announced the condition of these regions, but I, too,[75] have toured these same places, so that no part of the Earth should remain unknown to me.

31 Kosmas Indikopleustes, *Christian Topography,* 11. 80. 6–9: *Short nights in the north*

Pytheas of Massalia says, in his books *On Ocean,* that when he was present in the northernmost locations the barbarians who were there pointed out the 'bed of the Sun', because during the nights it was always present to them.

32 Stephanos of Byzantion ω 21: *The Ostiaioi*

Ostiones: a nation beside the western Ocean, whom Artemidoros refers to as Kossinoi but Pytheas as Ōstidaioi: 'To the left side of these are the Kossinoi, known as Ostiones, whom Pytheas designates Ōstidaioi'.[76]

---

[75] Reading *sed ⟨et⟩ ego* with Willis.
[76] An apparent quotation from Artemidoros (Ch. 18 below, no. 159). The lemma refers to Brittany.

PART THREE

HELLENISTIC PERIOD

~

(C. 323–30 BC)

Naxian Lykos died not on land, but on the main (*pontos*)
   saw ship and soul together meet destruction
as the merchant sailed from Aigina. Now he's a corpse
   in the drink (*hygrē*), but I, his tomb, carry a name in vain
and proclaim this word, ever true: flee from mixing
   with the sea (*thalassa*), sailor, while the Kids are setting!

Kallimachos of Kyrene, *Epigrams*, 18 (my translation)

9

DIKAIARCHOS OF MESSANA

(LATE 4TH C. BC)

D. Graham J. Shipley

An excellent researcher

(CICERO)

INTRODUCTION

Dikaiarchos son of Pheidias, from Messana (*Messina*) in Sicily, a younger contemporary of Aristotle and coeval of Theophrastos, is usually considered a philosopher (cf. **15** below); but a substantial proportion of his work, evidently carried out under the aegis of Aristotle's Lyceum or Peripatos (founded in 335 BC), displays geographical interests, mainly in physical geography and measuring the *oikoumenē* and its physical features.[1] Geography, indeed, was regarded as part of philosophy (3). The problem of seeing his geographical work clearly was bedevilled until modern times by the attribution to him of passages of text we now assign to Herakleides Kritikos and Dionysios son of Kalliphon (see the introductions to Chapters 11 and 20).[2] Most probably only one of his books, *Periodos ges* (*Circuit of the Earth*), was primarily dedicated to geography, within which his main interest was in what may be called physical geography.[3] This marks him out as a pioneer though, as such, a typical representative of the researchers working around Aristotle and Theophrastos. Perhaps because of his data-led approach, and because he did not explore the far west, he, unlike Pytheas (Chapter 8 above), commanded the respect of Polybios even though the historian believed he had miscalculated the distance from the Peloponnese to the Pillars of Herakles (4 §2). To judge from the surviving quotations, paraphrases, and citations, he did not include cultural and ethnographic information in his geographical work.[4]

Dikaiarchos' exact dates are hard to establish; the *Suda* implies, but only indirectly, that he lived around 336–332.[5] One of his non-geographical works certainly

---

[1] Most of Fortenbaugh and Schütrumpf 2000 deals with D.'s philosophy, but the final chapter (Keyser 2000) focuses on the geographical testimonia and fragments as a set (there are a few contestable points in his arguments). For recent introductions to D.'s work, see Dueck 2012, 95; Roller 2015, 105–8; Cataudella 2016, 126–31.

[2] Keyser 2000, 371.   [3] Keyser 2000, 371–2.   [4] Zhmud 2004.

[5] *Suda* s.v. Aristoxenos (Dik. fr. 3 Mirhady = fr. 2 Wehrli) dates the musical theorist Aristoxenos to 'the times of Alexander and those who came after, namely from the 111th Olympiad [336–332 BC]; a contemporary of Dikaiarchos the Messanian'.

postdated 325.[6] On a particular point he disagreed with Pytheas (4 §2), who probably made his voyage to north-western Europe in the 320s. There is indirect evidence (8) that may imply Dikaiarchos carried out observations of latitude, like Eudoxos and Pytheas, but with a new purpose: to measure the circumference of the Earth using calculations of latitude based on differences in the noonday shadow at the summer solstice; this would be in or after 309, when the city of Lysimacheia in the NE Aegean was founded.[7] If so, he may have been the first person to do so with that end in view. In effect, Dikaiarchos was using a meridian of longitude, though it seems to have been Eratosthenes that formalized it as such (see Eratosthenes 29 §7).

There is some kinship and common language between Dikaiarchos' work and the *periplous* known as Pseudo-Skylax (Chapter 7), written most probably in the mid-330s,[8] including a shared interest in long distances across the known world (4 §2); but it is not enough to assign the *periplous* to his hand with confidence, as he was probably quite young when it was written in the mid-330s. The calculation of vast west-to-east distances, such as from Gibraltar to Mt Imaos (probably the Himalayas or the Hindu Kush; 11), reveals a later stage of scientific knowledge than we see in Ps.-Skylax, with additional data resulting from Alexander the Great's expedition into western Asia (334–323). Dikaiarchos' major parallel of latitude through the Mediterranean became a baseline for subsequent investigators,[9] though Eratosthenes refined it and it was eventually superseded by the notion of the terrestrial and celestial equators as latitude zero.

Dikaiarchos entered into, or in some cases may have started, a wide range of debates. He surely knew Pytheas' views on the location of the Pillars of Herakles (5). Despite Pytheas' evidence from the Atlantic coasts, which had led him to identify the Moon's monthly cycle as the cause of the tides, Dikaiarchos wrongly linked them to the Sun instead (13). He believed that the *oikoumenē* was oblong (Agathemeros, 10, seems to have misunderstood him as having accepted Demokritos' view that the whole Earth, not just its inhabited portion, was oblong). He may, as we have noted, have attempted to reckon the dimensions of the terrestrial sphere long before Eratosthenes did so (8).

---

[6] D.'s chronology is examined in detail by Shipley 2012, 132–4. Sharples 2006 suggests a birth-date of *c*.375, but it is not clear that his adult life can be pushed back far before the 320s.

[7] Keyser 2000, 364, tries to show that D.'s visit to Lysimacheia can only have taken place when there was harmony between the Successor general Lysimachos and Ptolemy, then governor of Alexandria; but we have no reason to suppose military disputes impinged upon travellers. Equally, the phrase *cura regum*, 'by the patronage of kings' (7), does not necessarily require a date in or after 307/6, when the first of Alexander's Successors took the royal title; D. may have been assisted by men who later became kings. On Aristotle and others' estimates of the Earth's size, see Dueck 2012, 72.

[8] Shipley 2012.

[9] Keyser 2000, 367. Cataudella 2016, 131, regards this as D.'s key innovation. It is sometimes thought that D. referred to his central parallel as a *diaphragma* or 'partition': Irby 2012, 99; Salway 2012, 197; Cataudella 2016, 131, the last citing D. 10 (Agathemeros i. 5); but the term used there is 'a straight cut', *tomē eutheia* (τομὴ εὐθεία). Both terms recall Ps.-Skylax §113, part of the material appended to the *periplous*. 'Straight cut' by itself makes one wonder whether D. himself was the author of the endmatter, as he conceivably is of the *periplous* itself (Shipley 2012). On the central parallel, see also Dueck 2012, 95.

Like Hekataios, but unlike Aristotle, he believed incorrectly that the Nile flowed into Libyē from the Atlantic and out again at Egypt (14), perhaps resting his argument on the view that the Atlantic was higher than the Mediterranean (for the relative heights of seas, cf. Eratosthenes 14 ~ Hipparchos 19).[10]

A particularly fruitful exercise in which we know Dikaiarchos engaged was measuring the heights of mountains (2, 7, 9, 15) using one variety of the *dioptra*, a surveying instrument.[11] Once again he may have pioneered a new application of an existing technique.[12] Some of his data may be subject to a standard (observing?) error, though this has been overstated.[13]

Finally, it is possible that Dikaiarchos was the first to provide maps with his text, depending on how we interpret the Latin term *tabulae* (1 below) and whether Eudoxos of Knidos had done so earlier (see introduction to Chapter 6). Although it seems certain that maps were not in everyday use until the late hellenistic or Roman period (see Introduction, §V), the concept of a map as a graphic output to aid scientific explanation was well established long before Dikaiarchos' lifetime.

Wehrli's standard edition of all Dikaiarchos' testimonia and fragments is not entirely superseded by Mirhady's arrangement or by Keyser's chapter on Dikaiarchos' geography in the same volume.[14] The present chapter uses the fragments treated by Keyser together with the Kleomedes fragment (8) which he also discusses, but in chronological order.

SELECTED FURTHER READING

Cataudella, M. R. (2016), 'Some scientific approaches: Eudoxus of Cnidus and Dicaearchus of Messene', in S. Bianchetti *et al.* (eds), *Brill's Companion to Ancient Geography: The Inhabited World in Greek and Roman Tradition* (Leiden–Boston), 115–31.

*—— (forthcoming), 'Dicearco (2015)', in *FGrH* v.

*Keyser, P. T. (2000), 'The geographical work of Dikaiarchos', in W. W. Fortenbaugh and E. Schütrumpf (eds), *Dicaearchus of Messana: Text, Translation, and Discussion* (New Brunswick–London), 353–72.

---

[10] Keyser 2000, 369; Zhmud 2004.

[11] Keyser 2000, 355–6, discusses the range of instruments covered by this term. On the measurement of mountains, see Dueck 2012, 81–2. On the *dioptra*, see M. Lewis 2012, 132–40.

[12] One wonders whether the measurement of Acrocorinth's height which Strabo (8. 6. 21, C379 = Eudoxos 56 above) gives as 3½ st. (*c.*622 m; actual height today 1,880 ft = 573 m; Google Earth, 25 May 2020) derives from D., who had lived in the Peloponnese (1) and is credited with writing on Peloponnesian mountains (15). Acrocorinth would be not only an obvious target for a surveyor in view of its strategic importance, but relatively easy to survey because of its steep sides rising from not far above sea level, meaning that one could take readings from a point close by. Keyser 2000, 357, suggests that Sallust (*Histories*, fr. 2. 82 Maurenbrecher) may preserve D.'s measurement of Mt Olympos in Lykia, since it lies along his pan-Mediterranean parallel of latitude.

[13] Keyser 2000, 357, gives D.'s height for Mt Atabyrion as 8 st., whereas the text (2), if correct, says *less than* 8 st., which is closer to the true value; Keyser likewise omits 'less than' in considering Kyllene (see 2 again).

[14] Wehrli 1967; Mirhady 2000; Keyser 2000.

Shipley, D. G. J. (2012), 'Pseudo-Skylax and the natural philosophers', *Journal of Hellenic Studies*, 132: 121–38.

*Wehrli, F. (1967), *Dikaiarchos*, 2nd edn. Basel–Stuttgart.

Zhmud, L. (2004), 'Dikaiarchos aus Messene', in H. Flashar (ed.), *Philosophie der Antike* (Basel), 568–75.

TEXTS

1   Cicero, *Letters to Atticus,* 6. 2. 3 (*c.* late April 50 BC): *Whether all Peloponnesians have access to the sea*

For the view that all the states of the Peloponnese were on the coast,[15] I believed the *Tables* (*tabulae*)[16] of Dicaearchus, a man by no means negligible and even approved of by your own judgement. In the narrative of Chairon in the *Trophonian Tale*, he (*Dicaearchus*) upbraided the Greeks on many counts for being so dedicated to the sea, and he did not exclude any place in the Peloponnese. Although I liked this author, since he was *historikōtatos*[17] and had lived in the Peloponnese, I was surprised and got in touch with Dionysius. He, too, was initially perturbed; then, because he had as good an opinion of that Dicaearchan god[18] as you do of Gaius Vestorius and I of Marcus Cluvius, he had no hesitation in saying we should believe him. He was of the opinion that within Arkadia there was a certain place on the coast (*called*) Lepreum, whereas Tenea and Aliphera and Tritia (*Tritaia*) were *neoktista* (*newly founded*);[19] he checked this in the *Katalogos tōn neōn* (*Catalogue of Ships*), where there is no mention of those people. Therefore I translated that passage in its entirety from Dicaearchus.

2   Geminos, *Introduction to the Phenomena,* 17. 5: *Heights of mountains*

The height of Kyllene is less than 15 stades, as Dikaiarchos demonstrates, having measured it. The perpendicular of Atabyrios is less than 8 (?) stades.

3   Strabo 1. 1. 1, C1–2: *Dikaiarchos as a leading geographer*

We consider that geography is part of the business of a philosopher, if anything is. . . . For the first men bold enough to grasp it were such as Homer, Anaximandros of Miletos, Hekataios—his (*fellow*) citizen, as Eratosthenes also says—as well as Demokritos,

---

[15] i.e. that all the peoples of the Peloponnese had access to the sea. The question turns on Arkadia, which was landlocked apart from the Triphylian *poleis* including Lepreon; these joined the short-lived Arkadian league in the 360s BC, and the Lepreates still regarded themselves as Arkadian in the Imperial period (Pausanias 5. 5. 3). For the territory of Lepreon extending to the coast, see Ps.-Skyl. §44.

[16] Not necessarily maps; Shackleton Bailey 1968, 105, translates simply as 'accounts'.

[17] 'Most *historikos*', i.e. an excellent investigator (Shackleton Bailey 1968, 257 ad loc., suggests 'well-informed' or 'accurate'). Cic., writing to his Greek friend, uses Greek here and twice below.

[18] So Shackleton Bailey 1968, 104–5, reading *de deo* [*cum*] *isto Dicaearch⟨e⟩o* and making C. play upon Dikaiarcheia, 'the ancient name of Puteoli where Vestorius and Cluvius lived' (p. 257). Alternatively, read *de isto Dicaearcho*, lit. 'of yonder Dicaearchus', almost 'of the great D.'. Either way, this attests to D.'s high reputation. Is Dionysius our poet D. son of Kalliphon? For potential Ciceronian links, see Ch. 20, introduction.

[19] Tenea is in the territory of Corinth, Tritaia in Achaia. Though they are inland like Arkadian Alipheira, their relevance seems unclear.

Eudoxos, Dikaiarchos, Ephoros, and several others; and those who came after them, Eratosthenes, Polybios, and Poseidonios, were still philosophers (*practising geography*).

4   Strabo 2. 4. 1–3, C104–5: *Dikaiarchos' strengths and weaknesses*
Polybios,[20] in describing the land of (*chōrographōn*) Europe, says that he leaves aside the old (*writers*) but examines those who criticize them: Dikaiarchos, Eratosthenes— the latest who had practised geography—and Pytheas, by whom he says many were led astray. . . .

(2) . . . He (*Eratosthenes*) says it is much better to believe the Messanian (*i.e. Euhemeros*) than him (*Pytheas*);[21] for the former says he sailed to a single land, Panchaia, while Pytheas says he has observed all the northward part of Europe even as far as the end of the world; no one would believe even Hermes if he said that! Eratosthenes (*says Polybios*) calls Euhemeros a Bergaian[22] and believes Pytheas, yet not even Dikaiarchos believed those things—though 'not even Dikaiarchos believed' is laughable: as if it were appropriate for Eratosthenes to use that man as a standard upon whom he himself heaps so many criticisms.

With respect to the western and northern parts of Europe, I have already reported Eratosthenes' ignorance.[23] While we should forgive him and Dikaiarchos, since they had not observed those places, who could forgive Polybios and Poseidonios? Polybios is the one who calls those writers' conclusions about distances in those and many other places 'folk judgements', yet he does not elucidate the things for which he criticizes those writers.

(*Polybios says that*) Dikaiarchos reckons the distance in stades from the Peloponnese to the Pillars as 10,000 (*stades*), that to the head of the Adriatic as greater; and that he gives the distance towards the Pillars as far as the narrows (*at Sicily*) as 3,000, so the remainder, from the narrows to the Pillars, becomes 7,000. He (*Polybios*) says he leaves aside the 3,000 whether they are understood correctly or not, but certainly not the 7,000 whether one measures the coast or through the middle of the open sea (*pelagos*). . . . With the addition of the 3,000 from the Peloponnese to the Pillars (*he says*), the total—and this in a direct line—will be more than twice what Dikaiarchos stated,[24] while by his (*Dikaiarchos'*) own account he will need to make the figure to the head of the Adriatic still greater.

(3) 'Dear Polybios', one might say, 'just as the experience of these things that you have yourself stated gives a clear refutation of this untruth, . . . similarly both those

[20] Polyb. 34. 5. 1–6.
[21] See n. on Pytheas 6 above.
[22] 'Storyteller', Mirhady. See my n. 50 on Pytheas.
[23] At 2. 1. 41.
[24] Polybios is perhaps taking the Peloponnese–Adriatic section as part of the total; but it is not clear that D. did so.

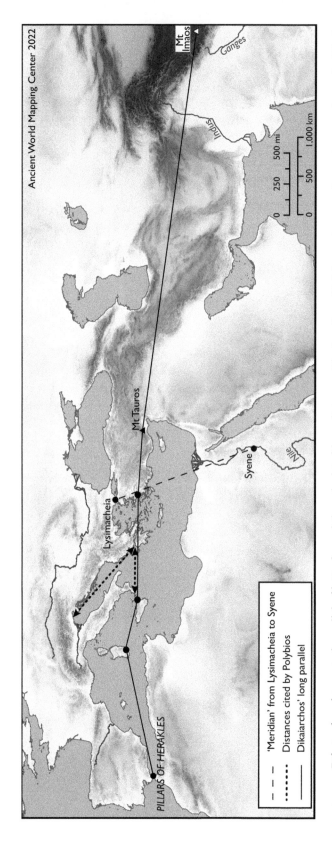

MAP 9.1. Dikaiarchos: his central parallel of latitude, and the calculated long distances. The location of Mt Imaos is approximate; it may refer to the Hindu Kush or the W extremity of the Himalayas.

Legend within map:

- – – – 'Meridian' from Lysimacheia to Syene
- ······· Distances cited by Polybios
- ——— Dikaiarchos' long parallel

Labels on map: Ancient World Mapping Center 2022; Mt Imaos; Ganges; Indus; Mt Tauros; Lysimacheia; Syene; Nile; PILLARS OF HERAKLES

Scale bars: 0 250 500 mi; 0 500 1,000 km

things are untruths as well: both what Dikaiarchos said, that the (*distance*) from the narrows to the Pillars is 7,000 stades, and what you believe you have proved.'[25]

5 Strabo 3. 5. 5, C170: *Location of the Pillars of Herakles*
Dikaiarchos, Eratosthenes, Polybios,[26] and the majority of the Hellenes show that the Pillars (*of Herakles*) are in the area of the Strait.

6 Pliny, *Natural History*, 1. 2 and 4–6: *Pliny's sources*
In the 2nd book are contained . . . from these authors: . . . foreign (*i.e. non-Roman*): . . . Dicaearchus . . .

In the 4th book are contained places, peoples, seas, towns, harbours, mountains, rivers, measurements, and peoples who exist or who existed . . . from these authors: . . . foreign (*i.e. non-Roman*): . . . Dicaearchus . . .

In the 5th book . . . (*the same*).
In the 6th book . . . (*the same*).

7 Pliny, *Natural History*, 2. lxv. 162: *Heights of mountains in relation to the Earth as a sphere*
It is, however, extraordinary that amid so great a level area of sea and fields a globe is produced. This view is also supported by Dicaearchus, one of the most learned of men, who measured mountains under the patronage of kings. Among these he reported that the highest was Pelium (*Pelion*) at 1,250 paces by calculation of the perpendicular, and that this value was negligible in relation to the entire spherical shape (*of the globe*).

8 Kleomedes, *Meteora* (*Caelestia*), 1. 5. 57–75: *Measuring the size of the Earth*[27]
Now if the Earth had a wide, flat form, the total diameter of the cosmos would be 100,000 (*stades*). For people in Lysimachia[28] have Draco above their heads, while Cancer lies above the area of Syene (*Aswan*);[29] and the fifteenth part of the meridian[30] running through Lysimachia and Syene is the circumference (*i.e. segment*) from Draco to Cancer, as is shown by sundials. One-fifteenth of the whole circle becomes one-fifth of the diameter.[31]

If, then, positing that the Earth is level, we extend perpendiculars onto it from the limits of the (*segment of*) circumference running from Draco to Cancer, they will make contact with the diameter which measures the meridian through Syene and Lysimachia.[32] The interval between the two perpendiculars will be 20,000 (*stades*), for it is 20,000 stades from Syene to Lysimachia. Since this distance is one-fifth of the total

---

[25] Cf. Polyb. 34. 6. 11–14.   [26] Polyb. 34. 9. 4.
[27] Kleomedes' date is very uncertain and may be summarized as AD 100 ± 200 years.
[28] Spelled thus here. For Kleomedes' errors, see Bowen and Todd 2004, 68 n. 16.
[29] At latitude c.24° N, approximately on the Tropic of Cancer (*c*.23½° N).
[30] sc. 24° of a great circle.
[31] A circle's diameter was conventionally taken to be one-third of its circumference (Bowen and Todd 2004, 68 n. 19).
[32] The reasoning is faulty: see Bowen and Todd 2004, 69 n. 21.

diameter, the whole diameter of the meridian will become 100,000 (*stades*). Having a diameter of 100,000, the cosmos will have a great circle of 300,000. In comparison with this the Earth, having the character of a point, is 250,000 (*in circumference*) while the Sun is many times greater, though amounting to a very small part of the heavens. How, then, can it fail to be clear that the Earth is not flat in nature?[33]

9   **Theon of Smyrna,** *On the Usefulness of Mathematics,* 3. 3: *Heights of mountains*
The surplus perpendicular (*i.e. difference in height*) of the highest mountains in relation to the lowest places on Earth is less than ⟨10 stades⟩, as Eratosthenes and Dikaiarchos say that they found. Such large quantities are observed mechanically by using *dioptrai*, which measure the values from distances.[34]

10   **Agathemeros** i. 2: *Shape of the oikoumenē*
The old writers drew the inhabited world as round, and believed that Hellas lay in the middle, with Delphi in the middle of Hellas as it contained the navel of the Earth. But Demokritos, a man of great experience, was the first to perceive that the Earth (*i.e. the inhabited part*) is oblong, with a length one and a half times its breadth. Dikaiarchos the Peripatetic agreed with this . . .

11   **Agathemeros** i. 5: *Dikaiarchos' central parallel of latitude*
Dikaiarchos, however, divides the Earth not with waters but with a straight line in the temperate zone, from the Pillars (*of Herakles*) through Sardo (*Sardinia*), Sicily, the Peloponnese, Ionia, Karia, Lykia, Pamphylia, Kilikia, and (*Mt*) Tauros[35] as far as Mt Imaos (*Himalaya?*). Of the areas (*thus defined*) he names one the northern, the other the southern.

12   **Martianus Capella,** *On the Marriage of Philology and Memory,* 6. 590–1: *Sphericity of the Earth*
(590) That the shape of the whole Earth is not flat, as those people think who liken it to the position of a rather wide disc, nor concave, as others claim who have said that rain falls 'into the lap of the earth', but round and indeed spherical, is asserted by Dicaearchus.   (591) For indeed, the rising and setting of stars would not be seen to be different according to the elevation or inclinations of the Earth if, with the works of the composition of the world being dispersed over plane surfaces, they shone at one and the same time above the lands and waters; or, again, if the rising of the sun as it emerged was hidden by the concave recesses of the more withdrawn land.

---

[33] D. is not named here, but Keyser associates the fragment with him.
[34] Cf. Eratosthenes 38 and nn. 11–12 above.
[35] A mountain range principally situated in mod. Turkey but extended by ancient geographers to link up with the Himalayas. D. may have been responsible for this idea (Dicks 1960, 122).

13   Stobaeus, *Anthology*, 1. 38. 2: *Cause of the tides*
How the ebb tide and high tide occur: ⟨Dikaiarchos of Mess⟩ana[36] himself attributes the cause to the Sun, which makes high tides occur in the open seas (*pelagē*) at whichever places on Earth it (*the Sun*) is, but pulls them away with it at the (*places*) from which it happens to have withdrawn. (*He says*) these things occur around the deflections (*of the wind*)[37] at dawn and midday.

14   Ioannes Lydus, *On Months*, 4. 107: *Cause of the Nile's rising*
But Dikaiarchos, in his *Periodos ges* (*Circuit of the Earth*), wishes the Nile's (*annual*) rising to be (*caused*) by the Atlantic sea (*thalatta*).

15   *Suda* δ 1062: *Life and works of Dikaiarchos*
Dikaiarchos son of Pheidias: a Sikeliotes (*Sicilian*) from the city of Messene (*Messina*). Pupil of Aristotle, philosopher, rhetorician, and geometrician. (*Wrote*) *Measurements of the Mountains in the Peloponnese*; *Life of Hellas* in three books. This man wrote the *Constitution of the Spartans*; and a law was enacted in Lakedaimon that each year the story should be read out at the office of the ephors and that the men of youthful age should listen; and this persisted for a long time.

---

[36] The attribution of this claim to D. depends on an emendation by Meineke which, though rejected by Curtius Wachsmuth 1884, 252, is generally accepted; the MS gives, implausibly '[—]*ēnios Mesēnios*', e.g. ⟨Eu⟩enios (?) of Messana (or Messene). The gap was left to allow a large initial letter or ligature (e.g. diphthong) to be inserted in red by the rubricator; W. prefers to restore 'Euenios' without the *ethnikon*.
[37] This sense is suggested by Keyser 2000, 370.

10

TIMOSTHENES OF RHODES

(ACTIVE 282–246 BC)

D. Graham J. Shipley

INTRODUCTION

First attested in the *Nikomedean Periodos* ('Ps.-Skymnos'; 1), Timosthenes, as we learn from later writers, was a naval commander in the service of Ptolemy II Philadelphos (r. 283/2–246 BC; 8, 16, 23) and the author of one or more navigational books of practical value. His younger contemporary Eratosthenes is said to have read his work (23). He may be identical with the Timosthenes who wrote sacred music for use at Delphi (8); and appears to have been not just a naval officer but an agent of high-level cultural politics on behalf of Ptolemy.[1]

The range of Timosthenes' writings is uncertain. The title most frequently mentioned is *Peri limenon* (*On Harbours*; 2), but we also hear of *Periploi* (*Circumnavigations*; 18), *Stadiasmos* or *Stadiasmoi* ('stade table(s)'; 24, cf. 23 §3), *Exegetikon* (*Commentary*; 35), and even his own epitome (précis) of his *Periploi*; 23. It is not clear that the first three are different from one another—the *Stadiasmos* may have been an abridgement of *Peri limenon* that outlived it,[2] of which it is possible (but unproven) that traces may survive in the late *Stadiasmos* (Chapter 31 below).[3] Many fragments or testimonia cannot be assigned to a particular work; few of those assigned to *On Harbours* come with the number of a particular book of that work (see 2 on book 5; 29 on book 6). It has also been doubted that the *Exegetikon* is by the same Timosthenes.[4]

Timosthenes was preceded in writing about harbours by a certain Timagetos in the early 4th century, of whose work very little is known.[5] He is, however, exceptional among known pre-Roman geographical writers in having compiled what was evidently very detailed nautical data, as witness the direct quotations informing us of a cove large enough for a single long ship (2), and of an offshore islet and a harbour for eight vessels (how precise a figure!) (27); or Strabo's indirect report that Timosthenes mentioned shipsheds at a port in Iberia (7). Sometimes he seems to mention mountains

---

[1] Meyer 2013, citing Hauben 1996, 225.   [2] Roller 2020b, 57.

[3] Arnaud 2017b identifies at least four sources for *Stad.*; Arnaud 2010, however, rejects a link with T. If any of the sort of detail we see in 2 and perhaps 27 below has been transmitted to *Stad.*, it has probably been interleaved and overlaid with a great deal of subsequent navigational experience.

[4] N. F. Jones 2010 believes it is by an Athenian of the same name; but see discussion below.

[5] Roller 2015, 79–80.

as aids to navigation (e.g. 27, 31). This detailed quality has led some to suggest that the work may have been a functional handbook for navigators.[6]

He is often cited today for information about winds, including his twelvefold wind-rose (18; cf. 3, 33), which embodied a refinement of Aristotle's scheme of ten or eleven winds (*Meteorologika*, 2. 6, printed as an appendix to the present chapter), itself a development from the work of Ephoros (see Introduction, §VI. 2. e). Referring to a diagram that evidently stood in his text, Aristotle gives the eight cardinal and ordinal winds, adding Thraskias (NNW) and Mesēs (NNE), but leaves the SSW point blank and identifies Phoinikias (SSE) as no more than a local name. A more complex array is offered slightly later by Aristotle's younger colleague Theophrastos, in his fragmentary *On Winds*, §62:[7]

> In Sicily they do not refer to Kaikias but to Apeliotes; but to some it seems not to be the same but different, in that the former darkens the sky, the other not. Some call Argestes Olympias, others Skirōn, but those in Sicily Derkias. (*Some*) call Apeliotes Hellespontias, but the Phoenicians call it Karbas, those in the Pontos Berekyntias.[8]

Timosthenes' scheme thus regularizes and supersedes those of both Aristotle and Theophrastos. It has been suggested that his is practical rather than theoretical,[9] but this seems a false opposition: as we shall argue, he is more than a merely practical instructor,[10] and his twelvefold scheme was followed or adapted by later writers.[11] Even functional works were normally embellished with material displaying the author's intellectual credentials in order to validate them. On the other hand, the enumeration of peoples living in the directions from which the various winds blow (18; Fig. 10.1), possibly following Ephoros' example,[12] is not necessarily evidence of cartographic psychology or a 'bird's-eye' viewpoint; a *tour d'horizon* mentality was probably more characteristic of physical navigation by land or by sea in a largely pre-cartographic era.[13]

The most interesting fragments betoken a keen eye for detail. *On Harbours* may have been in essence a genuine navigational handbook (unlike, for example, the 4th-century *periplous* by Ps.-Skylax, which is a desk-based exercise: see Chapter 7). It may have followed an anti-clockwise sequence, beginning with Egypt and the Red Sea, then rounding the coasts of the *oikoumenē* via Asia, the Black Sea, and Europe, returning along the North African coast.[14] Timosthenes sometimes communicates specific local directions (2; other relatively detailed extracts include 13 and 27) as well as longer sailing times and distances (15–16, 19–21). These extracts, surely indicative

---

[6] Roller 2015, 113.
[7] I have not taken account of the new edition of *On Winds* by Brodersen 2023b, 16–69.
[8] My translation.   [9] Meyer 2013.
[10] For the influence of T.'s wind rose upon the author of the *Stadiasmos* (Ch. 31 below), see Arnaud 2010. On winds, see also the introductions to Agathemeros (Ch. 29) and *Hypotyposis* (Ch. 35).
[11] Roller 2020b.
[12] Roller 2015, 82, notes that Ephoros had linked nations to wind directions.
[13] Cf. Shipley 2006.   [14] Meyer 2013.

of the distinctive character of his writings, are regrettably few, but they are enough to suggest that he, or his direct informants, had first-hand knowledge of many parts of those seas, though not necessarily all, as some critical sources imply (5, 23 §3). A case can be made for dating his expedition, or expeditions, to the years 275–268.[15] Islands both large and small are a recurrent feature,[16] both specific ones and as a category (13, 17, 19, 21, 27, 36), including land-forms that may appear to be islands (7), again tending to confirm the partly practical intention behind the work.

The connexion with Delphi has been doubted, despite Strabo's specifying the Timosthenes in question as a Rhodian (8). There is reason to think the 'Pythian Melody' was composed much earlier; but perhaps Timosthenes modified it or made a scholarly version,[17] or was the first to transcribe and publish it in literary form. For a naval commander to have produced literature and even composed music for public performance is not necessarily surprising, in view of Ptolemy II's extensive patronage of high culture.[18]

Thus it is not in any way discordant, either, that Timosthenes should enliven a technical treatise with notes on the local settings of Greek myths (25, 34, and 35),[19] or engage in the debate on the number and divisions of the continents, which unusually he made four in number by separating Egypt from Libyē (37, cf. 12). That he appears to have referred to the foundation legend of an important navigational landmark, the Hieron (sanctuary of the Twelve Gods) at the entrance to the Black Sea (34), and that this also featured prominently in the epic poem *Argonautika* by Apollonios, a fellow Rhodian, further suggests that Timosthenes was not just a navigator but a cultured and cultural figure. The fact that the scholiasts on Apollonios once specifically cite Timosthenes' *On Harbours* (31) makes his identification with the Timosthenes they cite elsewhere without an *ethnikon* likely. As coevals from the same *polis*, both moving in court circles at Alexandria, Timosthenes and Apollonios can be expected to have known and influenced each other. Giving greater weight to Timosthenes as a literary figure is, perhaps, easier if we suppose that he was a naval commander primarily in relation to his expeditions, rather than necessarily a supreme figure in Ptolemaic strategy.[20]

Strabo regards Timosthenes as strong but not outstanding in both mathematics and geography, like Eratosthenes (6); this in itself shows that he regarded Timosthenes as more than the author of a 'pilot'. It has been observed that his wind-rose was probably envisaged as centred upon Rhodes, itself a key point along Dikaiarchos' central Mediterranean parallel of latitude;[21] more speculatively, he may have been behind a

---

[15] Hauben 1996, 224–5.   [16] As remarked by Meyer 2013 on her F 22.
[17] Roller 2020b.   [18] Meyer 2013.
[19] If 35 is from our Timosthenes: see N. F. Jones 2010.
[20] Hauben 1996, 229–32, is inclined to see T. as something other than a supreme commander.
[21] Hauben 1996, 222 n. 6, citing Gisinger 1937, 1315, who notes that T. locates the Thracian Skythai towards the Aparktias wind, which would fit an imagined view from Rhodes; Meyer 2013, n. 4; Roller 2020b.

monumentalization of the wind rose in the city's urban layout, with the Colossus at its heart.[22] Be that as it may, it makes a coherent picture if we see Timosthenes as an intellectual, cultural, and political figure as well as a significant figure in Ptolemaic cultural policy. If he was not a major military executive, he was perhaps more of a scientist who was commissioned to produce a work both of literary prestige and utility to the state.

Timosthenes was not immune from the kind of controversial reception that we see tarnishing the reputation of other writers. Eratosthenes himself is criticized for following (4) and even plagiarizing him (23 §3). Like Pytheas, he may have been rebuked by Polybios for not knowing more about the far west, though the direct evidence for this (5) comes from Strabo, who has his own issues with Timosthenes (6); in fact, Timosthenes clearly knew enough about the west to discuss the walls and shipsheds of Karteia (7). He was perhaps a pioneer to the extent that, for the geographical areas he knew well, he blended practical detail of locations and distances with literary aspiration typical of early Ptolemaic Alexandria.

The Greek text translated here is that of Meyer.[23]

SELECTED FURTHER READING

Arnaud, P. (2010), 'Notes sur le Stadiasme de la Grande Mer (2): rose des vents, systèmes d'orientation et Quellenforschung', *Geographia antiqua*, 19: 157–62.

Davis, D. L. (2009), 'Commercial navigation in the Greek and Roman world', Ph.D. thesis. University of Texas at Austin. [Esp. ch. 4 (pp. 90–119).]

Meyer, D. (1998), 'Hellenistische Geographie zwischen Wissenschaft und Literatur: Timosthenes von Rhodos und der griechische Periplus', in W. Kullmann *et al.* (eds), *Gattungen wissenschaftlicher Literatur in der Antike* (Tübingen), 193–215.

*—— (2013), 'Timosthenes von Rhodos (2051)', in *FGrH* v.

Prontera, F. (2013), 'Timosthenes and Eratosthenes: sea routes and hellenistic geography', in K. Buraselis *et al.* (eds), *The Ptolemies, the Sea and the Nile: Studies in Waterborne Power* (Cambridge), 207–17.

Roller, D. W. (2020b), 'Timosthenes of Rhodes', in D. W. Roller (ed.), *New Directions in the Study of Ancient Geography* (Sarasota), 56–79.

On Aristotle, Meteorologika

Cohen, S. M., and Burke, P. (1990), 'New evidence for the dating of Aristotle Meteorologica 1–3', *Classical Philology*, 85. 2: 126–9. [Arguing for late 337 BC or after.]

*Lee, H. D. P. (1952), *Aristotle, Meteorologica*. [Loeb edition.] London–Cambridge, Mass.

*Louis, P. (1982), *Aristote, Météorologiques*, i: *Livres I et II*. ['Budé' edition.]

---

[22] Suggested only as an attractive possibility by De Callataÿ 2006, 39–40, 54–5. The evidence of shipwrecks shows that wind roses were not normally reified in material form, but 'were conceived primarily as mental constructs' (Davis 2009, 116).

[23] Meyer 2013. An alternative arrangement of the fragments, geographically ordered and translated with commentaries, is Roller 2020b.

TEXTS

These are presented in one sequence, as the uncertain attributions of some extracts to particular works makes any systematic grouping by title somewhat speculative. *On Harbours* is specified in **2, 4, 8** (in the last it is mentioned only in passing; Strabo may be drawing on another work), **22–3, 29**, and **31**; *Stadiasmos* or *Stadiasmoi* ('stade table(s)') in **23–4**; *Exegetikon* ('commentary') in **35**. The title *Periploi* (*Circumnavigations*; **18**) may refer to *On Harbours*.

Following the extracts she classifies as testimonia (here numbered **1, 4–6, 8, 11**, and **23**), Meyer's section headings assign **2–3, 7, 12, 14, 18, 22, 23** (part), **25–7, 29, 31, 33–4**, and **37** to *On Harbours*; **24** to *Stadiasmoi*; **9–10, 13, 15–17, 19–21, 28, 30**, and **36** to either *On Harbours* or *Stadiasmos*; **35** to *Exegetikon*; and **32** to either *On Harbours* or *Exegetikon*.[24]

1 *Nikomedean Periodos*, 109–20: *Timosthenes as a source*

> I shall now move to the start of my composition
110 > by setting out the writers by whose use
> I make my historical account reliable.
> For I have relied especially on the one
> who has most carefully written about geography,
> both zones (*of latitude*) and forms,[25] Eratosthenes;
> and Ephoros; and him who tells foundations
> in five books, Chalkidian Dionysios;
> and Demetrios, the writer from Kallatis;
> Sicilian Kleon, and Timosthenes
> (*who*) — — the position of the — —[26]
120 > and the (*fellow?*) citizen — —

2 Didymos, *On Demosthenes*, col. 11. 28–37: *Nikaia near Thermopylai*[27]
Nikaia is a city on the sea, 20 stades distant from Therm[o]pylai, about which Timosthen[e]s, in his work O[n] Harbours, book 5, speaks in this [way]: 'When one is conv[eyed by sail]ing from [Thermop]ylai for about [twenty st]ad[es, there is a c]ity, Nikaia; [but for a man on foot it is about fi]fty stades; [and about] five stades [from

---

[24] Roller, though not systematically listing extracts by work, assigns **3, 7, 14–18, 22, 24–34**, and by implication **10, 12–13, 20**, and **36** to *On Harbours*; implies that **21** is from *Stad.*; and connects **8** to *Exegetikon*.

[25] *schēmata*, referring to the *sphragides* or 'sealstones' into which Eratosthenes divided the *oikoumenē*.

[26] This line and the next three are largely illegible and their reconstruction endlessly contested; **119** may require a mention of the winds, or perhaps of Rhodes, T.'s home city.

[27] The text is preserved in a papyrus, from which words in square brackets are missing, restored by an editor.

this] [l]i[es] a [sa]ndy cape, which after fo[u]r stades [has] a minor anchorage (*hyphor-mos*) for a long [ship].'²⁸

3 Strabo 1. 2. 21, C29: *The wind rose*

There are those who say that there are two dominant winds, Boreas (*the north wind*)²⁹ and Notos (*the south wind*), and that the others differ from them only by a small deviation, that from the summer sunrises (*approx. north-east*) being Euros, that from the winter ones (*approx. south-east*) Apeliotes; that from the summer sunsets (*approx. north-west*) being Zephyros, that from the winter ones (*approx. south-west*) being Argestes. As witnesses to this idea of the two winds they invoke Thrasyalkes³⁰ and the Poet himself (*Homer*), who assigns the Argestes to Notos in 'the clearing (*argestēs*) Notos', and Zephyros to Boreas in 'Boreas and Zephyros, the two that blow from Thrace'.³¹

But Poseidonios says that none of those who were knowledgeable about these matters, such as Aristotle, Timosthenes, and Bion the astronomer, have handed down this view, but rather that the one from the summer sunrises is Kaikias, while the one diametrically opposite this, Lips, is from the winter sunset; and conversely that from the winter sunrise is Euros, while the opposite one is Argestes, and those in the middle are Apeliotes (*east*) and Zephyros (*west*).

4 Strabo 2. 1. 40, C92: *Timosthenes' errors*

But so great a plethora of errors are committed by Eratosthenes in these passages, and by Timosthenes, author of *Harbours*—whom he (*Eratosthenes*) praises above the rest of them, but whom he disagrees with and disproves in many respects—that I do not deem it worthwhile to dwell upon either of these authors, who commit so many errors of fact, nor upon Hipparchos.

5 Strabo 2. 1. 41, C93: *Gaps in Timosthenes' knowledge*

Let it now be said that both Timosthenes and Eratosthenes, and those even earlier than they, were completely ignorant of the Iberian and Keltic lands, and ten thousand times more so the Germanic and Brettanic lands; also the lands of the Getai and Bastarnai.³² They also fell into great ignorance when they reached the parts around Italy, the Adriatic, the Pontos, and the northerly ones beyond, even if these charges are perhaps (*overly*) censorious.

6 Strabo 2. 1. 41, C94: *Timosthenes' unreliability*

In a certain way he (*Eratosthenes*) is a mathematician among geographers and a geographer among mathematicians. Thus he offers points of attack to his opponents on both sides, indeed fair attacks in respect of this treatise (*my own*); both he and Timosthenes do so. Therefore there is no remaining need for us to examine them together, and we shall be satisfied with what has been said by Hipparchos.

---

²⁸ Presumably one of T.'s most characteristic passages.　　²⁹ But see **18** §7.
³⁰ Fr. 2 in Diels 1952.　　³¹ *Il.* 11. 306 and 21. 334 for the first quotation; 9. 5 for the second.
³² Peoples living NW of the Black Sea.

7 Strabo 3. 1. 7, C139–40: *Karteia beyond the strait of Gibraltar*
Lying between this (*Iberian*) coast, upon which the Baitis and the Anas discharge, and the furthest parts of Maurousia (*Mauretania*),[33] the Atlantic main pours in and forms the strait by the Pillars at which the inner sea joins the outer. Here is a mountain of those Iberians who are called Bastetanoi, whom people also call Bastouloi; this is Kalpe,[34] not great in area but great in height, and so lofty that from far away it appears to be an island. For those sailing from our sea into the outer one, it is on the right. Beside it at a distance of 40 stades is the city of Kalpe,[35] a noteworthy and ancient place which was once the naval base of the Iberians.[36] Some say it was a foundation by Herakles; among them is Timosthenes, who says that it was called Herakleia of old, and that a great circuit wall and shipsheds were displayed there.

8 Strabo 9. 3. 10, C421–2: *Timosthenes' authorship of the Pythian Melody*
There was instituted the ancient competition of the citharodes at Delphi, singing the paean to the god. The Delphians set this up. After the war of Krisa the Amphiktyones arranged a competition in horse-riding and one in gymnastics and called it Pythia. To the citharodes they added oboists (*aulētai*)[37] and lyre-players without singing, who produced the song called the Pythian Melody (*nomos*). There are five parts to it: 'Prelude', 'Exercise', 'Exhortation', 'Iambs and dactyls', and 'Pan-pipes'. The melody was written by Timosthenes, admiral of the second Ptolemy, who also composed *Harbours* in ten books. He seeks to celebrate through the song Apollo's fight against the serpent, presenting the prologue as the 'Prelude', the first test of the fight as the 'Exercise', the fight itself as the 'Exhortation', setting the reiteration of the paean over the victory as the 'Iamb-and-Dactyl' in those metres, the latter of which is integral to hymns whereas the iamb is for invectives, as in 'to iambize'; while the 'Pan-pipes' imitates the subduing of the beast, as if it is dying with, as it were, its final 'pipings'.[38]

9 Strabo 13. 2. 5, C618: *Islets off Lesbos*
At the strait between Asia and Lesbos there are about 20 islets, or 40 as Timosthenes says. Collectively they are called Hekatonnesoi (*The Hundred Isles*).

10 Strabo 17. 3. 6, C827: *Location of Metagonion*
A great cape (*of NW Africa*) also lies near the river (*Molochath*), as does Metagonion, a waterless and foul locality. The mountain running from the Koteis extends almost to here; the length from the Koteis to the frontiers of the Masaisylioi is 5,000 stades. Metagonion is on the mainland roughly opposite New Carthage; Timosthenes errs when he says it is opposite Massalia (*Marseille*). The crossing from Nea Karchedon

---

[33] For the scope of anc. Mauretania (wider and further E than mod. *Mauritania*), see Ch. 22, introduction.

[34] In the view of some ancient writers, this was the northern Pillar of Herakles.

[35] The early editor Casaubon substituted 'Karteia'.   [36] Cf. Markianos, *Peripl.* 2. 9.

[37] Often translated 'flautists'; but the *aulos* was usually a double-reeded pipe like an oboe (Howard 1893, esp. 21–8).

[38] The text here is disputed; I translate that of Radt.

(*New Carthage*) to Metagonion is 3,000 stades; but the coastal sailing to Massalia is more than 6,000.

11 Pliny, *Natural History*, 1. 4–6: *Pliny's sources*
In the 4th book are contained places, peoples, seas, towns, harbours, mountains, rivers, measurements, and peoples that exist or once existed. . . . from these authors: . . . foreign (*i.e. non-Roman*): . . . Timosthenes . . .[39]

> In the 5th book . . . (*the same*).
> In the 6th book . . . (*the same*).

12 Pliny, *Natural History*, 5. ix. 47: *Size of Asia*
Asia joins it (*Libyē*), and Timosthenes asserts that it extends from the Canopic mouth to the mouth of the Pontus, a distance of 2,638 miles.[40]

13 Pliny, *Natural History*, 5. xxxv. 129: *Size of Cyprus*
The Pamphylian sea has insignificant islands. The Cilician sea has one of the five largest: namely, Cyprus, which in its sunrise and sunset parts lies opposite Cilicia and Syria. It was once the seat of nine kingdoms. Timosthenes offers the figure of 427½ miles for its circuit; Isidorus gives 375. Its length between the two capes, Clides (*Kleïdes*) and Acamas (*Arnaoutis*), which is towards the sunset, is given by Artemidoros as 162½ miles, by Timosthenes as 200.

14 Pliny, *Natural History*, 6. v. 15: *Peoples of the Black Sea*
Below it is the region of Colica (*Kolike*) in the Pontos, in which the ranges of Caucasus are deflected towards the Rhipaean mountains, as has been said. On one side they descend to the Euxine and Lake Maiotis, on the other to the Caspian and the Hyrcanian sea. The other shores are inhabited by wild nations, the Melanchlaeni (*Black-cloaks*) and Coraxi (*Koraxoi*), with the city of Dioscurias adjoining the river Anthemus, now deserted but once so famous that Timosthenes could report that three hundred nations with different tongues came down into it; and at a later date business was conducted by our 130 interpreters.

15 Pliny, *Natural History*, 6. xxxiii. 163: *Dimensions of the 'Arabian gulf' (Red Sea)*
Now we shall follow the rest of the opposite coast of Arabia. Timosthenes has gauged the whole gulf (*the Red Sea*) as a voyage of 4 days lengthwise and 2 days across, while the narrows are 7½ miles (*in width*).

16 Pliny, *Natural History*, 6. xxxv. 183: *Length of Egypt*
In like manner they have offered various information about its (*Egypt's*) measurement. First Dalion, who was carried up far beyond Meroë; then Aristocreon, Bion, and Basilis; then the younger Simonides, who even lingered in Meroë for five years while he

---

[39] Pliny does not, in fact, name T. in book 4 (Roller 2020b, 79).
[40] A measurement of the Mediterranean coast of 'Asia', not of the entire continent.

wrote about Aethiopia.[41] For Timosthenes, commander of Philadelphus' fleets, while giving no measurement, offers a journey of 60 days from Syene to Meroë.

17 Pliny, *Natural History*, 6. xxxvi. 198: *Islands in the Indian Ocean*
That there are very many islands in the whole of this sea (*the western Indian Ocean*) is reported by Ephorus, and also by Eudoxus[42] and Timosthenes.

18 Agathemeros ii. 6–7: *The wind rose*

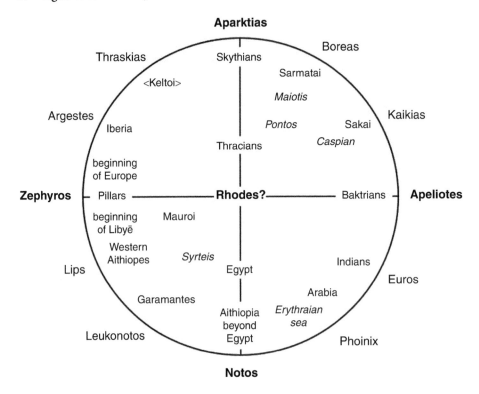

FIG. 10.1. Timosthenes' wind rose (D. G. J. Shipley).

(6) The winds that blow are, from the equinoctial[43] sunrise (*due east*), Apeliotes; from the equinoctial sunset (*west*), Zephyros; from the south, Notos; from the north, Aparktias.

⟨The easterly winds:⟩ from the summer turning-point (*solstice; approx. north-east*), Kaikias; next, from the equinoctial sunrise, Apeliotes; and from the winter one (*approx. south-east*), Euros.

The westerly winds: from the winter sunset (*approx. south-west*). Lips; from the equinoctial sunset, Zephyros again; from the summer sunset (*approx. north-west*), Argestes or Olympias, also known as Iapyx.

---

[41] On these Ptolemaic representatives, see Roller 2015, 110–11.
[42] See n. on Eudoxos of Knidos 75.
[43] Lit. 'equidiurnal'. See Introduction, §X. 3. b fin.

Next Notos and Aparktias, blowing opposite to one another.

Thus there are eight.[44]

(7) But Timosthenes, the author of the *Periploi* (*Circumnavigations*), says there are twelve. Between Aparktias and Kaikias he adds Boreas (*NNE*); between the Euros and Notos, Phoinix (*SSE*), also called Euronotos; between Notos and Lips, Leukonotos or Libonotos (*SSW*); between Aparktias and Argestes, Thraskias (*NNW*), also ⟨named⟩ Kirkios by those living around that area.[45]

He states that the nations living at the furthest points towards Apeliotes are the Baktrians;[46] towards Euros, the Indians; towards Phoinix (*lie*) the Erythraian sea[47] and Arabia; towards Notos, the Aithiopia that is beyond Egypt;[48] towards Leukonotos, the Garamantes beyond the Syrteis; towards Lips, the western Aithiopes, ⟨those⟩ beyond the Mauroi;[49] towards Zephyros, the Pillars (*of Herakles*) and the beginnings of Libyē and Europe; towards Argestes, Iberia, which is now Hispania; towards Thraskias, ⟨the Keltoi (*Celts*) and the neighbouring places; towards Aparktias⟩, those Skythians that are beyond the Thracians; towards Boreas, the Pontos, (*Lake*) Maiotis, and the Sarmatai;[50] towards Kaikias, the Caspian sea and the Sakai.

19 Agathemeros v. 20: *Dimensions of Sicily*

In what follows, we shall state the circumferences of the islands in our part of the world, taking them from Artemidoros, Menippos, and other reliable (*authorities*). . . . The circumference of Sicily, according to Timosthenes, is 4,740 stades; its form is a triangle with unequal sides,[51] and it has a crossing from Peloron Akron (*Monster Point*) to Italia of 12 stades. The side of the island from Peloron to Pachynos is 1,360 stades; that from Pachynos[52] to Lilybaion, 1,600 stades; according to Timosthenes, that from Lilybaion to Pelorias, 1,700 stades. From Lilybaion, the crossing to Aspis in Libyē is close to 1,500 stades.

20 Ptolemy, *Geography*, 1. 15. 3: *Distance from Africa to Sicily*

(*Marinos says that*) Pachynos is (*opposite*) Great Leptis, and the (*river*) Himera⟨s⟩ opposite Theainai, the distance from Pachynos to the Himera⟨s⟩ being about 400 stades in total, that from Leptis to Theainai above 1,500, from what Timosthenes records.[53]

---

[44] This paragraph seems to derive from Aristotle, *Mete.* 2. 6 (translated as an appendix to the present chapter); T.'s contribution may not begin until §7 below, since Agathemeros names him only there.

[45] i.e. in the NNW part of the *oikoumenē*. T. thus omits the ENE, ESE, WSW, and WNW directions.

[46] In NE Afghanistan.   [47] The western Indian Ocean and *Red Sea*.   [48] i.e. E. Africa.

[49] It was often believed that the Aithiopes occupied a swathe of N. Africa from the E coast to the W.

[50] On the Sarmatai, see Grumeza 2021.

[51] On the use of geometrical figures to describe landscapes, see Dueck 2005.

[52] The NE extremity of Sicily.

[53] Clearly the river Himeras on the S coast of Sicily is meant, not its homonym on the N coast (or the city of Himera, succeeded by Thermai Himeraiai, near it). Both rivers are named 'Himeras' (masculine) at Ptol. 3. 4. 3 and 3. 4. 2 respectively, so 'Himera' (feminine) here must be a MS error.

21   Ptolemy, *Geography,* 1. 15. 4: *Distances in the Nile Delta*
Similarly, he (*Marinos*) says the Chelidoniai (*islands; Beş Adalar*)[54] lie opposite Kanobos, but Akamas[55] opposite Paphos[56] and Paphos opposite Sebennytos,[57] the number of
stades from the Chelidoniai to Akamas also being put at 1,000 by him, but those from
Kanobos to Sebennytos at 290 by Timosthenes.[58]

22   Harpokration s.v. *eph' Hieron: Hieron on the Bosporos*
'Towards Hieron': Demosthenes (*uses this phrase*) in his oration *On the Trierarchy beyond the Legal Term*. It is a sanctuary of the Twelve Gods on the (*Thracian*) Bosporos,
as Timosthenes (*says*) in the (*books*) *On Harbours*.[59]

23   Markianos, *Epit. Men.* 2–3: *Gaps in Timosthenes' knowledge*[60]
2. . . . Those who in my view have investigated these matters intelligently are Timosthenes of Rhodes, who was chief helmsman of the second Ptolemy (*r. 283/2–246*); and
after him Eratosthenes, whom the officials of the Mouseion (*at Alexandria*) called Beta
(*Number Two*). . . .
    3. . . . For Timosthenes, when most parts of the sea were still unknown, since the
Romans had not yet conquered them in war, wrote treatises *On Harbours*, in which
he did not deal accurately with all the nations living round our sea. Of course, in
the European area his *periplous* of the Tyrrhenic (*Etruscan*) open-sea (*pelagos*) was
incomplete, and he was unable to obtain knowledge of the area around the strait of
Herakles (*straits of Gibraltar*), in respect of either our sea or the outer sea. In respect
of Libyē he encountered the same problem, in that he was ignorant of all the places
beyond Carthage and round the outer sea. From these ten books, an epitome in one
book has been made. Furthermore, he also wrote a summary of the so-called stade distances (*stadiasmoi*) in another, single book. In all these, however, he has been unable
to convey anything completely or clearly. But Eratosthenes of Kyrene—I don't know
what possessed him—transcribed Timosthenes' book, adding a few items but in such
a way that he did not even keep his hands off the prologue of the author mentioned,
but placed that at the start of his book in those very words.

24   Stephanos of Byzantion α 21: *Agathe in Liguria*
Agathe (*Good; Agde*): a city of the Ligyes (*Ligurians*) or Keltoi. . . . Timosthenes in the
Stadiasmos refers to it as Agathe Tyche (*Good Fortune*).

---

[54] Off Lykia, cf. Ps.-Skylax §100. 1. The Turkish name means 'five islands'.
[55] The NW cape of Cyprus.   [56] A city in SW Cyprus.
[57] Inland, in the E part of the Delta, cf. Ps.-Skyl. §106. 1. Marinos perhaps had in mind the mouth of
the Sebennytic branch of the Nile rather than the location of Sebennytos itself, some 50 mi (80 km)
upstream to the SW.
[58] An under-estimate (Roller 2020b).
[59] This is the Hieron (*hieron*, 'sanctuary', has become a place-name) at the entrance to the Black Sea;
see Index. The text has the definite article ('the') in a plural form, which would imply that *On Harbours*
comprised two or more volumes.
[60] Trans. J. B. Campbell.

25 Stephanos of Byzantion α 200: *Alexandria in the Troad*
Alexandreiai (*Alexandrias, plural*): . . . There is also a locality on the Trojan (*Mt*) Ida called Alexandreia, in which they say Paris judged the goddesses, as Timosthenes (*says*).

26 Stephanos of Byzantion α 357: *A river in the Troad*
Apia: . . . Demetrios (*of Magnesia*), however, says that there is also a river Apidanos in the Troad: 'discharging into the western sea', as Timosthenes (*says*).

27 Stephanos of Byzantion α 457: *Artake in Phrygia*
Artake: a city in Phrygia, a colony of the Milesians. Demetrios (*of Magnesia*) refers to it as an islet, as does Timosthenes, saying 'Artake, in one case, is a mountain in the territory of Kyzikos; in another, an islet a stade distant from the land; at this point a deep harbour exists for eight ships under the cape (*ankōn*) which the mountain causes to project from the shore'.

28 Stephanos of Byzantion χ 13: *Chalkeia in Libyē*
Chalkeia: a city in Libyē. (*Alexander*) Polyhistor (*mentions it*) in *Libyka*, 3rd (*book*). So does Timosthenes. When Polybios is criticizing him in the 12th (*book*), he writes thus:[61] 'he is wholly ignorant about Chalkeia: for it is not a city, but copper-works' (*chalkourgeia*).

29 scholion to Aeschylus, *Persians*, 305 (303): *Topography of Salamis (off Attica)*
'but Artembares': . . . Sileniai is a shore on Salamis, close to the cape called Tropaion (*Trophy*), as Timosthenes says in the 6th (*book*) of *On Harbours*.[62]

30 scholia AB to Theokritos, *Idylls*, 13. 22–3: *The Kyaneai*
'Who of the Kyaneai': (*Scholion A*) Karystios of Pergamon says that the Kyaneai (*Blue Rocks, or Clashing Rocks*) were named by humans, but the Gates of Phorkos by gods. Timosthenes says that at about 25 stades from Hieron[63] is a rocky islet, and that its capes are called the Kyaneai.[64] (*Scholion B*) The islet is (*said to be*) in Europe, but the cape in Asia; they are 25 stades from one another.

---

[61] Polyb. 12. 1. 5 (restored in the revised Loeb, Paton, Walbank, and Habicht 2011, 341). T.'s name is a correction from the 'Demosthenes' of the MS, for which there are parallels. Some have thought, nevertheless, that the scholar criticized by Polyb. was in fact Timaios (P. devotes part of book 12 to criticizing the Sicilian historian), but T. is also the subject of criticism by various authors and his name may remain (Billerbeck 2006–17, v. 79).

[62] The MSS texts of the scholia here read 'Timoxenos' (Dähnhardt 1894, 102–3), easily corrected to 'Timosthenes'.

[63] See **22, 34**.

[64] For other contributions to the debate about the Clashing Rocks that feature in the story of the Argonauts, see Index.

31 scholion B to Apollonios of Rhodes 2. 296–7: *A sanctuary on Kephallenia*
Strophades: . . . For there is a mountain (*called*) Ainos on Kephallenia, where there is a sanctuary of Zeus Ainesios which Kleon mentions in his *Periplous* and Timosthenes in his *Harbours*.

32 scholion Q to Apollonios of Rhodes 2. 498–527: *The name Sirius*
'Seirios' (*Sirius*): . . . Some say it is the star of Orion's dog, others that of Erigone's (*dog*), others that of Alkyoneus' (*dog*), others that of Isis' (*dog*), others that of Kephalos' (*dog*); and others say it is a proper name, as Timosthenes says.[65]

33 scholion V to Apollonios of Rhodes 2. 498–527: *The Etesian winds*
'For⟨ty⟩ days': some say the days of the Etesian winds are 40; others 50, as Timosthenes does. They begin to blow when the Sun is at the end of the Crab (*Cancer*), blow throughout the Lion (*Leo*), and cease two parts (*i.e. two-thirds*) of the way through the Virgin (*Virgo*).

34 scholion to Apollonios of Rhodes 2. 531–2: *Hieron on the Bosporos*
'An altar where the surf breaks opposite': he (*Apollonios of Rhodes*) says that on the opposite shore, in Asia, when they sailed over to it, they built an altar to the Twelve Gods.[66] Well, it is clear that it is in Europe: indeed, to this day there is the so-called Hieron (*Sanctuary*) on the opposite shore, in Europe. Timosthenes says the sons of Phrixos founded an altar of the Twelve Gods, but the Argonauts one of Poseidon.

35 scholion A to Apollonios of Rhodes 3. 846–7: *An epithet of Persephone*
'Daira sole-born': Daira is an elliptical form used because of the metre; for it is (*really*) Daëira. It refers to Persephone, as 'sole-born' indicates. . . . That they call Persephone Daira is assented to by Timosthenes in his *Exegetikon* (*Commentary*).[67]

36 scholion to Apollonios of Rhodes 4. 1712: *An island near Thera*
The island of Hippouris[68] is near Thera. Timosthenes mentions it . . .

37 scholion to Lucan 9. 411: *Egypt as a continent*
(*Of Libyē*) ''Tis the third part of the whole, if you would credit its repute ⟨entirely⟩': some have divided the world into two parts, as does Varro, that is, Asia and Europe; some into three, Asia, Europe, and Africa, as does Alexander; and some into four by adding Egypt, as does Timosthenes.[69]

---

[65] T., as elsewhere, evinces an interest in mythology which may be connected with navigation: the heliacal rising of Sirius coincides not only with the hottest season, but also with the onset of the Etesian (annual) winds (Meyer 2013 ad loc.), on which see **33**.

[66] Cf. **22, 30**.

[67] This extract = *BNJ* 354, also Timosthenes of Rhodes; but N. F. Jones, author of the *BNJ* entry, argues that this T. 'of Rhodes' was a different man and an Athenian.

[68] Roller 2020b: the islet of *Phtiní*, SE of Thera.

[69] T., a commander in Ptolemaic service, perhaps wished to compliment his king by picking up Hdt.'s ironic suggestion (2. 16) that the Delta should be a fourth continent.

APPENDIX: ARISTOTLE, *METEOROLOGIKA*, 2. 6

(363A 21–365A 14)

Vertical lines mark the beginning of a new column in the standard Bekker numbering.

38 (363a 21) Concerning their (*the winds'*) positions, and which are contrary to which, and which can possibly blow at the same time and which cannot, and moreover which there are and how many they happen to be, and additionally concerning their other features that happen not to have been stated in detail in the *Problems*:[70] (*of all this*) we shall now speak.

(363a 25) Concerning their positions, one must consider the words by using the diagram at the same time. In it has been drawn the circle of the horizon, so that it is intelligible; for which reason it is round. One must understand that is one of the two sections (*of the Earth*), the one inhabited by us: for it will be possible to divide the other in the same way. Let those things be defined as opposite in location that are most distant (*from one another*) in location, just as opposites in form are those most distant in form. Those things are most distant in location that lie opposite one another along a diameter.

(363a 34) Let the point marked *A* be the equinoctial[71] sunset (*due west*), | and let the point marked *B* be the location opposite this, the equinoctial sunrise. (*Let there be*) another diameter intersecting with this one at right angles; upon this, let the point marked *G* be the north (*arktos*); directly opposite this, let the point marked *H* be the south (*mesēmbria*). Let the point marked *F* be the summer sunrise (*northeast*), that marked *E* the summer sunset (*north-west*), that marked *D* the winter sunrise (*south-east*), and that marked *C* the winter sunset (*south-west*). From *F* let a diameter be drawn to *C*, and another from *D* to *E*. Then, since the things most distant in location are opposite in location, and the things (*opposite*) along a diameter are most distant, those winds must necessarily be contrary to one another that are along a diameter.

(363b 11) The winds are named as follows according to the situation of their locations: the Zephyros (*west wind*) (*blowing*) from *A*, for this is the equinoctial sunset. Opposite this, the Apeliotes (*east wind*) from *B*, for this is the equinoctial sunrise. The Boreas or Aparktias (*north wind*) from *G*: for here is the north (*arktos*). Opposite this, the Notos (*south wind*) from *H*: for this is the south (*notos*) from which it blows, and *H* is opposite *G*, as they are along a diameter. From *F* the Kaikias: for this is the summer sunrise. Its contrary is not that blowing from *E* but the Lips, from *C*: for that one blows from the winter sunset, opposite to this, for it lies along a diameter. From *D* the Euros: for this blows from the winter sunrise, being the neighbour of the Notos; for which

---

[70] The long book 26 of Aristotle's *Problems*, in 62 chapters, largely derived from Theophrastos, *On Winds*, is devoted entirely to the topic. The translation here follows the Greek of Louis's 'Budé' edition.
[71] Lit. 'equidiurnal'. See Introduction, §X. 3. b fin.

reason Euronotoi (*i.e. SSE winds*) are often said to blow. The contrary of this is not the Lips blowing from *C*, but that from *E*, which some call Argestes, some Olympias, others Skirōn; for this blows from the summer sunset, and it alone lies diametrically opposite.

(363b 26) These, then, are the winds that lie along a diameter and their contraries: but there are others against which there are no contrary winds. For from *I* (*blows the one*) they call Thraskias; for this is midway between Argestes and Aparktias. From *J*, the one they call Mesēs; for this is midway between Kaikias and Aparktias. The chord[72] *IJ* is almost the ever-visible (*circle*),[73] but not exactly. There are no contraries to these winds: either to Mesēs, for such a one would blow from *L*, which is (*opposite*) along the diameter; | or to Thraskias, for such a one would blow from *M*, for this is the point along the diameter; except that from this point there blows occasionally[74] a certain wind which those around that place call Phoinikias.

(364a 4) The most important and distinctive winds are these, and they are arranged in this way. The reason why there are more winds from the locations to the north than from those to the south is that the inhabited region (*oikoumenē*) lies towards that location, and that much more water and snow is propelled into this part because the part on the other side is under the Sun and its course. These (*substances*) melt into the ground and are warmed by the Sun, which necessarily causes the exhalation from the ground to become greater, and over a greater area.

(364a 13) Among the said winds, Boreas[75] is (*i.e. comprises*) chiefly Aparktias, but also Thraskias and Mesēs; but the Kaikias is shared between Apeliotes and Boreas. Notos is both the direct wind from the south (*mesēmbria*) and the Lips. Apeliotes is that from the equinoctial sunrise and the Euros; the Phoinikias is shared. Zephyros is both the direct wind and the one called Argestes.

(364a 19) Overall, some of these are called northerlies (*boreia*), others southerlies (*notia*). The westerlies (*zephyrika*) are assigned to Boreas, as they are colder since they blow from the west (*dysmai*). To Notos are assigned the easterlies (*apēliōtika*), as they are warmer since they blow from the east. People called them by these names (*sc. northerlies and southerlies*) because they were distinguished by cold, heat, and warmth. For those from the east are hotter than those from the west, because those from the east are under the Sun for a longer time, but it leaves those from the west more swiftly and approaches that location later.

---

[72] The word is *diametros*, but here meaning a shorter line between points on the circle not directly opposite one another.

[73] The circle defining the area of sky around the North Pole that is never below the horizon from a given location; also called by the Greeks the 'arctic circle' of a place.

[74] Or 'briefly' or 'locally' (*ep' oligon*).

[75] i.e. the group of northerly winds. This, and the rest of this passage, is either elliptical or illogical; but it is echoed by Ps.-Aristotle (Ch. 23 below), ch. 4, who likewise groups the winds into northerlies, easterlies, etc.

(364a 27) As the winds are arranged in this way, it is clear that contraries cannot blow at the same time, for they are along a diameter, so the other would be overcome and cease. But there is nothing to stop those not lying in such a relation to one another, such as F and D, (*from blowing at the same time*). For this reason, both may sometimes blow at the same time and be favourable (*for a ship heading*) to the same point, yet not (*blowing*) from the same point or with the same wind.

(364a 32) During opposite seasons, opposite winds mostly blow: for example, around | the spring equinox Kaikias and in general those from beyond (*i.e. north of*) the summer solstice (*i.e. the solstitial sunrise*); around the autumn equinox Lips winds; around the summer solstice Zephyros; and around the winter one Euros.

(364b 3) Those that most of all obstruct and stop the others are Aparktias winds, Thraskias winds, and Argestes winds; for as they have their origin closest (*to us*), these ones blow particularly often and strongly. This is the reason why they are the clearest of the winds: for as they blow from close by, they most of all overpower the other winds, and by blowing away the clouds that have gathered, they make a clear sky—unless, that is, they happen to be very cold at the same time, and then they are not clear, for if they are cold rather than big they freeze them (*the clouds*) rather than forcing them away. The Kaikias is not clear because it bends back upon itself; hence is spoken the proverb 'Bringing to himself as Kaikias does a cloud'.[76]

(364b 14) The veering of winds occurs when they stop and (*are followed by*) the ones adjoining them according to the relocation of the Sun, because what adjoins the beginning (*of a movement*) is most greatly moved, and the beginning of the winds moves in this way as the Sun does.

(364b 17) Contrary (*winds*) create either the same result or the opposite. For example, Lips and the Kaikias, which some call Hellespontias,[77] are moist while Argestes and Euros are dry; but the last is dry at the start but ends up watery.

(364b 21) The snowy (*wind*) is Mesēs, as is Aparktias, for these are coldest. The hail-producers are Aparktias, Thraskias, and Argestes. The heat-bringer is Notos, as are Zephyros and Euros. The sky is filled with clouds strongly by Kaikias, more thinly by Lips. Kaikias does so because of bending back upon itself, and because of being shared by Boreas and Euros, so that because it is cold it freezes the vaporous air and compacts it, but because it is easterly (*apēliōtikos*) in its location it contains much matter and vapour, which it forces forwards. The clear winds are Aparktias, Thraskias, and Argestes; the reason has been stated earlier. These, and Mesēs, are particularly characterized by lightning: for since they blow from close at hand they are cold, and lightning is caused by cold, for it is expelled by clouds as they coalesce. This is the reason why some of these same winds | are hail-producers, for they freeze things quickly.

---

[76] By turning up into the sky and down again: see Aristotle, *Problems*. 26. 1, 940a 18–34; also 26. 29, 943a 32–b 3, where the same proverb (an iambic pentameter) is quoted, as it is as by Theophrastos, *On Winds*, 37.

[77] This alternative name refers only to the Kaikias.

(365a 1) Hurricanes arise mostly in autumn, then in spring. Mostly (*they are*) an Aparktias, Thraskias, or Argestes. The reason is that hurricanes mostly arise when new winds fall upon winds already blowing; the cause of this, too, has been stated earlier.

(365a 6) For those living around the west, the Etesians veer from Aparktias winds to Thraskias, Argestes, and Zephyros winds—for the Zephyros belongs to the northerly winds[78]—beginning from the north and finishing further round. For those around the east, they veer (*from the north*) up to the Apeliotes.

(365a 10) Concerning winds, their first origin, their essence, and the features that occur in them collectively and individually, let that be our account.

[78] Some editors omit this phrase.

11

HERAKLEIDES KRITIKOS

(WRITTEN 279–239 BC)

D. Graham J. Shipley

To the memory of
Peter J. Rhodes (1940–2021)
φιλαθήναιος

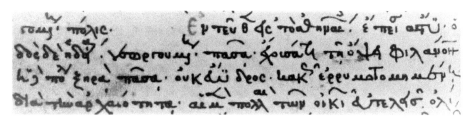

FIG. 11.1. Opening of the text of Herakleides Kritikos, p. 114 (detail).

INTRODUCTION

According to the scholarly consensus, the author we call Herakleides Kritikos ('the Critic') has left us parts (including the conclusion) of a prose work encapsulating insights into different *poleis* and regional communities in east-central mainland Greece. It was evidently written for a Greek audience in the middle decades of the 3rd century BC (there is no current consensus as to a more precise date).[1] He is a shadowy figure but represents a uniquely comic voice among the authors in the present volumes, and his text displays more literary features than most. Besides what we might call geographical material, characteristic of a *periēgēsis* or chorography, his main interest, at least in the longest fragment, appears to be in entertaining a (live?) audience.

Halfway down page 111 of the mid-13th-century manuscript D (which contains several of our geographers in unique copies; see Introduction) is the closing two-line title of the surviving portion of Isidoros of Charax (Chapter 23 below). After a small gap, a new text begins on the next line (l. 13), its first letter in red. After three pages of this we find another space, a red letter, and a mark in the margin: these indicate that the copyist was aware that one work had ended and another begun, but no closing title is given to the work just ended. Ten pages further on (at 124. 25) is the title *'Dikaiarchos'*

---

[1] Among recent commentators, Arenz favours the years 279–267 (the run-up to the Chremonidean war), McInerney 262–229 (during a period of Macedonian domination of Athens); Marcotte 1990, 3, favours 260–229 (following E. Fabricius 1890).

Cities and Witticisms' (*Dikaiarchou poleis kai skōmmata*), apparently referring to the text that has ended there, or to all of the preceding 13½ pages.[2]

At least some of this material, however, has nothing to do with Dikaiarchos (Chapter 9 above). It comprises two passages of verse, written out continuously as if they were prose, which we now rightly attribute to Dionysios son of Kalliphon (Chapter 20), and between these—here we come at last to the nub of the matter!—a passage of genuine prose. This short passage, buried within the fragments of the poem of Dionysios son of Kalliphon, is now credited to Herakleides Kritikos. Though continuous in the manuscript, it contains a clear rupture in content and is divided by editors into two parts, fragments 1 and 3 (A. 1 and 3 below); the latter contains the ending of a work, while the beginning is lost. Between these passages, editors now insert a text known as 'fragment 2' (A. 2 below), thought to be from the same work, found in a 15th-century manuscript (Parisinus graecus 571),[3] where it follows extracts from Strabo, again with no indication of a change of source. Given the different tone and content of the three passages, however, it cannot be certain that they are all from one work.

The authorship of the text is deduced from an account (B. 4 below) in a hellenistic work on marvels that includes details of a medicinal herb on Mt Pelion, explicitly attributed to one Herakleides Kretikos, 'Herakleides of Crete', which closely resembles A. 2 §5. Finally, editors emend the author's name to Herakleides Kritikos, 'the Critic'.[4]

The work (if correctly reconstructed) can perhaps be described as an early surviving example of chorography, a focused description of one or more regions (cf. Introduction, §III. 1. d). The writer of fragment 1 arranges his material like a *periplous* on land, or perhaps a *stadiasmos*: but pausing to sketch each *polis*, then announcing the move to the next one and giving a distance in stades. He uses a rich vocabulary and adopts characteristic stylistic devices such as a trio of successive adjectives (e.g. fr. 1 §1 on the theatre and then on the Athena sanctuary) or emphasis achieved through asyndeton (the omission of conjunctions, e.g. fr. 1 §1 'Three gymnasia, Akademia, Lykeion, Kynosarges . . . All kinds of festivals, diversions, relaxations . . . many leisure activities, continual spectacles'). He adopts, without a systematic philosophical framework, character tropes comparable to those in Theophrastos' *Characters* (a slightly earlier work),[5] evidently designed to amuse readers; as such, it is hard to know to what extent his acerbic judgements on certain groups are meant at all seriously.

The frequent quotations from poetry in fragment 1 strengthen the impression of a work intended to be declaimed before an audience, just as many moments in the text evoke theatrical ideas. As well as depicting an unusually lively range of features of life in the *poleis* of central Greece, such as dramatic entertainments and herbal healing,

---

[2] An actual witticism follows immediately, at the top of p. 125 in the MS: εὐτυχῶς Μαρκιανῷ (*eutychōs Markianōi*), 'Good luck to Markianos!'—the medieval copyist's own words, as he knew the end of his labour was nigh?—before the beginning of the *Nikomedean Periodos* (Ch. 17 below).

[3] Diktyon no. 50149 (the *Pinakes* entry does not record this extract).

[4] The MS of Apollonios (B. 4 below) reads *Krētikos*, 'of Crete', but Pfister 1951, 18–19, argues for *Kritikos*, 'the Critic'; Arenz 2006 and McInerney 2019 concur.

[5] McInerney 2019.

the three fragments tend to suggest economic well-being and prosperously cultivated landscapes, which coheres with what other evidence we have. The author of fragment 1 has a clear sense of the importance of trade in this region, and perhaps enunciates the mindset of a travelling businessman—even posing as a man with an eye for the ladies of important cities (Athens, fr. 1 §5; Thebes, fr. 1 §§17–19). It is hard to know whether his comments are not tongue in cheek, designed to amuse ironically by stating the opposite of what his audience knows to be true; his digs at Athenians' sense of superiority (fr. 3 §§2 and 7) are more obviously satirical.

After leaving Athens in a northerly direction and reaching Oropos at the frontier, the author makes a highly selective clockwise circuit (in text) of Boiotia: first travelling west to inland Tanagra and continuing to Plataiai (another frontier *polis*), then striking north to the principal city, Thebes, and from there north again, back to the coast of the Euboian gulf at Anthedon. The text thus omits important inland *poleis* such as Thespiai, Koroneia and Orchomenos, though he mentions the first two along with Onchestos and Haliartos in his closing remarks on the region (perhaps descriptions of these places have dropped out of the text). We do not know by what route he reached Mt Pelion in Magnesia, between Thessaly and the sea, though evidently a description of the recently founded *polis* of Demetrias stood immediately before it. Whether he described other places in Thessaly in any depth is unclear, for fragment 3 is taken up with a theoretical discussion of the meaning and extent of 'Hellas' and of its limits.

Like Pseudo-Skylax (Chapter 7), fragment 3 defines the river Peneios, the northern boundary of Thessaly, as the end of Hellas (or 'continuous Hellas' as Ps.-Skylax calls it at §33. 2 and §65. 2), thus excluding Macedonia.[6] Rather surprisingly, however, the author retrospectively locates the beginning of continuous Hellas in the Peloponnese, thus, uniquely among Greek geographical authors, excluding not only Epeiros (as does Ps.-Skylax) but also Akarnania and Aitolia, to say nothing of Western Lokris and Phokis. Since the work, if correctly reconstructed, ends with Thessaly, roughly half of it may be lost, covering the Peloponnese and presumably the Megarid and western Attica. We can only dream of what comic impressions it might have given us of the great cities of the Peloponnese, perhaps even Sparta.[7]

The authoritative edition of Pfister is complemented by the recent critical edition by Arenz, his chapter in *FGrH* v (both with German translation), and McInerney's lucid commentary with English translation.[8]

An interesting contrast may be drawn between Herakleides Kritikos and a fragment of an unknown author of similar date (*BNJ* 369), describing the Piraeus in some detail in rather different tone. This is appended to the chapter.

The Greek text translated is that of Arenz, with an exception at fr. 1 §25.

---

[6] The insistence that Thessaly belongs to Hellas is not necessarily evidence that the author was himself Thessalian, *pace* Arenz 2013. There is no evidence that any writers wished to deny the Thessalians this status: McInerney 2019.

[7] For an attempt to characterize life in the C3 Peloponnese, see Shipley 2018, esp. chs 4–5.

[8] Pfister 1951; Arenz 2006, summarized in Arenz 2013; McInerney 2007 (2nd edn McInerney 2019).

SELECTED FURTHER READING

*Arenz, A. (2006), *Herakleides Kritikos, Über die Städte in Hellas: eine Periegese Griechenlands am Vorabend des chremonideischen Krieges*. Munich.

*—— (2013), 'Herakleides Kritikos (2022)', in *FGrH* v.

Austin, M. M. (2006), *The Hellenistic World from Alexander to the Roman Conquest: A Selection of Ancient Sources in Translation*, 2nd edn. Cambridge. [Pp. 198–201 no. 101 (map, p. 201).]

McInerney, J. J. (2012), 'Heraclides Criticus and the problem of taste', in I. Sluiter and R. M. Rosen (eds), *Aesthetic Value in Classical Antiquity* (Leiden–Boston), 243–64.

*—— (2019), 'Herakleides Kritikos (369A)', in *BNJ²*.

*Pfister, F. (1951), *Die Reisebilder des Herakleides: Einleitung, Text, Übersetzung und Kommentar mit einer Übersicht über die Geschichte der griechischen Volkskunde*. Vienna.

*Sickinger, J. P. (2020), 'Anonymous Periegete (P. Haw., 80–81) (Anonymus periegeta) (369)', in *BNJ²*. [*P. Hawara* 80–81; see Appendix below.]

A. ON THE CITIES IN HELLAS

Headings are added.

1   Codex Parisinus supplément grec 443, pp. 114. 13–121. 23

ATHENS

1. From here one comes to the town of the Athenians. The road is pleasant, all the land is farmed, and it has a benevolent aspect to the sight. The city, however, is all dry, not well-watered, and the town-planning is bad on account of its age. The majority of the houses are cheap, and few are serviceable. On its being viewed by strangers, there would be instant disbelief that this was the city known by the name of the Athenians; but soon one would believe it. [—] most beautiful of those in the inhabited world: a notable theatre, great and admirable; an expensive sanctuary of Athena, visible from afar and worth seeing, the so-called Parthenon overlooking the theatre; it arouses great astonishment in those who view it.[9] The half-complete Olympieion[10] also evokes astonishment in respect of the plan of its construction, but it would be the best (*such temple*) if it were completed. Three gymnasia, Akademia, Lykeion, Kynosarges, all endowed with trees their ground is planted with grass. All kinds of festivals, diversions, relaxations from all kinds of philosophers, many leisure activities, continual spectacles.

---

[9] This is the earliest euphoric praise of the Parthenon temple, though like other ancient authors HK admires the sanctuary's wealth and generally spectacular appearance, rather than the sculptures that fascinate the modern viewer.

[10] The temple of Olympian Zeus, begun by the Peisistratid tyrants in C6, finished under Hadrian (r. AD 117–38).

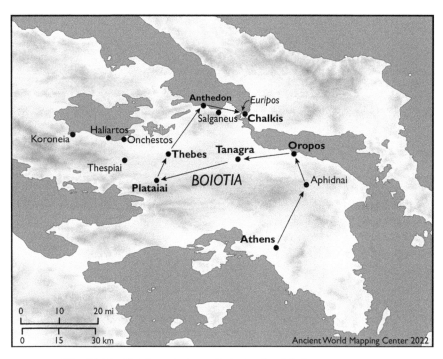

MAP 11.1. Herakleides Kritikos: Attica to Boiotia, simplified.

2. The products of the land are all beyond price and in the first rank for taste, though slightly scarce. But since foreigners spend time residing with each of them, a co-existence well coordinated with their desires, this distracts them from their intentions and creates a complaisant forgetfulness of their enslavement. By reason of its spectacles and leisure activities, as far as the common people are concerned, the city has no awareness of hunger but engenders forgetfulness about the supply of foodstuffs. For those with ready cash, no city is its peer in the matter of enjoyment. And the city has other pleasures in great numbers, for the cities near it are suburbs belonging to the Athenians.   3. Those occupying the city do well to secure great fame for every creative artist, casting their blessings upon all whom they happen to encounter—a wonderful lesson in how people are 'ceramic animals'.

4. Of the inhabitants some are Attic folk, others Athenians.[11] The Attic ones are over-particular in discourse, secretly hostile, denunciatory observers of foreign ways of life. The Athenian ones, on the other hand, are great-hearted, simple in their behaviour, authentic guardians of friendship. But certain speechwriters run around the city disturbing the foreign residents if they are rich; if the People ensnares them, it imposes

---

[11] HK is probably drawing a class distinction between the elite and the common folk, rather than between urban and rural inhabitants (McInerney 2019).

severe punishments upon them. The genuine Athenians are a harsh audience for the arts because they encounter them all the time.

5. All in all, just as the other cities differ from the countryside in the matter of enjoyment and the organization of life, so does the city of the Athenians surpass the other cities. One thing above all is to be guarded against: the courtesans, so that you don't fail to notice you are being sweetly destroyed. Lysippos' lines say:[12]

> If you haven't seen Athens, you're a log.
> If you've seen it but not chased it, an ass.
> If you delight in it and run away, a pack-ass.
> This is the Hellenic city that has a scent
> like roses even as it stinks.
> For the Halieia[13] gets my bile up,
> while the Haliac year makes me mad.
> When one of them says mildly 'the poplar
> is the Haliac crown', I choke
> so badly on their words that I desire
> to expire rather than persist in listening.
> Such is the darkness heaped upon foreigners.

OROPOS

6. From here to Oropos (*Skála Oropoú*) by way of Aphidnai and the sanctuary of Zeus Amphiaraos, for a walking man unladen, is a journey of nearly a day, uphill. But the multiplicity of hostelries, offering copiously the necessities of life and opportunities for rest, checks the travellers' tiredness from arising.[14]   7. The city of the Oropians is a possession of Thebes. The business of commerce has been nurtured (*here*) from time immemorial, as has the unsurpassable avarice of tax-men alongside their extreme wickedness. For they charge duty even on items which are intended to be imported to them.[15] Most of them are rough in their dealings, as they have eliminated the intelligent ones. Rejecting the Boiotians, they are 'Athenian Boiotians'.[16] These lines are by Xenon:[17]

> They're all tax-men (*telōnes*), all robbers.
> I wish an evil tax (*telos*)[18] would fall due for the Oropians!

---

[12] Lysippos was a C5 comic playwright, but the authenticity of the last nine lines is disputed.
[13] The Heliaia lawcourt.
[14] If there were any doubt about the continuing prosperity of central Greece under the early Successors, this passage should quell it. Cf. Shipley 2018, ch. 4.
[15] i.e. not yet brought in.
[16] Oropos periodically changed from an Athenian to a Boiotian *polis* and back again.
[17] Unidentified.   [18] Also meaning 'end'.

TANAGRA

8. From here to Tanagra is 130 stades. The road runs through olive-planted and densely wooded land, purifying one of all fear of thieves. The city is rough and upland; white in appearance like clay. It is very finely crafted in the entrances of the houses and their encaustic decoration. In edible crops from the land it is not very generous, but among the wine made in Boiotia it is in the first position.   9. Those living there shine brightly in their fortunes, but are frugal in their lifestyle. All of them are farmers, not labourers.[19] They are good at ensuring justice, trust, hospitality. From what they have, they prioritize giving to the needy among the citizens and to wanderers among immigrants, and freely give them a share; thus they are strangers to any unjust greed. It is the safest city for foreigners to stay in of those in Boiotia. One finds there a plain-speaking, rather severe condemnation of evil, because of the self-sufficiency and industry of the inhabitants.   10. A passion for any variety of self-indulgence is a thing I observed least of all in this city; it is, by and large, the cause of the greatest injustices among humankind. For where there is enough to live on, passion for gain does not flourish, and it is difficult for evil to arise among such people.

PLATAIAI

11. From here to Plataiai is 200 stades. The road is quiet, deserted, and rocky, extending up to Kithairon, and not particularly risky. The city, according to the comic playwright Poseidippos,[20] is as follows:

> There are two temples, a stoa, and the name,
> plus the bath-house and the fame of Serambos;
> mostly a headland, during the Eleutheria (*Freedom Festival*) it's a city.

The citizens have nothing to tell, other than that they are colonists of the Athenians, and that it was in their land that the battle of the Greeks and Persians occurred. They are 'Athenian Boiotians'.[21]

THEBES

12. From here to Thebes is 80 stades. The road is all smooth and level. The city lies in the middle of the land of the Boiotians, having a circumference of 70 stades. It is entirely flat, round in form, and like black earth in colour because it is old; but its town-plan is new because it has now been razed three times, as the histories say, on account of the heavy-handedness and pride of the inhabitants.   13. It is a good place

---

[19] Possibly a tongue-in-cheek remark, given the notable production of terracotta figurines at Tanagra.
[20] C3e writer of comedies.   [21] Like the Oropians, fr. 1 §7.

for maintaining horses; it is all well-watered, green and hilly, having the most gardens of all the cities in Hellas. For rivers flow through it, two in number, watering the whole of the plain below the city. Water is also borne invisibly from the Kadmeia,[22] carried in pipes created, they say, by Kadmos in olden times.

14. So much for the nature of the city. The people living it are great-hearted and admirable for their optimistic attitude to life; but bold, abusive, and proud; brawlers, indifferent to any stranger or citizen, and turning their back upon any form of justice. 15. In regard to disputed transactions, they do not reach a resolution by words, but by impetuously deploying violence with their hands; thus transferring to the process of justice the violent acts experienced at the hands of competitors in gymnasium contests. 16. This is why court cases between them are drawn out for at least thirty years. For he who makes mention of such a circumstance in the presence of the mass (*of citizens*), and does not straightaway remove himself from Boiotia but remains in the city for even a very short time, is not long afterwards discovered at night by those who do not wish the case to be concluded,[23] and punished with a violent death. Murders occur among them upon any excuse.[24]

17. It turns out, then, that the men have this character. But some among them are worthy of mention, great-hearted, worthy of total friendship. Their women, when one considers their stature, gait, movements, are the most elegant and good-looking of all the women of Hellas. Sophokles testifies to it:

> You speak to me of Thebes, the seven-mouthed gates,
> where alone the mortal women give birth to gods.

18. Their head is covered by their cloak (*himation*) in such a way that all their face seems to be constricted by a small mask. For only their eyes are showing, while the remaining portions of their face are entirely covered by the cloak. All of them wear cloaks that are white. 19. Their hair is fair, tied up on the top of the head, in what is called by locals a 'little torch'. Their shoe is slender, not deep, crimson in colour and low; it has eyelets, so that the feet appear almost naked. 20. In their social dealings they are not particularly Boiotian women, more like Sikyonian. Their speech is charming, but that of their menfolk is joyless and heavy.

21. The city is one of the best in which to spend the summer, for it has plentiful water that is cold, and also gardens. Its winds are kindly, and it has a green appearance, being productive of fruits and generous in regard to summer market produce. But it has no timber, and is one of the worst places in which to spend the winter, because of the rivers and the winds; indeed, it even endures snow and has a lot of mud.

---

[22] The low acropolis of the city.   [23] i.e. are prepared to start an on-going feud.

[24] HK's criticism of Theban public life echoes those of Aristotle, *Politics* 5. 3, and foreshadows those of Polybios 20. 4.

22. These lines are by Laon.[25] He writes in praise of them (*the Thebans*), not telling the truth: for when he was seized for adultery he was let go after buying off the injured party for a small consideration:[26]

Love the Boiotian man but never shun
the Boiotian lady: for he is noble, she adorable.

ANTHEDON

23. From here to Anthedon is 160 stades, a crooked wagon-road; the journey is through fields. The city is of no great size, and lies right upon the Euboian sea.[27] It has a marketplace entirely planted with trees and enclosed by double stoas. The city itself is well provided with wine and fine cuisine, but poorly endowed with grain because the land is woeful. 24. The inhabitants are nearly all fishermen making their living from hooks and fish, as well as from purple and sponges. They have grown old on beaches, seaweed, and huts; red in complexion and all slim, but the ends of their nails eaten away by their labours at sea; the majority passionate ferrymen and boat-builders, generally not working the land and possessing none, asserting that they are descendants of Glaukos the Man of the Sea, whom all agree was a fisherman.

OVERVIEW OF BOIOTIA

25. Such, then, is the character of Boiotia. For Thespiai has only the ambitious rivalry between its men[28] and (*some*) well-made statues;[29] nothing else. The Boiotians report the particular unfortunate characteristics that exist among them, saying that avarice dwells in Oropos, envy in Tanagra, competitiveness in Thespiai, violent arrogance in Thebes, greed in Anthedon, officiousness in Koroneia, in Plataiai boastfulness, fever in Onchestos, insensibility in Haliartos. The unfortunate characteristics of the whole of Hellas have flowed down into the cities of Boiotia. The line by Pherekrates[30] (*is*):

If you are in your senses, run away from Boiotia.

Such, then, is the character of the land of the Boiotians.

---

[25] C3 comic poet.

[26] For another adultery case at Thebes, where a conviction which was fair, but secured by a man's enemies in a partisan spirit, led to revolution, see Arist. *Pol.* 5. 6.

[27] Fossey 1988, 252 (map, 253), measures the roughly circular walled area of the city at *c*.600 × *c*.600 m (*c*.36 ha, *c*.90 acres).

[28] Or 'has no distinction other than its men' (McInerney, 2019), taking *philotimia* to be the result of competition rather than the rivalry itself.

[29] The MS reads 'not made' (*ou pepoiēmenous*), which is illogical unless aniconic images are meant. McInerney 2019 (following Müller in his n. at *FHG* ii. 259–60) prints *eu* for *ou* and translates as 'a few well-made statues', which is appropriate since Thespiai was the location of Praxiteles' *Eros* (Arenz 2013 ad loc., citing i.a. Strabo 9. 2. 25, C410, who says people used to visit Thespiai to see it). Paus. 9. 27. 5 mentions two other works by P. at Thespiai.

[30] C5 comic playwright.

CHALKIS

26. From Anthedon to Chalkis is 70 stades.[31] Up to Salganeus the road runs beside the shore, and is entirely level and gentle. On one side it extends to the sea, on the other it has a mountain by it, not high but with groves of trees and irrigated by water from springs.

27. The city of the Chalkidians is 80 stades (*in circumference*), greater than the road leading to it from Anthedon; all hilly and shaded, possessing water sources mostly salty, but one only a little salty though healthy in use and cold: namely, the one flowing from the fountain called Arethousa, which has the capacity to provide the flow from the spring to all those living in the city. 28. In the matter of public projects, too, the city is unusually well equipped with gymnasium, stoas, sanctuaries, theatre, paintings, statues, and the agora, whose location is unsurpassed with regard to the needs of business. 29. For the current from Salganeus in Boiotia and from the sea of the Euboians,[32] converging upon the same point at the Euripos, is borne past the very walls of the harbour; this turns out to be the location of the gateway to the trading-centre, and this is adjoined by the marketplace, which is wide and enclosed by three stoas. Since the harbour lies close to the marketplace, and the offloading of cargoes from ships is rapid, many is the man who sails into this trading-place. Indeed, the Euripos, having a double entrance, draws the trader into the city.

30. The whole of the territory is olive-planted. The sea is good too. The inhabitants are Hellenes not only by descent but also in their speech. They are at home in the sciences, fond of travelling, literate, bearing nobly the difficulties that have befallen them because of their homeland. Enslaved for a long time now, but free in their character, they have acquired a firm habit of bearing lightly what befalls them. This line is by Philiskos:[33]

Truly a city of noble Hellenes is Chalkis.

2   Codex Parisinus Graecus 571 (15th c.), fo. 430[r–v] (includes beginning of fr. 3)

MOUNT PELION

1. The mountain called Pelion is large and afforested, containing as many fruiting trees as is the case on lands with cultivated crops.[34] The greatest and most overgrown root of the mountain is 7 stades distant from the city (*Demetrias*) by water, 20 on foot. 2. The whole mountain is gentle, hilly, and productive. Every species of timber

---

[31] Travelling E, HK leaves Boiotia from its N limit.

[32] Perhaps meaning the coastal routes from the NW along the SW and SE sides of the gulf respectively; see Arenz's *FGrH* commentary ad loc.

[33] Comic playwright of c.C4e.

[34] The Pelion range is the main core of Magnesia, the long promontory running NW–SE and separating Thessaly from the sea.

grows on it, but it is particularly rich in beech, fir, Olympian maple, other maples, and also cypress and cedar. Flowers also grow on it: so-called wild lilies and rose campions.

3. There also grows, especially in its driest places, a plant that is also a root, that of the arum, which cures the bites of snakes and appears to be dangerous to them: those from the area where it grows, it drives far away by its smell; those that come close, it disables by casting them into a deep sleep; those that touch it, it kills by its smell.   4. Such is the power it possesses. By humans, however, it is perceived as sweet; for its scent is very like that of the thyme in flower. Given in wine, it heals those bitten by a snake of any sort.[35]

5. There also grows on the mountain the fruit of a thorny plant very like white myrtles.[36] When one pounds this with olive oil and rubs it on the body, one receives no sensation of the severest winter, or almost none; neither of burning in the summer. The medicine by its coagulation prevents the outside air from penetrating the body deeply.[37]   6. This fruit is rare, however, growing in ravines and in precipitous localities, so that one will hardly find it; and if someone does find it, they will not easily be able to take it; and if they try to take it, they risk tumbling from the rocks and being destroyed. Its power remains for a year; aged longer, it loses its own capacity.

7. Rivers flow through the mountain range, two in number: that called Krausindon and the Brychon;[38] the former watering the fields that lie under the crests of Pelion, the latter flowing beside the forest of Pelaia and discharging into the sea.

8. On the peak at the summit of the mountain is a cave, the one called Cheironion,[39] and a sanctuary of Zeus Aktaios. At the rising of the Dog (*Star*), during the maximum heat,[40] an ascent is made by the citizens who are most distinguished and in the prime of life, who are chosen in the presence of the priest. They are garbed in new fleeces of triple thickness, such is the cold that occurs on the mountain.

9. One side of the mountain extends along Magnesia and Thessaly, being turned towards the west wind and the setting of the sun. The other is inclined upon Athos and the gulf called Makedonikos, and has land that is all maritime and rougher than that turned to Thessaly.

10. The mountain is rich in medicaments,[41] and has many and varied potencies for those who know their appearance and are able to use them. It has a particular one with different and dissimilar powers.[42] The tree grows to a size of no more than a cubit (*c.18 inches, c.45 cm*) visible above ground; but in colour it is black. The root grows to the

---

[35] Aside from the magical properties attributed to it here, arum in various varieties is a medicinal herb with toxic properties (details in McInerney 2019 ad loc).

[36] This has not been definitively identified; McInerney 2019 ad loc. suggests a variety of alkanet and notes the ancient medicinal uses of myrtle itself.

[37] Cf. B. 4.

[38] Not attested elsewhere; according to McInerney, Pfister identifies the Krausindon as the *Méga* (sc. *Réma*) in SW Pelion, and the Brychon as one of the streams flowing E into the Aegean.

[39] After the centaur Cheiron, mentioned at §12 below.

[40] The heliacal rising (for this term, see n. above on *AWP* 2. 2) of Sirius takes place in August.

[41] As observed earlier by Theophrastos, *HP* 9. 15. 4.

[42] Unidentified; McInerney 2019 ad loc. suggests mullein (*Verbascum*).

same distance underground. 11. The root of it, pounded finely and shaped for application, drives out the pains of gout sufferers and prevents the tendons from becoming inflamed. The bark, pounded to a smooth consistency and drunk with wine, gives healing to those with bowel problems. The leaves, if pounded and applied to the linen cloth used by those with eye infections who are afflicted by discharge and are at risk of having their sight ruined, gently inhibit the persistent discharge, and as if in response to entreaty the discharge is no longer carried onto the eyes. 12. One family among the citizens (*of Demetrias*) knows of this power; they are said to be descended from Cheiron. Father hands it on and shows it to son, and thus the power is protected, since none other among the citizens knows it. It is an impiety for those who understand the medicines to help sufferers for gain; it must be free.

It turns out, then, that Pelion and Demetrias have this character.

3   Codex Parisinus supplément grec 443, pp. 121. 24–123. 19

THESSALY

1. I take the Peloponnese as the beginning of Hellas, and set its limit at the inlet of the Magnesians, ⟨Homolion, and the Thessalians⟩. Of course, some say those of us who number Thessaly as belonging to Hellas are ignorant; they are unacquainted with the truth of things. 2. For Hellas, which once was just a city in olden times, was named after Hellen son of Zeus and founded by him. It belonged to the land of the Thessalians, lying right between Pharsalos and the city of the Melitaians. For these people are Hellenes by ancestry, and use the Hellenic ways of speech that come from Hellen. The Athenians are those occupying Attica; they are Attic by ancestry and 'atticize' in their spoken language, just as the Dorians descended from Doros 'dorize' in their speech, those descended from Aiolos 'aiolize', and those from Ion son of Xouthos 'ionicize'.[43] So Hellas, whenever it existed, was in Thessaly, not in Attica.[44] The poet (*Homer*), anyhow, says:

> Myrmidones they were called, and Hellenes and Achaians.

He says Myrmidones are those dwelling around the Phthia in Thessaly; Hellenes the people mentioned a little above; and Achaians those who still today dwell in Meliteia, the Larissa called Kremaste, and Thebai Achaïides (*Achaian Thebes*), formerly called Phylake,[45] from which came Protesilaos who was in the expedition to Ilion (*Troy*).[46] Thus Hellas is both a city founded by Hellen, and a land. 3. Euripides testifies to it:[47]

> For Hellen, as they say, was born of Zeus.
> His son was Aiolos. Of Aiolos came Sisyphos,

---

[43] A literal translation, consistent with the preceding words, would be 'ionize'; but that has a scientific meaning.

[44] A dig at the Athenians' superiority complex; cf. §7.

[45] Also called Phthiotic Thebes, in the district of Thessaly called Achaia Phthiotis. Phylake appears in the Homeric Catalogue (see Prologue to these volumes, l. 695).

[46] Cf. *Iliad* 2. 681–711, in the Prologue.   [47] In his *Aiolos*.

Athamas, Kretheus, and he who into the streams
of Alpheios, god-maddened, cast the flame: Salmoneus.

4. It is Hellas, therefore, as we have stated just above, that Zeus' son Hellen founded, from which the expression 'to hellenize' (*hellēnizein, speak Greek*) takes its designation. Hellenes are the people descended from Hellen; these are Aiolos, Sisyphos, and moreover Athamas and Salmoneus, and the offspring born from them.   5. But while Hellas is now referred to, it does not exist. For I say that 'to hellenize' does not consist in discoursing correctly, but in the genesis of the speech; and this comes from Hellen. Hellas lies in Thessaly; therefore we shall say that those people inhabit Hellas and 'hellenize' in their speech.   6. If, with respect to its specific descent, Hellas belongs to Thessaly, it is also fair that in common use, as people are now named Hellenes, Thessaly should be part of Hellas.

7. That everything we have enumerated is Hellas is attested for us by the comic playwright Poseidippos,[48] who censures the Athenians because they declare that their own speech and their own city are those of Hellas. He puts it thus:

Hellas is one, the cities numerous.
You atticize whenever you use your own
speech; but we Hellenes hellenize.
Why, consorting with syllables and letters,
do you turn dexterity into unpleasantness?

8. In response to those who do not accept that Thessaly belongs to Hellas, or that the Thessalians, being descendants of Hellen, speak Greek, let the above be an adequate statement.[49] Having defined Hellas as extending up to the (*sea*) inlet of the Thessalians and to the Magnesians' (*city of*) Homolion,[50] and having made our exposition, we end our account.

B. OTHER TEXTS

4   Apollonios Paradoxographos, *Stories about Wonders*, 19

Herakleides Kritikos,[51] in the (*book*) *On the Cities in Hellas*, says that around Mount Pelion there grows a fruiting thorn-bush (*akantha*), and that if one pounds its fruit with olive oil and water and anoints one's body or that of another person with it, when it is winter, one will not feel the cold.

---

[48] Poseidippos of Kassandreia, writing in C3f.   [48] The quotation seems irrelevant to his point.
[50] Cf. Ps.-Skylax §65. 2, where the end of 'continuous Hellas' is the frontier between Thessaly and Macedonia.
[51] *Krētikos* ('Cretan') in the MS; Giannini adopts an earlier scholar's emendation, which Pfister and subsequent editors follow.

APPENDIX: ANONYMOUS DESCRIPTION
OF PIRAEUS (*BNJ* 369)

P. Hawara 80–1

Preceding Herakleides Kritikos in *BNJ* is a short text from the same era which merits close attention.[52] It is on a very damaged scrap of papyrus from the 1st century AD, containing remnants of a detailed description of the Piraeus composed probably in the 3rd century BC. While less literary and philosophical than fragments 1–3 above, and more focused on physical and monumental structures, it appears to include both historical and legendary material, and raises possibilities about the range of readers to whom written accounts of geography (in some sense of that word) were of interest in the early hellenistic period.[53]

The translation uses Sickinger's text. Square brackets indicate illegible or missing letters.

(fr. 1) [—] harbour [—] ship[yards? —] surrounded by others (?) [—] Now in Zea[54] a h[arbour —] containing shipsheds. T[o the so]uth a sundial [—] hour the sun casts ea[ch shadow].   (2) But in Moun[ichia] is [the fa]mous [sanctuary] of Artemis], surrounded by walls [—] Thrasymedes [—] setting aside [—] account [—] brought down [—].   (3) In total [— of Pir]aeus a wall ninet[y stades? — is en]closed [—] stades [—] hip[p-[55] —] work of [—]seus.[56]   (4) The forty stades bet[ween this and the town] are enclosed with wal[ls, a northern and] a southern. [These they call the Long] Legs, not without reason; [they are the] most reno[wned] in Europe.   (5) From [Phaleron?] there used to extend [beyond] Sikelia[57] for [five and thir]ty stades [a third wall, making the?] total amount [one hundred and fif?]teen, [—] deducted [—]. The city is the work of Theseus [—] synoikized [—]

(fr. 2) [—] dancers [—] dedications (?) [—] art [—] each [—] envy [—].[58]

---

[52] Sickinger 2020; first fully published by Wilcken 1910; original now lost. For its context, see McInerney 2019 (on Herakleides Kritikos), 'Biographical essay'.

[53] There seems to be nothing to link the two texts directly.

[54] One of the two smaller natural harbours at Piraeus.

[55] Possibly a reference to the town planner Hippodamos of Miletos (on whom see i.a. Shipley 2005, 356–65), or to a hippodrome.

[56] Perhaps Theseus is named here, as lower down.

[57] A hill in Athens, Paus. 8. 11. 12.   [58] This passage may describe a sanctuary.

12

ERATOSTHENES OF KYRENE

(C.280–C.200 BC)

D. Graham J. Shipley

Quite a gentle old age, not dark disease,
   snuffed you out. You fell into the sleep you deserved,
Eratosthenes, who meditated on the heights. Maternal
   Kyrene received you not into your fathers' graves,
Aglaos' son, still dear though veiled in foreign soil
   beside this margin of the shore of Proteus.

Dionysios of Kyzikos, in *Anthologia Graeca*, 7. 78
(BNJ 241 T 6)

INTRODUCTION

Eratosthenes of Kyrene (*Cyrene*) was born in the 280s or 270s BC and reportedly lived to the age of 80 or beyond.[1] As head of the Alexandrian library under Ptolemy III (r. 246–222), he made contributions to many fields; most relevant here are his efforts to improve on the cartographic methods of earlier pioneers, and his notional division of the inhabited portion of the globe (the *oikoumenē*) into separate topographical units. In later centuries he was remembered as a philologist and a poet, but above all for a single piece of research: the measurement of the size of the Earth, which he effected more rigorously than his predecessors. Though a renowned polymath, he was once nicknamed Beta ('Number Two')[2] because, though more learned overall than any other single scholar, he ranked only second in any given discipline; the tag has adhered but should not be taken seriously.

His early writings focused upon mathematics and historical chronology, and may have included the *Katasterismoi* (*Catasterisms*), which is extant and catalogues the constellations into which mythical figures have been turned.[3]

---

[1] See Roller 2015, 121–30, for an overview of E. His birthdate is given as Olympiad 126 = 276–273 by *Suda* ε 2898 s.v. Eratosthenes (*BNJ* 241 T 1 in Pownall 2009; appendix 2 no. 1 at Roller 2010, 269), but as *c*.285 by Roller 2010, ix. A floruit of 214/3 is given by Eusebios (*BNJ* 241 T 4) but is probably neither E.'s 40th year nor his date of death (Pownall ad loc.). The poignant epitaph by Dionysios of Kyzikos is quoted above.   [2] *Suda* s.v. Eratosthenes.

[3] The work survives in a confused tradition: Pàmias i Massana and Zucker 2013 accept the attribution to E.; Robinson 2013, 446–9, is more cautious.

Eratosthenes' calculated value for the circumference of the Earth was 252,000 stades (29 §7, 34, 41).[4] This was arrived at by measuring the difference between the sun's shadow at midday on the summer solstice at Syene (*Aswan*), where it was proved to be directly at the zenith as expected (61 §36), and comparing it with that at Alexandria some 525 miles (850 km) to the north. It is tempting to speculate that the support afforded by Ptolemaic patronage was the key difference between his measurement and earlier ones: Aristotle had estimated 400,000 stades (*On the Heavens*, 2. 14, 298a 15–17), while Dikaiarchos may have proposed 300,000 stades some years later (Dikaiarchos 8). Later Hipparchos would propose correcting Eratosthenes' figure to just less than 278,000 (Hipparchos 41). Eratosthenes appears to have set out his method in a dedicated treatise *On the Measurement of the Earth*, though the material is hard to sift from what appears to have been contained in book 2 of his *Geography*. As with several other authors in these volumes, the problem in assessing their geographical work is that their original writings do not survive.

To the two works already mentioned we can add books *On Good and Bad Things*, *Hermes* (a short epic poem), and of course the book that is our immediate concern, the *Geographia* or *Geographika*.[5] This was largely driven by the cartographic aims of improving on previous maps of the Earth and systematizing the use of latitude and longitude,[6] for example by developing further Dikaiarchos' concept of a central parallel of latitude (Chapter 9 above, e.g. no. 11; see 52 §33).[7] Though he is recognized today as the probable coiner of the word *geōgraphia*, Eratosthenes' own geography was superseded as knowledge increased. Indeed, for him more than for any author, we rely heavily on the assessment made by Strabo, though the latter's allusive writing style sometimes creates ambiguity over who he is citing or paraphrasing at any given moment.[8] At least one passage (the first part of 29), at any rate, is thought to be a virtual transcript of Eratosthenes' words, as the tone is unlike Strabo's own.[9] Generally, Strabo approves of him, with the exception of what he takes to be an insufficiently reverent attitude towards the geographical knowledge of Homer (3–9, 11, 19, 26), whom he sometimes calls simply 'the poet'. He criticizes Eratosthenes' over-credulous use of poor sources (12), but also defends him from criticisms by Hipparchos (e.g. 14, 48, 52).

The *Geographia* or *Geographika* was a largely desk-based piece of research, though the author (who came from Kyrene but worked in Alexandria) is known to have travelled to the Peloponnese (66) and evidently visited Rhodes (60). Book 1 (1–23) appears to have contained a discussion of Homeric geography, general considerations on the nature of the Earth, including the behaviour of tides and sea currents (14), and a

---

[4] See also e.g. Hipparchos 40a, 41; *Hypotyposis* §1. Dueck 2012, 72–3, discusses different estimates of the size of the Earth.

[5] Geus 2014–15, 6–7. Strabo 1. 1. 2, C15, cites the first as *On Good Things*.

[6] Geus 2002, ch. 8 (pp. 260–88); Geus 2007.

[7] See Roller 2015, 124–5 & n. 25; below, 52 §33. See also Dueck 2012, 95, on E.'s expansion of Dikaiarchos' use of parallel(s).

[8] Roller 2010, 16.   [9] Roller 2010, 21.

section on 'fantasies and fabrications' (15–23).[10] In book 2 (24–41), Eratosthenes turned to the shape of the Earth and its latitudinal zones, introducing the term *spondylos* (vertebra or spindle-whorl; 29–30) to characterize the curved surface of the inhabited portion or *oikoumenē*, and likening it to an outspread cloak (*chlamys*; 29 §6, 57). The third book (42–127) focused more, but not exclusively, on regional description, beginning from India in the east and moving west, and is considered innovative by reason of its organization in terms of geographical units rather than ethnic communities (e.g. 46).[11] Another homely metaphor, the *sphragis* or 'sealstone' (52 §22, 73), which in the Egyptian system also meant a surveyed parcel of land (possibly oblong with round corners), was used to describe the major geographical units making up the *oikoumenē* such as India (covered in 47–9, 52 §§19–22, 72, 77–81, 101), Ariane (52 §22, 80–1), and Mesopotamia (41, 52 §23–7, 86), but Eratosthenes may have considered it unworkable and does not appear to have used it systematically for places further west, if Strabo's treatment of the *Geography* is reliable in this respect.[12] The last part of the work turned to western and northern Europe including the British Isles (18, 25–6, 29, 52 §41), for which Eratosthenes used Pytheas, of whom Strabo (following Polybios) disapproves (18, 26 §5, 29 §8, 62).

The present chapter does not contain all of Eratosthenes' work, but is designed to represent his contribution in the area of geography. Roller's compendious translation and commentary on the geographical work (without Greek texts) supersedes earlier collections of material, of which the chief is Berger (still important).[13] The selection below is based on Roller (with some extracts truncated or combined); but, within each book of Eratosthenes' *Geography*, extracts are reordered by the date of their source and their sequence in that source.[14] Those from Strabo are adapted from Roller's 2014 translation, except for passages enclosed in raised points (·), which are mine.

SELECTED FURTHER READING

*Berger, H. (1880), *Die geographischen Fragmente des Eratosthenes*. Leipzig.

Blomqvist, J. (1992), 'Alexandrian science: the case of Eratosthenes', in P. Bilde *et al.* (eds), *Ethnicity in Hellenistic Egypt* (Aarhus), 53–75.

Fraser, P. M. (1972), *Ptolemaic Alexandria*. 3 vols. Oxford. [Pp. 175–207 cover important aspects.]

Geus, K. (2002), *Eratosthenes von Kyrene: Studien zur hellenistischen Kultur- und Wissenschaftsgeschichte*. Munich. [Detailed discussion of Eratosthenes.]

—— (2007), 'Die Geographika des Eratosthenes von Kyrene: Altes und Neues in Terminologie und Methode', in M. Rathmann (ed.), *Wahrnehmung und Erfassung geographischer Räume in der Antike* (Mainz am Rhein), 111–22.

McPhail, C., and Hannah, R. (2008–11), 'Eratosthenes' perception of the Caspian sea: a gulf or an inland sea?', *Orbis Terrarum*, 10: 155–72.

---

[10] These terms are used by Roller 2010, 22.   [11] Roller 2010, 24.   [12] Roller 2010, 26.
[13] Geus 2014–15 calls for a full edition.
[14] Geus 2011, reviewing Roller, comments that the allocation of certain extracts to particular works by E. is uncertain; and notes that some fragments could be added to R.'s collection.

*Pownall, F. (2009), 'Eratosthenes of Cyrene (241)', in *BNJ*. [Focuses on history, chronology; 11 testimonia, 57 non-geographical fragments (numbered 1–48), none included in the present chapter).]

Prontera, F. (2013), 'Timosthenes and Eratosthenes: sea routes and hellenistic geography', in K. Buraselis *et al.* (eds), *The Ptolemies, the Sea and the Nile: Studies in Waterborne Power* (Cambridge), 207–17.

—— (2017), 'The Indian Caucasus from Alexander to Eratosthenes', in C. Antonetti and P. Biagi (eds), *With Alexander in India and Central Asia: Moving East and Back to West* (Oxford), 212–21.

Roller, D. W. (2010), *Eratosthenes' Geography: Fragments Collected and Translated.* Princeton. [Some translations from Strabo are superseded by his 2014 volume.]

Zimmermann, K. (2002), 'Eratosthenes' chlamys-shaped world: a misunderstood metaphor', in D. Ogden (ed.), *The Hellenistic World: New Perspectives* (Swansea/London), 23–40.

GEOGRAPHIA OR *GEOGRAPHIKA*

BOOK 1

1   **Strabo** 1. 1. 1, C1–2: *Pioneers of geography*
·We consider that geography is part of the business of a philosopher, if anything is. . . . For the first men bold enough to grasp it were such as Homer, Anaximandros of Miletos, Hekataios—his (*fellow*) citizen, as Eratosthenes also says—as well as Demokritos, Eudoxos, Dikaiarchos, Ephoros, and several others; and those who came after them, Eratosthenes, Polybios, and Poseidonios, were still philosophers (*practising geography*).·[15]

2   **Strabo** 1. 1. 11, C7: *Pioneers of geography*
·What I have said may now be taken as evidence that Homer was the pioneer[16] of geography (*geōgraphia*). Those who followed him are conspicuously notable as men and as adherents of philosophy. The first two of them, after Homer, are said by Eratosthenes to have been Anaximandros, a close associate and fellow-citizen of Thales, and Hekataios of Miletos. (*He says that*) the former was the first to publish a geographical map (*pinax*),[17] while the latter left a treatise (*gramma*) which is inferred from his other writing (*graphē*) to be his.·[18]

---

[15] This, the beginning of Strabo's *Geography*, and his succeeding chapters on E.'s geographical predecessors (though S. focuses mainly on Homer), probably give a good indication of how E.'s own opening pages were structured (Roller 2010, 111).

[16] Lit. 'began (ἦρξεν–*ērxen*) geography'.

[17] On the meaning of *pinax*, see the Introduction, §V, and the Glossary. Cf. Hekataios 5 and 9–10 (in Ch. 3 above).

[18] E. probably discussed these predecessors more fully than Strabo (Roller 2010, 124).

3   Strabo 1. 2. 3, C15–17: *Homer's geography*

He (*Eratosthenes*) says that all poets attempt to amuse rather than teach. On the contrary, the ancients say that poetry is foremost a pursuit of knowledge, introduced into our life from youth, and which teaches with pleasure about character, emotion, and actions. Moreover, we say that only the poet is wise. For this reason the Hellenic cities educate their youth in poetry first of all, presumably not for the sake of mere amusement but to learn morality. Even musicians, teaching plucking, lyre playing, and pipe playing, claim this virtue, for they say that such an education improves character. One may hear this said not only by the Pythagoreans, but Aristoxenos[19] maintains the same thing. And Homer said that the singers were chastisers, as in the case of the guardian of Clytemnestra, 'whom Atreides, going to Troy, strictly commanded to guard his wife'.[20] Aigisthos was not able to prevail over her before 'he took the singer to a deserted island and left him there . . . and then willingly led her, willing, to his home'.[21]

Apart from this, Eratosthenes contradicts himself. Shortly before he said this, at the beginning of his geographical treatise, he says that from earliest times all of them (*the poets*) have eagerly placed themselves in the mainstream of that discipline. For example, whatever Homer learned about the Aithiopes he recorded in his poem, as well as about the Egyptians and Libyans. Yet insofar as Hellas and the neighbouring places are concerned, he elaborated excessively, saying that Thisbe is dove-rich, Haliartos is grassy, Anthedon is the farthest, and Lilaia is by the Kephissian springs, but he also never threw out a useless qualification.[22] Is someone who does this an entertainer or a teacher? By Zeus the latter, you say, but that which is beyond perception he (*Homer*) and others have filled with legendary marvels.

He (*Eratosthenes*) should have said that every poet writes for the sake of mere entertainment and teaching, but he said 'merely for entertainment and not for teaching'. He meddles still further when he asks how it contributes to the quality of the poet to become skilled in places or military command or farming or rhetoric or whatever else others might wish him to have acquired. ·Well, to seek to endow him (*Homer*) with everything is a thing one might attribute to a person transcending the bounds of ambition. Hipparchos says that if one were to attach to an Attic festival-wreath a quantity of apples and pears it could not support, that would be the same as attributing to him (*Homer*) every aspect of learning and every art.· You may be right, Eratosthenes, about that, but you are not right when you take away from him (*Homer*) his great learning, and declare that his creativity is the mythology of an old woman, who has been allowed to fabricate, as you say, whatever appears for her own amusement.

4   Strabo 1. 2. 7, C18: *Homer's geography*

But he (*Homer*) does not speak only of nearby places—as Eratosthenes says—those within Hellas, but also many far away. Homer tells myths more accurately than later

---

[19] Fr. Ia 305 in Kaiser 2010.   [20] *Od.* 3. 267–8.   [21] *Od.* 3. 270–2 (with omission).
[22] *Il.* 2. 502, 503, 508, and 523 (see Prologue).

mythological authors, not totally recounting marvels, but for the sake of knowledge, using allegory, revision, and popularity, especially concerning the wanderings of Odysseus, about which he (*Eratosthenes*) makes many mistakes, maintaining that the commentators and the Poet himself are nonsense.[23]

5 **Strabo 1. 2. 11–14, C21–3: *Homer's geography***
(11) Having set forth these preliminaries, it is necessary to ask what is meant by those who say that according to Homer the wanderings of Odysseus were around Sikelia (*Sicily*) and Italia.[24] This can be understood in two ways, one better and the other worse. The better is to accept that he believed the wanderings of Odysseus were there, and taking this as the truth, elaborated this assumption poetically. One could naturally say this about him, and one can find vestiges of the wanderings—and those of many others—not only around Italia but in the farthest regions of Iberia. The worse interpretation is to accept the elaboration as historical, because Okeanos, Hades, the cattle of Helios, hospitality by goddesses, transformations, large Kyklopes and Laistrygonians, the shape of Skylla, the distances sailed, and many other similar things are clearly writings about marvels. But it is not worth refuting someone who is so clearly in error about the Poet, as if one could not say that the return of Odysseus to Ithaca and the slaughter of the Suitors and the battle in the country between them and the people of Ithaca happened in that very way. It is also not proper to attack someone who interprets it correctly.

(12) Eratosthenes has confronted both of these reasons, but not well. In the second case, he believes that he (*Homer*) attempts to misrepresent something obviously false and unworthy of a lengthy discussion, and in the former, that all poets tell falsehoods and that their experience of places or the arts does not lead to virtue. Myths are related both about uninvented places, such as Ilion, Ida, and Pelion, and also about invented ones, such as where the Gorgons and Geryon are. He (*Eratosthenes*) says that those mentioned in the wanderings of Odysseus are also a construct, and that those who say they are not invented but substantiated are convicted of falsehood because they do not agree with one another. At any rate, some put the Seirenes on Pelorias (*Faro*),[25] and others on the Seirenoussai, more than 2,000 stades away—allegedly the three-headed promontory that separates the Kymaian and Poseidoniate gulfs. But this rock (*C. Sorrento*) is not three-pointed, nor does its summit come at all to a head, but a kind of elbow projects out, long and narrow, from the region of Syrrenton (*Sorrento*) to the strait of Kapria (*Capri I.*), having the sanctuary of the Seirenes on one side of the mountainous ridge. On the other, towards the Poseidoniate gulf, lie three deserted

---

[23] The debate over locations in the Homeric poems intensified in C3, with legendary locations tending to be placed further from Old Greece as maritime knowledge grew; E. was probably introduced to the debate by his teacher Zenon of Kition (Roller 2010, 114).
[24] This view is, however, held today: e.g. Roller 2015, 19. In this extract, it is not always possible to sift Strabo's argument from that of E.
[25] The NE cape of Sicily.

and rocky islets that are called the Seirenes.[26] The Athenaion is on the strait itself, from which the elbow is named.

(13) Moreover, even if those who have handed down the account of these places are not in agreement, frankly we should not throw out the entire account, since on the whole it may be more believable. As an example, I would ask whether it is said that the wanderings were around Sikelia or Italia, and that the Seirenes are somewhere around there. The one who says that they are in Pelorias disagrees with the one putting them on the Seirenoussai, but both of them do not disagree with someone saying that they are around Sikelia and Italia, yet provide him greater credibility, for although they do not point out the same place, nonetheless they do not depart from the region of Italia and Sikelia. If, then, someone were to add that a memorial of Parthenope, one of the Seirenes, is visible in Neapolis (*Naples*), there is even more credibility, although this is mentioning a third place. Moreover, Neapolis lies in this gulf (*Bay of Naples*), which Eratosthenes calls the Kymaian and which is formed by the Seirenoussai, and thus we can believe even more strongly that the Seirenes were around these places. The Poet did not learn about each accurately, nor do we seek accuracy from him, but nonetheless we do not assume that he learned to sing about the wanderings without (*knowing*) where or how they happened.

(14) Eratosthenes infers that Hesiod learned that the wanderings of Odysseus were throughout Sikelia and Italia, and believing this, recorded not only those places mentioned by Homer, but also Aitna (*Etna*), Ortygia[27]—the little island next to Syracuse— and Tyrrhenia (*Tuscany*),[28] yet Homer did not know them and did not wish to put the wanderings in known places. Are Aitna and Tyrrhenia well known, but Skyllaion and Charybdis, Kirkaion, and the Seirenoussai not at all? Is it fitting for Hesiod not to talk nonsense and to follow prevailing opinions, yet for Homer 'to shout forth everything that comes to his untimely tongue'? Apart from what has been said concerning the myth which it was fitting for Homer to relate about a place, most of the prose authors who repeat the same things, as well as the customary local reports about these places, can teach that these are not the fantasies of poets or even prose authors but vestiges of peoples and events.

6 Strabo 1. 2. 15, C24: *Homer's geography*
He (*Polybios*)[29] does not approve of the assertion by Eratosthenes, who says that one will find where Odysseus wandered when you find the cobbler who sewed up the hide of winds.[30]

---

[26] The three *Galli*, S of C. *Sorrento* (Roller 2018, 21). [27] Hesiod, fr. 98.
[28] *Theogony*, 1016: 'all the Tyrsenoi'. [29] This citation is designated Polyb. 34. 2. 11.
[30] E.'s point, made again in 7, was that Homer's geography in the *Odyssey* was not meant as a literal description (Roller 2010, 115). For Aiolos sewing up the bag of the winds, see *Od.* 10. 19–20.

7   Strabo 1. 2. 17, C25: *Homer's geography*

To fabricate everything is neither plausible nor Homeric. Everyone believes that his poetry is a scholarly treatise, not like Eratosthenes says, who commands us neither to judge the poems in regard to their thought, nor to seek history in them.

8   Strabo 1. 2. 18–19, C26: *Homer's geography*

When did a poet or prose author persuade the Neapolitans to make a memorial for Parthenope the Seirene, or those in Kyme, Dikaiarcheia, and at Vesuvius[31] for Pyriphleg-ethon, the Acherousian marsh, the oracle of the dead at Aornos, or Baios and Misenos, both companions of Odysseus?[32] It is the same with that about the Seirenoussai, the Strait, Skylla and Charybdis, and Aiolos. This must not be scrutinized carefully or considered without roots or a home, not attached to the truth or any historical benefit.

(19) Eratosthenes himself suspected this, for he says one might understand that the Poet wished to put the wanderings of Odysseus towards western places, but he set aside the idea because he had not learned about them accurately—or because he chose not to do so—in order to develop each element more cleverly and more mar-vellously. He (*Eratosthenes*) understands this correctly, but is wrong in regard to why it was done, since it was not for silliness but for a benefit.[33] Therefore it is proper that he should undergo examination both about this and also why he says that marvellous tales are told about faraway places because it is safe to tell falsehoods about them.

9   Strabo 1. 2. 20–4, C28–30: *Homer's geography*

(20) . . . The Poet spoke accurately: 'Boreas and Zephyros, the Thracian winds,'[34] but he (*Eratosthenes*) does not accept this correctly and quibbles about it, as if he (*Homer*) were speaking generally that the Zephyros blows from Thrace. Yet he is not speaking generally, but about when they come together on the Thracian sea around the Melas (*Black*) gulf,[35] which is a part of the Aigaion itself. For Thrace, where it touches Mace-donia, takes a turn to the south, and forms a promontory into the open sea (*pelagos*), and it seems to those on Thasos, Lemnos, Imbros, Samothrake, and the surrounding sea (*thalatta*) that the Zephyroi (*westerlies*) blow from there, just as for Attica they come from the Skironian rocks, because of which the Zephyroi, and especially the Arg-estes, are called the Skirones. Eratosthenes did not perceive this, although he suspected it. Nevertheless he told about the turn of the land that I have mentioned. He accepts it (*what Homer said*) as universal and then accuses the Poet of ignorance, in that the Zephyros blows from the west and Iberia, but Thrace does not extend that far.[36] . . .

---

[31] Or possibly Baiai; the name is corrupt in the Greek text.

[32] These two men are not, in fact, named in the *Odyssey* but in Lykophron's *Alexandra* (C2), ll. 694, 737 (Roller 2010, 118).

[33] Strabo exaggerates the degree of rationalism attributed to Homer by E., who appears to have grasped that Homer's purposes were entirely literary.

[34] *Il.* 9. 5.   [35] *Saros Körfezi* in the NE Aegean.

[36] Strabo accuses E. of pedantry; but it may be that he was discussing the Homeric passage as part of a general consideration of winds (Roller 2010, 124).

(21) . . . These are the corrections that are to be made at the beginning of the 1st (*book*) of the *Geographika* of Eratosthenes.

(22) Continuing in his assumption about the falsity of Homer, he (*Eratosthenes*) says that he does not even know that there are several mouths to the Nile, or its name, although Hesiod knows, for he records it.[37] Concerning the name, it is probable that it was not yet used in his time. In regard to the mouths, if they were unnoticed or only a few knew that there were several rather than one, it might be granted that he did not know this. . . .

(23) How they reproach him (*Homer*) about this island of Pharos is unreasonable, because he says it is in the open sea (*pelagia*), as if he were speaking from ignorance.[38] . . .

(24) There is the same mistake about his (*Homer's*) ignorance of the isthmus between the Egyptian sea and the Arabian gulf (*Red Sea*), in suggesting that he is wrong in speaking of 'the Aithiopes, divided in two, the farthest of men'.[39] It is correct to say this, and later writers do not rebuke him (*Homer*) justly.

10   Strabo 1. 2. 31, C38: *Changes in seas*
But the isthmus (*between the Mediterranean and Red Sea*) was also not navigable, and what Eratosthenes suggests is not correct. He believes that the breakout at the Pillars had not yet happened and that the inner sea joined the outer sea, and since it was higher, covered the isthmus, but when the breakout occurred it was lowered and thus uncovered the land around Kasion and Pelousion[40] as far as the Erythraian (*sea*).[41]

11   Strabo 1. 2. 37, C44: *Homer's geography*
Apollodoros (*of Athens*) agrees with those around Eratosthenes in censuring Kallimachos, because, although a scholar, he named Gaudos (*Gozo?*) and Korkyra (*Corfù*), in opposition to the Homeric assumption that the places where he says the wanderings occurred were located in the Outer Ocean.[42]

12   Strabo 1. 3. 1–2, C47–8: *Eratosthenes' use of poor authorities*
(1) Eratosthenes does not handle the following well: he discusses men not worthy of remembering, sometimes refuting them, and other times believing in them and using

---

[37] *Theogony*, 338. Homer calls the Nile the river Aigyptos (*Od.* 14. 258, 17. 427). If Strabo is speaking the truth, E. does seem to have written pedantically: Homer did not need to document the mouths of the Nile (cf. Roller 2010, 123).

[38] Pharos I. was less than a mile off the coast at Alexandria (before it was joined to the mainland in C3).

[39] *Od.* 1. 23. Despite his correct understanding that literary purposes were to the fore in Homer, E. again forgets that Homer did not need to document matters not germane to his story. Strabo appears to conflate two separate discussions here; the Aithiopes are divided because some of them were believed to live in West Africa.

[40] At the E limit of the Delta. See, further, **14** §13 below.

[41] 'Erythraian sea' denotes the western Indian Ocean and the mod. *Red Sea*.

[42] Kallimachos, fr. 13 in Pfeiffer 1949–53; Apollodoros (C2l): *BNJ* 244 FF 157d, 413, and 470. Cf. **19** §6 below. Kallimachos had been a researcher and poet at Alexandria in C3f. The controversy may largely have blown up in C2 rather than in E.'s lifetime (Roller 2010, 122–3).

them as authorities, such as Damastes[43] and others like him. Even if there is some truth in what they say, we should not use them as authorities or believe them. On the contrary, we should use only reputable men in this way, those who have generally been correct, and even if they have omitted many things, or not discussed them sufficiently, they have said nothing untrue. But to use Damastes as an authority is no different from invoking as an authority the Bergaian Euhemeros and the others that he (*Eratosthenes*) quotes in order to discredit their nonsense.[44] He tells one of his pieces of trash, that he (*Damastes*)[45] believes the Arabian gulf to be a lake, and that Diotimos the son of Strombichos, leading an Athenian embassy, sailed up the Kydnos from Kilikia to the Choaspes river, which flows by Sousa, arriving at Sousa on the fortieth day. He was told this by Diotimos himself. Then he wonders how it was possible for the Kydnos to cut across the Euphrates and Tigris and empty into the Choaspes.[46]

(2) One would not only disapprove of this, but also because he (*Eratosthenes*) says that the seas were not yet exactly known even in his own time, exhorting us not easily to believe people casually, and rendering at length the reasons that no one should be believed who tells mythic tales, for example about the Pontos and the Adriatic.[47] Yet he himself believes whomever he happens to encounter. Although he believed that the Issic gulf is the most easterly limit of our sea, a point at Dioskourias in the extreme recess of the Pontos is further east by about 3,000 stades, even from the measurement of stades that he himself records.[48] In discussing the northern and extreme areas of the Adriatic, he does not abstain from the fabulous. He also believes many stories about what is beyond the Pillars of Herakles, naming an island called Kerne and other places that are nowhere visible today,[49] concerning which I will also discourse later. He says that the earliest people sailed for piracy or commerce, and did not go into the open sea (*pelagizein*) but along the land, like Jason, who abandoned his ships and made an expedition from the Kolchoi as far as Armenia and Media.[50] Later he says that in antiquity no one dared to sail on the Euxeinos, or along Libyē, Syria, or Kilikia. Now if he means by 'in antiquity' those for whom there is no record in our time, I am not about to speak of them and whether they sailed or not. But if he means those who have been recorded, one would not hesitate to say that those in antiquity are shown to have made longer journeys, whether completed by land or sea, than those later, if we pay attention to what has been said.

---

[43] Damastes of Sigeion: see Introduction, §VI. 4. b.

[44] Bergaian: i.e. liar; cf. n. on Pytheas 6 above. Euhemeros: cf. n. on Pyth. 5.

[45] *BNJ* 5 F 8.

[46] Damastes of Sigeion (*BNJ* 5 F 8), C5l. Diotimos' mission to Sousa is feasible, but not by boat all the way (Roller 2010, 126).

[47] Strabo makes insufficient allowance for the progress in knowledge of these areas since E.'s day (Roller 2010, 126).

[48] But presumably E. did not regard the Black Sea as part of 'our sea' for this purpose (Roller 2010, 126).

[49] But Kerne was real: see Ch. 4, introduction, and n. on Ps.-Skyl. §112. 5 in Ch. 7.

[50] This variation on the Argonautic tale was perhaps a Hl distortion intended to magnify Alexander's achievements (Roller 2010, 127).

13   Strabo 1. 3. 3–4, C48–50: *Geological change*

(3) He (*Eratosthenes*) himself speaks of the great advance made in the knowledge of the inhabited world by those after Alexander and those in his own time, and then proceeds to a discussion about the shape, not of the inhabited world—which would have been more appropriate to his topic—but of the entire Earth. That must also be considered, but not out of its place. He says, then, that in its entirety it is spherical, not as if turned on a lathe, but having certain irregularities, and then he lists the numerous changes in its shape that occur because of water, fire, earthquakes, eruptions, and other such phenomena, but here also he does not preserve the arrangement. The spherical shape of the entire Earth results from the state of the whole, but the changes in form do not alter the Earth as a whole—such small things disappear in great things—although they create in the inhabited world differences from one time to another, with one and another cause.

(4) He says that this presents a particular issue, for why can one see mussel, oyster, and scallop shells in many places 2,000 or 3,000 stades from the sea and in the interior, as well as many lagoons, such as, he says, those around the temple of Ammon[51] and along the road of 3,000 stades to it? A large quantity of oyster shells and much salt is still found there today, and eruptions of salt water spring up to some height. In addition, pieces of wreckage from sea-going ships are visible, which they say have been thrown out of a chasm, and there are small columns with dolphins dedicated on them, having the inscription 'Of the Kyrenaian envoys'.

Then he says that he praises the opinion of Straton, the scientist,[52] and also that of Xanthos the Lydian. Xanthos says[53] that in the time of Artaxerxes (*I*) there was so great a drought that the rivers, lakes, and cisterns became dry, and he had often seen, far from the sea—among the Armenians, Matienoi, and in Lower Phrygia—stones like mollusc shells, sherds like combs, the outlines of scallop shells, and a salt lagoon. Because of this he (*Xanthos*) believed that the plains were once the sea.

Straton engages further in the matter of causes, for he says that he believes the Euxeinos at one time did not have its mouth below Byzantion, but the rivers which empty into it forced it and opened it up, so that the water came out of the Propontis and the Hellespont. The same thing (*says Straton*) occurred in our sea, for here the strait beyond the Pillars was broken through when the sea had been filled by the rivers and the former shallows were uncovered by this flooding. He suggests a cause: first, that the outer and inner seas have a different seabed, and that even today there is a certain undersea ridge running from Europe to Libyē, which shows that formerly the interior and exterior could not have been the same. Around the Pontos (*he says*) it is especially shallow—but the Cretan, Sicilian, and Sardinian seas are very deep—since the rivers flowing from the north and east are numerous, large, and fill it with sediment, but the

---

[51] At the oasis of Ammon in W. Egypt.   [52] Fr. 54 in Desclos and Fortenbaugh 2011.
[53] *BNJ* 765 F 12.

others remain deep; and that this is why the Pontic sea (*thalatta*; *Black Sea*)[54] is the sweetest and why it flows out towards the place that its bed slopes. He believes that the entire Pontos will fill up in the future, if such an influx continues. And even now (*he says*) the area on the left side of the Pontos is already covered with shallow water, such as at Salmydessos and the place called by sailors the *Stēthē* ('*Chests*'),[55] around the Istros, and the Skythian desert; and that perhaps the temple of Ammon was once on the sea but is now in the interior because there has been an outflow of the sea. He (*Straton*) suggests that the oracle with good reason became so famous and well known because it was on the sea, but since it is now so far removed from the sea there is no good reason for its fame and reputation. (*He says that*) in antiquity Egypt was covered by the sea as far as the marshes around Pelousion, Mount Kasion, and Lake Sirbonis (*L. Bardawil*); and that even today when the salty lands in Egypt are excavated, the holes are found to contain sand and mussel shells, as though the land had been submerged and all the territory around Kasion and the place called Gerrha had been covered with shallow water, so that it connected to the Erythraian gulf; and that when the sea gave way they were revealed, although Lake Sirbonis remained, but then it broke through so that there was a marsh; so that in the same way the shores of what is called Lake Moiris[56] resemble more the shores of the sea than the shores of rivers.[57]

One would admit that the greater part of the continents was once flooded at certain times and then uncovered again, and similarly the entire surface of the Earth that is now underwater is uneven, just as, by Zeus, that which is above water—on which we live—receives all the changes of which Eratosthenes himself speaks. Thus one cannot accuse Xanthos of saying anything unreasonable.[58]

14 **Strabo** 1. 3. 11–15, C54–7: *Seas, currents, and change*
(11) But he (*Eratosthenes*) is so ingenuous that even though a mathematician he will not confirm the opinion of Archimedes, who says in his *On Floating Bodies*[59] that all calm and quiet water appears to have a spherical surface, with the sphere having the same centre as the Earth. Everyone who has ever understood mathematics accepts this point of view. He (*Eratosthenes*) says that the inner sea is a single sea, but he does not believe that it has ever been constituted as a single surface, even in neighbouring places. He uses engineers as witnesses for this ignorance, although the mathematicians proclaim that engineering is a part of mathematics. He also says that Demetrios[60] attempted to cut through the Peloponnesian Isthmus to supply a passage for his forces to sail through, but was prevented by the engineers who measured carefully and reported

---

[54] An unusual term for the Black Sea, more usually Euxeinos Pontos.
[55] In the sense of 'torsos'.   [56] *Birket Qarun* in the Fayum Oasis, W of the Delta.
[57] As far as this point it is all the views of Straton, presumably summarized by E. and from him by Strabo.
[58] On the question of change in ancient geographical writing, see Introduction, §III. 4.
[59] Book 1, proposition 2.
[60] Demetrios I Poliorketes, Macedonian king dominant in Greece c.307/6–294.

that the sea level of the Corinthian gulf was higher than at Kenchreai,[61] so that if he were to cut through the intervening land, the entire strait around Aigina, as well as Aigina itself and the nearby islands, would be submerged and the sailing passage would not be useful. This (*he says*) is why narrow straits have strong currents, especially the narrows of Sicily which, he says, are similar to the high and low tides of the Ocean, with the flow changing twice each day and night, and like the Ocean there are two floodings and two withdrawals. He (*Eratosthenes*) says that similar to the flood tide is the current that goes down from the Tyrrhenic to the Sicilian sea, as though from a higher level, which is called 'the descending', and he agrees that it begins and ends at the same time as the high tides. (*He*) also (*says that*) it begins around the rising and setting of the moon and ceases when it reaches either meridian, that above the Earth or below the Earth; and that the one opposite to the ebb tide, called 'the outgoing', begins when the moon is at either meridian, just like the ebb tide, and ceases when it reaches the points of setting and rising.

(12) The flooding and ebbing of the tides has been sufficiently discussed by Poseidonios and Athenodoros.[62] Concerning the rushing back of straits, which is a more scientific discussion than appropriate in this treatise, it is sufficient to say that there is no single explanation for the currents in straits that corresponds to their form, for if so it would not be the case that the Sicilian changes twice a day, as he (*Eratosthenes*) says, and the Chalkidian seven times,[63] or that ·the (*strait*) at Byzantion exhibits no change, but persists in having an outflow (*ekrhous*) only from the Pontic ocean into the Propontis. As Hipparchos records, it sometimes used to undergo interruptions.· If there were a single explanation, the reason would not be what Eratosthenes says, that each sea has a different surface. This would also not be the case with rivers unless they have cataracts, but even having them, they do not flow back but continuously go lower. Thus it would not flow back, nor would it stand still and remain, even when flowing together, as there is not one level, but one that is higher and the other lower. This also happens because the stream and its surface are inclined. But who would say that the surface of the sea is inclined? This is especially because of the theory that the four bodies—which we would call elements—are made to be spherical. The water is not like the Earth, whose state has assumed a solid form, thus having permanent hollows and protuberances, but, through the effect of its weight, it is carried upon the Earth, having the kind of surface that Archimedes says.

(13) Adding to what he (*Eratosthenes*) has said about Ammon and Egypt,[64] he believes that Mount Kasion was once washed by the sea and that the entire region, where what is now called Gerrha is, was covered with shallow water since it was connected with the gulf of the Erythraian (*sea*) becoming uncovered when the seas came

---

[61] The port of Corinth on the Saronic gulf.
[62] *BNJ* 746 F 6b. Athenodoros was a C1 Stoic philosopher and an acquaintance of Cicero.
[63] At the Euripos channel between Euboia and the mainland of central Greece.
[64] See 13 §4 above.

together. To say that the place was covered with shallows and connected to the gulf of the Erythraian is ambiguous, since 'connected' means 'to be near' or 'to touch,' so that, if it is a body of water, one would flow into the other. I believe that the shallows came near to the Erythraian sea while the narrows at the point of the Pillars were closed, and the withdrawal happened because of the lowering of our sea due to the outflow at the Pillars. But Hipparchos argues that 'connected' is the same as our sea 'flowing into' the Erythraian, because of its filling up. Because of the outflow at the Pillars and our sea changing its direction, he demands to know why the Erythraian, which was flowing into it, remained at the same level and was not lowered. According to Eratosthenes himself (*he says*) the entire outer sea flows together and thus the western and Erythraian sea are one. Saying this, he insists that the sea outside the Pillars, the Erythraian, and even that which flowed together into it, have the same height.

(14) But Eratosthenes would say he has not reported that the flowing together with the Erythraian happened at the time of the filling, but only that they were near to one another. It does not follow that one sea that was kept together would have the same height and same surface, as this is not the case in ours, by Zeus, at Lechaion and around Kenchreai. Hipparchos indicates this in his treatise against him. Knowing that this is his opinion, let me speak on his own account against him and let him not presume that someone who says that the outer sea is one would agree that its level is also one.

(15) Saying that the inscription of the Kyrenaian envoys on the dolphin is false, he (*Hipparchos*) provides an implausible reason: that although the founding of Kyrene was in recorded times no one recorded that the oracle (*of Ammon*) was ever on the sea.[65] Even if no one reported this, we can infer from the evidence that the place was once on the coast, since the dolphins were erected and inscribed by the Kyrenaian envoys. He concedes that with the raising of the bed the sea flooded as far as the location of the oracle, somewhat more than 3,000 stades from the sea, but he does not concede that the raised level covered all of Pharos and most of Egypt, as if such a height were not sufficient to cover these also. He also says that if our sea were filled to such a level before the outbreak at the Pillars occurred, as Eratosthenes said, all of Libyē and most of Europe and Asia must first have been covered. He then adds that the Pontos (*Black Sea*) would have begun to flow together with the Adriatic in certain places, since because of the lie of the land the Istros (*Danube*) divides in the region of the Pontos and flows into each sea.[66] But the Istros does not have its source in the Pontos region, but on the contrary, in the mountains above the Adriatic. Moreover, it does not flow into each sea, but only into the Pontos, and it branches only around its mouths. In common with some of those before him he fails to understand his own ignorance, for they believed that a certain river with the same name as the Istros broke away and emptied

---

[65] The text is uncertain here, and consequently the import of the passage likewise (Roller 2010, 133–4).
[66] This view is first expressed at Ps.-Skyl. §20.

into the Adriatic, from which the people through whom it flows took their name,[67] and by this way Jason made his return voyage from Kolchis.

15   Strabo 1. 3. 22, C61–2: *The southern hemisphere*
I return to what is next, from which I was diverted. In regard to what Herodotos said, that there are no Hyperboreans because there are no Hypernotians,[68] Eratosthenes says that this argument is ludicrous and would be like the following sophistry: as if one were to say that there are none who rejoice at the misfortunes of others because there are none who rejoice at the good fortune of others. Moreover it so happens that there are Hypernotians, and anyway the Notos does not blow in Aithiopia but further down.

16   Strabo 1. 3. 23–1. 4. 1, C62: *Fantastical geographies*
3. (23) Next he (*Eratosthenes*) discusses those who clearly speak of fabricated and impossible things—some of which are in the form of myths and others in the form of history—concerning whom it is not worthy to mention. Yet in this subject matter he should not have considered those who are nonsensical.   4. (1) This, then, is his first discussion in the commentaries.[69]

17   Strabo 2. 1. 9, C70: *Fantastical peoples*
Especially worthy of disbelief are Deimachos[70] and Megasthenes,[71] for they write about the Enotokoitai (*Sleep-in-ears*), the Astomoi (*Mouthless*), and the Arrhinoi (*Noseless*), as well as the Monophthalmoi (*One-eyed*), Makroskeleis (*Long-legged*), and Opisthodaktyloi (*Backwards-fingered*).[72] They have also revived the Homeric tale about the battle between the cranes and Pygmaians, who, they said, were three *spithamai* (*handspans*) tall. There are also the gold-mining ants, and Pans with wedge-shaped heads, and snakes that swallow both cattle and deer along with their horns. Concerning these things, each refutes the other, as Eratosthenes says. For they were sent to Palimbothra—Megasthenes to Sandrakottos and Deimachos to his son Amitrochades—as ambassadors, and left such writings as reminders of their travels, persuaded to do so for whatever reason. Patrokles was not such a person at all,[73] and the other witnesses Eratosthenes used are not unreliable.[74]

---

[67] A reference to the *Istria* peninsula on the Adriatic.

[68] 'Hyperboreans', 'people beyond the north wind', were believed by some authors to live in NE Europe; Hdt. 4. 36, doubting their reality, ironically suggests that, if they exist, there must be 'people beyond the south wind' (*notos*) too. E. may have taken Hdt. too literally (Roller 2010, 137). Cf. Poseidonios 75 below.

[69] Editors take this to refer to the last part of book 1 of E.'s *Geographika*, devoted to fantasy geography. The Strabo passage continues with **25**.

[70] *BNJ* 716 F 5.   [71] *BNJ* 715 F 27a. For Megasthenes, see further Stoneman 2021.

[72] For such anatomically strange groups, see Skylax of Karyanda 8 and 14 above.

[73] Patrokles (*BNJ* 712) was an explorer sent out by the Seleukid kings (Roller 2015 115–17); see also e.g. Pajón Leyra and Bartoš 2020, esp. 88–9, 104.

[74] Deimachos of Plataiai (*BNJ* 716 Daimachos) was sent to India by the Seleukid king Antiochos I (r. 281–261). Megasthenes (*BNJ* 715) was there in C4l and wrote an *Indika*.

18   **Strabo** 2. 4. 1–2, C104: *Eratosthenes' reliance on Pytheas*
(1) .Polybios,[75] in describing the land of (*chōrographōn*) Europe, says that he leaves
aside the old (*writers*) but examines those who criticize them: Dikaiarchos, Eratosthenes—the latest who had practised geography—and Pytheas, by whom he says many
were led astray.·[76] (*Polybios says that*) he (*Pytheas*) asserted that he travelled over the
whole of Brettanike that was accessible, reporting that the circumference of the island
was more than 40,000 (*stades*), and also recorded matters about Thoule and those
places where there was no longer any land in existence—and neither sea nor air—but
something compounded from these, resembling a sea lung in which, he (*Pytheas*) says,
the earth, sea, and everything are suspended, as if it were a bonding for the whole,
accessible neither by foot nor by ship. He himself saw the lung but tells the rest from
hearsay. This is the report of Pytheas, and he adds that when he returned from there he
went along the entire ocean coast of Europe from Gadeira to the Tanaïs.
 (2) Now Polybios[77] says that this is unbelievable: how could someone who was a
private individual and poor have gone such distances by ship and foot? Eratosthenes
was at a loss whether to believe these things, but nevertheless believed him about Brettanike and the regions of Gadeira and Iberia. ·He (*Eratosthenes*) says it is much better to
believe the Messanian (*i.e. Euhemeros*)[78] than him (*i.e. Pytheas*);[79] for the former says he
sailed to a single land, Panchaia, while Pytheas says he has observed all the northward
part of Europe even as far as the end of the world; no one would believe even Hermes
if he said that![80] Eratosthenes (*says Polybios*) calls Euhemeros a Bergaian[81] and believes
Pytheas, yet not even Dikaiarchos believed those things—though 'not even Dikaiarchos believed' is laughable: as if it were appropriate for Eratosthenes to use that man as
a standard upon whom he himself heaps so many criticisms. With respect to the western and northern parts of Europe, I have already reported Eratosthenes' ignorance.[82]
While we should forgive him and Dikaiarchos, since they had not observed those places, who could forgive Polybios and Poseidonios? Polybios is the one who calls those
writers' conclusions about distances in those and many other places 'folk judgements',
yet he does not elucidate the things for which he criticizes those writers.·

19   **Strabo** 7. 3. 6–7, C298–300: *Homeric geography and fantasies*
(6) ·What Apollodoros has said in his preface to book 2 of *On Ships* (*i.e. the Homeric
catalogue*)[83] could only in the slightest degree be asserted. For he praises Eratosthenes
for saying that Homer and other early writers knew about Greek (*places*) but were

---

[75] Polyb. 34. 5. 1–6.
[76] On the problem of recovering the truth about Pytheas' journey from the biased assessment by
Polybios transmitted by Strabo, see introduction to Ch. 8.
[77] Polyb. 34. 5. 7–6. 10.   [78] BNJ 63.   [79] See n. on Pyth. 6 above.
[80] A bizarre argument (Roller 2010, 128). Euhemeros' journey was known to be a utopian fiction.
[81] 'Storyteller', Mirhady. See my n. 50 on Pytheas.   [82] At 2. 1. 41 (52 below, §41).
[83] BNJ 244 F 157a. Apollodoros of Athens wrote a work about the Homeric *Catalogue of Ships* (see
Prologue to these volumes). Strabo here represents E.'s views (perhaps in the last part of his 1st book,
dealing with imaginary geography) through Apollodoros' response to them.

seriously lacking in experience of those further off,· ignorant of long journeys, and ignorant of sea voyages. In support of this he (*Apollodoros*) says that Homer calls Aulis rocky, just as it is, Eteonos many-ridged, Thisbe dove-abundant, and Haliartos grassy,[84] but that neither he nor the others knew faraway places. There are about forty rivers that flow into the Pontos, but he does not mention even those that are the best known, such as the Istros, Tanaïs, Borysthenes, Hypanis, Phasis, Thermodon, or Halys. Moreover, he does not mention the Skythians, but creates certain 'noble Hippemolgoi' (*Mare-milkers*) or the Galaktophagoi (*Milk-eaters*) and the Abioi (*No-lifers*).[85] Concerning the Paphlagonians of the interior, his report is from those who approached these territories on foot, but he is ignorant of the coast, and naturally so. At that time the sea was not navigable and was called the Axenos (*Inhospitable*) because of its wintriness and the wildness of the peoples living around it, most of all the Skythians, who sacrificed strangers, ate their flesh, and used their skulls as drinking cups. Later, when the Ionians founded cities on its coast, it was called the Euxeinos. Moreover, he (*Homer*) is ignorant of matters concerning the Egyptians and Libyans, such as the rising of the Nile and the silting up of the sea—which he records nowhere—or the isthmus between the Erythraian and Egyptian seas, or Arabia, Aithiopia, and the Ocean, unless one should agree with the scholar Zenon when he wrote 'we came to the Aithiopes and Sidonioi and Arabes'.[86]

But this is not surprising for Homer, for those more recent than him have been ignorant of many things and tell of marvels. Hesiod speaks of the Hemikynes (*Half-dogs*), Megalokephaloi (*Long-heads*), and the Pygmaioi;[87] Alkman[88] about Steganopodes (*Webfoots*) and Aeschylus[89] about the Kynokephaloi (*Dog-heads*), Sternophthalmoi (*Eyes-in-Chests*), Monommatoi (*One-eyes*), and countless others. ·From these authors he goes on to those who talk about the Rhipaian mountains· and Mount Oguion, and the settlements of the Gorgons and the Hesperides, the Meropian land of Theopompos,[90] ·the city of Kimmeris in Hekataios· (*of Abdera*),[91] the Panchaian land of Euhemeros,[92] and Aristotle's river stones formed from sand but melted by rain. In Libyē there is the city of Dionysos that no one can find twice. He censures those who say that the wanderings of Odysseus were, according to Homer, around Sicily, for if so, one must say that although the wanderings were there, they were placed by the Poet in the Ocean for mythological reasons. Although (*he says*) others can be excused, Kallimachos[93] cannot be at all, in his pretence as a scholar, who says that Gaudos is the Island of Kalypso and Korkyra is Scheria.[94] He (*Apollodoros*) accuses others of being mistaken about Gerena, Akakesion, Demos in Ithaca, Pelethronion in Pelion,

---

[84] All named at *Il.* 2. 496–503 (in the Prologue).
[85] Generally thought to mean 'without livelihood'.
[86] Fr. 275 in von Arnim 1903–24; *Od.* 4. 84, emended.   [87] Fr. 101 in Most 2007.
[88] A Spartan poet of C7; this is fr. 148 in D. A. Campbell 1988.
[89] Frs 431, 441, and 434a in Radt 1985.   [90] Fr. *BNJ* 115 F 75d.
[91] *BNJ* 264 F 8. Hekataios of Abdera wrote in C4. See n. on Hekat. 6.   [92] *BNJ* 63 T 5c.
[93] Frs 13 and 470 in Pfeiffer 1949–53.   [94] Cf. **11** above.

and Glaukopion in Athens. To this he adds some minor things and then ceases, having transferred most of them from Eratosthenes, and which, as I have said previously,[95] are not correct.

In regard to Eratosthenes and him (*Apollodoros*), one must grant that the more recent writers are more knowledgeable than the ancient ones, but thus to go beyond moderation, particularly in regard to Homer, seems to me something for which they could justly be rebuked. Indeed one could say the opposite: that when they are ignorant themselves about these, this topic happens to be mentioned at the appropriate places as well as generally.

(7) I was speaking now about the Thracians: 'the hand-to-hand fighting Mysians and the noble Hippemolgoi, Galaktophagoi, and the Abioi, the most just of men',[96] wishing to compare what was said by myself and Poseidonios with them (*Eratosthenes and Apollodoros*). In the first case, the reasoning that they made is opposite to what they have proposed. They propose to demonstrate that those earlier were more ignorant of places far from Hellas than were those more recent, but they have shown the opposite, not only about far places, but also those within Hellas.

But, as I was saying, let us postpone the rest and observe that which is here: they say because of ignorance he (*Homer*) does not mention the Skythians or their cruelty towards strangers—they sacrifice them and eat their flesh, using their skulls for drinking cups—and because of whom the Pontos was called the Axenos, yet he creates certain 'noble Hippemolgoi, Galaktophagoi, and the Abioi, the most just of men', who are nowhere on Earth. How could there be the name 'Axenos' if they did not know about their savageness, and that they were the most (*savage*) of all? These are presumably the Skythians. Were not the Hippemolgoi beyond the Mysians, Thracians, and Getai, as well as the Galaktophagoi and the Abioi? Even now there are Hamaxoikoi (*Wagon-dwellers*) and Nomades (*Pasturers*), as they are called, who live off their animals and milk and cheese, especially that from horses, and do not know about storing things or trading, except goods for goods. How could the poet be ignorant of the Skythians if he spoke of certain Hippemolgoi and Galaktophagoi? At that time they were called the Hippemolgoi, and Hesiod is a witness to this, in the words that Eratosthenes quotes: 'Aithiopes, Ligyes, and also the mare-milking (*hippēmolgoi*) Skythians'.[97]

20 Strabo 11. 7. 4, C509–10: *Manipulation of geography for Alexander*
Many false things were further imagined about this sea because of the ambition of Alexander. Since it was agreed by all that the Tanaïs river separated Asia from Europe, and that which was between the sea and the Tanaïs, a greater part of Asia, had not fallen to the Macedonians, it was reported in such a way as to show that Alexander had conquered that region. They combined the Maiotic lake—which receives the Tanaïs—

---

[95] At 1. 2. 24.   [96] *Il.* 13. 5–6.
[97] Hesiod, *Catalogue*, fr. 98 in Most 2007. Once again, Strabo defends Homer from the charges levelled by E. and later by Apollodoros.

and the Caspian sea, calling it a lake, and insisting that there was a passage from one to the other so that each was a part of the other. Polykleitos[98] offers proofs that the sea is a lake—it produces serpents and the water is fairly fresh—and he judges that it is nothing other than the Maiotis because the Tanaïs empties into it. The Ochos and Oxos and many others come from the same Indian mountains from which the Iaxartes (*Syr Darya*) flows, which is the most northerly of all and, like the rest, empties into the Caspian sea. This (*the Iaxartes*) they named the Tanaïs, and as an additional proof that it was the Tanaïs of which Polykleitos spoke, they note that across the river the fir-tree exists and that the Skythians there use fir⟨wood⟩ arrows. This is their proof that the territory across the river is part of Europe and not Asia, for upper and eastern Asia do not produce the fir-tree. But Eratosthenes says that the fir-tree also grows in Indike and that Alexander built his ships there out of fir. Eratosthenes attempts to reconcile many other such issues, but let what I have said about them be enough.

21 Strabo 15. 1. 7, C687: *Attitude to myths*
Regarding the tales about Herakles and Dionysos, Megasthenes[99] and a few others consider them trustworthy, but most, including Eratosthenes, find them not to be trusted, but legendary, like the tales among the Hellenes.

22 Strabo 16. 2. 44, C764: *Changes in seas*
Eratosthenes says the contrary, that the territory (*around the Dead Sea*) formed a lake,[100] most of which was uncovered by an outbreak, as in Thessaly.

23 Arrian, *Anab.* 5. 3. 1–4: *Manipulation of geography for Alexander*
Let people take these things as they wish and disbelieve them or believe them. For I, at any rate, do not agree with Eratosthenes of Kyrene in every respect. He says that all the things attributed to the divine by the Macedonians were grossly exaggerated in the telling in order to add lustre to Alexander.[101] (2) An example is when he says the Macedonians saw a cave in (*the territory of*) the Parapamisadai and heard some local myth, or made it up themselves and put it about, that this was the actual cave where Prometheus was bound, where the eagle used to come to eat Prometheus' innards, and where Herakles arrived, killed the eagle, and freed Prometheus from his bonds. (3) He says that in their account the Macedonians displaced Mount Caucasus from the Pontos to the eastward parts of the Earth and the land of the Parapamisadai in the direction of the Indians, and that they called the mountain that was actually Parapamisos Kaukasos, all for the sake of Alexander's reputation—as if Alexander had actually come over the Caucasus. (4) In the land of the Indians themselves, (*he says*)

---

[98] *BNJ* 128 Polykleitos of Larisa (otherwise little known), F 7. On the political manipulation of geography, see **23** §3 below, and Introduction, §III. 3. k.

[99] *BNJ* 715 F 11a.

[100] Asphaltitis is the anc. name of the Dead Sea, though the text erroneously refers to L. Sirbonis a few lines above.

[101] Cf. **20**. See Roller 2015, 95 (cf. 102–3), on the persistent belief, in the Cl period, in an E–W range uniting the Tauros range in Asia Minor with the Caucasus.

they saw cows that had been branded with (*the sign of*) a club and took this as evidence that Herakles came to the Indians.

In the same way Eratosthenes does not believe what is said about the wanderings of Dionysos. For me, the tales about these matters must be left open.

BOOK 2

24   Strabo 1. 1. 8–9, C5–6: *The outer Ocean*
(8) That the inhabited world is an island must be assumed both from the senses and from experience. Everywhere that it has been possible for men to access the farthest points of the Earth, the sea has been found, which we call Okeanos. Wherever it is not possible to make use of the senses, reason shows it. The eastern side, that near the Indians, and the western, that near the Iberians and the Maurousians, can be completely sailed round in the southern or northern portions for a great distance. The remainder that has not been sailed by us up to today, because those who sailed round did not meet each other, is not so great, if one adds together the parallel distances accessible by us. It is not likely that the Atlantic open-sea (*pelagos*) is divided into two seas (*dithalatton*), separated by isthmuses so narrow that they prevent sailing round, but rather that it flows together and is continuous. Those who attempted to sail round but turned back say that it was not because they came upon some continent and were prevented from sailing beyond, reversing their direction, but because of the difficulties and the isolation, not that the sea became less open.[102] This agrees better with the properties of the Ocean concerning its ebbing and flooding. Everywhere the same characteristic or one not greatly varying is enough for the changes of height and diminution, as if one sea and one cause produced the movements.

(9) ·Hipparchos is not credible when he rebuts this view (*that the oikoumenē is surrounded by water*) on the grounds that the entire Ocean does not show similar characteristics, and that, even if this point were conceded, it would not follow from it that the entire encircling Atlantic open-sea (*pelagos*) was connected. For the dissimilar characteristics he cites Seleukos of Babylon as a witness.·

25   Strabo 1. 4. 1–2, C62–3: *Breadth of the oikoumenē*
(1) In his 2nd (*explanation*),[103] he (*Eratosthenes*) attempts to change the structure of geography and states his own assumptions. If there is any further correction, there must be an attempt to provide it. To introduce mathematics and physics into the topic is well considered, as also is the idea that if the Earth is spherical—just as the cosmos—it is inhabited all around, and other such comments. ·That it (*the Earth*) is as great as he (*Eratosthenes*) has said it is, is not accepted by later writers; nor do they commend the way in which he measures it. But for the purpose of locating the appearances (*of the heavenly bodies*) over each of the inhabited regions, Hipparchos nevertheless employs

---

[102] Cf. Introduction, §III. 3. g–h.
[103] This follows **16** and is taken to refer to the 2nd book of E.'s *Geographika*.

those distances upon the meridian through Meroë, Alexandria, and the Borysthenes (*Dnieper*), saying that they do not diverge far from the truth.· In what follows about its shape, where he proves at length that the nature of the Earth along with its watery portions is spherical, as are the heavens, he seems to be speaking irrelevantly, for brevity would be sufficient.

(2) In determining the width of the inhabited world,[104] he (*Eratosthenes*) says that from Meroë it is 10,000 stades along its meridian to Alexandria, and from there to the Hellespont about 8,100, then 5,000 to the Borysthenes, and then to the parallel that runs through Thoule,[105] which Pytheas says is six days' sail north of Brettanike and is near the Frozen Sea, an additional 11,500. Moreover, if we add 3,400 more beyond Meroë, so that we include the Egyptian island,[106] the Kinnamomophoros (*Cinnamon-bearing Land*) and Taprobane,[107] we have 38,000 stades.[108]

26 Strabo 1. 4. 5–8, C64–6: *Length of the oikoumenē*

(5) Since he (*Eratosthenes*) entirely missed its width, he was also compelled to miss its length. It is agreed by later sources as well as the most talented early ones that its known length is more than twice the known width; I am speaking of that from the extremities of Indike to the extremities of Iberia, and that from the Aithiopes as far as the parallel of Ierne. He has determined the previously mentioned width, that from the farthest Aithiopes to the parallel through Thoule, and has stretched the length more than necessary, so that he can make it more than the previously mentioned width. Moreover, he says that the narrowest part of Indike, up to the Indos river, is 16,000 stades—that which extends to the promontories is an additional 3,000 stades—and to the Caspian Gates[109] is 14,000, and then to the Euphrates 10,000, and from the Euphrates to the Nile 5,000, with an additional 1,300 as far as the Kanobic mouth, then 13,500 as far as Karchedon (*Carthage*), then as far as the Pillars at least 8,000, a total of 800 beyond 70,000 stades. Then it is still necessary to add the bulge of Europe outside the Pillars of Herakles, set against the Iberians and sloping to the west—no less than 3,000 stades—as well as all the promontories, especially that of the Ostidaioi, which is called Kabaion,[110] and the surrounding islands, the farthest of which, Ouxisame (*Ushant*), Pytheas says is three days' sail away. After mentioning these final places, which in their extent add nothing to its length, he adds the districts around the promontories, that of the Ostidaians and Ouxisame and the islands of which he speaks. All these places

[104] The geographers usually refer to the W–E dimension of the *oikoumenē* as its length and the N–S dimension as its width.

[105] That is, the parallel of latitude. Up to this point, the places listed are those deemed to lie on the same line of longitude, defined by E. as his prime meridian. Thoule, wherever it be placed, lies much further W than this.

[106] Two months' travel S from Meroë (Hdt. 2. 30–1). Cf. 57 below.

[107] i.e. the latitude of Taprobane (*Sri Lanka*), which lies much further E.

[108] As 26 §5 indicates, Strabo disagrees with E.'s reckoning of the N–S width of the *oikoumenē*. E.'s figure of 38,000 st. equates to *c.*4,750 mi (*c.*7,000 km).

[109] At the SE point of the Caspian.

[110] Western Brittany, or a cape of it (Roller 2010, 155).

are towards the north and are in Keltike, not Iberike, or rather they are fantasies of Pytheas. He (*Eratosthenes*) also adds to the previously mentioned length more stades, 2,000 to the west and 2,000 to the east, to keep the width from being more than half the length.

(6) He attempts to reassure us even further when he says that it is natural to make the interval from east to west greater, and natural that the inhabited world is longer from east to west, saying that 'we have stated, as do the mathematicians, that it joins together in a circle, touching itself with itself, so that, if not prevented by the size of the Atlantic open-sea, we could sail from Iberia to Indike along the same parallel—the part that remains beyond the previously mentioned interval, which is more than one-third of the distance—if the one through Athens, where we have made this stated measurement of stades from Indike to Iberia, is less than 200,000 stades'.[111] Yet he does not say this well. He might say this about the temperate zone, the one in our region,[112] according to mathematics, since it is only a portion of the inhabited Earth, yet concerning the inhabited Earth—since we call inhabited that which we inhabit and know—it is possible that in this same temperate zone there are two inhabited worlds, or more, especially near the circle through Athens that is drawn through the Atlantic open-sea. Moreover, by persisting in the proof of the spheroid shape of the Earth he receives the same criticism. Similarly, he does not stop disagreeing with Homer about the same things.

(7) Next, saying that there has been much written about the continents, and that some divide them by rivers, such as the Nile and Tanaïs—representing them as islands—and others by isthmuses, such as the one between the Caspian and Pontic seas or between the Erythraian and the Ekrhegma (*Break-out*)—saying that they are peninsulas—he says that he does not see how this examination can result in anything consequential, except for those living contentiously in the fashion of Demokritos. If there are no exact boundaries—as with Kolyttos and Melite[113]—such as standing-stones (*stēlai*) or enclosures, we can only say that 'this is Kolyttos and this is Melite',[114] but do not have the boundaries. It is for this reason that there are often disputes about districts, such as that between the Argives and Lakedaimonians about Thyrea,[115] or between the Athenians and Boiotians about Oropos.[116] The Hellenes named the three continents differently because they did not pay attention to the inhabited world, but only to their own area and what was directly opposite, the Karike (*Karia*), where there are now Ionians and their neighbours. In time, advancing still further, and learning more about territories, they have focused their division. Were those who first separated the three—so that we

---

[111] This appears to be a direct quotation from E. Roller 2010, 148, however, stresses Strabo's obscurity in parts of this passage.

[112] On the theory of zones, see Introduction, §III. 3. f.   [113] Two demes (parishes) of Athens.

[114] Two adjacent demes in the urban area of Athens. The point is that though their boundaries were not obvious they were distinct (Roller 2010, 150).

[115] A *polis* and its territory on the E coast of the Peloponnese.

[116] Cf. Herakleides Kritikos fr. 1 §§6–7.

begin with his (*Eratosthenes'*) last point, living contentiously but not in the fashion of Demokritos, but of him—the original men who sought to divide the Karians, lying opposite, from their own territory? Or did they conceive only of Hellas and Karia and the small amount that touched it, but not in the same way about Europe, Asia, or Libyē, and were those afterwards—travelling through enough to conceive of the outline of the inhabited world—the ones who divided it into three? How could they not have made the division of the inhabited world? Would someone speaking of three parts and calling each of the parts a continent not think of the whole from which he makes his division? But if he does not conceive of the inhabited world but makes his division of some part of it, of what part of the inhabited world would anyone have said that Asia was a part, or Europe, or a continent in general? These things have been said sloppily.

(8) Even more sloppily, he does not see what can be said about the practical result of the investigation of boundaries: to set forth Kolyttos and Melite and then to turn round to the opposite. If the wars about Thyrea and Oropos happened because of ignorance of the boundaries, then the separation of territories results in something practical. Or, in regard to districts, and, by Zeus, the various ethnic groups, is he saying that it is practical to divide them accurately, but for continents this is superfluous? But this is by no means less important, for there might be some great dispute among rulers—one holding Asia and the other Libyē—as to which possessed Egypt, specifically that which is called the Lower Territory of Egypt. If anyone were to dismiss this because of its rarity, nevertheless it must be said that the continents are divided according to a major distinction that relates to the entire inhabited world. In regard to this, there must be no concern—if the division is made according to rivers—that certain areas remain undefined, because the rivers do not extend as far as the Ocean and thus truly do not leave the continents as islands.[117]

27 Strabo 2. 1. 20, C77: *Latitude of Meroë*[118]
Regarding the latitude of Meroë, Philon,[119] who wrote about his voyage to Aithiopia, records that the Sun is at the zenith 45 days before the summer solstice, and also discusses the relationship of the gnomon to the shadows of both the solstices and equinoxes. Eratosthenes is closely in agreement with Philon.

28 Strabo 2. 3. 2, C97: *Zones of latitude*
If, as Eratosthenes says, that which lies under the celestial equator is temperate—and Polybios[120] agrees with this opinion, although he adds that it is the highest part, and because of this it is rainy, since in the Etesian season the clouds from the north frequently strike against the heights there—it would be much better to consider it a third, narrow, temperate zone, than to introduce two tropical ones.[121]

---

[117] This paragraph is very much Strabo ratiocinating, rather than a report of E.'s views.

[118] This extract sits within **52** §20.

[119] *BNJ* 670 F 2. Philon was a military commander under Ptolemy II (r. 283/2–246); see Pliny 37. xxxii. 108.

[120] Polyb. 34. 1. 16.   [121] Cf. Introduction, §III. 3. f.

29 **Strabo** 2. 5. 5–9, C112–16: *The circumnavigable oikoumenē; the 'spondylos' and the 'chlamys'*

(5) Let us assume that the Earth along with the sea is sphere-shaped and that one and the same surface contains the open seas (*pelagē*), for the projections on the Earth would be concealed because they are small in comparison with its great size and would escape notice.[122] Thus we call it 'sphere-shaped', not as if it were turned on a lathe nor as a surveyor would present it, but in order to perceive it, and this somewhat roughly. Let us consider it as five-zoned,[123] with the equator drawn as a circle on it, and another circle parallel to it bordering the cold region in the northern hemisphere, and another at right angles through the poles.[124]

Since the northern hemisphere contains two-fourths of the Earth, formed by the equator and the (*line*) passing through the poles, a four-sided area is cut off in each of them. The northern side is half of the parallel next to the pole, the southern side is half of the equator, and the remaining sides are sections of those (*lines*) passing through the poles, lying opposite to each other and equal in length. In either of these four-sided areas[125]—it would seem to make no difference which one—we say that our inhabited world is placed, washed all round by the sea and like an island. It has been said[126] that this can be shown through perception and reason. If anyone were not to believe this argument, it would make no difference to geography whether to make it an island or to admit what we understand from experience: that one can sail round both sides, from the east and the west, except for a few areas in the middle. Regarding these, there is no difference whether they are bounded by sea or uninhabitable land, for the geographer attempts to speak about the known parts of the inhabitable world (*oikoumenē*). He omits the unknown parts, as well as that which is outside it. It will suffice to join with a straight line the farthest limits of the coastal sailing (*paraplous*) on both sides and to fill completely the form of the so-called island.

(6) Let us suppose, then, that the island is in the previously mentioned quadrilateral. It is necessary to take as its size what it appears to be, removing our hemisphere from the entire size of the Earth, and from this its half, and then from it also the quadrilateral in which we say that the inhabited world lies. It is necessary to understand its shape by analogy and adapt its appearance to the hypotheses. But since the segment of the northern hemisphere that is between the equator and the polar parallel is in the shape of a *spondylos* (*spindle whorl*),[127] and since the polar parallel cuts the hemisphere

---

[122] The clear style of exposition here suggests a direct quotation or paraphrase from E. (Roller 2010, 144).
[123] On zones, see Introduction, §III. 3. f.
[124] i.e. a great circle of longitude dividing the N hemisphere into two.
[125] Bounded by lines of longitude to W and E, and by parallels of latitude to N and S.
[126] At 1. 1. 8 (24 §8 above).
[127] This would ordinarily mean a spherical or disc-shaped object, pierced for mounting on a spindle (whose rotation twists the thread as it forms). If disc-shaped, it may resemble a truncated cone or a section of a sphere flat above and below, i.e. tapering towards one surface; thus E., as paraphrased by Strabo, appears to mean 'the entire circumference of the earth between two parallels' (sc. of latitude), 'which Eratosthenes cut in half because the inhabited world was in only one hemisphere' (Roller 2010, 147).

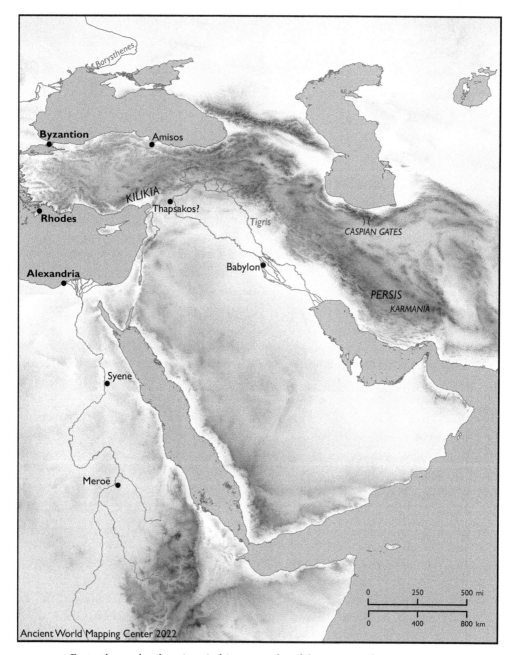

MAP 12.1. Eratosthenes: key locations in his geography of the eastern *oikoumenē*.

into two, and also cuts the spindle whorl in two, making the quadrilateral, it will be clear that the quadrilateral in which the Atlantic open-sea (*pelagos*) lies appears as half the spindle-whorl, and that the inhabited world is a *chlamys*-shaped (*cloak-shaped*)[128]

[128] Strabo does not explain what he means; it may have had the form of a rectangle with rounded corners (Roller 2010, 154). He goes into more detail at 57.

island in it, less than half the quadrilateral in size. This is clear from geometry, from the size of the sea that spreads around it—which covers the farthest point of the continents at both ends, contracting them to a tapering shape—and, third, from its great length and width. The former is 70,000 stades, limited for the most part by a sea that still cannot be crossed because of its size and desolation. The latter is less than 30,000 stades, bounded by areas that are uninhabitable because of heat or cold. The part of the quadrilateral that is uninhabitable because of heat has a width of 8,800 stades, and a maximum length of 126,000, which is half the equator [—] [*omission in original*] and the remainder may be more.

(7) ·What Hipparchos says is more or less consonant with these points. For he assumes the size of the Earth as stated by Eratosthenes, and therefore states that we must separate from this question our study of the inhabited world: for it will make little difference as regards the appearances of the heavenly bodies in each inhabited region whether the measurement is thus (*sc. as Eratosthenes said*) or as later writers have given it.· Since, according to Eratosthenes, the equator is 252,000 stades,[129] one-fourth of it would be 63,000. This is the distance from the equator to the pole, fifteen-sixtieths of the sixty (*intervals*) of the equator.[130] From the equator to the tropic is four-(*sixtieths*), and this is the parallel drawn through Syene (*Aswan*).[131] Each of these distances is computed from known measurements. The tropic lies at Syene because at the summer solstice there a gnomon has no shadow in the middle of the day. The meridian through Syene is drawn approximately along the course of the Nile from Meroë to Alexandria, which is about 10,000 stades. It happens that Syene lies in the middle of that distance, so that from there to Meroë is 5,000. Going in a straight line about 3,000 stades further south, it is no longer inhabitable because of the heat, so the parallel through these places, the same as the one through the Cinnamon-bearing Land,[132] must be put as the limit and the beginning of our inhabited world in the south.

Since it is 5,000 from Syene to Meroë, adding the other 3,000 the total would be 8,000 to the boundary of the inhabited world. But from Syene to the equator is 16,800—this is the four-sixtieths, with each of them 4,200—so the remainder would be 8,800 from the boundary of the inhabited world to the equator, and 21,800 from Alexandria. Again, everyone agrees that the sea route from Alexandria to Rhodes is in line with the course of the Nile, as well as the sailing route from there along Karia and Ionia to the Troad, Byzantion, and the Borysthenes (*Dnieper*). Taking, then, the known distances that have been sailed, they consider how the territories in a straight line beyond the Borysthenes are inhabitable and what the boundary is of the part of

---

[129] If a stade is *c.*607.3 ft (*c.*185.1 m; see Introduction, §IV. 1), this figure equates to 28,984 mi (46,645 km), as against the true (equatorial) figure of 24,902 mi (40,075 km); the excess is *c.*16.4 per cent. (Dicks 1960, 150, reckons the true value at 224,000 st., making the excess *c.*12.5 per cent.)

[130] E. divides the circle into sixtieths (each of 6°, in our terms), as the 360-degree system was not in use by Greek writers before C2 (Roller 2010, 151), when it was probably introduced by Hipparchos.

[131] *Aswan* is at latitude *c.*24° N; the Tropic of Cancer at *c.*23½° N.

[132] Probably in Somalia (Roller 2010, 152).

the inhabited world towards the north. The Rhoxolanoi, the farthest of the known Skythians, live beyond the Borysthenes, although they are further south than the remote peoples we know about north of Brettanike. The area lying beyond immediately becomes uninhabitable because of the cold. Further to the south of them are the Sauromatai[133] beyond the Maiotis (*Sea of Azov*) and the Skythians as far as the eastern Skythians.

(8) Now Pytheas of Massalia says that the region around Thoule, the most northerly of the Brettanides (*British Isles*), is the farthest, and that the circle of the summer tropic is the same as the arctic circle.[134] I have learned nothing about this from anyone else: whether there is a certain island called Thoule, or whether there is habitation up to where the summer tropic becomes the arctic. I believe that the northern boundary of the inhabited world is much further to the south. Nothing is described beyond Ierne, which lies to the north of Brettanike and near to it, where men are totally wild and live badly because of the cold, and thus I believe that the boundary is to be placed there.

·Given that the parallel through Byzantion goes roughly through Massalia, as Hipparchos says, relying upon Pytheas[135]—for he says that at Byzantion the ratio of the gnomon to its shadow is the same as Pytheas says it is in Massalia·—and with the one running through the Borysthenes about 3,800 from there, considering the distance from Massalia, the circle (*of latitude*) through the Borysthenes would fall somewhere in Brettanike. But Pytheas, who misleads men everywhere, is in error here. . . .

(9) If one were to add, to the distance from the Rhodia (*territory of Rhodes*) as far as the Borysthenes, a distance of 4,000 stades from the Borysthenes to the northern regions, this is a total of 12,700 stades, and that from the Rhodia to the southern limit of the inhabited world is 16,600, so the entire width of the inhabited world is less than 30,000 from south to north. The length is said to be about 70,000, that is, from west to east, from the extremities of Iberia to the extremities of Indike, measured in part by land journeys and in part by sea journeys. That this length is within the previously mentioned quadrilateral is clear from the relationship of the parallels to the equator, and thus the length is more than twice the width. It is said to be somewhat *chlamys*-shaped, for when we travel throughout its regions, a great contracting of width at the extremities is found, especially at the west.

30   Strabo 2. 5. 13, C118: *Whether the other hemisphere of the Earth in our latitudes is inhabited*

To describe accurately the entire Earth and the whole spindle whorl is another discipline, as is whether the spindle whorl is inhabited in its other fourth portion.[136] If it were, it would not be inhabited by ones like those among us, and it must then be

---

[133] These, and the Rhoxolanians just mentioned, were known in Strabo's time but probably not in E.'s.
[134] See n. on Pyth. 7 above.   [135] An error; see n. on Pyth. 2 above.
[136] i.e. in the other half-hemisphere. E. dismissed the question of the other 180° of longitude, W and E of our *oikoumenē*, as not being the province of geography.

considered another inhabited world, which is believable. But I must speak of what is in our own.

31 **Strabo** 2. 5. 42, C135: *Length of the prime meridian*
Eratosthenes says that these regions (*at the latitude of the mouth of the Borysthenes*) are a little more than 23,000 (*stades*) from Meroë, since it is 18,000 to the Hellespont and then 5,000 to the Borysthenes.[137]

32 **Geminos,** *Introduction to the Phenomena*, 15: *The five zones*
The surface of all the Earth, having a spherical form, is divided into five zones. Two of them are the ones in the area of the poles, which lie furthest from the passage of the Sun; they are called 'the frozen' (*mod. 'frigid'*), and ⟨are⟩ uninhabited because of the cold. They are bounded by the arctic circles in the direction of the poles. (2) The ones next to these, lying in a moderate relation to the passage of the Sun, are called 'the temperate'. They are bounded by the arctic and tropical circles in the heavens, and lie between these. (3) The remaining one is between the aforementioned (*zones*), lies right under the passage of the Sun, and is called the 'burned' (*mod. 'torrid'*). This one is divided by the equatorial circle on the Earth, which lies under the equatorial circle in the heavens. (4) Of the two temperate zones, the northerly one has come to be settled by the people in our inhabited world (*oikoumenē*). It is, on the best estimate, about 10,000 stades in length, and, again on the best estimate, half that in width.[138]

33 **Pliny,** *Natural History*, 2. lxxv. 183–lxxvi. 185: *When and where the Sun is overhead*
lxxv. (183) In a similar way they say that in the town of Syene, which is 5,000 stades upstream from Alexandria, in the middle of the day on the solstice no shadow is cast, and that a well dug for the purpose of this experiment became wholly illuminated. From this (*they say*) it becomes clear that at that time and in that place the Sun is overhead. Onesicritus writes that in India the same thing occurs at that time over the river Hypasis.[139] It is also accepted that in Berenice, a city of the Trogodytae,[140] and also 4,820 stades away at the town of Ptolemais belonging to the same nation[141]—the latter was founded by the side of the Red Sea for the first elephant hunts—the very same thing occurs on the 45th day before the solstice each year and during the same interval after it, while during those 90 days the shadows are cast southwards.

(184) Furthermore, at Meroë[142]—this island, the capital of the Aethiopes, is 5,000 stades from Syene and is a settled place on the river Nile—the shadows are eliminated twice a year, when the Sun occupies the 18th part (*i.e. degree*) of Taurus and the 14th part of Leo. . . .

---

[137] The distances are stated slightly differently in **25** §2 and **29** §§7–9.
[138] The last sentence could be a comment by Geminos (Evans and Berggren 2006, 208–9).
[139] The *Beas*, whose mouth is around the latitude of the Tropic of Cancer.
[140] On the Red Sea coast in S. Egypt.
[141] Further S, at *c.*19° N and thus within the Tropic of Cancer.   [142] At *c.*17° N.

(185) . . . lxxvi. Eratosthenes also announced that all over Trogodytice, for 45 days twice a year, the shadows fall the opposite way.

34   Pliny, *Natural History*, 2. cxii. 247–8: *Circumference of the Earth*
(247) . . . The total circumference was shown by Eratosthenes—an expert, of course, in the minutiae of all disciplines but surpassing others in this subject—to be 252,000 stades; I see he is esteemed by all. This measurement, in Roman measurement, makes 31,500 miles. The statement was bold and daring, but contained within such minute argument that it would be shameful to disbelieve it. ·Hipparchos, who is admired for his refutation of him and for his other careful work, adds just under 26,000 stades.·[143]

(248) Dionysodorus' reliability is another thing[144]—for I shall not remove this outstanding example of Greek inanity. He was from Melos, and renowned for his knowledge of geometry.[145] He died at a great age in his fatherland, and his female relatives conducted his funeral; the inheritance had come to them. While performing the rites in the days that followed, they are said to have found in the tomb a letter written to the gods in the name of Dionysodoros, which said that he had travelled from his tomb to the lowest point of the Earth, a distance of 42,000 stades. There was no lack of geometricians to interpret the letter as meaning that it had been sent from the centre of the Earth, which was the place the furthest downwards from the surface, and was the middle of the globe; from this followed the calculation that led them to declare the circumference to be 252,000 stades.

35   Pliny, *Natural History*, 6. xxxiv. 171: *The solstitial period at Berenice*
This is the region noted by us in our second book,[146] in which for 45 days up to the solstice and the same afterwards, at the sixth hour the shadows disappear, and at the remaining hours they fall southwards, while on other days they fall northwards. At Berenice, however, which we discussed first, at the sixth hour on the very day of the solstice the shadows are wholly eliminated, though nothing else unusual is observed. This is at a distance of 602[147] miles from Ptolemais. It was a matter of huge precedent and the site of a display of enormous intelligence,[148] the world being comprehended in that place: for it was here that Eratosthenes formed the idea of announcing the dimension of the Earth using the irrefutable reasoning of shadows.

---

[143] See n. on Hipparch. 41.

[144] Thus following Beaujeu and König; or 'Dionysodorus has a different creed', Rackham.

[145] He seems otherwise unknown, if he is not Dionysodoros of Kaunos (C3f).

[146] See **33** above.

[147] Mayhoff adds ½, followed by Rackham. It is 4,820 st. at Pliny 2. lxxv. 183, which at 8 st. per mile = 602½ miles. Brodersen and Desanges retain 602.

[148] *locusque subtilitatis inmensae*; alternatively, 'a passage of great precision', sc. in E.'s written work.

36 Pliny, *Natural History*, 12. xxx. 53: *Value of the schoinos*
In the calculation by Eratosthenes the *schoinos* turns out to be 40 stades, which is 5 miles; though others assign the value of 32 stades to single *schoinoi*.[149]

37 Agathemeros i. 2: *Proportions of the oikoumenē*
Demokritos, a man of great experience, was the first to perceive that the Earth (*i.e. the inhabited part*) is oblong, with a length one and a half times its breadth. Dikaiarchos the Peripatetic agreed with this; but Eudoxos (*made*) the length double the breadth, Eratosthenes more than double.

38 Theon of Alexandria, pp. 394–5: *Measuring the heights of mountains*
The perpendicular descending from the highest mountains to places lower down is shown by Eratosthenes, using *dioptrai* that measure from a distance, to be 10 stades.[150]

39 Ammianus Marcellinus 22. 15. 31: *Summer solstice at Syene and Meroë*
Next is Syene, in which at the time of the solstice—the point to which the Sun extends its summer passage—its rays, enveloping all vertical objects, do not permit shadows to reach outside those bodies themselves. If at that time a person sets a stake vertical, or sees a man or tree standing up, he will observe how the shadows are eliminated at the very limits of their outlines; just as is said to occur at Meroë, the nearest part of Aethiopia to the equinoctial circle, where for 90 days the shadows fall in the opposite sense to ours; this is why people call the inhabitants Antiskioi (*Countershadows*).[151]

40 Markianos, *Periplous* 1. 4: *Circumference of the Earth*
Eratosthenes of Kyrene says the greatest circumference of all the ⟨known⟩ Earth is 259,200 stades. Dionysios son of Diogenes has measured it similarly.[152]

41 *Anametresis tes oikoumenes* 1: *Dimensions of the oikoumenē*
One must realize that the whole Earth's circumference in stades is 2,035† myriads; the length of our inhabited (*part*) from the mouth of the Ganges as far as Gadeira is 8,308†; the width from the Ethiopian sea as far as the river Tanaïs (*Don*) is 3,500† stades; and the part between the Euphrates and the Tigris river, called Mesopotamon, has a dimension of 3,000 stades. This calculation (*anametrēsis*) was made by Eratosthenes, the most mathematical of the ancients.[153]

---

[149] The plural of *schoinos*. Hdt. 2. 6 makes the *schoinos* 60 st.; according to Strabo 17. 1. 24, C803–4, it ranges from 30 to 120. Geus 2011 suggests that this text belongs to another work than the *Geography*.

[150] This is similar but not identical to the statement by the earlier writer Theon of Smyrna at Dik. 9. Geus 2011 suggests that this refers to a text other than the *Geography*.

[151] Although this passage derives ultimately from E., he may not have used the perhaps derogatory term *antiskioi* (Roller 2010, 158–9).

[152] See n. on Markianos, *Peripl.* 1. 4 (in Ch. 34 below). Geus 2011 suggests that this refers to a text other than the *Geography*.

[153] This error-strewn passage is from a medieval copy of a late antique note on geography. For the full text, and nn. on the numbers here, see appendix to Ch. 36 below. Its interest for present purposes lies in the evidence that E. made measurements referring to Mesopotamia. Geus 2011 suggests that it refers to a work of E.'s other than the *Geography*.

BOOK 3

42   *Nikomedean Periodos,* 405–12: *An area of the Adriatic*

> Next the great Hyllic peninsula,[154]
> somewhat equal in size to the Peloponnese;
> they say that fifteen cities in that land
> are settled by Hylloi, who are Hellenes by race,
> for they took Herakles' son Hyllos as founder;
> 410   but people report that they were barbarized
> in time by the customs of nearby nations,
> as Timaios and Eratosthenes say.

43   Caesar, *Gallic War* 6. 24: *The Hercynian (Orkynian) forest*
Previously there was a time when the Galli exceeded the Germani in bravery and even started wars against them, and when, because of their large population and for want of farmland, they sent colonies across the Rhine. And thus the places in Germania that are most fertile, around the Hercynian forest—which was, I see, familiar by repute to Eratosthenes and certain Greeks, who call it 'Orcynian'—were taken and settled by the Volcae Tectosages.[155]

44   *Vita Arati* (anonymous life of Aratos of Soloi), 3 (p. 77. 3–8): *A city in Euboia*
Again, there is Athēnai (*Athens*) in Attica, but there is also one in Euboia called Athēnai Diades . . . While citizens from the Athēnai in Attica are called Athēnaioi, those from the one in Euboia are called Athēnētai, as Eratosthenes says in the 1st (*book*) of his *Geographoumena.*[156]

45   Strabo 1. 2. 20, C28: *The south coast of Thrace*
For Thrace, where it touches Macedonia, takes a turn to the south, and forms a promontory into the open sea (*pelagos*), and it seems to those on Thasos, Lemnos, Imbros, Samothrake, and the surrounding sea that the Zephyroi (*westerlies*) blow from there . . . Eratosthenes did not perceive this, although he suspected it. Nevertheless he told about the turn of the land that I have mentioned.

---

[154] The *Punta Planka* promontory in Croatia. For the Hylloi cf. Ps.-Skyl. §22. 2.

[155] Caesar's description that follows locates the forest in modern Austria and Czechia. He takes the opportunity to remind readers of his intellectual credentials while showing that he, unlike E., has seen the forest for himself and has greater knowledge of its nomenclature (assuming we are to understand 'Hercynian' as its local name).

[156] The importance of this fragment, from a Hl biography of the poet Aratos of Soloi, is in showing that E.'s work included information about central Greece. Athēnai Diades was an Athenian colony in N. Euboia (Roller 2010, 214).

46 Strabo 1. 4. 9, C66: *True and false classifications of humankind*
Near the end of his treatise he (*Eratosthenes*) refuses to praise those who separate all the number of humanity into two groups, Hellenes and barbarians, as well as those who advised Alexander to consider the Hellenes as friends but the barbarians as enemies. He says that it is better to make such a distinction between good and bad characteristics, for there are many bad Hellenes or urbane barbarians, such as the Indians or Arians, or, moreover, the Romans and Karchedonians (*Carthaginians*), who administer their governments so marvellously.[157] Because of this, Alexander ignored his advisers, embraced as many distinguished men as possible, and showed them kindness.

47 Strabo 2. 1. 1–3, C67–8: *The central parallel of the oikoumenē*
(1) In the 3rd (*book*) of the *Geographika*, establishing the plan of the inhabited world, he (*Eratosthenes*) divides it into two parts by a certain line from west to east, parallel to the line of the equator.[158] He takes as the extremities of this line the Pillars of Herakles in the west and in the east the farthest summits of the mountains that define the northern edge of Indike. He draws the line from the Pillars through the Sicilian strait and the southern summits of the Peloponnesos and Attica, as far as the Rhodia and the Issic gulf. Up to here, he says, the previously mentioned line runs through the sea and the adjacent land; in fact, it lies entirely along the length of our sea as far as Kilikia. Then it is thrown out as an approximately straight line along the entire Tauros mountain range as far as Indike,[159] for the Tauros runs in a straight line with the sea from the Pillars, dividing Asia lengthwise into two parts, making one the northern part and the other the southern: thus in a similar way it (*the Tauros*) lies on the parallel through Athens, as does the sea that comes from the Pillars as far as it.

(2) Having said this, he believes it necessary to correct the ancient geographical plan, for according to it the eastern portion of the mountains is greatly twisted towards the north, and Indike is drawn along further to the north than it should be. He offers as his primary proof that many agree the most southerly promontories of Indike rise opposite to the region around Meroë, as demonstrated by the climate and the celestial phenomena. From there to the northern part of Indike, at the Caucasian mountains, Patrokles[160]—who is believed to be most accurate both because of his reputation and because he is not uneducated as a geographer—says is 15,000 stades, which is about the same as from Meroë to the parallel through Athens. Thus the northern parts of Indike, which touch the Caucasian mountains, end at this latitude.

(3) Another proof he offers is that the distance from the Issic gulf[161] to the Pontic sea (*Black Sea*) is about 3,000 stades, going towards the north and the regions around Amisos and Sinope, equal to what is said for the width of the mountains.[162] From

---

[157] This comment is most likely Strabo's (Roller 2010, 220).
[158] Lit. 'to the equidiurnal' (i.e. equinoctial) 'line' (for 'equidiurnal', see Introduction, §X. 3. b fin.). For the notion of a central line of latitude, see Dik. 11 above. E. here corrects and refines it.
[159] See n. on Dik. 11 above.   [160] *BNJ* 712 F 2.   [161] At the SE corner of Turkey.
[162] E. thus corrects the earlier minimization of the width of Asia Minor: e.g. Ps.-Skyl. §102. 2.

Amisos, heading towards the equinoctial[163] sunrise, Kolchis is first, and then the pass to the Hyrkanian (*Caspian*) sea, and next the route to Baktra[164] and the Skythians beyond, having the mountains on the right. This line through Amisos, (*extended*) to the west, is thrown out through the Propontis and the Hellespont. From Meroë to the Hellespont is no more than 18,000 stades, as much as from the southern side of Indike to the parts around the Baktrians, adding 3,000 to the 15,000, part of which is due to the width of the mountains and part due to that of Indike.

48   **Strabo** 2. 1. 5, C69: *Patrokles' credibility*
I think that the argument (*of Hipparchos against Patrokles' credibility*)[165] can be corrected in many ways. First, although the former (*Eratosthenes*) used many testimonia, the latter (*Hipparchos*) says that only one was used, Patrokles. But who said that the southern promontories of Indike rise opposite to the regions of Meroë? Who said that from Meroë as far as the parallel of Athens was such a distance? Again, who said what the width of the mountains was, and that it was the same from Kilikia to Amisos? Who said that from Amisos through Kolchis and Hyrkania as far as Baktria and the regions beyond down to the eastern sea was in a straight line towards equinoctial east, along the mountains that are on the right? Or again that to the west this line was straight towards the Propontis and the Hellespont?[166] Eratosthenes takes all these things as established by those who had been in those places, for he studied many treatises, having them in abundance in a library as large as Hipparchos says that it was.

49   **Strabo** 2. 1. 7, C69: *Patrokles' credibility*
·Moreover, Hipparchos in his second treatise (*hypomnēma; i.e. book 2*) says that Eratosthenes himself attacks the reliability of Patrokles[167] on the basis of his (*Patrokles'*) disagreement with Megasthenes about the length of the side of Indike that is to the north—Megasthenes saying it is 16,000 stades,[168] Patrokles saying it is 1,000 shorter—and that he (*Eratosthenes*) starts from a particular *Anagraphē stathmōn* (*Record of Stopping-points*)[169] and disbelieves those writers because of their disagreement, adhering instead to the list.·

50   **Strabo** 2. 1. 10–11, C70–1: *Accuracy of meridians, parallels, and old maps*
(10) [—] if the meridian through Rhodes and Byzantion has been taken correctly, then the one through Kilikia and Amisos has also been taken correctly, since from many sources it is shown that lines are parallel if neither of them meets.

   (11) The voyage from Amisos to Kolchis is thus towards the equinoctial sunrise (*due east*)—which is shown by the winds, seasons, crops, and the sunrises themselves—as

---

[163] Lit. 'equidiurnal'. See Introduction, §X. 3. b fin.
[164] City in Baktria (NE Afghanistan).   [165] See **47** §2.
[166] Strabo means that these facts are established by other sources than Patrokles.
[167] *BNJ* 712 F 3.   [168] *BNJ* 715 F 6d.
[169] A list of points on recognized routes, with distances, evidently similar to that of Isidoros (Ch. 23 below) in Strabo's own day. Cf. **81** §8.

also are the pass to the Caspian and the route from there to Baktra. Often clarity and total agreement are more trustworthy than an instrument.[170]

·Hipparchos himself did not take the fact that the line from the Pillars to Kilikia is straight and runs to the equinoctial sunrise (*due east*) entirely from instruments and geometry, but trusted in sailors for the whole stretch from the Pillars to the Strait. Consequently he (*Hipparchos*) is even in error when he says:[171]

> Since we are unable to state either the ratio of the longest day to the shortest, or that of gnomon to shadow, for the mountain slope from Kilikia to the Indians, nor even say whether the obliquity (*of the slope*) runs along a parallel (*of latitude*), therefore we must leave it uncorrected, keeping it oblique just as the old maps (*pinakes*) present it.·

First, 'cannot say' is the same as withholding it, and someone withholding inclines neither way. When he exhorts that it be left alone, just like the ancients, he inclines that way. Rather he would be preserving his consistency if he advised one not to use geography at all, for we 'cannot say' what the positions are of the other mountains, such as the Alps, Pyrenaian, Thracian, Illyric, or Germanic. Who would believe that the ancients were more trustworthy than those more recent, since they made all those mistakes in map-drawing (*pinakographia*) that Eratosthenes has accused them of, none of which Hipparchos objected to?

51   Strabo 2. 1. 16, C74: *Climate as evidence of latitude*
Eratosthenes cites this epigram in the Asklepieion of the Pantikapaians,[172] on a bronze hydria that had been broken by the frost:

> If any person does not believe what can happen here,
>   let them look at this hydria and know.
> Not as an honourable dedication to the god but as proof
>   of a great winter, Stratios the priest presented it.

Since (*the climate*) in the region around the Bosporos cannot be compared to that in the places enumerated, not even with Amisos and Sinope—which, we would say, are more temperate—it could hardly lie parallel to the region around the Borysthenes and the farthest Kelts. Moreover, it could scarcely be at the same parallel as the region around Amisos, Sinope, Byzantion, or Massalia, which are agreed to be 3,700 stades further south.

---

[170] An interesting statement of scientific method: the *combination* of instrumental data and eye-witness reports is most convincing, as exemplified in the following sentence.

[171] The following words are in direct speech, and as such a verbatim quotation from Hipparchos; the rest of the paragraph is probably from H. too, apart from the mention of the 'Germanic' mountains (Roller 2010, 165).

[172] At Pantikapaion on the Kimmerian Bosporos, E of the Crimea.

52 Strabo 2. 1. 19–41, C76–94

Headings are added.

Deimachos' errors about India

(19) Moreover, he wishes to demonstrate that Deimachos[173] is an amateur and inexperienced in such things, for he believes that Indike lies between the autumnal equinox (*phthinopōrinē isēmeria*) and the winter tropic (*tropoi*)[174]—contradicting Megasthenes,[175] who says that in the southern portion of Indike the Bears are hidden[176] and shadows fall in the opposite direction. But he (*Deimachos*) believes that neither instance occurs anywhere in Indike, and thus in asserting this he speaks with ignorance, for it is ignorant to think that the autumnal differs from the vernal in terms of its distance from the tropic, because the circle and the sunrise are the same at both. Since the distance between the tropic of the Earth and the equator—where he had placed Indike—has been shown through careful measurement to be much less than 20,000 stades, this would turn out to be—even according to him (*Deimachos*)—exactly what he (*Eratosthenes*) believes, not what the former believes. If Indike were of that extent—or even 30,000—it could not fall within that distance, but if it is what he (*Eratosthenes*) says, it would fall within it. It is the same ignorance to say that nowhere in Indike do the Bears set or the shadows fall in the opposite direction, since it begins to happen as soon as one gets 5,000 (*stades*) from Alexandria. ·In the following statements, too, Hipparchos wrongly modifies what he (*Eratosthenes*) says· . . .

The latitudes of India

(20)[177] ·(*Hipparchos also says that*) Eratosthenes himself concurs almost exactly with Philon,[178] but that no one records the zone of latitude in Indike, not even Eratosthenes himself. (*Finally, Hipparchos says that*) if indeed the Bears both disappear (*i.e. set*) there, as they (*Eratosthenes and Philon*) think, relying on those who were with Nearchos,[179] it is not possible that Meroë and the capes of Indike lie on the same parallel.·[180] If Eratosthenes agrees with those asserting that both the Bears set, why is it that no one reports on the latitudes in Indike, not even Eratosthenes? For this discussion is about latitude. If he does not agree with them, let him be discharged from the accusation. And he does not agree, for when Deimachos[181] says that nowhere in Indike are the

---

[173] *BNJ* 716 (Daimachos) F 3.

[174] A few lines below, Strabo implicitly takes Hipparchos to task for adopting Deimachos' bizarre specification 'autumnal'. The 'winter tropic' is the Tropic of Capricorn (*c.*23½° S)—an error for 'summer tropic', Tropic of Cancer (*c.*23½° N). All of India is N of the equator. Deimachos (*BNJ* 716 Daimachos) is an obscure figure; we cannot tell whether it his error, Eratosthenes', or Hipparchos' (Roller 2018, 69–70).

[175] *BNJ* 715 F 7a.

[176] Not strictly true: in lower latitudes N of the equator, a great or lesser part of each of them is no longer circumpolar but rises and sets each day.

[177] **27**, from book 2, stands here in Strabo's text.   [178] *BNJ* 670 F 2.

[179] *BNJ* 133 F 16. Nearchos was Alexander's admiral: see Introduction, §VI. 2. h.

[180] Meroë is at *c.*16° N, the S tip of India at *c.*8° N.   [181] *BNJ* 716 (Daimachos) F 3.

Bears hidden, nor do the shadows fall in the opposite direction—which Megasthenes[182] does in fact assume—he (*Eratosthenes*) charges him (*Deimachos*) with ignorance. Thus the entire combination is false.[183] ...

(21) In what follows, attempting to prove these things, he (*Hipparchos*) says what has been refuted by me, or uses false assumptions, or imposes erroneous conclusions. Regarding the fact that from Babylon to Thapsakos is 4,800 stades, and 2,100 north to the Armenian mountains, one cannot conclude that from Babylon along its meridian to the northern mountains is more than 6,000. Eratosthenes does not say that it is 2,100 stades from Thapsakos to the mountains, but that there is a remainder that is unmeasured, and thus the following reasoning, from assumptions not proved, cannot be assumed. Eratosthenes nowhere declared that Thapsakos lies more than 4,500 stades north of Babylon.[184]

Eratosthenes' first two sealstones (India and Arianē)

(22) ... Following the thesis about the Tauros and the sea from the Pillars, he (*Eratosthenes*) divides the inhabited world into two parts by means of this line, calling them the northern part and the southern, and he attempts to divide each again into portions, insofar as possible, calling them *sphragides* ('sealstones').[185] He says that the first sealstone of the southern portion is Indike, and the second Ariane,[186] which are easy to sketch out, as he could render not only the width and length of both, but in a manner to show their shape, as a geometrician would. He says that Indike is rhomboidal because its sides are washed by the sea on the south and east—making shores without major gulfs—and the remainder by the mountains and the river, somewhat preserving there the rectilinear shape.

He (*Eratosthenes*) also sees that Ariane has three sides suitably formed for the creation of a parallelogram, although he cannot mark off the western side by points, because the peoples there alternate with one another,[187] yet he nevertheless indicates it by a sort of line from the Caspian Gates ending at the promontories of Karmania that touch the Persian gulf. He calls this side the western and that along the Indos the eastern, but he does not say that these are parallel, nor the others—the ones delineated by the mountain and by the sea—but merely (*calls them*) the northern and the southern.

---

[182] *BNJ* 715 F 7a.

[183] Strabo is of little help in disentangling the different sources here (Roller 2010, 176).

[184] See n. on §24 below.   [185] See introduction to chapter.

[186] E. probably extended the scope of Ariane from the area of *Herat* in mod. Afghanistan to the whole region from India to Mesopotamia (Roller 2010, 181).

[187] E., as reported by Strabo via Hipparchos here, was attempting to replace an ethnically organized geography with a geometric (Roller 2010, 184).

Eratosthenes' difficulties with his third sealstone (Mesopotamia)

(23) Thus he (*Eratosthenes*) renders the second sealstone by the form of a rough outline, but he renders the third sealstone much more roughly, for several reasons. First, as already mentioned, the side from the Caspian Gates to Karmania, common to the third and second sealstones, has not been defined distinctly, and then the Persian gulf breaks into the southern side, as he himself says. Thus he was forced to take the line from Babylon as if it were straight, through Sousa and Persepolis to the borders of Karmania and Persis, on which he was able to find a measured route, being in total of slightly more than 9,000 stades. This he calls the southern side but he does not say that it is parallel to the northern. It is clear that the Euphrates, by which he marks off the western side, is nothing like a straight line: after flowing from the mountains to the south it then turns towards the east and then back to the south until it empties into the sea. In showing the shape of Mesopotamia, which is created by the convergence of the Tigris and the Euphrates, and which resembles a rower's cushion[188]—as he says—he makes it clear that the river is not straight. Moreover, he does not have a complete measurement for the western side that is marked off by the Euphrates, and he says that he does not have how much further the distance is to Armenia and the northern mountains, as it is unmeasured. Because of all this he says that he represents the third portion very roughly. And he says that he collected the distances from many reports of those who had worked out the stopping points, some of which he says were without titles. . . .

(24) Thus he says that he has shown the third portion roughly, with a length of 10,000 stades from the Caspian Gates to the Euphrates, and in dividing it into portions he set down the measurements as he had found them already recorded, beginning in reverse from the Euphrates and its crossing at Thapsakos.[189] As far as the Tigris, where Alexander crossed it, he writes 2,400 stades, and then to the successive places through Gaugamela, the Lykos, Arbela, and Ekbatana, by which Darius (*III*) fled from Gaugamela to the Caspian Gates, he fills out with 10,000, having an excess of only 300 stades. This is how he measures out the northern side, not having placed it parallel with the mountains or with the line through the Pillars, Athens, and Rhodes. For Thapsakos is far away from the mountains, and the mountains and the route from Thapsakos come together at the Caspian Gates. These are the northern portions of the boundary.

---

[188] i.e. with a convex curve. E.'s necessary reliance on recorded road distances made it difficult to shoehorn the topography into his essentially rectangular *sphragis*.

[189] Though mentioned several times in this extract, Thapsakos' precise location remains unknown; it is not listed in the gazetteer to *Barr*. Located on the Euphrates E of *Gaziantep* in S-central Turkey by ToposText (https://topostext.org), at anc. Zeugma, as it is by Gawlikowski 1996; but further downstream, W of *Raqqah* in N-central Syria, by Pleiades (https://pleiades.stoa.org/ (both websites last accessed 30 January 2023). It is a Euphrates crossing at Xen. *Anab.* 1. 4. 11; see also Roller 2015, 70 & n. 72, 94–5 & n. 46. Cf. **52** §39 below.

(25) Having thus represented the northern side, he says that the southern cannot be taken along the sea because the Persian gulf breaks into it, but from Babylon through Sousa and Persepolis to the boundaries of Persis and Karmania it is 9,200 stades. He calls this the southern side, but he does not say that the southern is parallel to the northern. He says that the difference in length that occurs between the assumed northern and southern sides is because the Euphrates, having up to a point flowed to the south, turns more towards the east.

(26) Of the two flanking sides, he speaks about the western first. What it is like and whether it is one or two (*lines*) is considered uncertain. He says that from the Thapsakos crossing along the Euphrates to Babylon is 4,800 stades, and from there to the outlet of the Euphrates and the city of Teredon[190] is 3,000. From Thapsakos to the north it has been measured as far as the Armenian Gates and is about 1,100, but through the Gordyaioi and the Armenians it is unknown and thus omitted. The eastern side, that which goes through Persis lengthwise from the Erythraian (*sea*) somewhat towards Media and the north, he believes is no less than 8,000, and from certain promontories, over 9,000. The remainder through Paraitakene and Media to the Caspian Gates is about 3,000. The Tigris river and the Euphrates flow from Armenia to the south, and when they pass the mountains of the Gordyaioi they go round a great circle and enclose the large territory of Mesopotamia and then turn towards the winter sunrise (*south-east*) and the south, especially in the case of the Euphrates. It constantly becomes closer to the Tigris around the Wall of Semiramis and the village of Opis, from which it is only 200 stades. Flowing through Babylon, it empties into the Persian gulf. Thus it happens, he says, that the shape of Mesopotamia and Babylonia is like a cushion on a rowing bench.

(27) ·Concerning the third *sphragis* (*sc. Mesopotamia*), he (*Eratosthenes*) does indeed make certain other mistakes, which we shall consider, but not at all in the matters Hipparchos brings up against him. Let us see what he (*Hipparchos*) says. For in wishing to validate what he says at the start, that Indike must not be transferred further south as Eratosthenes adjudges, he says this can be made totally clear from the things he (*Eratosthenes*) himself brings up: for the latter says the third division (*meris*)[191] is delimited on its northern side by the line from the Caspian Gates to the Euphrates, which is of 10,000 stades; and subsequently adduces that its south side, the one running from Babylon to the mountains of Karmania, is a little more than 9,000, while the side towards the west, from Thapsakos along the Euphrates to Babylon, is 4,800 stades and then 3,000 to the outlets (*of the river*). As for the places north of Thapsakos, part has been measured up to 1,100 stades while the rest has not yet been measured.· . . .

---

[190] Somewhere near *Basra* in lower Mesopotamia, where the coast has advanced up to *c*.125 mi (*c*.200 km) since E.'s day (Roller 2010, 187).

[191] Strabo means the same as *sphragis*.

The western boundary of the second sealstone

(28) ... Yet Eratosthenes has not said that the line bounding the western side of Ariane lies on a meridian, nor that (*the line*) from the Caspian Gates to Thapsakos is at right angles with the meridian through the Caspian Gates, but rather (*mentions the line*) marked by the mountain—with which that from Thapsakos makes an angle—since it has been brought down from the same point as that from which the line at the mountain (*has been drawn*). Moreover, he has not said that the line to Babylon from Karmania is parallel to the line to Thapsakos.[192] ...

Hipparchos' objections to the second sealstone

(29) ... ·He (*Hipparchos*) asserts that if a straight line is understood as extended south from Thapsakos, and another perpendicular to this one from Babylon, there will be a right-angled triangle consisting of the side reaching from Thapsakos to Babylon, the perpendicular extended from Babylon to the meridian through Thapsakos, and the actual meridian through Thapsakos. He posits that the hypotenuse of this triangle is the direct line from Thapsakos to Babylon, which he states is 4,800 stades, while the perpendicular line from Babylon to the meridian through Thapsakos is a little more than 1,000, the value of the excess of the line to Thapsakos (*from the Caspian Gates*) over that to Babylon (*from the frontier between Carmania and Persia*).[193] From these points he also calculates that the other of the (*two*) sides on either side of the right angle is many times greater than the aforesaid perpendicular.

He also adds to this line the one running north from Thapsakos that terminates at the Armenian mountains. Of this, Eratosthenes said that one part had been measured and was of 1,100 (*stades*), while he leaves aside the unmeasured part; it is supposed to measure at least 1,000, with the result that both add up to 2,100. He (*Hipparchos*), adding this to the straight side of the triangle as far as the perpendicular line from Babylon, calculates that the distance from the Armenian mountains and the parallel (*sc. of latitude*) through Athens to the perpendicular from Babylon is many thousands, setting this perpendicular upon the parallel through Babylon. He shows, however, that the distance from the parallel through Athens to the parallel through Babylon is no greater than 2,400 stades, on the assumption that the entire meridian has the length in stades that Eratosthenes says it has. If this is true, then the mountains of Armenia and of the Tauros could not be on the parallel through Athens, as Eratosthenes claims, but according to Eratosthenes himself must be many thousands of stades further north.·

In addition, making further use of the demolished assumptions about the structure of the right-angled triangle, he (*Hipparchos*) takes something that is not given: that the hypotenuse in the right angle—the line straight from Thapsakos as far as Babylon—is within 4,800 stades.[194] But Eratosthenes says that the route is along the Euphrates,

---

[192] But E. did not assume that his *sphragides* were necessarily oriented N–S (Roller 2010, 184–5).
[193] The two explanatory parentheses are from Dicks 1960, 75. On this passage, see Dicks 1960, 130–5.
[194] Strabo here moderates Hipparchos' criticism of E.

and—stating that Mesopotamia along with Babylonia is enclosed by the great circle of the Euphrates and Tigris—he also says that most of the circumference is due to the Euphrates. Therefore the straight line from Thapsakos to Babylon would not be along the Euphrates or be anywhere near as many stades. Thus his (*Hipparchos'*) argument is destroyed.

Moreover, it has already been stated that granting two lines drawn from the Caspian Gates, one to Thapsakos and the other to the part of the Armenian mountains corresponding to Thapsakos—which Hipparchos himself has at least 2,100 stades from Thapsakos—they could not be parallel to each other or to that through Babylon—which Eratosthenes calls the southern side. He said that the route along the mountain had not been measured, yet he also said that from Thapsakos to the Caspian Gates has been, but he added that one is speaking roughly. Moreover, in wishing only to speak about the territory between Ariane and the Euphrates, there is no difference whether one or the other was measured. . . .

(30) . . . The following are the accusations that one might make against Eratosthenes.[195] Just as the cutting of a limb differs from (*the cutting*) of a part—because the former removes the parts that are by nature defined by certain joints or a conspicuous shape, about which it has been said 'cutting him limb from limb',[196] but the latter is in no such way—and just as we make use of the proper one, considering the time and necessity, thus in regard to geography it is necessary to cut what is examined into parts, yet imitating the cutting of a limb rather than at random. Therefore the significant and well-defined is removed, that which is useful for the geographer. It is well defined when it is possible (*to make use of*) rivers, mountains, or seas, people or peoples, or, whenever possible, a particular size or shape. Everywhere, instead of something geometrical, a simple (*definition*) is totally sufficient. For the size, it is sufficient to state its greatest length and width, as in the case of the inhabited world, a length of about 70,000 stades and a width of less than half its length. For the shape, you can compare it to a certain geometrical figure, such as Sicily to a triangle, or to other known figures, such as Iberia to a hide or the Peloponnesos to the leaf of a plane-tree. The larger (*the region*) that is cut up, the rougher the parts will conspicuously be.

Geometrical divisions

(31) He (*Eratosthenes*) has cheerfully divided the inhabited world into two parts by means of the Tauros and the sea extending to the Pillars. In regard to the southern portion, the borders of Indike have been well delimited in terms of a mountain, river, and sea, and by a single name—that of a single people—so that he correctly calls it four-sided and rhomboidal.

---

[195] Strictly speaking, this paragraph does not preserve any idea of E.'s, but it is interesting for Strabo's objection to his methods, as well as for S.'s comparison of the shapes of large regions to common objects (on which see Dueck 2005).

[196] *Od.* 9. 291.

More problems of the second sealstone

Ariane cannot easily be outlined because its western side is confused, but it is bounded by three sides, which are approximately straight, and also by its name, that of one people. But, as it has been determined, the third sealstone is completely undefined, for the common side between it and Ariane is confused, as I have said, and the southern side has been taken most sloppily, for it does not outline the sealstone, since it runs through the middle of it and many portions towards the south are left out. It also does not trace its greatest length, for the northern side is longer. The Euphrates is not the western side, even if it flowed in a straight line, since its extremities do not lie on the same meridian. How can this be the western rather than the southern? Apart from this, since the remainder to the Kilikian and Syrian sea is small, it is implausible that the sealstone could not be advanced to there, since Semiramis and Ninos are called Syrians. The former founded Babylon and made it the royal residence, and the latter (*founded*) Ninos as the metropolis of Syria. Moreover, up to the present the same language exists both outside and within the Euphrates, and to tear in two a most famous people by such a division, joining parts to foreign peoples, would be especially inappropriate.

Nor could he (*Eratosthenes*) say that he was forced to do this because of the size, for (*including the territory*) as far as the sea would not make it equal to Indike or Ariane, even adding that as far as the boundary of Fortunate Arabia and Egypt. It would have been much better to extend the third sealstone this far, saying that such (*territory*) as far as the Syrian sea has been added to it, so that the southern side is not as he said it was, nor as a straight line, but it extends as one sails straight along the Persian gulf with the Karmanian coast on the right as far as the mouth of the Euphrates, and touches the boundaries of Mesene and Babylonia, which is the beginning of the isthmus that divides Fortunate Arabia from the rest of the continent, and then crosses over it and comes as far as the recess of the Arabian gulf and Pelousion, and even to the Kanobic mouth of the Nile. This is the southern side; the remaining or western (*side*) would be from the Kanobic mouth as far as the Kilikian coast.

The fourth sealstone

(32) The fourth sealstone is composed of Eudaimon (*Fortunate*) Arabia,[197] the Arabian gulf, all Egypt, and Aithiopia. The length of this portion will be that bounded by the two meridians, one of which is drawn through its most westerly point and the other through the most easterly.[198] The width will be between two parallels, one of which is drawn through the most northerly point and the other (*through*) the most southerly, since the size of irregular figures whose sides make it impossible to determine their width and length must be determined in this way. . . .

---

[197] Roman Arabia Felix; the names refer to the luxury commodities traded between S. Asia and the Mediterranean world, of which Agatharchides and *PME* tell us much.

[198] Having wrestled with irregular forms in the third sealstone, E. surprisingly adopted a cardinally oriented scheme for the fourth (Roller 2010, 192).

Difficulty of dividing using parallels of latitude

(33) Eratosthenes takes the length of the inhabited world on the line through the Pillars, the Caspian Gates, and the Caucasus as if straight, and that of the third section on the one through the Caspian Gates and Thapsakos, and that of the fourth section on the one through Thapsakos and Heroönpolis[199] as far as the region between the mouths of the Nile, which must come to an end in the region around Kanobos and Alexandria, for the last mouth is there, called the Kanobic or Herakleotic. Whether or not he places these lengths straight with each other or as if making an angle at Thapsakos, it is clear from what he says that neither is parallel to the length of the inhabited world. He draws the length of the inhabited world straight from the Tauros through the sea as far as the Pillars on a line through the Caucasus, Rhodes, and Athens, and he says that from Rhodes to Alexandria, along the meridian through them, is not much less than 4,000 stades: thus the parallels through Rhodes and Alexandria would be this (*distance*) apart from one another. That at Heroönpolis is about the same (*as ⟨at⟩ Alexandria*), or somewhat further south, and thus the line intersecting that parallel and that of Rhodes and the Caspian Gates, whether straight or deflected, cannot be parallel to either. Thus he has not taken the lengths well, nor has he taken the portions stretching northward well.

Difficulties of the third sealstone: distances from Babylon

(34) . . . ·For he (*Hipparchos*) states that he (*Eratosthenes*) says the distance from Babylon to the Caspian Gates is 6,700 stades, and to the frontiers of Karmania and Persis more than 9,000, which is measured along a line running straight towards the equinoctial sunrise; and that this line is perpendicular to the shared side of the second and third 'seals', so that according to him (*Eratosthenes*) a right-angled triangle subsists with its right angle towards the frontiers of Karmania, its hypotenuse being shorter than one of the sides enclosing the right angle; so therefore he (*Eratosthenes*) assigns Persis to the second 'seal'.· But I have said[200] in regard to this that he (*Eratosthenes*) does not take (*the distance*) from Babylon to Karmania on a parallel, nor does he say that the straight line that separates the sealstones is a meridian, so he (*Hipparchos*) cannot speak against him.

·What he next adduces is not right either. For since he (*Eratosthenes*) had said it was so far from the Caspian Gates to Babylon, and to Sousa 4,900, and from Babylon to there 3,400.· . . .

Further problems of the third sealstone

·He then goes on to calculate that, according to these hypotheses, it will turn out that the meridian line through the Caspian Gates has its common point (*i.e. intersection*) with the parallel through Babylon and Sousa further west than the common point

---

[199] In NE Egypt, between the E limit of the Delta and the *Red Sea* (possibly at *Tell el-Maskhuta*).
[200] At §28 above. But the hypotenuse is always the longest side of a right-angled triangle.

of the same parallel and the straight line extending from the Caspian Gates to the frontiers of Karmania and Persis, by more than 4,400 stades; and that, in relation to the meridian line through the Caspian Gates, the line through the Caspian Gates and the frontiers of Karmania and Persis just about makes half a right angle and inclines to the midpoint between the south and the equinoctial sunrise (*due east*); and that the Indos river is parallel with this line, so that it does not flow to the south from the mountains as Eratosthenes says, but between that point and the equinoctial sunrise, as it is delineated in the old maps (*pinakes*).· . . . ·And it is without these points[201] that he (*Eratosthenes*) has stated that the form of Indike is rhomboid; and that as the eastward side diverges strongly towards the east—especially at the furthest promontory, which additionally advances more towards the south in comparison with the remainder of the coast—so, too, does the side adjoining the Indos.·

Distinguishing differences of latitude

(35) . . . ·Even so (*Hipparchos says*), he (*Eratosthenes*) demonstrates that deviations (*in latitude*) of 400 stades can be perceived, as in the case of the parallel through Athens and that through Rhodes.· Observing this is not something done by a single method, but there is one where the difference is greater and another where it is less.[202] Where it is greater, we can trust our eyes or the crops, or the temperature of the air in judging the latitude, but for the lesser there are instruments such as gnomons or *dioptrai*. Thus when taking the parallels of Athens with a gnomon, and that of Rhodes and Karia, the difference is perceptible, as is expected with so many stades. But, in a width of 3,000 stades and a length of 40,000 stades in the mountains and 30,000 in the sea, when someone makes a line from west to the equinoctial sunrise (*due east*), naming one part the southern and the other the northern, calling them 'the rectangle' and 'the sealstone,' he must understand what he means by these terms, as well as 'northern sides' or 'southern', and moreover 'western' and 'eastern'. If he disregards this, he is greatly in error and must be held to account—for it is just—but if it is merely slight, even if he disregards it, he should not be questioned. In this there is no refutation to be made against him (*Eratosthenes*). . . .

The problem of the length of the fourth sealstone

(36) . . . ·He rightly criticizes him (*Eratosthenes*) in that he identifies as the length of this section the line from Thapsakos as far as Egypt, as if a man should call the diagonal of a parallelogram its 'length'. For Thapsakos does not lie on the same parallel as the coast of Egypt, but they lie on parallels at a great distance from one another, while the line between Thapsakos and Egypt runs in a sort of diagonal and oblique manner. Where he is not correct is in expressing surprise that he (*Eratosthenes*) confidently says

---

[201] Or 'assumptions', Dicks.
[202] Again (cf. n. on **50** §11 above), E. favoured the combination of instrumental measurement and eye-witness reports.

the distance from Pelousion to Thapsakos is 6,000 stades when it is more than 8,000.·
. . . He (*Eratosthenes*) said that the route to Babylon from Thapsakos is 4,800 stades
and follows the Euphrates, this on purpose so that no one would take it as straight
or a measurement of the distance between two parallels. . . . ·For it certainly has not
been granted (*by Eratosthenes*) that from Babylon to the meridian through the Caspian
Gates is a distance of 4,800.· . . .

Difficulties of Eratosthenes' parallels and meridians

(37) This is not where one must criticize Eratosthenes, but we do say that his loose
magnitudes and figures must have some (*agreed*) measurement, and that in some
cases more must be conceded, in others less. Taking the width of the mountains that
stretch towards the equinoctial sunrise (*due east*)[203] as 3,000 stades, and similarly the
sea as far as the Pillars, one could agree more easily that the parallels drawn with the
same width lie on a single line, rather than those that intersect, and also in regard to
the ones that intersect within the same width rather than those that intersect outside.
Similarly (*considered*) are those lines that diverge without extending beyond the width,
rather than those extending beyond, and those with greater length rather than those
that are shorter. Thus the inequality of the length would be concealed, as well as the
dissimilarity of the figures. For example, if the width of the entire Tauros or the sea up
to the Pillars is 3,000 stades, we then perceive a parallelogram that marks the outline
of the entire mountain range and the previously mentioned sea. . . . But when he takes
(*the line*) from the Caspian Gates through the mountains themselves and also the one
that immediately diverges greatly from the mountains into Thapsakos, as if they led as
far as the Pillars on the same parallel, and again throws out (*a line*) from Thapsakos as
far as Egypt,[204] taking in this width, and then measures the length of the figure by this
length, he would seem to be measuring the lengths of the rectangle by the diagonal of
the rectangle. When it is not a diagonal but a deflected line, he would seem to err much
more, for it is a deflected line leading from the Caspian Gates through Thapsakos to
the Nile. . . .

(38) ·Another objection to Hipparchos is that, since he has laid a charge against
what Eratosthenes says, he should likewise have made some rectification of his errors,
as we are doing. But even if he has occasionally given thought to this, he commands
us to abide by the old maps, which require a great deal more rectification than does
the map of Eratosthenes. The proof he next attempts is equally shoddy. For he takes
as a premiss what has been concocted from things not granted, as we have demonstrated[205]—that Babylon is further east than Thapsakos by no more than 1,000 stades—
so that, even if it is concluded that it is further east by more than 2,400 stades, on the
basis that Eratosthenes states that from Thapsakos to the Tigris crossing by which

---

[203] Probably the Caucasus. Strabo is presumably again following Hipparchos' account of E.'s
argument. (Roller 2010, 168.)
[204] Which would run approx. SW (Roller 2010, 168).   [205] At §27 above.

Alexander crossed is a short cut of 2,400, while the Tigris and Euphrates encircle Mesopotamia, bearing east for a time, turning back south, and then approaching one another and also approaching Babylon—that is no extraordinary feature of his (Eratosthenes') account.·

Hipparchos' excessive criticism of Eratosthenes' parallels and meridians

(39) ·He (*Hipparchos*) is off key, too, in his next attempt, in which he wants to deduce that the road from Thapsakos to the Caspian Gates, which Eratosthenes has stated to be 10,000 stades, had not been measured in a straight line, as Eratosthenes says it had, and that the straight line is much shorter.[206] The attack he makes is of the following nature. He says that even on Eratosthenes' account the meridian through the Canopic mouth (*of the Nile*) and the one through the Kyaneai[207] (*Cyanean Rocks*) are the same, and that this stands apart from the one through Thapsakos by 6,300 stades, and the Kyaneai stand apart from Mount Kaspios—which lies above the transit to the Caspian open-sea (*pelagos*) from Kolchis—by 6,600. So, within 300 stades, it is the same distance from the meridian through the Kyaneai to Thapsakos as it is to Kaspios; in a way, therefore, Thapsakos and Kaspios lie on the same meridian. As a consequence, he says, the Caspian Gates are at the same distance from Thapsakos as they are from Kaspios, and their distance from Kaspios is much less than 10,000, which Eratosthenes says is their distance from Thapsakos; therefore their distance from Thapsakos is much less than 10,000 (*measured*) in a straight line, and therefore his (*Eratosthenes'*) 10,000 is a circuitous route even though he reckons as a straight line from the Caspian Gates to Thapsakos.·

I say to him (*Hipparchos*) that Eratosthenes makes his line loosely, as is proper in geography,[208] and also makes his meridians and lines to the equinoctial sunrise loosely, but he (*Hipparchos*) critiques them geometrically, as if each had been drawn with instruments. Yet he does not use instruments himself, rather taking the relationship of the perpendicular and parallel by guessing. This is one of his mistakes. Another is that he does not put down the measurements that were produced (*by Eratosthenes*) or put them to the test, but only those created by himself. ·For this reason, in the first place, while he (*Eratosthenes*) says the distance from the mouth (*of the Black Sea*) to Phasis was 8,000 stades, and adds the 600 from there to Dioskourias and the transit from Dioskourias to the Kaspios, which is five days—which according to Hipparchos himself can plausibly be said to be around 1,000 stades—and thus according to Eratosthenes the whole (*journey*) adds up to 9,600, he himself (*Hipparchos*) has cut this down and says that while it is 5,600 from the Kyaneai to Phasis it is a further 1,000 from there

[206] On Thapsakos, see n. on §24 above.
[207] The Wandering, Clashing, or Dark Blue Rocks near the entrance to the Black Sea, through which Jason's ship *Argo* passed.
[208] Hipparchos would disagree.

to Kaspios.· Thus it is not according to Eratosthenes that Kaspios and Thapsakos are essentially on the same meridian, but according to him (*Hipparchos*). . . .

Eratosthenes' account of Europe's promontories

(40) ·In the second treatise (*hypomnēma; i.e. book 2*), after taking up the same enquiry again about the frontiers in the Tauros region, which we have adequately discussed, he (*Hipparchos*) moves on to the northerly parts of the inhabited world. Next he expounds the statements of Eratosthenes concerning the places beyond the Pontos: namely, that three capes extend from the north, and that one of these has the Peloponnese upon it, the second is the Italian cape, and the third the Ligurian; and that both the Adriatic gulf and the Tyrrhenic are embraced by these. Having expounded this in a general fashion, he attempts to disprove the detailed statements made about them, and does so in a geometrical rather than geographical way. But so great a plethora of errors are committed by Eratosthenes in these passages, and by Timosthenes, author of *Harbours*—whom he (*Eratosthenes*) praises above the rest of them, but whom he disagrees with and disproves in many respects—that I do not deem it worthwhile to dwell upon either of these authors, who commit so many errors of fact, nor upon Hipparchos. For even he (*Hipparchos*) leaves aside some of their errors and does not correct others, but only refutes them on the basis that they have been spoken falsely or polemically.· Perhaps one could accuse him (*Eratosthenes*) of this because he says that there are three promontories of Europe, putting down that on which is the Peloponnesos as one, although it is split into many parts. Sounion makes a promontory, just like Lakonike (*Laconia*), which is not much less to the south than Maleai[209] and includes a notable gulf. And that from the Thracian Chersonesos (*Gallipoli peninsula*) up to Sounion cuts off the Melas (*Black*) gulf[210] and those as far as the Macedonian. Even if we were to overlook this, most of the distances are obviously wrong and prove that his ignorance of these places is excessive, without needing any geometrical proofs but only those that are obvious and can be immediately witnessed.

Eratosthenes' imperfect knowledge of certain regions

For example, the pass from Epidamnos (*Durrës*) to the Thermaic gulf (*gulf of Thessaloniki*) is more than 2,000 stades. He (*Eratosthenes*) says it is 900, and that from Alexandria to Karchedon is more than 13,000, although it is no more than 9,000 if Karia and Rhodes are on the same meridian as Alexandria, and the Strait is on the same one as Karchedon (*Carthage*). All agree that the voyage from Karia to the Strait is no more than 9,000 stades. In the case of a great interval, the meridian could be taken as the same as the more westerly one, that is, as far west as Karchedon is west of the Strait, but in 4,000 stades the error is manifest. And he places Rome on the same meridian as Karchedon, although it is more to the west, but he does not admit his excessive ignorance of these regions and of those on towards the west as far as the Pillars.

---

[209] Or Malea; the SE cape of the Peloponnese, in Laconia.   [210] W of *Gallipoli*.

The nature of Eratosthenes' work: summing up

(41) ·So, if Hipparchos was not writing geography but examining what was said in the *Geography* of Eratosthenes, it was appropriate for him to correct things more extensively in detail.· For our part, we have thought it necessary in each case to bring forth a proper discussion, not only in regard to where he is right, but especially where he hits a false note, both correcting and absolving him of the charges made against him by Hipparchos, as well as examining Hipparchos himself, whenever he has said something censorious. But in these cases, when I see that he (*Eratosthenes*) is completely off the mark and that he is accused justly, we assume that it is enough to correct what he said in his *Geographia*. Where the mistakes are continuous and on the surface, it is better not to record them, unless rarely and generally. This is what we will attempt to do in what follows.

·Let it now be said that both Timosthenes and Eratosthenes, and those even earlier than they, were completely ignorant of the Iberian and Keltic lands, and ten thousand times more so the Germanic and Brettanic lands; also the lands of the Getai and Bastarnai.[211] They also fell into great ignorance when they reached the parts around Italy, the Adriatic, the Pontos, and the northerly ones beyond, even if these charges are perhaps (overly) censorious.· In regard to remote areas, Eratosthenes says that he records the distances that have been handed down, but does not validate them, reporting them as they have been received, although at times adding 'by means of a more or less straight line'. One cannot put to a strict test those distances that do not agree with one another. ·That is what Hipparchos attempts to do, both in the above-mentioned instances and in the passage where he expounds the distances in the area of Hyrkania as far as Baktria and the nations beyond, and furthermore the distances from Kolchis to the Hyrkanian (*Caspian*) sea.·

In these matters he should not be scrutinized in the same way as with the continental coast and other places that are well known, and, moreover, as I said, it is not something geometric, but rather geographical. ·Having criticized, then, some of the Aithiopian statements, towards the end of his second of his treatises (*hypomnēmata*) written *Against the Geography of Eratosthenes*, he (*Hipparchos*) says that in the third the perspective will rather be mathematical though also to a degree geographical. Yet it seems clear to me that he does not even have a certain amount of geography, but that it is completely mathematical, although Eratosthenes has given him quite an excuse. Often he (*Eratosthenes*) slips into something too scholarly for the topic before him, and having slipped into something inaccurate, the conclusions that he makes are roughly done. ·In a certain way he (*Eratosthenes*) is a mathematician among geographers and a geographer among mathematicians. Thus he offers points of attack to his opponents on both sides, indeed fair attacks in respect of this treatise (*my own*); both he and

---

[211] Peoples living NW of the Black Sea.

Timosthenes do so. Therefore there is no remaining need for us to examine them together, and we shall be satisfied with what has been said by Hipparchos.·

53 **Strabo** 2. 2. 2, C95: *The prime meridian beyond Syene*
From Syene, which is on the boundary of the summer tropic, to Meroë is 5,000 (*stades*), and from there to the parallel of the Cinnamon-bearing Land, which is the beginning of the burned (*mod. 'torrid'*) zone, is 3,000. All of this distance is measurable, as it is travelled by sea and by land, but the remainder as far as the equator is shown to be 8,800 stades, by means of the measurement of the Earth made by Eratosthenes. The relationship of the 16,800 to the 8,800 would be that of the distance between the tropics to the width of the burned zone.

54 **Strabo** 2. 4. 2, C104: *Eratosthenes' knowledge of the west and north*
·With respect to the western and northern parts of Europe, I have already reported Eratosthenes' ignorance.[212] While we should forgive him and Dikaiarchos, since they had not observed those places, who could forgive Polybios and Poseidonios?·[213]

55 **Strabo** 2. 4. 4, C106–7: *Polybios' criticisms of Eratosthenes only partly justified*
Next, he (*Polybios*)[214] corrects the statements of Eratosthenes, in some cases correctly, but in others what he says is worse. For example, when he (*Eratosthenes*) says that from Ithaca to Korkyra is 300 (*stades*), he (*Polybios*) says that it is more than 900; (*Eratosthenes*) set down 900 from Epidamnos to Thessalonikeia, but he (*Polybios*) says it is more than 2,000. In these he is correct.

But when he (*Eratosthenes*) says that it is 7,000 from Massalia to the Pillars, which are 6,000 from Pyrene (*the Pyrenees*), he (*Polybios*) himself speaks in error in saying that it is more than 9,000 from Massalia and from Pyrene a little less than 8,000, for he (*Eratosthenes*) is nearer to the truth. Those today agree that if one cuts through the irregularities of the roads, the length of the whole of Iberia, from Pyrene to its western side, is no more than 6,000 stades.[215] But he (*Polybios*) puts the Tagos river at 8,000 in length from its source as far as its mouth, without any of its bends—this is not being geographical—but speaking of a straight line, although the sources of the Tagos are more than 1,000 stades from Pyrene.

On the other hand, he is correct when he proclaims that Eratosthenes is ignorant of Iberike, because he proclaims things that conflict with one another, such as when he says that the exterior as far as Gadeira is inhabited by the Galatai—if they do possess the western part of Europe as far as Gadeira—and then he forgets this and nowhere records the Galatai in his circuit of Iberia.[216]

---

[212] At 2. 1. 41 (52 §41 above).
[213] This repeats the end of **18** §2 above, but probably comes from book 3.
[214] Polyb. 34. 7. 1–7.
[215] Artemidoros 168 (if genuine) computes more than 7,000 st. from Pyrene to Gadeira.
[216] Down to E.'s time 'Iberia' was originally conceived of as including all territory W of the Rhône (Roller 2010, 212–13).

56 **Strabo** 2. 4. 8, C108: *The promontories of Europe*
Since Europe extends into a number of promontories, he (*Polybios*)[217] describes it better than Eratosthenes, although not adequately. The latter spoke of only three, the one going down to the Pillars, on which is Iberia, the one to the Strait, on which is Italia, and the third, down to Maleai, on which are all the peoples between the Adriatic and the Euxeinos and the Tanaïs.[218]

57 **Strabo** 2. 5. 14, C118–19: *The oikoumenē as a 'chlamys'*
The shape of the inhabited world is somewhat in the form of a *chlamys*,[219] whose greatest width is marked by the line through the Nile, with its beginning taken at the parallel through the Kinnamomophoros (*Cinnamon-bearing Land*) and the island of the fugitive Egyptians[220] as far as the parallel through Ierne. The length is at right angles, from the west through the Pillars and the Sicilian strait as far as the Rhodia and the Issic gulf, going through the Tauros that girdles Asia and ending at the eastern sea between the Indians and the Skythians beyond Baktriane. It is necessary to conceive of a certain parallelogram in which the *chlamys*-shaped form is engraved so that its greatest length agrees with and is equal to the length (*of the parallelogram*) and whose width agrees with (*and is equal to*) its width.

This *chlamys*-shaped form is the inhabited world. Its width, as we have said,[221] is bounded by the farthest sides of the parallelogram, which separate the inhabited and uninhabited parts from one another. These are, on the north, that through Ierne, and in the burned region, that through the Kinnamomophoros. Extending these to the east and west as far as the portions of the inhabited world that rise opposite to them would make a certain parallelogram, joining up with those at the extremities. It is clear that the inhabited world is within this because neither the greatest width nor length falls outside.

The form is *chlamys*-shaped because the extremities of its length taper on both sides and diminish its width, washed away by the sea. This is clear from those who have sailed round the eastern and western portions on either side. They proclaim that the island of Taprobane (*Sri Lanka*) is considerably further south than Indike, but nonetheless inhabited, rising opposite to the Island of the Egyptians and the land that bears cinnamon, and that the temperature of the air is about the same. The regions around the mouth of the Hyrkanian sea are further north than the ultimate part of Skythia beyond the Indians, and those around Ierne are still further. Similar things are said about the region beyond the Pillars, that the most western boundary of the inhabited world is the promontory of the Iberians called Hieron ('*Sacred*'),[222] which lies approximately on the line through Gadeira (*Cádiz*), the Pillars, the Sicilian strait, and the Rhodia.

---

[217] Polyb. 34. 7. 11–14. [218] Cf. n. to 52 §40. [219] Cf. 29 §6.
[220] Same as the 'Egyptian island', 25 §2. [221] At 2. 5. 6 (29 §6).
[222] C. St Vincent or possibly C. Trafalgar.

The *horoskopeia* (*time-measurers*),[223] the favourable winds in both directions, and the lengths of the longest days and nights (*are the same*), for the longest days and nights have 14½ equinoctial hours.[224]

58   **Strabo** 2. 5. 16, C120: *Eratosthenes' prime parallel and meridian*
Such being the shape of its entirety, it appears useful to take two straight lines, which cut across each other at a right angle, one going throughout the greatest width and the other the length. The first will be one of the parallels and the other one of the meridians. Then one should think of lines parallel to these on either side, which divide the land and the sea that we happen to use. Thus the shape will be somewhat clearer, as we have described, according to the length of the line, with different measurements for both the length and width, and the latitudes will be manifested better, both in the east and west as well in as the south and north.

59   **Strabo** 2. 5. 20, C123: *The Syrteis*
The smaller of the Syrteis (*gulf of Gabès*) is about 1,600 stades in circumference, with the islands of Meninx and Kerkina lying on either side of its mouth. Eratosthenes says that the Great Syrtis (*gulf of Sidra*) has a circuit of 5,000 and is 1,800 deep, from the Hesperides to Automala and the boundary between the Kyrenaia and the rest of Libyē.

60   **Strabo** 2. 5. 24, C125–6: *Distance from Rhodes to Alexandria*
The passage from Rhodes to Alexandria is about 4,000 stades with a north wind, but along the coast it is double that. Eratosthenes says that this is the estimate of sailors regarding the crossing of the sea. Some say this, and others do not shrink from saying 5,000, but he, using the shadow of a gnomon, found it to be 3,750.

61   **Strabo** 2. 5. 35–41, C132–4: *Places on Eratosthenes' prime meridian*
(35) ·Indeed, he (*Hipparchos*) says that for those dwelling upon the parallel through the Cinnamon-bearing Land, which is at a distance of 3,000 stades south of Meroë, with the equator 8,800 from it, their dwelling is almost halfway between the equator and the summer tropic at Syene; for Syene is 5,000 stades distant from Meroë. Among these people, the first, the Little Bear is enclosed entirely within their arctic circle and is always seen; for the bright star at the end of its tail, being the most southerly, is anchored upon the very arctic circle so that it touches the horizon.·[225] The Arabian gulf lies to the east and approximately parallel to the meridian discussed, and the Kinnamomophoros (*Cinnamon-bearing Land*) is where it empties into the outer sea, where they hunted the elephant in antiquity. Its parallel is outside (*the inhabited world*) and extends on one side somewhat to the south of Taprobane, or its farthest inhabitants, and on the other through southernmost Libyē.

---

[223] A device for measuring the time of day, but of uncertain type; presumably a sundial, gnomon, or water-clock (Hannah 2008, 68–70).

[224] For this notion of defining latitude by the length of the longest day, see n. on Pyth. 4.

[225] This was true in the late Hl period, when α UMi (Polaris) was slightly further from the Pole than the rest of the 'bear'; now, thanks to precession, Polaris is the Pole Star, very close to the pole.

(36) ·For those at Meroë and the Ptolemaïs in the Trogodytic land, the greatest day is 13 equinoctial hours. This dwelling-place is roughly midway between the equator and the (*parallel*) through Alexandria, apart from the 1,800 (*stades*) by which the distance to the equator is longer.· The parallel through Meroë passes on one side through parts that are unknown and on the other through the promontories of Indike. ·At Syene and at the Berenike on the Arabian gulf, in the Trogodytic land, the Sun at the summer solstice is overhead and the longest day is 13½ equinoctial hours. Almost all of the Great Bear appears on their arctic circle except for the legs, the end of its tail, and one of the stars in the rectangle.· The parallel through Syene passes, on one side, through the territory of the Ichthyophagoi (*Fish-eaters*) in Gedrosia and through Indike, and on the other side through territory almost 5,000 stades further south than Kyrene. . . .

(38) ·In the places approximately 400 stades south of the parallel through Alexandria and Kyrene, where the greatest day is 14 equinoctial hours, Arcturus stands overhead, declining slightly southwards. At Alexandria, the gnomon has the same ratio to its equinoctial shadow as 5 does to 3. These (*places*) are 1,300 stades further south than Carthage, at least if the gnomon (*there*) has the same ratio to its equinoctial shadow as 11 does to 7.· The parallel passes on one side through Kyrene, 900 stades south of Karchedon, and as far as the middle of Maurousia (*Mauretania*),[226] and on the other side through Egypt, Hollow Syria, Upper Syria, Babylon, Sousias, Persis, Karmania, and Upper Gedrosia, as far as Indike.

(39) ·In the places around the Ptolemaïs in Phoenicia, and around Sidon and Tyre, the greatest day is 14¼ equinoctial hours. These places are about 1,600 stades further north than Alexandria, and about 700 (*further north*) than Carthage. In the Peloponnese and around the middle of Rhodian territory, and around Xanthos in Lykia or the parts slightly further south, and also the parts 400 stades further south than the Syracusans' territory, there the greater day is 14½ equinoctial hours. These places are 3,640 stades from Alexandria ⟨and some 2,740 from Carthage⟩.· According to Eratosthenes, the parallel runs through Karia, Lykaonia, Kataonia, Media, the Caspian Gates, and the Indians along the Caucasus.

(40) ·In the parts around Alexandria in the Troad, at Amphipolis, at Apollonia in Epeiros, and places further south than Rome but further north than Neapolis (*Naples*), the greatest day is 15 equinoctial hours. This parallel lies about 7,000 stades north of that through Alexandria-by-Egypt; above 28,800 from the equator; 3,400 from the parallel through Rhodes; but 1,500 south of Byzantion, Nikaia, and the places around Massalia.· Somewhat to the north is the one through Lysimacheia, which Eratosthenes says passes through Mysia, Paphlagonia, the region around Sinope, Hyrkania, and Baktra.

(41) ·In the places around Byzantion the greatest day is of 15¼ equinoctial hours and the gnomon at the summer solstice has the ratio to its shadow that 120 has to 42

---

[226] For the scope of anc. Mauretania (wider and further E than mod. *Mauritania*), see Ch. 22, introduction.

less one-fifth.[227] These places are at a distance of around 4,900 stades from the parallel through the middle of Rhodian territory and about 30,300 from the equator. For those who sail into the Pontos and advance towards the north about 1,400 stades, the greatest day becomes 15½ equinoctial hours. These places are the same distance from the pole and the equator, and their arctic circle is at the zenith.·

62   Strabo 3. 2. 11, C148: *Places around Gadeira*
Eratosthenes says that the territory adjoining Kalpe is called Tartessis (*sic*), and that Erytheia is a blessed island. Artemidoros contradicts him and says that this is a falsehood by him, just like that the distance from Gadeira to the Hieron (*Sacred*) Promontory[228] is a five-day sail, although it is no more than 1,700 stades, that the tides terminate at that point, although they exist around the circuit of the entire inhabited world, that the northerly part of Iberia is an easier means of access to Keltike than sailing by the Ocean, and everything else that he (*Eratosthenes*) said while relying on Pytheas, because of the latter's false pretensions.

63   Strabo 3. 4. 7, C159: *Places in Iberia*
Between the branching of the Iber and the heights of Pyrene, on which the dedications of Pompeius are set up,[229] the first city is Tarrakon, which has no harbour but is situated on a bay and is sufficiently equipped with everything, today no less populated than Karchedon (*Carthage*). It is naturally suited for the residence of the commanders and is the metropolis, so to speak, not only of the territory within the Iber but much of that beyond. The Gymnesiai (*Balearic*) islands lie nearby, and Ebosos, all notable islands, which suggests that the position of the city is propitious. Eratosthenes says that it also has a naval station (*naustathmos*), but Artemidoros contradicts him, saying that it is not even fortunate enough to have an anchorage (*ankyrobolia*).

64   Strabo 3. 5. 5, C170: *Location of the Pillars of Herakles*
For this reason some believe that the peaks at the strait are the Pillars, others that they are at Gadeira, and others that they lie further outside Gadeira. Some assume that the Pillars are Kalpe and Abilyx—the mountain opposite in Libyē that Eratosthenes says is situated among the Metagonians, a nomadic people—and others that they are the islets near each (*mountain*), one of which is named Hera's Island. Artemidoros speaks of Hera's Island and her temple, and he mentions another, but neither Mount Abilyx or the Metagonian people. Some transfer the Planktai and Symplegades here, believing these to be the Pillars which Pindar[230] calls the Gadeirid gates, saying that they were the farthest point reached by Herakles. ·Dikaiarchos, Eratosthenes, Polybios, and the majority of the Hellenes show that the Pillars are in the area of the Strait.·

---

[227] i.e. 41⁴/₅; the ratio is thus *c*.2.92 : 1.   [228] Cape *St Vincent*, or possibly *Trafalgar*.
[229] This refers to Pompey's military campaign against Sertorius in the 70s BC.
[230] Fr. 256 in Maehler 1989.

65 **Strabo 5. 2. 6, C224:** *Visibility of Corsica and Sardinia*
Moreover, Eratosthenes is not correct when he says that neither Kyrnos nor Sardo can be seen from the mainland.

66 **Strabo 8. 7. 2, C384:** *Destruction of Helike*
Helike was submerged two years before Leuktra.[231] Eratosthenes says that he himself saw the place, and the ferrymen say that a bronze Poseidon stood upright in the strait, with a hippocamp in his hand, a danger to those fishing with nets.

67 **Strabo 8. 8. 4, C389:** *Rivers in the Peloponnese*
Eratosthenes says that around Pheneos[232] the river called the Anias makes a lake in front of the city and flows down into strainers called *zerethra*. When these are stopped up, the water at times overflows into the plains, but when they are opened up again, it comes out of the plains all together and empties into the Ladon and the Alpheios, so that even at Olympia the land around the sanctuary was once flooded and the lake was diminished. The Erasinos, flowing around Stymphalos,[233] goes under the mountain and reappears again in the Argive territory. Because of this Iphikrates,[234] when he was besieging Stymphalos and accomplishing nothing, attempted to block up the sinkhole with many sponges that he provided himself, but ceased because of a sign from Zeus.

68 **Strabo 10. 4. 5, C475:** *Distance from Africa to Crete*
Eratosthenes says that from the Kyrenaia (*territory of Cyrene*) to Kriou Metopon (*Ram's Brow; C. Krios*)[235] is 2,000 (*stades*) and less from there to the Peloponnesos.

69 **Strabo 11. 2. 15, C497:** *Names of the Caucasus*
Eratosthenes says that the Caucasus is called the Kaspios by those living there, perhaps derived from the Kaspioi.

70 **Strabo 11. 6. 1, C506–7:** *The Caspian sea*
The second portion begins from the Caspian sea, where the first comes to an end. The same sea is also called the Hyrkanian. It is necessary to speak first about the sea and the people living around it. It is the gulf that extends from the Ocean to the south, somewhat narrow at its entrance but becoming wider as it goes inland, especially around its innermost part, where it is about 5,000 stades.[236] Sailing from the entrance to the innermost part would be slightly more, since it nearly touches the uninhabited region. Eratosthenes says that the circuit of this sea was well known to the Hellenes, that the portion along the Albanoi and Kadousioi is 5,400 stades, the portion along the

---

[231] Helike was one of the, conventionally twelve, *poleis* of Achaia on the N coast of the Peloponnese, destroyed in a natural catastrophe in 373 (two years before the battle at Leuktra in Boiotia in which the Spartan–Lakedaimon army was defeated by the Thebans). See Introduction, §III. 4. b.

[232] A *polis* in N. Arkadia.   [233] A *polis* in NE Arkadia.

[234] Athenian general of C4e.   [235] The SW point of Crete.

[236] Strabo retails the common misconception that the Caspian was an inlet of the outer Ocean.

Anariakoi, Mardoi, and Hyrkanoi to the mouth of the Oxos river is 4,800, and from there to the Iaxartes (*Syr Darya*), 2,400.

71   Strabo 11. 7. 3, C509: *Rivers flowing into the Caspian*
The rivers flowing through Hyrkania are the Oxos (*Amu Darya*) and Ochos,[237] which empty into the sea. Of these, the Ochos also flows through Nesaia, but some say that the Ochos empties into the Oxos. Aristoboulos[238] says that the Oxos is the largest that he had seen in Asia, except those among the Indians. He also says that it is navigable—he and Eratosthenes took this from Patrokles[239]—and that many Indian goods come down it to the Hyrkanian sea, and from there are carried over to Albania[240] by means of the Kyros (*Kura*) river, brought down through the successive places to the Euxeinos (*Black Sea*).

72   Strabo 11. 8. 8–9, C513–14: *Peoples and distances in the north-east of the oikoumenē*
(8) Eratosthenes says that the Arachotoi and Massagetai are alongside the Baktrians to the west along the Oxos, and that the Sakai and Sogdianoi and all their lands lie opposite to Indike, although the Baktrians only for a small distance, as they are mostly along the Paropamisos (*Hindu Kush*). The Sakai and Sogdianoi are separated by the Iaxartes, and the Sogdianoi and Baktrioi by the Oxos, and the Tapyroi live between the Hyrkanoi and the Arioi. In a circuit round the sea, after the Hyrkanoi are the Amardoi, Anariakoi, Kadousioi, Albanoi, Kaspioi, and Ouitioi, and perhaps others, until the Skythians are reached. On the other side of the Hyrkanoi are the Derbikes, and the Kadousoi touch the Medes and the Matianoi below Parachoathras.[241]

(9) He says that these are the distances: from (*Mt*) Kaspios to the Kyros is about 1,800 stades, and then to the Caspian Gates 5,600, to Alexandria among the Arioi (*Herat*) 6,400, then to the city of Baktra, also called Zariaspa, 3,870, then to the Iaxartes river, to which Alexander came, about 5,000, a total of 22,670.

He also says that the distances from the Caspian Gates to the Indians are as follows: they say it is 1,960 to Hekatompylos, to Alexandria among the Arioi 4,530, then to Prophthasia in Drange 1,600—others say 1,500—then to the city of the Arachotoi 4,120, then to Ortospana and the meeting of three roads from Baktra, 2,000, and then to the borders of Indike 1,000, a total of 15,300. It must be believed that the length of Indike is a distance in a straight line, that from the Indos as far as the eastern sea.

73   Strabo 11. 12. 4–5, C522: *Armenia and Media*
(4) . . . Thus we place Media, in which the Caspian Gates are, within the Tauros, as well as Armenia.   (5) According to me, then, these peoples would be towards the north, but Eratosthenes, who made the division into a southern part and a northern,

---

[237] Not certainly identified (see Roller 2010, 204–5). The Oxus does not flow into the Caspian, but into the *Aral sea*.
[238] *BNJ* 139 F 20. Aristoboulos of Kassandreia was an early historian of Alexander the Great.
[239] *BNJ* 712 F 5. See n. on 17 above.   [240] An area of the E. Caucasus.
[241] E.'s source may have been Patrokles (Roller 2010, 204).

calling some of his previously mentioned 'sealstones' northern and others southern, declares that the Caspian Gates are the boundary between the two latitudinal regions. Reasonably, he would declare the southern part that which is more southerly than the Caspian Gates, stretching towards the east, among which are Media and Armenia, and the northern part the more northerly, since this happens regardless of the distribution of sections. But perhaps it did not occur to him that no part of either Armenia or Media is south or outside of the Tauros.

74 **Strabo** 11. 14. 7–8, C529: *Rivers of western Asia; the Tigris*
(7) There are a number of rivers in the territory, the best known of which are the Phasis (*Rioni*) and the Lykos (*Kelkit Çay?*), which empty into the Pontic sea—Eratosthenes has wrongly put down the Thermodon (*Terme Çay*) instead of the Lykos—the Kyros and Araxes (*Aras*) into the Caspian, and the Euphrates and Tigris into the Erythraian.
(8) . . . The Tigris rushes from this mountainous territory near the Niphates, and keeps its flow unmixed because of its quickness, from which comes its name, since the Medes call an arrow a *tigris*. And while it has many types of fish, there is only one type in the lake. Around the innermost recess of the lake the river falls into a pit and flows underground for some distance, coming up around Chalonitis. From there it goes down towards Opis and the so-called Wall of Semiramis, leaving the Gordyaioi and all Mesopotamia on the right, but the Euphrates, on the contrary, has the same territory on the left. Coming near to one another and producing Mesopotamia, the former runs through Seleukeia to the Persian gulf and the latter through Babylon, which I said somewhere in my discussion against Eratosthenes and Hipparchos.[242]

75 **Strabo** 14. 2. 29, C663–4: *Eratosthenes' central parallel*
The places lying in a straight line as far as Indike are the same in Artemidoros as Eratosthenes. Polybios[243] says that in regard to this the latter must be trusted, who begins from Samosata in Kommagene, which lies at the crossing and at Zeugma, saying that it is 450 stades to Samosata from the boundaries of Kappadokia around Tomisa across the Tauros.[244]

76 **Strabo** 14. 6. 4–5, C683–4: *Cyprus*
(4) Why should one wonder at the poets, especially those who were totally eager about their manner of expression, when one compares what Damastes says,[245] who gives the length of the island (*Cyprus*) as running from north to south, from Hierokepia, as he says, to Kleides?[246] Nor is Eratosthenes correct, although complaining about him, when he says that Hierokepia is not in the north, but the south. It is not in the south, but the west, as it lies on the western side, where Paphos and Akamas are.[247] Such is the location of the position of Cyprus.

---

[242] At 52 §26.   [243] Polyb. 34. 13.
[244] Apart from the distance given, the other material here may be post-Eratosthenic (Roller 2010, 190).
[245] *BNJ* 5 F 10.   [246] For Damastes, see n. on 12 §1 above.
[247] A *polis* and a cape, respectively.

(5) It is not inferior to any other island in excellence, for it is good in wine and good in olives, and sufficient in grain for its use. There are abundant copper mines at Tamassos, in which chalcanthite (*copper sulphide*) is produced, and also verdigris of copper, useful for its medicinal purposes. Eratosthenes says that formerly the plains were overrun with woods, and thus there were thickets spread over them that were uncultivated. Mining helped this a little, since the trees would be cut down to burn the copper and silver, and in addition there was shipbuilding, for sailing on the sea was safe through sea power. Yet because it was not possible to prevail, those wishing or able were allowed to cut them down and to possess the cleared land as private property, tax free.

77 Strabo 15. 1. 10–11, C688–9: *Form of India*

(10) ... From my former discussion,[248] that which was expounded by Eratosthenes in the summary of the 3rd (*book*) of his *Geographika*, concerning what was believed to be Indike when Alexander invaded, particularly seems most trustworthy. The Indos was the boundary between it and Ariane, which is to the west and was then a Persian possession. Later the Indians held much of Ariane, having taken it from the Macedonians.

(11) This is what Eratosthenes says about it: Indike is bounded on the north, from Ariane to the eastern sea, by the extremities of the Tauros, whose various parts the inhabitants call the Paropamisos, Emodon, Imaon, and other names, but the Macedonians call it the Kaukasos (*Caucasus*). On the west is the Indos river, and the southern and eastern sides, much larger than the others, are thrust into the Atlantic open-sea (*pelagos*).

Thus the shape of the territory becomes rhomboidal, with each of the larger sides having the advantage over the opposite sides by 3,000 stades, which is as much as the promontory common to the eastern and southern coast thrusts out equally on either side beyond the remaining shore. The western side from the Kaukasian mountains to the southern sea is said to be about 13,000 stades, along the Indos river to its outlets. Thus the opposite—eastern—side, adding the 3,000 to the promontory, will be 16,000 stades. These are the least and greatest widths of the territory. The length is from west to east, and one may speak with certainty about it as far as Palibothra (*Pataliputra*), for it has been measured with lines (*schoinoi*), and there is a royal road of 10,000 stades. Beyond, it is known only by guess, by means of the voyage from the sea on the Ganges river as far as Palibothra, which would be about 6,000 stades. The entire extent, at least, is 16,000 stades, which Eratosthenes says that he took from the most trusted record of stopping points.[249] ⟨Megasthenes⟩[250] agrees, although Patrokles[251] says 1,000 less. The fact that the promontory thrusts out further west into the sea adds to this distance, and these 3,000 stades make the greatest length. This is how it is from the outlets of the Indos river along the successive shore to the previously mentioned promontory and the eastern boundary. Those living there are called the Koniakoi.

---

[248] At 2. 1. 1 (47 §1 above).   [249] Cf. **49**.   [250] *BNJ* 715 F 6c.   [251] *BNJ* 712 F 3b.

78 **Strabo** 15. 1. 13–14, C690: *Rivers of India; location of Sri Lanka*

(13) All of Indike is watered by rivers, some of which flow into the two largest, the Indos and the Ganges, and others empty into the sea through their own mouths. All begin in the Caucasus[252] and first run towards the south, and although some continue in the same direction, especially those that join the Indos, others turn towards the east, such as the Ganges. It flows down from the mountains and when it reaches the plain it turns towards the east and flows past Palibothra, a very large city, and then continues towards the sea and a single outlet. It is the largest of the Indian rivers. The Indos empties by two mouths into the southern sea, encompassing the land called Patalene, similar to the Egyptian Delta. It is because of the rising of vapours from these rivers and the Etesian winds, as Eratosthenes says, that Indike is inundated by summer rains and the plains become lakes. At the time of the rains, flax and millet are sown, and in addition sesame, rice, and *bosmoron*.[253] In the winter season there are wheat, barley, pulse, and other edible crops unknown to us. Almost the same animals that are in Indike appear in Aithiopia and throughout Egypt, and there are the same ones in the Indian rivers except the hippopotamus, although Onesikritos[254] says that this horse is also there. The people in the south are the same as the Aithiopes in colour, but in regard to eyes and hair they are like the others; because of the moisture in the air their hair is not curly. Those in the north are like the Egyptians.[255]

(14) They say that Taprobane (*Sri Lanka*) is an island in the Ocean, seven days' sail to the south from the southernmost part of Indike, the territory of the Koniakoi. Its length is 8,000 stades, towards Aithiopia, and it has elephants. This is what Eratosthenes reports.

79 **Strabo** 15. 1. 20, C693: *Fertility of Indike*

Megasthenes[256] demonstrates the prosperity of Indike through its two-yearly harvests and crops, as Eratosthenes also says, who mentions the winter sowing and that of the summer, as well as the rain.[257] He says that no year is found to be without rain in both seasons, resulting in prosperity with the earth never barren. There are many fruit trees and plant roots, especially the large reeds that are sweet both by nature and when boiled, since the water is warmed by the sun, both that falling on account of Zeus and in the rivers. In a way, then, he wishes to say that what is called by others ripening— whether of fruits or juices—they call heating, and this is as effective as using fire to produce a good taste. In addition, he says that the branches of trees used in wheels are flexible, and for the same reason wool (*i.e. cotton*) blooms on some.

---

[252] As erroneously designated by Alexander's geographers: see **20**.
[253] A variety of millet.   [254] *BNJ* 134 F 7.
[255] Here E. probably combined information from Alexander's captains Nearchos (*BNJ* 133), Onesikritos (*BNJ* 134), as well as from Megasthenes (*BNJ* 715) and Deimachos (*BNJ* 716 Daimachos).
[256] *BNJ* 715 F 8.   [257] Evidently Megasthenes was quoted from E. (Roller 2010, 180).

80 **Strabo** 15. 2. 1, C720: *Location of Ariane*

Ariane is after Indike, the first portion subject to the Persians after the Indos river and the upper satrapies outside the Tauros, bounded on the south and north by the same sea and the same mountains as Indike, and the same river, the Indos, from which it stretches towards the west as far as the line drawn from the Caspian Gates to Karmania, so that its shape is a quadrilateral.[258] The southern side begins at the outlets of the Indos and at Patalene and ends at Karmania and the mouth of the Persian gulf, having a promontory stretching considerably to the south, and then making a turn into the gulf towards Persis. First there are the Arbians, named like the Arbis river, which is the boundary between them and the next people, the Oreitai. They have a seacoast of 1,000 stades, as Nearchos says.[259] This is a part of the Indians. Then there are the Oreitai, an autonomous people. The sail along the seacoast is 1,800 stades; along the next peoples, the Ichthyophagoi (*Fish-eaters*), 7,400; and along the Karmanian territory as far as Persis, 3,700: so that the total is 12,900.

81 **Strabo** 15. 2. 8–9, C723–4: *Boundaries of Ariane*

(8) The southern side of Ariane is the location of the coast and islands that lie above it and nearby, those of the Gedrosians and Oreitai. It is large, and Gedrosia extends into the interior until it touches the Drangai, Arachotoi, and Paropamisadai, concerning which Eratosthenes has spoken as follows, for I cannot say it any better: he says that Ariane is bordered on the east by the Indos, on the south by the Great Ocean, on the north by the Paropamisos and the mountains continuing up to the Caspian Gates, and on the west by the same boundaries that separate Parthyene from Media and Karmania from Paraitakene and Persis.[260]

The width of the territory is the length of the Indos from the Paropamisos to its outlets, 12,000 stades, although some say 13,000, and the length from the Caspian Gates is recorded in the treatise *Asiatikoi stathmoi* (*Asiatic Stopping-points*) in two ways.[261] As far as Alexandria of the Arioi, from the Caspian Gates through Parthyaia there is one route, and then there is a straight route through Baktriane and over the mountain pass into Ortospana to the meeting of three roads from the Baktrians, which is among the Paropamisadai. The other route turns slightly from Aria towards the south to Prophthasia in Drangiane, and the rest of it then goes back to the Indian boundaries and the Indos. This route through the territory of the Drangai and Arachotoi is longer, 15,300 stades in its entirety. If one were to remove 1,300, the remainder would be a straight line and the length of the territory would be 14,000. The sea coast is not much less, although some increase it and in addition to the 10,000 add Karmania with 6,000, including the gulfs or the sea coast of Karmania within the Persian gulf. The name Ariane is extended to a certain part of Persis and Media as well as to the Baktrians

---

[258] See further **81** §8, and n. on **52** §22 above.

[259] *BNJ* 133 F 24.

[260] The information here is fuller than in **80**.

[261] Cf. the similar work mentioned in **49**.

and Sogdianoi towards the north, who speak roughly the same language, only slightly different.

(9) The arrangement of the peoples is as follows: along the Indos are the Paropamisadai, above whom is the Paropamisos. Then, towards the south, are the Arachotoi, and next towards the south the Gedrosenoi along with the others on the seacoast, and with the Indos lying alongside all of these. Part of these places along the Indos are possessed by certain Indians, but formerly were Persian. Alexander took them away from the Arioi and established his own foundations, and Seleukos (*I*) Nikator gave them to Sandrakottos, concluding an intermarriage and receiving 500 elephants in return. Lying to the west of the Paropamisadai are the Arioi, and the Drangai (*are west*) of the Arachotoi and Gedrosenoi, but the Arioi also lie to the north of the Drangai, as well as to the west, almost encircling a small part of them. Baktriane lies to the north of Aria and then there are the Paropamisadai, through whom Alexander passed over the Caucasus pushing towards Baktra. To the west, next to the Arians, are the Parthyaioi and the territory around the Caspian Gates, and to the south is the Karmanian desert, and then the rest of Karmania and Gedrosia.

82 Strabo 15. 2. 14, C726: *Karmania*
Karmania is the last place on the seacoast from the Indos, although much further north than the outlet of the Indos. Its first promontory, however, stretches to the south, towards the Great Ocean, making the mouth of the Persian gulf, along with the promontory extending from Fortunate Arabia, which is in view, and it bends towards the Persian gulf until it touches Persis.

83 Strabo 15. 3. 1, C727: *Persis and its peoples*
According to Eratosthenes, the length of the territory (*Persis*) towards the north and the Caspian Gates is about 8,000 stades, or 9,000 advancing by certain promontories, and the remainder to the Caspian Gates is no more than 2,000. The width, in the interior, from Sousa to Persaipolis (*Persepolis*), is 4,200 stades, and from there to the border of Karmania an additional 1,600. The tribes (*phyla*) living in the country are the so-called Pateischoreis, the Achaimenidai, and the Magoi, who have chosen a certain holy life, but the Kyrtoi[262] and Mardoi are piratical, and the others are farmers.

84 Strabo 16. 1. 12, C741: *Lakes in Mesopotamia (?)*
Eratosthenes, mentioning the lakes near Arabia, says that when the water is unable to exit, it opens underground passages and flows underground as far as the people of Hollow (*Koile*) Syria, pressing into the region of Rhinokoroura and Mount Kasion, creating lakes and pits there.[263]

---

[262] The name is possibly present in mod. 'Kurds', though they are usually equated with the anc. Kardouchoi. The name may mean 'humped' or 'hunchbacks'.
[263] The passage is confused; no such lakes can be identified (Roller 2010, 198).

85 **Strabo** 16. 1. 15, C743: *Asphalt in Babylonia*

A large amount of asphalt is produced in Babylonia, about which Eratosthenes says that the liquid kind, which is called naphtha, is found in Sousis, but the dry kind, which can be solidified, is in Babylonia. There is a fountain of the latter near the Euphrates, and at the time of flooding by snow-melt it fills and overflows into the river. Large lumps are formed that are suitable for structures of baked brick.

86 **Strabo** 16. 1. 21–2, C746–7: *Mesopotamia*

(21) Mesopotamia is named from what it is.[264] As I have said,[265] it lies between the Euphrates and Tigris, and thus the Tigris washes only its eastern side, and the Euphrates its western and southern. To the north is the Tauros, which separates Armenia from Mesopotamia. The greatest distance that they are apart from one another is towards the mountains, and this would be the same as Eratosthenes has said, 2,400 (*stades*), from Thapsakos—where the ancient bridge over the Euphrates was—to the crossing of the Tigris where Alexander himself crossed. The least is slightly more than 200 somewhere around Seleukeia and Babylon. The Tigris flows through the lake called Thopitis,[266] through the middle of its width, and going to the opposite edge sinks under the earth with a great noise and upward blasts.[267] It is invisible for a distance, and then appears again not far from Gordyaia. It thus runs through it so vehemently, as Eratosthenes says, that although it is generally salty and without fish, this part is sweet, with a strong current, and full of fish.

(22) The contracting of Mesopotamia goes on for a great length, somewhat like a boat, with the Euphrates making most of the circumference, and it is 4,800 stades from Thapsakos as far as Babylon, as Eratosthenes says. From Zeugma in Kommagene, where Mesopotamia begins, to Thapsakos is no less than 2,000 stades.

87 **Strabo** 16. 3. 2–6, C765–7: *The Persian gulf*

(2) The Persian gulf (*Persikos kolpos*) is also called ·'the sea (*thalatta*) beside the Persians'.· Eratosthenes says the following about it: he says that its mouth is so narrow that from Harmozai (*Hormuz*), the promontory of Karmania, one can look across to that of Makai in Arabia. From its mouth the right-hand coast, being curved, is at first turned slightly to the east from Karmania, and then bends towards the north, and afterwards towards the west as far as Teredon and the mouth of the Euphrates. It consists of the Karmanian coast, and part of the Persian, Sousian, and Babylonian, about 10,000 stades, concerning which I have already spoken.[268] From there to its mouth is the same distance. This, he says, is according to Androsthenes of Thasos,[269] who sailed

---

[264] From *mesos* 'middle' + *potamos* 'river'. The name may have been devised by E. (Roller 2010, 189).

[265] At 11. 14. 2.

[266] Probably L. *Van*, though it is not the source of the Tigris (Roller 2010, 190).

[267] One of many Greek anecdotes about rivers vanishing underground and reappearing; cf. **67**, and Juba 4 below.

[268] At 15. 2. 14 (**82** above).   [269] *BNJ* 711 F 2.

with Nearchos and also by himself.[270] Thus it is clear that this sea is only slightly smaller than the Euxeinos sea (*Black Sea*). He (*Eratosthenes*) says that he (*Androsthenes*), who sailed round the gulf with an expedition, said that beyond Teredon—having the continent on his right and sailing along the coast—is the island of Ikaros (*Failaka*), with a temple on it sacred to Apollo and an oracle of Tauropolos.[271]

(3) After sailing along Arabia for 2,400 stades there is the city of Gerrha,[272] lying on a deep gulf, where Chaldaians exiled from Babylon live. The land is salty and they have houses of salt, and since flakes of salt come away because of the heat of the sun and fall off, they sprinkle the walls with water and keep them solid. The city is 200 stades from the sea. The Gerrhaioi trade mostly by land for Arabian goods and aromatics. In contrast Aristoboulos[273] says that the Gerrhaioi generally travel on rafts to Babylonia for trade, sailing up the Euphrates to Thapsakos with their goods, and distributing them to everywhere by land from there.[274]

(4) Sailing further, there are other islands, Tyros (*Bahrain*) and Arados, that have temples like those of the Phoenicians. Those living there say that the islands and cities with the same names are Phoenician settlements. These islands are ten days' sail from Teredon and one day from the mouth at the promontory of Makai.

(5) Both Nearchos[275] and Orthagoras[276] say that the island of Tyrine[277] lies towards the south on the Ocean at a distance of 2,000 stades, and the grave of Erythras is visible on it, a large mound planted with wild palms. He was king of that region and left the sea named after himself. They say that this was pointed out to them by Mithropastes son of Arsites the satrap of Phrygia, who had been exiled by Darius (*III*) and passed his time on the island, joining them when they landed in the Persian gulf and through them attempting to return home.

(6) Along the entire coast of the Erythraian sea are trees in the depths that are like laurel and olive, completely visible at low tide but completely covered at high tide, although the land lying above is without trees, thus intensifying the peculiarity.[278] Concerning the region of the Persian sea, which, as I have said, forms the eastern side of Fortunate Arabia, this is what Eratosthenes has said.

88 **Strabo 16. 4. 2–4, C767–9: *Arabia***
(2) But I return to the views of Eratosthenes, who sets forth what he knows about Arabia.[279] He says, concerning its northerly or desert part—which is between Fortunate Arabia, the land of the people of Hollow Syria, and that of the Ioudaians (*Judaeans*) as

---

[270] Androsthenes (*BNJ* 711) appears to have been E.'s main source here (Roller 2010, 193).
[271] For an historical interpretation of the archaeology of *Failaka*, see Stavrou 2021.
[272] Possibly near *al-Jubayl* (Saudi Arabia): Roller 2010, 194.   [273] *BNJ* 139 F 57.
[274] Cf. Agatharch. 89a–c; 104ac.   [275] *BNJ* 133 F 27.   [276] *BNJ* 713 F 5.
[277] Probably in fact Ōgyris, cf. Juba 22; location unknown (Roller 2010, 194).
[278] Cf. Schneider 2017 on the mangroves of the Red Sea.
[279] E.'s account is the earliest reasonably full description of Arabia, and may be based on his own travels (Roller 2010, 195). Cf. the later account in Agatharchides book 5.

far as the inner recess of the Arabian gulf: namely, that from Heroönpolis,[280] which is the inner recess of the Arabian gulf near the Nile—to the Petra of the Nabataeans ⟨it is . . . stades, and from Petra⟩ to Babylon 5,600 stades. All this land is towards the summer sunrise, via the adjacent Arabian tribes: the Nabataeans, Chaulotaioi, and Agraioi.

Beyond these is Fortunate (*Eudaimon, sc. Arabia*), which extends for 12,000 stades towards the south as far as the Atlantic open-sea (*pelagos*). The first people there, beyond the Syrians and Ioudaioi, are farmers. Beyond these the land is very sandy and wretched, with a few palm trees, a thorny plant, and the tamarisk, with water from digging, just as in Gedrosia. The Skenitai (*Tent-dwelling*) Arabians possess it, who are camel-herders. The extremities, towards the south, rising opposite to Aithiopia, are watered by summer rains and have two sowings, like Indike, and the rivers are consumed by plains and lakes. It is fertile and abundant in honey production.[281] It has plenty of fatted animals except for horses, mules, and pigs; and all kinds of birds except geese and chickens. The four most numerous peoples living in the extremity of the previously mentioned territory are the Minaioi, in the district towards the Erythraian sea, whose largest city is Karna or Karnana; next to these are the Sabaioi, whose metropolis is Mariaba; third are the Kattabaneis, extending to the narrows and the crossing of the Arabian gulf, and whose royal seat is called Tamna; and, farthest towards the east are the Chatramotitai, whose city is Sabata.

(3) All are monarchies and prosperous, beautifully furnished with temples and palaces. Their houses are like those of the Egyptians regarding the joining of the beams. The four districts have more territory than the Egyptian Delta. No child succeeds to the kingship of his father: rather it is the child of a distinguished person who was the first born after the accession of the king. At the same time that someone accedes to the throne, the pregnant wives of distinguished men are recorded and guards are placed. The son who is born first to one of them is by law adopted and raised in a royal fashion to be the successor.

(4) Kattabania produces frankincense, and Chatramotitis myrrh, and these and other aromatics are traded with merchants. They come there from the Ailanoi, arriving in Minaia in 70 days. Ailana is a city on the other recess of the Arabian gulf, the one opposite Gaza called the Ailanites, as I have already said.[282] The Gerrhaioi, however, arrive at Chatramotitis in 40 days.

The part of the Arabian gulf along the side of Arabia, beginning at the Ailanites recess, was recorded by those around Alexander, especially Anaxikrates,[283] as 14,000 stades, although this is said to be too much. The part opposite Trogodytike, which is on the right when sailing from Heroönpolis, as far as Ptolemaïs and the elephant-hunting

---

[280] See n. on 52 §33.   [281] The description is of *Yemen* (Roller 2010, 196).
[282] At 16. 2. 30.
[283] Otherwise unknown, but evidently the leader of the expedition sent here by Alexander (Theophrastos, *HP* 9. 4. 4; Arrian, *Indike*, 43. 7).

territory, is 9,000 stades to the south and slightly towards the east, and then, as far as the narrows, 4,500 somewhat more to the east.

The narrows (*Bab el-Mandab*) towards Arabia are created by a promontory called Deire (*Ras Siyyan*), and a small town with the same name, in which the Ichthyophagoi (*Fish-eaters*) live. Here, it is said, there is a pillar of Sesostris the Egyptian that records his crossing in hieroglyphics.[284] It appears that he was the first to subdue the Aithiopis and Trogodytike, and then he crossed into Arabia and proceeded against all Asia. Because of this, what are called the fortifications (*charakes*) of Sesostris[285] are identified everywhere, as well as reproductions of temples to the Egyptian gods. The narrows at Deire contract to 60 stades, yet these are not called the narrows now. As one sails further along, where the passage between the continents is about 200 stades, there are six islands that come in succession and fill up the crossing, leaving extremely narrow passages through which boats carry goods across, and these are called the narrows. After the islands, the next sailing, following the bays along the land that bears myrrh towards the south, and east as far as the land that bears cinnamon, is about 5,000 stades. It is said that until now no one has gone beyond this region.[286] There are not many cities on the coast, but many beautiful settlements in the interior.

This, then, is the account of Eratosthenes about Arabia.

89   Strabo 17. 1. 1–2, C785–6: *The Nile*

(1) In making the rounds of Arabia, I have included the gulfs that tighten it up and make it a peninsula—the Persian and Arabian—and at the same time I have gone round parts of Egypt and Aithiopia, that of the Trogodytai and those beyond them as far as the Cinnamon-bearing Land. The remainder that touches these peoples must be set forth, the regions around the Nile. Afterwards I will go across Libyē, which is the last topic of the entire *Geographia*. The assertions of Eratosthenes must also be expounded.

(2) He says that the Nile is 900 or 1,000 stades west of the Arabian gulf, and is similar to the shape of a backward letter nu (*N*), for, he says,[287] after flowing from Meroë towards the north for about 2,700 stades, it turns back towards the south and the winter sunset (*i.e. south-west*) for about 3,700 stades, and after coming almost opposite the location of Meroë and projecting far into Libyē, it makes the second turn and is carried 5,300 stades north to the great cataract, turning aside slightly towards the east, then 1,200 to the smaller one at Syene, and then 5,300 more to the sea.

There are two rivers that empty into it, which come from certain lakes to the east and encircle Meroë, a good-sized island. One of these is called the Astaboras, flowing

---

[284] *hiera grammata*, lit. 'sacred letters'.

[285] Cf. Hdt. 2. 102–22, 137, for Greek popular beliefs about this pharaoh.

[286] The present time referred to is probably that of E. (Roller 2010, 197), not of Strabo, by whose day more was known of these areas, as *PME* shows (Ch. 25 below).

[287] The sentences as far as 'summer rains' are attributed to Artemidoros by the 'Munich fragment' (Artem. 168 below).

on the eastern side, and the other the Astapous—although some call it the Astasobas, saying that another is the Astapous, flowing from certain lakes to the south, and that the latter makes almost the entire straight body of the Nile, created by being filled with summer rains.[288]

Seven hundred stades above the confluence of the Astaboras and the Nile is Meroë, a city with the same name as the island. There is another island above Meroë which is held by the Egyptian fugitives who revolted at the time of Psammetichos (II),[289] called the Sembritai, which means 'foreigners'. They are ruled by a woman but are subject to those in Meroë. In the lower districts on either side of Meroë, along the Nile towards the Erythraian, live the Megabaroi and Blemmyeis, subject to the Aithiopes and bordering the Egyptians.

Along the sea are the Trogodytai. The Trogodytai opposite Meroë lie ten or twelve days' journey from the Nile. On the left side of the course of the Nile in Libyē live the Noubai (*Nubians*), a large group of people who begin at Meroë and extend as far as the bends, not subject to the Aithiopes but divided into a number of separate kingdoms. The extent of Egypt along the sea from the Pelousiac to the Kanobic mouth is 1,300 stades. Eratosthenes has these things.

90   Strabo 17. 1. 19, C802: *Egyptian treatment of strangers*
Eratosthenes says that banishment of foreigners is common among all barbarians, but the Egyptians are censured for this because of the tales concerning Bousiris. Those *(living)* later wish to accuse this place of inhospitality, but, by Zeus, there was no king or tyrant named Bousiris. Moreover, this is quoted as a reproach: 'To go to Egypt, a long and painful journey'.[290] The lack of harbours adds greatly to the problem, and also that one could not enter the single existing harbour, the one at Pharos, because it was guarded by shepherds who were pirates, and who would attack those coming to anchor. The Karchedonians (*Carthaginians*) would drown any foreigner who sailed past them to Sardo or the Pillars.[291] Because of this most things about the west are not believed. Moreover, the Persians would deceitfully guide ambassadors over circuitous roads and through difficult places.

91   Strabo 17. 3. 1–2, C824: *Libyē*
(1) Next I will speak about Libyē, which is the remaining part of the entire *Geography*. I have previously said much about it,[292] but now additional appropriate matters must also be mentioned, adding what has not previously been said.[293]

---

[288] Cf. Juba 4 below.   [289] Cf. 25 §1, 57.

[290] *Od.* 4. 483.

[291] Polybios 3. 22 records an early Carthaginian treaty forbidding Romans from sailing W of Sardinia. This passage comes from the last part of E.'s third book (Roller 2010, 219–20).

[292] At 2. 3. 4 and 2. 4. 3.

[293] This passage reflects the era of E. or an earlier time, not Strabo's own; has not been updated to reflect the fall of Carthage or the *Libyka* of Juba (Ch. 22 below) (Roller 2010, 200). It may reflect a C4 traveller who could also have informed Ps.-Skylax (Roller l.c.), though the latter may have worked from an alternative version of Hanno (see Ch. 4, introduction).

Those who have divided the inhabited world into continents have divided it un-equally, for the division into three parts suggests three equal ones, but Libyē is so much lacking in being a third part of the inhabited world that even if it were combined with Europe it would not seem to be equal to Asia. Perhaps it is smaller than Europe, and greatly so in regard to its importance, for much of the interior and of the coast along the Ocean is desert, dotted with small settlements that are for the most part scattered and nomadic.

In addition to the desert, it abounds in wild beasts that drive (*the inhabitants*) away even from areas capable of habitation, and it occupies much of the burned zone. How-ever, all of the coast opposite us—that between the Nile and the Pillars—is prosper-ously settled, especially that part subjected to the Karchedonians (*Carthaginians*),[294] although even here portions are found without water, such as those around the Syrteis, Marmaridai, and the Katabathmos (*'Descent'; at Sollum*).

It (*Libyē*) is in the shape of a right-angled triangle as conceived on a level surface, having as its base the sea-coast opposite us from Egypt and the Nile as far as Maur-ousia (*Mauretania*)[295] and the Pillars. The side perpendicular to this is that which is formed by the Nile as far as Aithiopia and extended by us to the Ocean, and the hy-potenuse to the right angle is the entire coast of the Ocean between the Aithiopes and the Maurousioi. What is at the extremity of the previously mentioned triangle, lying somewhat within the burned (*i.e. torrid*) zone, we can only speak about from conjec-ture because it is inaccessible, so we cannot speak of the greatest width of the land, although we have said in a previous section[296] this much: going south from Alexandria to Meroë, the royal capital of the Aithiopes, is about 10,000 stades, and from there in a straight line to the boundaries between the burned and inhabited regions is another 3,000. At any rate, this should be put down as the greatest width of Libyē—13,000 or 14,000 stades—with its length slightly less than double that. This then is the totality of Libyē, but I must speak about each (*region*), beginning from the western parts, the most famous.

(2) Here live those whom the Hellenes call the Maurousioi, and the Romans and locals the Mauroi, a numerous and prosperous Libyan nation (*ethnos*) on the strait opposite Iberia. Here also is the strait called the Pillars of Herakles, of which I have often spoken. Going outside the strait at the Pillars, having Libyē on the left, there is the mountain that the Hellenes call Atlas and the barbarians Dyris. Something pro-jects from it farthest towards the west of Maurousia, called the Koteis.[297] Nearby is a small town above the sea that the barbarians call Trinx, but Artemidoros calls it Lynx

---

[294] Strabo uses an aorist middle participle, γενομένη, to describe the part that 'became' subject to Carthage, which had been destroyed in 146; as such, it is ambiguous as between 'is' and 'was', and may be a carry-over from E.'s own phrasing. Roller 2010, 200, suggests that the lack of detail about the N coast W of Cyrene may reflect Carthaginian control in the C3, when E. wrote.

[295] For the scope of anc. Mauretania (wider and further E than mod. Mauritania), see Ch. 22, intro-duction.

[296] At 1. 4. 2.   [297] Cf. Kotes in Ps.-Skyl. §112. 1.

and Eratosthenes Lixos.[298] It lies across the strait from Gadeira, 800 stades across the sea, which is about as far as each lies from the strait at the Pillars. To the south of Lixos and the Koteis lies the gulf called Emporikos (*Trading*), which has settlements of Phoenician merchants.

The entire sea-coast encompassed by this gulf is indented, according to the triangle shape that I have outlined, but the gulfs and projections should be removed. One must conceive that the continent becomes larger to the south and east.[299] The mountain that extends through Maurousia from the Koteis as far as the Syrteis is inhabited, both it and the others that are parallel, first by Maurousioi but deep within the territory by the most numerous of the Libyan peoples, who are called the Gaitouloi.

92   Strabo 17. 3. 8, C829: *Lixos*

Artemidoros disagrees with Eratosthenes because the latter says that a certain city near the western extremities of Maurousia is Lixos rather than Lynx, that there are a large number of Phoenician cities that have been destroyed and of which there are no traces to be seen, that the air among the western Aithiopes is brackish, and that the air at the hours of daybreak and the afternoon is thick and misty.

93   Pliny, *Natural History*, 3. v. 75: *Names of seas*

But Eratosthenes calls the area (*of water*) between the ocean's mouth and Sardinia the Sardoan (*Sardoum mare*), from there to Sicily the Tyrrhenian (*Tyrrhenum*), from this sea to Crete the Sicilian (*Siculum*), and from this the Cretan (*Creticum*).

94   Pliny, *Natural History*, 5. vi. 39: *A distance in N. Africa*

Eratosthenes declares that the distance from Kyrene to Alexandria, by land journey, is 525 miles.

95   Pliny, *Natural History*, 5. vi. 40: *Length of the Mediterranean*

Agrippa (*stated*) the length of all of Africa from the Atlantic, including Lower Egypt, as 3,040 (*miles*).[300] Polybios and Eratosthenes, who are regarded as most careful, have made the distance from the Ocean to Great Carthage 1,100 miles, and from there to Canopus, the nearest mouth of the Nile, 1,688 miles.[301]

96   Pliny, *Natural History*, 5. vii. 41–2: *Islands off N. Africa*

These seas (*sc. off Libyē*) do not contain particularly many islands. The most renowned is Meninx, 25 miles long and 22 wide, which is called Lotophagitis by Eratosthenes. It has two towns: Meninge on the side towards Africa, and Phoar on the other.[302] It lies 1,500 (*double*) paces (*i.e. 1½ miles*) from the right-hand promontory of the Lesser Syrtis. 100 miles from it, against the left hand, is Cercina with a free city of the same name; it is 25 miles long and half as wide at its maximum, but no more than 5 miles

---

[298] Cf. Hanno §6; Ps.-Skyl. §112. 3.

[299] The ancients had no notion of the length of southern Africa, believing that the coast ran E from what we call W. Africa to the Indian Ocean.

[300] 3,000 Rackham.   [301] 1,628 Rackham.   [302] So Desanges; alternatively, Thoa.

wide at its end. Towards Carthage the diminutive Cercinitis is joined to it by a bridge. (42) About 50 miles from them is Lepadusa, 6 miles long; soon come Gaulos, then Galata whose soil kills scorpions, that detestable beast of Africa.

97 Pliny, *Natural History*, 5. ix. 47: *Extent of Asia*
Asia joins it (*Libyē*), and Timosthenes asserts that it extends from the Canopic mouth to the mouth of the Pontus, a distance of 2,638 miles; but Eratosthenes says that from the mouth of the Pontus to the mouth of Maeotis is 1,545 miles.

98 Pliny, *Natural History*, 5. xxxiii. 127: *Vanished nations in Asia*
From Asia various nations have perished: according to Eratosthenes the Solymi, Leleges, Bebryces, Colycantii, and Tripsedi.

99 Pliny, *Natural History*, 6. i. 3: *Breadth of Black Sea*
Certain writers have made the measure[303] of the Pontus from the Bosporus to Lake Maeotis 1,438½ miles, but Eratosthenes 100 less.

100 Pliny, *Natural History*, 6. xv. 36: *Dimensions of the eastern Black Sea*
Eratosthenes sets the measure (*of the Pontos*) on the east and south, via the coast of Cadusia and Albania, at 5,400 stades; from there via the Anariaci, Amardi, and Hyrcani to the mouth of the river Zonus, 4,800 stades; from this to the mouth of the Jaxartes (*Syr Darya*), 2,400 stades. The total of these makes 1,575 miles.[304]

101 Pliny, *Natural History*, 6. xxi. 56: *Form of India*
The Hemodi mountains rise up and the nation of the Indians begins, which not only borders the eastern sea but also the southern one that we have named the Indic. The part (*of the Indian nation*) that is turned to the east is extended in a straight area as far as a bend, and by the beginning of the Indian sea it amounts to 1,875 miles. From there the part that bends south occupies 2,475 miles, as Eratosthenes records, as far as the river Indus, which is the end of India on the west.

102 Pliny, *Natural History*, 6. xxiv. 81: *Dimensions of Taprobane*
Eratosthenes announced that the measurement (*of Taprobane*) is 7,000 stades in length and 5,000 in width; and that there are no cities, but 750 villages.

103 Pliny, *Natural History*, 6. xxviii. 108: *Form of Erythraian sea*
It (*the Erythraian sea*) is divided into two gulfs. That lying on the east is called Persian and is 2,500 miles in circuit, as Eratosthenes reports; on the opposite side is Arabia, whose length is 1,500 miles. Again, it is surrounded by the other gulf, named Arabic (*Red Sea*); the (*part of*) Ocean that flows into it they call Azanius. Some have made the Persian gulf 5 (*miles*) in breadth at its entrance, others 4. It is agreed that from this to the innermost part of gulf is almost 1,125 (*miles*) by a direct course, and that its situation is in the form of a human head.

---

[303] i.e. circumference.   [304] That is, 12,600 st., which divided by 8 gives 1,575.

104 Pliny, *Natural History*, 6. xxxiii. 163: *Dimensions of the 'Arabian gulf' (Red Sea)*
Now we shall follow the rest of the opposite coast of Arabia. Timosthenes has gauged
the whole gulf (*the Red Sea*) as a voyage of 4 days lengthwise and 2 days across, while
the narrows are 7½ miles (*in width*). Eratosthenes gives 1,200 from the mouth along
either side; . . .

105 Arrian, *Anabasis*, 5. 6. 2–3: *The parts of Asia*
(2) The southward part of Asia being divided into four, Eratosthenes makes the largest
part the land of the Indians, as does Megasthenes . . . and the smallest part is that area
which the river Euphrates confines, towards our inner sea. The two parts confined
between the river Euphrates and the Indos, if combined, hardly merit comparison
with the land of the Indians.   (3) The land of the Indians (*they say*) is confined, in
the direction of the east and the Apeliotes wind (*and*) as far as the south, by the Great
Sea; the Caucasus mountain confines its northward part as far as its junction with the
Tauros; while the river Indos cuts off the part towards the west and the Iapyx (*WNW*)
wind as far as the Great Sea. The majority of it is a plain; and this, they suppose, was
accumulated by the rivers.

106 Arrian, *Indike*, 3. 1–5: *Size of India*
(1) In my view, Eratosthenes of Kyrene may be more reliable than any other, because
Eratosthenes had an interest in the circuit of the Earth.   (2) This man says that from
the Tauros mountain,[305] where the Indos has its sources, as one proceeds along this
very river Indos as far as the Great Sea and the outflows of the Indos, the side of the
land of the Indians (*i.e. its NW border*) reaches 13,000 stades.   (3) He understands
the side opposite these (*outflows*), from the same mountain to beside the eastern sea
(*i.e. the NE border*), not to be merely equal to this side but—since a cape projects (*here*)
a long way into the open sea (*pelagos*), this cape extending to about 3,000 stades—for
him the side of the country of the Indians towards the east would be about 16,000 stades.   (4) For him, this constitutes the breadth of the land of the Indians. He says he is
recording its length from west to east, as far as the city of Palimbothra, which has been
measured in *schoinoi*—for it is a royal road—and that it extends to 10,000 stades; but
that the places beyond are not so certain: (5) and those who have recorded rumours
say that, including the cape extending into the open sea (*pelagos*), it reaches about
10,000 stades, so that (*he says*) the length of the land of the Indians would be around
20,000 stades.

107 Ammianus Marcellinus 22. 8. 10–13: *Length of the Black Sea coasts*
Its (*the Black Sea's*) total coastal navigation, as if it were an insular circuit, has been
measured as 23,000 stades, as Eratosthenes declares and also Hecataeus, Ptolemy,
and other most detailed investigators of this sort of knowledge.[306] It is formed into

---

[305] Some geographers extended the Tauros range to join the Himalayas.
[306] For the continuation of this extract, see Hekat. 60.

the appearance of a Skythian bow when strung, on which all of geography concurs. ... (13) But the two outermost points of the bow, (one) on each side, are represented by the two Bospori, placed in opposite regions to one another, namely the Thracian and the Cimmerian.

108 scholion A to Apollonios of Rhodes 2. 399–401: *The river Phasis*
The Phasis runs from the mountains of Armenia, as Eratosthenes says, but issues into the sea beside the Kolchoi.

109 scholion A to Apollonios of Rhodes 2. 1247: *The Caucasus*
'Even of the Caucasian (*mountains*)': the ones designated Kaukasia are said by Eratosthenes to be near the sea designated Kaspiane (*the Caspian*).

110 scholion B to Apollonios of Rhodes 4. 131–5: *A river in the Black Sea*
'Beyond Titenian Aia': the river Titenos, after which the land of Titenis has been called, is noted by Eratosthenes, *Geography*.

111 scholion B to Apollonios of Rhodes 4. 282–91: *The mouth of the Danube*
Eratosthenes, in book 3 of his *Geographika*, (says the Istros) flows from desert places, and surrounds the island of Peuke (*Pine I.*).

112 scholion to Apollonios of Rhodes 4. 310: *Peuke Island*
'three-barbed': Eratosthenes, in book 3 of his *Geographika*, says it is a three-cornered island in the Istros, equal (*in size*) to Rhodes, and is called Peuke on account of having many pines.

113 scholion to Apollonios of Rhodes 4. 1215: *Peoples of the Adriatic*
Skylax says the Nestaioi are an Illyric nation: 'from these there is a coastal sailing into the gulf [— *distance missing?* —]'. And Eratosthenes, in book 3 of his *Geographoumena*, says, 'After the Illyrians (*are*) the Nestaioi, beside whom is the island of Pharos, a colony of the Parians'.[307]

114 scholion to Euripides, *Medea* 2: *The Clashing Rocks*
The Symplegadai are called Synormadai by Simonides; but Eratosthenes, in his *Geographoumena*, says that the voyage is narrow and crooked, which is why sailors imagine the closing together of the rocks.

115 Proclus, *On the Timaeus*, 1. 37b (on Plato, *Timaeus* 22a): *The cause of the Nile flood*
But others say that the Nile is swollen by certain rains that pour out into it, as has been stated explicitly by Eratosthenes.

---

[307] Ps.-Skyl. §23. 1, a rare citation of the *periplous*. Its misattribution to Skylax evidently took place before this scholion was composed.

116   Stephanos of Byzantion α 44 Agraioi: *An Arabian nation*
Agraioi: an Arabian nation . . . There is another nation, near the Akarnanians, as Thucydides (*says*) in (*the*) 3rd (*book*). . . . They are also called Agraëis, as by Eratosthenes.[308]

117   Stephanos of Byzantion α 254: *A place in Bithynia*
Amaxa: a place in Bithynia, as Eratosthenes (*says*).

118   Stephanos of Byzantion α 493: *The Mesopotamian Assyrians*
Assyria: a territory around Babylon. . . . They are also called Assyrikoi, also Assyres in Eratosthenes.

119   Stephanos of Byzantion α 547: *An Epeirote nation*
Autariatai: a Thesprotic nation. (*Other authors mention it*) . . . also Eratosthenes.[309]

120   Stephanos of Byzantion γ 8 Gangra: *A place in Paphlagonia*
Gangra (*singular*): a *polis* ⟨in Paphlagonia⟩, feminine. . . . But Eratosthenes refers to it as neuter (*plural*), Gangra.

121   Stephanos of Byzantion δ 143: *A city in Illyria*
Dyrrhachion: an Illyric *polis*. . . . Eratosthenes, 3rd (*book*) of *Geographoumena*: 'Following these, there live the Taulantioi. (*There is*) a Hellenic *polis*, Epidamnos, on the peninsula called Dyrrhachion; and the rivers Drilōn and Aoös, near which the tombs of Kadmos and Harmonia are pointed out.'

122   Stephanos of Byzantion ι 123 Ichnai: *A city in Macedonia*
Ichnai: a city in Macedonia. . . . But Eratosthenes refers to it as Achnai.

123   Stephanos of Byzantion τ 39: *A city in Kilikia*
Tarsos: a most renowned *polis* in Kilikia. . . . Eratosthenes ⟨says the appellation came to the city from Zeus Tersios, so called by those living there. Others, however, call it⟩ Tersos . . . The citizen is a 'Tarseus'; but Eratosthenes also calls him a 'Tarsenos'.

124   Stephanos of Byzantion τ 52: *An Alpine nation*
Tauriskoi: a nation in the area of the Alpeia mountains (*Alps*). . . . Eratosthenes, using an epsilon, refers to them as Teriskoi, who are also called Tauroi.

125   Tzetzes (Isaak or Ioannes), *On Lykophron, Alexandra*, line 1285
'The Symplegades Rocks': . . . But Eratosthenes calls them Synormadai; he says they are hidden and concealed (*and lie*) near the Euxeinos Pontos; that is, around the strait.

126   Eustathios, *On Dionysios Periegetes* line 867: *Origin of a city name*
But Eratosthenes says that appellation of the *polis* (*of Tarsos*) is from Zeus Tersios, as he is called by the people there.

---

[308] E. is probably referring to the second instance, but conceivably to the first.
[309] Cf. Pajón Leyra 2021 for an anonymous history of this people, antedating E.

127   Eustathios, *On Homer, Iliad* 2. 612: *Observations on Arkadia*

You must realize that in the books of Pausanias it is given that *Arkas kynē* ('*Arkas dog-skin cap*') was used to mean an Arkadian felt hat, because it probably had some point of difference as compared with similar items; and that a certain *phellos* (*cork-oak*) was called *Arkas*, and that Eratosthenes says that among the Arkadians a *phellos* is something between a *prinos* (*evergreen oak*) and a *drys* (*deciduous oak*), and that some call it *thēlyprinos* ('*female oak*').[310]

---

[310] Geus 2011 attributes this fragment to E.'s work *On Comedy*.

13

MNASEAS OF PATARA

(ACTIVE C.225–C.200 BC)

Daniela Dueck

INTRODUCTION

This is what we know with a relatively high degree of probability: Mnaseas, from Patara in Lykia, lived in the second half of the 3rd century B C and was a pupil of Eratosthenes. He composed two works in Greek: one known as *Periplous* (*Circumnavigation*) or *Periegesis* (*Guided Tour*), the other *On Oracles*, which included a collection of texts and some interpretations. Only fragments of both works survive,[1] though the citations of Mnaseas are relatively plentiful in comparison with some other hellenistic geographers, indicating that he was a figure of some importance.

Mnaseas' provenance is mentioned only in several of the allusions to his work and not in a uniform way: either *Patreus* (Πατρεύς), a man from Patrai in the west of Achaia in the northern Peloponnese, or *Patareus* (Παταρεύς), a man from Patara in Lykia, now in south-western Turkey. Although there is no firm ground for choosing one over the other, the modern tendency to prefer Patara relies, first, on the fact that this version appears in more reliable sources, including the earliest allusion to Mnaseas in a papyrus excerpt dated to the 3rd century B C.[2] Another consideration is the cultural and political situation of both cities in the early hellenistic period: Patrai, though a co-founder of the Achaean league in or about 280, was recovering after two military defeats around that date,[3] whereas Patara is thought to have been prospering under the patronage of the early Ptolemies, who renamed it Arsinoë.[4]

Mnaseas' date is based on two hints: the same 3rd-century papyrus excerpt, which forms a *terminus post quem* for his life, and the *Suda's* mention of a Mnaseas who was one of the pupils of Eratosthenes (*c*.280–*c*.200).[5] No other solid chronological marker is preserved in the contents of the fragments.

---

[1] The most updated and comprehensive discussion of M.'s biography and works is Cappelletto 2003, 13–39, and the following is based on some of his notions.

[2] *P. Oxy.* 13. 1611 fr. 2 (fr. 54 Cappelletto), l. 121: Μνα[σέας ὁ] Παταρ[εὺς ἐ]ν τῷ[ι Περὶ χ]ρησμῶ[ν], 'Mna[seas] of Patar[a i]n th[e *On O*]racl[e]s'.

[3] Shipley 2018, 55, 56.

[4] In addition, *Patareus* is slightly preferable on the principle of *lectio difficilior*: it is less likely to have been introduced as an error for the simpler word *Patreus*.

[5] *Suda* s.v. Eratosthenes: 'Mnaseas, Menandros, and Aristis were pupils of his'.

Mnaseas' geographical work is identified by some of the quoting sources as a *periplous* (circumnavigation), as a *periēgēsis* (guided tour), or in the plural as *periēgēseis*. There are also allusions to parts within the work devoted to each of the three continents—Europe, Asia, and Libyē—and within them to books. These sporadic hints enable us to construct the following: Mnaseas wrote a *periplous* of the inhabited world, divided into three parts (*periēgēseis*), each corresponding to one of the continents. The first was *On Europe*, which included some introductory remarks to the entire work and was composed of at least three books; the second part, *On Asia*, included at least two books; and *On Libyē* probably more than one book.

The fragments below are ordered according to this general scheme, starting with the ones attributed with certainty to the section *On Europe* and ending with excerpts attributed to Mnaseas but with no clear indication or hint as to their context within the original geographical work. The 53 fragments are mostly short and indirect allusions; this situation disturbs the possibility of arriving at firm conclusions regarding the scope, style, content, and sources of the complete work at the time. Therefore, any comment made on their basis should be taken cautiously and may no less reflect the interests of the quoting sources. It is, for instance, apparent that many allusions to Mnaseas appear in short lexical collections or in various scholia. Nevertheless, and with this deficiency in mind, one may see that fewer than half of the fragments include clear geographical information such as topographic, ethnographic, and toponymic details, while most of them deal mainly with mythography, genealogies, and etymologies.

Other than glimpses of well-known myths, there are several instances showing that Mnaseas preserved some unique versions of mythology, for instance his allusion to Apollo's death (10) or the ancestry of the Stymphalidai (23). The quoting sources sometime notice Mnaseas' exceptional approach, indicating that it is 'peculiar' (using the adverb *idiōs*, 23) or 'rather unusual' (*xenikōteron*, 26). All these mythographic details should not mislead us into believing that Mnaseas was interested mainly in mythology for its own sake, for they may be understood as originating in a geographical work as part of some introductory remarks on earlier phases of the physical world, or along the lines of the descriptive tradition of local myths.

At the same time, the fragments reflect Mnaseas' geographical interests, for instance his reference to a lesser-known Dodona in Thessaly (17); his allusions to local worship in Samothrake (21), among the Getai (19), or in Syria (31). Mnaseas dealt with ethnonyms (42) and toponyms (45), and was also interested in marvels, such as talking fish (14).

As a general inspiration, Eratosthenes' teaching must have left a mark on his student, although given the present state of the fragments it is impossible to pinpoint specific influences. We hear only once about one of Mnaseas' sources, Xanthos of Lydia, who composed a *Lydiaka* and who delivered some details on the final fate of Atargatis, the Syrian goddess (31). Other than this, one may only discern some general tendencies such as the traditional division of the work according to continents and what seems to be a rationalistic approach to myths along the lines of Euhemeristic notions.

Mnaseas' fragments have appeared in an earlier and incomplete collection by Müller,[6] and much later in another by Cappelletto, whose volume is most comprehensive, thorough, and accurate. However, his thorough approach includes an assemblage of all variations and a maximalistic approach to each fragment with its wider context of reference. In order to focus straightforwardly on Mnaseas, I have chosen in some cases to leave out some of the additional details and to offer only what should be attributed to him with a higher degree of certainty. Extracts are here reordered by date within each subsection (scholia appearing last within each).

SELECTED FURTHER READING

Bollansée, J., Haegemans, K., and Schepens, G. (2008), 'Mnaseas of Patara (215–175 BCE)', *Encyclopedia of Ancient Natural Scientists*, 559.

*Cappelletto, P. (2003), *I frammenti di Mnasea*. Milan.

Laqueur, R. (1932), 'Mnaseas 6', *Pauly–Wissowa, Realencyclopädie der classischen Altertumswissenschaft*, xv. 2, 2250–2.

PERIPLOUS OR *PERIEGESIS*

ON EUROPE

Book 1

1 Harpokration s.v. Hippia Athena
'Hippia Athena': . . . Mnaseas, in (*the*) 1st (*book*) of *Europe*, says that Athena Hippia is the daughter of Poseidon and Koryphe daughter of Okeanos, and that she was the first to build a chariot and therefore called Hippia (*of Horses*).

2 Fulgentius, *Mythologies*, 2. 16
She (*Diana*) is said to have fallen in love with the shepherd Endymion for one of two reasons. One is because Endymion was the first man to discover the track of the Moon, and since then he, who did nothing in his life besides study this repetition, slept for thirty years, just as Mnaseas writes in the 1st book of *On Europe*.

Book 3[7]

3 Athenaios 4. 47, 158c
I know that the sister of Odysseus, the most prudent and wisest of men, was called Phakē (*Lentil*), whom some others call Kallisto, as Mnaseas of Patrai tells in (*the*) 3rd (*book*) of *Europiaka* (*European Matters*).

---

[6] *FHG* iii. 149–58.   [7] No specific allusion to book 2 survives.

4   Athenaios 7. 47, 296b–c

Mnaseas, in (*the*) 3rd (*book*) of *Europiaka* (*European Matters*), traces his (*Glaukos'*) ancestry to Anthedon[8] and Alkyone and says that, being a sailor and an excellent diver, he was called Pontios (*of the sea*), and that after he carried off Symē, the daughter of Ialysos and Dotis, he sailed away to Asia and settled in the desert island near Karia[9] and called it Symē after his wife.

5   Athenaios 12. 40, 530c

Not only Sardanapallos pampered himself, but so did Androkottos the Phrygian.[10] For he also wore brightly coloured dress and adorned himself more charmingly than a woman, as Mnaseas says in (*the*) 3rd (*book*) of *Europe*.

6   Stephanos of Byzantion ε 6

Engelanes: a nation in Illyria, the same people as the Encheleai,[11] as Mnaseas (*says*) in (*the*) 3rd (*book*) of the *Periegeseis*.[12]

Book number uncertain

7   Herodian, *General Prosody* book 7, fr. 42

Kandyos: Mnaseas mentions it in his book *On Europe*.[13]

8   Aelian, *On the Nature of Animals*, 17. 44 (46)

Mnaseas, in his work *On Europe*, says that there is a temple of Herakles and his wife, of whom the poets sing as the daughter of Hera.

9   Ammonios, *On the Difference between Similar Words*, §333

Didymos . . . says, 'There are those who say that the Nereids differ from the daughters of Nereus, and that the latter are considered to be his genuine daughters by Doris while the former, born from other mothers, are now commonly called Nereids; also, the genuine ones are six in number and the others are more numerous. These things Mnaseas says in this manner in his work *On Europe*.'

10   Fulgentius, *Explanation of Obsolete Words*, 2

Vispillones are said to be porters . . . Mnaseas, however, writes in his work *On Europe* that after Apollo was defeated and killed by Jupiter he was carried to his burial by *vispillones*.

---

[8] Anthedon in Boiotia was the birthplace of the sea-god Glaukos.

[9] Between Rhodes and Karia.

[10] Otherwise unknown, and may be a corrupted form of Sandrokotos who was an Indian king, but this contradicts his definition as a Phrygian.

[11] The Encheleioi in Illyria dwelling to the N of L. Lychnidos.

[12] Note the plural form *Periegeseis*, 'guided tours'.

[13] Perhaps an ethnonym, or some form (*kandys*) of a Persian dress or city, but the European context poses a problem. The source of the new fragment of Herodian is Hunger 1967, 11 no. 42.

11 Photios, *Lexikon* s.v. Praxidike

Praxidike: . . . Mnaseas, in his *On Europe*, says that from Soter (*Saviour*)[14] and his sister Praxidike (*Enforcer of Justice*) were born a son, Ktesios (*Protector of Property*), and his daughters Homonoia (*Unity*) and Arete (*Virtue*), who were called 'Praxidikai' after their mother.

12 scholion C **to Theokritos,** *Idylls,* 1. 64

Mnaseas, in his work *On Europe*, says that Boukolion is the son of Pan, and that from his name comes the verb 'to tend cattle' (*boukolein*).

Probable fragments

13 Zenobios, *Proverbs* 2. 67[15]

'Boulias judges': this proverb is said about those who always delay and hold over decisions. For, as Mnaseas says, Boulias son of Hekale was an Athenian, and when the Eleians disputed with the Kalydonians they handed him their case, thinking that they would stay until there was a decision. And this Boulias knew this and listened to both sides, and then delayed his decision until he died.

14 Athenaios 8. 3, 331d

Mnaseas of Patrai in his *Periplous* says that the fish in the river Kleitor[16] utter sounds, although Aristotle[17] has said that only the parrotfish and the squeaker[18] can utter sounds.

15 Arnobius, *Against the Nations,* 3. 37

Mnaseas is the author who says that the Muses are the daughters of Tellus (*Earth*) and Coelus (*Sky*)[19] . . . Ephoros contributes that they are three in number;[20] Mnaseas, whom we mentioned, four; Myrsilos introduces seven;[21] Krates asserts eight;[22] Hesiod brings it to an extreme by providing nine Muses with their names.[23]

16 Stephanos of Byzantion α 151

Akanthos: a Thracian city[24] surrounded by shrubs of acanthus, beyond Mt Athos, named after them, or after a certain man (*named*) Akanthos, as Mnaseas (*says*).

17 Stephanos of Byzantion δ 146

Dodona: . . . There are double Dodonas: this one (*in Epeiros*) and the one in Thessaly,[25] just as others and also Mnaseas (*say*).

---

[14] A title of Zeus.

[15] The name 'Bounas' is corrected on the basis of the shorter version of the same entry at 2. 86.

[16] In Arkadia, falling into the R. Aroarios, near the town of Kleitor.

[17] *History of Animals,* 535 b 14–536 a 3.

[18] Lit. 'river-pig', identified by Thompson 1947, 214, with the schall (*Synodontis schall*); it can denote any member of the family *Mochokidae*. (Information supplied by the Press's anonymous reader.)

[19] Equivalent to Latin *caelus*, 'sky'.   [20] *BNJ* 70 F 222.

[21] *BNJ* 477 F 7b.   [22] Probably Krates of Mallos.

[23] *Theogony,* 76–9, 915–17.   [24] Barr. 51 B 4, near the Athos promontory.

[25] Dodona in Epeiros; the allusion to another Dodona in Thessaly probably follows an exegetic Homeric tradition.

18   Stephanos of Byzantion δ 151

Dotion: a city in Thessaly²⁶ . . . Mnaseas (*says it was named*) after Dotos son of Pelasgos.

19   Photios, *Lexikon*, s.v. Zamolxis

Zamolxis: . . . Mnaseas ⟨says⟩ that Kronos is honoured by the Getai²⁷ and called Zamolxis.

20   *Epimerismoi Homerikoi* s.v. Mousa

'Muse': the three are called after one. Mnaseas says that the Muses are three in all, Mousa, Thea, and Hymno;²⁸ and that Thea is mentioned in the *Iliad*, 'The wrath sing, Thea (*goddess*)';²⁹ Mousa in the *Odyssey*, 'Tell me, O Mousa, of the man';³⁰ and Hymno in the *Palamedeia*.³¹ . . .

21   scholion B to Apollonios of Rhodes 1. 916–18

In Samothrake people are initiated into the mysteries of the Kabeiroi, as Mnaseas says.

22   scholion to Apollonios of Rhodes 2. 675

'of the Hyperborean people': . . . and Mnaseas says that now the Hyperboreans are called Delphians.

23   scholion A to Apollonios of Rhodes 2. 1052–7

Mnaseas says peculiarly that the Stymphalidai are the daughters of a certain hero named Stymphalos and a woman named Ornis (*Bird*), and that Herakles killed them because they did not accept him hospitably and defeated the Moliones.

24   scholion B to Apollonios of Rhodes 4. 263–4

'Arkadians who lived earl⟨ier⟩': . . . Mnaseas says that Proselenos (*Before-the-Moon*)³² was king of the Arkadians.³³

25   scholion to Euripides, *Phoenissae* 651

'and about him the curly ivy': . . . Mnaseas tells that after the Kadmeian palace was struck with thunderbolts, ivy grew round the pillars hiding him (*Dionysos*), so that the baby might not in any way die that day. And because of that the god is called Perikionios (*Surrounded with Pillars*) among the Thebans.

26   scholion to Euripides, *Rhesos* 36

'Pan, Kronos' son': . . . Mnaseas explains these things about Pan in a most unusual way: either that he is the son of Kronos or that his ancestry is traced of old to Aither—they

---

²⁶ There is the Dotion plain near Larissa in Thessaly, *Barr.* 55 D 1, and a city in S. Chios, *Barr.* 56 C 5.

²⁷ Between Dacia and Moesia Inferior.

²⁸ But see 15, where M. is said to have mentioned four Muses. For the Epimerismoi, see n. on Hekataios 59. The present extract is at Cramer 1835, 277–8; Dyck 1995, 499–500 (μ 64).

²⁹ Iliad, 1. 1.   ³⁰ Odyssey, 1. 1.

³¹ Probably the last part of the *Cypria*, a lost work in the 'Epic Cycle'.

³² Note the etymology connected with the Moon (Selene). On the notion of Arkadians as older than the Moon, see Dueck 2020, esp. 137–8 on this extract.

³³ Cf. Eudoxos of Knidos 69 in Ch. 6 above.

said that the very old ones are named Kronoi or Kronioi—or, being the son of Zeus, he is named after his grandfather, just as Achilles is called Aiakides (*son of Aiakos*).[34]

27   scholion B to Homer, *Odyssey*, 18. 85

'to King Echetos': Echetos was the son of Bouchetos, and after him a city in Sicily is named Bouchetos.[35] He is said to be a tyrant of the Sicilians. He hurt the locals in every manner, but the foreigners he maimed and destroyed. His perversion was so intense that also those who lived afar, every time they wanted to punish someone and to kill him in a special way, they sent to Echetos. For he invented many devices for injury. This is why, when the people could not endure this cruel tyranny, they stoned him to death. The story is found in Mnaseas and Marsyas.[36]

28   scholion G to Pindar, *Olympian Odes,* 10. 34

In the war against Augeas, Herakles fled after the Molionidai caught him, and because of this he was angry with them and stationed his army near Kleonai,[37] says Mnaseas of Patara.

29   scholion A to Pindar, *Pythian Odes,* 4. 106

'the oracle of the bee (*melissa*) raised up':[38] . . . Some said that those (*nymphs*) who live around the temples are also called Melissai; Mnaseas of Patara explains saying that after they stopped eating flesh, the men persuaded them to take their food from the trees, and at that time one of them, Melissa, found a honeycomb and was the first to eat honey, and she also mixed it with water and drank it, and she taught the others, and she called the creatures (*of the honeycomb*) *melissai* after her, and set great protection (*over them*). He says that these things happened in the Peloponnese.

ON ASIA

Book 1

30   scholion B to Apollonios of Rhodes 1. 1126–31

'Idaean dactyls':[39] . . . As Hellanikos says, they were called the Idaean Dactyls because, encountering Rhea on Mount Ida, they greeted the goddess and took hold of her fingers. But according to Mnaseas in the 1st (*book*) of *On Asia*, they are called Idaean Dactyls after their father Daktylos and their mother Ida.

Book 2

31   Athenaios 8. 37, 346d–e

Mnaseas in (*the*) 2nd (*book*) of *On Asia* says so: 'It seems to me that Atargatis[40] was a cruel queen and ruled the peoples severely, so much that she ordered them not to eat

---

[34] Although Aiakos is Peleus' father and Achilles' grandfather.
[35] Otherwise unknown. There is a Bouchetion in Epeiros.   [36] *BNJ* 135/136 F 19.
[37] *Barr.* 58 D 2, in Argolis near Nemea.   [38] Pindar is referring to the oracle at Delphi.
[39] The legendary companions of the Great Mother.   [40] Also known as Dea Syria or Derketo.

fish, but to bring them to her because of her fondness for that food' . . . Proceeding a little further he again says, 'Atargatis, as Xanthos of Lydia[41] says, was captured by Moxos the Lydian[42] and was drowned with her son Ichthys (*Fish*) in the lake near Askalon because of her hubris, and was eaten up by the fish'.

Probable fragments

32   Josephus, *Jewish Antiquities* 1. 93
. . . also Hieronymus the Egyptian, who wrote the *Phoenician Antiquities*,[43] and Mnaseas, and many others mention these (*the Flood and the Ark*).

33   Josephus, *Against Apion* 1. 216–17
Moreover, in addition to those already mentioned, Theophilos, Theodotos, Mnaseas, Aristophanes, Hermogenes, Euhemeros and Konon, Zopyrion, and perhaps many others—for I have not read all the books—have mentioned us (*the Jews*), and not merely in passing.

34   Josephus, *Against Apion* 2. 112
He (*Apion*) scorns again such pious men by adding Mnaseas to his story. He says that Mnaseas has told that when the Jews carried on for a long time their war against the Idumaeans, one person from an Idumaean city called Dorii,[44] who worshipped Apollo in this city and whose name was Zabidos, came to the Jews and promised to bring them Apollo, the god of the people of Dorii, who would come to our temple if they all withdrew. The entire Jewish crowd believed him. But Zabidos made a wooden instrument and put it round his body and inserted in it three rows of lamps. Thus he walked about, so that he looked to those standing at a distance like stars passing over the Earth. 'The Jews, amazed by the surprising spectacle, remained at a distance keeping quiet. And Zabidos in this deep silence passed into the sanctuary, and tore away the golden head of the pack-ass—for so he has cleverly written—and went quickly back to Dora.'

35   Zenobios, *Proverbs* 2. 106
Artemis of Perga: she is worshipped by beggars and wanderers. The goddess, too, is thought always to beg and wander, as Mnaseas tells.

36   Harpokration s.v. Saboi
'Saboi': . . . Mnaseas of Patrai says that Sabazios is the son of Dionysos.

37   Stephanos of Byzantion δ 18
Dardanos: a city in the Troad, the former Teukris. Mnaseas says, 'Dardanos, carrying the Palladion from the temple of Athena, came to Samothrake from Si[—][45] together with his siblings Harmonia and Iasion, and there Kadmos son of Agenor became his friend, and after Telephaë died Kadmos married Harmonia and sent Dardanos to Asia together with

---

[41] *BNJ* 765 F 17a.   [42] Mythical king of Lydia.   [43] *BNJ* 787 F 2.
[44] The first part of this passage is preserved in Latin, hence the spelling.
[45] Name incomplete in the MSS.

his friends against Teukros the Trojan. And Teukros recognized Dardanos and gave him his daughter Bateia and, while he was dying, the kingdom. And he (*Dardanos*) founded a city, Dardanos, and called the region Dardania, which was earlier called Teukris.'

38   scholion to Apollonios of Rhodes 1. 131
'and with him went Hylas': the lover of Herakles and the son of Theiodamas the Dryopian. And Mnaseas says so also.

39   scholion to Homer, *Iliad*, 19. 291–2
According to Mnaseas the son of Briseis was Eëtion.

40   scholion D to Homer, *Iliad*, 20. 234
'the gods caught him (*Ganymedes*)': Mnaseas says that he was carried off by Tantalos and after he fell during a hunt, he was buried in the Mysian Olympos near the temple of Olympian Zeus.

41   scholion to Lucian, *Zeus Rants* (*Zeus tragodos*) 6
'into (*the*) agora': . . . Mnaseas of Patara calls Priapos Hermaphroditos.

42   scholion C to Theokritos 13. 75
Mnaseas says that the Kolchoi are so called after Kolchos son of Phasis.[46]

ON LIBYĒ

43   Hesychios s.v. *Barkaiois ochois*
In chariots of Barke: in Libyan ones. For these men were enthusiastic about horse-breeding. And people say that they were also the first who were taught by Poseidon to prepare chariots, and by Athena to drive them, as Mnaseas says in his (*books*) *On Libyē*.

Probable fragments

44   Pliny, *Natural History*, 37. xi. 38
Mnaseas calls a place in Africa Sicyon and (*mentions*) a river Crathis[47] flowing into the Ocean from a lake, in which birds live that he calls Meleager's Daughters (*meleagridae*) and Penelopes (*penelopae*). Here it (*amber*) is formed in the same manner as described above.

45   Zenobios, *Proverbs* 3. 25
'There is no city of slaves': this proverb is said in order to indicate rarity, but Sosikrates says that it is a city in Crete, and Mnaseas says that in Libyē there is another city called Doulopolis (*Slave City*).[48]

---

[46] The R. Phasis (*Rioni*?) is in the region of the Kolchians.

[47] Also mentioned by Ps.-Skylax §112. 3, where the MS has 'Krabis'. Pliny's spelling may be influenced by the well-known R. Krathis in Italy (Ps.-Skyl. §13. 5; Paus. 8. 15. 9). For full discussion, see Shipley 2019, 214–15. There is another R. Krathis in Arkadia (Paus. 7. 25. 11–13; 8. 15. 9, etc.; *Barr.* 58 C1, D 2). For the Meleagrid birds (guinea fowl?), see Ps.-Skyl. §112. 1; Shipley 2019, 212.

[48] Dulopolis = Akanthos, Pliny 5. xxix. 104; or a region in Egypt: Olympianos (Oulpianos?), *BNJ* 676 F 1. A similar version is at Gaisford 1836, 81 no. 675 (which also contains Artemidoros 161),

46 scholion A to Apollonios of Rhodes 2. 498–527
Mnaseas says that she (*the nymph Kyrene*) came to Libyē of her own free will and was
not carried over by Apollo.

Uncertain book of Periplous

47 Photios, *Lexikon,* s.v. *pythou chelidonos*
'find out from the swallow' (*chelidōn*): a proverb after a certain man named Chelidon, a
theologian and an interpreter of marvels and one who examines the future, as Mnaseas
of Patrai says in his *Periplous.*

Possible fragments of Periplous

48 Plutarch, *On Isis and Osiris* 37 (*Moralia* 365f)
I leave out Mnaseas, who associates Dionysos and Osiris and Sarapis with Epaphos.

49 Herodian, *General Prosody* book 11 (263. 35–264. 1 Lentz)
Ioura:[49] Mnaseas mentions it.

50 Athenaios 7. 62, 301d
Mnaseas of Patrai says, 'Of Ichthys (*Fish*) and his sister Hesychia (*Tranquility*) were
born Galene (*Serenity*), Myraina (*Sea-eel*), and *ēlakatēnes* (*large sea-fishes*)'.

51 scholion to Aeschylus, *Persians,* 747 (745)
'who . . . the Hellespont': . . . he calls this (*the Hellespont*) 'sacred' (*hieron*) because a
temple of Zeus was founded there, as Mnaseas says.

52 scholion to Dionysios Thrax 6
Dosiades[50] says that they (*the letters*) were invented in Crete. But Aeschylus[51] says that
Prometheus invented them . . . and Mnaseas says that Hermes (*invented them*), and
others say someone else.

53 scholion C to Homer, *Iliad,* 15. 336
'his stepmother Eriopis': like the poet, Hellanikos[52] too says that Eriope is the mother
of Aias (*Ajax*). But Pherekydes in his 5th (*book*)[53] and Mnaseas in his 8th[54] say that
Alkimache is his mother, and the poet of the *Naupaktika*[55] says that she has two names.

as follows: '"There is no city of slaves": there is a city in Libyē called Doulon Polis (*Slaves' City*), as
Mnaseas of Patrai says; and (*he says*) that the man crying out for freedom said, "There is no city either
of slaves or free".'

---

[49] Possibly the European chain of mountains, *Barr.* 18 D 3.   [50] *BNJ* 458 (Dosiadas) F 6.
[51] *Prometheus Bound,* 460.   [52] *BNJ* 4 F 121.   [53] *BNJ* 3 F 24.
[54] The text is unclear and no conclusion as to the number of books in M.'s work may be gained.
[55] A lost C6 Greek epic poem; see M. L. West 2003, 274–83.

14

SKYMNOS OF CHIOS

(EARLY 2ND C. BC)

D. Graham J. Shipley

INTRODUCTION

The hellenistic author Skymnos of Chios evidently wrote, in the Ionic dialect, a work in at least 10 books which one author calls *Periplous Asias* (*Circumnavigation of Asia*; **1**), probably the same as *Asia* (**4**). He also expounded information about Europe in a work cited as *Europe* or *On Europe* (**6–8**), which apparently had at least 6 or possibly 16 books (**8**). Ancient works, especially before the late antique period, did not necessarily have original or stable titles, so it may be that only a single work, with 16 or more books grouped into continental sequences, is in question. The whole, or the European part, may have begun with the Cyclades or the Adriatic (**7**); either would be an unorthodox starting-point and may indicate an anti-clockwise geographical sequence. Five of the nine quotations that we have concern the Black Sea (**2–4, 8**). We do not know whether it covered Libyē. Pytheas and he give Britain the same circumference (**5**, cf. Pytheas **6**); other fragments indicate an interest in colonial origins and ancestries (e.g. **1, 3–4, 6**) as well as mythic geography (**8**) and botany (**5**).

Skymnos may be taken as an example of the class of extremely fragmentary authors, other examples of whom are discussed in the Introduction (§VI. 4). He is indeed a shadowy figure. It is unclear whether he reported his own travels or merely collected information from previous writers, perhaps for instructional purposes. He is not cited by any later geographer; there is one potentially contemporary citation (**5**), by Apollonios the Paradoxographer, active no later than the early 2nd century BC. Skymnos appears to have made use of the work of the late 4th-century traveller Pytheas (Chapter 8 above; **1** below), and possibly the 3rd-century authors Timaios and Eratosthenes (for the latter, see Chapter 12).[1] If not identical with, he should be a relative of, the 'Skymnos son of Apelles of Chios' who was appointed a *proxenos* of the Delphians around 185/4.[2]

In the 17th century, Lucas Holsten (1596–1661) and Isaac Vos (1618–89) proposed that Skymnos wrote the incomplete *Nikomedean Periodos* (Chapter 17 below),[3] whose

---

[1] Orth 2011b.

[2] *Syll.*³ 585; *FGrH* 2047 T 1. The name Skymnos on a C2 bronze coin of Chios suggests that the author or a relative was a mint official (Mavrogordato 1916, 315; also Fraser and Matthews 1987, 408, together with six homonyms from Chios dated C5–C1).

[3] See Marcotte 2000b, clvi and 36.

author's name must have stood at the end of the poem in one of the lost quaternions of manuscript D. The identification was later refuted,[4] but the sobriquet 'Pseudo-Skymnos' unfortunately became standard for the *Iambics*—even though the use of 'Pseudo-' followed by any name whatsoever was unwarranted, since no pre-modern evidence names Skymnos, or indeed any writer, as its author. The poem is now dated to the late 2nd or early 1st century BC, half a century or more after Skymnos' lifetime. Despite the paucity of evidence for him and his work, he is worth including in a collection of geographers not least because of this lingering association with the *Iambics*.

The translation of the fragments follows the Greek text of Orth, except for **8**. Within each book of Skymnos' work, extracts are in chronological order (with scholia placed last for uncertainty).

SELECTED FURTHER READING

Gärtner, H. A. (2006), 'Scymnus [1]', in *Brill's New Pauly*.
Gisinger, F. (1927), 'Skymnos 1', *Pauly–Wissowa, Realencyclopädie der classischen Altertumswissenschaft* [2]iii. 1. 661–87.
*Orth, C. (2011), 'Skymnos (2047)', in *FGrH* v.

PERIPLOUS (CIRCUMNAVIGATION)

ASIA

1 Herodian, *On the Unique Word* 1. 19. 4–8: *An unusual river name*
Is (*sic*) is the name given to a river in Herodotos;[5] it has a long iota. Similarly, Skymnos in book 10 of his *Circumnavigation of Asia* has been found to say, 'There follows Kelenderis, a city of the Samians, and a sanctuary of Hera beside the city, with a grove; the river Is emerges (*here*) beside the sea'.[6]

2 Stephanos of Byzantion α 413: *An island in the Black Sea*
Areos Nesos (*Ares' Island; Giresun Adası*): beside the Kolchoi in the Pontos. Skymnos, in *Asia*.[7]

3 Stephanos of Byzantion ε 123: *An island in the Kimmerian Bosporos*
Hermonassa (*Taman*): a small island bearing a city, in the Kimmerian Bosporos; a colony of the Ionians, according to (*Dionysios*) the Periegete.[8] Skymnos also calls this (*island*) Hermoneia.

---

[4] Holsten's views from 1630 and 1641 are documented by Meineke 1846 viii–xvi; and refuted at xvi–xxii.
[5] Hdt. 1. 179, referring to Babylon.   [6] This location is in southern Asia Minor.
[7] Called Aretias at Arrian 16. 4.   [8] At l. 552.

4   scholion A to Apollonios of Rhodes 4. 277–8: *Egypt and the Black Sea*
Thus those (*sc. Kolchoi*) in Skythia are also descendants of the Egyptians, as Apollonios says.[9] Skymnos, too, says in his *Asia* that the Kolchoi are colonists of the Egyptians.

EUROPE

5   Apollonios Paradoxographos, *Stories about Wonders* 15: *Great Britain*
Skymnos of Chios says that the island of Brettanike (*Great Britain*) is 40,000 stades in circuit, and that in it the vegetation grows without seeds: for example, the olive-trees have no stones, neither does the grape have a pip; nor do plants similar to these.[10]

6   Stephanos of Byzantion α 21: *A city in Gaul*
Agathe (*Good; mod. Agde*): a city of the Ligyes (*Ligurians*) or Keltoi. Skymnos, however, says it is (*a city*) of the Phokaians, in the *Europe*.[11]

7   Stephanos of Byzantion π 56: *Paros in the Adriatic*
Paros: . . . There is another Paros (*or Pharos; Hvar*), an island of the Libyrnoi, as Skymnos of Chios says in (*the*) 1st (*book*) of *Periegesis*.

8   scholion B to Apollonios of Rhodes 4. 282–91: *The divided Danube and the Argonauts' return journey*
'Calling him Istros': he (*Apollonios*) says the Istros (*Danube*) runs down out of the Hyperboreans and the Rhipaian mountains . . . and that when it is between the Skythians and Thracians it divides: †and that one stream discharges into the sea on our side, while the other emerges into the Pontic sea, the other into the Adriatic gulf†.[12] . . . Skymnos, in book ⟨1⟩6 of his work *On Europe*, says that the Istros runs from uninhabited places in a single (*stream*).[13] No one reports that the Argonauts sailed into our sea along these (*the branches of the Istros*), apart from Timagetos, whom Apollonios (*of Rhodes*) follows. For Skymnos (*says*) they sailed by way of the Tanaïs into the Great Sea,[14] and came from there into our sea; and he digresses, saying that, in fact, on arriving at the mainland the Argonauts carried the *Argo* on roof-beams until they arrived at the sea.[15]

---

[9] Also Hdt. 2. 103–5 and other authors. 'Those' evidently refers to Kolchians (as in Hdt. 2. 104), not to peoples of Skythia as a whole.

[10] Pytheas 6 (from Strabo, quoting Polybios) gave the same measurement for Great Britain's circumference. Although Orth 2011b considers the statement about olives fanciful, it may derive from an accurate report about the olive-tree failing to reproduce in the cool climate of the British Isles.

[11] It is is located E of *Narbonne* (Orth 2011b).

[12] Cf. Eratosthenes 14 above. The text of scholion B is confused; various rearrangements have been suggested.

[13] Or 'says only this: that the Istros runs from uninhabited places'.

[14] Usually the outer Ocean; the scholiast may believe it is possible to sail into the Tanaïs from the Black Sea and out at the other end. Skymnos may have referred, however, to the Black Sea.

[15] For variant versions of the story of the Argonauts, see Dueck 2012, 26–7.

15

AGATHARCHIDES OF KNIDOS, ON THE ERYTHRAIAN SEA

(WRITTEN C.145 BC)

*Stanley M. Burstein and D. Graham J. Shipley**

INTRODUCTION

Contemporary scholars view *On the Erythraian Sea* (*Peri tēs Erythras thalassēs*)[1] by Agatharchides of Knidos as a uniquely important work for three reasons. First, it is the only hellenistic historical work besides the *Histories* of Polybios of which substantial portions of the original Greek text survive (though in adaptation). Second, it is the only extant example of a hellenistic ethnographic text. Third, it is the main source of information for Greek knowledge of the Red Sea basin. It is unfortunate, therefore, that so little is known about Agatharchides' life.

The evidence for Agatharchides' biography is limited to a few comments in the *Geography* of Strabo (*BNJ* 86 T1) and in *On the Erythraian Sea* (*BNJ* 86 T3), and the review of *On the Erythraian Sea* in Codex 213 of the *Bibliotheke* of the 9th-century AD scholar and patriarch of Constantinople Photios (*BNJ* 86 T2). These bits of information suggest that Agatharchides was probably born about 200 BC in Knidos in south-western Anatolia, and that sometime in the early 2nd century he migrated to Egypt, where he entered the household of an official and adviser of Ptolemy VI named Kineas, who made Agatharchides his 'protégé' (*threptos*). Kineas probably also introduced him to another important Ptolemaic official, the Peripatetic scholar and diplomat Herakleides Lembos, whom he served as personal secretary and reader and whom he also probably assisted in the compilation of his works. It was probably also as a result of his connection to Herakleides that Agatharchides became familiar with the Peripatetic ideas that he employed in *On the Erythraian Sea*.

According to Photios, Agatharchides eventually became a grammarian and, thanks to the patronage of Herakleides, a well-known figure in the intellectual life of Alexandria. It was probably also Herakleides who facilitated his access to the royal archives, which Agatharchides (*BNJ* 86 T3) claimed to have used in composing *On*

---

[*] SB is primarily responsible for the introduction and notes, GS for the translation; but this has also been a collaborative undertaking.

[1] A., like others, uses 'Erythraian sea' for both the modern Red Sea and the northern Indian Ocean, though, as the end of the work shows (A. 2 below, §112), he managed to cover only the former.

the Erythraian Sea. About the rest of his life, all that is known is that Agatharchides claimed that he stopped working on that work because of old age and disturbances in Egypt, and that in Athens a Hellenized Persian named Boxos told him a story about Erythras, the eponym of the Erythraian sea. The most likely interpretation of these facts is that Agatharchides was one of the intellectuals whom Ptolemy VIII drove into exile in 145 because of their support for his rival for the Egyptian throne, Ptolemy VII, and that he spent at least part of the remainder of his life in Athens.

Agatharchides' literary activity was considerable. Besides *On the Erythraian Sea* and two large histories, which are discussed below, Photios lists six other works in his Codex 213 (*BNJ* 86 T2): an epitome (précis) of the 4th-century BC poet Antimachos of Kolophon's *Lyde* (a poetic anthology of love stories from Greek mythology); a book on friendship; and, although the text is corrupt, probably two collections of excerpts, one from writers on natural and human phenomena, and another from histories. Photios also mentions an abridgement of *On the Erythraian Sea* in one book, but it is not clear if this work was by Agatharchides or by a later writer. Likewise, *On the Trogodytai* in five books may only be an alternative title for *On the Erythraian Sea*. Unfortunately, nothing beyond their titles is known about these works.

Agatharchides was best known in antiquity, however, as an historian. Traditionally, scholars have believed that his historical oeuvre consisted of three works. Two were large histories: *On Affairs in Asia* (*Ta kata tēn Asian* or *Asiatika*) in ten books; and *On Affairs in Europe* (*Ta kata tēn Eurōpēn* or *Europiaka*) in forty-nine books, which together formed a universal history that surveyed world history, possibly down to Agatharchides' own time. It was his third and final work—*On the Erythraian Sea*—that Agatharchides considered his unique contribution to scholarship because he expected it to become the authoritative account of the southern portion of the *oikoumenē*. In it he treated in five books the history, ethnography, and geography of the Red Sea and its hinterlands; and unlike his other two histories—which, like other ancient universal histories, were primarily syntheses of the works of earlier historians—*On the Erythraian Sea* was based on the accounts of Ptolemaic military officers and explorers, both their original reports that were preserved in the royal archives in Alexandria and the published versions of them.

Recently, however, two scholars, Didier Marcotte and Walter Ameling, have offered radically different interpretations of the place of *On the Erythraian Sea* in the corpus of Agatharchides' historical works. Although their theories differ in detail, both agree in arguing that it was not an independent work but an integral part of a larger universal history: Marcotte maintaining that it was part of *On Affairs in Asia*, which would have been organized ethnographically instead of chronologically, and Ameling that it formed the introduction to a single work that included both *On Affairs in Asia* and *On Affairs in Europe*. Evaluation of these theses would require a full analysis of *On the Erythraian Sea* for which there is no room here. However, Agatharchides' statement in book 5 of this work that he had 'recorded in five books the situation concerning the tribes located in the south as they were in our time' after having written many works about Europe and Asia (A. 2 below, §112, from Photios *On the Erythraian Sea*),[2] and his description of his goal in writing *On the Erythraian Sea* as doing for the south what other historians had done for the northern, eastern, and western portions of the *oikoumenē* (2 §65, again from Photios), combined with the fact that there are no references to the supposed 'unified work' in the sources, strongly support the traditional view that he wrote three separate historical works.

Unfortunately, only the most general reconstructions of *On Affairs in Asia* and *On Affairs in Europe* are possible. With regard to the *Asia*, the fact that Egypt and Aithiopia were treated in book 2,[3] the reign of Alexander in book 8,[4] and Alexander's successors, the Diadochoi, in books 9 and 10[5] suggests that it was organized in accordance with the theory of the succession of Asian world empires, presumably beginning with the Assyrian empire in book 1 and ending, as such histories usually did,[6] with the establishment of the fourth empire by Alexander and his successors. The citation by Diodoros of Sicily (*Library of History*, 3. 11. 2) of Agatharchides' *Asia* alongside the *Geographoumena* of the late 2nd-century BC writer Artemidoros of Ephesos (Chapter 18 below) comes at the end of a lengthy passage describing Aithiopia and Egypt (part of which can be found below as Artemidoros 44 *b*). The next 37 chapters of Diodoros' third book (12–48) are incorporated into the present Chapter (interleaved within 2), as they draw upon book 5 of *On the Erythraian Sea*. Other material covered in Agatharchides' *Asia* included a lengthy description of the Nile, for which Diodoros (1. 32–41 = *BNJ* 86 F 19) is again the evidence (citing Agatharchides at 1. 41. 4).

As for *On Affairs in Europe*, all that can be said for certain is that the death of Magas of Kyrene in 250 BC was treated in book 16, the Spartan revolution in books 27–30, and the reign of Philip V of Macedonia in books 31–8, and that the treatment of the second half of the 3rd century occupied at least twenty-two books. It is not improbable, therefore, that the work continued *On Affairs in Asia*, beginning with the end of the wars of the Diadochoi. Any more detailed reconstruction, however, must be considered speculative.

The transmission of *On the Erythraian Sea* is complex. Although no manuscript of the work survives, three witnesses to it are extant, two direct and one indirect. The most important of the direct witnesses is Codex 250 of Photios' *Bibliotheke*, which contains extensive excerpts from books 1 and 5. The other direct witness is chapters 12–48 of Diodoros' third book, which are derived from book 5 of *On the Erythraian Sea*. As with all collections of excerpts, however, both groups reflect the interests of their excerptor. So the bulk of Photios' excerpts from book 1 are devoted to Agatharchides' refutation of the historicity of Greek myth and to a speech ascribed to a

---

[2] F 111 Burstein.   [3] Diodoros 3. 11. 1–3 (*BNJ* 86 F 1).
[4] Athenaios 4. 42. 155c–d (*BNJ* 86 F 2).
[5] Book 9: Phlegon of Tralles, *On Long-livers*, 2 (*BNJ* 86 F 4 = 257 F 37). Book 10: Athenaios 12. 55. 539b–d (*BNJ* 86 F 3).
[6] Cf. Diodoros 1. 3. 3.

Ptolemaic adviser, as would be expected of a Byzantine theologian with a strong interest in rhetoric; while he omitted long narratives such as the long account of the capture of a python in his excerpts from book 5. Likewise, Diodoros, who was interested
in Agatharchides' information on Aithiopia, omits non-ethnographic material, such
as the preface on how to write effectively about suffering that one did not experience,
while harmonizing Agatharchides' style with that of the rest of the *Library of History*.
Diodoros prefers long descriptive passages over more technical discussions, and tends
to soften Agatharchides' criticisms of the Ptolemies, for example in the section on
the Nubian mines. By contrast, Strabo's evidence for Agatharchides' text is indirect,
abridging in book 16 of his *Geography* the account of the Red Sea by Artemidoros
(Chapter 18 below), who, while largely preserving Agatharchides' wording, had reorganized book 5 as a *paraplous* (coastal sailing) and supplemented it with new information acquired between the composition of *On the Erythraian Sea* in the mid-2nd
century BC and the end of that century.

Less certain is the genre of *On the Erythraian Sea*. Although it is usually included
in corpora of the minor Greek geographers and no attributable fragments survive of
books 2–4, the evidence points to the work being historical in character. Specifically,
the discussions of the origin of the name of the Erythraian sea and the beginnings of
Ptolemaic activity in Nubia in the fragments of book 1, and the reference to a now lost
account of elephant hunting in the fragments of book 5 (§86b, from Diodoros), suggest that the first four books of the work treated the history of Ptolemaic activity in
the Nile valley south of Egypt and the Red Sea, probably beginning with the Nubian
campaign of Ptolemy II in the 270s BC. Book 5 treated comprehensively the history
and cultural geography of both the African and Arabian coasts of the Red Sea and
their hinterlands, based on the reports of 3rd-century Ptolemaic explorers preserved at
Alexandria or their rewritten and published accounts; and interpreted their accounts
of the peoples of the region in accordance with the evolutionary scheme proposed
by the late 4th-century Peripatetic Dikaiarchos (Chapter 9 above), who argued that
societies developed in three stages based on their adaptation to their environment:
food collecting, pastoralism, and agriculture. In Agatharchides' version of Dikaiarchos' scheme, the first stage was represented by the Ichthyophagoi (*Fish-eaters*), the
second by the Trogodytai, and the third by the Sabaioi. It has been argued also that
Agatharchides uses what he sees as malfunctioning societies, such as those who elim-
inate their weaker members (e.g. 2 §64b), as a protreptic to philosophical reflection on
the part of readers.[7]

Survival is not necessarily secure evidence of significance. In an important study
of the nature of Greek historiography, Hermann Strasburger treated Agatharchides
as one of the major figures of hellenistic historiography, arguing that he restored the
Herodotean tradition of universalism and was a major influence on Poseidonios.[8]

---

[7] Schneider 2006.   [8] Strasburger 1966, 88–92.

The evidence, however, suggests a different conclusion. Of the 22 fragments of Agatharchides' two big histories, 15 come from a single source, Athenaios' *Deipnosophistai* (*Philosophers at Dinner*), and none from a source later than the early 3rd century A D. The situation is somewhat different with regard to *On the Erythraian Sea*, which did become, as Agatharchides hoped, the main source for all later Greek and Roman accounts of the geography and ethnology of the Red Sea and its hinterlands. Few writers, however, seem to have consulted it directly; the latest (other than Photios) is Aelian in the early 3rd century A D, who used it in his *On the Characteristics of Animals* (B. 6–7). Most writers, such as Strabo and Pliny the Elder, accessed its information through intermediary sources such as the *Geographoumena* of Artemidoros. Finally, it is striking that Agatharchides is not cited in the *Ethnika* of Stephanos of Byzantion despite the obvious relevance of his work, and that there is no article on him in the *Suda*. It is probable, therefore, that, despite the existence of a codex of *On the Erythraian Sea* in 9th-century Constantinople, Agatharchides was not a widely read author in antiquity and had little influence on the development of Greek historiography.

Diodoros and Photios are translated from the 'Budé' editions;[9] the extract from Strabo book 16 (B. 3 below) follows Radt.[10] Several emendations have been adopted from Lucarini's recent study.[11] Some thirty further emendations to the Greek of Photios, reflected in this translation, will be published in the Oxford Classical Texts edition of that author by N. G. Wilson.[12]

SELECTED FURTHER READING

Alonso-Nuñez, J.-M. (1997), 'Approaches to world history in the hellenistic period: Dicearchus [sic] and Agatharchides', *Athenaeum*, n.s. 75. 1: 53–67.

Ameling, W. (2008), 'Ethnography and universal history in Agatharchides', in T. C. Brennan and H. I. Flower (eds), *East and West: Papers in Ancient History presented to Glen W. Bowersock* (Cambridge, Mass.), 13–59.

Burstein, S. M. (1989), *Agatharchides of Cnidus, On the Erythraean Sea*. London.

*—— (2009), 'Agatharchides of Knidos (86)', in *BNJ*.

—— (2021a), 'Greek and Roman views of ancient Nubia', in G. Emberling and B. Beyer Williams (eds), *The Oxford Handbook of Ancient Nubia* (Oxford), 697–711.

—— (2021b), 'The African encounter with Greece', *Acta Classica*, 64: 48–71.

Canfora, L., Micunco, S., Bianchi, N., and Schiano, C. (2016) with M. R. Acquafredda *et al.*, *Fozio, Biblioteca*. Pisa.

Engels, J. (2004), 'Agatharchides von Knidos' Schrift Über das Rote Meer', in H. Heftner and K. Tomaschitz (eds), *Ad fontes! Festschrift für Gerhard Dobesch zum 65. Geburtstag am 15. September 2004* (Vienna), 179–92.

Gozzoli, S. (1978), 'Etnografia e politica in Agatarchide', *Athenaeum*, 56: 54–79.

---

[9] Diod. 3: Bommelaer 1989. Phot. 250: Henry 1974.
[10] Radt 2001–11, vol. viii. [11] Lucarini 2020, 221–4.
[12] A complete Italian translation of Photios is now available: Canfora, Micunco *et al.* 2016.

Huntingford, G. W. B. (1980), *The Periplus of the Erythraean Sea: By an Unknown Author*. London. [Excerpts from Photios' Agatharchides at pp. 177–97.]

Leon, M. L. S. (1981), 'En torno a la transmision de la obra de Agatarqides', *Hispania antiqua*, 11–12: 183–95.

Marcotte, D. (2001), 'Structure et caractère de l'œuvre historique d'Agatharchide', *Historia*, 50. 4: 385–435.

Peremans, W. (1967), 'Diodore de Sicile et Agatharchide de Cnide', *Historia*, 16: 432–55.

A. *ON THE ERYTHRAIAN SEA*

Headings added.

1 **Photios**, *Bibliotheke*, codex 250, pp. 441b 16–445b 36[13]

(441b 16–19). Two accounts[14] by Agatharchides have been read: the 1st and 5th of *On the Erythraian Sea and Other Surprising Facts*, with divisions by chapter.

BOOK 1

From the 1st account of *On the Erythraian Sea*:

The Name of the Sea

1. (441b 20–30) He (*Agatharchides*) says that the Ptolemy (*II*) who succeeded the son of Lagos (*Ptolemy I*) arranged for the hunting of elephants, but also of similar animals, and by his forethought brought together into one dwelling those divided by Nature.[15] One must examine what the historian says here. For even before the Ptolemies people used many tame elephants, even in war, such as Poros of India who fought a war against Alexander, and not a few others. Alternatively (*he means*) that this Ptolemy was the first to devote close attention to this hunting, or the first after Alexander, or the first of the kings of Egypt.[16]

2. (441b 31–44). He also says the Erythraian sea did not draw its name from the fact that the mountains to the west of the so-called Arabian gulf (*Arabios Kolpos; mod. Red Sea*), when the piercing and scorching ray of the sun strikes them, give the appearance of burning coal, while on the east side sandbanks, reddish and earth-like, have spread out along many stades of the coast there. In no way has it been called 'red' because of this circumstance. For even if the coastal sailing is narrow, with crests and banks dominating the whole gulf on each side, and even if the light of the sun falling from both land masses into the channel makes the sea look similar to the dry land—an

---

[13] Although divided into the traditional section numbers (which mostly match those of Burstein 1989, this text from Phot. is continuous, not an assemblage of 'fragments'.

[14] *logoi*, i.e. books (cf. n. 10).   [15] For Ptolemy II's animal collecting see Hubbell 1935.

[16] Phot.'s last alternative is the correct interpretation of A.'s intention. For elephant hunting under Ptolemy II, see Burstein 2008. The fullest treatment of elephants in Greece and Rome is Scullard 1974.

appearance that is observed by all but not comprehended by all—(*nevertheless*) it was not, he says, because of this that the sea received the name, even though that seemed to be the case to many before him.[17]

3. (442a 4–10) That is the first, though untrue, account of the cause. The second, which is similar, has it that in that region the rising sun does not, as among us, strike the channel with bright rays but with rays resembling blood, as a result of which the sensation makes the image of the sea reddish for observers, and from this it was named Red.

4. (442a 11–21) The third account is the Argolic one, which is, he says, great in boldness but empty of proof. For the historians associated with Deinias, adopting like him the liberty that comes from poetic licence, say that Perseus came from Argos to Aithiopia—then called Kephenia—to rescue the daughter of Kepheus; and that relocating from there to the Persians he let the Persians share his name, after one of his descendants, but fathered a son called Erythras, and from him gave the appellation to the sea. That is the Argolic conceit about the Erythraian sea.[18]

5. (442a 21–43) The fourth account, and the true one, is the one he (*Agatharchides*) learned from a Persian: Boxos was his name, he says; this man became Hellenic in language and thought, leaving his fatherland and making a life in Athens. The account of the Persian has it thus: there existed a certain man who was highly esteemed for his boldness and wealth, Erythras by name, Persian by race and a son of Myozaios, and living not far from the sea but opposite islands which were then uninhabited—not so now, but during the Median supremacy, for it was then that Erythras was well known. He took up residence at Pasargadai in the winter, but in spring he relocated to his own estate, needing to do so for a number of reasons including contributing a certain enhancement to his life by such a change. This man had a rather large stable of grazing animals, which were ambushed by lions, who killed some of them. Those that survived, becoming frenzied through fear at what they saw, rushed into the sea and, since there was by chance quite a strong breeze off the land, they were caught by the current in their excited state. At first they swam along beside the land; but since their terror did not decrease they changed course and finally just managed to escape onto the island opposite. One of the herdsmen, a young man of unusual boldness, crossed over with them by holding on to the shoulders now of one animal and then of another.

(442a 44–b 24) So Erythras, looking for his grazing animals which were not visible, was the first person in those parts to make a raft, which was appropriate in size and sturdy in power. Gauging that the wind was favourable and appropriate, he launched it into the channel. The wave drove him quickly forward and he found his horses, and found the stable-boy. Amazed at the island, he also founded a town upon a convenient harbour. From the land opposite he brought over those who could not make a living and made a city; and from there he civilized the other islands, which were

---

[17] Cf. Artemidoros 98 (Strabo) §20.   [18] Cf. ibid. §20.

uninhabited, with settlements of people. So great a reputation among many people did he derive from his deeds that they all named the sea in that region, which is of boundless size, Erythraian right down to our time.

This is where the differences in the causes of the name lie: for there is a great divergence between saying 'Erýthra sea' ('*sea of Erythras*') and 'Erythrá (*Red*) sea', since the one signifies the man who ruled the sea, while the other refers to the redness of its reported nature. The account, he (*Agatharchides*) says, that attributes the appellation to the colour is false—for the sea is not red—whereas the one that attributes it to the overlord is true, as the Persian story makes credible.[19]

Myth and history

6. (442b 24–8) He (*Agatharchides*) judges, too, that the Persians did not receive their name from one of the descendants of Perseus, though many say so; for those people do not call themselves *Pérsas*, paroxytone (*with an acute accent on the penultimate syllable*), but *Persâs*, with the perispomenon (*circumflex*) placed at the end.

7. (442b 29–443a 19) He pays serious attention to disposing of the story of Perseus as false on many other grounds, and adds the following. Other than in tragedy, Perseus has not embarked on a military campaign, putting on a mask and holding his sickle. As for what happens next, you should turn to an actor and chorus to solve matters of controversy and make a story, as most people have admitted. Let us survey in brief the most important of these things. There was the centaur, Geryones, the Cyclops, Chryses, Circe, Kalypso, the Minotaur, Scylla, the Chimaira, Pegasos, the Laistrygonians, Cerberus, Glaukos (*the Man*) of the Sea, Atlas, Proteus, Nereus, the Nereïdai, and the sons of Alōëus who grew to be 9 fathoms tall and 9 cubits wide. Moreover, according to Hesiod there was initially a golden race, then a silver, finally a bronze. Again, horses were born that conversed with Achilles about the future, a Sphinx that set the puzzle to the sons of the Thebans, the Sirens who sang to destroy those who heard them, Niobe and Polydektes who turned into stone out of fear. In addition, those who sailed with Odysseus were turned from men into pigs, but from pigs into the condition of men. And Tantalos was honoured for his good sense and was a dining-companion of the gods, but was punished for his intemperance by being borne into the air. Others descended into Hades by choice: some to consult dead seers on behalf of the living, others to marry Persephone by force as she was lonely. There was a golden fleece upon a sheep, apple-trees grew in Libyē bearing golden apples, a living creature endured an entire life awake, and Boreas and Notos (*the north and south winds*), along with the others, were stifled by being shut up in a wineskin.

(443a 19–41) On top of this, Pasiphaë had sex with a bull, Tyro with a river, both having a bed that was alien to no race. Philomela exchanged her form for that of a nightingale, Tereus that of a hoopoe, and Hekabe changed her nature to that of a guard-dog. Additionally, Io was born the daughter of a river, but in the horned shape of a frenzied

---

[19] Cf. ibid. §20.

cow she flew over the Pontic open-sea (*pelagos*), and from her the Bosporos takes its name. Kaineus the Lapith was originally born a virgin and a woman, but grew up and turned into a man, eventually being planted in the earth by the Centaurs and beaten with oars, still upright and alive. Leda, instead of what a woman is supposed to give birth to, produced a kind of egg from which was formed that *eidos* (*shape*)[20] over which battles were fought—I mean Helen. When Helle and Phrixos came to the strait on a ram that used its feet to fly, they gave the name of Hellespont to the sea on either side. Herakles in a basin sailed the open seas (*pelagē*) where the worst storms happen, passed through Libyē, a land unsown, unwatered, and uncharted, all on his own and relieved Atlas of the vast world—not under orders, but performing a kindness.

(443a 41–b 14) The mountains and rocks, for love of music, obeyed Orpheus while he played his lyre. The flesh of the cattle of Helios (*the Sun*), as it was being baked, uttered words comprehensible to humans. Those who had passed beyond life went through all kinds of chatter with Odysseus at leisure, and he knew their particular character from that of a formless shade; he observed some of them as they drank blood even though they had no inner organs and no throat; others being scared of the iron though no longer capable of being wounded; others rolling a stone when their bodies had long since been burned; some judging other dead men without any crime occurring; and, to cap it all, forms of non-existent persons sailing in a ferry with Charon as captain and steersman, in case they suffer an accident and require a second funeral.

(443b 14–20) And Alkestis, Protesilaos, and Glaukos died and came to life again: she after being brought back (*from the dead*) by Herakles, the second by the love of his wife, and the third by the seer buried with him. But the earth received the body of the living Amphiaraos along with his horses and chariot.

(443b 20–7) There is more: serpents' teeth were sown by Kadmos, and from them arose armed soldiers fighting one another. Talos, the guard of Minos, travelled all the way round Crete three times in a day, huge as it was, but unlike all animate beings he had his mortal part in his ankle; while there was no means of ending the life of Minos unless one poured boiling water over him.

(443b 28–444a 6) Additionally, an aged ram, subjected to spells by Medea, became young again, while at the hands of the Peliades their father, Pelias, was boiled so that he would become young. The Phorkides, three aged women using a single eye, spent their life inseparable from one another, taking turns fairly. Those living in Arkadia and Attica were earth-born and came into being in an unnatural way. The woman sacrificed at Aulis plainly appeared alive among the Tauroi; the one cast into the sea in the Peloponnese by her father, Akrisios, landed on the coast of the Seriphians uninjured and with her baby. The man already overpowered by Menelaos in single combat was carried off suddenly, to reappear in his chamber ready for intercourse, having forgotten all his terrors. The Timber Container (*Wooden Horse*) was constructed not to

---

[20] In some versions of the Trojan war, not Helen but an *eidōlon* ('image') of her went to Troy.

capture a city but to betray the companions of Odysseus and Neoptolemus; a variant that ascribes vast silliness to the artist who built it, the brave men who got into it, and those who received it into their city.

(444a 6–17) As well as these things, it is said that despite placing on his own shoulders the vast heaven and all the gods dwelling in it, Atlas sired the so-called Atlantides, which is impossible. We are told that Ocean encircles the entire inhabited world, guarding it and holding it together with its currents; and Hesiod says that beyond it dwell the Gorgons. Some of the heroes maintain the unaffected continuance of their bodies unaffected for all time in the Isles of the Blessed, which no one has investigated authoritatively. These things convert belief into doubt, and provide even a lot of women with grounds for well-founded mockery.

(444a 17–22) How can we accept that one of the gods was reared despite being stitched into a thigh? That a female deity employed Zeus's head as a womb? That another was generated without a father—I refer, of course, to Hephaistos—or that the sun made east into west, and west into east, because of the actions of Atreus against Thyestes?

(444a 22–32) In addition, Apollo and Poseidon served a year as labourers in the construction of Troy, but were deprived of pay and fodder for their cattle, meeting with terrible threats from Laomedon. Dionysos, pursued by Lykourgos, ran into the sea in fear and fled to Thetis. Moreover, a beauty contest was set up between the goddesses, and each of them tried to corrupt the judge with her particular gifts to make him disregard justice; yet what eventually ensued from his judgement benefited none of them.

(444a 32–42) The immensity of Athena shrank to the size of a swallow; the majesty of Zeus was contracted to that of a swan; the beauty of Demeter was converted into the most ill-favoured arrangement. Zeus, regarded as the greatest, was conspired against by a very close relative, his wife's brother, but saved by his most hated foes—I mean the Titans, who sprang from their chains, from the darkness, and from their prison in it; and having done him a favour by terrifying the associates of Poseidon, they willingly went back down to Acheron and the place of Hades.

(444a 42–b 9) We have Aphrodite being wounded by a mortal actor; Ares being bound by Otos and Ephialtes; Hades, in the place where he exercised kingly rule, shot with the bow by Herakles and experiencing the greatest agonies; Hephaistos thrown from the heights in heaven and carried to Lemnos in a desperate condition; and enormous anvils tied to Hera's feet when she was hung up by Zeus.

(444b 9–19) All in all, we see the gods committing adultery, being struck with thunderbolts, having club feet, habitually thieving, being weaker than humans, casually using verbal abuse, treating others unjustly, complaining, and rising above none of the passions by which we are being oppressed when we call upon the gods. People who tell such monstrous tales stand far aside from the truth, and should not be judged worthy to purvey such a version of truth to others. For reasons of this kind, and many of them, Agatharchides demotes the question of Perseus to the category of similar legends, and does not concede that the Erythraian (*sea*) is called after his son.

8. (444b 20–34) He says that the man who reduces the liberties of the mythographer to factual clarity exposes himself to refutation.[21] But if anyone does away with his refutation, he will leave no more worthless class (*of narrative to be refuted*), credibility having been lost. 'So for what reason do I not criticize Homer for narrating the argument between Zeus and Poseidon, for which the author can offer no credibility? Why do I not censure Hesiod for daring to portray the birth of the gods; or criticize Aeschylus for being deceived over many matters and for writing much that cannot be condoned; or accuse Euripides for endowing Archelaos with the deeds of Temenos, or presenting Teiresias as having lived for more than five generations? Nor do I lead forward for punishment the others who employ impossible constructions in their dramas. The reason is that every poet aims at winning our souls rather than at the truth.'[22]

India and Egypt

9. (444b 35–7) He says that the Indian land breeds elephants;[23] as does Aithiopia, which shares a frontier with the borderlands of the Thebans (*of Egypt*); and so does Libyē.[24]

10. (444b 38–40) Four regions have enclosed Egypt: from the north the open sea (*pelagos*), from the east and west deserts, and from the south the Aithiopes.

How Ptolemy (II?) was urged to attack Nubia

11. (444b 41–445a 5) 'The account is severe but promotes security. It is presented not for the sake of pain but of protection. It has taken the element of pleasure out of the words so that by appreciating the charm of reality we shall never opt for the worse rather than the better; or, by Zeus and the other gods, so that we shall not miss things that lie in between those two.

12. (445a 6–11) 'Without an effort, it is hard to protect a private individual's estate that is somewhat abundant; so can you hope to keep hold of an inheritance of so many things, and of such a kind, without a real contest? Especially as you know that the law protects one who possesses the former, whereas the iron takes the latter away from a weaker party.

13. (445a 12–15) 'For a long time', he says, 'we have grasped that it is opportunity that seals and loosens the friendships of potentates, and that your own lack of leisure

---

[21] Taking ἐλέγχων as gen. pl. of ἔλεγχος 2 m., not a participle (*contra* Henry).

[22] A. is alluding to Eratosthenes' assertion (Strabo 1. 1. 10, C6–7; 1. 2. 3, C15–16) that poets aim for 'amusement, not instruction' (see Erat. 3). The point of A.'s critique was not to deny the historicity of Greek heroes but to reject the idea that myths as told by the poets could provide reliable historical or geographical information.

[23] For elephant hunting in S. Asia, see now Trautmann 2015.

[24] A brief summary of A.'s account of the techniques of elephant-hunting in these three areas may be preserved by Pliny in B. 4 below.

gives an impetus now to one man, now to another to enhance and worsen the affairs of each side.

14. (445a 15–21) 'The man who continually curries favour by what he says, going beyond what is actually permitted by the facts, is deceived in many respects; but the man who, during crises of this kind, brings in his own friends to share in the decision process will not be without a supporter to reinforce his own inclination. Who is so unreflective as to wish to discover what his own view is by asking someone else, and to take as an adviser on uncertain issues one who will (*simply*) back up his own desires?

15. (445a 22–8) 'For if the man who is lord of so many good things is stronger than the desire of those trying to use force against him, I can regard as blessed the authority of the possessor of these things, but am unable to take his advantages from him by using force of weapons. How hapless is it, then, to divert action into empty profession and pay heed to unclear hopes rather than clear dangers?

16. (445a 28–32) '"But the Aithiopes will frighten the Hellenes." How so? By their blackness and their different form? Such apprehension does not outlast our childhood years; and in wars and great contests, affairs are settled not by appearance and colour but by boldness and generalship.

17. (445a 33–b 13) 'From that day when Fortune made me the guardian of your person, when you were very young, and of the entire kingdom, right from that day I placed a great task upon myself. And what was this? To combat and make life difficult for those who would speak (*only*) to please you. My first priority was to divest you not of your power but of your ignorance, in order that you might enjoy all these great goods with intelligence and not go astray. For I aimed at this with a father's goodwill that is directed at the passage of time, not a flatterer's dishonesty that speaks to the present. For I know, being older and having gained experience of many matters, that it is because of those who apply themselves to flattering people in pre-eminent positions that even the greatest kingdoms were totally overthrown—that of Cassander, that of Lysimachos, that of Alexander, mighty though it was, that of the Medes, that of the Syrians, and that of the Persians, so that no seed of their race has been left behind. Not without reason: for nothing is more unstable or insecure than a young man who, because of his age, is ignorant of much but is praised for his mistakes. Alexander, at any rate, while undefeated in arms, was very weak in his personal dealings: for he was captivated whenever he was praised, and when he was called "Zeus" he did not consider he was being made fun of but being honoured. He desired the impossible, but had forgotten his nature.

18. (445b 14–23) 'When a demagogue speaks to the many, not taking the stance of a friend but that of a flatterer, the impulse of the crowd, adopting as its counsellor a man who simply confirms its error, overturns the city. For blame falls not only upon those responsible, but also on those to whom envy may have opened a way for blame to enter. To put it another way: blame overcomes not only those responsible but sometimes

also those who rise above an accusation, whenever envy lets fly a sharp arrow and takes down first the man who did not deserve this fate.'

War in Aithiopia

19. (445b 24–9) Amid the dangers of war the Aithiopes use long bows but arrows that are short. Upon the end of the reed shaft, instead of iron, a stone of elongated form is firmly set, bound with sinews; it is exceedingly sharp and dipped in deadly poisons.

20. (445b 30–6) $_{II.1}$Ptolemy, he says, gathered 500 horsemen from Hellas for his war against the Aithiopes.[25] Those destined to brave the first danger and exercise command, a body numbering 100, he clad in special armour: for he issued them and their horses with clothes of felt which the people of that land name *kasai*, such that they hide all of the body apart from the eyes.[26]

BOOK 5

2   Photios, *Bibliotheke,* **codex 250 = 445b 36–460b 16, and Diodoros of Sicily,** *Bibliotheke historikē,* 3. 11. 4–48. 5

(445b 36–7) From the 5th *History Concerning the Erythraian Sea* by Agatharchides:

Prologue: good and bad rhetoric

21. (445b 38–446a 2). Many men, he (*Agatharchides*) says, among statesmen and those who have written poetry, have been undecided as to how one who is away from danger should narrate appropriately the calamities overwhelming certain persons. The manner should not be too explicit unless one can base it on a suitable reason for describing things explicitly.

(446a 2–15) Olynthos and Thebes, both renowned cities, were plundered by Alexander and Philip, who then demolished them to their foundations. The terrible character of what had been committed, coming upon people unexpectedly, also instilled in many of the Hellenes a great anxiety about wider affairs and provided not a few of the orators with a starting-point for writing in order to display the story of the catastrophe fittingly. So some have talked about this event in allegorical fashion and in language that appears excessive; others in a more serious way, while not avoiding customary practice and using literal expression amid the horrors. We shall present you with examples of each type, so that you may observe their character by comparison and find which of them spoke better and which the contrary, by the very results of your examination.

---

[25] For the view that the war in question was the Aithiopian war of Ptolemy II and that the preceding speech was supposedly delivered by a *sōmatophylax* (bodyguard) of Ptolemy II, see Burstein 1986 ~ Burstein 1995. The subscript fragment no. is that assigned in Burstein 1989.

[26] Cf. Burstein 2012a on the cavalry of Kush; *kasai* is not a Semitic word but a form of the name of Kush.

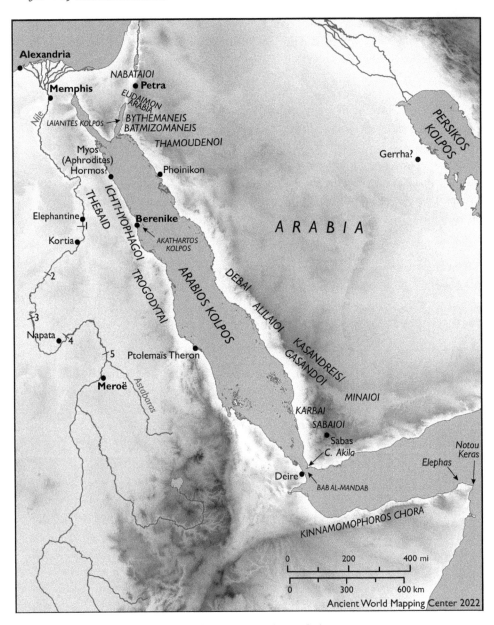

MAP 15.1. Agatharchides: principal regions, peoples, and places.

(446a 15–37) Thus Hegesias,[27] who mentions the destruction several times, is cheap. For wishing in no way to discourse fittingly for the events, but being compelled to display elegance about a grave matter, he achieves his ambition to a certain degree, but misses the mark in respect of the value of his subjects. He is caught out in his own

---

[27] Hegesias of Magnesia-by-Sipylos, was a C4/C3 historian and orator, later regarded as an exponent of the florid 'Asianic' style (Weißenberger 2006).

words, such as 'We have earned a name, forsaking a city'. Consider it: it evinces no feeling at all, but focuses on his meaning and makes us search for what he is saying. For where one produces hesitation as to one's view, one has removed power from the words. Why? Because that which is spoken and fully understood may also capture one's emotion, but he who fails in clarity is also short on force. Next he makes a similar statement about the Thebans: 'The place with the greatest voice has been made voiceless by the calamity'. And again on the Olynthians: 'I went out from a city of ten thousand; turning back, I saw it no more'. What were you searching for? The spoken word, subordinated to that kind of meaning, has made our understanding stray from the topic. He who utters a lament must put away sophistication and show the thing in which the emotion dwells, if he wishes not to make decoration of speech but to address the reason for the calamity.

(446a 37–b 19) We must, however, move to another case. 'Think, Alexander, that Epameinondas too is seeing the ruins of the city and, by his presence, comes to you as a suppliant alongside me.' The appeal is immature, the metaphor harsh, and the melancholy nature of the deed unspoken. Again: 'Colliding with a king's madness, the city has become more piteous than a tragic play.' This seems to have been devised with anything in view but what is fitting for a sophist, so it makes no contact with the topic. For I judge that it is difficult for the language of mockery to tackle difficult situations. Again: 'What need to mention the Olynthians and the Thebans, how they have suffered and died city by city?' Here is another, similar case that cleaves to unseemly flattery and silliness: 'By razing Thebes, Alexander, you have done a deed that would be like Zeus removing the Moon from its heavenly region; for I reserve the sun for Athens. For these two cities were the eyes of Hellas; hence I am in distress about the former. For one of these eyes has been struck out: the city of the Thebans.' Through these words the sophist seems to me to be making a joke, not grieving for the fate of the cities. He seems to be looking for a way to bring his oration to a close as quickly as he can, rather than how to bring the emotion into view through clear expression.

(446b 19–25) Another, similar case: 'The cities nearby wept for the city, seeing that what was before was no more.' Well, if a man had spoken these sentences to the Thebans and Olynthians on the occasion of their capture, in order to express sympathy, I believe they would have laughed at the writer and supposed him to be, in a way, more unfortunate than they.

(446b 25–447a 2) Let us touch upon another kind of (utterance) as we expound the same sophist: 'Terrible it is that the land that gave birth to the Sown Men is unsown.' But that is not how Demosthenes put it, whose view he has modified and made worse; for Demosthenes writes that it is terrible that Attica has become a 'sheep-rearing' land when it was the first place to bring forth domesticated crops for other people. But he (Hegesias), in saying that it is terrible that the land that gave birth to the Sown Men has become unsown, has taken the opposition from the names, not from the reality. Hence he exhibits the utmost coldness, as does Hermesianax[28] when he praises Athena in this way: 'For it is right that, having been born from the head of Zeus, she should possess the headship of happiness'. Similarly this: 'Who could make Cyrus's permission invalid (*akyros*)?' This is also similar: 'How would a place become untrodden (*abatos*) because a bramble-bush (*batos*) lay around it?' All such things, says Agatharchides, are worthless. Well, if he (*Hegesias*) said them in order not to arouse pity, then his position is close to what it should be; but if he did so using all kinds of discourse, he misdirected himself in his judgement.

(447a 2–16) Moreover, he (*Agatharchides*) adds other cases similar to those mentioned, bringing the same accusation to bear. For example, 'The Thebans were turned over in the battle against the Macedonians, to a number greater than ten thousand'.[29] What a wonderful impression: so many people unexpectedly 'turned over'! And again: 'The city having been razed, the men endure the misfortunes of their children; the women were transported to Macedonia, after burying the city in a way'. Another similar one: 'The phalanx of the Macedonians, after forcing its way within the wall by its weapons, killed the city'. There the burial of a city; here death. For the rest, we have only to add a funeral procession and recite an epigram and the deed is concluded. Moreover, says Agatharchides, we have gone through most of this man's elegance—let me not appear too bitter by saying 'madness'.

(447a 17–28) Among those who have spoken with clarity and an elaboration suitable to their speeches on the same subject, he (*Agatharchides*) also brings in Stratokles as follows: 'Ploughed and sown is the town of the Thebans, who alongside you contested the war against Philip'. At the same time, he (*Agatharchides*) says, he has expounded the suffering of the city distinctly, and has mentioned the friendship of these unlucky people; for horror set out with kindness generally makes expressions of pity more weighty. After Stratokles he likewise brings in Aischines, who said, 'A city which was our neighbour has vanished from the middle of Hellas'. With great skill, says Agatharchides, he uses the metaphor to signal the speed of the loss, and fixes the dangers in place by showing his listeners that the one who suffered shares a border with them.

(447a 29–36) But Demosthenes, he (*Agatharchides*) says, changing the target of his words to Alexander, has explained it thus: 'He dug up the city from its foundations, so that he did not even leave the ash in the hearths. He distributed the children and wives of those who had led Hellas among the barbarians' tents'. Bitterly, plainly, and briefly he removed excess from the visions, but did not forget the clarity that teaches the reality.

(447a 36–447b 5) Again, the same orator said of the Olynthians: 'Olynthos, Methone, Apollonia, and thirty-two of the cities in Thrace—all these has he destroyed so violently that it is not even easy for those who go there to say whether they were ever inhabited'. Indicating the multitude of the cities, he moved on to the calamity suffered

---

[28] Hermesianax of Kolophon was an early Hl epigrammatist; but these quotations are in prose, so may be from an unknown writer—probably not the H. 'of Cyprus' cited by Ps.-Plutarch (ch. 26 below, §§2. 3; 12. 4; 24. 1), who may well be fictitious.

[29] Here we revert to quotations from Hegesias.

by the men, so that the extreme piteousness of the paradox he set out might evoke the listeners' emotion all the more.

He (*Agatharchides*) gives these and similar cases, including some from other writers; and while he commends some of them, he marks down writers associated with Hegesias and the examples taken from them.

The Nubian gold mines

22. (447b 6–20) (*He says*) that from the town of Memphis to the Thebaid there are five intervening nomes (*nomoi, provinces*) of nations with a populous character: first the Herakleopolite, second the Lykopolite, third the Oxyrhynchite, fourth the Hermopolite, and fifth the one that some call Phylake (*Guard-post*) and others Schedia (*Raft*). In the last one, charges are levied on goods brought from upstream, and they pay the fee. When one goes above the said places, the beginning of the Thebaid is Lykon Polis, then Aphrodites Polis, and additionally Panon, then Thoinis, after this Bopos, beyond which is Diospolis which they call the Small. After the province called Tentyrites is the city named Apollonos Polis (*Apollo's City*), above which is Koptos, then Elephantine, then the land of the Aithiopes, whose first (*city*) is Kortia. The places from Memphis to Aithiopia have thus been told.

23. (*a*) (447b 21–33) (*He says*) that near the Erythraian sea, by which the Nile makes many deviations and distributaries, it nevertheless at that point conspicuously turns a corner; in the right-hand course of its angles it makes its great bend. From the open sea (*pelagos*) a mighty gulf extends into the mainland, so that the area separating the waters—the salt and the drinkable—takes on a composition similar to clay. Beside the said sea, not far away, there occur certain of the so-called noble (*rocks*) containing a large number of minerals.[30] These are exceedingly dark in colour, but produce outgrowths of marble[31] within them, such that anything competing with it is left behind, as the whiteness admits of no comparison.

Diodoros 3. 11. 4–48. 5[32]

(*b*) (3. 11. 4–12. 1). 11. (4) Concerning the Aithiopes dwelling towards the west, we shall remain satisfied with the things we have said; but concerning those (*Aithiopes*) lying towards the south and the Erythraian sea, we shall go through them in turn; and it

---

[30] The main gold-mining area in Lower Nubia was located E of the Nile in the *Wadi Allaqi* and the *Wadi Gabgaba*. The region was entered at the S end of the Dodecaschoinos, *c.*75 mi (120 km) S of *Aswan*. A comprehensive account of its archaeology is provided by Alfredo Castiglioni, Angelo Castiglioni, and Vercoutter 1995. The specific mines cannot be identified, though comparable ones were operational in Egypt from C4d to at least C3s (Redon, Faucher, and Versnel 2017); cf. Faucher 2018 for the longer history of Egyptian gold-mining.

[31] Probably quartz.

[32] The extracts from Photios codex 250 (a continuous text) are here interleaved with those from Diod. 3. Since Diod.'s testimony, though based on direct reading of A., is less full and evidently less close to the original (see chapter introduction), it should be regarded as of secondary importance and is accordingly printed in smaller type. Subscript numbers of the forms $_{50H}$ and $_{50M}$ are those of sections of Phot. in Henry 1974 and Müller's *GGM*, respectively, indicated only if they differ from those in Burstein 1989.

seems fitting to us first to go through the preparation of gold that takes place in these locations.   12. (1) For around the furthest parts of Egypt and those parts of Arabia and Aithiopia that border upon it, there is a place with many great gold-mines, a lot of metal being gathered with great hardship and cost. The earth is dark by nature and contains seams and veins of marble (*probably quartz*) which are of unusual whiteness and exceed in brightness all the substances shining around them. Those managing the mining operations prepare the gold by using a multitude of working people.

24. (*a*) (Phot. 447b 34–40) (*He says*) that those whom the utmost ill fortune overtakes are taken away by the tyranny to the harshest servitude in the gold mines; some enduring distress together with their wives and children, others without the said persons. So, having described their suffering in tragic terms, so as to leave no room for any misfortune to be more extreme, he (*Agatharchides*) reports the nature of the labour in search of the gold.

(*b*) (Diod. 3. 12. 2–3) (2) For those persons condemned for wickedness and those made prisoners in war, also those who have been entangled in unfair accusations and consigned to prisons because of (*others'*) anger—sometimes themselves alone, sometimes with their whole family—the kings of Egypt gather up all these people and deliver them to the mining of gold, simultaneously exacting punishment from the convicted and exacting vast income from the labourers.   (3) Those delivered (*to the mines*), being large in number but all bound with fetters, stick at their tasks continuously both by day and during the whole night, taking no rest at all and zealously confined against any escape: for garrisons are set over them, composed of barbarian soldiers using various languages, so that no one is able to corrupt any of those supervising them by companionship or any friendly conversation.

25. (*a*) (Phot. 447b 40–448a 20). Those steep parts of the mountains where gold occurs, which have an extremely hard consistency, they burn with wood and render porous with fire, and thus move the enterprise forward. They cut up the pieces released by the rock with iron quarry-tools.[33] A craftsman, leading the others, divides up the stone. When this man points out the galleries to the mineworkers, the entire task is distributed according to the obligations of the unfortunate men, in the following way. (448a 7) The strongest and the young men break up the marble-bearing ground with iron hammers, using not skill but force in the strike. They cut a number of underground passages through the rock, not straight but sometimes turning up above the gold-bearing stone, sometimes below it, sometimes deviating to the left, and sometimes in a crooked and twisted fashion similar to tree-roots. The men do the mining with lamps tied to their foreheads, following something like a whitish vein. Often, after making the posture of their body conform (*to the passage*), they drop the fragments on the floor, not because of their own habit or ability but to put it within sight of the overseer, who never separates criticism from a blow.

---

[33] The reference is to fire-setting in which a fire is kindled against a rock face and then the heated rock is fractured by rapid cooling with water or vinegar.

(b) (Diod. 3. 12. 4–6)   (4) After burning the hardest of the gold-containing earth with intense fire, and making it porous, they carry forward the working of it with their hands. The stone thus released, which is capable of yielding to modest labour, is laboured on by tens of thousands of luckless persons.   (5) The craftsman who separates the rock leads the whole operation and points it out to the workers. Among those consigned to this unhappy fate, those superior in bodily strength strike the marbled stone with iron hammers, not applying skill to their tasks but force. They cut underground passages—not in a straight line but according to how the crevice of the glinting rock lies.   (6) As they spend their time in the dark because of the bends and crookedness of the diggings, these men carry around lamps constructed upon their foreheads. Often reshaping their body according to the rock's configuration, they drop the quarried fragments on the floor. They labour at this job without interruption, in response to the heavy-handedness and blows of the supervisor.

26. (a) (Phot. 448a 20–39) The very young boys climb down into the passages dug by those men, collect the mass of chippings with great effort, and take them outside the entrances. From them the older workers, and most of the infirm ones, take over the stone; they carry it to the so-called 'overseers'. Those are the ones aged less than thirty and strong in body; they take stone mortars and grind it (the rock) intensively with an iron pestle. Having caused the greatest morsel to be of similar size to a vetch seed, in that same hour they measure it out to others. Here is the labour of the women who have been taken away with their men or parents: for a number of mills stand in a row, into which they throw the sorted rock. Three women stand on each side, three to one pole, clad in such unseemly fashion that they cover only (?)[34] their private parts, and perform the grinding. They grind until the measure assigned to them has passed through to the place where flour is collected. All these people, subject to the said share of fortune, hold death to be more desirable than their life.

(b) (Diod. 3. 13. 1–3) (1) The very young boys, climbing down through the passages to the hollowed-out places in the rock, laboriously send up the rock that is being thrown down piece by piece, and take it to the place in the open air outside the entrance. Those over (sic) thirty years old take from them a specified measure of the quarried material in stone mortars, and pound it with iron pestles until they have worked it into the size of a vetch seed.   (2) From these men the women, and the older ones among the men, receive the vetch-sized rock and place it onto several mills set in a row. Standing beside the handles in twos and threes, they grind it until they have worked the measure given to them into the consistency of flour. As no care for their bodies is available to them, and clothing to enclose their shame is not available to them either, there is no one who, if he saw them, would not pity the luckless ones for their excessive suffering.   (3) For none of them enjoys any concession or even rest—not the sick, not the lame, not the aged, not the weakness of woman—all are forced by blows to stick at their tasks until, owing to their torment, they die in their oppression. For this reason the unlucky people always regard the future as more to be

---

[34] This contradicts Diod. in §26b; possibly the text is at fault here.

feared than the present because of their excessive punishment, and look forward to death as more desirable than living.

27. (*a*) (Phot. 448a 39–b 18) From the female sex, the worked product is taken over by men called *selangeis*. These are craftsmen capable of bringing the king's requirements to a conclusion. Their task is like this: they place the milled marble[35] upon a board which is wide and planed to a flat surface; it is not set in a straight position but at a slight slope. Next, pouring on water, they rub it with their hands, at first lightly and then more strongly. Thus, I believe, the earthen part is dissolved and flows away in the manner that the arrangement of boards is intended to cause, while the dominant and strong part remains unmoved upon the wood. After washing the material several times with the waters, the so-called *selangeus* takes soft, dense sponges and applies them gently to the marble. By pressing a little, he takes off the light, porous material which gets caught in the holes, removes it from the cavity and discards it. The heavy, glinting material he leaves separated out upon the board; it is less moveable by reason of the heavy quality of its underlying nature.

> (*b*) (Diod. 3. 14. 1–2) (1) In the final stage, the craftsmen take over the milled rock and bring everything to completion. For they rub the worked marble upon a flat, slightly inclined board, while pouring water over it. Next, the earthen part is dissolved by the moisture and flows down the inclined board, while the part containing the gold remains on the wood owing to its heaviness. (2) They do this many times, at first rubbing it lightly with their hands but afterwards pressing upon it lightly with sponges full of holes and taking up the porous, earthen part through these until the gold-dust becomes pure.

28. (*a*) (Phot. 448b 18–30) In this way the *selangeus*,[36] after thoroughly cleaning the pieces of gold-dust, hands them to the smelters. (448b 19) These men, after taking the collected gold according to its measure and weight, put it in a ceramic vessel. They mix into it, in proportion to its quantity, a piece of lead, some grains of salt, a small amount of tin, and some husks of barley. Next, placing over it a well-attached cover and greasing it all round, they bake it in a kiln for five days and the same number of nights, allowing no interruption. On the following day they apply moderate cooling to the fired (*material*) and transfer it into a vessel; they find nothing left of the things that were put in with the gold, only the melted lump of gold, which has undergone a small loss because of the dust.[37]

> (*b*) (Diod. 3. 14. 3–4) (3) Finally, other craftsmen, taking the collected gold according to measure and weight, put it in ceramic jars. They mix in, in proportion to its quantity, a

---

[35] Again, probably quartz.

[36] Exact meaning unknown, but clearly the technical term for a gold-washer.

[37] This description combines elements of amalgamation, in which gold or silver is separated from any base metal by being alloyed with lead, and cupellation, in which gold is separated from silver using salt. Bran, a reducing agent, would lower the rate of oxidation. Tin was probably intended as a hardener. The 'small loss' may have been the result of absorption of silver chloride by the crucible.

piece of lead, some grains of salt, and additionally a little tin and some husks of barley. Making a well-fitted lid and greasing it thoroughly with clay, they bake it in a kiln for five days and the same number of nights without interruption.   (4) Then, having allowed it to cool, they find none of the other things in the vessels but gain pure gold, a small loss having occurred.

29. (*a*) (Phot. 448b 30–449a 10) The loss of many personnel in the mines conveys our account towards its aforementioned result: indeed, nature itself demonstrates that it has come to pass that gold's creation is laborious, its preservation insecure, the desire for it very great, its employment situated between pleasure and pain, and its working, in a way, the most ancient of its kind. (448b 37) For the nature of the mines was discovered by the first kings of the place; but at one time it ceased operation, when a multitude of Aithiopes[38] converged on Egypt and garrisoned its cities for many years—people say the Memnoneia were also built by them—and once again when the Medes and Persians were the rulers.[39] (449a 2–10) In our time, indeed, there are found in the gold-mines created by those people bronze chisels, since at that time the use of iron was not yet known; but also unbelievable masses of human bones. What probably happened is that not a few collapses occurred in the porous, flaking underground passages; such was the size of the diggings, even extending to the very sea in their deepest lateral parts.

> (*b*) (Diod. 3. 14. 4–5) (4 *contd*) The working of gold that takes place around the further parts of Egypt is completed with such mighty toil of such a kind;   (5) for nature itself, I think, makes it obvious how gold involves a laborious birth, a difficult safeguarding, the greatest desire, and a utility midway between pleasure and pain. The finding of these mines is absolutely ancient, given that it was accomplished by the old kings.

Ichthyophagoi (Fish-eaters)

30. (*a*) (Phot. 449a 11–17) (*He says*) that beside the southern latitude of Egypt there are four very populous tribes: the one associated with rivers, which sows sesame and millet; the one living around lakes, which is dedicated to the reed and to soft plants; the one that wanders at random and governs its life by flesh and milk; and the one that goes out from the coast and hunts for fish.

> (*b*) (Diod. 3. 14. 6). Of these nations living on the coast of the Arabian gulf and Trogodyt-ike, as well as the part of Aithiopia towards the midday and the south wind, we shall now attempt an account.

---

[38] The reference is to the kings of the 25th dynasty, who ruled Egypt from 747 to 663, when they were driven back into Nubia by the Assyrians. In the Hl period, Memnonia was a generic term for various Egyptian monuments supposedly built by Memnon, son of Dawn and king of the Aithiopians, including most notably the 'Labyrinth', the mortuary temple of Seti I at Abydos (Strabo 17. 1. 42, C813; Pliny 5. xi. 61).

[39] The Persians ruled Egypt from 525 to 404 and again from 343 to 332.

31. (*a*) (Phot. 449a 17–28) This race (*the fish-hunting one*) has no cities, no territories, and no sign of other artificial construction, but is, according to some, the most populous among these races. For the whole area from the Autaioi, who are settled in the inner recess of the gulf that happens to be terminated by the Great Sea (*outer Ocean*), as far as India and Gedrosia, and furthermore Karmania and the Persians and the islands lying before the said races, is occupied everywhere by Ichthyophagoi (*Fish-eaters*).[40] They themselves are naked, possess women in common, and the making of children is communal. They have a natural knowledge of pleasure and pain, but import into it not even the least sense of impropriety or goodness.

> (*b*) (Diod. 3. 15. 1–2) (1) The first people we shall speak of are the Ichthyophagoi (*Fish-eaters*) living on the coast from Karmania and Gedrosia to the extreme inner end located on the Arabian gulf. This gulf extends an unbelievable distance into the interior and is surrounded by two mainlands towards its opening: on one side by Eudaimon Arabia (*Fortunate Arabia*), on the other by Trogodytike.   (2) Some of these barbarians live their life totally naked and have their women and children in common, as they do their domesticated animals; since they operate with only a natural understanding of pleasure and pain, they acquire no sense of impropriety or goodness whatsoever.

32. (*a*) (Phot. 449a 28–b 9) For these people the deep offshore waters are all alien to their life, and likewise the waters adjoining long beaches; for such ground[41] offers no abundant hunting of fish or any similarly formed species. All the said folk have their dwellings spread out beside rocky shores with deep hollows, uneven valleys, narrow channels, and crooked branching streams. When such places suited to their need exist, they set up solid rocks upon the hollow place, in such a manner as to be narrow [—].[42] (449a 37) Whenever, therefore, the tide comes in from the open sea (*pelagos*) to the land—which it does twice each day, towards the ninth hour and the third—the sea covers over all the rocky shore, forcefully bringing with it from the strait to the beach a substantial number of fish which for a time remain by the coast, wandering about the sheltered spots to find food.[43] When the ebb-tide comes on, the liquid flows away through the stones and valleys, rushing to the lower point, but the fish left behind in the depressions become ready prey and nourishment for the Ichthyophagoi.

> (*b*) (Diod. 3. 15. 3–4) (3) They have their dwellings not away from the sea but beside the rocky shores, by which there are not only deep valleys but also irregular gorges and extremely narrow channels naturally divided by crooked side-ways. Since these (*branches*) have come into being in a manner befitting the needs of the locals, they have heaped up

---

[40] 'Fish-eaters' is a generic term used by historians and geographers to characterize various peoples living along the coasts of the Indian Ocean, Persian gulf, and Red Sea whose primary but not necessarily sole source of food was fish. In A.'s adaptation of Dikaiarchos' sequence of cultural development, they represented the first stage, that of food-collecting.

[41] *Sic*, χέρσος ('dry') being used here of an area of shallow water, if the text is right.

[42] A word is probably missing in the Greek.

[43] The correct order of the times is preserved by Diod. in §32 (*b*). The third hour is *c*.8 a.m., the ninth hour *c*.2 p.m.

the side-ways and exits with huge stones with which, as if with nets, they practise fishing. (4) For whenever the sea tide moves up violently onto the dry land—which it does twice a day, around the third hour and approximately the ninth—the sea washes over the rocky shore and covers it all. With its violent, large waves it carries with it towards the dry land an unbelievable multitude of all sorts of fish. These at first stay inshore, wandering about the sheltered spots and hollows to find food; but when the time for the ebb tide comes, the liquid flows away gradually through the heaped-up stones and gorges, but the fish are left behind in the hollows.[44]

33. (a) (Phot. 449b 9–13) Well, the other fish, as we said, are easily defeated; but when dogfish, the larger seals, sea-scorpions, sea-eels, and any of that sort of species fall in, the encounter is fraught with danger.

(b) (Diod. 3. 15. 5–7) (5) At this point the mass of the locals, with children and women, gather at the rocky shores as if acting on a single command. The barbarians are then separated into their respective contingents, and each group moves to its own place while shouting in an extraordinary manner as if some sudden hunt has fallen upon them. (6) Then the women with the children bring together the smaller ones among the fish and those that are closer to land, and throw them on the ground; but the men whose bodies are in their prime apply their hands to those fish which are difficult to subdue on account of their size; for giant fish are being driven out of the open sea (*pelagos*), not only sea-scorpions, sea-eels, and dogfish but even seals and many such creatures, strange to behold and with strange names. (7) These they defeat despite having no skilfully designed weapons, but spear them using sharp goats' horns and cut them with broken rocks. For need educates Nature, which is appropriately adapted to the available opportunities to achieve the hoped-for utility.

34. (a) (Phot. 449b 13–30) Whenever they catch any quantity, they carry it over to the rocks that face south, which are intensely hot, and cast it upon them. Leaving them for a short time, they turn them all onto their other side. Then, when they have taken hold of them by the tail and shaken the whole weight by this end, the entire fleshy portion, broken up by the said heating process, falls off; but the men pile up the spiny part there, with the result that from a faraway point they are seen as hills of great size. Collecting the flesh of the fish on a flat rock, they tread it intensively for a long time, mixing in the fruit of the Christ-thorn (*paliouros*); when this is mixed in, the whole becomes much more like glue and seems to play the part of a seasoning or filling. After working it with their feet for an adequate period, they shape it into elongated bricks and put them back in the sun. When these have acquired dryness, they sit down and celebrate a meal: not with moderation and norms, but according to the wish and pleasure of each.

(b) (Diod. 3. 16. 1–4) (1) Whenever they have collected a multitude of fish of all kinds, they carry off what they have caught and bake them all upon those of the rocks that slope towards the south, which are intensely hot because of the excessive burning. Leaving them for a short time they turn them, and then taking hold of them they shake the whole

---

[44] Cf. Artem. 98 (Strabo) §13, at location 32c.

weight; (2) and the fleshy portions, broken up by the heat, fall away, but the spiny parts are thrown into one place and form a great pile, being collected to serve a need of which we shall tell a little later. After this, they place the fleshy parts on a particular smooth rock, tread it carefully for an adequate period, and mix in the fruit of the Christ-thorn; (3) for when this is thoroughly worked in the whole substance becomes like glue, and this appears to play the part of a seasoning for them. At the last stage, they press the well-trodden material into elongated bricks and put them in the sun; when these are properly dried out, they sit and celebrate a meal: not with moderation and norms, but according to each one's own wish; to circumscribe their enjoyment they have (*only*) their natural appetite. (4) For they use constantly available stores, ready at all times, as if Poseidon has taken over the job of Demeter.[45]

35–6. (*a*) (Phot. 449b 31–450a 8) $_{35-6H}$ (*He says*) that in the face of sudden storms that deprive them of the hunting of fish, they devise something of the following sort. Wandering all along the nearby coast, they gather mussels. They happen to be of the greatest size, so much so that to those who have not seen them their exceeding size is unbelievable. They have the raw flesh with which to make good the shortage at this stage. While the necessary fish remains available to them, they collect the said mussels and feed them on fresh seaweed and the heads of the smaller fish, after putting them into pits. When a time of shortage besets them, it is claimed, they use these for food. If on any occasion both food supplies should fail, they pick out from the pile of spiny parts the moist, fresh ones and break them off joint by joint. Then, cutting some up in a rocky spot and working on others with their teeth, they adopt the same character as those wild animals that live in dens.

> (*b*) (Diod. 3. 16. 4–7) (4 *contd*) But sometimes such a great wave rolls from the open sea (*pelagos*) to the dry land, submerging the rocky shores for many days in its violence, that no one is able to go near those places. (5) For this reason, around these times, as they lack food, they first gather the mussels, which are of such a size that some that are found weigh four *minai*. They fracture the shells by throwing rather large stones on them, and eat the meat in them raw; the taste being comparable to oysters. (6) Whenever, by reason of the succession of winds over a longer period, the ocean happens to be full and the intractable circumstance prevents their usual fish-hunting, if the food from the mussels is scarce they resort to the pile of spines: (7) for from this they choose the succulent and fresh ones among the spines, break them apart joint by joint, and working on some with their teeth. The hard ones they smash with stones, then prepare them and eat them up, showing a similar behaviour to those wild animals that live in dens.[46]

37. (*a*) (Phot. 450a 9–16) The drink they consume is much more wondrous. Over four days they are engaged in (*fish*)-hunting, disorganized songs, and the kind of social occasions that occur for the sake of play. Nothing diverts them, because of the convenience of their food supply. But when the fifth day comes on, they move off into the

---

[45] Cf. ibid. 34c.   [46] Cf. ibid. 35c.

uplands in search of drink, to the gathering-places of the nomads, at which the latter water their animals. The expedition occurs in the evening.

(*b*) (Diod. 3. 17. 1–2) (1) They are well provided with dry food in the manner previously mentioned, but they employ moist food in a surprising and altogether incredible way. For they persist in (*fish*)-hunting for four days, celebrating meals all together with merriment and diverting one another with their disorganized songs. Moreover, at this time they sleep with any women they encounter in order to sire children, for they are relieved of any occupation by the labour-free nature and easy accessibility of their food supply. (2) But on the fifth day they hasten to the uplands all together in search of drink, where there are gathering-places of fresh water at which the nomads water their flocks of nurslings.[47]

38. (*a*) (Phot. 450a 16–22) On reaching the nomads' watering-places, they stand round the hollow place in a ring. Then, leaning their hands upon the earth and kneeling down, they drink like cattle; not making just one effort to relieve (*their thirst*) but resting frequently between drinks. After filling their bellies with liquid as if they were jars, they go away laboriously towards the sea.

(*b*) (Diod. 3. 17. 3–4) (3) This expedition of theirs is similar to those of herds of cattle, with everyone giving voice, not coherently but merely producing noise. As for the children, the mothers carry the infants in their arms throughout, while those weaned from the milk are carried by their fathers, and those aged more than five years go ahead with the parents in a spirit of play, filled with joy as if setting off for the most pleasurable enjoyment. (4) For the nature of these people, being undistorted, regards the satisfaction of wants to be the greatest good, and pursues none of the imported pleasures.[48] And when they draw near to the watering-places of the nomads and their bellies are filled with the drink, they come back, travelling with difficulty because of the weight.[49]

39. (*a*) (Phot. 450a 22–32) Upon returning, each man tastes neither fish nor anything else on that day, but lies stuffed and breathless, so that in his heaviness he is somewhat like a drunken man. From the following day, however, he comes back to the said mode of living. And this circular movement recurs throughout their life, while they give no thought to any occupation or anxiety about any matter. They succumb to few diseases because of the simplicity of their lifestyle; but they take away from the length of their years in proportion as they have a less toilsome mode of life than others do.

(*b*) (Diod. 3. 17. 5) On that day they taste nothing, but each man lies stuffed and breathless, altogether comparable to a drunken man. But on the next day they turn back again to their diet of fish; and in this manner their mode of living takes its circular course among them for all the duration of their life. Those occupying the coast within the straits live thus, succumbing to diseases on few occasions because of the simplicity of their diet; but are much more short-lived than the people among us.[50]

---

[47] Cf. ibid. fr. 37c.   [48] Diod.'s view here differs from A.'s.
[49] Cf. Artem. 98 (Strabo) §13, at location 38c.
[50] Diod. (using Artem.) over-simplifies what Phot. records A. as saying.

40. (*a*) (Phot. 450a 33–40) Those Ichthyophagoi who have their dwellings within the straits[51] are occupied in this way; but those who possess the outer coast are perpetually endowed with this kind of prey. They require absolutely no moisture: for as they consume the fish while it is succulent, so that it is not much different from raw meats, they look for no kind of drink and do not even have any concept of that sort of thing. They bear without pain the things that fate has handed them from the start.

> (*b*) (Diod. 3. 18. 1–2) (1) The life of those who possess the coast outside the gulf, however, has developed in a much more surprising way than these people's, as if they have a nature immune from thirst and sensation. For having been displaced by fate from the inhabited places into the desert, they are well provided for fish-hunting but do not pursue moist food. (2) For they consume the fish while it is succulent and not much different from raw meats, and do not pursue anything like moist food by way of drink, and do not even have any concept of it; but love the mode of living originally allocated to them by fate, regarding prosperity to be (*simply*) the removal of what gives pain through deprivation.

41. (*a*) (Phot. 450a 41–450b 11) (*He says*) that those living in the said regions, besides what has been said,[52] do not have a similar concept to ours of what are, among us, the greatest evils. For they do not flee the iron raised against them, or get roused by insults; nor do those not enduring such things share the anger of those who are enduring them. If some such action is directed towards them by foreigners, they look intently at the action and keep nodding their head, but convey not the slightest awareness of what normally passes from person to person. 'Whence', says the writer, 'I believe they do not have a ⟨spoken or⟩ written language familiar to them, but direct all the affairs of their life by custom and signs, by noises and imitative demonstration.'[53]

> (*b*) (Diod. 3. 18. 3–6) (3) The most surprising thing of all is that they exceed all people in lack of sensitivity to the extent that the account is difficult to believe. Yet many traders, among those sailing from Egypt via the Erythraian sea up to today, have frequently sailed to the land of the Ichthyophagoi and agree in their explanations of what we have already said about the insensitive people. (4) And the third Ptolemy,[54] the one that was zealous in the matter of hunting the elephants that exist in this land, sent out one of his friends,[55] Simmias by name, to inspect the land. This man, despatched

---

[51] The straits of *Bab al-Mandab*, where the Red Sea joins the Indian Ocean.

[52] The repetition reflects the Greek.

[53] The emergence of language in connection with the development of social life was a commonplace of Greek anthropological thought (cf. Cole 1967, 32–3). In A.'s scheme the 'insensitive' Fish-eaters represent the lowest stage of human development before the emergence of the most basic social institutions. Simmias' reference to their passivity even when their children and women are attacked suggests that 'first contact' was probably brutal.

[54] Ptolemy III Euergetes (r. 246–221).

[55] 'Friend' in hellenistic monarchies designated a member of the royal entourage with personal access to the king. Simmias is otherwise unknown, but his report was probably the ultimate source of A.'s account of the peoples of the African coast of the Red Sea.

with the appropriate support, described accurately—according to Agatharchides, the Knidian historian—the nations along the coast.

So he (*Simmias*) says that the nation of the Insensitive Aithiopes makes no use of drink whatsoever, nor does their nature pursue it, for the aforementioned reasons. (5) Overall, he shows, they neither hold converse with those of other nations, nor does the alien appearance of those who sail to their country affect the locals; but regarding them intently they keep their senses unmoved as if no one was there. Not even if one has drawn one's sword and made a stroke with it have they run away; nor were they aroused by submitting to insults or blows; and the mass of people did not share the anger of those who are enduring them, but sometimes they remained impassive in their behaviour while children and women were being cut to pieces in their sight, making no expression of anger or, on the other hand, pity. (6) On the whole, they remained calm before the most astonishing horrors, looking intently upon what is being performed, and nodding their head at each thing that occurs. Hence people say that they use no language, but by imitative demonstration with the hands they signify each thing that pertains to their requirements.

42. (*a*) (Phot. 450b 12–19) He says that those dwelling near the un-thirsting Ichthyophagoi, as if an inviolable treaty had been set up between themselves and the seals, do not themselves injure seals and are not harmed by them; but each race conserves the other's quarry and does not lay plots against the hunter. Thus they coexist with each other, in a way that could scarcely be found among people living alongside other people.

(*b*) (Diod. 3. 18. 7) And the most wondrous thing of all is that seals cohabiting with these races carry out fish-hunting by themselves in a similar manner to the people. Likewise, these two races exhibit the greatest trust to one another in the matter of their sleeping-places and the safety of their offspring: for no injury is committed in the co-existence of creatures of different tribes, which occurs peacefully and with total circumspection. So this way of life, while it is surprising, has been preserved from ancient times by these races, whether by habituation over time or whether it has been adapted under the pressure of compelling necessity.

43. (*a*) (Phot. 450b 20–7) Some of the Ichthyophagoi, he says, employ caves as living-quarters; not turned towards the south, on account of the breathless heat, but turned away from it. Others (*dwell*) under the ribcages of fish, placing seaweed upon them. Others tie the tops of olive-trees to each other and then use them as living-quarters. He says this olive-tree bears a fruit very comparable to the sweet-chestnut.

(*b*) (Diod. 3. 19. 1–4) (1) These nations do not all use dwellings in a similar way, but inhabit different ones in accordance with the particular circumstances. For some dwell in caves, especially those that are orientated towards the north, in which they cool themselves owing to the depth of the shadow and the breezes that circulate; for those facing the south, which have a temperature like ovens, are inaccessible to humans because of the excessive burning. (2) Those who are ill-provided with caves facing north gather the ribcages of the monsters thrown up by the open sea (*pelagos*), and since there is a plentiful supply of these they weave the ribcages together from each side, facing each other, and weave fresh seaweed through them. As the chamber gets roofed over, they take their ease during the most oppressive heat, for natural necessity instructs them in a self-taught skill. (3) The third manner of building living-quarters among the Ichthyophagoi is of the following sort. Large numbers of olive-trees grow around these places, and while the parts around their roots are inundated by the sea, they have dense foliage and bear a fruit like the sweet-chestnut. (4) Weaving these together and making continuous shade, they inhabit these peculiar tents. Spending time on land and sea at the same time, they lead their lives happily, avoiding the sun by means of the shade of the branches, while compensating for the natural burning of those places by the continual dashing of the waves and setting their bodies at leisure by the circulating breaths of the welcome winds.[56]

44. (a) (Phot. 450b 27–41) The fourth race of Ichthyophagoi has the following type of dwelling. A mighty load of sand has been heaped up from time immemorial, like a mountain. This whole heap has been felted hard by the continual beating of waves, so that—being a uniform mass and having a single nature, by reason of the combination and intermingling of the sand—it never shifts its position. So they dig out man-sized underground passages, leaving in place the mass at the summit, to be a reinforcement and to roof it over as a result of the said compression, while constructing lengthy tunnels in the lower ground, which have been bored through into one another on all sides. For a certain time they make light-holes on the side towards the wind and stay there quietly; but whenever the tide comes in, they prepare everything for the hunt, as has been told earlier.

(b) (Diod. 3. 19. 4–5) (4 *contd*) We must also speak of the fourth category of (*their*) encampment (*skēnōsis*). (5) From time immemorial a mighty load of sea-wrack[57] has been heaped up, comparable to a mountain. This, felted by the continual striking of the swell, has a solid character, interwoven with sand. In these elevations, therefore, they dig man-sized underground passages, leaving the place at the summit as a roof, while underneath they make lengthy tunnels which have been cut through into one another. Cooling themselves in these, they make themselves untroubled, while during the dashing of the waves they leap out and get busy hunting fish; but when the ebb-tide occurs, they celebrate their catch and withdraw together into the aforementioned passages.[58]

45. (a) (Phot. 450b 41–451a 3) They do not think those that die are worth any attention; they possess an understanding that is immune to the pity that comes from judgement. Hence they leave them to lie, cast aside, until the next ebb-tide conveys them into the sea as food for fish.

(b) (Diod. 3. 19. 6) Those that die they bury only around the moment of ebb tide, leaving them cast aside, and when the high tide comes they throw the bodies into the sea. Hence, turning their own interment into nutriment for the fish, they have a life-style that distinctively turns full circle for all time.[59]

---

[56] Cf. Artem. 98 (Strabo) §13, at location 43c.
[57] Phot. above refers to sand here, but the explanation that follows is consistent with sea-wrack.
[58] Cf. Artem. 98 (Strabo) §14, at location 44c. [59] Cf. ibid. 45c.

46. (*a*) (Phot. 451a 4–16) He says that some of those who feed off the sea, as well as other properties, also have this more surprising feature, one not easy to admit to reasoned confidence. For neither is it possible to determine from where they arrived at the place in which they dwell, nor how they did so, with a smooth rock contiguous with it above, cliffs to the side blocking any entrances, and ⟨the open sea (*pelagos*)⟩ bounding it on the side facing it. It is completely impossible to reach the place on foot, as I said; likewise inaccessible to rafts for want of those that we have. In these circumstances, he says, the only remaining view is that they are sprung from this spot, have inherited no memory of their first siring, and are aboriginal,[60] just as certain of the so-called physical scientists have determined.

(*b*) (Diod. 3. 20. 1–3) (1) But one race of Ichthyophagoi has dwellings of such a sort as to provoke great uncertainty in those zealous to investigate such things: for some of them have established themselves among precipitous gorges into which it was originally impossible for people to penetrate, since a high rock, everywhere precipitous, overhangs them, while to the sides inaccessible crags deny any entrances, while the open sea (*pelagos*) delimits the remaining side. It is impossible to get through to the place on foot, but they do not use rafts at all and they exist without any concept of the boats known among us.   (2) As such difficulty surrounds them, it only remains to say that they exist as autochthonous people who have had no beginning to their origin as a race but have always been there through all time, in the way that certain natural philosophers demonstrated for all natural phenomena.   (3) But since, in such matters, understanding is unattainable by us, there is nothing to stop those making the largest number of demonstrations being the ones who know the least, given that the credibility of the words may persuade the ear but by no means find out the truth.

47. (*a*) (Phot. 451a 17–451b 1) He says that beyond the narrows that enclose Arabia and the land opposite lie scattered islands, all low-lying, small in size, in number too great to tell, and generating no produce, either domesticated or wild, to support life. They are distant from the said mainland by around 70 stades, and are turned towards the open sea (*pelagos*) that appears to extend alongside India and Gedrosia. Here no swell arises, but each island being set in front of another takes the surf upon its promontories. They appear to have the best of all airs.

(451a 26) People inhabit these islands in modest numbers, and live life as follows. In the open sea (*pelagos*) lying beside them, extremely rough and stormy, occur a multitude of turtles of unbelievable width and size, which we all agree are sea-turtles. By night, these occupy the depths; but by day they come in to the quiet, calm place among the islands and sleep. They do this on the surface,[61] facing the sun, resembling fully fitted ferry-boats. At this point in time the locals, using skill, speed, and ropes, cast them onto the dry land and feed upon all the flesh inside—after baking them for a short time in the burning heat—but use their shells in setting up their tents, setting them the right way up in high places as if they were huts. They have also used them

---

[60] *aei hyparchontes*, lit. 'always in existence'.   [61] Or 'high up on the beach'.

for sea crossings and for watering, so that for the said people the same thing is a ship, a house, a container, and food.

> (b) (Diod. 3. 21. 1–5) (1) We must also speak of the so-called Chelonophagoi (*Turtle-eaters*) and the manner in which they make the whole arrangement of their life. For there are islands in the ocean, lying near the mainland; plentiful in number but small in size and low-lying, and possessing no produce, either domesticated or wild. In them, because they are tightly grouped, no swell arises, the surf being broken up around the capes of the islands. A multitude of sea-turtles spends its days around these places, taking refuge in the protection of the calm water. (2) In the nights, these spend time in the depths, busy with grazing; but in the days they frequent the sea in the middle of the islands and sleep afloat with their shells towards the sun, taking on an appearance very comparable to capsized boats;[62] for they are of exceptional size, and no smaller than the smallest fishing-boats. (3) But during this time the barbarians inhabiting the islands silently swim towards the turtles and approach them on each side; then while one group presses down the other lifts up, until the creature is upside-down. (4) Next, those on each side steer the whole weight of it, so that the creature cannot turn and, with the aid of its natural capacity, escape into the deep. One man, holding a long rope and tying it to the tail, swims to land and goes before the creature to drag it onto dry land, those who originally made the attack helping to convey it. (5) When they have conveyed it out onto the island, they bake all the inner parts for a short time in the sun and celebrate a meal; but they use the shells, which are shaped like boats, to sail over to the mainland, something they do for the purpose of getting water; but also for their living-quarters, placing them the right way up in high places. Thus nature seems to have endowed them, through one benefaction, with the satisfaction of many needs: for the same gift is to them food, a container, a house, and a ship.[63]

48. (a) (Phot. 451b 2–10) (*He says*) that at no great distance from the said race are people, modest in number, with the following lifestyle: they live off the sea-monsters thrown up onto the land. If such a food supply is scarce, as often occurs, they work through the shortage by using the cartilage and the ends of the ribs; albeit with difficulty, they nevertheless assuage it.

Those, he says, are all the races of Ichthyophagoi that we have detected, though there are a myriad others that have eluded our knowledge.

> (b) (Diod. 3. 21. 6) (6) Not far distant from these people, the coast is the possession of barbarians who have an insecure life. For they are nourished by the sea-monsters stranded on dry land. Sometimes they have an abundance of food because of the size of the animals that are found; but at other times there are intervals when they are in a bad way for want of them. At that time they are compelled by scarcity to work with the cartilage from the old bones and the material that grows from the ends of the ribs.
>
> Such are the many races of the Ichthyophagoi and such is the way of life they practise, to tell it in outline.

---

[62] Phot. implies they are not upturned.   [63] Cf. Artem. 98 (Strabo) §14, at location 47c.

49. (Phot. 451b 11–30) Whereas our life (*he says*) subsists among excess and necessities, the said races of Ichthyophagoi have rejected all unnecessary things, but fall short in none of the proper ones, he says. They decide in favour of the direct road to life, not the one that misapplies thinking to nature. For having no longing to acquire power, they are not affected by any ambitious and unhappy competitiveness. As they do not desire over-abundance, they do not do many unnecessary things to others or suffer many such things. Not setting up great hatreds aimed at harming an enemy's person, they are not overwhelmed by the ill-fortune of their relatives. Since they do not sail, over-straining their existence for the sake of profit, they do not measure pain by the mishaps of life. Rather, needing few things, they also regret few things: they possess a sufficiency and seek nothing more. Each of us is troubled not by what is unknown, if it is not present, but by what is wanted, if it comes later than the moment at which the desire drives us. Therefore he who has everything he wishes will be happy by the reckoning of nature, not that of thought. (*These people*) are not put right by laws: why be enslaved by commands, when one has the capacity to judge rightly without the written word?

Minor peoples

50. (Diod. 3. 22. 1–4) (1) The coast alongside Babylonia[64] connects with a civilized, well-planted land. So large a multitude of fish do the locals have that those who consume them cannot easily get the better of the abundance. (2) For along the beaches they put close-set reeds interwoven with one another, so that their appearance is similar to a net set beside the sea. All along the work there are closely spaced doors, woven to look like baskets and equipped with hinges easily released for movements in both directions. These doors are opened by the swell as it moves up onto the land during the time of high tide, but closed when it pours back on the ebb tide. (3) For this reason it happens that each day, when the sea is at high tide, the fish are all carried out of the deep water and plunge through the doors; when it retreats, they are unable to flow out with the liquid because of the weaving of the reeds. Hence it is sometimes possible to see piles of gasping fish building up beside the ocean; those assigned to this work, by continuously picking them out, gain abundant enjoyment and large incomes. (4) But some of those who spend their time about these places, the land here being a low-lying plain, dig straight ditches from the sea for many stades up to their private residences; they install plaited gates at the extremities and open them as the tide begins to rise, but when it falls and goes in the other direction they close them. Then, as the sea flows away through the interstices in each gate while the fish are left behind in the ditches, they store them and take as many as they choose and at whatever time they wish.

51. (*a*) (Phot. 451b 31–452a 11) $_{50H}$ After the Ichthyophagoi (*he says*), alongside the river Astabaras—which runs through Aithiopia and Libyē but is much slighter than the

---

[64] A. appended to his account of the Fish-eaters on the W side of the Indian Ocean these observations from the Asiatic side. The African coast continues at §51a.

Nile,[65] and by adding its own force to the greater stream it makes, by flowing round it, an island, Meroë[66]—so alongside the said river, on both edges, lives a throng of people that are not numerous but have the following lifestyle. They dig up the roots of the reeds from the adjoining marsh, then wash them clean and cut them up piece by piece with stones. Making it smooth and glue-like, they shape it into lumps of cake, though less than hand-sized, then bake it lightly and have this for sustenance. They also have an inescapable evil in the form of marsh lions that attack them; and during the rising of the Dog (*Sirius*) an immeasurable multitude of mosquitoes arises, which has such power that the people depart for the moist conditions of the marshes, and remain there out of sight. Even the lions are driven away by them: not so much harmed by their bite, though it is annoying, as incapable of enduring the strange sound of their call. But let these things be told for the sake of paradox; for what is stranger than that lions should give way to mosquitoes while humans are saved by this threat?

> (*b*) (Diod. 3. 23. 1–3) (1) Having gone through those living along the coast from Babylonia as far as the Arabian gulf, we shall go through the nations that succeed them. For all about the part of Aithiopia above Egypt, along the river called Asa[67] lives the nation of the Rhizophagoi (*Root-eaters*). For the barbarians, digging up the roots of reeds in the nearby (*places*),[68] wash them zealously, and having made them clean they cut them with stones until the worked material becomes smooth and glue-like. Then they shape hand-sized masses and bake them in the sun. They live all their life employing this food. (2) While possessing, however, uninterrupted and abundant supplies of this food and keeping the peace with one another, they have a multitude of lions making war upon them: for, as the surrounding air is fiery, lions often frequent their area, coming out of the desert for the sake of shade, or in some cases to hunt smaller animals. For this reason, those of the Aithiopes who come out of the wetlands are occasionally consumed by these animals: for they are incapable of resisting the ferocity of the lions, having no aid from weapons. Their race would eventually have been wholly wiped out if nature had not spontaneously created a certain form of assistance. (3) For surprisingly, during the rising of the Dog (*Sirius*), though no period of calm occurs around these places, a multitude of mosquitoes gathers, exceeding in power the familiar sort; it is so great that the people escape to the marshy lakes and come to no harm, but the lions all flee from these places, simultaneously afflicted with their bite but also overwhelmed by the sound of their call.[69]

---

[65] The Astabaras is the *Atbara*, which joins the Nile downstream from, and *c*.55 mi (*c*.90 km) NE of, Meroë.

[66] Actually, the 'island of Meroë' is not a true island as believed by Eratosthenes (Strabo 17. 1. 2, C786 = Erat. 89 §2) and later Greek and Roman geographers, since it is not fully surrounded by water.

[67] An error for 'Astabaras'.

[68] Rhodoman, an early editor, suggested adding 'marshes' (ἑλῶν) to match the corresponding passage of Photios, but Bommelear ad loc. does not adopt this.

[69] Cf. Artem. 98 (Strabo) §§8–9, at location 51c.

52. (*a*) (Phot. 452a 12–40) _{51H}He says that the race of Hylophagoi (*Wood-eaters*) and that of those who feed on seeds live near those mentioned.[70] The latter exhibit only a small variation from the former: for in the summertime they feed on the fruit falling from the trees, and at other times gather a plant growing in shady vales, solid in character and putting out a stem like those of the so-called brassicas. The former group feeds on the soft part of woody plants; and these people sleep at night when they have chosen a place to serve as a fortification and guard-post against the wild animals in the area. As soon as the sun is up, they go up into the trees with their children and wives, seeking to occupy the highest twigs rapidly; and there, squeezing the juice from the softest wood, they feed easily. Through all their life they have achieved such capability that their climbing is unbelievable to see: not only the tension of their hands, fingers, and feet but also, straightforwardly, of the remaining limbs. For they jump effortlessly from one branch to another, and often take boughs away from one another in the most precarious positions, and make such a spectacle that the man who sees it is himself astonished but does not even dare to tell of it to those who have not experienced it. They reduce every juicy bough with their teeth and digest it easily in their stomach. The body of one who slips from above, owing to its slimness, does not suffer an impact that is heavy. These people are all naked; they own children and wives common to all; but they make war on one another over localities. Most expire from being oppressed by hunger, as around the age of fifty cataracts overrun their eyes.

(*b*) (Diod. 3. 24. 1–4) (1) Adjacent to these people are those called the Hylophagoi (*Wood-eaters*) and the Spermatophagoi (*Seed-eaters*). Of these, the latter feed themselves without effort in summertime by gathering the fruit falling from the trees, of which there is a lot; but at other times they supply themselves with the tenderest part of the branching herb[71] that grows in shaded places where vales meet; for as it is solid in character and has a stem similar to the so-called brassicas, it remedies the lack of essential food. (2) But the Hylophagoi with their children and wives come out for the purpose of finding food, go up into the trees, and supply themselves with the softer branches. Through continuous practice, they make the climb to the very ends of the boughs in such a way that what happens is unbelievable: for they jump from one tree to another in a similar way to birds, and make the ascent onto the thinnest boughs without danger. (3) As they are outstanding in slimness and lightness of body, whenever they slip with their feet they grip instead with their hands; and if they happen to fall from a height they suffer nothing because of their lightness. And by reducing each juicy bough with their teeth, they digest it without effort in their stomach. (4) These people always live naked of any clothing, and therefore own women in common and regard the children who are born as common to all; but they wage war upon one another about localities, armed with wands, and warding off their opponents with these they tear apart those they have got the better of. Most of them die

---

[70] In fact, these were probably bands of chimpanzees (cf. McDermott 1938, 69–70, 108).
[71] βοτάνη–*botanē*; I use 'herb' to distinguish it from Phot.'s πόα–*poa*, 'plant'.

worn out by hunger, when their eyes develop cataracts and their body is deprived of the indispensable use of this sense.[72]

53. (*a*) (Phot. 452a 41–452b 7) ₅₂ₕ After the said people (*he says*) are the ones called Kynegetai (*Hunter Folk*) by those in the area. Because of the population of wild animals to which the area gives rise in great numbers, these people camp in the trees but hunt the animals by ambushing them, and thus create their diet. They have a great knowledge of archery. But whenever they are short of a quarry, they make good their lack (*of food*) with the skins of those previously caught, by wetting the hides, casting them onto lightly burning embers, baking them in the ashes, and then removing them to be shared out.

> (*b*) (Diod. 3. 25. 1–5) (1) The next area of land is occupied by the Aithiopes called Kynegoi (*Hunters*). They are modest in numbers and have the lifestyle that belongs to their name. For as their land is populated with animals and totally wretched, and moreover has few streams of spring-water, they lie down to sleep on the trees for fear of the animals; but around the time of dawn, with their weapons, they frequent the places where water collects, hide themselves in the woodland, and look out from the trees.   (2) During the time of burning heat a multitude of wild cattle, leopards, and the other animals arrive for the drinking-water and, because of the exceeding heat and their thirst, impetuously apply themselves to the liquid until they are quite full. When the animals become heavy and slow, the Aithiopes leap down from the trees and, using fire-hardened wooden clubs and stones, as well as arrows,[73] overpower them easily.   (3) They employ these hunting techniques in companies and eat the flesh of the animals they have caught; and while occasionally they are killed by the fiercest creatures, mostly they get the better of their superior force through cunning.   (4) But if ever they are short of the animals which they hunt, they wet the skins of those taken earlier and place them onto a low fire; they then bake them in the ashes to remove the hair, share out the skins, and make good their lack (*of food*) by eating them out of necessity.   (5) They train the very young boys to shoot at a mark and give food only to those who succeed. Hence they become adults wonderful for their good aim, being taught in the best way—by the pains of hunger.[74]

54. (*a*) (Phot. 452b 8–23) ₅₃ₕ After the said people (*he says*), at a great distance from them and extending further to the west, are those who make their living from the hunting of elephants. They watch for the passing of the animals from the tree in which they sit, and then seize the tail with their hands, use their feet to climb onto the left thigh, and employ repeated blows, from a suitable axe that they have ready, to cut through the right hamstring. They bring the axe down so strenuously with one hand, and hold on so hard with the other, that it is as if their soul was a prize to be won: for they must either kill or perish, the critical moment presenting no other possible conclusion. And when the creature falls before the attack and the loss of blood, the

---

[72] Cf. Artem. 98 (Strabo) §9, at location 52c.
[73] Cf. the fire-hardened weapons of the Aithiopes, Ps.-Skylax §112. 9.
[74] Cf. Artem. 98 (Strabo) §9, at location 53c.

fellow hunters approach the fallen one and, even while the animal is still alive, cut away the portions of flesh from its rear parts and celebrate a meal, waiting in this manner for the eventual death of the exhausted creature.

(b) (Diod. 3. 26. 1–4) (1) Towards the western parts of this land, at a great distance, are hunters called Elephantophagoi (*Elephant-eaters*). For occupying bushy places, dense with trees, they observe the entrances and by-ways of the elephants by making their lookouts in the highest trees. They do not attack the herds of these animals, as they have no hope of achieving their end; but lay their hands upon those travelling one by one, undertaking surprising and daring deeds.   (2) For when the creature passes and comes to the right of the tree in which a watchman happens to be hidden, as soon as it is passing by the place he grabs its tail with his hands and uses his feet to brace himself against the left thigh. With the axe fastened round his shoulders, which is of the lightness for delivering a one-handed but exceedingly sharp blow, he takes this in his right hand and cuts through the right hamstring, landing repeated blows and controlling his own body with his left hand. They bring a surprising alacrity to their work, as if the prize to be won was each man's soul; for the only options are to get the better of the creature or die oneself, as the circumstance admits of no other outcome.   (3) The hamstrung creature sometimes, through difficulty of movement, is unable to turn, leans upon the place where it has suffered hurt, and destroys the Aithiopian together with itself; but sometimes it squeezes the man against a rock or tree, pressing with its weight until it kills him.   (4) But some of the elephants, in extreme pain, so far from warding off their attacker, begin to flee over the plain until the man, still mounted on it and striking the same place, cuts through the tendons with his axe and makes the creature go limp. When the creature falls down, they run together in their companies and, while it is still alive, cut the portions of flesh from the rearward limbs and celebrate a meal.[75]

55. (Phot. 452b 23–34) ₅₄H Well, those are the people who, taking extreme risks, are elephant-hunters; others, however, hunt them in the following way. Three men, carrying one bow and several arrows impregnated with the bile of snakes, take up a position in a thicket beside the routes of the animals. So when the creature comes along, the first man handles the bow, putting his foot upon it, while the other two, drawing the string with all their might, let fly the missile, picking a single target in the middle of the animal's side, so that passing through the enclosing flesh it severs and injures the convex parts (*i.e. the belly*):[76] whence this mighty animal, struck and torn apart, is undone and falls down.[77]

56. (a) (452b 34–453a 15) ₅₅H There is a third race of Elephantophagoi (*Elephant-eaters*). When the elephants have filled themselves up with pasture and wish to turn to sleeping, they do not fall upon the ground and sleep, but lean themselves against the stoutest and tallest trees, in such a way that their two legs nearest the tree-trunk rest lightly on

---

[75] Cf. ibid. §10, at location 54c.   [76] A noun may be missing in the Greek.
[77] Cf. Artem. 98 (Strabo) §10, at location 55b.

the ground, while their flank receives the whole weight of their body and is supported by the natural (*strength*) of the wood. In this manner they achieve, not a true sinking into sleep, but the pretence thereof. The reason is that deep sleep involves great anguish for them, for if one of them should fall down its destruction will follow at once because of its natural weakness.[78]

The people who make their living from the pursuit of these animals range over the thickets and note the animal's sleeping-place. They then saw into the rear part of the tree, to the point where it does not entirely bend over, nor is it left in a very strong state with much strength,[79] but remains standing under light pressure. The creature comes from grazing and leans upon the usual location of its sleeping-place, but falls over suddenly when the wood breaks. Thus it is available to the hunters, a meal all prepared: for they cut portions of flesh from its rear parts and cause it to lose its blood. Once it is dead, they divide its limbs according to the need of each man.

> (*b*) (Diod. 3. 27. 1–4) (1) But some of those dwelling nearby hunt the elephants without danger, subduing their strength by skill. For this creature, whenever it is replete from grazing, usually descends into sleep, while having a different arrangement in this matter from the other quadrupeds: (2) for it cannot put its whole weight onto the ground using its knees, but while leaning against a tree it achieves its rest through sleep. For this reason the tree, since the creature often leans against it, is rubbed and full of mud. Additionally, the area around it carries footprints and many signs by which those Aithiopes who search for these things can recognize the elephants' *sleeping-places.* (3) So when they light upon such a tree they saw into it at ground level until it would take only a little push to cause its collapse. Then, disguising the signs of their own presence, they quickly depart, anticipating the creature's arrival. The elephant, towards evening, full up after grazing, comes down to its usual sleeping-place; but having leant down with all its weight it is immediately thrown to the ground by the rapid motion of the tree. Having fallen on its back it remains lying there through the night, because its bodily character is not designed for standing up. (4) The Aithiopes who sawed into the tree approach as soon as day comes and after killing the creature without any danger they camp around the place, and stay there until they have consumed the fallen one.[80]

57. (Phot. 453a 16–21) [56H] Ptolemy king of Egypt[81] (*he says*) requested these hunters to abstain from the killing of elephants so that he could take them alive, and promised them many wonderful things; but not only did he not persuade them, but he heard them give the answer that they would not even take his entire kingdom in exchange for their existing way of life.

58. (*a*) (453a 22–31) [57H] In a westerly direction from these hunters (*he says*), whom the nomads habitually call the Unclean, the land is occupied by a subdivision of the

---

[78] A. believes that an elephant, once fallen, cannot stand up; this is untrue (Henry ad loc.).

[79] The repetition ('strong . . . strength') is justified by that in the Greek.

[80] Cf. Artem. 98 (Strabo) §§10–11, at location 56c.   [81] Probably Ptolemy II.

Aithiopes who are called the Simoi (*Snub-nosed*). To the south is a not very large nation, the so-called Strouthophagoi (*Ostrich-eaters*), who hunt these birds with skill and
cunning, using clubs, and live off them.[82] They feed on their flesh and use their skins as
garments and bedding. As they have war waged upon them by the Simoi, they use the
horns of gazelles as weapons, for they are large and good for cutting; the land produces
this creature in large masses.

(*b*) (Diod. 3. 28. 1–6) (1) In the parts to the west of these races live the Aithiopes designated Simoi (*Snub-nosed*). In the parts inclined towards the south, the race of Strouthophagoi (*Ostrich-eaters*) manages the land; (2) for among them there is a certain species
of bird with a nature combined with that of a land creature. This lacks nothing in size
compared with the largest deer, but has been designed by nature to have a long neck, and
sides that are round and feathered; it also has a weak, small head but is extremely strong
in the thighs and legs, the foot being cloven. (3) This (*creature*) is unable to fly above
the ground because of its weight, but runs the fastest of all animals, scarcely touching the
ground with the points of its feet; and particularly when it lifts up its wings against the
force of the wind, it slips away just like any ship under sail. It wards off those pursuing it
by using its feet to sling hand-sized stones in a surprising manner. (4) When it is being
pursued in calm weather, however, its wings rapidly become soaked in sweat and it is
unable to exploit the advantages of its nature, so it is easily caught and captured. (5) As
these creatures exist across this land in a multitude too great to tell, the barbarians devise
all sorts of schemes for hunting them. Many are easily captured, and they use their flesh
in their diet and their skins for clothing and bedding. (6) When war is made upon
them by the Aithiopes named Simoi, they face every danger in confronting those attacking them, using gazelles' horns as weapons of defence: being large and good for cutting,
these offer great assistance, for across the land there is an abundance of these owing to the
multitude of animals that have them.[83]

59. (*a*) (Phot. 453a 32–b 1) [58H] Not far distant from the said people (*he says*) are the
Akridophagoi (*Locust-eaters*). The nation is shorter than the others, slight in form, and
unusually dark. Around the spring equinox, when the Libes (*SW winds*) and Zephyroi
(*westerlies*) blow with immense force in their land, a multitude, too great to tell, of
locusts arrives with the wind from the unexplored land. They are not much different
from birds in the power of their flight, but are very different in body. The people are
nourished by this creature at all times: among other things, they even consume them
in pickled form. They hunt these creatures with smoke, bringing them to ground out
of the air.

(453b 1–15) These people are said to be light and rather keen-footed, but live no more
than forty years as they partake entirely of dry food. They die more miserably than
they live: for at the moment when old age draws near, winged varieties of lice are born
in their bodies, similar in shape to ticks but less long than those that appear on dogs.

---

[82] Phot. and Diod. omit A.'s account of the hunting mimicry used by the Strouthophagoi, which is,
however, preserved in Artem. 98 (Strabo) §11, at location 58c.
[83] Cf. ibid.

They begin from the chest and belly, but are immediately distributed over the whole person.[84] The people are initially in a similar condition to those irritated by scabies, but subsequently inflict painful abrasions upon themselves. Next, as the disease draws to its climax, with the breaking out of the creatures and the discharging of thin fluids, there comes a point where the unfortunates endure unbearable irritation. Thus, whether having their bodily fluids, their diet, or the air as the cause of the evil, they perish.[85]

(b) (Diod. 3. 29. 1–7) (1) A short way from these people, the Akridophagoi (*Locust-eaters*) occupy the places adjacent to the desert. These are smaller people than the others, slim in build, and exceedingly black. In their land during the spring season, strong Zephyroi (*westerlies*) and Libes (*SW winds*) propel out of the desert a multitude of locusts too great to tell. These are different from others in size, and the colour of their wing looks unpleasant and dirty.   (2) As a result, the people have abundant food throughout their life, as they practise their hunting in a special way. For beside their land for many stades extends a ravine of substantial depth and width. This they fill with wild wood, which is plentiful in this land. Next, when the aforementioned winds begin to blow and clouds of locusts are carried towards them, they divide between them all the space in the ravine and burn the vegetation in it.   (3) Since a lot of bitter smoke is produced, the locusts, as they fly over the ravine and are choked by the bitterness of the smoke, fly only a short distance before falling to the ground. Their annihilation takes place over several days, so that large piles grow up. As the land contains a great deal of salt, all the people bring this over to the massive piles and soak them thoroughly in the proper manner. Thus they give them an attractive taste and make possible their long-term storage.

(4) They have this diet, therefore, based on these creatures in both the short and the long term; for they do not rear cattle, live close to the sea, or possess any other support at all. They are light in their bodies and very keen-footed, but are entirely short-lived, given that the longest-lived among them do not get beyond forty years.   (5) They not only have a surprising end to their life but the most unfortunate of all: for when old age draws near, winged lice are born in their bodies, not only unusual in form but also wild and totally unpleasant in appearance.   (6) The evil begins in their belly and torso, but spreads over all their frame in a short time. The sufferer at first, like one irritated by scabies, is zealous to scratch in moderation, as the disease combines pleasure with its pains; but subsequently, as more of the animals that are born come up to the surface, a mass of thin fluid is discharged which carries a perfectly intolerable irritation.   (7) For this reason the one caught up in the disease lacerates himself more forcefully with his nails, emitting great groans; but with the tearing action of his hands such a great multitude of the insects comes out that people who try to remove them achieve nothing, with one appearing after another as if from a container pierced in many places. So these people terminate their life with such an

---

[84] *prosōpon* originally meant 'face', but from late Hl times could mean 'person', 'body'. 'Face' (Fr. *visage*, Henry) does not seem likely here, given the 'but'; possibly Phot. has altered A.'s wording.

[85] The reference is probably to guinea-worm (*Dracunculus medinensis*) infestation. The worms, which can grow to 5 feet in length, enter the body as a result of drinking water containing their eggs. For a vivid account of the illness, see Bruce 1790, 37–9. Plutarch preserves more clearly A.'s description of the worm's behaviour (B. 5 below).

unfortunate breakdown of their body; whether it is because of their unusual diet or the air that they meet with such a reversal of fortune.[86]

60. (*a*) (Phot. 453b 18–34) _{59H} There is, he says, an extensive land neighbouring the Akridophagoi, which has pasture of outstanding variety but is totally empty and untrodden by all those dwelling around. In the beginning it did not lack a human race, but now it does so because of an unbelievable multitude of scorpions and poisonous spiders, which some name the Four-jaws; for they say that this species proliferated as the result of an episode of heavy rain. The inhabitants were unable to resist the evil; but owing to the flight of those evading it, who chose safety from pestilence in preference to their fatherland, from that time the land was left empty of the race of humans. Similarly, (*there has been*) a multitude of country mice as has occurred three times in Italy, and sparrows devouring the seeds as in Media, and frogs as in the area of the Autariatai; and cities have been relocated because of the proliferation of lions, as in Libyē; and many other unforeseen misfortunes have overtaken many lands and emptied them of settlers.

(*b*) (Diod. 3. 30. 1–4) (1) Alongside this nation runs a land that is extensive in size and good in terms of the variety of its pasture, but is empty and completely untrodden. Originally it was not lacking in the race of humans, but in later times, as a result of an unseasonal episode of heavy rain, it gave forth a multitude of poisonous spiders and scorpions. (2) For they report that so great a multitude of the said animals proliferated over the place that the resident people at first began, as a whole community, to kill each of these natural enemies; but when the multitude was not overcome and their bites were bringing speedy deaths to those that were struck down, they renounced their fathers' country and mode of life, and fled from the area.

One should not wonder at what is said, or distrust it, for we have accepted many more surprising events than these, all over the inhabited world, on the basis of true history. (3) For in Italy a multitude of country mice, engendered in the plains, drove certain people out of the land of their fathers. Across Media, numbers of sparrows, too numerous to tell, proliferated over the region and, by causing the people's seed-crops to disappear, compelled them to migrate to alien places. The so-called Autariatai were forced by frogs, which took on their original formation in the clouds and fell to earth in place of the usual rain, to leave behind their fatherlands and take refuge in the very place in which they have now become settled. (4) Indeed, who has not written the history, among the Labours completed by Herakles to win the prize of immortality, of the one numbered among them during which he expelled from the Stymphalian lake the multitude of birds that proliferated at it? And across Libyē certain cities were evacuated when a multitude of lions invaded from the desert. So let these cases suffice in answer to those who are inclined

---

[86] For the Akridophagoi, Cf. Artem. 98 (Strabo) §12, at location 59c. The infestation described is probably myiasis rather than the effects of the guinea worm described by Plutarch (see previous n., and Marcotte 2021).

to disbelieve the accounts because of their surprising nature. But now we shall again move to the next part of the account following the aforementioned matters.[87]

61. (a) (Phot. 453b 35–454a 4) ₆₀ₕ The last people, he says, among those living towards the south are those whom the Hellenes call Kynamolgoi (*Dog-milkers*) but their neighbours call, as one might say, Agrioi Barbaroi (*Wild Barbarians*). These are long-haired and wear exceptional beards. They rear many large dogs, in a similar manner to the Hyrkanians, and use these to hunt the Indian cattle that arrive in their land and appear in a multitude too great to tell, from the summer solstice until midwinter. Additionally, they milk the dogs' bitches and are nourished by their milk, as well by the hunting of other animals. Such is the character of the last races towards the south.

(b) (Diod. 3. 31. 1–4) (1) The extreme regions of the parts towards the south are occupied by men callled Kynamolgoi (*Dog-milkers*) by the Hellenes, but in the language of the neighbouring barbarians Agrioi (*Wild Men*). These wear long beards and rear packs of savage dogs well adapted to the needs of their lifestyle. (2) For from the start of the summer solstice until midwinter, Indian cattle, in a multitude too great to tell, frequent their land from a cause that is unclear: for no one knows if they are being made war upon by many flesh-eating creatures whom they are fleeing, or are leaving behind their own areas for lack of food or some other circumstance that Nature, which gives birth to all surprising things, has created but which the race of humans is incapable of understanding with the mind. Well, lacking the strength to overcome the multitude (*of cattle*) by themselves, they send the dogs against them and by carrying out the hunt using these they get the better of huge numbers of the creatures. Of those they capture, some they eat up at once while others they place in salt and store away. As they also hunt many other creatures through the ferocity of the dogs, their lifestyle is founded upon meat-eating.

(4) So the last races among those living towards the south, though they have the shape of humans, have the lifestyle of animals; but it remains to explain two nations, the Aithiopes and the Trogodytai. We have written up our account of the Aithiopes elsewhere,[88] however, and will now talk about the Trogodytai.[89]

Trogodytai

62. (a) (Phot. 454a 5–32) ₆₁ₕ The affairs of the Trogodytai[90] are as follows. Their political organization is classed as a tyranny,[91] but their women and children are held in

---

[87] Cf. Artem. 98 (Strabo) §12, at location 60c.

[88] The reference to A.'s having already discussed the Aithiopians is probably not to a lost section of *On the Erythraian Sea* but to his account of the island of Meroë in book 2 of *On Affairs in Asia*, excerpts from which are preserved by Diod. (3. 5–11 = *BNJ* 86 F 1 and 673 F 21) and indirectly by Strabo (17. 2. 1, C821 = *BNJ* 673 F 22a) on the basis of book 8 of the *Geographoumena* of Artemidoros. Cf. Burstein 1986, 22–3.

[89] Cf. Artem. 98 (Strabo) §10, at location 61c.

[90] Many MSS of Photios, Diodoros, and Strabo read 'Troglodytai', 'Hole–dwellers'. However, Ptolemaic sources (e.g. *OGIS* 70. 4; 71. 3; Householder and Prakken 1945), and the note in the *Chrestomathia Straboniensia* (*GGM* ii. 629), to the effect that Strabo omitted the letter lambda in the term, ensure that Trogodytai is the correct form. Its meaning is unknown.

[91] 'Tyrant' is the term used in Hl and Roman texts to designate a tribal chieftain or local headman subject to the overlordship of another ruler.

common, though the tyrant's wife is the only one with whom one may not consort, and the penalty imposed upon anyone that dares to do so is to pay one sheep. Their lifestyle is as follows.[92] During their winter—that is, in the season of the Etesian winds—when the god afflicts their land with violent rains, they live off blood and milk, mixing them together and stirring them in lightly warmed vessels. But when the summer sets in, they inhabit the swampy districts and fight one another for cattle fodder. They consume their older herd-animals and the sick ones, killing them through the agency of butchers whom they call the Uncleansed.

(454a 18) These people endow no person with the title of parent, but rather a bull and a cow, calling him Father and her Mother, and similarly with a ram and a ewe, for the reason that they gather their food each day not from their parents but from those animals. They also have drinks: the great mob of people use an extract of Christ-thorn, but the tyrants drink the preparation of a certain flower; it resembles low-grade grape-syrup. Though they happen to be naked as to the rest of their body, they are girdled about their loins with animal skins. As for the genitals, it is usual for other Trogodytai to be circumcised, like all Egyptians; but the custom of those whom the Hellenes call the Koloboi (*Docked*) is to remove with razors, while they are infants, the whole part that undergoes circumcision among other peoples; whence they have acquired the said title.

(*b*) (Diod. 3. 32. 1–33. 1) 32. (1) So the Trogodytai are designated Nomads by the Hellenes; while they have a pastoral (*nomadikos*) lifestyle based on their herds, they form political communities ruled by tyrants. They hold both their children and their women in common, except for one woman, that of the tyrant: from anyone who consorts with her, the tyrant exacts the penalty of a fixed number of sheep.

(2) During the period of the Etesian winds, when heavy rainstorms occur in their country, they are nourished by blood and milk, mixing these and boiling them for a short time. Afterwards, however, when the pasture dries up because of the excessive heat, they take refuge in the marshy places and fight intensely against one another over the pasture-land.

(3) They consume the older animals and those that are beginning to fall ill, and are nourished at all times by these. For this reason they attach the term 'parent' to no human, but to a bull and a cow, and also to a ram and a ewe, calling the former fathers and the latter mothers, because their everyday sustenance is always provided by these, not by those who have sired them. The ordinary people employ as their drink an infusion of Christ-thorn, but for the rulers (*their*) drink is prepared from a certain flower; it resembles the worst kind of grape-syrup known among us. They accompany their herds of animals and travel from one land to another, shunning the idea of lingering in the same places.

(4) They are all naked as to their bodies except for their loins, which they cover with animal skins; as for the genitals, all the Trogodytai are circumcised similarly to the Egyp-

---

[92] Trogodytai is the generic term for transhumant pastoralists living in the eastern desert and Red Sea, whose modern descendants are probably the Beja peoples who inhabit the same regions. They represent the second stage in A.'s adaptation of Dikaiarchos' scheme of social development.

tians, except for those called Koloboi (*Docked*) after what happens to them: for these people, alone among those occupying the land within the straits, have the whole part cut off with razors, when infants, that undergoes circumcision among the remaining peoples.

33. (1) For weaponry, those of the Trogodytai called Megabareis have rounded shields of untanned oxhide and a club with iron-covered knobs; but the others use bows and spears.[93]

63. (Phot. 454a 33–4) $_{62H}$ The author, though an atticist, uses the word *kamara*.

64. (*a*) (454a 35–454b 29) $_{63H}$ The Trogodytai, he says, have the following practice concerning those who have passed away. Having tied the neck to the legs using withies of the Christ-thorn, they next place (*the body*) upon a mound and throw hand-sized stones at it with mockery and laughter, until the shape of the deceased is hidden away. After that, they put a goat's horn on top and are dismissed, being now free from emotion and altogether merry. Thus, he says, they deal with funerals intelligently, if indeed it is a sign of understanding not to cause themselves grief about people no longer in pain. The hostilities, fights, and wars that occur over the pasture when it suddenly grows—for they do not fight over anything else—are resolved by the older women, who come between them and with calming words restrain their excited spirits.

(454b 8) They do not, he says, go about sleeping in the way other humans do. They have a multitude of domesticated animals following them round; having tied bells to the horns of all the males so that the sound of them may drive away wild animals, when night comes they herd their valuable possessions into pens and place hurdles made from palm-trees on top. The women with their children get up onto these, but the men set fires around in a ring; singing certain ancestral stories, they thus keep sleep at bay; for in many circumstances where necessity requires it, careful usage overcomes nature.

(454b 18) Whenever any persons on whom old age—the debt that all must pay—is heavy are no longer able to accompany the flocks, they put a cow's tail round those persons' necks and pull the loop tightly behind their throat, releasing them from life. But if any of them were to try to go past his (*appointed*) end, any willing bystander, as one relieving him of his reluctance with kindness, may give him advice together with censure of his conduct, and send him off along the same road. It is not only those growing old that they remove out of life, but also those whom persistent disease, or the maiming of a limb, has rendered useless for the task of following the herds.

(*b*) (Diod. 3. 33. 2–6) (2) They are dedicated to wholly unusual burials: for after binding the bodies of the deceased with withies of the Christ-thorn they attach the neck to the legs, and placing the corpse upon a certain raised ground they throw hand-sized stones at it while laughing, until by heaping them about with the stones they hide the bodies away. Finally they place a goat's horn on it and are dismissed, gaining no fellow-feeling. (3) They make war against each other not, in a similar way to the Hellenes, out of

---

[93] Cf. Artem. 98 (Strabo) §17, at location 62c.

anger or because of any other accusations, but over the pasture as it periodically grows up. In their combats they first throw stones at each other until some are wounded; for the rest of the time they resort to a contest of bows. Many die in an instant, given that they shoot with a good aim because they are trained in these matters and have for a target a man naked of any protective armour. (4) The battle is resolved by the older women, who jump in between them and are treated with respect, for their custom prevents them from striking these women in any manner; hence, as soon as they appear, they stop shooting.

(5) Those who through old age are unable to accompany the flocks use a cow's tail, which they fix tightly round their own neck, to release themselves willingly from life. But if a person tries to postpone death, anyone who wishes has the power to put the loop round him, as one acting in kindness, and with a word of advice deprive him of life. (6) Similarly, it is their custom to remove from life those maimed or affected by diseases resisting a cure. For they think it the greatest of evils for a person to love life who is incapable of doing anything worth living for. Hence it is possible to observe that the Trogodytai are perfect in body and still strong in the prime of life, given that none of them exceeds sixty years.[94]

65. (Phot. 454b 30–6) [64H] The whole inhabited world, as he (*Agatharchides*) says, being encircled in four parts—I mean east, west, north, and south—the westward parts have been covered by Lykos and Timaios, the eastward by Hekataios and Basilis, the northward by Diophantos and Demetrios,[95] and the southward—a burdensome task, as he rightly says—by ourselves.[96]

66. (Diod. 3. 33. 7–34. 4) [65M] 33. (7) About the Trogodytai we have said enough; but if any reader should disbelieve these accounts because of their foreignness and the surprising nature of the ways of life reported, he should place beside one another in his mind the air of Skythia and that in the Trogodytike and see the differences between the two; then he will not disbelieve what is reported.

34. (1) For so great is the variation in the airs in our region, compared with those reported, that the difference, considered point by point, is unbelievable. (2) For in some places the greatest rivers are frozen by the exceeding cold, and the ice withstands armies that cross it as well as the advance of heavy-laden wagons; wine and the other liquids are frozen so that they are cut up with knives; and things still more wondrous—people's extremities fall apart when clothing rubs them, their eyes grow dim, fire gives no protection, and even bronze statues are cracked. At some seasons, because of the thickness of the clouds, they say, no lightning or thunder occurs in those regions. Many other things more

[94] Cf. ibid. 64c.

[95] Lykos of Rhegion (*BNJ* 570), wrote histories of Libya and Sicily in C4l/C3e. Timaios of Tauromenion (*BNJ* 566) wrote a history of Sicily and a biography of Pyrrhos, king of Epeiros, in C3f. Hekataios is probably H. of Abdera (*BNJ* 264), who in C4l wrote what became the standard Hl history of Egypt. Basilis (*BNJ* 718) wrote a book on India and possibly another on Aithiopia in C3 or C2. Diophantos (*BNJ* 805) wrote a work entitled *Pontika*, dealing with the peoples of the Black Sea, prior to C2m. Demetrios of Kallatis (*BNJ* 85) wrote during C3l or C2 a history of Asia and Europe in 20 books.

[96] The variation in word order seems likely to be A.'s own.

surprising than these are brought about that are unbelievable to those who know nothing of them, but insupportable to those who have gained experience of them.

(3) Around the further parts of Egypt and the Trogodytike, because of the excessive heating caused by the sun at the midday period, bystanders cannot even see each other because of the dense concentration occurring in air. They are all incapable of walking without footwear, since blisters arise immediately on those going unshod. (4) As for their drink, if a person does not promptly satisfy his thirst they swiftly die, since the heat rapidly consumes the nature of the liquids in the body. In addition, whenever someone places comestibles of any kind in a bronze vessel with water and places it in the sun, it is swiftly cooked without fire and wood.

67. (a) (Phot. 454b 37–455a 14) $_{66H}$ No large space (*he says*) spans and separates the very different lifestyles of humankind. For out of Lake Maiotis (*Sea of Azov*)[97] many people carried on cargo vessels have reached the Rhodians' harbour on the tenth day, from where at the same season they have arrived at Alexandria on the fourth day; sailing up-river from here against the stream, they might arrive in Aithiopia in a further ten days without difficulty. Thus, from an excess of cold to the maximum heat (*the interval*) is no more than five and twenty days, for those conveyed without interruption. All the same, while the distance between places is of this scale, humans display such unsurpassable differences from one another in their lifestyle, customs, and air that one group will not believe what is usual and normal among another, nor could they tolerate at all things without which others would not even choose to live. Thus every familiar behaviour carries a particular, powerful spell; and the harshness of the environment is defeated by time, which welcomes into life one's earliest moments.

(b) (Diod. 3. 34. 5–8) (5) All the same, those inhabiting both the said lands do not even wish to escape the excessive evils that happen to them, but on the contrary to renounce their life voluntarily in order not to be forced to experience a different existence and way of life. (6) In this way every familiar land casts a particular, individual spell; and Time, which takes over the prime of life from infancy, overcomes the sufferings caused by the airs. (7) No great interval of distance separates such marked variations towards both extremes: for from Lake Maiotis, beside which dwell some of the Skythians, planted among frost and exceedingly cold conditions, many of those voyaging in cargo vessels running with the wind have sailed into Rhodes on the tenth day, from which they descend upon Alexandria on the fourth day; and from here, sailing along the Nile, many have descended upon Aithiopia on the tenth day. Thus from the chilled parts of the inhabited world to the hottest parts is no more than twenty-four days' sailing for those conveyed continuously. (8) For this reason, the change in the airs being great over a small distance, it is in no way surprising that both their mode of living and their lives, but also their bodies, should differ greatly from those among us.

---

[97] Skythia and Aithiopia as representing the climatic extremes of human habitation are a commonplace of Greek theory of how climate influences human behaviour (cf. Isaac 2004, 65–72).

Animals

68. (Diod. 3. 35. 1) ₆₇ₘ Since we have gone through the chief points of the nations and ways of life that seem surprising, we shall go through the animals found across the areas under discussion, one by one.

69. (Phot. 455a 15–19) ₆₈ₕ The lions in the region of Arabia, he says, are smoother-skinned and braver, but have a regular colour like those reared in Babylonia. Their hair is so gleaming that the yellowness of their neck shines in a similar manner to gold.

70. (455a 20–3) ₆₉ₕ Most of those called 'ants' do not vary from the rest at all in appearance, but have a form of genitals that is turned the opposite way to others.[98]

71. (455a 24–8) ₇₀ₕ The leopards are not as those in the regions near Karia and Lykia are: they are long-bodied and much more capable of suffering injuries and pains. In ferocity they differ as much from the others as a wild animal from a domestic.[99]

72. (*a*) (455a 29–455b 2) ₇₁ₕ The rhinoceros (*he says*) yields nothing ⟨in fierceness⟩[100] to the elephant, but is inferior in height. It has a colour comparable to cheap boxwood; likewise the surface of its hide ⟨is strong⟩.[101] It wears an upturned horn at the ends of its nostrils,[102] which is similar in strength to iron; whenever it encounters a rock it arms itself by throwing forward its chest; but on meeting an elephant—an animal with which it contends over pasture throughout its life—it ducks beneath its belly and slashes up into the round flesh with its horn, causing it to lose blood at once. One may see numerous elephants that have died in this way. But if it happens that the rhinoceros fails to make contact with the belly, instead it is often itself disabled by being struck with the trunk and tusks, and thus undone: for a great contrast exists in their power and strength.

(*b*) (Diod. 3. 35. 2–3) (2) For there is a creature which is called a 'nose-horn' (*rhino-kerōs*) because of this attribute. In ferocity and strength it is similar to an elephant, but in height it is lower. The hide it possesses is very strong, and its colour is that of boxwood. At the ends of its nostrils it carries a horn that is upturned in shape and comparable to iron for strength. (3) Always competing with the elephant over pasture, it whets its horn on one of the rocks, and when it meets the said animal it ducks under its belly and slashes up into the flesh with its horn as if with a sword. By employing this mode of battle it causes the animals to lose blood and destroys many of them. But whenever the elephant avoids the attack under its belly it seizes the rhinoceros with its trunk first, overcoming it easily by striking it with its tusks and by its superior strength.[103]

---

[98] Cf. Artem. 98 (Strabo) §15, at location 70b.   [99] Cf. B. 7 below.
[100] Adopting ⟨ἀλκῇ⟩ (Lucarini 2020, 222).   [101] Adopting ⟨ἰσχυρὰν⟩ (Lucarini 2020, 222).
[102] There is no satisfactory explanation of A.'s erroneous claim that the rhinoceros has only one horn since, unlike the Indian rhinoceros, both African species, the white and the black rhinoceros, have two horns. Curiously, although the geographer Artemidoros claimed to have seen a rhinoceros in Alexandria (cf. Artem. 98 (Strabo) §15, at location 72c), he copied A.'s description without correction.
[103] Cf. Artem. 98 (Strabo) §15, at location 72c.

73. (Phot. 455b 3–8) _{72H}Among the Trogodytai (*he says*), there occurs what the Hellenes call the *kamelopardalis* (*giraffe*), possessing a kind of compound form in terms of its formation and nature. For it has the dappled character of a leopard but the stature of a camel, as well as enormous speed; and such a neck that it can milk its sustenance from the tree-tops.[104]

74. (*a*) (455b 9–14) _{73H}Sphinxes, 'dogheads', and *kēpoi*,[105] he says, are despatched to Alexandria from the Trogodytike and Aithiopia. Sphinxes are similar to those represented in paintings, except that they are hairy all over and are tame and gentle in spirit. They possess great cunning, and latch onto regular instruction so well that people wonder at the grace of all their actions.

> (*b*) (Diod. 3. 35. 4) The sphinxes occur in the areas of Trogodytike and Aithiopia. In shape they are not unlike those in paintings, and differ only in their hairiness; they have tame, more cunning spirits and accept regular instruction.

75. (*a*) (Phot. 455b 15–22) _{74H}The 'doghead'[106] is the very picture of an ugly human body with a dog's face. It gives out a sound similar to moaning; it is exceedingly wild and perfectly impossible to tame. It has a severe appearance because of its eyebrows and eyes. That is true of the male; the female's role is to wear her womb outside her body and live her entire life in that state.

> (*b*) (Diod. 3. 35. 5) Those named dogheads are comparable to ugly humans, and emit a human moaning with their voices. These creatures are born wild and totally impossible to tame, and have a rather severe look on account of their eyebrows. An altogether individual feature of the females is to carry the womb outside the body at all times.

76. (*a*) (Phot. 455b 22–5) _{75H}The *kēpos* (*lit.* 'garden') has a face similar to a lion's, a body like a panther's, and a stature like a gazelle's. It takes its name from its variegated form.

> (*b*) (Diod. 3. 35. 6) The so-called *kēpos* has been given its name on account of the beautiful and smooth development of its entire body. It has a face similar to a lion and carries its remaining body comparably to a panther, apart from its size, which equates to a gazelle.

77. (*a*) (Phot. 455b 25–456a 2) _{76H}Among all the creatures that have been reported, the most wild and most difficult to subdue is the race of flesh-eating bulls.[107] This has a size more substantial than that of domesticated ones and surpasses them in speed; it is exceptionally red. Its mouth opens wide as far as its ears, but its eye appears shinier than a lion's. At other times it moves its horns around in a comparable manner to its ears, but when engaged in battle it raises them stiffly. It has hair whose direction is contrary to that of other animals. This animal attacks the fiercest ones and hunts all

---

[104] Cf. ibid. §16, at location 73b.

[105] Lit. 'gardens', but written *kēboi* in Artem. 98 (Strabo) §16, at location 74c.

[106] The Hamadryas baboon (*Papio hamadrayas*), the sacred animal of the Egyptian god Thoth, was imported to Egypt in large numbers during the 1st millennium BC (D. Kessler 2001).

[107] If the animal is not mythical, then this is most likely a confused account of the African buffalo (*Syncerus caffir*).

other creatures, but it especially damages the herds of the local people. It is the only animal that cannot be wounded by spearhead or bow; hence no one has been strong enough to bring it under control, though many have dedicated themselves to this. On falling into a digging or some similarly clever device, however, it rapidly gets suffocated by its own fury. This animal is justly deemed by the Trogodytai to have the ferocity of a lion, the speed of a horse, and the force of a bull; and never to submit to the iron.

(b) (Diod. 3. 35. 7–9) (7) Of all the said animals, the wildest and totally unconquerable is the flesh-eating bull. This is greater in stature than domesticated bulls, but in the speed of its feet it lacks nothing compared with a horse. Its mouth opens wide up to its ears; it has an exceedingly red colour. It has eyes shinier than a lion's, which flash by night, and horns partaking of an unusual nature: for at other times it moves them in a comparable manner to its ears, but in battles it raises them stiffly. The direction of its hair is contrary to other creatures.   (8) The animal is unusual in ferocity and power, given that it attacks the fiercest creatures and makes its diet from eating the flesh of the defeated. It also destroys the flocks of the local people, and fights in an astonishing manner against whole bands of shepherds and packs of dogs.   (9) Its skin is even said to be invulnerable; at any rate, though many have dedicated themselves to catching and bringing it under control, no one has been strong enough. But on falling into a digging, or being subjugated by some other trick, it gets suffocated by its own fury and in no manner does it exchange its freedom for the kind treatment which being tamed would bring. For this reason the Trogodytai deem this animal the strongest, given that its nature has been endowed with the ferocity of a lion, a horse's speed, and the force of a bull; and is not defeated by the strongest nature of all things, that is, iron.[108]

78. (a) (Phot. 456a 3–14) ₇₇ₕ The thing in Aithiopia which he says is named *krokottas* is like a compound of wolf and dog,[109] but wilder than both and much more fearsome by reason of its face and paws. In ferocity it is wondrous, and it is more powerful than other animals in teeth and belly: for it easily breaks up all sorts of bone and, once it is broken up, it has swiftly devoured it with its inexplicable digestive processes. Some people tell us that the creature imitates human language; but they do not convince us. Those informants add that the creatures call people by name during the night, and when these persons come near, believing the voice to be human, they swiftly jump on them and devour them.

(b) (Diod. 3. 35. 10) What is called by the Aithiopes *krokottas* has a nature mixed from those of a dog and a wolf, but its wildness is more terrifying than both these. It stands above all creatures for its teeth: for it crushes easily any size of bone, and what it swallows its belly digests in a surprising manner. Some of those who tell surprising tales report falsely that this creature imitates the language of humans; but they do not convince us.[110]

---

[108] Cf. Artem. 98 (Strabo) §16, at location 77c.

[109] Probably the spotted hyena (*Crocuta crocuta*).

[110] Cf. Artem. 98 (Strabo) §16, at location 78c; and *PME* 50. For Müller's extract 79, from Aelian, see **B. 6** below.

80. (a) (Phot. 456a 15–32) $_{78H}$ There are, he (Agatharchides) says, surprisingly large snakes of wondrous species in these places,[111] all of which survive by hunting. Of all those that have appeared to human view, he says, the greatest has been 30 cubits long. But every snake, he says, including the largest, becomes tame when oppressed and tormented by lack of necessities. Indeed, the one he says he saw, when its food was continuously rendered scarce, both became humble in spirit and developed a stronger appetite for food. At this point, the people cast sacrificed animals into its cage to satisfy its lust, and thus rendered the wild creature tame and gentle. As a result, none of all the other animals was regarded as either tamer or more terrifying. This, I believe, is probable when such circumstances face tamed creatures; but resistance is met with torment, surrender with nurture. All animals learn self-control not by understanding the consequence of better behaviour, but because the memory has been cross-woven by experience.[112]

> (b) (Diod. 3. 36. 1–37. 9) 36. (1) All kinds of species of snakes, of unbelievable size, are observed (here), according to those dwelling near the desert infested by animals. For certain people who purport to show that they have seen snakes 100 cubits long could justly be understood, by not only ourselves but all other people, to be telling lies. For they join onto this suspect claim even more surprising things, saying that, as the land is a plain, whenever the greatest of the animals are coiled up they make eminences with their wound-up coils which from a distance appear similar to a hill. (2) One might not easily concur with the size of the aforesaid animals; but we shall make a description of the greatest ones that have come into view and have been conveyed to Alexandria in certain suitable containers, adding as well the arrangements for hunting them.
>
> (3) For the second Ptolemy, being zealous in the matter of hunting elephants and granting vast bonuses to those who achieved surprising captures of the fiercest creatures, also spent a great deal of money on this appetite. He obtained numerous war-elephants and caused other animals with hitherto unseen and strange natures to be brought within the knowledge of the Hellenes. (4) Hence certain hunters, seeing the king's greatheartedness in the matter of bonuses, once they had assembled into an adequate quantity, judged that they should gamble with their lives and hunt one of the great snakes and convey it back alive to Ptolemy in Alexandria. (5) Though the venture was great and strange, Fortune collaborated with their designs and obtained an appropriate conclusion to the matter. They spotted one of the snakes, 30 cubits long, lingering around pools of water. The rest of the time it kept its coiled body motionless; but during the arrivals of creatures frequenting the place because they were thirsty, it would suddenly rise up, clutch with its mouth the creatures that had appeared, but wind their bulk in its coils, so that the fallen one had no way of escaping.

---

[111] Although the size of the snake is greatly exaggerated, the creature is most likely the African rock python (Python sebae).

[112] I take ἐναλλάξ–enallax, 'alternately', to refer to the warp and weft lying at 90 degrees.

Thus, the creature being lengthy and lazy in character, they expected to master it with nooses and cords. First they went up to it boldly with this in mind, carrying all the necessary equipment prepared;   (6) but when they approached it they were ever more assailed by fear, observing its blazing eye; its tongue licking in all directions; then the exceptionally loud noise it made because of the coarseness of its scales as it went through the trees and rubbed its sides on them; the unnatural size of its teeth; the wild appearance of its mouth; and the surprising stature of its coiled body.   (7) For this reason, losing the colour from their faces in their fear, they nervously put the nooses upon its tail, but the animal, as soon as the rope made contact with its body, turned upon them terrifyingly with a huge blast of breath, reared up above the first man's head, grabs him with its mouth, and began to devour his flesh while he was still alive. It drew the second man to itself with its coil as he ran away, wound itself round him, and began to crush his belly in its grip. The rest, terror-struck, sought safety in flight.

37. (1) Still they did not give up the chase, as the favour and bonus (*they expected*) from the king exceeded the risks of which they had learned in making the attempt. By their passion for their craft, and by cunning, they got the better of that which could scarcely be vanquished by force, by creating a device like this: they prepared a round object woven of stout reeds, similar in shape to lobster-pots but capable by its size and spatial capacity of containing an animal of such bulk.   (2) So they scouted out its lair, the time of its departure for feeding, and that of its returning back. Then, as soon as it set off for its usual pursuit of the other kinds of animals, they built over the existing mouth of its lair with rather large stones and earth, but dug an underground passage near its lair and inserted the woven trap into it opposite the mouth, so that it should be possible for the animal to make its entrance without difficulty.   (3) At the time of the creature's return they got ready archers and slingers, and additionally a large number of horsemen, and moreover trumpeters and other such resources. At the moment when the animal came close to them it lifted up its neck higher than the horsemen, but those gathered together for the hunt dared not approach it, having taken warning from the calamities that had befallen them earlier; but managed to strike it from a distance, with many hands aiming at one large target, and struck fear into the creature through the appearance of the horsemen and the multitude of fierce dogs, not to mention the sound made by the trumpets.

(4) For this reason, as it began to withdraw to its own lair, they closed in upon it just enough not to irritate it further; but when it came close to the passage that had been built over, they made a great noise with their weapons and instilled confusion and fear through the appearance of the crowds of people and the trumpets. The animal was unable to find the entrance; but, made fearful by the onset of the hunters, it took refuge in the mouth constructed nearby.   (5) When the woven trap was being filled up by the unwinding of its coils, certain of the hunters flew towards it before it knew, and before the snake could turn for the exit they laid hold of the (*trap's*) mouth, which was long and craftily made with such rapid action in view. Dragging out the woven trap and putting poles beneath it, they lifted it up quite high.   (6) The animal, cooped up in a confined space against its nature, emitted an extraordinary hissing and, with its teeth, pulled at the reeds enclosing it. As it swayed in every direction it created the expectation in those

carrying it that it was about to jump out of the carefully crafted device containing it; hence, in their terror, they placed the snake on the ground and began stabbing the animal's tail area to draw its attention away from tearing with its teeth to the feeling of pain in those parts.

(7) After transporting it to Alexandria they gave it to the king as gift: a surprising sight, and disbelieved by those who only heard about it. Wearing down the animal's ferocity by lack of food, they gradually rendered it tame, with the result that its growing docility became a matter for wonder. (8) Ptolemy distributed suitable bonuses to the hunters and continued to feed the tamed snake, offering a great and most surprising sight to foreigners who turned up in the kingdom. (9) For this reason, as a snake of such a size has come before the sight of all, it is unworthy to disbelieve the Aithiopes or to assume that what is repeated over and over by them is a fable. For they make it known that snakes of such size are seen about their land that they not only consume cows, bulls, and other creatures of similar size, but even confront elephants in combat.[113] By winding their coils round their legs they impede their natural movement, but then raise their neck above the trunk; they place their head opposite the elephants' eyes, so that with the fiery power of their own eyes they project their lustre in a manner similar to lightning, thus blinding the sight of the elephants; and wrestling them to the ground they eat the flesh of those creatures they have got the better of.[114]

The African Coast of the Red Sea

81 (Diod. 3. 38. 1–5) [79M] (1) We have now thoroughly and adequately examined matters concerning Aithiopia, Trogodytike, and the adjacent land as far as the part that is uninhabited on account of the heat; and also the coast beside the Erythraian sea and the Atlantic open-sea (*pelagos*) that inclines to the south. Now we shall make a description of the part left behind—I refer to the Arabian gulf—partly drawing our material from the royal records (*hypomnēmata*) in Alexandria, and partly by learning from eye-witnesses.[115] ... (4) The gulf designated Arabian has its innermost part opening upon the ocean that lies to the south. Extending for very many stades in length,[116] it has its innermost part defined by the extremities of Arabia and Trogodytike. It has a width at its mouth and its innermost part of around 16 stades, but a run of one day for a long ship from the harbour of Panormos to the mainland opposite. Its greatest width is by Mount Tyrkaios and the island of Maria[117] in a bad (*part of the*) open sea

[113] The theme of pythons fighting elephants was probably of African origin and widespread in antiquity (cf. Hofmann 1970).

[114] Cf. Artem. 98 (Strabo) §16, at location 80c.

[115] Cf. §112. The reference to royal records suggests that Diod. has taken over A.'s wording here. The next words, describing how knowledge of the world was expanded through Roman power down to Diod.'s own time, are omitted.

[116] Ancient estimates of the length of the Red Sea vary widely. Eratosthenes (Strabo 16. 4. 4, C768–9, cf. Roller 2018, 923–4) gave a figure of 14,000 st. (*c*.1,750 mi, *c*.2,820 km) on the basis of the report of Anaxikrates, probably a navigator sent to explore the coasts of Arabia by Alexander. The actual length, however, is 1,380 mi (2,220 km).

[117] Makaria, emended by Müller.

(*pelagos*), given that the mainlands cannot be seen from one another.   (5) From here the breadth continuously draws closer, having its convergence towards the mouth. In many places the coastal sailing of the gulf includes long islands which have narrow straits between them but a strong and violent current.

82. (*a*) (Phot. 456a 33–41) ₈₀ₕ As there are, he says, many wonderful things lying far from the familiar regions, I shall go through those places that are worth recalling.

(456a 35) From Arsinoë,[118] the first thing as one runs along the right-hand mainland is hot springs being forced out through several channels from a high rock into the sea, and having narrow passages. (*The springs*) are not of fresh water but of bitter saltiness and from a source of that nature. Next after the lake is a confluence with the Nile, its channel flowing down through various cavities into the hollowest place.[119]

> (*b*) (Diod. 3. 38. 5–39. 1) 38. (5 *contd*) Such, in outline, is the position of this gulf; but we shall begin from the furthest places at this innermost part, and go through the coastal sailing of the mainlands on each side, and the most notable distinguishing features along them. First we shall take the right-hand part, whose coast the nations of the Trogodytai possess, as far as the desert.
>
> 39. (1) So as people are conveyed from the city of Arsinoë along the right-hand mainland, many waters fall out of the rock into the sea in many places; they have a taste of bitter saltiness.[120]

83. (*a*) (Phot. 456b 1–10) ₈₁ₕ Near the lake, a mountain the colour of red ochre, overlooking a rather large plain, is revealed. It exhibits no special feature, other than that it displays such a colour from the summit of its peak that the eyes of those who stare at it are often damaged. Succeeding this, there follows a great harbour which was previously called Myos Hormos (*Mussel Anchorage*) and was then named Aphrodites (Hormos) (*Aphrodite's Anchorage*).[121] Three islands lie in front of these places; ⟨two⟩ are densely planted with olive-trees, while one is less thickly wooded but nurtures a multitude of the so-called Meleagrides (*guinea-fowl*).

> (*b*) (Diod. 3. 39. 1–2) (1) . . . As one runs past these springs, above a large plain lies a mountain that has the colour of red ochre and injures the sight of those who stare at it for a long time. Under the extremity of the highlands lies a harbour that has a crooked entrance, named Aphrodites (Limen) (*Aphrodite's Harbour*). (2) Beyond this lie three islands, of which two are full of olive-trees and fig-trees, while one is inferior in the quantity of the said trees but has a multitude of the birds named Meleagrides (*guinea-fowl*).[122]

---

[118] Also known as Kleopatris. Arsinoë was named after the wife of Ptolemy II and founded *c.*270/69 at the S end of the canal leading from the Nile to the Heroönpolitan gulf (cf. Cohen 2006, 308–9).

[119] The 'lake' has not been mentioned. 'Flowing down' translates ὑπορρέοντος, suggested for ὑπερθέοντος by Lucarini 2020, 222.

[120] Cf. Artem. 98 (Strabo) §5, at location 82c.

[121] Myos Hormos, modern *Quseir al-Qadim*, was in C1l and the early Principate the principal departure point for ships bound for the Indian Ocean (Roller 2018, 925–6).

[122] Cf. Artem. 98 (Strabo) §5, at location 83c.

84. (*a*) (Phot. 456b 10–30) ₈₂ₕ Adjoining these is a gulf which they call Akathartos (*Uncleansed*). When one has sailed past it, there is an island lying in a midsea position, with a length of around 80 stades, which they call Ophiodes (*Snake Island*).[123] Formerly it abounded in all sorts of serpents, but in our time it is free of these. In this island, he (*Agatharchides*) says, occurs the so-called topaz: this is a transparent stone comparable to glass, which delivers a pleasing look of gold. Those who live on the island, protecting and gathering this stone by royal command, acquire the precious stone in the following way.

(456b 20) During the night, they go round the island in turn, holding bowls of all sizes. The stone in the rocks is overpowered by the light during the daytime, and not clearly seen, being overpowered by the light because of its oppressive power, but when darkness sets in it shines forth on every side in whichever place it exists. The guard who saw it has placed round the glittering object, as a marker, a vessel of the same size as that of the observed phenomenon; then he returns by day and, cutting out a portion of rock of equal breadth to the aforementioned bowl,[124] he hands it over to craftsmen capable of polishing it.

(*b*) (Diod. 3. 39. 3–40. 7) 39. (3) After these places is a fairly large gulf, the one called Akathartos (*Uncleansed*). Beside it is an exceedingly lofty peninsula, across whose neck, being narrow, they convey boats to the sea on the other side. (4) When one has been conveyed past these places, there lies an island that in terms of distance is a midsea one, but in length extends about 80 stades. It is called Ophiodes (*Snake Island*), and in olden times it used to be full of all sorts of terrifying serpents, from which indeed it acquired this designation; but in subsequent times, under the kings in Alexandria, it was so zealously tamed that none of the creatures that previously existed is seen in it any longer. (5) But we must not leave aside the reason for the zeal for taming it: for there is found in this island the so-called topaz, which is a pleasing transparent stone, comparable to glass and presenting a wondrous golden appearance.

(6) For this reason it (*the island*) is kept inaccessible to other people, anyone who sails to it being punished with death by the guards based there. These men, being few in number, have a luckless life: for in order that not a single stone shall be stolen, no boat whatsoever is left on the island, while those sailing past keep their course far from it for fear of the king. And though the provisions conveyed thither quickly run out, others are totally unavailable in the locality. (7) For this reason, whenever only a small amount of food is left, all the people of the village sit and wait for people conveying provisions to sail in; if these are slow to come, they are driven to the extremity of their hopes. (8) The aforementioned stone, occurring in the rocks, is not seen in the daytime because of the oppressive power (*of daylight*), but is overpowered by the light of the sun; but when night

---

[123] *Gazirat Zabarjad* (*St John's I.*), 32 mi (51 km) SE of *Ras Banas* (cf. Wainwright 1946). The 'topaz' is periodotite. The Ptolemies maintained similar administrative control of other islands in the Red Sea (Pliny 6. xxxiv. 169). See now Marcotte 2020.

[124] Following the suggestions ἰσοπλατῆ . . . ⟨σκαφίδι⟩ of Lucarini 2020, 223.

comes on it shines forth in the darkness and is clear from a distance in whatever place it lies.   (9) The island guards, after sharing out the places by lot, watch over them and, as a marker, they place round any stone that is seen a vessel of the same size as that of the glittering stone. Making their rounds in the daytime, they cut out the place in the rock that was marked and hand it over to those who, through their craft, are capable of polishing properly what is handed to them.

3. 40. (1) When one has sailed past these places, many nations of Ichthyophagoi occupy the coast, and also many nomad Trogodytai. Beside these peoples are found mountains of all different sorts, as far as a harbour designated Soterias (*Of Safety*), which got this naming from the first Hellenes to sail to it, who reached safety here.   (2) From these parts the gulf begins to take on a convergence and make a curve towards the region of Arabia. Because of the particular character of the places, it has transpired that the nature of the land and sea are unusual: (3) for the mainland is seen to be low, with no rising ground lying above it on any side, while the sea contains shoals and is not found to exceed 3 fathoms. In colour it is totally green; this, they say, occurs not because the liquids are naturally such, but because of the mass of wrack and seaweed showing under the water.

(4) For oared ships the place is comfortable, rolling its swell from no great distance, and presents an immeasurable quantity of fish to hunt. But ships carrying elephants, sitting deep owing to their weight and heavy-laden with equipment, bring great and fearful dangers to those sailing in them.   (5) For since they run with sails set and often press on in the night because of the force of the winds, they are sometimes shipwrecked by falling against rocks, and sometimes fall onto shoal bars. The sailors are then unable to disembark because the depth is greater than the height of a man, and when, despite working to save the vessel with spars, they achieve nothing, they throw out everything except the food. As even so they fail to gain safety, they fall into great difficulty since there is no island, no cape on the mainland, and no other ship to be seen nearby; for these places are totally inhospitable and have few people being conveyed through them on ships.   (6) More than these evils, the swell in an instant casts up so great a mass of sand against the hull of the ship, and builds it into a mound in a surprising manner, than the area encircling is covered over with it and the vessel is bound to the dry land as if by design.

(7) Those that have fallen upon such a mishap at first complain in a modest way to the unhearing solitude, not having totally despaired of eventual safety; for often the swell of the tide rose up high for such men and, as if it were a god that had appeared, preserved those in extreme danger; but when the aforementioned help from the gods does not ensue, and the available food runs short, the strong ones throw the weaker into the sea so that the remaining essential supplies may hold out, for the few, over a greater length of days. But in the end, having erased all hope from their mind, they are destroyed in a much worse fashion than those who died earlier: for some have surrendered their spirit in an instant to Nature that gave them it; while others, after splitting their death between many sufferings, endure prolonged adversities in meeting the ruin of their life.[125]

---

[125] Cf. Artem. 98 (Strabo) §§5–6, at location 84c.

85. (*a*) (Phot. 456b 31–457a 10) ₈₃H After this point the open sea (*pelagos*) is so shallow that it is measured at no more than 2 fathoms. On all sides it is green, not from the nature of the liquid but from the wrack and seaweed showing through. This is why it contains an uncountable multitude of 'sea-dogs'. For the same reason the said passage becomes well suited to a long ship and to vessels with oars: for it has no waves—rolling its swell from no great distance—and offers unbelievable numbers of fish to hunt. But the evil fate of the elephant ships[126] provokes great pity for the sufferers on the part of those observing it. For the wave has suddenly launched the boats either onto a rock or driven them onto an area of shoal, and made safety unattainable for the crews. Hence at first the crews are seized by great lamentation, but do not despair in expectation of the better outcome, for the tide has saved some men stranded in this way when it lifts them off with great masses (*of water*) that swell up suddenly out of the sea. But when the available food runs low they suffer myriad misfortunes and eventually are all consumed either by hunger or, unable to bear the protracted hunger, by the sword, or simply by throwing themselves into the sea.

> (*b*) (Diod. 3. 40. 8–9) (8) The vessels so piteously robbed of their passengers endure for a long time, gradually being covered over on every side, as if they were cenotaphs. They still have their masts and yard-arms raised on high, moving those who see them from afar to pity and sympathy for those who have perished. For it is the decree of the king that they should leave such mishaps of the dead to signal to sailors those places that engender destruction.
>
> (9) A story has been handed down among the Ichthyophagoi who live nearby which keeps preserved the rumour among their ancestors: that on the occasion of a strong ebb-tide the whole area of the gulf that gives the impression of looking green was turned into land, as the sea fell away into opposed parts and the dry land in the depths was revealed; then an extraordinarily high tide came back in, and put back the strait in its previous arrangement.[127]

86. (*a*) (Phot. 457a 11–30) ₈₄H He says that the parts up to the Tauroi (*Bulls*)[128] and Ptolemaïs[129] have been investigated, but further than these it (*the sea*) undergoes an unusual transition. For the parts beyond no longer lie to the south, but turn ever more towards the east, and throw shadows onto the northern part lying opposite for up to two hours. Moreover, the area is inundated by rivers which reveal their sources to be from the so-called Psebaia mountains. The part of the land extending into the interior is filled with elephants, rhinoceroses, bulls, and pigs; but the part coming down to the strait is all crowded with islands, by nature unproductive but full of birds of unrecorded kinds.

---

[126] No description of the elephant transports survives, although the reference to them sailing with 'sails set' suggests that they were not galleys. A letter of 224 BC indicates that facilities for building and repairing elephant transports existed at Berenike (*P. Petrie* II 40 [a], III 53 [g]).

[127] Cf. Artem. 98 (Strabo) §7, at location 85c.   [128] Mountains or (as in *b*) promontories.

[129] Ptolemaïs of the Hunts, probably modern *Aqiq*, was a self-supporting settlement founded by Ptolemy II *c.*270 to serve as a base for hunting elephants (Cohen 2006, 341–3; Roller 2018, 927).

(457a 23) As to the area beyond here, the sea is deep and navigable, but contains monsters so large as to distress anyone that sees them; however, no one has actually expired other than those who have involuntarily fallen onto the back-fins of one through not knowing about the said animals. For they cannot even boldly chase sailors, since the animals' eyes are blinded whenever they make their face appear out of the sea.

(b) (Diod. 3. 41. 1–4) $_{85M}$ (1) From these places the coastal sailing from Ptolemaïs to the Tauroi promontories was told earlier when we reported the elephant hunts of Ptolemy.[130] From Tauroi, however, the coast turns back towards the east. At the summer solstice the shadows fall southwards until the second hour, contrary to what is the case among us.   (2) The land also contains rivers flowing from the mountains designated Psebaian; and is divided up by large plains bearing unbelievably large mallows, nasturtiums, and palm-trees. It also produces fruits of all kinds with a mild taste and are unknown among us.   (3) The land stretching into the interior is full of elephants, wild bulls, lions, and many other kinds of fierce animals. The strait is divided up by islands producing no cultivated fruits but species of birds that are special and wonderful in appearance.   (4) The next area of sea is totally deep and bears all kinds of monsters of surprising size; they do not, however, trouble humans unless a person involuntarily falls onto the back-fins of one of them: for they are unable to pursue sailors, given that during their emergence from the sea their eyes are blinded by the light around the sun.

These parts, then, of the Trogodytike are the most extreme known; they are circumscribed by the peaks that people name the Psebaia.

The Arabian Coast of the Red Sea

87. (Diod. 3. 42. 1–4) (1) Taking up again the other part of the opposite coast, that inclining towards Arabia, we shall go through it, beginning from the innermost part (of the gulf). This is named Poseidion, because Ariston founded an altar to Poseidon Pelagios after being sent by Ptolemy to spy out the part of Arabia lying beside the ocean.   (2) Next after its innermost recess is a coastal place highly esteemed by the locals because of the benefit gained from it. It is named Phoinikōn (Palm-grove) and has an exceedingly fruitful quantity of this plant, unusually good for enjoyment and luxury.   (3) All the nearby land is short of spring-water and, because of its inclination towards the south, has a fiery character. Hence the tree-rich place, lying in the parts least inhabited by humans yet providing food, has understandably been treated as sacred by the barbarians. For no small number of springs and streams of water appear in it, which are in no way inferior to snow in coldness;

---

[130] This reference, also preserved in a slightly different form by Photios, is to a section of one of the lost books of On the Erythraean Sea in which the Ptolemaic elephant hunting programme was described. Artemidoros, as preserved by Strabo (16. 4. 7–10, C770–2), inserted the geographical portions of Agatharchides' account of Ptolemaic elephant hunting in his paraplous of the African coast of the Red Sea. Diodoros' cross-reference here should refer back to 3. 18. 4 (§41 (b) above), 'where, however, there is no mention of either Ptolemaïs or the Promontories of the Tauri' (Oldfather 1935, 207); an indication of how Diod. has compressed information from his first-hand reading of Agatharch. Strabo, however (16. 4. 7–8, C770–1, part of B. 3 below), does mention Ptolemaïs and the Tauroi, evidently drawing on the same lost passage of Agatharch.

these make the areas of ground on either side green and totally pleasant. (4) There is also an altar of solid stone, old in years and bearing an inscription in ancient, unknown letters. A man and a woman supervise the sanctuary, holding their sacred position for life. The people dwelling here are long-lived and make their sleeping-places in the trees for fear of the animals.[131]

88. (Phot. 457a 31–3) _{86H} The area that can be seen inland from the Phoinikōn (*Palm Grove*), he says, is occupied by a variety of high rocks, but below the parts running down to the sea lies a long, narrow beach.

89. (*a*) (457a 33–457b 2) _{87H} Connected to the said coast is a place they gave the name Nessa (*Duck*) from the profusion of that creature. This Nessa lies close to an extremely well-wooded promontory; if viewed in a straight line, it extends towards the so-called Petra (*Rock*)[132] and to Palaistine, to which the Gerrhaioi,[133] Minaioi,[134] and all the Arabs occupying settlements nearby bring their frankincense, so it is said, and their loads of items connected with fragrances from up-country.

> (*b*) (Diod. 3. 42. 5) When one sails past the Phoinikōn, there is an island near a promonto-ry of the mainland named Phōkōn Nesos (*Seals' Island*) from the creatures that have their quarters on it. For so great a multitude of these animals lingers in these places that those who see them are in wonder. The promontory of the island that lies in front of it also lies opposite the so-called Petra (*Rock*) and Palaistine; for it is to this land, as the story goes, that the Gerrhaioi and Minaioi bring frankincense and other perfume-related cargoes from the so-called Upper Arabia.[135]

> 90. (Diod. 3. 43. 1–5) _{88M} (1) The next coastal area[136] was occupied by Maranitai in olden times, but after that by Garindaneis, neighbours of theirs. They took the land in some such way as this: in the Phoinikōn that was mentioned above, there was a quadrennial festival to which those dwelling round about used to come in order to make sacrifices of well-bred camels to the gods of the sanctuary, and to convey to their fatherlands some of the waters from it, because the story had been handed down that this drink engendered good health for those who consumed it. (2) When for these reasons the Maranitai came down to the festival, the Garindaneis put to the sword those left behind in their land, while those returning from the festival they ambushed and destroyed. Having emptied the land of settlers, they divided into plots the plains, which produced crops and abundant pasture for their flocks. (3) This coast has few harbours and is divided by frequent large moun-tains, from which, with its varied colours of all kinds, it offers a wonderful sight to those sailing past it.

[131] Cf. Artem. 98 (Strabo) §18, at location 87b.
[132] Petra, located at *Selah* in Jordan, was the religious and political centre of the Nabataeans.
[133] Gerrha was located in E. Arabia and was the centre for the trans-shipment of goods from the Persian gulf, reaching the Mediterranean in Syria or at Gaza in Palestine. Cf. Groom 1981, 194–7, for the role of Gerrha in the incense trade.
[134] The kingdom of Ma'in in Yemen controlled the caravan routes through which incense was brought to the Mediterranean at Gaza from the C4 until its conquest by Saba *c*.120 BC.
[135] Cf. Artem. 98 (Strabo) §18, at location 89c.   [136] Of the Sinai peninsula.

(4) When one has sailed past this land, the Laianites gulf (*i.e. Ailanites; gulf of Aqaba*] comes next, which is surrounded by many villages of the Arabs designed Nabataians. These occupy a large part of the coast, and no small part of the land extending into the interior. They have a people whose number is too great to tell, and herds of domestic animals in unbelievable multitudes.   (5) In olden times they went on observing justice and being content with the food they gained from their animals; but later, when the kings[137] from Alexandria made the strait navigable to traders, they began to attack those who were shipwrecked, constructed pirate ships, and plundered sailors, imitating the wildness and law-breaking of the Tauroi of the Pontos.[138] After this, on being captured in the open sea (*pelagioi*) by four-banked ships, they were fittingly punished.[139]

91. (*a*) (Phot. 457b 3–14) [89H] After the so-called Laianites gulf (*he says*), about which the Arabs dwell, is the country of the Bythemaneis, which is extensive and takes the form of a plain all well-watered and deep (*in vegetation*) though only with dog's-tooth grass, lucerne, and man-sized lotus. The entirety of its produce is limited to this; it has no other crops. Hence there are many wild camels in the land, many herds of deer and gazelles, many flocks of sheep, and a number of mules and cattle too great to tell. With these blessings is interwoven a contrasting evil, for the country also supports a multitude of lions, wolves, and leopards, so that the natural advantage of the land is the reason for its inhabitants' ill-luck.

(*b*) (Diod. 3. 43. 6–7) (6) After these places lies a land that is well-watered plain and, because of the springs flowing through it in all directions, produces dog's-tooth grass, lucerne, and also man-sized lotus. Because of the mass and quality of the pasture, it produces not only a multitude of herd animals of all kinds, too great to tell, but also wild camels and even deer and gazelles.   (7) Against the multitude of creatures reared there, herds of lions, wolves, and leopards come frequently from the desert. Against them the herdsmen are obliged, both day and night, to do battle with animals on behalf of their flocks. Thus the good fortune of the land is a cause of ill fortune to its inhabitants, because Nature overall gives to humans, together with good things, things that do harm.[140]

92. (*a*) (Phot. 457b 15–19) [90H] After this succession of shores is a gulf orientated into the heart of the land, not less than 500 stades deep. Those dwelling within the gulf are called Batmizomaneis and are hunters of creatures of the mainland.

(*b*) (Diod. 3. 44. 1–2) (1) When one has sailed past these plains, there follows a gulf of a surprising nature. For it is orientated into the heart of the land, but in length it extends to 500 stades. It is shut in by cliffs of wondrous size, and has a crooked mouth that is

---

[137] The most probable date for the campaign against Nabataean pirates is during the reign of Ptolemy II (285–246).

[138] A non-Greek people, whose home was in the S. Crimea, and who were notorious as pirates and for their supposed custom of sacrificing captured Greeks to their goddess known as the Parthenos, whom Greeks identified with Artemis. The most influential ancient depiction of them is that found in Euripides' drama *Iphigenia in Tauris*.

[139] Cf. Artem. 98 (Strabo) §18, at location 90b.   [140] Cf. ibid. 91c.

hard to escape from, since a rock projecting into the sea occupies the entrance, so that it is possible neither to sail into the gulf nor to sail out.   (2) During the onset of the current and changes in the wind, the waves falling onto the rocky shore make churning, rough water in every direction around the projecting rock. Those occupying the land by the gulf, named Banizomeneis, gain their food by hunting and by eating the flesh of land creatures. A most holy sanctuary has been founded there, very much esteemed by all Arabs.[141]

93. (*a*) (Phot. 457b 19–24) ₉₁ₕFollowing the said land are three islands forming several harbours, of which they call the first one the Sacred Isle of Isis, the second Soukabya, and the third Salydo. All are deserted and shaded by olive-trees, not the kind that occurs among us but the ones growing in those places.

> (*b*) (Diod. 3. 44. 3) Next after the aforementioned coast three islands lie off it, forming several harbours. Of these the first is reported to be sacred to Isis and is deserted, but has stone foundations of old houses and standing stones incised with barbarian letters. Similarly, the others are deserted; but all are densely covered with olive-trees different from those among us.[142]

94. (*a*) (Phot. 457b 25–31) ₉₂ₕ After the offshore islands it is possible to see a long, stony shore; the land belongs to the Thamoudenoi Arabs.[143] The coastal sailing along it amounts to more than 1,000 stades and is the hardest of all, for there is (*nothing,*) neither a harbour with good anchorage (*limēn euormos*) nor a roadstead at anchor (*salos ep' ankyras*), no sheltering gulf, no sort of breakwater as an urgent refuge to receive the seafarer.

> (*b*) (Diod. 3. 44. 4) (4) ₉₃ₘ After these islands a shore with cliffs lies beside one, which is difficult to sail beside for around 1,000 stades, for no harbour or roadstead (*salos*) is available to mariners, and no mole capable of offering sailors in difficulties the run-in that they need.[144]
>
> 95. (3. 44. 4–45. 1) 44. (4 *contd*)A mountain lies beside this (*sea*), which has sheer rocks around its summit that are terrifyingly high, but by its feet are sharp reefs densely clustered in the sea, and behind them ravines that have been undercut and are crooked.   (5) As these have been bored through into one another and the sea has some depth, the waves, now breaking, now rushing back, emit a noise similar to loud thunder. When the waves are dashed upon the great rocks they stand up high and create a wondrous quantity of foam; and when they are swallowed in the hollows they present a terrifying convulsion so that people who involuntarily go close to these places virtually die before their time through fear.   (6) This coast is held by the Arabs called Thamoudenoi.

---

[141] Cf. ibid. 92c.   [142] Cf. ibid. 93c.
[143] From the C5 BC to C5 AD, the Thamoud were the head of a confederation centred in the N. Hejaz, but whose territory extended into the interior of Arabia, where they controlled a number of towns.
[144] Cf. Artem. 98 (Strabo) §18, at location 94c.

The next part is occupied by a rather large gulf, off which lie scattered islands with an appearance like the so-called Echinades. After this coast there follow sand-dunes of immeasurable length and breadth, of a black colour. (7) After these appears a peninsula with the finest harbour among those recorded in histories, named Charmouthas; for under an extraordinary mole orientated towards the west (*Zephyros*) is a gulf not only wonderful in shape but also superior in value by far to others. For beside it extends a thickly covered mountain forming a circle on all sides for 100 stades. It has an entrance of two *plethra* (*c.200 feet*) and offers a calm harbour for 2,000 ships. (8) More than these features, it is exceedingly well-watered since a rather large river flows out into it; and in the middle it has a well-watered island which is even capable of accommodating garden plots. All in all, it is most comparable to the harbour of Carthage designated Kothon, about which we shall attempt to go through its virtues one by one at the appropriate time. A multitude of fish gathers in it from the Great Sea because of the calmness and sweetness of the waters flowing into it.

45. (1) When one sails past these places, five mountains, distant from one another, extend up high and have summits converging at a breast-shaped rock, resulting in an image similar to the pyramids in Egypt. Next is a gulf of circular form surrounded by great promontories. Midway along its diameter stands a trapezium-shaped hill upon which three temples of wondrous height have been founded for gods unknown to the Hellenes, but revered pre-eminently by the local people.[145]

96. (*a*) (Phot. 457b 31–5) $_{94H}$ After these places, though not coming immediately but after some others, extends an extremely well-watered shore and the mountain named Laimos. The length of the circumference it displays is too great to tell, but it is girdled with thickets of all kinds of woodland.

(*b*) (Diod. 3. 45. 3) After these places extends a watery shore enclosed by freshwater streams from springs. Along it is a mountain named Chabinos, densely covered with all sorts of thickets.

97. (*a*) (Phot. 457b 36–458a 5) $_{95H}$ The neighbouring area to the mountainous tract (*he says*) is occupied by the Debai; some are nomads, some farmers. A river runs through the middle of the land; it is tripartite in form and brings down gold-dust, and thus has such a conspicuous gleam[146] that the mud that gathers beside its outlets glitters from afar.[147] Those inhabiting the place are inexperienced in such work, but are exceedingly hospitable—though not to all people but to those who pass over[148] from the Peloponnese and Boiotia, on account of a certain legendary story about Herakles.

---

[145] Cf. ibid. 95b.   [146] Reading διάλαμψιν for δαψίλειαν with Lucarini 2020, 223.
[147] The reference is to the region near the modern Saudi Arabian port of *al-Qunfundha* in the SW portion of the Arabian peninsula. That gold from this region was already known in Egypt during the reign of Ptolemy II is suggested by the reference to gold from Arabian mountains in the *Stones* segment of the recently discovered book of poems by Poseidippos (*P. Mil. Vogl.* viii. 309, no. 7; trans. in Nisetich 2005, 18 no. 7; also discussed in the same volume by Bing 2005, 125–7).
[148] Reading διαβάλλουσι for διεκβάλλουσι with Lucarini 2020, 223.

(*b*) (Diod. 3. 45. 3–5) (3 *contd*) The dry land next to the mountain land is occupied by the Arabs called Debai. (4) These people breed camels and employ the usefulness of this creature for all the greatest things in life. For they fight against their enemies from them, and by organizing the transportation of their cargoes on their backs they easily accomplish everything. They drink the milk of these animals to feed themselves, and travel over the whole land upon racing camels. (5) Down through the middle of their land runs a river that brings down so much visible gold-dust that at its outlets the mud glitters as it is carried along. The locals are totally inexperienced in the working of gold, but are hospitable—though not to all those who arrive, but only to those from Boiotia and the Peloponnese on account of some old kinship of Herakles with their nation, which they report they have received from their ancestors in story form.[149]

98. (*a*) (Phot. 458a 6–27) ₉₆ₕ The neighbours of these people are the Alilaioi and the Kasandreis (?);[150] they have a country wholly unlike the aforementioned ones. For the atmosphere is not chilled, dry, or torrid but exhibits soft, thick cloud from which seasonal rains and storms arise even during summer. The greater part of the land is extremely productive but not all of it benefits from cultivation, the people being rather inexperienced; though by excavating for gold in the flaking underground passages[151] they find a lot of it: not the kind that is melted from gold-dust using knowledge and skill, but the spontaneously occurring kind that, because of this feature, is called 'fireless' by the Hellenes. Its slightest form is the size of a fruit-stone, the middling size that of a medlar stone, and the largest such as to be compared to walnuts. Piercing a hole in it, they wear it round their wrists and round their necks, alternating with translucent stones. They also transport it to their neighbours, selling it cheaply: for they take bronze for three times the weight of gold, iron for twice the weight of gold. Silver has the worth of ten portions of gold, the value being adjusted according to ubiquity or shortage.[152] In these matters, life always looks not to nature but to need.

(*b*) (Diod. 3. 45. 6–8) (6) The next land is settled by Arabs, the Alilaioi and Gasandoi. It is not fiery as those nearby are, but is often covered over by soft, thick clouds; from these arise heavy rains and seasonal storms, and they make the summertime temperate. The land is very productive and superior in virtue, but does not enjoy the possible level of management through the people's lack of experience. (7) Finding gold in natural underground passages beneath the earth, they gather a lot of it—not the kind that is melted from gold-dust but the self-generated kind known from this circumstance as 'fireless'. In terms of size, the slightest form is similar to a fruit-stone, but the largest not far short of a walnut. (8) They wear it round their wrists and round their throats, pierced and alternating with translucent stones. As this species of gold occurs everywhere among them,

---

[149] Possibly suggested to Greeks by the similarity between Debai and Thebat (*Thebes*). Cf. Artem. 98 (Strabo) §18, at location 97c.

[150] Or Γασανδοί as in Diod.? Müller notes they are Κασσανῖται in Ptol. Burstein adds *Gasani* from Pliny and links to *Wadi Ghazan*.

[151] As at §29.

[152] Yemen is, in fact, poor in iron deposits. The statement at §98b that the trade was on an equal basis appears to be an arbitrary modification of A.'s text by Diod.

while bronze and iron are scarce, they exchange these goods with traders on a basis of equality.[153]

99. (*a*) (Phot. 458a 27–b 15) ₉₇ₕ Adjoining these men are the Karbai, occupying the mainland; then comes a harbour with deep water close inshore, at which several springs arise.

(458a 29) The next neighbours are the race of the Sabaioi, the largest of those in Arabia and enjoying all kinds of blessings.[154] For their country bears all things that, among us, support life, while the inhabitants' bodies are rather remarkable. They have provided themselves with multitudes of domestic animals too great to tell. A scent overhangs the whole coast, creating for those that come there a divine delight surpassing words: for alongside the sea itself grow much balsam, cassia,[155] and a certain other plant that, when fresh, possesses the sweetest joy for the eyes, but becomes rapidly faded as it ages, so that the virtue of the plant is obscured before the power of the species can be transmitted to us.

(458b 1) Over the interior continuous, large thickets stand in rows:[156] for lofty trees rise up—myrrh and frankincense,[157] additionally cinnamon, palm, reed, and other such (*species*)—so that no word can convey the reality that is presented to those who have a chance to examine the species with their senses. It does not give the stored-up, old enjoyment of spices, or that which is detached from the solid thing that gave it birth and nourished it, but that which flowers in its divine and perfect condition and emits the wondrous thing through its own natural characteristics. Thus many reach a point where they forget mortal blessings and suppose they are receiving ambrosia, casting around for a name for the phenomenon to fit its overwhelming character.

(*b*) (Diod. 3. 46. 1–5) (1) After those peoples come those named Karbai, and after these the Sabaioi, the most populous of the Arabic nations. They possess the so-called Eudaimon Arabia (*Fortunate Arabia*),[158] which bears the majority of what, among us, are good things, and brings forth a multitude of all kinds of animals, too great to tell. A natural fragrance occupies it all, because almost all the first-rate scents grow without interruption across the land. (2) For by the coast grow the so-called balsam, cassia, and a certain other plant of a particular nature: this, when it is fresh, offers the most gentle joy to the eyes, but when it has aged it becomes rapidly faded. (3) In the interior there are well-grown thickets in which are great trees of frankincense and myrrh, and in addition to these palm, reed, cinnamon, and the others that have a similar fragrance to them. For it is not possible to count

---

[153] Cf. Artem. 98 (Strabo) §18, at location 98c.

[154] Until C1 A D the kingdom of Saba (Biblical Sheba) in mod. Yemen was the dominant state in S. Arabia. Its wealth was derived from its central role in the caravan trade in incense to the Mediterranean.

[155] Cassia and cinnamon are both products of trees of the laurel family, and are actually native to S. and E. Asia, not Arabia as was believed by ancient geographers, probably because they were transshipped to the Mediterranean by caravans from S. Arabia.

[156] Reading στοιχοῦσι for στείχουσι with Lucarini 2020, 223.

[157] Myrrh and frankincense are gum resins gathered from shrubs of the genus *Commiphora* and trees of the genus *Boswellia* respectively, both of which are found in Arabia and NE Africa.

[158] The ancient term for SW Arabia, especially modern Aden.

the properties of each or their natures, on account of their multitude and the exceedingly strong scent gathered from them all. (4) For the fragrance appears to be a divine thing and beyond words, meeting and stirring each person's senses.

It even causes those sailing beside this place, though they be far removed from the dry land, not to be deprived of such pleasure. For in the summertime, when the wind blows off the land, it happens that the fragrances exhaled by the myrrh-trees and other such ones permeate to the nearby parts of the sea. For it does not have the laid-up, old character of spices as they are among us, but the fresh power that is in perfect condition in the flower and permeates to the most refined points of the sense. (5) For as the breeze bears the efflux of the most fragrant (*plants*), and falls upon those sailing towards the coast in gentle intensity, and moreover a healthy and special mixture of the best ones. For neither has the fruit been cut and thus exhaled its own perfection; nor has it undergone storage in alien vessels; but is at its most youthful hour, presenting the pure shoot of its divine nature. Thus those partaking of its particular quality believe that they are enjoying the legendary ambrosia, because they can find no other suitable designation for the overwhelming character of the fragrance.[159]

100. (*a*) (Phot. 458b 15–24) 98H All over the thickets of the fragrant trees there occurs a species of snake, the most unusual of all. It is as if Fortune begrudged abundant successes and interwove the harmful with the good in order that no one, approaching the height of insolence like a Titan and despising the divine, should adopt an attitude of pride over their success in relation to good things, but rather that they should be educated by the juxtaposition and memory of contrasting things. The species of snake has a purple colour, a length roughly that of a finger-to-thumb span, and a bite that is incurable if it makes one bleed above the hips. It strikes its blow while swaying high in the air.

> (*b*) (Diod. 3. 47. 1–2) (1) But not complete or free from envy did Fortune make the prosperity with which she endowed these people. Rather, to such great gifts as these she yoked a harmful thing that will warn those who, through a succession of good things, become accustomed to despise the gods. (2) For around the most fragrant thickets exists a multitude of snakes; they have a purple colour, the length of a finger-to-thumb span. They inflict bites that are totally incurable; and they bite while jumping towards one, and while swaying up high[160] they make the skin bleed.[161]

101. (*a*) (Phot. 458b 24–39) 99H Among these Sabaians the scent of the fragrant trees is sharpest but the pleasure incomplete: for the uninterrupted experience from childhood moves the sense less and renders it duller, no alteration occurring in their lifestyle. Moreover, they are unable to train their life so that it is equably tranquil, since their body is perfused by an undiluted, incisive force which makes porous[162] the appropriate

---

[159] Cf. Artem. 98 (Strabo) §19, at location 99c.
[160] Reading παλλόμενοι as in the equivalent passage of Phot., rather than ἁλλόμενοι.
[161] Cf. Artem. 98 (Strabo) §19, at location 100c.
[162] Reading ἀραίουσης for ἀγούσης with Lucarini 2020, 224.

level of congestion so as to drive it to the utmost lassitude. At that point, by fumigating for a short time with pitch and goatsbeard, they use such substances to remove the strongly fragrant excess of the influence and, by thus combining it with a substance that appears to give pain, they somewhat restrain the harmful effect of the pleasure. Thus every natural advantage, if governed by moderation and right order, moves life forward; but when deprived of commensurability and due season, it does not make its possession beneficial.

> (b) (Diod. 3. 47. 3) A particular thing occurs among the locals concerning those weakened in body by chronic disease. Since their body is perfused by an undiluted, incisive substance and the aggregation of particles is concentrated in the pore, a lassitude ensues that is hard to remedy. For this reason they fumigate such persons with pitch and goatsbeard, militating against the excess of the fragrance with contrary substances. For beauty, moderated by quantity and right order, assists and delights humans; but when it misses proportionality and the appropriate season, it causes its gift to be of no benefit.[163]

102. (a) (Phot. 458b 39–459a 8) $_{100H}$ The town of the Sabaioi, displaying the appellation of the whole nation, lies on a not very large mountain and is by far the finest of those in Arabia. It is called Sabas.[164] The man who is king of the whole nation receives a privilege from the populace that is, on the one hand, full of honour but, on the other, a very poor lot: full of honour, in that he gives orders to many people and does what he wants according to his judgement and without responsibility; poor, in that, on taking over the role of superintendent, he cannot even come back out of the palace. If he disobeys, he suffers stoning at the hands of everyone in accordance with an ancient oracular response. So his superiority is harmful to him.

> (b) (Diod. 3. 47. 4) (4) The mother-city of this nation is the one they call Sabai, and is founded on a mountain. They have kings who succeed one another by birthright;[165] to them the masses allot honours mixed with both goods and evils. For they appear to have a blessed life, as they give orders to everyone and undergo no accounting of their deeds; but they are thought unlucky in so far as they are not permitted ever to come out from the palace. If they disobey, they suffer stoning at the hands of the mob in accordance with some ancient oracular response.[166]

103. (Phot. 459a 8–25) $_{101H}$ Among the men, those concerned with spending their time in lingering at home scarcely behave more valiantly than the female sex, being feminized by continuous leisure. The other men practise everything relating to war, work the entire land, and travel from the house by employing their rather large rafts. Among other things, they especially traffic the fragrant fruit growing away from the sea which

---

[163] Cf. Artem. 98 (Strabo) §19, at location 101c.
[164] The correct form is Sabai, as preserved by Diod.
[165] A. may have been correcting Eratosthenes, who, according to Strabo (16. 4. 3, C768), maintained that their kings succeeded by adoption from within specific social groups.
[166] Cf. Artem. 98 (Strabo) §19, at location 102c.

in Arabic is called *larimna*; it possesses the most fragrance of all the incenses; this species is said to prevail against bodily illness in general.[167] As the country bears no other wood, they are forced to burn cinnamon and cassia for their daily needs and for the remaining necessities of life: so inequitably has Fortune shared her possessions, granting to some a lack of crucial things, to others a multitude of them. More than a few of the Sabaioi also use leather conveyances, the tide teaching the use of them, even though they pass their time in luxury.[168]

104. (*a*) (459a 25–b 5) [102H] No race appears to be more prosperous than the Sabaioi and the Gerrhaioi, who dispense anything from Asia and Europe that falls into the class of specialities. It is these people that have made Ptolemy's Syria rich in gold.[169] It is they that have built up profitable trade for the Phoenicians' love of work, and ten thousand other things. Their extravagance exists not only in wonderful metalwork and different varieties of drinking-cups, but also in the scale of their couches and tripods, and includes the superiority of the other items that are present at home among us, since many of these people, it seems likely, have obtained a kingly level of provision. He says they have made numerous gilded and silver columns for themselves; moreover, their ceilings and doors are distinguished by jewelled drinking-bowls set close; similarly, the intercolumniations make a fine sight. All in all, the degree by which their fortunes surpass those of others is vast. Well, these things are reported about their life-style down to our own times. But if they did not dwell in a place far distant from those who turn[170] their (*military*) forces in all directions, these lords of their own mansions would instead subsist as managers of others' goods; for indolence is incapable of ensuring freedom for any significant period of time.

(*b*) (Diod. 3. 47. 5–8) (5) This nation surpasses not only the neighbouring Arabs, but even all other people, in wealth and in one luxury after another. For in the exchanges and sales of cargoes, among all people who practise trade for the sake of the silver gained from exchanges they take away the highest price for the slightest amounts. (6) For this reason, since they have not been plundered for long ages because of their remoteness, and since a mass of both gold and silver has flooded over them—especially at Sabai, in which lies the palace—they have worked vessels of all kinds in silver and gold, silver-footed couches and tripods, and other furniture of unbelievable luxury: colonnaded courts with mighty columns, some gilded, others bearing silvered images on their capitals. (7) Having decorated their ceilings and doors with jewelled drinking-bowls set close, they have made the whole construction of their houses, feature by feature, a source of wonder for its luxuries: for they created some parts from silver and gold, others from ivory and the most magnificent stones, or from other things most valued among people. (8) But these people

---

[167] This last comment refers only to *larimna* (Henry).

[168] Cf. Artem. 98 (Strabo) §19, at location 103b.

[169] Since the Ptolemies lost control of Koile Syria, essentially ancient Palestine, Phoenicia, and S. Syria, in the fifth Syrian war (200–197 BC), A.'s characterization of the area as 'Ptolemy's Syria' suggests that he used a C3 source for his information on the incense trade.

[170] Reading τρεπόντων for στρεφόντων with Lucarini 2020, 224.

also enjoyed unshaken prosperity through many periods because they are totally alienated from those who, because of their own avarice, regard another's wealth as Hermes' gift to themselves.[171]

105. (a) (Phot. 459b 6–14) ₁₀₃ₕ Alongside this land the sea looks white, like a river, so that one is truly astonished as to the cause of this phenomenon. Beside the land are prosperous islands[172] in which the cattle are all white, but horns do not grow on any of the females. In these islands it is possible to see trading ships from adjoining lands lying at anchor, mostly from where Alexander established his naval station beside the river Indos, but not a few from Persis, Karmania, and all the neighbouring lands.

(b) (Diod. 3. 47. 8–9) (8 contd) . . . The sea beside these people looks white in colour, so that people wonder at the surprising feature and search for the cause of what oc-curs. (9) Prosperous islands lie near here, with unfortified towns in which all the do-mesticated animals have a white colour; and on their females no horn grows at all. Traders sail into these islands from all directions, but especially from Potana,[173] which Alexander founded beside the river Indos, wishing to have a naval station upon the coast beside the ocean.

So concerning this land and those dwelling in it, we shall be content with what we have said.

106. (a) (Phot. 459b 15–23) ₁₀₄ₕ Among these people, wondrous things take place in the heavens, including what occurs around the (Great) Bear. For from (the month of) Maimakterion that is observed by the Athenians,[174] none of the seven stars makes an appearance until the first watch; in Poseideon until the second; and so on in the succeeding months. Of the other stars, the planets are invisible, while some stars have greater weight and others do not make their settings and risings at the established times.

(b) (Diod. 3. 48. 1–2) (1) But we must not leave out the surprising things seen in the heav-ens in these places. Most wondrous is what is reported to occur around the Bear, which creates great uncertainty among those travelling on ships. For from the month that the Athenians call Maimakterion, they say none of the seven stars in the Bear is seen until the first watch, in Poseideon until the second, and little by little during the successive months they become impossible for those travelling on ships to observe. (2) And of the others, (they say) some of those that are named planets are bigger than among us, while others do not make the same risings and settings.

107. (a) (Phot. 459b 23–460a 7) ₁₀₅ₕ In the places beyond Ptolemaïs, they say, the ap-pearance of the sun is unique and altered. First of all, whereas in our region we see

---

[171] Cf. Artem. 98 (Strabo) §19, at location 104c.

[172] Probably the island of Socotra. 'Prosperous islands' is probably derived from Sanskrit *Sukhatarad-vipa*, 'The Most Pleasant Island' (cf. Basham 1968, 230). The discovery of over 200 graffiti in the Hoq cave on Socotra in Greek, Sabaean, but mostly in Prakrit is clear evidence of Socotra's role in the trade between the Red Sea and India (Evers 2017, 134–42).

[173] The reference is to the port of Patala, near mod. *Hyderabad*, which Alexander founded in 325.

[174] Fifth month of the Athenian calendar, approx. November.

light without the sun for a long time at dawn, followed by sunrise, this is not so. Rather, while the dark night[175] is present, the sun suddenly has shone out, and day never comes before one sees the sun. Second, the sun as it comes up appears from the middle of the open sea (*pelagos*). Third, as it does so it looks exactly like the fieriest coal, but throws out great sparks: some into the circular shape of the shining body, others outside it. Fourth, they say the sun does not have a disc-shaped form, but is at first like a wide column, its extremities giving a slightly fatter impression as if it were a head. Fifth, at this point no beam or ray shines upon either the earth or the sea until the first hour, and it is a fire without light in the dark; but when the second hour commences, the whole star rises up and is rendered shield-shaped, casting the impression and illumination of this form upon the earth and the open sea (*pelagos*) in such an unusual and fiery manner that the exceedingly remarkable extents of both are believed to be vast. Sixth, in the evening, they say, the contrary change is observed in the sun: for after it shows that it has sunk beneath the earth, it subsequently shines for no less than three hours; they believe that this is the most enjoyable time of day in the region where they dwell.

> (*b*) (Diod. 3. 48. 2–5) (2 *contd*) . . . And the sun does not, as among us, begin to emit light shortly before its own rising, but when it is still dark night it appears and shines out with surprising suddenness. (3) Hence in those places the day never begins before the sun has been seen. They also say that when it appears from the middle of the open sea (*pelagos*) it is seen to be similar to the most fiery coal and to throw out great sparks. In form it does not appear conical, as we believe it to be, but comparable to a pillar with a slightly thicker appearance at its head. In addition, it creates neither brightness nor rays until the first hour, but an unshining fire appears in the darkness. When the second begins, however, it becomes shield-shaped and casts a sheer, exceedingly fiery light. (4) At its setting, the contrary events occur in regard to it: for it seems to watchers to light up the heavens with unusual rays for not less than two hours, or—as Agatharchides of Knidos wrote—three. (*They say*) this period is most pleasurable to the locals, as the heat is decreased by the setting of the sun.

> 108. (3. 48. 5) ₁₀₆M As for the winds, the Zephyroi (*westerlies*) and Libes (*SW winds*), as well as the Argestai (*NW winds*) and Euroi (*east winds*), blow just as they do among other peoples; but the Notoi (*south winds*) neither blow in Aithiopia nor are known of at all. But in Trogodytike and Arabia they are exceedingly hot, so that they set forests on fire and bring lassitude to the bodies of those who try to take refuge in the shade within their huts. The Boreas (*north wind*), however, could justly be thought the best, permeating to every place in the inhabited world and remaining cold.

109. (Phot. 460a 8–22) ₁₀₇H This writer (*Agatharchides*), speaking of the tides, offers different causes but discounts all of them as containing no truth. 'It is easy to see that all these (*ideas*) contain drivel and can be shamed into silence; they have grasped nothing that could offer help in the said (*inquiry*).' Next, after adding other words in the same sense, he resumes again: 'Hence, concerning the tide, earthquake, winds, lightning,

---

[175] σκοτίας can be adj. or noun.

and all such things, we relinquish the causes of their occurring to those who are better equipped than we are to do it easily. We have demonstrated what events give rise to obvious calamities by learning from those who know; and are zealous to find out more credible ones than these in the matter of a surprising subject, but could not possibly endure to communicate them as a true report.'

110. (460a 23–35) $_{108H}$ He says that in the aforementioned strait an uncommon thing happens to the olive-trees. When it is high tide they are all covered over, but when the ebb tide occurs they flower continuously in the sea. A certain plant is growing there, in the deep water among the reefs, similar to the black reed; those dwelling in that place say it is Isis' hair, aiming to confer a simple-minded assurance upon a mythical invention. What happens is that when it is knocked by the waves it bends in many directions, as its whole outer part is soft and similar to those of other plants; but if one cuts it off and displays it in the open air, the severed portion at once grows harder than iron.

111. (460a 36–b 2) $_{109H}$ He says that, along with many other fish that spawn in the said places and have unusual characteristics, there is one fish that is exceedingly dark and the size of a man, which they call the Aithiopian on account of its face having a snub-nosed appearance. Because of this resemblance, those who have caught one initially think it wrong to either sell or consume it, but as time goes on they do both and (*feel that they*) are doing nothing sinful.

112. (460b 3–16) $_{110H}$ 'The affairs of the nations lying towards the south, as they exist in our time, have now been carefully investigated by us in five books; but about the islands in the open sea (*pelagos*) that were observed later, and the successive nations therein, and all the fragrant substances that the Trogodytike bears, we have resigned ourselves to abandoning an account of all this. Our time of life is incapable of enduring the effort, when many things have been composed by us about Europe and Asia. Neither do the monographs convey an accurate picture on account of the revolts in Egypt. But one who has encountered these matters piece by piece, and has crafted his investigations in suitable language, and takes the decision to pursue mighty fame through hard work—he will not renounce the task.'[176]

B. OTHER TEXTS

3   Strabo 16. 4. 5–15, C769–74:[177] *From books 1–4*

(5) $_{II.2}$ Artemidoros states that the promontory of Arabia lying opposite Deire is called Akila, and that the men in the area of Deire have the end of their penis docked. As

---

[176] This = Burstein's *BNJ* 86 T 3. The passage is also summarized in B. **8**, at 171a 15–27.
[177] The information in this passage, including the names of hunting-stations and other locations, probably derives not from the 5th and last book (cf. §112 above) of *On the Erythraian Sea* but from an earlier book (i.e. one of books 1–4), since none of it appears in the passages of Diod. and Phot. based on book 5. The complete text of Strabo 16. 4. 5–20, C769–79, is printed as Artem. 98 in Ch. 18 below.

you sail from Heroönpolis along Trogodytike, there is a city named Philotera after the sister of the second Ptolemy; it is a foundation by Satyros, the man sent to inquire after elephant hunting and explore Trogodytike.⌋ . . .

(7) . . . ₁₁.₃ Next are the Tauroi (*Bulls*), two mountains which, from afar, present an appearance somewhat like animals. Then there is another mountain which has a sanctuary of Isis, founded by Sesostris. Next is an island well planted with olives but washed over by the sea. After this is Ptolemaïs, beside the area for elephant hunting, a foundation of Eumedes who was sent by Philadelphos for the hunting. He covertly built a ditch and circuit wall round the peninsula, but then cultivated the men who would have impeded him and made them into friends instead of enemies.⌋

(8) Between these places there discharges a tributary of the river called Astaboras, which has its source in a lake; it discharges partially, but most of it enters the Nile. Next are six islands called the Latomiai (*Quarry Islands*); and after these the so-called Sabaïtic mouth, with a fort in the interior, a foundation by Tosouchos. Next a harbour called Elaia, and Straton's Island. Next the harbour of Saba, and an elephant-hunting station which has the same name. The territory inland from these places is called Tenessis. The Egyptians exiled by Psammetichos (*II*) hold it, who are surnamed Sembritai as if they are incomers. They are ruled by a woman, under whose authority also lies Meroë, which is an island in the Nile close to these places.[178] Above this is another island, not far away, in the river; it is a settlement of those same exiles. From Meroë to our sea, for a lightly laden man, is a journey of fifteen days. . . .

(9) . . . After Elaia are Demetrios's Lookouts and Konon's Altars. . . . After Konon's Altars is the harbour of Melinos, and above it is the so-called Koraos's Fort, with the hunting-station of Koraos, and another fort, and several hunting-stations. Next is Antiphilos's Harbour and the Kreophagoi (*Meat-eaters*) who live beyond it, who have the end of their penis docked; their women are also cut in the Ioudaic (*Jewish*) way.

(10) . . . Subsequent to Antiphilos's Harbour is the so-called harbour called Kolobōn Alsos (*Grove of the Mutilated*); and the city of Berenike, the one by Sabai; and Sabai itself, quite a large city. Next is Eumenes's Grove, above which lies the city of Darada and the elephant-hunting station known as Pros tōi Phreati (*By-the-Well*). . . .

(13) After Eumenes's Harbour,[179] as far as Deire and the narrows by the six islands, the Ichthyophagoi (*Fish-eaters*) and Kreophagoi (*Meat-eaters*) live, as do the Koloboi (*Mutilated*), as far as the interior. There are several places to hunt elephants here, some

It comprises the passages printed here interleaved with much additional material ultimately originating in Ag.'s book 5 but likewise taken by Strabo directly from its reworking by Art.; that material complements Diod. and Phot., but in a different order probably determined by Art. It is not always possible to distinguish what Art. found in Ag. from what he added. For the subscript fragment numbers here, see p. 385 n. 25.

---

[178] This sentence presumably reflects the situation in Strabo's day.

[179] Strabo has not named this place in the preceding sections; it may be at the same location as Eumenes's Grove (above).

unimportant cities, and islets off the coast. Most people are nomads; farmers are few. Among some of them grows the styrax (*gum-tree*) in no small amount. . . .

(14) . . . Next in succession lie three of the islands, known as Chelonon Nesos (*Isle of Turtles*), Phokon Nesos (*Isle of Seals*), and Hierakon Nesos (*Isle of Hawks*). All this coast has palm-trees, olive-trees, and laurels; not only the part within the straits but also much of the exterior portion. There is also a certain island called Philip's Island, opposite which lies the place called Pythangelos's Elephant-hunting Station. Next is the city and harbour of Arsinoë, and after these places is Deire. Beyond these lies elephant-hunting territory. The land next beyond Deire is scent-bearing: the first part is the one that produces myrrh, and this belongs to the Ichthyophagoi and Kreophagoi; it also grows the persea-tree and the Egyptian mulberry. Beyond it lies the elephant-hunting territory of Lichas. In many places there are pools of rainwater; when they dry up, the elephants use their trunks and tusks to dig wells and discover water. Upon this coast, as far as the promontory of Pytholaos, there are two fairly large lakes: one of salt water, which they call Thalassa (*The Sea*); one of fresh, which supports hippopotamuses and crocodiles, as well as papyrus round its edge. Ibises are also seen round about this place. At this point the people near the cape (*sic*) of Pytholaos are whole in body.

After these people is the Frankincense-bearing Land;[180] here is a cape and a sanctuary possessing a poplar grove. In the interior is a certain district called Potamia Isidos (*River-land of Isis*), and another called Neilos (*Nile*); both have myrrh and frankincense growing alongside them. There is also a particular cistern filled with the waters from the mountains; and after these places are Leontos Skopē (*Lion's Lookout*) and Pythangelos's Harbour. The next area grows pseudo-cassia. Then in succession are several river-lands with frankincense growing alongside them, and some rivers as far as the Kinnamomophoros (sc. *Chora; Cinnamon-bearing Land*). The river that defines this land also bears a great amount of rush reed.[181] Next is another river, and Daphnous harbour, and the so-called Potamia Apollonos (*River-land of Apollo*), which in addition to frankincense grows myrrh and cinnamon; the last is more plentiful round about the places inland. Next is Elephas (*Elephant*), the mountain, extending out to sea; then a channel; and successively Psygmou Limen (*Drying-place Harbour*), a large one, and the so-called Hydreuma Kynokephalon (*Watering-place of the Kynokephaloi, Dog's-heads*); and the last promontory of this coast, Notou Keras (*Horn of the South*).[182] As one rounds this in a southward direction, he[183] says, we possess descriptions neither of any harbour nor of places beyond it, because there is no further knowledge of the area.

---

[180] Some of this section probably reflects the addition of material by Artem. to what he found in Agatharchides.

[181] φλοῦς: 'flowering rush' Loeb; but LSJ inconclusive; Montanari 'bark'; we translate Radt's *Binsenschilf*.

[182] *keras* here meaning an extremity of a land, not an inlet of the sea; identified with *Ras el-Kheil*, Bucciantini 2012, in the region now called the Horn of Africa.

[183] Probably Artemidoros, but we cannot be sure (Roller 2014, 721 n. 1).

(15) On the next stretch of coast there are columns and altars of Pytholaos, Lichas, Pythangelos, Leon, and Charimortos, beside the well-known coast from Deire to Not-ou Kerōs (*Horn of the South*); but the distance is not known. . . .

4   Pliny, *Natural History*, 8. viii. 24–5: *Elephant-trapping in India and Africa*[184]
(24) In India they are captured when a driver riding one of the tamed ones catches a solitary wild one[185] and draws it away from the herd by beating it. Once it becomes tired, he crosses over onto it and controls it no differently from the previous animal.

Africa captures them in pits. When one of them wanders into it, the other (*men*) at once collect branches, roll down massive stones, build ramps, and attempt with all their might to drag it out. (25) Previously the (*Macedonian*) kings, with the aim of taming them, would use cavalry to force them into a manmade dell—deceptive by reason of its great length—and, once they were shut within the banks and ditches, tamed them with hunger. The proof was when (*an elephant*) calmly took a branch when a man offered it.

5   Plutarch, *Symposiaka*, 8. 9. 16 (*Moralia* 733b 5–c 1): *Guinea-worm*[186]
Those falling ill in the area of the Erythraian sea, as Agatharchidas (*sic*) has reported, have various novel and unreported symptoms. These included small serpents (*i.e. guinea worms*) that ate through their thighs and arms and emerged there; but when one touched them they went in again, coiled themselves up, and caused intolerable inflammations in the muscles. No one knew this sickness before, nor did it occur afterwards among other peoples, but only among these people, like many other (*sicknesses*).[187]

6   Aelian, *On the Nature of Animals*, 5. 27: *Horned pigs*
Agatharchides says that in Aithiopia the pigs have horns.[188]

7   Aelian, *On the Nature of Animals*, 17. 41 (43): *Leopards in Asia Minor*
The Karian and Lykian leopard is not bold, nor is it a strong jumper; but it is long in body, and when wounded by spears and lances it is resistant and does not succumb easily to the iron.[189]

---

[184] See n. to §9 above. This citation must refer to book 1 of *On the Erythraian Sea*.

[185] 'with iron', Burstein; but Loeb, König, and Thayer read *ferum* 'wild'.

[186] See nn. to §59 (*a*)–(*b*) above. The work is conventionally called *Quaestiones convivales* (*Table-talk* in the Loeb edition).

[187] This report, citing Agatharchides, should refer to the area from Ptolemaïs Theron to the Tauroi at the S entrance to the Red Sea (strait of *Bab al-Mandab*), an area A. did not cover in book 5, and must therefore derive from an earlier book (Marcotte 2021, 106). See n. on A. 2 §59 (*b*) above.

[188] This is fr. 79 in Burstein 1989, 125. Henry (who omits it) notes that Müller places this after §78 but that its placement is uncertain.

[189] This (fr. 71b in Burstein 1989, 118) is part of a passage (17. 40–5) where Aelian repeats descriptions of various animals that we have seen above; this information about leopards may also derive from Agatharchides book 5.

8   Photios, *Bibliotheke*, cod. 213, pp. 171a 6–b 17: *Photios' appraisal*

(171a 6–15) An historical (*work*) by Agatharchides was read, though some name him Agatharchos. This man had Knidos as his fatherland, and his art showed him to be a scholar. Herakleides of the Lembos,[190] whose secretary and reader he was, ensured he became well known on account of his services to him. He was also an apprentice of Kineas.   (2)   We know this man wrote *Affairs in Asia* in 10 books; and his *History of Affairs in Europe* extends to 49; but 5 books also investigate all of the Erythraian (*sea*) and the parts around it.

(171a 15–27) He makes mention of all the said writing at the end of the 5th account[191] (*of the last work*), when (*he says*) he has ceased to write for various reasons, among them being that the state of being old would predispose him to redundancy.[192]   (3)   There are some, however, who say he has composed additional treatises, of which we know nothing as yet. They say he drew up an epitome of what he had written about the Erythraian sea in 1 book, and indeed 5 books about the Trogodytai, but also an epitome of the *Lydē* of Antimachos, and another epitome of those who had written collections of writings *On Remarkable Winds*, and drew up *Selections from Histories* and *On the Company of Friends*.

(171a 27–39) (4) From what we have learned of the man by going through his work, he is grandiloquent and sententious, taking pleasure in the scale and worth of his writing more than other writings, but neither introducing choice words at all, nor proceeding by using commonplace words at all points, or creating words himself, but—being a craftsman in the use of words if anyone else is—he achieves a diction that delivers a certain novelty of appearance without using novel words. He introduces the effect so appropriately that innovation does not appear as innovation and yields no less clarity than do customary words.   (5)   He makes statements that display good sense and energy.

(171a 39–b 12) He moves subtly into figures of speech, organizing—in a manner as excellent as anyone's—sweetness, beguiling words, and things that relax the soul, and sowing it through all his writing without one's noticing. Whatever leads to a figure of speech he utters in a form that conveys nothing unpleasant. What effects this for him is not the substitution of words in itself, but the transition and alteration between one sort of material and another by using a certain wise, calm handling: for he takes a noun instead of a verb, but swaps a verb for a noun; he enlarges words into sentences while compressing a sentence into a noun phrase; of all the writers we know, he is second to none in effectiveness. He is also an enthusiast for Thucydides in the richness[193] and

---

[190] Usually called Herakleides Lembos, he served Ptolemy VI Philometor (r. 180–164 and 163–145).

[191] i.e. book; the word in Greek is *logos* 'account' or 'narrative'.

[192] Cf. §112.

[193] A reference to their style rather than their number, as Photios only knew books 1 and 5 of *Erythraian Sea*.

organization of speeches, but in no way second to him in grandeur of his words while surpassing the other man in clarity.

(171b 12–17) Such, then, is the character of the man, and the fame he enjoys comes from his use of language; and if an opinion lacking in sobriety has not endowed him with the title in rhetoric, nevertheless he seems to me to appear clearly in no way inferior to the grammarians or the orators, because of what he writes and teaches.[194]

[194] Here codex 213 of Photios ends.

16

HIPPARCHOS OF NIKAIA

(ACTIVE 162–128 BC)

D. Graham J. Shipley

To the memory of
Caroline M. Fraser, physicist
(1955–96)

INTRODUCTION

Hipparchos was a citizen of the Greek city of Nikaia in Bithynia, on the south coast of the Black Sea, but carried out his main researches chiefly at Rhodes (rather than Alexandria), between 162 and 126 BC or later.[1] Best known as an astronomer, he also went beyond Eudoxos, Dikaiarchos, and Eratosthenes in the rigorous application of mathematics to Earth measurement and large-scale mapping, particularly through the development of refined models of latitude and longitude.

Hipparchos developed spherical trigonometry[2] (though probably not stereographic projection),[3] was probably the first Greek scholar to introduce the term *klima* (lit. 'inclination') to refer to latitude, was the first to adopt the Babylonian 360-degree system (40 §34), and catalogued around 850 stars with their celestial coordinates (7, 11).[4] His commentary on Aratos of Soloi's astronomical poem *Phainomena* is extant.[5] The comparison of measurements over such a long period, including those of his predecessors, led him to the discovery of the precession of the equinoxes[6] (Ptolemy of Alexandria, *Syntaxis*, 3. 1). Other astonishing achievements included measuring the duration of the solar year to within a few minutes. He formulated long-term predictions of celestial events (6, 8) as well as, allegedly, weather events (9), and appears to have observed a comet—or possibly the planet Uranus (7).[7] The predictive power of his astronomy made it attractive to those practising astrology (7–8, 10); there was in any case no real boundary between those sciences. He also appears to have proposed a method for determining longitude by using information about eclipses (15).[8]

---

[1] Dicks 1960, 1–8. General overview: Roller 2015, 131–3.   [2] Hübner 2006.
[3] See n. to **46**.   [4] For a pilot study towards a reassessment, see Gysembergh 2019.
[5] New edition, with the first modern translation (in French): Aujac 2020b.
[6] Or, as it is now somewhat confusingly called by the International Astronomical Union, 'precession of the equator' (IAU 2006 Resolution B1, www.iau.org/static/resolutions/IAU2006_Resol1.pdf).
[7] Bourtembourg 2013. At its brightest, the planet is in principle just visible to the naked eye.
[8] Geus 2016, 151 n. 6, notes that Dicks's standard edition omits a fragment of Pappos of Alexandria,

Hipparchos' star catalogue was based partly on data assembled by Eratosthenes, but in the area of geography he criticized Eratosthenes as insufficiently rigorous; he was able, indeed, to improve his predecessor's figure for the circumference of the Earth (41), though the correction he made was a little too much.[9] He also criticized him in a work in three books, *Against the Geography of Eratosthenes*; the critical attitude is already documented in the earliest attestation of Hipparchos, a letter by Cicero (1). This was his main piece of research on geography, and it is known mainly through Strabo, who generally defends Eratosthenes against Hipparchos while recognizing that the later scholar was rigorous (15); that he had a positive view of Homer's geographical understanding (13, 16) despite inaccuracies in the poems (17); and that he was not attempting to write geography as such but correcting his predecessor's errors (3). This process of refinement was the reason why Eratosthenes' geographical research was relatively soon superseded (see Chapter 12, introduction). Some of Strabo's objections to Hipparchos are based on reasonable judgement, such as about the existence of a unified outer Ocean, which Hipparchos seems to have regarded as unproven; it was a logical position to hold, but in Strabo's view it was unreasonably sceptical (14).[10] But there is no doubt that Hipparchos' exact use of zones of latitude and triangulation was a sound replacement for Eratosthenes' imprecise *sphragides* or 'parcels' of the Earth's surface; a model which Eratosthenes himself did not apply systematically, perhaps recognizing its shortcomings. Strabo's objections themselves, in some cases, rested upon an imperfect understanding of Hipparchos' methods.[11]

The translation is based on the Greek and Latin of Dicks,[12] which remains the authoritative treatment of Hipparchos' geographical work, pending Geus's new edition forthcoming in *FGrH*.[13] Many of the extracts may also be found under Eratosthenes (Chapter 12 above). In view of the number of extracts attributable to *Against the Geography of Eratosthenes*, other testimonia have been gathered into a section which stands first.

SELECTED FURTHER READING

*Dicks, D. R. (1960), *The Geographical Fragments of Hipparchus*. London.
Dueck, D. (2012), with K. Brodersen, *Geography in Classical Antiquity*. Cambridge. [Esp. pp. 92–7.]

in its Armenian version, which attests that H. referred to the historical lunar eclipse of 331, observed at both Arbela (*Erbil* in mod. Iraqi Kurdestan) and Carthage; see eventually Geus forthcoming. On the determination of longitude, and the difficulty therein, see Introduction, §III. 3. d; Dueck 2012, 96–7.

[9] Dicks 1960, 43.
[10] Hübner 2006 gives a good assessment of where Strabo is harsh but also where his criticism is justified.
[11] Shcheglov 2005.   [12] Dicks 1960.
[13] Geus forthcoming will include the Armenian fragment of Pappos (n. 5 above). At Geus 2016, 151 n. 6, Geus also recommends omitting Dicks's F 41 (44 below) and F 63 (46).

Hübner, W. (2006), 'Hipparchos [6]', in *Brill's New Pauly*.

Roller, D. W. (2015), *Ancient Geography: The Discovery of the World in Classical Greece and Rome*. London–New York. [Esp. pp. 131–3.]

Shcheglov, D. A. (2005), 'Hipparchus on the latitude of southern India', *Greek, Roman and Byzantine Studies*, 45. 4: 359–80.

A. TESTIMONIA

1   Cicero, *To Atticus* 2. 6 (59 BC): *His criticisms of Eratosthenes*

My mind altogether shies away from writing. Even the *geōgraphika* that I had decided upon are a big job, so strongly is Eratosthenes, whom I had set myself to use, criticized by Serapion[14] and by Hipparchos.

2   Strabo 1. 2. 1–2, C14–15: *A key source for Strabo*

Since it is not worth debating philosophy with all of them, it is good to do so with Eratosthenes, Hipparchos, Poseidonios, Polybios, and others of the same kind.   (2)   First, however, one must examine Eratosthenes, juxtaposing at the same time the opposing argument of Hipparchos against him.

3   Strabo 2. 1. 41, C93: *Not writing geography as such*

So, if Hipparchos was not writing geography but examining what was said in the *Geography* of Eratosthenes, it was appropriate for him to correct things more extensively in detail.

4   Strabo 8. 1. 1, C332: *Not a geographer as such*

Others incorporated some discussion of such matters into their work on nature and on mathematics, such as Poseidonios and Hipparchos.

5   Strabo 12. 4. 9, C566: *Notable compatriots*

Men worthy of note for their learning have been born in Bithynia: Xenokrates the philosopher;[15] Dionysios the dialectician;[16] Hipparchos, Theodosios,[17] and his sons, (*all*) mathematicians.

6   Pliny, *Natural History*, 2. ix. 53: *Predictive achievements*

After these writers, Hipparchus predicted the course of both heavenly bodies (*the Sun and Moon*) for 600 years.[18] His work encompassed the months of the nations (*gentes*),

---

[14] Serapion (of Antioch or Alexandria), astronomer and astrologer, was later than H., and was perhaps his pupil; Cicero probably knew H.'s work only through him (Dicks 1960, 107).

[15] From Chalkedon; third head of Plato's Academy (339/8–314).

[16] Philosopher from Megara (C5l–C4e).   [17] *c.*100 BC; noted for his work on geometry.

[18] Including lunar eclipses (less probably solar): Dicks 1960, 108–9. But note that Pliny sees H. as a major figure in fields beyond astronomy.

days and hours, the locations of places, and the appearance of populations.[19] Time testifies[20] that in so doing he was nothing less than a participant in Nature's designs.

7   Pliny, *Natural History*, 2. xxiv. 95: *Achievements as an astronomer*
This same Hipparchus has never been praised adequately as the one whom no one surpassed in demonstrating the kinship between the constellations and humans, and that our souls are part of heaven.[21] He captured a new, different star born in his own lifetime,[22] and was led, by its movement in the place where it shone, to wonder whether this might not occur quite often and whether even those stars we think are fixed might not be moving.

Accordingly he dared to do something that would be improper even for a god: to number the constellations for those who would come after him, and mark each star by name using specially devised instruments. These allowed him to identify the location and size magnitude of each individual star, so that on this basis it could easily be determined not only whether they died and were born, but also whether certain ones actually moved across the heavens and were displaced, and likewise whether they grew and diminished. Thus in his legacy the heavens were left to all people, if someone were to be found to take possession of that inheritance.

8   Sextus Empiricus, *Against the Professors*, 5 (*Against the Astrologers*), 1: *Two kinds of 'astrologia'*
My purpose is to investigate astrology, also known as mathematics: not, that is, the perfect kind comprising arithmetic and geometry, since we have contradicted the men belonging to those sciences; nor the predictive capacity seen in adherents of Eudoxos, Hipparchos, and the like, which some also call 'astronomy', for this involves the observation of phenomena in the same way as agriculture and steersmanship, from which it is possible to prophesy droughts and heavy rain, plagues and earthquakes, and other such environmental changes.

Rather (*I contradict*) the casting of horoscopes, which the Chaldaeans decorate with more solemn titles, announcing themselves as mathematicians and astrologers: they exercise intricate influence over life, but entrench a deeply fortified superstition within us, and do not permit us to operate on the basis of true reason.

9   Aelian, *On the Nature of Animals*, 7. 8: *Weather forecasting in his home city*
Hipparchos, too, in the reign of the tyrant Hieron,[23] caused surprise by sitting in the theatre dressed in leather because he had advance knowledge of the imminent storm

---

[19] Or possibly their longitudes (a possibility raised by Rackham in a footnote); or the appearance of the sky from their respective regions (following Beaujeu and König).

[20] *aevo teste*, 'with time as witness'; translated similarly by Beaujeu and König; or 'on the evidence of his contemporaries', Rackham.

[21] Pliny probably consulted H.'s ideas only second-hand by Poseidonios and Roman writers (Dicks 1960, 109).

[22] Opinions differ on whether this was a nova or a comet (Dicks 1960, 110).

[23] Otherwise unknown (Dicks 1960, 106).

from the sky even though it was clear. Hieron felt admiration for him and rejoiced with the Nikaians of Bithynia on having Hipparchos for a citizen.

10 *Catalogus codicum astrologorum Graecorum*, v. 1, p. 205: *His value to astrology*[24]
Those who documented the efficacy of (*the stars'*) activity almost on a daily basis . . . (*include*) Hipparchos in Bithynia. Writings are reported by each of the aforementioned men about the ⟨power⟩ of the fixed stars ⟨and⟩ the efficacy of their activity.

11 Servius, *On Vergil, Georgics* 1. 137: *His work on constellations*
'He made the numbers and names': . . . For Hipparchus wrote about the constellations and even preserved the memory of every single one:[25] how many bright stars it had, how many of the second brightness, and how many dim ones. According to this, however, while the constellations are well recorded, he neglected the number of the stars as if it were well known.

12 *Suda* ι 521: *Hipparchos' literary works*
Hipparchos of Nikaia, a philosopher, born under the consuls.[26] He wrote *On the Phainomena of Aratos*, *On the System of the Fixed Stars and Catasterism*,[27] *On the Moon's Monthly Movement in Latitude*, and *Against Eratosthenes*.[28]

B. *AGAINST THE GEOGRAPHY OF ERATOSTHENES*

BOOK 1

13 Strabo 1. 1. 2, C2: *Homer as the founding geographer*
First, it has been rightly understood by me and those before me, one of whom is Hipparchos, that Homer is the pioneer of geographical experience.[29]

14 Strabo 1. 1. 9, C5–6: *Whether the oikoumenē is an island*
Hipparchos is not credible when he rebuts this view (*that the oikoumenē is surrounded by water*) on the grounds that the entire Ocean does not show similar characteristics, and that, even if this point were conceded, it would not follow from it that the entire

---

[24] This text is dated C4s AD.
[25] Practically impossible even for the naked-eye stars, which number around 6,000; his catalogue may have contained around 1,000 (Dicks 1960, 111).
[26] Since the whole entry is corrupt (Dicks 1960, 105), it is possible that the names of two Roman consuls, used as a dating formula, have dropped out.
[27] Reading καταστερισμοῦ with Toomer, followed by *Suda On Line* (Whitehead and Roth).
[28] Reading κατ' Ἐρατοσθένους for the ungrammatical καὶ εἰς τὰς ἀρίστους ('to the best men' but with feminine article) as *Suda On Line* implies, though the editors note Adler's suggestions εἰς ἀστερισμούς ('on constellations') and εἰς ἀστερίσκους ('on small stars').
[29] H. was more critical of Homer than Strabo allows: see e.g. 16–17.

encircling Atlantic open-sea (*pelagos*) was connected. For the dissimilar characteristics he cites Seleukos of Babylon as a witness.[30]

15   Strabo 1. 1. 12, C7: *Latitude and longitude*
In any case, it has frequently been said that one needs multiple expertise in approaching these matters. Hipparchos does well, in his work against Eratosthenes, to teach that although geographical enquiry belongs to any man, be he a private person or a lover of learning, it is impossible to grasp it without heavenly matters and the assessment of eclipse observations. For example, it is not possible to grasp whether the Alexandria by Egypt is further north or further south than Babylon, or by what distance, without the inspection of the zones of latitude (*klimata*).[31] Similarly, one could not know accurately which places are associated to a greater or lesser extent with the east or with the west unless from comparisons of eclipses of the sun and moon.[32] This is his view.

16   Strabo 1. 2. 3, C16: *A warning about Homeric geography*
Well, to seek to endow him (*Homer*) with everything is a thing one might attribute to a person transcending the bounds of ambition. Hipparchos says that if one were to attach to an Attic festival-wreath a quantity of apples and pears it could not support, that would be the same as attributing to him (*Homer*) every aspect of learning and every art.[33]

17   Strabo 1. 2. 20, C27: *Where Homer is accurate*
In the Catalogue (*of Ships*) he (*Homer*) does not mention the cities in the correct sequence—indeed, it was unnecessary to do so—but he mentions the nations (*ethnē*) in their correct sequence. He does the same with distant places: 'Wandering to Cyprus, Phoenicia, and the Egyptians, I came to the Aithiopes and Sidonioi and Eremboi, and to Libyē.'[34] The same observation is made by Hipparchos.

18   Strabo 1. 3. 12, C55: *The current in the Bosporos*
The (*strait*) at Byzantion exhibits no change, but persists in having an outflow (*ekrhous*) only from the Pontic ocean into the Propontis.[35] As Hipparchos records, it sometimes used to undergo interruptions.[36]

---

[30] A C2 astronomer and predecessor of H., from Seleukeia on the Erythraian sea. Strabo is motivated by his desire to uphold the Homeric view of an all-encompassing Ocean; it was true, as it happens, but H. raised an important point about differences between seas, presumably including their levels.

[31] On *klimata*, see n. to 40 §34.   [32] See Introduction, §III. 3. d.

[33] Eratosthenes had criticized Homer's lack of geographical expertise; Strabo disagrees, and Hipparchos takes a balanced view.

[34] *Od.* 4. 84–5.

[35] This is an element in the theory that the Black Sea had burst through in the past to forge a connection with the Mediterranean (Dicks 1960, 116).

[36] Cf. **21.**

19   Strabo 1. 3. 13–15, C55–7: *Connexions between the Black Sea, Red Sea, and Mediterranean*

(13) Eratosthenes adds to what he has said about Ammon and Egypt the fact that Mt Kasios would appear to have been surrounded by sea, and that all the area where the so-called Gerrha now lies[37] formed shallows in every part and adjoined the gulf of the Erythraian (*sea*), but was uncovered when the sea came together.[38] The statement that the aforesaid region forms shallows and adjoins the Erythraian gulf is ambiguous; for 'adjoin' signifies both proximity and contact, so that if one were speaking of water it would mean that the one was connected with the other. Therefore I take it that the shallows approached the Erythraian sea as long as the narrows at the Pillars were closed at the extremity, but that when those were breached the retreat (*of the water*) took place, our sea being lowered because of the outflow (*ekrhysis*) at the Pillars.

Hipparchos, however, takes 'adjoin' to mean the same as our sea becoming connected with the Erythraian because of being filled up; and criticizes the idea that our sea, being altered in that sense by the outflow (*ekrhysis*) at the Pillars, could possibly fail to cause an alteration in the Erythraian, which was connected with it, and keep the same level and not be lowered. For according to Eratosthenes himself the entire outer sea is connected, so that the western (*sea*) and the Erythraian sea are one. After saying this, he adduces what follows from it: that the sea outside the Pillars, the Erythraian, and the one that has become connected with it, have the same height.

(14) But Eratosthenes says[39] that he has not stated this—that it (*our sea*) became connected with the Erythraian because it filled up—but only that it approached it, and that it does not follow that, because there is one connected sea, it has the same height and the same level; that is not the case with ours or, by Zeus, with that at Lechaion and that around Kenchreai.[40] Hipparchos himself notes this fact in his work against him (*Eratosthenes*).[41] . . .

(15) He (*Hipparchos*) says that the inscription by the sacred envoys of Kyrene on the dolphins is not genuine; but gives a reason that is not credible, (*namely*) that while the foundation of Kyrene is reported (*as having taken place*) in times that are remembered, no one has a memory of the oracular shrine ever being by the sea. What does it matter that no one reports it? From the evidence that leads us to deduce that the locality was once on the coast, the dolphins were (*in fact*) dedicated and the inscription was made by sacred envoys of Kyrene.[42] (*Hipparchos*) agrees that the sea, when raised

---

[37] Not the Gerrha in Arabia, but a place in NE Egypt (Dicks 1960, 118).

[38] i.e. the Atlantic and Mediterranean were united. This passage is also Erat. 14 above.

[39] That is, Strabo (who is confused here) considers that Eratosthenes *would* say this in response (Dicks 1960, 117–18).

[40] The harbours of Corinth, on the gulf of Corinth and the Saronic gulf respectively.

[41] Strabo deploys a pedantic point about the difference between 'adjoin' and 'approach' in order to defend Eratosthenes (Dicks 1960, 117–18). In fact, the *Red Sea* was higher than the Mediterranean (Juba 23 below).

[42] On this extract, see Erat. 14 above.

up along with the raising of the sea-bed, flooded the places as far as the oracle, which are a little over 3,000 stades distant from the sea. He does not, however, agree that the rise was so great as to cause all of Pharos and the majority of Egypt to be covered; as if so great an elevation was not capable of flooding these parts too. He also says that if the sea on our side had been filled up to the level stated by Eratosthenes before the breach at the Pillars, then all of Libyē and the majority of Europe and Asia must previously have been hidden. In addition to this, he adduces that the Pontos would have been connected to the Adriatic in certain places, since the Istros divides in the area around the Pontos and flows into each sea because of the lie of the land. But the Istros does not have its origin in the regions around the Pontos, but instead beyond the mountains beyond the Adriatic; nor does it flow into each sea but only into the Pontos, dividing only at these mouths. He has shown ignorance with the same ignorance (*sic*) as some of those before him, who understood there to be a homonymous river Istros discharging into the Adriatic after dividing from it, and that the race of the Istroi through whom it flows take their name from it, and that Jason made his voyage back from the Kolchoi along this river.[43]

20 Pomponius Mela 3. 7. 7: *Taprobane*
That Taprobane is either an extremely large island or the first part of another continent is stated by Hipparchos.

21 Eustathios, *On Dionysios Periegetes* line 473: *The current at the Bosporos*
Of these straits, that at Byzantion has only an outflow (*ekrhous*) with no upward flow. Hipparchos records that it has been known to exhibit interruptions or even stop flowing.[44]

BOOK 2

22 Strabo 2. 1. 4, C68–9: *Unreliability of Patrokles*
Hipparchos opposes this judgement, attacking the reliability of the arguments. For in his view Patrokles is not reliable given that two others testify against him: Deimachos[45] and Megasthenes,[46] who say that at some points 20,000 stades is the distance from the sea in the south, at others 30,000. He cites this view of theirs, and notes that the old maps (*pinakes*) concur with them. Indeed, he thinks that having to rely on Patrokles alone is an unreliable approach; it entails leaving aside those who differ from him so greatly in their testimony, and correcting the old maps on this specific ground rather than leaving them as they are until we have more reliable knowledge about them.[47]

---

[43] This paragraph is part of a discussion in Strabo about how the Mediterranean forced its way out into the Atlantic; but Strabo presents it confusingly (Dicks 1960, 120–1). For the divided *Danube*, cf. Skylax of Karyanda 8.

[44] Cf. **18.**   [45] *BNJ* 716 (Daimachos) T 3.   [46] *BNJ* 715 T 5.

[47] This extract is part of a consideration by Strabo of whether India has been placed too far N (Dicks 1960, 122).

23   **Strabo** 2. 1. 7, C69–70: *Unreliability of Patrokles*

Moreover, Hipparchos in his second treatise (*hypomnēma; i.e. book* 2) says that Eratosthenes himself attacks the reliability of Patrokles[48] on the basis of his (*Patrokles'*) disagreement with Megasthenes[49] about the length of the side of Indike that is to the north—Megasthenes saying it is 16,000 stades, Patrokles saying it is 1,000 shorter— and that he (*Eratosthenes*) starts from a particular *Anagraphē stathmōn* (*Record of Stopping-points*)[50] and disbelieves those writers because of their disagreement, adhering instead to the list. If (*says Hipparchos*) Patrokles is unreliable here because of this disagreement, even though the difference is (*only*) one of 1,000 stades, all the more should we think him unreliable when the difference is one of 8,000 stades between him and two men who agree with one another: they say the width of India is 20,000 stades, he 12,000.[51]

24   **Strabo** 2. 1. 11–12, C71: *Hipparchos' errors over latitude*

(11) … Hipparchos himself did not take the fact that the line from the Pillars to Kilikia is straight and runs to the equinoctial[52] sunrise (*due east*) entirely from instruments and geometry, but trusted in sailors for the whole stretch from the Pillars to the Straits (*of Gibraltar*).[53] Consequently he (*Hipparchos*) is even in error when he says:

> Since we are unable to state either the ratio of the longest day to the shortest, or that of gnomon to shadow, for the mountain slope from Kilikia to the Indians, nor even say whether the obliquity (*of the slope*) runs along a parallel (*of latitude*), therefore we must leave it uncorrected, keeping it oblique just as the old maps (*pinakes*) present it.[54]

…   (12) The statements that follow are also full of great difficulties. Consider, for example, that if one were not to modify the statements that the capes of Indike rise up opposite the area around Meroë,[55] and that the distance from Meroë to the mouth (*of the Hellespont*) at Byzantion is around 18,000 stades, but were to reckon 30,000 from the southern Indians as far as the mountains, many illogicalities would occur.

25   **Strabo** 2. 1. 19–20, C76–7: *Hipparchos' misrepresentation of Eratosthenes, and further errors over latitude*

(19) In the following statements, too, Hipparchos wrongly modifies what he (*Eratosthenes*) says: first, in seeing a reference to the summer tropic instead of the winter one; then in believing that in mathematical matters one should not use a witness who has no astronomy.[56] …

---

[48] *BNJ* 712 F 3.   [49] *BNJ* 715 F 6d. For Megasthenes, see further Stoneman 2021.
[50] Cf. Erat. 49.
[51] H. pointed out the inconsistency on Eratosthenes' part of downgrading Patrokles as a source while selectively using his data (Dicks 1960, 124).
[52] Lit. 'equidiurnal'. See Introduction, §X. 3. b fin.
[53] See n. on Erat. 50.   [54] On this extract, see Dicks 1960, 124–5.
[55] Strabo reports that H. objected to Eratosthenes' placing of Meroë and the tip of India on the same latitude. He was right to do so. On this extract, see Dicks 1960, 125.
[56] On this extract, see Dicks 1960, 125–8; on 25–31 as whole, his pp. 125–44.

(20) Next, then: if we suppose that the most southerly parts of Indike rise up opposite the area around Meroë, as many have said and believed, we have shown that the consequences are illogical. But since Hipparchos says nothing against this hypothesis at this point, but subsequently in his second treatise (*hypomnēma; i.e. book 2*) does not agree with it, it is necessary to examine this account too. What he says is that, if places rise up opposite one another and lie on the same parallel, in cases where there is great distance between them we cannot know this very thing—that the places are on the same parallel—without comparing the zones of latitude (*klimata*) in each of the places. Now, as for the zone of latitude (*klima*) at Meroë, (*he says*) that Philon,[57] who composed *The Voyage to Aithiopia*, records that forty-five days before the summer solstice the sun is directly overhead; he also states the ratios of the gnomon to both the solstitial and the equinoctial shadows. (*He also says that*) Eratosthenes himself concurs almost exactly with Philon, but that no one records the zone of latitude in Indike, not even Eratosthenes himself. (*Finally, he says that*) if indeed the Bears both disappear (*i.e. set*) there, as they (*Eratosthenes and Philon*) think, relying on those who were with Nearchos,[58] it is not possible that Meroë and the capes of Indike lie on the same parallel.[59]

26 Strabo 2. 1. 21–2, C77–8: *Hipparchos' errors over Eratosthenes' first three 'sealstones'*
(21) In what follows, attempting to prove these things, he (*Hipparchos*) says what has been refuted by me, or uses false assumptions, or imposes erroneous conclusions. Regarding the fact that from Babylon to Thapsakos[60] is 4,800 stades, and 2,100 north to the Armenian mountains, one cannot conclude that from Babylon along its meridian to the northern mountains is more than 6,000. Eratosthenes does not say that it is 2,100 stades from Thapsakos to the mountains, but that there is a remainder that is unmeasured, and thus the following reasoning, from assumptions not proved, cannot be assumed. Eratosthenes nowhere declared that Thapsakos lies more than 4,500 stades north of Babylon.

(22) Next, continuing to plead on behalf of the old maps (*pinakes*), he (*Hipparchos*) brings up things that are not said by Eratosthenes about the third *sphragis* ('sealstone'),[61] but conveniently for himself moulds the assertion so as to favour an elegant refutation.

---

[57] *BNJ* 670 F 2. Philon was a Ptolemaic commander.   [58] *BNJ* 133 F 16.
[59] Dicks 1960, 125–7, shows that Strabo's objections to H. do not bear examination.
[60] For the location of Thapsakos—a key point in ancient geographical theory—possibly at Zeugma, see n. to Erat. 52 §24. On this extract, see Dicks 1960, 130–5.
[61] Strabo has not yet explained Eratosthenes' notion of *sphragides* ('sealstones') as a term for major regions of the *oikoumenē* (see Ch. 12, introduction); he does so a few lines further on in this section (2. 1. 22, quoted above as Erat. 52c). The first three *sphragides* are India, Ariane, and Mesopotamia respectively.

27 **Strabo** 2. 1. 27, C80–1: *Criticism of Eratosthenes' third 'sealstone'*
Concerning the third *sphragis* (*sc. Mesopotamia*), he (*Eratosthenes*) does indeed make
certain other mistakes, which we shall consider, but not at all in the matters Hipparchos brings up against him. Let us see what he (*Hipparchos*) says. For in wishing to
validate what he says at the start, that Indike must not be transferred further south as
Eratosthenes adjudges, he says this can be made totally clear from the things he (*Eratosthenes*) himself brings up: for the latter says the third division (*meris*)[62] is delimited
on its northern side by the line from the Caspian Gates to the Euphrates, which is of
10,000 stades; and subsequently adduces that its south side, the one running from Babylon to the mountains of Karmania, is a little more than 9,000, while the side towards
the west, from Thapsakos along the Euphrates to Babylon, is 4,800 stades and then
3,000 to the outlets (*of the river*). As for the places north of Thapsakos, part has been
measured up to 1,100 stades while the rest has not yet been measured. Since, therefore,
as he (*Hipparchos*) says, the northern side of the third division is around 10,000, while
the line parallel to it, running straight from Babylon as far as the eastern side, has been
calculated to be a little more than 9,000, it is evident that Babylon is a little over 1,000
further east than the crossing at Thapsakos.

28 **Strabo** 2. 1. 29, C81–2: *Objections to Eratosthenes' second 'sealstone'*
He (*Hipparchos*), taking these things as given and having shown, as he supposes, that
according to Eratosthenes Babylon is further east than Thapsakos by a little more
than 1,000 stades, once more moulds an assumption for himself as a basis for the
next demonstration. He asserts that if a straight line is understood as extended south
from Thapsakos, and another perpendicular to this one from Babylon, there will be a
right-angled triangle consisting of the side reaching from Thapsakos to Babylon, the
perpendicular extended from Babylon to the meridian through Thapsakos, and the
actual meridian through Thapsakos. He posits that the hypotenuse of this triangle is
the direct line from Thapsakos to Babylon, which he states is 4,800 stades, while the
perpendicular line from Babylon to the meridian through Thapsakos is a little more
than 1,000, the value of the excess of the line to Thapsakos (*from the Caspian Gates*)
over that to Babylon (*from the frontier between Karmania and Persia*).[63] From these
points he also calculates that the other of the (*two*) sides on either side of the right
angle is many times greater than the aforesaid perpendicular.

   He also adds to this line the one running north from Thapsakos that terminates at
the Armenian mountains. Of this, Eratosthenes said that one part had been measured
and was of 1,100 (*stades*), while he leaves aside the unmeasured part; it is supposed
to measure at least 1,000, with the result that both add up to 2,100. He (*Hipparchos*),
adding this to the straight side of the triangle as far as the perpendicular line from
Babylon, calculates that the distance from the Armenian mountains and the parallel

---

[62] Strabo, or H., here uses an alternative term to *sphragis*; he does so again at **30**. On this extract, see
Dicks 1960, 130–5.
[63] The two explanatory parentheses are from Dicks 1960, 75. On this extract, see Dicks 1960, 130–5.

(*sc. of latitude*) through Athens to the perpendicular from Babylon is many thousands, setting this perpendicular upon the parallel through Babylon. He shows, however, that the distance from the parallel through Athens to the parallel through Babylon is no greater than 2,400 stades, on the assumption that the entire meridian has the length in stades that Eratosthenes says it has. If this is true, then the mountains of Armenia and of the Tauros could not be on the parallel through Athens, as Eratosthenes claims, but according to Eratosthenes himself must be many thousands of stades further north.

29   Strabo 2. 1. 34–5, C86–7: *Further criticism of Eratosthenes' third 'sealstone'*
First, however, let us return to Hipparchos and look at what he goes on to say. For, once more moulding assumptions for himself, he dismantles geometrically things that his opponent (*Eratosthenes*) said only sketchily. For he states that he (*Eratosthenes*) says the distance from Babylon to the Caspian Gates is 6,700 stades, and to the frontiers of Karmania and Persis more than 9,000, which is measured along a line running straight towards the equinoctial sunrise; and that this line is perpendicular to the shared side of the second and third 'seals', so that according to him (*Eratosthenes*) a right-angled triangle subsists with its right angle towards the frontiers of Karmania, its hypotenuse being shorter than one of the sides enclosing the right angle; so therefore he (*Eratosthenes*) assigns Persis to the second 'seal'. . . .[64]

What he next adduces is not right either. For since he (*Eratosthenes*) had said it was so far from the Caspian Gates to Babylon, and to Sousa 4,900, and from Babylon to there 3,400, once more beginning from the same hypotheses he (*Hipparchos*) says an obtuse triangle subsists between the Caspian Gates, Sousa, and Babylon with the obtuse angle at Sousa and the lengths of its sides as expounded above. He then goes on to calculate that, according to these hypotheses, it will turn out that the meridian line through the Caspian Gates has its common point (*i.e. intersection*) with the parallel through Babylon and Sousa further west than the common point of the same parallel and the straight line extending from the Caspian Gates to the frontiers of Karmania and Persis, by more than 4,400 stades; and that, in relation to the meridian line through the Caspian Gates, the line through the Caspian Gates and the frontiers of Karmania and Persis just about makes half a right angle and inclines to the midpoint between the south and the equinoctial sunrise (*due east*); and that the Indos river is parallel with this line, so that it does not flow to the south from the mountains as Eratosthenes says, but between that point and the equinoctial sunrise, as it is delineated in the old maps (*pinakes*). . . .

And it is without these points[65] that he (*Eratosthenes*) has stated that the form of Indike is rhomboid; and that as the eastward side diverges strongly towards the east—especially at the furthest promontory, which additionally advances more towards the south in comparison with the remainder of the coast—so, too, does the side adjoining the Indos.

---

[64] On this extract, see Dicks 1960, 135–8.   [65] Or 'assumptions', Dicks.

(35) He (*Hipparchos*) says all these things in geometric terms, but does not examine them in a reliable way. Having imposed these terms upon himself,[66] he lets himself off, saying that if the examination involved only small distances he would condone them, but that since it appears to fail by thousands of stades it is not to be condoned. Even so (*he says*), he (*Eratosthenes*) demonstrates that deviations (*in latitude*) of 400 stades can be perceived, as in the case of the parallel through Athens and that through Rhodes.

30 **Strabo 2. 1. 36, C88–9:** *Criticism of Eratosthenes' fourth 'sealstone'*
He (*Hipparchos*) gives a better account of the fourth section (*meris*), but imposes the same censoriousness and an insistence on the same or similar hypotheses. He rightly criticizes him (*Eratosthenes*) in that he identifies as the length of this section the line from Thapsakos as far as Egypt, as if a man should call the diagonal of a parallelogram its 'length'. For Thapsakos does not lie on the same parallel as the coast of Egypt, but they lie on parallels at a great distance from one another, while the line between Thapsakos and Egypt runs in a sort of diagonal and oblique manner. Where he is not correct is in expressing surprise that he (*Eratosthenes*) confidently says the distance from Pelousion to Thapsakos is 6,000 stades when it is more than 8,000. (*Hipparchos*)—accepting the proof that the parallel through Pelousion is further south than the one through Babylon by more than 2,500 stades, and that according to Eratosthenes, as he thinks, in relation to the one through Babylon, the one through Thapsakos is further north by 4,800—says the total is more than 8,000. . . .[67]

For Hipparchos himself has shown that, on the contrary, Babylon happens to lie further east than Thapsakos by more than 1,000 stades. . . .

This not being granted, his (*Hipparchos'*) next statement is also empty. He purports to show that, given a right-angled triangle existing between Pelousion, Thapsakos, and the intersection of the parallel through Pelousion and the meridian through Thapsakos, one of its (*sides*) enclosing the right angle, that upon the meridian, will be greater than that under (*i.e. subtended by*) the right angle (*i.e. the hypotenuse*),[68] namely the (*side*) from Thapsakos to Pelousion. Empty, too, is the statement that is linked to this, being concocted on the basis of an assumption that has not been conceded. For it certainly has not been granted that from Babylon to the meridian through the Caspian Gates is a distance of 4,800. It has been demonstrated by us that Hipparchos has concocted this from things not conceded by Eratosthenes. In order that what he (*Eratosthenes*) has granted be made invalid, he has taken it that it is a distance of over 9,000 from Babylon to the line thus drawn from the Caspian Gates (*as Eratosthenes has said*) to the frontiers of Karmania, and would then show the very same thing.

---

[66] i.e. the use of *sphragides*, 'sealstones'. For Strabo, a strictly mathematical or geometrical analysis of Eratosthenes' arguments is unfair; but he effectively concedes that H. did allow for a margin of error of 400 st., questioning E.'s data only when the discrepancies were larger (Dicks 1960, 129–30).

[67] On this extract, see Dicks 1960, 130–5; 138–41.

[68] H. means that Eratosthenes' dimensions create an impossibility, as a right-angled triangle always has the hypotenuse as its longest side. Strabo thinks H.'s argument unfounded.

31 Strabo 2. 1. 38–40, C90–2: *Excessive criticism of Eratosthenes; the latter's account of Europe*

(38) Another objection to Hipparchos is that, since he has laid a charge against what Eratosthenes says, he should likewise have made some rectification of his errors, as we are doing. But even if he has occasionally given thought to this, he commands us to abide by the old maps, which require a great deal more rectification than does the map of Eratosthenes. The proof he next attempts is equally shoddy. For he takes as a premiss what has been concocted from things not granted, as we have demonstrated[69]—that Babylon is further east than Thapsakos by no more than 1,000 stades—so that, even if it is concluded that it is further east by more than 2,400 stades, on the basis that Eratosthenes states that from Thapsakos to the Tigris crossing by which Alexander crossed is a short cut of 2,400, while the Tigris and Euphrates encircle Mesopotamia, bearing east for a time, turning back south, and then approaching one another and also approaching Babylon—that is no extraordinary feature of his (*Eratosthenes'*) account.[70]

(39) He (*Hipparchos*) is off key, too, in his next attempt, in which he wants to deduce that the road from Thapsakos to the Caspian Gates, which Eratosthenes has stated to be 10,000 stades, had not been measured in a straight line, as Eratosthenes says it had, and that the straight line is much shorter. The attack he makes is of the following nature. He says that even on Eratosthenes' account the meridian through the Canopic mouth (*of the Nile*) and the one through the Kyaneai (*Cyanean Rocks*) are the same, and that this stands apart from the one through Thapsakos by 6,300 stades, and the Kyaneai stand apart from Mount Kaspios—which lies above the transit to the Caspian open-sea (*pelagos*) from Kolchis—by 6,600. So, within 300 stades, it is the same distance from the meridian through the Kyaneai to Thapsakos as it is to Kaspios; in a way, therefore, Thapsakos and Kaspios lie on the same meridian. As a consequence, he says, the Caspian Gates are at the same distance from Thapsakos as they are from Kaspios, and their distance from Kaspios is much less than 10,000, which Eratosthenes says is their distance from Thapsakos; therefore their distance from Thapsakos is much less than 10,000 (*measured*) in a straight line, and therefore his (*Eratosthenes'*) 10,000 is a circuitous route even though he reckons as a straight line from the Caspian Gates to Thapsakos. . . .

For this reason, in the first place, while he (*Eratosthenes*) says the distance from the mouth (*of the Black Sea*) to Phasis was 8,000 stades, and adds the 600 from there to Dioskourias and the transit from Dioskourias to the Kaspios, which is five days—which according to Hipparchos himself can plausibly be said to be around 1,000 stades—and thus according to Eratosthenes the whole (*journey*) adds up to 9,600, he himself (*Hipparchos*) has cut this down and says that while it is 5,600 from the Kyaneai to Phasis it is a further 1,000 from there to Kaspios. . . .

---

[69] At 2. 1. 27 (27 above).   [70] On this extract, see Dicks 1960, 129–30, 143–4.

(40) In the second treatise (*hypomnēma; i.e. book 2*), after taking up the same enquiry again about the frontiers in the Tauros region, which we have adequately discussed, he (*Hipparchos*) moves on to the northerly parts of the inhabited world.[71] Next he expounds the statements of Eratosthenes concerning the places beyond the Pontos: namely, that three capes extend from the north, and that one of these has the Peloponnese upon it, the second is the Italian cape, and the third the Ligurian; and that both the Adriatic gulf and the Tyrrhenic (*Etruscan*) are embraced by these. Having expounded this in a general fashion, he attempts to disprove the detailed statements made about them, and does so in a geometrical rather than geographical way. But so great a plethora of errors are committed by Eratosthenes in these passages, and by Timosthenes, author of *Harbours*[72]—whom he (*Eratosthenes*) praises above the rest of them, but whom he disagrees with and disproves in many respects—that I do not deem it worthwhile to dwell upon either of these authors, who commit so many errors of fact, nor upon Hipparchos. For even he (*Hipparchos*) leaves aside some of their errors and does not correct others, but only refutes them on the basis that they have been spoken falsely or polemically.[73]

32 Strabo 2. 1. 41, C94: *Hipparchos' approach to Eratosthenes*
That is what Hipparchos attempts to do, both in the above-mentioned instances and in the passage where he expounds the distances in the area of Hyrkania as far as Baktria and the nations beyond, and furthermore the distances from Kolchis to the Hyrkanian (*Caspian*) sea.[74] ... Having criticized, then, some of the Aithiopian statements, towards the end of the second of his treatises (*hypomnēmata*) written *Against the Geography of Eratosthenes*, he (*Hipparchos*) says that in the third the perspective will rather be mathematical though also to a degree geographical.

... In a certain way he (*Eratosthenes*) is a mathematician among geographers and a geographer among mathematicians. Thus he offers points of attack to his opponents on both sides, indeed fair attacks in respect of this treatise (*my own*); both he and Timosthenes do so. Therefore there is no remaining need for us to examine them together, and we shall be satisfied with what has been said by Hipparchos.

BOOK 3

33 Strabo 1. 1. 21, C12: *Hipparchos' astronomical data*
Nor need we be so exact as to know everything about co-risings in all locations, co-settings, co-culminations, elevations of the poles, the constellations[75] at the zenith,

---

[71] This is evidence for the scope of book 2.   [72] Ch. 10 above.
[73] Strabo has had to admit the justice of H.'s criticisms of Eratosthenes' account of the W and N of the *oikoumenē*, but repeats his unreasonable objection to H.'s use of geometrical arguments (Dicks 1960, 144–5).
[74] On this extract, see Dicks 1960, 144–6.   [75] *sēmeia*; or 'points', as Dicks and Roller have it.

and all other such things one may encounter according to alterations in horizons and differences in the arctic circles,[76] whether they be a matter of vision or of nature.[77]

34 **Strabo** 1. 4. 1, C62: *Eratosthenes' calculation of the Earth's circumference*
That it (*the Earth*) is as great as he (*Eratosthenes*) has said it is, is not accepted by later writers; nor do they commend the way in which he measures it. But for the purpose of locating the appearances (*of the heavenly bodies*) over each of the inhabited regions, Hipparchos nevertheless employs those distances upon the meridian through Meroë, Alexandria, and the Borysthenes (*Dnieper*), saying that they do not diverge far from the truth.[78]

35 **Strabo** 1. 4. 4, C63: *Questions of latitude*
That the parallel (*of latitude*) through the Borysthenes is the same as that through Brettanike is conjectured by Hipparchos and others, from the fact that the one through Byzantion is the same as that through Massalia. For the ratio stated by Pytheas between the gnomon and its shadow at Massalia is the same as that which Hipparchos says he has found at Byzantion at the identical season.[79]

36 **Strabo** 2. 1. 12–13, C71–2: *Further questions of latitude*
First of all, if the same parallel passes through Byzantion as through Massalia—just as Hipparchos has stated, relying upon Pytheas[80]—and if the same meridian passes through Byzantion as through the Borysthenes, a fact that Hipparchos declares to be true; and if he also declares that the distance from Byzantion to the Borysthenes is 3,700 stades: thus the distance would be the same from Massalia to the parallel through the Borysthenes, which would also run through the Ocean-facing part of Keltike. For as people travel roughly this far they meet the Ocean.

(13) Again, as we know the Cinnamon-bearing Land to be the last inhabited place southwards, and according to Hipparchos himself the parallel through it is the start of the temperate zone, and of the inhabited zone, and lies around 8,800 stades from the equator; then, since he says the parallel through Borysthenes is 34,000 stades distant from the equator, the remaining stades from the (*parallel*) bounding the burnt (*i.e. torrid*) and the temperate (*zones*) to that through the Borysthenes and Ocean-facing Keltike would be 25,200.

37 **Strabo** 2. 1. 18, C75:[81] *Northerly latitudes in the British Isles*
Hipparchos, anyhow, says that at the Borysthenes and in Keltike, during all the nights of summer, the sun is partially lit up (*sic*) as it moves in a contrary direction from setting to rising; and that at the winter solstice the sun rises at most 9 cubits (*pēcheis; i.e. 18°*).[82] Among the people that are at a distance of 6,300 from Massalia—whom he

[76] As defined for each latitude: see n. on Pytheas 7.
[77] Although Strabo disdains the detailed data he lists for geographical purposes, this is a good indication of the detail in H.'s work, especially his star catalogue (cf. Dicks 1960, 164–5).
[78] For the method Eratosthenes employed to refine the circumference of the Earth, see Erat. 29 §7.
[79] Cf. **39**. See nn. on Pyth. 2.   [80] See **35**; on this and **36**, **39–40**, see Dicks 1960, 178–83.
[81] See nn. on Pyth. 4.   [82] For 1 cubit = 2° in astronomy, see n. to Pyth. 4.

(*Hipparchos*) understands still to be Keltoi, but who I think are Brettanoi, 2,500 stades further north than Keltike—this occurrence is much more notable. In the winter days the sun rises at most 6 cubits (*12°*), but only 4 (*8°*) for the people at a distance of 9,100 stades from Massalia, and less than 3 (*6°*) for the people beyond them. According to our account these people would be far further north than Ierne (*Hibernia, i.e. Ireland*). But he (*Hipparchos*), relying on Pytheas, locates this inhabited region among places further south than Brettanike, and says that there the longest day is 19 equinoctial hours, but 18 where the sun rises 4 cubits.[83] He says they lie at a distance of 9,100 stades from Massalia. So the southernmost Brettanoi are further north than they.

38 **Strabo** 2. 5. 7, C113: *Hipparchos' adopts Eratosthenes' calculation of the Earth's size*
What Hipparchos says is more or less consonant with these points. For he assumes the size of the Earth as stated by Eratosthenes, and therefore states that we must separate from this question our study of the inhabited world: for it will make little difference as regards the appearances of the heavenly bodies in each inhabited region whether the measurement is thus (*sc. as Eratosthenes said*) or as later writers have given it.

39 **Strabo** 2. 5. 8, C115: *Northern latitudes*
Given that the parallel through Byzantion goes roughly through Massalia, as Hipparchos says, relying upon Pytheas—for he says that at Byzantion the ratio of the gnomon to its shadow is the same as Pytheas says it is in Massalia.[84]

40 **Strabo** 2. 5. 34–43, C131–5: *Zones of latitude*
(34) The remaining task is to talk about the zones of latitude (*klimata*).[85] . . . For specialists in astronomy this must be done more fully, as Hipparchos did. For he composed, as he says himself, the changes occurring in the heavenly bodies for each place on the Earth that is among those assigned to our quarter of it: I refer to those places from the equator as far as the north pole. . . . But it suffices to expound the noteworthy and simpler of those (*differences*) he notes if we suppose, as he (*Hipparchos*) does, that the size of the Earth is 252,000 stades, as Eratosthenes also makes it.[86] For there will be no great difference, compared with this, in the distances between the inhabited zones in respect of the (*heavenly*) appearances. Indeed, if one were to divide the great circle of the Earth into 360 sections,[87] each of the sections will be 700 stades.[88] He (*Hipparchos*) applies this measurement to the distances proposed to be taken upon the aforesaid meridian through Meroë. He begins from those dwelling upon the equator. For the

---

[83] For latitude expressed in terms of the length of the longest day, see n. on Pyth. 4.
[84] Cf. **35**.
[85] It was probably H. who introduced the use of *klima* ('inclination', 'slope') in this sense: see detailed discussion in Dicks 1960, 154–64.
[86] See Erat. 29 §7.
[87] The passage of H. here summarized by Strabo was the first occurrence of the 360-degree system in Greek scholarship (Dicks 1960, 148–9).
[88] Approx. 80 mi (130 km) at 8 st. to the mile and 185 m to the stade; in reality 1° of longitude at the equator (where the Earth's circumference is greatest; it is not a perfect sphere) equates to *c.*69 mi (*c.*111 km).

remainder, he goes through the inhabited zones in successive steps of 700 stades along the aforementioned meridian, attempting to state the (*heavenly*) appearances relating to each of them. For us, however, a beginning should not be made at that place. . . . But we must begin, like Hipparchos, from the southern parts.

(35) Indeed, he (*Hipparchos*) says that for those dwelling upon the parallel through the Cinnamon-bearing Land, which is at a distance of 3,000 stades south of Meroë, with the equator 8,800 from it, their dwelling is almost halfway between the equator and the summer tropic at Syene; for Syene is 5,000 stades distant from Meroë. Among these people, the first, the Little Bear is enclosed entirely within their arctic circle[89] and is always seen; for the bright star at the end of its tail, being the most southerly, is anchored upon the very arctic circle so that it touches the horizon.[90] . . .

(36) For those at Meroë and the Ptolemaïs in Trogodytike, the greatest day is 13 equinoctial hours. This dwelling-place is roughly midway between the equator and the (*parallel*) through Alexandria, apart from the 1,800 (*stades*) by which the distance to the equator is longer.[91] . . . At Syene and at the Berenike on the Arabian gulf (*Red Sea*), in Trogodytike, the sun at the summer solstice is overhead and the longest day is 13½ equinoctial hours. Almost all of the Great Bear appears on their arctic circle except for the legs, the end of its tail, and one of the stars in the rectangle. . . .

(38) In the places approximately 400 stades south of the parallel through Alexandria and Kyrene, where the greatest day is 14 equinoctial hours, Arcturus stands overhead, declining slightly southwards. At Alexandria, the gnomon has the same ratio to its equinoctial shadow as 5 does to 3. These (*places*) are 1,300 stades further south than Carthage, at least if the gnomon (*there*) has the same ratio to its equinoctial shadow as 11 does to 7. . . .

(39) In the places around the Ptolemaïs in Phoenicia, and around Sidon and Tyre, the greatest day is 14¼ equinoctial hours. These places are about 1,600 stades further north than Alexandria, and about 700 (*further north*) than Carthage. In the Peloponnese and around the middle of Rhodian territory, and around Xanthos in Lykia or the parts slightly further south, and also the parts 400 stades further south than the Syracusans' territory, there the greater day is 14½ equinoctial hours. These places are 3,640 stades from Alexandria ⟨and some 2,740 from Carthage⟩. . . .

(40) In the parts around Alexandria in the Troad, at Amphipolis, at Apollonia in Epeiros, and places further south than Rome but further north than Neapolis (*Naples*), the greatest day is 15 equinoctial hours. This parallel lies about 7,000 stades north of that through Alexandria-by-Egypt; above 28,800 from the equator; 3,400 from the parallel though Rhodes; but 1,500 south of Byzantion, Nikaia, and the places around Massalia. . . .

---

[89] For the notion of local 'arctic circles', see n. on Pyth. 7 §8.
[90] On changes in the night sky since antiquity, see n. on Erat. 61 §35.
[91] For discussion of this passage, see Dicks 1960, 172–94.

(41) In the places around Byzantion the greatest day is of 15¼ equinoctial hours and the gnomon at the summer solstice has the ratio to its shadow that 120 has to 42 less one-fifth (*i.e.* $41^4/_5$; *the ratio is thus c.2.92 to 1*). These places are at a distance of around 4,900 stades from the parallel through the middle of Rhodian territory and about 30,300 from the equator. For those who sail into the Pontos and advance towards the north about 1,400 stades, the greatest day becomes 15½ equinoctial hours. These places are the same distance from the pole and the equator, and their arctic circle is at the zenith; upon it lies the star on the neck of Cassiopeia, while that on the right elbow of Perseus is slightly further north.

(42) In the places lying about 3,800 stades north of Byzantion the greatest day is 16 equinoctial hours; therefore Cassiopeia revolves within their arctic circle. These places are around the Borysthenes and the southern parts of Lake Maiotis, and lie at a distance of about 34,100 (*stades*) from the equator. The northward part of the horizon, during nearly all the nights of summer, is partially illuminated by the sun as its light moves in a contrary direction, all the way from west as far as east.[92] For the summer tropic lies one-half plus one-twelfth (*i.e.* $^7/_{12}$) of a zodiacal sign (*i.e. 17° 30'*)[93] from the horizon, so that at midnight the sun stands the same distance from (*sc. below*) the horizon. Where we live, too, even before dawn and after the evening, being such a distance from (*i.e. below*) the horizon, it illuminates the air around the east and the west. In the winter (*days; sc. in those parts*), the sun rises at most 9 cubits. . . . In the places that are about 6,300 stades from Byzantion and are further north than Lake Maiotis, during the winter days the sun rises at most 6 cubits and the greatest day is 17 equinoctial hours.

(43) The regions beyond, now approaching the zone that is uninhabitable by reason of the cold, are no longer useful to the geographer. He who wishes to learn about them, and about such other heavenly phenomena as Hipparchos has talked of—but which we have left aside because they are too transparent to be part of the business before us—let him acquire the knowledge from him.

41 **Pliny**, *Natural History*, 2. cxii. 247: *Circumference of the Earth*
Hipparchos, who is admired for his refutation of him (*Eratosthenes*) and for his other careful work, adds just under 26,000 stades (*to the circumference of the Earth as calculated by Eratosthenes*).[94]

---

[92] Or possibly 'from setting (*dysis*) as far as rising (*anatolē*)' (ὑπὸ τοῦ ἡλίου ἀπὸ δύσεως ἕως καὶ ἀνατολῆς), but the absence of the definite articles suggests that here the two terms are directional markers. For solar terms as directions, see Shipley 2021b.

[93] One zodiacal sign being 30° ($^1/_{12}$ of a circle).

[94] Since Strabo at **34** and **38** states that H. accepted Eratosthenes' figure for the circumference of the Earth, this is probably a mistake by Pliny: Dicks 1960, 153.

42   Ptolemy, *Geography*, 1. 7. 4: *The constellation Ursa Minor*
It has been handed down by Hipparchos that the most southerly star in the Little Bear
(*Ursa Minor*), the last one in its tail, lies at a distance of 12²/₅ degrees from the pole.[95]

43   Ptolemy, *Geography*, 1. 7. 9: *Stars visible from the Equator*
He himself (*Marinos*) brings up that he has gathered, through mathematical accounts,[96]
that for those dwelling under the equator the whole of Orion appears before the summer solstice; and that the Dog (*Sirius*) begins to rise before Procyon for those dwelling
under the equator, and from them as far as Syene.

44   Ptolemy, *Syntaxis mathematica*, 1. 67. 22–68. 6: *Size of the zone between the tropics*
We have adopted the (*section of*) circumference from the most northerly extreme to
the most southerly, namely the section between the tropics, as being in all cases 47°
plus more than ⅔° and less than ½° + ¼° (*i.e.* ¾°).[97] The resulting calculation is nearly
the same ratio as that of Eratosthenes, which Hipparchos also made use of; for the
section between the tropics is approximately 11 of the units of which the meridian
contains 83.[98]

45   scholion to Ptolemy, **Geography** 1. 3. 3: *Method of calculating the Earth's circumference*
For in many cases, indeed most, places do not form a straight line, which is impossible
(*sc. on a sphere*). Employing a segment of circle, however, one can say what ratio the
intervening distance has to the Great Circle drawn upon it (*the Earth*). As has been
attested by Hipparchos and by Ptolemy himself, if we take the (*places*) at the zenith and
the distances between them in degrees, we shall find what ratio a distance has to the
great circle, and likewise to (*a great circle*) upon the Earth. For the circle in the heavens
and that inscribed upon the Earth will have the same circumference (*in degrees*). Let
there be (*an arc of*) a circle AB in the heavens and (*an arc of*) a circle CD inscribed
upon the Earth. Let E and F be the given places (*on the Earth*), and let the places at the
zenith be G and H, whose locations we shall find if we extend forwards the line of the
circle. For by finding the distance of the stars from one another in degrees using the
meteōroskopion,[99] we shall now have the distances (*of places on the Earth*) from one

---

[95] See discussion at Dicks 1960, 170–1. On the movement of stars since antiquity, see n. 90 to 40 §34.
[96] i.e. taken over from an earlier authority, probably Hipparchos (Dicks 1960, 169–70, who notes that
the phenomena here were determined by calculation, not observation).
[97] The result of the first calculation is between 47⅔° and 47¾°, i.e. from 47° 40′ to 47° 45′. Dividing it by
2 gives the latitude of either tropic (equal to the inclination of the ecliptic) as between 23° 50′ and 23° 52′.5.
[98] i.e. ¹¹/₈₃ of 360° = c.47° 42′ 39″, which being divided by 2 is 23° 51′ 19″.5. The obliquity of the ecliptic, in fact, changes: in Eratosthenes' day it was c.23° 43′ 40″; slightly less in H.'s, c.23° 42′ 55″ (Dicks
1960, 168); at epoch AD 2000 it was c.23°.439107 (= c.23° 26′ 21″) (Wittmann 1979). Both scholars
were working with a value that was slightly too high; this affected their calculations of latitude, which
were based on identifying the point further N than which the sun is never directly overhead.
[99] An instrument for measuring the positions of 'things on high' (*meteōra*), i.e. heavenly bodies. The
word 'distance', only implied in Dicks's text, is adopted from two MSS by Tsiotras 2018, 273 (*apparatus
criticus*, 274). Likewise, 'no longer' (below) follows T.'s text.

another in stades. If we are in the given places and identify the objects at the zenith using the instrument, we shall find that they also have the same distance between them on the Earth, according to how many stades each underlying degree contains; and there will no longer be any need to reckon the ratio in relation to the circumference of the whole Earth. This will be the case even if the given journey is not direct or perfectly straight.[100]

46 Synesios, *Letter to Paeonius* 5. 1–11 (*'On the Gift of the Astrolabe'*): *Stereographic projection*
The unfolding of a spherical surface that preserves ratios in a modification of shapes is a thing that the ancient writer Hipparchos wrote about in a vague fashion. He was the first to make the attempt on this speculation. But we—if it is not too grand a statement for us—have woven it right to the hem and have finished it, after the problem had been ignored for the majority of the intervening period. The mighty Ptolemy and the inspired band of his successors were keen only to embrace the use of it to the extent that the sixteen stars presented it as adequate for the night-time clock; these were the only ones that Hipparchos reorganized and installed on the instrument.[101]

---

[100] This is a later formulation of Poseidonios' method, effectively a theorization of that of Eratosthenes. The qualification at the end amounts to an admission that distance measurements and directions could not be perfectly accurate (see Dicks 1960, 149–52).

[101] Synesios describes (in vague terms) an instrument such as a map of the heavens or 'astrolabic clock of the Vitruvian type' (though probably not a planispheric astrolabe). In his exhaustive discussion, Dicks 1960, 194–207 (quotation at 202), doubts whether the passage is evidence that H. invented stereographic projection.

17

THE *NIKOMEDEAN PERIODOS* ['PSEUDO-SKYMNOS']

OR *IAMBICS TO KING NIKOMEDES*
(APOLLODOROS OF ATHENS? PAUSANIAS OF DAMASCUS?)
(127/6–74 BC)

D. Graham J. Shipley

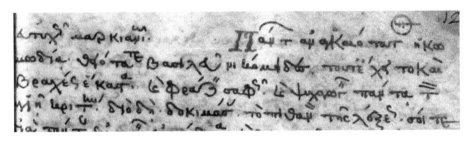

FIG. 17.1. Opening of the *Nikomedean Periodos*, p. 125 (detail).

INTRODUCTION

This didactic poem in Greek, now truncated, is the earliest surviving verse exposition of Greek geography (apart from the Homeric Catalogue of Ships: see the Prologue to these volumes) and the first known didactic poem in the flexible metre known as comic iambics.[1] Conventionally but misleadingly called 'Ps.-Skymnos' since the 17th century, it should more properly be called by some such title as 'The anonymous iambics for King Nikomedes', or less cumbersomely the *Nikomedean Periodos* (*Nik.* for short).[2]

The poem is dated by the name of its dedicatee, who must be one of the last three independent rulers of Bithynia in north-western Asia Minor: Nikomedes II (r. 149–127/6 BC), III (r. 127/6–94), and IV (r. 94–74). Given that the poet compliments his patron on being the last virtuous king (ll. 50–1), a date after the end of the Attalid dynasty of Pergamon in 133 is implied. Since he congratulates the king on his father's having had the aid of the god Apollo (via his oracle at Didyma in Ionia) to set the kingdom

---

[1] Marcotte 2000b, 24–5.

[2] Hence the name *Auctor* ('author') *ad Nicomedem regem*, adopted by Diller 1952, and his abbreviation 'Nic.' Roller 2022b adopts *The King Nikomedes Periodos*, which could be misunderstood as meaning that the king composed it. The attribution to Skymnos of Chios was merely a scholarly suggestion of the early modern period, later discounted (see introduction to Chapter 14); but the name 'Pseudo-Skymnos' has persisted. This is unfortunate: the truncated copy of the work in MS D would have carried its title and author's name at the end, so that there is no surviving claim of authorship to deny, let alone any evidence of a link with Skym., who is in any case too early. Ryan 2007 examines the problems caused by the obsolete sobriquet, proposing that we call the author Anonymus Parisinus Londiniensisque.

in order, the honorand can hardly be Nikomedes II, who had his father, Prousias II, put to death; he is surely, therefore, Nikomedes III or Nikomedes IV, giving a range of 127/6–74.[3]

Attempts to narrow the date range further are bound up with the attempt to identify the poem's author, a question that remains unresolved.[4] In the early era of printed editions, it was suggested that he was Skymnos of Chios,[5] but this was disproved. One suggestion, not so far taken up, is that the author is a certain Semos of Delos.[6] Marcotte, editor of the most comprehensive study, suggests the major figure of Apollodoros of Athens,[7] who was at one time under the patronage of Attalos II of Pergamon (r. 158–138), not far from Bithynia. Yet the opening verses obliquely but unmistakably commend Apollodoros (ll. 16–49) for presenting his historical work in the same metrical form; in this respect Apollodoros was indeed a pioneer, but the fulsome praise would then be self-praise. The identification of Apollodoros remains the one suggested by the principle of Ockham's razor, simply because Strabo (14. 5. 22, C677) specifically says Apollodoros wrote a *Ges periodos* in comic iambics.[8] Does Apollodoros as author leave himself unnamed to avoid the imputation of self-praise?

Others have found further reasons to contest Marcotte's identification,[9] such as by maintaining that the poem is a forgery masquerading as Apollodoros' work.[10] If Apollodoros' name could reliably be detected in the evanescent traces of line 123, would it disprove Marcotte's thesis? Not if we suppose a kind of irony, a pretence of detachment, even humour; but in any case the reading is itself uncertain.[11] We should not

[3] Marcotte 2000b argues for Nikomedes III, Braund 2019a for Nikomedes IV.

[4] Marcotte 2000b, 7–16, narrows the range to *c*.130–110/09; but his key argument—that when the poem was written book 4 of Apollodoros of Athens' *Chronika*, covering the period from 144/3 onwards, had not yet been published—depends on establishing whether a quotation from A. by the C1 author Philodemos echoes l. 21 of the poem or is echoed by it; on which point, certainty seems unattainable. Boshnakov 2004 favours *c*.120.

[5] See n. 2 above.   [6] Boshnakov 2004.

[7] Marcotte 2000b, 42–4 (cf. Marcotte 1990, 43–4).

[8] This is to be distinguished from A.'s *Peri ges* (*On the Earth*), whose definite and possible fragments are assembled by Marcotte 2000b, 266–70: up to 28, all from Steph. Byz.; twelve explicitly cite book 2 of *Peri ges*, while fr. 12 (Steph. Byz. *v* 20 Nastos) cites book 2 of *Periegesis* (Meineke 1849, 478, l. 11, adopts the emendation *Peri ges*, which Billerbeck prints silently; Marcotte retains *Periegesis* silently; Williams 2018, on *BNJ*[2] 244 F 320, retains and discusses, but miscites Strabo 14. 5. 22, C677, as saying A. wrote a *Periegesis*—S. says *Ges periodos*). Marcotte finds correspondences between the fragments of *Peri ges* and *Nik.*

[9] e.g. Boshnakov 2004, 43–53.

[10] Thus Bravo 2009, esp. ch. 1 (pp. 1–29), with review by Leroy 2011.

[11] Bravo 2009, 7–17, detects the name; but see doubts expressed by Fleischer 2020, 22–3. My own inspection of detailed colour and UV photographs, kindly supplied by M. Christian Förstel (Bibliothèque Nationale de France), confirms some of the letters read by Bravo (who in turn confirms some of the readings by Miller, Letronne, Haase, and Müller in C19), but not, as yet, the name of Apollodoros. The lines in question were already partly illegible by the year 1505 (Bravo, p. 7). Hanigan and Kynaston 2023 also doubt Bravo's readings, propose that a line is missing after 126 (they offer a tentative reconstruction), and argue that the author here acknowledges Timaios as a major source more fully than was previously apparent.

overlook, however, a possibility which Marcotte rightly leaves open:[12] that the poet is the otherwise unknown Pausanias of Damascus, on the basis of an elegant observation by Diller which remains tempting. The suggestion seems supported by the fact that one of the authors who appear to cite this Pausanias comments that he is said to have written 'poetically', though one cannot be sure that this is intended to imply that he wrote in verse.[13] On the other hand, the very existence of Pausanias of Damascus has been cast into doubt on palaeographic grounds.[14]

The author, whoever he be, begins with the lengthy dedication that establishes his credentials (ll. 1–108). This is followed by an introduction (ll. 109–38) explaining his working method and naming the authors upon whom he has drawn; only eight names survive out of what was once a longer list in the passage that includes the damaged lines 119–25. Finally, beginning from the area of Gibraltar, he makes a tour of the north side of the Mediterranean and eventually enters the western Black Sea, soon after which the continuous text breaks off after line 747. Lines 87–8 express a division into Europe and Asia which may hint that the poem was divided into two books.[15]

As is the case with several other works in the present volumes, this continuous passage is preserved only in one manuscript: the last 19 pages (125–43) of codex 'D' of the geographers (see Introduction, §VIII. 2. b). Additional excerpts referring to the Black Sea are found in the late antique Pseudo-Arrianic *Euxine* (Chapter 36 below), easily betrayed by their iambic metre—though they occur in the opposite geographical sequence since the late *Euxine* describes the Pontos anti-clockwise. Diller and others attempt to use these snippets of verse to construct several hundred more lines of the

---

[12] As does Korenjak 2003. Boshnakov 2004, in his edition of the Black Sea section of the work, suggests as author the little-known Semos of Delos and/or Elis (*BNJ* 396), credited with two *periploi* (circumnavigations) by the *Suda*; but Semos lived around 200 BC.

[13] Ioannes Malalas cites 'Pausanias the chronographer' several times, including *Chronographia*, p. 204 ll. 7–8 Dindorf: 'the same most wise Pausanias has also written many other things poetically' (*poiē-tikōs*); attributed, however, to P. of *Antioch* by Asirvatham 2012 (*BNJ* 854 F 10, last line). This passage is not cited by Diller 1952, 177 (addenda), or by Diller 1955.

[14] Diller 1955 points out that when the Byzantine scholar-emperor Constantine VII Porphyrogenne-tos cites the geographical authors he consulted to verify a fact (*De thematibus*, 1. 2; Greek quoted in Diller 1952, 177 (addenda), with his earlier discussion), his list (apart from Strabo, whom he names first, and unspecified others) ends with 'Pausanias of Damascus' and seems to match the order of the texts in codex D, an earlier copy of which CP almost certainly used. D, as we have it, ends with the present poem, whose author's name probably stood after its end, which is missing. The suggestion is thus that CP found P.'s name there. Note the caution of Marcotte 1990, 42–3; Marcotte 2000b, 38–40. Asirvatham 2012 examines the suggestion, by Christ, Schmid, and Stahlin 1924, 759 n. 2 ~ Christ 1890, 577 n. 5, that CP skipped a few words and that we should read 'Pausanias ⟨of Antioch and Niko-laos⟩ of Damaskos' (Nikolaos is cited elsewhere by CP). Diller was aware of that idea (1955, 276 n. 41), and regards both Palmer's suggestion of *Mazakēnos* for *Damaskēnos*, and (less justifiably?) Christ's, as 'violent alterations'; but Asirvatham improves C.'s supplement ⟨*Antiocheus*⟩ to ⟨*Antiochēnos*⟩, the similarity of the latter to *Damaskēnos* providing an occasion for confusion (by *saut du même au même*) and thus removing P. of Damaskos from the circles of the world. P. of Antioch cannot replace him as a candidate for authorship of *Nik.*, for he postdates the accession of Claudius (*FGrH* 854 F 11). If Christ's theory is right, the question of authorship remains open. (Dueck 2008b accepts the attribution to P. of Damascus.)

[15] Korenjak 2011.

poem,[16] but this risks giving a misleading impression of near-completeness; Marcotte's arrangement into separate fragments is preferable.[17] These take us almost all the way round the Black Sea, back to the entry point. The preservation of this material in the *Euxine* necessarily does not extend to the last portion of the poem, which presumably continued its clockwise progress round the Mediterranean via Asia Minor, the Levant, and Egypt, returning to the Pillars of Herakles. An original text of some 1,500–2,000 lines may be imagined.

Acutely aware of the need to pay respect to traditional geographical enumerations while establishing his own originality, the poet shows that he has absorbed lessons from his wide reading. He refers frequently to foundation myths, occasionally citing one of his authorities. After initially following the example of Pseudo-Skylax[18] and others in dividing Mediterranean space into ethnic units, while aware of Eratosthenes' innovation in moving away from this practice (cf. Eratosthenes 46 above),[19] at line 470 he signals a change, stating that in the case of the Greek homeland he will adopt the practice of Ephoros of Kyme (*c.*400–330), the founder of universal history, and arrange his material not by ethnic community but by state.[20] The poet's response to Ephoros varies, however, as between the western and eastern portions of the surviving narrative, reflecting the poet's wish to please King Nikomedes; while the rhetorical purpose of the work, to honour a patron, determines that he is less affected by nostalgia for the lost glories of Greece than by a desire to base a legitimation of the Bithynian dynasty on the invocation of respectable authorities.[21]

Apollodoros and the present author adopted comic iambics because they allow longer successions of short syllables than do formal iambics (the metre of, for example, speeches in Athenian tragedies) and are thus more amenable to the inclusion of place-names. A literary work rather than a technical treatise on geography, the poem does not strictly follow a coastal 'route' but veers inland at certain points.[22] It acquires historical importance from its assertion of the Mediterranean supremacy of Rome (ll. 231–5); though this claim is less important, perhaps, the closer we date the work to the 70s BC. It is also one of the earliest geographical works to equate 'Great Greece', *Megalē Hellas*, with *Italia* (l. 304) or southern Italy—Magna Graecia in Latin—which was the part of Italy best known to the Greeks and whose coasts were most heavily settled by them. The poem's emphasis on autopsy (ll. 128–36) as a foundation for credibility

---

[16] Notably by Diller 1952, 166–76, ll. 748–1026.

[17] Followed by Korenjak 2011. Bravo 2009, xxiii, urges a bolder approach; I prefer M.'s practice of assigning more weight to the evidence of primary MSS.

[18] Did he know the Ps.-Skylax *periplous* under its original author's name? Is that author named in the surviving lines, or was he named in the damaged ll. 119–25?

[19] On the influence of Eratosthenes on *Nik.*, see Geus 2002, 285–6.

[20] Marcotte 2000b, 62.

[21] Bianchetti 2014. Marcotte 1990, 40, observes that *Nik.* describes Greece as it was before his day (citing Müller *GGM* i, p. lxxviii; N. G. L. Hammond 1967, 515–17).

[22] Korenjak 2011, with fold-out sketch map following p. 10.

is also notable,[23] and implies that the author was widely travelled. Drawing as it does upon the work of Eratosthenes, the text can be used, with caution, to help reconstruct the chronology of early Greek settlement in the West, as least as believed by the Greeks.

The relationship between the *Iambics* and other works, such as those of Apollodoros and Avienus, continues to stimulate discussion,[24] as do the poet's references to foundation dates of colonies.[25] The work has prompted intricate analyses of its relationship with earlier writings: the figure of Odysseus, for example, has been found to loom large in the subtext of the poem and its role of compliment to a king.[26] It is also one of the few texts in the present book that has a highly developed aesthetic—the other main example is the polished Homeric hexameters of Dionysios Periegetes (Chapter 28)—though some more 'factual' writings, even the laconic Ps.-Skylax (Chapter 7), can be seen to exhibit a deliberate choice of linguistic effects in places, and thus to have their own 'poétique'.[27] As the first elaborate verse work on the Greeks' geographical outlook upon their world, it justifies the author's claim to be a pioneer; but its legacy in the literary and geographical tradition was negligible except for the late antique Pseudo-Arrianic *Euxine*.[28]

Earlier scholarship has been superseded by the comprehensive study of Marcotte, whose lengthy introduction explores the poem's relationship to other hellenistic works as well as questions of genre, the poet's organization of his material, and his frequent use of specific historical chronology.[29] The translation (loosely in English iambic pentameters) follows Marcotte's Greek text and his arrangement of fragments (though renumbered). Double quotation marks " " indicate phrases within the prose of the Pseudo-Arrianic *Euxine* that are confidently identified as coming from the lost portion of the poem, though many further phrases may also be taken from it, as the reader may verify by comparing Chapter 36.

SELECTED FURTHER READING

Bianchetti, S. (2014), 'Aspetti di geografia eforea nei Giambi a Nicomede', *La parola del passato*, 69: 394–400; 751–80.

Boshnakov, K. (2004), *Pseudo-Skymnos (Semos von Delos?), Τὰ ἀριστερὰ τοῦ Πόντου: Zeugnisse griechischer Schriftsteller über den westlichen Pontosraum*. Stuttgart. [On the western Black Sea.]

Bravo, B. (2009), *La Chronique d'Apollodore et le Pseudo-Skymnos: érudition antiquaire et littérature géographique dans la seconde moitié du IIe siècle av. J.-C.* Leuven. [With reviews by P. Leroy, *BMCR* 2011.01.27; M. Mund-Dopchie, *L'Antiquité classique*, 80. 1 (2011), 270–2.]

---

[23] Korenjak 2003, 18.

[24] See notably Bravo 2009, ch. 3 (pp. 112–58, and generally on the poems' representation of a past maritime world.

[25] See e.g. De Boer 2006 and Avram 2009 on the Black Sea; Bats 2009 on Gaul; Mele 2009 and Mele 2016 on Italy; Bereti, Consagra *et al.* 2013 on the Adriatic.

[26] Jessica Lightfoot 2020a, esp. 394–409.   [27] Marcotte 2000b, lxx.

[28] Marcotte 2000b, 90–3. The character of Zenothemis' work (Introduction, §VI. 4 b fin.) is uncertain.

[29] Boshnakov 2004 focuses only on the western Black Sea; Korenjak 2003, with a translation but no Greek text, aims chiefly at introducing the work to a wider German-speaking readership.

Diller, A. (1952), *The Tradition of the Minor Greek Geographers*. Lancaster, Pa.–Oxford. [Ch. 6 (pp. 165–76) on the fragments.]

Hunter, R. L. (2006), 'The prologue of the periodos to Nicomedes ("Pseudo-Scymnus")', in M. A. Harder *et al.* (eds), *Beyond the Canon* (Leuven), 123–40.

*Korenjak, M. (2003), *Die Welt-Rundreise eines anonymen griechischen Autors ('Pseudo-Skymnos')*. Hildesheim.

—— (2003), 'Textkritische und interpretatorische Bemerkungen zu Pseudo-Skymnos', *Philologus*, 147. 2: 226–37.

*—— (2011), 'Pseudo-Skymnos (2048)', in *FGrH* v.

Lightfoot, Jessica (2020a), '"Not enduring the wanderings of Odysseus": poetry, prose, and patronage in Pseudo-Scymnus's Periodos to Nicomedes', *Transactions of the American Philological Association*, 150. 2: 379–413.

*Marcotte, D. (2000), *Introduction générale; Ps.-Scymnos, Circuit de la terre*. Paris. ['Budé' edition.]

A. CONTINUOUS TEXT

Codex Parisinus supplément grec 443, pp. 125. 1–143. 26

Headings are added.

PREFACE

Of all things the following is most essential for comedy
to possess, O most divine King Nikomedes:[30]
the capacity to express each thing briefly and clearly,
and to enchant in all respects the man who is a sound judge.
So, after proving the style was plausible,
I aimed at making contact with you through it,
and enjoying a brief discussion. I have laboured
to render this assembled outline composition
beneficial, intending to proffer its utility,
10   through you, to all who desire to pursue learning.
So, wishing first to expound clearly to you
the justification of the whole composition,
I require few words devoted to the preamble:
for it is my resolve, in Laconian fashion,
to speak of great matters in the shortest compass.
    What I have to write is this: in honour of the kings
in Pergamon—whose glory, even after death,

---

[30] For the dedicatee's identity and the significance of the poet's choice of the comic iambic metre, see introduction to chapter.

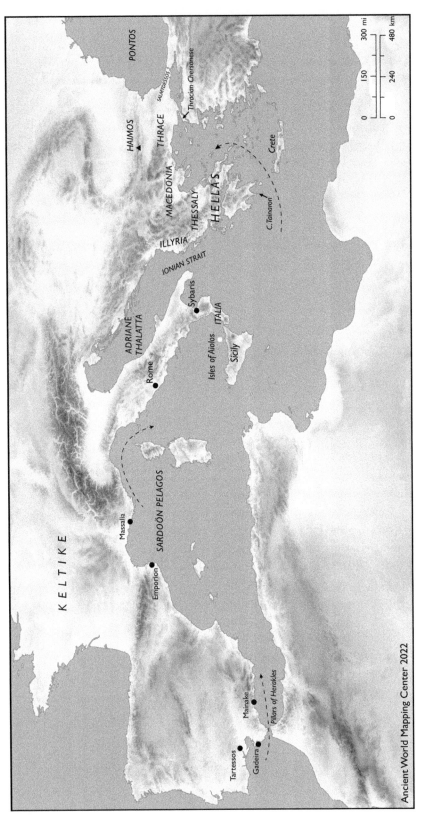

MAP 17.1. *Nikomedean Periodos:* narrative sequence and selected places.

Ancient World Mapping Center 2022

       remains alive among us for all time[31]—
       one of the true Attic philologists,[32]
20   having listened to Diogenes the Stoic
       and passed a lengthy time with Aristarchos,[33]
       composed a chronological record that went
       from the capture of Troy down to our present lifetime.
       Forty years he expounded in addition
       to a thousand,[34] in definite fashion, enumerating
       captures of cities, displacements of army camps,
       relocations of nations, expeditions by barbarians,
       assaults and passages by naval forces,
       contests held, alliances, treaties, battles,
30   deeds of kings, lives of famous men,
       exile, expeditions, abolition of tyrannies—
       a summary of all that has been told confusingly.
       He chose to expound this summary in verse,
       indeed the comic metre, for the sake of clarity,
       realizing that thus it would be easily memorized.
       He took a simile imagined from real life:
       as if a man wished to pick up and carry
       a loose pile of wood, he would not be able
       to hold it easily, but tied together would be easier;
40   so one cannot pick up disconnected language
       quickly, but if it is contained in metre
       one can grasp it unerringly and faithfully.
       For it has a certain grace running through it,
       when history and language are woven in verse.
           That author, gathering the headlines of chronology,
       yielded them to the favour of Philadelphos.[35]
       They ran through the whole inhabited world,
       bestowing undying glory upon Attalos,
       who received the dedication of the treatise.
50   But I, hearing that you, alone of all
       the kings of today, exhibit kingly virtue,
       desired to make a trial upon myself,

[31] The last Macedonian king of the Attalid dynasty at Pergamon, Attalos III, had died in 133 leaving his kingdom to the Roman People.

[32] Apollodoros of Athens; see introduction to chapter.

[33] Aristarchos of Samothrace, head of the Library at Alexandria in C2m. On this line, see n. 4.

[34] Eratosthenes had dated the fall of Troy to 1184/3 BC. On the poem's relationship to Apollodoros' *Chronika*, see n. 4.

[35] Attalos II Philadelphos, king of Pergamon 159–138.

to come to you and see what a king is,
so I can report back to others myself.
Therefore, as adviser to my project I selected
the one who earlier rectified the affairs
of the kingdom for your father, as we hear;
one genuinely honoured by you, O king,
in all matters; I mean Apollo of Didyma,

60   giver of oracles, leader of the Muses.
So, trusting almost totally in him,
I came to your hearth at your command, which you
had almost declared public for lovers of learning.
May the god lay his hand upon my choice!
     From things recorded by some in scattered fashion,
I have written for you, in summary, the colonies,
foundations of cities, and almost all over the Earth
those places that are sailable and passable.
Of these things, those that are distinct and clear

70   I shall précis and expound summarily;
while such of them as are not clearly known
my account will present in detail part by part.
Thus, O King, you shall have the delineation
of all the inhabited world in concise form:
the properties and courses of great rivers;
the position of the two continents part by part;
in each of them, which cities belong to Hellenes;
who founded them, at what times dwelt within them,
both those of one nation and the aboriginal;

80   what races of barbarians are their neighbours,
which of the latter are called mixed, which nomadic,
which are peaceable, which are most inhospitable
in customs and barbaric in ways ⟨and⟩ deeds;
which of the nations are greatest and richest in men;
what laws and ways of life each nation has;
which trading-cities are the most successful;
the position of all the islands beside Europe,
⟨and⟩ then the ones that lie alongside Asia;
the city foundations handed down within them;

90   in short, an exposition of all places
and the whole circuit in a few short verses.
     He that listens will not just take pleasure,
but take from it the benefit of learning

—if nothing else, they say—where he is on the Earth,
and in which places lies his fatherland,
to which inhabitants it once belonged,
and with which kinds of cities it claims kinship.
To state it briefly: without undertaking
what the myths call the Wandering of Odysseus,
100 but remaining blessedly in his own land,
he shall know not only the variegated life
of humans, but all nations' towns and laws.[36]
My composition, finding you its most
distinguished founder and its kindest champion,
shall pass through studious childbed into life.
It shall declare your fame, O King, to all,
as it is sent about from place to place,
and to those after declare your good repute.
 I shall now move to the start of my composition
110 by setting out the writers[37] by whose use
I make my historical account reliable.
For I have relied especially on the one
who has most carefully written about geography,
both zones (*of latitude*) and forms,[38] Eratosthenes;
and Ephoros;[39] and him who tells foundations
in five books, Chalkidian Dionysios;[40]
and Demetrios, the writer from Kallatis;[41]
Sicilian Kleon,[42] and Timosthenes[43]
(*who*) — — the position of the — —
120 and the (*fellow?*) citizen — —
  — — — — — —

---

[36] A clear allusion to the first lines of the *Odyssey*. Possibly νόμους–*nomous* ('laws') should be νόους–*noöus* ('minds') in light of *Od.* 1. 3 'knew their mind'. Conversely, νόμον 'law' was an ancient variant for νόον 'mind' in that line of *Od.* (Marcotte ad loc.).

[37] Marcotte 2000a, 155, notes that the word for 'writer' (*syngrapheus*) should denote prose authors, not poets.

[38] *schēmata*, referring to the *sphragides* or 'sealstones' into which Eratosthenes divided the *oikoumenē*.

[39] Ephoros of Kyme in Aiolis (C4; *BNJ 70*), author of a universal history arranged thematically rather than in strict chronological fashion.

[40] Dionysios of Chalkis (perhaps C4, see Bucher 2016, F 11; or C2, see Korenjak 2003, 16 n. 24) wrote a book on city foundations.

[41] A C3 historian and geographer.

[42] Little-known author of a *periplous*; see Meyer forthcoming. Marcotte 2000a, 155, suggests Leon.

[43] See Ch. 10 above.

— — — — — — [44]

— — places —

— also following (?) Kallisthenes[45] — —

— — — — — certain — and

Timaios, a Sicilian from Tauromenion,[46]

and from the things composed by Herodotos.

    Also what I have examined with much labour,

bringing the reliability of an eye-witness.

130   I am an observer not only of Hellas

or the little towns lying about Asia,

but a researcher into the Adriatic

and those, in turn, around the Ionian (*sea*);

I have visited the frontiers of Tyrrhenia,[47]

the bounds of Sicily and those to the west,

and the greater part of Libyē and Carthage.

Assembling most of these, I shall begin;

and first I shall arrange the places in Europe.

---

[44] These lines are largely illegible and their reconstruction contested. Line 119 may require a mention of the winds or perhaps of Rhodes. Marcotte 2000b, 109 n. 17, believes that ll. 120–2 almost certainly named Theopompos of Chios and Hekataios of Abdera (or Teos), in which case l. 120 would imply that the poet was from one of those cities. In the view of Korenjak 2003, 17, however, the list of authorities probably contained no further names. After re-examining the MS, Bravo 2009, 7–17, reconstructs ll. 119–26 thus (my translation):

> I [learn]ed the position of [all the inhabited worl]d;
> and [I chose (?) as guide] my fellow citizen
> Apollodoros, known to everyone,
> while endeavouring to investigate some places
> inserted into the catalogue in the *Iliad*.
> Similarly, I have taken [as guide(s)?] Kallisthenes
> and K[leitar]ch[os? and on] certain points
> Timaios . . .

Leroy 2011, reviewing Bravo, is sceptical about 'Apollodoros' and other new readings; but a few of B.'s readings seem confirmed by my own prolonged inspection of online images of the MS, and of other study images in colour kindly supplied by M. Christian Förstel in 2021. Few letters, however, can be identified beyond doubt. See, further, n. 46 below.

[45] The historian of Alexander the Great (*c*.370–327) may have written a *periplous* (Marcotte 2000b, 156), but such a work is cited only in scholia to Apollonios of Rhodes (*BNJ* 124 F 6 on 1. 1037; F 7 on 2. 672), which may really refer to K.'s *Deeds of Alexander*.

[46] Early Hl historian who composed his major works at Athens (*BNJ* 566). Hanigan and Kynaston 2023, with persuasive syntactical arguments, posit a missing line after 126, reconstructing it (as 126a) to give (in my words) '⟨who reports some things, writing in accordance with Ephoros⟩ from among the things composed by Herodotos, but has examined other things with much labour, bringing the reliability of an eye-witness'. *NP* thus credits Timaios more fully than scholars have appreciated.

[47] Etruria (*Tuscany*).

IBERIA

The mouth that leads to the Atlantic sea (*thalatta*)
140   is said to be a hundred and twenty stades (*long*).
The land enclosing it nearby is, first,
the cape of Libyē; the other, that of Europe.
the islands lying either side of these
are roughly thirty stades from one another,
and are called by certain persons the Pillars
of Herakles. Near one of these is a Massaliot
city, called Mainake;[48] this has the furthest position
of all of the Hellenic cities in Europe.
150   When one has rounded the cape that is opposite
the setting sun, there is a voyage of a day,
after which there follows the island called
Erytheia; altogether short in length
and having herds of cattle and other animals
and some resembling both the Egyptian bulls
and the Thesprotian ones in Epeiros.
They say this place has westward Aithiopes[49]
as settlers, a colony having been made.
    Quite close to this there is a city which took
160   a colony of Tyrian traders: it is ⟨called⟩
Gadeira,[50] where the story is that great
sea-monsters are born. After this, with two days' voyage
completed, is a successful trading-place:
Tartessos it is called, a famous city,
with river tin out of the Keltic land
brought in, and gold, and quantities of copper.

KELTIKE

The next land is known as Keltike,
as far as the sea that is lying beside Sardo;[51]
this is the largest nation towards the west.
170   For the land within the sunrises is mostly
settled by Indians, that by the midday sun

---

[48] The poet refers too soon to places E of Gibraltar, to which he presently returns; he appears to confuse this Carthaginian foundation with Malake (*Malaga*), which is closer to the strait (Korenjak 2011).
[49] For 'western Aithiopes' cf. Ps.-Skyl. §112. 5–12, and the Index.
[50] *Cádiz.*   [51] Sardinia.

by Aithiopes, lying near the south wind's breath;
the west wind's place as far as summer sunsets
the Keltoi hold; that by the north wind Skythai.
　　Indians dwell between the summer and winter
sunrises; Keltoi, conversely, it is said,
under the equinoctial and ⟨summer⟩ sunset.[52]
So the four nations are equal in their crowds
and in their masses of inhabitants:

180　　the Aithiopes' and Skythians' land is larger,
though with a great amount of desert, since
the one has more fiery parts, the other wet.
　　The Keltoi have customs of Hellenic kind,
having close relations to Hellas because of
receiving those who come as guests among them.
They organize assemblies using music,
prizing it thanks to the calming power it has.
The last place lying in their territory
is the so-called column ⟨of Briareus?⟩;[53] mighty high,

190　　extending a cape in the wavy open sea (*pelagos*).
There dwelling, in the places near the column,
are the Kelts who come to an end, being furthest off,
both †Enetoi and of those within the Adriatic
extending to the Istros†.[54] They say that from here
the Istros takes the origin of its current.

SARDINIAN SEA

In places lying by the open sea (*pelagos*) of Sardo[55]
live Libyphoenicians, who took a colony
out of Carthage. Next, the story goes,
Tartessioi have the land; then their neighbours,

200　　the Iberians. There lie above these places
the Bebrykes. Next and below there follow
the maritime Ligyes[56] and the Hellenic cities

---

[52] i.e. between W and NW. 'Equinoctial' is *isēmerinēs*, lit. 'equidiurnal'; see Introduction, §X. 3. b fin. This passage echoes Timosthenes 18 (the poet cites him at l. 118 above).

[53] The text is corrupted; the name of Briareus, one of the legendary Giants, is suggested by Marcotte 2000b, 165.

[54] Another corrupt passage, which however, clearly posits some kinship between the Celts of the *Fin-isterre* region and the peoples of the inner Adriatic. The Enetoi may be the similarly named people of l. 387 (in the mod. *Veneto* region), though the accentuation varies (as it does in Ps.-Skyl. §§19–20).

[55] The poet refers to the westernmost basin of the Mediterranean.　　[56] Ligurians.

which Massaliot Phokaians colonized:
first Emporion, ⟨and⟩ in second place Rhode;
the latter founded by the then sea lords,
the Rhodioi, after whom the Phokaian founders
of Massalia,[57] coming to Iberia, took Agathe[58]
and Rhodanousia,[59] beside which flows the great river
Rhodanos.[60] Massalia then follows,

210   a very great city, colony of the Phokaians.
It was in Ligystine[61] that they founded
this city, a hundred and twenty years, they say,
before the battle that took place at Salamis.
This is how Timaios narrated the foundation.
Next after this is Tauroëis, and nearby
the city of Olbia, and Antipolis, the furthest.[62]
    After Ligystine are the Pelasgoi,[63]
who earlier came and settled here from Hellas,
holding the land in common with Tyrrhenoi.

220   Tyrrhenia was founded when Lydian Tyrrhenos,
Atys' son, once came to the Ombrikoi.[64]
In the strait lie islands in the open sea (*pelagiai*):
Kyrnos[65] and Sardo—said to be the largest
after the isle of Sicily—and those formerly
called Seirenides[66] and Circe's Islands.[67]

226   Above the Pelasgoi are the Ombrikoi
(*at least 1 line missing*)
— — — ⟨the Latinoi⟩,

227   whom Latinos founded, born of Odysseus
and Circe; and the Ausones, holding an inland
place, it seems were unified by Auson,

230   the child born of Odysseus and Kalypso.
Among these nations is the city of Rome,
which has a name the rival of its power;
a common star for the whole inhabited world,
in Latine.[68] Romulus founded it, they say,
putting on it this name taken from himself.

---

[57] *Marseille.*   [58] *Agde.*   [59] Unlocated.   [60] *Rhône.*
[61] Liguria. The MS gives the commoner form *Ligystikē*, which Marcotte corrects (here and at 217) to *Ligystinē*, noting Steph. Byz.'s entry for that name and Lykophron, *Alexandra*, 1356.
[62] Tauroëis is unlocated; Olbia was near *Hyères*; Antipolis is *Antibes.*
[63] An ancestral people of the Greeks, Hdt. 1. 56–8; see the study by Sourvinou-Inwood 2003.
[64] Umbrians.   [65] Corsica.   [66] 'Siren Isles'; cf. Erat. 5 §§12–14.
[67] Perhaps the promontory of Kirkaion (*Monte Circeo*).   [68] Latium.

After the Latinoi a city among the Opikoi,[69]
lying close to the so-called Lake Aornos,[70]
Kyme.[71] Formerly Chalkidians colonized it,
then Aiolians. Here is displayed the underground
240   oracle of Cerberus; and to it, they say,
came Odysseus, making his return from Circe.
From this Kyme, lying by Aornos,
Neapolis[72] had its foundation after an oracle.
    Beside these people live the Saunitai,[73] following
upon the Ausones. After these, lying inland,
dwell both the Leukanoi[74] and the Kampanoi.[75]
Adjoining these, again, are the Oinotrioi
as far as the land named Poseidonias,
which they say the Sybaritai colonized once;
250   and Elea, city of Massaliotai and Phokaians,
which the Phokaians founded as they fled
during the Persian wars. The city of Phokaia,
lying in Asia, was well supplied with men.
    In the strait of Tyrrhenia there lie
islets, seven in number, not far from Sicily,
which they refer to as the Isles of Aiolos.[76]
One of them is called Hiera,[77] and with reason:
for burning fires appear from out of it,
visible to all from a distance of some stades,
260   with expulsions of fiery anvils to a height,
the works of hammers and their iron clash.
There is one of them that has a Dorian colony;
its name is Lipara, kindred city to Knidos.

SICILY

Next is the very fortunate island of Sicily.
They say that formerly barbarian masses
of different tongues from Iberia possessed it.
Because of this land's different-sided nature,
it was called Trinakria[78] by the Iberians,
but in time was renamed Sikelia[79] again
270   in the reign of Sikelos; then it received Hellenic

---

[69] The Osci or Oscans.   [70] Avernus.   [71] Cumae.   [72] *Naples.*   [73] Samnites.
[74] Lucanians.   [75] Campanians.   [76] *Lipari* Is.   [77] 'Sacred Isle'.
[78] 'Triple Cape'.   [79] Sicily.

cities, they say, after the Trojan events,
in the tenth generation after, when Theokles
received a fleet from the Chalkidians; by race
he was from Athens; and the story goes
that Ionian settlers, then Dorians, joined in.
When strife occurred among them, the Chalkidians
founded Naxos, the Megarians Hybla,
and the Dorians seized Epizephyrion
in Italia. Taking these last with him, Archias
280   the Corinthian, with the Dorians, founded a city
that took its name from the lake it borders on:
Syrakousai, as it is now called by its people.
    After this, from Naxos the ⟨city of⟩ Leontine,
and the city positioned opposite Rhegion
and lying on the strait of Sicily, Zankle,
had colonies, as did Katane and Kallipolis.
From these, in turn, two further cities were settled,
and these are called Euboia and Mylai;
then Himera follows, then Tauromenion;
290   all these are cities of Chalkidians.
The Dorians, again, it is necessary to state:
the Megarians founded Selinous, the Geloans
Akragas, but Messene[80] the Ionians from Samos,
and the Syrakosioi the one called Kamarina:
but they themselves razed it to its foundations
after it had been settled six and forty years.
These, then, are the cities of Hellenic kind:
but the rest of the settlements[81] are barbarian,
the Carthaginians having fortified the places.

MAGNA GRAECIA

300   Italia is adjacent to Oinotria;
previously it had mixed barbarians in it,
and took its name from the man who was king there,
Italos; later it was referred to as
'Great Hellas to the West', after its colonies;
at any rate, it has maritime cities of the
Hellenic kind: Terina first, colonized
by the Krotoniates earlier, ⟨and⟩ nearby

---

[80] *Messina.*   [81] sc. those in Sicily.

Hipponion and Medma, which the Lokroi founded.
Next are the Rheginoi and the city of Rhegion,

310 where the shortest crossing to Sicily for a sailor
is found; the Chalkidians appear to have been
the colonists of Rhegion. The so-called
Epizephyrian Lokrians lie nearby.
They say these were the first people with written
laws, which Zaleukos appears to have enjoined;
they are colonists from the Opountian Lokrians,
but some say from the Lokrians in Ozolai.
There follows upon these people, first, Kaulonia,
which had a colony from out of Kroton;

320 ⟨and⟩ from the valley[82] lying very near
the city, this one later took its name
and, over time, was renamed as Kaulonia.
Next after this, a city most successful
and well-populated of old, Kroton,
which Myskelos the Achaian seems to have founded.
After Kroton, Pandosia and Thourioi;
sharing a border with these is Metapontion.
They say the founders of all these cities were
Achaians coming from the Peloponnese.

330 Next is the largest one in Italia, Taras,[83]
called by the name of a certain hero, Taras,
colonist from Lakedaimon; a successful city.
For the Partheniai founded this of old,
a lucky site, strong, a natural success;
drawn in by two harbours, like an island,
it has a sheltered landing for any ⟨ship⟩.
There was a city, greatly celebrated
in hymns; large, weighty, rich, and beautiful,
which from the river Sybaris was named

340 Sybaris, famous colony of Achaians.
It almost had ten myriads[84] of townsmen
and was provisioned with very great abundance.
Lifted up beyond all human measure,
they destroyed their famous city, men and all,
not learning to bear well an excess of good things.
For it is said they no longer would observe

---

[82] *aulōn.*   [83] Tarentum.   [84] i.e. 100,000.

the consequences of Zaleukos' laws;
that having chosen luxury and a lazy life
they progressed, in time, to arrogance and satiety;

350   that they were eager to dissolve the contest
of the Olympia and to abolish the honours
due to Zeus upon the following pretext:
they held a gymnastic contest with vast rewards
at the same time as that of the Eleians,[85] so that
any man, induced by the prizes, might hasten
to descend upon them and leave Hellas behind.
The Krotoniatai, located nearby,
captured them by force after a short time,
after they had remained untroubled in every way

360   for one hundred and ninety more than twenty ⟨years⟩.

IONIAN SEA AND ADRIATIC

Immediately after Italia lies the Ionian
strait.[86] Extending down towards the entrance
there dwell Iapygians, after them Oinotrians
and Brentesion,[87] harbour town of the Messapians.
     Across from these are the Keraunian mountains.
⟨To the west of⟩ the Messapians dwell the Ombrikoi,
who are said to have chosen a delicate way of life,
living in a fashion most like the Lydians.
     Then there is the so-called Adrianē sea.[88]

370   Theopompos[89] writes up the position of this:
forming an isthmus together with the Pontic,
it has islands most similar to the Cyclades,
among which are the so-called Apsyrtidai
and Elektridai, as well as the Libyrnidai.[90]
They report that around the Adriatikos gulf
there live a mass of barbarians in a circle,
nearly a hundred and fifty myriads,[91]
possessing very fine and fertile land;
for they say that even the animals bear twins.

380   The air over these people changes as compared
with the Pontic, despite the latter being nearby:

---

[85] Olympia lay in the region of Elis in the NW Peloponnese.   [86] *poros*, 'channel'.
[87] *Brindisi.*   [88] Adriatic.   [89] Theopompos of Chios, C4 historian.
[90] Cf. similar names at Ps.-Skyl. §21. 1–2.   [91] i.e. 1½ million.

for it is not snowy or excessively chilled,
but remains thoroughly wet at all times;
it is sharp and chaotic in respect of changes,
particularly in summer, and takes hits
from waterspouts, lightning-bolts, and the so-called
typhoons. Of the Enetoi there are about fifty
cities lying in it (*the gulf*), at the head,
whose people, they say, came out from the Paphlagonians'

390   land, and settled round the Adrias.
Here the Eridanos[92] bears finest amber,
which, they say, is tears made stone, translucent
exudation of the black poplar tree;
for some people say that once upon a time
the lightning strike on Phaëthon took place here,
wherefore all the masses of inhabitants
⟨both⟩ dress in black and put on mourning costume.

    After the Enetoi follow the Thracians called Istroi.
There are two islands lying alongside them,

400   which appear to bear the finest kind of tin.
Above these are the Ismenoi and Mentores.[93]

    The land lying close to these is occupied
by the Pelagones and Libyrnoi.

    Attached to these is the nation of the Boulinoi;
next the great Hyllic peninsula,
somewhat equal in size to the Peloponnese;[94]
they say that fifteen cities in that land
are settled by Hylloi, who are Hellenes by race,
for they took Herakles' son Hyllos as founder;

410   but people report that they were barbarized
in time by the customs of nearby nations,
as Timaios and Eratosthenes say.

    Beside them is an island, Issa by name,
that has a colony from the Syracusans.[95]

ILLYRIA

After these extends the Illyrian land,
containing many nations. For they say

---

[92] River *Po*.   [93] Mentorides, Ps.-Skyl. §21. 2.
[94] Similarly, Ps.-Skyl. §22. 2. On this passage, see Čače 2015, 19–22.
[95] On the region in the preceding lines, cf. Ps.-Skyl. §22–3.

there are numerous masses of Illyrians, and that some
hold the interior wherein they dwell,
others the coast within the Adrias;
420   and that, while some are subject to kingly powers,
some subject even to monarchies,
others are autonomous. They are said to be
extremely pious, very just, hospitable,
enamoured of a sociable disposition,
devoted to a very orderly life.
    Lying not far from these is Pharos island,
a foundation of the Parians, and the so-called
Melaina Korkyra,[96] which the Knidians settled.
This territory has a certain lake,
430   quite large, and called Lychnitis by the people.
Adjacent is an island where some say
Diomedes' life failed him when he came;
whence the island's name is Diomedeia.[97]
    Beyond these people are the barbarian Brygoi.
By the sea is Epidamnos, a Hellenic
city, which Korkyra seems to have founded.
Beyond the Brygoi the so-called Encheleioi[98]
dwell, whom Kadmos once ruled over.
Adjacent is the city of Apollonia,
440   foundation of Korkyraians and Korinthians;
and Hellenic Orikos, a coastal city;
Euboians have founded it while they are returning
from Ilion, borne to this place by the winds.

EPEIROS

Next the barbarian nations of Thesprotoi
and Chaones, occupying no great space.
Korkyra island is here, by Thesprotia.
After the Thesprotoi dwell the so-called Molottoi,
whom Pyrrhos once upon a time brought here,
child of Neoptolemos; also Dodona, oracle
450   of Zeus, which is a Pelasgic foundation.
In the interior are mixed barbarians
who are said to live adjacent to the oracle.

---

[96] 'Black' Corcyra (*Korčula*).   [97] On Diomedes in the Adriatic, see e.g. Zweifel 2012.
[98] Cf. Hekat. 40; Ps.-Skyl. §25.

After the Molottoi is Ambrakia, a colony
of the Korinthians; the elder child of Kypselos[99]
founded it, Gorgos. Next the so-called Argos
Amphilochikon; this seems to have been founded
by Amphilochos, son of Amphiaraos the seer.
    Beyond these places barbarian neighbours dwell.
On the coast is the city of Anaktorion,
460   which Akarnanians and Korinthians founded.
After that is Akarnania, some of whom (*sic*),
they say, were settled here by Alkmeon,
while others were founded by his son Akarnas.
A number of islands also lie by here:
Leukas among the first, Corinthian foundation;
next the Kephallenians' isle, and Ithaca
nearby, and Zakynthos lying quite close
to the Peloponnese. Next, extending towards
the Acheloös, the so-called Echinades.[100]

WESTERN MAINLAND GREECE

470   Now we shall go through Hellas once again,
showing in summary form the places round it,
arranged by nation (*ethnikōs*) as by Ephoros.
    After the Akarnanians is Aitolia,
which took its colony from out of Elis:
for the Kouretes[101] earlier dwelt in it,
but Aitolos, coming from Elis, named it
Aitolia, expelling those other people.
By Rhion lies the city of Naupaktos,
which the Dorians with Temenos have founded.
480   Next from the Aitolians, the Lokrians live beside them,
the ones they call the Ozolai, being colonists
from those Lokrians who face towards Euboia.
Delphi is attached to these, following next,
and the Pythic oracle, most undeceitful.
    Next the Phokians, whom Phokos synoikized,
it seems, descending once with Korinthians;
his ancestry is traced to Ornytos, Sisyphos' son.

---

[99] Tyrant of Corinth in C6; see esp. Hdt. 5. 92.
[100] *Il.* 2. 626 (see Prologue to these volumes); Ps.-Skyl. §34. 3.
[101] Mythical dancers worshipping Kybele.

Neighbouring this land lies that of Boiotia,
a very great territory, lucky in its position:
490   for it alone has use of three seas, they say.
Some of its harbours fortunately look
to the midday sun, towards the Adrias[102]
and the Sicilian trading-place, others to Cyprus
and the voyage down to Egypt and the islands—
these places are located around Aulis,
and among them the city of Tanagra lies,
and beyond this in the interior Thespiai—
and the third, outside the run by Euripos,
comes to the Macedonians' and Thessalians' land;
500   by it is the coastal city of Anthedon.
Thebai is the greatest city of Boiotia.
     Adjacent lies Megara, a Doric city:
for the entirety of Dorians made it a city,
most of them Korinthians and Messenians.
They say that when he became lord of Onchestos
Megareus put this name on it, from himself.
The land of Megaris marks the end of Boiotia.
     The Korinthian gulf is next following,
and that of Kenchreai; these draw in the isthmus
510   to a narrow form, framed each side by mainland.

PELOPONNESE, CRETE, AEGEAN ISLANDS

Then the Peloponnese is lying next,
possessing deep sea-gulfs and many capes:
Maleas, the greatest one,[103] called Tainaron;
here is a sanctuary of Poseidon, most fitting
for the god, established here by the Lakones.
Now the northern parts of the Peloponnese
are held by the Sikyonians and those that formerly
had settled at Corinth, a most renowned city,[104]
and by others, the Achaians; the limits towards evening
520   and the west wind by Eleians and Messenians;
the part by the midday sun and the southern zone
by Lakones and Argives; to the rising sun

---

[102] The Adriatic.   [103] Reading μεγίστην with Korenjak.
[104] 'Formerly' confirms that the poem dates after 146 BC.

by those of the cities that occupy the Akte.[105]
In the interior are the Phleiasia
and the Arkadian nation, greatest of these.
 They say the Arkadians are aboriginal.
Later Aletes settled the Korinthians,
Phalkes Sikyon, Tisamenos Achaia,
while Oxylos acted as the leader of
530 Elis, Kresphontes led Messenia,
Eurysthenes and Prokles Lakedaimon;
in Argos it was Kissos and Temenos with him,
of those around the Akte Agaios, they say,
and Deïphontes, Temenos' son-in-law.
 The isle of Crete lies facing the Peloponnese,
great in size and also very successful,
extending from Maleia,[106] cape of Lakonike,
lengthwise into the open sea (*pelagos*) to Dorian
Rhodos, and inhabited almost from
540 the beginning by numerous crowds and cities.
The oldest settlers that it has are those
among them who are called the Eteocretans.
It is said that Cretans were the first to rule
over the Hellenic sea and seize the island
cities, and Ephoros has said that they
synoikized some of them; and says
the island is named after a certain Kres,
an aboriginal who became a king;
and is a day's voyage from Lakonike.
550   Astypalaia, amid the Cretan strait,
is a colony of the Megarians,
an island in the open sea (*pelagia*); by Lakonike
is Kythera; after these, by Epidauros,
the island once referred to as Oinone,
which Aiakos later seized, changing its name
to Aigina after Aigine the Asopid.
And near this Salamis, where the story is
that Telamon son of Aiakos once was king.
 Next comes Athens. This city, they say, first gained
560 Pelasgians as settlers, those who, the story goes,

---

[105] 'Headland'; the Argolis or Argolid.
[106] For metrical reasons, the poet uses the feminine Maleia in place of the masculine Maleas (see l. 513).

were called Kranaoi; then the Kekropidai,
when Kekrops held the kingship; in later times,
when Erechtheus was the leader of the city,
it gained its appellation from Athena.
Herodotos tells these stories in his writing.
    When one has rounded Sounion, after Attica
lies the island of Euboia, in former times,
they say, called Makris[107] on account of its form;
then, in time, taking the name of Euboia[108]
570   from the daughter of Asopos of that name.
They say that at one time mixed Lelegians,
were the first people to live together in it,[109]
but Erechtheus' son Pandoros crossed from Attica
and founded the greatest city in it, Chalkis;
Aiklos, Athenian by race, founded Eretria,
Kothos Kerinthos in the salt sea,
the Dryopes the city named Karystos;
while Hestiaia is a Perrhaibian foundation.
    Lying near it are the following islets: Skyros,
580   Peparethos, Skiathos. Of these, the Cretans
who once crossed from Knossos with Staphylos
synoikized Peparethos and the island
lying near to it, Ikos; while Skyros and Skiathos
were synoikized, so the story goes, by Pelasgiots
crossing from Thrace. When all these became deserted,
the Chalkidians synoikized them again.

EASTERN MAINLAND GREECE

Opposite Euboia the Lokrians are settled.
Their first ruler, they say, was Amphiktyon
son of Deukalion; the next by blood
590   was Itonos; then Physkos, who sires (*sic*) Lokros,
and named the Leleges Lokrians after himself.
    Next after these the Dorians have small cities,[110]
Erineos, Boion, and Kytinion,
very ancient, also Pindos which follows;
all these did Doros, born of Hellen, settle.

---

[107] 'Long (Island)'.   [108] Reading Εὐβοίας with Korenjak.
[109] Marcotte prints συκοίκους, evidently a misprint for συνοίκους (which appears in TLG).
[110] In the confined region of Dōris, supposed homeland of all Dorian peoples.

All Dorians are colonists from these people.
    Next beside these is the city of Herakleia,
which the Laconians settled in earlier time,
sending ten thousand settlers to Trachis.
600   Next in line is Pylaia by the coast;
the Amphiktyonian gathering occurs there.
    The Maliac gulf lies within the corner,
where the city of Echinos lies, founded by Echion
the Sown,[111] and other cities of the Malians.
    Next are the coastal Phthiotic Achaians.
while the Magnetes live around Pelion.
    Beyond these is a land most rich in pasture,[112]
possessing very mighty and productive
plains, and Larisa, a most successful
610   city, and many others. Through the city
flows the Peneios, a great river, passing
towards the narrows of Tempe and by Pelion
the deep lake which is called Boibeïs.
    Bordering on Thessaly is Athamania,
the adjacent Dolopian and Perrhaibian nations,
and the Ainianes, who appear to have been
born of Haimones, Lapiths, and Myrmidons.

BEYOND THESSALY

Beyond Tempe is the territory of
the Macedonians, lying next by Olympos.
620   They say the earth-born Makedon was its king.
The nation of the Lynkestoi and that of the
Pelagones lie there, by the Axios,
and that of the Botteatai by the Strymon.
    In the interior there are many cities,
of which Pella and Beroia are most famous.
On the coast lie Thessalonike and Pydna.
After one has rounded the cape that is called
Aineia, there is the former foundation of the
Korinthians, Potidaia, a Doric city,
630   afterwards renamed as Kassandreia.
In the interior one called Antigoneia;

---

[111] *Spartos*, i.e. one of those born of the dragon's teeth sown by Kadmos; nothing to do with Sparta.
[112] Thessaly.

later comes the city that was Olynthos,
which Philip the Macedonian[113] uprooted,
capturing it by the spear. After the Olynthia
Arethousa, and Pallene lying on an isthmus;
the story is that this city, once called Phlegra,
was settled by the giants who fought the gods;
later the Pelleneans, after starting
out from Achaia, named it after themselves.

640   Next comes the gulf that is called Toronic,
where once there a lay a city, Mekyberna;
next Torone, homonymous with the places.

    Then Lemnos, in the open sea (*pelagia*), Hephaistos' nurse,
which Thoas son of Dionysos first settles;[114]
after this it took an Attic colony.

    When one sails past Athos there is a coastal city,
Akanthos, colony of the Andrians,
beside which a cut ditch is displayed,
seven stades long: it is said that Xerxes cut it.[115]

650   Next Amphipolis. The Strymon, a great river,
flows beside this, running as far as the sea
by the so-called 'Dances of Nereids' there.
On it in the interior lies Berga,
the homeland of Antiphanes, who wrote
the unbelievable, a joke of mythic history.
After Amphipolis, the former city of Oisyme
that belonged to Thasians, later to Macedonians,
(*when it was*) named after the Macedoness[116] Emathia.

    Next Neapolis and the isle of Thasos,
660 founded earlier, the story goes, by barbarians,
then by Phoenicians who crossed over from Asia
with Kadmos and Thasos; Thasos also took
its name from Thasos,[117] the name it has today.

    The more remote land, as far as the Pontic
Istros,[118] is held by the Thracians who reach there.
Those who lie on the coast possess a city,
Abdera, named after the Abderos
who earlier founded it; later he seems to have been

---

[113] Philip II, father of Alexander the Great.
[114] The author adopts the 'historic' present tense here.   [115] Hdt. 7. 23–4.
[116] This name I have coined to translate the rare term *Makessa*.
[117] i.e. from the man of that name.   [118] *Danube.*

destroyed by the horses of Diomedes,
670   killers of strangers. Teians synoikized it
after fleeing during the Persian events.
On the other side of this there lies a river
called Nestos. In the parts towards the east,
taking its name from the Bistonian
Thracians, is a long lake called Bistonis.
Next Maroneia, where history has it that
the Kikones settled long ago, those in Ismaros;
later this became a Chian foundation.
        Opposite is Samothrake, Trojan island,
680   with a mixed-up population of settlers;
for earlier, some say, the Trojans were in it.
The daughter of Atlas who is called Elektra
gave birth to Dardanos and Iasion;
of these, they say, Iasion committed
a sacrilege against Demeter's statue,
was struck a blow by divine lightning, and died.
Earlier Dardanos had left these places
and founded, on the lower slopes of Ida,[119]
a city called Dardanis after himself.
690   The Samothracians, Trojans by descent
but with the surname 'Thracian' from the place,
remained in the place because of piety.
Once, during a famine, the Samians
supported them; then they received some fellow
settlers from Samos and accepted them.
        ⟨And⟩ after Maroneia lies Ainos city,
which has Aiolian settlers from Mitylene.
        The so-called Thracian Chersonese[120] lies after,
along which is the first city, Kardia,
700   originally founded by Milesians
and Klazomenians, and again by Athenians
when Miltiades laid hold of the Chersonesians.
Next is Lysimacheia, this founded
by Lysimachos as a city named after himself.
Then there is Limnai of the Milesians;
then Alopekonnesos, Aiolians' city;
then Elaious, having an Attic colony,

---

[119] A syllable is missing; perhaps we should add δὲ ('and') after ὑπωρείαις, matching the syntax of 687.
[120] *cherrhonēsos* meaning 'peninsula', mod. *Gelibolu/Gallipoli*.

which Phrynon (?) appears to have synoikized.
After that are Sestos and Madytos, lying
710   on the strait, foundations of the Lesbians.
Next is the city of Krithote, and Paktyë;
they say Miltiades also founded these.
    After the Chersonese, Thrace extends in the
Propontis; there is a colony of Samians,
Perinthos. Next in order is Selymbria,
which the Megarians founded before Byzantion.
Next the Megarians' successful Byzantion.

THE BLACK SEA

After these is the Pontos,[121] whose situation
seems to have been researched most carefully
720   by the writer from Kallatis, Demetrios.[122]
We shall go through its places part by part.
    Near the Pontic mouth there lies the land
of the Byzantines, which is called Philia.
Then a certain shore called Salmydessos
extends for seven hundred stades; very marshy,
difficult to anchor on, and wholly
harbourless, a place most hostile to ships.
Attached to it is a cape with a good harbour,
Thynias, the furthest place in Astic[123] Thrace,
730   after which is a neighbouring city, Apollonia.
The founders of this city, some fifty years
before the reign of Cyrus, were Milesians
after their arrival at this place.
For they sent many colonies from Ionia
to the Pontos, which was previously called Axenos[124]
because of the attacks by the barbarians,
but they caused it to take a new name, Euxeinos.[125]
    And at the feet of the mountain known as Haimos[126]
there is a city called Mesembria,[127]
740   bordering on the Thrakian and Getic land;
Kalchedonians[128] and Megarians settled this

---

[121] Black Sea.   [122] Cf. l. 117.   [123] Named after the Astai, Marcotte 236.
[124] 'Inhospitable'.   [125] 'Hospitable'.   [126] The Great Balkan range (*Stara Planina*).
[127] *Nesebur*.
[128] From the Megarian colony of Kalchedon (*Kadıköy*), opposite Byzantion, on the Kimmerian Bosporos.

when Darius sent his force against the Skythai.
A mighty mountain rises above it, Haimos,
comparable to Cilician Tauros in size
and in extension of the places lengthwise;
for from the Krobyzoi[129] and the Pontic boundaries
it projects as far as the Adriatic places.

The continuous text ends here.

B. FRAGMENTS

All the following extracts, apart from **3**, are from the Pseudo-Arrianic *Circumnavigation of the Black Sea* (*Eux.*; see Chapter 36). They are listed in the order in which they are believed to have stood in *Nik.*, reversing their order in *Eux.* (with the exception of nos **19–21**).

Words in double quotation marks " " are in iambic metre, and are designated by Marcotte as quotations from *Nik.* preserved within *Eux.* (travelling in the other direction round the Black Sea), though not all sequences of words consistent with iambic metre are so marked. Line-divisions within quotations from *Nik.* are indicated by |. Words added by the compiler of *Eux.* in the later 6th c. AD are in square brackets [ ].

For notes on the fragments from *Eux.*, see the relevant sections of Chapter 36; section numbers of *Eux.* follow Podossinov (where those of Diller differ, they are distinguished by 'P.' and 'D.'). Marcotte's fragment numbers may be found by consulting the Concordance.

1   Pseudo-Arrian, *Circumnavigation of the Black Sea,* §109
The Milesians are founding Odessos when Astyages ruled Media; and in a circle around it, it has the Thracian Krobyzoi.

2   Stephanos of Byzantion δ 90
Dionysou polis (*Dionsyos' City*): in the Pontos; the former Krounoi (*Springs*), (*so called*) from the discharge of the waters; "later, the Dionysiac statue having fallen | out of the sea onto the place", it was named thus.[130]

3   Pseudo-Arrian, *Circumnavigation of the Black Sea,* §107
(*Dionysopolis*) "was first named | Krounoi through the outflow of the nearby waters"; next it was renamed Matiopolis; and next the statue of Dionysos having fallen from the sea onto the place "they say it was in turn called Dionysopolis". | Lying "on the frontier of the land of the Krobyzoi and Skythai, | it has mixed Hellenic settlers".

4   Pseudo-Arrian, *Circumnavigation of the Black Sea,* §105
(*The township of Bizonē*) some say is barbarian, "others that it came into being as a colony of Mesembria".

---

[129] A Thracian people.
[130] Recognized as lines from *Nik.* by Vossius (Marcotte 2000b, 133r). Since Steph. Byz. invariably cites his source, it appears the authorship of the iambics was already unknown in C6 AD.

5 Pseudo-Arrian, *Circumnavigation of the Black Sea*, §103
Kallatis, a colony of the Herakleotai that came into being according to an oracle: "and they founded this when | Amyntas took over the rule of the Macedonians".

6 Pseudo-Arrian, *Circumnavigation of the Black Sea*, §101
Tomeoi, "being a colony of the Milesians, | was settled by Skythai" †in a circle round about†.

7 Pseudo-Arrian, *Circumnavigation of the Black Sea*, §99
(*The city of Istros*) took its name from the river; and this city "the Milesians are founding when the army | of the barbarian Skythai crossed into Asia, | pursuing the Kimmerians from the Bosporos".

8 Pseudo-Arrian, *Circumnavigation of the Black Sea*, §97
(*The river Istros*), also called Danoubis, comes down from the western places "making its outflow in five mouths"; but splitting into two it also flows into the Adriatic. It is also "recognized", actually, as far as "Keltike, | and persists all the time, even in summer; | for in the winter it is increased and filled | by the rains that occur" †and by the snow, as they say, taking the inflows of the generated frosts, but in summer† "it emits a stream that is exactly equal; | and it also has islands lying within itself, | numerous and of great size, so the story goes, | of which the one that lies between the sea | and the mouths" is no lesser in size than Rhodes. It is called Peuke because of the multitude of pines there; then immediately after it, lying in the open sea (*pelagia*), is the aforementioned Achilles' Island.

9 Pseudo-Arrian, *Circumnavigation of the Black Sea*, §94
(*Achilles's Island*) "has also a tame multitude of birds", a sacred sight to people who arrive. From this it is not possible to see land, even though it is distant from land 400 stades, 53⅓ miles, as indeed Demetrios (*of Kallatis*) writes.

10 Pseudo-Arrian, *Circumnavigation of the Black Sea*, §92
(*From the river Tyras to the mouth of the Istros called Psilon*), these people are Thracians and immigrant Bastarnai.

11 Pseudo-Arrian, *Circumnavigation of the Black Sea*, §91
(*The river Tyras; Dniester*), being deep and nourishing in pastures for flocks, "has resources for traders" in fish | "and for cargo ships it offers a safe voyage upstream. | A city sharing its name with the river lies here, | Tyras", said to be a colony of the Milesians.

12 Pseudo-Arrian, *Circumnavigation of the Black Sea*, §98
(*The river Borysthenes*) "is the most serviceable of all, | bearing many great monsters and the crops | that grow here and pastures for herd animals. | They say the

flow of its stream is navigable | for forty days; though in its upper parts | it is unnavigable" and not passable, "for it is blocked by snow and frosts". At the confluence on the Hypanis and Borysthenes †with their two rivers† a city was founded, formerly called Olbia but after that again called Borysthenes by Hellenes. The Milesians are founding this during the Median empire. It has an upstream voyage of 240 stades from the sea, by the river Borysthenes. [The river is now called Danapris; the distance is 32 miles.]

13   Pseudo-Arrian, *Circumnavigation of the Black Sea,* §87
The Achilleian Racetrack, which is a beach—that is, a shore—is truly long and narrow.

14   Pseudo-Arrian, *Circumnavigation of the Black Sea,* §82
In this land in Taurike "some say that after her abduction" Iphigeneia came here from Aulis; the Tauroi are dense with crowds of people, "and are devoted to a life on the land, a pastoral one, | but in cruelty they are barbarians, murderers, | placating the divinities with their impieties. | The so-called Taurike Chersonesos | is attached to these, and has a Hellenic city | which Herakleiots and Delians colonized | after an oracle came to the Herakleiots | who lived in Asia within the Kyaneai" that they should settle the Chersonese together with the Delians.

15   Pseudo-Arrian, *Circumnavigation of the Black Sea,* §80
(*In Theudosia*), it is said, exiles from the people of the Bosporos, too, once settled.

16   Pseudo-Arrian, *Circumnavigation of the Black Sea,* §79
(*The city of Kimmerikon:*) opposite in the sea are rocky islands, not very large, two in number, a little distant from the mainland.

17   Pseudo-Arrian, *Circumnavigation of the Black Sea,* §78
The last place in Europe, on the very mouth of Lake Maiotis, is Pantikapaion, named a royal residence by the people of the Bosporos. Above these people, Skythike is barbarian; "it is bordering upon the unlived-in land, | and is a land unknown to all the Hellenes. | The first people by the Istros are the Karpides, | says Ephoros; the Aroteres" (*Ploughmen*) are "further off, | and the Neuroi, as far as the empty, frozen land. | Towards the east, when one leaves the Borysthenes" river, they say that in so-called Hylaia "the inhabitants are Skythai; then the Georgoi (*Farmers*) follow above these, | then again emptiness over a wide place, | and beyond this the nation of the Anthropophagoi (*Man-eating*) Skythai", and beyond these again a desert follows. "Across the Pantikapes, the nation of the Limnaioi (*Lake-men*) | and several others not having their own names | but with the surname Nomadic, very pious; | none of them would be unjust to a living person; | house-carriers, it has been said, they feed | upon the milk" from the Skythian milk-mares, "their way of life involves declaring property | and social relations to be common to all. | They say wise Anacharsis was born of those | Nomadics that are by far the most pious of all".

18   Pseudo-Arrian, *Circumnavigation of the Black Sea,* §78

(*Ephoros has said that*) "some also came to Asia | and settled in it, whom in fact they call | Sakai"; and he says the most conspicuous (*race*) is that of the Sauromatai, (*then*) the Gelones, "and third | the race of the Agathyrsoi, as they are named". Taking its name from the Maiotai, "lying next is the Maiotis lake" into which the Tanaïs (*Don*), "taking the current from the river Araxes, | is mingled, as Hekataios of Teos[131] said, | or, as Ephoros reports, from a certain lake | whose limit is unstated. It (*the Tanaïs*) debouches, | with double-mouthed stream, into the so-called Maiotis | and (*then*) into the Kimmerian Bosporos".

19   Pseudo-Arrian, *Circumnavigation of the Black Sea,* §74

The river Tanaïs, which is the frontier of Asia, cutting each continent apart, is possessed, first, by Sarmatai, continuing for 2,000 stades, which becomes 250 miles; next after the Sarmatai is the race of Maiotai called Iazamatai, as Demetrios has said, after whom lake Maiotis is called; but as Ephoros calls it, the nation of the Sauromatai. The Amazons mingled with these "Sauromatai, they say, when once they came" from the battle that took place around the Thermodon; after them the Sauromatai were surnamed Gynaikokratoumenoi (*Woman-ruled*).

20   Pseudo-Arrian, *Circumnavigation of the Black Sea,* §77

"As you sail out of the mouth, the city of Kimmeris (*or Kimmerikon*),[132] | called after the barbarian Kimmerioi"; it is a foundation by the tyrants of the Bosporos; "and Kepos (*or Kepoi*),[133] colonized by Milesians".

21   Pseudo-Arrian, *Circumnavigation of the Black Sea,* §76

"Next is Hermonassa, and Phanagoreia, | which they say the Teians founded at some date; | and Sindikos Harbour, having for its founders | Hellenes who came out from nearby places. | These cities have their sites enclosed within" an island (*i.e. peninsula*) "beside Maiotis as far as the Bosporos; | it occupies a large amount of plain-land, | in part impassable by reason of marshes | and rivulets, by lagoons in the further part, | which form within the sea and in the lake".

22   Pseudo-Arrian, *Circumnavigation of the Black Sea,* §66

(*So from Hermonassa as far as Sindikos Harbour*) certain Maiotai live alongside, called the nation of the Sindoi, after whom Sindike is named. These Sindoi are barbarians, but civilized in their customs. After the Sindoi are the Kerketai called Toritai, a just and reasonable nation, very dedicated to nautical matters. After the Kerketai, the land bordering on these is held by Achaians, "whom they say, being Hellenes by race", are called the Barbarized Achaians. For they say that once the Orchomenian host "of Ialmenos, and the Minyans, sailing | in full strength from Ilion, by the breaths" of the wind of the Tanaïs "came perforce into the Pontic area, | barbarian land; thus forced into exile, |

---

[131] A mistake (by the author of *Nik.*?) for Abdera.   [132] On the *Taman* peninsula.
[133] On the gulf of *Taman.*

they are outside the law and, in their customs, | strongly malevolent towards the Hellenes". Many of the Achaians are enemies of the Kerketai.

23 Pseudo-Arrian, *Circumnavigation of the Black Sea*, §51
The nation of the Heniochoi (*Charioteers*) hates foreigners. Some say these people were called Heniochoi after Amphitos and Telchis, the charioteers of Polydeukes (*Pollux*) and Kastor. "These men appear" to have arrived in the expedition with Jason, but "to have settled around these places | after being left behind, so the myth says". Beyond the Heniochoi and inland lies the Kaspia, "as the sea is called, which has living around it | horse-eating (*hippophaga*) races of barbarians; | the frontiers of the Medes are close to it".

24 Pseudo-Arrian, *Circumnavigation of the Black Sea*, §45
(*The river Phasis*) has a current "that runs down out of Armenia, near which | Iberians live who once were relocated | from Iberia to Armenia. As one goes into" a river "to the left of the Phasis", there lies beside it a Hellenic city of the Milesians, called Phasis, into which it is said sixty nations come down, all using different tongues, "among whom they say that some from India" and Baktria have come together, both barbarian. Between these the Koraxic land is barbarian; the places following it are the so-called Kolike, the nation of Melanchlainoi, and that of the Kolchoi.

25 Pseudo-Arrian, *Circumnavigation of the Black Sea*, §37
(*From Trapezous to Pharnakia, anciently Kerasous, there lived formerly*) the nation called the Makrones (*Long Men*) or Makrokephaloi (*Long-heads*).

26 Pseudo-Arrian, *Circumnavigation of the Black Sea*, §35
(*From Pharnakia, anciently Kerasous, to Kotyoros there lived formerly*) the nation called the Mosynoikoi (*Hut-dwellers*), with harsh customs, most barbaric in their deeds; "for, it is said, they all reside in lofty | towers of wood, but everything they do | is always done in public; while their king, | bound and shut away within a tower, | watches with care—his tower is the one | with the highest roof of all—but those who guard him | ensure that all of his commands are lawful; | if he transgresses, he receives a punishment"—the greatest, they say, as they give him no food.[134]

27 Pseudo-Arrian, *Circumnavigation of the Black Sea*, §34
(*Pharnakia was called Kerasous of old; this, too, is a colony of Sinope*), founded †by which an empty place is lying, opposite which† extends an island called Ares's Isle.

28 Pseudo-Arrian, *Circumnavigation of the Black Sea*, §33
(*From Kotyoros almost as far as Polemonion there lived formerly the nation of the Tibarenoi*), sharing space [—] "to play, loving to laugh in every fashion", having judged that this is the greatest blessing.

---

[134] The Greek of this last 'line' does not seem to scan quite perfectly, and αὐτοῦ seems odd: why not αὐτόν?

29 Pseudo-Arrian, *Circumnavigation of the Black Sea*, §27

(*The city of Amisos*), lying in the land of the Leukosyroi,[135] (*is*) a colony of the Phokaians: for being settled four years earlier than Herakleia it received an Ionian founding; and by this city is the neck of Asia that is almost the narrowest, "passing through | to the Issic gulf (*g. of Issos/Alexandretta/İskenderun*) and Alexandroupolis, | founded by the Macedonian; it has a road | of seven days in total to Kilikia". For it is said that the most isthmus-like part of Asia "draws together into the corner around it (*the city*); | but Herodotos seems not to know it, saying | that a straight road of five days exists | from Kilikia, as he reports in his writing", to Sinope, a city further on.[136] "The peninsula, comprising almost the best locations | in Asia, has fifteen races, three Hellenic: | the Aiolic, next the Ionic, and the Doric"; but otherwise the rest of the mixed peoples are barbarian. "There live here Kilikians, Lykians, and in addition | Karians and maritime Mariandynoi | and Paphlagonians and Pamphylians; | Chalybes in the interior, Kappadokians near them, | and those that hold Pisidia, and Lydians, | and in addition Mysians and Phrygians."

30 Pseudo-Arrian, *Circumnavigation of the Black Sea*, §25

(*The river Halys*), being 300 stades distant from Amisos, running between the Syroi[137] and Paphlagonians, debouches into the Pontos.

31 Pseudo-Arrian, *Circumnavigation of the Black Sea*, §22

Sinope is named after one of the Amazons living nearby who occupied it of old; they were kindred of the Syroi. "After that, it is said, those Hellenes who came over | against the Amazons, Autolykos and Phlogios, | who followed Deïleon and were Thessalians". Next Abron (*sic*), by race a Milesian; he appears to have been killed by Kimmerians. "After the Kimmerians in turn, Kretines of Kos", and those who had become exiles from the Milesians. This people are founding it when the army of the Kimmerians overran Asia.

32 Pseudo-Arrian, *Circumnavigation of the Black Sea*, §18

(*Cape Karambis*); (*after it*) a high mountain falling steeply into the sea, the so-called Kriou Metopon (*Ram's Brow; C. Sarych*), distant from Karambis the voyage a night and a day.

33 Pseudo-Arrian, *Circumnavigation of the Black Sea*, §16

(*The city of Amastris:*) "they say Phineas ruled over these places, | son of Phoinix the Tyrian".[138] In later times an expedition of Milesians came from Ionia and founded these cities, "which Amastris later brought together | into Amastris, a city of this name she founded | upon this site. She is reported as | the Persian Oxathres' daughter, the story goes, | and Herakleian" tyrant Dionysios' wife.

---

[135] Not 'White Syrians' but a distinct group; cf. n. on fr. 26.
[136] Hdt. 2. 34. See n. on Ps.-Skyl. §102. 2.   [137] *Sic*, not 'Syrians', cf. n. on fr. 25.
[138] Not formatted by Marcotte as a quotation from *Nik.*, but he clearly understands it so.

34 **Pseudo-Arrian,** *Circumnavigation of the Black Sea,* §14
(*The river Parthenios*) is sailable, descending with a very quiet current. In it, so the story goes, "there is a very famous bath of Artemis".

35 **Pseudo-Arrian,** *Circumnavigation of the Black Sea,* §10
Herakleia is "a foundation of the Boiotians | and Megarians; they are founding this within | the Kyaneai, starting out from Hellas | at the times when Cyrus took control of Media".

36 **Pseudo-Arrian,** *Circumnavigation of the Black Sea,* §8
(*The river Hypios*) has upon it an inland city called Prousias.

37 **Pseudo-Arrian,** *Circumnavigation of the Black Sea,* §7
(*The river Sangarios*), running from the land about the Thynoi and from Phrygia, debouches through the Thynian territory.

38 **Pseudo-Arrian,** *Circumnavigation of the Black Sea,* §6
(*The island of Apollonia*) has within it a city called Thynias, a colony of the Herakleiots.

18

ARTEMIDOROS OF EPHESOS

(C.104–100 BC)

D. Graham J. Shipley

INTRODUCTION

ARTEMIDOROS AND HIS WORK

Artemidoros' geographical work is usually cited under its Greek title *Geographoumena* (*Things Treated Geographically*).[1] It was, to judge from the fragments we have, a comprehensive prose description of the known world, illustrated with cultural digressions and informed by the systematic enumeration of local distance measurements—some perhaps in Roman miles, the rest in traditional Greek stades. It was heavily drawn upon by later writers, and its reputation was high, though it is less clear that Artemidoros was methodologically innovative.

In work from five hundred years after his time, the scholar Markianos of Herakleia (**120** below; Chapter 34 below) lists the geographers he regards as most reliable, followed by those he rates as most accurate of all ('after' the others, but only in a chronological sense): namely Artemidoros—to whom, further on, he assigns the very first place—Strabo, and Menippos. Giving details he gives for none of the others, he notes that Artemidoros lived around the 169th Olympiad (104–100 BC) and travelled extensively in the Mediterranean and beyond the Pillars of Herakles, where 'he saw the island of Gadeira (*Cádiz*) and *some parts* of the external sea, which they call Ocean'. We also have evidence from Strabo (**89**) that Artemidoros represented his home city of Ephesos on an embassy to Rome; elsewhere (**1**) Strabo expatiates upon Ephesos' involvement in the foundation of Massalia at such length that one may wonder whether Artemidoros is not his source.

While, in Markianos' view, Artemidoros' work 'falls short of an accurate geographical description', he says he 'covered with proper diligence the circumnavigation of the sea *within* the strait of Herakles *and the measurement of this*', and 'seems to have written very clearly and accurately the circumnavigation *of our sea*' (my emphases). So important was Artemidoros that Markianos made an abridgement (*epitome*) of his eleven books, preserving the sequence of the material but adding information 'from other old writers ... so as to produce a reasonable geographical account *but a complete*

---

[1] For general overviews of A., see Dueck 2012, 57–8; Roller 2015, 134–5.

circumnavigation (*periplous*)'. The various qualifications italicized above are significant, as we shall see.

In assessing whether Markianos' high estimation is justified, we may take cognizance of no fewer than 58 citations of Artemidoros by Strabo—almost as many as he makes of Poseidonios, only Eratosthenes among geographers receiving more mentions. In no case, however, does Strabo specify which book of the *Geographoumena* he is using. He refers to Artemidoros as an example of how later geographers correct earlier (81), and often supports him implicitly or explicitly (e.g. 3, 60, 72, 77), but also criticizes him on occasion (e.g. 67–9, 96; perhaps unjustifiably at 59).

There are also 14 citations of Artemidoros by Pliny the Elder in his *Natural History* (4–7, 105–14).[2] A much larger number are found in the *Ethnika* compiled by the 6th-century AD grammarian Stephanos of Byzantion (or rather in its surviving 10th-century precis), who cites only Hekataios, Strabo, and Pausanias more often among geographers. Of his 78 citations of Artemidoros (11–30, 32–7, 39–43, 45–51, 53–7, 123–57), 19 are explicitly to Markianos' epitome rather than to the work itself (14, 16–17, 26, 48, 129, 131, 139, 141–4, 147–9, 151, 155–6, 164); it is clear, however, that Stephanos also consulted the complete *Geographoumena* (see 11 for book 1, 21 for book 2, and so on).[3]

The *Geographoumena* is Artemidoros' only definite work. The Imperial-period writer Athenaios (115) seems to imply that he wrote an *Ionian Memoranda* (*Iōnika hypomnēmata*), but this may have been no more than a digression within the *Geographoumena* or an extract from that work.[4] Some have read Stephanos of Byzantion's references to an 'epitome of 11 books' as implying that Artemidoros made an abridgement of his own work, long before Markianos compiled one;[5] current scholarship, however, accepts only the latter. Another misconception in earlier generations was that the passages of an epitome preserved with Markianos' introduction are from his epitome of Artemidoros; they are now recognized as parts of his epitome of Menippos (and are printed in Chapter 21 below).

THE ARTEMIDOROS PAPYRUS

Given how often he is cited by Strabo, Pliny, and Stephanos, and given Markianos' high opinion, extraordinarily little had been written about Artemidoros in modern times until the publication, from 1998 onwards, of the controversial Artemidoros Papyrus (167). This substantial fragment of a papyrus roll, some 8 feet (*c*.2.5 m) wide and over a foot (*c*.30 cm) high, contains two passages of text in slightly different handwriting,[6] one or both of which may derive from the *Geographoumena*, as well as a sketch map

---

[2] Not including the listings of A. in Pliny's table of contents (104).
[3] Hammerstaedt 2012.   [4] Banchich 2019.   [5] The view of Stiehle 1856, 240, 243.
[6] On the differences in handwriting, see van Minnen 2009, 172.

possibly representing part of the Iberian peninsula,[7] and sculptural and animal drawings in two or more hands.[8]

The authenticity of the papyrus has been challenged, resulting in a highly polarized debate: the minority camp claiming it is the latest known invention by the notorious, but learned, 19th-century forger Constantine Simonides;[9] the other, the majority, being persuaded that it is genuine (at least in some sense) and important, but taking widely different views of its precise nature.[10] Ion beam analysis proves that the ink is organic and probably carbon-based, and thus compatible with an ancient date, though a 19th-century forger might conceivably have prepared a successful imitation. Radiocarbon testing, more conclusively, demonstrates that the papyrus itself was made in 40 BC–AD 130 (at the 95 per cent confidence level), which equates to AD 45 ± 85 years; this does not, of course, prove that it was not written and drawn on much later,[11] though specialists agree that the writing of the textual passages is of this date.[12] Digital techniques have also confirmed changes to the order of the fragments previously argued for on textual grounds.[13]

Although an Italian court ruled in 2018 that the work was indeed a 19th-century forgery, albeit using ancient papyrus,[14] the scholarly debate seems likely to continue. A recent study by a sceptic argues that the supporters of the papyrus's validity have been forced to cede ever more ground as new issues, both external and internal, have been raised.[15] On the other hand, the same is true of the doubters: many objections to authenticity were quickly rebutted or refuted, or were met by refinement of the original editors' views. It has been shrewdly observed that the onus is on the sceptics to prove their case, and that, in the absence of any incontrovertible scientific proof of a modern date (which seems unlikely to be forthcoming, as radiocarbon dating of the ink would be too destructive), it is wrong to exclude considerations of form and content from the assessment of authenticity.[16]

In fact, various features of the texts can be regarded as compatible with an early date, including specialized vocabulary some of which the doubters had previously argued could not be earlier than the late antique period; while other features seem to

---

[7] But note the caution of Talbert 2009, 62–3; Talbert 2012c.

[8] Multiple hands for the drawings: van Minnen 2009, 174.

[9] Persistently argued by Canfora (e.g. Canfora 2013) and summarized by Janko 2009 (whose comparison of the writing to a known forgery by Simonides is, however, unconvincing, also the view of D'Alessio 2009, 30; Marcotte 2010, 341). For a brief restatement of J.'s views, see Janko 2022.

[10] Three conferences generally supportive of the genuineness of the papyrus have taken place: Gallazzi, Kramer, and Settis 2010; Gallazzi, Kramer, and Settis 2012; Adornato 2016. For a balanced, but generally positive, appraisal, see the carefully considered papers in Brodersen and Elsner 2009. Rathbone 2012 gives a vigorous defence of authenticity.

[11] Fedi, Carraresi et al. 2010; cf. Marcotte 2010, 338.

[12] Luppe 2008; D'Alessio 2009, 30; van Minnen 2009.

[13] Tarte 2012, confirming D'Alessio 2009.

[14] See e.g. Giustetti 2018; Giustetti 2019; Ronchey 2018; anon. 2019. Objections to the verdict, and the process, were immediately voiced: e.g. Wasserman 2018.

[15] Condello 2018.   [16] Marcotte 2010.

preclude any possible involvement of Simonides, including the format of some of the numbers in the descriptive section.[17]

On the other hand, the first part of the papyrus text, with a theoretical discussion of geography and the role of the geographer, is thought by some scholars to be by an author other than Artemidoros;[18] a recently proposed date is around the turn of the Christian era.[19]

The last sentence of the text states that 'no one has observed' the Atlantic coast beyond Cape Artabra (*Ortegal*), the north-west tip of Spain; this has been held to contradict Markianos, but he does not claim that Artemidoros saw anything specific beyond Gadeira (as the qualifications italicized in §1 above suggest).[20] Markianos' statement may be a slight upon Pytheas (Chapter 8 above), but we have no direct evidence that Pytheas made a detailed report on the coast of northern Spain or western France; he may simply have sailed across the Bay of Biscay.

IMPLICATIONS OF THE PAPYRUS

If the Artemidoros Papyrus is not a forgery, what is it? While the text in the columns iv–v may very well be a summary of Artemidoros' description of Iberia, this stands or falls independently of the attribution of columns i–iii, part of a more theoretical manifesto for geographical practice; though this could also be hellenistic, as it is thought to exhibit the influence of Stoic philosophy.[21] The Iberian section is unlikely to be of late antique date, or derivative from Markianos' epitome of Artemidoros; it is more likely a summary made not long after Artemidoros' lifetime.[22] Either it or Artemidoros' original text was consulted by the Byzantine emperor Constantine VII Porphyrogennetos (r. AD 913–59; see **31**, from which part of **167** has been completed). The representational drawings undoubtedly reflect a later reuse of the papyrus roll. The apparent map cannot conclusively be divorced from Artemidoros' work, but does not necessarily represent any part of Iberia.[23] The most important section for present purposes, therefore, is the geographical account of the Iberian peninsula in columns iv–v.

Among the reasons why the debate has not been resolved to the satisfaction of all is that we know so little about Greek literary prose in Artemidoros' lifetime, and even

[17] The use of the obsolete Greek letter sampi (ϡ) as an abbreviation for 'thousands', seen in columns 4–5, is rare, but occurs at Didyma and Priene—close to Artemidoros' home city of Ephesos—before falling out of use elsewhere in the late Hl or early Roman period. Crucially, this use of sampi was not understood until 1907 (Luppe 2008), so Simonides could not have known of its epigraphic use (Hammerstaedt 2009); cf. Marcotte 2010.

[18] '[P]erhaps the person who commissioned this roll of excerpts rather than the scribe himself', D'Alessio 2009, 40. The attribution of this passage to another author is supported by Lucarini 2015, 16 n. 16.

[19] Lucarini and Scermino 2018; Lucarini and Scermino 2019. The authors suggest that this passage shows the influence of the Ps.-Aristotelian *De mundo* (Ch. 24 below).

[20] Lucarini 2017.   [21] Sedley 2010; Marcotte 2010, 346–60.

[22] One alternative theory is that the papyrus is 'a miscellaneous compilation of the early Imperial period'; D'Alessio 2009, 30.

[23] Marcotte 2010, 363–6.

less about the development of maps designed to accompany texts before the work of Ptolemy (2nd century AD), so that the lack of direct parallels for particular features of the papyrus is not necessarily proof of a later date. It may be that it is simply, now, the earliest evidence for these and other features; for 'the history of ancient cartography will always necessarily be a study of hapaxes'; that is, *hapax legomena*, words that occur only once in surviving evidence.[24]

If the papyrus is genuine, it confirms—by using terms such as 'outline', *perigraphē*—that Artemidoros adopted a cartographic perspective which built upon that of Eratosthenes, and used detailed measurements in places, as Markianos claims. The long distances in column v may reveal more of his practice than has been realized: no other Greek geographer gives sea distances to the nearest stade (other than extremely short ones). Only Pseudo-Skylax's paragraph on Attica (§57) is comparable in its sequence of distances; while they are only to the nearest 10 stades, they may derive not from sailing estimates but from the more accurate measurement of coastal routes by surveying or pacing.[25]

Of the 22 distances in the passage, all (or all bar 1) are multiples of two,[26] while all but 3 or 4 are divisible by four. Of the first 15 distances up to Cape Hieron (*Sanctuary*),[27] the south-western tip of Iberia, 8 are also multiples of eight, as are 3 or 4 of the 7 thereafter. But while 11 of the first 15 are not divisible by ten, all but 1 (or possibly all) of the last 7 are. This suggests that *two different kinds of data* have been combined: one for the coast up to Hieron, one for the remainder. Those beyond Hieron, given to the nearest ten stades, are typical of coastal distances estimated on the basis of sailing experience. For the stretch up to Hieron, (*a*) if they were originally in miles, some of them must have ended in a fraction (½ or ¼ mile);[28] they all appear to have been converted into stades at the rate of eight to the mile,[29] whether by Artemidoros or by a later copyist or epitomator (at some date up to when the papyrus was written). (*b*) If they were originally in stades, it appears they were converted into miles (rounded to the nearest ¼ mile, 2 stades) and then back into stades, with the result that each was an even number; this could have happened before Artemidoros wrote or later.

Lists in miles could possibly have antedated Artemidoros, as the Spanish provinces were created before his lifetime and roads began to be built there from the 2nd century

[24] Marcotte 2010, 356: 'une histoire de la cartographie antique sera toujours, par nécessité, une étude de hapax'.

[25] Shipley 2010.

[26] The possible exception is the penultimate distance, from the river 'Benis' to C. Artabra in NW Iberia. The editors read ϡμ (940) followed by the trace of an indeterminate letter. If that letter is a numeral and not part of a word, the distance must be 941 to 949; but since no other distance in the passage is an odd number, it was surely 942, 944, 946, or 948.

[27] Cape *St Vincent*, or possibly *Trafalgar*.

[28] Up to C. Hieron, those equivalent to distances in miles ending in ¼ or ¾ are Kalpe to Menestheos Limen (86 st., 10¾ miles) and Onoba to Mainoba (78 st., 9¾ miles). On the Atlantic stretch, the only such distance is Obleuion to Benis (110 st., 13¾ miles).

[29] 8 st. (of 185 m each) to the Roman mile was the usual equivalence: Pothecary 1995, 67.

BC—and sometimes marked with milestones then or later (as southern Gaul from Narbo to the Rhône had been by the late 3rd century).[30] It has been observed that Roman conquest concretized Iberia and allowed Polybios, followed by Artemidoros, to construct its geography.[31] Already by Polybios' lifetime the Romans had measured a central portion of the route from southern Spain to Italy (Polyb. 3. 39. 8, reporting in stades), the part from Narbo to the Rhône, marking every eighth stade.[32] By the end of the 2nd century they could have measured the whole route. To this extent, it would not be surprising if Artemidoros accessed distances in a Roman form. On the other hand, the Roman roads in eastern Spain cut across country, some way inland, and there is no evidence that land surveyors ever measured coasts as such. Since Artemidoros' distances here are generally greater than corresponding ones in other sources, they probably derive ultimately from sailing estimates; their affinity with distances in miles may be an artefact of source transmission, in the manner described above.[33] It is more likely that conversion took place during post-publication recopying, perhaps under the influence of the registers of distances in miles that clearly existed by the time of Pliny (whose lifetime falls within the date range during which the papyrus roll was made); or earlier, for one may readily suppose that land surveys accelerated during Augustus' residence at Tarraco in 27–24 BC.[34]

ARTEMIDOROS REASSESSED

Although, even on the provisional assumption of authenticity, neither of the texts on the Papyrus need contain the work of Artemidoros in its original state, the Iberian fragment tends to support Markianos' view of the high quality of Artemidoros' account of 'our sea', particularly 'within the strait of Herakles', and is consistent with his knowing of only 'some parts' of the outer sea well. If the coastal measurements, comprising mainly long distances between widely separated points, are typical of Artemidoros' original work (of which we cannot be sure), they could explain why Markianos felt the need for more detail in a 'complete circumnavigation'.

More informative, however, are the quotations which were already known before the discovery of the Papyrus. They suggest that the structure of the *Geographoumena* exhibited some originality. From the 6 explicit citations of book 1 (9, 11, 13, 15, 19–20, all but one from Stephanos), it is clear that it was not limited to a particular part of

---

[30] Polyb. 3. 39. 8, quoted in Introduction, §VI. 2. g. The phrase is accepted as genuine by Walbank 1957–79, i. 373, noting that P. could have inserted it as late as *c.*118 BC (and that he regularly reckons 8⅓ st. to the mile).

[31] Cruz Andreotti 2016, 280–5; 289.   [32] Kolb 2016, 233.

[33] The editors of the papyrus compare A.'s distances with those for the same coasts given by other authors, and generally find that his are longer; they take this as a sign that they were coastal sailings reflecting the curves of the shore, whereas others, especially Pliny's, are inland distances along the shorter Via Domitia. See Gallazzi, Kramer, and Settis 2008, 116–33. They do not, however, consider the evident change from one kind of number to another at C. Hieron.

[34] Roller 2010, 212.

the world. Its wide range of attested examples, though mostly drawn from the western Mediterranean, may indicate that it included (as we might expect) a general introduction to geography, possibly including the theoretical text in columns i–iii of the papyrus. A descriptive account, arranged by region, may not have begun until book 2, where all the citations (21–31) refer to the Iberian peninsula. None of books 3–11 (32–57) has more than four citations, but it is clear that the normal progress eastward from the Pillars of Herakles was observed, reaching Greece in book 5 and the European side of the Black Sea in book 6. At this point, however, Artemidoros adopted a novel 'route'. While several predecessors had encompassed the whole *oikoumenē* clockwise—an exception being Eratosthenes (Chapter 12), who organized his account from east to west—Artemidoros departed from previous models, not completing a clockwise circuit but beginning again from the west with Libyē (book 7) and moving east to the Levant (books 9–10) to end with the Asian shore of the Black Sea and Asiatic Skythia (book 11). The two east–west sequences may imply a conceptual division of *oikoumenē* into Europe and Asia (the latter including Libyē), such as we see in, for example, Hekataios.

On the basis of this, one may assign the remaining genuine fragments (58–166, not including the disputed papyrus, 167) to their appropriate book, though scholars have done so in slightly different ways; we cannot, after all, be sure where Artemidoros divided one book from another, and some places from different regions were mentioned in the general discussion in book 1. Of particular interest are the fragments referring to Trogodytike on the east coast of Africa (98 §5–14), and to Arabia (130); these may have been grouped with Egypt and Aithiopia in book 8.

As the plentiful citations of his work show, Artemidoros' work was wide-ranging. He certainly saw it as the geographer's duty to update and correct his predecessors (Eratosthenes at 60, 63, 108; also Hekataios at 165 and Polybios at 2, 67, 77), a trait Strabo associates with him (81). He appears to have known the text we call Ps.-Skylax (29). We do not know how widely he travelled, other than that, starting from his home city of Ephesos (of whose history he seems proud, 88), he travelled the length of the Mediterranean (including to Rome, 89) and some way north along the Atlantic coast (58–9, probably also 67–8); perhaps even south along Morocco (101–3), where his meteorological observations may be first-hand.

The gathering of detailed information was a particular strength of Artemidoros, it seems, and may partly explain why he is cited so often. Judging by the citations, he was in the habit of listing or giving the total number of towns in a region (65, 85, 92) and the number of islands in a group (9, 83, 106). Like his predecessors since the 4th century, he gave a best estimate for the west–east length of the *oikoumenē* (4 §242, 5) as well reckoning major distances within it (4 §§243–6, 6–7, 72–4, 91, 93, 95, 97, 105). Pliny cites him for exact distances in miles or fractions of miles (e.g. 4, 7, 107), and we have suggested that not all such distances need have been in stades originally.[35] Artemidoros was interested in the dimensions of islands (8 §20, 38, 65, 83), including the circumferences of Crete (82), and Taprobane (49), as well as the 'near-island' of the Peloponnese (75).

Artemidoros was prone to digressions, in Markianos' view (120); but the critic may be seeking, in contradiction to his good opinion of Artemidoros elsewhere, to disparage his manner of writing a *periplous* in order to prepare the reader for his own. He may have had in mind Artemidoros' habit of discussing the interiors of land masses (e.g. 30, 36, 85; cf. 44 §10), not just their coastal transects. Artemidoros evidently knew Egyptian topography in some detail (45–7), whether at first hand we do not know, and clearly supplied detailed coastal itineraries, for example of the Levant (48, 51) as well as, if the Papyrus is genuine, Iberia (167). Enriching geography with ethnographic colour was not new, and Artemidoros, as with Ephesos (88), seems to have had a keen interest in local customs (e.g. 52 on Lykia; 64 on Keltiberian women's dress; 68 on rituals), the origin myths of cities (20, 22, 36) and peoples (86), and the definition of and relationships between different peoples (30; 98 §§18–19, where he may be drawing on Agatharchides; 133, 162). He is frequently cited by encyclopaedic authors for explanations of names (3, 32, 117, 136, 155, 157–8), and surprisingly often for variant or alternative forms of them (123–4, 126, 130, 133–5, 138, 140, 146, 151–3), though this may reflect changing nomenclature in the generations after he wrote.

As noted above, synthetic work on Artemidoros has been very limited until recently,[36] and scholarship has tended to under-estimate his achievement. The most recent full collections of testimonia and fragments are from 1838 and 1856; neither includes a full commentary.[37] The tide began to turn with the publication of the Papyrus,[38] and 2010 saw a substantial entry in *Brill's New Jacoby*.[39] Two full studies are now under way: a recent monograph on Artemidoros includes a new collection of the fragments of book 1 as a pilot for a full edition.[40]

For the present chapter, a new arrangement of all the extracts has been constructed. For book 1 (1–20), it follows the recent pilot edition by Schiano mentioned above. For books 2–11 (21–57), it includes fragments for which a book number is given in the primary evidence, whether or not it is questionable.[41] These are followed by fragments without a stated book number (58–166). Within each section, extracts are arranged in date order and then by sequence in their original context. The texts on the

---

[35] The distance of 991½ miles at 4 does not match the data in the Papyrus.

[36] Though see the overview by Cruz Andreotti 2016, 285–9 (focused on Iberia), who recognizes A.'s importance for later authors and sees him as interested in defining territories and describing culture groups, not only in the scientific approach characteristic of the earlier Hl period.

[37] Stiehle 1856; Hoffmann 1838, 221–88.

[38] The original full publication is Gallazzi, Kramer, and Settis 2008. It was soon followed by three conferences dedicated to further investigation: Gallazzi, Kramer, and Settis 2010; Gallazzi, Kramer, and Settis 2012; Adornato 2016.

[39] Banchich 2010, revised as Banchich 2019.

[40] Schiano 2010. A complete collection of testimonia and fragments, with Italian translation, is being prepared for *FGrH* v (no. 2008) by Silvia Panichi.

[41] In one case (142), the book number in the source has been discounted, with a high degree of confidence.

Artemidoros Papyrus are included as an Appendix (167),[42] followed by the probably spurious 'Munich fragment' (168). The extracts from Strabo are adapted from Roller's translation, except for passages enclosed in raised points (·), which are mine.

SELECTED FURTHER READING

Billerbeck, M. (2009), 'Artemidorus' Geographoumena in the Ethnika of Stephanus of Byzantium: source and transmission', in Brodersen and Elsner (below), 65–87.

Engels, J. (2012), 'Artemidoros of Ephesos and Strabo of Amasia: common traditions of Greek cultural geography and Strabo's decisive importance in the history of reception of Artemidoros' Geographoumena', in C. Gallazzi et al. (eds), *Geografia e cartografia* (Intorno al papiro di Artemidoro, 2) (Milan), 139–55.

*Hoffmann, S. F. W. (1838), 'Fragmente der Geographie des Artemidorus', in his *Die Iberer im Westen und Osten: eine Ethnographische Untersuchung* [. . .] (Leipzig), 221–88. [Includes material not in Stiehle's edition.]

*Panichi, S. (forthcoming), 'Artemidoros von Ephesos (2008)', in *FGrH* v.

*Schiano, C. (2010), *Artemidoro di Efeso e la scienza del suo tempo*. Bari. [Includes pilot edition of book 1.]

*Stiehle, R. (1856), 'Der Geograph Artemidorus von Ephesos', *Philologus*, 11. 2: 193–244. [Still the latest attempt at a comprehensive collection of 'fragments', but outdated.]

The Artemidoros Papyrus

From a vast range of bibliography (some cited in the footnotes above).

Adornato, G. (ed. 2016), *I disegni* (Atti del convegno internazionale del 4 febbraio 2011 presso il Gabinetto Disegni e Stampe degli Uffizi, Firenze) (Intorno al Papiro di Artemidoro, 3). Milan.

Brodersen, K., and Elsner, J. (eds 2009), *Images and Texts on the 'Artemidorus Papyrus': Working Papers on P.Artemid.* Stuttgart. [Clear discussions giving a good orientation.]

Canfora, L. (2008), with L. Bossina et al., *Il papiro di Artemidoro*. Rome–Bari. [The classic sceptical statement.]

—— (ed. 2008), *The True History of the So-called Artemidorus Papyrus: A Supplement*. Bari. [Concise and accessible statement of the sceptics' position.]

*Gallazzi, C., Kramer, B., and Settis, S. (eds 2008), *Il papiro di Artemidoro (P. Artemid.).* 2 vols. Milan. [The *editio princeps*.]

——, ——, and —— (eds 2010), *Contesto culturale, lingua, stile e tradizione* (Atti del convegno internazionale del 15 novembre 2008 presso la Scuola Normale Superiore di Pisa) (Intorno al papiro di Artemidoro, 1). Milan.

——, ——, and —— (eds 2012), *Geografia e cartografia* (Atti del convegno internazionale del 27 novembre 2009 presso la Società Geografica Italiana, Villa Celimontana, Roma) (Intorno al papiro di Artemidoro, 2). Milan.

Marcotte, D. (2010), 'Le papyrus d'Artémidore', *Revue d'histoire des textes*, n.s. 5: 333–71. [Judicious overview, accepting the text as genuine.]

---

[42] The supposed Munich fragment of Artemidoros on the Nile (in codex Monacensis graecus 287), which may derive rather from Eratosthenes via Strabo, is included as Appendix 2 to the present chapter (168).

TEXT

BOOK 1

1 Strabo 4. 1. 4–5, C179–80:[43] *The cult of Artemis of Ephesos*
(4) Massalia (*Marseille*) is a Phokaian foundation, situated on a rocky place. Its harbour is at the foot of a theatre-shaped rock that looks to the south. It, as well as the entire city, is well fortified, although it is considerable in size. The Ephesion is located on the headland, as well as the sanctuary of Delphinian Apollo. It is common to all Ionians but the Ephesion is a temple to the Ephesian Artemis.

It is said that when the Phokaians departed from their home, an oracle was delivered to them that they should use on their voyage a guide taken from Ephesian Artemis, and thus some of them went to Ephesos to ask how they could be provided with what the goddess had commanded. In a dream the goddess stood beside Aristarche, one of the most honoured of women, and ordered her to go away with the Phokaians, taking a copy of the sacred image of the sanctuary. When this was done and the settlement was finally made, they established the sanctuary, and especially honoured Aristarche by appointing her priestess. In their cities settled away from home, this goddess is honoured everywhere first of all, and they preserve the representation of the *xoanon*,[44] and observe all other customs as in the mother city.

(5) . . . Later, however, they prevailed through their bravery and acquired some of the surrounding plains, with the same strength by which they founded cities and their frontier strongholds in Iberia against the Iberians, where they established the ancestral rites of Ephesian Artemis, so that they would sacrifice in the Hellenic manner, as well as Rho⟨danousia[45] and⟩ Agathe (*Agde*)—against the barbarians living around the Rhodanos (*Rhône*) river—and Tauroention, Olbia,[46] Antipolis (*Antibes*), and Nikaia (*Nice*), founded against the Sallyes and the Ligyes (*Ligurians*) living in the Alps. . . .

Formerly they were particularly fortunate in all things, especially their friendship with the Romans, in regard to which one may detect many signs. Moreover, the *xoanon* of Artemis that is on the Aventine was made by the Romans in the same manner as that dedicated by the Massaliotes.[47]

2 Strabo 4. 1. 8, C183: *The Rhône*
Concerning the mouths of the Rhodanos (*Rhône*), Polybios[48] finds fault with Timaios,[49] saying that there are not five mouths but two mouths. Artemidoros says three.

---

[43] Included in book 1 by Schiano 2010. Although the passage does not name Artemidoros, these parts may well derive from his personal knowledge of the city, his home *polis*.
[44] A non-figurative representation of a deity carved in wood.
[45] Roller notes that the MSS read *rhoē*, 'flow' or 'current', and suggests a place-name stood here.
[46] Tauroention (cf. Tauroëis in *Nikomedean Periodos* 215) is unlocated; Olbia is near *Hyères*.
[47] This is particularly likely to be information from Artemidoros, given his diplomatic mission to Rome on behalf of Ephesos (89 below).
[48] Polyb. 34. 10. 5.   [49] *BNJ* 566 F 70.

3   Strabo 4. 1. 11, C185: *Cities in southern Gaul*

In between are the cities of Auenion (*Avignon*), Arausion (*Orange*), and Aëria (*Barry?*), which, Artemidoros says, is actually 'aerial' (*aëria*) because it is located on a great height.

4   Pliny, *Natural History*, 2. cxii. 242–6: *Length and breadth of the oikoumenē*[50]

(242) As was stated (*earlier*), our part of the Earth, which I am discussing—swimming, as it were, in the surrounding Ocean—extends furthest from sunrise to sunset: that is to say, from India to the Pillars of Hercules dedicated at Gades (*Cádiz*) it is 8,578 miles in the judgement of Artemidorus, but 9,818 in that of Isidorus.[51] Artemidorus adds a further distance from Gades by the circuit of the Sacred Cape to the promontory of Artabrum (*C. Ortegal?*), where the face of Hispania runs out furthest: namely 991½ miles.[52] (243) The measurement follows a double route:

> from the Ganges river and its entrance, where it discharges into the eastern Ocean, via India and Parthyene to the city of Myriandrus (*İskenderun*) in Syria, situated in the Issic gulf, 5,215 (*miles*);
>
> from there via the shortest voyage to the island of Cyprus, to Patara in Lycia, Rhodes, the island of Astypalaea in the sea of Carpathos, to Taenarum in Laconia, Lilybaeum on Sicily, and Caralis on Sardinia, 2,113;
>
> then to Gades, 1,250;
>
> which measurement makes the total miles from the eastern sea **8,578**.

(244) Another route, which is more secure and enables one to stay inland to the greatest extent, (*is*):

> from the Ganges to the Euphrates river, 5,169;
>
> from there to Mazaca (*Kayseri*) in Cappadocia, 244;
>
> from there via Phrygia, Caria, and Ephesus, 499;
>
> from Ephesus via the Aegean open-sea (*pelagus*) to Delos, 200;
>
> to the Isthmus, 212½;
>
> from there by land ⟨and by the Laconian sea⟩ and Corinthian gulf to Patrae in the Peloponnese, 90;
>
> to Leucas, 87½;

---

[50] These paragraphs and **8** below both present Artemidoros' data, Pliny using miles and giving less detail. Martianus Capella (C5 AD), *Nupt.* 6. 611, 613, and 615–16 Cristante *et al.*, are frs 19–21 of the *Epitome* in Hoffmann 1838, but are not included here as the first two closely match Pliny §242, the third §246.

[51] The first part of §242 is repeated almost verbatim by Dicuil (C8 AD), *De mensura*, 5 (see Tierney and Bieler 1967); it is included by Hoffman as fr. 22 of the *Epitome* (cf. also his p. 273 n.).

[52] At 8 st. to the mile, this exactly matches the figure of 7,932 st. at Agathemeros iv. 16 (Ch. 29 below). The Loeb edition (Rackham 1938) gives several of the distances in the remainder of this passage differently, but Beaujeu 1951, Thayer (in Lacus Curtius, on line), and the most recent edition (Winkler and König 1997) gives them as here. R. also omits '79 miles' at the end of §245.

to Corcyra, the same;

to Acroceraunia, 82½;

to Brundisium, 87½;

to Rome, 360;

to the Alps, as far as the village of Scingomagus, 519;

via Gallia to the Pyrenaean mountains (*at*) Illiberis, 468;

to the Ocean and the coast of Hispania, 831;

by the crossing to Gades, 7½.

This measurement, by Artemidoros' reckoning, makes **8,945** (*miles*).

(245) But the width of the Earth from the southern position to the north is roughly one-half less: for Isidorus it amounts to **5,462** (*miles*), which makes plain how much the warming on this side, and the freezing conditions on the other, have removed; though I do not consider that there is a deficit in these lands, or that the Earth does not have the shape of a sphere, but that the uninhabitable parts on each side are unknown. This measurement runs:

from the shore of the Aethiopic ocean, at the point where it is scarcely inhabited, to Meroë, 625 (*miles*);

from there to Alexandria, 1,250;

to Rhodes, 584;

to Cnidus, 87½;

to Cos, 25;

to Samos, 100;

to Chius, 94;

to Mytilene, 65;

to Tenedus, 119;

to Cape Sigeum, 12½;

to the mouth of the Pontus, 312½;

to Cape Carambis, 350;

to the mouth of the Maeotis, 312½ (*sic*);

to the entrance of the Tanaïs, 275.

This route can be made 79 miles less by using short cuts across the sea.

(246) From the entrance of the Tanaïs, the most careful authors have perpetrated no exaggerations. Artemidorus adjudged that the places beyond were unknown, though

he admitted that the nations of the Sarmatae resided around the Tanaïs. Isidorus added 1,250 (*miles*) up to Thyle (*Thoule*), which is an interpretation based on divine foresight.

5   Pliny, Natural History, 4. xxxvii. 121: *Length of Europe*
With the tour of Europe complete, a reckoning must now be given, so that nothing may be inconvenient for those who desire knowledge. Artemidorus and Isidorus have presented (*the distance of*) 8,714 (*miles*) from the Tanaïs to Gades. Polybius wrote that the width of Europe from Italy to the Ocean is 1,250,[53] though in his day its (*Europe's*) size had not been ascertained.[54]

6   Pliny, Natural History, 5. vi. 40: *Length of Africa*
Agrippa (*stated*) the length of all of Africa from the Atlantic, including Lower Egypt, as 3,040 (*miles*).[55] Polybios and Eratosthenes, who are regarded as most careful, have made the distance from the Ocean to Great Carthage 1,100 miles, and from there to Canopus, the nearest mouth of the Nile, 1,688 miles.[56] Isidorus (*has given*) 3,697[57] from Tingis to Canopus, Artemidorus 40 miles less than Isidorus.[58]

7   Pliny, Natural History, 5. ix. 47: *Length of Asia*
Asia joins it (*Libyē*), and Timosthenes asserts that it extends from the Canopic mouth to the mouth of the Pontus, a distance of 2,638 miles; Eratosthenes (*reports*) that from the opening of the Pontus to the mouth of the Maeotis is 1,545; but Artemidorus and Isidorus (*give*) the whole from Egypt to the Tanaïs as 5,013 miles and 750 paces (*i.e. ¾ mile*).[59]

8   Agathemeros iii. 10, iv. 15–19, and v. 20: *Dimensions of parts of the oikoumenē; its length and breadth; islands in the Mediterranean*[60]

iii. (10) The circumnavigation of Europe, from the outflows of the river Tanaïs (*Don*) as far as the Pillars of Herakles, is 69,709 stades.[61]

That of Libyē from Tingis as far as the Canopic mouth (*of the Nile*), 29,252 stades.[62]

Of Asia from Kanobos to the river Tanaïs, with the gulfs, the coastal sailing is **40,111** stades.[63]

. . .

iv. (15) The length of the inhabited world from the Ganges to Gadeira (*Cádiz*) is **68,545 stades,** as follows:[64]

---

[53] So Zehnacker and Silberman, following Mayhoff; 1,543 Winkler; 1,150 Rackham.
[54] Cf. **8** iii. 10, from Agathemeros. This and the next extracts contain distances which are taken from Artemidoros.
[55] 3,000 Rackham.   [56] 1,628 Rackham.   [57] 3,519 Rackham.
[58] Cf. **8** iii. 10.   [59] Cf. **8** iii. 10.
[60] Stiehle includes Agathem. i. 5 (on Sardinia and Corsica) as a fragment of Artem. (48a ~ 50 ~ 118 St.), assigning it to book 4. It is not included in book 1 by Schiano. The whole of Agathem. iii (§§8–15), detailing the major gulfs of the world—Mediterranean/Black Sea, Persian, Caspian, and Arabian—may also derive from Artemidoros (Leroy 2018, introduction; commentary ad locc.).
[61] Cf. **4** §§242–3.   [62] Cf. **5.**
[63] Cf. **6.** The next sentence (the end of §10) is not included in book 1 by Schiano; but §§11–14 on seas and inlets (which may be read in Ch. 29) are possibly also based on Artemidoros.
[64] iv. 15–19 and **4** above both present A.'s data more fully here.

From the river Ganges as far as Myriandros (İskenderun) in the gulf of Issos,[65] **41,725 stades,** as follows:

> from the Ganges to the outflows of the river Indos, 16,000 stades;
>
> from the Indos to the Caspian Gates, 15,300;
>
> to the Euphrates, 10,050;
>
> to Myriandros, 375 stades.

(16) From Myriandros to Gadeira, **26,820 stades,** as follows:

> from Myriandros to Kleïdes (*The Keys*) on Cyprus, 1,400 stades;
>
> to the promontory of Akamas,[66] 1,300 stades;
>
> to the Chelidoniai (*islands; Beş Adalar*)[67] via the Pamphylian open-sea (*pelagos*), 1,900 stades;
>
> to Patara, 800 stades;
>
> to Rhodes, 700 stades;
>
> to Astypalaia via the Karpathian (*open-sea*), 140† stades;
>
> to Tainaron, 1,950 stades;
>
> to Pachynos[68] in Sicily, 4,600 stades;
>
> to Lilybaion via the Libyan open-sea (*pelagos*), 1,520 stades;
>
> to Karalis in Sardinia via the Tyrsenian open-sea (*pelagos*), 1,800 stades;
>
> to Gadeira, sailing beyond the Gymnasiai islands (*Balearic*), 10,000 stades.

From Gadeira via Hieron (*Sacred*) Promontory[69] to the harbour of Artabra, 7,932 stades.[70]

> Altogether these make **76,477.**

(17) Or in another manner:

> from the Ganges as far as the river Euphrates, 41,350;
>
> from the Euphrates to Mazaka (*Kayseri*) among the Kappadokians, 1,950 stades;
>
> from Mazaka via Phrygia Paroreia (*beside the Mountains*), Great (*Phrygia*),[71] and Karia as far as Ephesos, 3,990 stades;

Altogether from the Ganges to Ephesos, **47,290 stades.**

> From Ephesos to Delos via the Aegean, 1,600 stades;
>
> to the Isthmus, 1,700 stades;
>
> from the Isthmus via the Corinthian gulf to Patrai, 720 stades;

---

[65] *Gulf of Alexandretta or gulf of İskenderun.*   [66] The NW cape of Cyprus.
[67] The Turkish name means 'five islands'.   [68] The NE cape of Sicily.
[69] Cape *St Vincent*, or possibly *Trafalgar.*
[70] At 8 st. to the mile, this exactly equals Pliny's 991½ miles: see 4 §242.
[71] The former is part of the latter, Strabo 12. 8. 13, C576.

to Leukas, 700 stades;

to Kerkyra, 700 stades;

to the Akrokeraunian mountains, 660 stades;

to Brentesion (*Brindisi*), 700 stades;

from Brentesion, for a man travelling on foot, as far as Rome, 2,880 stades;

from Rome to the Alps as far as Skingomagos, located under the Alps, 4,152 stades;

next via Keltike as far as the city of Illigyris, ⟨3,744 stades;

from Illigyris⟩ via the inns as far as Gadeira (*Cádiz*), 6,654 stades;

and the voyage across to Gadeira, 60 stades.

Altogether from the Ganges to Gadeira, **71,560 stades.**

(18) The breadth of the inhabited world from the Aithiopic sea (*East Atlantic*)[72] to Meroë, 5,000 stades.

From Meroë to Alexandria, 10,000 stades.

From Alexandria to the river Tanaïs (*Don*), **11,056**†—for the parts above the mouths of the Tanaïs to the north are unknown—as follows:

from Alexandria to Lindos on Rhodes, 4,500 stades;

to Thoanteion, as you sail with Rhodes on your right, 400 stades;

to Telos, 160 stades;

to Lakter in Koan territory, 120 stades;

to Drepanon in Koan territory, 100 stades;

to Arkitis island, 230 stades;

to (*the*) Korsiai (*islands*), 100;

to Ampelos in Samian territory, 30 stades;

to Argennon †via the Aegean†, 500 stades;

to Korynaion in Erythraian territory, 270 stades;

to Phlion†, the tip of Chios, 50 stades;

to Melaneus, the tip of Lesbos, 450 stades;

to Sigrion on Lesbos, 500 stades;

to Tenedos island, 450 stades;

to Sigeion, 100 stades;

to the mouth of the Pontos, 2,500 stades;

to Karambis, 2,800 stades;

to the mouth of Maiotis, 2,500 stades;

to the Tanaïs, 2,200 stades.

[72] The name 'Aithiopic sea' for the great bight off West Africa reflects the belief that the Aithiopes extended from coast to coast of 'Libyē' (Africa). Cf. Index s.v. Western Aithiopes.

(19) Or in another manner, from city to city:

From Alexandria to Rhodes, 4,670 stades;

to Knidos, 700 stades;

to Kos, 200 stades;

to Samos, 800 stades;

to Chios, 750 stades;

to Mytilene, 520 stades;

to Tenedos, 950 stades;

to Sigeion, 100 stades;

to the mouth of the Pontos, 2,500 stades;

to Karambis, 2,800 stades;

to the mouth of Maiotis, 2,500 stades;

to the river Tanaïs, 2,200 stades.

Altogether from Alexandria to the Tanaïs, **18,690 stades.**

v. (20) Finally we shall tell the circumferences of the islands in our region, taking them from Artemidoros, Menippos, and other trustworthy writers.

Gadeira is 120 stades in length, 16 in breadth. The crossing by the Pillars of Herakles is narrowest (*here*), at 80 stades.

In the Iberian open-sea (*pelagos*) are the islands called Pityoussai: the larger, inhabited one is 300 stades long, the lesser one 100 stades.

Of the Gymnasioi, which the Carthaginians called Baliariai—for their slingers are likewise called Baliareis—the larger is 1,200 stades in length and 400 stades in breadth; the lesser is 300 stades (*long*).

Those bearing the name Stoichades lie in succession directly in front of the cities of the Massalians; the greater are three in number, but two small ones are close to Massalia itself.[73]

Sardo (*Sardinia*) has a form like that of a footprint, and is hollow in the middle; its length is 2,200. Kyrnos (*Corsica*) is close to Sardo but much more undistinguished; it is less than half the length of Sardo. The point of departure for Sardo and Kyrnos (*Corsica*) is Popoulonion (*Populonium*) in Tyrsenia (*Etruria*); the crossing is 1,200 stades.

According to Timosthenes, the circumference of Sicily is 4,740 stades, its form that of a scalene triangle. It has a crossing from Peloros Point to Italy of 12 stades. The side of the island from Peloros to Pachynos is 1,360 stades; from Pachynos to Lilybaion 1,600 stades; according to Timosthenes, from Lilybaion to Pelorias (*Peloros*) 1,700 stades. From Lilybaion the voyage across to Aspis in Libyē is close to 1,500 stades.

---

[73] Cf. **9.**

9 *Oxyrhynchos Papyrus* xxiv. 2694, lines 18–32 = scholion to Apollonios of Rhodes 4. 554: *The number of the Stoichades Is.*
'[S]toichade[s]': according to what it said, three St[o]ichades exist [—] four, as Artemidoros says in book 1 of his *Geographika*. For they lie as if on a single straight line and [—]beside it [—] being three [—] island actually lies in the [—] of Massalia.[74]

10 **Markianos**, *Periplous*, 2. 19: *Narbonese Gaul*
We have clearly expounded the circumnavigation of Narbonesia (*Gallia Narbonensis*) in the *Epitome* of Artemidoros' *Geography* or *Periplous* (*Circumnavigation*), even if the aforementioned Artemidoros did not make a distinction between places in ⟨Keltogalatia and in⟩ Iberia.

11 **Stephanos of Byzantion** β 148: *A city in Illyria*
Bounnos: a city in Illyria. The *ethnikon* is Bounnios; as Artemidoros (*says*) in (*the*) 1st (*book*) of *Geographoumena*.

12 **Stephanos of Byzantion** γ 50: *A Ligurian city*
Genoa: a city of the Ligyres, now called [—], as Artemidoros (*says*). The *ethnikon* is Genoates.

13 **Stephanos of Byzantion** δ 45: *A city in Italia*
Dekiēton: a city in Italia.[75] The *ethnikon* is Dekiētai, as Artemidoros (*says*) in (*the*) 1st (*book*) of *Geographoumena*.[76]

14 **Stephanos of Byzantion** δ 58: *A Ligurian city*
Dertōn: a city of the Ligyres. Artemidoros, in *Epitome of the Eleven* (*books*): 'The city called Dertōn'. The *ethnikon* is Dertonios, like Antronios.

15 **Stephanos of Byzantion** κ 4: *A colony of Massalia*
Kabelliōn: a city (*belonging to*) Massalia.[77] Artemidoros, in (*the*) 1st (*book*) of *Geographoumena*. The *ethnikon*, of local type, is Kabellionesios, like Tarrakonesios; but in the Greek form Kabellionites, like Tarrakonites.

16 **Stephanos of Byzantion** λ 61: *The Ligurian nation*
Ligyres (*Ligurians*): a nation adjoining the Tyrrhenoi (*Etruscans*). Artemidoros, in *Epitome of the Eleven* (*books*): 'From the river Ligyros'.

17 **Stephanos of Byzantion** μ 94: *A city in Gaul*
Mastramele: a city and lake in Keltike (*Gallia*). Artemidoros, in the *Epitome of the Eleven* (*books*).

---

[74] Cf. **8** v. 20 above. Raschieri 2007 notes that A. is the only source to give the number of the islands as four.

[75] Schiano 2010, 41 and 43, places this E of the *Rhône*.

[76] Stiehle emends to 'book 4'.   [77] Schiano 2010, 41, places it E of the *Rhône*.

18 Stephanos of Byzantion ν 13: *A city in Gaul*
Narbōn: trading-place and Keltic city. . . . But Markianos refers to it as Narbonesia.

19 Stephanos of Byzantion σ 116: *A river in Gaul*
Sekoanos (*Saône*): a river of the Massaliotai, from which (*comes*) the *ethnikon* Sekoanoi, as Artemidoros (*says*) in (*the*) 1st (*book*).[78]

20 Stephanos of Byzantion τ 53: *Foundation of a city in Gaul*
Tauroëis: a Keltic (*Gallic*) city, a colony of the Massalietai.[79] The citizens (*are*) Tauroëntioi. Apollo[doros . . . *words missing* . . . Artemi]doros, in (*the*) 1st (*book*) of *Geographoumena*, says that the ship that conveyed the founders of the city had a bull for its figurehead; they were lost from the expedition of the Phokaians, were brought to this spot by the emblem of the ship, and founded the city.

BOOK 2

21 Stephanos of Byzantion α 6: *A city in Iberia*
Abdera: two cities. . . . The second city is in Iberia, near Gadeira, as Artemidoros (*says*) in (*the*) 2nd (*book*) of *Geographoumena*.[80]

22 Stephanos of Byzantion η 13: *A city in Iberia*
Hemeroskopeion ('*Viewpoint*'; *Dénia?*): a city of the Keltiberoi, a colony of the Phokaians. Artemidoros, 2nd narrative (*logos*)[81] of *Geographoumena*.

23 Stephanos of Byzantion ι 19a: *Iberias*[82]
Iberiai (*Iberias*), two: the one by the Pillars of Herakles, (*named*) after the river Iber; the other Iberia is beside the Persians.[83] The *ethnikon* (*is*) 'Iber'. And from the genitive 'Iberos' (*come*) 'Iberikos' and 'Iberos'.[84] . . .

24 Stephanos of Byzantion κ 81: *A city in Iberia*
Karthaia: . . . There is also a Kartaia (*sic*) in Iberia, about which Artemidoros (*writes*) in (*the*) 2nd (*book*) of *Geographoumena*.

25 Stephanos of Byzantion κ 92: *An island off Akarnania*
Karnos: an island in Akarnania.[85] Artemidoros, 2nd (*book*) of *Geographoumena*. The *ethnikon* is Karnios.

---

[78] Schiano 2010, 41, places it E of the *Rhône*.   [79] Schiano 2010, 41, places it E of the *Rhône*.

[80] The geographical divisions between A.'s books are not always certain, but he began his *periplous* of the *oikoumenē* in the W, as many of the extracts attributed to book 2 make clear. For this Abdera, cf. **61**.

[81] i.e. the 2nd book.   [82] Cf. **31**; **167** column iv.   [83] E of the Black Sea.

[84] Both masculine adjectives. This entry in the surviving C10 abridgement of the *Ethnika* does not cite A., but has been reconstructed by editors using **31** below, which cites A. twice and is agreed to be based on Stephanos' unabridged entry, now lost. Cf. also Markianos **15**.

[85] Cf. Ps.-Skylax §34. 2.

26 Stephanos of Byzantion μ 35: *A city in Iberia*

Malake (*Málaga*): a city in Iberia. Markianos, in (*the*) 2nd (*book*) of the *Epitomai*[86] of Artemidoros. The *ethnikon* is Malakitanos.

27 Stephanos of Byzantion ν 37: *A city and river in Illyria*

Nestos: a city and river in Illyria. The *ethnikon* is Nestios, as Artemidoros (*says in the*) 2nd (*book*) of *Geographoumena*; and the territory is Nestis.

28 Stephanos of Byzantion τ 208: *An island (?)*

Tropis: an island. Artemidoros, in (*the*) 2nd (*book*) of *Geographoumena*.[87]

29 Stephanos of Byzantion ψ 1: *A city in Lakonike*

Psamathous (*Sandy*): a city in Lakonike. Artemidoros, 2nd (*book*) of *Geographoumena*: 'For after Tainaron there follows the city of Psamathous'. The *ethnikon* is Psamathountios and Psamathousios, like Selinountios and Selinousios.[88]

30 Stephanos of Byzantion ω 16: *A city in Iberia*

Orisia: a city in Iberia. The *ethnikon* is Oritanos. Artemidoros, in (*the*) 2nd (*book*) of *Geographoumena*, says, 'For both peoples occupy the coast and certain places in the interior; first the Oritanoi, and the large cities among them are Orisia and Kastalōn'.[89]

31 Constantine Porphyrogennetos, *De administrando imperio,* 23[90]
On Iberia and Hispania

Iberiai (*Iberias*), two: . . . Artemidoros, in the 2nd (*book*) of the *Geographoumena*, says they are divided thus: 'From the Pyrenaian mountains inland as far as the places by Gadeira (*Cádiz*) is called both Iberia and Hispania synonymously. It has been divided by the Romans into two provinces [—] all the (*land*) stretching from the Pyrenaian mountains up to Kaine Karchedon (*New Carthage*) and the springs of the Baitis (*Guadalquivir*); in the second province, the (*places*) up to Gadeira and Lysitania.'[91] . . . And Artemidoros in (*the*) 2nd (*book*) of the *Geographoumena* (*says*), 'Those Iberes who live by the sea use the script of the Italians'.

BOOK 3

32 Stephanos of Byzantion β 62: *A people of Iberia*

Belitanoi: the same people as the Lysitanoi, as Artemidoros (*says*) in (*the*) 3rd (*book*) of *Geographoumena*.

---

[86] Steph. Byz., if correctly transmitted, is inconsistent in referring to Markianos' summary of A.'s 11-book work: sometimes calling it *Epitome of the Eleven*, but here referring to the passages summarizing particular books as if they were distinct works.

[87] Schiano 2010, 35–6, argues that this is not an island (*nēsos*) but refers to the keel (*tropis*) of a ship (*nēos*), and has been taken from one of the accounts of historical events which A. included in his geographical work.

[88] Psamathous is near the tip of the Tainaron peninsula (*Máni*); cf. Ps.-Skyl. §46. 1.

[89] See n. on **33**.   [90] Cf. **23**; **167** column iv.

[91] See n. on **23**. The passage containing this extract is agreed to be based on the original, unabridged text of Steph. Byz.'s entry 'Iberiai', and also partly matches the Artemidoros Papyrus (**167**).

33   Stephanos of Byzantion κ 118: *A city in Iberia*
Kastalōn: the largest city in Ōritania, as Artemidoros (*says*), 3rd (*book*) of *Geographoumena*.[92] The *ethnikon* is Kastalonites, like Askalonites and Tarrakonites.[93]

BOOK 4

34   Stephanos of Byzantion τ 20: *A city in Crete*
Tanos: a city in Crete, as Artemidoros (*says*) in (*the*) 4th (*book*) of *Geographoumena*. The *ethnikon* is Tanios.[94]

35   Stephanos of Byzantion τ 63: *A city in Italia*
Teanon: a city in Italia, as Artemidoros (*says*), 4th (*book*) of *Geographoumena*. The ethnikon is Teanos.

36   Stephanos of Byzantion τ 120: *A city in Italia*
Tibyris (*Tibur*): a city in Italia. Artemidoros, 4th (*book*) of *Geographoumena*: 'There is also in the interior Tibyra, which originally came into existence as a Hellenic city, 147 stades distant from Rome'. The *ethnikon* is Tibyrtinos.

37   Stephanos of Byzantion φ 107: *A people of Italia*
Phrourentanoi (*Frentani*): a nation in Italia. Artemidoros, 4th (*book*) of *Geographoumena*.

BOOK 5

38   Porphyrios, *De antro Nympharum*, §4:[95] *Kephallenia and Ithaca*
Those that have considered that the cave, and everything he told about it, is pure invention by the poet appear to have written about the local history in a rather lazy manner; but those that have written about geography—well, among them the Ephesian Artemidoros writes in the most excellent and accurate fashion, in the fifth (*book*) of the composition gathered by him into eleven (*books*), as follows: 'eastward from the harbour of Panormos on Kephallenia, at a distance of 12 stades, is the island of Ithaca, (*measuring*) 85 stades, narrow and lofty, with a harbour called (*the harbour*) of Phorkys. There is a shore in this (*harbour*), and there lies a cave sacred to the Nymphs, where it is said Odysseus was set ashore by the Phaiakians'.[96]

---

[92] Meineke's *apparatus criticus* suggests book 2 rather than 3, on the basis of 30 above.
[93] This and **30** should be from the same book of A., both places being in the same region.
[94] If A. mentioned Tanos in its normal place, it should perhaps have been in book 5, which included parts of Greece and its islands (cf. **39** on a cape of Mt Ida in Crete). Tanos might be thought an error for Itanos, but there are coins with the legends Tan(itōn) and Tanit(ōn) (Billerbeck 2006–17, vol. iv ad loc.).
[95] Section number as in Seminar Classics 609 1969, p. 6.   [96] See *Od.* 13. 96–121.

39 **Stephanos of Byzantion** φ 10: *A cape of Corfù*
Phalakrai: a cape of (*Mt*) Ida, which has nothing living on it because of snow and ice, but has become bare. . . . There is also a cape Phalakron on Kerkyra (*Corfù*), as Artemidoros says in (*the*) 5th (*book*) of *Geographoumena*.

BOOK 6

40 **Stephanos of Byzantion** π 43: *A cape in the southern Black Sea*
Parthenios: a river flowing in the middle of the city of the Amastrianoi. . . . There is also a cape near Herakleia, which Artemidoros mentions in (*the*) 6th (*book*) of *Geographoumena*.[97]

BOOK 7

41 **Stephanos of Byzantion** ε 129: *A cape in Libyē*
Erythra: the sea (*of that name*). . . . There is also a Cape Erythra in Libyē, as Artemidoros (*says*), 7th (*book*) of *Geographoumena*.[98]

42 **Stephanos of Byzantion** ι 84: *A city in Libyē*
Hipponesos: a city in Karia. . . . There is also one in Libyē, as Artemidoros (*says*) in (*the*) 7th (*book*). The *ethnikon* is Hipponesios.

43 **Stephanos of Byzantion** λ 85: *An island off Libyē*
Lopadoussa (*Lampedusa*): an island off Thapsos in Libyē, as Artemidoros (*says*), 7th (*book*) of *Geographoumena*. The *ethnikon* is Lopadoussaios.

BOOK 8

44 (*a*) **Strabo** 17. 2. 1–5, C821–4: *Aithiopian customs*[99]
(1) In the previous portion many things were said about the Aithiopes, so that it could be described at the same time as Egypt. One can say that the extremities of the inhabited world, which lie alongside what is not temperate and is uninhabitable because of the heat or cold, must be deficient and inferior to that which is temperate, which is clear from the lifestyle and the lack of necessities of the inhabitants. They live a hard life, are naked, and are mostly nomads. Their domestic animals—sheep, goats, and cattle—are small, and their dogs are small although fast and belligerent. Perhaps people have imagined and fabricated the Pygmaioi on the basis of the small

---

[97] Book 6 appears to have dealt with Asia Minor.
[98] All three fragments from book 7 concern Libyē (N. Africa) other than Egypt.
[99] This passage has a better claim than Diodoros 3. 5–11 (*b* below) to reflect Artemidoros closely (it is the only time D. cites A.). A. is incorporating material from Agatharchides (probably from the *On Affairs in Asia*) but we cannot separate the two threads. For related material, see **98–100**.

stature of these (*the animals*), since no man worthy of belief has recorded seeing them.

(2) They (*the Aithiopes*) live on millet and barley, from which they make a drink. For oil they use butter and fat. They do not have fruit trees except for a few palms in the royal gardens. Some of them have grass as food, as well as soft twigs, lotus, and the roots of reeds. They also use meat, blood, milk, and cheese.

They revere their kings as gods, who are generally shut up in their homes. Meroë is their greatest royal residence, a city having the same name as the island, which they say is like an oblong shield in shape. It is said that its size—perhaps exaggerated—has a length of about 3,000 stades, and its width is about 1,000. It has many mountains and large thickets, and is inhabited by nomads, hunters, and farmers. There are copper mines, iron mines, and gold, and varieties of precious stones. It is surrounded on the Libyan side by large dunes, on the Arabian by continuous cliffs, and up in the south by the confluence of rivers: the Astaboras, Astapous, and Astasobas. Towards the north is the onward stream of the Nile, as far as Egypt, along the previously mentioned windings of the river.[100] The houses in the cities have walls of split palm woven together, or of brick. They excavate salt, as do the Arabians. The palm, persea, ebony, and carob are the abundant plants. They hunt elephants, lions, and leopards. There are also the elephant-fighting serpents and many other wild animals, who flee for refuge from the more burning and arid regions to those that are moist and marshy.

(3) Psebo lies above Meroë, a large lake having a rather well-settled island. Since the Libyans have what is on the western bank of the Nile, and the Aithiopes on the opposite side, they dominate in turns the islands and the riverine territory, each being driven out by the other and giving way to whomever is stronger.

The Aithiopes use bows of four cubits that are wooden and hardened in the fire.[101] The women are armed, and most of them have a copper ring through the lip of their mouth. They wear sheepskin—as they do not have wool—and their sheep are hairy like goats. They are naked, or are girdled with sheepskins of well-woven hair. They believe in an immortal god—the cause of everything—and also a mortal one, who is unnamed and not manifest. For the most part they consider their benefactors and kings to be gods, and of these the kings are the common saviours and guardians of all, and as private individuals are the same, in a special sense, to those who have experienced good things from them. Some of those in the burned regions are considered without gods. They say that they hate the sun and speak badly of it when they look at its rising, since it burns them and makes war on them, and they flee for refuge into the marshes. Those in Meroë revere Herakles, Pan, Isis, and some other barbarian god. Some throw the dead into the river, others pour glass round them and keep them, and some bury them around the sanctuaries in clay coffins. They call upon them in oaths, and consider them the most sacred of all.

---

[100] At 17. 1. 2.   [101] Cf. the fire-hardened weapons of the Aithiopes at Ps.-Skyl. §112. 9.

They appoint as kings those who are unusual in their beauty, their keeping of cattle, courage, or wealth. The priest had the highest rank at Meroë in antiquity, and would command the king, sometimes sending a messenger (*to tell him*) to kill himself, and appointing another in place of him. Later one of the kings brought this custom to an end by going with armed men to the sanctuary, where the golden temple is, and cutting the throats of all the priests. It is also an Aithiopian custom that if one of the kings is mutilated in any part of his body, those closest around him undergo the same thing, and they die with him. Because of this the king is guarded especially well by them. This is sufficient about the Aithiopes.

(4) There must be added to the Egyptian account what is peculiar to it. There is the so-called Egyptian bean, from which the *kibarion* comes, and papyrus, which is only here and among the Indians. The persea is only here and among the Aithiopes, a large tree with fruit that is sweet and also large. There is also the mulberry that produces the fruit called a *sykomoros*, which resembles a fig, although it is not valued for its taste. There is also the *korsion*, a sweet fruit like a pepper but a little larger. There are many fish in the Nile, of different types, that are special and indigenous. The best known are the *oxyrhynchus*, *lepidotos*, *latos*, *alabes*, *korakinos*, *choiros*, and *phagrorios* (also called the *phagros*), and also the *silurus*, *kitharos*, *thrissa*, *kestreus*, *lychnos*, *physa*, and *bous* (*ox*). The shellfish include a large snail that makes a sound like a frog croaking. Egyptian indigenous animals include the ichneumon and the asp, which is peculiar in regard to others. There are two kinds, one of which is a handspan (*spithamē*)[102] in length and causes death quickly, and the other is nearly a fathom (*orguia*), as Nikandros, who wrote the *Theriaka*, stated.[103] Among the birds are the ibis and the Egyptian hawk, which is tame like the cat when compared to those elsewhere. The night raven here is also distinctive, for among us it is the size of an eagle and makes a deep sound, but in Egypt it is the size of a jackdaw and makes a different sound. The ibis is the tamest, and is like a stork in shape and size. There are two colours, one of which is like the stork and the other completely black. Every road intersection in Alexandria is full of them, and they are useful in a way, but in another way they are not useful. They are useful because they pick out every wild animal as well as the by-products from the meat and food shops, but they are inconvenient because they eat everything and are unclean, and only with difficulty can they be kept away from clean things and anything that is not polluted.

(5) The statement of Herodotos is also true, that it is an Egyptian custom to knead mud with the hands, but the dough for bread-making with the feet.[104] *Kakeis* is a special kind of bread that stops the bowels, and the *kiki* is a fruit that is sown in the fields, from which oil is pressed for lamps, and which is used by almost everyone in the region, and also as an unguent for those who are poorer and more hard-working, both men and women. *Koukina* is Egyptian wickerwork from some plant similar to

---

[102] See Glossary.　　[103] Nicander, *Theriaka*, 168–9.　　[104] Hdt. 2. 36.

rushes or palms. They prepare beer in a peculiar way: it is common to many, but the preparation varies among each. Most zealously they raise all children who are born and circumcise the males and cut the females, as is the custom among the Ioudaioi (*Jews*), who were originally Egyptians, as we said in that section.[105]

Aristoboulos[106] says that because of the crocodiles no fish comes up from the sea into the Nile except the *kestreus*, *thrissa*, and dolphin: the dolphin because it is stronger, and the *kestreus* because it is escorted by *choiroi* along the banks through a natural affinity. The crocodiles keep away from the *choiroi*, since they are round and have spines on their heads that are dangerous to the animals. The *kestreus* runs up in the spring, carrying its offspring, but comes down in groups to give birth a little before the setting of the Pleiades. This is when they are captured, since their groups are surrounded by nets. Such a reason can also be conjectured in the case of the *thrissa*. This is it for Egypt.

(*b*) **Diodoros** 3. 5. 1–11. 2: *Aithiopia (and Egypt)*[107]

> 5. Among the customs of the Aithiopes, more than a few seem to differ markedly from those found among other people, particularly as regards the choosing of kings. For the priests pick out the best men from among themselves, but then the mass of the people choose, from among those listed, the one whom the god, when being carried round in a celebration in conformity with a particular custom, selects. At once (*the people*) perform obeisance and honour him as a god, since his rule has been ordained by decision (*pronoia*) of the divine power.   (2) The man chosen lives his life in the manner prescribed by the laws, and performs other actions according to ancestral custom. He bestows no benefaction or punishment upon anyone in violation of the lawful ordinance originally adopted by them (*the Egyptians*). Their custom is that he shall not enforce death upon any of his subjects, even if a man has been convicted of a capital crime and evidently deserves punishment; instead he sends one of his servants to the offender bearing a token of death, and when the man sees the sign he immediately goes off to his own house and expels himself from life. It is absolutely impermissible to go into exile from one's own land into a neighbouring one, and cancel the penalty through expulsion from one's homeland, as happens among the Hellenes.   (3) This is why they tell of one man who, after the fatal token was sent to him by the king, proposed to go into exile from Aithiopia; but when his mother realized and tied her girdle round his neck, he did not dare to lay hands on her by any means, but endured strangulation until he died, so as not to leave behind an even worse disgrace to his kinfolk.

---

[105] At 16. 2. 34.   [106] *BNJ* 139 F 39.

[107] Book 8 concerned Egypt. At the end of this lengthy passage on Aithiopia (3. 11. 2), Diod. names his most valued sources on Egypt (the subject of his own book 2) and Aithiopia as (i) book 2 of Agatharchides' historical work *On Asia* and (ii) Artemidoros book 8. He evidently consulted both directly, but may have under-estimated the extent to which Art. relied on Ag. See Burstein 2012b, first extract (Diod. 3. 11. 1–3), *contra* Marcotte 2001. As Diod. does not distinguish different sources in §§1–10, however, we cannot tell which material is from which author. Nor does he cite Ag. or Art. in book 2. The Strabo passage at (*a*) above has a better claim to reflect Art. closely; accordingly, Diod.'s text is indented and printed in smaller type. (I am grateful to Stanley Burstein for discussion of these passages.)

6. The most surprising thing of all is what happens regarding the kings' passing. For at Meroë the priests who busy themselves with worshipping and honouring the gods, and form a very large and authoritative group, whenever the notion comes into their minds, send a messenger to the king and order him to die: (2) for (*they say*) the gods have given this response to them and the instruction of the immortals may not be disregarded in any way by one of mortal nature. They also express additional reasons, such as will be accepted in plain understanding by one whose nature has been reared in an ancient practice that is hard to erase, and has no argument he can deploy even against injunctions that are not ineluctable. (3) So during remote times the kings used to pay heed to the priests, not forced by weapons or violence but overpowered in their reasonings by their very superstition; but in the time of the second Ptolemy the king of the Aithiopes, Ergamenes, after partaking of Hellenic education and practising philosophy, was the first who was brave enough to ignore the matter: for adopting an attitude worthy of kingship he crossed with his soldiers into the impenetrable place where the golden temple of the Aithiopes used to stand, slaughtered the priests, cancelled the custom, and reorganized matters in accordance with his own preference.

7. They said that their law about the king's friends, surprising though it is, remains valid down to our own times. For they say that the Aithiopes have the custom that when the king becomes disabled in any part of his body, from any cause whatsoever, every one of his usual associates sacrifices this same part by choice. For they consider that it would be shameful if, after the king had been disabled in his leg, his friends should still be uninjured and not all accompany him on his excursions in a similarly lame condition; and that it would be illogical if steadfast friendship should mourn and grieve together with him, and likewise share in all other good and bad things, but not join him in his bodily pain. They even say it is usual for the companions to die willingly at the same moment as the kings, and that this death is distinguished and a testimony of genuine friendship. This (*they say*) is why it is not easy for a plot against the king to be laid among the Aithiopes, since every one of his friends takes forethought equally for the king's safety and their own. Such, then, are the laws among the Aithiopes who live in their mother-city or who possess the island of Meroë[108] and the territory near Egypt.

8. But there are also numerous other races of the Aithiopes: some occupying the land beside the river Nile on both banks and the islands in the river, others possessing the neighbouring part of Arabia,[109] and others established in the inland parts of Libyē. (2) Most of these people, and particularly those living beside the river, are dark in colour, have snub-nosed faces, and are curly-haired. In spirit they are totally wild, displaying animal characteristics, though less so in their spirit than in their practices: for besides being dirty all over their body they likewise keep their nails extremely long in a similar way to wild animals. They also have little to do with kindness towards one another. (3) Speaking in a harsh voice, while possessing none of the things that other peoples practise in order to make life cultivated, they thus exhibit a vast difference from

---

[108] For Meroë, see Agatharch. 51a (Phot.) and appendix at §8 (Strabo); and see Index.
[109] sc. across the *Red Sea*.

our own customs. (4) Some of them are armed with shields of untanned oxhide and short spears; others with javelins, but no thongs, and sometimes with wooden bows 4 cubits (*6 feet*) long which they shoot while setting their foot against them, but once the arrows are spent they carry on fighting with wooden clubs. They also arm the women, though defining a set age limit for them; it is the law that most of the women should bear a bronze ring on the lip of their mouth. (5) Some of the people use no clothing at all, living a life of nakedness forever and only equipping themselves against the burning heat by making something with their own hands from whatever lies around them. Some, however, cut off the tails from the rear end of their sheep and use them to cover their midriff, as if to give some covering to their private parts. Some use the skins of their cattle, though there are some who cover their body down to the middle with aprons which they weave from hair, as their sheep yield no wool on account of the distinctive nature of the country. (6) For food, some of them use what fruit they find growing in the waters; it springs up spontaneously around the lakes and marshy places. Others prune the branches with the softest foliage, and shade their body with them to cool down in the middle of the day. Some sow sesame and lotus, while some are sustained by the softest roots of reeds. Not a few have practised archery intensively, and shoot down birds with accurate aim, with which they make good the deficiency of nature; but the majority have a lifelong diet of meat, milk, and cheese from their flocks.

9. Concerning the gods, those (*Aithiopes*) who dwell upstream from Meroë have two views. They understand that some of them (*the gods*), including the sun, the Moon, and the whole universe, have an immortal and imperishable nature, but think that others partake of mortal nature and have earned the honours due to immortals because of their goodness and their benefactions to humans. (2) So as they revere Isis and Pan, and in addition Herakles and Zeus, they believe the race of humans enjoys benefactions most of all from them. But a few of the Aithiopes do not believe that there are any gods whatsoever: thus they blaspheme against the sun at its rising, saying it is their worst enemy, and take refuge in the marshy places. (3) They also have divergent customs with regard to those of them that die. For some throw them into the river and send them off that way, believing this to be the best kind of burial. Others pile up glass round (*the dead person*) in their house and keep watch, believing that the faces of those who die must not fail to be acknowledged by their kinfolk, and that family relatives should not forget their close kin. Others again place (*the dead*) into ceramic urns and inter them in a circle around their sacred places, deeming that an oath taken over these (*remains*) is the most powerful. (4) Some of them hand their kingships to the best-looking men, thinking that both sole rule and beauty are gifts of Fortune; others present the position of ruler to the most meticulous herdsmen, and suppose that they alone will take the best care of their subjects; some distribute this honourable role to the richest men, thinking that only these men will be capable of helping the common folk because of their ready supply of resources; and there are others who choose as kings those who are outstanding in courage, judging that those most capable in war are the only ones worthy of receiving first prize.

10. In the territory lying beside the Nile in Libyē there is an area outstanding in excellence: for it produces plentiful, varied food and against the burning heat it offers easy assistance in the form of refuges in the marshes. As a result, this place is

intensely fought over by the Libyes and the Aithiopes, who persist in fighting wars about it with each other.   (2) Into it there regularly comes a mass of elephants from up-country, as certain people say, because of the plentiful and good-tasting pasture. This is because wonderful marshes extend along the edges of the river, and a great deal of varied food grows in them.   (3) Therefore, when they taste the rush and the reed, they remain there because of the sweet food and destroy the livelihood of the people, who are consequently forced to escape from these places and become tent-dwelling nomads; in sum, defining their homeland by what benefits them.   (4) The herds of wild animals mentioned earlier (*sometimes*) abandon the inland territory for lack of food, since the plants that grow suddenly in the ground all dry up, for because of the excessive heat and lack of water from springs or rivers, the food supply becomes tough and scarce.   (5) According to some, snakes of marvellous size and number breed in the so-called Wild Animal Land; they attack the elephants near the pools of water. Bravely resisting (*the elephant*), they cause their coils to be wrapped round their legs, and finally exert themselves continually in order to bind them tightly in those fetters, to the point where the animals, which by now have foamed (*at the mouth*), collapse under their own weight. Then they (*the snakes*) assemble and eat the flesh of the fallen creature, overpowering it easily because the animal has difficulty moving.   (6) There remains the mystery of why they do not accompany the elephants to the aforementioned land beside the river and thus pursue their usual food; they (*the Aithiopes*) say that snakes of this size shun the level ground in the territory and make their dens in ravines on the lower slopes that suit their length, and in caves with deep parts, which is why it is out of the question for them to leave their accustomed places that give them an advantage. For all animals' natures are self-taught. About the Aithiopes and their land, then, that is all we (*wish to*) say.

11. It is necessary for us to discriminate among the writers, in that many of them have written about Egypt and Aithiopia—some of them trusting in false rumour, others devising many things on their own initiative for the purpose of entertaining—and it would be right to disbelieve them.   (2) So Agatharchides of Knidos, in the 2nd book of *On Asia*, and the composer of geographies Artemidoros of Ephesos in the 8th book, and various others from among the inhabitants of Egypt, have researched the majority of the things we have already mentioned and are successful at nearly all points.

45   Stephanos of Byzantion ψ 2: *A district of Egypt*
Psebo: a territory in the interior of Egypt. . . . But Artemidoros, in (*the*) 8th (*book*) of *Geographoumena*, says it is a lake. The *ethnikon* is Pseboïtes, like Saboïtes.

46   Stephanos of Byzantion ψ 3: *A village in Egypt*
Psenako: a village in the Athribite nome, as Artemidoros (*says*) in (*the*) 8th (*book*) of *Geographoumena*.

47   Stephanos of Byzantion ψ 22: *A city in Egypt*
Psochemmis: a small city in Egypt. Artemidoros, in (*the*) 8th (*book*) of *Geographoumena*: 'And on the right-hand side are Perikermis, Thalabaude, and Psochemmis'. The *ethnikon* is Psochemmites, for the reason given in the (*entry on*) Psittachemmis.

BOOK 9[110]

48   Stephanos of Byzantion δ 150: *A city in Phoenicia*
Doros: a city in Phoinike. . . . Artemidoros also knows of the city of Dora, in *Epitome of the Eleven (books):* 'Immediately afterwards is Straton's Tower; next in (*Phoinike*) is Dora, a small city lying on a place resembling a peninsula, where Mt Karmelos begins'. And the same in (*the*) 9th (*book*) of *Geographoumena*.[111]

49   Stephanos of Byzantion τ 26: *Sri Lanka*
Taprobane (*Sri Lanka*): a very large island in the Indian sea . . . which in the old days was called Simoundou[112] but now Salike. The length of the voyage is [—], being seven times 1,000 stades, and its width is 500. Artemidoros, too, says the same things, 9th (*book*) of *Geographoumena*.

50   Stephanos of Byzantion υ 51: *A city in Parthia*
Hysia: a city in Boiotia. . . . There is another, the royal seat of the Parthyaioi (*Parthians*); Artemidoros, 9th (*book*) of *Geographoumena*.[113]

51   Stephanos of Byzantion ψ 7: *A coastal area of south-east Asia Minor*
Pseudokorasion: an extensive shore between Korykos ⟨and⟩ the territory of Seleukeia that lies beside the Isauroi. Artemidoros, 9th (*book*) of the *Geographoumena*: 'When one has passed this place, another shore follows, 3 stades long, crescent-shaped, (*with a*) minor anchorage (*hyphormos*), called Pseudokorasion'.

BOOK 10

52   Athenaios 8. 8, 333f–334a: *A spring in Lykia*
Artemidoros, in the 10th (*book*) of the *Geographoumena*, says it is claimed by the locals (*in Lykia, the subject of the preceding passage*) that a spring of fresh water arises (*here*), from which whirlpools (*dinai*) come into being, and that large fish occur in this revolving location. Those who sacrifice to these fish skewer the first-fruits of their sacrifices on wooden spits, namely boiled and baked meat, barley-cakes, and loaves. The harbour and this locality are named Dinos.

53   Stephanos of Byzantion ι 69: *A place in Rhodes*
Ixiai: in the plural, a settlement (*chōrion*) in Rhodos, (*named*) from the harbour of Ixos. Also Ixios Apollo, as Artemidoros (*says*), 10th (*book*) of *Geographoumena*.

---

[110] Agathem. v. 26 on Cyprus is also assigned to this book by Stiehle (as fr. 118).
[111] Book 9 has brought us into the Levant.
[112] For the variation Simoundou/Palaisimoundou, see n. to Mark. *Periplous*, 1. 1 (in Ch. 34 below).
[113] If the text is correct, this Boiotian place must have been mentioned out of sequence.

54   Stephanos of Byzantion κ 90: *A city in Phoenicia*
Karnē: a city in Phoinike. . . . But Artemidoros in the 10th book says, 'There is Karnos, following that Paltos, and next the city of Gabala'.[114]

55   Stephanos of Byzantion τ 79: *A cape in Lykia*
Telmissos: a city in Karia. . . . There is also a cape in Lykia called the following: Telmissias, as Artemidoros (*says*) in (*the*) 10th (*book*) of *Geographoumena*.

BOOK 11

56   Stephanos of Byzantion κ 167: *A place in northern Asia Minor*
Korokondame: near Sinope. Artemidoros, 11th (*book*) of *Geographoumena*.

57   Stephanos of Byzantion χ 18: *An island in the Thracian Bosporos*
Chalkitis (*Copper Island*): an island opposite Chalkedon, with a copper mine. Artemidoros, in (*the*) 11th (*book*) of *Geographoumena*, says, 'When one has sailed 110 stades beside the mainland from Akritas,[115] there lies a cape called Hyris, and the island of Pityodes (*Pine I.*) lies beside it, and another island called Chalkitis, and another named Prota (*First*). From this to the so-called city of Chalkitis is 40 stades.'[116]

EXTRACTS LACKING BOOK NUMBER

strabo

58   Strabo 3. 1. 4, C137–8: *Observations at C. Hieron in Iberia*
The cape (*C. Hieron*)[117] itself projects into the sea, and Artemidoros compares it to a ship—having been at the place, as he says—with three islets assisting in the resemblance, one having the form of a prow and others, which have reasonable minor anchorages (*metrioi hyphormoi*) like cat-heads.[118] Concerning Herakles, there is no sanctuary of his to be seen—Ephoros is wrong about this[119]—nor an altar, or none to any other of the gods. But in many places there are stones in groups of three or four, which, according to a hereditary custom, are rotated by those visiting, and then are moved back after libations are offered. It is not lawful to sacrifice there, or to set foot there at night, for they say that the gods possess it at that time; and those who come to visit spend the night in a nearby village and go there in the daytime, taking water because it is waterless.

---

[114] Stiehle emends the book number to 9. For Paltos, cf. **148**.
[115] Billerbeck's emendation for 'When one has sailed 110 st. from Akritas towards the east (Euros)'. See also n. on Menippos 7 in Ch. 21 below.
[116] Book 11 perhaps covered the Black Sea.   [117] Cape *St Vincent*, or possibly *Trafalgar*.
[118] *Epōtides*, in the nautical sense: 'beams projecting like ears on each side of a ship's bows, whence the anchors were let down', LSJ.
[119] *BNJ* 70 F 130.

59 **Strabo** 3. 1. 5, C138: *Sunset at C. Hieron in Iberia*

But Artemidoros says that the setting sun (*on the coast at Gadeira*) is a hundred times larger, and that night falls immediately. In examining his analysis, however, one must understand that he could not have seen this at the Hieron Promontory, for he says that no one may set foot there at night and thus no one sets foot there at sunset if night happens immediately. And there is no other place on the coast (*for this*), since Gadeira is also on the Ocean. Moreover Poseidonios and many others contradict him.[120]

60 **Strabo** 3. 2. 11, C148–9: *Western Iberia*

Eratosthenes says that the territory adjoining Kalpe is called Tartessis, and that Erytheia is the Fortunate Island. Artemidoros contradicts him and says that this is a falsehood by him, just as the distance from Gadeira to the Sacred Promontory is a five-day sail, although it is no more than 1,700 stades;[121] that the tides terminate at that point, although they exist around the circuit of the entire inhabited world; that the northerly part of Iberia is an easier means of access to Keltike than sailing by the Ocean, and everything else that he (*Eratosthenes*) said while relying on Pytheas, because of the latter's false pretensions.

61 **Strabo** 3. 4. 3, C157: *A temple in Baitike*

After this is Abdera (*Adra, Spain*), itself a Phoenician foundation.[122] Above these places in the mountainous country, Odysseia is pointed out, with a sanctuary of Athena in it, as Poseidonios has said, as well as Artemidoros and Asklepiades of Myrleia.[123]

62 **Strabo** 3. 4. 3, C157: *The Lotus-eaters*

And in regard to Libyē, some have believed—paying attention to the merchants among the Gadeiritai (*men of Cádiz*)—as Artemidoros says, that those living beyond Maurousia next to the western Aithiopes are called the Lotophagoi (*Lotus-eaters*), eating the lotus, a kind of herb and root, and they do not need to drink, or have anything, because of the aridity. They extend as far as the territory of Kyrene.

63 **Strabo** 3. 4. 7, C159: *Places in Iberia*

Between the branching of the Iber and the heights of Pyrene, on which the Dedications of Pompeius are set up, the first city is Tarrakōn, which has no harbour but is situated on a bay and is sufficiently equipped with everything, today no less populated than Karchedon (*Carthage*). It is naturally suited for the residence of the commanders and is the metropolis, so to speak, not only of the territory within the Iber but much of that beyond. The Gymnesian (*Balearic*) islands lie nearby, and Ebosos, all notable islands, which suggests that the position of the city is propitious. Eratosthenes says that it also has a naval station (*naustathmos*), but Artemidoros

---

[120] Even if Strabo is right, A. may have heard the story locally.
[121] In the Artemidoros Papyrus (**167**) the total distance is 1,884 st.
[122] Cf. **21**.   [123] *BNJ* 697 F 7.

contradicts him, saying that it is not even fortunate enough to have an anchorage (*ankyrobolia*).[124]

64   Strabo 3. 4. 17, C164: *Keltiberian women*[125]
One would consider the ornaments of some of the women ⟨*of the Keltiberians*⟩ to be barbaric in form, as Artemidoros reports. He says that they wear iron neckpieces that are curved like a beak over the top of the head, projecting far in front of their foreheads, and, if they wish, they draw their veil down over these beaks so that it spreads into a sunshade for their face, considering this an ornament. They also have a *tympanion* (*lit.* 'little drum') around them, going round the skull and binding the head as far as the ear lobe, but somewhat thrown back on the top and sides. Others strip away the hair on the front of their head so that it shines more than the forehead, and others place a small rod about a foot high on top, twist their hair round it, and then wrap it with a black covering.

65   Strabo 3. 5. 1, C167: *The Gymnesiai islands*
The larger of the Gymnesiai has two cities, Palma and Polentia, one of which, Polentia, is in the east and the other in the west. The length of the island is a little less than 600 stades and its width 200; but Artemidoros says that both the width and length are twice as great.

66   Strabo 3. 5. 5, C170: *The Pillars of Herakles*
Some assume that the Pillars are Kalpe and Abilyx, the mountain opposite in Libyē that Eratosthenes says is situated among the Metagonioi, a nomadic nation; and others that they are the islets near each (*mountain*), one of which is named Hera's Island. Artemidoros speaks of Hera's Island and her temple, and he mentions another, but neither Mount Abilyx nor the nation of the Metagonioi.

67   Strabo 3. 5. 7, C172: *A spring at Gadeira*
Polybios[126] says that there is a spring in the Herakleion at Gadeira that has a descent of only a few steps to drinkable water, and that it acts in reverse to the ebb and flow of the sea, ceasing at the time of the flood and filling at the ebb. The reason for this is that the air driven out of the depths of the Earth to the surface, if covered by a flood with the approach of the sea, is cut off from its proper outlets and goes back into the interior, blocking up the passages of the spring and creating a lack of water. When it is made bare again, the passages of the spring are set free, so that it gushes forth easily. Artemidoros speaks against him and gives his own reason, recalling the opinion of Silanos the historian,[127] but he does not seem to me to have said anything worth recording, since both he and Silanos are laymen in these matters.

---

[124] This passage concerns Tarraco, as Hoffmann 1838, 224 fr. 12, sees—not Ebusos, as in Stiehle 1856, 204–5.
[125] Discussed by Schiano 2010, 120–6, esp. 120.   [126] Polyb. 34. 9. 5–7.
[127] *BNJ* 175 F 9.

68 Strabo 4. 4. 6, C198: *Two Ravens harbour*

What Artemidoros said about ravens is more fabulous. He wrote that there is a certain harbour on the Ocean called Duo Korakes (*Two Ravens*), in which two ravens are seen, whose right wings are somewhat white. Those who have disputes about things come here, put a wooden plank at the place, and then separately throw barley cakes. The birds fly in and eat some and scatter others. The one whose barley cakes are scattered wins. What he says about this is rather fabulous, but that about Demeter and Kore is more believable, for he says that there is an island near Brettanike on which there are religious ceremonies concerning Demeter and Kore similar to those on Samothrake.

69 Strabo 5. 2. 6, C224: *Sardinia and Corsica*

Moreover, Eratosthenes is not correct when he says that neither Kyrnos nor Sardo can be seen from the mainland, nor is Artemidoros who says that both are in the open sea within 1,200 stades, for even if this were the case for some, they could not be seen by me at such (*a distance*), or were not seen clearly, especially Kyrnos.[128]

70 Strabo 5. 4. 6, C245: *The Lokrinos gulf in Campania*

Some say that this (*the Lokrinos gulf*) is Lake Acherousia, but Artemidoros that it is Aornos.

71 Strabo 6. 1. 11, C261–2: *The Tarantine gulf*

This (*the Iapygian cape*) is said to be the mouth of the Tarantinos (*Tarantine*) gulf. The sail round the gulf is remarkable: 240 miles, as the Chorographer[129] says, or 380 [—] Artemidoros, and lacking as much in the width of the gulf.

72 Strabo 6. 2. 1, C267: *Distances from Sicily*

Artemidoros, however, in saying that it is 4,600 from Pachynos to Tainaron and 1,130 from the Alpheios to the Pamisos, seems to me to provide a reason why his statement does not agree with the one who said that it was 4,000 to the Alpheios from Pachynos.[130]

73 Strabo 6. 3. 9–10, C283–5: *Apulia*

(9) From Barion (*Bari*) to the Aufidus river, on which is the trading-place (*emporion*) of the Kanysitai (*Canusians*), is 400 (*stades*), with the sail up to the emporium 90. Also nearby is Salapia (*Salpi*), the seaport of the Argyrippenoi. . . . It seems that Sipous (*Sipontum*) was founded by Diomedes, and it is about 140 stades distant from Salapia. It was named Sepious in Greek because of the cuttlefish (*sēpiai*) cast up by the waves. Between Salapia and Sipous is a navigable river and a large lagoon. Produce, especially grain, is brought down from Sipous on both. . . . Lying in front of this gulf is

---

[128] They might, however, be descried from clouds over them.

[129] Fr. 43 in Klotz 1930–1. Strabo occasionally cites this authority, who is not identified.

[130] Strabo is discussing the dimensions of Sicily and distances to and from it, including the voyage across open water to mainland Greece. Pachynos is the NE corner of Sicily; Tainaron the S point of the Peloponnese. The river Alpheios emerges in Eleia W of Olympia; the Pamisos is the principal river of Messenia.

a promontory, Garganon (*Gargano*), that extends 300 stades towards the coast into the open sea. When one goes round the cape there is the small town of Ourion and off the cape are the Diomedeian islands (*Tremiti*). . . . (10) These distances are laid down as according to Artemidoros. The Chorographer[131] says that from Brentesion (*Brindisi*) as far as Garganon is 165 miles, but Artemidoros gives a greater distance. The former says that it is 254 miles from there, but Artemidoros has 1,250 stades to the Aisis near Ankon (*Ancona*), which is much less.

74 Strabo 7 fr. 22a: *Long distances in SE Europe*
From Perinthos[132] to Byzan⟨tion⟩ is 630 (*stades*), and from the Hebros and Kypsela[133] to Byzantion, as far as the Kyaneai,[134] is 3,100, as Artemidoros says. ⟨The⟩ entire length from the Ionian gulf (*southern Adriatic*) at Apollonia, as far as Byzantion, is 7,320. Polybios[135] adds 180 more, since he adds one-third of a stade to the 8 stades to a mile.

75 Strabo 8. 2. 1, C335: *Circuit of the Peloponnese*
The perimeter (*of the Peloponnese*), not following the gulfs, is 4,000 stades, according to Polybios.[136] Artemidoros adds 400. Following the gulfs it is more than 5,600.

76 Strabo 8. 6. 1, C367: *Coastal cities of eastern Laconia*
And the fortress of Minoa (*Monemvasia*), which has the same name as the one in the Megaris; and Limera Epidauros, as Artemidoros says.

77 Strabo 8. 8. 5, C389: *Cape Maleai*
Polybios says that from Maleai[137] north to the Istros (*Danube*) is about 10,000 stades, but Artemidoros not unreasonably corrects it, saying that it is a journey of 1,⟨4⟩00 to Aigion from Maleai, and from there to ⟨Kirrha⟩[138] a voyage of 200, and from there through Herakleia[139] [—] a journey of 500, then to Larisa [—] 340, then through the outlets of the Peneios 240 [—], to Thessalonikeia 660, then through ⟨Eidom⟩ene, Stoboi,[140] and the Dardanioi 3,000 (?).[141] [—] Yet according to him (*Artemidoros*) it is 6,500 from Thessalonikeia. The reason is that it was not measured by the short route, but a random one that was taken by a certain commander.

---

[131] Fr. 44 in Klotz 1930–1.

[132] Perinthos is on the N shore of the Propontis. Strabo is discussing long distances in Italy and the Balkans, incl. what appears to be the length of the Via Egnatia (Roller 2018, 420). His observation about Polybios' long mile of 8⅓ st. (= Polyb. 34. 12. 9–10) implies that A. used 8 st. to the mile.

[133] The lower Hebros forms the land frontier between mod. Greece and Turkey, W of the *Gallipoli* peninsula in Thrace. Kypsela (*İpsala*) is a town some 20 mi (32 km) inland on the left (E) bank.

[134] The Dark Blue or Clashing Rocks at the entrance to the Black Sea.　　　[135] Polyb. 34. 12. 9–10.

[136] Polyb. 34. 12. 11.　　　[137] Also called Malea. This extract = Polyb. 34. 12. 12.

[138] If this name is correct, it is the port (also Krisa) below Delphi on the N side of the gulf of Corinth; a regular crossing-point for a journey from the Peloponnese to central Greece.

[139] Perhaps Herakleia in Trachis, in Malis on the E seaboard of central Greece.

[140] Eidomene is inland, up the r. Axios (*Vardar*) from *Thessaloníki*, with Stoboi further upstream.

[141] The extract = Polyb. 34. 12. 12. The text of Strabo here is imperfect and the numbers uncertain (Roller 2014, 384 n. 22).

78   Strabo 9. 5. 8, C433: *Coastal cities of east-central Greece*
Thus Sophokles[142] calls Trachis Phthiotic. Artemidoros places Halos on the coast, situated outside the Maliac gulf, but as Phthiotic. He goes from there towards the Peneios, and places Pteleon after Antron, and then Halos, 110 stades distant from Pteleon.

79   Strabo 9. 5. 15, C436: *The gulf of Pagasai*
Artemidoros places the Pagasitic gulf further away from Demetrias and among the places subject to Philoktetes. He says that the island of Kikynethos and a small town with the same name are in the gulf.

80   Strabo 10. 2. 21, C459–60: *Aitolian Chalkis*
After the (*river*) Euenos is Mount Chalkis, which Artemidoros calls Chalkia, then Pleuron, and then the village of Halikyrna, with Kalydon lying 30 stades above it in the interior. . . . This is what Artemidoros says about the mountain, whether it is Chalkis or Chalkia, placing it between the Acheloös and Pleuron; but Apollodoros (*of Athens*),[143] as I have previously said,[144] has Chalkis and Taphiassos above Molykreia, and says that Kalydon is located between Pleuron and Chalkis. Perhaps one should assume that there are two, one near Pleuron called Chalkia and the other near Molykreia called Chalkis.

81   Strabo 10. 3. 5, C465: *Progressive corrections in geography*
Such is Ephoros, but he is better than many others. Polybios praises him enthusiastically and says that Eudoxos (*of Knidos*)[145] did well in regard to Hellenic matters, but Ephoros was the best at examining foundations, kinship, migrations, and founders; and he (*Polybios*) also says that 'we will show things as they are, concerning both the position of places and the distances between them, for this is most suitable for chorography'.[146] But, Polybios, you introduce popular assertions about distances—not only those outside Hellas but also Hellenic ones[147]—and must submit to examination by Poseidonios, Artemidoros, and a number of others.

82   Strabo 10. 4. 3, C474–5: *Circuit of Crete*
Sosikrates[148] . . . determined its (*Crete's*) length at more than 2,300 stades and its width [—] so that its (*Crete's*) circuit would be more than 5,000 stades. Artemidoros says that it is 4,100. Hieronymos[149] says that the length is 2,000, and the width irregular, and thus would say that the circuit is larger than that of Artemidoros.

83   Strabo 10. 5. 3, C485: *The Cyclades*
Originally they (*the Cyclades*) were said to have been twelve, but more were added. At any rate, Artemidoros enumerates them, saying about Helene (*Makrónisos*) that it is long, extending from Thorikos to Sounion, about 60 stades in length. He says that the so-called Cyclades begin from here. He names Keos, which is nearest to Helene, and

---

[142] Fr. 1110 in Radt 1999.   [143] *BNJ* 244 F 203.   [144] At 10. 2. 4.
[145] Fr. 328 in Lasserre 1966 (not in Chapter 6 above).   [146] Polyb. 34. 1. 3–6.
[147] i.e. within Greece.   [148] *BNJ* 461 F 5.   [149] *FGrH* 154 F 18.

after it Kythnos, Seriphos, Melos, Siphnos, Kimolos, Prepesinthos, and Oliaros; and in addition Paros, Naxos, Syros, Mykonos, Tenos, Andros, and Gyaros. I consider all these to be among the twelve except for Prepesinthos, Oliaros, and Gyaros.[150]

84   Strabo 11. 2. 14, C496–7: *A harbour in the Black Sea*
The voyage from Korokondame is straight towards the east, and the Sindian harbour and city is in 180 stades. Then, in 400 (*stades*) is what is called Bata, a village and harbour. It is believed that Sinope lies almost opposite the coast towards the south, just as Karambis is said (*to be opposite to*) Kriou Metopon (*Ram's Brow; C. Sarych*). After Bata, Artemidoros speaks about the coast of the Kerketai, which has minor anchorages (*hyphormoi*) and villages for about 850 stades. Then there is that of the Achaioi, for 500 stades, then that of the Heniochoi, for 1,000 stades, and the Great Pityous [—] 360 [stades] as far as Dioskourias. The historians of Mithridatic affairs—those with whom one must agree the most—first mention the Achaioi, then the Zygoi, then the Heniochoi, then the Kerketai, Moschoi, Kolchoi, the Phtheirophagoi (*Louse-eaters*) who are above them, the Soanës, and other lesser peoples around the Caucasus.[151]

85   Strabo 12. 7. 2, C570: *Cities in Pisidia*
Artemidoros says that the Pisidian cities are Selge, Sagalassos, Petnelissos, Adada, Timbriada, Kremna, Tityassos, Amblada, Anaboura, Sinda, Aarassos, Tarbassos, and Termessos. Some of these are completely in the mountains and others reach as far as the foothills on either side, to Pamphylia and Milyas, bordering on the Phrygians, Lydians, and Karians, all peaceful people although towards the north.

86   Strabo 12. 8. 1, C571: *Mysia*
Mysia is in a similar situation (*to Phrygia*), with the Olympene[152]—continuous with Bithynia and Epiktetos, and which Artemidoros says was settled by Mysians from across the Istros—as well as that around the Kaikos and Pergamene[153] as far as Teuthrania and the outlets of the river.

87   Strabo 13. 3. 5, C622: *Coast of Aiolis*
According to Artemidoros, one goes from Kyme to Adai, and then, after 40 stades there is the cape called Hydra, which, along with the opposite cape, Harmatous, forms the Elaitic gulf.

88   Strabo 14. 1. 22–3, C640–1: *The temple of Artemis at Ephesos*
Chersiphron was the first architect of the temple of Artemis, and then someone else enlarged it. When a certain Herostratos set it on fire, they built another and better one, having collected the ornaments of women and their own property, and disposing of the earlier columns. The proof of what happened is in the decrees from that time.

---

[150] Evidently not Helene either, which would make thirteen. Ps.-Skyl. §58. 1 includes Helene among the Cyclades.
[151] Many of these places are named in Arrian's *Periplous* (Ch. 27) and *Eux.* (Ch. 36).
[152] The area around Mt Olympos in Mysia.   [153] The territory of Pergamon.

Artemidoros says that because Timaios of Tauromenion[154] was ignorant of them—and was envious and argumentative, because of which he was called Epitimaios (*Fault Finder*)—he says that they provided for the restoration of the sanctuary from Persian funds deposited there. But there was nothing deposited at that time, and even if there had been, they would have been burned along with the temple. After the fire, who would have wished to have things deposited there, when the roof had been destroyed and the sacred precinct was open to the air? Alexander suggested that he would pay the Ephesians for both past and future expenses, if he were credited on the inscription, but they were unwilling, and they would have been far more unwilling to acquire a reputation for sacrilege and robbery. He (*Artemidoros*) praises the Ephesian who said to the king that it was not proper for a god to construct a dedication to gods.

(23) After the completion of the temple, which he says was the work of Cheirokrates, the same man who built Alexandria and who suggested to Alexander that he put his likeness on Athos—pouring an offering from a vessel into a bowl—and make two cities, one on the right of the mountain and the other on the left, with a river flowing from one to the other: after the temple (*was completed*) the large number of dedications were obtained by the honour given the artists, but almost the entire altar was filled with the works of Praxiteles.

89 Strabo 14. 1. 26, C642: *Artemidoros' diplomatic mission*
After the outlet of the Kaÿstros is a lake that overflows from the sea—called Selinousia—and next there is another that flows together with it, both providing a large income. Although these were sacred, the kings took them away from the goddess, but the Romans gave them back. Again the tax collectors forcibly appropriated the duties for themselves, and Artemidoros was sent on an embassy, as he himself says, and received the lakes back for the goddess and also won at Rome a judgement against the Herakleotis,[155] which was in revolt. In return the city (*of Ephesos*) erected a golden image of him in the sanctuary.[156] In the deepest recess of the lake is the sanctuary of the King, which they say was established by Agamemnon.

90 Strabo 14. 2. 10, C655: *Circuit of Rhodes*
The island (*of Rhodes*) has a circuit of 920 stades.[157]

91 Strabo 14. 2. 29, C663: *The Rhodian peraia; the route through Karia*
Artemidoros says that going from Physkos on the Rhodian shore to Ephesos it is 850 stades as far as Lagina, and then another 250 to Alabanda, and 160 to Tralleis. But the road to Tralleis is at the crossing of the Maiandros (*Meander*), about the middle of the route, at the boundaries of Karia. In its entirety, from Physkos to the Maiandros along the Ephesos road, it is 1,180. Again, from the Maiandros next going the length of Ionia

---

[154] *BNJ* 566 F 150b.   [155] The territory of Herakleia.
[156] Cf. **1** for information about Ephesos which is thought to derive from A.
[157] Although Artemidoros is not named, Stiehle includes this as a fr. because the distance matches that in Agathem. i. 5.

on the same road, it is 80 from the river to Tralleis, and then 140 to Magnesia, 120 to Ephesos, 320 to Smyrna, and less than 200 to Phokaia and the boundaries of Ionia. Thus the straight length of Ionia would be, according to him, slightly more than 800.

There is a sort of common road used by everyone travelling from Ephesos towards the east, and he goes along it. To Karoura, the frontier of Karia towards Phrygia, through Magnesia, Tralleis, Nysa, and Antiocheia, is a route of 740 stades. The Phrygian part is through Laodikeia, Apameia, Metropolis, and Chelidonia. At the beginning of the Paroreios is Holmoi, about 920 stades from Karoura, and at the end of the Paroreios near Lykaonia, through Philomelion, is Tyriaion, which is slightly more than 500. Then there is Lykaonia, as far as Koropassos, through Laodikeia Katakekaumene (*the Burnt*), in 840. From Koropissos in Lykaonia to Garsaoura, a small town in Kappadokia situated on its border, is 120. Then to Mazaka (*Kayseri*), the metropolis of the Kappadokians, through Soandos and Sadakora, is 680, and from there to the Euphrates as far as Tomisa, a place in Sophene, through Erpha, a small town, is 1,440. The places lying in a straight line as far as Indike are the same in Artemidoros as in Eratosthenes.

92   **Strabo** 14. 3. 3, C665: *Cities in Lykia*
Artemidoros says that the six largest (*cities*) were Xanthos, Patara, Pinara, Olympos, Myra, and Tlos, located near the pass to Kibyra.

93   **Strabo** 14. 5. 3, C670: *Places in Kilikia*
Nagidos is the first city after Anemourion. Then there is Arsinoë, which has a by-anchorage (*prosormos*),[158] and then the locality (*topos*) of Melania, and Kelenderis, a city having a harbour. Some put this, not Korakesion, as the beginning of Kilikia, among whom is Artemidoros. He says that from the Pelousiac mouth it is 3,650 stades to Orthosia, 1,130 to the Orontes river, to the Gates that follow 520, and to the Kilikian borders 1,900.

94   **Strabo** 14. 5. 16, C675: *Rivers in Kilikia*
After the Kydnos is the Pyramos, which flows from Kataonia and which I have mentioned previously.[159] Artemidoros says that from there to Soloi is a straight voyage of 500 stades.

95   **Strabo** 14. 5. 22, C677: *The 'isthmus' of Asia Minor*
The same ignorance (*about the shape of Asia Minor*) remains even if one were to reduce the distance of the isthmus to the least possible—one-half of the total, or 1,500 stades— as those who are the most deceived say, as well as Artemidoros; but this does not bring it together enough to create a triangular form.[160]

---

[158] This rare term is used by Strabo only with reference to a cove on Samos (14. 1. 19, C639) and then for a few places in Lykia and further E (14. 3. 8, etc.). It is not clear that it always denotes a small refuge, but I have chosen to distinguish it with a special term.
   [159] At 12. 2. 4.   [160] On the 'isthmus' of Asia Minor, cf. Ps.-Skyl. §102. 2 & n.

96 Strabo 15. 1. 72, C719: *The river Ganges*

Artemidoros says that the Ganges river flows down from the Emoda mountains to-wards the south, and when it comes to the city of Gange it turns towards the east as far as Palibothra and the outlet to the sea. He calls one of its tributaries the Oidanes. It produces crocodiles and dolphins. He says certain other things but they are confused and unpolished and should not be considered.

97 Strabo 16. 2. 33, C760: *Distances around Phoenicia*

Such is Phoinike (*Phoenicia*). Artemidoros says that it is 3,650 stades to Pelousion from Orthosia, going through the gulfs, and from Melainai or Melaniai in Kilikia, near Kelenderis, to the common boundary of Kilikia and Syria, it is 1,900. From there to the Orontes is 520, and then it is 1,130 to Orthosia.

98 Strabo 16. 4. 5–20, C769–79:[161] *East Africa*

Trogodytike

(5) ·$_{II.2}$Artemidoros states that the promontory of Arabia lying opposite Deire is called Akila, and that the men in the area of Deire have the end of their penis docked. As you sail from Heroönpolis along Trogodytike, there is a city named Philotera after the sister of the second Ptolemy; it is a foundation by Satyros, the man sent to inquire after elephant hunting and explore Trogodytike. $_{82c}$Then there is another city, Arsinoë; and then an outflow of hot waters which are bitter and salty, which issue into the sea by a particular high rock. $_{83c}$Nearby is a mountain the colour of red ochre, in a plain. Then there is Myos Hormos (*Mussel Anchorage*), which is also called Aphrodites Hormos (*Aphrodite's Anchorage*), a great harbour with its entrance crooked. Three islands lie before it: two shaded by olive-trees and one less shady and full of Meleagrides (*guinea-fowl*). $_{84c}$Next in order is the Akathartos (*Uncleansed*) gulf, which itself lies beside the Thebaid, like Myos Hormos, and is genuinely 'uncleansed', for it has been made rough by underwater hogsbacks and reefs, and by winds that are mostly stormy winds. Here, he says, the city of Berenike has been founded, at the inner end of the gulf.[162]

(6) After the gulf is the island called Ophiodes (*Snake Island*), from the circum-stance that it is so; the king liberated it from the serpents both because the people an-choring their ships here were being killed by the creatures, and because of the topazes: this is a transparent stone that glitters with a light like gold, although by day it is not

---

[161] This passage of Strabo can be deemed a fragment of Artemidoros, whom Strabo consulted directly (cf. first n. on **44** (*b*) above). It evidently contains, however, much material drawn by Art. from Agath-archides (see Ch. 15 no. 4), though we cannot usually tell which this is and what is added by Art. He rearranged the sequence to suit his expository aims, as may be seen from Burstein's section numbers from his earlier edition of Ag. (Burstein 1989), which I print in subscript type (e.g. $_{II.2}$ or $_{82c}$) and which are often out of sequence here. (Where such a passage is not immediately followed by another, its end is indicated by $_{J}$.) See also the map to Ch. 15, which includes places named in this passage.

[162] Founded by Ptolemy II, at the innermost point of Foul Bay, *c.*260 km E of Aswan, Berenike was the principal Red Sea port from C3 BC to its abandonment in C6e AD (cf. Cohen 2006, 320–5; Sidebotham 2011).

easy to see, for it is outshone, but collectors can see it at night. They enclose it with a pot as sign, and with the coming of day they dig it up. There used to be an association of people charged with guarding this deposit of stone and its collection, who were provisioned by the kings of Egypt.⌐

(7) ₈₅꜀After this island, there are many races of Ichthyophagoi (*Fish-eaters*) and Nomads. Next is Soteiras Limen (*Saviour-goddess's Harbour*), which was named from the circumstance that certain commanders were saved from great perils here. After these places there is a pronounced alteration in the coast and the gulf: for it happens that the coastal sailing is not rough any more, and in a certain manner approaches Arabia. The open sea (*pelagos*) is shallow to the depth of about two fathoms; its surface is grass-grown, with wrack and seaweed showing through it, which increases near the strait, where even trees grow in the water alongside them. The strait also has a multitude of sea-dogs. ₁₁.₃ Next are the Tauroi (*Bulls*): two mountains which, from afar, present an appearance somewhat like animals. Then there is another mountain which has a sanctuary of Isis, founded by Sesostris. Next is an island well planted with olives but washed over by the sea. After this is Ptolemaïs, beside the area for elephant hunting, a foundation of Eumedes who was sent by Philadelphos for the hunting. He covertly built a ditch and circuit wall round the peninsula, but then cultivated the men who would have impeded him and made them into friends instead of enemies.⌐

(8) Between these places, there discharges a tributary of the river called Astaboras, which has its source in a lake; it discharges partially, but most of it enters the Nile. Next are six islands called the Latomiai (*Quarry Islands*); and after these the so-called Sabaitic mouth, with a fort in the interior, a foundation by Tosouchos. Next a harbour called Elaia, and Straton's Island. Next the harbour of Saba, and an elephant-hunting station which has the same name. The territory inland from these places is called Tenessis. The Egyptians exiled by Psammetichos (*II*) hold it, who are surnamed Sembritai as if they are incomers. They are ruled by a woman, under whose authority also lies Meroë, which is an island in the Nile close to these places.[163] Above this is another island, not far away, in the river; it is a settlement of those same exiles. From Meroë to our sea, for a lightly laden man, is a journey of fifteen days. ₅₁꜀Around Meroë there is also the confluence of the Astaboras with the Astapos, and that of the Astasobas with the Nile.

(9) Beside these places are the Rhizophagoi (*Root-eaters*) and Heleioi (*Marsh-folk*), named from the fact that they cut roots from the adjoining marsh using stones, shape them into cakes, heat them in the sun, and consume them. These districts support lions; but in the days around the rising of the Dog (*Sirius*) the animals are driven away from these places by great mosquitoes. ₅₂꜀There are also Spermophagoi (*Seed-eaters*) near here, who when the seeds are used up live off tree-nuts, which they prepare in a similar way to how the Rhizophagoi prepare their roots.⌐ After Elaia are Demetrios's

---

[163] This sentence (omitted by Burstein 1989, 137) presumably reflects the situation in Strabo's day.

Lookouts and Konon's Altars. ₅₃c Inland from here grow masses of Indian reeds, and the area is called Korakios' Land. In the interior there used to be a settlement, Endera, of light-armed fighters using reed-bows and fire-hardened arrows;[164] they shoot animals mainly from trees, though sometimes from the ground. Among them is a multitude of wild cattle, and they live by eating the meat of these and the other beasts; but when they can catch nothing they bake dry hides on charcoal and are content with that as food. They have a custom of setting up an archery contest for the adolescent boys.⌡ After Konon's Altars is the harbour of Melinos, and above it is the so-called Koraos's Fort, with the hunting-station of Koraos, and another fort, and several hunting-stations. Next is Antiphilos's Harbour and the Kreophagoi (*Meat-eaters*) who live beyond it, who have the end of their penis docked; their women are also cut in the Ioudaic (*Jewish*) way.

(10) ₆₁c Further beyond these towards the south are the Kynamolgoi (*Dog-milkers*), also called Agrioi (*Wild Men*) by the locals. These are long-haired and long-bearded; they breed quite large dogs, with which they hunt the Indian cattle that come here from the nearby territory, either driven by wild animals or by lack of pasture; their arrival is from the summer solstice to the middle of winter.⌡ Subsequent to Antiphilos's Harbour is the so-called harbour called Kolobon Alsos (*Grove of the Mutilated*); and the city of Berenike, the one by Sabai; and Sabai itself, quite a large city. Next is Eumenes's Grove, above which lies the city of Darada and the elephant-hunting station known as *Pros tōi Phreati* (*By-the-Well*). ₅₄c The Elephantophagoi (*Elephant-eaters*) live here, who practise their hunting as follows. When from the trees they first spy a herd moving through the wood, they do not attack it, but instead they secretly approach from the rear the ones that wander off from the herd, and hamstring them. ₅₅b Some, however, also kill them using missiles dipped in snake bile; this form of archery is carried out by three men: two of them advance on foot holding a bow, while the other draws the bowstring. ₅₆c Still others note the trees against which the animals are accustomed to rest, approach from the other direction, and partially cut through the trunk; so when the animal approaches and leans against it, the tree falls and so does the animal, and it cannot get up because its legs have each an unjointed bone which will not bend; so the men leap down from the trees and cut it to pieces. ₅₈c The Nomads call the hunters the Akathartoi (*Uncleansed*).

(11) Beyond these places is the not very large nation of the Strouthophagoi (*Ostrich-eaters*), among whom there are birds the size of deer which cannot fly but can run fast, like 'ostrich-camels' do. They hunt these birds. Some use bows. Others, concealed in skins of the birds, hide their right hand in the neck portion, which they move in the same way the creatures move their neck; with their left hand they scatter seed from a pouch fastened beside them, and use this to entice the creatures, forcing them into gullies where club-wielders are standing by, who beat them to death. These folk dress

---

[164] For these, cf. Ps.-Skyl. §112. 10.

in the skins of the birds, and lay them out as bedclothes. The so-called Simoi (*Snub-nosed*) Ethiopians make war on these folk using gazelle's horns as weapons.

(12) _{59c} Living next to these places are a people who are blacker than the others, shorter, and very short-lived, the Akridophagoi (*Locust-eaters*); for they rarely surpass forty years as their flesh becomes filled with wild creatures. They live off locusts, which the springtime Libes (*SW winds*) and Zephyroi (*westerlies*), blowing strongly, drive together into these places. They throw wood that will smoke into ravines and make it smoulder . . . for (*the locusts*), flying over the smoke, cannot see and fall down. Chopping them up with salt, they make cakes and consume them. _{60c} Beyond these places lies a great empty zone which contains plenty of pastures but has been abandoned because of the multitude of scorpions and the poisonous spiders called *tetragnathoi* (*four-jaws*); at one time these gained the upper hand and brought about a total evacuation by the people.」

(13) After Eumenes's Harbour,[165] as far as Deire and the narrows by the six islands, the Ichthyophagoi (*Fish-eaters*) and Kreophagoi (*Meat-eaters*) live, as do the Koloboi (*Mutilated*), as far as the interior. There are several places to hunt elephants here, some unimportant cities, and islets off the coast. Most people are nomads; farmers are few. Among some of them grows the styrax (*gum-tree*) in no small amount. _{32c} The Ichthyophagoi collect the fish on the ebb tide; _{34c} they cast them onto the rocks and bake them in the sun, and then, having baked them hard, they pile up the spiny parts but tread the flesh and make it into cakes; these they leave in the sun once more, then eat them. _{35c}During a storm, if they are unable to collect the fish, they chop up the heaped-up spines, make them into cakes, and eat those; they also suck on the new bones. Some of them keep shellfish whose flesh they fatten by putting them into little streams and sea-pools and throwing in small fish as food; then, when they are short of fish, they eat the shellfish. They also have many kinds of fish-farms, whose produce they distribute. _{37c} Some of those living on the waterless coast area go up with all their families to the watering-places every five days, with chanting of paeans, _{38c} cast themselves face down, and drink like oxen till their stomach is like a drum, and then go back to the sea again. _{43c} They live in caves, or in huts covered with beams and joists made of the bones of sea-monsters and the spines (*of fish*), completed with olive foliage.

(14) _{47c} The Chelonophagoi (*Turtle-eaters*) use the shells of those animals as roofs, since they are large enough to be sailed in.[166] _{44c} Since a lot of seaweed is thrown up and makes high and lofty heaps, some of these people excavate these and live beneath them. _{45c} They throw their dead to the fish as food, and they are taken by the tides.」 Next in succession lie three of the islands, known as Chelonon Nesos (*Isle of Turtles*), Phokon Nesos (*Isle of Seals*), and Hierakon Nesos (*Isle of Hawks*). All this coast has palm-trees, olive-trees, and laurels; not only the part within the straits but also much of the exterior portion. There is also a certain island called Philip's Island, opposite

---

[165] Strabo has not mentioned this place, but it may be at the same location as Eumenes's Grove in §10.
[166] On this passage, see Burstein 1989, 85 n. 1.

which lies the place called Pythangelos's Elephant-hunting Station. Next is the city and harbour of Arsinoë, and after these places is Deire. Beyond these lies elephant-hunting territory. The land next beyond Deire is scent-bearing: the first part is the one that produces myrrh, and this belongs to the Ichthyophagoi and Kreophagoi; it also grows the persea-tree and the Egyptian mulberry. Beyond it lies the elephant-hunting territory of Lichas. In many places there are pools of rainwater; when they dry up, the elephants use their trunks and tusks to dig wells and discover water. Upon this coast, as far as the promontory of Pytholaos, there are two fairly large lakes: one of salt water, which they call Thalassa (*The Sea*); one of fresh, which supports hippopotamuses and crocodiles, as well as papyrus around its edge. Ibises are also seen round about this place. At this point the people near the cape (*sic*) of Pytholaos are whole in body.

After these people is the Frankincense-bearing Land;[167] here is a cape and a sanctuary possessing a poplar grove. In the interior is a certain district called Potamia Isidos (*River-land of Isis*), and another called Neilos (*Nile*); both have myrrh and frankincense growing alongside them. There is also a particular cistern filled with the waters from the mountains; and after these places are Leontos Skopē (*Lion's Lookout*) and Pythangelos's Harbour. The next area grows pseudo-cassia. Then in succession are several river-lands with frankincense growing alongside them, and some rivers as far as the Kinnamomophoros (*sc. Chora; Cinnamon-bearing Land*). The river that defines this land also bears a great amount of rush reed.[168] Next is another river, and Daphnous harbour, and the so-called Potamia Apollonos (*River-land of Apollo*), which in addition to frankincense grows myrrh and cinnamon; the last is more plentiful round about the places inland. Next is Elephas (*Elephant*), the mountain, extending out to sea; then a channel; and successively Psygmou Limen (*Drying-place Harbour*) a large one, and the so-called Hydreuma Kynokephalon (*Watering-place of the Kynokephaloi, Dog's-heads*); and the last promontory of this coast, Notou Keras (*Horn of the South*).[169] As one rounds this in a southward direction, he (*Artemidoros?*) says, we possess descriptions neither of any harbour nor of places beyond it, because there is no further knowledge of the area.

Animals of East Africa

(15) On the next stretch of coast there are columns and altars of Pytholaos, Lichas, Pythangelos, Leon, and Charimortos, beside the well-known coast from Deire to Notou Kerōs (*Horn of the South*); but the distance is not known. [70b] The land teems with elephants and those lions called 'ants'; these possess genitals turned the wrong way and have a colour like gold; they are smoother than those in Arabia. [72c] The land also produces fierce leopards and rhinoceroses; the latter are not, as Artemidoros carelessly

---

[167] Some of this section probably reflects the addition of material by A. to what he found in Agatharchides.

[168] *phlous*, 'flowering rush', Loeb; but LSJ is inconclusive; 'bark' in Montanari 2015.

[169] *keras* here meaning an extremity of a land, not an inlet of the sea (see Glossary); identified with *Ras el-Kheil*, Bucciantini 2012, in the region now called the Horn of Africa.

says, slightly smaller than elephants, even though he says he saw one in Alexandria, but roughly similar in height, on the basis of the one seen by me.⌐ Nor is their colour comparable to boxwood, but rather to the elephant; and they are the size of a bull. Their form is very close to that of a wild boar, especially in the face except for the nose, which is an upturned horn harder than any bone; it uses it as a weapon as a wild boar does its tusks. It also has two calluses, like the coils of snakes, running round it from spine to stomach; one is towards the back of the neck, the other towards the loins. I state these things on the basis of the one seen by me; but he (*Artemidoros*) additionally clarifies that the creature is particularly an enemy of the elephant over grazing: it ducks underneath it with its face and slices open the stomach, unless it is seized first by the trunk and tusks.

(16) ₇₃ᵦ In these parts there also occur camelopardalises (*giraffes*), but they have no similarity to a leopard. For the variegated nature of their skin is more like fawn-skins marked with striped stains. Furthermore, their rear parts are lower than their fore-parts, so that they seem to be sitting on their tail-end, which has the height of an ox, while the front legs are as long as those of camels. The neck is raised straight up to a height, carrying a head very much more elevated than a camel's. Because of this asymmetry, I do not think the creature can have so great a speed as Artemidoros says, who states that it is unsurpassed. But neither is it a wild animal, rather it is domesticated; for it displays no wildness. ₇₄c There also occur, he says, sphinxes, *kynokephaloi* (*dog's-heads*), and *kēboi* (*lion-monkeys*) possessing the face of a lion while the rest of their body is that of a panther; they are as big as a gazelle. ₇₇c There are also wild flesh-eating bulls, in size and weight greatly exceeding those among us, and with flame-coloured skin. ₇₈c The *krokouttas* is a mix of wolf and dog, he states;⌐ but what the Skepsian, Metrodoros, says in his book *On Custom* is in the nature of a myth, and not to be heeded as far as these creatures are concerned. ₈₀c Artemidoros has also stated that there are snakes with a length of 30 cubits which overcome elephants and bulls;⌐ in this respect he is cautious, for the Indian ones are more mythical, as are the Libyan ones upon which grass is said to grow.

Trogodyte nomads

(17) ₆₂c The life of the Trogodytai is nomadic. Each community is ruled by a tyrant, and they share their wives and children, except for the tyrants: for him who corrupts the tyrant's wife, the penalty is one sheep. They carefully apply black paint round their eyes as women do,[170] and round their neck are shells against magic charms. They fight wars about pasture, initially shoving with their hands, then using stones, and when an injury occurs they also use arrows and knives; but the women resolve the conflict by going forward between them and presenting them with their pleas. Their diet is meat and bones chopped up, mixed together, wrapped in skins, and then baked. It can also be prepared in many other ways by the cooks, whom they call 'the uncleansed'. So they

---

[170] Retaining Radt's ⟨ὡς⟩.

are not only flesh-eaters but bone-eaters and skin-eaters too; and they even mix blood and milk together and consume them. For the majority their drink is an extract of the Christ-thorn (*paliouros*), but for the tyrants it is milk and honey, the honey being expressed from a certain flower. Winter, for them, is when the Etesian winds blow—for they do experience rain—but it is summer the rest of the year. They are lightly armed, wear skins, and carry clubs. Not only are they docked (*koloboi*), but some are also circumcised in the manner of Egyptians. The Aithiopes who are the Megabaroi also fix iron knobs on their clubs, and use lances and shields of untanned ox-skin; the other Aithiopes (*use*) bows and spears. ₆₄꜀ Some of the Trogodytai bury the dead by binding the necks of the corpses to their legs with withies of Christ-thorn; then they joyfully pelt them with stones, laughing all the while, until they have hidden away the sight of the body. Then they put a goat-horn[171] on it and depart. For they travel by night after hanging bells upon the male cattle, in order to deter wild animals with the noise. They also employ torches and bows against the wild animals, and stay awake through the night for the sake of their flocks, singing a particular song at the fireside.

The Arabes

(18) ₈₇ᵦ Having said all these things about the Trogodytai and the adjoining Ethiopians, he (*Artemidoros*) returns to the Arabians. The first ones he discusses are those at the edge of the Arabian gulf, lying opposite the Trogodytai. He begins from Poseidion, and says that it lies further in than the mouth of the Ailanitic gulf; and that next to Poseidion is a well-watered palm grove which is highly esteemed because all the land round about is burning hot, waterless, and without shade. Here the productivity of the date-palms is wonderful. In charge of the grove are a man and a woman, designated by descent. They wear skins and feed upon the dates; they also make tree-houses and sleep there because of the multitude of wild animals. ₈₉꜀ Next in succession is Seals' Island, so named from the multitude of these creatures. Near it is a promontory which extends to the Petra of the so-called Nabataean Arabs and the land of Palaistine, into which the Minaioi, Gerrhaioi, and all the peoples living nearby bring consignments of spices. ₉₀ᵦ Next is another coast, formerly called that of the Maranitai, some of whom were farmers, others tent-dwellers; but now it is called that of the Garindaioi. The latter killed the former by trickery: for they attacked them as they celebrated a certain quadrennial festival. They destroyed the worshippers and, pursuing the others, treated them horribly.

Next is the Ailanites gulf and the land of the Nabataeans, a land abounding in people and pasture. They also occupy islands lying in front and nearby. Formerly they lived quietly, but later used rafts to commit piracy against people sailing out of Egypt; they paid the penalty when an army came upon them and pillaged their land. ₉₁꜀ Next in succession is a plain well provided with trees and water, and full of all kinds of domesticated animals including mules; there is also a multitude of wild camels, deer, and

---

[171] I differentiate between *keras aigeion* here and *aigos keras* above.

gazelles in it, with lions, leopards, and many wolves. In front of it lies an island called Dia. ₉₂c Next is a gulf of about 500 stades, enclosed by mountains and an entrance that is difficult to pass through. Around it live hunting men whose quarry is land animals. ₉₃c Next are three uninhabited islands full of olive-trees; not the kind we have but the local sort which we call Ethiopian, whose sap also has medicinal potency. ₉₄c Then in succession are a stony beach, and after it a rugged shore that is difficult to sail along for about 1,000 stades for want of harbours and anchorages (*ankyrobolia*); for a rugged, high mountain runs along here. Next there are craggy foothills reaching to the sea, which, during the Etesian winds and the rains that come at that time, present a risk from which there is no rescue. ₉₅b Next is a gulf containing a scatter of islands, and connected with it three extremely high banks of black sand. After these is the harbour of Charmothas, measuring roughly 100 stades round; it has a narrow entrance dangerous to any boat, and a river flows into it with a well-wooded and cultivable island midstream. ₉₇c Next is a rugged coast, and after this certain gulfs and the territory of nomads who make their living from camels: for they fight upon them, travel upon them, and are nourished by consuming their milk and meat. A river flows through their land, bearing gold-dust, but they do not know how to work it. They are called the Debai; some are nomads, some farmers.⌐ I do not say most of the names of the nations, by reason of their obscurity and the absurd way they sound. ₉₈c Adjoining them are tamer men occupying a more temperate land, for it is both well-watered and shady. Gold can be mined among them—not gold-dust, but small lumps requiring little cleaning; their slightest size is that of a fruit-stone, the middling size that of a medlar, and the largest that of a walnut. Piercing these alternately with translucent stones, they make chains by stringing them on linen thread, and place them round their throats and wrists. They also sell the gold to their neighbours for a reasonable price, exchanging three times as much for bronze, twice as much for ⟨iron, and ten times as much for⟩ silver, because of their inexperience in its working and a shortage of the things they get in return, the need for which is more essential to their life.

The Sabaioi

(19) ₉₉c Contiguous with this area (*says Artemidoros*) is the most blessed land of the Sabaioi, a very extensive nation among whom occur myrrh, frankincense, and cinnamon; on the coast there is also balsam and a certain other strongly scented plant with a smell that vanishes quickly. ₁₀₀c There are also fragrant palms, reeds, and snakes a finger-to-thumb span in length which are purple in colour; they can spring as high as your flank[172] and have an incurable bite. ₁₀₁c Because of the plentiful produce, the people are idle and indifferent to their lifestyle. Most of them, the common folk, sleep upon the roots of trees which they cut off. Being made sleepy by the sweet perfumes, they keep themselves awake with by burning asphalt and goatsbeard as incense. ₁₀₂c The city of the Sabaioi, Mariaba, lies on a well-wooded mountain. It has a king with authority

---

[172] Or 'as far as a hare', Roller.

over judgements and other matters. It is unlawful for him to go out of the palace, or the crowds will stone him to death immediately on the basis of a certain oracle. [103b] He and those around him live in womanly luxury, but the masses practise either farming or the trade in spices, both local and from Ethiopia. They sail through the straits in search of them upon leather boats. ⟨Each group of neighbours in turn receives the cargoes and hands them on to the one next along, as far as Syria and Mesopotamia.⟩[173] So great is the quantity of these things that in place of brushwood and firewood they use cinnamon, cassia, and the rest. Among the Sabaioi there also occurs *larimnon*, a most sweet-smelling incense. [104c] As a result of trade, these people and the Gerrhaioi are the richest of all people. They have a copious array of gold and silver objects—couches, tripods, and mixing-bowls as well as drinking-cups and the luxurious character of their houses: for even their doorways, walls, and roofs are decorated with ivory, gold, and silver all studded with gems.⌋ That is what he (*Artemidoros*) has said about these people; the other things he presents are in part similar to what Eratosthenes tells us and in part taken from other historians.

Colour of the Erythraian sea

(20)[174] [2b]For (*it is said by Artemidoros that*) some people call this sea 'Erythra' after the colour that appears by reflection, whether from the sun when overhead or from the mountains that are made red from the burning heat. While both opinions are held, [5b] (*he says that*) Ktesias of Knidos[175] reports that there is a spring of reddened and red-ochre-like water issuing into this sea; and that Agatharchides, his fellow-citizen, who had it from a certain Boxos, Persian by race, tells of a certain Persian called Erythras. When a herd of horses was forced out of the land by a lioness who was seized with frenzy, were driven as far as the sea, and migrated to a certain island, he was the first to construct a raft and cross over to the island. Seeing that it was a fine place to settle, he took the herd back to Persis and sent colonists to this and the other islands, and to the coast, and caused the open sea (*pelagos*) to bear his own name. [4b] Others (*says Artemidoros*) show that Erythras was a son of Perseus and ruled over these places. The distance from the narrows of the Arabian gulf (*Red Sea*) to the furthest part of the Cinnamon-bearing Land is said by some to be 5,000 stades; it is not stated clearly whether this is southwards or eastwards. It is also said that emerald and beryl occur in the gold-mines. There are also fragrant salts among the Arabs, according to Poseidonios.·

99   Strabo 17. 1. 18, C801: *The Menelaïte nome in Egypt*
After Kanobos is the Herakleion, which has a sanctuary of Herakles. Then there is the Kanobic mouth and the beginning of the Delta. That on the right of the Kanobic

---

[173] This sentence follows 'roots off trees which they cut off' above, but is moved here by Radt.
[174] This passage, like the preceding paragraph, may be from A. (Roller 2014, 725 n. 4, regards it as uncertain); if it is, he is evidently using Agatharchides.
[175] *FGrH* 688 F 66 (not yet in *BNJ*).

canal is the Menelaïte nome, from the brother of the first Ptolemaios and not—by Zeus!—from the hero, as some including Artemidoros say.

100 Strabo 17. 1. 24, C803–4: *The Nile delta*
This is the description from Alexandria to the head of the Delta. Artemidoros says that the sail up is 28 *schoinoi*, which is 840 stades, calculating the *schoinos* at 30 stades. When I made the voyage different measurements were used by different people, in giving the distance in *schoinoi*, so that 40 stades or even more was agreed upon, according to the places.

That the measure of the *schoinos* among the Egyptians is uncertain was made clear by Artemidoros himself in the following: he says that from Memphis to the Thebais each *schoinos* is 120 stades, and from the Thebais to Syene 60. He also says that sailing up from Pelousion to the head (*of the Delta*) is 25 *schoinoi*, or 750 stades using the same measurement. The first canal, going from Pelousion, is the one that fills the lakes called Kata ta Helē (*At the Marshes*), which are two and lie on the left of the great river above Pelousion, in Arabia. He also speaks of other lakes and canals in the same portions outside the Delta. There is also the Sethroite nome by the second lake, which he numbers as one of the ten in the Delta.

101 Strabo 17. 3. 2, C825: *Trinx near Mt Atlas*
Nearby (*to the Koteis promontory*) is a small town above the sea that the barbarians call Trinx, but Artemidoros calls Lynx and Eratosthenes Lixos.[176]

102 Strabo 17. 3. 8, C829:[177] *Artemidoros' errors regarding the far west*
Artemidoros disagrees with Eratosthenes because the latter says that a certain city near the western extremities of Maurousia is Lixos rather than Lynx, that there are a large number of Phoenician cities that have been destroyed and of which there are no traces to be seen,[178] that he says the air among the western Aithiopes is brackish, and that the air at the hours of daybreak and the afternoon is thick and misty. How can this be in places that are dry and very hot? But he (*Artemidoros*) speaks much worse about these places. He recounts that certain wanderers, the Lotophagoi (*Lotus-eaters*), would inhabit the waterless (*regions*) and eat the lotus, a kind of herb and root, and because of it they do not need to drink. They extend as far as the places above Kyrene. Those who are there also drink milk and eat meat, although they are at the same latitude.

103 Strabo 17. 3. 10, C830: *Rivers in Libyē*
I do not know whether Poseidonios tells the truth when he says that only a few small rivers flow through Libyē, for those mentioned by Artemidoros between Lynx and Karchedon, he says, are numerous and large.

---

[176] For Lixos, cf. Hanno §§6–11; Ps.-Skyl. §112. 3–4.
[177] Cf. Eratosthenes 91 §2, from an earlier passage of Strabo.
[178] Cf. perhaps Hanno §§1–2; 5; 8.

SOURCES LATER THAN STRABO (104–59)

104   Pliny, *Natural History,* 1. 2–7 and 36: *Pliny's sources*
In the 2nd book are contained . . . from these authors: . . . foreign (*i.e. non-Roman*): . . .
Artemidorus of Ephesus . . .

In the 3rd book are contained places, peoples, seas, towns, harbours, mountains,
rivers, measurements, and peoples who exist or who existed . . . from these authors:
. . . foreign: Artemidorus[179] . . .

In the 4th book are contained places, peoples, seas, towns, harbours, mountains,
rivers, measurements, and peoples who exist or who existed . . . from these authors:
. . . foreign: . . . Artemidorus . . .

In the 5th book . . . (*the same*).

In the 6th book . . . (*the same*).

In the 7th book (*on the human race*) are contained . . . from these authors: . . . foreign: . . . Artemidorus . . .

In the 36th book are contained the natures of stones . . . from these authors: . . . foreign: . . . Artemidorus . . .

105   Pliny, *Natural History,* 4. xii. 77: *The Black Sea*
But between the two Bospori, the Thracian and the Cimmerian, by a direct voyage,
on the authority of Polybios the distance is 500 (*miles*). However, the circuit of the
whole Pontus is 2,150, on the authority of Varro and the old writers in general. Nepos
Cornelius adds 350. Artemidorus makes it 2,919 miles.[180]

106   Pliny, *Natural History,* 5. x. 59: *Syene*[181]
It (*the Nile*) begins to be under Egyptian jurisdiction where Aethiopia ends, at Syene.
This is the name of a peninsula which has a circuit of 1,000 (*double*) paces (*1 mile*),
where there is a fort on the Arabian side (*of the Nile*); opposite are the four islands of
Philae, 600 (*miles*) from the division of the Nile, from which point on, as we have said,
the area is called the Delta. This distance is given by Artemidorus, who says there are
250 towns in it.

107   Pliny, *Natural History,* 5. xxxv. 129: *Dimensions of Cyprus*
The length between the two capes (*of Cyprus*), Clides (*Kleïdes*) and Acamas—the latter
being in the west—is 162½ (*miles*) according to Artemidorus, or 200 according to
Timosthenes.

108   Pliny, *Natural History,* 6. xv. 36–7: *The Caspian*
For it (*the Caspian*) breaks into the opposite parts of Asia from the Scythic ocean.
While it is called by several names of peoples, it is most renowned under two: Caspium
and Hyrcanium. Clitarchus thinks this sea is no lesser than the Pontus Euxinus. Eratos-

---

[179] Listed first in this instance.   [180] 2,119 in Loeb.
[181] Martianus Capella (C5 AD), *Nupt.* 6. 676 Cristante *et al.*, is included by Hoffmann 1838 as fr. 73, but
closely replicates this passage and is not included here.

thenes sets its measurement on the eastern and southern side, via the coast of Cadusia and Albania, at 5,400 stades; from there via the Anariaci, Amardi, and Hyrcani to the entrance of the river Zonus at 4,800 stades; and from this to the entrance of the Iaxartes (*Syr Darya*) at 2,400, which sum amounts to 1,575 miles. From this Artemidorus subtracts 25 miles.

109 Pliny, *Natural History*, 6. xxii. 70: *Rivers of India*
Artemidorus reports that there is a distance of 2,100 (*miles*) between the two rivers (*Ganges and Indus*).

110 Pliny, *Natural History*, 6. xxxii. 156: *The gulf of Aqaba*
The innermost gulf in which dwell the Laeanitae, who have given their name to it. . . . Our own writers have written the name of the gulf as Laeaniticus, others as Aelaniticus, Artemidorus as Alaeniticus, Juba as Leaniticus.

111 Pliny, *Natural History*, 6. xxxiii. 163–4: *Dimensions of the 'Arabian gulf' (Red Sea)*
Now we shall follow the rest of the opposite coast of Arabia. Timosthenes has gauged the whole gulf (*the Red Sea*) as a voyage of 4 days lengthwise and 2 days across, while the narrows are 7½ miles (*in width*). Eratosthenes gives 1,200 from the mouth along either side; Artemidoros gives 1,750 on the Arabian side, (164) but on the Trogodytic side 1,137½[182] as far as Ptolomais (*i.e. Ptolemaïs*).

112 Pliny, *Natural History*, 6. xxxv. 183: *From Syene to Meroë*
For Timosthenes, commander of Philadelphus' fleets, while giving no measurement, offers a journey of 60 days from Syene to Meroë. Eratosthenes gives 625 miles, Artemidoros 600, Sebosus 1,675 from the furthest end of Egypt. Hence the aforementioned (*scholars—Eratosthenes and Artemidoros—give*) the distance as 1,250.[183]

113 Pliny, *Natural History*, 7. ii. 30: *Taprobane*
Artemidorus (*says*) that in the island of Taprobane people enjoy a very long life with no weakness of body.

114 Pliny, *Natural History*, 36. xvii. 79: *The Pyramids*
Those who have written about them (*the Pyramids*) are . . . Artemidorus . . . There is no agreement among all of them regarding who they were made by, the creators of such huge vanity having been, by a most equitable fortune, consigned to oblivion.

115 Athenaios 3. 76, 111d: *Ionian bread*
'Chopped': a variety of bread among the Ionians; Artemidoros of Ephesos says so in *Iōnika hypomnēmata* (*Ionian Memoranda*).[184]

---

[182] This distance varies in the MSS; I follow Desanges 2008, 1; Brodersen 1996, 114–15 and 234, gives 1,187½; Rackham 1942, 461, 1,184½.

[183] On the complex relations between these distances, see the long note at Desanges 2008, 144–7.

[184] Repeated, without book title, in the *Epitome* of Athenaios, 2. 1. 24; more briefly still by Hesychios, *Lexikon*, κ 3119. This is the only fragment of Art. included in *FGrH* i–iii (Banchich 2010); *FGrH* v does not include Art.

116   Harpokration s.v. *Ganos kai Ganiada: Settlements in Thrace*
'Ganos and Ganias': . . . They are Thracian settlements, according to Artemidoros.

117   Hesychios s.v. *Skyria dikē: Achilles on Skyros*
Skyrian justice: Artemidoros in particular says, 'It is called Theseus' End: for they say that after fleeing to Skyros he was there thrown over a precipice'.

118   Hesychios s.v. Talantion: *A place called Talantion*
Talantion: a place. Artemidoros.

119   Markianos, introduction to *Epitome of Menippos*, 3–4[185]
3. After most of these writers,[186] Artemidoros of Ephesos the geographer, and Strabo, who combined geography and circumnavigation (*periplous*), and Menippos of Pergamon, who wrote about sea crossings, are in my view more accurate than all those mentioned above. . . . Artemidoros of Ephesos the geographer, who lived around the 169th Olympiad,[187] sailed out round the largest part of the inner sea, our sea, and saw the island of Gadeira and some parts of the external sea, which they call Ocean. It falls short of an accurate geographical description; but in eleven books he covered with proper diligence the circumnavigation of the sea within the strait of Herakles and the measurement of this, and so seems to have written very clearly and accurately the circumnavigation of our sea.

4. Now, I placed Artemidoros of Ephesos ahead of all those mentioned, and I made an epitome of his eleven books, adding from other old writers material that was lacking while keeping the arrangement of the eleven books, so as to produce a reasonable geographical account but a complete *periplous*.

120   Markianos, *Periplous*, 1. 1: *Artemidoros' starting-point; cities in Aithiopia*
1. [—] ⟨Within the Pillars of Herakles⟩ lies a sea whose western end is marked by the Ocean surrounding the Earth, which makes its inflow at the so-called Herakleian strait—the circumnavigation of this was composed by the geographer Artemidoros of Ephesos, to the best of his ability, in the eleven books of the *Geography*. We, however, leaving aside the superfluous digressions by the previously noted man in these books, and also the Aithiopian cities of the barbarians, made the circumnavigation for ourselves, in summary form, very clearly and with the precise addition of supplementary discoveries, in order that nothing might be lacking that could contribute to perfect clarity for those studying this aspect of geography.[188]

121   Markianos, *Periplous*, 2. 4: *Mt Kalpe*
For those at Mt Kalpe, which lies inward from the Herakleian narrows, say that this is the Pillars; but those at Gadeira (*say that*) the island is, as does Artemidoros the geographer.

---

[185] Adapted from Campbell's translation in Ch. 21 below.
[186] He means 'after' in the chronological sense.   [187] 104–100 BC.
[188] Cf. the similar statement of Mark. *Periplous*, 2. 2 (in Ch. 34 below).

122 Pseudo-Arrian, *Circumnavigation of the Black Sea*, 92: *Distances in the NW Black Sea*

Altogether, from the river Borysthenes as far as the river Tyras, 810 stades, 108 miles;[189] and from Cherson to the river Tyras, 4,110 stades, 548 miles.

Artemidoros the geographer writes that from the city of Cherson up to the river Tyras, with the circumnavigation of the gulf of Karkinitis, is 4,420 stades, 589⅓ miles.

From the river Tyras to the area of Neoptolemos, 120 stades, 16 miles.

From Neoptolemos to Kremniskoi, 120 stades, 16 miles.

Artemidoros the geographer says that from the river Tyras to Kremniskoi is 480 stades, 64 miles.

From Kremniskoi as far as the (*Places*) of Antiphilos, 330 stades, 44 miles.

From Antiphilos to the mouth of the river Istros called Psilon, 300 stades, 40 miles. These people are Thracians and immigrant Bastarnai.

123 Stephanos of Byzantion α 4: *A cape in the Hellespont*

Abarnos: a city, territory, ⟨and⟩ cape in the territory of Parion. . . . There is also a city, a territory, and a cape. The form Aparnis with a pi has also been found, as in Artemidoros the geographer.

124 Stephanos of Byzantion α 36: *A city in Italy*

Ankōn (*Ancona*): a city of the Pikentinoi. The *ethnikon* is Ankonios. . . . Ankonites is also said, as by Artemidoros.

125 Stephanos of Byzantion α 39: *A city in Gaul*

Agnotes: a nation in Keltike (*Gaul*) beside the Ocean, as Artemidoros (*says*).

126 Stephanos of Byzantion α 92: *A cape in Aiolis*

Aiga: a cape in Aiolis, as in Strabo: 'which they now call Kane and Kanai'. Artemidoros said the nominative was Aix, against the analogy.[190]

127 Stephanos of Byzantion α 239: *An island near Massalia*

Alonis: an island and city (*belonging to*) Massalia, as Artemidoros (*says*). The *ethnikon* is Alonites.

128 Stephanos of Byzantion α 462: *A peninsula in Akarnania*

Artemita: a Tyrrhenic island (*i.e. in the Tyrrhenic sea*) . . . But Artemidoros says that (*there is*) a peninsula near the outflow of the Acheloös river called Artemita.

129 Stephanos of Byzantion α 496: *A nation in Thrace*

Astai: a nation in Thrace. Artemidoros, in *Epitome of the Eleven* (*books*).

---

[189] These conversions into miles were added in C6 AD by the author of the Pseudo-Arrianic *Euxine* (Ch. 36 below).

[190] Cf. **158**. Steph. Byz. is making a point about Aiga or Aix and related names in the next two entries, Aigaion Pelagos (the Aegean sea) and Aigai (name of various *poleis*).

130   Stephanos of Byzantion α 522: *An Arabian nation*
Atramitai: a nation in Fortunate Arabia (*Arabia Felix*). . . . Artemidoros calls them Atramotitai.

131   Stephanos of Byzantion α 579: *Islands in the Adriatic*
Apsyrtides: islands towards the Adriatic. . . . Artemidoros, in *Epitome*, reports a city ⟨and⟩ an island of Apsyrtos.

132   Stephanos of Byzantion β 59: *An island off Laconia*
Belbina: a Laconian city. Pausanias, 8th (*book*). Artemidoros refers to it as an island.

133   Stephanos of Byzantion β 144: *An Illyrian city*
Boulinoi: a nation in the area of Illyria. But Artemidoros refers to it not as a nation, but as Bouline, a city, whose *ethnikon* (*is*) Boulinos.

134   Stephanos of Byzantion γ 18: *A Libyan nation*
Gaitouloi: a nation in Libyē. Artemidoros refers to them as Gaitylioi.

135   Stephanos of Byzantion γ 75: *A city in Thrace*
Gigonos: a city in Thrace. . . . But Artemidoros of Ephesos refers to this as Gigonis.

136   Stephanos of Byzantion γ 119: *A Phoenician city*
Gynaikospolis (*Woman's City*): a city of the Phoinikes. . . . There is also another in Egypt. But Aristagoras, not much younger than Plato, says that it was named thus for three reasons: because, when the enemy fell upon it and the men were absent, the women took charge of the war; or because a certain wife of a provincial governor, when her children were robbed by the king, armed herself together with the children, hunted down the king, and defeated him; or because, when the men of Naukratis were sailing upstream along the river and were blocked from disembarking by the rest of the Egyptians, the latter were struck with cowardice and failed to block them. Artemidoros also says these things.

137 Stephanos of Byzantion δ 77: *Two of the Aiolian islands*
Didyme (*Twin*): one of the Aiolian islands. . . . But Artemidoros refers to two islets (*called*) Didyma.

138   Stephanos of Byzantion ε 161: *A city in Lokris*
Eupalia: a city in Lokris, which Artemidoros refers to as Eupalion.

139   Stephanos of Byzantion θ 22: *A place in Phrygia*
Themisonion: a settlement in Phrygia. Artemidoros, in *Epitome*.

140   Stephanos of Byzantion ι 115: *A city on Crete*
Istros: a city on Crete, which Artemidoros refers to as Istrōn.

141   Stephanos of Byzantion κ 307: *An island near Kythera*
Kōthōn: an island not far from Kythera. Artemidoros, in *Epitome of the Eleven* (*books*).

142   Stephanos of Byzantion κ 234: *A city in Lykia*
Krya: a city in Lykia. Artemidoros, in *Epitome of the Eleven* (*books*).[191] The *ethnikon* is
Kryeus: 'There are also other islands of the Kryeis, namely Karysis and Alina'.

143   Stephanos of Byzantion λ 36: *An island off Africa*
Laodamanteia: an island in Libyē. Artemidoros, in *Epitome of the Eleven* (*books*).

144   Stephanos of Byzantion λ 119: *An island off Thessaly*
Lōs: an island near Thessaly. . . . Artemidoros, in *Epitome of the Eleven* (*books*).

145   Stephanos of Byzantion μ 243: *An island in Ionia*
Myonesos: an island between Teos and Lebedos. . . . But Artemidoros refers to it as a
settlement (*chōrion*).

146   Stephanos of Byzantion μ 253: *A city in the Taurike Chersonesos*
Myrmekion: a small city in Taurike. . . . But Artemidoros refers to it as Myrmekia.

147   Stephanos of Byzantion ξ 12: *A city in Libyē*
Xouches: a city in Libyē, Artemidoros in *Epitome of the Eleven* (*books*). The *ethnikon*
is Xouchites.

148   Stephanos of Byzantion π 7: *A city in Syria*
Paltos: a city in Syria. Artemidoros, in *Epitome*.[192]

149   Stephanos of Byzantion σ 242: *A city in Sardinia*
Solkoi (*Sulci*): a city in Sardo, as Artemidoros (*says*) in *Epitome*: 'from Karalis up to
Solkoi'.

150   Stephanos of Byzantion σ 263: *A city in northern Italy*
Spina: a city in Italia, as Eudoxos and Artemidoros (*say*). The *ethnikon* is Spinates . . .
There is also a river called Spinos.

151   Stephanos of Byzantion τ 66: *A city in Illyria*
Tegestra, neuter: a city in Illyria near Akyleia (*Aquileia*). But Artemidoros, in *Epitome
of the Eleven* (*books*), knows it as Tergestron and as a village: 'from the village of Tergestron and the head (*of the gulf of Trieste*) to the Adriatic is 5,029 stades'.

152   Stephanos of Byzantion τ 159: *A territory in Iberia*
Tourdetania: a territory in Iberia. . . . But Artemidoros calls it Tourtytania, and the
inhabitants Tourtoi and Tourtytanoi.

153   Stephanos of Byzantion τ 233: *An island in the Erythraian sea*
Tyros: . . . Moreover, an island by the Erythraian sea, which Artemidoros calls Tylos,
using a lambda.

---

[191] The text of Stephanos reads ἐν ἐπιτομῆς α', 'in *Epitome*'s 1st (*book*)', but S. nowhere else gives a book
number within Markianos' epitome of A. I translate the emendation proposed by Schiano 2010, 50–1.
[192] Cf. **54**; also *Stadiasmos* §130.

154 Stephanos of Byzantion φ 36: *A Libyan nation*
Pharousioi: a Libyan nation. Dionysios (*Periegetes*) mentions them, as does Artemidoros.

155 Stephanos of Byzantion φ 69: *A city in Macedonia*
Philippoi: a city in Macedonia, the former Krenides. Artemidoros, in *Epitome of the Eleven* (*books*): 'And the city of Philippoi, Krenides of old. When Philip came to help the Krenitai, who were having war waged upon them by Thracians, he named (*it*) Philippoi'.

156 Stephanos of Byzantion φ 76: *A city on an Adriatic island*
Phlanōn: a city and harbour at the island of Apsyrtos. Artemidoros, in *Epitome of the Eleven* (*books*): 'after Aloös is the harbour of Phlanōn and the city of Phlanōn, and all this gulf is called the Phlanōnikos'.

157 Stephanos of Byzantion ω 21: *A nation in Brittany*
Ostiones: a nation beside the western Ocean, whom Artemidoros refers to as Kossinoi but Pytheas as Ōstidaioi: 'To the left side of these are the Kossinoi, known as Ōstiones, whom Pytheas designates Ōstidaioi'.[193]

158 Constantine Porphyrogennetos, *De thematibus*, 1. 42. 9: *Cape Aix*
There is a certain cape in Aiolis that the locals call Aix, from which the open sea (*pelagos; i.e. the Aegean*) has received the name that it has, as Artemidoros says.[194]

159 Tzetzes (Isaak or Ioannes), *On Lykophron, Alexandra*, 633: *The Gymnesiai islands*
Gymnesiai: two islands near the Tyrsenis (*sic; Etruria*). . . . Artemidoros also mentions them.

UNDATED SOURCES (160–6)

160 *Epimerismoi Homerikoi* s.v. *cheiros: The river Eir*[195]
cheiros (*Hand*): . . . For there is a river Eir, which Artemidoros mentions in *Geographoumena*.

161 *Proverb in Bodleian manuscript*: *A foundation by Philip II*[196]
'There is no city of slaves': . . . And Artemidoros says that Philip founded the one called Ponērōn Polis (*Rogues' City*), in which he used to confine all the rogues as a punishment.

---

[193] A quotation from A. citing Pytheas (= Pyth. 32).   [194] Cf. **126.**
[195] For the *Epimerismoi*, see n. on Hekataios 59. The present extract is at Cramer 1835, 440; Dyck 1995, 743 (χ 30). It discusses monosyllables ending in -*eir* (*cheiros* being the genitive singular of *cheir*, 'hand').
[196] From a C15 manuscript published by Gaisford 1836, 81 no. 675. See also n. to Mnaseas 45.

162 scholion B to Apollonios of Rhodes 2. 946–54: *The 'White Syrians' of the southern Black Sea*
That some people call the Assyrioi Leukosyroi (*White Syrians*) is also stated by Artemidoros.

163 scholion A to Apollonios of Rhodes 2. 963–5: *'White Syria' in the southern Black Sea*
'Halys' and 'Iris': rivers in Leukosyrike (*White Syria*). He (*Apollonios*) has also mentioned the 'cape' near Themiskyra above . . . This, as I said, is followed by the so-called Cape Herakleios, which Artemidoros among others mentions, upon which the sanctuary of Herakles has been founded.

164 scholion C to Apollonios of Rhodes 3. 854–9: *The Caspian*
Artemidoros investigates the Caspian sea in the *Epitome* of the *Geographoumena*. It is near the Ocean, and by it lies the nation named Kaspion, which shares a frontier with the Persians.

165 scholion B to Apollonios of Rhodes 4. 257–62: *The Argonauts' return route*
But Hekataios of Miletos (*says*) that from the Phasis (*Rioni*) they (*the Argonauts*) went through to the Ocean, then from there into the Nile, and thence into our sea. But the Ephesian Artemidoros says this is a falsehood: for the Phasis does not meet the Ocean, but runs down from mountains.[197]

166 scholion to Dionysios Periegetes, line 14: *The mouths of the Tanais*
Artemidoros says the two mouths of the Tanaïs are 7 stades distant from each other [—] for one of them flows into Lake Maiotis, the other into Skythia.[198]

APPENDIX 1: THE ARTEMIDOROS PAPYRUS

167

COLUMNS I–III[199]

(*i. 1*) He who aspires to apply himself to geography must make a demonstration [of all] his knowledge, balancing[200] his own soul for this business through a more [effect]ive will towards this profession, and making himself ready, according to the power of (*his*) virtue, by the (*10*) voluntary tools of his soul. For it is no ordinary effort that is capable

---

[197] Another version, but with A.'s name missing, is Hekat. 18.   [198] The text is uncertain.

[199] Based on the original text and translation by the editors (Gallazzi, Kramer, and Settis 2008, 196–7 (ed. pr.), with consideration of revisions proposed by Condello 2011 and the works of van Minnen 2009 and Marcotte 2010. Angle brackets indicate words added to those in the papyrus by editors; square brackets are used selectively to indicate some supplements and damaged letters. Column and line numbers are indicated in the form (*i. 1*).

[200] Or 'shaping'.

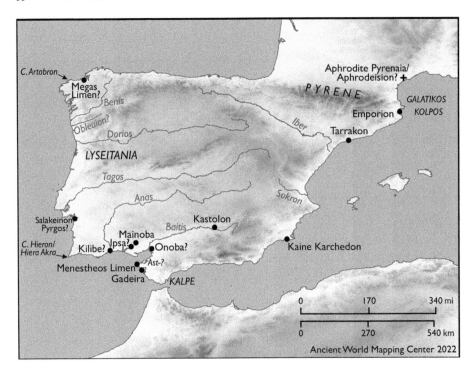

MAP 18.1. Artemidoros Papyrus: Iberia.

of struggling alongside this science. For I am ready to set it (*geography*) beside philosophy, that most divine (*thing*), as being nearly equal to it. For if geography is silent, it talks through its particular doctrines. And why not? It wields around itself the many assorted weapons that are closest (*to it*), (20) in face of the laboured work that occurs with (*the acquisition of*) knowledge.

For one professes to steer throughout one's life, with polished and frequent thinking, for the doctrines of philosophy; so that, wielding that Atlantean[201] load of those who worthily practise philosophy, one may (*nevertheless*) hold the load without fatigue, and may embrace (30) one's own soul as it is fatigued by nothing and is no longer weighed down; (*and professes*) all the more to have an appetite for the matter, since one's soul and will are in no way at rest, and to be awake, looking round at everything, by night and by day, adding to one's own load good things more numerous than what one is obliged (*to take on*). For Man[202] (40) is spread over the cosmos, and collaboratively dedicates all of himself to the virtuous precepts of the most godlike Muses, in order that the godlike form of [ph]ilos[ophy] (*ii. 1*) may make Man [most s]ac[red] in virtue.

Likewise the geographer, after coming to the mainland (*ēpeiros*) of a territory (*chōra*) and having previously understood the vessel[203] of the land lying beside him

---

[201] i.e. like that of Atlas, who holds up the world.
[202] I translate ὁ ἄνθρωπος, literally 'the male human being'.
[203] *kytos*, meaning 'vessel' in the sense of 'container', not 'ship'. Cf. Marcotte 2010, 358.

and those of other [kinds]—many years of painstaking labour having previously been dedicated by him—once established (*there*), ought (*10*) to broaden his soul to fit the land under consideration, looking round at many things and contrasting his specific intellectual starting-points: whether to begin with a certain part of the land or encounter it as a whole as befits a man with [no k]n[ow]l[edge], and having approached it with his intellect[204] to establish the manner of gaining understanding (*20*) and make a start from this. (*Then*) he shall receive [guarant]ees, from those who respect geography and do not look down upon it, that he himself is within it[205] (*though*) lapped, as in a ship, by waves of contrasting conjectures. Therefore he will helplessly remain (*as he is*), and act thus, and will need . . . in a bad . . . [— *ii. 29–43 and iii. 1–19 very fragmentary* —] . . . (*30*) geography . . . (*31*) way . . . (*iii. 1*) look forward . . . (*4*) sacred . . . (*5*) harbour . . . (*6*) cape . . . (*7*) note . . . (*8*) research . . . (*9*) show . . .

COLUMNS IV–V

(*iv. 1*) [From the Pyrenaian mountains as far as] the [places b]y Ga[deira][206] (*Cádiz*) and the zones (*klimata*) further inland, the whole land is called synonymously Iberia and Hispania, but it has been divided by the Romans into two provinces (*eparcheiai*). In the first province is all the (*land*) stretching from the Pyrenaian mountains up to Kaine (*10*) Karchedon (*Nova Carthago, New Carthage*) and Kastol[ōn] and the springs of the (*river*) Baitis (*Guadalquivir*). In the other province are the (*places*) up to Gadeira, and all the (*places*) about Lyseitania.

The character (*physis*) of the land has a total outline (*perigraphē*) of this kind.[207] For P[yrene] has divided [Kel]tike [and Iberia], and [one extremi]ty protrudes[208] int[o] our land, inclined (*20*) towards the southern (*notios*) side, the one ⟨towards⟩ the south (*mesēmbria*).[209] But the other limit, turned away t[owards] the north, projects forward a long way into the Ocean. As for the (*places*) to the sides of this (*sc. Pyrene*), some are inclined towards the east (*ēōs*), from which [pla]ces a substantial amount of Keltike is observed; others [tow]ards the west, from which places [a similar amount] of Iberia is observed.

These things being (*30*) established, three sides of the land must be conceived, which enclose Iberia: one stretching from the Py[renaian] mountains as far as Gadeira, and this is the one extending beside our sea, the one w[ithin] the Pillars of Herakles, and parallel to the zones [to the] south. (*v. 1*) The second side, washed by the open sea (*pelagos*) at the Ocean and bearing towards the north (*arktoi*), extends along up to (*the area*) towards the west (*hespera*) and connects with the third side that lies in the west

---

[204] Reading τ[ῷ] νῷ with van Minnen 2009, 170, rather than π[ό]νῳ ed. pr. Van Minnen takes the subjunctives in ii. 18 and 20 to be part of the construction that begins at ii. 14.

[205] i.e. master of it.　　　[206] Cf. **31** (also **23** for this paragraph).

[207] *Perigraphē* may imply a cartographic perspective.

[208] 'Protrudes': if this passage is genuinely by Artemidoros, it may be the first topographical use of ἔκκειμαι–*ekkeimai*; and 'our land' should mean Greece.

[209] The sentence combines two words for 'south' in a way difficult to parallel.

(*dysmai*), in which it is the case that Lyseita[nia lies] and the so-called Hieron (*Sacred*) Promontory and all the localities around Gadeira. Beside the very parts bordering upon Pyr[ene], some parts of Iberia deviate towards the (*10*) east and form the outline (*perigraphē*) of a somewhat sizeable gulf extending up to the mountains that (*we have*) shown.[210] This (*gulf*) also connects with the Galatic gulf.

And the whole form of [Ibe]ria is of this kind; but now we shall undertake its coastal sailing (*paraplous*) in summary, in light of the distances between localities, understood in a general fashion (*katholikōs*).[211]

For from the promontory of Aphrodite Pyrenaia as far as the city of [Em]porion, a colony of the Phokaians, (*is*) [632 s]t[ades].[212]

From this to the city of (*20*) Tarrakōn (*Tarragona*), 1,[5]08.

From here to the river Iber (*Ebro*), less than 92.

From this to the river Sokrōn, 1,048.

From here to the new [K]arch[edon], 1,240.

From Karchedon, up to Mt [Kalp]e, 2,020.

From this as far as Gade[ira], 544.

All the (*stades*) from Pyrene [and] the Aphrodeision (*sanctuary of Aphrodite*) as far as Gadeira, 7,084. And continuing after Gadeira to the tower and harbour of Menestheus[213] it is 7,170.

From this [to the] second [m]out[h] of the Ast[..],[214] 120.

After this, to the river Baitis (*Guadalquivir*), 84.

(*30*) After this, to Onoba, 280.

From here to Mainoba, 78.

After this to the city of Ipsa, 24.

After this to the outpourings of the An[as] there are, in the projected straight line (*to*) where the city of Kilibe is, 36 stades.

After the outflows of the Anas, there follows the limit of the Hiera (*Sacred*) Cape and, to the furthest place (*on it*), stades 992.

When people have rounded the promontory (*and made*) for the tower of (*the*) Salakeinoi, there are stades 1,200.

And from here to the mouth of the river Tagos, 320.

From this to the river Do[rios] (*Douro*), (*40*) 1,300.

---

[210] Micunco 2007, 400–1, detects incoherence in ll. 7–12.

[211] Presumably Artemidoros (if this is genuine) means he has selected important long staging-points.

[212] It seems unparalleled in Hl texts for sea distances not to be given to the nearest 10 or even 100 st., with the exception of Attica in Ps.-Skylax where coastal lengths may have been measured on land (Shipley 2010).

[213] Luppe 2008, 689, takes this to be a lighthouse. See Introduction, §III. 3. j.

[214] Cf. Astan at Mark. *Periplous* 2. 9.

After this there pours in (?), at 180 stades, [the] river Obleuiōn;[215] this is surnamed the river of Lethe (*Forgetting*) and of Lim[aia?] (*Hungry?*).[216]

After this, to the river Ben[i]s, 110.[217]

From this to the cape of Artabra (*Ortegal*), 940.

From this to Megas Limen (*the Great Harbour*), 40 [stades].

T[he re]s[t of th]e coast no one has obser[ved].[218]

APPENDIX 2: THE 'MUNICH FRAGMENT'

168 Codex Monacensis 287, fos. 161ᵛ–162ʳ: *The Nile*

This supposed fragment of Artemidoros is found in a manuscript in Munich dated to *c*.1550–1600.[219] It names Artemidoros as its source, and on the basis of Berger's publication of 1804 it was included by Hoffmann and Stiehle in their collections of fragments; both attributing it to Artemidoros' 8th book (see 44–7 above).[220] Diller, however, has shown that the text cannot be from Artemidoros and is a late medieval, garbled version of material from Strabo 17 taken by him from Eratosthenes (translated above at Eratosthenes 89).[221] It is included here, however, for completeness' sake and in order to take the opportunity to offer corrections to the text.[222]

[215] As Hillgruber 2019, 115, points out, this confirms Xylander's conjecture that Strabo's *Belion* (3. 3. 4) conceals *Obliouiōn*. (Similarly, Marcotte 2010, 353 n. 63.) As Hammerstaedt 2013, 143–4, points out, the word *obleivio* ('forgetting', synonymous with Greek Lethe) was current in C2 Latin; the passage also fits the existence of two Hispaniae, which was true only from 138 to 27 BC, so *obleivio* could have been given as a name to a river by the time of Artemidoros' visit. Appian, *Iberike* (*Civil Wars*, 6), lxxii. 304, reports that in 137 BC Sextus Iunius Brutus (i.e. Decimus Iunius Brutus Callaicus, cf. Velleius Paterculus 2. 5. 1) became the first Roman general to cross the Lethe. M. L. West 2009, 98, shows that the Hispanic geography is not, *contra* Canfora, incompatible with A.'s date.

[216] Its mod. name is *Limia*.

[217] Not 120 as in the translation in ed. pr.; also the opinion of van Minnen 2009, 171.

[218] Pytheas had probably travelled this way by sea in C4l (see introduction to Ch. 7), though he may not have measured the coast in detail.

[219] Codex Monacensis graecus 287 (https://daten.digitale-sammlungen.de/~db/0004/bsb00049971/images/), fos. 161ᵛ–162ʳ (Hoffmann and Stiehle miscite the MS number as 387). Nigel Wilson advises me that a date in C16, perhaps C16s, is likelier than the C15 which earlier editors suggested. I am grateful to Kai Brodersen for locating an online version of F. X. Berger 1804; to Silvia Panichi for referring me to Diller 1969; and especially to Mr Wilson for detailed discussion of the text, as well as to Anne Sackett and Joseph Shipley for the realization that the general sense of the last paragraph is clearly that people use the water because it is clean, having deposited its silt during the flood. (The tables of contents for the MS in the 'Pinakes' and the Munich databases omit this item; but the MS has its own table of contents in a later hand that includes 'Artemidori geographi de Nilo'.)

[220] F. X. Berger 1804; fr. 66 H.; fr. 90 St. Stiehle notes close similarities with the material from Erat. at Strabo 17. 1. 2, C786 (Erat. 89 in this vol.), 17. 1. 7–8, C793 (not in the present vol.; probably St. is thinking of the statement near the end of 17. 1. 7 that the Nile is cleaner in early summer, but there is no close similarity), and 17. 1. 14, C799.

[221] Diller 1969, 29.

[222] In the last paragraph, reprinted by Hoffmann and Stiehle unchanged from Berger's text, I adopt the following emendations: πέμψιν cod. : πρόληψιν Berger : πέψιν Wilson. | τοῦτο ἄν (*sic*) ἀποροῦσι cod.: τοῦτο ἀναποροῦσι Berger: τούτου Wilson εὐποροῦσι Shipley. | ἀπορεῖν cod., Berger: ἀπορρεῖν (or ἀποχωρεῖν?) Shipley. | διηδές cod.: διηθὲς Berger: διειδὲς Wilson.

TRANSLATION

From Artemidoros the geographer, *On the Nile*: the Nile, flowing from the south and the places around Meroë, runs towards the north. After passing through 2,700 stades, it turns its current back again in a southerly direction, after making an angle; and it runs in this manner, diverted towards the winter sunsets (*south-west*), for 3,700 stades. After drawing level with the places around Meroë and advancing far into Libyē, it makes another curve to the north; and thus is diverted towards the east and arrives at the great cataract (*after*) 5,300 stades. Up to the next cataract by Syene and the city of Elephantine, it makes 1,200 stades. Up to its outlet into our sea, 5,300 stades. So the total of the stades is ⟨18,200⟩.[223]

Rivers also debouch[224] into the Nile: one running from the south, called Astaboras—a distributary[225] of this runs into the Erythraian sea; another from the mountains of the east and of Arabia;[226] and a third, Astosobas. So they say that these are the 'fillers up'[227] of the Nile, as they are increased by summer rains.[228]

It is important to know that the Nile makes two mouths. One of them, the one oriented towards the west and running towards the north, is called Kanobikon. The other, diverging towards the summer sunrises (*north-east*), is called Pelousiakon.[229]

The Nile flows into[230] a certain place and makes a lake above Alexandria, named Mareotis, which is extremely large; this actually has a width of 150 stades and a length of 270 stades. Within itself it contains eight islands.[231] Because of the healthful waters of the Nile and the temperate airs, that place enjoys great good fortune.

Indeed, most of the experts on the universe (*kosmos*) say that there is no water in the (*land*) under Heaven like that of the Nile for health, digestion, and bodily vigour; and they are well provided with this because a great deal of sediment flows from it: for they say that when the sediment and its dirt are cleaned to a large extent by the rising (*of the river*), it (*the water*) becomes clear and healthful.

---

[223] Stiehle explains in his n. *b* that 18,200 is Eratosthenes' figure.
[224] προσεισβολοῦσι, a rare, perhaps unique word.   [225] ἀπόσπασμα.
[226] The latter is patently impossible.   [227] εἰσπληροοῦντες.
[228] So far, this passage resembles the beginning of Strabo 17. 2. 1, C821.
[229] No other source limits the mouths of the Nile to two (I owe this observation to Silvia Panichi).
[230] προσρέει, another rare word (cf. Hdt. 1. 62).
[231] The preceding two sentences resemble the end of Strabo 17. 1. 14, C799.

19

POSEIDONIOS OF APAMEIA

(c.135–c.51 bc)

*Katherine J. Clarke**

INTRODUCTION

Few scholars or intellectuals of the hellenistic period could rival the vast scope and expertise of Poseidonios of Apameia. Standing on a par with Aristotle and Eratosthenes as one of the greatest polymaths of the Classical world, Poseidonios spanned a subject range that included physics in its broadest sense of natural philosophy, cosmology, meteorology, gods and heroes; ethics; philosophical logic; science in terms of both mathematical and physical geography; travel texts; history and ethnography. The fact that none of his works, written in Greek, survives intact surely represents one of the greatest imaginable losses to the history of ideas. Nevertheless, the few hundred extant fragments, preserved as citations by later writers such as Strabo, Seneca, Athenaios, and Diogenes Laërtios, offer tantalizing glimpses into the intellectual treasure trove that the works of Poseidonios must have comprised. Furthermore, the references to Poseidonios in over a hundred testimonia by authors such as Cicero, Galen, Plutarch, and Macrobius indicate the wide scope of his readership and influence.

One obvious difficulty that should be addressed head-on is the fragmentary nature of all of Poseidonios' extant work.[1] The loss of context for the vast majority of fragments renders their full comprehension and appreciation elusive, as does the notorious problem of what precisely constitutes a fragment.[2] Furthermore, the dominance of certain source-authors, such as Athenaios, no doubt offers a very skewed sense of the range of interests of the original works. Without Athenaios, for example, we would not possess a single fragment of Poseidonios' *History* with the title and book number cited. One author is thus solely responsible for our construction of the skeletal framework of that monumental piece of writing, and it is an author with a very specific and idiosyncratic set of interests.[3] In terms of 'geographical' fragments, this dominance accounts for the fact that the ethnographic material preserved concerns almost

* I should like to thank Graham Shipley not only for his initial invitation to participate in this project, but also for his considerable patience while I have been distracted by administrative and other commitments, and his generous help in preparing the translations and securing permissions.

[1] On the problem of fragmentary texts, see Lenfant 1999.   [2] On this see Brunt 1980.
[3] See Clarke 2007, for the methodological difficulties in extracting the content, thought and structure of P.'s work from source authors. In the case of Athenaios, 'il ne s'agit pas de domination, il s'agit de monopole', p. 291.

exclusively food and eating customs, to a degree which may not accurately reflect Poseidonios' own preoccupations.

Another complication is the unevenness of scale among the fragments. While many comprise the tiniest of snippets, small details cited by a later writer, others are far more extensive. Again, this has particular relevance for understanding the geographical fragments. While many are small notes on, observations concerning, or explanations of specific phenomena in physical or human geography, others constitute major excursuses on the nature of the geographical enterprise, its scope and limitations, and the broader configuration and coherent functioning of the inhabited world. The geographer Strabo in particular not only preserves extracts of Poseidonios through citations throughout his own geographical work, but also devotes a significant part of his opening books to a critique of geography as a discipline, in which Poseidonios is one of the most significant figures to be discussed. This brings the benefits of a much more protracted 'fragment', and one which is contextualized within the wider development of geographical thought.

The question of contexts naturally leads us to consider the various frameworks within which Poseidonios was operating. Born at Apameia on the river Orontes in Syria around 135 BC, his education took place in Athens at the feet of Panaitios, head of the Stoic school of philosophy, which determined the frequent designation by later authors of Poseidonios as 'from the Stoa', in spite of the fact that he seems to have been eclipsed by Chrysippos as representative of that school of thought. Poseidonios settled to teach in Rhodes, yet another intellectual hotspot and hub of the hellenistic Mediterranean, and his works must span the six or more decades between this point, around 110, and his death around 51. His cosmopolitan outlook was further enhanced by extensive travels which encompassed southern Spain, southern Gaul, mainland Italy, Sicily, Dalmatia, Greece, North Africa, and the Near East. Thus the intellectual diversity of his formative milieux was matched by a range of geographical experience that few could match.

Poseidonios' scholarly output is an exceptional but natural product of his position in time and space. The ecumenical nature of his professional milieu and his own mobility around the Mediterranean world are influences complemented by Poseidonios' moment in history, flourishing as he did in the aftermath of Rome's expansion of power across that Mediterranean world, driving its gradual coalescence into what Polybios had described as a 'corporate whole'. Poseidonios' On the Ocean (Peri tou Ōkeanou) and History (Historia), difficult though they are to characterize given the paucity of fragments, seem to have complemented each other in providing an account of the inner and outer seas, the encircling Ocean and the Mediterranean, in a telling reflection of the increasingly coherent world of Roman power.[4] But, although Poseidonios' most influential works were those focused on history and geography, his provenance

---

[4] On this, see Clarke 1999, ch. 3. Villani 2009, offers another view on the relationship between these different bodies of water as part of P.'s world-view.

'from the Stoa' should also not be forgotten, nor his cosmological research.[5] Bringing Polybios' 'corporate whole' into the still broader, even panoptic, frame of the inhabited world as a cosmological phenomenon and a philosophical concept would be Poseidonios' monumental contribution to the developing understanding of geography as a discipline, and of geographical thought as fundamentally embedded in the study of the physical and human worlds in their broadest interpretation.

The vastness of scope in Poseidonios' geographical, intellectual, and subject range is key to understanding his significance in the history of ideas, but also to underpinning a generous interpretation of what constitutes 'geography' for this author. In selecting which fragments of his work to include in this collection of geographical texts, the guiding principle has been breadth rather than narrowness. The fragments are grouped here under six main headings:

1. *The principles and practice of geography* (1–19). Poseidonios' work *On the Ocean*, known to us only through Strabo's critique, with its discussion of tides, climatic zones, circumnavigations, and the wider configuration of the inhabited world, sits square within the scope of physical geography and occupies prime position in this section. Complementing this are many citations in Strabo and other authors which concern the physical layout of the world, including its relationship to celestial phenomena.

2. *Geology* (20–32). Poseidonios' interest in the physical make-up of the Earth itself, including phenomena such as earthquakes and volcanoes, extends here to the materials which comprise its substance—rocks and metals. Fragments concerning the human interface with the fabric of the Earth in the fields of mining, or the moral corruption associated with precious metals, are included here, although they neatly illustrate the close interplay between physical and human geography in Poseidonios' understanding of the world as the habitat of human beings; such fragments could equally well have been placed among the ethnographic material in the final section.

3. *Hydrology* (33–46). From land we turn to various bodies of water. Here the focus is naturally more clearly on the physical phenomena of tides, floods, and the circumferences of seas, and it is hard to imagine that some of this material did not originally belong to the work *On the Ocean*, although the imprecise citation habits of most of Poseidonios' source-authors leave that impossible to prove. Nevertheless, some of the fragments included here also have a strong human aspect, such as the tidal wave which drowned the troops of Tryphon of Apameia, leaving them covered with piles of fish.

4. *Geographical observations*, cited mainly by Strabo (47–58). In addition to his extensive critique of Poseidonios and his position in the history of geographical thought, Strabo also cites Poseidonios' geographical observations frequently throughout his *Geography* on matters such as sunsets, flora and fauna, and the shape of geographical units. (A citation by Athenaios is also included.) This section enables us to see the

---

[5] Reinhardt 1926, although almost a century old, remains valuable for its treatment of P.'s broader sense of an organic universe. Comparatively recent is K. Schmidt 1980.

564 • 19 POSEIDONIOS

importance of Poseidonios as a physical geographer for the author who would write the only large-scale descriptive geography to survive from the classical world.

5. *Geography in the 'History'* (59–64). This offers another opportunity to see Poseidonios' geographical thought through the eyes of a single source-author, this time Athenaios, who, as noted above, is the only author to cite the *History* by title and book number. What emerges above all else is the importance of geographical material, ranging from produce to dining habits, in a work of history. The integrated nature of the geographical and historical enterprises should not cause surprise,[6] but it is worth introducing a note of caution here, since the food-related slant in these fragments must surely be owed in part to their preservation as part of Athenaios' *Deipnosophistai* (*Philosophers at Dinner*), and it should be assumed that a far wider range of geographical material would have suffused Poseidonios' *History* had we more sources which cited the provenance of passages cited.

6. *Other extracts concerning peoples and places* (65–75). The final section contains a wide selection of mostly ethnographic passages cited by Strabo, Athenaios, and various scholarly commentators, again illustrating Poseidonios' interest in the inhabited world as the home of human beings and the relationship between man and his environment.

These categories facilitate a distinction between Poseidonios as, on the one hand, the object of Strabo's critique, a renowned geographical thinker in his own right, a major representative of the genre, and one who amply fulfilled Strabo's own definition of geography as the business of the philosopher (Strabo 1. 1. 1, C1–2; see 1); and, on the other hand, the source of many observations and theories which would be drawn upon by later writers in support or otherwise of their own propositions, or simply as a treasure trove of knowledge. Throughout, the importance of reading the world as Poseidonios did, through multiple scholarly and interpretative lenses, in order to achieve the fullest possible understanding of the inhabited world as not only a physical entity, both terrestrial and celestial, but also the habitat of human beings, is paramount.[7] Strabo claimed that 'what lies beyond our inhabitable world is not for the geographer to consider' (2. 5. 34), a wide enough scope to claim for the subject, one might think. Poseidonios, the extraordinary polymath whose expertise and knowledge spanned even beyond Strabo's world, nevertheless still had as his core mission the understanding of the cosmic order in relation to the existence, behaviour, and ethics of man. It is no surprise that Strabo found here so much to interest him and to admire.

The standard edition of Poseidonios' fragments is by Edelstein and Kidd (below), from which the extracts presented below have been selected and re-translated by the present author with the exceptions of (*a*) **46**, adapted from Kidd, and (*b*) passages from Strabo, which are either adapted from Roller's version[8] or, if enclosed within raised points (·), translated by Graham Shipley.

Within each section, extracts are arranged by date.

---

[6] On this see Clarke 1999, *passim.*
[7] Boechat 2018, for P. as innovative in drawing together scientific and descriptive geographies.
[8] Roller 2014. Reproduced with the permission of the translator and Cambridge University Press.

SELECTED FURTHER READING

Boechat, E. M. B. (2018), 'Geographical systems in the first century BC: Posidonius' F 49 E-K and Vitruvius' On Architecture VI 1. 3–13', *Prometeus*, 11: 37–61.

Clarke, K. (1999), *Between Geography and History: Hellenistic Constructions of the Roman World*. Oxford. [Esp. ch. 3 (pp. 129–92).]

—— (2007), 'Les fragments de Posidonios chez Athénée', in D. Lenfant (ed.), *Athénée et les fragments d'historiens: actes du colloque de Strasbourg (16–18 juin 2005)* (Paris), 291–302.

*Dowden, K. (2013), 'Poseidonios (87)', in *BNJ*².

*Edelstein, L., and Kidd, I. G. (1989), *Posidonius*, 2nd edn, i: *The Fragments*. Cambridge. [Texts in Greek and Latin.]

*Kidd, I. G. (1988), *Posidonius*, ii: *The Commentary*. Cambridge.

*—— (1999), *Posidonius*, iii: *The Translation of the Fragments*. Cambridge.

Laffranque, M. (1964), *Poseidonios d'Apamée: essai de mise au point*. Paris.

Marcotte, D. (1998), 'La climatologie d'Ératosthène à Poséidonios: genèse d'une science humaine', in G. Argoud and J.-Y. Guillaumin (eds), *Sciences exactes et sciences appliquées à Alexandrie* (Saint-Étienne), 263–77.

Reinhardt, K. (1926), *Kosmos und Sympathie: neue Untersuchungen über Poseidonios*. Munich.

Schmidt, K. (1980), *Kosmologische Aspekte im Geschichtswerk des Poseidonios*. Göttingen.

Villani, D. (2009), 'La Méditerranée, l'Océan et l'oikouménè dans l'œuvre de Posidonius et à travers le personnage de Pompée', *Pallas*, 79: 283–93.

Yarrow, L. M. (2005), *Historiography at the End of the Republic: Provincial Perspectives on Roman Rule*. Oxford.

A. PRINCIPLES AND PRACTICE OF GEOGRAPHY

1   Strabo 1. 1. 1, C1–2: *Nature of geography*[9]

·We consider that geography is part of the business of a philosopher, if anything is. . . . For the first men bold enough to grasp it were such as Homer, Anaximandros of Miletos, Hekataios—his *(fellow)* citizen, as Eratosthenes also says—as well as Demokritos, Eudoxos, Dikaiarchos, Ephoros, and several others; and those who came after them, Eratosthenes, Polybios, and Poseidonios, were still philosophers (*practising geography*).·[10] Great learning, which alone makes such a work possible, is attained by no one other than someone who carefully examines both human and divine matters,

---

[9] Strabo's geographical tradition seems dominated by scientific figures, such as a selection of Presocratic cosmologists, and Hl scholars such as Eratosthenes and Eudoxos of Knidos. However, Strabo's placing of Homer at the head of this scholarly tradition, and his introduction of Polybios as Poseidonios' direct predecessor, make clear the much broader intellectual context within which geographical thought developed, particularly suited to the polymathic interests of Poseidonios.

[10] This, the beginning of Strabo's *Geography*, and his succeeding chapters on Eratosthenes' geographical predecessors (though S. focuses mainly on Homer), probably give a good indication of how E.'s own opening pages were structured (Roller 2010, 111).

knowledge of which, it is said, is scholarship. Thus the manifest usefulness (*of geography*) for political activities and for those of commanders, as well as the understanding of the heavens and things on the earth and sea—animals, plants, and fruits, whatever is to be seen in each place—assumes the same type of man as the one who gives consideration to the art of life and happiness.

2 **Strabo** 2. 2. 1–2. 3. 8, C94–104: *Poseidonios' geography*

Theory of zones

2. (1) Let us see what Poseidonios says in his *On the Ocean*.[11] In it he seems to concern himself for the most part with geography, as is fitting, but also somewhat mathematically.[12] It is not out of place to treat a few things that he has said, some of it now, and the remainder in the sections, as it occurs, and to have a certain standard. It is proper in geography to assume that the Earth as a whole is sphere-shaped—just as the heavens—and to accept what follows from this assumption: that there are five zones.[13]

(2) Poseidonios says that the division into five zones originated with Parmenides,[14] but he represents the extent of the burned (*torrid*) zone at almost twice its width, (*lying*) between the tropics, exceeding both of the tropics, and with its edge in the temperate zones. Aristotle defines this zone as that between the tropics, and the temperate zone as that between the tropics and the arctic circles.[15] He (*Poseidonios*) justly objects to both: the burned is said to be that which is uninhabitable because of heat—considering the Aithiopes beyond Egypt—and more than half the width of what is between the tropics is uninhabitable, if that which the equator divides from the other is half the entire width. From Syene, which is on the boundary of the summer tropic, to Meroë is 5,000 (*stades*), and from there to the parallel of the Cinnamon-bearing Land, which is the beginning of the burned zone, is 3,000. All of this distance is measurable, as it is travelled by sea and by land, but the remainder as far as the equator is shown to be 8,800 stades, by means of the measurement of the Earth made by Eratosthenes. The relationship of the 16,800 to the 8,800 would be that of the distance between the tropics to the width of the burned zone. If the smallest of the more recent measurements of the Earth is introduced—which Poseidonios calculates at around 180,000 (*stades*)—this shows that the burned zone is half of what is between the tropics, or slightly more

---

[11] This is our fullest set of insights into the content and approaches of P.'s work *On the Ocean*, although many other unassigned fragments could appropriately have found a place in this work.

[12] An interesting distinction between geographical and mathematical approaches, but the combination is characteristic of many Hl geographers, such as Hipparchos.

[13] The importance of P.'s theory of climatic zones in this work indicates a strong element of mathematical geography and a clear interest in the relationship between celestial and human phenomena, such as physical characteristics. The range of intellectuals cited in this section illustrates how fundamental but contestable the division of the earth into climatic zones was considered to be.

[14] Fr. 43 in Graham 2010.

[15] Arist. *Mete.* 2. 5, implied especially at 362a 31–4 and 362b 25–363a 13.

than half, but in no way equal to it. How could someone distinguish the temperate zones, which are unchanging, by means of the arctic circles, which are not visible to all nor the same everywhere? That the arctic circles are not visible to everyone would not be of use in his refutation, because they must be visible to everyone living in the temperate zone, those alone for whom 'temperate' is used. It is well taken that it is not the same way everywhere, but changeable.

(3) Dividing the Earth into zones, he (*Poseidonios*) says that five are useful for celestial matters. Two of them—those that are beneath the poles and (*extend*) as far as the arctic tropics—have shadows all round. The two that are next, as far as those living under the tropics, have shadows in only one direction, and the one between the tropics has shadows both ways. But in regard to human affairs there are two additional narrow ones below the tropics, which have the sun overhead for about half a month and are divided in two by the tropics. These zones have a certain unusual quality, as they are peculiarly without rain, and are sandy and barren except for silphium and certain fiery fruits that are burned up. There are no nearby mountains that the clouds hit against and make rain, nor do rivers flow through them. Because of this they produce (*inhabitants*) with curly hair, crumpled horns, prominent lips, and flat noses, for their extremities are twisted. The Ichthyophagoi (*Fish-eaters*) also live in these zones. He says that it is clear that these things are peculiar to these zones, since those further south have a more temperate environment and a more fruitful and better-watered land.

3. (1) Polybios[16] makes six zones, two falling under the arctic circles and two between these and the tropics, and two between them and the equator. Yet it seems to me that the division into five zones is natural and geographical: natural in regard to the heavens and the conditions of the atmosphere, and in regard to the heavens, because of the shadows all round, the shadows in only one direction, and the shadows both ways. This is the best way to distinguish them. One can also determine the appearances of the stars, and thus by a kind of rough division they undertake their alterations. In regard to the conditions of the atmosphere—because the conditions are judged in regard to the sun—they are affected by three significant differences that influence animals, plants, and everything else beneath the air or in it: too much heat, a lack of it, or a moderate amount. These conditions are properly determined by the division into zones, for the two chilled ones suggest the absence of heat, and indicate a single quality to the atmosphere, the temperate ones are similar in having a single moderate quality, and the remaining single burned one has the remaining (*condition*).

It is clear that this division is geographical. Geography seeks to determine by boundaries the section of the temperate zone in which we live. On the west and east the limit is the sea, but on the south and north it is the air, for in between it is temperate enough for plants and animals, but beyond it is disagreeable, because of an excess or lack of heat. Because of these three distinctions it is necessary to make the division

---

[16] Polyb. 34. 1. 14.

into five zones. The sphere of the Earth is cut in two by the equator, into the northern hemisphere, where we are, and the southern, indicating the three distinctions. At the equator and the burned zone it is uninhabitable because of heat, and at the pole because of cold, but the middle (*regions*) are temperate and inhabitable. Whoever adds the (*zones*) beneath the tropic does not apply the analogy of these five, or make use of a similar distinction (*diaphora*), but seems to have zones that employ national distinctions (*ethnikai diaphorai*): for one is the Aithiopic (*zone*), another the Skythian and Keltic,[17] and the third the intermediate.

(2) Polybios[18] is not correct in making the boundary of some of his zones the arctic circles: the two that fall under them and the two between them and the tropics. It has been stated that variable signs cannot define invariables. The tropics must not be used as the boundaries of the burned zone, which also has already been said. Clearly when he divides the burned zone into two parts, he does not appear to have been moved by any careless thought, since because of this we naturally use the equator to divide the entire Earth in two: the northern hemisphere, and the southern. It is clear that the burned zone is divided according to this sectioning, conveniently making each of the hemispheres composed of three entire zones, each corresponding to the one in the other hemisphere. Such sectioning makes a division into six zones, but the other not at all. If, at any rate, the Earth were cut in two through the poles, each of the hemispheres—the western and eastern—could not easily be cut into six zones, but five would be sufficient, for the similarity of the two sections of the burned zone, which are created by the equator and their contiguousness, makes sectioning of them superfluous and unnecessary. Although the temperate and cold zones are alike in form, they are not contiguous. Thus, if the entire Earth is conceived as such hemispheres, it is sufficient to divide it into the five.

If, as Eratosthenes says, that which lies under the celestial equator is temperate—and Polybios[19] agrees with this opinion, although he adds that it is the highest part, and because of this it is rainy, since in the Etesian season the clouds from the north frequently strike against the heights there—it would be much better to consider it a third, narrow, temperate zone, than to introduce two tropical ones. In agreement is what Poseidonios has recorded in regard to these matters: that the horizontal movement of the sun is quicker, and also that from east to west, for movement at the same speed is quicker where the circle is greater.

(3) Poseidonios resists Polybios[20] for saying that the inhabited region under the equator is the highest,[21] for (*he himself says that*) no high point appears on a sphere because of its uniformity, and it is not mountainous under the equator, but rather a

---

[17] These peoples are three of the four stock representatives of different quarters of the inhabited world. See *Nik.* 167–74 for the Kelts as inhabiting the west, the Indians the east, the Aithiopes the south, and the Skythians the north.

[18] Polyb. 34. 1. 15.   [19] Polyb. 34. 1. 16.   [20] Polyb. 34. 1. 17.

[21] i.e. the celestial equator. Here, as elsewhere, P. is seen to be in lively debate with other intellectuals on both geographical and other issues—both theoretical and factual.

plain at a level that is about equal with the surface of the sea; and that the rains that fill the Nile come from the mountains of Aithiopia. Although he (*Poseidonios*) said these things, he is in agreement elsewhere, saying that he suspects that there are mountains under the equator and that the clouds from both temperate zones strike against them and make the rains. Yet the inconsistency is obvious. But if one admits that it is mountainous under the equator, something else seems to emerge, for they say that the Ocean flows all round. How, then, can they place mountains at its centre, unless they intend to speak of certain islands? However this may be, it falls outside the subject of geography, and perhaps it should be given to someone who proposes a treatise on the Ocean.

(4) Recording those who are said to have circumnavigated Libyē, he (*Poseidonios*) says that Herodotos believes that certain men sent by Darius[22] accomplished the circumnavigation, and that in a dialogue Herakleides of Pontos[23] also has a Magos who has come to the court of Gelon assert that he has circumnavigated (*it*).

Eudoxos of Kyzikos

saying that these are unattested, he discusses a certain Eudoxos of Kyzikos, an envoy and *spondophoros* for the festival of Kore who is reported to have come to Egypt at the time of the second Euergetes (*Ptolemaios VIII*). He became associated with the king and those around him, especially in the matter of the voyages up the Nile, for he was inclined to wonder at unusual places, about which he was not uninformed. It happened that a certain Indian was brought to the king by the guards of the Arabian recess, who said that he had been found half dead, the only survivor of a ship, but who he was and where he came from was unknown, since they did not understand his language. He was given to those who could teach him Hellenic. When he had learned it, he described how, while sailing from Indike, he was shipwrecked due to an error, and although he was saved, he lost his shipmates through starvation. Upon being disbelieved he offered to lead an expedition to the Indians with those selected by the king, among whom was Eudoxos.

He sailed with presents and came back with a return cargo of aromatics and precious stones, some of which the rivers bring down with pebbles and others that are found by digging, solidified from liquid just as our own crystals. But he was deceived in his hopes since Euergetes took the entire cargo. After he died, his wife Kleopatra (*III*) succeeded to the rule, and Eudoxos was sent out again by her with greater preparations. On his return he was driven by winds beyond Aithiopia. Carried to certain places, he won over the people by sharing grain, wine, and preserved fruit—for they

---

[22] As noted by Roller, the circumnavigation of Libyē referred to by Herodotos at 4. 42 is that organized by Necho. Strabo seems to have conflated and confused the various attempts at this circumnavigation noted by H., including an unsuccessful bid by the Persian Sataspes, sent by Xerxes (4. 43), and the expeditions down the Indus sponsored by Darius himself (4. 44).

[23] Fr. 139 in Schütrumpf 2008.

had no such things—and in return obtained water and guides. He also recorded some of their words. He found the end of a prow, in wood, from a shipwreck, which had a horse carved on it, and he found out that this wreckage had come from those sailing from the west, and took it with him when he returned on his journey home. Safely back in Egypt, with Kleopatra no longer reigning, but her son, he again had everything taken away from him, for it was discovered that he had stolen many things. He brought the end of the prow to the market and showed it to the ship-owners, who realized that it belonged to the Gadeiritai (*men of Cádiz*), for although their merchants sent out large ships, poor men would have small ones that they called 'horses' from the devices on the prows, and would sail in fishing voyages round Maurousia as far as the Lixos river. Some of the ship-owners recognized that the end of the prow was from one that had sailed rather far beyond the Lixos river and had not survived.

Putting all this together, Eudoxos realized that a circumnavigation of Libyē was possible. He went home, and gathering all his property he set forth. First he went to Dikaiarcheia and then Massalia (*Marseille*), and then successive coastal places as far as Gadeira (*Cádiz*). Everywhere he made a great amount of noise and conducted business. Constructing a large ship along with two rowed barges like those used by pirates, he put on board music girls, physicians, and other artisans and set sail to Indike, driven on the high seas by the Zephyroi (westerly winds). When his companions tired of the cruise, he unwillingly sailed with a fair wind towards the land, fearing the flood and ebb of the tides. And what he feared actually happened, for the ship ran aground, although gently, so that it was not completely broken apart and they were able to save the cargo and most of the wood onto land. From this he was able to construct a third ship, equal in size to a penteconter (*50-oared ships*), and sailed until he came upon people who spoke the same language that he had formerly recorded. He also learned that these men were related to the other Aithiopes and that they were neighbours to the kingdom of Bogos (*I*).

Giving up on the voyage to the Indians, he turned back, and while sailing along the coast he saw an island that was well watered and well wooded but deserted, and made note of it. Safely coming to Maurousia (*Morocco*), he disposed of his boats and went on foot to Bogos, and advised him to take on the sea expedition, but his friends prevailed upon him to the contrary, suggesting that they feared the land might be exposed to intrigue if the route to it were shown to outsiders who might wish to attack it.

When he (*Eudoxos*) learned that it was said he was being sent forth on the announced expedition, but in fact was going to be abandoned on some deserted island, he fled to Roman-controlled territory and then crossed over to Iberia. Again he constructed a rounded ship and a long penteconter, the former to cross the open sea and the latter to explore the coast. He placed on board agricultural instruments, seeds, and builders and set forth on the same coastal sailing. He planned, if the cruise were delayed, to spend the winter on the island that had been previously observed, and to use the seed and its harvest to complete the cruise that he had planned from the beginning.

(5) 'Thus I', he (*Poseidonios*) says, 'have brought the account of Eudoxos to this point.[24] What happened later, those from Gadeira and Iberia probably know.' Yet he says that from all this it is shown that the inhabited world is encircled by the Ocean flowing round it:

> the bonds of a continent do not surround him,
> but he pours forth boundlessly, and nothing defiles him.[25]

Poseidonios is wonderful in all of this, for he believes the circumnavigation of the Magos, of which Herakleides spoke,[26] to be unsubstantiated, as well as those sent by Darius whom Herodotos records.[27] Nevertheless he puts this Bergaian tale in the category of truth, even though it was either fabricated by him or believed from others who fabricated it. First, what can be believed about the Indian's reversal of fortune? The Arabian gulf is narrow like a river, and its length is around 15,000 stades as far as its mouth, which is completely narrow itself. It is unlikely that the Indians sailing outside of it were pushed aside into the gulf while off course—for the narrowness of the mouth would have shown that they were about to go off course—and if they went into the gulf on purpose there would be no excuse about being off course or the uncertain winds. How could they allow all of them except one to be destroyed by starvation? Having survived, how was he able to guide the ship alone, which was not small, since it was of a size capable of crossing the open sea? How could he learn the language so quickly, well enough to persuade the king that he could lead the expedition? Why did Euergetes have a scarcity of that type of leader, since that sea was already known to many? And why did the *spondophoros* and envoy of the people of Kyzikos leave his city and sail to Indike? Why was he entrusted with so important a commission? When he returned, everything was taken from him, contrary to his expectations, and he was in disgrace, so why was he entrusted with a greater shipment of presents? When he returned again and was carried beyond Aithiopia, why did he decide to write down the language, and why did he learn where the piece of prow from the fishing boat had been washed ashore? To learn about this shipwreck sailing from the west would be no accomplishment, since he was about to sail from the west on his return home.

Going, then, to Alexandria, when it was discovered that he had appropriated many things, why was he not punished, but went around questioning ship-owners and

---

[24] Here we find a turning point in the articulation of this passage. Having related at length the narrative of Eudoxos of Kyzikos' travels, Strabo now claims that P. deduces some geographical consequences, not least the existence of an all-encircling Ocean, one of the mainstays of Homeric geography. S. is quick to critique this conclusion as a Bergaian tale (Antiphanes of Berge was famed for implausible stories), and proceeds with an extensive sequence of questions to undermine P.'s theory; it seems likely that, if P. did maintain the idea of the encircling Ocean, he did so on the basis of further scientific evidence, perhaps involving tidal uniformity, rather than simply this inconclusive story. However, this extract does offer a tantalising glimpse into the striking combination of sober mathematical theory with lively story-telling in *On the Ocean*.

[25] The lines are possibly from Eratosthenes' *Hermes* (Kidd 1988, 250, on F 49).

[26] Herakleides of Pontos, fr. 139 in Schütrumpf 2008.   [27] Hdt. 4. 42.

showing them the part of the prow? And was not the one who recognized it wonderful? And the one who believed him even more wonderful, as he went back home on such a hope, and then made a change of residence to beyond the Pillars? But he could not have set sail from Alexandria without permission, especially if he had appropriated royal property. He also would have been unable to sail out secretly, since the harbour and other exits were barred by a guard, such as we know still remains today—I have lived in Alexandria for a long time—although at present, with the Romans in control, it is loosened, but the royal guard was much stricter. Then, when he had gone to Gadeira and built a ship in his royal manner and sailed away, and the ship had been wrecked, how could he have built a third boat in a desolate place? And why, when he continued his voyage and found the western Aithiopes who had the same language as the eastern, did he not attempt to complete the remainder of the cruise—being so frivolous in his fondness of travelling abroad and having the expectation that the unknown remaining portion was small—but gave it up and desired that the expedition be at the hands of Bogos (I)? How did he learn about the plot that was secretly contrived against him? And what was the advantage to Bogos to destroy the man when he could merely have sent him away? Even if he had anticipated the scheme, how could he have fled to safe places?

Although there is nothing impossible in each case, it is difficult and unlikely even with some good fortune. But he always happened to have good fortune, although he was constantly in danger. Having escaped from Bogos, why was he not afraid to sail again along the coast of Libyē when he had preparations capable of settling an island? This is not so far from the fabrications of Pytheas, Euhemeros, and Antiphanes. They can be pardoned, however, since this is what they practise, like conjurors, but how can he (*Poseidonios*) who is precise and a scholar, essentially the first contender, be pardoned? He does not do this well.[28]

Changes in levels of the Earth

(6) The rising and settling that the Earth undergoes at times, and the changes due to earthquakes and other similar things, which we have enumerated, are correctly laid out by him (*Poseidonios*).[29] It is good that he cites Plato[30] on this, and it is possible that the matter of the island of Atlantis is not fabricated. Concerning this, he reports that Solon—having learned it from the Egyptian priests—said that it once existed but

---

[28] This damning judgement on P.'s geographical expertise, setting him alongside notoriously unreliable sources, seems strange given Strabo's avowed admiration for him elsewhere.

[29] *On the Ocean* thus clearly included some discussion of changes resulting from earthquakes, although such material appeared in other works too. The wide scope of topics summarized in the rest of the passage—migrations, the length of the inhabited world, geographical determinism, and continental divisions—indicates, if nothing else, what a diverse work this must have been, in reflection of P.'s own breath of expertise and global vision.

[30] Plato, *Timaios* 24d–25d.

disappeared and was of a size no smaller than a continent. And he (*Poseidonios*) thinks it is better to say it in that way than how its maker made it disappear, as the Poet did with the Achaian wall.[31]

Cimbrian Migrations

He also infers that the Kimbroi (*Cimbri*) and their relatives were driven out of their homeland because of an approach of the sea that happened all at once.

Length of the Oikoumenē

Also, he suggests that the length of the inhabited world—about 70,000 stades—is half of the entire circle on which it is taken, so that, he says, someone sailing from the west along its width will come to the Indians in the same number of thousands (*of stades*).

The continents: human versus environmental geography

(7) He (*Poseidonios*) attempts to find fault with those who divided the continents in such a way—rather than by using (*divisions*) parallel to the equator, which would show the variations in animals, plants, and the atmosphere—because some of them approach the cold (*zone*) and others the burned, and thus the continents are virtually zones. But then he changes again and withdraws his judgement, again approving of the division, thus making it an arbitrary question that serves no purpose.

Like the differences of nationality or language, such an arrangement is not because of foresight, but due to accident and chance. Arts, qualities, and capabilities, once they have begun, are for the most part strong in any latitude whatsoever, and even in spite of the latitudes. Thus some customs of a people are natural, and others due to training. It is not by nature that the Athenians are fond of learning and the Lakedaimonians[32] are not, or even the nearer Thebans, but rather by training. The Babylonians and Egyptians are scholars not by nature but by practice and habit. The abilities of horses, cows, and other animals are not only because of their location but their training. But he confuses this.

Agreeing on the division of continents as it now is, he uses the example that the Indians differ from the Aithiopes in Libyē, for the former are better developed physically and are less burned by the dryness of their atmosphere. This is why Homer, speaking about all of them, divides the Aithiopes into two, 'some where Hyperion (*the Sun*) sets and others where he rises',[33] ⟨But Krates writes 'these where Hyperion sets, and those where he rises'.⟩[34] Yet to introduce another inhabited world, which Homer did not know about,

---

[31] *Il.* 12. 13–33.   [32] The collective name for the Spartans and their free dependants.
[33] *Od.* 1. 24.   [34] Fr. 37 in Broggiato 2001.

is to be a slave to hypothesis, and he (*Poseidonios*) says that it is necessary to emend it to 'both where Hyperion departs', or where he declines from the meridian (*mesēmbrinon*).

(8) First, the Aithiopes near Egypt are themselves divided in two, for some are in Asia and others in Libyē, and not different from one other. Homer divided the Aithiopes into two not because he knew that they were physically similar to the Indians—for Homer probably did not know anything about the Indians, since not even (*Ptolemaios VIII*) Euergetes, according to the tale of Eudoxos, knew about Indike or the voyage to it—but rather because of the division that we discussed previously.[35] We have also discussed[36] the reading suggested by Krates, and there is no difference which way it is read. But he (*Poseidonios*) says that there is a difference, and it is better to emend it to 'both where he departs'. How is this different from 'where he sets'? The entire section from the meridian to the setting is called 'the setting', just like the semicircle of the horizon. This is what Aratos means in 'where the extremities of the settings and the risings mix with one another'.[37] If the reading of Krates is better, it must be said that the one of Aristarchos is also.

Conclusion

So much for Poseidonios. Many of his points we treat appropriately in what follows, especially geographical matters. What is more about nature must be examined elsewhere, or not considered. There is much inquiry into causes by him, in imitation of Aristotle, that our school avoids because of the concealment of causes.

3   Strabo 2. 5. 14, C119: *Observation of the star Canopus at Gadeira*
Similar things are said about the region beyond the Pillars,[38] that the most western boundary of the inhabited world is the promontory of the Iberians called Hieron (*Sacred*), which lies approximately on the line through Gadeira (*Cádiz*), the Pillars, the Sicilian strait, and the Rhodia.[39] The *horoskopeia* (*time-measurers*) the favourable winds in both directions, and the lengths of the longest days and nights (*are the same*), for the longest days and nights have 14½ equinoctial[40] hours. Occasionally on the coast around Gadeira one can see ⟨Canopus⟩. Poseidonios says that from a high house in a city about 400 stades from these places one can see a star which he considered to be Canopus itself,[41] as those who had gone a short distance south of Iberia agreed that they had seen it, as is also the case from examinations on Knidos,[42] since the

---

[35] At 1. 2. 26.   [36] At 1. 2. 24.   [37] *Phainomena* 61–2.

[38] That is, the so-called Pillars of Herakles at the strait of Gibraltar.

[39] The territory of Rhodes.   [40] Lit. 'equidiurnal'. See Introduction, §X. 3. b fin.

[41] A good example of Poseidonian autopsy or eye-witness testimony. P. clearly travelled quite extensively in Spain, although the majority of extant examples relate to time spent at or near Gadeira (*Cádiz*). His point of reference is strikingly vivid in its specificity and immediacy, taking the reader imaginatively not only to the city of Gadeira, but to the viewpoint of a tall house within it.

[42] A Greek city in SW Asia Minor, home to one of the great figures of scientific geography in the late Cl age, Eudoxos of Knidos (Ch. 6 above).

observatory of Eudoxos is not much higher than the houses. It is said that he saw the star Canopus from there, and Knidos is on the Rhodian latitude, as are Gadeira and the nearby coastline.

4 Strabo 2. 5. 43, C135–6: *Klimata and the gnomon*
Also stated better is what Poseidonios says about the Periskioi (*Shadow-abouts*), Amphiskioi (*Shadow-both-ways*), and Heteroskioi (*Shadow-either-ways*).[43] Nevertheless this must be recounted in order to make the concept understandable, as well as in what way it is useful for the geographer, and in what way it is useless. The issue is about the shadows of the sun, and the sun, as it is perceived, is carried along a parallel, as is the cosmos. Thus when each revolution of the cosmos produces a day and a night, because at one time the sun is carried above the Earth and at another under the Earth, they are considered Amphiskioi or Heteroskioi. The Amphiskioi are those whose shadows at noon—when the sun is from the south, according to the angle of the gnomon related to the underlying surface—fall at times in one way, and at times in the opposite way when the sun has gone round to the opposite. This occurs only with those who live between the tropics. The Heteroskioi are those (*whose shadows*) always fall towards the north, as with us, or towards the south, as with those living in the other temperate zone. This is the result for everywhere that the arctic circle is smaller than the tropic. When the former is larger, the Periskioi begin, as far as those beneath the pole. There the sun is carried above the Earth through the entire revolution of the cosmos, and it is clear that the shadow will be carried in a circle round the gnomon. This is why he (*Poseidonios*) called them (*people in the far north*) Periskioi, although they do not exist in regard to geography. That region is uninhabitable because of cold, as we have already said in the comments against Pytheas. Thus one should not consider the size of this uninhabitable region, beyond the fact that those who have the tropic as arctic circle fall below the circle delineated by the pole of the zodiac, according to the revolution of the cosmos, assuming that the distance between the equator and the tropic is four-sixtieths of the greatest circle.

5 Strabo 8. 1. 1, C332: *Poseidonios' geography scientific rather than descriptive*
Having gone over the western portions of Europe—those surrounded by the Inner and Outer Sea—I have systematically covered all the barbarian peoples in it as far as the Tanaïs, but not much of Hellas. I will now discuss the rest of the geography of Hellas. Homer was the first to examine it, followed by a number of others, who have written particularly *On Harbours*, *Periploi*, and *The Circuit of the Earth*, or such others, in which Hellas is included. Still others have published the topography of the continents in separate portions of their general historical works, as Ephoros and Polybios did. ·Others incorporated some discussion of such matters into their work on nature and

---

[43] A fascinating passage in which a pseudo-ethnography of imaginary peoples defined by how their shadows fall is linked to a discussion of zone theory and classification.

on mathematics, such as Poseidonios and Hipparchos.[44]. It is easy to decide about these others, but one must consider the statements of Homer critically.

6   Strabo 10. 3. 5, C465: *Progressive corrections in geography*

Such is Ephoros,[45] but he is better than many others. Polybios praises him enthusiastically and says that Eudoxos[46] did well in regard to Hellenic matters, but Ephoros was the best at examining foundations, kinship, migrations, and founders, and he (*Polybios*) also says that 'we will show things as they are, concerning both the position of places and the distances between them, for this is most suitable for chorography'.[47] But, Polybios, you introduce popular assertions about distances—not only those outside Hellas but also Hellenic ones[48]—and must submit to examination by Poseidonios, Artemidoros, and a number of others.[49]

7   Strabo 11. 1. 5–6, C491–2: *Isthmuses*

(5) Passing from the topic of Europe to that of Asia in geography, the northern is the first of the two divisions, and thus one must begin with it. Its first (*portion*) is around the Tanaïs, which we have established as the boundary between Europe and Asia. This, in a way, is a sort of peninsula, surrounded on the west by the Tanaïs river and the Maiotis as far as the Bosporos and the coast of the Euxeinos that ends at Kolchis, on the north by the Ocean as far as the mouth of the Caspian sea, and on the east by the same sea as far as the boundary region of Albania and Armenia where the Kyros and Araxes rivers empty; the latter flowing through Armenia and the Kyros through Iberia and Albania. On the south it is from the outlet of the Kyros as far as Kolchis, about 3,000 stades from sea to sea through the Albanians and Iberians, and thus it is said to be an isthmus. Those who have pulled the isthmus together, such as Kleitarchos[50]—who says that it is flooded from either sea—are not worthy of mention. Poseidonios says that the isthmus is 1,500 (*stades*), as much as from Pelousion (*Port Said*) to the Erythraian (*sea*). 'I believe', he says, 'that from the Maiotis (*Sea of Azov*) to the Ocean it is not much different.'

(6) Yet I do not know how he can be trusted about uncertain things when he speaks so unreasonably about what is visible,[51] even though he was a friend of Pompey, who made an expedition against the Iberians and the Albanians as far as both seas, the Cas-

---

[44] It is interesting to see P. classified here primarily as a scientific geographer in contrast to the writers of periegetic texts and historians, given his authorship of both types of work (if *On the Ocean* may be considered in some form periegetic at least in concept and content).

[45] Strabo has just discussed Ephoros' evidence on the relationship between Eleians and Aitolians (*BNJ* 70 F 122a).

[46] Fr. 328 in Lasserre 1966.   [47] Polyb. 34. 1. 3–6.   [48] i.e. within Greece.

[49] The notion of an accumulating critical tradition of geographical thought comes through clearly here. It is interesting that Strabo cites P. in this teleological progression not only for theoretical plausibility but also for actual accuracy of content.

[50] *BNJ* 137 F 13.

[51] Strabo is rightly alarmed at P.'s vast underestimate of the Caucasian isthmus, which is the focus of Strabo's attention at the time.

pian and the Kolchian. At any rate, they say that when Pompey came to Rhodes, about to go to war against the pirates—immediately afterward he was to set forth against Mithridates (*VI*) and the peoples as far as the Caspian[52]—he happened to be present at a lecture by Poseidonios, and when leaving asked if he had any suggestions. He replied 'always be the best and pre-eminent above all'.[53] In addition to this he (*Poseidonios*) wrote a history of him, and because of this he should have been more considerate of the truth.

8   Strabo 17. 1. 21, C803: *Isthmuses*
The isthmus between Pelousion and the recess at Heroönpolis is 1,000 stades, but Poseidonios says that it is less than 1,500.

9   Pliny, *Natural History,* 6. xxi. 57–8: *Orientation and climate of India*
(57) . . . Posidonius has measured it (*India*) from the summer sunrise (*i.e. north-east*) to the winter rising (*south-east*), determining that it is opposite Gallia, which he was measuring from the summer sunset (*south-west*) to the winter sunset (*north-west*) and entirely towards the west wind (*in relation to India*). And that consequently the contrary blowing of that wind benefits India and it becomes healthy, as he has taught by convincing argument. (58) It has a different appearance to its sky, and different star risings. The year has a double summer and a double harvest. In the midwinter period between those, it has the blowing of the etesian winds; during our winter, however, the breezes are light there and the sea navigable. It has countless races and cities, if one wished to investigate them all.[54]

10   Kleomedes, *Meteora* (*Caelestia*), 1. 4. 90–131 Todd: *The torrid zone*
(90) Since, as we have stated, the sun approaches the tropics and departs from them quite slowly, and consequently lingers for rather a long time in their vicinity; and since the places below them are not uninhabited, neither are those further in (*i.e. towards the equator*)—for Syene lies under the summer circle (*i.e. tropic*) and Aithiopia further in from it—Poseidonios, taking his keynote from these facts, additionally understood all the latitudinal zone (*klima*) under the (*celestial*) equator to be temperate.[55]

---

[52] A reference to the expedition of Pompey the Great against Mithradates in 66 BC under the *lex Manilia*, but in fact the visit to Poseidonios' lecture in Rhodes was the previous year. Strabo appears slightly confused in his arguments against Poseidonios here, and the chronology of Pompey's autopsy of certain areas is askew with his mention in relation to Poseidonios and this particular geographical problem. The connection in Strabo's mind seems to be that Poseidonios and Pompey were friends and therefore should have shared, even retrospectively, geographical knowledge.

[53] *Il.* 6. 208, 11. 784.

[54] P.'s account of India (see also **14**) is positive and somewhat idyllic, with a double harvest, moderate weather, and prosperity in terms of peoples and places. This sits in dissonance from the idea of India as one of the extremities of the inhabited world, although the double harvests of India had already been observed by Megasthenes and Eratosthenes (Strabo 15. 1. 20, C693).

[55] P.'s interest in zone theory recurs frequently in the unassigned fragments (**10–11, 13, 18–19, 53**), but is explicitly ascribed only to *On the Ocean* at **2 §2. 1**.

(95) And since the well-regarded natural philosophers had asserted that there are five zones on the Earth, he himself asserted that the one they said was 'burned' (*i.e. the torrid zone*) was inhabited and temperate.

(98) For, he says, as the sun spends rather a long time in the area of the topics but the places under them are not uninhabited, neither are those further in than them, how could it not be the case that the places under the equator were not much more temperate? For the sun approaches them quickly and withdraws again with equal speed and does not linger in that zone. And, he says, that, since the night there is equal to the day, (*how could it not be the case that*) it has a duration commensurate with the (*required*) cooling ⟨of the air⟩?

(105) And since this air is in the midmost and deepest part of the shadow, rains and winds will also occur with the capacity to cool the air; for continuous rains are recorded as descending upon Aithiopia in summer, especially at its height, from which the Nile is also understood to be filled up in summer.[56]

(109) That, then, is the direction of Poseidonios' thought. In addition, if that is the case for the places under the equator, the seasons will necessarily occur twice a year in those parts, since, of course, the sun is twice situated overhead there and makes two equinoxes.

(113) Those speaking against this opinion of Poseidonios say that, on the one hand, as far as concerns the sun spending rather a long time in the tropics, this view of Poseidonios must be sound.

(115) On the other hand, the sun withdraws again rather a long way from the tropics, and thus the air under them is cooled rather a lot, and the zones are capable of being inhabited; but it withdraws from the equator, which is midway between the tropics, only a short way and makes a quick return to it.

(119) Moreover, the places under the tropics receive the etesian winds from the frozen (*i.e. frigid*) zones, and these moderate the sun's burning by cooling the air; but these are unable to penetrate as far as the equator, (*or*) if they do they will become hot and burning from the length of their journey under the sun.

(124) As for the fact that the night is equal to the day, this by itself could have no capacity to cool the air there, since the sun possesses untold power and emits its ray towards this zone in a wholly vertical and intense form, as it makes no significant declination from it.

(128) It is understood by the natural philosophers that the majority of the Great Sea has been placed in this latitudinal zone and exists in this central location to nourish the stars. Thus, it seems, Poseidonios in this point seems to go in the wrong direction.[57]

---

[56] P.'s participation in the ongoing debates about the flooding of the Nile is seen also in S42 and at 2 §3. 3, in the one extract explicitly assigned to *On the Ocean*, raising the question of whether this work was quite extensively used as a treasure-trove of Hl scientific theory.

[57] Kleomedes' extensive and detailed critique of P.'s theory on the inhabitability of the torrid zone reveals both that P. was viewed with considerable seriousness by scientific writers and that his arguments were by no means adopted without scrutiny.

11 Kleomedes, *Meteora (Caelestia),* 1. 7. 1–50: *Circumference of the Earth*

Concerning the size of the Earth, several opinions have arisen among the natural philosophers, but better than the others are that of Poseidonios and that of Eratosthenes.[58] The latter demonstrates its (*the Earth's*) size through a geometric (*i.e. geodesic*) approach;[59] that of Poseidonios is simpler. Each of them adopts certain hypotheses and, from the consequences of these hypotheses, reaches the proofs. We shall speak first of those of Poseidonios.

(8) He says that Rhodes and Alexandria lie under the same meridian. Meridian circles (*mesēmbrinoi kykloi*) are those drawn through the heavenly poles and through a point that lies overhead for persons standing on the Earth. Well, the poles are the same for all, but the overhead point is different for different people. Hence an infinite number of meridians are capable of being drawn. So Rhodes and Alexandria lie under the same meridian, and the distance between the cities is agreed to be 5,000 stades. Let it be assumed that this is the case. All the meridians are among the great circles of the cosmos, as they divide it into two equal parts and are drawn through both its poles.

(18) Now, these things being assumed to be the case, Poseidonios next divides the zodiac, which is equal to the meridians—since it too divides the cosmos into two equal parts—into 48 parts, dividing each of its twelfths (*i.e. zodiacal signs*) into four. Now, if the meridian through Rhodes and Alexandria has been divided into the same 48 parts as the zodiac, its sections are equal to the aforementioned sections of the zodiac. For when equal quantities have been divided into equal parts, these parts must be equal to the parts of the (*previously*) divided ones.

(27) Now, these things being first assumed to be the case, Poseidonios next says that the star called Kanobos (*Canopus*) is the brightest one to the south, on the steering-oar of *Argo*. This star is not visible at all in Hellas; hence Aratos does not even mention it in the *Phainomena*. As one travels from north to south, it acquires its visibility at Rhodes, where on being sighted it straightaway sinks below the horizon as the heavens revolve. But when we sail the 5,000 stades from Rhodes and are in Alexandria, this star, when it exactly culminates, is found to have an elevation above the horizon of one-quarter of a zodiacal sign; that is, one-forty-eighth of the meridian through Rhodes and Alexandria. Now the section of the same meridian that lies above the distance between Rhodes and Alexandria must be one-forty-eighth of it, because the horizon of the Rhodians is at a distance of one-forty-eighth of the zodiacal circle from that of

[58] P. is seen here as an influential participant in one key challenge for Hl scientists, namely calculating the size of the Earth, and it is striking to find his method deemed clearer than that of Eratosthenes, who was renowned for his own calculation. The two scientific geographers are clearly seen here as comparable in terms of expertise and authority. Both use a similar method of choosing two places on the same meridian (Alexandria and Syene for Eratosthenes; Alexandria and Rhodes for P., perhaps betraying his adoption of the latter as his home) and calculating the distance between the two points by using the position of a celestial body (the sun and the star Canopus, respectively) in relation to the two places, from which the entire circumference can be extrapolated.

[59] See Bowen and Todd 2004 ad loc. for this meaning.

the Alexandrians. Therefore, since the part of the Earth that lies under this section is agreed to be 5,000 stades, those (*parts*) lying under the other sections are also 5,000 stades.

(44) And thus the great circle of the Earth is found to be four and twenty myriads (*240,000, sc. stades*), if those from Rhodes to Alexandria are 5,000; if they are not, (*the figure will be*) in proportion to the (*actual*) distance. This is Poseidonios' approach to the size of the Earth, but that of Eratosthenes has a more geodesic approach and is agreed to be somewhat less clear.

12 **Agathemeros i. 2:** *Shape of the oikoumenē*
Demokritos, a man of great experience, was the first to perceive that the Earth (*i.e. the inhabited part*) is oblong, with a length one and a half times its breadth. Dikaiarchos the Peripatetic agreed with this; but Eudoxos (*made*) the length double the breadth, Eratosthenes more than double; Krates made it a semicircle, Hipparchos a trapezium, others the shape of a tail. Poseidonios the Stoic made it sling-shaped: broad in the middle from south to north, narrow to east and west, but broader towards the Euros (*south-east wind*), in the parts towards India.[60]

13 **Achilles Tatius,** *Introduction to Aratos' Phainomena,* 31: *Number of zones*
Parmenides of Elea was the first to put forward a convincing theory of zones. But there was much disagreement over their number amongst those who came after him. For some said there were six, such as Polybios and Poseidonios, both of whom split the torrid zone into two parts, but others accepted that there were five, such as Eratosthenes and many others, whom we ourselves have followed.

14 **Solinus,** *Collection of Memorable Things,* 52. 1–2: *Orientation and climate of India*
India begins from the Emoda mountains (*Himalayas*), stretching from the Mediterranean to the eastern sea, a most healthy country because of the westerly breeze. It has summer twice a year, it gathers in two harvests, and enjoys summer rather than winter winds. Poseidonios located it opposite Gaul.[61]

15 **Eustathios,** *On Homer, Iliad* 7. 446: *Shape of the oikoumenē*
And that, according to Homer, the whole Earth is boundless, that is, it is spherical and circular. But Poseidonios the Stoic and Dionysios say that the inhabited world is sling-shaped, while Demokritos says it is oblong and Hipparchos that it is shaped like a trapezium.

---

[60] P. clearly forms the culmination of this catalogue with the longest and most elaborate entry. It is interesting, given his strong scientific base, that he is cited on the shape of the inhabited world not in terms of geometrical figures, but in terms of comparison with a sling (Strabo 2. 5. 9, C116, uses the image of a cloak) which is then orientated in terms of celestial coordinates, and further clarified in relation to the SE wind and to India. His 'sling' is thus quite precisely located within other geographical frameworks. See also **15–16**.

[61] Cf. **9**. Mommsen 1895 prints *a Medis montibus* but notes that Salmasius (Saumaise) altered the name to *Emoda* on the evidence of Pliny 6. xxi. 56 (see Erat. 101).

16 **Eustathios,** *On Dionysios Periegetes* line 1 (p. 217): *Shape of the oikoumenē*
This (*that the oikoumenē is circular and surrounded by Ocean*) is not true, as it seemed to Herodotos also, when he said that he did not accept those who asserted that the world was circular, as if drawn by a pair of compasses. He (*Dionysios*) notes as a correction 'not completely circular throughout', but clearly elongated, as will be said, like a sling. For the inhabited world is also shaped like this, so Poseidonios thinks.

For this reason also the inhabited world is split into two cones, as Dionysios will say in what follows. Of these, one completes Asia, and the other evens off Europe and Libyē. Of this inhabited sling kind of shape, the sharp corners point towards the east and the west, which he calls 'the paths of the sun', and the broader part lies towards the north and to the south. And so, with the two cones being base-to-base, the sharp ends of the cones lie to the east and west, while the breadth of the bases faces south and north.

17 **Julian of Ascalon,** *Metrological Table:*[62] *Definition of the mile and parasang*
The mile, according to the geographers, Eratosthenes and Strabo, is 8¼ stades.[63] However, according to the prevailing custom of measurement nowadays it is 7½ stades or 750 fathoms or 1,500 paces or 3,000 feet. It is necessary to recognize that today's mile is 750 geometric fathoms, or 875 simple; since 100 geometric fathoms equals 116⅔ simple fathoms.[64]

The parasang is a Persian unit of measurement, but it is not universally held to be the same. Most people consider it to be 40 stades, but Xenophon counts it as 30 stades, and still others count it as 60 stades. Some people consider it even larger, according to Strabo citing the erudite Poseidonios as the authority for his calculation.[65]

18 **Proclus,** *On the Timaeus,* 4. 277d–e (on Plato, *Timaeus* 40a–b): *Elevation of Canopus at Rhodes and Alexandria*
Plato assigned such a movement to the fixed stars. But those such as Ptolemy and Hipparchos before him, who, trusting in observations, gave these stars also a retrograde movement round the zodiacal axis to the extent of one degree every hundred years, ought first to be aware that the Egyptians, who were using observations well before them, and the Chaldaeans who, even earlier still, before they had observations, were taught by the gods, thought the same as Plato about the movement of fixed stars. . . . In addition to them, the phenomena themselves are enough to persuade anyone with eyes. For it is clear that, if the fixed stars moved round the zodiacal pole with a retrograde movement, no small part of the Bear constellation would have to set in those

---

[62] On this problematic text, preserved in different variants, see Geiger 1992, superseding Kidd 1988, 729–31, and Diller 1950.

[63] Strabo 7. 7. 4, C322. 8¼ is probably a mistake for 8⅓ (Kidd). The term *ourgiai* is more usually *orguiai.*

[64] 116⅔ is an obvious correction for the '112' of the MSS. Several other figures in this extract have been corrected.

[65] Strabo 11. 11. 5, C518. Kidd notes that our text of S. does not, in fact, cite P.; but P.'s authority over points of detail and accuracy is visible in many passages (e.g. 6). Here his range of expertise is also stressed—he is erudite in many fields (πολυμαθής–*polymathēs*).

regions; but since the times of Homer it has been called 'ever-bright', and similarly in our times it would have had to have moved more than 15 degrees, and Canopus would no longer appear about the axis of the equator, making a small circle above the horizon for those in the third climatic zone, but shaving the horizon for those in Rhodes, as Poseidonios says.[66] But surely not. The Bear constellation is ever-bright and Canopus retains its same position. So the retrograde movement of fixed stars, which is much bandied about among them, is not true.

19 Symeon Seth, *On the Usefulness of the Heavenly Bodies*, 44: *The torrid zone*
In any case, still now those who live at the equator benefit sufficiently from a temperate climate because of the changing course of the sun, as Poseidonios relates and as those who have come from those regions to our latitudes have told us.[67] Secondly, not only the land under that parallel would have been uninhabitable, but also those nearby because of the excessive nature of the temperature and the lingering of the sun, and this applies as far as 20 degrees away or even more. And the lands after these would have been very few and extremely narrow, that had some small share in a temperate climate. They would all have been useless and unable to produce ripe harvests, with no winter because of the retreat of the sun, and no summer because of its proximity, nor spring because of the lack of winter leading the way, nor autumn because of the lack of summer in advance. The lands beyond these would have been utterly uninhabitable because of the excessive cold not only for men, but also for all living things, nothing short of the Kimmerians.[68] And the whole Earth would have remained uninhabitable on account of the extreme conditions and unsuitability brought by such a movement.

B. GEOLOGY, ETC.

20 Strabo 1. 3. 16, C58: *Earthquakes*
Poseidonios says that in Phoenicia a city above Sidon was swallowed up because of an earthquake, and also that almost two portions of Sidon collapsed, but not all at once, so that not many people were killed. The same activity extended over the whole of Syria, but somewhat moderately. It crossed over to some of the islands, both the Cyclades and Euboia, so that the spring of Arethousa, a fountain in Chalkis, failed, although many days later it gushed out of another mouth. Earthquakes did not cease in parts of the

---

[66] This should be read alongside S11 and P.'s method for estimating the circumference of the earth, which involved the position of the star Canopus (α Carinae) in relation to Alexandria and Rhodes in turn.

[67] For P.'s theories on inhabitability of the torrid zone, see 2 (e.g. §2. 2); 10. Note here the combination of theoretical science and the eye-witness evidence of travellers.

[68] The Kimmerians were a stock far-northern people, sometimes associated with the Kimbroi, but well-known from Herodotos' account of Skythia in book 4.

island until a chasm in the earth opened in the Lelanton plain that vomited a river of fiery mud.[69]

21   Strabo 3. 2. 9, C146–7: *Metals in Spain*
Poseidonios, in his praise of the quantity and quality of the mines, does not desist from his customary rhetoric,[70] inspired by the exaggerations. He says that he does not disbelieve the story that once when the thickets had burned up the earth melted—since it contained silver and gold ore—and boiled over the entire surface, because every mountain and every wooded hill is money, preserved by a bountiful fortune. He says that in general anyone who has seen these regions would call them eternal treasuries of nature, or the infinite storehouse of a government. The land is not only rich, but rich underneath, he says, and for them it is truly not Hades but Ploutos who lives in the regions beneath the earth. This is what he says about these things, in a graceful manner, using much of his language as if from a mine.

In speaking of the diligence of the miners, he furnishes (*Demetrios*) the Phalerian,[71] who says that in the Attic silver mines the men dig as intensively as if they expected to bring up Ploutos. Thus he (*Poseidonios*) makes it clear that their effort and industriousness are similar, cutting the passages at an angle and deep, and the rivers that they encounter in them are often drawn out by the Egyptian screw. Yet the whole situation is never the same for them as for those in Attica, since he says their mining of the latter is like the riddle: 'what they took up, they did not take, and what they had, they lost'. But for those (*in Tourdetania*) it is exceedingly profitable, since one-fourth of that brought out of the earth by the copper miners is copper, and certain private silver miners can take out a Euboian talent in three days. He says that tin is not found on the surface, despite what the historians repeat over and over, but by digging. It is produced both among the barbarians beyond the Lysitanoi (*Lusitanians*) and in the Kassiterides islands, and is carried to Massalia from the Brettanikoi. He says that among the Artabroi, who are in the furthest north-west of Lysitania, the earth blooms with silver, tin, and white gold; it is mixed with silver. This earth is carried by the rivers, and women scrape it away with shovels and wash it in sieves of woven baskets. This is what he says about mining.

22   Strabo 6. 2. 3, C268–9: *Etna*
Aitna (*Mt Etna*) is located right above Katane (*Catania*), which shares most of the effects of the craters, as lava streams are carried down nearly into the Katanaia (*territory of Katane*). A story is repeated there concerning piety, about Amphinomos and

---

[69] P. here offers a rare description of the extremely far-reaching effects of an earthquake, noting, with characteristic precision, the different manifestations of this seismic event in Syria across the eastern Mediterranean.

[70] Strabo indicates that the high rhetorical style of this passage, with elevated language, mythological allusions and word-play, is by no means atypical of P.'s writing. Parallels for the hints at morality in P.'s comments on mining are to be found at **31–2** on the ethical impact of gold and silver.

[71] *BNJ* 228 F 35a.

Anapias, who lifted their parents on their shoulders and saved them, carrying them away from disaster. When, according to Poseidonios, the region around the mountain is shaken, the Katanaia is deeply covered with ashes. The ashes are an affliction at the moment but are beneficial to the territory at later times, making it productive for the vine and capable of bearing good fruits, as elsewhere it is not good for wine. The roots that have been nourished by the ash-bearing fields make the herds so fat, they say, that they choke, because of which blood is drawn from their ears every four or five days, which, as I have said,[72] also occurs near Erytheia. When the lava changes to a solid, the surface of the earth becomes stone to a sufficient depth, so chat quarrying is necessary for those wishing to uncover the original surface. When the rock in the craters melts and is thrown up, the liquid flows over the summit and black mud flows over the mountain. Upon taking a solid form it becomes millstone, keeping the same colour as when it flowed. Ash is created when the stones are burned, as from wood. Just as ash from wood produces rue (*pēganon*), thus the ash from Aitna has some advantage suitable for the vine.

23 Strabo 7. 5. 8, C316: *Bitumen*

In the territory of the Apolloniatai[73] in a certain place called the Nymphaion, a rock that produces fire, and warm bituminous springs flow beneath, seemingly because the bituminous lumps are burned. There is a mine of it nearby on a hill, and what is dug out is filled up again in time, for the earth thrown into the excavation is turned into bitumen, as Poseidonios says.[74] He also speaks of ampelite, the bituminous earth that is mined at Seleukeia in Pieria, as a remedy for infested vines. When rubbed with oil, it kills the animals before they can climb the shoots of the roots. This was also discovered on Rhodes when he was serving as *prytanis* (*a senior magistrate*),[75] but it needed more oil.

24 Strabo 11. 9. 1, C514: *Rhagai*

From the Caspian Gates to Rhagai[76] is 500 stades, as Apollodoros (*of Artemita*) says,[77] and to Hekatompylos, the Parthyaian (*i.e. Parthian*) royal seat, is 1,260. They say that Rhagai (*Fissures*) was named from the earthquakes that occur there, because of which numerous cities and 2,000 villages were ruined, as Poseidonios says.[78]

---

[72] At 3. 5. 4.   [73] Apollonia lies on the Illyrian seaboard in modern Albania.

[74] Note that P.'s detailed observations of a natural marvel are combined with aetiological theory involving the interaction between minerals, soil type, and plant cultivation.

[75] P.'s holding of the key magistracy on Rhodes, that of *prytanis*, is remarkable for one who was not even a native citizen. The date of this magistracy is unclear. This mention brings to life the multi-faceted figure of P. as a high-profile political office-holder, engaged in his adopted community, at the same time as both practical and theoretical scientist.

[76] Rhagai is just S of Tehran in Iran.   [77] *BNJ* 779 F 5a.

[78] Although P. is cited here for the number of cities and villages in Parthia destroyed by earthquakes, it is possible that the explanation for the name of Rhagai is also his, given his interest elsewhere in etymologies (65, 71).

25   **Strabo** 13. 1. 67, C614–15: *Bricks*

They say that in Pitane bricks float on water, as also occurs on an islet in Tyrrhenia (*Tuscany*), for the earth is lighter than an equal bulk of water, so it floats. Poseidonios says that in Iberia he saw bricks moulded from a clayey earth, by which silver plate is cleaned, and they floated.[79]

26   **Strabo** 16. 1. 15, C743: *Naphtha*

A large amount of asphalt is produced in Babylonia, about which Eratosthenes says that the liquid kind, which is called naphtha, is found in Sousis, but the dry kind, which can be solidified, is in Babylonia. . . . Others say that the liquid kind also occurs in Babylonia. . . . Poseidonios says that some of the naphtha springs in Babylonia are white while others are black, and that some of those, I mean those that are white, have liquid sulphur—these attract the flames—and the black have liquid asphalt, which is burned in lamps instead of oil.[80]

27   **Strabo** 16. 2. 42–3, C764: *Asphalt in the Dead Sea*

(42) . . . The asphalt is a lump of earth that is moistened by heat which comes up and is dispersed, and then changes again into a hard solid substance because of the cold, which is the kind of water that the lake has. Then it must be cut and chopped, and it floats on the surface because of the nature of the water, due to which, as we said, there is no need for divers, and no one going into it can be immersed but is raised up. They sail to the asphalt on rafts, and cut it up and carry away as much as they can.

(43) Such is the way that it happens. Poseidonios says that the people are sorcerers and pretend to be enchanters, using urine and other foul liquids, which they pour over the asphalt and then squeeze.[81] It then solidifies and is cut. But it is possible that there is something useful in urine, such as *chrysokolla*, which is produced in the bladder when there are stones and in the urine of children.

28   **Strabo** 16. 4. 20, C779: *Aromatic salt*

·There are also fragrant salts among the Arabs, according to Poseidonios.·

29   **Seneca the Younger,** *Natural Questions* 6. 21. 2: *Classification of earthquakes*

According to Posidonius there are two types of earthquake. Each has its own name: one is *succussio* (*a violent shock from below*), when the earth is shaken and moved both upwards and downwards; the other is *inclinatio* (*leaning*), by which it rocks to one side or the other like a ship.

---

[79] Although P. is, as an expert on Spain, cited by Strabo for the Iberian parallel, it seems likely that he also knew about the floating bricks found in Pitane (on the Elaitic gulf in W. Turkey).

[80] P. here offers a remarkably detailed set of observations on the different properties of liquid naphtha (petroleum) as opposed to dry bitumen.

[81] This is a classic instance of the tension between superstitious and scientific explanations.

30   Seneca the Younger, *Natural Questions* 6. 24. 6: *Sidon*

Thucydides says that around the time of the Peloponnesian war, the island of Atalanta was crushed, either entirely or at least the majority of it. If you believe Posidonius, the same happened to Sidon. Nor is there any need for authorities to back this up: for we ourselves recall that when lands are torn asunder by internal movement locations are split apart and plains cease to exist.

31   Athenaios 6. 23–5, 233d–234c: *Corrupting effect of gold and silver*[82]

(23) By way of example, to be sure, there are places where this kind of metal is found on the surface, since, in the extremities of the inhabited world, even ordinary streams bring down grains of gold which women or physically feeble men rub with sand and sift, and after washing it they bring it to the melting-pot. This is the case among the Elouettioi (*Helvetii*),[83] as my friend Poseidonios says,[84] and among some other Keltoi.

Furthermore, the mountains which used to be called Rhipaia,[85] then later named Olbia, and today Alpia—part of Galatia—flowed with silver whenever a forest fire broke out spontaneously. However, the majority of this metal is found by deep and laborious mining according to Demetrios of Phaleron, since greed hopes to draw up from the recesses of the Earth Plouton (*Pluto*) himself. Indeed, in a piece of wit, he declares that 'men often let go of visible benefits for the sake of what is uncertain; but they fail to get what they expected, and let fall what they had, unfortunate in the manner of a riddle'. (24) But the Lakedaimonians, as Poseidonios also relates, were hindered by their customs from importing silver or gold into Sparta or acquiring them, they nevertheless did acquire them, but they deposited them with their neighbours the Arkadians. They then proceeded to make enemies of them instead of friends, in order that because of this hostility their disobedience might escape close scrutiny. It is said, to be sure, that the gold and silver which had formerly been in Sparta was dedicated to Apollo in Delphi, but Lysander brought it into the city for public use, and became the source of many evils. At any rate, there is a story that Gylippos, who liberated the Syracusans, starved himself to death because he had been convicted by the ephors of embezzling some of the money introduced by Lysander. It was not easy for a mere mortal to treat lightly what had been dedicated to a god and acknowledged, I suppose, as his ornament and possession.

(25) Among the Keltoi the so-called Skordistai, though they do not import gold into their own land, nevertheless do not pass silver by when they are pillaging other people's land and committing injustices. This tribe is a remnant of those Keltoi who attacked the Delphic oracle under the command of Brennos, but a leader named Bathanattos resettled them in the regions round the Istros (*Danube*); from him also the road by

---

[82] On this see Moret 2012.   [83] The Helvetii lived roughly where modern Switzerland is.

[84] An explicit sign of Athenaios' affiliation with 'my' Poseidonios.

[85] 32 suggests that this identification of the mythical Rhipaian mountains with the Alps stems from P. See 75 for another example of mythical geography (the location of the Hyperboreans) being located here.

which they returned home is called the Bathanattia, and they call his descendants Bathanattoi still even today. These men too have forsworn gold and do not bring it into their native towns, because through it they have suffered many terrible ills; but they do use silver, and for its sake commit many terrible acts. And yet surely they ought not to have banished the particular type of metal that was stolen, but rather the impiety which committed the sacrilege.[86] For if they had not brought silver into their country, then they have been doing wrong with respect to bronze and iron; or, again, if even these were not found among them, then they would be continually raging in war in order to steal food and drink and other necessities.

32 Eustathios, *On Homer, Odyssey* 4. 89: *Corrupting effect of gold and silver*
Let it be known that the abundance of the aforementioned metals from the more re-mote parts of the non-Greek world, is not unpersuasively composed for Menelaos, if it is true. And the man who reported that at the extremities of the inhabited world even ordinary streams bring down grains of gold is indeed truthful. As for India, let it be passed over in silence. But he says that the ancient Rhipaia mountains in Galatia, later the Olbia, but now the Alpia or Alpeis, according to Poseidonios, when forest fire erupted, spontaneously flowed with silver. The majority of this is found by deep and laborious mining, according to Demetrios of Phaleron.

C. HYDROLOGY, ETC.

For the scope of Poseidonios' *On the Ocean*, see **2**.

33 Strabo 1. 1. 7, C4: *Homer's Okeanos and tides*
A further indication of his assiduousness is that he (*Homer*) was not ignorant of the flood tide and the retreat of the Ocean, speaking of 'the Ocean flowing back'[87] and 'three times a day it goes up, and three times it is swallowed back'.[88] Even if it is 'three times' and not 'twice'—perhaps he strayed from the record or there is an error in the text—the idea is the same. 'Soft-flowing'[89] also has some suggestion of the flood tide, which has a gentle approach without a totally violent flow. Poseidonios conjectures that when he (*Homer*) speaks of the covering of the headlands and the laying of them bare, as well as saying that the Ocean is a river, and (*speaks of*) its flow, he is describ-ing the flood tide. His first suggestion is good but the second is not, for the approach of the flood tide is not like the flow of a river, and the retreat is even less similar.[90]

---

[86] The observation that it is neither gold nor silver that has a corrupting effect but rather the acquis-itive behaviour associated with them offers a good example of P.'s breadth of thinking, combining ethnography, history, and ethics.
[87] *Il.* 18. 399; *Od.* 2. 65.   [88] *Od.* 12. 105.   [89] *Il.* 7. 422; *Od.* 19. 434.
[90] P.'s interest in tides is evident in the extant fragments (33–4, 36–7). This is hardly surprising in the author of a work entitled *On the Ocean*. Note also, as elsewhere in these extracts from P., the persistent interest in the exposition of Homeric geography (see also Introduction, §VI. 1. a, §VI. 3, §VI. 4. c fin., etc.).

34 Strabo 1. 1. 8–9, C5–6: *General*

(8) ... This[91] agrees better with the properties of the Ocean concerning its ebbing and flooding. Everywhere the same characteristic—or one not greatly varying—is enough for the changes of height and diminution, as if one open sea (*pelagos*) and one cause produced the movements.

(9) ·Hipparchos is not credible when he rebuts this view (*that the oikoumenē is surrounded by water*) on the grounds that the entire Ocean does not show similar characteristics, and that, even if this point were conceded, it would not follow from it that the entire encircling Atlantic open sea (*pelagos*) was connected. For the dissimilar characteristics he cites Seleukos of Babylon as a witness.· For further discussion about the Ocean and the flood tides we put forth Poseidonios and Athenodoros,[92] who have examined the matter sufficiently. In regard to this, I say that at present it is better to assume this homogeneity, and that the heavenly bodies will better be held together by the rising of vapour if the moisture is scattered all around.

35 Strabo 1. 3. 9, C53–4: *Sea of Sardinia*

Thus it is possible that the open sea could be completely silted up, beginning at its shore, if the influx from the rivers were continuous. This would happen even if we were to assume that the Pontos is deeper than the Sardinian open-sea (*pelagos*), which is said to be the deepest that has been measured, about 1,000 *orguiai* (*fathoms*), as Poseidonios says.[93]

36 Strabo 1. 3. 12, C55: *Tides, etc.*

The flooding and ebbing of the tides has been sufficiently discussed by Poseidonios and Athenodoros.[94] Concerning the rushing back of straits, which is a more scientific discussion than appropriate in this treatise, it is sufficient to say that there is no single explanation ...

37 Strabo 3. 3. 3–4, C153: *Lusitania*

Its (*Lusitania's*) length is 3,000 stades and its width much less, created between the eastern side and the coast that lies opposite. The eastern side is high and rugged, but the territory lying below is all plain as far as the sea, except for a few mountains that are not large. Because of this Poseidonios says that Aristotle[95] is incorrect in saying that this and the Maurousian (*Moroccan*) coasts are the reason for the flood and ebb

---

[91] The notion, which Strabo has just discussed, that the Atlantic is a single sea, not divided by some land mass.

[92] *BNJ* 746 F 6a.

[93] 1,000 fathoms is notionally 10 stades, a little over a mile. Although P. is only explicitly ascribed the point concerning the depth of the Sardinian sea, it is quite likely that the notes concerning silting and the comparison with the Black Sea were also his. This a rare allusion to measuring the depth of the sea, presumably with a weighted rope or with chains. Kidd ad loc. (his F 221), seems to doubt the report; but see the Introduction, §III. 3. e.

[94] *BNJ* 746 F 6b.

[95] Fr. 680 in Rose 1967.

tides,[96] and that the flowing back of the sea is because of the height and ruggedness of the capes, which thus receive the waves strongly and give them back with equal force. It is in fact the contrary—for the most part it is sandy and low—as he (*Poseidonios*) says correctly.

(4) The land of which we speak is prosperous with large and small rivers flowing through it, all of which come from the eastern parts and are parallel to the Tagos. Most of them can be sailed upstream and have large amounts of gold dust. The best known of the rivers beyond the Tagos are the Mounda, which can be sailed upstream short distances, and similarly the Ouakoua (*Vacua*). After these is the Durius, which flows from far away and passes Numantia and many other Keltiberian and Ouakkaian settlements. It is navigable by large boats for about 800 stades inland. Then there are other rivers. After them, there is the Lethe, which some call the Limaia and others the Belion. It also flows from the Keltiberians and the Ouakkaioi, and after it is the Bainis—some say Minios—the largest by far of those in Lysitania, navigable inland for 800 stades. Poseidonios says that it flows from the Kantabroi. An island lies off its mouth, and there are two breakwaters for anchorages. The nature of these rivers is worthy of praise, because they have high banks that are sufficient to receive the sea within its channel at high tide, without overflowing or wandering into the plains. This was the limit of Brutus' campaign, although further on there are many other rivers, parallel to those mentioned.

38   Strabo 3. 5. 7–9, C172–5: *Wells at Gadeira; Seleukos of Babylon*
(7) Polybios[97] says that there is a spring in the Herakleion at Gadeira (*Cádiz*) that has a descent of only a few steps to drinkable water, and that it acts in reverse to the ebb and flow of the sea, ceasing at the time of the flood and filling at the ebb. The reason for this is that the air driven out of the depths of the Earth to the surface, if covered by a flood with the approach of the sea, is cut off from its proper outlets and goes back into the interior, blocking up the passages of the spring and creating a lack of water. When it is made bare again, the passages of the spring are set free, so that it gushes forth easily. Artemidoros speaks against him and gives his own reason, recalling the opinion of Silanos the historian,[98] but he does not seem to me to have said anything worth recording, since both he and Silanos are laymen in these matters.

Poseidonios notes that this account is false and says that there are two wells in the Herakleion and a third in the city.[99] When drawing water from the smaller one it immediately fails, but upon leaving it for an interval the water fills up again. Water can be

---

[96] P. is engaged in criticism of Aristotle over the explanation of a particular tidal phenomenon involving the water courses between Spain and Morocco, a key area in Mediterranean geography, where the Mediterranean and Atlantic (or inner and outer seas) come into contact.

[97] Polyb. 34. 9. 5–7.

[98] *BNJ* 175 (Silenos) F 9.

[99] Another example of P.'s critical engagement with the scientific theories of predecessors, here on the subject of the wells at *Cádiz*.

drawn from the larger one for the entire day—although it does diminish, as happens to all wells—yet it fills at night if water is no longer drawn. Since the ebb tide often happens at the time that it is completely full, the locals foolishly believed in the reverse activity. Thus the account that he relates has been believed, and we have accepted it among the paradoxes that are repeated over and over.

I have heard that there are other wells, some in the gardens in front of the city and others within it, but because of the bad condition of the water it is common to have water cisterns in the city. Whether any of these wells demonstrates the conjecture of the reversal, I do not know. If it happens in this way, it must be admitted that the causes are a matter of difficulty. It is reasonable that it is as Polybios says, and also reasonable that some of the passages of the spring, moistened from the outside, become relaxed and thus give the water a sideways overflow, rather than forcing it up along the original channel into the spring. If, as Athenodoros[100] says, it happens that the flood and ebb tides are similar to inhalation and exhalation, then certain flowing waters that naturally have passages discharging out into the open—which we call the mouths of fountains or springs—and other passages are drawn together into the depths of the sea, and assist in raising it, so that at flood tide when the exhalation occurs, they abandon the proper channel and then withdraw again into their proper channel when it (*the sea*) makes its withdrawal.

(8) I do not know why Poseidonios—who otherwise represents the Phoenicians as clever—can charge them with foolishness here rather than sharpness. The day and night is measured by the revolution of the sun, at one time below the Earth and at another visible above the Earth. He says that the movement of the Ocean is controlled by the circuit, like that of the heavenly bodies, since it is daily, monthly, and yearly, in accordance with the Moon. When it is above the horizon at the height of a zodiacal sign, the rise of the sea begins to be seen, visibly approaching the land until its (*the Moon's*) culmination.[101] But with the declining of the heavenly bodies, the sea withdraws little by little until the Moon is at the height of a zodiacal sign above its setting. It then remains at the same place for some time, until the Moon touches its point of setting, and even beyond, until it moves beneath the Earth as much as a zodiacal sign below the horizon. Then (*the sea*) rises again until (*the Moon*) is at the meridian below the Earth, and then withdraws until the Moon goes round to the east and is a zodiacal sign from the horizon. It then remains until (*the Moon*) has risen to a zodiacal sign above the Earth, and then (*the sea*) approaches again. This, he says, is the daily circuit.

Regarding the monthly (*movement*), (*he says*) that the ebb and flood are largest around the conjunction, and then diminish up to when (*the Moon*) is cut in half, increase again around the full moon, and diminish again until the waning half. From then until the conjunction it increases, and the increase is magnified because of the

---

[100] *BNJ* 746 F 6c.

[101] 'Culmination' (*mesouranēsis*, 'mid-heavening') is the moment when a celestial body such as the Moon or a star is due south and at its highest point in the observer's field of view.

time and speed. In the case of the annual (*movement*), he says that he learned about them from those in Gadeira, who said that at the time of the summer solstice the withdrawal and approach increase the most. He conjectures that they diminish from the solstice to the equinox, and then increase until the winter solstice. Then they diminish up to the spring equinoxes and then increase up to the summer solstice.

These periods occur each day and night, with the sea coming up and retreating twice during both these times together, in an order during both the day and night time. Yet how is it that the filling of the well happens often during the ebb tides but the lack of water is not so often? Or often but not the same number of times? Or the same number of times, for are the Gadeiritai not capable of observing closely what happens every day, but observing closely the yearly period from something that happens only once a year? Yet that he (*Poseidonios*) believes them is clear from his additional conjecture, that the diminutions and the subsequent increases are from one solstice to another solstice, each returning back to the other. And the other matter is not reasonable either, that they closely observed things but did not see what happened, yet believed in what did not happen.

(9) He (*Poseidonios*) says that Seleukos—the one from the Erythraian sea—speaks of a certain anomaly in this regularity according to the differences of the zodiacal signs. If the Moon is in the equinoctial zodiacal sign, the properties are uniform, yet in the solstitial (*sign*) they are irregular in terms of both quantity and speed, but in each of the others it is in proportion to (*the Moon's*) nearness. He (*Poseidonios*) says that he spent several days in the Herakleion at Gadeira at the summer solstice around the time of the full moon, yet was unable to see the annual differences.[102] Nevertheless around the conjunction of that month he observed at Ilipa a major difference in the pushing back of the Baitis in relation to what had happened previously. Formerly it did not wet the banks halfway, yet at this time the water overflowed to the point that the soldiers drew water there; Ilipa is about 700 stades from the sea. The plains at the sea were deeply covered by the flood tide as far as 30 stades so that the islands were cut off. The height of the foundation—both of the temple in the Herakleion and of the mole that lies in front of the harbour of Gadeira—was, he says, measured as being covered only by 10 cubits (*pecheis*) of water. If one were to double this (*for the earlier increases*), one thus could present the impression produced by the greatness of the flood tide in the plains.

This condition is recorded to be common along the entire circuit of the Ocean, but he says that the Iber is unique and peculiar, for it floods without rain or snow when the north wind is excessive, and the cause of this is the lake through which it flows, since it is driven from the lake by the winds.

---

[102] The importance of autopsy (eye-witness experience) in P.'s scientific explanations of geographical phenomena (here his theory of tides) is a recurring theme and reinforces the importance of travel alongside scholarly endeavour in the development of ancient geography.

39 **Strabo** 4. 1. 7, C182–3: *A stony plain*

The previously mentioned coast has another marvel in addition to the dug mullets, which is even somewhat greater and will be discussed. Between Massalia (*Marseilles*) and the outlets of the Rhodanos (*Rhône*) is a plain (*Plaine de la Crau*), 100 stades distant from the sea and the same in diameter, and circular in shape.[103] It is called Lithodes (*Stony*) from its characteristics. It is full of stones that can be held in the hand, having *agrostis* (*dogstooth grass*) growing beneath them, which is exceptional pasturage for livestock. Standing in the middle of it are water, salt springs, and salt. All of the territory that lies beyond is towards the wind that is carried across the plain and rushes down, the Melamboreion ('*Dark Northerly*'), which is violent and shuddering. At any rate, they say that the stones are swept and rolled along, and that people are thrown from their vehicles and stripped of weapons and clothing by the force of the wind.

Aristotle says that because of the earthquakes called boilers (*brastai*)[104] the stones are thrown up into view and fall together in the hollows of the region. But Poseidonios says that since it was a lake it solidified during the surging of waves, and because of this it was divided into many stones, just like pebbles in rivers and stones on the shore, and due to this similarity they are smooth and the same size. The causes have been described by both. Both arguments are plausible. By necessity the stones that have come together have not changed from liquid to solid individually. Nor were they formed from the successive fracturing of great rocks. What was clearly hard to explain, Aeschylus, observing carefully or taking it from elsewhere, removed into myth. At any rate, Prometheus, describing to Herakles the roads from the Caucasus to the Hesperides, says:

> You will come to the fearless army of the Ligyans
> and not find fault with battle there, I clearly know, as you are
> courageous. Yet it is fated that your missiles will fail
> you there, and you will not be able to choose
> any stone from the earth, since the entire region is soft.
> Seeing you at a loss, Zeus will have pity on you
> and provide a cloud with snowy round stones
> that will shadow the ground. These you will throw
> and thus easily break through the Ligyan army.[105]

Would it not have been better, says Poseidonios, for him (*Zeus*) to have thrown the stones at the Ligyans himself and to bury them all, rather than to make Herakles need

---

[103] The *Plaine de la Crau* was, as this passage indicates, already by the time of Aeschylus seen as a geographical marvel. P. is seen to be deliberately rejecting the mythological explanation for one grounded in scientific observation and theory.

[104] Cf. Ps.-Aristotle 4 (Ch. 24 below).

[105] Aeschylus, *Prometheus Unbound*, fr. 199 in Radt 1985.

so many stones? Yet he needed so many if the crowd was exceedingly numerous, and thus the writer of myth is more believable than the one who demolishes the myth.

40 Strabo 5. 1. 8, C214–15: *River Timavus*
In the very recess of the Adriatic is a sanctuary of Diomedes that is worthy of recording, the Timauon. It has a harbour, a remarkable grove, and seven springs of drinkable water that empty immediately into the sea in a wide and deep river. Polybios says that all but one are salt water, and the natives have named the place the Source and Mother of the Sea. But Poseidonios says that the Timauos is a river which comes from the mountains and empties into a pit, is carried underground for about 130 stades, and makes its outlet into the sea.[106]

41 Strabo 6. 2. 11, C277: *A volcano*
Poseidonios says that in his own memory,[107] about the time of the summer solstice, the sea between Hiera and Euonymos was seen to be raised to an extraordinary height and remained puffed up for some time, continuously and without a pause, and then subsided. Those who dared to sail into it saw dead fish driven by the current, and some of them were stricken because of the heat and odour, and fled. One of the little boats came rather near, and some of those in it were thrown out, and the others barely escaped to Lipara and at times became senseless like epileptics, later regaining their own reason. Many days later mud was seen appearing on the sea, and fire, and smoke, and dark flames broke out in many places. Later it solidified and became as hard as millstone. The commander of Sicily, Titus Flamininus, made this known to the Senate, which sent (*a delegation*) to make sacrifices to the gods of the underworld and the seas, both on the islet and in the Liparai.[108]

42 Strabo 17. 1. 5, C790: *The Nile*
Starting from such things, it is astonishing that they (*ancient writers*) did not have clear information then about the rains, since the priests rather officiously report in the sacred books whatever reveals any extraordinary information and then store it away. They should have investigated—if they did anything at all—what is investigated still today: why the rains fall in summer and not in winter, and why in the southernmost portions but not in the Thebais and the region around Syene. That the rising is from the rains need not have been investigated, nor did this need such witnesses as Poseidonios

---

[106] The underground river systems of this part of Italy to the N of Trieste were notoriously complex and ripe for geographical as well as poetic attention (cf. e.g. Vergil, *Aeneid* 1. 244–6, on the mouths of the Timauos, Lat. *Timavus*).

[107] The date of this eruption is likely to be 126 BC. P. offers a remarkably detailed description of the sequence of events surrounding this volcanic eruption in the sea around the Liparaean Is.

[108] The procedure for how this event is reported to the senate in Rome, and the details of their response, sending a purificatory delegation, offers a vivid insight into Roman administration in the Mediterranean.

mentions.[109] He says Kallisthenes[110] states that the reason is the summer rains, something taken from Aristotle,[111] and he from Thrasyalkes of Thasos, one of the ancient natural philosophers,[112] and he from someone else, and he from Homer, who calls the Nile 'fallen from Zeus': 'back to the river of Egypt, fallen from Zeus'.[113]

43   Strabo 17. 3. 10, C830: *Rivers in Libyē*[114]

I do not know whether Poseidonios tells the truth when he says that only a few small rivers flow through Libyē, for those mentioned by Artemidoros between Lynx and Karchedon (*Carthage*), he says, are numerous and large. The statement is more truthful in regard to the interior, and the former says the reason for this is that no rain falls in the northern portions, just as they say about Aithiopia. Because of this, pestilence often occurs due to the droughts, as the lakes are filled with mud and locusts are common. He further says that the eastern regions are moist, for the sun passes quickly when rising but the western ones are dry because it turns back there. Moisture and dryness are a matter of abundance or scarcity of water, as well as the effect of the sun. He wishes to speak about the effect of the sun, which everyone defines by the northern or southern latitude. Moreover, the eastern and western regions—speaking in regard to the inhabitable areas—differ according to each habitation and the change in horizons, so that it is not possible to speak generally in regard to an incomprehensible number (*of places*) as to whether the western are moist and the eastern dry. Yet if he were to make such statements about the entire inhabited world and such extremities as Indike and Iberia, perhaps he could make such a decision. But what plausibility is there in giving such a cause? In the revolution of the sun, which is continual and incessant, what would be the turning back? The speed of its movement is everywhere equal. Moreover, it is contrary to perception to say that the extremities of Iberia or Maurousia—those in the west—are the driest places of all, for they have a temperate atmosphere and are greatly abundant in water. And if the turning back is taken to mean that it is the last above the inhabited world there, how does this relate to the aridity? For there, and in the other parts of the inhabited world in the same latitude, it departs for an equal time of night and then returns again and warms the earth.

44   Seneca, *NQ* 2. 26. 4–7: *A volcano*

(4) Why not? Ancestral memory, as Poseidonios has transmitted it, recalls that, when an island rose up in the Aegean sea, the sea foamed during the day and smoke poured from the depths of the sea.[115] Night finally brought forth fire, not continuously but

---

[109] This is interesting not only for P.'s engagement in one of the great debates of ancient geography—why the Nile floods—but also for his scholarly practice of attempting to trace the development of a particular explanation.

[110] *BNJ* 124 F 12b.   [111] Fr. 246 in Rose 1886.

[112] Thrasyalkes fr. 1 in Diels and Kranz 1959–60.   [113] *Od.* 4. 581.

[114] On this fragment, see Shcheglov 2006.

[115] This can be identified as the small island of Hiera in the *Santorini* group of volcanic islands. The later emergence of Thia (see next n.), with which the passage in Seneca is primarily concerned, clearly triggered memories of the earlier eruption mentioned by P. It is striking to see his record described

flashing intermittently like lightning, as often as the heat underground overcame the weight of water lying on top of it.   (5) Then rocks were hurled up and stones, mostly intact, which the blast had driven out before they were burned, but some destroyed and turned to the lightness of pumice. Finally, the peak of a burned mountain broke out and afterwards that rock gained in height and grew to the size of an island.

(6) The same thing happened in living memory when Valerius Asiaticus was consul for a second time.[116] Why have I recalled this? So that it may be clear that fire does not entirely die out even when it is covered by sea, nor is its force prevented from bursting out by the weight of a vast body of water. Asclepiodotus, the pupil of Posidonius, tells that it was a depth of 200 feet that the fire had to rend apart before it emerged.   (7) Now, if that vast force of water could not suppress the force of the flames, as it pressed up from the deep, how much less could the thin and dewy moisture of clouds control fire?

45   Athenaios 8. 7, 333b–d: *Syria*
I know that Poseidonios from the Stoa said the following about a great quantity of fish: 'When Tryphon of Apameia, who had seized the Syrian kingdom and was being attacked by Sarpedon, the general of Demetrios, near the city of Ptolemais, Sarpedon, left abandoned, retreated to the interior with his own special soldiers. Tryphon's men, having been successful in battle, were heading along the sea-shore, when suddenly a sea-wave reared right up in the air to an amazing height and then crashed down to the ground and immersed them all, drowning them underwater.[117] But as the wave retreated, it left behind a huge pile of fish with the corpses. When Sarpedon's men heard about the disaster, they hastened to the bodies of their enemies, and carried off a wealth of fish and made sacrifices to Poseidon, the god of the rout, near the suburbs of the city.'

46   Priscianus Lydus, *Solutions to Chosroës,* 6: *The Red Sea (western Indian Ocean)*[118]
The following question too is asked: why is it that the Red Sea[119] diurnally flows and ebbs, and how do flood tides vary through the Moon; and why is it said that the sea does not increase in volume in flood tides, nor decrease in ebb? Nor again are flood tides brought about by the force of the wind, nor ebb tides by their lack. This is also clear because although great rivers flow into the sea without feedback, no addition of sea-water is apparent.

---

as *maiorum nostrum memoria* (lit. 'the memory of our ancestors'), indicating either that his sources included informal community memory, or that Seneca misrepresents the nature of P.'s note.

[116] The mention of the current consul allows us to identify this with certainty with the emergence of the island of Thia in AD 46.
[117] This miraculous event could possibly have been included in P.'s *Histories,* but would equally well find a place as a *paradoxon* in *On the Ocean,* illustrating the difficulty in assigning fragments to different works.
[118] This text survives only in a poor Latin version. The translation here is lightly adapted from Kidd 1999, 287–94, with the permission of Cambridge University Press.
[119] *Rubrum mare* in the surviving Latin version; i.e. the Erythraian sea or western Indian Ocean.

On the ebb and flow tides in the Red Sea, and such behaviour that occurs in the external Ocean and in other parts of our sea, there are great differences of opinion among the ancients. But from all of them, those who seem to have collected the causes of this behaviour are the Stoic Posidonius, the Assyrian,[120] and those who agree with him, whose opinion has the approval of Arrian. They say that the outer Ocean moves in relation to the cycle of the Moon; the inner sea behaves in unison, for joined only at the Pillars of Hercules it is affected sympathetically as a harbour is by the sea, and receives other special motions.

Posidonius declares that the behaviour of Ocean by the Sicilian straits is also moved four times in relation to the Moon. When the Moon rises to meridian, the sea is borne from west to east and is called the 'descending' current, that is from the Tyrrhenic sea to the Sicilian sea as far as Dungheap[121] at Taurominium (*Taormina*). When the Moon descends from the meridian, the water turns and flows from its eastern limit to the west, and is called the 'outgoing' current. But it is weaker than the first flow ... For the first one sweeps with a strong current, as you would expect, since from the Pillars of Hercules there is a great rush of Ocean because of its narrow path, the land forcing it in. Again the Moon from its sinking goes to the opposite sub-meridian, and the flood tide of the 'descending' current rises. From the opposite meridian the Moon returns to its rising, and again the 'outgoing' current is created.

This happens also with regard to the outer sea: four motions in a complete cycle of the Moon. Flood tides occur in the Moon's advance to the meridian, ebb in her sinking and descents to the horizon. The same phenomenon is observed in gulfs, in the Red Sea in the south, and the Hyrcanian sea in the north and among the people of Gadira (*Cádiz*)....[122]

There occurs also outside the Mediterranean a phenomenon of the Great Sea (*outer Ocean*), such that a flood in much of the mainland and islands reaches 70 stades, as the writer Strabo says, getting it from Posidonius; fields are covered in sea water by flooding to 30 stades, leaving islands; it retreats and leaves quickly dry land, occupied up to that time with water and sailable on.[123]

Each day there are two ebb and flow tides, as I said, in succession. Flood tides which happen monthly much exceed daily tides. At the quarters there is less difference between high and low water; but at full moon and at conjunction it rises into a great sea and much land is flooded with very fast current. There is also a proportionate cycle

---

[120] i.e. Syrian.

[121] This is the literal meaning of *kopria*; Kidd (in a footnote) interprets as 'The shipwreck coast'.

[122] 'In the omitted passage, Priscianus adds that flood tides occur not only at the diurnal lunar meridian, but also on a monthly cycle at full moon and conjunction. He then cites some notorious water phenomena which behave oddly for reasons other than the influence of the heavenly bodies: the Euripus passage, the Hellespont, and Arethusa, the well at Syracuse.' (Kidd's note.)

[123] A garbled version of Strabo 3. 5. 9, C174–5 (Kidd); see **38** §9 above.

each year thus: at each of the solstices there are lower tides and a slower flow; but at equinoxes, the same sort of thing happens as at full and new moons.[124]

Flow tides do not begin immediately at the actual rising of the moon, but only gradually as the moon rises in the heavens; nor again does the culmination of flood tide occur when the moon reaches precise meridian, but gradually as the moon inclines towards another part; and a little after, the water ebbs again until the moon reaches a sign of the zodiac above the horizon of its sinking. Then the water stays put in the same place as long as it takes the moon to reach its own sinking, and still more so until the motion of the Moon reaches a sign of the zodiac below the Earth's horizon. The same phenomena are observed of lunar motion beneath the Earth in relation to the Moon's elevation of one sign from the horizon and flow and ebb tides. But at new moon and full moon extensive flood tides occur, but moving from conjunction and full moon. The annual account is similar: so the floodings proceed in order, with the flow turning to ebb by starting to flow back on itself, and then in sequence mount back on the land.[125]

Tidal flow is so powerful that it even turns great rivers in the opposite direction. They say that this happens to the river Rhenus (*Rhine*) flowing from the country of the Keltoi, and again to other rivers in Spain and Britain. For in Britain, they say, the river named the Tamessa (*Thames*) for four days is reversed, filled up from the sea by the flood tide, so that it seems to be flowing from the sea, going back in the opposite direction.

So Posidonius, the Stoic, seeking out the causes of these things, inasmuch as he became a personal investigator of this kind of reflux, noticed that the Moon was the cause rather, not the sun. For he said that the sun's heat is pure and of the highest grade; so it removes any moisture whatsoever from land or sea, and soon destroys it by fire. But the Moon's heat is not pure but weaker and feebler, and for that reason it is more fertile for earthly things. It cannot consume whatever it encounters, but only raises moisture and makes waves, displacing with its heat, but not reducing because of the weakness of its heat and greater humidity—that is the reason why anything warmed by the Moon putrefies. So when water is warmed in a kettle with a medium heat, at first it swells, rises and overflows, but apply a pure flame and the water is consumed and falls. So too the Great Sea suffers the same effects from the sun, as water in the kettle from too much heat; but from the moon, whatever follows from a weak and initial warmth.

So thus also the water of the sea follows the cycle of the moon, as when the moon is risen and thus weak, there are flood tides, when it turns to the west the sea turns with it in ebb; and the very same process happens when the moon goes under the Earth each day. In the monthly account also the size of the flow corresponds to the quality of the moon, so the maximum rise of water occurs at full moon and conjunction, since

---

[124] 'This is the important information, correctly giving highs at the equinoxes, not at the solstices; and it appears to come from Posidonius' (Kidd).

[125] The translation is uncertain.

at those points the quality of the moon is great; for at full moon the whole of it turned towards the Earth is shining from the sun; at conjunction, illuminated from above by the sun, it offers by its fullness an equal force of quality on what is on the Earth; but when cut in half, it is dim for sea effects. And in the same way each time the moon goes below the Earth, the sequence of flows is none the less, with flood-tide certainly rising by the same lunar system. And he says that a reason for the flowing together of waters is also the cyclical nature of water; so waves follow the moon rising in a semicircular pattern.

And in the same way the cause of annual flood tides is the moon in the equinoxes. For in each of the equinoxes when the sun is in Aries and the Claws,[126] the quality of the moon at the same hour combining with the sun is great; and for that reason if there is a full moon in either of the equinoctial forms, the sun leads it to the opposite. Posidonius reveals that the Great Sea also is at its highest flow in the cycle at the equinox. For at that point the moon, either in conjunction with the sun or at the full, and at its maximum elevation above the sea, has its highest flood tides; but when the sun enters other signs of the zodiac, then when the moon comes into Aries or Libra, it is neither full nor in conjunction. But this also can be from the nature of the moon at that time of year: for it is warm and moist, and it is from those qualities that the water rises. Winter equally follows this moisture certainly,[127] but summer is the opposite of moist;[128] spring and autumn however are noticeably moist and warm. And so the moon too is very like these. But flood tide reaches prime when the moon is at the meridian, and the flows are increased still more when it has passed the mid-point; for in the position on both sides they are stronger through the greater connection of the moon. . . .[129]

Well the nature of water is like that, and not only in the Great Sea but in very many other places too. He maintains[130] that there are tales of a lake like that where if you tie up a man and throw him in, or a beast of burden, they float on top, says he, and don't sink or even cleave the water. The lake is so bitter and salty that no fish survive in it; where you wash clothes by shaking them after wetting. It is clear that this is so because brine creates a dense substance with an earthy quality at its core. There is another lake in the region of the Palaestini, often called the Asphalt lake, and also named the Dead Sea[131] as nothing lives in it; bitumen is produced from it. And in other places in the world, rivers or springs have a natural salty current, and some are warm and turbulent.[132] So the cause of all this has been said to be a fiery element inherent or produced in them, because burnt earth produces different forms of effluence depending

---

[126] Lat. *Brachia*, now part of the constellation Scorpius (β and δ Scorpii) but anciently part of Libra.
[127] 'But it is cold, not warm' (Kidd).   [128] 'Although warm' (Kidd).
[129] There follows an incomprehensible passage; then discussions of evaporation as offsetting the flow of water from rivers into the sea, and of why the sea is salty, which rely directly or indirectly on Arist. *Mete.* (Kidd).
[130] Despite these words, the next passage is based on Arist. *Mete.* 2. 3, 359a 18–24 (Kidd).
[131] Kidd points out that the lake just described is in fact the modern Dead Sea; this one is unknown.
[132] This and the next sentence are a version of Arist. *Mete.* 2. 3, 359b 4–21 (Kidd).

on the degree of combustion [—] is imbued with such qualities through which water is conveyed and filtered, and if originally sweet, or if it is naturally produced from such effusion, in some cases becomes vinegary, in others bitter, and again boils in the heat and turmoil. Research is full of such places gathered from different sources, such as the well said to be in the region of Cissia Persica[133] that is like that. Its effusions offer a variety of aspects. For it is bitumen oil, which they call naphtha, but liquid naphtha.[134] This is how there are such differences in draught liquid.

D. OBSERVED GEOGRAPHY

47   **Strabo** 3. 1. 5, C138: *Sunsets at sea*

These things are possible and must be believed, but not so much what he has said that is in agreement with the common masses. Poseidonios says the masses report that along the Ocean the sun is larger when it sets, with a noise resembling the hissing of the sea, quenching as it falls into the depths, but this is false, as well as that night comes immediately after sunset. For it is not immediate, but a little later, just as on the other large seas. Where it sets into the mountains, the day continues for a long time after sunset because of the indirect light, but there (*on the sea-coast*) it does not follow quickly, although the darkness does not occur immediately, just as it does not in the great plains. Yet it appears to be larger on the seas both at setting and rising, because a great amount of vapour rises from the water. Thus the rays seem broader, as if refracted through a glass, just as when the setting or rising of the sun or the moon is seen through a dry thin cloud, and thus the star appears somewhat red. He says that he proved this false during the thirty days he stayed at Gadeira and carefully observed the sunset.[135] But Artemidoros says that the setting sun (*on the coast at Gadeira*) is a hundred times larger, and that night falls immediately. In examining his analysis, however, one must understand that he could not have seen this at the Sacred Promontory, for he says that no one may set foot there at night and thus no one sets foot there at sunset if night happens immediately. And there is no other place on the coast (*for this*), since Gadeira is also on the Ocean. Moreover Poseidonios and many others contradict him.

48   **Strabo** 3. 4. 3, C157: *A temple in Baitike*

After this is Abdera (*Adra in Spain*), itself a Phoenician foundation. Above these places in the mountainous country, Odysseia is pointed out, with a sanctuary of Athena in it, as Poseidonios has said, as have Artemidoros and Asklepiades of Myrleia.[136]

---

[133] '[T]he area north of the Persian Gulf' (Kidd).   [134] Or white naphtha (Kidd).

[135] P.'s basing of his scientific theory on personal observation or autopsy gives it clear priority, in Strabo's view, over Artemidoros' unobserved speculation, recalling the importance of autopsy in historiography also.

[136] *BNJ* 697 F 7.

49 **Strabo** 3. 4. 15, C163: *Iberian fauna*

The rivers have beavers, but their castoreum does not have the same strength as that from the Pontos, for the medicinal quality of that from the Pontos is unique, as is the case in many other matters. For example, as Poseidonios says, Cypriot copper is the only type that produces cadmian stone, chalkanthite, and spodium.[137] Poseidonios says it is unique to Iberia that the crows are black and that the Keltiberian horses, which are somewhat dappled, change their colour when transferred to Further Iberia. They are similar to the Parthian, for they are faster and run better than the others.

50 **Strabo** 3. 5. 5, C169–70: *Gadeira and Pillars of Herakles*

In telling such stories about the founding of Gadeira, the Gaditanoi remember a certain oracle, which, they say, ordered the Tyrians to send a settlement to the Pillars of Herakles.[138] Those who were sent in order to reconnoitre believed that when they came to the strait at Kalpe the capes that formed the strait were the end of the inhabited world and of the expedition of Herakles, and this was what the oracle had called the Pillars. They took possession of a certain place on this side of the narrows, which is now the city of the Exitanoi, and sacrificed there, but the victims were not favourable so they went back. In time, those who were sent later went on about 1,500 stades outside the strait to an island sacred to Herakles, lying near the Iberian city of Onoba, and believing that the Pillars were here they sacrificed to the god, but again the victims were not favourable and they went back home. On the third expedition those who came founded Gadeira, and they located the temple on the eastern part of the island but the city on the western.[139]

For this reason some believe that the peaks at the strait are the Pillars, others that they are at Gadeira, and others that they lie further outside Gadeira. Some assume that the Pillars are Kalpe and Abilyx—the mountain opposite in Libyē that Eratosthenes says is situated among the Metagonioi, a nomadic people—and others that they are the islets near each (*mountain*), one of which is named Hera's Island. Artemidoros speaks of Hera's Island and her temple, and he mentions another, but neither Mount Abilyx or the nation (*ethnos*) of the Metagonioi. Some transfer the Planktai and Symplegades here, believing these to be the Pillars which Pindar[140] calls the Gadeirid Gates, saying

---

[137] Cyprian copper was known for its medicinal qualities, but here the passage in Strabo relates to the particular qualities of fauna rather than metallurgy. That P. is cited in succession on two very different branches of science hints not only at the breadth of his scholarly expertise, but also possibly at Strabo's methods of citation—did he pick up the point about copper, while consulting a text of P. for the salient detail on animal characteristics?

[138] Gadeira is *Cádiz*; Strabo uses both Gaditanoi and Gadeiritai for their citizens. The Pillars of Herakles formed a key part of the real and imaginative geography of the ancient world, marking the meeting-point of the Mediterranean and Atlantic realms; it is particularly important for P. as the link between the inner sea and the outer Ocean. Many *periplous* texts took them as their start and end (e.g. Ps.-Skylax).

[139] These memories recorded at Gadeira, apparently in Strabo's time, invite comparison with the purportedly C5 voyage (possibly later or non-genuine) preserved under the name of Hanno (Ch. 4 above).

[140] Fr. 256 in Maehler 1989.

that they were the furthest point reached by Herakles. ·Dikaiarchos, Eratosthenes, Polybios,[141] and the majority of the Hellenes show that the Pillars (*of Herakles*) are in the area of the strait.· But the Iberians and Libyans say that they are at Gadeira, for the region around the straits does not resemble pillars. Others say that they are believed to be the bronzes of eight cubits (*oktapēcheis*) in the Herakleion at Gadeira on which the expenses of constructing the sanctuary are inscribed. Those who have ended their voyage and come to sacrifice to Herakles make it loudly known that this is the end of land and sea. Poseidonios believes this is the most plausible explanation and that the oracle and the many expeditions are a Phoenician falsehood.[142]

51 Strabo 3. 5. 10, C175: *Trees in Spain*
He (*Poseidonios*) mentions a tree at Gadeira (*Cádiz*)[143] that has branches which bend to the ground, and whose leaves are often sword-shaped and 8 cubits (*pēcheis*) long but four fingers wide. Around Nea Karchedon[144] there is a tree whose thorns produce a bark from which most beautiful material is woven. I know of one in Egypt that is similar to that in Gadeira in regard to the bending down of the branches, but different as to the leaves and its lack of fruit, for he says (*the one in Gadeira*) has (*fruit*). Thorn material is also woven in Kappadokia, but it is a low-growing herb that produces the thorn from which the bark occurs, not a tree. In regard to the tree at Gadeira, it is also recorded that milk flows from a branch that is broken, but the cutting of the root produces a red liquid. This is it about Gadeira.

52 Strabo 4. 1. 14, C188: *The isthmus of Gaul*
Tolosa (*Toulouse*) is located on the narrowest part of the isthmus that separates the Ocean from the sea at Narbon (*Narbonne*), which Poseidonios says is less than 3,000 stades (*across*).[145]

53 Strabo 6. 2. 1, C265–6: *The form of Sicily*
Sicily is triangular in shape, and because of this it was formerly Trinakria (*Three Capes I.*), although later this was changed and it was more euphoniously called Thrinakia. Its shape is determined by three capes, Pelorias, which along with Kainys and the Pillar of the Rheginoi (*the people of Rhegion*) makes the Strait; Pachynos, which is exposed to

[141] Polyb. 34. 9. 4.
[142] P.'s contribution to the lively scholarly debate over this most important geographical and mythological location is confined to the final comment in terms of explicit attribution. However, it seems likely that much of the preceding discussion, setting out different explanations for the Pillars—some referring to geographical features, some to elements in the temple of Herakles (or Melkart), some based on literary tradition—was part of P.'s narrative. It is interesting to see his scepticism concerning the account of the local inhabitants, and his general preference for explanations backed by observation above those based on legend.
[143] This strange plant seems to be the dragon tree, with its extraordinary red resin, still to be found in the Canary Is.
[144] New Carthage (*Cartagena*) in SE Spain, showing that P. travelled more widely in Spain than only to *Cádiz*, mentioned in several fragments. The tree is generally assumed to be the dwarf palm.
[145] As in 7–8, we find P.'s interest in the length of isthmuses adduced; as before, his estimate is largely inaccurate.

the east and is washed by the Sicilian sea, looking towards the Peloponnesos and the passage to Crete; and, third, Lilybaion, that next to Libyē, looking both towards it and the winter sunset. Of the sides, which are marked off by the three capes, two of them are moderately concave and the third—the one reaching from Lilybaion to Pelorias—is convex and the longest, 1,700 stades, as Poseidonios says,[146] although he adds 20. Of the others, the one from Pachynos to Lilybaion is longer than the other, and the shortest is that next to the Strait and Italia—the one from Pelorias to Pachynos—about 1,130 stades.

Poseidonios reports that the sail round is 4,400 stades. In the *Chorographia*[147] the distances are said to be greater, divided into portions and in miles: from Pelorias to Mylai, 25, the same from Mylai to Tyndaris, from there to Agathyrnon 30, the same to Alaisa, and again the same to Kephaloidion; these are small towns. To the Himeras river, which flows through the middle of Sicily, 18, and then to Panormos 35, to the *emporion* of the Aigestians 32, and the remainder to Lilybaion 38. Then, going round it to the adjoining side, it is 75 to the Herakleion, and to the *emporion* of the Akragantinoi 20, and another 20 [—] to Kamarina, and then to Pachynos 50. Then back along the third side to Syracuse it is 36, to Katane 60, then to Tauromenion 33, then to Messene 30. On foot it is 168 from Pachynos to Pelorias, and on the Oualerian road (*via Valeria*) from Messene to Lilybaion is ⟨2⟩35. Some are more general, such as Ephoros,[148] saying that the sail round is 5 days and nights.

Poseidonios, marking off the island by latitudes, places Pelorias towards the north, Lilybaion towards the south, and Pachynos towards the east. Yet by necessity—since the latitudes are defined by the shape of a parallelogram—the inscribed triangles, especially those that are unequal and none of whose sides fits onto (*a side*) of the parallelogram, would not fit to the latitudes because of their slant.

54   Strabo 6. 2. 7, C273: *Sicilian strongholds*
Poseidonios says that Syracuse and Eryx are like two *akropoleis* (*citadels*) by the sea,[149] and Enna lies between both of them above the encircling plains.

55   Strabo 16. 2. 4, C749–50: *Organization of Seleukis*
Seleukis (*in Syria*) is the best of the previously mentioned portions, and is called *tetrapolis* (*land of four cities*), and is one because of the prominent cities in it. . . . The Seleukis, with the *tetrapolis*, was divided into four satrapies, as Poseidonios says, the same as Koile (*Hollow*) Syria, although Mesopotamia was only one.

---

[146] Strabo cites P. here only for the length of one side and of the island's perimeter, but it is possible that some of the other common techniques here, such as the use of geometrical shapes to bring geographical features to the mind's eye, were present in P.'s account also. On comparing geographical areas to geometrical shapes, see Dueck 2005.

[147] Fr. 13 in Klotz 1930–1.   [148] *BNJ* 70 F 135.

[149] This comment from P. on the geography of Sicily probably came in the context of the C2 slave revolts. It is striking that he adopts the same imagery of the *acropolis* as Polybios (3. 54. 2: the Alps, the *acropolis* to Italy; 5. 8. 6: Thermos, the *acropolis* to all Aitolia; 18. 40a: Ephesos, the *acropolis* to anyone with designs on Ionia and the Hellespontine cities) to designate lofty locations, although the truly precipitous site of Eryx is far more appropriately described in this way than that of Syracuse.

56   **Strabo** 16. 2. 17, C755: *A monster in Koile Syria*
The first of the plains from the sea is called the Makras or Makra (*Long*) plain. Poseidonios records that a dead serpent was seen here whose length was about a *plethron* (*c.100 feet*), and so thick that horsemen positioned on either side could not see one another. Its gaping mouth admitted someone on horseback, and each of its horny scales was larger than an oblong shield.[150]

57   **Strabo** 17. 3. 4, C827: *Apes in North Africa*
(*Maurousia has*) many very large apes, about which Poseidonios says that when he was sailing from Gadeira to Italia he was carried close to the Libyan coast and saw a forest projecting into the sea full of these animals, some in the trees and others on the ground.[151] Some had their young and were giving them their breast, but he laughed when he saw some with heavy breasts, some with bald heads, and others ruptured or showing other such injuries.

58   **Athenaios** 1. 51, 28d: *Vines at Damascus*
That the king of Persia used to drink only Chalybonian wine. Poseidonios says that this could also be found in Damascus in Syria, where the Persians had transplanted the vines.

E. FROM THE *HISTORY*

(In the order of Poseidonios' books, not Athenaios' text.)

59   **Athenaios** 14. 61, 649d: *Pistachios in Syria and Arabia*
Poseidonios from the Stoa writes in the 3rd (*book*) of the *Histories* as follows: 'Arabia and Syria produce both the *perseion* and the so-called *bistakion* (*pistachio*).[152] The latter sends forth fruit like a bunch of grapes, whitish-grey and large, somewhat like teardrops, which fall upon each other like grapes, but inside it is greenish and less tasty than the seeds of a pine-cone, although more fragrant.'

60   **Athenaios** 6. 84, 263c–d: *Subjection of Mariandynoi to the people of Herakleia*
Poseidonios from the Stoa says, in the 11th (*book*) of the *Histories*, 'Many who are not able to stand up for themselves because of their weakness of intellect hand themselves over to the service of the more intelligent, so that they may get from them provision for their needs and give them in return through their own persons whatever service

---

[150] The implausible size of this monster verges on the territory of paradoxography. It is noteworthy that P. distances himself from any claim to its authenticity.

[151] This piece of explicit autopsy, drawing on a voyage made by P. along the North African coast (Maurousia is perhaps better known as ancient Mauretania, roughly modern Morocco) from Gadeira (*Cádiz*), offers a rare personal insight reinforced by the mention of his humorous response.

[152] The identification of the *perseion* is problematic. It may refer to the *persikon* or peach (Pliny 15. xiii. 44).

they can manage.[153] In this way the Mariandynoi were subordinated to the Herakleiotai, promising to serve them permanently as long as the Herakleiotai provided what they needed, and stipulating in addition that none of them would be sold outside the territory of the Herakleiotai, but only in their own land.'

61   Athenaios 5. 46, 210e–f: *Impact of environment on Syrians*
'And everyone in Syria, so they say, because of the abundance provided by the land, used to hold large frequent gatherings free from the misery of life's necessities, with the result that they were continually enjoying sumptuous feasts.'[154]

62   Athenaios 4. 36–7, 151e–152f: *Celtic ethnography*
Poseidonios from the Stoa in the *Histories* which be put together in a manner consonant with the philosophy which he had adopted,[155] in recording many habits and customs from many peoples, says, 'The Keltoi serve their food with hay thrown underneath and on wooden tables which are slightly raised from the ground.[156] The food is a small amount of bread, and a great deal of meat boiled in water and roasted on charcoal or spits. They eat these cleanly, but with a lion's appetite, taking whole joints in both hands and gnawing bits off, and if there is a bit which is hard to tear off, cutting it off with a small knife, which lies close by with its sheath in its own box. Those who live by rivers and by the inner and outer sea also eat fish, and these are roasted with salt and vinegar and cumin. The last they also sprinkle into their drink. They do not use olive oil because of its scarcity, and because it seems to them unusual and unpleasant.

'Whenever more people dine together, they sit in a circle; and the mightiest sits in the middle like the leader of a chorus, distinguished from the others either through his coolness in war or through birth or wealth. The host sits next to him, and the rest in order according to the value of their rank on either side. And those who bear the shields stand behind, and the spear-bearers sitting opposite in a circle feast together like their masters.

'Those who serve the drink carry it round in vessels like spouted cups, made either of pottery or of silver. For truly the platters on which they serve the food are similar to these, with others bronze and others baskets of wood or wicker.

---

[153] An excellent example of convergence between P.'s historical, ethnographical, and ethical interests. The Mariandynoi lived in territory on the S shore of the Black Sea, in which the C6 Megarian colony of Herakleia was to be found.

[154] This is a standard piece of environmental determinism, which was so characteristic of the ancient geographical tradition from at least Herodotos and the Ionian scientists onwards. Kidd assigns this extract to book 16 of the *History*.

[155] This notion of a historical work composed in a way which was aligned with the author's philosophical stance is difficult to interpret. There is nothing particularly 'Stoic' about the passage which follows. Kidd assigns this extract to book 23 of the *History*.

[156] The focus in this passage on dining and entertainment can easily be motivated by the fact that they are cited by Athenaios and act as a reminder of how strongly influenced by patterns of citation we are in our reception of fragmentary authors.

'The drink among the wealthy is wine brought from Italy or from the land of Massilia (*Marseilles*), and this is generally unmixed, but sometimes a little water is added. Among the poorer people a beer is made from wheat, with honey added, and most drink it on its own. It is called *korma*. They sip from the same drinking-cup a little at a time, no more than a cupful (*kyathos*); but they do this rather often. The slave-boy carries it round to the right and to the left; and so they distribute it. And they worship the gods turning to the right.'

Furthermore, when Poseidonios relates the wealth of Luvernius, the father of Bituis, who was taken from power by the Romans,[157] he says that, attempting to win the favour of the mob, he was carried round in a chariot across the countryside; and that he scattered gold and silver to the thousands of Keltoi who accompanied him; and that he made a square enclosure of 12 stades, in which he filled up vats with expensive drink and prepared such a mountain of food that those who wanted could for several days come in and enjoy what had been prepared with continuous service. And he says that, after he had fixed the closing day of the feast, a native poet came and, on meeting him, sang a song in honour of his eminence, but lamented his own lateness; and that Luvernius was delighted and asked for a little bag of gold and threw it to him as he ran alongside. The man, when he took it, sang again, saying that the tracks on the ground where his chariot went brought forth gold and benefits for men. This, then, is what he (*Poseidonios*) recounted in the 23rd (*book*).

63   Athenaios 9. 8, 369c–d: *Turnips and carrots grown in Dalmatia*
Poseidonios from the Stoa, in the 27th (*book*) of the *Histories*, says about Dalmatia that there are uncultivated turnips and wild carrots.

64   Athenaios 4. 39, 153e: *German diet*
The Germans,[158] as Poseidonios relates in the 30th (*book*), serve meat roasted in joints for breakfast and drink milk and unmixed wine.

F. OTHER HISTORICAL EXTRACTS

65   Strabo 1. 2. 34, C41–2: *The Eremboi*
Much has been said about the Eremboi, and those who believe that he (*Homer*) said 'Arabians' are most persuasive. Our Zenon writes it thus: 'I came to the Aithiopes and

---

[157] Bituis was deposed during the Roman victory over the Averni and Allobroges in 121 BC, though P.'s interest is in Luvernius' wealth rather than the historical context; we are not to assume that the encounter with the Celtic bard took place in 121 (Clarke 1999, 364).

[158] P.'s treatment of NW Europe seems to have been quite extensive and clearly appeared in both *On the Ocean* (see 2 §3. 6 and 69 on the Kimbrian migrations) and the *Histories*, as here. The relationship between the two treatments in these two works is unclear, but his keen interest in the more remote inhabitants of the known world reinforces his ecumenical compass. See Dobesch 1995.

Sidonioi and Arabes'.[159] But it is not necessary to alter the wording, which is old. A better reason is that they changed their name, something that is frequent and manifest among all peoples. It is careless to make changes of certain letters.

What Poseidonios says seems to be better, with the etymology from the kinship of the peoples and their communality. For the nation (*ethnos*) of the Armenians, that of the Syrians, and that of the Arabians display a great kinship (*homophylia*), both in their language and their lives and physical characteristics, particularly where they are adjacent. It is clear that Mesopotamia is where these three peoples come together, and their similarity is particularly manifested. Considering the latitudes, there is a great difference between those towards the north and south and the Syrians in the middle, but common conditions prevail, and the Assyrians and Arimanioi somewhat resemble both each other and the others. He (*Poseidonios*) infers that the names of these peoples are similar to each other, for those whom we call Syrians are called Aramaioi by the Syrians themselves, and there is a resemblance between this (*name*), and that of the Armenians, Arabians, and Eremboi.[160] Perhaps the ancient Hellenes called the latter the *Arabes*, with the etymology connecting them. Thus most derive it from *eis tēn eran embainein* (*to go into the earth*), which they later changed to the clearer 'Troglodytai' (*Hole-dwellers*). These are the Arabians who are on that side of the Arabian gulf that inclines towards Egypt and Aithiopia.

66   Strabo 3. 4. 13, C162–3: *The Keltiberians*
Polybios,[161] in discussing the peoples and places of the Ouakkaioi and Keltiberians, includes Segesama and Interkatia with the other cities. Poseidonios says that Marcus Marcellus exacted a tribute of 600 talents from the Keltiberians,[162] from which one may conjecture that there were many Keltiberians and that they were well supplied with wealth, although they live in rather poor territory. But when Polybios says[163] that Tiberius Gracchus destroyed 300 cities, he (*Poseidonios*) ridicules him, saying that the man did this to gratify Gracchus, calling towers 'cities', just as in triumphal processions.[164] Perhaps what he says is not to be disbelieved, for both generals and historians are easily led into such a falsehood, adorning their deeds.

---

[159] Fr. 275 in von Arnim 1903–24; *Od.* 4. 84, altered.

[160] This fragment should be read in conjunction with 71 and 73, as a classic exposition of Homeric geography: namely, one of the puzzles of the wanderings of Menelaos. The Eremboi were the source of much scholarly controversy, a debate which P. enthusiastically joined, combining etymology with ethnology to underpin his solution.

[161] Polyb. 34. 9. 13.

[162] Keltiberia was in N-central Spain. The tribute which P. claims was exacted by M. Marcellus (152/1 BC) is a vast amount; hence Strabo's deduction concerning the wealth of the area.

[163] Polyb. 25. 1. 1.

[164] This offers a fascinating insight into the critical reception of one historian by another.

67   **Strabo** 3. 4. 17, C165: *Ligurian women*

Poseidonios says that in Ligystike (*Liguria*)[165] his host, Charmoleon, a Massaliote man (*from Marseille*), described that he had hired both men and women for digging, and that one of the women, having birthing pains, left her work for a nearby place, and after giving birth returned immediately to her work so that she would not lose her pay.[166] He saw that she was working in pain, but did not know the reason until later. When he did learn it he sent her away, giving her the pay. She carried the infant to a little spring, washed and swaddled it with what she had, and took it safely home.

68   **Strabo** 5. 2. 1, C218: *Liguria*

Let the second (*part of Italia*) be Ligystike that is within the Apennines, situated between the Keltike just spoken about and Tyrrhenia (*Tuscany*), which has nothing worthy of describing except that they live in villages, tilling and digging rough land, or rather quarrying it,[167] as Poseidonios says.

69   **Strabo** 7. 2. 1–2, C292–4: *Cimbrian migrations as a result of tides*

(1) Concerning the Kimbroi (*Cimbri*),[168] some things said about them are not correct, and others are most unbelievable. One cannot accept that the reason they became wanderers and brigands is because, while living on a peninsula, they were driven out of the place by a great flood-tide. Today they have the territory they formerly had, and they sent their most sacred cauldron to Sebastos (*Augustus*) as a gift, seeking his friendship and an amnesty for their previous offences, and when they were considered worthy they went away. It is absurd that because of something that is natural and eternal which occurs twice a day they became angry and left the place. It seems a fiction that an excessive flood-tide occurred once, for when the Ocean is affected in this way it is ordered and periodic. Whoever said that the Kimbrians took up arms against the flood-tide is also not correct; nor is it that the Kelts, trained to be fearless, submitted to the inundation of their homes and then rebuilt them, or that they suffered greater destruction by water than in war, as Ephoros says.[169] The regularity of the flood-tides, and the knowledge about the territory that could be inundated, would make such absurdities improbable. Since it happens twice each day, how could they not understand and believe at once that the flowing back was natural and harmless and that it occurred not only among them but everywhere along the Ocean? Kleitarchos is also in error, for he says that the horsemen, seeing the advance of the sea, rode away and were almost overtaken in flight.[170] We have observed that the onset does not advance with such a speed, but the sea comes imperceptibly, and also what occurs daily and is fresh in the

---

[165] This refers to the area around the gulf of Genoa.

[166] The hardiness of the inhabitants seems to be reflected in, or perhaps determined by, the harshness of the terrain mentioned in the next fragment.

[167] This seems to be a mild joke on P.'s part, suggesting that the ground was so hard that it needed to be mined rather than dug.

[168] A people in northern Germany or Denmark.   [169] *BNJ* 70 F 132.

[170] *BNJ* 137 F 26.

memory of those coming near to it, even before they see it, would not have created such fear as to cause them to flee, as if it had happened unexpectedly.

(2) Poseidonios is right in finding fault with the historians about these things. He conjectures—not badly—that the Kimbroi, who were brigands and wanderers, made an expedition as far as around the Maiotis, and that the Kimmerian Bosporos was named after them, being the same as Kimbrikos, since the Hellenes named the Kimbroi the Kimmerioi. He also says that the Boïoi formerly lived in the Herkynian forest, and that the Kimbroi attacked this place but were driven away by the Boïoi and went down the Istros (*Danube*) to the Skordiskoi Galatai, then to the Teuristai and Tauriskoi, who were also Galatai, and then to the Elouettioi (*Helvetii*), who were peaceful men rich in gold. When the Elouettioi saw that the wealth obtained through brigandage exceeded their own, they—especially the Tigyrenoi and Toÿgenoi—became so excited that they rushed forth with them. All of them were put down by the Romans,[171] both the Kimbroi themselves and those who had joined with them, some after they had crossed the Alps into Italia, and others while still beyond the Alps.

70 Strabo 7. 3. 2–4, C295–7 and 7. 3. 7, C300: *The Mysians and the Iliad*
(2) The Hellenes assumed that the Getai were Thracian. They lived on either side of the Istros (*Danube*), as did the Mysoi (*Mysians*), who were also Thracian—those who are today called Moisoi. The Mysians who today live between the Lydians, Phrygians, and Trojans originated from them. The Phrygians themselves are Briges, a Thracian nation (*ethnos*), as are also the Mygdones, Bebrykes, Maidobithynoi, Bithynoi, Thynoi, and, I believe, the Mariandynoi. All these have completely abandoned Europe, although the Mysians remain. Poseidonios seems to be correct in conjecturing that Homer names the Mysians in Europe when he says:[172]

> he turned back his shining eyes
> and looked far away to the land of the horse-herding Thracians
> and the hand-to-hand-fighting Mysians.[173]

If one were to accept this as the Mysians in Asia, the statement would not hang together. When one turns the eyes away from the Trojans towards the Thracian land, to connect it with these Mysians—who are not 'far away' but have a common boundary with the Troad and are located behind and on either side of it, separated from Thrace by the 'broad Hellespont'[174]—would only be done by someone who confuses the continents and does not understand the wording. 'He turned back' generally means to the rear,

---

[171] In 101 BC.

[172] With this sentence, Strabo resumes his own voice rather than reporting what P. says. The exposition of Homeric geography, including the correct location and identification of groups who appear in the Homeric epics, was clearly a major preoccupation for Hl scholars such as P. The Mysians were not alone in proving problematic, partly due to large-scale migrations and the consequent location of peoples of the same name in different locations, but P. seems clear here that Homer referred to the Mysians in Europe.

[173] *Il.* 13. 3–5.   [174] *Il.* 7. 86; *Od.* 24. 82.

and he who transfers his view from the Trojans to those who are in their rear or along their side transfers it rather far, but not at all to (*his own*) rear. One can produce as witness the fact that he (*Homer*) connected to them the Hippemolgoi (*Mare-milkers*), Galaktophagoi (*Milk-drinkers*), and Abioi, who are the wagon-dwelling Skythians and Sarmatai. Today, too, these nations (*ethnē*), as well as the Bastarnic ones, are mixed together with the Thracians—mostly those (*Thracians*) outside the Istros but also those within it—as are the Keltic ones: the Boïoi, Skordiskoi, and Tauriskoi. Some call the Skordiskoi Skordistai, and say that the Tauriskoi are Ligyriskoi† and Tauristai.

(3) Poseidonios says that the Mysians abstain from living things, including domesticated animals, out of piety. They use honey, milk, and cheese, and live peacefully, because of which they are called 'god-fearing' and *kapnobatai* (*Smoke-goers*).[175] Some of the Thracians live apart from women and are called the Ktistai (*Founders*), and because of their honoured status are dedicated to the gods and live in freedom from fear. The Poet speaks collectively of all these peoples as 'the noble Hippemolgoi, the Galaktophagoi, and the Abioi, most just of men'.[176] (*Poseidonios says*) he (*Homer*) calls them *abioi* (*Lifeless*) especially because they live apart from women, believing that such a deprived life is only half-complete, just as the house of Protesilaos was half-complete because it was deprived;[177] and that the Mysians are 'hand-to-hand fighters' because they were un-subdued, like all good warriors; and that it is necessary to write, in book 13,[178] 'hand-to hand-fighting Moisoi' instead of 'Mysoi'.   (4) It is perhaps superfluous to change the wording that has been popular for so many years, for it is much more believable that they were called Mysians from the beginning but changed their name †also now†. One might accept the 'Abioi' not so much as those who were deprived, but as those without hearths who lived in wagons. For the most part, injustices are created in regard to contracts and a high esteem for property, so it is reasonable that those who live cheaply on few resources would be called the most just. In fact, the philosophers who place justice nearest to moderation strive most of all for self-sufficiency and frugality, and thus going beyond these limits will push some of them into Cynicism. Regarding the statement that they live deprived of women, he indicates nothing of this sort, particularly with the Thracians and those among them who are Getai. . . . Thus, to believe that the womanless Getai are particularly reverent is clearly contrary to reason. A feeling for the divine is especially strong among these people, from what Poseidonios and other histories generally say, and should not be disbelieved. . . .

(7) I was speaking now about the Thracians: 'The hand-to-hand fighting Mysians and the noble Hippemolgoi, the Galaktophagoi, and the Abioi, most just of men',[179] wishing to compare what was said by myself and Poseidonios with them (*Eratosthenes and Apollodoros of Athens*). In the first case, the reasoning that they made is opposite to what they have proposed. . . .

---

[175] The meaning of the word is regarded as uncertain, though it clearly combines 'smoke' and 'go'.
[176] *Il.* 13. 5–6.   [177] *Il.* 2. 701.   [178] At l. 5.   [179] *Il.* 13. 5–6 again.

71 **Strabo 16. 4. 27, C784–5:** *The Eremboi*

When the Poet says, 'I came to the Aithiopes and Sidonioi and Eremboi',[180] they are at a loss whether one should speak of the Sidonioi as certain inhabitants on the Persian gulf, from whom the Sidonioi near us[181] were settlers—just as they record certain island-dwelling Tyrioi there, and Aradioi,[182] saying that those among us were settlers—or whether they are the Sidonioi themselves. The inquiry about the Eremboi is more serious, for one must suspect either that the Troglodytai are meant, as do those who force the etymology from *eis tēn eran embainein*—that is, 'to go into the earth'—or that they are the Arabians. Our Zenon changed it to 'and to the Sidonioi and Arabes'.[183] Poseidonios, more plausibly, writes, with only a small change, 'and Sidonioi and Aramboi', as though the Poet called the present Arabians thus, the same as they were named by others in his time. He (Poseidonios) also says that there were three tribes situated adjacent to each other that show a racial identity (*homogeneia*) with each other because they are called by similar names: the Armenioi (*Armenians*), Aramaioi, and Arambioi.[184] Just as one can accept that they were divided into three tribes, according to the differences in latitude, which always vary, thus they used a number of names instead of one. Those who write 'Eremnoi' (*Dark People*) are not believable, for that is more a characteristic of the Aithiopes. The Poet also speaks of the Arimoi,[185] which, as Poseidonios says, must be accepted, not as in some place in Syria or Kilikia or some other land, but in Syria itself, for those there are Aramaioi, although perhaps the Hellenes called them Arimaioi or Arimoi. The changes in names, especially among the barbarians, are many, just as Dariekes is called Dareios (*Darius*), Pharziris Parysatis, and Athara Atargatis, yet Ktesias calls her Derketo.[186]

72 **Athenaios 2. 24, 45f:** *The Carmani*

One should not drink toasts in the way that the Karmanians do,[187] according to Poseidonios. For, as he alleges, as a mark of friendship they open the veins in their faces and, mixing the blood that drips down with their drink, they quaff it, believing it to be the ultimate sign of friendship to taste of each other's blood. And after this imbibing, they anoint their heads with perfume, particularly that distilled from roses, but if not, then from apples, in order to ward off any effect from the drink and avoid harm from the fumes of the wine.

---

[180] *Od.* 4. 84. On this passage, see Verlinsky 2019, 27–30.
[181] That is, the people of Sidon in Phoenicia.
[182] The people of Tyros and Arados, respectively.
[183] Fr. 275 in von Arnim 1903–24, i.
[184] This return by Strabo in book 4 of his *Geography* to a Homeric problem which he has already expounded in book 1 (**65** above), adducing P.'s testimony again, is indicative of P.'s centrality to Strabo's interpretation of Homeric geography.
[185] *Il.* 2. 783.   [186] *FGrH* 688 F 1d.
[187] Karmania corresponded to the SE part of Iran and was well known from the Alexander historians Nearchos and Onesikritos.

73 Eustathios, *On Homer, Iliad* 2. 782: *Homer's Arimoi*

(*Strabo*) says elsewhere that, according to Poseidonios, Arimoi is not a place in Syria or Kilikia, but refers to Tyria itself, that is the area around Tyre. For the people there are Arimaioi.

74 Eustathios, *On Homer, Iliad* 13. 6: *German habits*

Poseidonios relates that the Germans for their *arista* or *ariston*—that is to say *brōma* (*lunch*)—eat meat roasted in joints, and drink their wine unmixed. . . . (*Other authorities are cited.*) . . . And so, this is what Poseidonios and Pindar say. And this too is from the geographer (*Strabo*).

75 scholion to Apollonios of Rhodes 2. 675: *Hyperboreans*

Herodotos[188] says that the Hyperboreans did not exist at all, since, if there are any such people as Hyperboreans, then there are certainly also Hypernotians.[189] But Poseidonios says that the Hyperboreans do exist, and that they live in the region of the Italian Alps.[190]

---

[188] At 4. 36.   [189] See n. on Erat. 15.

[190] The Italian Alps seem a slightly odd location for these representatives of the region 'beyond the North wind'. It is worth noting P.'s identification elsewhere (**31** §23; **32**) of another mythical element, the Rhipaia mountains, in the Alps.

20

DIONYSIOS SON OF KALLIPHON

(EARLY TO MID-1ST C. BC)

D. Graham J. Shipley

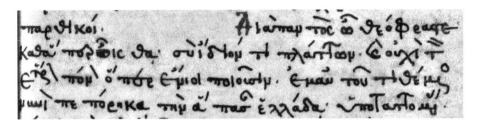

FIG. 20.1. Opening of the text of Dionysios son of Kalliphon, p. 111 (detail).

INTRODUCTION

The two surviving passages of this Greek geographical poem, whose scope is limited to the Greek homeland and islands, are found in manuscript 'D' (folios 111. 10–114. 13 and 123. 20–124. 25; for 'D', see Introduction, §VIII. 2. b), either side of two prose passages now attributed to Herakleides Kritikos (his fragments 1 and 3; see Chapter 11 above). They are laid out as if they were continuous prose, not in lines of verse; but their metrical form, the comic iambic pentameter—the same as that of the *Nikomedean Periodos* ('Pseudo-Skymnos'; Chapter 17)—is easily identified. The first passage contains 109 lines, the second 41; there is a clear hiatus between them in terms of content. The first passage begins with a prologue of 23 lines, which defines the poem's scope as Hellas in its entirety and is followed by an economical account of mainland Greece in coastal sequence, beginning in the north-west and reaching Megara. The second fragment begins with Crete and describes the Aegean islands before breaking off at the erroneous title, purportedly defining all three of the texts, 'Dikaiarchos, *Description of Hellas*'. The hiatus between fragments 1 and 2 is probably not large; the narrator has travelled—in words—briskly, and has evidently made a similar choice to Pseudo-Skylax (Chapter 7), who inserts Crete (§47) as a digression part-way through his account of the Peloponnese. One may hazard an estimate that roughly half of the poem survives.

The author shows knowledge of the *Chronika* of Apollodoros of Athens (late 2nd century BC), and of Artemidoros, active around 100 (Chapter 18). On the basis of presences and absences within the poem, it can be confidently dated to the early or mid-1st century. First, it does not mention two prominent cities in western Greece that were founded by Augustus in the late 1st century (Nikopolis and Patrai). Second, the first place it names, and upon which it dwells for several lines, is the *polis* of Ambrakia (l. 24), which was to be synoikized into the said Nikopolis. Third, it refers to the *ethnos* of the Dolopes (l. 62), which Augustus dissolved. While none of these three points is itself conclusive, cumulatively they suggest a date before the end of the Roman civil wars. Less decisively, the poet's use of the adjective 'great' to describe Thebes (l. 94), followed by a statement of the length of its 5-mile circuit of walls (l. 95), has been thought to indicate a date before the Roman general Sulla sacked that city in 86, reducing it to village-like proportions; but the lines could be a later gesture towards Thebes's eminent place in Greek mythology. For similar reasons, the allusion to the temple of Apollo on Delos (l. 141), while it may refer by default to the most famous one on the island—built by the Athenians but sacked by Mithradates' forces in 88—does not give a conclusive *terminus ante quem*.[1] Both the last points could even be tacit hints that ancient Hellenic culture in the homeland will endure, come what may.

The author's name is certain, being given by an acrostic in the first 23 lines (replicated in this translation): *Dionysiou tou Kalliphōntos*, 'Of Dionysios (son) of Kalliphōn'. He is otherwise unknown; but his father's name, Kalliphōn, is relatively rare, and in the last two centuries BC it occurs most often at Athens.[2] Notable bearers of it include a philosopher who, on the evidence of Cicero, was active before 129/8.[3] Another is an Athenian exile who successfully asked Sulla to spare the lives of the survivors of his siege of the city in 86 (Plutarch, *Sulla*, 14. 5). Whether either of these men is identical with the other, or with our poet's father, cannot be known; but the onomastic evidence makes it a strong possibility that Dionysios was an Athenian from an intellectual family. He may even be the Stoic rhetorician of that name whose lectures Atticus, Cicero's correspondent, attended around 50,[4] and who, like our poet, has been thought to show the influence of Apollodoros; but the name Dionysios is a common one, and judgement should be reserved.[5] In fact, certain allusions in the poem, such as the exaggeration of Athens' importance in Cretan affairs (ll. 116–17), likewise suggest that the author was an Athenian,[6] or at least living at Athens. The onomastic evidence reinforces this Athenian connexion, while not supplying a firm identification.

An awareness of Stoicism is suggested by Dionysios' use of terms such as 'discourse' (*diatribē*, l. 7).[7] He displays a knowledge of the rhetorical terminology discussed by Aristotle in the *Metaphysics*, especially in the prologue (the cluster of terms includes *hexēs*, 'successive(ly)', l. 5; *emmetrōs*, 'proportionately', l. 10);[8] and adopts the language of the *Metaphysics* and *Physics* to express division and contiguity.[9] Despite his promise

---

[1] I follow the dating criteria offered by Marcotte 1990, 34–8, 203–4, except on these points.

[2] An online *LGPN* search (16 June 2020) produced 65 occurrences of the name Kalliphon in all periods, excluding men with no known *ethnikon*; 30 are from Athens; of the 12 from the C2 and C1, 8 are Athenian.

[3] The key testimony is Cicero, *Academica*, 2 (= *Lucullus*), 45. 139, who reports that Karneades defended an opinion of Kalliphon. Karneades died in 129/8. Fortenbaugh and White 2004, 119 n. 2, citing White 2002, 90 n. 47, believe Kalliphon was a C2 Peripatetic.

[4] Cic. *Tusc.* 2. 11. 26.

[5] See discussion by Marcotte 1990, 39 n. 39. Could D. be the authority to whom Cicero referred the conundrum of Arkadian access to the sea (see Ch. 9 no. 1)?

[6] Marcotte 1990, 32 n. 21, 38, 177, 203–4.　　　[7] Marcotte 1990, 39–40.

[8] Marcotte 1990, 39, 80–4.　　[9] Marcotte 1990, 201.

not to take credit for other writers' work (ll. 1–3), he names only one source, Phileas,[10] whom he cites for the limits of continuous Hellas (ll. 31–8; cf. Ps.-Skylax §§33. 2 and 65. 2, who also uses Phileas, though silently). What he does do, however, is to recast his sources' words, not simply parrot them.[11] Specific details appear to be drawn from the Homeric Catalogue of Ships (see Prologue to these volumes), for the Ionian islands;[12] from Ps.-Skylax, for north-western Greece[13] and Crete;[14] from Apollodoros, for the location of Okalea;[15] and from Artemidoros, for the length of Ithaca.[16]

In using comic iambics for a didactic work—one that is framed as educational—Dionysios consciously imitates his renowned and recent predecessor Apollodoros, as does the author of the *Nikomedean Periodos* (Chapter 17) around the same date as our poet or not many years before. His aspiration to brevity (ll. 10–11) is amply fulfilled, to the extent that he gives few details except where he chooses to let his eye linger. Unlike Ps.-Skylax, he gives few measurements; most of the dozen he includes are clustered in the first half of the surviving text. Half of them concern the lengths of islands (ll. 51, 112) or distances by land (ll. 28, 40–1, 95, 104); there is only a handful of coastal lengths; neither does he give any sizes of islands or distances in the Aegean passage (ll. 130–50). In short, he forgoes most of the opportunities to give sailing distances that his material offers; perhaps recognizing that older information had become out of date owing to geopolitical changes.[17] He also eschews scientific consistency in so far as he mixes distances in days and nights with those in stades, even for the same part of Greece.

Dionysios' verse is not finely polished; rather, he has scientific and instructional aims.[18] It is unclear what his intended audience was, apart from the dedicatee, a certain Theophrastos (the name is too common to allow identification). Less 'literary' than most so-called didactic poems, but still imbued with a certain ingenuity in the re-encoding of varied data from earlier writers and thus in a display of learning, the work nevertheless falls short of a consistent scientific account, to judge from the surviving extracts. Although it has been thought to be aimed at 'a demanding public',[19] it remains, perhaps, a private communication—a shared tribute to Old Greece, expressing an understated resistance to the impact of Rome? Certainly it appears to have left no legacy.

---

[10] Probably C5; the sparse evidence for Phileas is collected by González Ponce 2013b.
[11] Marcotte 1990, 29–33.
[12] e.g. ll. 50–2, describing some islands as belonging to the Kephallenians, cf. *Il*. 2. 631; also adapted by Artemidoros, as we know from Porphyrius (no. 38 in Ch. 18 below). See Marcotte 1990, 201–2.
[13] Lines 27–32 ~ Ps.-Skylax §33. 2.   [14] Lines 111–25 ~ Ps.-Skyl. §47. 2.
[15] e.g. l. 99 ~ *BNJ* 244 F 197 = Steph. Byz. ω 7 Okalea.
[16] Line 51 ~ Artem. fr. 55 St. = my no. 38 (cf. n. 12 above). On these points, see Marcotte 1990, 202–3.
[17] Marcotte 1990, 203.   [18] Marcotte 1990, 19; Marcotte 1990, 198.
[19] Marcotte 1990, 198: 'un public exigeant'.

There is surprisingly little modern scholarship on Dionysios. Marcotte's exhaustive commentary supersedes earlier work, and little has been added to the discussion since its publication. This translation follows his skilfully revised Greek text.

SELECTED FURTHER READING

Counillon, P. (2001), 'Les Cyclades chez les géographes grecs', in *Les Îles de l'Égée dans l'Antiquité = Revue des études anciennes*, 103. 1–2: 11–23.

*Marcotte, D. (1990), *Le Poème géographique de Dionysios, fils de Calliphon: édition, traduction et commentaire*. Louvain.

TEXT

FRAGMENT 1

Codex Parisinus supplément grec 443, pp. 111. 10–114. 13
Headings are added.

Introduction

> Dear Theophrastos, always, as you know,
> I fashion my own work, not representing
> Others' toil as mine, as some men do.
> Now I have provided the whole of Hellas;
> Under this the successive cities are arranged;
> Structured with artistry, Hellenic, too,
> In giving an adequate discourse for those capable
> Of perceiving each part correctly. For the things
> Uttered in many words by the old writers,
> 10   These shall be said in brief, proportionate verse,
> Of which there is an adequate, strong power. I
> Understand that the most renowned cities are
> Known to lie safely in their proper place for us:
> As groves, rivers, islands, sea crossings, and harbours,
> Like the races said to exist in the Peloponnese
> Locally bordering on one another,
> In order that nothing escape you in all of it,
> PHrased and set out clearly and agreeably;
> Of everything the memory you may recall.
> 20   Not a dull enterprise, but lively, you should find
> This treatment; so apply yourself entirely
> Over these things at length, and earnestly;
> Share your love of learning with me, as ever.

HELLAS

Western Central Greece

> In Hellas the first city is Ambrakia,
> said to be a colony of the Corinthians.
> It was settled midway along the gulf
> known as Ambrakikos, at a distance from
> the sea of eighty stades.[20] There is a famous
> sanctuary of Athena in it, and a closed

30   harbour. The whole land is called Dryopis.
> Hellas appears to be at its most continuous[21]
> from Ambrakia onwards. The limit of it is found
> at the river Peneios,[22] as Phileas writes,[23]
> and the Magnesians' mountain called Homole.
> But some say Macedonia belongs
> to Hellas, and that Phileas ignorantly
> separated it, and that this is obvious
> to those lovers of learning who are most ambitious.[24]
> However, I shall proceed to the rest of my story.

40   From Ambrakia to Thessaly is a journey
> of three days. The former has a river
> called Aratthos, issuing into the sea,
> and beside it is a mountain called the Sacred.
> The coastal sailing in stades is a hundred and twenty.
> After this region are the so-called Oreitai;[25]
> next, the Amphilochians; here is the Argos called
> Amphilochikon. After them the Akarnanes:
> these folk have several cities including Leukas,
> after which is a great gulf leading to the Isthmus.

50   In it lie the isles of the Kephallenes;
> ⟨among them⟩ Ithaca—eighty stades (*long*), narrow,
> with a high peak and three harbours—follows;
> in the area beyond, Aitolia, they live.

[20] This sentence recalls Ps.-Skyl. §33. 1; the next seven lines §33. 2.
[21] For the notion of 'continuous' Hellas, cf. Ps.-Skyl. §33. 2, §65. 2, and nn. there.
[22] The river forming the boundary between Thessaly and Macedonia on the E side of Greece.
[23] For Phileas, see Introduction, §VI. 4. b.
[24] Having begun his tour of Greece in *periplous* style, D. at once subverts expectations by dwelling on what would be the destination of his entire journey and raising, but leaving unresolved, the controversial question of Macedonia's Hellenic status. The transitions into and out of this passage are rather abrupt—as are several of those to new regions, which frequently begin in the middle of a line, even with the last foot of a line as at 99 (contrast e.g. the *Nikomedean Periodos*).
[25] 'Mountain People'.

A sanctuary called Herakles' is here,[26]
another Aphrodite's. The land has a river,
the Acheloös. Two days and two nights
is the coastal sailing.[27]

Central Greece

Next follows Aitolia,
in which lies the city of Pleuron and a sanctuary
sacred to and named after Athena.
60   Next Kalydon, [—] Echinades islands,
and the river Euenos, flowing out of Pindos.
These people[28] live to the south of the Dolopians;
the coastal sailing of this land, one day.
Next after this, the so-called Lokris lies;
in it a city, Naupaktos. Next lies
the great harbour and city of Tolophon.
After Tolophon is the river named Hylaithos;
they say that this flows out of Aitolia.
the whole coastal sailing is not even a day.
70   These people[29] live to the south of Aitolia;
in former times they had been called Leleges.
    After that ⟨are⟩ the Phokians, known for prophecies;
by them, the Krisaian plain. Going up from Kirrha,
there lies the city of Delphi and a sanctuary,
in which is the oracle; and Parnassos, a great
and shaded mountain; next follows the Nymphs'
Korykian cave. Then the city of Antikyra
and the river Kephisos, the one flowing out of Phokis.
The coastal sailing of this is not a whole day.
80   In the interior are the city of Kyparissos,
and Larisa, and after it Daulis.
            The Boiotian land
lies beyond the Phokians, lying towards
the east from the Phokian land; and there are
two famous mountains, one called Helikon,
the other Kithairon. Next the city of Oropos
and a sanctuary, not distant from the sea:
that of Amphiaraos, with a temple and a precinct;
and Aulis, city of the Boiotians, with a harbour

---

[26] Sc. in Leukas.   [27] Of Akarnania.   [28] i.e. the Aitolians.   [29] The Lokrians.

90	and Artemis' holy sanctuary, its founder said to be Agamemnon. Then a promontory which is called Emperesion; then the Euripos. Anthedon has
92	a harbour, the Anthedonios; not long after
92*	[— — — — —] (*line missing*)
93	Tanagra lies in the interior, a very fine city. (*Then*) great Thebes, with a circumference of forty stades and then another three; the city of Kopai, and Orchomenos; after these two the city of Lebadeia and a shrine of Trophonios, where they say the oracle came into being. Next is Okalea city, and Medeon. And next
100	after this lies Thespia; following next is the place named as Plataiai; beyond these lies the city of Nisa. The length of the land of Boiotia, it is said, is five hundred stades, ⟨but⟩ two hundred and seventy is its breadth. For rivers it has, first, the so-called Ismenos and the Asopos; and well-watered plains lying beside them.
108a	Next the land of the Megarians[30]
108b	[— — — — —] harbour,
109a	silted up, lies here, and the so-called Lechaion,[31]
109b	a *polis*. [—]

FRAGMENT 2

Codex Parisinus supplément grec 443, pp. 123. 20–124. 25

Crete, Aegean Islands

110	Crete is an island lying beside Kythera, lapped by the waves.[32] The extent of it is almost two thousand five hundred stades; of all (*islands*) it is furthest out in open sea (*pelagiōtatē*) and is perfectly narrow. In it, three races of Hellenes took a colony: one from the Lakedaimonians, next from the Argives, then that by the Athenians; and it has barbarian

[30] Here in the MS a line of prose reads 'From here is the beginning of the Peloponnese'.
[31] We have entered the Korinthia in the lacuna; Lechaion is the N harbour of Corinth.
[32] The account of Crete echoes the W–E, zigzag progression of Ps.-Skyl. §47. 2.

indigenous races. They say that in Crete is a city,
Phalasarna, lying towards the setting sun,
120   having a closed harbour and a sanctuary
sacred to Artemis, and that the goddess is called
Diktynna. Then the so-called Aptaraia
in the interior; following next, Knosos;
to the south, Gortyna; and there are other cities
in Crete, which it is laborious to spell out.
For rivers it has Lethaios, then the so-called
Didymoi,[33] then Mainomenos;[34] following them
Kedrisos, Amphimelas, and Messapolis;
Mount Diktynnaion bearing towards the west.
130   The islands of the Cyclades we see
lying beyond Geraistos, to the south
from Euboia, enclosing the open sea (*pelagos*)
that is called Myrtoan; and yet partaking
completely of the land of Attica.
Near Sounion, first, lies Keos the four-citied,
an island and a harbour. There follows Kythnos,
both island and city; Seriphos and its harbour;
next is Siphnos; following it Kimolos,
which possesses two harbours; and after this
140   the holy isle called Delos, with a harbour
and temple of Apollo. Next there follows
Mykonos. After this Tenos and its harbour,
and Andros isle, by Geraistos, with a harbour.
These are the Cyclades.[35]
                Others are called
the Sporades, among them Melos, then
not far away the isle of Thera, then not far
is Ios, then Naxos, after it Pelasgian
Skyros—off Euboia we see it lying.
From this one it is no great distance to
150   the isle of Peparethos, called three-citied.
[— *text breaks off* —]

---

[33] The 'Twin' rivers.   [34] The 'Raging' river.
[35] On how D. integrates a periplographic narrative structure with a Hl conception of the Mediterranean as made up of a plurality of seas, see Counillon 2001b, 19–21.

21

MENIPPOS OF PERGAMON

(ACTIVE C.26/5 BC)

J. Brian Campbell

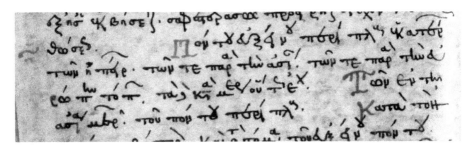

FIG. 21.1. Opening of Markianos' epitome of Menippos, p. 56 (detail).

INTRODUCTION

What we have of the Greek writings of Menippos of Pergamon appears in manuscript D (see the Introduction, §VIII. 2. b) in an *epitome* (précis), also in Greek, made by Markianos around AD 400. In a preface addressed to his friend Amphithalios (part at A. 1 below; full text in Chapter 34), Markianos describes three of his own works: (1) an *epitome* of Artemidoros; (2) an account of the Outer Sea (see Chapter 34); and finally (3) an edition of Menippos' work. Of these, (1) and (2) were earlier works, and in §6 of the preface Markianos gives a summary of Menippos which is in line with the text that follows in D. Earlier scholarship took that text to be the *epitome* of Artemidoros (Chapter 18 above), but it is now clear that this text is actually the *epitome* of Menippos' *periplous* in which he described the Black Sea and Mediterranean in three books. Markianos claims to have edited Menippos' text and made some additions, though there is little sign of substantial alterations. Some additional quotations appear in Stephanos of Byzantion (B. 4–8 below).

Long before Markianos worked with Menippos' writings, the latter's work had been used by Agathemeros in the 2nd century AD (3; Chapter 29), who includes Menippos among authors 'worthy of trust' (*axiopistoi*). It is possible that he was one source for Arrian's *Periplous*, written in the 130s (Chapter 27); this is not certain, however, as the similarity of subject matter may account for the resemblance. Similarities have been observed between Menippos' work and the anonymous *Stadiasmos* (Chapter 31), whose original version may have dated from his lifetime or shortly after.[1] We have

---

[1] Diller 1952, 149–50; Medas 2013.

a more precise, earlier date for Menippos as a result of a poem addressed to him by Krinagoras of Mytilene, who we know visited Rome in 26/5 BC as part of an embassy (2). The epigram may contain evidence that Menippos put together the collection of geographical writings which, in Markianos' hands, became the second great geographical corpus and the original version of manuscript D.[2]

Menippos' *Periplous* embraces Asia, Europe, and Libyē (North Africa) starting at the mouth of the Black Sea; the surviving text provides a circumnavigation of the Euxine, and the lost portion will have described the coastline of Europe to the strait of Herakles (*strait of Gibraltar*) before crossing to Africa and traversing the southern coast of the Mediterranean. In his geographical survey Menippos treats capes and natural phenomena, towns, settlements, ports including the type of ship for which they were suitable, rivers, and the boundaries of provinces and regions. Presentation is formulaic and, as far as we can tell, lies within the normal confines of *periploi* of this type. Sites are briefly described with any unusual characteristics, and intervening distances are noted in stades.

Diller also prints a text which he presents as a further part of Menippos' *Periplous*.[3] However, this is merely reconstructed from those parts of the text of the Pseudo-Arrianic *Periplous of the Euxine* (*Eux.*) that he believes were taken from Menippos' work.[4] This approach is circular and unsafe, and therefore his reconstruction is not translated in this edition. (The relevant passages in *Eux.* are marked ^m in Chapter 36 below.)[5]

SELECTED FURTHER READING

Dilke, O. A. W. (1985), *Greek and Roman Maps*. London. [Pp. 141–4.]

Diller, A. (1952), *The Tradition of the Minor Greek Geographers*. Lancaster, Pa.–Oxford. [Ch. 5 (pp. 147–64).]

Dueck, D. (2012), with K. Brodersen, *Geography in Classical Antiquity*. Cambridge. [Pp. 58–9, 113.]

*González Ponce, F. J. (2008b), *Periplo de Hanón y autores de los siglos VI y V a.C.* Zaragoza. [Edition and translation of *Epit. Men.* 1–5 at pp. 50–69 (Greek text based on Müller, *GGM*).]

Medas, S. (2013), 'Contenuti nautici nel "Periplo del mare interno" di Menippo di Pergamo', in F. Raviola (ed.), *L'indagine e la rima: scritti per Lorenzo [Braccesi]* (Rome), 985–96.

---

[2] Marcotte 2000b, cxxii.   [3] Diller 1952, 154–6.   [4] Diller 1952, 148.

[5] The apparent citation of M. at Steph. Byz. χ 45 s.v. Chitone is false: for παρὰ Μενίππῳ we should read Παρμενίων, 'Parmenion' (Müller, *GGM* i. 573 n.) or Παρμένων, 'Parmenon' (Meineke 1849, 694, followed by Billerbeck).

A. MARKIANOS' *EPITOME* (EXTRACT)[6]

1

TABLE OF CONTENTS

⟨Epitome by Markianos of Herakleia of the *Periplous of the Inner Sea* (*Periplous tēs entos thalassēs*) which Menippos of Pergamon wrote in three books.[7]

Preface.

Contents of the First Book of the *Epitome*: Introduction. Circumnavigation (*periplous*) of the Pontos Euxeinos in both continents, including places both in Asia and in Europe. The details are as follows: Circumnavigation of the parts of Asia in the Pontos. Circumnavigation of Bithynia from the sanctuary of Zeus Ourios. Circumnavigation of Paphlagonia. Circumnavigation of the two Pontoi. . . . Circumnavigation of the parts of Europe in the Pontos. . . . Circumnavigation of the Thracian Bosporos and the Propontis and the Hellespont of both continents. The details are as follows: Circumnavigation of parts of Asia from the sanctuary of Zeus Ourios. . . . Circumnavigation of the parts in Europe.

Contents of the Second Book of the *Epitome*: Circumnavigation of the remaining parts of Europe from the Hellespont to the strait of Herakles and the island of Gadeira. The details are as follows: . . .

Contents of the Third Book of the *Epitome*: Circumnavigation of Libyē from the strait of Herakles. The details are as follows: . . . Circumnavigation of Asia from the boundary of Libyē to the Hellespont mentioned above. The details are as follows:⟩ Coastal sailing (*paraplous*) from Kane or Aigaia to Adramytion.[8] The distances between cities by land. Coastal sailing from Adramytion to Lekton. Circumnavigation of the Troas to Sigeion.

MARKIANOS' PREFACE (PART)

(For the full text of Markianos' preface, see Chapter 34 below, section C. The parts most relevant to Menippos are replicated here.)

3. Next to most of these writers, Artemidoros of Ephesos the geographer, and Strabo, who combined geography and circumnavigation, and Menippos of Pergamon, who

---

[6] From manuscript D, Codex Parisinus supplément grec 443, pp. 49 l. 4–p. 60 l. 22.

[7] As far as the third mention of the Hellespont below, the table of contents is purely Müller's reconstruction, based on the material in the text that follows. The gap in MS D where the sixth quaternion (set of sixteen pages) was lost is followed by the beginning of the quaternion numbered ζ' (7) at the mention of Kana.

[8] Cf. n. 5. The surviving portion of Markianos' epitome of Menippos begins here, at the top of p. 49 of MS D (the previous quaternion being lost). We begin with the preserved end of Mark.'s table of contents.

wrote about sea crossings (*diaploi*), are in my view more accurate than all those mentioned above. . . . Menippos of Pergamon himself treated the circumnavigation of the inner sea in three books, and produced an account combining history and geography.

4. . . . When I saw that the majority of old writers either did not mention the outer sea at all or only to a limited degree, and since even this description was obscure and not in harmony with the truth, I gave my own scrutiny to the entire eastern and south-ern ocean of both continents, Africa and Asia, from the Arabian gulf (*Red Sea*) as far as the nation of the Sinai.[9] I also included in two books the *periplous* of the western and northern ocean and the parts of both Europe and Africa. Since I learned that Menip-pos too offered a reasonable account to his readers from his own volumes, but had not carefully explained everything, I appended a great deal of material that had been left out, and furthermore added clarity in respect of places and descriptions of peoples, which usually provide a complete understanding for readers, and made an account in three volumes. However, I did not take away the author's paternity from this work, nor did I claim for myself someone else's work, just as I did not suppress the name of Arte-midoros when he set out everything carefully, but I wrote the names of these authors in the books so that I should seem to have done nothing wrong in respect of the gods of writing, giving the epitomes of these works and corrections which resulted from my own efforts a clear designation, so that those who read them cannot fail to recognize what was written by those authors and the material added by me or thought worthy of careful correction.

. . . 6. Menippos has divided up the circumnavigation of the three continents, Asia, Europe, and Libyē (*Africa*), in the following way. He withheld and dealt with in a sepa-rate circumnavigation the Hellespont and Propontis, with the Thracian Bosporos and furthermore the Euxeinos Pontos on both continents, Asia and Europe: first the Pon-tos, after that the Thracian Bosporos and the Propontis along with the Hellespont. He made the start of the circumnavigation of both continents from the sanctuary called Zeus Ourios,[10] which is situated right at the mouth of the Pontos. After this, starting from the remaining parts of Europe he circumnavigates all of it up to the strait of Herakles and the island of Gadeira (*Cádiz*). Then, crossing to the mainland opposite at the strait of Herakles, that is, to Libyē, he sails round this area too and adds to it the circumnavigation of Asia up to the Hellespont, which I mentioned above. The entire arrangement of the circumnavigation has the following plan: it will go through each part in turn and receive correction to make it clearer, as mentioned above.

---

[9] For the Sinai, cf. Mark. *Peripl.* 1. 12 and n.   [10] The settlement was called Hieron: see §7.

CIRCUMNAVIGATION OF THE PONTOS EUXEINOS IN BOTH CONTINENTS, AND OF PLACES BOTH IN ASIA AND IN EUROPE

The details are as follows.[11]

Circumnavigation of the sea of the parts in Asia

7. Near the Thracian Bosporos and the mouth of the Euxeinos Pontos in the right-hand parts of Asia, which belong to the province (*ethnos*) of the Bithynians, lies a place called Hieron (*Sanctuary*), in which is a temple named Zeus Ourios. This place is the point of departure for those sailing towards the Pontos. For someone sailing into the Euxine and keeping Asia on the right, and sailing round the remaining part of the province of the Bithynians that faces the Pontos, the *periplous* is as follows.

Circumnavigation of ⟨the part of⟩ Bithynia ⟨by the Pontos⟩

8. From the sanctuary of Zeus Ourios to the river Rhebas is 90 stades.[12]

From the Rhebas to Cape Melaina (*Black*) is 150 stades.

⟨From Cape Melaina to the river Artane and the place there is 150 stades⟩.[13] It has a small harbour suitable for small craft, and an islet lies nearby which shelters the harbour.

From the river Artane to the river Psillion and the place ⟨is 140 stades.

From the river Psillion to the harbour at Kalpa and the river⟩ is 210 stades.[14] This is a trading-place of the people of Herakleia, and it has a river and a fine harbour.

From the river Kalpa to the island of Thynias is 60 stades.

From the island of Thynias to the Sangarios, a navigable river, is 200 stades.

From the river Sangarios to the river Hypios is 180 stades.

From the river Hypios to the city of Dia is 60 stades; it also has a minor anchorage (*hyphormos*).

From the city of Dia to the river Elaion and the trading-place is 90 stades.

From the river Elaion to the river Kaleps (*i.e. Kalēs*) and the trading-place is 120 stades.

From the river Kaleps (*i.e. Kalēs*) to the very large city of Herakleia is 80 stades.

From Herakleia to the city of Apollonia in Europe, lying opposite in the nation of the Thracians, is 1,000 stades.[15]

All the (stades) from the sanctuary of Zeus Ourios to the city of Herakleia amount to 1,530.

To someone sailing directly from Hieron to the city of Herakleia is 1,200 stades.

---

[11] This is Markianos' summary, and the next sentence is probably his.
[12] Many of the names in this passage also occur in Arrian's *Periplous* (Ch. 27 below) and the derivative *Eux.* (Ch. 36), where modern equivalences are noted.
[13] Added by Müller from Arr. §12. 3.   [14] Added by Müller based on *Eux.*
[15] Müller notes that the number of stades should be 2,000 to fit better with the actual distance of 225 mi (*c.*360 km). However, *Eux.* §11 also has 1,000 st.

From Herakleia to Poseideion, where there is a roadstead (*salos*), is 110 stades.

From Poseideion to the river Oxines is 90 stades; here is an anchorage (*hormos*) for small craft.

From the Oxines to Sandarake is 40 stades; here is an anchorage for ships.

From Sandarake to Krenides is 20 stades; here is an anchorage for ships of medium size.

From Krenides to the place called Psylla is 20 stades.

From the place called Psylla to the city of Tios and the river Billaion is 90 stades. This river forms the boundary of Bithynia. Beyond this belongs to Paphlagonia. Some, however, wish the river Parthenion to be the boundary between Bithynia and Paphlagonia.[16]

All the stades from Herakleia to the city of Tios and the river Billaion amount to 370.

Circumnavigation of Paphlagonia

9. All the seaboard parts of Paphlagonia happen to lie along the Pontos. The parts of Bithynia previously mentioned near the Pontos, which come before this part, are situated on the Thracian Bosporos and the Astakenian gulf and along the Propontis right up to the river Rhyndakos.

From Tios to the river Psilis is 60 stades.

From the Psilis to the river Parthenion is 70 stades.

From the Parthenion to the city of Amastris and the river is 90 stades.

All the stades from Tios to Amastris amount to 220.

From Amastris to the place called Kromna is 150 stades.

From Kromna to the place called Kytoros is 90 stades; here there is a roadstead.

⟨From Kytoros to Aigialos is 60 stades.⟩[17]

From Aigialos to the city of Klimax is 50 stades.

From Klimax to the place called Timolaion is 60 stades.

From the place called Timolaion to Karambis, a huge and lofty promontory, is 100 stades. Opposite Cape Karambis is situated in Europe the huge promontory which is called Kriou Metopon (*Ram's Brow; C. Sarych*).

From Cape Karambis to the village of Kallistratia is 20 stades.

From Kallistratia to the locality (*called*) Garion is 80 stades.

From the locality called Garion to the city of Abonouteichos, now called Iounopolis (*i.e. Ionopolis*),[18] is 120 stades.

From Abonouteichos to the small town of Aiginetes and the river is 160 stades.

---

[16] Strabo 12. 3. 5, C542, and Arr. §13, make the Parthenion river the boundary.

[17] Added by Müller on the basis of Arr. §14.

[18] Since the name Ionopolis appeared first in the time of Marcus Aurelius, this may be an addition by Markianos.

From Aiginetes to the village of Kinolis and the river—it has a minor anchorage at the place called Antikinolis—is 60 stades.

From Kinolis to the village of Stephane is 150 stades; there is an anchorage (*hormos*) here.

From Stephane to the place called Potamoi is 120 stades; there is an entrance for small craft to Potamoi.

From the place called Potamoi to Syrias, a narrow cape, is 120 stades.

After Cape Syrias there is a bay; someone sailing into it comes to the village of Armene and a large harbour, a distance of 50 stades. Beside the harbour is a river named Ochosbanes.

From Armene to the city of Sinope is 50 stades. There is situated at the outskirts an islet called Skopelos. It has a way through for smaller ships, though bigger ships must sail round it and in this way reach the city. For those who sail round the island there is an additional distance of 40 stades.

From cape Karambis the distance for someone sailing straight to Sinope is **700 stades.**

All the stades from Amastris to Sinope amount to **1,450.**[19]

From Herakleia to Sinope is 2,040 stades. From Hieron to Sinope is **3,570 stades.**

From Sinope to the river Euarchos is 80 stades; this river forms the boundary of Paphlagonia and the following area, Kappadokia. For the ancients wished Kappadokia to stretch right to the Euxeinos Pontos; some called them Leukosyroi. Now, however, after Paphlagonia the places up to the frontier of the barbarian regions are properly called Pontos. It has been divided into two provinces.[20]

Circumnavigation of the two Pontoi[21]

10. From the river Euarchos to the place called Karousa is 70 stades; it has a harbour in winds from the west.[22]

From the place called Karousa ⟨to Gourzoubathe is 60 stades.

From Gouzoubathe⟩ to the place called Zagoros is 120 stades.

From the place called Zagoros to the river Zalikos (*i.e. Zalekos*) and the village, which has no harbour, is 120 stades.

From the river Zalikos (*i.e. Zalekos*) to the navigable river Halys is 150 stades.

From the river Halys to the lake and roadstead above it, which is called Naustathmos, is 120 stades.

---

[19] The stades in the text amount to 1,440 or 1,480 for those sailing round the island.

[20] Two provinces of Pontos would not suit the situation in the time of Menippos when the W part of Pontos was attached to Bithynia, and this may be an addition by Markianos, as may the heading that follows.

[21] i.e. the two provinces; see preceding n.

[22] Diller 1952, 159, wonders if westerly winds were the only ones to blow in the Euxine; Menippos may mean that the harbour provided a safe anchorage when winds blew from the W.

From Naustathmos to another lake called Konopion, without a harbour, is 120 stades.

From Konopion to the city of Amisos is 150 stades.

All the stades from Sinope to Amisos amount to **950**.[23]

From Hieron to Amisos is **4,520 stades.**

From Amisos to the river Lykastos is 20 stades.

From Lykastos to the village and river Chadision is 150 stades.

⟨From Chadision to the river Iris is 100 stades⟩ [—].[24] (*The manuscript breaks off at this point*).[25]

B. OTHER TEXTS

2 Krinagoras, in *Anthologia Graeca*, 9. 559

> My voyage aims at Italy: I'm summoned to my friends,
>> from whom I've been a long time absent now.
> I seek a *periplous* to be my guide and bring me
>> to the Cyclades and ancient Scheria.
> So, Menippos, assist me, my friend and writer of the expert
>> circuit,[26] you who know all about geography.

(trans. Graham Shipley)

3 Agathemeros v. 20

Finally we shall tell the circumferences of the islands in our region, taking them from Artemidoros, Menippos, and other trustworthy writers.

4 Stephanos of Byzantion ε 123

Hermonassa (*Taman*): a small island bearing a city, in the Kimmerian Bosporos; a colony of the Ionians, according to (*Dionysios*) the Periegete. Skymnos also names this (*island*) Hermoneia. Strabo in (*the*) 7th (*book*) says it is a village (*kōmē*). But Menippos in *Periplous of the Two Pontoi* (*describes it as*) a settlement (*chōrion*) belonging to Trapezous. But Hekataios and Theopompos describe it as a city (*polis*).

---

[23] The total of stades in the text is 930.

[24] This sentence is restored from Arr. §15 and Steph. Byz.

[25] Diller 1952, 160, attempts to recover more of the text of M. by using the anonymous *Periplous of the Euxine* (Chapter 36 below), which probably employed M. as a source; see the introduction to this chapter.

[26] Marcotte 2000b, cxxii, sees a reference to the collection of geographical writings assembled by M. and later expanded by Markianos (see Introduction, §VIII. 2. b).

5   Stephanos of Byzantion ν 13

Narbōn: trading-place and Keltic city. . . . But Markianos refers to it as Narbonesia.

6   Stephanos of Byzantion ν 59

Nikopolis: a city in Epeiros, as Markianos (*says*).

7   Stephanos of Byzantion χ 9

Chaldia: a territory in Armenia. Menippos in (*the*) *periplous* of the two Pontoi: 'right up to these barbarians is the Pontic kingdom,[27] and the (*places*) beside Tibarēniē and Chaldiē and Sannikē'.

8   Stephanos of Byzantion χ 15

Chalkedon: . . . Menippos, too, in *Periplous of Bithynia*: 'From the sanctuary of Zeus Ourios and the mouth of the Pontos, for someone keeping the mainland on the left and sailing towards the city of Chalkedon, it is 120 stades, and from this to Akritas 60 stades.'[28] [The same (*writer refers to*) the island of Chalkitis.][29] It was called after the nearby river Chalkis, as all the historians say.

9   Constantine Porphyrogennetos, *De thematibus*, 10. 9 ~ Stephanos of Byzantion σ 155

Sikelia (*Sicily*): the island was formerly named Sikania and then called Sikelia, as Hellanikos relates in book 2 of *The Priestesses of Hera*: 'At the same time the Ausones, under the leadership of Sikelos, were driven out of Italy by the Iapyges. Crossing over to the island, which was then called Sikania, they settled round Mount Aitna (*Etna*), along with Sikelos, their king, who established a kingdom there. Setting out from there, the said Sikelos came to rule over this entire island, which was thereafter called Sikelia after this very man.' Menippos, too, says the same things.[30]

10   Constantine Porphyrogennetos, *De thematibus*, 1. 2

. . . the *thema* (*province*) called the Armeniakon . . . Neither does Strabo mention such a nomenclature . . ., nor does Menippos, who wrote the *stadiasmoi* of the whole *oikoumenē*, nor even Skylax the Karyandene, nor any other one among those who have written histories, nor Pausanias of Damascus (?) himself.[31]

---

[27] Corrected from Billerbeck.

[28] Billerbeck 2006–17, v. 80, notes a suggestion that this distance should be 160 st., but does not adopt it.

[29] Billerbeck excises these words as belonging to entry χ 18 (Artemidoros 57 in Ch. 18).

[30] Constantine Porphyrogennetos based this account on the unabridged text of Steph. Byz., now lost; in the surviving epitome, the entry on Sikelia (σ 155) is a précis of the same information. CP's work deals with the provinces of the empire and discusses their origin and development. Müller comments that this fragment is evidence that Menippos included historical information in his geography. Jacoby plausibly reads ταὐτά, 'the same things', for ταῦτα, 'these things'.

[31] For the otherwise unknown 'Pausanias of Damascus', see Ch. 17, introduction; another author of that name may have stood here.